PISA

PISA 2015 Results (Volume V)

COLLABORATIVE PROBLEM SOLVING

OECD
BETTER POLICIES FOR BETTER LIVES

This work is published under the responsibility of the Secretary-General of the OECD. The opinions expressed and arguments employed herein do not necessarily reflect the official views of the OECD member countries.

This document, as well as any data and any map included herein, are without prejudice to the status of or sovereignty over any territory, to the delimitation of international frontiers and boundaries and to the name of any territory, city or area.

The statistical data for Israel are supplied by and under the responsibility of the relevant Israeli authorities. The use of such data by the OECD is without prejudice to the status of the Golan Heights, East Jerusalem and Israeli settlements in the West Bank under the terms of international law.

Please cite this publication as:
OECD (2017), *PISA 2015 Results (Volume V): Collaborative Problem Solving*, PISA, OECD Publishing, Paris.
http://dx.doi.org/10.1787/9789264285521-en

ISBN (print) 978-92-64-28550-7
ISBN (PDF) 978-92-64-28552-1

Series: PISA
ISSN (print): 1990-8539
ISSN (on line): 1996-3777

Corrigenda to OECD publications may be found on line at: www.oecd.org/publishing/corrigenda.

Foreword

For as long as there have been societies, people have had to work with others. As the world becomes even more interconnected, it will need more people who know how to collaborate. Do today's students have the skills it takes to work with others? Do they know how to listen to other people, how to act as part of a team to achieve a goal?

There have been few attempts to assess how well students collaborate with one another. The PISA 2015 collaborative problem-solving assessment is the first large-scale test of its kind. The assessment finds that, as expected, students who do well in the core academic subjects of science, reading and mathematics, also tend to do well in collaborative problem solving; and girls outperform boys in every participating country and economy. But there are large differences between countries in their students' mastery of the specific skills needed for successful collaboration; and, on average across OECD countries, not even one in ten students can handle problem-solving tasks that require them to maintain awareness of group dynamics, take the initiative to overcome obstacles, and resolve disagreements and conflicts.

As workplaces around the globe are demanding – and paying higher wages for – people with well-honed social skills, schools need to do more to help their students develop these skills. They can do so through regular course work, through organised physical education activities, and by creating learning environments where diversity is celebrated, where students' relationships with both their peers and their teachers are strengthened, and where students are encouraged to share their ideas and participate in class.

This report is the product of a joint effort between the countries participating in PISA, the national and international experts and institutions working within the framework of the PISA Consortium, and the OECD Secretariat.

The development of this volume was led by Andreas Schleicher and Yuri Belfali and guided by Francesco Avvisati and Miyako Ikeda. This volume was drafted by Jeffrey Mo with Alfonso Echazarra and edited by Marilyn Achiron. Day-to-day management was performed by Giannina Rech. Hélène Guillou provided statistical and analytical support with the help of Judit Pál. Rose Bolognini co-ordinated production and Fung Kwan Tam designed the publication. Administrative support was provided by Claire Chetcuti, Juliet Evans, Thomas Marwood, Lesley O'Sullivan and Hanna Varkki. Additional members of the OECD PISA and communications teams who provided analytical and communications support include Peter Adams, Guillaume Bousquet, Cassandra Davis, Tue Halgreen, Bonaventura Francesco Pacileo, Mario Piacentini, Michael Stevenson and Sophie Vayssettes.

To support the technical implementation of PISA, the OECD contracted an international consortium of institutions and experts, led by Irwin Kirsch of the Educational Testing Service (ETS). Overall co-ordination of the PISA 2015 assessment, the development of instruments, and scaling and analysis were managed by Claudia Tamassia of ETS; development of the electronic platform was managed by Michael Wagner of ETS. Development of the science and collaborative problem-solving frameworks, and adaptation of the frameworks for reading and mathematics, were led by John de Jong and managed by Catherine Hayes of Pearson. Survey operations were led by Merl Robinson and managed by Michael Lemay of Westat. Sampling and weighting operations were led by Keith Rust and managed by Sheila Krawchuk of Westat. Design and development of the questionnaires were led by Eckhard Klieme and managed by Nina Jude of the Deutsches Institut für Pädagogische Forschung (DIPF).

Art Graesser chaired the expert group that guided the preparation of the collaborative problem-solving framework and instruments. This group also included Eduardo Cascallar, Pierre Dillenbourg, Patrick Griffin, Chee Kit Looi and Jean-François Rouet. The expert group that guided the preparation of the science assessment framework and instruments was chaired by Jonathan Osborne and also included Marcus Hammann, Sarah Howie, Jody Clarke-Midura, Robin Millar, Andrée Tiberghien, Russell Tytler and Darren Wong. Charles Alderson and Jean-Francois Rouet assisted in adapting the reading framework, and Zbigniew Marciniak, Berinderjeet Kaur and Oh Nam Kwon assisted in adapting the mathematics framework. David Kaplan chaired the expert group that guided the preparation of the questionnaire framework and instruments. This group included Eckhard Klieme, Gregory Elacqua, Marit Kjærnsli, Leonidas Kyriakides, Henry M. Levin, Naomi Miyake, Jonathan Osborne, Kathleen Scalise, Fons van de Vijver and Ludger Woessmann. Keith Rust chaired the Technical Advisory Group, whose members include Theo Eggen, John de Jong, Jean Dumais, Cees Glas, David Kaplan, Irwin Kirsch, Christian Monseur, Sophia Rabe-Hesketh, Thierry Rocher, Leslie A. Rutkowski, Margaret Wu and Kentaro Yamamoto.

The development of the report was steered by the PISA Governing Board, chaired by Lorna Bertrand (United Kingdom) and Michelle Bruniges (Australia), with Jimin Cho (Korea), Maria Helena Guimarães de Castro (Brazil), Dana Kelly (United States), Sungsook Kim (Korea), and Carmen Tovar Sanchez (Spain) as vice chairs. Annex C of this volume lists the members of the various PISA bodies, including Governing Board members and National Project Managers in participating countries and economies, the PISA Consortium, and the individual experts and consultants who have contributed to PISA in general.

Editorial

Successes and failures in the classroom will increasingly shape the fortunes of countries. And yet, more of the same education will only produce more of the same strengths and weaknesses. Today's students are growing up into a world hyperconnected by digitalisation; tomorrow, they'll be working in a labour market that is already being hollowed-out by automation. For those with the right knowledge and skills, these changes are liberating and exciting. But for those who are insufficiently prepared, they can mean a future of vulnerable and insecure work, and a life lived on the margins.

Schools need to prepare students for change that is more rapid than ever before, for jobs that have not yet been created, for societal challenges that we can't yet imagine, and for technologies that have not yet been invented. In today's schools, students typically learn individually, and at the end of the school year, we certify their individual achievements. But the more interdependent the world becomes, the more it needs great collaborators and orchestrators. Innovation is now rarely the product of individuals working in isolation; instead, it is an outcome of how we mobilise, share and integrate knowledge. These days, schools also need to become better at preparing students to live and work in a world in which most people will need to collaborate with people from different cultures, and appreciate a range of ideas and perspectives; a world in which people need to trust and collaborate with others despite those differences, often bridging space and time through technology; and a world in which individual lives will be affected by issues that transcend national boundaries.

We are born with what political scientist Robert Putnam calls "bonding social capital", a sense of belonging to our family or other people with shared experiences, cultural norms, common purposes or pursuits. But it requires deliberate and continuous effort to expand our radius of trust to strangers and institutions, to create the kind of bridging social capital through which we can share experiences, ideas and innovation, and build a shared understanding among groups with diverse backgrounds and interests. Societies that nurture bridging social capital and pluralism have always been more creative, as they can draw on and bring to bear the best talent from anywhere, build on multiple perspectives, and nurture creativity and innovation.

PISA has a long history of assessing students' problem-solving skills. A first assessment of cross-curricular problem-solving skills was undertaken in 2003; in 2012, PISA assessed creative problem-solving skills. The evolution of digital assessment technologies has now allowed PISA to carry out the world's first international assessment of collaborative problem-solving skills, defined as the capacity of students to solve problems by pooling their knowledge, skills and efforts with others.

As one would expect, students who have stronger science, reading or mathematics skills also tend to be better at collaborative problem solving because managing and interpreting information, and the ability to reason are always required to solve problems. The same holds across countries: top-performing countries in PISA, like Japan, Korea and Singapore in Asia, Estonia and Finland in Europe, and Canada in North America, also come out on top in the PISA assessment of collaborative problem solving.

But individual cognitive skills explain less than two-thirds of the variation in student performance on the PISA collaborative problem-solving scale, and a roughly similar share of the performance differences among countries on this measure is explained by the relative standing of countries on the 2012 PISA assessment of individual, creative problem-solving skills.

There are countries where students do much better in collaborative problem solving than what one would predict from their performance in the PISA science, reading and mathematics assessments. For example, Japanese students do very well in those subjects, but they do even better in collaborative problem solving. The same holds for students in Australia, Korea and New Zealand. Students in the United States also do much better in collaborative problem solving than one would expect from their average performance in reading and science, and their below-average performance in mathematics. By contrast, students in the four Chinese provinces that took part in PISA (Beijing, Shanghai, Jiangsu and Guangdong) do well in mathematics and science, but come out just average in collaborative problem solving. Likewise, in Lithuania, Montenegro, the Russian Federation, Tunisia, Turkey and the United Arab Emirates, students punch below their weight in collaborative problem solving. In a nutshell, while the absence of science, reading and mathematics skills does not imply the presence of social and emotional skills, social skills are not an automatic by-product of the development of academic skills either.

The results show that some countries do much better than others in developing students' collaborative problem-solving skills, but all countries need to make headway in preparing students for a much more demanding world. An average of only 8% of students can handle problem-solving tasks with fairly high collaboration complexity that require them to maintain awareness of group dynamics, take the initiative to overcome obstacles, and resolve disagreements and conflicts. Even in top-performer Singapore, just one in five students attains this level. Still, three-quarters of students show that they can contribute to a collaborative effort to solve a problem of medium difficulty and that they can consider different perspectives in their interactions.

Similarly, all countries need to make headway in reducing gender disparities. When PISA assessed individual problem-solving skills in 2012, boys scored higher in most countries. By contrast, in the 2015 assessment of collaborative problem solving, girls outperform boys in every country, both before and after considering their performance in science, reading and mathematics. The relative size of the gender gap in collaborative problem-solving performance is even larger than it is in reading.

These results are mirrored in students' attitudes towards collaboration. Girls reported more positive attitudes towards relationships, meaning that they tend to be more interested in others' opinions and want others to succeed. Boys, on the other hand, are more likely to see the instrumental benefits of teamwork and how collaboration can help them work more effectively and efficiently. As positive attitudes towards collaboration are linked with the collaboration-related component of performance in the PISA assessment, this opens up one avenue for intervention: even if the causal nature of the relationship is unclear, if schools foster boys' appreciation of others and their interpersonal friendships and relationships, then they might also see better outcomes among boys in collaborative problem solving. It is all very well for boys to understand that teamwork can bring benefits, but in order to work effectively in a team and achieve something in a collaborative fashion, boys must be able to listen to others and take their viewpoints into account. Only in this manner can teams make full use of the range of perspectives and experiences that team members offer.

Those attitudes do not just vary between the genders; they vary across countries too. Students in Portugal value relationships more so than students in other countries, and the picture is also positive in Costa Rica, Singapore and the United Arab Emirates. Students in these countries are especially likely to agree that they are good listeners, that they enjoy seeing their classmates be successful, that they take into account what others are interested in, and that they enjoy considering different perspectives. To some extent, that variation in attitudes might be shaped by cultural factors well beyond school walls; but policy makers should note that they are not written in stone.

There also seem to be factors in the classroom environment that relate to those attitudes. PISA asked students how often they engage in communication-intensive activities, such as explaining their ideas in science class; spending time in the laboratory doing practical experiments; arguing about science questions; and taking part in class debates about investigations. The results show a clear relationship between these activities and positive attitudes towards collaboration. On average, the valuing of relationships and teamwork is more prevalent among students who reported that they participate in these activities more often. For example, even after considering gender as well as students' and schools' socio-economic profile, students who reported that they explain their ideas in most or all science lessons were more likely to agree that they are "a good listener" (in 46 of 56 education systems) and students also agreed that they "enjoy considering different perspectives" (in 37 of 56 education systems). So there is much that teachers can do to facilitate a climate that is conducive to collaboration.

Many schools can also do better in fostering a learning climate where students develop a sense of belonging, and where they are free of fear. Students who reported more positive student-student interactions score higher in collaborative problem solving, even after considering the socio-economic profile of students and schools. Students who don't feel

threatened by other students also score higher in collaborative problem solving. In contrast, students who reported that their teachers say something insulting to them in front of others at least a few times per year score 23 points lower in collaborative problem solving than students who reported that this didn't happen to them during the previous year.

It is interesting that disadvantaged students see the value of teamwork often more clearly than their advantaged peers. They tend to report more often that teamwork improves their own efficiency, that they prefer working as part of a team to working alone, and that they think teams make better decisions than individuals. Schools that succeed in building on those attitudes by designing collaborative learning environments might be able to engage disadvantaged students in new ways.

The inter-relationships between social background, attitudes towards collaboration and performance in collaborative problem solving are even more interesting. The data show that exposure to diversity in the classroom tends to be associated with better collaboration skills. For example, in some countries students without an immigrant background perform better in the collaboration-specific aspects of the assessment when they attend schools with a larger proportion of immigrant students. So diversity and students' contact with those who are different from them and who may hold different points of view may aid in developing collaboration skills.

Finally, education does not end at the school gate when it comes to helping students develop their social skills. It is striking that only a quarter of the performance variation in collaborative problem-solving skills lies between schools, much less than is the case in the academic disciplines. For a start, parents need to play their part. For example, students score much higher in the collaborative problem-solving assessment when they reported that they had talked to their parents after school on the day prior to the PISA test, and also when their parents agreed that they are interested in their child's school activities or encourage them to be confident.

PISA also asked students what kinds of activities they pursue both before and after school. Some of these activities – using the Internet/chat/social networks; playing video games; meeting friends or talking to friends on the phone; and working in the household or taking care of family members – might have a social, or perhaps antisocial, component to them. The results show that students who play video games score much lower, on average, than students who do not play video games, and that gap remains significant even after considering social and economic factors as well as performance in science, reading and mathematics. At the same time, accessing the Internet, chatting or using social networks tend to be associated with better collaborative problem-solving performance, on average across OECD countries, all other things being equal.

In sum, in a world that places a growing premium on social skills, a lot more needs to be done to foster those skills far more systematically across the school curriculum. Strong academic skills will not automatically also lead to strong social skills. Part of the answer might lie in giving students more ownership over the time, place, path, pace and interactions of their learning. Another part of the answer can lie in fostering more positive relationships at school and designing learning environments that benefit students' collaborative problem-solving skills and their attitudes towards collaboration. Schools can identify those students who are socially isolated, organise social activities to foster constructive relationships and school attachment, provide teacher training on classroom management, and adopt a whole-of-school approach to prevent and address bullying. But part of the answer lies with parents and society at large. It takes collaboration across a community to develop better skills for better lives.

Andreas Schleicher

Andreas Schleicher
Director for Education and Skills

Table of contents

BOXES

FIGURES

TABLES

Executive summary

Today's workplaces demand people who can solve problems in concert with others. But collaboration poses potential challenges to team members. Labour might not be divided equitably or efficiently, with team members perhaps working on tasks they are unsuited for or dislike. Conflict may arise among team members, hindering the development of creative solutions. Thus, collaboration is a skill in itself.

There have been few attempts to assess how well students collaborate with one another. With its first ever assessment of collaborative problem solving, PISA 2015 addresses the lack of internationally comparable data in this field, allowing countries and economies to see where their students stand in relation to students in other education systems. Some 52 countries and economies participated in the collaborative problem-solving assessment (32 OECD countries and 20 partner countries and economies).

WHAT THE DATA TELL US

Student performance in collaborative problem solving

- Students in Singapore score higher in collaborative problem solving than students in all other participating countries and economies, followed by students in Japan.
- On average across OECD countries, 28% of students are able to solve only straightforward collaborative problems, if any at all. By contrast, fewer than one in six students in Estonia, Hong Kong (China), Japan, Korea, Macao (China) and Singapore is a low achiever in collaborative problem solving.
- Across OECD countries, 8% of students are top performers in collaborative problem solving, meaning that they can maintain an awareness of group dynamics, ensure team members act in accordance with their agreed-upon roles, and resolve disagreements and conflicts while identifying efficient pathways and monitoring progress towards a solution.
- Collaborative problem-solving performance is positively related to performance in the core PISA subjects (science, reading and mathematics), but the relationship is weaker than that observed among those other domains.
- Students in Australia, Japan, Korea, New Zealand and the United States perform much better in collaborative problem solving than would be expected based on their scores in science, reading and mathematics.

Student demographics and collaborative problem solving

- Girls perform significantly better than boys in collaborative problem solving in every country and economy that participated in the assessment. On average across OECD countries, girls score 29 points higher than boys. The largest gaps – of over 40 points – are observed in Australia, Finland, Latvia, New Zealand and Sweden; the smallest gaps – of less than 10 points – are observed in Colombia, Costa Rica and Peru. This contrasts with the PISA 2012 assessment of individual problem solving, where boys generally performed better than girls.
- Performance in collaborative problem solving is positively related to students' and schools' socio-economic profile, although this relationship is weaker than the relationship between socio-economic profile and performance in the three core PISA subjects.

There are no significant performance differences between advantaged and disadvantaged students, or between immigrant and non-immigrant students, after accounting for performance in science, reading and mathematics. But girls still score 25 points higher than boys after accounting for performance in the three core PISA subjects.

Students' attitudes towards collaboration

- Students in every country and economy have generally positive attitudes towards collaboration. Over 85% of students, on average across OECD countries, agree with the statements "I am a good listener", "I enjoy seeing my classmates be successful", "I take into account what others are interested in", "I enjoy considering different perspectives", and "I enjoy co-operating with peers".
- Girls in almost every country and economy tend to value relationships more than boys, meaning that girls agree more often than boys that they are good listeners, enjoy seeing their classmates be successful, take into account what others are interested in and enjoy considering different perspectives.
- Boys in the majority of countries and economies tend to value teamwork more than girls, meaning that boys agree more often than girls that they prefer working as part of a team to working alone, find that teams make better decisions than individuals, find that teamwork raises their own efficiency and enjoy co-operating with peers.
- Advantaged students in almost every country and economy tend to value relationships more than disadvantaged students, while disadvantaged students in most countries and economies tend to value teamwork more than advantaged students.
- After accounting for performance in the three core PISA subjects, gender, and socio-economic status, the more students value relationships, the better they perform in collaborative problem solving. A similar relationship is observed the more that students value teamwork.

Student activities, school policies and collaboration

- Attitudes towards collaboration are generally more positive as students engage in more physical activity or attend more physical education classes per week.
- Students who play video games outside of school score slightly lower in collaborative problem solving than students who do not play video games, on average across OECD countries, after accounting for performance in the three core PISA subjects, gender, and students' and schools' socio-economic profile. But students who access the Internet, chat or social networks outside of school score slightly higher than other students.
- Students who work in the household or take care of other family members value both teamwork and relationships more than other students, as do students who meet friends or talk to friends on the phone outside of school.

Collaborative schools

- On average across OECD countries, students who reported not being threatened by other students score 18 points higher in collaborative problem solving than students who reported being threatened at least a few times per year. Students also score 11 points higher for every 10 percentage-point increase in the number of schoolmates who reported that they are not threatened by other students.
- Students score higher in collaborative problem solving when they or their schoolmates reported that teachers treat students fairly, even after accounting for their performance in science, reading and mathematics.

What PISA results imply for policy

Education systems could help students develop their collaboration skills. Physical education, for example, provides many natural opportunities to embed collaborative activities and to develop social skills and attitudes towards collaboration. Results also show that exposure to diversity in the classroom is associated with better collaboration skills.

This report also shows that fostering positive relationships at school can benefit students' collaborative problem-solving skills and their attitudes towards collaboration, especially when these relationships involve students directly. Schools can organise social activities to foster constructive relationships and school attachment, provide teacher training on classroom management, and adopt a whole-school approach to prevent and address school bullying. Parents can also make a difference, as collaboration begins at home.

Reader's guide

Data underlying the figures

The data referred to in this volume are presented in Annex B and, in greater detail, including some additional tables, on the PISA website (www.oecd.org/pisa).

Three symbols are used to denote missing data:

c There are too few observations or no observation to provide reliable estimates (i.e. there are fewer than 30 students or fewer than 5 schools with valid data).

m Data are not available. These data were not submitted by the country or were collected but subsequently removed from the publication for technical reasons.

w Data have been withdrawn or have not been collected at the request of the country concerned.

Country coverage

The PISA publications (PISA 2015 Results) feature data on 72 countries and economies, including all 35 OECD countries and 37 partner countries and economies (see Map of PISA countries and economies in "What is PISA?").

This volume in particular contains data on 57 countries and economies (including all 35 OECD countries and 22 partner countries and economies) that participated in the computer-based assessment, of which 52 participated in the collaborative problem-solving assessment (including 32 OECD countries and 20 partner countries and economies).

The statistical data for Israel are supplied by and under the responsibility of the relevant Israeli authorities. The use of such data by the OECD is without prejudice to the status of the Golan Heights, East Jerusalem and Israeli settlements in the West Bank under the terms of international law.

Two notes were added to the statistical data related to Cyprus:

Note by Turkey: The information in this document with reference to "Cyprus" relates to the southern part of the Island. There is no single authority representing both Turkish and Greek Cypriot people on the Island. Turkey recognises the Turkish Republic of Northern Cyprus (TRNC). Until a lasting and equitable solution is found within the context of the United Nations, Turkey shall preserve its position concerning the "Cyprus issue".

Note by all the European Union Member States of the OECD and the European Union: The Republic of Cyprus is recognised by all members of the United Nations with the exception of Turkey. The information in this document relates to the area under the effective control of the Government of the Republic of Cyprus.

B-S-J-G (China) refers to the four PISA-participating Chinese provinces of Beijing, Shanghai, Jiangsu and Guangdong.

For Malaysia, results based on students' or school principals' responses are reported in a selection of figures (see Annex A4).

International averages

The OECD average corresponds to the arithmetic mean of the respective country estimates. It was calculated for most indicators presented in this report.

In this publication, the OECD average is generally used when the focus is on comparing characteristics of education systems. In the case of some countries, data may not be available for specific indicators, or specific categories may not apply. Readers should, therefore, keep in mind that the term "OECD average" refers to the OECD countries included in the respective comparisons. In cases where data are not available or do not apply for all sub-categories of a given population or indicator, the "OECD average" may be consistent within each column of a table but not necessarily across all columns of a table.

In tables showing two OECD averages, a number label is used to indicate the number of countries included in the average:

OECD average-35: Arithmetic mean across all OECD countries.

OECD average-32: Arithmetic mean across OECD countries that participated in the collaborative problem-solving assessment.

OECD average-31: Arithmetic mean across OECD countries that participated in the ICT questionnaire.

OECD average-28: Arithmetic mean across OECD countries that participated in the ICT questionnaire and the collaborative problem-solving assessment.

OECD average-12: Arithmetic mean across OECD countries that participated in the parent questionnaire.

OECD average-11: Arithmetic mean across OECD countries that participated in the parent questionnaire and the collaborative problem-solving assessment.

Rounding figures

Because of rounding, some figures in tables may not add up exactly to the totals. Totals, differences and averages are always calculated on the basis of exact numbers and are rounded only after calculation.

All standard errors in this publication have been rounded to one or two decimal places. Where the value 0.0 or 0.00 is shown, this does not imply that the standard error is zero, but that it is smaller than 0.05 or 0.005, respectively.

Reporting student data

The report uses "15-year-olds" as shorthand for the PISA target population. PISA covers students who are aged between 15 years 3 months and 16 years 2 months at the time of assessment and who are enrolled in school and have completed at least 6 years of formal schooling, regardless of the type of institution in which they are enrolled, whether they are in full-time or part-time education, whether they attend academic or vocational programmes, and whether they attend public or private schools or foreign schools within the country.

Reporting school data

The principals of the schools in which students were assessed provided information on their schools' characteristics by completing a school questionnaire. Where responses from school principals are presented in this publication, they are weighted so that they are proportionate to the number of 15-year-olds enrolled in the school.

Focusing on statistically significant differences

This volume discusses only statistically significant differences or changes. These are denoted in darker colours in figures and in bold font in tables. See Annex A3 for further information.

Changes in the PISA methodology

Several changes were made to the PISA methodology in 2015:

- **Changes in scaling procedures** include:
  - Change from a one-parameter model to a hybrid model that applies both a one- and two-parameter model, as appropriate. The one-parameter (Rasch) model is retained for all items where the model is statistically appropriate; a more general 2-parameter model is used instead if the fit of the one-parameter model could not be established. This approach improves the fit of the model to the observed student responses and reduces model and measurement errors.
  - Change in the treatment of non-reached items to ensure that the treatment is consistent between the estimation of item parameters and the estimation of the population model to generate proficiency estimates in the form of plausible values. This avoids introducing systematic errors when generating performance estimates.
  - Change from cycle-specific scaling to multiple-cycle scaling in order to combine data, and retain and aggregate information about trend items used in previous cycles. This change results in consistent item parameters across cycles, which strengthen and support the inferences made about proficiencies on each scale.

- Change from including only a subsample for item calibration to including the total sample with weights, in order to fully use the available data and reduce the error in item-parameter estimates by increasing the sample size. This reduces the variability of item-parameter estimation due to the random selection of small calibration samples.
- Change from assigning internationally fixed item parameters and dropping a few suspect items per country, to assigning a few nationally unique item parameters for those items that show significant deviation from the international parameters. This retains a maximum set of internationally equivalent items without dropping data and, as a result, reduces overall measurement errors.

The overall impact of these changes on trend comparisons is quantified by the link errors. As in previous cycles, a major part of the linking error is due to re-estimated item parameters. While the magnitude of link errors is comparable to those estimated in previous rounds, the changes in scaling procedures will result in reduced link errors in future assessment rounds. For more information on the calculation of this quantity and how to use it in analyses, see Annex A5 from Volume I and the *PISA 2015 Technical Report* (OECD, 2017).

- **Changes in population coverage and response rates.** Even though PISA has consistently used the same standardised methods to collect comparable and representative samples, and population coverage and response rates were carefully reviewed during the adjudication process, slight changes in population coverage and response rates can affect point estimates of proficiency. The uncertainty around the point estimates due to sampling is quantified in sampling errors, which are the major part of standard errors reported for country mean estimates. For more information, see Annexes A2 and A4.
- **Change in test design** from 13 booklets in the paper-based design to 396 booklet instances. Despite the significant increase in the number of booklet types and instances from previous cycles, it is important to bear in mind that all items belonging to the same domain were delivered in consecutive clusters. No student had more than one hour of test questions related to one domain only. This is an improvement over the existing design, which was made possible by computer delivery. It strengthens the overall measurement of each domain and each respondent's proficiency.
- **Changes in test administration.** As in PISA 2000 (but different from other cycles up to 2012), students in 2015 had to take their break before starting to work on test clusters 3 and 4, and could not work for more than one hour on clusters 1 and 2. This reduces cluster position effects. Another change in test administration is that students who took the test on computers had to solve test questions in a fixed, sequential order, and could not go back to previous questions and revise their answers after reaching the end of the test booklets. This change prepares the ground for introducing adaptive testing in future rounds of PISA.

In sum, changes to the assessment design, the mode of delivery, the framework and the set of science items were carefully examined in order to ensure that the 2015 results can be presented as trend measures at the international level. The data show no consistent association between students' familiarity with ICT and with performance shifts between 2012 and 2015 across countries. Changes in scaling procedures are part of the link error, as they were in the past, where the link error quantified the changes introduced by re-estimating item parameters on a subset of countries and students who participated in each cycle. Changes due to sampling variability are quantified in the sampling error. The remaining changes (changes in test design and administration) are not fully reflected in estimates of the uncertainty of trend comparisons. These changes are a common feature of past PISA rounds as well, and are most likely of secondary importance when analysing trends.

The factors below are examples of potential effects that are relevant for the changes seen from one PISA round to the next. While these can be quantified and related to, for example, census data if available, these are outside of the control of the assessment programme:

- **Change in coverage of PISA target population.** PISA's target population is 15-year-old students enrolled in grade 7 or above. Some education systems saw a rapid expansion of 15-year-olds' access to school because of a reduction in dropout rates or in grade repetition. This is explained in detail, and countries' performance adjusted for this change is presented in Chapters 2, 4 and 5 in Volume I.

- **Change in demographic characteristics.** In some countries, there might be changes in the composition of the population of 15-year-old students. For example, there might be more students with an immigrant background.
- **Change in student competency.** The average proficiency of 15-year-old students in 2015 might be higher or lower than that in 2012 or earlier rounds.

Abbreviations used in this report

% dif.	Percentage-point difference	Index dif.	Index difference
Dif.	Difference	S.D.	Standard deviation
ESCS	PISA index of economic, social and cultural status	S.E.	Standard error
ICT	Information and communications technology	Score dif.	Score-point difference
ISCED	International Standard Classification of Education		

Definition of immigrant students in PISA

PISA classifies students into several categories according to their immigrant background and that of their parents:

Non-immigrant students are students whose mother or father (or both) was/were born in the country or economy where they sat the PISA test, regardless of whether the student himself or herself was born in that country or economy. In this chapter, these students are also referred to as **"students without an immigrant background"**.

Immigrant students are students whose mother and father were both born in a country/economy other than that where the student sat the PISA test. In this chapter, they are also referred to as **"students with an immigrant background"**. Among immigrant students, a distinction is made between those born in the country/economy of assessment and those born abroad:

- **First-generation immigrant students** are foreign-born students whose parents are also both foreign-born.
- **Second-generation immigrant students** are students born in the country/economy where they sat the PISA test and whose parents were both foreign-born.

In some analyses, these two groups of immigrant students are, for the purpose of comparison, considered along with non-immigrant students. In other cases, the outcomes of first- and second-generation immigrant students are examined separately. PISA also provides information on other factors related to students' immigrant background, including the main language spoken at home (i.e. whether students usually speak, at home, the language in which they were assessed in PISA or another language, which could also be an official language of the host country/economy) or, for first-generation immigrant students, the number of years since the student arrived in the country where he or she sat the PISA test.

Further documentation

For further information on the PISA assessment instruments and the methods used in PISA, see the *PISA 2015 Technical Report* (OECD, 2017).

This report uses the OECD StatLinks service. Below each table and chart is a URL leading to a corresponding Excel™ workbook containing the underlying data. These URLs are stable and will remain unchanged over time. In addition, readers of the e-books will be able to click directly on these links and the workbook will open in a separate window, if their internet browser is open and running.

What is PISA?

"What is important for citizens to know and be able to do?" In response to that question and to the need for internationally comparable evidence on student performance, the Organisation for Economic Co-operation and Development (OECD) launched the triennial survey of 15-year-old students around the world known as the Programme for International Student Assessment, or PISA. PISA assesses the extent to which 15-year-old students, near the end of their compulsory education, have acquired the key knowledge and skills that are essential for full participation in modern societies. The assessment focuses on the core school subjects of science, reading and mathematics. Students' proficiency in an innovative domain is also assessed (in 2015, this domain is collaborative problem solving). The assessment does not just ascertain whether students can reproduce knowledge; it also examines how well students can extrapolate from what they have learned and can apply that knowledge in unfamiliar settings, both in and outside of school. This approach reflects the fact that modern economies reward individuals not for what they know, but for what they can do with what they know.

PISA is an ongoing programme that offers insights for education policy and practice, and that helps monitor trends in students' acquisition of knowledge and skills across countries and in different demographic subgroups within each country. PISA results reveal what is possible in education by showing what students in the highest-performing and most rapidly improving education systems can do. The findings allow policy makers around the world to gauge the knowledge and skills of students in their own countries in comparison to those in other countries, set policy targets against measurable goals achieved by other education systems, and learn from policies and practices applied elsewhere. While PISA cannot identify cause-and-effect relationships between policies/practices and student outcomes, it can show educators, policy makers and the interested public how education systems are similar and different – and what that means for students.

WHAT IS UNIQUE ABOUT PISA?

PISA is different from other international assessments in its:

- **policy orientation**, which links data on student learning outcomes with data on students' backgrounds and attitudes towards learning, and on key factors that shape their learning, in and outside of school, in order to highlight differences in performance and identify the characteristics of students, schools and education systems that perform well
- **innovative concept of "literacy"**, which refers to students' capacity to apply knowledge and skills in key subjects, and to analyse, reason and communicate effectively as they identify, interpret and solve problems in a variety of situations
- **relevance to lifelong learning**, as PISA asks students to report on their motivation to learn, their beliefs about themselves, and their learning strategies
- **regularity**, which enables countries to monitor their progress in meeting key learning objectives
- **breadth of coverage**, which, in PISA 2015, encompasses all 35 OECD countries and 37 partner countries and economies.

Box A. PISA's contributions to the Sustainable Development Goals

The Sustainable Development Goals (SDGs) were adopted by the United Nations in September 2015. Goal 4 of the SDGs seeks to ensure "inclusive and equitable quality education and [to] promote lifelong learning opportunities for all". More specific targets and indicators spell out what countries need to deliver by 2030. Goal 4 differs from the Millennium Development Goals (MDGs) on education, which were in place between 2000 and 2015, in the following two ways:

- Goal 4 is truly global. The SDGs establish a universal agenda; they do not differentiate between rich and poor countries. Every single country is challenged to achieve the SDGs.
- Goal 4 puts the quality of education and learning outcomes front and centre. Access, participation and enrolment, which were the main focus of the MDG agenda, are still important, and the world is still far from providing equitable access to high-quality education for all. But participation in education is not an end in itself; what matters for people and economies are the skills acquired through education. It is the competence and character qualities that are developed through schooling, rather than the qualifications and credentials gained, that make people successful and resilient in their professional and personal lives. They are also key in determining individual well-being and the prosperity of societies.

In sum, Goal 4 requires education systems to monitor the actual learning outcomes of their young people. PISA, which already provides measurement tools to this end, is committed to improving, expanding and enriching its assessment tools. For example, PISA 2015 assesses the performance in science, reading and mathematics of 15-year-old students in more than 70 high- and middle-income countries. PISA offers a comparable and robust measure of progress so that all countries, regardless of their starting point, can clearly see where they are on the path towards the internationally agreed targets of quality and equity in education.

Through participation in PISA, countries can also build their capacity to develop relevant data. While most countries that have participated in PISA already have adequate systems in place, that isn't true for many low-income countries. To this end, the OECD PISA for Development initiative not only aims to expand the coverage of the international assessment to include more middle- and low-income countries, but it also offers these countries assistance in building their national assessment and data-collection systems. PISA is also expanding its assessment domains to include other skills relevant to Goal 4. In 2015, for example, PISA assesses 15-year-old students' ability to solve problems collaboratively.

Other OECD data, such as those derived from the Survey of Adult Skills (a product of the OECD Programme for the International Assessment of Adult Competencies [PIAAC]) and the OECD Teaching and Learning International Survey (TALIS), provide a solid evidence base for monitoring education systems. OECD analyses promote peer learning as countries can compare their experiences in implementing policies. Together, OECD indicators, statistics and analyses can be seen as a model of how progress towards the SDG education goal can be measured and reported.

Source: OECD (2016), *Education at a Glance 2016: OECD Indicators*, OECD Publishing, Paris, http://dx.doi.org/10.1787/eag-2016-en.

WHICH COUNTRIES AND ECONOMIES PARTICIPATE IN PISA?

PISA is now used as an assessment tool in many regions around the world. It was implemented in 43 countries and economies in the first assessment (32 in 2000 and 11 in 2002), 41 in the second assessment (2003), 57 in the third assessment (2006), 75 in the fourth assessment (65 in 2009 and 10 in 2010), and 65 in the fifth assessment. A total of 72 countries and economies participated in PISA 2015.

In addition to all OECD countries, the 2015 survey was conducted in:

- **East, South and Southeast Asia**: Beijing, Shanghai, Jiangsu and Guangdong (China), Hong Kong (China), Indonesia, Macao (China), Malaysia, Singapore, Chinese Taipei, Thailand and Viet Nam
- **Central, Mediterranean and Eastern Europe, and Central Asia**: Albania, Bulgaria, Croatia, Georgia, Kazakhstan, Kosovo, Lebanon, Lithuania, the former Yugoslav Republic of Macedonia, Malta, Moldova, Montenegro, Romania and the Russian Federation

- **The Middle East:** Jordan, Qatar and the United Arab Emirates
- **Central and South America:** Argentina, Brazil, Colombia, Costa Rica, Dominican Republic, Peru, Puerto Rico, Trinidad and Tobago, Uruguay
- **Africa:** Algeria and Tunisia.

Map of PISA countries and economies

OECD countries

Australia	Korea
Austria	Latvia
Belgium	Luxembourg
Canada	Mexico
Chile	The Netherlands
Czech Republic	New Zealand
Denmark	Norway
Estonia	Poland
Finland	Portugal
France	Slovak Republic
Germany	Slovenia
Greece	Spain
Hungary	Sweden
Iceland	Switzerland
Ireland	Turkey
Israel	United Kingdom
Italy	United States
Japan	

Partner countries and economies in PISA 2015

Albania	Lithuania
Algeria	Macao (China)
Argentina	Malaysia
Brazil	Malta
B-S-J-G (China)*	Moldova
Bulgaria	Montenegro
Colombia	Peru
Costa Rica	Qatar
Croatia	Romania
Cyprus[1]	Russian Federation
Dominican Republic	Singapore
Former Yugoslav Republic of Macedonia	Chinese Taipei
Georgia	Thailand
Hong Kong (China)	Trinidad and Tobago
Indonesia	Tunisia
Jordan	United Arab Emirates
Kazakhstan	Uruguay
Kosovo	Viet Nam
Lebanon	

Partner countries and economies in previous cycles

- Azerbaijan
- Himachal Pradesh-India
- Kyrgyzstan
- Liechtenstein
- Mauritius
- Miranda-Venezuela
- Panama
- Serbia
- Tamil Nadu-India

* B-S-J-G (China) refers to the four PISA participating Chinese provinces: Beijing, Shanghai, Jiangsu, Guangdong.

1. Note by Turkey: The information in this document with reference to « Cyprus » relates to the southern part of the Island. There is no single authority representing both Turkish and Greek Cypriot people on the Island. Turkey recognises the Turkish Republic of Northern Cyprus (TRNC). Until a lasting and equitable solution is found within the context of the United Nations, Turkey shall preserve its position concerning the "Cyprus issue".

Note by all the European Union Member States of the OECD and the European Union: The Republic of Cyprus is recognised by all members of the United Nations with the exception of Turkey. The information in this document relates to the area under the effective control of the Government of the Republic of Cyprus.

WHAT DOES THE TEST MEASURE?

In each round of PISA, one of the core domains is tested in detail, taking up nearly two-thirds of the total testing time. The major domain in 2015 was science, as it was in 2006. Reading was the major domain in 2000 and 2009, and mathematics was the major domain in 2003 and 2012. With this alternating schedule of major domains, a thorough analysis of achievement in each of the three core areas is presented every nine years; an analysis of trends is offered every three years.

The *PISA 2015 Assessment and Analytical Framework* (OECD, 2017a) presents definitions and more detailed descriptions of the domains assessed in PISA 2015:

- **Science literacy** is defined as the ability to engage with science-related issues, and with the ideas of science, as a reflective citizen. A scientifically literate person is willing to engage in reasoned discourse about science and technology, which requires the competencies to explain phenomena scientifically, evaluate and design scientific enquiry, and interpret data and evidence scientifically.
- **Reading literacy** is defined as students' ability to understand, use, reflect on and engage with written texts in order to achieve one's goals, develop one's knowledge and potential, and participate in society.
- **Mathematical literacy** is defined as students' capacity to formulate, employ and interpret mathematics in a variety of contexts. It includes reasoning mathematically and using mathematical concepts, procedures, facts and tools to describe, explain and predict phenomena. It assists individuals in recognising the role that mathematics plays in the world and to make the well-founded judgements and decisions needed by constructive, engaged and reflective citizens.
- **Financial literacy** is defined as the knowledge and understanding of financial concepts and risks, and the skills, motivation and confidence to apply such knowledge and understanding in order to make effective decisions across a range of financial contexts, to improve the financial well-being of individuals and society, and to enable participation in economic life.
- **Collaborative problem-solving literacy** is defined as the capacity of an individual to effectively engage in a process whereby two or more agents attempt to solve a problem by sharing the understanding and effort required to come to a solution and pooling their knowledge, skills and efforts to reach that solution.

Box B. Key features of PISA 2015

The content

- The PISA 2015 survey focused on science, with reading, mathematics and collaborative problem solving as minor areas of assessment. PISA 2015 also included an assessment of young people's financial literacy, which was optional for countries and economies.

The students

- Approximately 540 000 students completed the assessment in 2015, representing about 29 million 15-year-olds in the schools of the 72 participating countries and economies.

The assessment

- Computer-based tests were used, with assessments lasting a total of two hours for each student.
- Test items were a mixture of multiple-choice questions and questions requiring students to construct their own responses. The items were organised in groups based on a passage setting out a real-life situation. About 810 minutes of test items for science, reading, mathematics and collaborative problem solving were created, with different students taking different combinations of test items.
- Students also answered a background questionnaire, which took 35 minutes to complete. The questionnaire sought information about the students themselves, their homes, and their school and learning experiences. School principals completed a questionnaire that covered the school system and the learning environment. For additional information, some countries/economies decided to distribute a questionnaire to teachers. It was the first time that this optional teacher questionnaire was offered to PISA-participating countries/economies. In some countries/economies, optional questionnaires were distributed to parents, who were asked to provide information on their perceptions of and involvement in their child's school, their support for learning in the home, and their child's career expectations, particularly in science. Countries could choose two other optional questionnaires for students: one asked students about their familiarity with and use of information and communication technologies (ICT); and the second sought information about students' education to date, including any interruptions in their schooling, and whether and how they are preparing for a future career.

HOW IS THE ASSESSMENT CONDUCTED?

For the first time, PISA 2015 delivered the assessment of all subjects via computer. Paper-based assessments were provided

for countries that chose not to test their students by computer, but the paper-based assessment was limited to questions that could measure trends in science, reading and mathematics performance.[1] New questions were developed for the computer-based assessment only. A field trial was used to study the effect of the change in how the assessment was delivered. Data were collected and analysed to establish equivalence between the computer- and paper-based assessments.

The 2015 computer-based assessment was designed as a two-hour test. Each test form allocated to students comprised four 30-minute clusters of test material. This test design included six clusters from each of the domains of science, reading and mathematics to measure trends. For the major subject of science, an additional six clusters of items were developed to reflect the new features of the 2015 framework. In addition, three clusters of collaborative problem-solving items were developed for the countries that decided to participate in that assessment.[2] There were 66 different test forms. Students spent one hour on the science assessment (one cluster each of trends and new science items) plus one hour on one or two other subjects – reading, mathematics or collaborative problem solving. For the countries/economies that chose not to participate in the collaborative problem-solving assessment, 36 test forms were prepared.

Countries that chose paper-based delivery for the main survey measured student performance with 30 pencil-and-paper forms containing trend items from two of the three core PISA domains.

Each test form was completed by a sufficient number of students, allowing for estimations of proficiency on all items by students in each country/economy and in relevant subgroups within a country/economy (such as boys and girls, and students from different social and economic backgrounds).

The assessment of financial literacy was offered as an option in PISA 2015 based on the same framework as the one developed for PISA 2012.[3] The financial literacy assessment lasted one hour and comprised two clusters distributed to a subsample of students in combination with the science, reading and mathematics assessments.

To gather contextual information, PISA 2015 asked students and the principal of their school to respond to questionnaires. The student questionnaire took about 35 minutes to complete; the questionnaire for principals took about 45 minutes to complete. The responses to the questionnaires were analysed with the assessment results to provide both a broader and more nuanced picture of student, school and system performance. The *PISA 2015 Assessment and Analytical Framework* (OECD, 2017a) presents the questionnaire framework in detail. The questionnaires from all assessments since PISA's inception are available on the PISA website: www.oecd.org/pisa/.

The questionnaires seek information about:

- students and their family backgrounds, including their economic, social and cultural capital
- aspects of students' lives, such as their attitudes towards learning, their habits and life in and outside of school, and their family environment
- aspects of schools, such as the quality of their human and material resources, public and private management and funding, decision-making processes, staffing practices, and the school's curricular emphasis and extracurricular activities offered
- context of instruction, including institutional structures and types, class size, classroom and school climate, and science activities in class
- aspects of learning, including students' interest, motivation and engagement.

Four additional questionnaires were offered as options:

- **a computer familiarity questionnaire**, focusing on the availability and use of information and communications technology (ICT) and on students' ability to carry out computer tasks and their attitudes towards computer use
- **an educational career questionnaire**, which collects additional information on interruptions in schooling, on preparation for students' future careers, and on support for language learning
- **a parent questionnaire**, focusing on parents' perceptions of and involvement in their child's school, their support for learning at home, school choice, their child's career expectations, and their background (immigrant/non-immigrant)
- **a teacher questionnaire**, new to PISA in 2015, that will help establish the context for students' test results. Additionally, a parallel questionnaire in this cycle asked science teachers to describe their teaching practices, focusing on teacher-directed teaching and learning activities in science lessons, and on a selected set of enquiry-based activities. The teacher questionnaire given to science teachers also asked about the content of the school's science curriculum and how it is communicated to parents.

The contextual information collected through the student, school and optional questionnaires is complemented by system-level data. Indicators describing the general structure of education systems, such as expenditure on education, stratification, assessments and examinations, appraisals of teachers and school leaders, instruction time, teachers' salaries, actual teaching time and teacher training are routinely developed and produced by the OECD (e.g. in the annual OECD publication, Education at a Glance). These data are extracted from *Education at a Glance 2016* (OECD, 2016), *Education at a Glance 2015* (OECD, 2015) and Education at a Glance 2014 (OECD, 2014) for the countries that participate in the annual OECD data collection that is administered through the INES Network. For other countries and economies, a special system-level data collection was conducted in collaboration with PISA Governing Board members and National Project Managers.

WHO ARE THE PISA STUDENTS?

Differences between countries in the nature and extent of pre-primary education and care, in the age of entry into formal schooling, in the structure of the education system, and in the prevalence of grade repetition mean that school grade levels are often not good indicators of where students are in their cognitive development. To better compare student performance internationally, PISA targets students of a specific age. PISA students are aged between 15 years 3 months and 16 years 2 months at the time of the assessment, and have completed at least 6 years of formal schooling. They can be enrolled in any type of institution, participate in full-time or part-time education, in academic or vocational programmes, and attend public or private schools or foreign schools within the country. (For an operational definition of this target population, see Annex A2.) Using this age across countries and over time allows PISA to compare consistently the knowledge and skills of individuals born in the same year who are still in school at age 15, despite the diversity of their education histories in and outside of school.

The population of PISA-participating students is defined by strict technical standards, as are the students who are excluded from participating (see Annex A2). The overall exclusion rate within a country was required to be below 5% to ensure that, under reasonable assumptions, any distortions in national mean scores would remain within plus or minus 5 score points, i.e. typically within the order of magnitude of 2 standard errors of sampling. Exclusion could take place either through the schools that participated or the students who participated within schools (see Annex A2, Tables A2.1 and A2.2).

There are several reasons why a school or a student could be excluded from PISA. Schools might be excluded because they are situated in remote regions and are inaccessible, because they are very small, or because of organisational or operational factors that precluded participation. Students might be excluded because of intellectual disability or limited proficiency in the language of the assessment.

In 30 out of the 72 countries and economies that participated in PISA 2015, the percentage of school-level exclusions amounted to less than 1%; it was 4.1% or less in all countries and economies. When the exclusion of students who met the internationally established exclusion criteria is also taken into account, the exclusion rates increase slightly. However, the overall exclusion rate remains below 2% in 29 participating countries and economies, below 5% in 60 participating countries, and below 7% in all countries except the United Kingdom, Luxembourg (both 8.2%) and Canada (7.5%). In 13 out of the 35 OECD countries, the percentage of school-level exclusions amounted to less than 1% and was less than 3% in 30 OECD countries. When student exclusions within schools are also taken into account, there were 7 OECD countries below 2% and 25 OECD countries below 5%. For more detailed information about school and student exclusion from PISA 2015, see Annex A2.

WHAT KINDS OF RESULTS DOES PISA PROVIDE?

Combined with the information gathered through the tests and the various questionnaires, the PISA assessment provides three main types of outcomes:

- basic indicators that provide a baseline profile of the knowledge and skills of students
- indicators derived from the questionnaires that show how such skills relate to various demographic, social, economic and education variables
- indicators on trends that show changes in outcomes and distributions, and in relationships between student-level, school-level, and system-level background variables and outcomes over time.

WHERE CAN YOU FIND THE RESULTS?

This is the last of five volumes that present the results from PISA 2015. It describes and contextualises the results of the 2015 collaborative problem-solving assessment. The volume begins by explaining how PISA assessed collaborative problem solving. It then provides an international comparison of student performance in collaborative problem solving and examines how various demographic factors are related to performance. Attitudes towards collaboration are then covered, followed by an analysis of student activities and school practices that are related to performance in and attitudes towards collaboration. The volume concludes with a discussion of whether collaborative environments at school, at home, and within the community are related to skills in and attitudes towards collaboration.

The other four volumes cover the following issues:

- *Volume I: Excellence and Equity in Education* provides a detailed examination of student performance in science and describes how performance has changed over previous PISA assessments. It also explores students' engagement with and attitudes towards science, including their expectations of working in a science-related career later on. An overview of student performance in reading and mathematics in 2015 is also provided, along with a description of how performance in those subjects has evolved over previous PISA assessments. The volume defines and discusses equity in education, focusing particularly on how socio-economic status and an immigrant background are related to students' performance in PISA and to their attitudes towards science.
- *Volume II: Policies and Practices for Successful Schools* examines how student performance is associated with various characteristics of individual schools and concerned school systems. The volume first focuses on science, describing the school resources devoted to science and how science is taught in schools. It discusses how both of these are related to student performance in science, students' epistemic beliefs, and students' expectations of pursuing a career in science. Then, the volume analyses schools and school systems and their relationship with education outcomes more generally, covering the learning environment in school, school governance, the selection and grouping of students, and the human, financial, educational and time resources allocated to education. Trends in these indicators between 2006 and 2015 are examined when comparable data are available.
- *Volume III: Students' Well-Being* describes how well adolescent students are learning and living. This volume analyses a broad set of indicators that, collectively, paint a picture of 15-year-old students' home and school environments, the way students communicate with family and friends, how and how often they use the Internet, their physical activities and eating habits, their aspirations for future education, their motivation for school work, and their overall satisfaction with life.
- *Volume IV: Students' Financial Literacy* examines 15-year-old students' understanding about money matters in the 15 countries and economies that participated in this optional assessment. The volume explores how the financial literacy of 15-year-old students is associated with their competencies in science, reading and mathematics, with their socio-economic status, and with their previous experiences with money. The volume also offers an overview of financial education in schools in the participating countries and economies, and provides case studies.

Volumes I and II were published in December 2016. Volume III was published in April 2017 and Volume IV was published in May 2017.

The frameworks for assessing science, reading, mathematics, financial literacy and collaborative problem solving in 2015 are described in the *PISA 2015 Assessment and Analytical Framework* (OECD, 2017a).

Technical annexes at the end of this volume describe how questionnaire indices were constructed, and discuss sampling issues, quality-assurance procedures, the reliability of coding, and the process followed for developing the assessment instruments. Many of the issues covered in the technical annexes are elaborated in greater detail in the *PISA 2015 Technical Report* (OECD, 2017b).

A selection of data tables referred to in the analyses is included at the end of the respective volume in Annex B1, and a set of additional data tables is available on line (www.oecd.org/pisa/). A Reader's Guide is also provided in each volume to aid in interpreting the tables and figures that accompany the report. Data from regions within the participating countries are included in Annex B2.

Notes

1.The paper-based form was used in 15 countries/economies including Albania, Algeria, Argentina, the former Yugoslav Republic of Macedonia, Georgia, Indonesia, Jordan, Kazakhstan, Kosovo, Lebanon, Malta, Moldova, Romania, Trinidad and Tobago, and Viet Nam, as well as in Puerto Rico, an unincorporated territory of the United States.

2. The collaborative problem-solving assessment was not conducted in the countries/economies that delivered the PISA 2015 assessment on paper, nor was it conducted in the Dominican Republic, Ireland, Poland, Qatar and Switzerland.

3. The financial literacy assessment was conducted in Australia, Belgium (Flemish Community only), Beijging, Shanghai, Jiangsu, Guangdong (China), Brazil, seven Canadian provinces, Chile, Italy, Lithuania, the Netherlands, Peru, Poland, the Russian Federation, the Slovak Republic, Spain and the United States.

References

OECD (2017a), *PISA 2015 Assessment and Analytical Framework: Science, Reading, Mathematic, Financial Literacy and Collaborative Problem Solving,* revised edition, PISA, OECD Publishing, Paris, http://dx.doi.org/10.1787/9789264281820-en.

OECD (2017b), *PISA 2015 Technical Report,* OECD Publishing, Paris.

OECD (2016), *Education at a Glance 2016: OECD Indicators,* OECD Publishing, Paris, http://dx.doi.org/10.1787/eag-2016-en.

OECD (2015), *Education at a Glance 2015: OECD Indicators,* OECD Publishing, Paris, http://dx.doi.org/10.1787/eag-2015-en.

OECD (2014), *Education at a Glance 2014: OECD Indicators,* OECD Publishing, Paris, http://dx.doi.org/10.1787/eag-2014-en.

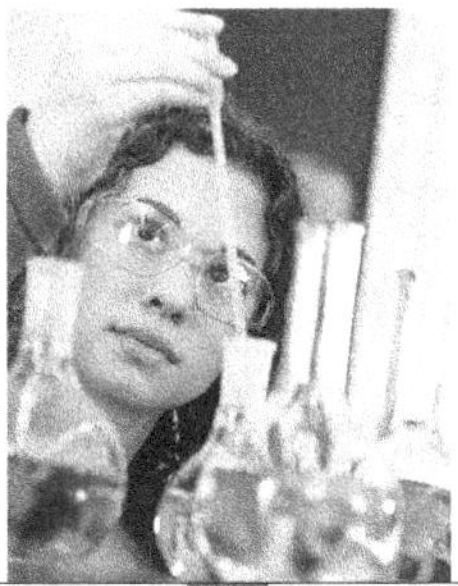

1

Overview: Collaborative problem solving

Today's workplaces demand people who can solve problems in concert with others. The increase in jobs requiring a high level of social skills has been accompanied by an increase in the wages for such jobs, suggesting that there is higher demand from employers for such skills instead of simply a surplus of workers who hold such skills. For example, wages have risen by over 20% for jobs that require high social skills but low mathematics skills, suggesting that social skills are increasingly of value to employers.

The importance of collaboration extends beyond the workplace. Many human activities involve groups of people, from a variety of physical and artistic endeavours to living in harmony with one's neighbours. Almost everyone relies on interactions with other individuals to do what he or she cannot do alone. Collaboration skills are essential to facilitating such interactions.

Collaborative problem solving has several advantages over individual problem solving: labour can be divided among team members; a variety of knowledge, perspectives and experiences can be applied to solve the problem; and team members can stimulate each other, leading to enhanced creativity and a higher quality of the solution. But collaboration also poses potential challenges to team members. Labour might not be divided equitably or efficiently, with team members perhaps working on tasks they are unsuited for or dislike. Conflict may also arise among team members, hindering the development of creative solutions. Collaboration is thus a skill in itself.

Yet in most countries and economies, collaboration is not explicitly taught in schools; rather, it is acquired through the teaching of other subjects. For example, students are often asked to perform group work in traditional academic subjects, and are also given chances to interact with one another in a variety of other contexts in other activities and classes, such as physical education class, music class, or extracurricular sports teams.

There have been few attempts to assess how well students collaborate with one another. Hence, PISA 2015 decided to assess 15-year-old students' ability to collaborate in order to solve problems. By doing so, PISA aims to address the lack of internationally comparable data in this field, allowing countries and economies to see, for the first time, where their students stand in relation to students in other education systems. Some 52 countries and economies participated in the collaborative problem-solving assessment (32 OECD countries and 20 partner countries and economies). The data were adjudicated in and results are presented for 51 of these countries and economies.

PISA 2015 defines collaborative problem-solving competency as the capacity of an individual to effectively engage in a process whereby two or more agents attempt to solve a problem by sharing the understanding and effort required to come to a solution and pooling their knowledge, skills and efforts to reach that solution. In the PISA assessment, one agent is the student whose performance is being evaluated; all other agents are computerised simulations. This allows the assessment to control the behaviour of the other agents in order to isolate the collaborative problem-solving ability of the student being evaluated. Had the student been in a group with other students, his or her performance would have depended on the ability of the other students and the pre-existing relationships between them.

All questions in the assessment were either multiple choice or involved moving icons into the appropriate slot; there were no free-response questions. Since it was an interactive assessment, students were required to respond to each question before moving onto the next and could not skip or omit questions. Collaboration was assessed through students' responses in their interactions with computer-based agents.

PISA summarises 15-year-olds' performance in collaborative problem solving on a single performance scale. Since collaborative problem solving was a new domain in PISA 2015, the OECD average performance was set at 500 score points and the standard deviation across OECD countries at 100 score points. This established the benchmark against which each country's collaborative problem-solving performance was compared.

Singapore outperforms all other participating countries in collaborative problem solving.

Singapore is the highest-performing country in collaborative problem solving, with a mean score of 561 points. The second highest-performing country is Japan, with a mean score of 552 points. Both of these countries score over half of a standard deviation, on average, above the OECD average score. Singapore scores significantly higher than every other country/economy, and Japan scores significantly higher than every other country/economy except Singapore.

Thirteen other OECD countries – Korea (538 points), Canada (535 points), Estonia (535 points), Finland (534 points), New Zealand (533 points), Australia (531 points), Germany (525 points), the United States (520 points), Denmark (520 points), the United Kingdom (519 points), the Netherlands (518 points), Sweden (510 points) and Austria (509 points) – and three East Asian partner countries and economies – Hong Kong (China) (541 points), Macao (China) (534 points) and Chinese Taipei (527 points) – score above the OECD average on the PISA collaborative problem-solving scale.

A gap of 129 score points separates the highest-scoring OECD country, Japan (552 score points), and the lowest-scoring OECD country, Turkey (422 score points), a difference of well over one standard deviation. Likewise, 180 score points separate the mean scores of the highest- and lowest-performing countries and economies in the collaborative problem-solving assessment – Singapore (561 score points) and Tunisia (382 score points). This gap corresponds to almost two standard deviations or two proficiency levels (Figure V.3.3 and Table V.3.2).

Across OECD countries, 8% of students are top performers in collaborative problem solving, but 6% of students do not even attain Level 1 proficiency.

To help interpret what students' scores mean in substantive terms, the scale is divided into five proficiency levels. Four of these (Levels 1 to 4, with Level 1 as the lowest level and Level 4 as the highest) are described based on the skills needed to successfully complete the items that are located within them; the last (below Level 1) is defined based on the absence of these skills.

Students proficient at Level 4 on the collaborative problem-solving scale can successfully carry out complicated problem-solving tasks with high collaboration complexity. They maintain an awareness of group dynamics and ensure that team members act in accordance with their agreed-upon roles, while simultaneously monitoring progress towards a solution of the given problem. They take initiative and perform actions or make requests to overcome obstacles and to resolve disagreements and conflicts. Students who perform at Level 4 are also referred to as "top performers" in the rest of this report.

Across OECD countries, 8% of students perform at this level. More than one in five students in Singapore (21%) and between 15% and 16% of students in Australia, Canada and New Zealand perform at this level. These four countries are also among the top-performing countries and economies in collaborative problem solving. By contrast, in two OECD countries and in seven partner countries, fewer than one in 100 students performs at Level 4; and in Tunisia, fewer than one in 1 000 students performs at this level (Figure V.3.6 and Table V.3.1).

Students proficient at Level 3 on the collaborative problem-solving scale can complete tasks with either complex problem-solving requirements or complex collaboration demands. They can recognise the information needed to solve a problem, request it from the appropriate team member, and identify when the provided information is incorrect. These students can perform multi-step tasks that require integrating multiple pieces of information.

Across OECD countries, 36% of students are proficient at Level 3 or higher. Level 3 was the most common proficiency level in 10 of the 51 countries/economies with adjudicated data from the collaborative problem-solving assessment (Figure V.3.6 and Table V.3.1).

Students proficient at Level 2 on the collaborative problem-solving scale can contribute to a collaborative effort to solve a problem of medium difficulty. They can communicate with team members about the actions to be performed and they can volunteer information not specifically requested by another team member.

Across OECD countries, 72% of students perform at Level 2 or higher. This is the most common proficiency level in 28 of the 51 countries and economies with comparable data. However, in two OECD countries and eight partner countries, a majority of students cannot complete Level 2 items successfully (Figure V.3.6 and Table V.3.1).

Students proficient at Level 1 can complete tasks with low problem difficulty and limited collaboration complexity. They tend to focus on their individual role within the group, but with support from team members, these students can help find a solution to a simple problem.

Across OECD countries, 94% of students reach this level of collaborative problem-solving proficiency. However, in Tunisia, almost one in four students (25%) fails to reach this level of proficiency. More than one in five students in Brazil (21%) and more than one in six students in Montenegro and Peru (both 18%) are likewise not proficient at Level 1. Level 1 is the most common proficiency level in 13 of the 51 countries/economies with available data (Figure V.3.6 and Table V.3.1).

The PISA 2015 collaborative problem-solving assessment was not designed to assess either elementary collaboration skills or elementary problem-solving skills. Hence, there were insufficient items to fully describe performance that fell below Level 1 on the collaborative problem-solving scale. Across OECD countries, 6% of students score below Level 1 on the proficiency scale (Figure V.3.6 and Table V.3.1).

Performance in collaborative problem solving is strongly related to performance in the core PISA subjects of science, reading and mathematics.

A comparison of the mean scores in collaborative problem solving, science, reading and mathematics shows that the same countries/economies – Canada, Hong Kong (China), Japan, Korea and Singapore – are found at the top of each set of rankings. Indeed, scores in the four domains are highly correlated. On average across OECD countries, student performance in collaborative problem solving shows a correlation of 0.77 with performance in science, 0.74 with performance in reading, and 0.70 with performance in mathematics. These numbers are lower – and thus the correlations are slightly weaker – than the pairwise correlations between scores in the core PISA subjects, which range from 0.80 to 0.88 (Figure V.3.7). The link between student scores in collaborative problem solving, science, reading and mathematics is strongest in Bulgaria, the United Arab Emirates and the United States and weakest in Costa Rica, the Russian Federation (hereafter "Russia") and Tunisia. In these latter three countries, however, correlations between performance in collaborative problem solving and performance in each of the three core PISA subjects still exceed 0.55 (Table V.3.4).

Top/low performers in the core PISA subjects also tend to be top/low performers in collaborative problem solving.

Another way to see the relationship is by looking at the extent to which top or low performance in the three core PISA domains predicts performance in collaborative problem solving. In science, reading and mathematics, top performers are defined as those students who perform at Level 5 or 6, while low performers are those students who perform below the baseline proficiency level, Level 2. In collaborative problem solving, top performers are defined as those students who perform at Level 4, while low performers are those students who perform below Level 2.

Some 44% of top performers in science, 39% of top performers in reading, and 34% of top performers in mathematics are also top performers in collaborative problem solving, on average across OECD countries (Table V.3.3a). Some 55% of students who are top performers in all three core PISA subjects (all-round top performers) are also top performers in collaborative problem solving (Figure V.3.8). This proportion is particularly large in Australia, Canada, New Zealand, Singapore, the United Kingdom and the United States, where over 69% of students who are all-round top performers are also top performers in collaborative problem solving. It may be that the development of collaborative problem-solving skills in these countries is more strongly linked to the development of science, reading and mathematics literacy; in other words, the development of cognitive and social skills in these countries takes place simultaneously.

By contrast, in Brazil and Chile, fewer than one in three all-round top performers score at the highest level in collaborative problem solving. This may imply that collaborative problem-solving skills in these countries are developed independently of skills and literacy in the three core PISA subjects. However, the share of top performers in these countries is very small: 0.6% in Brazil and 1.2% in Chile.

Similar relationships are observed among low performers. On average across OECD countries, 74% of low performers in science, 74% of low performers in reading, and 67% of low performers in mathematics are also low performers in collaborative problem solving. Some 83% of low performers in all three core subjects (all-round low performers) are also low performers in collaborative problem solving. Hence, it may be that a certain level of functional literacy in the three core domains is a pre-requisite for performance in collaborative problem solving (Figure V.3.8).

In Bulgaria, Montenegro, Tunisia, Turkey and the United Arab Emirates, over 93% of students who are all-round low performers are also low performers in collaborative problem solving. By contrast, in Germany, Japan and Korea, less than 75% of all-round low performers are low performers in collaborative problem solving. This is likely due to the particularly low scores of low performers in the former group of countries: the average student who is an all-round low performer in Tunisia scores lower in these domains than the average student who is an all-round low performer in Japan. Another interpretation is that that collaborative problem-solving skills might be more "fundamental", that is, developed in all students, regardless of ability, in the latter three countries, while they might be more dependent on basic literacy skills in the former five countries.

Most of the variation in student performance is observed within schools.

There is considerable variation in collaborative problem-solving performance within each country/economy, most of which is observed within schools. On average across OECD countries, the variation in student performance that is observed within schools amounts to 75% of the OECD average variation in student performance. The remaining variation (24%) is due to differences in student performance between schools (Table V.4.1a).

The variation in collaborative problem-solving performance between schools can be partly attributed to differences in the composition of schools and in the school policies and practices that may develop or foster student performance in collaborative problem solving.

Collaborative problem-solving performance is closely correlated to performance in the three core PISA subjects. Many school and neighbourhood factors foster the development of collaboration and problem-solving skills, just as they create the conditions for any type of learning. Differences in student performance in science, reading and mathematics accounted for 62% of the variation in student performance in collaborative problem solving, on average across OECD countries. In other words, on average, 38% of the differences in how students perform in the collaborative problem-solving assessment is unique to collaborative problem solving (Table V.4.1b).

At the same time, a larger fraction of the within-school differences in collaborative problem-solving performance (46% on average across OECD countries) cannot be accounted for by differences in performance in the core PISA subjects (Table V.4.1b). This suggests that differences in the experiences, personalities and opportunities among students attending the same school are the most likely explanations for the remaining differences in performance in collaborative problem solving, after performance in science, reading and mathematics has been accounted for.

Girls significantly outperform boys in every country and economy that participated in the collaborative problem-solving assessment.

Girls outperform boys in collaborative problem solving by 29 score points (515 points compared with 486 points, on average across OECD countries). Indeed, in every country/economy that participated in the collaborative problem-solving assessment, girls significantly outperform boys. The differences are greatest in Australia, Finland, Latvia, New Zealand and Sweden, where girls score over 40 points higher than boys, on average. Girls outperform boys by less than 10 points in Colombia, Costa Rica and Peru, but these differences are still statistically significant (Figure V.4.3).

On average across OECD countries, girls are 1.6 times more likely than boys to be top performers (Level 4) in collaborative problem solving, while boys are 1.6 times more likely than girls to be low achievers (below Level 2). The difference is even starker when examining students who score below Level 1: boys are 2.2 times more likely to score at this level than girls. In no country or economy are boys more likely than girls to be top performers, and in every country or economy are boys more likely than girls to be low performers (Table V.4.2).

After accounting for performance in the three core PISA subjects, girls still outperform boys in collaborative problem solving by 25 score points, on average across OECD countries, and this performance gap is significant and in favour of girls in every country and economy that participated in the assessment (Table V.4.3b).

These findings contrast with the gender differences observed in individual problem solving as discussed in *PISA 2012 Results: Creative Problem Solving* (OECD, 2014). In that assessment, boys scored 7 points higher than girls in individual problem solving, on average across OECD countries, and were 1.5 times more likely than girls to be top performers. Although different groups of students were measured in 2012 and 2015 and the assessments are not directly comparable to one another, the results suggest that it is the collaborative component of the PISA 2015 collaborative problem-solving assessment that favours girls.

The relationship between socio-economic status and performance is weaker in collaborative problem solving than in the three core PISA subjects.

Unsurprisingly, socio-economic status – as measured in PISA by the PISA index of economic, social and cultural status (ESCS) – relates positively to performance in problem solving, as it does to performance in all domains assessed in PISA. But the relationship between socio-economic status and performance differs across domains.

In general, the percentage of the variation in performance explained by socio-economic disparities at both the student and school levels is similar for science (the average across the OECD countries that participated in the collaborative problem-solving assessment is 23%), reading (22%) and mathematics (23%). But this relationship is weaker in collaborative problem solving than in the three other domains (Figure V.4.7). Still, even in collaborative problem solving, about 15% of the variation in performance can be explained by differences in socio-economic status. A higher position on the PISA index of economic, social and cultural status might be associated with greater academic enrichment opportunities, leading to disparities in performance in the cognitive domains. But opportunities to collaborate and co-operate arise in all social and economic contexts, which could reduce the extent to which socio-economic status is related to performance in collaborative problem solving.

The relationship between collaborative problem-solving performance and socio-economic status is positive in almost every country/economy that participated in the assessment; but the score-point improvement associated with a one-point increase in the PISA index of economic, social and cultural status is smaller in collaborative problem solving than in science, reading and mathematics. A one-point increase in students' socio-economic status is associated with a 13-point improvement in collaborative problem-solving performance, compared to between 17 and 19 points in the three core PISA subjects. A one-point increase in schools' socio-economic profile is associated with a 59-point improvement in collaborative problem-solving performance compared to an improvement of between 66 and 73 points in the three core PISA subjects (Table V.4.13e and Figure V.4.8).

Immigrant students tend to score lower in collaborative problem solving than students without an immigrant background.

In many countries and economies, children of immigrants are more at risk of low performance in academic subjects than the children of parents who were born in the country or economy. A gap in collaborative problem-solving performance between immigrant and non-immigrant students is also observed: on average across OECD countries, the children of immigrants score 36 points lower than non-immigrant students. However, in Macao (China), Singapore and the United Arab Emirates, immigrant students score better than non-immigrant students in collaborative problem solving (Table V.4.14a). The largest gaps in performance among countries where at least 6.25% of students are immigrants are observed in Denmark, where immigrant students score more than 60 points lower than students without an immigrant background, and in Austria, Belgium, France and Sweden, where immigrant students score between 50 and 60 points lower.

Performance differences related to immigrant background are no longer observed after accounting for performance in the three core PISA subjects.

A majority of 15-year-olds in almost all PISA-participating countries and economies reported positive attitudes towards co-operating with others.

The PISA 2015 student questionnaire asked students whether they strongly agree, agree, disagree, or strongly disagree with eight statements related to their attitudes towards collaboration:

- I prefer working as part of a team to working alone.
- I am a good listener.
- I enjoy seeing my classmates be successful.
- I take into account what others are interested in.
- I find that teams make better decisions than individuals.
- I enjoy considering different perspectives.
- I find that teamwork raises my own efficiency.
- I enjoy co-operating with peers.

In almost all OECD and partner countries and economies, the majority of students reported that they either agree or strongly agree with these statements. In fact, there are only two exceptions: only 48% of students in Turkey and 44% of students in Montenegro reported that they agree or strongly agree with the statement "I prefer working as part of a team to working alone".

Responses to these eight statements are combined into two indices of co-operation that reflect the valuing of relationships and teamwork (Figure V.5.3). Each index is standardised to have a mean of 0 and a standard deviation of 1 across OECD countries.

Students in Portugal have the highest index of valuing relationships (0.37) among all OECD and partner countries and economies, followed by Costa Rica, the United Arab Emirates and Singapore, all three of which have average indices of valuing relationships greater than 0.30 (Figure V.5.4). Students in these countries are especially likely to agree that they are good listeners, that they enjoy seeing their classmates be successful, that they take into account what others are interested in and that they enjoy considering different perspectives.

Students in Portugal also have the highest index of valuing teamwork (0.32) among OECD countries; however, the average student in the Dominican Republic has an index of valuing teamwork of 0.51 – over half a standard deviation above

the average student in OECD countries. These students are those who most prefer working as part of a team to working alone, who find that teams make better decisions than individuals, who find that teamwork raises their own efficiency and who enjoy co-operating with peers.

On average across OECD countries, the correlation between the indices of valuing relationships and teamwork is 0.41 (Table V.5.12). Countries with a high mean value on one index also tend to have a high mean value of the other index.

Girls and boys differ in what they value when it comes to collaborating with others.

Girls were significantly more likely than boys to agree or strongly agree with the four statements that comprise the index of valuing relationships. For example, on average across OECD countries, girls were 5.3 percentage points more likely than boys to report that they agree or strongly agree that "[they] are a good listener" (Figure V.5.5). Moreover, this difference is significant and in favour of girls in 54 of 56 countries; in the two other countries, the difference is not significant. Gender differences are most pronounced in Italy and Latvia, where there is a 10 percentage-point gap (Table V.5.4a).

By contrast, boys were significantly more likely than girls to report that they agree or strongly agree with the four statements that comprise the index of valuing teamwork (Figure V.5.5). The difference is most pronounced for the statement "I prefer working as part of a team to working alone", with which boys were 5.1 percentage points more likely than girls to agree or strongly agree. This difference is significant and in favour of boys in 38 of 56 countries; it is significant and in favour of girls in only one country: Beijing-Shanghai-Jiangsu-Guangdong (China) (hereafter "B-S-J-G [China]") (a 4.1 percentage-point gap). The gender gap is widest in Canada, Iceland and Sweden, where it exceeds 10 percentage points (Table V.5.4b).

Socio-economic status is associated with differences in students' attitudes towards collaboration.

There are significant differences related to socio-economic status in the propensity to agree or strongly agree with each statement. Advantaged students were 6.1 percentage points more likely than disadvantaged students to report that they agree or strongly agree with the statement "I take into account what others are interested in"; 5.7 percentage points more likely to agree or strongly agree with the statement "I enjoy considering different perspectives"; 4.8 percentage points more likely to agree or strongly agree with the statement "I am a good listener"; and 1.4 percentage points more likely to agree with the statement "I enjoy seeing my classmates be successful" (Figure V.5.6). These four statements comprise the index of valuing relationships.

By contrast, disadvantaged students were 7.5 percentage points more likely than advantaged students to agree or strongly agree with the statement "I find that teamwork raises my own efficiency"; 5.5 percentage points more likely to agree or strongly agree with the statement "I prefer working as part of a team to working alone"; 5.2 percentage points more likely to agree or strongly agree with the statement "I find that teams make better decisions than individuals"; and 1.0 percentage points more likely to agree or strongly agree with the statement "I enjoy co-operating with peers". These four statements comprise the index of valuing teamwork.

The data indicate that advantaged students were more likely to report that they agree or strongly agree that they engage in co-operative activities that do not directly involve personal gain, while disadvantaged students were more likely to report that they agree or strongly agree that teamwork brings benefits. A similar dichotomy is observed between girls and boys.

The relationships between students' attitudes towards collaboration and their performance in collaborative problem solving are remarkably consistent across countries.

Are students who have more positive attitudes towards collaboration also better able to solve problems collaboratively? Within-country differences in student performance related to self-reported attitudes towards collaboration are remarkably consistent across countries and economies (Figure V.5.8 and Tables V.5.2a to V.5.2h). On average across OECD countries, students who reported that they agree or strongly agree with the statements that comprise the index of valuing relationships score better than those who reported that they disagree or strongly disagree with those statements. The performance gap varies from 38 points for the statement "I take into account what others are interested in" to 26 points for "I enjoy seeing my classmates be successful."

By contrast, students who reported that they agree or strongly agree with the statements comprising the index of valuing teamwork score below students who reported that they disagree or strongly disagree with those statements, on average across OECD countries. For example, the performance gap related to the statement "I find that teamwork raises my own efficiency" is 22 points, while the gap related to the statement "I prefer working as part of a team to working alone" is 17 points.

But other patterns are observed after accounting for performance in the three core PISA subjects (science, reading and mathematics). There is a positive association between agreeing or strongly agreeing with any of the items related to attitudes towards collaboration – both the items that comprise the index of valuing relationships and those that comprise the index of valuing teamwork – and relative performance in collaborative problem solving (Figure V.5.8).[1] These positive associations persist after accounting for gender, and students' and schools' socio-economic profile. On average across OECD countries, students who agree or strongly agree with the statements in the index of valuing relationships perform between five and eight points higher in collaborative problem solving after accounting for performance in the three core PSIA subjects, gender, and students' and schools' socio-economic profile, while they perform between two and five points higher if they agree or strongly agree with the statements in the index of valuing teamwork.

Hence, it appears that positive attitudes towards collaboration – whether for altruistic reasons or for the benefit of one's own success in a collaborative project – are associated with the distinctively collaborative aspects of solving problems collaboratively. Students who perform at lower levels of proficiency are more likely to recognise the effectiveness of collaboration. However, a positive disposition towards collaboration, even if it is for the benefits to oneself that collaboration can bring, is still associated with better performance in collaborative problem solving when comparing students with similar performance in science, reading and mathematics.

Participation in physical activities has a limited relationship with students' ability to collaborate with others.

Many studies have tried to discover a link between participation in sports and academic performance, with inconclusive results. PISA 2015 asked students to report the number of days during which they engaged in moderate physical activity (such as walking, climbing stairs or riding a bike to school) for at least 60 minutes per day, or vigorous physical activity (such as running, cycling, aerobics, soccer and skating) for at least 20 minutes per day during the week before the PISA assessment. PISA also asked students how often, on average, they attend physical education classes each week during the school year.

Students who engage in moderate physical activity two or more days per week score higher in the collaborative problem-solving assessment than students who engage in such activity fewer than two days per week (Figure V.6.1 and Table V.6.1a). Students who attend one or two days of physical education class per week score highest in collaborative problem solving (Figure V.6.2, Tables V.6.1c and V.6.2c). These students score around 20 points higher than students who do not attend any physical education class, on average across OECD countries. However, students who participate in four days of physical education class per week score at least 31 points lower in collaborative problem solving than those who take part in one or two classes per week, and 10 points lower than those who do not take part in any physical education class.

After accounting for performance in science, reading and mathematics, there are few significant differences in performance on the collaborative problem-solving assessment related to the number of days in an average week during which a student engages in moderate physical activity (Table V.6.3a). However, additional days of vigorous physical activity beyond two days per week are associated with successively lower relative performance scores in collaborative problem solving (after accounting for performance in the three core PISA subjects) (Table V.6.3b).

Most differences in relative performance associated with the number of days that a student attends physical education class per week are not significant across OECD countries. The greatest differences are found among students who attend four or five days of physical education class per week, who score over five points lower in collaborative problem solving than students who attend fewer days of physical education class per week, but who have similar scores in science, reading and mathematics (Table V.6.3c). In other words, students' collaboration-specific skills are observed to decrease above a certain threshold of vigorous physical activity or attendance in physical education classes.

How students spend their time before and after school can be related to their performance in collaborative problem solving.

PISA 2015 asked students whether they participated in a variety of activities both before and after school on the most recent school day prior to sitting the PISA assessment. Several of these activities might have a social – or perhaps antisocial – component to them: using the Internet/chat/social networks; playing video games; meeting friends or talking to friends on the phone; and working in the household or taking care of family members.

Students who play video games score, on average, 32 points lower than students who do not play video games; and students who talk to their friends on the phone or meet their friends score 23 points below students who do not.

In no country or economy do students who played video games, or who met their friends or talked to them on the phone on the last school day prior to the PISA assessment score significantly better than those who did not engage in those activities (Figure V.6.5, Tables V.6.7b and V.6.7c).

This gap remains significant after accounting for performance in science, reading and mathematics. The relative score of students who play video games outside of school is 15 points below that of students who do not play video games, on average across OECD countries; after also accounting for gender and students' and schools' socio-economic profile, the gap is still significant but only 4 score points wide (Figure V.6.5, Table V.6.7b).

By contrast, accessing the Internet, chat or a social network was associated with a seven score-point improvement in collaborative problem-solving performance, on average across OECD countries (Figure V.6.5). This relationship in favour of students who accessed these forms of communication was observed in 23 out of 51 countries/economies. This performance gap exceeds 35 score points in Brazil, Colombia and Norway (Table V.6.7a).

After accounting for performance in science, reading and mathematics, gender, and students' and schools' socio-economic profile, a significant gap of six score points in collaborative problem-solving performance is still observed across OECD countries in favour of students who had accessed the Internet, chat, or social networks outside of school (Figure V.6.5). Thisgap is significant and in favour of students who had accessed such media in 13 of 51 participating countries and economies, and is over 15 points wide in the Czech Republic and Germany. By contrast, the performance gap is significant and in favour of students who had not accessed such media only in the United States, where it is 10 score points wide (Table V.6.7a).

Students interacted with computer agents in a virtual interface in this assessment, a process that is more akin to using electronic forms of communication than talking to friends on the telephone or seeing them outside of school. Students who use the Internet, chat or social media outside of school might therefore have an advantage in the assessment.

Student truancy appears more related to students' attitudes towards being and working with others, in general, than to their collaboration-specific skills.

On average across OECD countries, students who had skipped a whole day of school in the two weeks prior to the PISA test score 39 points below those who had not skipped a whole day of school in collaborative problem solving (Table V.6.9a). The difference is particularly stark in B-S-J-G (China), Japan, Korea, Slovenia and Chinese Taipei, where it exceeds 65 score points. In no country/economy do students who had skipped a whole day of school during that period perform better on the collaborative problem-solving assessment than students who had not.

The significant relationships related to truancy and lateness vanish after accounting for student performance in science, reading and mathematics, gender, and students' and schools' socio-economic profile: there is no longer any difference in collaborative problem-solving performance between students who had and those who had not skipped a whole day of school, skipped some classes or arrived late for school. It therefore appears that there is no association between student truancy and lateness, and the distinctively collaborative aspects of collaborative problem solving. This may lend support to the hypothesis that students choose to play truant from school because of factors related to their academic performance and how they view school itself, as opposed to their ability to collaborate with classmates.

Students who play truant or arrive late for school are also less likely to have positive attitudes towards collaboration. On average across OECD countries, students who had skipped at least one day of school or had skipped some classes in the two weeks prior to sitting the PISA assessment have significantly lower values on both the index of valuing relationships and the index of valuing teamwork. Students who had arrived late for school have a lower index of valuing relationships, but there is no difference observed in the index of valuing teamwork. After accounting for gender, and students' and schools' socio-economic profile, students who play truant or arrive late for school have lower indices of both valuing relationships and valuing teamwork (Figure V.6.7).

The largest gaps in attitudes towards collaboration are seen when considering the statements that are included in the index of valuing relationships, which are closely related to valuing others' opinions and success. It thus appears that there is a particularly strong relationship between the decision to play truant and the extent to which a student values friendships and interpersonal relationships.

Students who had not played truant or who had not arrived late for school had lower indices of valuing relationships and teamwork when they attended schools where more of their classmates were truant or late for school, after accounting for gender, and students' and schools' socio-economic profile (Tables V.6.11a-c).

Attendance at pre-primary school is associated with more positive attitudes towards collaboration later on.

Some 95% of 15-year-old students, on average across OECD countries, had attended some form of pre-primary school. Results from the PISA 2015 collaborative problem-solving assessment and student questionnaire show that students who had attended pre-primary school score 29 points higher than students who had not attended pre-primary school. A significant difference is observed in 21 of the 47 countries for which data are available (Table V.6.12a). In no country or economy is the gap significant in favour of students who had not attended pre-primary school.

On average across OECD countries, there is no significant relationship between attendance at pre-primary school and the distinctive aspects of collaborative problem solving, indicating that the performance gap described above reflects the relationship between collaborative problem-solving performance and performance in science, reading and mathematics. Attendance at pre-primary school has no discernible effect on the unique aspects of collaborative problem solving (or what one would attribute to collaboration skills as opposed to general academic proficiency) ten years later. In fact, after accounting for performance in the three core PISA subjects, a significant advantage in collaborative problem-solving performance among students who had attended pre-primary school is observed only in Norway (11 score points) and Russia (12 score points), while a significant disadvantage among students who had attended pre-primary school is found in the United States (11 score points) (Figure V.6.8).

On average across OECD countries and after accounting for gender, and students' and schools' socio-economic profile, students who had attended pre-primary school have significantly higher values on the indices of enjoying and valuing co-operation and were more likely to agree or strongly agree with all of the items that comprise these two indices. Students who had attended pre-primary school were between two and five percentage points more likely than those who had not attended to agree or strongly agree with each of the statements that are related to attitudes towards collaboration, after accounting for gender, and students' and schools' socio-economic profile. For instance, they were 4.7 percentage points more likely to agree that they "prefer working as part of a team to working alone", a gap that widens to over 15 percentage points in the Czech Republic and France. They were also 4.0 percentage points more likely to agree that they "take into account what others are interested in", a gap that grows to over 10 percentage points in the Czech Republic, Germany and Luxembourg (Table V.6.13).

Thus, attendance at pre-primary school is positively correlated with positive attitudes towards collaboration, and while attendance at pre-primary school is also positively correlated with performance in collaborative problem solving, this relationship disappears once performance in science, reading and mathematics is accounted for. These results provide some support to the idea that pre-primary schools develop socialisation skills and positive attitudes towards co-operating with others that can have a lasting impact.

Students who are regularly asked to discuss their work in class tend to have more positive attitudes towards collaboration.

The PISA 2015 student questionnaire asked students about how often certain activities occur during science class. Four of these activities were identified as being communication-intensive: explaining one's ideas in science class; spending time in the laboratory doing practical experiments; arguing about science questions; and taking part in class debates about investigations.

Significant relationships between these activities and attitudes towards collaboration are observed both on average across OECD countries and in many other countries and economies. On average across OECD countries, the indices of valuing relationships and teamwork are higher among students who reported that they participate in these activities in most or all lessons than among those who reported that they participate in these activities in only some lessons or never/hardly ever.

Students who are given opportunities to explain their ideas in most or all lessons were two to six percentage points more likely to agree or strongly agree with each of the statements regarding attitudes towards collaboration. This difference is observed in most countries and economies. For example, after accounting for gender, and students' and schools' socio-economic profile, in 46 of the 56 countries and economies that administered the student questionnaire on computer, students who reported that they explain their ideas in most or all science lessons were more likely to agree that they are "a good listener"; in 37 out of 56 countries and economies, these students also agreed that they "enjoy considering different perspectives" (Tables V.6.15a-d).

Figure V.1.1 ■ Snapshot of performance in collaborative problem solving and attitudes towards collaboration

Countries/economies with a mean performance/relative performance **above** the OECD average
Countries/economies with a mean performance/relative performance not significantly different from the OECD average
Countries/economies with a mean performance/relative performance **below** the OECD average

	Collaborative problem solving						
	All students	Relative performance[1]	Boys	Girls	Gender difference (boys - girls)	Index of valuing relationships	Index of valuing teamwork
	Mean score	Score dif.	Mean score	Mean score	Score dif.	Mean index	Mean index
OECD average-32	**500**	**3**	**486**	**515**	**-29**	**0.01**	**0.00**
Singapore	561	16	552	572	**-20**	0.32	0.27
Japan	552	23	539	565	**-26**	-0.22	-0.03
Hong Kong (China)	541	15	523	559	**-36**	-0.04	0.05
Korea	538	20	522	556	**-33**	-0.02	0.14
Canada	535	10	516	555	**-39**	0.11	0.00
Estonia	535	8	522	549	**-27**	0.03	-0.10
Finland	534	7	511	559	**-48**	-0.08	-0.22
Macao (China)	534	11	515	553	**-38**	-0.15	0.01
New Zealand	533	20	513	553	**-41**	0.01	0.07
Australia	531	23	511	552	**-41**	0.09	0.01
Chinese Taipei	527	5	513	541	**-28**	0.22	0.37
Germany	525	14	510	540	**-30**	0.15	0.14
United States	520	22	507	533	**-26**	0.13	0.06
Denmark	520	14	509	530	**-21**	0.01	-0.12
United Kingdom	519	12	503	536	**-34**	-0.04	-0.04
Netherlands	518	8	504	531	**-27**	-0.18	-0.26
Sweden	510	9	489	531	**-42**	0.05	-0.19
Austria	509	13	498	521	**-24**	0.24	0.19
Norway	502	-5	487	518	**-30**	0.11	-0.23
Slovenia	502	-10	484	521	**-36**	-0.04	0.02
Belgium	501	-4	489	514	**-25**	-0.06	-0.11
Iceland	499	15	485	512	**-27**	-0.09	-0.20
Czech Republic	499	3	486	512	**-26**	-0.20	0.00
Portugal	498	-5	489	507	**-19**	0.37	0.32
Spain	496	-1	485	508	**-22**	0.19	0.15
B-S-J-G (China)	496	-17	486	508	**-22**	0.01	0.39
France	494	-7	480	508	**-29**	-0.07	0.11
Luxembourg	491	2	478	504	**-25**	0.03	0.00
Latvia	485	-9	465	505	**-40**	-0.30	-0.14
Italy	478	-11	466	489	**-23**	-0.14	0.02
Russia	473	-22	460	486	**-25**	-0.25	-0.18
Croatia	473	-12	459	486	**-27**	0.01	0.21
Hungary	472	-10	459	485	**-26**	-0.03	-0.02
Israel	469	-11	459	481	**-22**	0.24	-0.03
Lithuania	467	-15	453	482	**-29**	0.16	0.33
Slovak Republic	463	-7	448	478	**-30**	-0.34	-0.12
Greece	459	-10	444	475	**-31**	0.03	0.18
Chile	457	-3	450	464	**-14**	0.08	0.21
Cyprus[2]	444	-6	424	464	**-40**	0.07	0.10
Bulgaria	444	-10	429	461	**-31**	-0.03	-0.07
Uruguay	443	-6	434	451	**-17**	0.11	0.20
Costa Rica	441	4	437	445	**-7**	0.35	0.34
Thailand	436	2	416	451	**-35**	0.10	0.37
United Arab Emirates	435	-14	416	454	**-38**	0.32	0.45
Mexico	433	-1	426	440	**-14**	0.16	0.23
Colombia	429	-4	425	433	**-8**	0.05	0.23
Turkey	422	-19	411	434	**-23**	0.00	-0.04
Peru	418	2	414	421	**-7**	-0.08	0.09
Montenegro	416	-18	403	429	**-26**	-0.05	-0.09
Brazil	412	-9	402	421	**-18**	-0.04	0.20
Tunisia	382	-18	375	387	**-12**	0.12	0.43
Ireland	m	m	m	m	m	0.03	0.04
Poland	m	m	m	m	m	-0.21	-0.06
Switzerland	m	m	m	m	m	0.19	0.22
Dominican Republic	m	m	m	m	m	0.27	0.51
Qatar	m	m	m	m	m	0.12	0.23

1. Relative scores are the residuals obtained from a pooled linear regression, across all participating countries/economies, of the performance in collaborative problem solving over performance in science, reading and mathematics.
2. Note by Turkey: The information in this document with reference to Cyprus relates to the southern part of the Island. There is no single authority representing both Turkish and Greek Cypriot people on the Island. Turkey recognises the Turkish Republic of Northern Cyprus (TRNC). Until a lasting and equitable solution is found within the context of the United Nations, Turkey shall preserve its position concerning the "Cyprus issue".
Note by all the European Union Member States of the OECD and the European Union: The Republic of Cyprus is recognised by all members of the United Nations with the exception of Turkey. The information in this document relates to the area under the effective control of the Government of the Republic of Cyprus.
Note: At the country/economy level, differences that are statistically significant are marked in bold (see Annex A3).
Countries and economies are ranked in descending order of the mean collaborative problem-solving score.
Source: OECD, PISA 2015 Database, Tables V.3.2, V.3.9a, V.4.3a and V.5.1.
StatLink http://dx.doi.org/10.1787/888933615724

Students who reported more positive relationships with other students score higher in collaborative problem solving.

The relationships that students establish with their schoolmates should be particularly relevant for the type of interpersonal skills evaluated in the collaborative problem-solving assessment. PISA asked students about their sense of belonging at school and about their experiences with bullying, and asked principals about the phenomena that hinder student learning. Students feel mostly positive about their relationships with their schoolmates. On average across OECD countries, about four in five students agreed that they seemed to be liked by other students and make friends easily at school; a slightly larger proportion disagreed that they feel lonely at school (Figure V.7.2). An even greater majority reported that they are never, or almost never, threatened or hit or pushed by other students.

Overall, students who reported more positive student-student interactions score higher in collaborative problem solving (Table V.7.3). On average across OECD countries, students who agreed that other students seem to like them score 9 points higher in collaborative problem solving, after accounting for students' and schools' socio-economic profile. Students also score considerably higher in collaborative problem solving when they reported that they are never, or almost never, threatened (18 points) or hit or pushed (14 points) by other students. In fact, in almost every school system, students who are not threatened by other students score higher in collaborative problem solving.

More positive student-student interactions at the school-level are always associated with better student performance, even those negatively related to collaborative problem solving performance at the student level. For instance, on average across OECD countries, for every 10 percentage-point increase in the number of schoolmates who reported that they are never, or almost never, hit or pushed by other students, student performance in collaborative problem solving increases by 11 score points.

After accounting for student performance in science, reading and mathematics – that is, among students who perform similarly in these core PISA subjects – students score higher in collaborative problem solving when they, or more of their schoolmates, reported that they are never, or almost never, threatened, hit or pushed by other students (Table V.7.4). Students also score higher when more of their schoolmates agreed that other students seem to like them, disagreed that they felt lonely at school, or reported that other students never, or almost never, make fun of them.

Parents' engagement with school, and students' relationships with their parents and teachers are all associated with performance in collaborative problem solving.

On average across the OECD countries that distributed the parent questionnaire, students score higher in collaborative problem solving, after accounting for the socio-economic profile of students and schools, when their parents socialise more with their children's school friends and their parents, and also when they feel comfortable talking to more school staff (Table V.7.13). In addition, students who reported that their teachers say something insulting to them in front of others at least a few times per year score 23 points lower in collaborative problem solving than students who reported that this never, or almost never, happened to them during the previous 12 months (Table V.7.18).

Most associations between the quality of student-teacher relationships and collaborative problem-solving scores disappear once scores in science, reading and mathematics are accounted for (Table V.7.19). This suggests that the quality of student-teacher relationships is as important for learning how to solve problems collaboratively as for acquiring knowledge and skills in science, reading and mathematics. However, when students, or their schoolmates, believe they have been treated unfairly, their relative performance in collaborative problem solving is significantly lower. For instance, in 25 out of 47 education systems, students who reported that their teachers never, or almost never, discipline them more harshly than other students score higher in collaborative problem solving, after accounting for their performance in the core PISA subjects, than students who reported they are disciplined more harshly at least a few times per year (Figure V.7.8).

On average across OECD countries, students score higher in collaborative problem solving when they, their parents, their schoolmates or their schoolmates' parents reported more positive student-parent relationships, after accounting for the socio-economic profile of students and schools (Table V.7.23). For instance, students score 19 points higher in the collaborative problem-solving assessment when they reported that they had talked to their parents after school on the day prior to the PISA test; and on average across the OECD countries that distributed the parent questionnaire, students score five points higher in collaborative problem solving when their parents strongly agreed that they are interested in their child's school activities or encourage them to be confident (Figure V.7.10 and Table V.7.23).

WHAT THE RESULTS MEAN FOR POLICY

Results from the PISA collaborative problem-solving assessment show that a very small proportion (9%) of the differences in students' performance, after accounting for performance in science, reading and mathematics, is observed between schools. This would seem to indicate that no matter which school parents send their children to, their children have the opportunity to develop strong collaboration skills. However, PISA data cannot discern whether this is because schools are more equitable in providing learning opportunities for collaborative skills, or whether collaboration skills are mainly developed outside schools.

Education systems can foster collaboration skills and attitudes in existing subjects or courses, or through new programmes, as Singapore did with its *Project Work* programme. The OECD is collecting information on how collaboration and co-operation are incorporated into school curricula through its *Education 2030* project.

Physical education, for example, is one subject that naturally provides many opportunities to embed collaboration activities and to develop social skills and attitudes towards collaboration. Collaboration is vital to many activities in physical education class, most obviously team sports.

Results also show that exposure to diversity in the classroom is associated with better collaboration skills. Students without an immigrant background perform better in the collaboration-specific aspects of the assessment when they attend schools with a larger proportion of immigrant students. Education systems could investigate whether, in their own context, diversity and students' contact with those who are different from them and who may hold different points of view can aid in developing collaboration skills.

This report also shows that fostering positive relationships at school can benefit students' collaborative problem-solving skills and their attitudes towards collaboration, especially when these relationships involve students directly. Students who establish more positive relationships with peers, teachers and parents tend to score higher in collaborative problem solving, and so do other students in the school. The good news is that most students, teachers and principals report a positive learning environment in their schools. However, too many students report that they feel isolated at school, are bullied repeatedly or are treated unfairly by teachers. Schools can identify those students who are socially isolated, organise social activities to foster constructive relationships and school attachment, provide teacher training on classroom management, and adopt a whole-school approach to prevent and address school bullying. Parents can also make a difference, as collaboration begins at home.

Note

1. Relative collaborative problem-solving performance is calculated by an ordinary least squares regression of collaborative problem-solving performance over performance in science, reading and mathematics. In Chapter 3, the regression is performed at the international level in order to rank countries and economies. In Chapters 4, 5, 6 and 7, the regression is performed at the individual country or economy level, as the focus is on factors related to differences in performance within each country/economy. This results in an average residual of 0 for each country/economy.

Reference

OECD (2014), *PISA 2012 Results: Creative Problem Solving: Students' Skills in Tackling Real-Life Problems (Volume V)*, PISA, OECD Publishing, Paris, http://dx.doi.org/10.1787/9789264208070-en.

2

What is collaborative problem solving?

This chapter introduces the PISA 2015 assessment of collaborative problem solving. It provides the rationale for assessing collaborative problem-solving competence in PISA and introduces the innovative features of the 2015 assessment, particularly in contrast to the individual problem-solving assessment of PISA 2012. The framework for the assessment is discussed and sample items are presented.

In the long history of humankind (and animal kind, too) those who learned to collaborate and improvise most effectively have prevailed.

Charles Darwin

Today's workplaces demand people who can solve non-routine problems – that was the rationale for assessing individual problem solving in PISA 2012. However, today's workplaces also demand people who can solve problems in concert and collaboration with others by combining their ideas and efforts. Collaborative problem solving has several advantages over individual problem solving: labour can be divided among team members; a variety of knowledge, perspectives and experiences can be applied to try to solve the problem; and team members can stimulate each other, leading to enhanced creativity and a higher quality of the solution.

However, collaboration also poses potential challenges to team members. Labour might not be divided equitably or efficiently, with team members perhaps working on tasks for which they are unsuited or that they dislike. Some group members may not contribute their fair share to the team, while others may prioritise their own goals over the team's goals. Conflict may arise between team members, hindering the development of creative solutions. Finally, team members might not effectively co-ordinate tasks, resulting in a loss of time and reduced productivity. The potential is rife for poor communication, unhappy and resentful team members, and an inefficient use of resources. Successful collaboration, therefore, requires a concerted and constructive effort from all parties and is a skill in itself.

There is an ever-increasing demand for collaboration skills in modern workplaces. In the 20th century, there was a high and increasing wage premium related to educational attainment: those with university degrees were paid more than those with only a high school diploma, and the difference in wages between these two groups increased over the latter half of the century (Autor, Levy and Murnane, 2003; Murnane, Willett and Levy, 1995). This was attributed to an increase in employer demand for those in service, sales-related, professional and managerial/administrator positions. The skills needed to succeed in these fields were, for much of the twentieth century, the cognitive skills associated with those one obtained through a university degree.

However, Autor, Levy and Murnane (2003) and Deming (2015) further found that the skills for which there was the greatest increase in demand in the last decades of the 20th century were non-routine analytical skills (i.e. those involved in problem solving) and, to an even larger extent, non-cognitive (or social) skills, including collaboration skills. By contrast, those skills for which demand decreased were routine manual and cognitive skills. Increasing automation is expected to further reduce the demand for such routine skills while simultaneously raising the demand for those complex skills that cannot be automated.

Deming (2015) also found that, in the United States, jobs requiring a high level of both mathematics and non-cognitive skills grew by 7.2 percentage points (as a share of the US labour force) between 1990 and 2012. Jobs requiring a low level of mathematics skills but a high level of social skills grew by 4.6 percentage points over the same period. However, jobs requiring a high level of mathematics skills but a low level of social skills – including many jobs in the fields of science, technology, engineering and mathematics (or STEM fields) – fell by 3.3 percentage points between 1990 and 2012.

The increase in the number of jobs requiring a high level of social skills has been accompanied by an increase in the wages for such jobs, suggesting that there is higher demand from employers for such skills instead of simply a surplus of workers who hold such skills. While hourly wages for jobs that require high mathematics proficiency but low social skills have increased by 5.9% between 1980 and 2012, they have increased by 26% for jobs that require both high mathematics proficiency *and* high social skills (Deming, 2015). Moreover, wages have risen by over 20% for jobs that require high social skills but low mathematics skills, suggesting that social skills are increasingly of value to employers.[1]

The importance of collaboration extends beyond the workplace. A great number of human activities take place in groups, from a variety of physical and artistic endeavours to living in harmony with one's neighbours. More generally, as John Donne said, "No man is an island": almost every human relies on interactions with other individuals to do what he or she cannot do for him or herself or do alone. These activities range from essential tasks like obtaining food, clothing or shelter, to organising large celebrations, to simply agreeing with one's friends and family as to where to go and what to do while on vacation. Collaboration skills are essential to facilitating such interactions.

Co-operation and collaboration are also important beyond the individual level. A variety of actors must collaborate to propose, pass and implement the laws that govern a country, and groups of interested people must work together to advocate for their ideas on a scale greater than what could be achieved by any individual in the group. For instance,

trade unions have relied on collaboration between its members to achieve higher pay, obtain better working conditions, and ensure more stringent health and safety standards. Likewise, restorative justice requires victims, offenders and society at large to collaborate and compromise in order to determine how an offender can best atone for his or her offense.

Many contemporary issues, such as trade, migration, climate change, intellectual property protection and the fight against tax avoidance and profit shifting, go beyond the local or national level and require co-operation between countries at the international level. For example, 196 countries signed the Paris Agreement regarding greenhouse gas emissions in 2015 as part of a concerted global effort to limit global warming, while the European Union gives its individual member countries a greater united voice in world affairs. Organisations including the OECD (which produces PISA), the G20, and the United Nations provide a space for countries to discuss and attempt to resolve global problems. Although it is ostensibly countries that collaborate in these situations, it is humans who negotiate each of these agreements and deals. "No man is an island" is also figuratively, if not literally, true for countries and other groups of humans.

TEACHING AND ASSESSING COLLABORATIVE PROBLEM-SOLVING SKILLS

Some education systems across the world are beginning to adapt their curricula and instruction to equip their students with collaboration skills (Griffin and Care, 2015; Hesse et al., 2015). One concrete example of such a pedagogical programme is Project Work, introduced for grade 11 students in Singapore in 2000 to "provide students with the opportunity to synthesise knowledge from various areas of learning, and critically and creatively apply it to real-life situations" (MOE, 2017).[2] Four learning outcomes were identified: knowledge application, communication, independent learning and collaboration. For the latter learning outcome, students "acquire collaborative skills through working in a team to achieve common goals".

However, in most countries and economies, collaboration is not a skill that is explicitly taught in schools but is rather acquired through the teaching of other subjects. For example, students are often asked to perform group work in traditional academic subjects (such as the three core PISA domains), and are also given chances to interact with one another in a variety of other contexts in other activities and classes, such as physical education class, music class, or extracurricular sports teams.

There have been few attempts to assess how well students collaborate with one another. This may be partly due to the lack of an obvious measure for how well one has collaborated. For example, in Singapore's Project Work, students are assessed in the learning outcomes of knowledge application (generating, developing and evaluating ideas and information in order to execute project tasks) and communication (presenting ideas clearly and coherently in both written and oral form). Collaboration and independent learning, which are skills developed and used on the way to completing their project tasks, are not assessed (MOE, 2017).

Hence, PISA 2015 decided to assess 15-year-old students' ability to collaborate in order to solve problems. By doing so, PISA aims to address the lack of internationally comparable data in this field, allowing countries and economies to see, for the first time, where their students stand in relation to students in other education systems in these skills. Within-country analyses will give policy makers the information they need to enable them to develop programmes to improve their students' collaboration and interpersonal skills. PISA thus seeks to address the lack of knowledge about which factors, policies and practices are related to the development of collaboration skills.

HOW PISA 2015 DEFINES COLLABORATIVE PROBLEM SOLVING

PISA 2015 defines collaborative problem-solving competency as:

> *the capacity of an individual to effectively engage in a process whereby two or more agents attempt to solve a problem by sharing the understanding and effort required to come to a solution and pooling their knowledge, skills and efforts to reach that solution.*

The PISA 2015 framework publication (OECD, 2017a) discusses the definition in full. Some of the key elements are discussed immediately below; other elements will be described in the following section on the more detailed framework of the assessment.

... the capacity of an individual ...

Collaboration necessarily requires the presence of at least two agents – after all, one cannot collaborate on his or her own. The success of the collaborative process can be evaluated at the collective level: How well did the group solve the problem? How well did group members work together? How well did the group manage conflict? Indeed, one of the advantages of collaboration is that the end result often exceeds the sum of each group member's individual contribution (Blaney et al., 1977; Laughlin et al., 2006; Schwartz, 1995), and such synergies can only be evaluated at the group level.

However, PISA measures individual competency and, in the context of collaborative problem solving, measures the ability of individuals to work in collaborative settings. Although the performance of an individual in collaborative problem solving depends on the group in which he/she finds himself/herself, he/she also has a certain baseline ability to collaborate with others. By varying, in a controlled manner, the characteristics of the group members with whom an individual collaborates, an overall assessment of the individual's collaborative problem-solving competency can be made.

... whereby two or more agents ...

As mentioned above, collaboration always involves the interaction of two or more agents working together. These agents must be theoretically capable of performing all of the actions involved in collaborative problem solving, such as communicating, reacting to others' actions and statements, advancing the task at hand, and managing group organisation.

The agents may be humans or computerised simulations of humans. In the PISA assessment, one agent is the student whose performance is being evaluated; all other agents are computerised simulations. This allows the assessment to control the behaviour of the other agents in order to isolate the collaborative problem-solving ability of the student being evaluated (Graesser et al., 2018; Kreijns, Kirschner and Jochems, 2003; Rosen and Rimor, 2009). Had the student been in a group with other students, his or her performance would have depended on the ability of the other students and the pre-existing relationships between the students. The use of computer agents also broadens the range of groups and situations that can be created, hence ensuring that all components of the framework (discussed below) are examined. Logistically, computer agents also allow for rapid scoring of students' results and avoid the need to co-ordinate communication between students in a time-limited situation. As a result, the PISA collaborative problem-solving framework favoured the use of computer-simulated agents. Box V.2.1 discusses the concerns in using computer agents instead of human agents when measuring collaborative problem-solving competence.

Box V.2.1. **The use of computer agents instead of human agents when measuring collaborative problem-solving competence**

In the PISA 2015 collaborative problem-solving assessment, the student test-taker interacts with computer agents instead of other human agents. The use of other human agents is impractical: student performance depends on the agents with whom the student interacts, and as human agents are unpredictable, students would need to interact with a large variety of other humans to be certain to place the students in a variety of collaborative environments. The other students would also need to be comparable across schools and countries.

Computer agents allow the assessment to precisely control and vary the characteristics of the other agents with whom students interact. The assessment can thus test a variety of aspects of students' collaborative problem-solving competency within 30-minute clusters.

However, in the workplace and in society at large, students are generally required to interact with other humans. The question therefore arises: Does the PISA 2015 assessment accurately measure students' ability to collaborate with other humans? Do the computer agents faithfully proxy for humans?

A study investigating these questions was carried out by the University of Luxembourg in classrooms in Germany and in cognitive laboratories at the University of Luxembourg (Herborn, Mustafic and Greiff, forthcoming; Herborn et al., forthcoming). In the classroom studies, four PISA collaborative problem-solving units were re-formatted by replacing one of the computer agents with a human agent partner who could select his or her response from a set of prepared responses, similar to what the human test-taker would see. Only the human test-taker was scored. Prior to starting the unit, students were informed whether they were interacting with a human or a computer agent. A statistically significant yet small difference in scores was observed between students who interacted with a computer agent and students who interacted with a human agent; this difference was deemed too small to be relevant from a practical standpoint.

In the cognitive laboratories, students were instructed to think aloud as they completed one of the original units used in the PISA 2015 assessment (with computer agents) and one re-formatted unit (with a human agent). Each student completed these units individually, i.e. in his or her own space, without direct contact with other humans/human agents. It was found that teachers' opinions of their students' collaboration skills were significantly and moderately well correlated with students' performance in the original and re-formatted collaborative problem-solving units.

...

The re-formatted units included at least two other agents: one human agent and at least one computer agent. Anecdotal evidence from students indicates that they were unable to distinguish which of the agents was the human agent, likely because their responses were all prepared.

Hence, although students collaborated with computer agents instead of real human agents in the PISA 2015 collaborative problem-solving assessment, any differences between the two types of agents were difficult to discern. There are no pertinent differences between the use of human and computer agents in the context of electronic collaboration where students cannot write their own individual responses.

With improvements in technology, more and more collaboration takes place in virtual settings: people find themselves increasingly working with others located on different floors, in different companies and organisations, and in other cities and countries. The PISA 2015 collaborative problem-solving assessment is thus particularly pertinent to the changing face of how humans collaborate in the twenty-first century.

Students also performed a collaborative problem-solving unit face-to-face with another human agent in the cognitive laboratories, where they could freely formulate their responses. This unit was evaluated by independent observers. It was found that students' performance in the original and re-formatted units, both of which took place in a virtual, computer-based setting, was a moderately good predictor of their performance in the face-to-face collaboration units with another human. Hence, the PISA 2015 collaborative problem-solving assessment is informative about students' performance in real-life collaboration scenarios, where they directly collaborate with other humans.

... attempt to solve a problem ...

A student's collaborative problem-solving ability is, as the name implies, assessed in scenarios where he or she must solve a problem. In this context, a problem is not necessarily a cognitive task, such as setting up a sustainable fish farm, planning the construction of a bridge, or writing a persuasive letter. Instead, it may be communicating with other agents, delegating roles to other agents, ensuring that the group remains focussed on the task at hand, or evaluating whether other agents have performed their assigned tasks, among other examples. All of these actions are directed towards the ultimate goal. In the case of the released unit described at the end of this chapter, *Xandar*, the goal is to answer questions in a simulated contest, and the problem-solving process incorporates all of the steps towards the final goal.

Collaborative problem-solving ability is not measured solely by whether the problem was successfully solved; for example, in the case of *Xandar*, it is not measured solely by how well students perform in the contest. Instead, assessment is continuous throughout the unit and incorporates all of the student's interactions with and responses to the computerised agents. Each response is indicative of how the student has chosen to interact and collaborate with the other agents in that particular situation.

THE PISA 2015 FRAMEWORK FOR ASSESSING COLLABORATIVE PROBLEM-SOLVING COMPETENCE

The PISA 2015 framework for assessing collaborative problem-solving competence guided the development of the assessment and sets the parameters for reporting results. The framework identifies two major components to collaborative problem solving: the cognitive and general problem-solving aspects common to individual problem solving (as examined in PISA 2012) and the collaborative aspects unique to collaborative problem solving.

As in PISA 2012, four processes in individual problem solving were identified:

- ***exploring and understanding:*** exploring the problem situation by observing it, interacting with it, searching for information and finding limitations or obstacles; and demonstrating understanding of the information given and the information discovered while interacting with the problem situation
- ***representing and formulating:*** using tables, graphs, symbols or words to represent aspects of the problem situation; and formulating hypotheses about the relevant factors in a problem and the relationships between them to build a coherent mental representation of the problem situation
- ***planning and executing:*** devising a plan or strategy to solve the problem; executing the strategy; and perhaps clarifying the overall goal and setting subgoals
- ***monitoring and reflecting:*** monitoring progress; reacting to feedback; and reflecting on the solution, the information provided with the problem or the strategy adopted.

Unique to PISA 2015 are three collaborative problem-solving competencies:

- ***establishing and maintaining shared understanding:*** identifying the knowledge and perspectives that other group members hold and establishing a shared vision of the problem states[3] and activities
- ***taking appropriate action to solve the problem:*** identifying the type of collaborative problem solving-related activities that are needed to solve the problem and carrying out these activities to achieve the solution
- ***establishing and maintaining team organisation:*** understanding one's own role and the roles of other agents, following the rules of engagement for one's role, monitoring group organisation, and facilitating the changes required to optimise performance or to handle a breakdown in communication or other obstacles to solving the problem.

These three collaborative problem-solving competencies are crossed with the four individual problem-solving processes to form a matrix of twelve specific skills, as illustrated in Figure V.2.1 below.[4] Each item within the collaborative problem-solving evaluation assesses one (or sometimes more than one) of these specific skills. The assessment as a whole is developed to measure all 12 specific skills over the various tasks.

Figure V.2.1 ▪ **Skills evaluated in the PISA 2015 collaborative problem-solving assessment**

		Collaborative problem-solving competencies		
		(1) Establishing and maintaining shared understanding	**(2) Taking appropriate action to solve the problem**	**(3) Establishing and maintaining team organisation**
Problem-solving processes	(A) Exploring and understanding	(A1) Discovering perspectives and abilities of team members	(A2) Discovering the type of collaborative interaction to solve the problem, along with goals	(A3) Understanding roles to solve the problem
	(B) Representing and formulating	(B1) Building a shared representation and negotiating the meaning of the problem (common ground)	(B2) Identifying and describing tasks to be completed	(B3) Describing roles and team organisation (communication protocol/rules of engagement)
	(C) Planning and executing	(C1) Communicating with team members about the actions to be/being performed	(C2) Enacting plans	(C3) Following rules of engagement (e.g. prompting other team members to perform their tasks)
	(D) Monitoring and reflecting	(D1) Monitoring and repairing the shared understanding	(D2) Monitoring results of actions and evaluating success in solving the problem	(D3) Monitoring, providing feedback and adapting the team organisation and roles

No assumption is made that the processes and competencies involved in solving a particular problem are sequential or that all of the processes and competencies listed are involved in solving a particular problem. As individuals confront, represent and solve problems in a collaborative group setting, they may move to a solution in a way that transcends the boundaries of a linear, step-by-step model. Nevertheless, each item in the PISA 2015 collaborative problem-solving assessment is intended to have one of these processes and one of these competencies as its main focus.

Although reasoning skills were not explicitly used to organise the domain, each of the individual problem-solving processes and collaborative problem-solving competencies draws upon one or more of them. In understanding a problem situation, the solvers may need to distinguish between facts and opinion; in formulating a solution, they may need to identify relationships between variables; in selecting a strategy, they may need to consider cause and effect; and, in reflecting on results, they may need to critically evaluate assumptions and alternative solutions.

Likewise, in establishing and maintaining shared understanding, students may need to determine which group member possesses each piece of information and what remains unknown; in taking appropriate action to solve the problem, they may need to analyse various possible ways to proceed towards the solution and determine how best to do so; and in establishing and maintaining team organisation, students may need to evaluate group dynamics and judge whether each group member is correctly following his or her assigned role and tasks. However, the PISA 2015 collaborative problem-solving assessment does not explicitly set out to assess cognitive reasoning skills. Thus, the level of cognitive demand is intended to be lower than that in the three core subjects of science, reading and mathematics.

Similarly, while each item targets one or more of the four individual problem-solving processes, these processes are not the focus of the PISA 2015 collaborative problem-solving assessment. Items were designed so that they required a low or intermediate level of proficiency in individual problem solving, so as to more explicitly measure proficiency in collaborative problem solving.

There are two key dimensions common to both individual and collaborative problems: the problem context and the nature of the problem situation. These two dimensions are described in Box V.2.2.

Box V.2.2. **Dimensions common to both individual and collaborative problems**

The PISA 2012 individual problem-solving assessment defined a problem in part by both the problem context, or how familiar a student is likely to be with the problem, and the problem situation, or the extent of the information to which a student has access at any given moment while solving the problem (OECD, 2013). These concepts are used again in the PISA 2015 collaborative problem-solving assessment (OECD, 2017a).

In the framework developed for the 2012 assessment, the problem context is composed of both its setting and its content (OECD, 2013). The setting of a problem may be either technology-based (e.g. controlling or troubleshooting a technological device) or not technology based (e.g. route planning, scheduling or decision making); private (relating directly to the student and his/her immediate circle, such as planning a party) or public (relating to the student's community or to society at large, such as choosing the best location to build a school); and school or non-school. The content of a problem refers to the topics covered in the problem. These may be one of the other PISA domains (science, reading, mathematics or financial literacy) or other subjects, such as civics, politics or sports.

One aspect of the problem situation is whether all of the information is present at the outset, in what are termed static problems, or whether students must delve into the problem to obtain additional information necessary for solving the problem, in what are known as dynamic or interactive problems. The other aspect of the problem situation is how clearly defined the problem is. Problems where the goals, possible actions, and problem states are clearly specified are known as well-defined problems. By contrast, ill-defined problems may have multiple goals and underspecified problem states and actions.

Problems that are solved collaboratively are, by nature, more likely to be interactive rather than static: team members rely on and learn from other team members during the course of solving the problem. Problems that require collaboration to solve are also more likely to be ill-defined (from the point of view of participants), as team members can neither control nor predict what other team members will do.

The collaborative aspect of the assessment adds several new dimensions to each problem. Perhaps the most obvious change between the individual and collaborative problem-solving assessments is that in 2015, students work in teams, and hence team composition is a new dimension to be considered. The group might be composed of just the student being evaluated and one collaborative agent, or it might be a larger group that includes the student being evaluated and multiple other agents. Team members might have the same or different roles and actions available to them.[5]

A new aspect of the problem situation is the type of collaboration required. PISA uses several different types of collaborative problem-solving tasks, including:

- **jigsaw or hidden-profile tasks,** where each group member is given different information or skills. Groups need to pool each member's information and skills together in order to solve the problem and hence collaboration among group members is required. Moreover, group members are dependent on one another to arrive at the solution; no single member can achieve the solution on his or her own, and a group member who chooses not to participate can jeopardise the achievement of the group's goal
- **consensus-building tasks,** where a group must agree on a decision after considering the views, opinions and arguments of all group members. A successful solution will involve all group members contributing their ideas and the careful yet efficient consideration of all such ideas. However, some group members may dominate the conversation and not allow for all ideas to be aired, while other group members may not be willing to disagree with what has already been said, potentially leading to "group think"
- **negotiation tasks,** where not all group members share the same individual goals. They must negotiate in order to achieve, in the best-case scenario, a win-win situation that satisfies both their individual goals and the goals of the group.

Jigsaw/hidden-profile tasks are primarily group co-ordination tasks, while consensus-building and negotiation problems are both primarily group decision-making tasks. A final type of collaborative problem is group production tasks, where the group must create a deliverable, such as a design for a new product or a written report. However, as the PISA 2015 collaborative problem-solving assessment was completely automated, it did not include any production tasks with open-ended products.

The type of collaboration might change over the course of a unit. For example, a unit may begin as a jigsaw task as team members try to work out what other team members know and can perform. Once this has been established, the unit may become a consensus-building task or a negotiation task as team members work to make some sort of final decision. It is also common for the problem situation (see Box V.2.2) to change over the course of the unit, particularly with jigsaw tasks. Problems may start out as dynamic as team members discover what other members know and may then become static once all of the information has been shared.

THE DESIGN AND DELIVERY OF THE PISA 2015 COMPUTER-BASED ASSESSMENT OF COLLABORATIVE PROBLEM SOLVING

While there has been much research on how to assess individual problem-solving competency and tools have been developed for conducting such assessments, PISA 2015 is the first large-scale, international assessment that tries to evaluate competency in collaborative problem solving.

Science is the major domain of the PISA 2015 assessment, meaning that each student received two 30-minute clusters (also known as booklets) of science tasks. Students also received two more 30-minute clusters chosen from among the other three domains: reading, mathematics and collaborative problem solving. These two additional clusters may have been chosen from the same domain or from different domains. Three collaborative problem-solving clusters were designed for the study.

Each collaborative problem-solving cluster comprises several units, which are interactive scenarios that students must work through while interacting with programmed computer agents. Units in the collaborative problem-solving assessment typically require between 5 and 20 minutes to complete and were time-limited. Each unit may be composed of multiple parts, or large, coherent subdivisions of the unit, and each part includes several items, which are the individual actions taken by students that change the state of the problem.[6] Most actions in this assessment require the student to select one response out of four possible options while in a conversation with the computer agents; some require students to provide a solution to a problem using information gathered with the other agents, generally by clicking on a region in the visual display area. Each unit consisted of between 10 and 30 individual items.

Each item can be classified as targeting one of the 12 specific skills in the collaborative problem-solving matrix (Table V.2.1), and thus as targeting one of the 3 collaborative problem-solving competencies and one (or more) of the 4 individual problem-solving processes. However, small sample sizes in each country did not allow for the creation of subscales in each of the competencies and processes. Annex A of the *PISA 2015 Technical Report* (OECD, 2017b) identifies the skills, competencies, and processes targeted by each item.

As noted earlier, student performance in collaborative problem solving depends on the other members in the collaborating group. A complete assessment of performance in this domain therefore requires that students interact with different types of agents in different types of group situations. For example, certain units and tasks may require students to supervise the work of other agents, while other units and tasks may require students to follow the direction set by a computer agent. Likewise, some groups may be more collaborative than other groups. The degree to which the other team members collaborate can be precisely controlled as they are computerised agents.

One potential pitfall of an interactive testing environment is that students who select different options may end up in different problem states. For example, students with high collaborative problem-solving proficiency may quickly incorporate information from and the perspectives of other team members, while students with low collaborative problem-solving skills may never obtain the required input from other team members and set off on a tangent that does not lead to a solution. This presents problems when trying to be consistent in measuring students' collaborative problem-solving abilities.

To overcome such problems, a "rescue agent" can intervene when students choose actions that do not represent a step towards solving the problem. The rescue agent, who is one of the computerised agents, can bring the problem back to the desired state by, for example, giving the student another chance to request the missing information, asking for the missing information himself/herself, or providing the missing information himself/herself. In this way, students always end up at the same problem state no matter what actions they take, and thus they are always faced with the same items. This is illustrated in the next section, which presents the released unit, *Xandar*.

SAMPLE COLLABORATIVE PROBLEM-SOLVING ITEMS

One full unit included in the PISA 2015 main survey is described below. A screenshot of the stimulus information is provided, together with a brief description of the context of the unit. This is followed by a screenshot and description of each item from that unit. The unit described below is also available for viewing on line at www.oecd.org/pisa/test/. The interactive nature of the unit *Xandar* can best be appreciated by trying to solve the items oneself.

Sample unit: XANDAR

In the unit *Xandar*, a three-person team consisting of the student test-taker and two computer agents takes part in a contest where it must answer questions about the fictional country of Xandar. The questions are evenly divided between Xandar's geography, people and economy. This unit involves decision-making and coordination tasks, requires consensus-building collaboration, and has an in-school, private, and non-technology-based context.

Figure V.2.2 ▪ **XANDAR: Introduction**

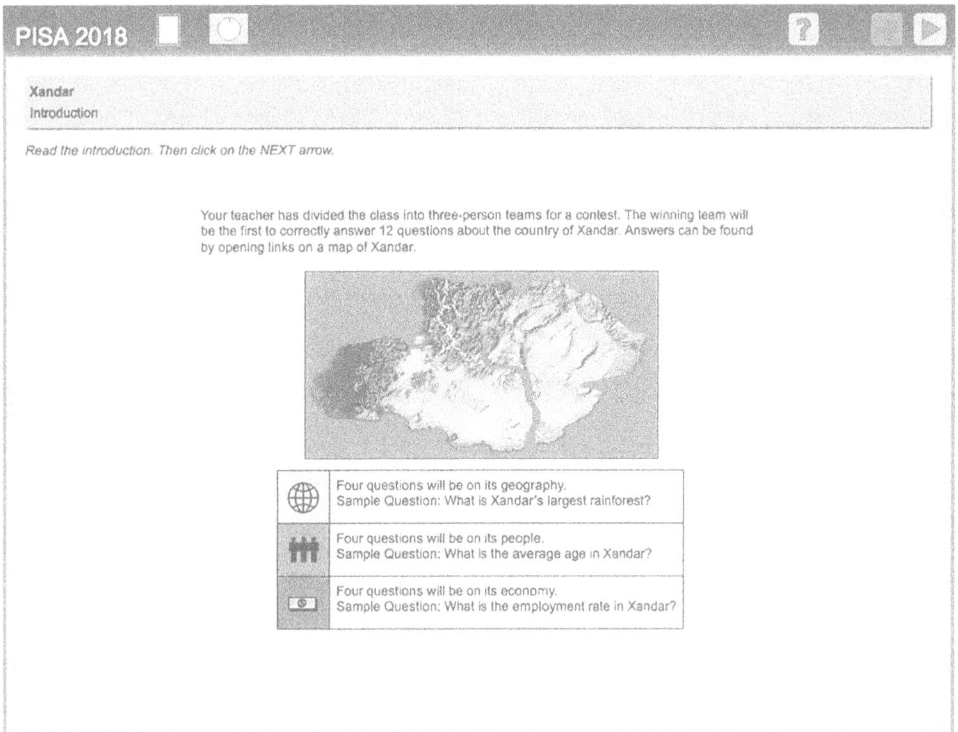

The unit consists of four independent parts; all parts and all items within each part are independent of one another. No matter which response a student selects for a particular item, the computer agents respond in a way so that the unit converges. All students are hence faced with an identical version of the next item.

Xandar: Part 1 – Agreeing on a Strategy

In Part 1 of *Xandar*, the student is familiarised with how the contest will proceed and in particular, the chat interface and the task space (buttons that students can click and the scorecard that monitors team progress). The teacher has asked teams to put off searching for questions and answers until the contest begins and instead to discuss how to approach the contest. The student has been assigned to work in a team with agents named Alice and Zach.

The first item of Part 1 requires students to click "Join the Chat" instead of clicking any of the buttons in the task space ("Geography", "People" or "Economy"). This item is classified as (C3) *following the rules of engagement*, requiring students to display the (C) *planning and executing* individual problem-solving process and the (3) *establishing and maintaining team organisation* collaborative problem-solving competency.

Figure V.2.3 ▪ **XANDAR: Part 1, Item 1**

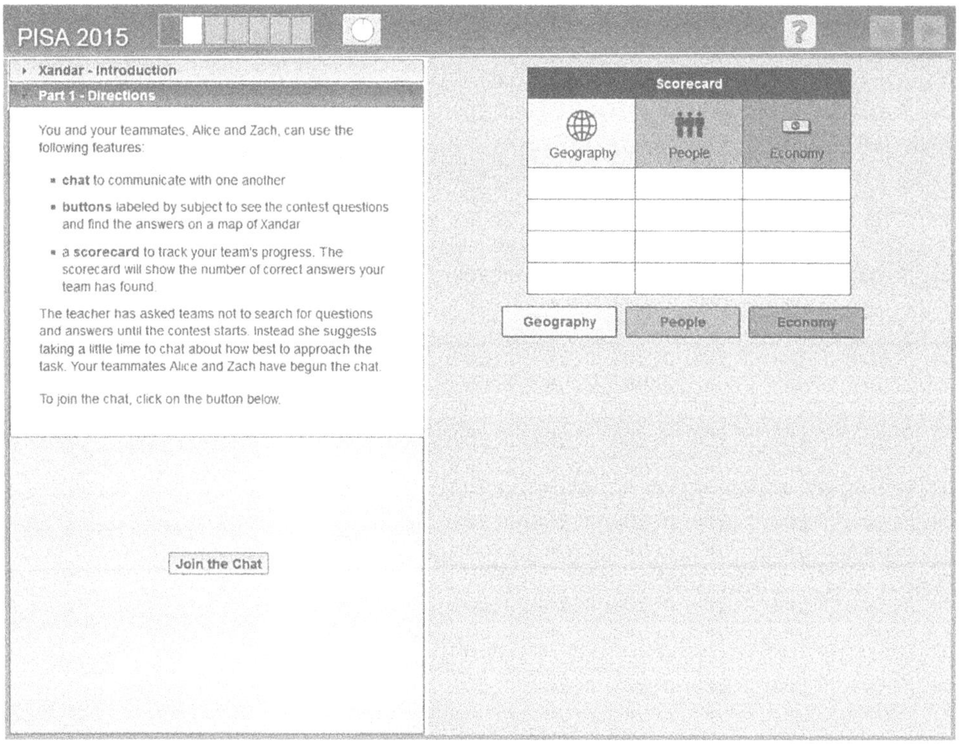

Figure V.2.4 ▪ **XANDAR: Part 1, Item 2**

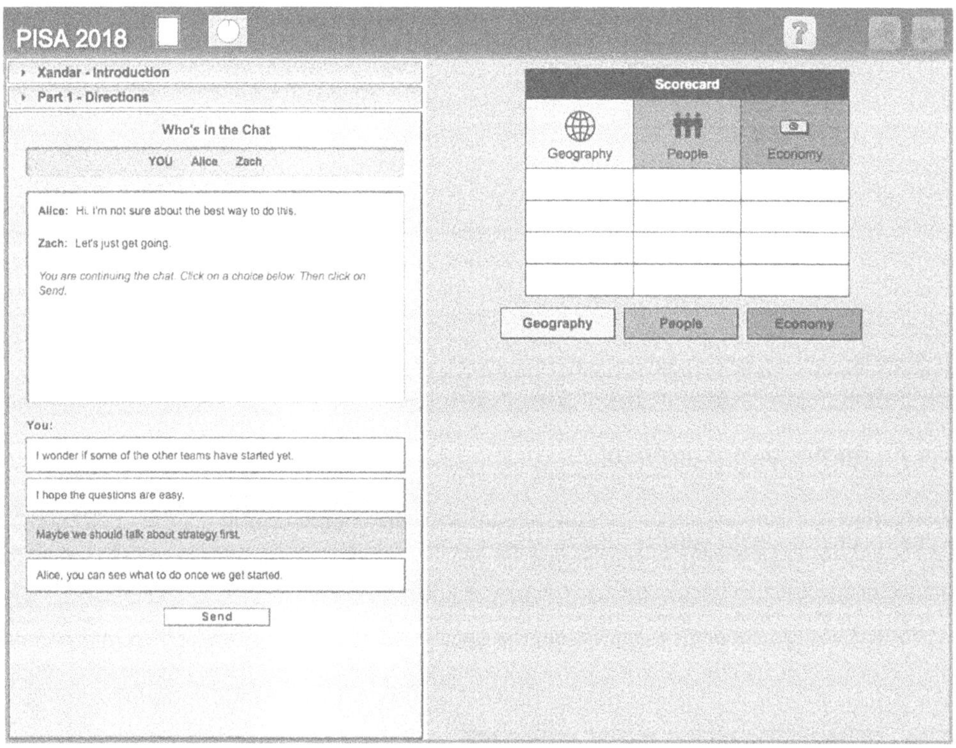

The second item in this part requires students to continue the conversation in a chat with Alice and Zach regarding how to proceed. Zach indicates that he wants to go ahead and start answering questions without a strategy, and the credited response from the student states his or her preference for developing a strategy. The skill evaluated in this item is (C1) *communicating with team members about the actions to be/being performed,* which synthesises the (C) *planning and executing* individual problem-solving process and the (1) *establishing and maintaining shared understanding* collaborative problem-solving competency.

Regardless of the student's response to Part 1, Item 2, Alice mentions her desire for a strategy, followed by Zach reminding the team of how the winning team is determined without describing a strategy *per se*. The student must once again choose between four response options. The credited response to this item, Part 1, Item 3, advances the problem-solving situation by focusing the discussion on the development of a strategy. This item requires (B1) *building a shared representation and negotiation the meaning of the problem* skills, involving the (B) *representing and formulating* individual problem-solving process and the (1) *establishing and maintaining shared understanding* collaborative problem-solving competency.

Alice, regardless of the student's response to Part 1, Item 3, continues to press for a collaborative strategy. Zach reiterates an individual strategy for winning the contest that does not take account of the collaborative nature of the contest. The student's credited response to this item, Part 1, Item 4, proposes this collaborative strategy. This is also a (B1) *building a shared representation and negotiation the meaning of the problem* item, which requires the (B) *representing and formulating* individual problem-solving process and the (1) *establishing and maintaining shared understanding* collaborative problem-solving competency.

Figure V.2.5 ▪ **XANDAR: Part 1, Item 3**

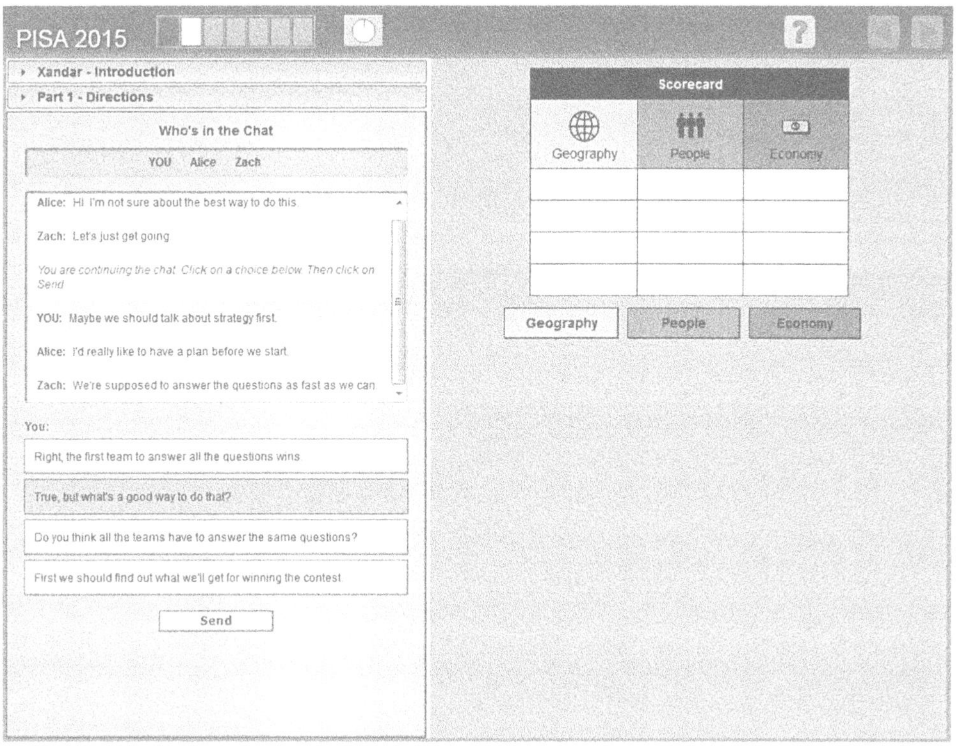

Regardless of how the student responded to Part 1, Item 4, Alice states that it would be self-defeating if they were to look for answers to the same questions at the same time. The credited response to the next item, Part 1, Item 5, identifies the concrete strategy the team should use: each team member will be responsible for one of the subjects. This item is classified as (B3) *describe roles and team organisation (communication protocol/rules of engagement)*, and involves the (B) *representing and formulating* individual problem-solving process and the (3) *establishing and maintaining team organisation* collaborative problem-solving competency. Part 1 ends here.

Figure V.2.6 ▪ **XANDAR: Part 1, Item 4**

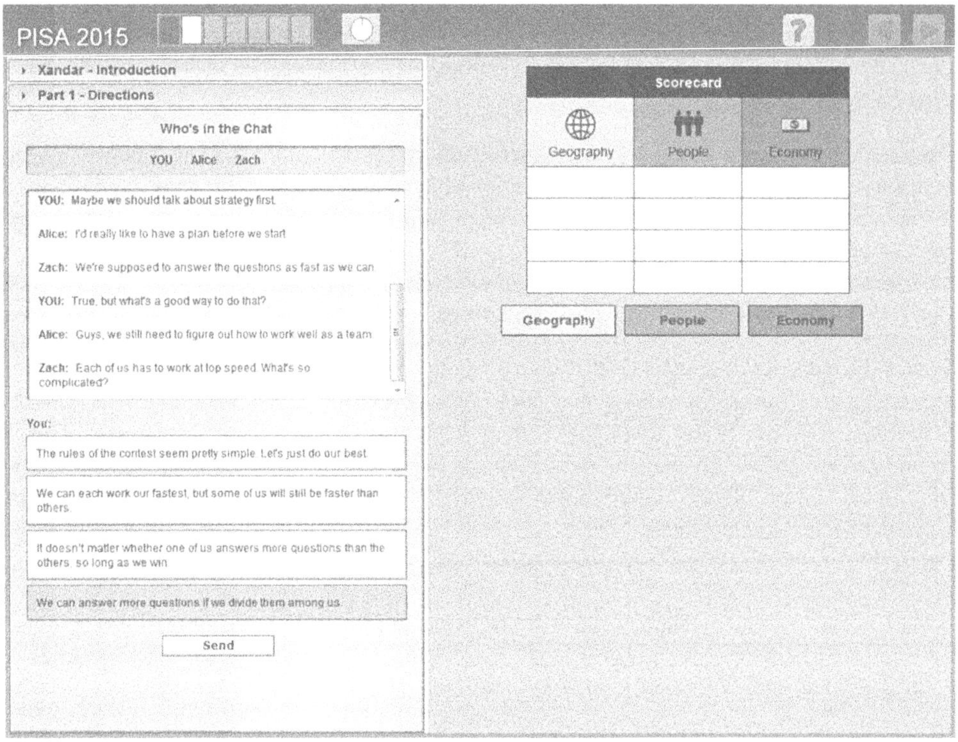

Figure V.2.7 ▪ **XANDAR: Part 1, Item 5**

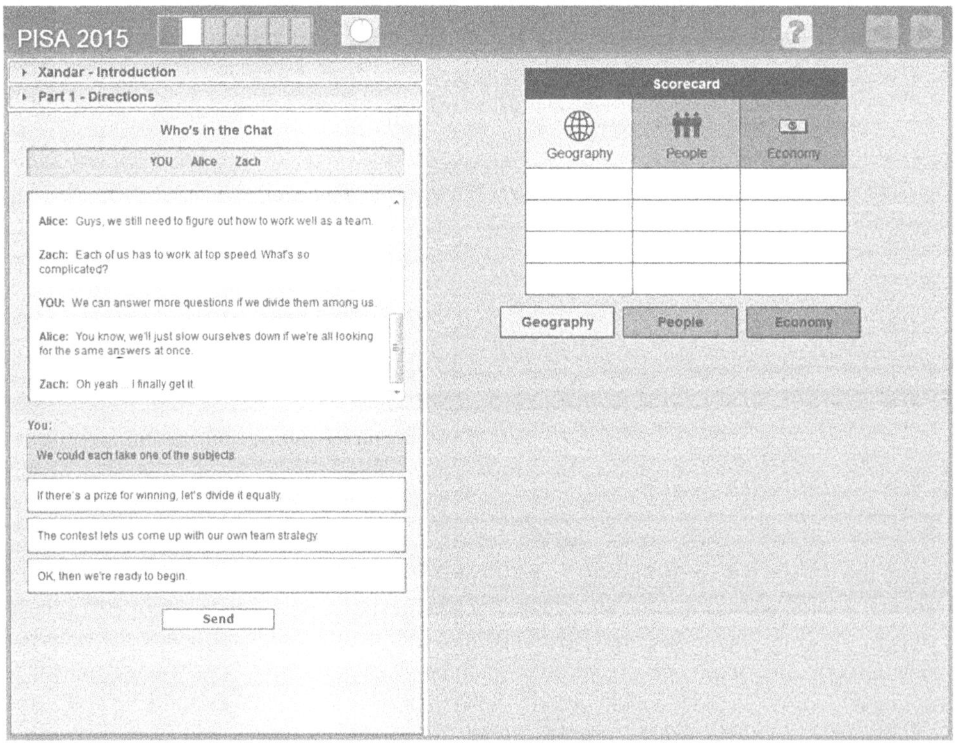

Xandar: Part 2 – Reaching a Consensus Regarding Preferences

At the beginning of Part 2, students are informed that each group member will be responsible for the questions in one subject area, regardless of how they responded to Part 1, Item 5. In Part 2, the team members will apportion the subject areas among themselves.

Figure V.2.8 ▪ **XANDAR: Part 2**

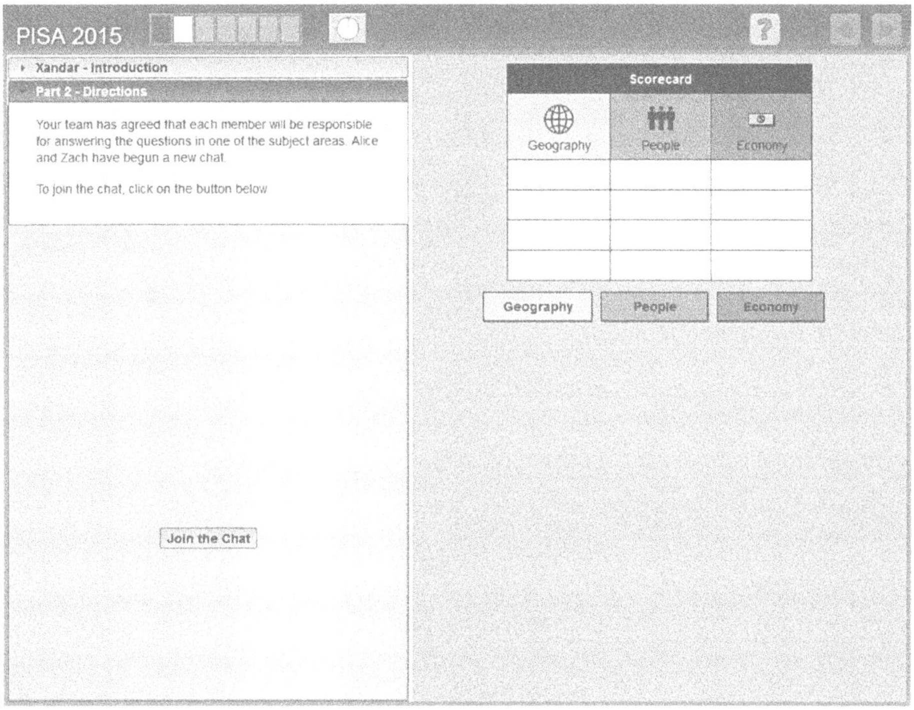

Figure V.2.9 ▪ **XANDAR: Part 2, Item 1**

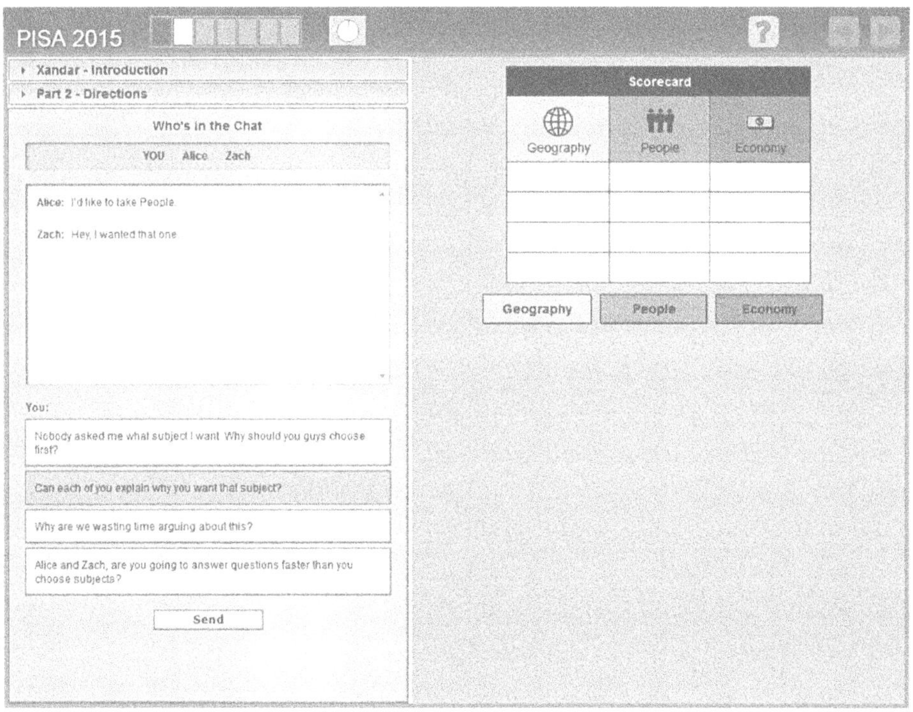

At the beginning of Part 2, both Alice and Zach show their preference for taking the subject "People". The credited response to the first item of this part, Part 2, Item 1, has the student, although not in the role of team leader, helping to resolve this disagreement. This response displays the (A1) *discovering perspectives and abilities of team members* skill, which involves the (A) *exploring and understanding* individual problem-solving process and the (1) *establishing and maintaining shared understanding* collaborative problem-solving competency.

Figure V.2.10 ▪ **XANDAR: Part 2, Item 2**

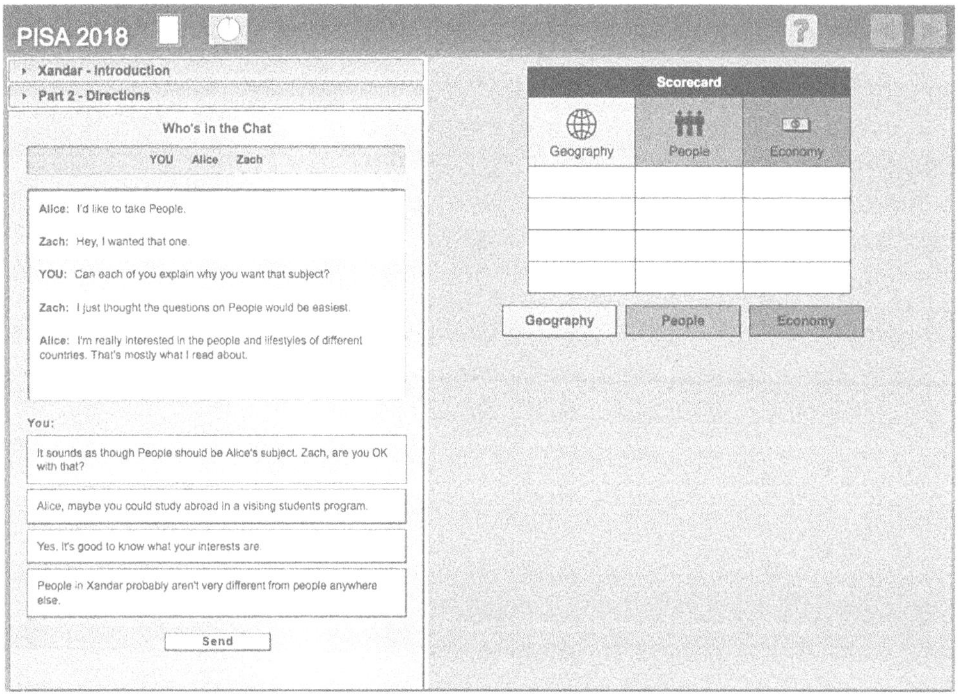

Figure V.2.11 ▪ **XANDAR: Part 2, Item 3**

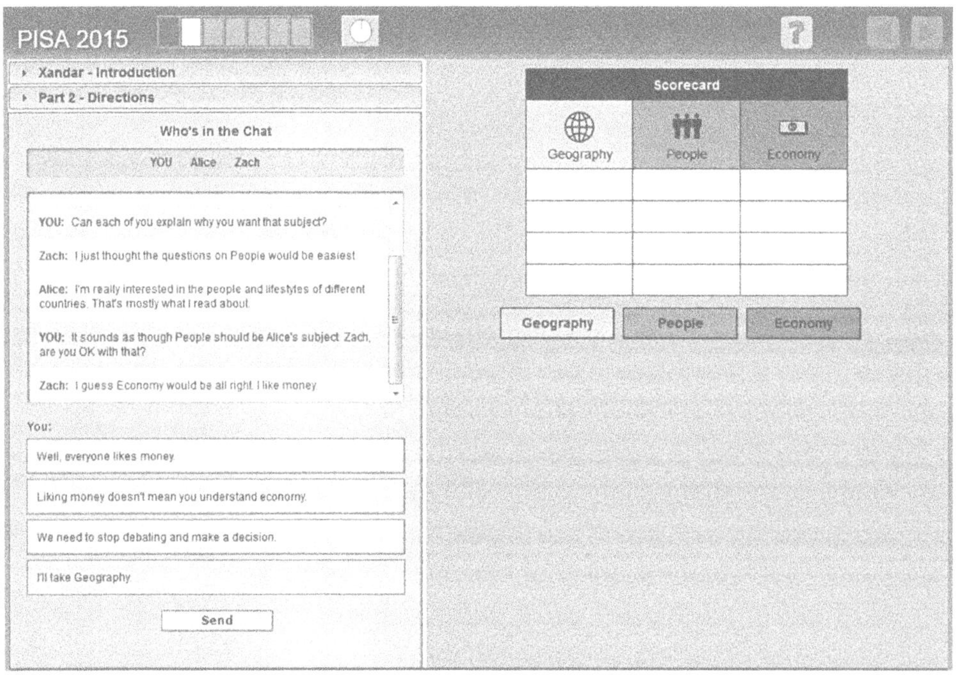

Alice and Zach give reasons as to why they both want to answer questions on "People", regardless of whether the student explicitly asked for them or not in Part 2, Item 1. The student, continuing to resolve the disagreement, is credited with a correct response to the next item, Part 2, Item 2, if he or she advances the problem and uses the information provided by Alice and Zach to assign the subject "People". This item is classified as (B3) *describe roles and team organisation (communication protocols/rules of engagement)*, combining the (B) *representing and formulating* individual problem-solving process and the (3) *establishing and maintaining team organisation* collaborative problem-solving competency.

Alice has been assigned a subject area and Zach has now claimed a second subject area. The collaborative response to Part 2, Item 3 requires the student to claim the last subject area for him or herself. Although this might not, at first glance, appear to be collaborative, claiming the last subject area implicitly confirms that the other two subject areas have already been assigned to Alice and Zach. This item tests (B3) *describe roles and team organisation (communication protocol/rules of engagement)* skills, which involve the (B) *representing and formulating* individual problem-solving process and the (3) *establishing and maintaining team organisation* collaborative problem-solving competency. Part 2 ends here.

Xandar: Part 3 – Playing the Game Effectively

At the beginning of Part 3, students know that their assigned subject area is "Geography", regardless of whether they claimed it for themselves in Part 2, Item 3. In Part 3, they must enter the contest and answer questions regarding Xandar's geography.

Figure V.2.12 ▪ **XANDAR: Part 3, Item 1**

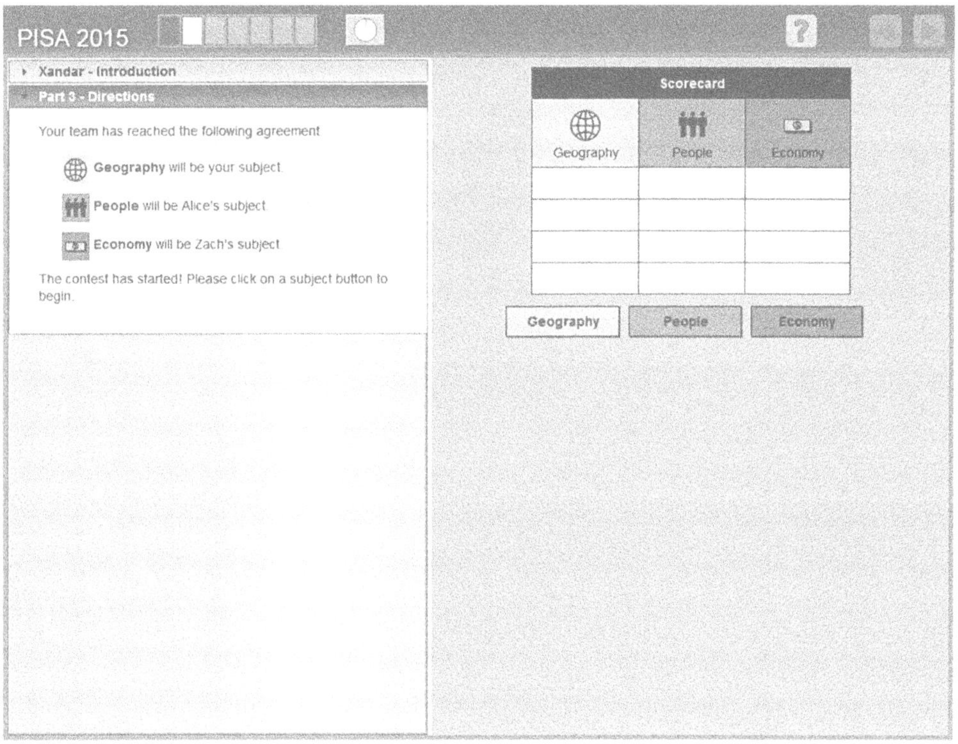

The student is requested to start the contest, with a reminder in the chat interface that he or she has been assigned to answer questions about geography. To begin, the student must click on one of the buttons in the task space; the student is credited with a correct response for Part 3, Item 1 if he or she clicks on the button that says "Geography". In this item, students can exhibit the (C3) *following rules of engagement* skill, which combines the (C) *planning and executing* individual problem-solving process and the (3) *establishing and maintaining team organisation* collaborative problem-solving competency.

Regardless of which button the student clicked, he or she is next presented with a screen that instructs students how to proceed with the contest: he or she must click on icons in the task space to obtain answers to questions about Xandar's geography.

Figure V.2.13 ▪ **XANDAR: Part 3, Item 2, Screen 1**

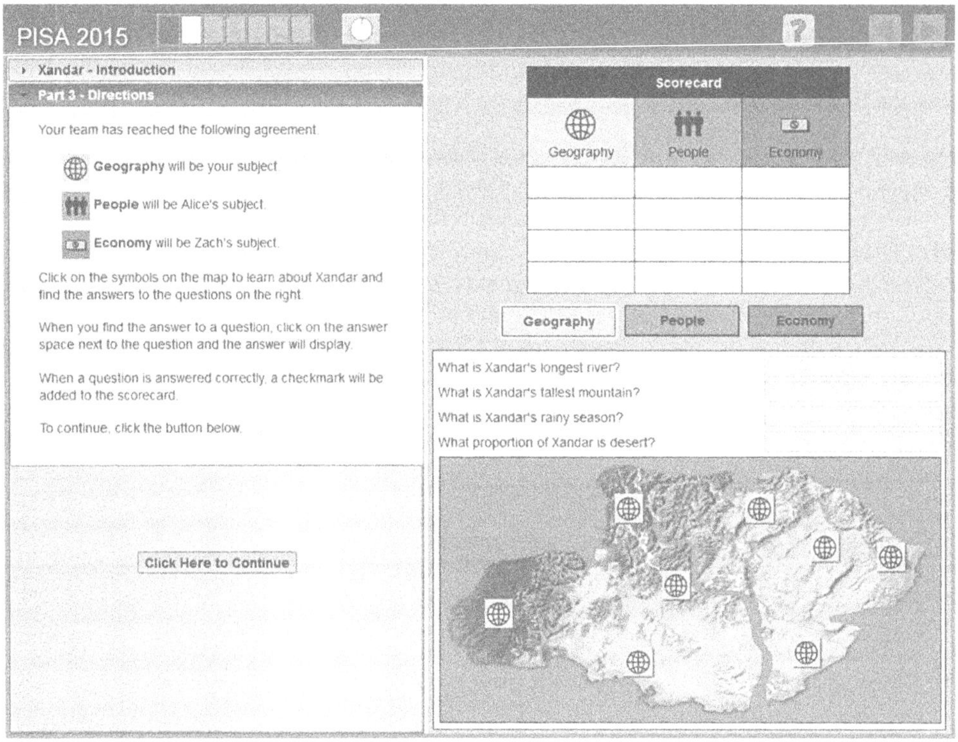

Figure V.2.14 ▪ **XANDAR: Part 3, Item 2, Screen 2**

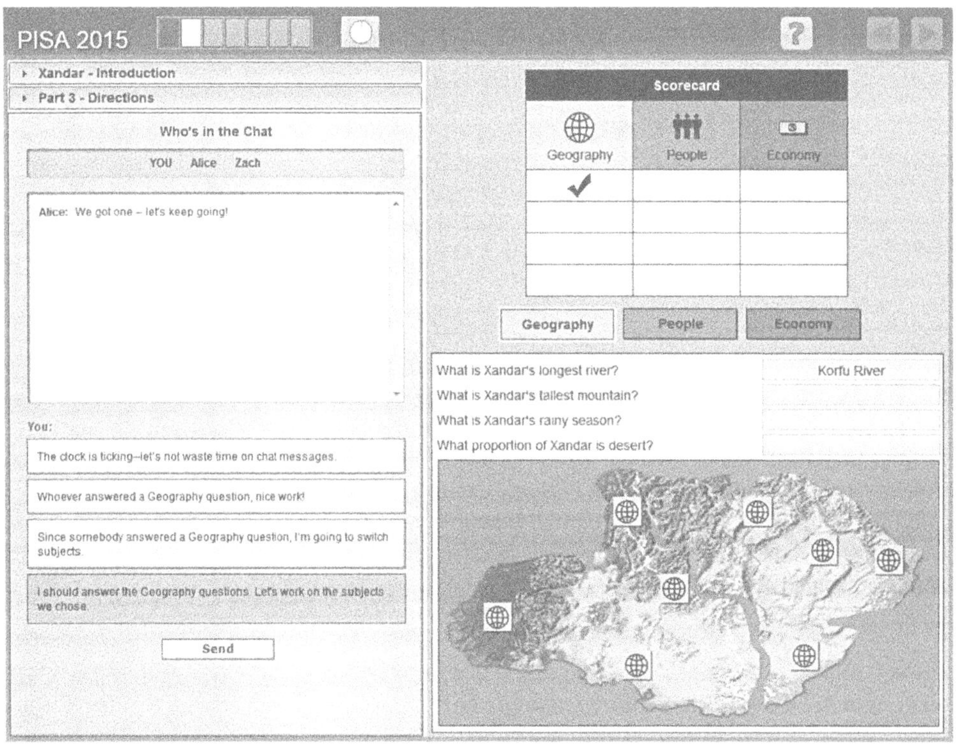

After clicking the "Click Here to Continue" button but before the student has a chance to click on one of the icons on the map of Xandar, a checkmark is placed on the scoreboard to indicate that one of the questions on Xandar's geography has been answered. Alice makes a remark to this effect in the chat interface. In Part 3, Item 2, students must then come up with an appropriate response. While one might be tempted to celebrate the progress made in the contest, the item actually tests to see whether the student has observed that the previously-agreed rules of engagement – that the student himself or herself should be the team member to answer the questions related to geography – are not being followed. This item therefore assesses the (D1) *monitoring and repairing the shared understanding* skill, which combines the (D) *monitoring and reflecting* individual problem-solving process and the (1) *establishing and maintaining shared understanding* collaborative problem-solving competency.

The student, regardless of how he or she responded to Part 3, Item 2, now continues with the contest by clicking on icons in the task space. No matter which icon is clicked, the statement "10 percent of Xandar is desert" pops up; students must then click on the blank space next to the question "What proportion of Xandar is desert?" in order for "10 percent" to show up and a checkmark to be recorded on the scoreboard. Students are not required to manually enter in their answers to questions regarding Xandar.

Figure V.2.15 ▪ **XANDAR: Part 3**

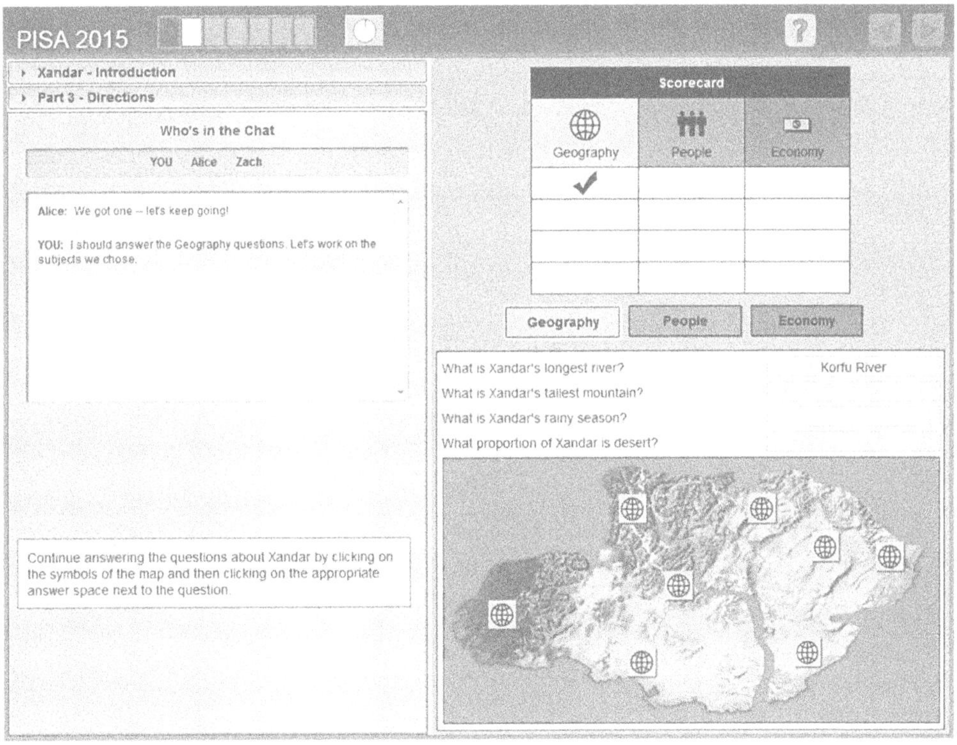

After answering this item, students are interrupted and informed that they have made progress in some, but not in all, subjects, and that Alice has sent another message. This is the end of Part 3.

Xandar: Part 4 – Assessing Progress

Part 4 picks up from Part 3 and requires students to evaluate their progress and fix any problems that have resulted.

Alice asks the team about its progress. In the credited response to Part 4, Item 1, the student provides, as accurately as possible, a response to Alice's question. This item is classified as (D2) *monitoring the results of actions and evaluating success in solving the problem*, which requires students to display the (D) *monitoring and reflecting* individual problem-solving process and the (2) *taking appropriate action to solve the problem* collaborative problem-solving competency.

Figure V.2.16 ▪ **XANDAR: Part 4, Item 1**

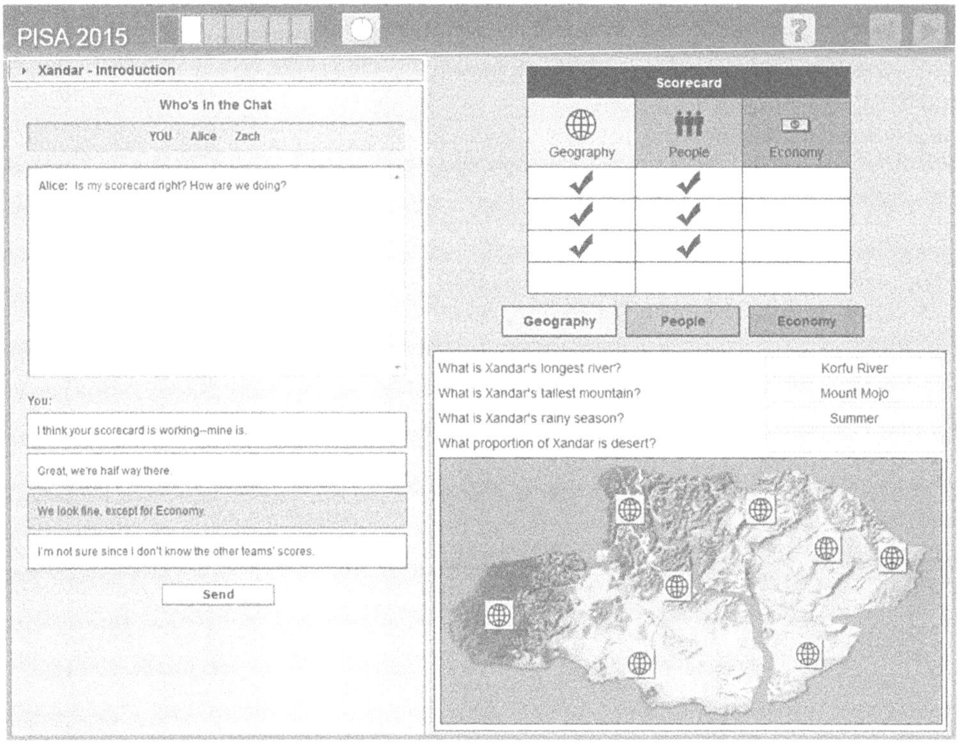

Figure V.2.17 ▪ **XANDAR: Part 4, Item 2**

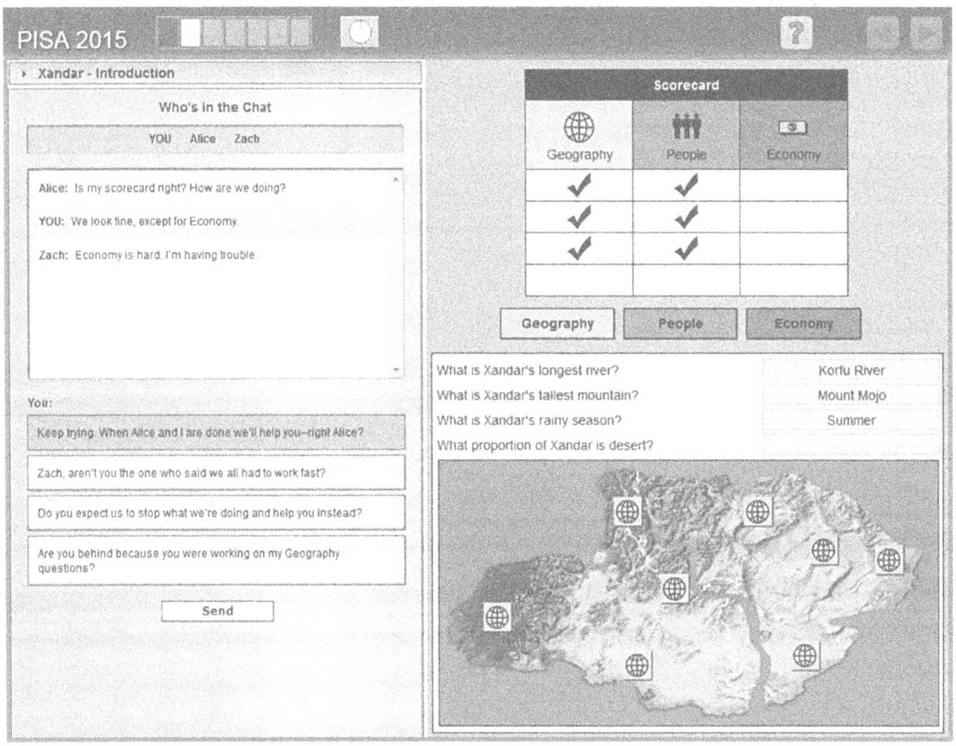

Regardless of the student's answer, Zach responds that he is having trouble with the questions in his assigned subject area, economy. In Part 4, Item 2, the student must choose the best response among the four possible options, which is the only one that encourages Zach and proposes how the student and Alice might help him. It also maintains team organisation by ensuring that the roles previously agreed – that each team member works on his or her assigned subject area first – are still followed. (D3) *Monitoring, providing feedback and adapting the team organisation and roles* skills are evaluated by this item, which thus also evaluates the (D) *monitoring and reflecting* individual problem-solving process and the (3) *establishing and maintaining team organisation* collaborative problem-solving competency.

Figure V.2.18 ▪ **XANDAR: Conclusion**

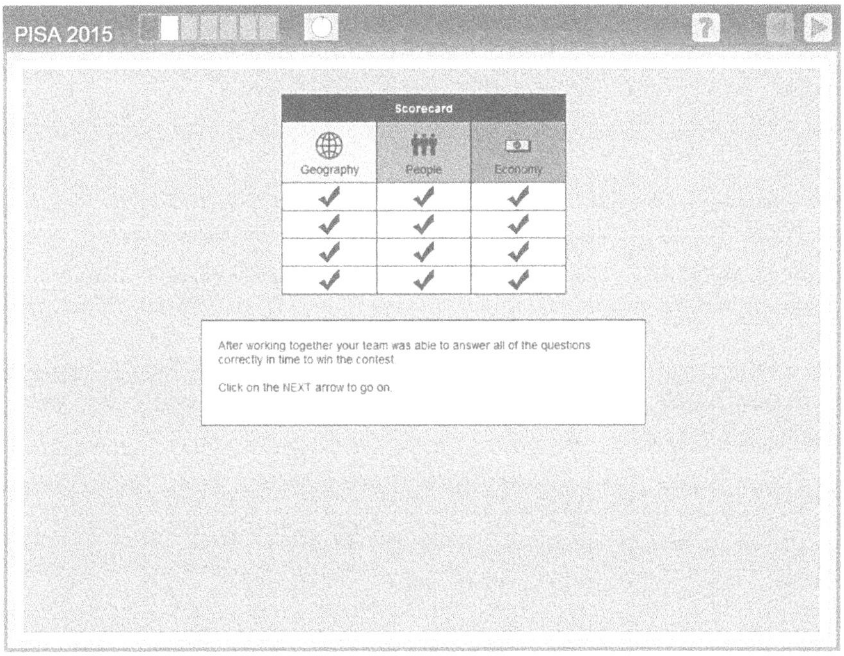

Finally, regardless of how the student responded to Part 4, Item 2, he or she is informed that his or her team won the contest by answering all of the questions correctly. The unit ends here.

Notes

1. This is not to say that social skills are more valued than mathematics and other cognitive skills. Indeed, the median salary of those who rank in the top 10 percent of cognitive skills in the United States was $67 000, while that of those who rank in the top 10 percent of non-cognitive skills was $52 000. These numbers are an average of salaries in 2000, 2002 and 2004 for a sample who were first collected in 1981 and tested between the ages of 35 and 48 (Schanzenbach et al., 2016).

2. Most students in Singapore who sit the PISA assessment will have attended only grades 7 through 10, where project work is infused into the rest of the curriculum.

3. The problem state at any given point during the problem-solving process includes all of the conversation and actions that have already taken place, all of the information and perspectives accumulated up to that point, and all of the possible actions that may be taken in the future.

4. The twelve specific skill cells have been labelled with a letter-number combination referring to the rows (individual problem-solving processes, represented by a letter) and columns (collaborative problem-solving competencies, represented by a number) for ease of cross-referencing later in this report and in related materials.

5. Team members, while sharing the same goals, may have different status levels, which is another new dimension to collaborative problem solving not observed in individual problem solving. However, the PISA 2015 collaborative problem-solving assessment did not include any units where team members had different status levels.

6. In some cases, responses from multiple actions were combined into one unit for statistical reasons, such as high correlation between the actions.

References

Autor, D.H., F. Levy and **R.J. Murnane** (2003), "The skill content of recent technological change: An empirical exploration", *The Quarterly Journal of Economics*, Vol. 118/4, pp. 1279-1333, https://doi.org/10.1162/003355303322552801.

Blaney, N.T. et al. (1977), "Interdependence in the classroom: A field study", *Journal of Educational Psychology*, Vol. 69/2, pp. 121-128.

Deming, D.J. (2017), "The growing importance of social skills in the labour market", *The Quarterly Journal of Economics*, Vol. 132/4, pp. 1593-1640, https://doi.org/10.1093/qje/qjx022.

Graesser, A.C. et al. (2018), "Challenges of assessing collaborative problem solving", in Care, E., P. Griffin and M. Wilson (eds.), *Assessment and Teaching of 21st Century Skills: Research and Applications*, Springer International, Cham, Switzerland.

Griffin, P. and **E. Care** (2015), "ATC21S Method", in Griffin, P. and E. Care (eds.), *Assessment and Teaching of 21st Century Skills: Methods and Approach*, pp. 3-33, Springer, Dordrecht, the Netherlands.

Herborn, K., M. Mustafic and **S. Greiff** (forthcoming), "An unspoilt broth by PISA 2015 cooks: Students' collaborative problem-solving results predict performance in real-life conditions", *manuscript submitted for publication.*

Herborn, K. et al. (forthcoming), "Collaborative problem solving in PISA 2015: Can computer-agents replace humans?", *manuscript submitted for publication.*

Hesse, F. et al. (2015), "A framework for teachable collaborative problem solving skills", in Griffin, P. and E. Care (eds.), *Assessment and Teaching of 21st Century Skills: Methods and Approach*, pp. 37-56, Springer, Dordrecht, the Netherlands.

Kreijns, K., P.A. Kirschner and **W. Jochems** (2003), "Identifying the pitfalls for social interaction in computer-supported collaborative learning environments: A review of the research", *Computers in Human Behavior*, Vol. 19/3, pp. 335-353, https://doi.org/10.1016/S0747-5632(02)00057-2.

Laughlin, P.R. et al. (2006), "Groups perform better than the best individuals on letters-to-numbers problems: Effects of group size", *Journal of Personality and Social Psychology*, Vol. 90/4, pp. 644-651, http://dx.doi.org/10.1037/0022-3514.90.4.644.

Murnane, R.J., J.B. Willett and **F. Levy** (1995), "The growing importance of cognitive skills in wage determination", *The Review of Economics and Statistics*, Vol. 77/2, pp. 251-266, http://doi.org/10.2307/2109863.

OECD (2017a), *PISA 2015 Assessment and Analytical Framework: Science, Reading, Mathematic, Financial Literacy and Collaborative Problem Solving*, OECD Publishing, Paris, http://dx.doi.org/10.1787/9789264281820-en.

OECD (2017b), *PISA 2015 Technical Report*, OECD Publishing, Paris.

OECD (2013), *PISA 2012 Assessment and Analytical Framework: Mathematics, Reading, Science, Problem Solving and Financial Literacy*, OECD Publishing, Paris, http://dx.doi.org/10.1787/9789264190511-en.

Rosen, Y. and **R. Rimor** (2009), "Using a collaborative database to enhance students' knowledge construction", *Interdisciplinary Journal of E-Learning and Learning Objects*, Vol. 5, pp. 187-195.

Schanzenbach, D.W. et al. (2016), *Seven Facts on Noncognitive Skills from Education to the Labour Market*, The Hamilton Project, Washington, DC, www.hamiltonproject.org/assets/files/seven_facts_noncognitive_skills_education_labor_market.pdf.

Schwartz, D.L. (1995), "The emergence of abstract dyad representations in dyad problem solving", *The Journal of the Learning Sciences*, Vol. 4/3, pp. 321-354, http://dx.doi.org/10.1207/s15327809jls0403_3.

Singapore Ministry of Education (MOE) and **University of Cambridge Local Examinations Syndicate (UCLES)** (2017), "Project Work: Higher 1 (2017)", www.moe.gov.sg/docs/default-source/document/education/syllabuses/english-language-and-literature/files/pw-syllabus.pdf, accessed June 16, 2017.

3

Performance in collaborative problem solving

This chapter explains how PISA measures students' collaborative problem-solving skills. It defines the five proficiency levels on the collaborative problem-solving scale and describes what students who attain those levels can do. The chapter also examines the relationship between student performance in collaborative problem solving and performance in the three core PISA subjects – science, reading and mathematics – and the links between collaborative problem solving and individual problem solving. It concludes with a discussion of the extent to which students' experiences with ICT are related to their performance in this computer-based assessment.

A note regarding Israel

The statistical data for Israel are supplied by and under the responsibility of the relevant Israeli authorities. The use of such data by the OECD is without prejudice to the status of the Golan Heights, East Jerusalem and Israeli settlements in the West Bank under the terms of international law.

How well do 15-year-old students work in groups to solve problems and achieve pre-set goals? The PISA 2015 computer-based assessment of collaborative problem solving uses scenarios with which 15-year-olds are likely to be familiar in order to measure their ability to collaborate with others. Test problems included items requiring only simple or moderate problem-solving ability. As such, the assessment focused as much as possible on students' collaboration skills, as opposed to their problem-solving skills, which were evaluated in PISA 2012. Some 52 countries and economies participated in the collaborative problem-solving assessment (32 OECD countries and 20 partner countries and economies).

What the data tell us

- Students in Singapore score higher in collaborative problem solving than students in all other participating countries and economies, followed by students in Japan.
- On average across OECD countries, 28% of students are able to solve only straightforward collaborative problems, if any at all. By contrast, fewer than one in six students in Estonia, Hong Kong (China), Japan, Korea, Macao (China) and Singapore is a low achiever in collaborative problem solving.
- Across OECD countries, 8% of students are top performers in collaborative problem solving, meaning that they can maintain an awareness of group dynamics, ensure team members act in accordance with their agreed-upon roles, and resolve disagreements and conflicts while identifying efficient pathways and monitoring progress towards a solution.
- Collaborative problem-solving performance is positively related to performance in the other assessed domains, but the relationship is weaker than that observed among performance in those other domains.
- Students in Australia, Japan, Korea, New Zealand and the United States perform among the best in collaborative problem solving, on average, compared to students in other countries who show similar performance in science, reading and mathematics.

HOW THE PISA 2015 COLLABORATIVE PROBLEM-SOLVING RESULTS ARE REPORTED

The previous chapter introduces the concept of collaborative problem-solving competence that underlies this assessment. This section discusses how an overall measure of collaborative problem-solving competence was derived from students' answers to questions that measure different types of collaborative problem-solving skills. It then describes how 15-year-olds were classified into five proficiency levels, one of which comprises those students who score below the lowest described level and whose proficiencies could not be identified.

How the assessment was analysed and scaled

Six units were developed and used for the PISA 2015 collaborative problem-solving assessment. Each unit involved a scenario with multiple individual items that students had to work through, all of which led to the resolution of the scenario. In the case of the released unit, *Xandar*, students had to work together to answer as many questions as possible in a simulation of an in-class contest. Units were presented in their entirety to students and were organised into three separate clusters, each of which required 30 minutes to complete. All students who participated in the collaborative problem-solving assessment completed two clusters of science and either one or two additional clusters of collaborative problem solving.

There were no free-response items in the collaborative problem-solving assessment. All items required students to make a multiple-choice selection among various ways to respond to their team members, or to move icons into the appropriate slot or click an option in the visual display area. Since it is an interactive assessment, students were required to respond to each item before moving onto the next item and could not skip or omit items.[1] Collaboration was assessed through student responses in their interactions with one or more computer-based agents. Data from a total of 117 items from these six units were used to analyse and scale performance in collaborative problem solving.

The relative difficulty of each item included in the assessment can be estimated by the proportion of students who answered each question correctly, with smaller proportions of correct answers indicating greater difficulty. Items were then arranged in increasing order of difficulty along a single dimension. The 117 problem-solving items included in the PISA 2015 assessment thus spanned a wide range of difficulty.

Conversely, a student's proficiency relative to the assessment can be estimated from the test questions that he or she answered correctly, taking into account the difficulty of these questions. His or her proficiency in the domain can then be reported on the same scale that measures the questions' difficulty.

Estimates of student proficiency reflect the items students would be expected to successfully complete. Students are likely to be able to complete items that are at or below the difficulty level associated with their own position on the scale.[2] Conversely, they are unlikely to be able to complete questions above the difficulty level associated with their position on the scale. Figure V.3.1 illustrates how this probabilistic model works.

Figure V.3.1 ▪ **Relationship between questions and student performance on a scale**

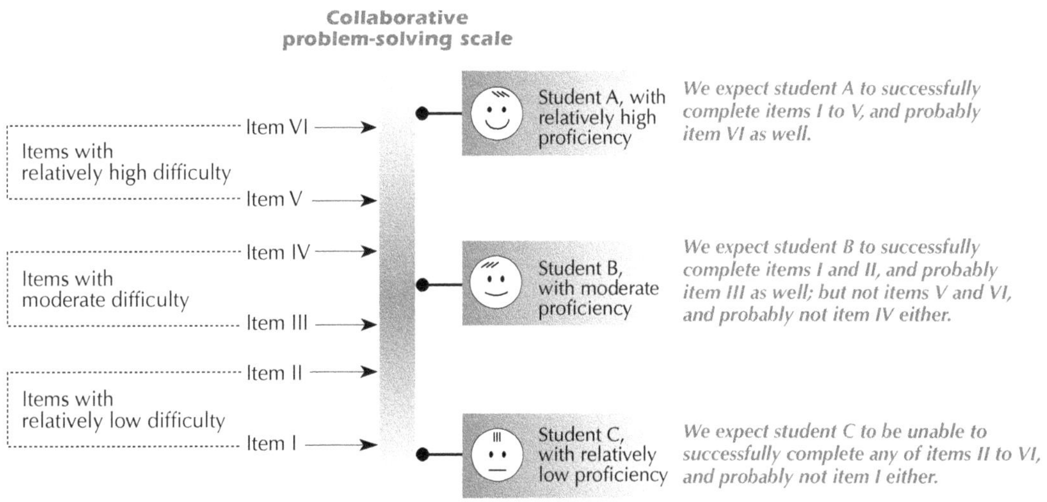

The further a student's performance is located above a given question on the proficiency scale, the more likely he or she will be able to successfully complete the question. Similarly, the further a student's performance is below a given question, the lower the probability that the student will be able to successfully complete the question.

The location of student proficiency on this scale is set relative to the particular group of questions included in the PISA collaborative problem-solving assessment. However, just as the sample of students who participated in PISA in 2015 was drawn to represent all 15-year-old students in the participating countries and economies, the individual questions used in the assessment were selected to provide a comprehensive representation of the PISA 2015 definition of collaborative problem-solving competence.

A profile of PISA collaborative problem-solving questions

Xandar, one of the six units from the PISA 2015 assessment of collaborative problem solving, was released to the public in order to illustrate the skills examined by the PISA collaborative problem-solving framework and to show how performance was measured. This unit, with several individual items, is presented at the end of Chapter 2 (Figures V.2.2 to V.2.18).

Figure V.3.2 shows where these items are located on the described proficiency scale. Items included in the same unit can span a range of difficulty; the released unit, *Xandar*, contains items in each difficulty level. All units covered a broad section of the PISA problem-solving scale.

A few items included in the test were associated with difficulty levels below Level 1. Among the released items, one asked students to simply click a box saying "Join the Chat" in order to continue with the assessment. The number of items that fall below Level 1 is not sufficient to adequately describe the skills that students who perform below Level 1 possess. However, including such items, which most students in even the lowest-performing countries and economies can complete, is one way to ensure that all countries and economies can learn from the assessment results. PISA 2015 thus not only measures proficiency in collaborative problem solving at different levels, but can also capture some of the basic components of collaborative problem-solving skills.

Figure V.3.2 ▪ **Map of selected collaborative problem-solving questions from the released unit *Xandar***

Level	Lower score limit	Part	Item	Question difficulty (in PISA score points)
4	640	3	2	992
		4	1	730
3	540	2	1	598
		4	2	593
2	440	2	3	537
		1	4	524
			2	502
			3	471
1	340	1	5	434
		2	2	381
		3	1	357
Below Level 1	N/A	1	1	314

Box V.3.1 presents the major differences between easy and difficult items and links them to students' progress in collaborative problem solving.

Box V.3.1. **How students progress in collaborative problem solving**

As students acquire proficiency in collaborative problem solving, they learn to handle increasingly complex demands. What these demands are and what it means for students to become better at collaborative problem solving can be inferred by comparing the easier tasks at the bottom of Figure V.3.2 to the harder tasks shown above them.

The PISA 2015 collaborative problem-solving assessment was based on a framework (OECD, 2017a) described in Chapter 2 of this report, which defined the domain and how competency in the domain could be evaluated. In order to measure students across a range of competency levels, the items used in the assessment must also span these competency levels.

Philpot et al. (2017) identify a variety of characteristics that affected the difficulty of the items in the PISA 2012 individual problem-solving assessment, including the distance from the goal and the reasoning skills required; the amount of information and how it is represented; the number of constraints and conditions; and the unfamiliarity and complexity of the system. Additional determinants of item difficulty were identified in the framework for the PISA 2015 collaborative problem-solving assessment, related to the three collaborative problem-solving processes (OECD, 2017a):

(1) Establishing and maintaining shared understanding. In the easiest tasks, students work in small teams to solve a well-defined problem that has a clear goal. Much of the information required is already explicitly stated, and the other agents in the problem will prompt the student to provide information or to perform actions. As the item becomes more difficult, students are faced with increasingly ill-defined problems that have vague goals. Navigating this uncertainty in order to understand and then attain the problem goal becomes part of the problem-solving activity. Groups become larger and more information is hidden or not explicitly stated at the beginning, thus requiring students to initiate communication with the other agents to obtain the required knowledge.

(2) Taking appropriate action to solve the problem. The easiest tasks have a clear, well-defined goal and are cast in a familiar, concrete setting. Students start from a point that is one or two steps away from the eventual goal, which can be attained with only minimal input from the other agents. They also have a limited number of possible actions and do not come across any unexpected complications. Other agents' actions are explicitly identified. Tasks that are harder to solve take place in more abstract settings or refer to unfamiliar objects. The goal is less easily identified and students must perform a large number of actions in order to attain this goal. The student's actions become increasingly interdependent on the actions of other group members, which are less and less explicit.

...

(3) Establishing and maintaining team organisation. In tasks at the bottom of the difficulty scale, students interact with co-operative group members who volunteer information about their own actions and motivations. In more difficult problems, students must ask for or else ascertain the actions and motivations of the other group members, who may be less forthright or lack the desire to work collaboratively towards the goal. Students must also monitor the group dynamic, keep agents on track, and manage conflict between them.

Initially, students may be able only to solve problems cast in familiar settings with few possible actions and that are not dependent on other agents, as in Part 1, Item 1 and Part 3, Item 1 of *Xandar*, where they need only to click on a button to start the rest of the unit. As students develop their collaborative problem-solving proficiency, the complexity of the problems that they can solve grows. In an item of moderate difficulty, such as in Part 1, Items 2, 3 and 4 of *Xandar*, students must advance the problem in a collaborative manner by engaging the other agents and responding to their comments and inputs. Finally, the most difficult items, such as Part 3, Item 2 and Part 4, Item 1 of *Xandar*, require students to synthesise information not explicitly mentioned – for example, the status of the students' progress in the contest as shown in the scorecard – and to then adjust the group's problem-solving strategy in order to get back on track towards attaining the goal (see Chapter 2 for a more detailed description of items).

WHAT STUDENTS CAN DO IN COLLABORATIVE PROBLEM SOLVING

PISA summarises student performance in collaborative problem solving on a single scale that provides an overall assessment of 15-year-old students' collaborative problem-solving competence. Results for this overall performance measure are presented below, covering both the average level of performance in problem solving in each country/economy and the distribution of collaborative problem-solving proficiency. The remainder of the report will analyse factors that relate to the observed performance.

Average level of proficiency in collaborative problem solving

This section uses students' average scores to summarise the performance of countries and economies in collaborative problem solving, both relative to each other and to the OECD mean. Since collaborative problem solving was a new domain in PISA 2015, the OECD average performance was set at 500 score points and the standard deviation across OECD countries at 100 score points. This established the benchmark against which each country's collaborative problem-solving performance in PISA 2015 was compared.[3,4]

Figure V.3.3 shows each country's/economy's mean score and allows readers to see for which pairs of countries/economies the differences in the means shown are not statistically significant. The data on which Figure V.3.3 is based are presented in Annex B. In each row, the countries/economies listed in the column on the right are those whose mean scores are not sufficiently different to be distinguished with confidence from the mean score of the country/economy in the middle column. When interpreting mean performance, only those differences among countries and economies that are statistically significant should be considered (Box V.3.2). For all other cases, Country A scores higher than Country B if Country A is above Country B in the list in the middle column; Country A scores lower than Country B if Country A is below Country B in the middle column. For example, while the Netherlands clearly ranks above Austria, the performance of Sweden cannot be distinguished with confidence from that of either Austria or the Netherlands.

Box V.3.2. What is a statistically significant difference?

A difference is called statistically significant if it is highly unlikely that such a difference could be observed in the estimates based on samples, if it were the case that no true difference existed between the populations.

The results of the PISA assessments for countries and economies are estimates because they are obtained from samples of students, rather than a census of all students, and because they are obtained using a limited set of assessment tasks, not the universe of all possible assessment tasks. When the sampling of students and assessment tasks is done with scientific rigour, it is possible to determine the magnitude of the uncertainty associated with the estimate. This uncertainty needs to be taken into account when making comparisons so that differences that could reasonably arise simply due to the sampling of students and tasks are not interpreted as differences that actually hold for the populations.

Figure V.3.3 ▪ Comparing countries' and economies' collaborative problem-solving performance

Statistically significantly **above** the OECD average
Not statistically significantly different from the OECD average
Statistically significantly **below** the OECD average

Mean score	Comparison country/economy	Countries and economies whose mean score is NOT statistically significantly different from the comparison country's/economy's score
561	Singapore	
552	**Japan**	
541	Hong Kong (China)	Korea, Canada, Estonia, Finland
538	**Korea**	Hong Kong (China), Canada, Estonia, Finland, Macao (China), New Zealand
535	**Canada**	Hong Kong (China), Korea, Estonia, Finland, Macao (China), New Zealand, Australia
535	**Estonia**	Hong Kong (China), Korea, Canada, Finland, Macao (China), New Zealand, Australia
534	**Finland**	Hong Kong (China), Korea, Canada, Estonia, Macao (China), New Zealand, Australia
534	Macao (China)	Korea, Canada, Estonia, Finland, New Zealand, Australia
533	**New Zealand**	Korea, Canada, Estonia, Finland, Macao (China), Australia, Chinese Taipei
531	**Australia**	Canada, Estonia, Finland, Macao (China), New Zealand, Chinese Taipei, Germany
527	Chinese Taipei	New Zealand, Australia, Germany, United States, Denmark
525	**Germany**	Australia, Chinese Taipei, United States, Denmark, United Kingdom, Netherlands
520	**United States**	Chinese Taipei, Germany, Denmark, United Kingdom, Netherlands
520	**Denmark**	Chinese Taipei, Germany, United States, United Kingdom, Netherlands
519	**United Kingdom**	Germany, United States, Denmark, Netherlands
518	**Netherlands**	Germany, United States, Denmark, United Kingdom, Sweden
510	**Sweden**	Netherlands, Austria, Norway
509	**Austria**	Sweden
502	**Norway**	Sweden, Slovenia, Belgium, Iceland, Czech Republic, Portugal, Spain, B-S-J-G (China)
502	**Slovenia**	Norway, Belgium, Iceland, Czech Republic, Portugal, B-S-J-G (China)
501	**Belgium**	Norway, Slovenia, Iceland, Czech Republic, Portugal, Spain, B-S-J-G (China)
499	**Iceland**	Norway, Slovenia, Belgium, Czech Republic, Portugal, Spain, B-S-J-G (China), France
499	**Czech Republic**	Norway, Slovenia, Belgium, Iceland, Portugal, Spain, B-S-J-G (China), France
498	**Portugal**	Norway, Slovenia, Belgium, Iceland, Czech Republic, Spain, B-S-J-G (China), France
496	**Spain**	Norway, Belgium, Iceland, Czech Republic, Portugal, B-S-J-G (China), France
496	B-S-J-G (China)	Norway, Slovenia, Belgium, Iceland, Czech Republic, Portugal, Spain, France, Luxembourg
494	**France**	Iceland, Czech Republic, Portugal, Spain, B-S-J-G (China), Luxembourg
491	**Luxembourg**	B-S-J-G (China), France
485	**Latvia**	
478	**Italy**	Russia, Croatia, Hungary, Israel
473	Russia	Italy, Croatia, Hungary, Israel, Lithuania
473	Croatia	Italy, Russia, Hungary, Israel, Lithuania
472	**Hungary**	Italy, Russia, Croatia, Israel, Lithuania
469	**Israel**	Italy, Russia, Croatia, Hungary, Lithuania, Slovak Republic
467	Lithuania	Russia, Croatia, Hungary, Israel, Slovak Republic
463	**Slovak Republic**	Israel, Lithuania, Greece, Chile
459	**Greece**	Slovak Republic, Chile
457	**Chile**	Slovak Republic, Greece
444	Cyprus[1]	Bulgaria, Uruguay, Costa Rica
444	Bulgaria	Cyprus,[1] Uruguay, Costa Rica, Thailand, United Arab Emirates
443	Uruguay	Cyprus,[1] Bulgaria, Costa Rica, Thailand
441	Costa Rica	Cyprus,[1] Bulgaria, Uruguay, Thailand, United Arab Emirates
436	Thailand	Bulgaria, Uruguay, Costa Rica, United Arab Emirates, Mexico, Colombia
435	United Arab Emirates	Bulgaria, Costa Rica, Thailand, Mexico, Colombia
433	**Mexico**	Thailand, United Arab Emirates, Colombia
429	Colombia	Thailand, United Arab Emirates, Mexico, Turkey
422	**Turkey**	Colombia, Peru, Montenegro
418	Peru	Turkey, Montenegro, Brazil
416	Montenegro	Turkey, Peru, Brazil
412	Brazil	Peru, Montenegro
382	Tunisia	

1. Note by Turkey: The information in this document with reference to "Cyprus" relates to the southern part of the Island. There is no single authority representing both Turkish and Greek Cypriot people on the Island. Turkey recognises the Turkish Republic of Northern Cyprus (TRNC). Until a lasting and equitable solution is found within the context of the United Nations, Turkey shall preserve its position concerning the "Cyprus issue".

Note by all the European Union Member States of the OECD and the European Union: The Republic of Cyprus is recognised by all members of the United Nations with the exception of Turkey. The information in this document relates to the area under the effective control of the Government of the Republic of Cyprus.

Countries and economies are ranked in descending order of mean collaborative problem-solving performance.

Source: OECD, PISA 2015 Database, Table V.3.2.

StatLink http://dx.doi.org/10.1787/888933615743

Figure V.3.4 [Part 1/2] ▪ **Collaborative problem-solving performance among participating countries/economies**

	Collaborative problem-solving scale					
			Range of ranks			
			OECD countries		All countries/economies	
	Mean score	95% confidence interval	Upper rank	Lower rank	Upper rank	Lower rank
Singapore	561	559 - 564			1	1
British Columbia (Canada)	561	550 - 573				
Japan	552	546 - 557	1	1	2	2
Massachusetts (United States)	549	537 - 561				
Alberta (Canada)	543	531 - 554				
Hong Kong (China)	541	535 - 547			3	5
Korea	538	533 - 543	2	5	3	7
Canada	535	531 - 540	2	6	4	10
Estonia	535	530 - 540	2	6	4	10
Finland	534	529 - 539	2	7	4	10
Macao (China)	534	531 - 536			5	10
Quebec (Canada)[1]	534	525 - 543				
Nova Scotia (Canada)	533	524 - 542				
New Zealand	533	528 - 538	3	7	5	11
Ontario (Canada)	532	523 - 541				
Australia	531	528 - 535	4	7	7	11
Prince Edward Island (Canada)	529	517 - 541				
Chinese Taipei	527	522 - 531			10	13
North Carolina (United States)	525	514 - 535				
Germany	525	519 - 530	7	10	10	14
Newfoundland and Labrador (Canada)	521	513 - 530				
England (United Kingdom)	521	515 - 527				
United States	520	513 - 527	8	12	11	16
Denmark	520	515 - 525	8	12	12	16
United Kingdom	519	514 - 524	8	12	12	16
Flemish community (Belgium)	519	513 - 524				
Madrid (Spain)	519	512 - 526				
Manitoba (Canada)	519	508 - 529				
Netherlands	518	513 - 522	9	12	13	16
New Brunswick (Canada)	517	507 - 528				
Castile and Leon (Spain)	517	509 - 525				
Northern Ireland (United Kingdom)	514	507 - 521				
Scotland (United Kingdom)	513	508 - 518				
Bolzano (Italy)	512	498 - 527				
Sweden	510	503 - 516	12	15	16	19
Austria	509	504 - 514	13	15	17	19
Saskatchewan (Canada)	508	501 - 515				
Navarre (Spain)	505	492 - 518				
Catalonia (Spain)	505	496 - 514				
Norway	502	497 - 507	14	19	18	24
Slovenia	502	499 - 505	15	19	19	23
Belgium	501	496 - 506	15	20	19	25
Trento (Italy)	500	494 - 505				
Iceland	499	495 - 504	15	21	19	26
Aragon (Spain)	499	487 - 511				
Czech Republic	499	494 - 503	16	22	19	26
Portugal	498	493 - 503	16	22	20	27
Lombardia (Italy)	498	487 - 509				
Castile-La Mancha (Spain)	497	489 - 505				
Spain	496	492 - 501	17	22	22	27
Wales (United Kingdom)	496	489 - 503				
B-S-J-G (China)	496	488 - 504			20	28

* See note 1 under Figure V.3.3.
1. Results for the province of Quebec in this table should be treated with caution due to a possible non-response bias.
Notes: OECD countries are shown in bold black. Partner countries and economies are shown in bold blue.
Regions are shown in black italics (OECD countries) or blue italics (partner countries).
Countries and economies are ranked in descending order of mean collaborative problem-solving performance.
Source: OECD, PISA 2015 Database, Table V.3.2.
StatLink http://dx.doi.org/10.1787/888933615762

Figure V.3.4 [Part 2/2] ■ **Collaborative problem-solving performance among participating countries/economies**

	Collaborative problem-solving scale					
			Range of ranks			
			OECD countries		All countries/economies	
	Mean score	95% confidence interval	Upper rank	Lower rank	Upper rank	Lower rank
Asturias (Spain)	496	475 - 517				
La Rioja (Spain)	495	477 - 513				
Galicia (Spain)	494	483 - 505				
France	494	489 - 499	19	23	24	28
German-speaking community (Belgium)	493	480 - 505				
Comunidad Valenciana (Spain)	492	485 - 500				
Luxembourg	491	488 - 494	22	23	27	28
Balearic Islands (Spain)	488	477 - 499				
Murcia (Spain)	486	476 - 496				
Latvia	485	480 - 489	24	24	29	29
Cantabria (Spain)	485	469 - 501				
Canary Islands (Spain)	484	474 - 494				
Basque Country (Spain)	484	474 - 493				
Andalusia (Spain)	483	474 - 491				
French community (Belgium)	479	471 - 487				
Italy	478	473 - 483	25	26	30	32
Dubai (UAE)	477	473 - 481				
Extremadura (Spain)	474	465 - 483				
Bogotá (Colombia)	474	464 - 483				
Russia	473	467 - 480			30	34
Croatia	473	468 - 478			30	34
Hungary	472	468 - 477	26	27	31	35
Israel	469	462 - 476	26	28	31	36
Lithuania	467	463 - 472			33	36
Região Autónoma dos Açores (Portugal)	467	461 - 473				
Slovak Republic	463	458 - 467	27	29	35	37
Greece	459	452 - 466	28	30	36	38
Chile	457	452 - 462	29	30	37	38
Medellín (Colombia)	453	444 - 462				
Manizales (Colombia)	451	444 - 459				
Cyprus*	444	441 - 448			39	42
Bulgaria	444	437 - 452			39	43
Campania (Italy)	443	432 - 453				
Uruguay	443	438 - 447			39	42
Costa Rica	441	436 - 446			39	43
Cali (Colombia)	440	432 - 449				
Thailand	436	429 - 442			42	46
United Arab Emirates	435	430 - 440			42	45
Mexico	433	428 - 438	31	31	43	46
Colombia	429	425 - 434			45	47
Sharjah (UAE)	429	411 - 448				
Turkey	422	416 - 429	32	32	46	48
Abu Dhabi (UAE)	422	413 - 430				
Peru	418	413 - 423			47	49
Montenegro	416	413 - 418			48	50
Brazil	412	407 - 416			49	50
Ajman (UAE)	412	401 - 423				
Fujairah (UAE)	402	388 - 416				
Ras Al Khaimah (UAE)	400	382 - 417				
Umm Al Quwain (UAE)	394	382 - 406				
Tunisia	382	378 - 385			51	51

* See note 1 under Figure V.3.3.
1. Results for the province of Quebec in this table should be treated with caution due to a possible non-response bias.
Notes: OECD countries are shown in bold black. Partner countries and economies are shown in bold blue.
Regions are shown in black italics (OECD countries) or blue italics (partner countries).
Countries and economies are ranked in descending order of mean collaborative problem-solving performance.
Source: OECD, PISA 2015 Database, Table V.3.2.
StatLink http://dx.doi.org/10.1787/888933615762

Figure V.3.3 lists each participating country and economy in descending order of its mean collaborative problem-solving score (left column). The values range from a high of 561 points for partner country Singapore to a low of 382 points for partner country Tunisia. Countries and economies are also divided into three broad groups: those whose mean scores are statistically around the OECD mean (highlighted in dark blue), those whose mean scores are above the OECD mean (highlighted in pale blue), and those whose mean scores are below the OECD mean (highlighted in medium blue).

Because the figures are derived from samples, it is not possible to determine a country's precise rank among the participating countries and economies. However, it is possible to determine, with confidence, a range of ranks in which the country's performance lies (Figure V.3.4).

Singapore is the highest-performing country in collaborative problem solving, with a mean score of 561 points. The second highest-performing country is Japan, with a mean score of 552 points. Both of these countries score over half of a standard deviation, on average, above the average level of students in other OECD countries. Singapore scores significantly higher than every other country/economy, and Japan scores significantly higher than every other country/economy except Singapore.

Thirteen other OECD countries – Korea (538 points), Canada (535 points), Estonia (535 points), Finland (534 points), New Zealand (533 points), Australia (531 points), Germany (525 points), the United States (520 points), Denmark (520 points), the United Kingdom (519 points), the Netherlands (518 points), Sweden (510 points) and Austria (509 points) – and three East Asian partner countries and economies – Hong Kong (China) (541 points), Macao (China) (534 points) and Chinese Taipei (527 points) – score above the OECD average on the PISA collaborative problem-solving scale.

Eight countries – Beijing-Shanghai-Jiangsu-Guangdong (China) (hereafter "B-S-J-G [China]"), Belgium, the Czech Republic, Iceland, Norway, Portugal, Slovenia and Spain – score around the OECD mean of 500 points.

There is a gap of 129 score points between the highest-scoring OECD country, Japan (552 score points), and the lowest-scoring OECD country, Turkey (422 score points), a difference of well over one standard deviation. Less than 10% of students in Japan perform below the mean score in Turkey while only roughly 5% of students in Turkey perform at or above the mean score in Japan (Table V.3.2).

Likewise, 180 score points separate the mean scores of the highest- and lowest-performing countries and economies in the collaborative problem-solving assessment – Singapore (561 score points) and Tunisia (382 score points). This gap corresponds to almost two standard deviations or two proficiency levels. Fewer than one in 20 students in Estonia, Hong Kong (China), Japan, Korea and Singapore performs at or below the mean of the lowest-performing country (Table V.3.2).

How collaborative problem-solving proficiency levels are defined in PISA 2015

PISA 2015 provides one overall collaborative problem-solving proficiency scale, drawing on all the questions in the collaborative problem-solving assessment. The collaborative problem-solving scale was constructed to have a mean score of 500 among OECD countries, with about two-thirds of students across OECD countries scoring between 400 and 600.[5] To help interpret what students' scores mean in substantive terms, the scale is divided into five proficiency levels. Four of these (Levels 1 to 4) are described based on the skills needed to successfully complete the items that are located within them; the last (below Level 1) is defined based on the absence of these skills.

Level 1 is the lowest described level and corresponds to an elementary level of collaborative problem-solving skills; Level 4 corresponds to the highest level of collaborative problem-solving skills. As explained above, students with a score within the range of Level 1 are expected to complete most Level 1 items successfully but are unlikely to be able to successfully complete items at higher levels. By contrast, students with scores in the Level 4 range are likely to be able to successfully complete any item included in the PISA assessment of collaborative problem solving.

Students at the different levels of proficiency in collaborative problem solving

Figure V.3.5 expounds on what students at four of the levels of proficiency in collaborative problem solving can typically do. These summary descriptions are based on the detailed analysis of task demands within each level; Chapter 2 provides such an analysis for the released unit, *Xandar*. The distribution of student performance across proficiency levels in each country/economy is shown in Figure V.3.6.

Figure V.3.5 ▪ **Summary descriptions of the four levels of proficiency in collaborative problem solving**

Level	Score range	What students can typically do
4	Equal to or higher than 640 score points	At Level 4, students can successfully carry out complicated problem-solving tasks with high collaboration complexity. They can solve complex problems with multiple constraints, keeping relevant background information in mind. These students maintain an awareness of group dynamics and take actions to ensure that team members act in accordance with their agreed-upon roles. At the same time, they can monitor progress towards a solution and identify obstacles to overcome or gaps to be bridged. Level 4 students take initiative and perform actions or make requests to overcome obstacles and to resolve disagreements and conflicts. They can balance the collaboration and problem-solving aspects of a presented task, identify efficient pathways to a solution, and take actions to solve the given problem.
3	540 to less than 640 score points	At Level 3, students can complete tasks with either complex problem-solving requirements or complex collaboration demands. These students can perform multi-step tasks that require integrating multiple pieces of information, often in complex and dynamic problems. They orchestrate roles within the team and identify information needed by particular team members to solve the problem. Level 3 students can recognise the information needed to solve a problem, request it from the appropriate team member, and identify when the provided information is incorrect. When conflicts arise, they can help team members negotiate a solution.
2	440 to less than 540 score points	At Level 2, students can contribute to a collaborative effort to solve a problem of medium difficulty. They can help solve a problem by communicating with team members about the actions to be performed. They can volunteer information not specifically requested by another team member. Level 2 students understand that not all team members have the same information and can consider differing perspectives in their interactions. They can help the team establish a shared understanding of the steps required to solve a problem. These students can request additional information required to solve a problem and solicit agreement or confirmation from team members about the approach to be taken. Students near the top of Level 2 can take the initiative to suggest a logical next step, or propose a new approach, to solve a problem.
1	340 to less than 440 score points	At Level 1, students can complete tasks with low problem complexity and limited collaboration complexity. They can provide requested information and take actions to enact plans when prompted. Level 1 students can confirm actions or proposals made by others. They tend to focus on their individual role within the group. With support from team members, and when working on a simple problem, these students can help find a solution to the given problem.

Proficiency at Level 4

Students proficient at Level 4 on the collaborative problem-solving scale can successfully carry out complicated problem-solving tasks with high collaboration complexity. They maintain an awareness of group dynamics and ensure that team members act in accordance with their agreed-upon roles, while simultaneously monitoring progress towards a solution of the given problem. They take initiative and perform actions or make requests to overcome obstacles and to resolve disagreements and conflicts. Students who perform at Level 4 are also referred to as "top performers" in the rest of this report.[6]

Part 3, Item 2 of *Xandar* is an example of a Level 4 item. It requires students first to recognise that one of the other team members has answered a question that he or she was supposed to answer. Students must then remind their team members that they should act in accordance with the roles hitherto agreed upon, instead of complimenting the student who correctly answered the wrong question. While the latter response develops a collaborative dynamic among team members, the credited response does so while also advancing towards a solution to the problem.

Across OECD countries, 8% of students perform at this level, although student proficiency varies among countries. More than one in five students in Singapore (21%) and between 15% and 16% of students in Australia, Canada and New Zealand perform at this level. These four countries are also among the top-performing countries and economies in collaborative problem solving (Figure V.3.4). Indeed, every country whose mean performance in collaborative problem solving is above the OECD average also has a larger-than-average proportion of students who perform at Level 4.[7]

In contrast, in two OECD countries and in seven partner countries, fewer than 1 in 100 students performs at Level 4; and in Tunisia, fewer than 1 in 1 000 students performs at this level (Figure V.3.6 and Table V.3.1).

Figure V.3.6 ▪ **Proficiency in collaborative problem solving**

Percentage of students at the different levels of collaborative problem-solving proficiency

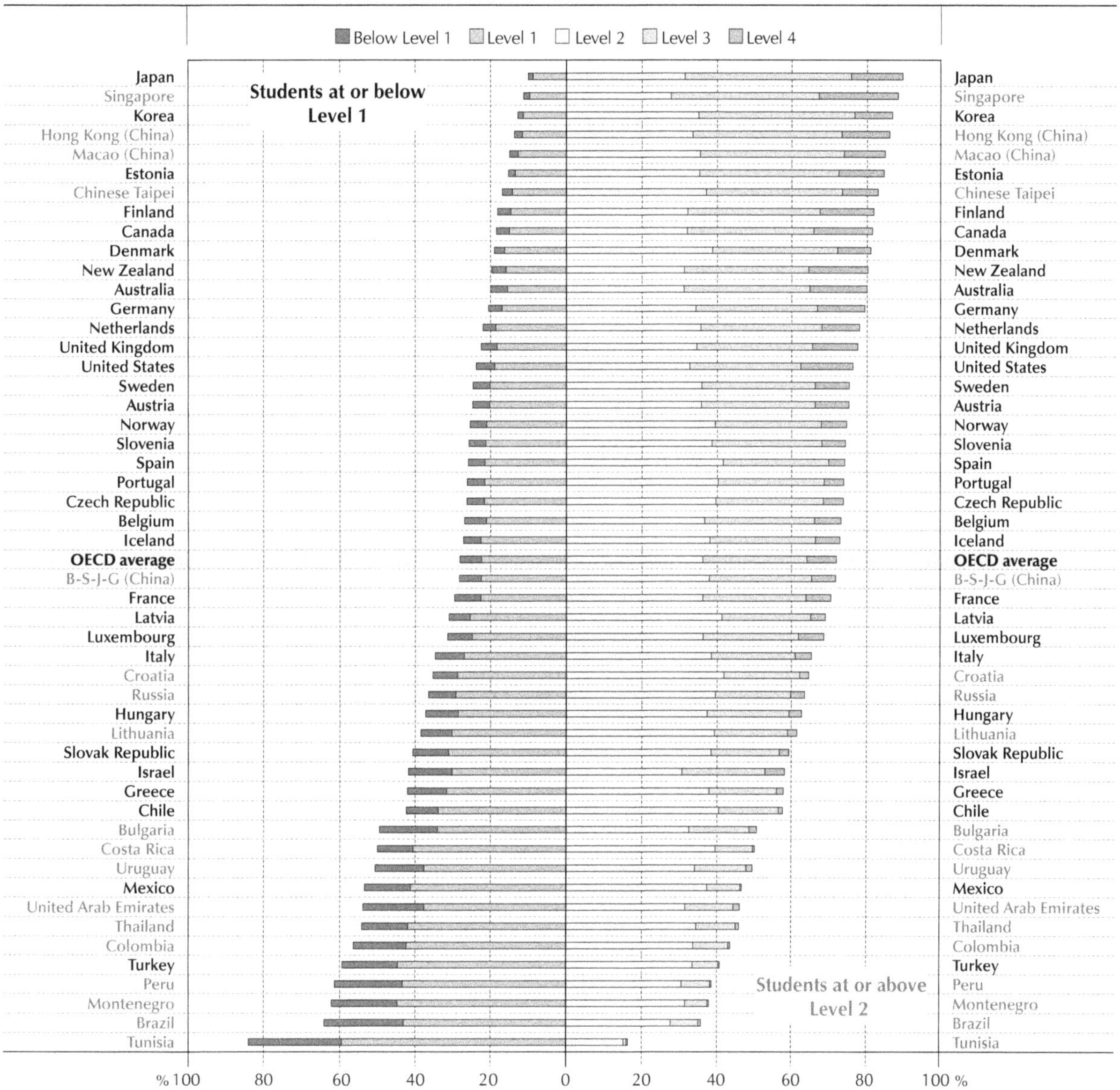

Countries and economies are ranked in descending order of the percentage of students at Level 2, 3 or 4 in collaborative problem solving.

Source: OECD, PISA 2015 Database, Table V.3.1.

StatLink http://dx.doi.org/10.1787/888933615781

Proficiency at Level 3

Students proficient at Level 3 on the collaborative problem-solving scale can complete tasks with either complex problem-solving requirements or complex collaboration demands. They can recognise information needed to solve a problem, request it from the appropriate team member, and identify when the provided information is incorrect. These students can perform multi-step tasks that require integrating multiple pieces of information.

Part 4, Item 2 of *Xandar* is an example of a Level 3 task. Students must recognise that Zach, one of the team members, needs help and then come up with a suggestion as to how to help him while simultaneously attending to their own tasks.

As students proficient at Level 4 can also complete Level 3 items, the following discussion uses "proficient at Level 3 or higher" synonymously with "can sucessfully complete a Level 3 item". The same terminology will be used below to refer to the cumulative proportions at lower levels.

Across OECD countries, 36% of students are proficient at Level 3 or higher. In Hong Kong (China), Japan, Korea and Singapore, more than one in two students are capable of completing Level 3 items, and just under one in two students (over 45%) in Australia, Canada, Estonia, Finland, Germany, Macao (China), New Zealand and Chinese Taipei performs at Level 3 or higher. In every country that performs significantly above the OECD mean, the proportion of students proficient at Level 3 or higher is also above the OECD mean (Figure V.3.6 and Table V.3.1).

Level 3 was the most common proficiency level in 10 of the 51 countries/economies with adjudicated data from the collaborative problem-solving assessment.[8] By contrast, in two OECD countries and five partner countries, fewer than one in ten students performs at Level 3 or higher. In Tunisia, fewer than one in 100 students can successfully complete a Level 3 item (Figure V.3.6 and Table V.3.1).

Proficiency at Level 2

Students proficient at Level 2 on the collaborative problem-solving scale can contribute to a collaborative effort to solve a problem of medium difficulty. They can communicate with team members about the actions to be performed and they can volunteer information not specifically requested by another team member.

Part 2, Item 3 of *Xandar* is one example of a Level 2 task. Alice and Zach, the other two team members, have already chosen their subject areas. The student must process this information and signal that they have done so by stating that they will choose the remaining subject area.

Across OECD countries, 72% of students perform at Level 2 or higher. In Hong Kong (China), Japan, Korea, Macao (China) and Singapore, over 85% of 15-year-olds are proficient at Level 2 or higher; in a further seven countries/economies – Australia, Canada, Denmark, Estonia, Finland, New Zealand and Chinese Taipei – over 80% of 15-year-olds achieve this level of competence. This is the most common proficiency level in 28 of the 51 countries and economies with comparable data. However, in two OECD countries and eight partner countries, a majority of students cannot complete Level 2 items successfully (Figure V.3.6 and Table V.3.1).

Proficiency at Level 1

Students proficient at Level 1 can complete tasks with low problem difficulty and limited collaboration complexity. They tend to focus on their individual role within the group, but with support from team members. When working on a simple problem, these students can help find a solution to the problem.

Part 3, Item 1 of *Xandar* is an example of a Level 1 problem. Students are told or reminded (depending on how they finished Part 2) that their subject area is geography, and that the other team members have been assigned the other two subjects. Focusing on their own role in the group, they must then click the correct button – the "Geography" button – to get started.

Across OECD countries, 94% of students reach this level of collaborative problem-solving proficiency. However, in Tunisia, almost one in four students (25%) fails to reach this level of proficiency. More than one in five students in Brazil (21%) and more than one in six students in Montenegro and Peru (both 18%) are likewise not proficient at Level 1. Level 1 is the most common proficiency level in 13 of the 51 countries/economies with available data (Figure V.3.6 and Table V.3.1).

Proficiency below Level 1

The PISA 2015 collaborative problem-solving assessment was not designed to assess either elementary collaboration skills or elementary problem-solving skills. Hence, there were insufficient items to fully describe performance that fell below Level 1 on the collaborative problem-solving scale.

Across OECD countries, 6% of students score below Level 1 on the proficiency scale. Between one in 50 students and one in 100 students in Estonia, Hong Kong (China), Japan, Korea and Singapore score below Level 1 (Figure V.3.6 and Table V.3.1).

HOW COLLABORATIVE PROBLEM-SOLVING PERFORMANCE RELATES TO PERFORMANCE IN SCIENCE, READING AND MATHEMATICS

A comparison of the mean scores in collaborative problem solving, science, reading and mathematics shows that the same countries/economies – Canada, Korea, Hong Kong (China), Japan and Singapore – are found at or near the top of each set of rankings. Thus, one may wonder to what extent the collaborative problem-solving assessment measures collaboration skills as opposed to general cognitive skills.

Scores in the four domains are indeed highly correlated, as shown in Figure V.3.7. On average across OECD countries, student performance in collaborative problem solving shows a correlation of 0.77 with performance in science, 0.74 with performance in reading, and 0.70 with performance in mathematics. These numbers are lower than the pairwise correlations between scores in the core PISA subjects, which range from 0.80 to 0.88. Collaborative problem-solving outcomes, while still closely related to outcomes in science, reading and mathematics, appear to be slightly less strongly related to these core subject outcomes than these core subject outcomes are related to each other.

Figure V.3.7 ▪ **Correlations among performance in collaborative problem solving and in core PISA subjects**

OECD average

Correlation between:			
Mathematics	**Reading**	**Science**	...and...
0.70	0.74	0.77	**Collaborative problem solving**
	0.80	0.88	**Mathematics**
		0.87	**Reading**

Source: OECD, PISA 2015 Database, Table V.3.4.

The link between student scores in collaborative problem solving, science, reading and mathematics is strongest in Bulgaria, the United Arab Emirates and the United States and weakest in Costa Rica, the Russian Federation (hereafter "Russia") and Tunisia. In these latter three countries, however, correlations between performance in collaborative problem solving and performance in each of the three core PISA subjects still exceed 0.55 (Table V.3.4).

Another way to see the relationship is by looking at the extent to which top or low performance in the three core PISA domains predicts performance in collaborative problem solving. In science, reading and mathematics, top performers are defined as those students who perform at Levels 5 or 6, while low performers are those students who perform below the baseline proficiency level, Level 2. In collaborative problem solving, top performers are defined as those students who perform at Level 4, while low performers are those students who perform below Level 2.[9]

Some 44% of top performers in science, 39% of top performers in reading, and 34% of top performers in mathematics are also top performers in collaborative problem solving, on average across OECD countries (Table V.3.3a). Some 55% of students who are top performers in all three core PISA subjects (all-round top performers) are also top performers in collaborative problem solving (Figure V.3.8). This proportion is particularly large in Australia, Canada, New Zealand, Singapore, the United Kingdom and the United States where over 69% of students who are all-round top performers are also top performers in collaborative problem solving.

By contrast, in Brazil and Chile, fewer than one in three all-round top performers score at the highest level in collaborative problem solving. This may imply that collaborative problem-solving skills in these countries are developed independently of skills and literacy in the three core PISA subjects. However, the share of top performers in these countries is very small: 0.6% in Brazil and 1.2% in Chile.

Similar relationships are observed among low performers, although there is greater observed overlap. On average across OECD countries, 74% of low performers in science, 74% of low performers in reading, and 67% of low performers in mathematics are also low performers in collaborative problem solving. Some 83% of low performers in all three core subjects (all-round low performers) are also low performers in collaborative problem solving. Hence, it may be that a certain level of functional literacy in the three core domains is a pre-requisite for performance in collaborative problem solving (Figure V.3.8).

In Bulgaria, Montenegro, Tunisia, Turkey and the United Arab Emirates, over 93% of students who are all-round low performers are also low performers in collaborative problem solving. By contrast, in Germany, Japan and Korea, less than 75% of all-round low performers are low performers in collaborative problem solving. This is likely due to the particularly low scores of low performers in the former group of countries: the average student who is an all-round low performer in Tunisia scores lower in these domains than the average student who is an all-round low performer in Japan. Another interpretation is that collaborative problem-solving skills might be more "fundamental", that is, developed in all students, regardless of ability, in the latter three countries, while they might be more dependent on basic literacy skills in the former five countries.

Figure V.3.8 ▪ **Top performers and low achievers in four PISA subjects**

Percentage of top performers/low achievers in collaborative problem solving among all-round top performers/low achievers in the three core PISA subjects

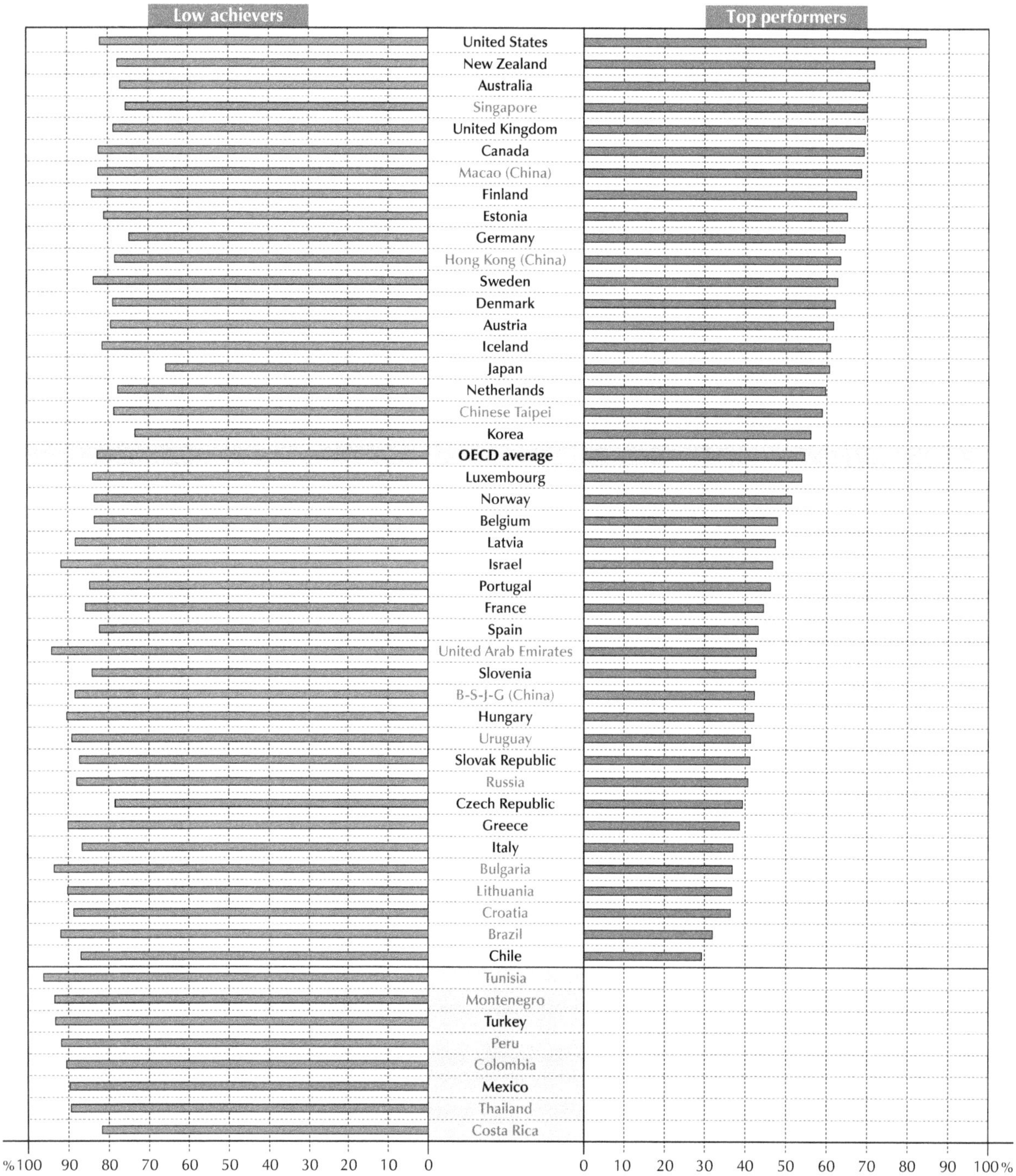

Notes: Top performers in collaborative problem solving are students who score at Level 4. All-round top performers score at Level 5 or 6 in science, reading and mathematics.

Low achievers in collaborative problem solving score below Level 2. All-round low achievers score below Level 2 in science, reading and mathematics.

Due to sample size limitations, the proportion of top performers for the eight countries at the bottom of the figure could not be accurately determined.

Countries and economies are ranked in descending order of the proportion of top performers in collaborative problem solving among all-round top performers in the three core PISA subjects.

Source: OECD, PISA 2015 Database, Tables V.3.3a and V.3.3b.

StatLink http://dx.doi.org/10.1787/888933615800

Mean performance across countries is more closely correlated than individual student performance. Across OECD countries, the correlations between mean country collaborative problem-solving scores and mean country scores in the three core domains are between 0.87 and 0.96, while the correlations between mean country scores within the three core domains are between 0.95 and 0.98. Education systems that are strong in one domain thus appear also to be strong in other domains, although individual students may have strengths and weaknesses in particular areas.

Relative performance in collaborative problem solving

As discussed above, performance in collaborative problem solving is closely linked to performance in the three core PISA domains of science, reading and mathematics. In order to isolate the distinctive aspects of collaborative problem-solving ability, scores in collaborative problem solving were regressed over scores in the three core domains. Each student's relative performance – his or her performance in collaborative problem solving after accounting for proficiency in science, reading and mathematics – was then calculated.[10] This calculation pooled data from all PISA-participating countries and economies and thus allowed for the ranking of countries and economies by their average relative performance.[11]

Although the average relative performance across all students pooled over all countries/economies is, by definition, equal to zero, the average relative performance in OECD countries is slightly positive at three score points, indicating that students in OECD countries have, on average, higher collaborative problem-solving skills than students in participating partner countries/economies who perform similarly in the three core domains.

Figure V.3.9 shows each participating country and economy in order of its mean relative collaborative problem-solving performance. The values range from a high of 23 points for OECD country Japan to a low of -22 points for partner country Russia. Countries and economies are also divided into three broad groups: those whose mean relative scores are statistically around the OECD mean (pale blue bars), those whose mean relative scores are above the OECD mean (medium blue bars), and those whose mean relative scores are below the OECD mean (dark grey bars). The range and variation of relative scores are noticeably smaller than that of raw performance scores. One way to interpret such scores is to say that, on average, students in Japan perform 0.23 standard deviations better than expected given their scores in science, reading and mathematics. Another interpretation is that based on their collaborative problem-solving performance, students in Japan score below expected in science, reading and mathematics.

Australia, Japan, Korea, New Zealand and the United States are among the highest-performing countries in terms of relative performance in collaborative problem solving. Students in these countries score between 20 and 23 points higher in collaborative problem solving, on average, than would be expected given their science, reading and mathematics scores (Figure V.3.9).

Ten other OECD countries – Iceland (15 points), Denmark (14 points), Germany (14 points), Austria (13 points), the United Kingdom (12 points), Canada (10 points), Sweden (9 points), Estonia (8 points), the Netherlands (8 points) and Finland (7 points) – and three partner countries/economies – Singapore (16 points), Hong Kong (China) (15 points) and Macao (China) (11 points) – score above the OECD average in relative performance in collaborative problem solving (Figure V.3.9).

Six countries – Costa Rica, the Czech Republic, Luxembourg, Peru, Chinese Taipei and Thailand – score around the OECD average of three points in relative performance in collaborative problem solving.

There is a gap of 42 score points between the relative performance of the highest-scoring OECD country, Japan (23 score points) and the lowest-scoring OECD country, Turkey (-19 score points), a difference of 42% of a standard deviation in raw performance. Some 66% of students in Japan perform better in collaborative problem solving than would be expected given their science, reading and mathematics scores, while only 35% of students in Turkey do so (Table V.3.9a). Similar results are observed in the poorest-performing country, the partner country Russia, where only 36% of students perform better in collaborative problem solving than would be expected given their performance in the three core PISA domains.

There are notable differences between country comparisons of raw and relative scores in collaborative problem solving. For instance, while Chinese Taipei ranks above the OECD average in raw performance scores, it does not differ significantly from the OECD average in relative performance. Students in Belgium, B-S-J-G (China), Norway, Portugal, Slovenia and Spain, while at the OECD average in raw collaborative problem-solving scores, score below the average once accounting for their science, reading and mathematics performance. These differences may be explained by students in these countries being weaker in the uniquely collaborative aspects of the assessment than students in countries that perform similarly in science, reading and mathematics. Explained another way, students in these countries perform particularly strongly in science, reading and mathematics without a correspondingly higher performance in collaborative problem solving.

Figure V.3.9 ▪ **Countries' and economies' relative performance in collaborative problem solving**

Score-point difference between actual and expected performance in collaborative problem solving

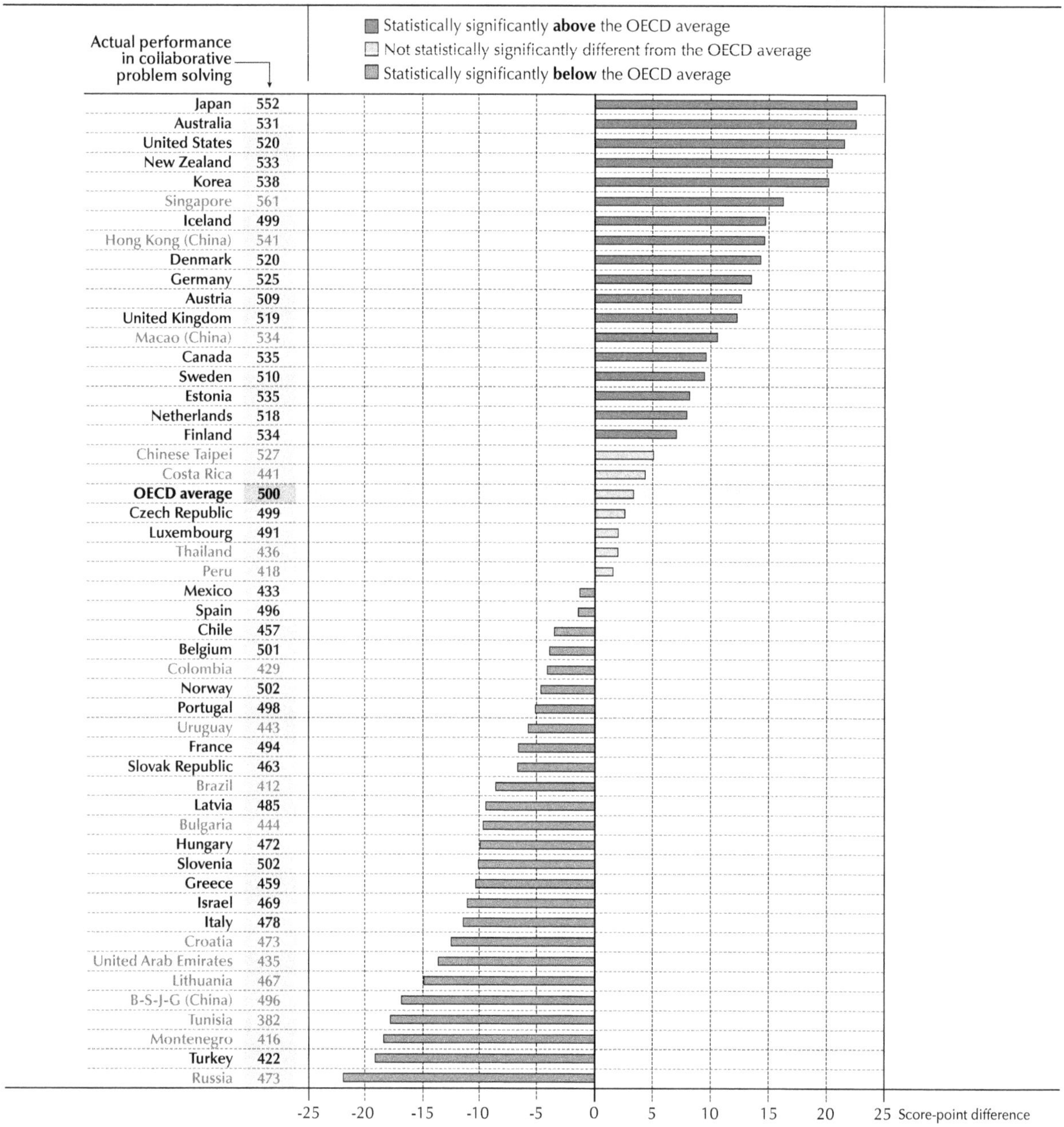

Note: A student's relative performance in collaborative problem solving is defined as the residual obtained upon an ordinary least-squares regression of the student's performance in collaborative problem solving over his or her performance in science, reading and mathematics. The regression is performed at an international level, pooling data from all countries and economies that participated in the collaborative problem-solving assessment.

Countries and economies are ranked in descending order of the relative performance in collaborative problem solving.

Source: OECD, PISA 2015 Database, Tables V.3.2 and V.3.9a.

StatLink http://dx.doi.org/10.1787/888933615819

By contrast, some countries/economies perform better when considering their relative performance. In Iceland, students ranked at the OECD average in raw performance, but were above the OECD average when considering relative performance. Moreover, in Costa Rica, Luxembourg, Peru and Thailand, students performed below the OECD average in their raw collaborative problem-solving scores but at the OECD average once accounting for scores in the other three domains. In these countries, students have stronger skills in the uniquely collaborative aspects of the assessment than would have been expected given their science, reading and mathematics performance. Conversely, they perform worse in science, reading and mathematics than their collaborative problem-solving scores would have suggested.

THE LINKS BETWEEN COLLABORATIVE PROBLEM SOLVING AND INDIVIDUAL PROBLEM SOLVING

PISA 2015 measured collaborative problem solving, which, as described in Chapter 2, is modelled on three competencies related to collaboration and four processes related to problem solving. As a result, a student's performance in collaborative problem solving is not purely a measure of his or her collaboration skills but also reflects his or her ability to use collaboration to resolve a problem or work towards a goal.

Individual problem solving was measured in the innovative domain in PISA 2012. Figure V.3.10 plots the raw performance scores of countries/economies that participated in both the individual problem-solving assessment in 2012 and the collaborative problem-solving assessment in 2015. There is a strong positive correlation (as measured by an r^2 of 0.85 among all countries and economies, and 0.70 among OECD countries) between the mean scores in the two assessments. Countries that performed well in individual problem solving in PISA 2012 also tend to perform well in collaborative problem solving in 2015. This might be expected, due to the cognitive skills and the problem-solving processes common to both assessments.

Figure V.3.10 ■ **Performance in individual problem solving (PISA 2012) and in collaborative problem solving (PISA 2015)**

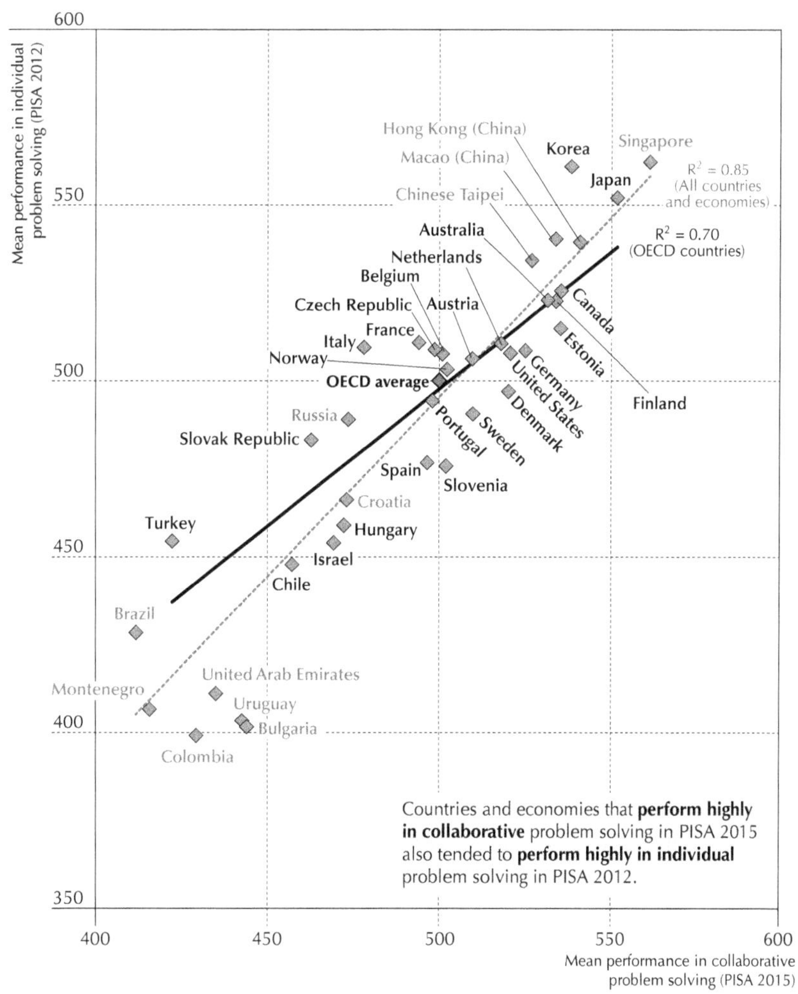

Note: Only those countries and economies with available data or valid results for the PISA 2012 assessment of individual problem solving and the PISA 2015 assessment of collaborative problem solving are shown.
Source: OECD, PISA 2015 Database, Table V.3.2, and PISA 2012 Database, Table V.3.2, from *PISA 2012 Results: Creative Problem Solving (Volume V)*.
StatLink http://dx.doi.org/10.1787/888933615838

As described above and in *PISA 2012 Results: Creative Problem Solving (Volume V)* (OECD, 2014), students' general level of ability, as reflected in their performance in science, reading and mathematics, is also highly correlated with their performance in both individual and collaborative problem solving. Relative scores for problem solving, calculated (as for collaborative problem solving) from the residuals on a regression of performance in creative problem solving against performance in the three core PISA subjects, were calculated using data from PISA 2012. Countries'/economies' mean relative scores in individual problem solving and collaborative problem solving are plotted against each other in Figure V.3.11.

Relative scores in collaborative problem solving are weakly and positively correlated with relative scores in individual problem solving (Figure V.3.11), with an r^2 of 0.23. This drop in the correlation coefficient after accounting for performance in science, reading and mathematics indicates that much of the relationship between scores in the two types of problem solving was due to their common relationship with the cognitive elements also displayed in the science, reading and mathematics assessments.

Figure V.3.11 ▪ **Relative performance in individual problem solving (PISA 2012) and in collaborative problem solving (PISA 2015)**

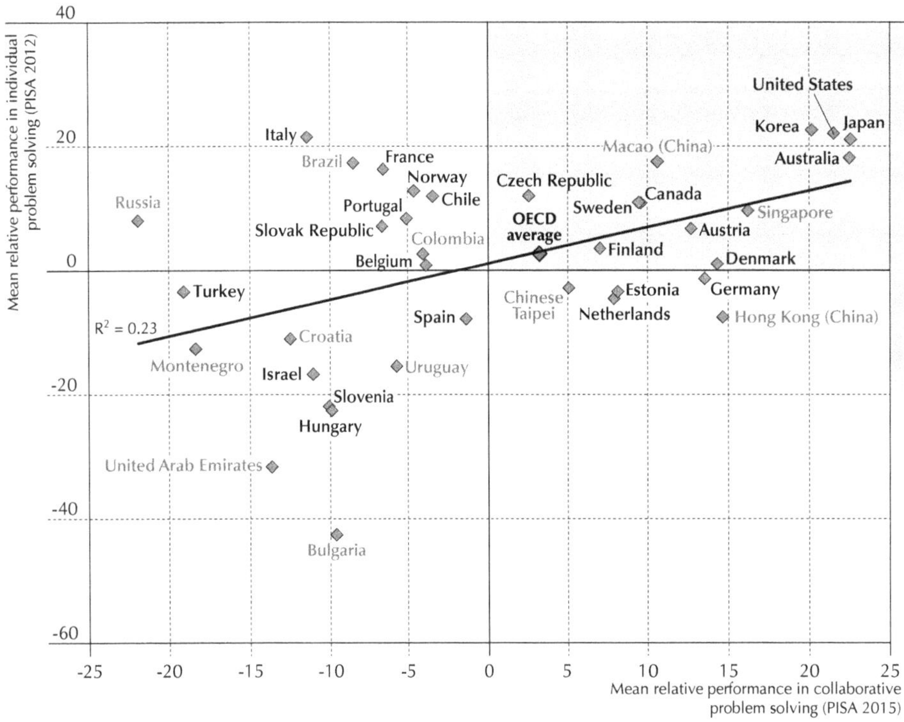

Countries and economies that **perform highly in collaborative problem solving** in PISA 2015 after accounting for performance in the three core domains also tended to **perform highly in individual problem solving** in PISA 2012 after accounting for performance in the three core domains.

The relationship is weaker than it is before accounting for performance in the three core domains.

Note: Only those countries and economies with available data or valid results for the PISA 2012 assessment of creative problem solving and the PISA 2015 assessment of collaborative problem solving are shown.
Source: OECD, PISA 2012 and PISA 2015 Databases, Tables V.3.9a and V.3.9b.
StatLink http://dx.doi.org/10.1787/888933615857

The remaining correlation between the relative scores includes the problem-solving elements that are common to both assessments. Its weaker magnitude also indicates, however, that relative scores in collaborative problem solving measure something distinct from relative scores in individual problem solving. This supports the idea that the three collaborative problem-solving competencies described in Chapter 2 exist and can be measured, and that collaborative problem solving is a skill in its own right, distinct from individual problem solving.

It is important to remember that the general trends mentioned above compare different students: 15-year-olds in 2012 versus 15-year-olds in 2015. The cognitive skills and (individual) problem-solving capabilities of students in 2015 may be different from those of students in 2012. Indeed, PISA measures trends in the three core domains, and many countries/economies show noticeable performance changes in these domains even over a three-year period.

However, on the assumption that three-year trends in most countries are small, these correlations are indicative of a likely relationship between individual (pure) problem solving and collaborative problem solving, the latter of which combines aspects of both pure problem-solving and collaboration skills.

THE INFLUENCE OF COMPUTER DELIVERY ON PERFORMANCE IN COLLABORATIVE PROBLEM SOLVING

The PISA 2015 collaborative problem-solving assessment is interactive and hence could only be delivered in a computer-based format. It was assumed that almost all 15-year-old students in 2015 were familiar with computers and other information and communications technology (ICT), especially in countries that chose to conduct the assessment on computer. However, the extent to which students use and are comfortable with computers and ICT equipment might have affected their performance in the collaborative problem-solving assessment compared to their performance on a similar test conducted in a different medium.

In an optional questionnaire on ICT familiarity administered in 43 out of the 52 countries/economies that assessed students' performance in collaborative problem solving, students were asked to report on the extent to which they use ICT at school and their self-perceived comfort with ICT. Their responses are summarised in Box V.3.3.

Box V.3.3. **Indices related to students' use of and familiarity with ICT**

The ICT questionnaire in PISA 2015 was administered in 46 of the 57 OECD and partner countries/economies that participated in the computer-based assessment; in addition, the questionnaire was administered in schools in the United Kingdom outside of Scotland.[12] It asks students about the availability of, their use of, and attitudes towards computers and other forms of ICT.

Since students completed the collaborative problem-solving assessment on the computer, their performance may be related to their use and familiarity with computers and ICT. Two ICT indices in particular were thought to be relevant to performance in the assessment:

- The index of the use of ICT at school. Students were asked how often they used digital devices for the following activities while at school: online chatting; using e-mail; browsing the Internet; downloading, uploading or browsing material from the school's website or Intranet; posting work onto the school's website; playing simulations; practicing and drilling, such as for learning foreign languages or mathematics; doing homework; and doing group work and communicating with other students.
- The index of students' self-reported ICT competence. Students were asked to what extent they agreed or disagreed that: they feel comfortable using digital devices that they are less familiar with; they can give advice if friends or relatives want to buy new digital devices or applications; they feel comfortable using digital devices at home; they think they can solve problems they come across with digital devices; and they can help friends or relatives who have a problem with digital devices.

Indices were normalised to an average of 0 and a standard deviation of 1 across OECD countries. As these are self-reported indices, there is cultural bias in how students respond, with students in some countries/economies being more likely to respond positively even if the underlying trait, such as the level of ICT use in school, is the same.

Students in Australia, Denmark, Sweden, and Thailand reported the highest use of ICT at school, with average indices over 0.50 (or over half a standard deviation above the OECD average); students in the East Asian countries of B-S-J-G (China), Japan and Korea reported the lowest use of ICT at school, with average indices below -0.50 (Table V.3.10a).

Self-reported ICT competence is found to be particularly high in Australia, Denmark, France, Ireland, New Zealand, Portugal, Sweden and the United Kingdom (excluding Scotland), where the index was between 0.20 and 0.40. This index was particularly low in the three East Asian countries of B-S-J-G (China), Japan and Korea, where it was between -0.49 and -1.00 (Table V.3.10b).

On average across OECD countries, students who rank between the 25th and 75th percentiles in the index of ICT use at school (i.e. those in the second and third quarters in their country/economy) perform better than students who use ICT at school the most (those in the top quarter) or the least (those in the bottom quarter). Moreover, students who use ICT the most in their school score 29 points lower in collaborative problem solving, on average, than students who use ICT the least. In Bulgaria, Greece, Israel, Latvia, Lithuania and Portugal, this gap is over 50 score points. Only in Australia and Japan, both of which are among the top countries/economies in collaborative problem solving, do students who report that they use ICT the most in school perform better than students who say they use ICT the least (Figure V.3.12, Table V.3.11a).

Students who reported that they use ICT the most frequently (those in the top quartile of ICT use at school in their country/economy) are only 60% as likely as other students to be top performers in collaborative problem solving. In Bulgaria, Greece and Lithuania, these students are less than 20% as likely as other students to be top performers in collaborative problem solving (Table V.3.11a).

Greater dependence on ICT may reduce the time students spend interacting and co-operating with each other, and thus may reduce their opportunities to learn how to collaborate, how to interpret the nuances of human communication, or how to compromise and consider others' opinions. Students might spend much of their time in a one-on-one "interaction" with education software, perhaps being distracted by it, thereby disengaging from the group (Heflin, Shewmaker and Nguyen, 2017).

Particularly infrequent use of ICT at school is often found in socio-economically disadvantaged schools. As is discussed in the next chapter, this is associated with lower performance in collaborative problem solving. Because of the cross-sectional and non-experimental nature of the variation in ICT use, the relationship between ICT use and performance in collaborative problem solving is not necessarily one of cause and effect.

By contrast, students' self-reported ICT competence is found to be positively related to performance in collaborative problem solving. Students who rank in their country's top quarter of self-reported ICT competence score 11 points higher in collaborative problem solving than students who rank in their country's bottom quarter, on average across OECD countries. The difference is especially large (more than 40 score points) in Bulgaria, Colombia and Lithuania. Only in Belgium do students who reported being highly competent in ICT score worse in collaborative problem solving (Table V.3.11b).

Figure V.3.12 ▪ **Index of ICT use at school and performance in collaborative problem solving**

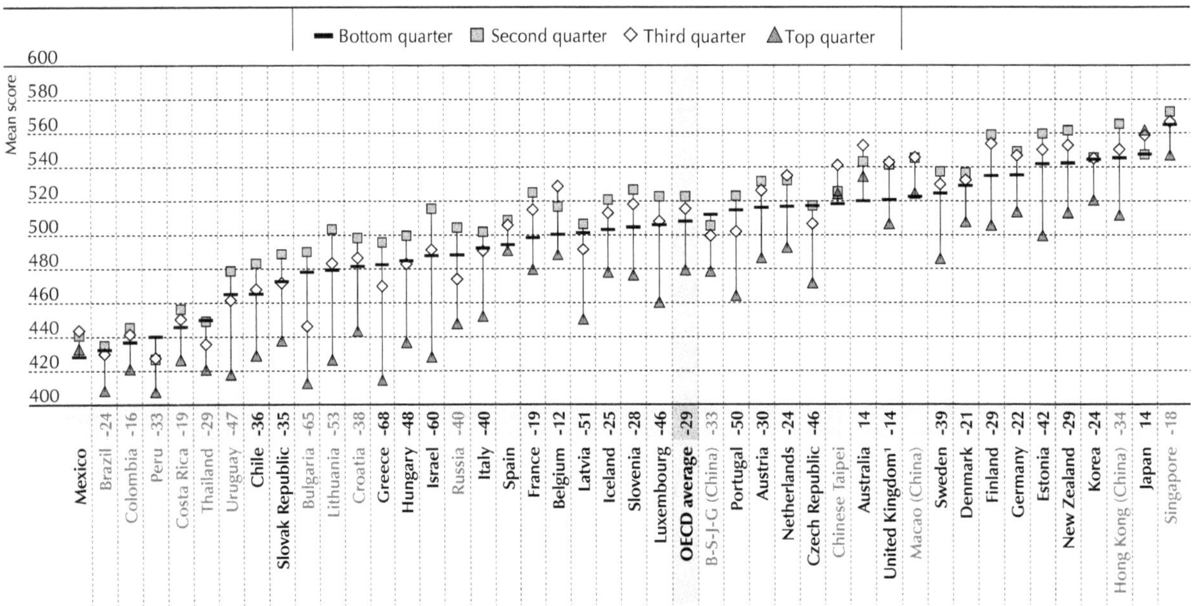

1. Only the United Kingdom subnational entities of England, Northern Ireland and Wales participated in the ICT questionnaire.

Notes: Statistically significant score-point differences in collaborative problem-solving performance between students in the top and bottom quarters of the index of ICT use at school are shown next to the country/economy name (see Annex A3).

Countries and economies are ranked in ascending order of the performance in collaborative problem solving among students in the bottom quarter of the index of ICT use at school.

Source: OECD, PISA 2015 Database, Table V.3.11a.

StatLink http://dx.doi.org/10.1787/888933615876

The index of self-reported ICT competence was normalised to have an average of 0 and a standard deviation of 1 across OECD countries. On average across all OECD countries that distributed the ICT questionnaire, 13% of 15-year-old students have an index of self-reported ICT competence that is below -1.00. Fewer than 7% of students in Denmark, Ireland, Portugal and the United Kingdom (excluding Scotland) reported such low ICT competence, while students in B-S-J-G (China), Japan and Korea were the most likely to report low ICT competence, with more than 20% of students in these countries so reporting (Figure V.3.13 and Table V.3.12).[13]

On average, students whose index of self-reported ICT competence was below -1.00 were 19% more likely to be low performers and scored, on average, 18 points below students with a higher index of self-reported ICT competence. Students with low self-reported ICT competence in Croatia, Hong Kong (China), Hungary, Lithuania and the United Kingdom (excluding Scotland) had a notably higher likelihood (over 40%) of being low performers. Only in Germany were students with an index of self-reported ICT competence below -1.00 less likely to be low performers than students with a higher index (Figure V.3.13 and Table V.3.12).

Figure V.3.13 ▪ **Low performance in collaborative problem solving and self-reported ICT competence**

Increased likelihood that students whose index of self-reported ICT competence is below -1.00 are low performers compared to those whose index is above -1.00

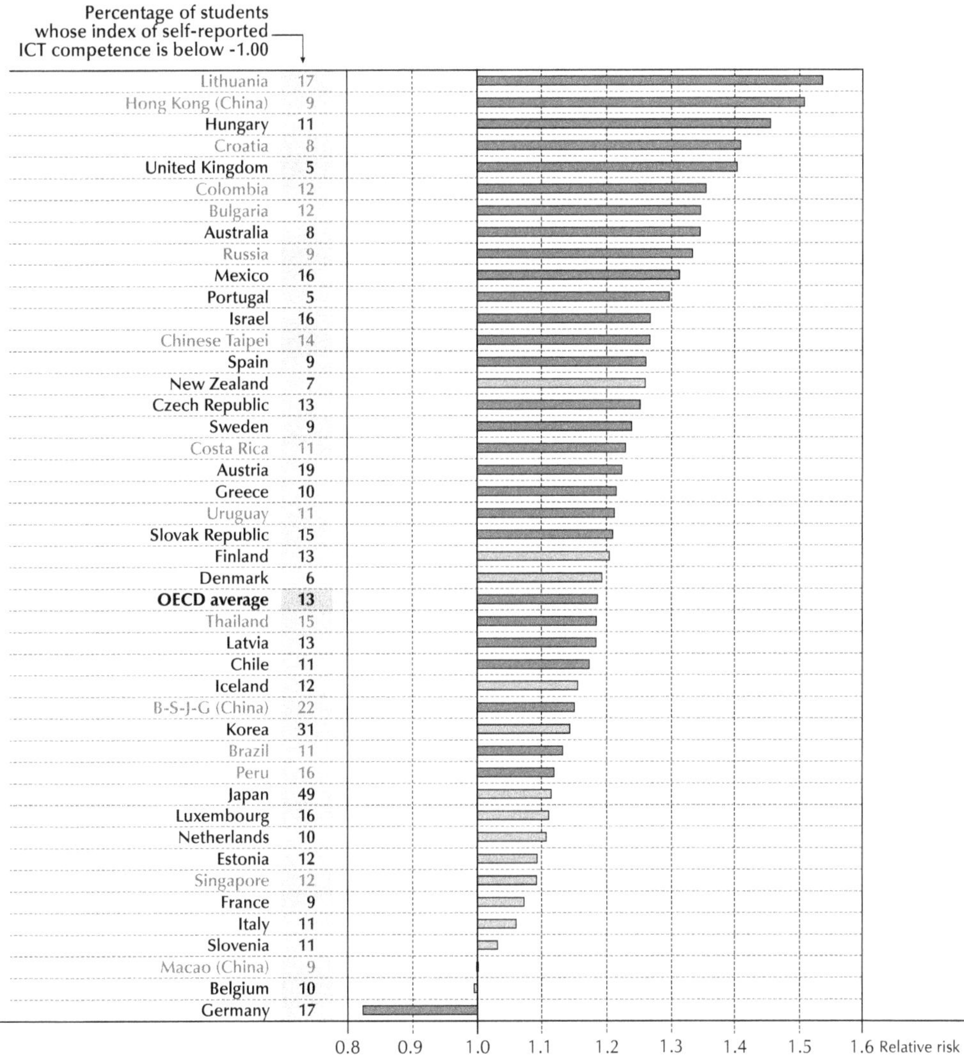

Note: Statistically significant relative risk is shown in a darker tone (see Annex A3).

Countries and economies are ranked in descending order of the increased likelihood that students whose index of self-reported ICT competence is below -1.00 are low performers in collaborative problem solving compared to students whose index is above -1.00.

Source: OECD, PISA 2015 Database, Table V.3.12.

StatLink http://dx.doi.org/10.1787/888933615895

Hence, low self-reported competence in ICT is associated with poor performance in collaborative problem solving. It may be that low ICT competence hinders performance, or that there is a threshold in ICT competence below which certain levels of performance in collaborative problem solving are less likely to be observed. However, the direction of the association cannot be ascertained from this analysis. Moreover, the correlation between ICT competence and performance is low: ICT competence explains only 0.6% of the variation in collaborative problem-solving performance.

If low self-reported ICT competence hinders performance in the computer-based collaborative problem-solving assessment, it should also hinder performance in the science, reading and mathematics assessments as those assessments are also delivered via computer. To analyse whether ICT competence is related to performance in the distinctly collaborative aspects of the collaborative problem-solving assessment, Figure V.3.14 shows the relationship between self-reported ICT competence and relative performance, defined as the residual in a regression of performance in the collaborative problem-solving domain over performance in the science, reading and mathematics domains.

Figure V.3.14 ▪ **Students' self-reported ICT competence and relative performance in collaborative problem solving**

Score-point difference between students whose index of self-reported ICT competence is above -1.00 and those whose index is below -1.00

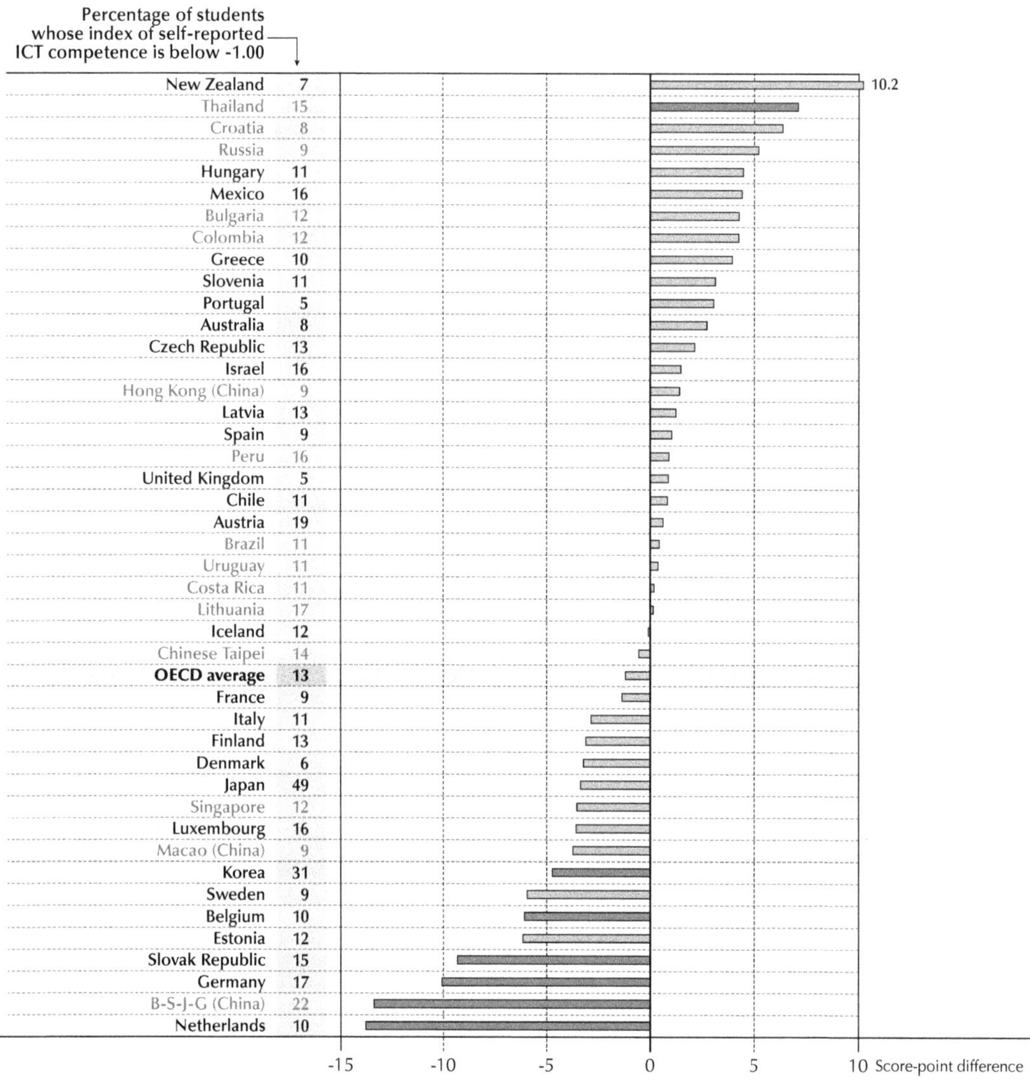

Note: Statistically significant score-point differences are shown in a darker tone (see Annex A3).

Countries and economies are ranked in descending order of the score-point difference in the relative performance in collaborative problem solving between students whose self-reported ICT competence is above -1.00 and those whose index is below -1.00.

Source: OECD, PISA 2015 Database, Table V.3.12.

StatLink http://dx.doi.org/10.1787/888933615914

On average across OECD countries, there is no significant difference in relative performance between students whose index of self-reported ICT competence is above -1.00 and those whose index is below -1.00. A significant difference at the country level was observed only in Thailand, where students with a higher index had higher relative scores; and in Belgium, B-S-J-G (China), Germany, Korea, the Netherlands and the Slovak Republic, where students with a higher index had lower relative scores. In general, therefore, students' ICT competency did not have a strong relationship with their performance in the distinctly collaborative aspects of the assessment; any relationship could be accounted for through the cognitive skills shown in their science, reading and mathematics assessments (Table V.3.12).

Collaboration today increasingly takes place in a virtual environment, using technology that gives people sitting on different continents the ability to interact in real time. The PISA 2015 collaborative problem-solving assessment mirrors how 15-year-old students will have to collaborate in the near future. While education systems should still aim to improve their students' ICT skills, the collaborative aspects of this assessment show little relationship to students' comfort with ICT.

Notes

1. In certain situations, after a pause of 60 or 90 seconds, students who had not selected a response were moved onto the next step in the simulation; such inactivity was recorded as an incorrect response.

2. In particular, a student has a probability of 0.62 of correctly answering an item at the same point on the scale as his or her own ability level. The width of each proficiency level (to be described below in the main text) is set so that, for a test composed entirely of questions spread uniformly across a level, all students whose scores fall within that level would be expected to answer at least half of the questions correctly. In particular, students who are at the lower score limit for a level are expected to respond correctly to 52% of the questions at this level, while students who are at the upper score limit for a level are expected to respond correctly to 70% of the questions at this level.

3. PISA scores are represented on a scale whose units do not have a substantive meaning (unlike physical units, such as metres or grams) but are set in relation to the variation in results observed across all test participants. There is theoretically no maximum or minimum score in PISA; rather, the results are scaled to have approximately normal distributions, with means around 500 and standard deviations around 100. In statistical jargon, a one-point difference on the PISA scale therefore corresponds to an effect size of 1%, and a 10-point difference to an effect size of 10%.

4. Numerous studies have attempted to identify the score-point difference equivalent to a progression of one grade level in school, or the increase in score as a student moves from, for instance, grade 9 to grade 10. This cannot be ascertained from a single PISA cycle, as 15-year-old students enrolled in grade 9 are not equivalent to 15-year-old students enrolled in grade 10 due to selection effects. Instead, two types of studies can provide a better measure of the grade-equivalence of PISA scores: longitudinal follow-up studies, where the same students who sat the PISA test are re-assessed later in their education, and cross-sectional designs, where representative samples of students are compared across adjacent age groups and grades. Unfortunately, neither of these studies was available for the PISA 2015 collaborative problem-solving assessment.

5. Technically, the mean score in collaborative problem solving across OECD countries was set at 500 points and the standard deviation at 100 points, with the data weighted so that each OECD country contributed equally. The average standard deviation of the problem-solving scale across OECD countries, as reported in the Appendix tables, is less than 100 score points because it is computed as the arithmetic average of the within-country standard deviations. This reported measure does not include the performance variation between countries. The standard deviation of 100 used for standardising scores, on the other hand, is a measure of overall variation within and between OECD countries.

6. Top performers in science, reading and mathematics are defined as those students who achieve at Level 5 or 6 in those domains. As only four levels of proficiency were defined in collaborative problem solving, top performers in collaborative problem solving were defined as those students who achieve the top level of performance, Level 4.

7. This statement and similar statements in the following sections do not consider potential error margins in the percentage of students who perform at each level. In other words, the percentage of students who perform at Level 4 in these countries is not necessarily significantly higher than the percentage of students who perform at Level 4 on average in OECD countries.

8. This statement does not consider potential error margins in the percentage of students who perform at each level. In other words, the percentage of students who perform at Level 3 in these 10 countries is not necessarily significantly higher than the percentage of students who perform at Level 2 on average in OECD countries.

9. Top performance and low achievement are defined independently and represent a different set of skills for each subject. Moreover, while Levels 5 and 6 represent top performance in the core subjects, only four proficiency levels were defined for collaborative problem solving, and only Level 4 represents top performance in that subject. Hence, top performance and low achievement are not equivalent across different subjects.

10. A linear ordinary least squares regression of performance in collaborative problem solving over performance in science, reading and mathematics was performed. Thus, a student's predicted performance in collaborative problem solving was ascertained from his or her performance in science, reading and mathematics. The student's relative performance was then defined as his or her actual performance in collaborative problem solving minus his or her predicted performance in collaborative problem solving, or in other words, the residual of the regression. One of the properties of the regression, to ensure that the predictions are not biased, is that the average residual (or relative performance) is equal to 0. Student weights were adjusted so that all countries and economies contributed equally to the regression.

11. By contrast, other analyses conducted in this report and in other PISA reports typically analyse data for each country/economy separately. This would have resulted in an average residual for each country/economy of 0 and made impossible the ranking of countries/economies on the basis of their relative collaborative problem-solving score. However, in the rest of this report (Chapters 4, 5, 6 and 7), where the focus is on differences between individuals within the same country, relative scores are calculated at the country level and then regressed over other potential explanatory variables, such as demographic characteristics or school practices, as it is the change in relative score that is of interest, not the absolute value of the relative score.

12. Five countries that administered PISA 2015 on the computer did not participate in the collaborative problem-solving assessment. Among these five countries, four (the Dominican Republic, Ireland, Poland and Switzerland) administered the ICT questionnaire.

13. Self-reported indices from students in Japan and Korea are amongst the lowest across PISA-participating countries and economies, likely attributable to cultural factors. Please see *PISA 2015 Results: Students' Well-Being* (OECD, 2017b) for further information.

References

Heflin, H., J. Shewmaker and **J. Nguyen** (2017), "Impact of mobile technology on student attitudes, engagement, and learning", *Computers and Education*, Vol. 107, pp. 91-99, http://dx.doi.org/10.1016/j.compedu.2017.01.006.

OECD (2017a), *PISA 2015 Assessment and Analytical Framework: Science, Reading, Mathematic, Financial Literacy and Collaborative Problem Solving*, OECD Publishing, Paris, http://dx.doi.org/10.1787/9789264281820-en.

OECD (2017b), *PISA 2015 Results (Volume III): Students' Well-Being*, OECD Publishing, Paris, http://dx.doi.org/10.1787/9789264273856-en.

OECD (2014), *PISA 2012 Results: Creative Problem Solving (Volume V): Students' Skills in Tackling Real-Life Problems*, OECD Publishing, Paris, http://dx.doi.org/10.1787/9789264208070-en.

Philpot, R. et al. (2017), "Factors that influence the difficulty of problem-solving items", in *The Nature of Problem Solving: Using Research to Inspire 21st Century Learning*, OECD Publishing, Paris, http://dx.doi.org/10.1787/9789264273955-11-en.

4

Student demographics and performance in collaborative problem solving

This chapter examines performance differences within countries and economies that can be related to the demographic and social characteristics of students and schools. The factors considered include students' gender, socio-economic status and immigrant background. The impact of student diversity on performance in collaborative problem solving is also discussed.

How does performance in collaborative problem solving relate to gender, socio-economic status and immigrant background? How do these differences compare to those observed in the three core PISA domains of science, reading and mathematics? This chapter aims to identify some of the factors that can explain the variation in performance in collaborative problem solving, both before and after accounting for performance in the three core PISA subjects.

What the data tell us

- Some 38% of the variation in students' collaborative problem-solving performance can be attributed to factors unique to collaboration; the remaining 62% is shared with factors common to performance in science, reading and mathematics.
- Girls perform significantly higher than boys in collaborative problem solving in every country and economy that participated in the assessment. On average across OECD countries, girls scored 29 points higher than boys; the largest gaps of over 40 points were observed in Australia, Finland, Latvia, New Zealand and Sweden, while the smallest gaps of fewer than 10 points were observed in Colombia, Costa Rica and Peru.
- Performance in collaborative problem solving improves as students' and schools' socio-economic profile improves, although this relationship is weaker than the relationship between socio-economic profile and performance in the three core PISA subjects.
- Non-immigrant students score 36 points higher in collaborative problem solving than immigrant students, on average across OECD countries.
- No significant performance difference remains between advantaged and disadvantaged students, or between immigrant and non-immigrant students, after accounting for performance in science, reading and mathematics. However, girls still perform 25 points higher than boys after accounting for performance in the three core PISA subjects.

VARIATION IN STUDENT PERFORMANCE IN COLLABORATIVE PROBLEM SOLVING

Variation in student performance within countries/economies

As discussed in Chapter 3 (Figure V.3.6 and Table V.3.1), there is considerable variation in collaborative problem-solving performance within each country/economy.[1]

The standard deviation summarises the distribution of performance among 15-year-olds within each country/economy in a single number (Table V.3.2). By this measure, the smallest variation in problem-solving proficiency is found in Tunisia, with a standard deviation of 59 score points, and Costa Rica, Mexico, Montenegro and Turkey, with standard deviations of under 80 score points. Among top-performing countries, both Japan and Korea have narrow spreads of performance (standard deviations of 84 and 85 score points, respectively).

At the other end of the spectrum, Australia, Canada, Finland, France, Germany, Israel, New Zealand, the United Kingdom and the United States have the largest variations in collaborative problem-solving proficiency, with standard deviations of over 100 score points. The differences in performance in these countries are therefore wider than would be expected in a diverse population of students across all 32 OECD countries that participated in the collaborative problem-solving assessment.

Variations in student performance within and between schools

The variation in performance within countries can be divided into a measure of performance differences between students in the same school, and a measure of performance differences between groups of students from different schools. Figure V.4.1 shows the total variance in performance within each country/economy divided into its between-school and within-school components.[2]

The data show that there is substantial variation in collaborative problem-solving results both within and between schools. On average across OECD countries, the variation in student performance that is observed within schools amounts to 75% of the OECD average variation in student performance. The remaining variation (24%) is due to differences in student performance between schools (Table V.4.1a).[3]

The variation in collaborative problem-solving performance between schools is a measure of how large "school effects" are. These school effects can be partly attributed to differences in the composition of schools and in the policies and practices that may develop or foster student performance in collaborative problem solving. The variation related to school demographics is discussed in this chapter; the variation related to policies and practices is discussed in Chapter 6.

As noted in the previous chapter, collaborative problem-solving performance is closely correlated to performance in the three core PISA subjects. Many school and neighbourhood factors foster the development of collaboration and problem-solving skills, just as they create the conditions for any type of learning. The importance of these common influences can be quantified and accounted for by separating the variation in problem-solving performance across students into a component that is shared with science, reading and mathematics performance, from a residual component, called the variation in relative performance, that measures the variation among students of similar performance in reading, mathematics and science.[4]

Figure V.4.1 ▪ **Variation in collaborative problem-solving performance between and within schools**

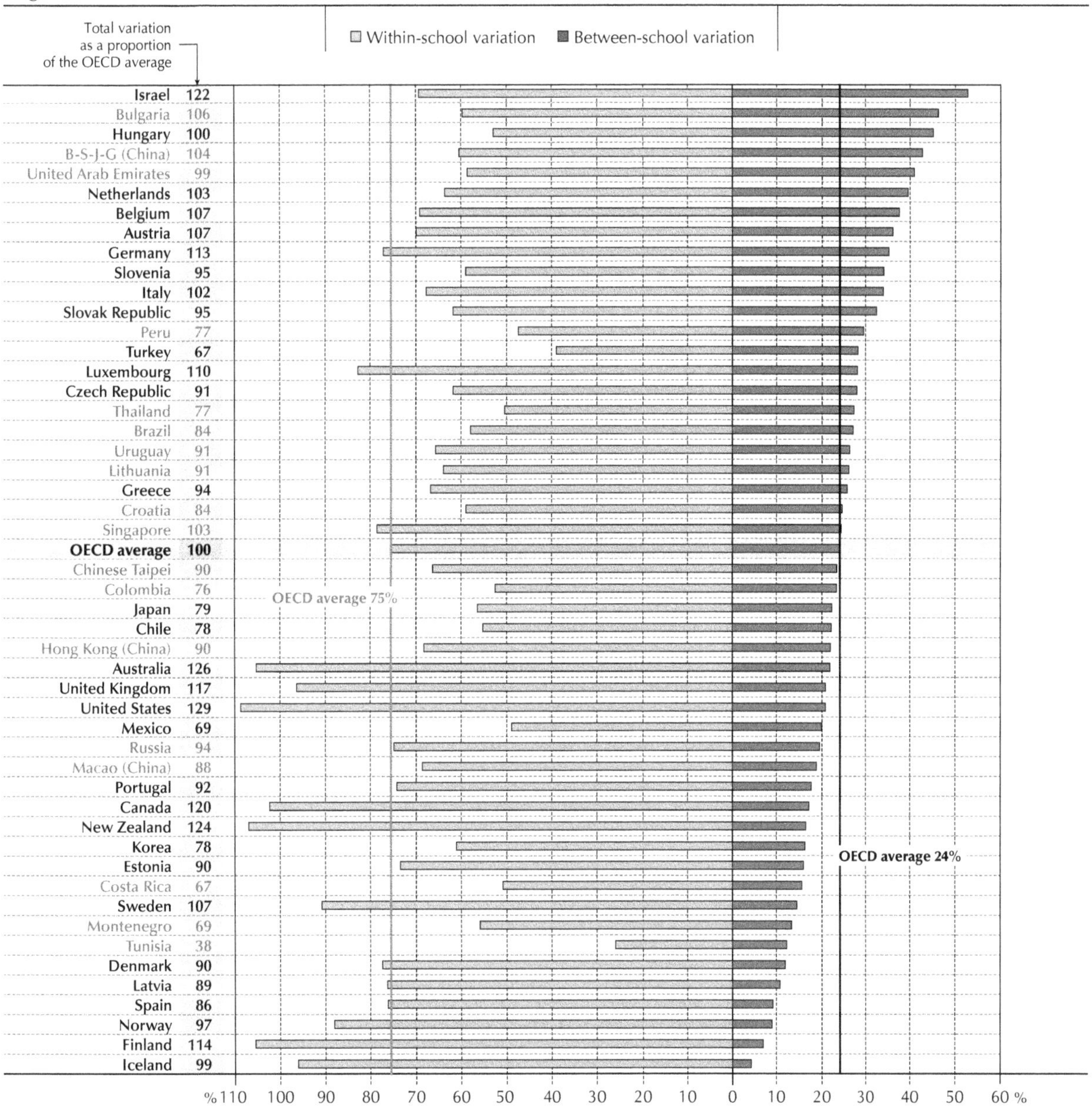

Countries and economies are ranked in descending order of the between-school variation in collaborative problem-solving performance, as a percentage of the total variation in performance across OECD countries.

Source: OECD, PISA 2015 Database, Table V.4.1a.

StatLink http://dx.doi.org/10.1787/888933615933

Differences in student performance in science, reading and mathematics accounted for 62% of the variation in student performance in collaborative problem solving, on average across OECD countries. In other words, on average, 38% of the differences in how students performed in the collaborative problem-solving assessment were not related to common cognitive factors that also dictated performance in the science, reading and mathematics assessments. This 38% of the variation is therefore unique to collaborative problem solving. In Bulgaria, less than 30% of the performance variation in collaborative problem solving is unique to collaborative problem solving (and not shared with the three core domains), while this figure was over 50% in Costa Rica and Tunisia (Table V.4.1b).

This reduction in the total variation in collaborative problem-solving performance was largely due to the between-school component of the variation, which decreased by 86%, on average across OECD countries, after accounting for performance in science, reading and mathematics. The decrease was particularly pronounced – more than 95% – in Bulgaria, Hungary, Luxembourg and Macao (China). In these countries, students in schools with high average scores in science, reading and mathematics also perform well in collaborative problem solving. This may be because schools in these countries develop their students' collaborative problem-solving skills simultaneously with the cognitive and disciplinary skills tested in the science, reading and mathematics assessments. It might also be due to demographic factors across schools that influence performance in collaborative problem solving and in the three core domains in the same way. Once performance in the three core subjects is accounted for, the between-school variation in relative student performance accounts for only 9% of the total variation in relative student performance (compared to the 25% of total variation before performance in the three core subjects is accounted for) (Tables V.4.1a and V.4.1b).

At the same time, a significant but smaller fraction of the within-school differences in collaborative problem-solving performance (46% on average across OECD countries) cannot be accounted for by differences in performance in the core PISA subjects. This fraction exceeds 60% in Slovenia, Tunisia and Turkey. Within-school variation accounts for 91% of the total between- and within-school variation in relative performance (Table V.4.1b). This suggests that differences in the experiences, personalities and opportunities among students attending the same school are the most likely explanations for the remaining differences in performance in collaborative problem solving, after performance in science, reading and mathematics has been accounted for.

Differences in the variation in performance in collaborative problem solving and in science

Figure V.4.2 compares the variation in student performance between schools in science and collaborative problem solving. To do so, it plots the intra-class correlation, defined as the proportion of between-school variation as a percentage of the overall within- and between-school variation. A higher intra-class correlation implies greater between-school variation, where schools have more of an impact on the performance of individual students.

On average across OECD countries, 25% of the overall within- and between-school variation in collaborative problem-solving performance is observed between schools.[5] This is smaller than the 30% of overall variation in science performance observed between schools (Figure V.4.2 and Table I.6.9 from PISA Volume I). In other words, there is relatively less between-school variation in collaborative problem-solving performance than in science performance. This means that the school a student attends is less predictive of his or her performance in the collaborative problem-solving assessment than of his or her performance in the science assessment.

The intra-class correlation for collaborative problem-solving performance is particularly low in the Nordic countries of Finland, Iceland and Norway, where less than 10% of the total variation in collaborative problem-solving performance can be explained by differences between schools (Figure V.4.2). All three of these countries perform at or above the OECD average, with Finland ranked between second and seventh among all OECD countries (see Figures V.3.3 and V.3.4 in Chapter 3).

By contrast, the intra-class correlation for collaborative problem-solving performance is above 40% in Beijing-Shanghai-Jiangsu-Guangdong (China) (hereafter "B-S-J-G [China]"), Bulgaria, Hungary, Israel, Turkey and the United Arab Emirates (Figure V.4.2). With the exception of B-S-J-G (China), all of these countries perform below the OECD average in collaborative problem solving (Figure V.3.3).

In most OECD and partner countries and economies, the intra-class correlation for collaborative problem-solving performance is less than that for science performance, indicating that at the level of the individual country or economy, the school that a student attends is more predictive of his or her performance in science than of his or her performance in collaborative problem solving (Figure V.4.2).[6] However, this is not the case in Israel (37% vs 43%), and to a lesser extent in Iceland, Norway, Peru, the Russian Federation (hereafter "Russia") and Thailand. In these countries, school effects are larger in collaborative problem solving than in science.

Figure V.4.2 ▪ **Index of intra-class correlation in collaborative problem-solving and science performance**

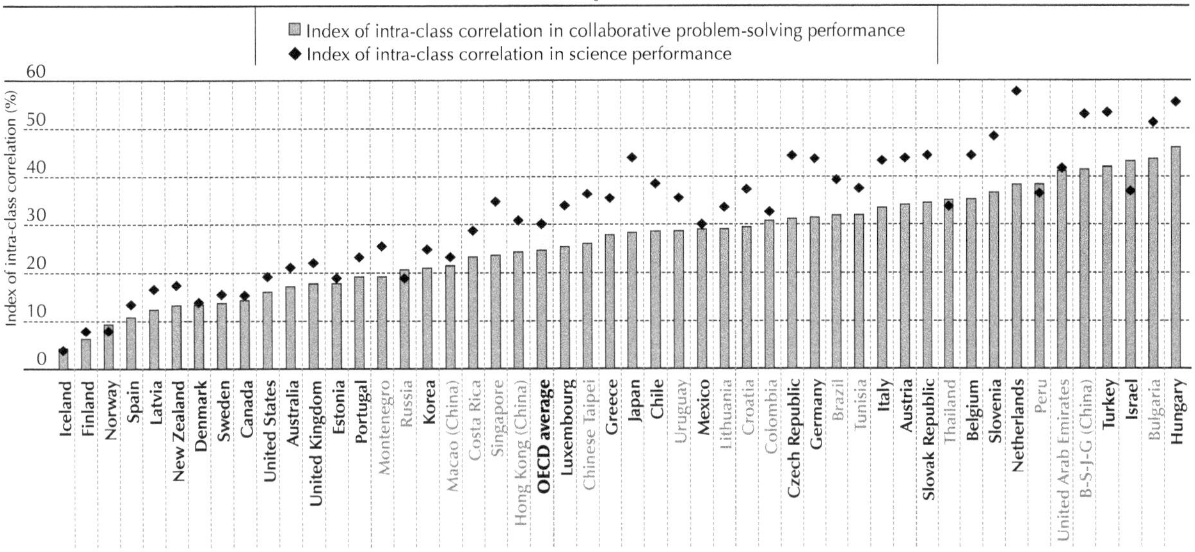

Notes: The intra-class correlation is the variation in student performance between schools, divided by the sum of the variation in student performance between schools and the variation in student performance within schools, and multiplied by 100.

Only countries and economies with available data for collaborative problem-solving and science performance are shown.

Countries and economies are ranked in ascending order of the index of intra-class correlation in collaborative problem-solving performance.

Source: OECD, PISA 2015 Database, Tables I.6.9 and V.4.1a.

StatLink http://dx.doi.org/10.1787/888933615952

DIFFERENCES IN COLLABORATIVE PROBLEM SOLVING RELATED TO GENDER

PISA 2015 Results (Volume I) (OECD, 2016) examines gender differences in science, reading and mathematics performance. Unlike the assessments of the core PISA subjects, the PISA 2015 collaborative problem-solving assessment is not a measure of individual differences in academic aptitude; rather, it aims to quantify interpersonal skills. Given that boys and girls are raised differently and face different societal expectations, the genders are likely to develop different collaboration skills by the age of 15.

Schmitt et al. (2008) found gender differences in the Big Five personality traits (openness to experience, conscientiousness, extraversion, agreeableness and neuroticism) across a variety of cultures. Co-operative and collaborative behaviour is often explained through agreeableness and conscientiousness.[7] Students who are agreeable are willing to compromise, while students who are conscientious take the perspectives of other group members into consideration and display responsibility towards others and towards solving the problem.

Women were significantly more agreeable and more conscientious than men in most countries. Among the 55 countries the researchers examined, women were more agreeable than men in 34 countries; only in Korea were men found to be significantly more agreeable than women. Likewise, women were more conscientious than men in 23 countries, while men were more conscientious than women only in India and Botswana (Schmitt et al., 2008). In most countries, the sample was comprised of college students, although some countries also included subjects from the general community.

Figure V.4.3 plots the mean performance of boys and girls in collaborative problem solving and shows the difference in their performance. Girls outperform boys in collaborative problem solving by 29 score points (515 points compared with 486 points, on average across OECD countries). Furthermore, in every country/economy that participated in the collaborative problem-solving assessment, girls significantly outperform boys. The differences are greatest in Australia, Finland, Latvia, New Zealand and Sweden, where girls score over 40 points higher than boys, on average. Girls outperform boys by less than 10 points in Colombia, Costa Rica and Peru, but these differences are still statistically significant.

The standard deviation in collaborative problem-solving performance among boys is also greater (96 score points) than that among girls (91 score points) (Table V.4.3a), similar to what is observed in all subjects tested in PISA. This difference is significant and positive in 24 out of the 51 countries and economies that participated in the collaborative problem-solving assessment. It is greatest in Macao (China), where the standard deviation among boys was 11 points greater than the standard deviation among girls. In no country did girls' performance show a higher standard deviation than boys' performance.

Figure V.4.3 ▪ **Gender differences in collaborative problem-solving performance**

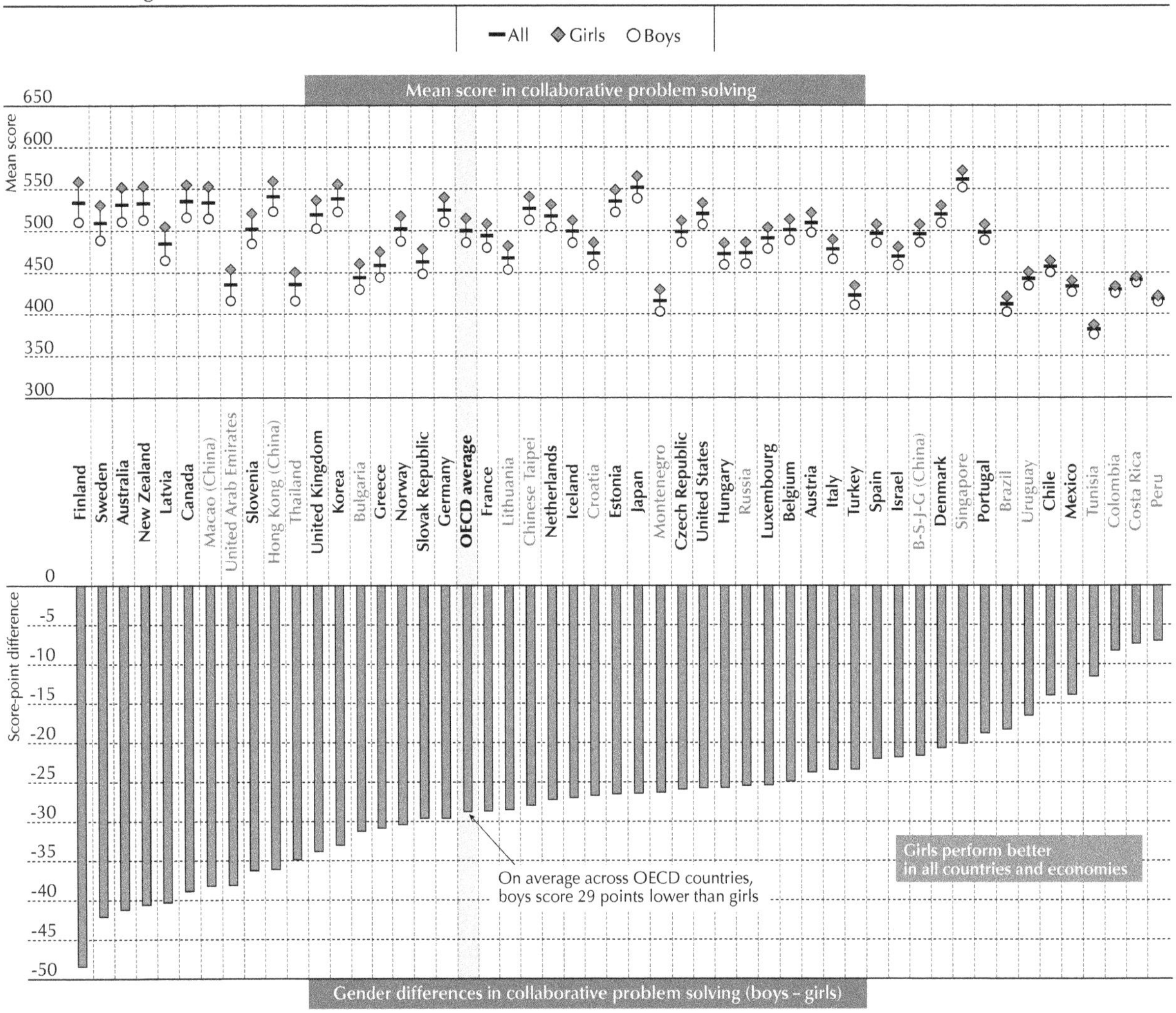

Note: All gender differences in collaborative problem-solving performance are statistically significant (see Annex A3).
Countries and economies are ranked in ascending order of the score-point difference in collaborative problem-solving performance between boys and girls.
Source: OECD, PISA 2015 Database, Tables V.4.1a and V.4.3a.
StatLink http://dx.doi.org/10.1787/888933615971

A greater standard deviation and lower mean performance among boys strongly implies that more boys than girls are found at the bottom range of the performance scale, both across OECD countries and in most countries/economies. This can be seen in Figure V.4.4, which plots the distribution of the scores of boys and girls in OECD countries. Boys have a greater density than girls at lower scores, while the opposite is observed at higher scores. On average across OECD countries, girls are 1.6 times more likely than boys to be top performers (Level 4) in collaborative problem solving, while boys are 1.6 times more likely than girls to be low achievers (below Level 2). The difference is even starker when examining students who score below Level 1: boys are 2.2 times more likely to score at this level than girls. In no country or economy are boys more likely than girls to be top performers, and in every country or economy, boys are more likely than girls to be low performers (Table V.4.2).

These findings contrast with the gender differences observed in individual problem solving as discussed in *PISA 2012 Results: Creative Problem Solving (Volume V)* (OECD, 2014). In that assessment, boys scored 7 points higher than girls in individual problem solving, on average across OECD countries, and were 1.5 times more likely than girls to be top performers. Although different groups of students were measured in 2012 and 2015 and the assessments are not directly comparable to one another, the results suggest that it is the collaborative component of the PISA 2015 collaborative problem-solving assessment that favours girls.

Figure V.4.4 ▪ **Distribution of proficiency in collaborative problem solving, by gender**
OECD average

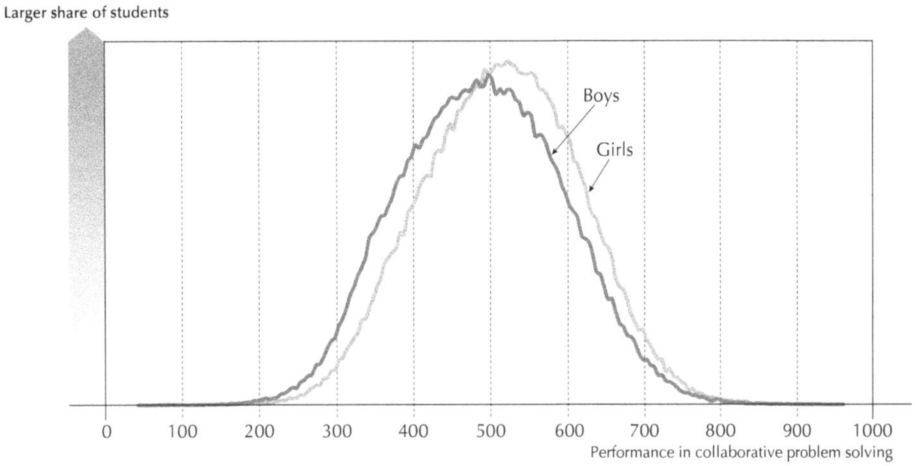

Note: This figure is a histogram of performance using an interval size of five score points.
Source: OECD, PISA 2015 Database.
StatLink http://dx.doi.org/10.1787/888933615990

How gender differences in collaborative problem-solving performance compare to gender differences in science, reading and mathematics performance

The larger variation in performance among boys, compared to the variation observed among girls, is not unique to collaborative problem solving; it is observed across all PISA assessments. The performance variation observed among boys is between 6 and 9 points wider than that among girls in the three core domains (Table V.4.3a and Tables I.2.7, I.4.7 and I.5.7 from PISA Volume I).

Given that the variation in scores differs both across countries and across subjects, absolute differences in performance related to gender may not be directly comparable across countries. For example, although girls might outperform boys by 20 score points in two different countries, this gap is more substantial when the standard deviation in the entire population of students is only 40 score points than when it is 100 score points, as gender differences explain a larger proportion of the overall variation in performance in the former country.

The gender effect size in each country/economy is thus calculated as the gap between the mean performance of boys and girls divided by the standard deviation in performance among all students in the country/economy. Gender effects will therefore be stronger in countries with low standard deviations in performance.[8] In the example above, the country with a 40 score-point standard deviation in performance will have a larger gender effect size than the country with a 100 score-point standard deviation.

By this measure, the average gender effect size across OECD countries is -0.30; in other words, girls outperform boys by an average of 30% of a within-country standard deviation (Figure V.4.5). As is the case with absolute (score-point) gender gaps in performance, these gender effects are significant and in favour of girls in every country and economy that participated in the PISA 2015 collaborative problem-solving assessment. Gender effects are particularly large in Finland, where girls outperform boys by 48% of a standard deviation. In Latvia, Macao (China), Sweden, Thailand and the United Arab Emirates, girls also outperform boys by over 40% of a standard deviation. By contrast, girls outperform boys by less than 10% of a standard deviation in the Latin American countries of Colombia, Costa Rica and Peru (Table V.4.5).

Across the core subjects assessed by PISA, gender differences in mean performance vary greatly. Girls outperform boys in reading but boys outperform girls in mathematics and science. The advantage of girls in reading is 28% of the standard deviation in performance, on average across OECD countries, while the advantage of boys in science is 4% and in mathematics 9% of the standard deviation (Table V.4.5 and Figure V.4.5).[9] The gender effect between boys and girls is also significantly more pronounced in favour of girls in collaborative problem solving than in reading.

Given the high correlations between performance in the three core PISA subjects and performance in collaborative problem solving, and the far larger magnitude of the gender effect in reading than in either science or mathematics, it might be tempting to view gender differences in collaborative problem-solving performance as related to gender differences in reading. But the gender gaps are still large and significant in favour of girls after accounting for performance in science, reading and mathematics (Table V.4.3b). In other words, girls' advantage in reading literacy does not fully explain their advantage in collaborative problem solving.

Figure V.4.5 ■ **Gender differences in collaborative problem-solving, science, reading and mathematics performance**

Gender differences (boys-girls) expressed as a percentage of the within-country standard deviation in performance

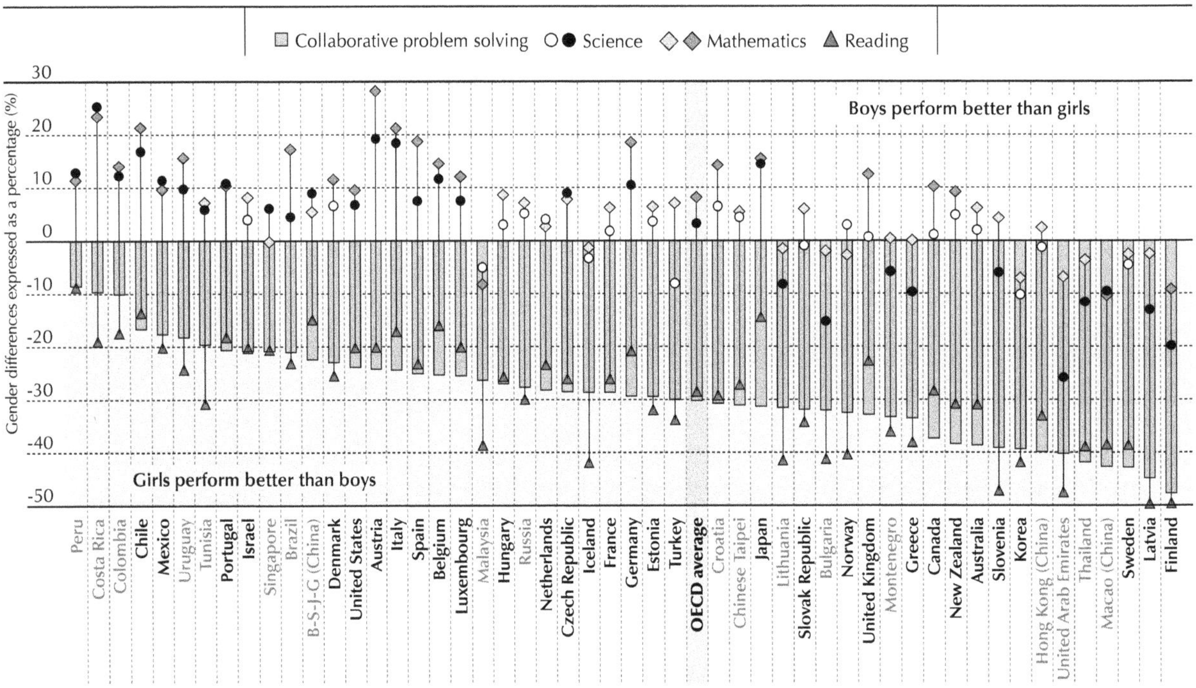

Notes: Statistically significant gender differences are shown in a darker tone. All gender differences in collaborative problem-solving and reading performance are statistically significant (see Annex A3).
The figure reports negative percentages when girls perform better than boys.
Countries and economies are ranked in descending order of the difference between boys and girls in collaborative problem-solving performance.
Source: OECD, PISA 2015 Database, Table V.4.5.
StatLink http://dx.doi.org/10.1787/888933616009

After accounting for performance in the three core PISA subjects, girls still outperform boys in collaborative problem solving by 25 score points, on average across OECD countries, and this performance gap is significant and in favour of girls in every country and economy that participated in the assessment (Table V.4.3b). The difference is largest in Australia, Austria, Canada, Germany, Italy and New Zealand, where girls outperform boys by over 30 score points after accounting for performance in the three core domains. However, in, Bulgaria, Costa Rica, Iceland, Malaysia, Peru, Tunisia and the United Arab Emirates, the difference is only between 10 and 15 score points.

Related gender differences have been observed across a variety of cultures. For example, Guiller and Durndell (2006) found that female university students in Scotland are more likely than their male counterparts to make positive statements, attenuated statements (i.e. statements with qualifiers or statements posed as questions), and to agree with their group partners when taking part in online discussion groups, while male students are more likely to use authoritative and negative language. Strong performance in the PISA 2015 collaborative problem-solving assessment is not synonymous with agreement and using hedging or apologetic language, as some of the released items in the unit *Xandar* required students to monitor and correct group members' actions. However, the credited responses in the released units generally did involve the use of non-aggressive language to advance the situation.

Other studies have examined boys and girls working in same-sex pairs and groups and found that although boys might have been more efficient in completing tasks and emphasised finding the necessary information as quickly as possible, girls exhibited more co-operative behaviour, talked to each other more, and often showed more enthusiasm about the task (Burdick, 1996, with American high school students; Large, Beheshti and Rahman, 2002, with Canadian 11-year-olds; Leong and Al-Hawamdeh, 1999, with Singaporean 11-year-olds).

Gender differences might be even more pronounced in face-to-face instances of collaborative problem solving, where students must decode the facial and emotional responses of their group members. Girls have been found to be more receptive to and better at interpreting nonverbal cues than boys (Hall and Matsumoto, 2004; Klein and Hodges, 2001; Rosip and Hall, 2004), which might give them an advantage when interacting with people.

Figure V.4.6 ▪ **Gender differences in relative performance in collaborative problem solving**

Differences in collaborative problem-solving performance (boys-girls) after accounting for performance in science, reading and mathematics

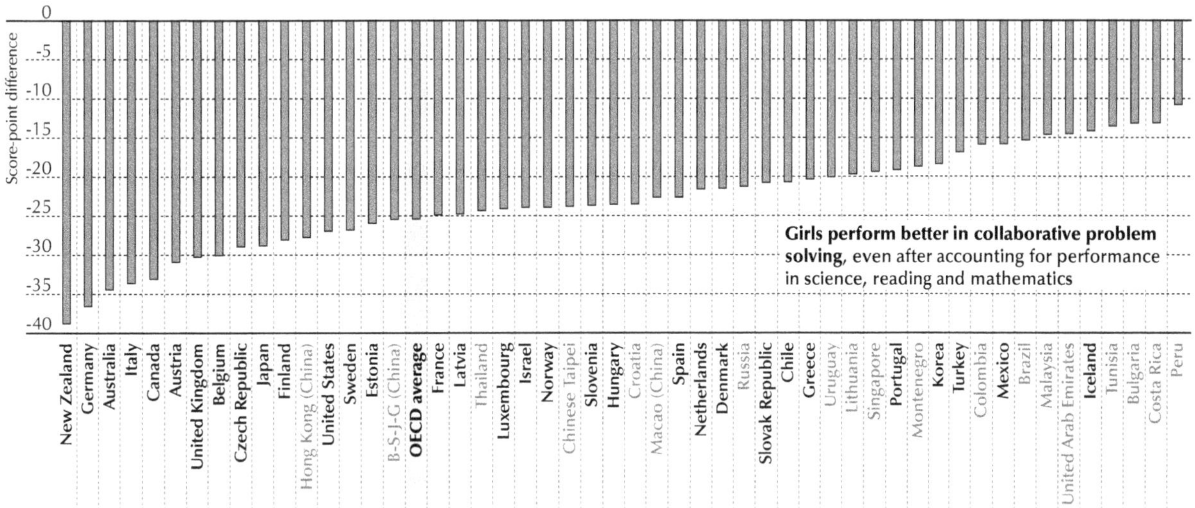

Note: All gender differences are statistically significant (see Annex A3).

Countries and economies are ranked in ascending order of the score-point difference in relative collaborative problem-solving performance between boys and girls.

Source: OECD, PISA 2015 Database, Table V.4.3b.

StatLink http://dx.doi.org/10.1787/888933616028

Most research on the interplay between gender and collaboration has focussed on same-gender or mixed-gender groups of students who interact in person. However, in the PISA 2015 collaborative problem-solving assessment, a student interacted with two or more computer agents who, while having been assigned names that reflect a certain gender, are not physically identifiable as boys or girls. This raises questions about the extent to which the gender of one's group members matters when collaborating in an online and somewhat anonymous environment. Unfortunately, this is beyond the scope of the data available from the PISA 2015 assessment, as the computer agents always included at least one boy and one girl, eliminating any variation in group composition.

THE RELATIONSHIP BETWEEN PERFORMANCE IN COLLABORATIVE PROBLEM SOLVING AND SOCIO-ECONOMIC STATUS

Unsurprisingly, socio-economic status – as measured in PISA by the PISA index of economic, social and cultural status (ESCS)[10] – relates positively to performance in problem solving, as it does to performance in all domains assessed in PISA. But does the relationship between socio-economic status and performance differ across domains?

In general, the percentage of the variation in performance explained by socio-economic disparities at both the student and school levels is similar for science (the average across OECD countries that participated in the collaborative problem-solving assessment is 23%), reading (22%) and mathematics (23%).[11] Figure V.4.7 shows that this relationship is weaker in collaborative problem solving than in the three other domains. Still, even in collaborative problem solving, about 15% of the variation in performance can be explained by differences in socio-economic status. A higher position on the PISA index of economic, social and cultural status might be associated with greater academic enrichment opportunities, leading to disparities in performance in the cognitive domains. However, opportunities to collaborate and co-operate arise in all social and economic contexts, which could lead to a reduction in the extent to which socio-economic status is related to performance in collaborative problem solving.

Figure V.4.7 ▪ **How well socio-economic status predicts performance in four PISA subjects**
Percentage of variation in performance explained by students' and schools' socio-economic profile

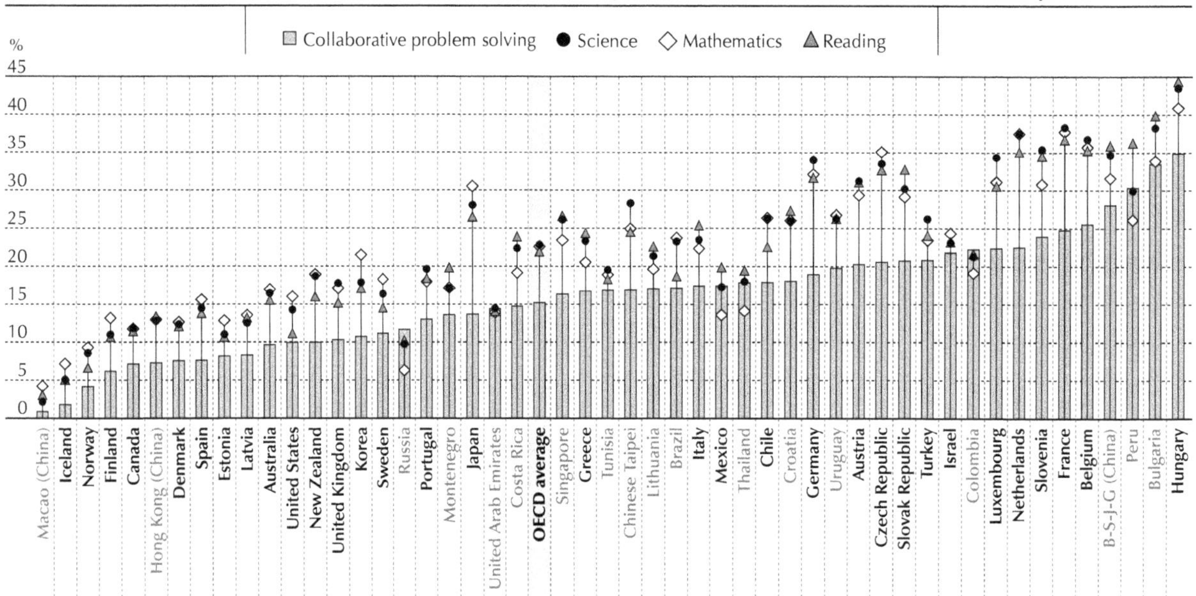

Note: The socio-economic status is measured by the PISA index of economic, social and cultural status (ESCS).
Countries and economies are ranked in ascending order of how well socio-economic status predicts performance in collaborative problem solving.
Source: OECD, PISA 2015 Database, Table V.4.13f.
StatLink http://dx.doi.org/10.1787/888933616047

The relationship between socio-economic status and science performance is stronger than that between socio-economic status and collaborative problem-solving performance in 43 out of 51 countries/economies for which data are available. In the remaining countries, the difference in the strengths of the relationships is not statistically significant (Table V.4.13f).

On average across OECD countries, a one-unit increase in a student's socio-economic status – while holding the school socio-economic profile constant – is associated with an increase in his or her collaborative problem-solving score of 13 points, while a one-unit increase in the average socio-economic profile of the student's school is associated with a 59 score-point increase in his or her score (Figure V.4.8 and Table V.4.13e). In other words, within the same school, students score 13 score points higher, on average, when their socio-economic status is one unit higher. However, for two students with the same socio-economic status, there is a 59 score-point increase in collaborative problem-solving performance if the school socio-economic profile is also one unit higher.[12]

The relationship between collaborative problem-solving performance and socio-economic status is positive in almost every country/economy that participated in the assessment. In Hong Kong (China), Hungary, Macao (China), the Netherlands and Slovenia, the relationship between collaborative problem-solving performance and student socio-economic status is insignificant when simultaneously accounting for school socio-economic profile. In other words, in these countries and economies, there is no significant relationship between collaborative problem-solving performance and student socio-economic status within schools, but there are differences between schools with different socio-economic profiles.

Figure V.4.8 ▪ **Impact of socio-economic status on performance in collaborative problem solving and in science**

Score-point difference associated with a one-unit increase in students' and schools' socio-economic profile[1]

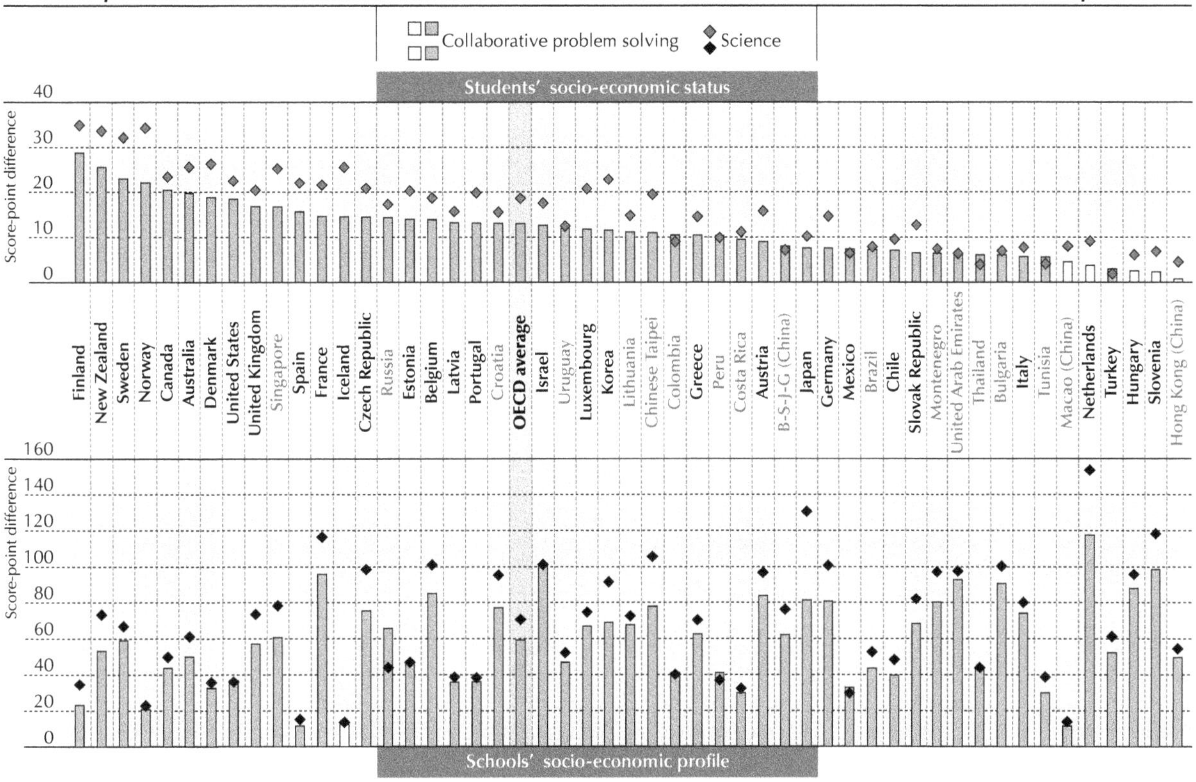

1. The socio-economic profile is measured by the PISA index of economic, social and cultural status (ESCS).

Notes: Statistically significant score-point differences are shown in a darker tone (see Annex A3).

All score-point differences in science performance are statistically significant.

Countries and economies are ranked in descending order of the score-point difference in collaborative problem-solving performance associated with students' socio-economic status.

Source: OECD, PISA 2015 Database, Table V.4.13e.

StatLink http://dx.doi.org/10.1787/888933616066

By contrast, in Iceland, the relationship between collaborative problem-solving performance and school socio-economic profile, when simultaneously accounting for student socio-economic status, is insignificant. In other words, in Iceland, there are no significant between-school differences in collaborative problem-solving performance related to socio-economic status. All such differences can be attributed to disparities between students in the same school.

The score-point improvements associated with a one-point increase in the PISA index of economic, social and cultural status are smaller in collaborative problem solving than in science, reading and mathematics. On average across OECD countries (that participated in the collaborative problem-solving assessment), a one-point increase in students' socio-economic status is associated with a 13-point improvement in collaborative problem-solving performance, compared to between 17 and 19 points in the three core PISA subjects. A one-point increase in schools' socio-economic profile is associated with a 59-point improvement in collaborative problem-solving performance compared to between 66 and 73 points in the three core PISA subjects (Table V.4.13e and Figure V.4.8).

The weaker magnitude of the relationship is also reflected in the socio-economic effect size, which scales the score-point difference associated with differences in socio-economic status by the variation in performance observed in each country. In other words, socio-economic status is associated with a smaller increase in performance in collaborative problem solving, relative to the performance of other students in the same country or economy, than in the three core PISA subjects. The one exception is in Russia, where the school socio-economic effect size in collaborative problem solving is significantly larger than that in science and mathematics. There, a one-unit increase in school socio-economic profile results in a relatively larger improvement in collaborative problem-solving performance than in science and mathematics performance (Table V.4.13e).

It is not immediately obvious whether differences in collaborative problem-solving performance related to socio-economic status are unique to the domain or whether they are common across the three core PISA domains. The relationships between the distinctive aspects of collaborative problem solving and socio-economic status can be elucidated using the relative scores in collaborative problem solving after accounting for performance in science, reading and mathematics.

On average across OECD countries, there is no significant difference in collaborative problem-solving performance between advantaged and disadvantaged students – defined as those students who are in the top and bottom quarter of socio-economic status within a country – once performance in science, reading and mathematics has been accounted for (Figure V.4.9).

Figure V.4.9 ▪ **Relative performance in collaborative problem solving, by socio-economic status**

Percentage of advantaged[1] and disadvantaged[2] students who score higher than expected in collaborative problem solving, based on their performance in science, reading and mathematics

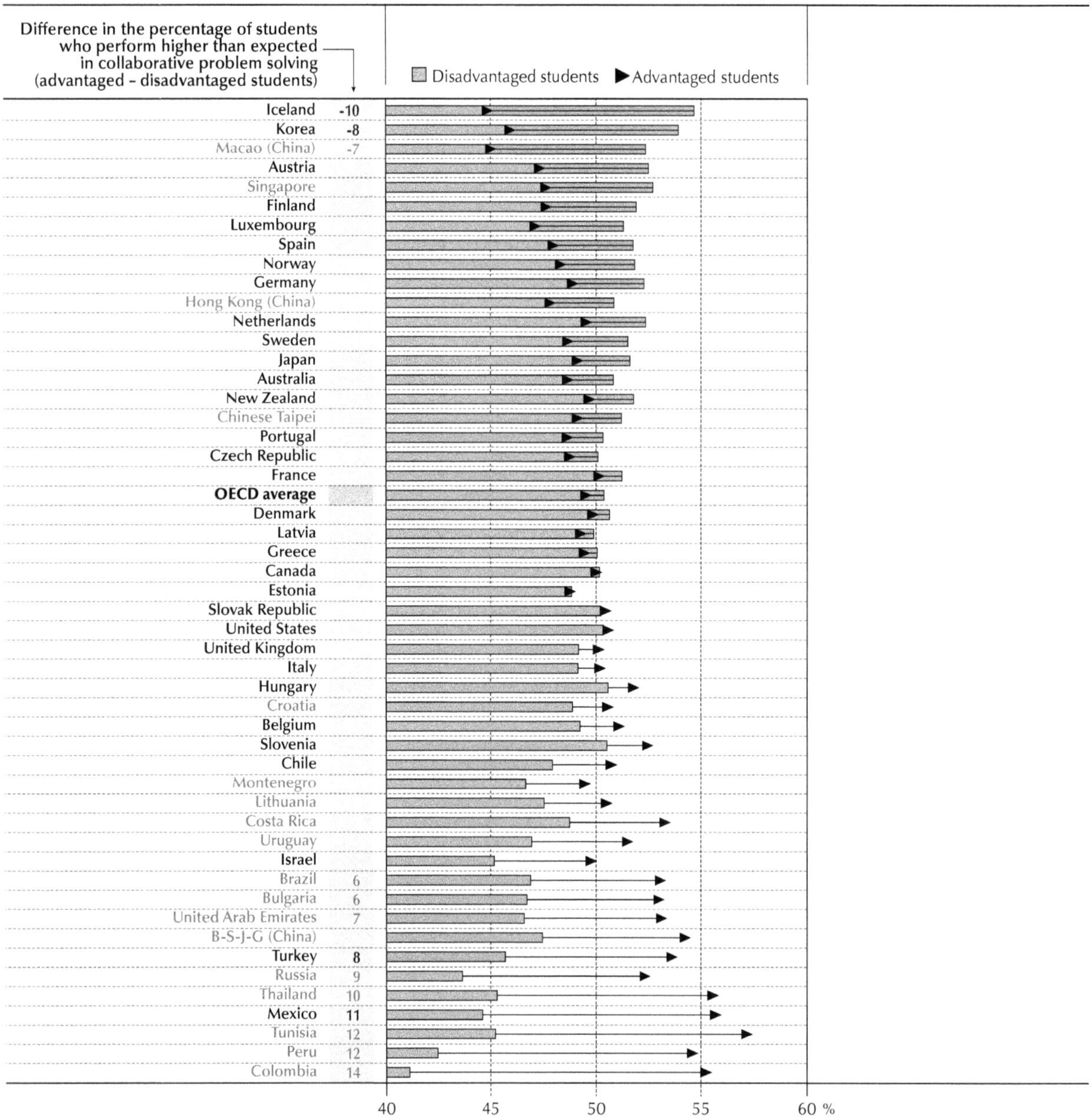

1. Advantaged students are those who rank in the top quarter nationally of the PISA index of economic, social and cultural status (ESCS).
2. Disadvantaged students are those who rank in the bottom quarter nationally of the PISA index of economic, social and cultural status (ESCS).

Countries and economies are ranked in ascending order of the difference between advantaged and disadvantaged students who score higher than expected in collaborative problem solving (advantaged – disadvantaged), based on their scores in science, reading and mathematics.

Source: OECD, PISA 2015 Database, Table V.4.10.

StatLink http://dx.doi.org/10.1787/888933616085

Some 50% of both advantaged and disadvantaged students perform better in collaborative problem solving than would have been expected on the basis of their science, reading and mathematics scores. Significant differences are observed in Iceland, Korea and Macao (China), where disadvantaged students are between 7 and 10 percentage points more likely than advantaged students to perform above expectations; and in Brazil, Bulgaria, Colombia, Mexico, Peru, Russia, Thailand, Tunisia, Turkey and the United Arab Emirates, where advantaged students are between 6 and 15 percentage points more likely than disadvantaged students to perform above expectations.

IMMIGRANT BACKGROUND AND COLLABORATIVE PROBLEM-SOLVING PERFORMANCE

In many countries and economies, children of immigrants are more at risk of low performance in academic subjects than the children of parents who were born in the country or economy. A gap in collaborative problem-solving performance between immigrant and non-immigrant students is also observed: on average across OECD countries, the children of immigrants score 36 points lower than non-immigrant students. However, in Macao (China), Singapore and the United Arab Emirates, immigrant students score better than non-immigrant students in collaborative problem solving (Table V.4.14a). The largest gaps in performance are observed in Denmark, where immigrant students score more than 60 points lower than non-immigrant students, and in Austria, Belgium, France and Sweden, where immigrant students score between 50 and 60 points lower than non-immigrant students.[13]

Figure V.4.10 ▪ **Performance in collaborative problem solving, by immigrant background**

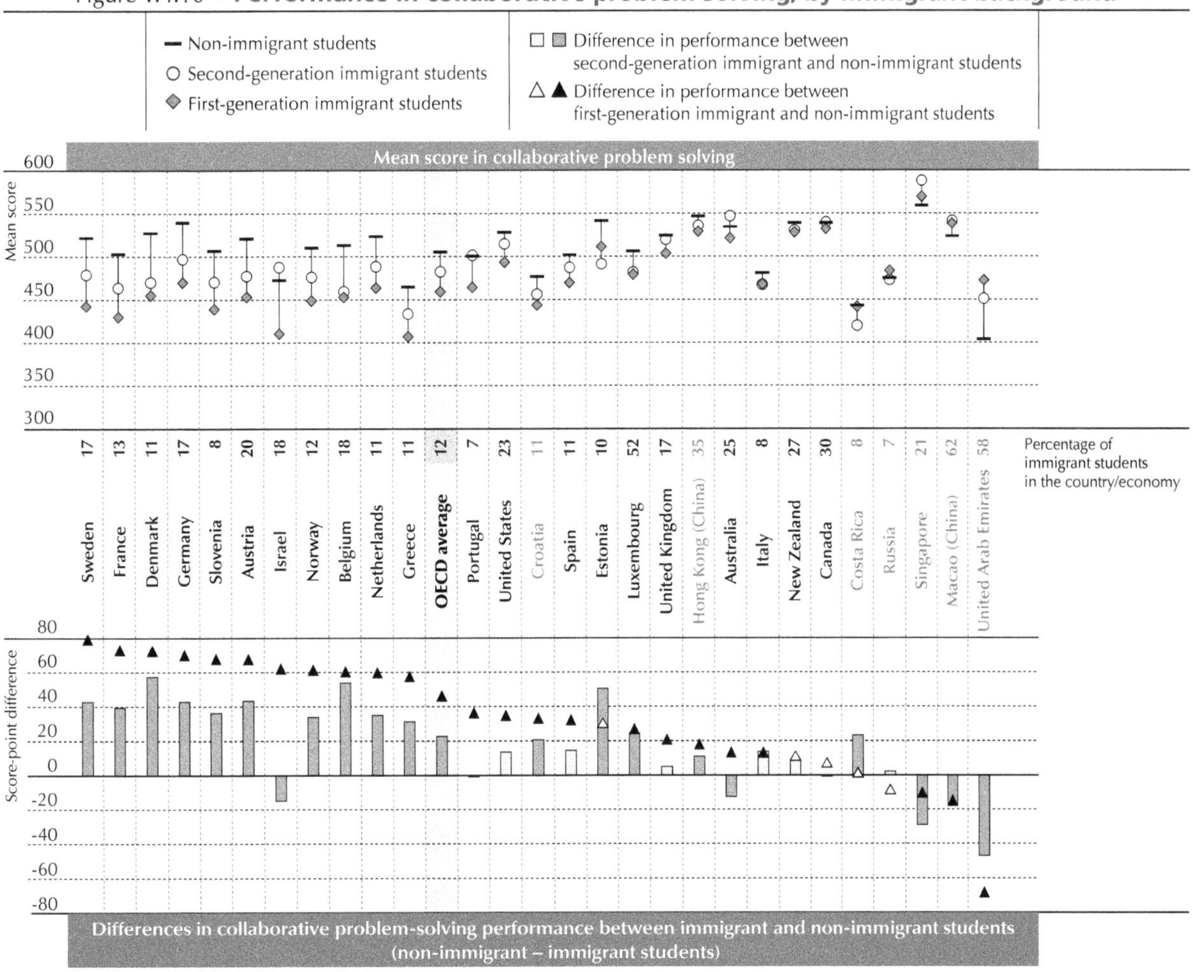

Notes: Only countries and economies where the percentage of immigrant students is higher than 6.25% in 2015 are shown.

Statistically significant differences between first- and second-generation immigrant students and non-immigrant students are shown in darker tones (see Annex A3).

Countries and economies are ranked in descending order of the score-point difference in collaborative problem solving between first-generation immigrant students and non-immigrant students.

Source: OECD, PISA 2015 Database, Table V.4.14a.

StatLink http://dx.doi.org/10.1787/888933616104

Performance differences are particularly large between non-immigrant and first-generation immigrant students, where the average gap across OECD countries is 46 score points. In comparison, non-immigrant students score 23 points higher in collaborative problem solving than second-generation immigrant students (Figure V.4.10).

Performance differences related to immigrant background are observed even after accounting for gender and socio-economic status. After accounting for these two factors, immigrant students still score 26 points below non-immigrant students, on average across OECD countries. A 14-point performance gap remains after further accounting for the language spoken at home.

However, accounting for performance in science, reading and mathematics produces inconclusive results. On average across OECD countries, there is no significant difference between immigrant and non-immigrant students after accounting for performance in the three core PISA subjects. Immigrants in Canada, Denmark, Estonia and Norway still perform worse than non-immigrant students, while in Italy and Luxembourg, they perform better than non-immigrant students. The significant performance gap in favour of immigrant students in Macao (China), Singapore and the United Arab Emirates disappears as immigrant students in these countries also perform better in science, reading and mathematics (Figure V.4.11). These results imply that in many participating countries and economies, a large part of the difference in collaborative problem-solving performance between immigrant and non-immigrant students can be attributed to factors related to differences in performance in science, reading and mathematics and not to factors unique to collaborative problem solving.

Figure V.4.11 ■ **Relative performance in collaborative problem solving, by immigrant background**

Score-point difference in collaborative problem-solving performance between immigrant and non-immigrant students who perform similarly in science, reading and mathematics

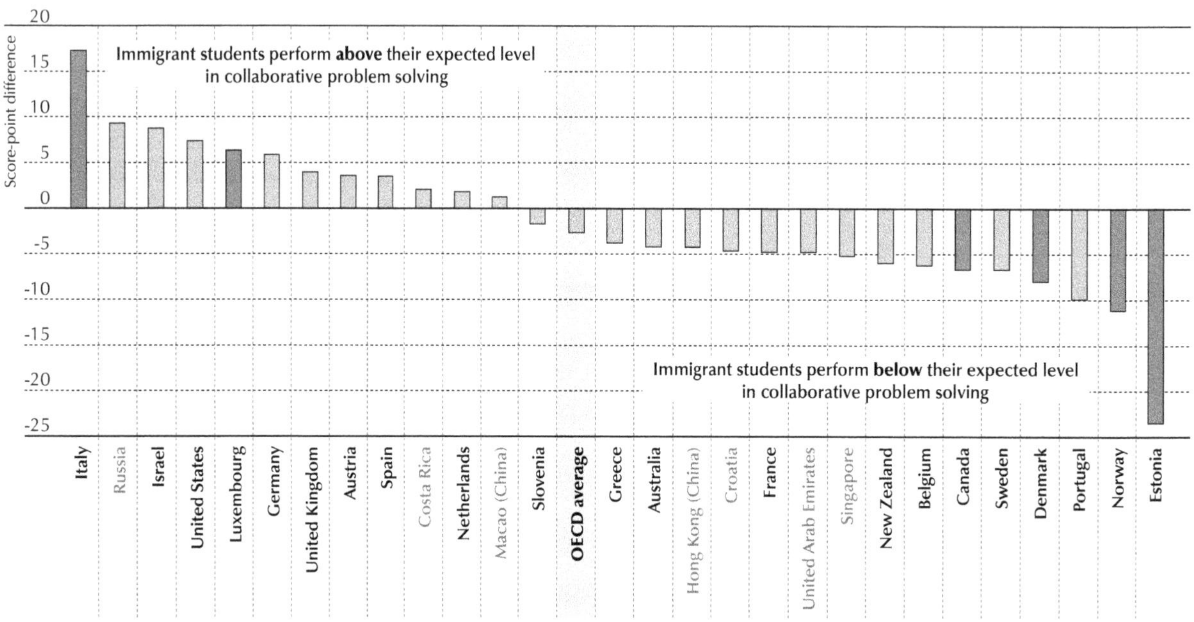

Notes: Only countries and economies where the percentage of immigrant students is higher than 6.25% in 2015 are shown.
Statistically significant differences are shown in a darker tone (see Annex A3).
Countries and economies are ranked in descending order of the score-point difference in collaborative problem-solving performance between immigrant and non-immigrant students who perform similarly in science, reading and mathematics.
Source: OECD, PISA 2015 Database, Table V.4.14b.
StatLink http://dx.doi.org/10.1787/888933616123

The immigrant effect, as calculated by dividing the performance gap between immigrant and non-immigrant students by the standard deviation in performance in each country and for each subject, is 0.38 standard deviation, on average across OECD countries, for collaborative problem solving. This is below the immigrant effect size observed in science (0.47 standard deviation), reading (0.42 standard deviation) and mathematics (0.42 standard deviation).[14] In other words, the relative difference in performance between immigrants and non-immigrants is significantly larger in science, reading and mathematics performance than in collaborative problem-solving performance (Table V.4.17a).

DIVERSITY WITHIN SCHOOLS AND PERFORMANCE IN COLLABORATIVE PROBLEM SOLVING

A student's performance in collaborative problem solving is not necessarily only related to his or her own characteristics. Collaboration and co-operation are practical skills that students develop through interactions with other students. It is possible that students who are exposed to a variety of backgrounds unlike their own might develop a greater range of interpersonal skills and perform better in the PISA 2015 collaborative problem-solving assessment. Such diversity in backgrounds might include both socio-economic and immigrant diversity.

On average across OECD countries, the average non-immigrant student attends a school where 10%[15] of 15-year-old students are immigrant students (Table V.4.22). This proportion varies from over 40% of students in Luxembourg and Macao (China) and over 30% in Hong Kong (China) and Qatar to less than 0.5% of students in B-S-J-G (China), Japan, Korea, Peru, Poland and Chinese Taipei. In addition, immigrant students are not distributed uniformly across schools in a system. In schools that are in the top quarter in their country in the concentration of immigrant students, a non-immigrant student attends a school where an average of 23% of the students are immigrants; but in schools that are in the bottom quarter in this measure, only 1.5%[16] of the students are immigrants.

Figure V.4.12 ▪ **Performance in collaborative problem solving, by concentration of immigrants in school**

Difference in collaborative problem-solving performance between the top and the bottom quarters of the concentration of immigrant students

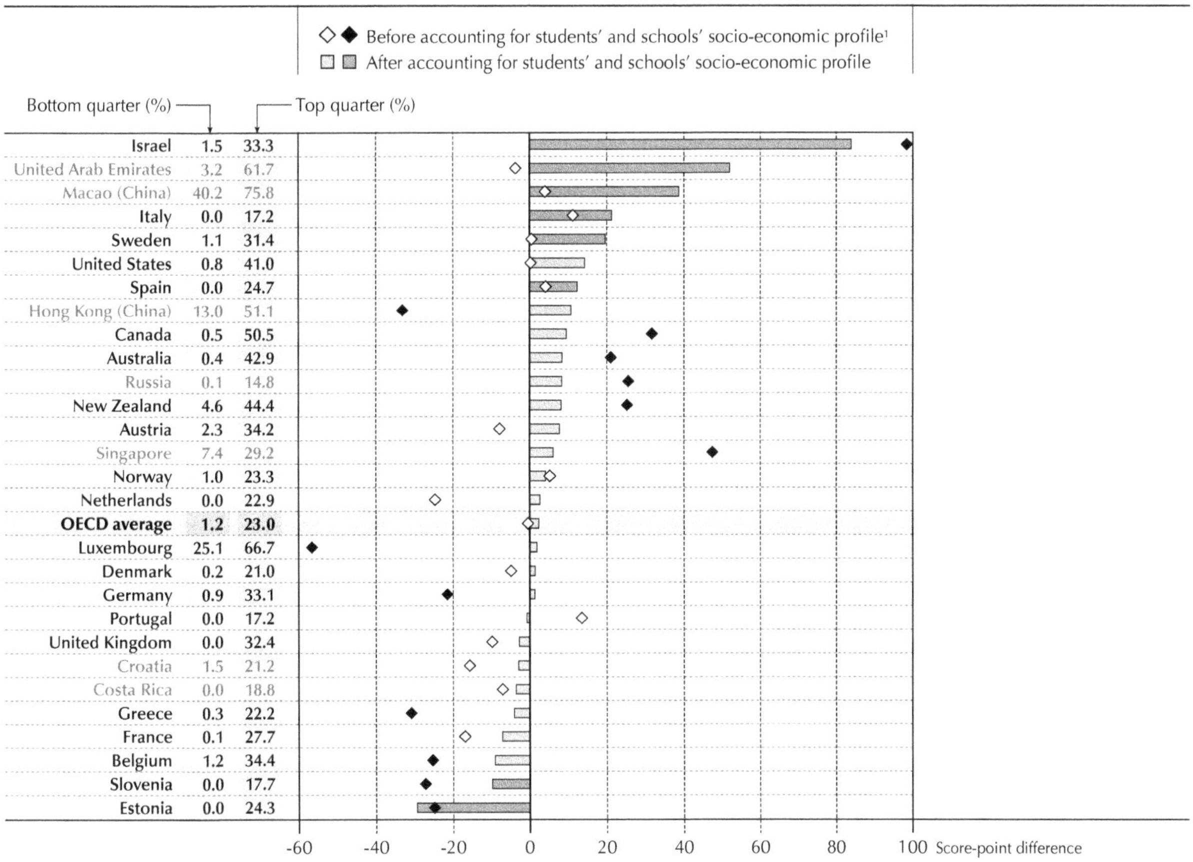

1. The socio-economic profile is measured by the PISA index of economic, social and cultural status (ESCS).

Notes: The school-level proportion of immigrant students is the proportion of students in each school who have an immigrant background.

The percentages of students in the top and the bottom quarters of the concentration of immigrant students are shown next to the country/economy name.

Only countries and economies where the percentage of immigrant students is higher than 6.25% are shown.

Statistically significant score-point differences are shown in a darker tone (see Annex A3).

Countries and economies are ranked in descending order of the difference in collaborative problem-solving performance, after accounting for students' and schools' socio-economic profile.

Source: OECD, PISA 2015 Database, Table V.4.22.

StatLink http://dx.doi.org/10.1787/888933616142

On average across OECD countries, there is no difference in the performance of non-immigrant students between those in schools with large numbers of immigrant students and those in schools with low numbers of immigrant students (Figure V.4.12). However, this difference becomes significant after accounting for performance in science, reading and mathematics: non-immigrant students in a more diverse environment score higher than their non-immigrant peers with similar performance in science, reading and mathematics but in a less diverse environment. At the country level, the difference after accounting for performance in the three core subjects is significant only in Israel and Russia, both of which have sizeable immigrant populations (Table V.4.22).

Perhaps surprisingly, given the paucity of significant results regarding immigrant concentration in schools, non-immigrant students who speak the language of assessment at home perform worse in collaborative problem solving if they attend schools with large numbers of students who do not speak the test language at home (Table V.4.23). On average across OECD countries, there is a 15-point gap in favour of students exposed to less linguistic diversity, before accounting for gender and students' and schools' socio-economic profile. The gap is particularly large in Belgium, Bulgaria, Italy and Singapore, where it exceeds 50 points. However, the gap is reduced to only 3 points after accounting for gender and students' and schools' socio-economic profile, indicating that it is not linguistic diversity itself but rather the tendency that such diversity is correlated to a lower socio-economic profile that accounts for much of this performance discrepancy. In Canada, Sweden and the United Arab Emirates, greater linguistic diversity at school is associated with higher collaborative problem-solving performance among non-immigrant students who speak the test language at home, after accounting for gender and students' and schools' socio-economic profile.

Similar results are seen when diversity is measured as the school-level variation in socio-economic status, or the proportion of advantaged or disadvantaged students, or students with special needs in individual schools (Tables V.4.20, V.4.21a, V.4.21b and V.4.24). There appears to be no significant relationship between diversity and the uniquely collaborative aspects of the collaborative problem-solving assessment, after the relationship between diversity and socio-economic profile has been accounted for.[17]

Notes

1. Scores in collaborative problem solving were scaled so as to set the mean across all OECD countries at 500 score points and the standard deviation across all OECD countries at 100 score points. This standard deviation combines the within-country variation in performance with the between-country variation in mean performance. As OECD countries differ in mean collaborative problem-solving performance, the within-country variation in performance is therefore expected to be, for most countries, below 100 score points.

2. The standard deviation in performance within a country/economy is the square root of the variation (also called the variance) of performance in the country/economy.

3. Due to the unbalanced and clustered nature of the data, the sum of the between- and within-school components of variation in performance, as an estimate from a sample, does not necessarily add up to the total variation in performance.

4. Relative collaborative problem-solving performance is calculated by an ordinary least squares regression of collaborative problem-solving performance over performance in science, reading and mathematics. In Chapter 3, the regression is performed at the international level in order to rank countries and economies. In Chapters 4, 5, 6 and 7, the regression is performed at the individual country or economy level, as the focus is on factors related to differential performance within each country/economy. This results in an average residual of 0 for each country/economy.

5. The 25% in this paragraph refers to the ratio of the between-school variation and the sum of the within-school and between-school variation. The 24% referenced earlier is the ratio of the between-school variation and the total variation. Due to the unbalanced and clustered nature of the data, the total variation does not equal the sum of the within- and between-school variations.

6. The significance of the difference in the intra-class correlations in collaborative problem-solving and science performance has not been formally tested.

7. "Collaboration" and "co-operation" are used synonymously throughout this report.

8. This may also make for a fairer comparison between countries at different ends of the performance scale. In particular, countries with low mean performance might have lower standard deviations as they will have few high-achieving students, while countries with higher mean performance will have higher standard deviations because in addition to having large numbers of top performers, they will often have significant numbers of lower performers. As a result, countries with low mean performance will typically have smaller gaps between different groups of students. This is normalised by dividing by the standard deviation.

9. On average across the OECD countries that participated in the collaborative problem-solving assessment, boys out-performed girls by 3% of the standard deviation in science and 8% of the standard deviation in mathematics.

10. The PISA index of economic, social and cultural status (ESCS) is derived from several variables related to students' family background: parents' education, parents' occupations, a number of home possessions that proxy for material wealth, and the number of books and other educational resources available in the home.

11. On average across all OECD countries, disparities in students' and schools' socio-economic profile explain 22% of the variation in science, reading and mathematics performance.

12. The score-point increase associated with school socio-economic profile is noticeably larger than that associated with student socio-economic status. However, a one-point increase in school socio-economic profile is equivalent to a one-point increase in each student's socio-economic status, entailing a more wide-reaching change in demographics.

13. PISA only presents data for countries where at least 1 in every 16 students (or 6.25% of students) have an immigrant background.

14. On average across all OECD countries, the immigrant effect size related to performance in science was 44% of a standard deviation in performance. The immigrant effect sizes related to performance in reading and mathematics were 40% and 39% of a standard deviation, respectively.

15. On average across the OECD countries that participated in the collaborative problem-solving assessment, non-immigrant students attend schools in which 9% of students are immigrants.

16. On average across the OECD countries that participated in the collaborative problem-solving assessment, students in schools that are in the bottom quarter of the concentration of immigrant students attend schools in which 1.2% of students are immigrants.

17. The correlation between school-level diversity in students' socio-economic status and school-level socio-economic status is -0.32, on average across OECD countries. In other words, schools that have greater levels of socio-economic diversity also tend to be worse off. The negative correlation is particularly strong in Ciudad Autónoma de Buenos Aires (Argentina), Israel, Luxembourg, Qatar and Singapore, where it is stronger than -0.70. Hence, accounting for students' and schools' socio-economic profile will already remove much of the variation in school-level socio-economic diversity.

References

Burdick, T.A. (1996), "Success and diversity in information seeking: Gender and the information search styles model", *School Library Media Quarterly*, Vol. 25/1, pp. 19-26.

Guiller, J. and **A. Durndell** (2006), "'I totally agree with you': Gender interactions in educational online discussion groups", *Journal of Computer Assisted Learning*, Vol. 22/5, pp. 368-381.

Hall, J.A. and **D. Matsumoto** (2004), "Gender differences in judgments of multiple emotions from facial expressions", *Emotion*, Vol. 4/2, pp. 201-206, http://dx.doi.org/10.1037/1528-3542.4.2.201.

Klein, K.J.K. and **S.D. Hodges** (2001), "Gender differences, motivation, and empathic accuracy: When it pays to understand", *Personality and Social Psychology Bulletin*, Vol. 27/6, pp. 720-730, https://doi.org/10.1177/0146167201276007.

Large, A., J. Beheshti and **T. Rahman** (2002), "Gender differences in collaborative Web searching behaviour: An elementary school study", *Information Processing & Management*, Vol. 38/3, pp. 427-443, https://doi.org/10.1016/S0306-4573(01)00034-6.

Leong, S.C. and **S. Al-Hawamdeh** (1999), "Gender and learning attitudes in using Web-based science lessons", *Information Research*, Vol. 5/1.

OECD (2016), *PISA 2015 Results (Volume I): Excellence and Equity in Education*, OECD Publishing, Paris, http://dx.doi.org/10.1787/9789264266490-en.

OECD (2014), *PISA 2012 Results: Creative Problem Solving (Volume V): Students' Skills in Tackling Real-Life Problems*, OECD Publishing, Paris, http://dx.doi.org/10.1787/9789264208070-en.

Rosip, J.C. and **J.A. Hall** (2004), "Knowledge of nonverbal cues, gender, and nonverbal decoding accuracy", *Journal of Nonverbal Behaviour*, Vol. 28/4, pp. 267-286, https://doi.org/10.1007/s10919-004-4159-6.

Schmitt, D.P. et al. (2008), "Why can't a man be more like a woman? Sex differences in Big Five personality traits across 55 cultures", *Journal of Personality and Social Psychology*, Vol. 94/1, pp. 168-182, http://dx.doi.org/10.1037/0022-3514.94.1.168.

5

Students' attitudes towards collaboration

This chapter describes responses to the student questionnaire, in which students were asked about eight facets of their attitudes towards collaboration. The chapter then looks at differences in these attitudes between different groups of students, and the relationship between attitudes towards collaboration and other attitudes towards learning and school discussed in *PISA 2015 Results (Volume III): Students' Well-Being* (OECD, 2017). It concludes by examining the relationship between attitudes towards collaboration and performance in the PISA 2015 collaborative problem-solving assessment.

Do students enjoy working with other students? Do they listen well to others? If students will be increasingly required to collaborate and co-operate with others in order to achieve goals in their professional and personal lives, then schools can help students develop not just the interpersonal skills needed to work together, but also positive attitudes towards collaboration.

What the data tell us

- Students in every country and economy have generally positive attitudes towards collaboration. Over 85% of students, on average across OECD countries, agree with the statements "I am a good listener", "I enjoy seeing my classmates be successful", "I take into account what others are interested in", "I enjoy considering different perspectives", and "I enjoy co-operating with peers".
- Girls in almost every country and economy tend to value relationships more than boys, while boys in a majority of countries and economies tend to value teamwork more than girls.
- Advantaged students in almost every country and economy tend to value relationships more than disadvantaged students, while disadvantaged students in most countries and economies tend to value teamwork more than advantaged students.
- Attitudes towards collaborative problem solving are generally positively but weakly correlated with indices of well-being.
- Students who value relationships tend to perform higher in the collaborative problem-solving assessment, while students who value teamwork tend to perform worse. However, once performance in the science, reading and mathematics assessments, gender, and students' and schools' socio-economic profile is accounted for, both students who value relationships and students who value teamwork tend to perform better in collaborative problem solving.

ATTITUDES TOWARDS COLLABORATION

The PISA 2015 student questionnaire asks students whether they strongly agree, agree, disagree, or strongly disagree with eight statements related to their attitudes towards collaboration:

- I prefer working as part of a team to working alone.
- I am a good listener.
- I enjoy seeing my classmates be successful.
- I take into account what others are interested in.
- I find that teams make better decisions than individuals.
- I enjoy considering different perspectives.
- I find that teamwork raises my own efficiency.
- I enjoy co-operating with peers.

On average across OECD countries, the percentage of students who reported that they agree or strongly agree with these statements ranges from 67% for "I prefer working as part of a team to working alone" and 70% for "I find that teamwork raises my own efficiency" to 87% for "I am a good listener," "I enjoy considering different perspectives", and "I enjoy co-operating with peers", and 88% for "I enjoy seeing my classmates be successful" (Figure V.5.1). It is not possible to determine the extent to which these responses reflect whether students actually hold these attitudes towards collaboration or whether they act accordingly in real life.

In almost all OECD and partner countries and economies, the majority of students reported that they either agree or strongly agree with these statements. In fact, there are only two exceptions: only 48% of students in Turkey and 44% of students in Montenegro reported that they agree or strongly agree with the statement "I prefer working as part of a team to working alone". However, in Korea, 95% of students reported that they agree or strongly agree that "[they are] a good listener"; in Portugal, Thailand and Uruguay, over 95% of students agreed or strongly agreed that "[they] enjoy seeing [their] classmates be successful"; in Singapore, 95% of students agreed or strongly agreed that "[they] enjoy considering different perspectives"; and in Thailand, 96% of students agreed or strongly agreed that "[they] enjoy co-operating with peers".

Figure V.5.1 ▪ Attitudes towards collaboration

Legend
Less than half of students
From 50% to 75% of students
More than 75% of students

		Percentage of students who agreed/strongly agreed with the following statements							
		Items comprising the index of valuing relationships				Items comprising the index of valuing teamwork			
		I am a good listener	I enjoy seeing my classmates be successful	I take into account what others are interested in	I enjoy considering different perspectives	I prefer working as part of a team to working alone	I find that teams make better decisions than individuals	I find that teamwork raises my own efficiency	I enjoy co-operating with peers
OECD	Australia	88	92	91	91	66	74	72	89
	Austria	89	83	88	81	69	75	67	87
	Belgium	85	91	86	89	66	71	63	85
	Canada	89	90	89	90	67	72	70	87
	Chile	87	90	80	90	72	75	81	93
	Czech Republic	92	78	86	86	72	76	67	89
	Denmark	91	91	86	89	65	67	61	90
	Estonia	88	89	92	87	62	72	71	81
	Finland	91	86	92	79	63	72	60	83
	France	86	87	83	88	71	72	76	85
	Germany	90	82	89	81	66	72	65	92
	Greece	85	90	87	91	72	83	76	89
	Hungary	84	87	85	88	74	77	67	86
	Iceland	82	87	79	89	58	63	65	87
	Ireland	85	93	89	89	68	74	72	88
	Israel	92	91	88	83	64	73	64	88
	Italy	85	85	78	91	71	74	71	88
	Japan	77	86	78	67	66	80	54	89
	Korea	95	82	89	91	76	83	84	87
	Latvia	81	84	81	82	69	71	66	82
	Luxembourg	86	84	84	83	68	71	67	85
	Mexico	89	93	84	93	70	82	83	90
	Netherlands	89	91	94	81	64	63	68	84
	New Zealand	83	91	89	90	70	76	73	90
	Norway	88	88	92	89	60	66	56	84
	Poland	88	83	79	88	74	71	69	85
	Portugal	93	96	93	94	72	83	81	95
	Slovak Republic	78	78	84	83	72	74	70	81
	Slovenia	82	92	90	84	69	75	71	89
	Spain	93	90	85	92	67	75	72	93
	Sweden	87	87	90	86	58	63	67	83
	Switzerland	87	88	88	86	73	76	72	91
	Turkey	86	83	76	88	48	71	79	81
	United Kingdom	87	89	88	87	68	74	72	86
	United States	90	93	86	91	69	75	74	87
	OECD average	**87**	**88**	**86**	**87**	**67**	**73**	**70**	**87**
Partners	Brazil	84	94	84	87	71	80	83	94
	B-S-J-G (China)	87	89	89	91	87	86	89	93
	Bulgaria	88	87	80	89	67	73	74	82
	Colombia	90	93	79	84	68	83	77	94
	Costa Rica	89	95	84	94	71	82	78	93
	Croatia	93	92	77	87	76	81	79	90
	Dominican Republic	88	90	84	83	74	82	82	94
	Hong Kong (China)	90	85	90	92	71	80	77	84
	Lithuania	86	85	77	88	73	79	80	86
	Macao (China)	84	85	86	89	69	74	80	84
	Montenegro	83	95	81	84	44	76	74	90
	Peru	90	85	78	91	68	79	77	91
	Qatar	85	92	75	87	62	80	83	88
	Russia	91	78	84	82	72	68	70	80
	Singapore	92	91	92	95	73	82	80	92
	Chinese Taipei	92	91	92	93	85	84	85	91
	Thailand	90	98	93	89	83	91	87	96
	Tunisia	89	94	74	87	78	84	86	92
	United Arab Emirates	88	93	86	91	69	87	86	91
	Uruguay	84	96	82	90	70	80	75	93

Source: OECD, PISA 2015 Database, Table V.5.1.

StatLink http://dx.doi.org/10.1787/888933616161

Students' responses to these eight statements are positively correlated to one another (Figure V.5.2). The highest correlations are observed between the statement "I find that teamwork raises my own efficiency" and the following three statements: "I prefer working as part of a team to working alone" (0.43 across OECD countries), "I find that teams make better decisions than individuals" (0.39 across OECD countries), and "I enjoy co-operating with peers" (0.39 across OECD countries).

Figure V.5.2 ▪ **Correlations among attitudes towards collaboration**

OECD average

Correlation between:							
I am a good listener	I enjoy seeing my classmates be successful	I take into account what others are interested in	I find that teams make better decisions than individuals	I enjoy considering different perspectives	I find that teamwork raises my own efficiency	I enjoy co-operating with peers	...and...
0.04	0.11	0.09	0.33	0.09	0.43	0.38	I prefer working as part of a team to working alone
	0.20	0.20	0.07	0.19	0.09	0.12	I am a good listener
		0.31	0.16	0.21	0.16	0.23	I enjoy seeing my classmates be successful
			0.16	0.25	0.14	0.19	I take into account what others are interested in
				0.16	0.39	0.31	I find that teams make better decisions than individuals
					0.18	0.19	I enjoy considering different perspectives
						0.39	I find that teamwork raises my own efficiency

Source: OECD, PISA 2015 Database, Table V.5.11.

StatLink http://dx.doi.org/10.1787/888933616180

Responses to these eight statements are combined into two indices of co-operation, as shown in Figure V.5.3, that reflect the valuing of relationships and teamwork.[1] The four statements that comprise the index of valuing relationships are related to altruistic interactions, when the student engages in collaborative activities not for his or her own benefit: "I am a good listener"; "I enjoy seeing my classmates be successful"; "I take into account what others are interested in"; and "I enjoy considering different perspectives". By contrast, three of the four statements that comprise the index of valuing teamwork are related to what teamwork, as opposed to working alone, can produce: "I prefer working as part of a team to working alone"; "I find that teams make better decisions than individuals"; and "I find that teamwork raises my own efficiency" (Figure V.5.3).

Each index is standardised to have a mean of 0 and a standard deviation of 1 across OECD countries. Students in Portugal have the highest index of valuing relationships (0.37) among all OECD and partner countries and economies, followed by Costa Rica, the United Arab Emirates and Singapore, all three of which have average indices of valuing relationships greater than 0.30 (Figure V.5.4). Students in Portugal also have the highest index of valuing teamwork (0.32) among OECD countries; however, the average student in the Dominican Republic has an index of valuing teamwork of 0.51 – over half a standard deviation above the average student in OECD countries. On average across OECD countries, the correlation between the indices of valuing relationships and teamwork is 0.41 (Table V.5.12). The correlation between the mean indices of valuing relationships and teamwork at the country level among OECD countries is 0.58: countries with a high mean value on one index also tend to have a high mean value of the other index.

Figure V.5.3 ▪ **Indices of co-operation**

Index of valuing relationships	Index of valuing teamwork
I am a good listener	I prefer working as part of a team to working alone
I enjoy seeing my classmates be successful	I find that teams make better decisions than individuals
I take into account what others are interested in	I find that teamwork raises my own efficiency
I enjoy considering different perspectives	I enjoy co-operating with peers

Figure V.5.4 ■ **Indices of valuing relationships and valuing teamwork**

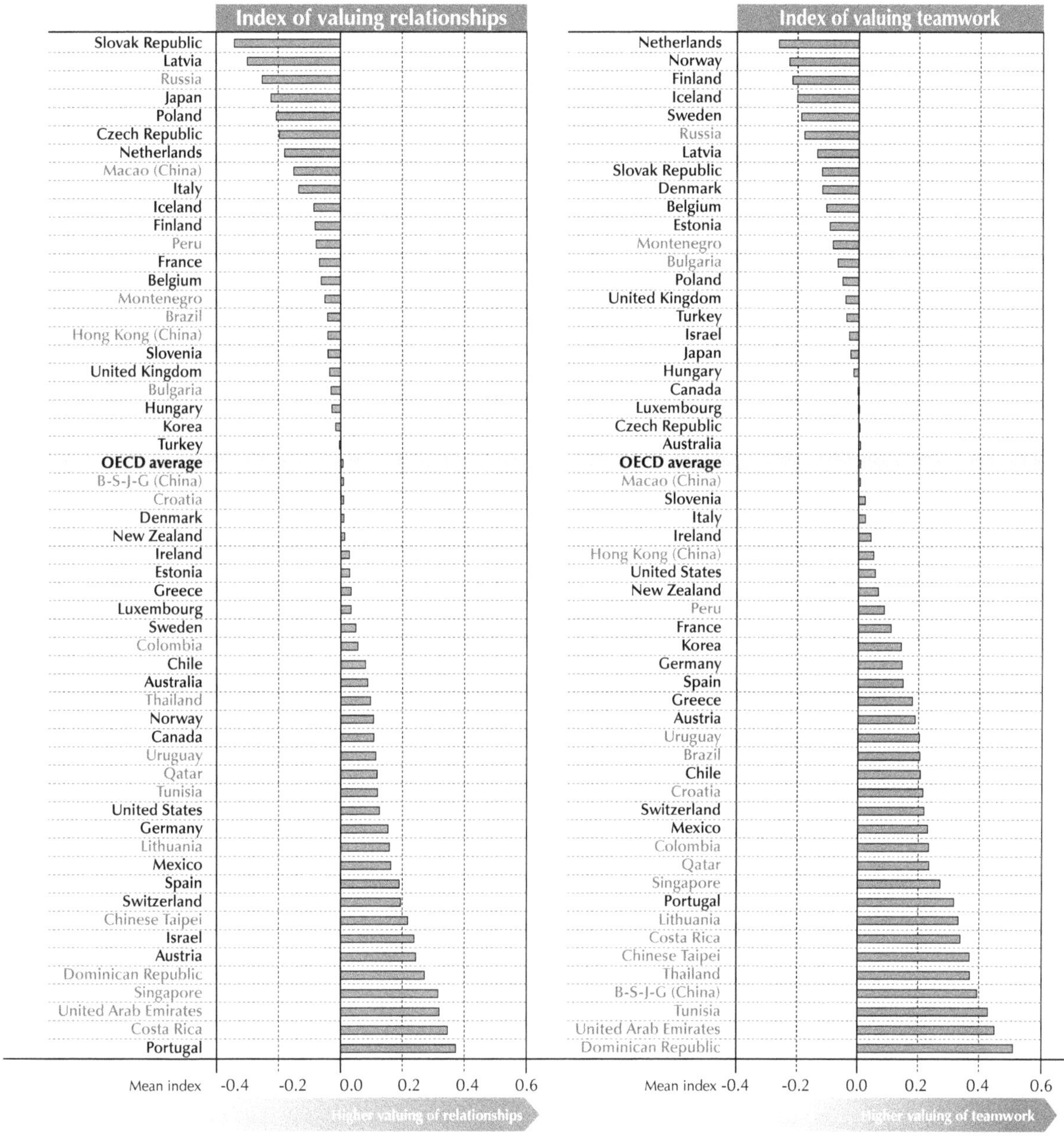

Countries and economies are ranked in ascending order of each index.
Source: OECD, PISA 2015 Database, Table V.5.1.
StatLink http://dx.doi.org/10.1787/888933616199

WITHIN-COUNTRY DIFFERENCES IN ATTITUDES TOWARDS COLLABORATION

Table V.5.3 shows a breakdown of the variation in attitudes towards collaboration in the countries and economies that participated in the PISA 2015 collaborative problem-solving assessment. Some 97% and 98%, respectively, of the variation in the indices of valuing relationships and valuing teamwork lie within schools. In other words, differences across schools account for only 3% of the differences in the index of valuing relationships and only 2% of the differences in the index of valuing teamwork. Student-level variation, not school-level variation, thus explains most of the observed differences in attitudes towards collaboration. This may reflect that students' frame of reference in reporting their attitudes lies within the familiar environment of their schools. Variation related to student demographics is examined next, while variation related to student behaviours and activities, and school policies and practices, is explored in Chapter 6.

Gender differences in attitudes towards collaboration

Cross-country comparisons of attitudes towards collaboration are difficult to interpret given the cultural differences between countries and economies. Such cultural differences are, to a certain extent, eliminated when examining differences in students' attitudes within countries.[2,3]

One such within-country comparison is between boys and girls. Girls were significantly more likely than boys to agree or strongly agree with the four statements that comprise the index of valuing relationships. For example, on average across OECD countries, girls were 5.3 percentage points more likely than boys to report that they agree or strongly agree that "[they] are a good listener" (Figure V.5.5). Moreover, this difference is significant and in favour of girls in 54 of the 56[4] countries that conducted the collaborative problem-solving assessment; in the two other countries, the difference is not significant. Gender differences are most pronounced in Italy and Latvia, where there is a 10 percentage-point gap (Table V.5.4a).

By contrast, boys were significantly more likely than girls to report that they agree or strongly agree with the four statements that comprise the index of valuing teamwork (Figure V.5.5).[5] The difference is most pronounced for the statement "I prefer working as part of a team to working alone", with which boys were 5.1 percentage points more likely than girls to agree or strongly agree. This difference is significant and in favour of boys in 38 of 56 countries; it is significant and in favour of girls in only one country: Beijing-Shanghai-Jiangsu-Guangdong (China) (a 4.1 percentage-point gap). The gender gap is widest in Canada, Iceland and Sweden, where it exceeds 10 percentage points (Table V.5.4b).

Figure V.5.5 ▪ **Gender differences in attitudes towards collaboration**

Difference in the percentage of boys and girls who agreed/strongly agreed with the following statements about collaboration, OECD average

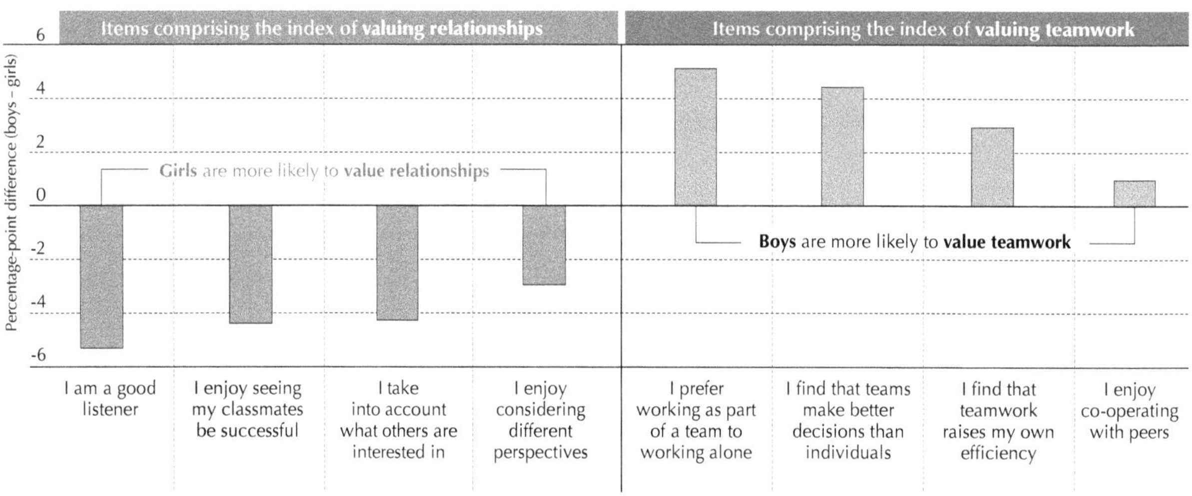

Note: All differences are statistically significant (see Annex A3).
Source: OECD, PISA 2015 Database, Tables V.5.4a and V.5.4b.
StatLink http://dx.doi.org/10.1787/888933616218

The consistent cross-country gender differences observed in responses to these eight statements differ from Wang et al. (2009), who find no significant gender differences in teamwork (whether reported by students themselves, by teachers, or through responses to hypothetical situations) in a United States high school.

Differences in attitudes towards collaboration, by socio-economic status

Figure V.5.6 shows differences in attitudes towards collaboration related to socio-economic status across OECD countries. The figure plots the difference in the percentage of students in the top national quarter of socio-economic status, as measured by the PISA index of economic, social and cultural status, and the percentage of students in the bottom national quarter of socio-economic status who reported that they either agree or strongly agree with each statement. Students in the top quarter of socio-economic status are referred to as advantaged students, while students in the bottom quarter are referred to as disadvantaged students.

Figure V.5.6 ▪ **Socio-economic differences in attitudes towards collaboration**

Difference in the percentage of advantaged and disadvantaged students who agreed/strongly agreed with the following statements about collaboration, OECD average

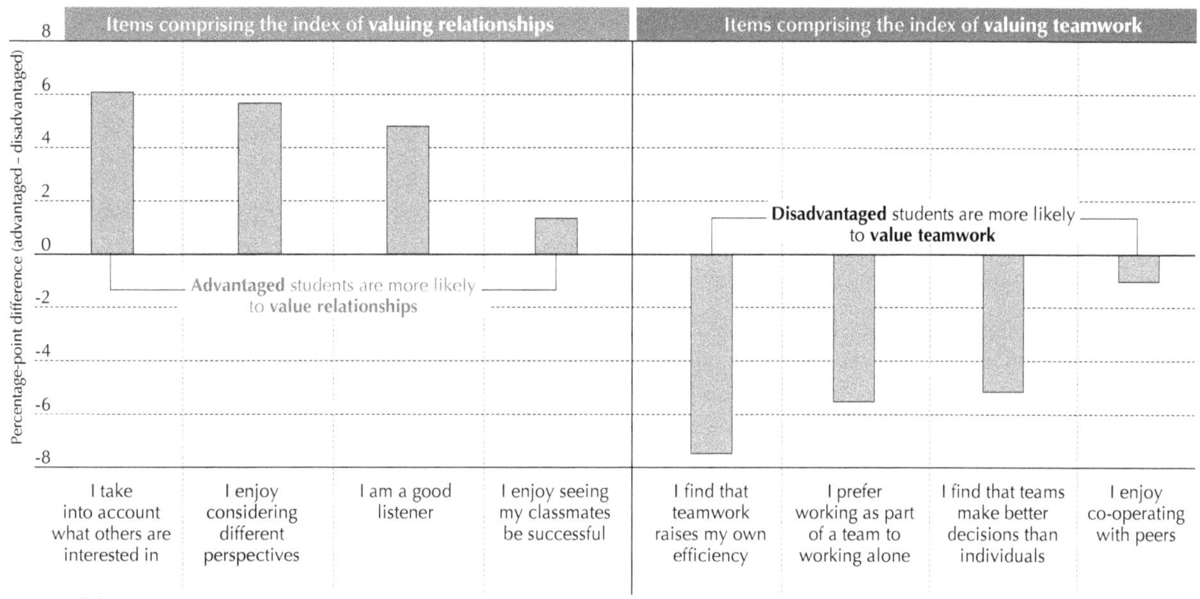

Notes: All differences are statistically significant (see Annex A3).

A socio-economically disadvantaged (advantaged) student is a student in the bottom (top) quarter of the PISA index of economic, social and cultural status (ESCS) in their country/economy.

Source: OECD, PISA 2015 Database, Table V.5.6a.

StatLink http://dx.doi.org/10.1787/888933616237

Significant differences related to socio-economic status in the propensity to agree or strongly agree with each statement are observed. Across all OECD countries, advantaged students were 6.1 percentage points more likely than disadvantaged students to report that they agree or strongly agree with the statement "I take into account what others are interested in"; 5.7 percentage points more likely to agree or strongly agree with the statement "I enjoy considering different perspectives"; 4.8 percentage points more likely to agree or strongly agree with the statement "I am a good listener"; and 1.4 percentage points more likely to agree with the statement "I enjoy seeing my classmates be successful" (Figure V.5.6 and Table V.5.6a). These four statements comprise the index of valuing relationships.

These results are consistent with some recent literature, which shows that those of higher socio-economic status tend to self-report higher levels of empathy (Varnum et al., 2015), which might be related to valuing relationships with others, and a variety of other positive traits, including honesty, sense of humour and friendliness (Varnum, 2015). However, most of the literature seems to suggest that it is students of lower socio-economic status who more commonly exhibit behaviour consistent with co-operation and consideration of others (Pitt and Robinson, 2017). For example, in the United States, university students who were the first in their family to attend university were more likely to be other-focused (as opposed to self-oriented) than university students whose parents had also attended university. These first-generation university students performed worse academically when universities were portrayed as an independent environment where everyone had to make his or her own way, but performed as well as other students when universities were portrayed as an interdependent environment or a community (Stephens et al., 2012). Intriguingly, brain scans show that those of higher socio-economic status actually display reduced neural responses of empathy (Varnum et al., 2015). It appears that those of higher socio-economic status might overstate the degree to which they display certain positive attributes, with the same outcome as if they displayed higher levels of social desirability.

By contrast, disadvantaged students were 7.5 percentage points more likely than advantaged students to agree or strongly agree with the statement "I find that teamwork raises my own efficiency"; 5.5 percentage points more likely to agree or strongly agree with the statement "I prefer working as part of a team to working alone"; 5.2 percentage points more likely to agree or strongly agree with the statement "I find that teams make better decisions than individuals"; and 1.0 percentage point more likely to agree or strongly agree with the statement "I enjoy co-operating with peers" (Figure V.5.6 and Table V.5.6a). These four statements comprise the index of valuing teamwork.

The data indicate that advantaged students were more likely to report that they agree or strongly agree that they engage in co-operative activities that do not directly involve personal gain, while disadvantaged students were more likely to report that they agree or strongly agree that teamwork brings benefits.[6] A similar dichotomy is observed between girls and boys.

THE RELATIONSHIP BETWEEN ATTITUDES TOWARDS COLLABORATION AND OTHER ATTITUDES

PISA 2015 Results (Volume III): Students' Well-Being (OECD, 2017) analyses a variety of well-being indicators based on data from the student questionnaire. What is the relationship between such well-being indicators and attitudes towards collaboration? Are students who have a greater sense of well-being also predisposed to co-operating and collaborating with others?

There is a weak but positive correlation between the indices of valuing relationships and valuing teamwork with the self-reported degree of life satisfaction and the index of achievement motivation (Table V.5.12). These latter two measures of well-being are both positive measures: a higher value in each index is associated with a greater sense of well-being.

In particular, 15-year-old students across OECD countries were significantly more likely to report that they agree or strongly agree with almost all of the statements regarding collaboration described above if they also agreed or strongly agreed with the statements regarding their motivation to achieve. For instance, students in every country and economy were more likely to report that they agree with each of the statements that comprise the index of valuing relationships if they reported that they agree or strongly agree that they "want to be able to select from among the best opportunities available when [they] graduate"[7] (Table V.5.13b). On average across OECD countries, there is a gap of over 13 percentage points in responses to each of the items that comprise the index of valuing relationships between students who agreed or strongly agreed with and students who disagreed or strongly disagreed with the statement "I want to be able to select from among the best opportunities available when I graduate".

The only exception observed is that students were at least one percentage point less likely to report that they agree or strongly agree that they "prefer working as part of a team to working alone" if they agree or strongly agree that they "want to be one of the best students in [their] class" (Table V.5.13b).

Likewise, both indices are weakly but positively correlated with the index of sense of belonging at school and weakly but negatively correlated with the index of exposure to bullying. The former is another positive measure of well-being, while the latter is a negative measure of well-being, where a higher value is considered to be a weaker sense of well-being (Table V.5.12). Hence it appears that a greater disposition towards collaboration goes hand-in-hand with indicators of social well-being.

However, both indices are weakly but positively correlated with the index of schoolwork-related anxiety, which is another negative measure (Table V.5.12). This might be related to the positive correlation between, for example, achievement motivation and anxiety, as discussed in *PISA 2015 Results (Volume III): Students' Well-Being* (OECD, 2017). Hewitt and Flett (1991) define self-oriented perfectionists as those who set high standards for themselves and frequently evaluate their own behaviour and performance. Such self-oriented perfectionists have been found to score higher in some measures of anxiety, such as worry, but lower in other measures of anxiety, such as lack of confidence or being distracted and preoccupied by other thoughts (Stoeber, Feast and Hayward, 2009). They have also been found to show high levels of social connection, as measured through trust and empathy, and low levels of hostility towards others (Stoeber et al., 2017). These self-oriented perfectionists might therefore tend to have more positive attitudes towards co-operation yet at the same time higher levels of anxiety.

THE RELATIONSHIP BETWEEN ATTITUDES TOWARDS COLLABORATION AND COLLABORATIVE PROBLEM-SOLVING PERFORMANCE

Previous chapters present student performance in the PISA 2015 collaborative problem-solving assessment, while this chapter presents student-reported attitudes towards collaboration. Is there a relationship between the two? Are students who have more positive attitudes towards collaboration also better able to solve problems collaboratively?

Figure V.5.7 plots a country or economy's mean score in collaborative problem solving against its mean index of valuing relationships or valuing teamwork. No correlation was observed between performance and the index of valuing relationships ($r^2 = 0.00$). However, a slight negative correlation (with $r^2 = 0.11$) was observed between performance and the index of valuing teamwork. Due to cross-cultural differences in how students report their attitudes towards collaboration, it is difficult to interpret the relationship between indices of collaboration and collaborative problem-solving performance at the mean country/economy level.

Figure V.5.7 ▪ **Performance in collaborative problem solving and the indices of valuing relationships and valuing teamwork**

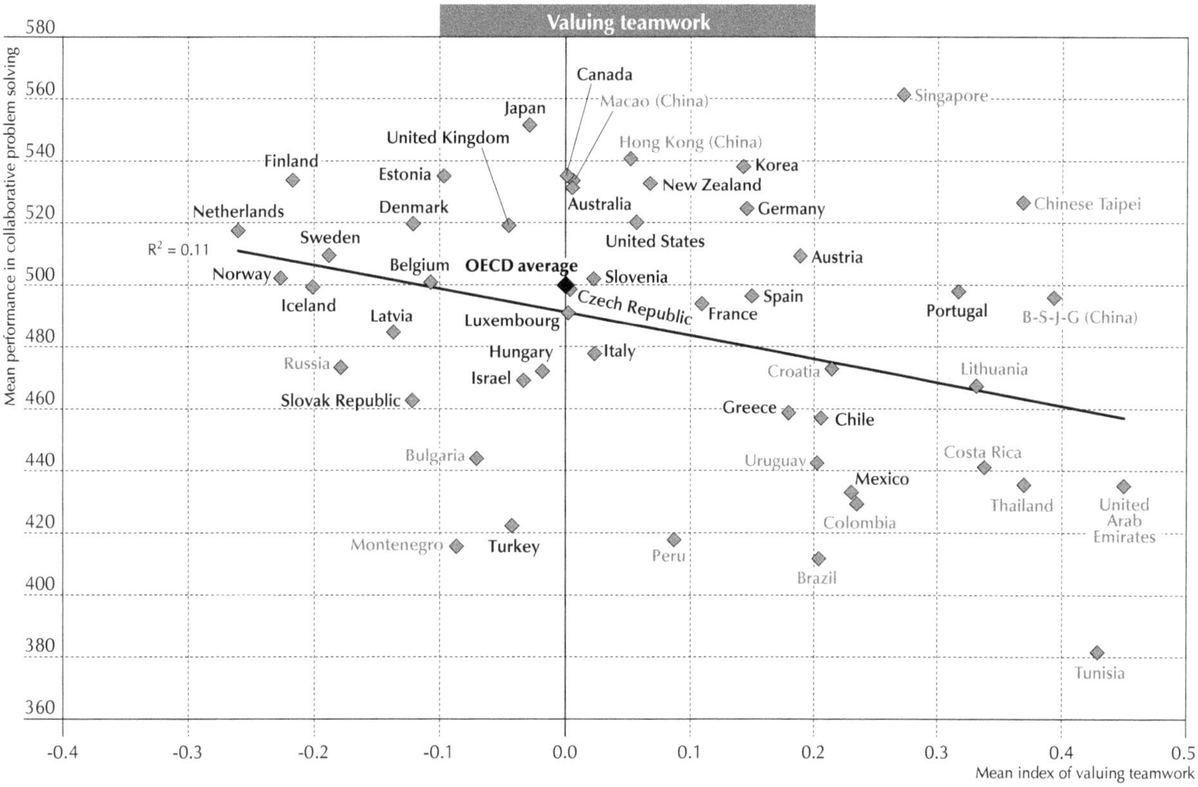

Source: OECD, PISA 2015 Database, Tables V.3.2 and V.5.1.

StatLink http://dx.doi.org/10.1787/888933616256

On the other hand, significant relationships can be found when examining within-country differences in student performance related to self-reported attitudes towards collaboration. On average across OECD countries, students who reported that they agree or strongly agree with the statements that comprise the index of valuing relationships score better than those who reported that they disagree or strongly disagree with those statements. The performance gap varies from 38 points for the statement "I take into account what others are interested in" to 26 points for "I enjoy seeing my classmates be successful" (Figure V.5.8).

By contrast, students who reported that they agree or strongly agree with the statements that comprise the index of valuing teamwork score below students who reported that they disagree or strongly disagree with those statements, on average across OECD countries. For example, the performance gap related to the statement "I find that teamwork raises my own efficiency" is 22 points, while the gap related to the statement "I prefer working as part of a team to working alone" is 17 points (Figure V.5.8). The direction of the performance gaps related to each statement is also remarkably consistent across countries and economies (Tables V.5.2a to V.5.2h).

Figure V.5.8 ▪ **Attitudes towards collaboration and performance in collaborative problem solving**

Score-point difference in performance between those who agreed/strongly agreed with each statement and those who disagreed/strongly disagreed with the statement, OECD average

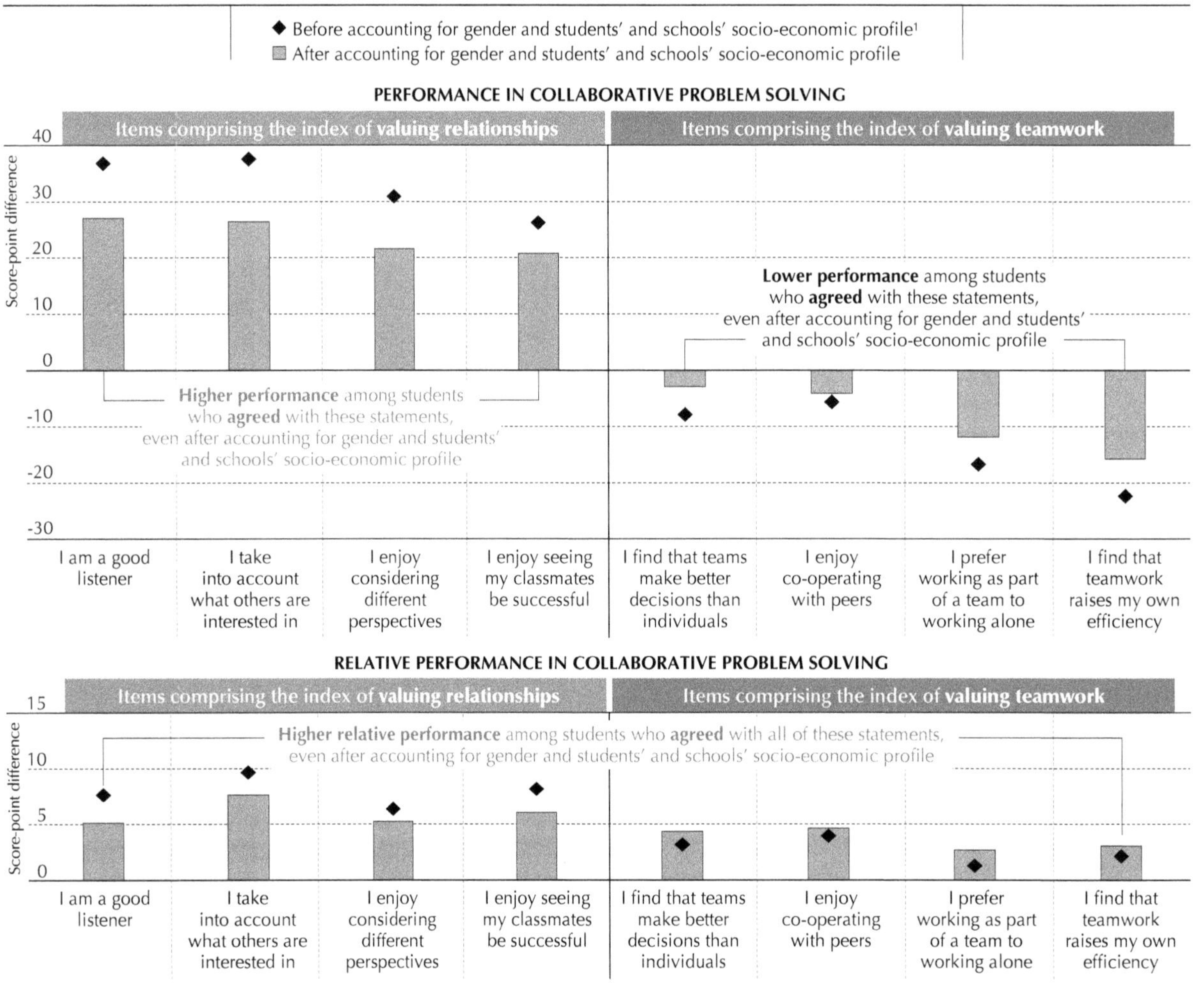

1. The socio-economic profile is measured by the PISA index of economic, social and cultural status (ESCS).

Notes: All differences are statistically significant (see Annex A3).

Relative performance refers to the residual performance, attributable to purely "collaborative problem-solving" competencies, after accounting for performance in science, reading and mathematics in a regression performed across students internationally.

Statements about attitudes towards collaboration are ranked in descending order of the score-point difference in collaborative problem solving between students who agreed/strongly agreed with and those who disagreed/strongly disagreed with the above statements.

Source: OECD, PISA 2015 Database, Tables V.5.2a-h.

StatLink http://dx.doi.org/10.1787/888933616275

Accounting for gender and both students' and schools' socio-economic profile tends to reduce the performance gap for all statements, although it does not change the direction of the gap: students who agreed or strongly agreed with the statements in the index of valuing relationships, and students who disagreed or strongly disagreed with the statements in the index of valuing teamwork still perform better in collaborative problem solving (Figure V.5.8). The reduction in the performance gap is somewhat to be expected, given the relationships in performance, attitudes, and gender and socio-economic profile. For example, girls tend to perform better than boys in the collaborative problem-solving assessment and tended to agree or strongly agree more often to the statements comprising the index of valuing relationships. Since students who agreed or strongly agreed with these statements also perform better in the collaborative problem-solving assessment, accounting for gender should reduce the score-point difference associated with agreeing to these statements.

But other patterns are observed after accounting for performance in the three core PISA subjects (science, reading and mathematics). There is a positive association between agreeing or strongly agreeing with any of the items related to attitudes towards collaboration – both the items that comprise the index of valuing relationships and those that comprise the index of valuing teamwork – and relative performance in collaborative problem solving (Figure V.5.8).[8] These positive associations persist after accounting for gender, and students' and schools' socio-economic profile. On average across OECD countries, students who agree or strongly agree with the statements in the index of valuing relationships perform between five and eight points higher in collaborative problem solving after accounting for performance in the three core PSIA subjects, gender, and students' and schools' socio-economic profile, while they perform between two and five points higher if they agree or strongly agree with the statements in the index of valuing teamwork.

The direction of the performance gaps between students who responded that they agree or strongly agree and students who responded that they disagree or strongly disagree with each statement was fairly consistent across countries and economies. For example, the strongest positive association is observed with the statement "I take into account what others are interested in" (Figure V.5.8). After accounting for performance in the three core PISA subjects, gender, and students' and schools' socio-economic profile, students who reported that they agree or strongly agree with this statement score eight points higher than those who reported that they disagree or strongly disagree with the statement. This difference is significant and in favour of students who reported that they agree or strongly agree in 20 of the 52 countries that participated in the PISA 2015 collaborative problem-solving assessment, and is over 20 points[9] in Estonia and New Zealand. Only in Colombia is the difference significant and in favour of students who reported that they disagree or strongly disagree with the statement "I take into account what others are interested in" (Figure V.5.9 and Table V.5.2d). Similar results are seen for the other items in the index of valuing relationships.

Figure V.5.9 ▪ **Taking into account others' interests and performance in collaborative problem solving**

Difference in collaborative problem-solving performance between students who agreed/strongly agreed with the statement "I take into account what others are interested in" and those who disagreed/strongly disagreed with that statement

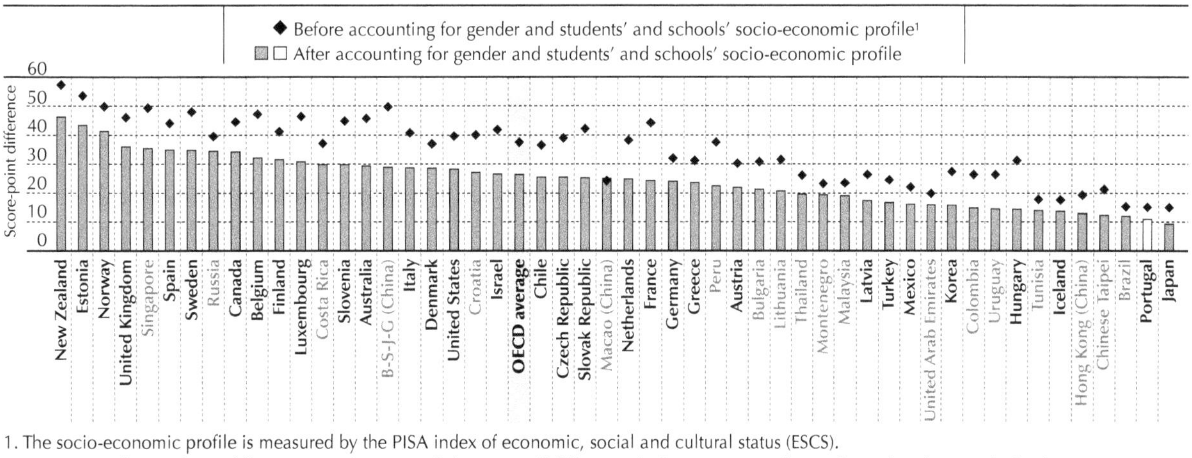

1. The socio-economic profile is measured by the PISA index of economic, social and cultural status (ESCS).

Note: Statistically significant differences are shown in a darker tone. All differences before accounting for gender and students' and schools' socio-economic profile are statistically significant (see Annex A3).

Countries and economies are ranked in descending order of the score-point difference between students who agreed/strongly agreed with the statement above and students who disagreed/strongly disagreed, after accounting for gender and students' and schools' socio-economic profile.

Source: OECD, PISA 2015 Database, Table V.5.2d.

StatLink http://dx.doi.org/10.1787/888933616294

Performance gaps related to items in the index of valuing teamwork are also fairly consistent across countries. As one example, students in 20 out of 52 countries who reported that they agree or strongly agree that "[they] find that teams make better decisions than individuals" perform better in the collaborative problem-solving assessment, after accounting for performance in the three core PISA subjects, gender, and students' and schools' socio-economic profile. The gap is 4 score points, on average across OECD countries, and more than 10 score points in Croatia and Portugal. Only in Tunisia is this difference significant and in favour of students who reported that they disagree or strongly disagree with this statement (Figure V.5.10 and Table V.5.2e).

Hence, it appears that positive attitudes towards collaboration – whether for altruistic reasons or for the benefit of one's own success in a collaborative project – are associated with the distinctive aspects of solving problems collaboratively. Students who perform at lower levels of proficiency are more likely to recognise the effectiveness of collaboration. However, a positive disposition towards collaboration, even if it is for the benefits to oneself that collaboration can bring, is still associated with better performance in collaborative problem solving when comparing students with similar performance in science, reading and mathematics.

Figure V.5.10 ▪ **Finding that teams make better decisions and performance in collaborative problem solving**

Difference in collaborative problem-solving performance between students who agreed/strongly agreed with the statement "I find that teams make better decisions than individuals" and those who disagreed/strongly disagreed with that statement, after accounting for performance in science, reading and mathematics

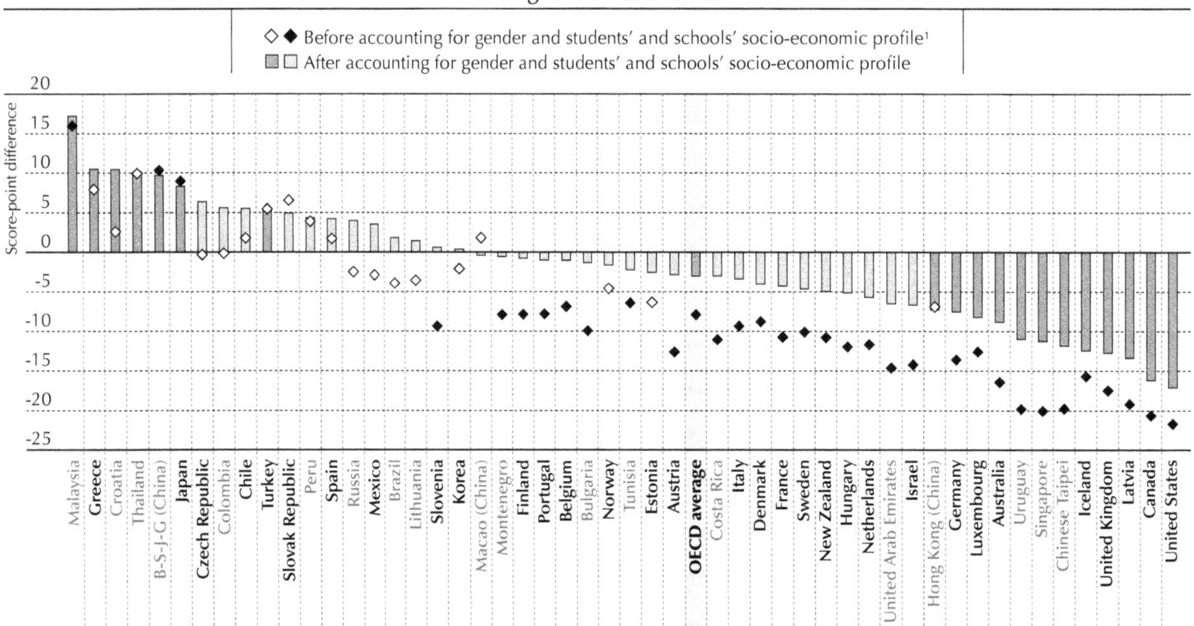

1. The socio-economic profile is measured by the PISA index of economic, social and cultural status (ESCS).

Note: Statistically significant differences are shown in a darker tone (see Annex A3).

Countries and economies are ranked in descending order of the score-point difference between students who agreed/strongly agreed with the statement above and students who disagreed/strongly disagreed, after accounting for gender and students' and schools' socio-economic profile.

Source: OECD, PISA 2015 Database, Table V.5.2e.

StatLink http://dx.doi.org/10.1787/888933616313

Notes

1. The four highly-correlated items described in the previous paragraph are indeed the constituent components of the index of valuing teamwork.

2. Examining differences within countries/economies allows for the elimination of country/economy-specific response patterns common across all subgroups in the country/economy. For example, if all students in Country A with a certain latent trait (e.g. a certain actual "level" of valuing relationships) *report* a higher index of valuing relationships than students in Country B with the same latent trait, comparisons of the reported trait are biased. However, within-country differences between subgroups in Country A and Country B may still be meaningful.

However, subgroups in each country/economy may also respond differently. For example, boys and girls may be socialised differently, leading to boys systematically reporting a higher or lower index than girls when their latent traits are actually identical. There is no way to determine the extent of such systematic differences from PISA data. If the systematic differences are common across countries, though, international comparisons can still be made.

3. Cross-country comparisons of attitudes are difficult due to cultural differences. As these cultural differences may still exist between non-immigrant and immigrant students who reside in the same country or economy, this chapter will not discuss immigrant-related differences in attitudes. Data on these differences are available in Tables V.5.8a to V.5.8d.

4. Although 57 countries and economies participated in the computer-based assessment in 2015, the coverage of data from Malaysia on attitudes was too small to ensure comparability.

5. Although girls are significantly likelier to agree or strongly agree with the statements that comprise the index of valuing relationships, and boys are significantly likelier to agree or strongly agree with the statements that comprise the index of valuing teamwork, it is still possible for responses to all eight statements to be positively correlated. Both boys and girls who value relationships are more likely to value teamwork; the difference lies in their average proclivity to agree to each statement.

6. Separate analyses, not presented in the text, show that the relationship between various measures of school-level diversity in socio-economic status and attitudes towards collaboration is generally not significant, both on average across the OECD and in individual countries/economies.

7. There are two exceptions: in Korea and Portugal, students who agree or strongly agree that they "want to be able to select from among the best opportunities available when they graduate" and those who disagree or strongly disagree to this statement are statistically as likely to agree or strongly agree that they "enjoy seeing [their] classmates be successful".

8. Relative collaborative problem-solving performance is calculated by an ordinary least squares regression of collaborative problem-solving performance over performance in science, reading and mathematics. In Chapter 3, the regression is performed at the international level in order to rank countries and economies. In Chapters 4, 5, 6 and 7, the regression is performed at the individual country or economy level, as the focus is on factors related to differences in performance within each country/economy. This results in an average residual of 0 for each country/economy.

9. Differences in relative performance in collaborative problem solving are typically smaller than differences in raw (actual) performance in collaborative problem solving as much of the variation in the former set of scores is eliminated after accounting for performance in the three core PISA subjects.

References

Hewitt, P.L. and **G.L. Flett** (1991), "Perfectionism in the self and social contexts: Conceptualisation, assessment, and association with psychopathology", *Journal of Personality and Social Psychology*, Vol. 60/3, pp. 456-470, http://dx.doi.org/10.1037/0022-3514.60.3.456.

OECD (2017), *PISA 2015 Results (Volume III): Students' Well-Being*, OECD Publishing, Paris, http://dx.doi.org/10.1787/9789264273856-en.

Pitt, P.K. and **A.R. Robinson** (2017), "Social class and prosocial behavior: Current evidence, caveats, and questions", *Current Opinion in Psychology*, Vol. 18, pp. 6-10, https://doi.org/10.1016/j.copsyc.2017.06.003.

Stephens, N.M. et al. (2012), "Unseen disadvantage: How American universities' focus on independence undermines the academic performance of first-generation college students", *Journal of Personality and Social Psychology*, Vol. 102/6, pp. 1178-1197, http://dx.doi.org/10.1037/a0027143.

Stoeber, J., A.R. Feast, and **J.A. Hayward** (2009), "Self-oriented and socially prescribed perfectionism: Differential relationships with intrinsic and extrinsic motivation and test anxiety", *Personality and Individual Differences*, Vol. 47/5, pp. 423-428, https://doi.org/10.1016/j.paid.2009.04.014.

Stoeber, J. et al. (2017), "Perfectionism, social disconnection, and interpersonal hostility: Not all perfectionists don't play nicely with others", *Personality and Individual Differences*, Vol. 119, pp. 112-117, https://doi.org/10.1016/j.paid.2017.07.008.

Varnum, M.E.W. (2015), "Higher in status, (even) better-than-average", *Frontiers in Psychology*, Vol. 6, https://doi.org/10.3389/fpsyg.2015.00496.

Varnum, M.E.W. et al. (2015), "Social class affects neural empathic responses", *Culture and Brain*, Vol. 3/2, pp. 122-130, https://doi.org/10.1007/s40167-015-0031-2.

Wang, L. et al. (2009), "Assessing teamwork and collaboration in high school students: A multimethod approach", *Canadian Journal of School Psychology*, Vol. 24/2, pp. 108-124, http://dx.doi.org/10.1177/0829573509335470.

6

Student activities, school practices and collaboration

This chapter considers various student activities that might be related to students' attitudes towards collaboration and their ability to solve problems collaboratively. These factors include students' participation in physical activity and attendance in physical education classes, their out-of-school activities, whether they play truant or arrive late for school, and their attendance at pre-primary school.

A note regarding Israel

The statistical data for Israel are supplied by and under the responsibility of the relevant Israeli authorities. The use of such data by the OECD is without prejudice to the status of the Golan Heights, East Jerusalem and Israeli settlements in the West Bank under the terms of international law.

The previous chapters examine how demographic factors are related to attitudes towards collaboration and performance in collaborative problem solving. Many of these factors are beyond the direct control of students, teachers or school systems. For example, schools often must accept any student who lives within designated boundaries and they cannot change the gender balance or immigrant population in their student body.

What can be done, then, to improve attitudes towards collaboration and performance in collaborative problem solving? This chapter examines the relationship between both of these outcomes and various student activities and behaviours and school policies and practices, including many of the factors discussed in *PISA 2015 Results (Volume II): Policies and Practices for Successful Schools* (OECD, 2016). As much of the variation in collaborative problem solving performance and in attitudes is found within schools and not between schools (Table V.5.3), the focus will primarily be on student activities and behaviours as most school-level policies and practices are expected to have only a limited relationship with collaboration.

Most of the student demographic factors analysed in Chapter 4 were found not to be unique to performance in collaborative problem solving; they were also observed in student performance in science, reading and mathematics. This chapter thus also attempts to identify those elusive factors that are related to skills specific to collaboration.

What the data tell us

- Attitudes towards collaboration are generally more positive as students engage in more physical activity or attend more physical education classes per week.
- Students who play video games outside of school score slightly lower in collaborative problem solving than students who do not play video games, on average across OECD countries, after accounting for performance in the three core PISA subjects, gender, and students' and schools' socio-economic profile. On the other hand, students who access the Internet, chat or social networks outside of school score slightly higher than other students.
- Students who work in the household or take care of other family members value both teamwork and relationships more than other students, as do students who meet friends or talk to friends on the phone.
- Students who had attended pre-primary school show more positive attitudes towards collaboration, after accounting for gender and socio-economic status.

PHYSICAL ACTIVITY

Many studies have tried to discover a link between participation in sports and academic performance, with inconclusive results. For instance, the United States Centers for Disease Control and Prevention (2010) analysed 50 studies showing that physical activity might have a positive, and at least does not have a negative, impact on academic performance. No comprehensive and quantitative studies were found that investigated the relationship between participation in sports and collaborative and co-operative behaviour. However, Pascarella and Smart (1991) found that participation in intercollegiate athletics among men at American colleges was related to both improved leadership skills and social development. There is also some evidence of a relationship between participation in sport and lower antisocial behaviour in adolescents (Mahoney, 2000; Mahoney and Stattin, 2000), increased social functioning in adolescents (Snyder et al., 2010), and increased co-operation among shy children (Findlay and Coplan, 2008).

PISA 2015 asked students to report the number of days during which they engaged in moderate physical activity[1] or vigorous physical activity[2] during the week before the PISA assessment. PISA also asked students how often, on average, they attend physical education class each week during the school year.[3]

On average across OECD countries, students engage in just under five days of moderate physical activity and just under four days of vigorous physical activity in a typical week (Tables V.6.1a and V.6.1b). There is some variation between countries, although students in all countries are, on average, physically active. The average student in Tunisia and the United Arab Emirates engages in moderate physical activity 3.5 times in a typical week (i.e. one out of every two days), while the average student in Denmark, Germany, the Netherlands, Norway and Poland engages in moderate physical activity over 5.5 times in a typical week. Similarly, the average student in Macao (China) engages in vigorous physical activity three times in a typical week, while his or her counterpart in Iceland engages in vigorous physical activity five times a week.

Students attend physical education class twice a week, on average across OECD countries (Table V.6.1c). In Costa Rica, Hong Kong (China) and Ireland, the average student attends physical education class around once a week, while in Hungary and Poland, the average student attends more than three physical education classes per week.

Performance in collaborative problem solving

There is, on the whole, a positive relationship between the number of days per week that students engage in moderate physical activity during the week prior to the PISA assessment and performance in collaborative problem solving. Students who engage in moderate physical activity two or more days per week score higher in the collaborative problem-solving assessment than students who engage in such activity fewer than two days per week (Figure V.6.1, Table V.6.1a). These trends differ slightly between boys and girls. The better performance among boys is seen only after attaining a threshold of five days of moderate physical activity. The improved performance among girls is observed after attaining a threshold of two days of moderate physical activity and continues to increase with the number of days of physical activity until it peaks at six days per week.

By contrast, students score by and large similarly in collaborative problem solving regardless of the number of days during which they engage in vigorous physical activity, except for those students who engage in these activities every day of the week. On average across OECD countries, these students score 29 points below students who did not engage in any vigorous physical activity during the week prior to the PISA test (among girls, 16 score points separate the two groups; among boys, the gap is 27 points wide) (Figure V.6.1, Tables V.6.1b and V.6.2b).[4]

Figure V.6.1 ▪ **Physical exercise and performance in collaborative problem solving, by gender**
Collaborative problem-solving performance, OECD average

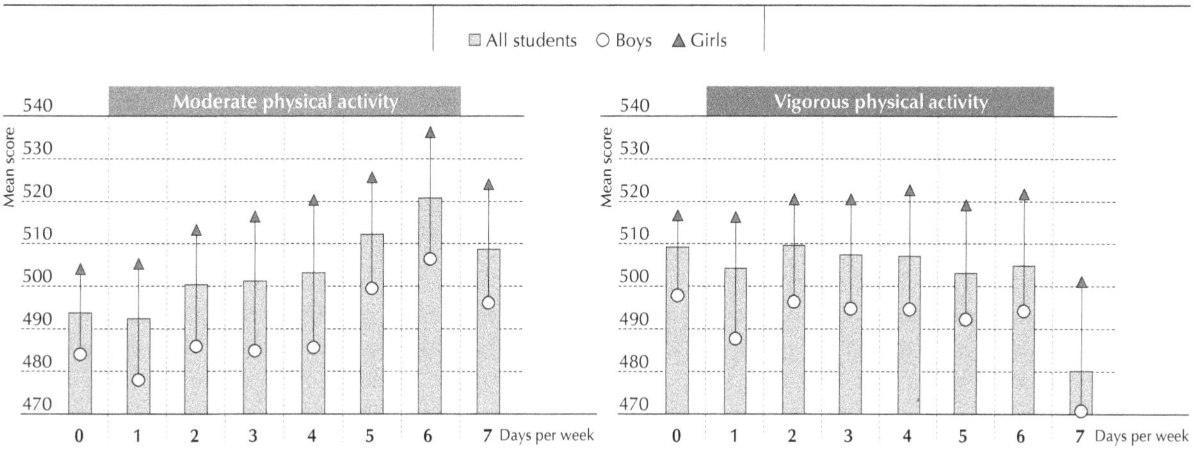

Notes: Moderate physical activities include walking, climbing stairs or riding a bicycle to school for at least 60 minutes per day.
Vigorous physical activities are those that make the student sweat and breathe hard, such as running, cycling, aerobics, soccer or skating, for at least 20 minutes per day.
Source: OECD, PISA 2015 Database, Tables V.6.1a and V.6.1b.
StatLink http://dx.doi.org/10.1787/888933616332

Students who attend one or two days of physical education class per week score highest in collaborative problem solving (Figure V.6.2, Tables V.6.1c and V.6.2c). These students score around 20 score points higher than students who do not attend any physical education class, on average across OECD countries. However, students who participate in four days of physical education class per week score at least 31 points lower in collaborative problem solving than those who take part in one or two classes per week, and 10 points lower than those who do not take part in any physical education classes. Students who participate in five days of physical education class per week score around 55 points lower than those who take part in one or two classes per week, and 33 points below those who do not take part in any physical education classes. Similar trends are observed among boys and girls.

However, performance in the three core PISA subjects of science, reading and mathematics follows similar patterns with respect to the frequency of physical activity and attendance at physical education classes. To what extent are these performance differences attributable to general cognitive performance, and to what extent are they representative of true differences in collaboration and interpersonal skills?

Figure V.6.2 ■ **Physical education class and performance in collaborative problem solving, by gender**

Collaborative problem-solving performance, OECD average

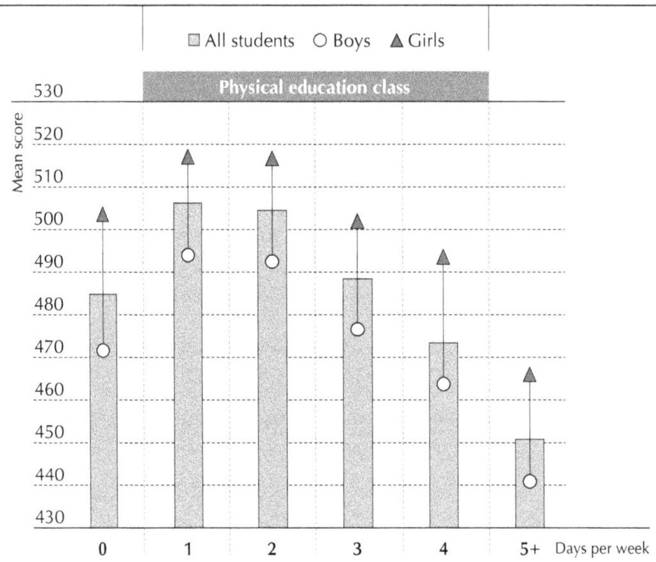

Source: OECD, PISA 2015 Database, Table V.6.1c.

StatLink http://dx.doi.org/10.1787/888933616351

After accounting for performance in science, reading and mathematics, there are few significant differences in performance on the collaborative problem-solving assessment related to the number of days in an average week during which a student engages in moderate physical activity (Table V.6.3a). Any significant differences observed on average across OECD countries are not consistently observed across individual countries and economies. However, additional days of vigorous physical activity beyond two days per week are associated with successively lower relative performance scores in collaborative problem solving (after accounting for performance in the three core PISA subjects) (Table V.6.3b).

Most differences in relative performance associated with the number of days that a student attends physical education class per week are not significant across OECD countries. The greatest differences are found among students who attend four or five days of physical education class per week, who score over five points lower in collaborative problem solving than students who attend fewer days of physical education class per week, but who have similar scores in science, reading and mathematics (Table V.6.3c). In other words, students' collaboration-specific skills are observed to decrease above a certain threshold of vigorous physical activity or attendance in physical education classes.

Attitudes towards collaboration

Students who participate in moderate or vigorous physical activity more often during the week tend to have more positive attitudes towards collaboration, as shown in Figures V.6.3 and V.6.4. The index of valuing relationships seems to increase progressively as students engage in more days of moderate physical activity. It increases up to a threshold of two days per week of vigorous physical activity, after which it remains relatively constant.[5]

There is also a continuous increase in the index of valuing teamwork with the number of days that students engage in vigorous physical activity. Students who do not engage in any vigorous physical activity during an average week are almost one-third of a standard deviation lower on that index than students who engage in vigorous physical activity every day of the week (Table V.6.4b). The relationship with moderate physical activity is less clear-cut. There appears to be a general increase in the index of valuing teamwork as students engage more frequently in moderate physical activity, although the trend is not monotonic.

The index of valuing teamwork increases progressively with the number of days of physical education class that students attend. On average across OECD countries, students who attend physical education class every day of the school week have an index of valuing teamwork 0.23 unit higher than students who do not attend any physical education class (Figure V.6.4). The index of valuing relationships, however, is highest among those students who participate in physical education class one or two days per week.

Figure V.6.3 ▪ **Physical exercise and attitudes towards co-operation, by gender**
OECD average

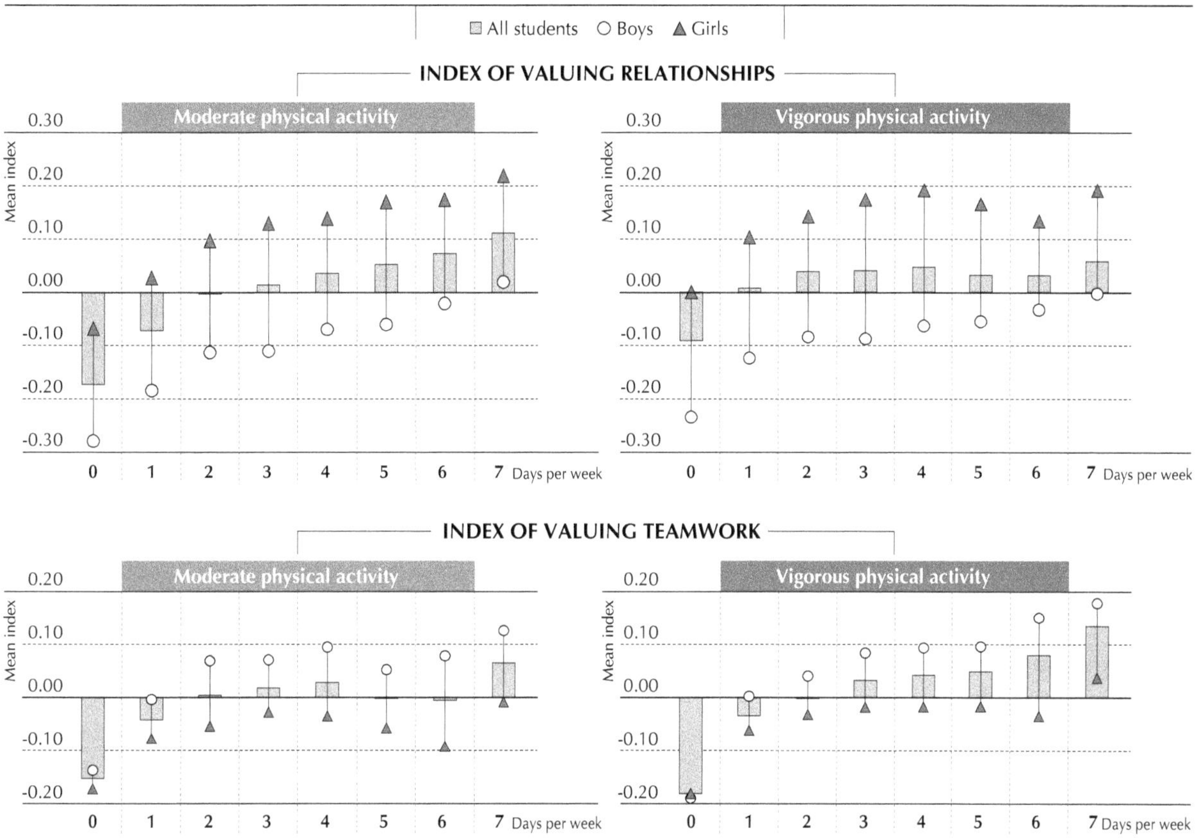

Notes: Moderate physical activities include walking, climbing stairs or riding a bicycle to school for at least 60 minutes per day.
Vigorous physical activities are those that make the student sweat and breathe hard, such as running, cycling, aerobics, soccer or skating, for at least 20 minutes per day.
Source: OECD, PISA 2015 Database, Tables V.6.4a and V.6.4b.
StatLink http://dx.doi.org/10.1787/888933616370

Figure V.6.4 ▪ **Physical education class and attitudes towards co-operation, by gender**
OECD average

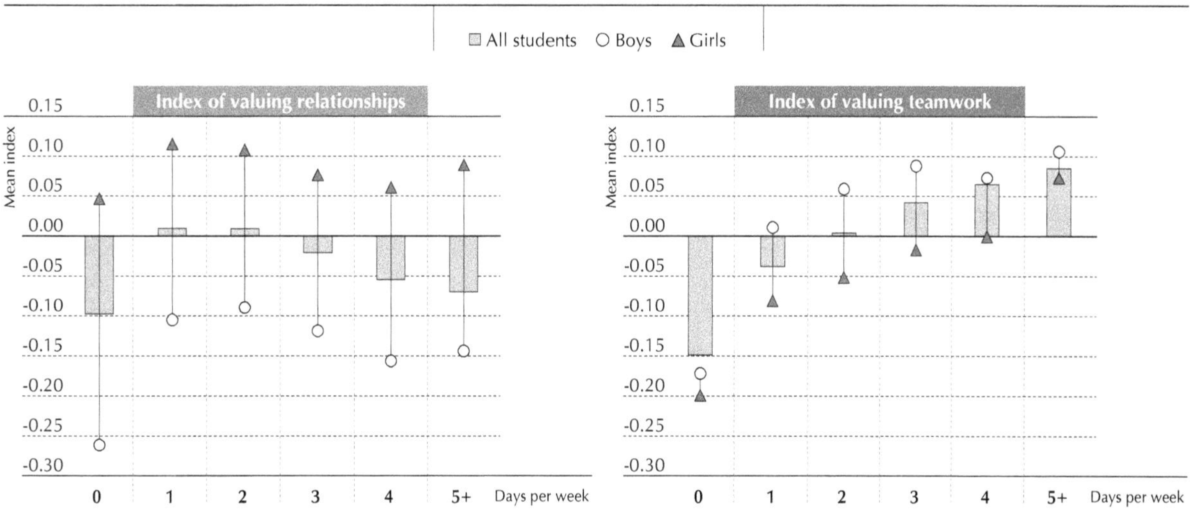

Source: OECD, PISA 2015 Database, Table V.6.4c.
StatLink http://dx.doi.org/10.1787/888933616389

Students were not asked whether they participate in individual or team sports, a factor that affects the interpretation of these results. Caution is also advised when comparing results that involve different measures of physical activity and exercise. Physical education class in school might be voluntary or obligatory. PISA did not ask students how long their physical education classes lasted, so some students might have had fewer days of longer physical education classes, while other students might have had more days of shorter physical education classes. Moderate or vigorous physical activity includes exercise and sport in which students participate both during and outside of school hours. Hence, the various measures of physical activity are neither necessarily interchangeable nor comparable.

STUDENT ACTIVITIES OUTSIDE OF SCHOOL

PISA 2015 asked students whether they participated in a variety of activities before or after school on the most recent school day prior to sitting the PISA assessment. Several of these activities might have a social – or perhaps antisocial – component to them: using the Internet/chat/social networks; playing video games; meeting friends or talking to friends on the phone; and working in the household or taking care of family members.

These questions measure what occurs on only one particular school day and may not accurately describe a student's general level of participation in any of these activities. However, the four activities described above generally require minimal dedicated effort – they can be performed at home, without having to go to a special location – and hence are likely to be performed on a regular, almost daily basis by those who partake in them. Hence, asking students whether they participated in these activities on the most recent school day is likely to elicit responses that show whether they participate in these activities on most school days.[6]

Performance in collaborative problem solving

Playing video games

On average across OECD countries, a negative association is observed between performance in collaborative problem solving and playing video games. Students who play video games score 32 points lower, on average, than students who do not play video games (Figure V.6.5). This gap is also significant and in favour of those who do not play video games in 50 out of the 51 participating countries and economies; it is largest in Israel and the United Arab Emirates, where students who play video games score 58 points in collaborative problem solving below students who do not play video games. Only in Costa Rica is there a non-significant gap between these two groups of students (Table V.6.7b).

This gap remains significant after accounting for performance in science, reading and mathematics. The relative score of students who play video games outside of school is 15 points below that of students who do not play video games, on average across OECD countries; after also accounting for gender and students' and schools' socio-economic profile, the gap is still significant but only 4 score points wide (Figure V.6.5, Table V.6.7b). The fall in collaborative problem-solving performance associated with playing video games is particularly large in Israel, Thailand and the United States, where it is over 10 score points (after also accounting for gender and students' and schools' socio-economic profile).

The reduction of the performance gap in collaborative problem-solving between students who play and those who do not play video games, after accounting for performance in the three core PISA subjects, can be largely attributed to cognitive aspects common to all four assessments. Likewise, boys play video games more often than girls and boys perform worse in collaborative problem solving; accounting for gender thus narrows the performance gap. However, the gap still remains significant after accounting for all of these variables, which indicates that there are still unexplained factors that might be behind this relationship.

Accessing the Internet, chat or social networks

By contrast, accessing the Internet, chat, or social networks outside of school is associated with higher performance in collaborative problem solving. On average across OECD countries, students who access such online communication media score seven points above students who did not in the collaborative problem-solving assessment (Figure V.6.5). At the country level, the gap is significant and in favour of students who accessed such media in 23 of the 51 countries and economies, and is over 35 score points wide in Brazil, Colombia and Norway. In six countries and economies, the gap is significant but in favour of students who did not access such media, with the widest such gap – 35 score points – observed in the United States (Table V.6.7a).

After accounting for performance in science, reading and mathematics, gender, and students' and schools' socio-economic status, a significant gap of six score points in collaborative problem-solving performance is still observed across OECD countries in favour of students who had accessed the Internet, chat, or social networks outside of school (Figure V.6.5).

Figure V.6.5 ▪ **Activities outside of school and performance in collaborative problem solving**

Difference in collaborative problem-solving performance between students who reported that they had engaged in these activities before or after school and those who reported that they had not, OECD average

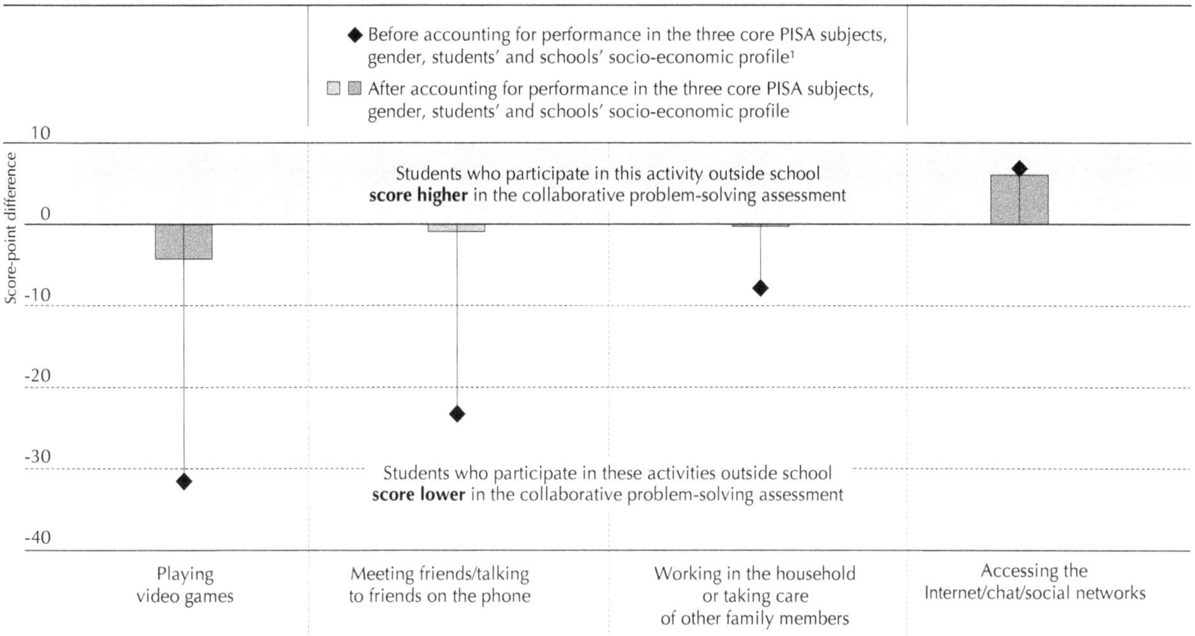

1. The socio-economic profile is measured by the PISA index of economic, social and cultural status (ESCS).

Notes: Score-point differences that are statistically significant are shown in a darker tone. All differences before accounting for performance in the three core PISA subjects, gender, and students' and schools' socio-economic profile are statistically significant (see Annex A3).

Students were asked whether they had engaged in these activities before or after school on the most recent school day prior to the PISA assessment.

Activities are ranked in ascending order of the score-point difference in collaborative problem solving, after accounting for performance in the core PISA subjects, gender, and students' and schools' socio-economic profile.

Source: OECD, PISA 2015 Database, Tables V.6.7a-d.

StatLink http://dx.doi.org/10.1787/888933616408

This gap is significant and in favour of students who had accessed such media in 13 of the 51 participating countries and economies, and is over 15 points wide in the Czech Republic and Germany. By contrast, the performance gap is significant and in favour of students who had not accessed such media only in the United States, where it is 10 score points wide (Table V.6.7a).

These forms of media are all accessed via the computer or another form of information and communications technology (ICT), much in the same way that the PISA 2015 collaborative problem-solving assessment was conducted. Hence, students who participate in these activities outside of school might already be more familiar with the idea of and have more experience in interacting with others in a virtual environment. Accessing these forms of media may also be relevant to how students might collaborate virtually after they leave school.

Other out-of-school activities

Students who met friends or talked to friends on the phone performed below students who did neither in the collaborative problem-solving assessment. Likewise, students who worked in the household or took care of family members performed worse in collaborative problem solving than students who did not do so. However, after accounting for performance in science, reading and mathematics, gender, and students' and schools' socio-economic status, no significant different in performance between the groups of students remained (Figure V.6.5).

Attitudes towards collaboration

Meeting friends or talking to friends on the phone, and accessing the Internet, chat or social networks

Participation in each of the activities described above is associated with a significant change in students' attitudes towards collaboration. First, students who met friends or talked to friends on the phone outside of school are located higher on the index of valuing relationships (by 0.07 unit after accounting for gender and socio-economic status, on average across OECD countries) and much higher on the index of valuing teamwork (by 0.29 unit after accounting for gender and socio-economic status, on average across OECD countries) than students who did not do so (Table V.6.8a).

Indeed, the index of valuing teamwork was higher among students who met friends or talked to friends outside of school in 54 out of the 57 countries that administered the PISA assessment on the computer.

Students who met friends or talked to friends on the phone outside of school were particularly more likely to report that they prefer working as part of a team to working alone (11 percentage-point difference, after accounting for gender and socio-economic status); that they find that teamwork raises their own efficiency (11 percentage-point difference); and that they enjoy co-operating with peers (9 percentage-point difference). The largest gaps are found in the Russian Federation (hereafter "Russia"), where students who met friends or talked to friends on the phone outside of school were 22 percentage points more likely to report that they prefer working as part of a team; 19 percentage points more likely to report that they find that teamwork improves their own efficiency; and 19 percentage points more likely to report that they enjoy co-operating with peers (Table V.6.8a).

Similar results are observed for students who access the Internet, chat or social networks outside of school. After accounting for gender and socio-economic status, these students have an index of valuing teamwork 0.19 unit higher than students who do not access such communications media, on average across OECD countries, although their index of valuing relationships is a relatively small 0.02 unit below that of students who do not access such communications media (Table V.6.8b).

As with meeting friends or talking to friends on the phone, students who access the Internet, chat or social networks outside of school are also significantly more likely to say that they prefer working as part of a team to working alone (by 8 percentage points); that they enjoy co-operating with peers (by 8 percentage points); and that they find that teamwork raises their own efficiency (by 7 percentage points) (Table V.6.8b).

Meeting friends, talking to friends on the phone, and using the Internet, chat or social networks are all ways to develop and nurture relationships with others. It might therefore seem surprising that these activities are associated with a greater difference in how students value teamwork compared to how they value relationships. However, the relationships are not causal and an explanation for these relationships cannot be ascertained from data from PISA.

Working in the household and taking care of family members

Students who work in the household or who take care of family members value both relationships and teamwork more than students who do not engage in these activities. On average across OECD countries, these students are 0.19 unit higher on the index of valuing relationships and 0.16 unit higher on the index of valuing teamwork than other students, after accounting for gender and students' and schools' socio-economic profile. Moreover, a significant difference is observed in almost every country and economy that administered the PISA 2015 assessment on the computer. Students in Latvia, Lithuania and New Zealand were particularly more likely to value both relationships and teamwork if they work in the household or take care of family members (Table V.6.8d).

As mentioned earlier, it is impossible to determine causality, if a causal relationship between the variables exists. Students who value relationships and teamwork might be more likely to help out around the house. However, it might also be that students who, out of necessity, help out around the house develop an appreciation of the interpersonal relationships and teamwork required to make a family work successfully.

Playing video games

Playing video games is also associated with students' attitudes towards teamwork. On average across OECD countries, and after accounting for gender and students' and schools' socio-economic profile, students who play video games outside of school have a higher index of valuing teamwork than students who do not play video games (a 0.04-unit gap), with students in Bulgaria, Hungary, Italy, Portugal and the United Arab Emirates particularly more likely to value teamwork (a gap of over 0.10 unit). Many video games, especially multiplayer games where players in different physical locations connect to a network, require players to work together on the same team towards the same goal. This may develop or require positive dispositions towards teamwork.

However, students who play video games have a lower index of valuing relationships (a 0.05-unit gap), on average, than other students. Students in Greece, Iceland, Lithuania, Montenegro, Norway, Peru, Spain, Switzerland and Turkey were particularly less likely to value relationships (a gap of over 0.10 in the index). Meaningful relationships with others are not necessarily fostered in video games, where players often interact through virtual avatars and not face-to-face with others (Table V.6.8c).

STUDENT TRUANCY

Students may play truant from school or be late for school for a variety of reasons, including a lack of motivation, interest or desire to be in school (Allen-Meares, Washington and Walsh, 2000; Read, 1983), poor enforcement of disciplinary penalties for truancy (Epstein and Sheldon, 2002), poor academic performance (Henry, 2007; Strickland, 1998) or because they do not enjoy spending time with their classmates or in the school environment (Buist, 1980; Croft and Grygier, 1956; Nielsen and Gerber, 1979). Truancy and lateness may be manifestations of the rejection of this stable environment, where students learn subject matter, develop cognitive skills, and nurture friendships and relationships with others.

In particular, Reid (1984) found that Welsh students who often played truant from school displayed neurotic and antisocial behaviour to a larger extent than students who did not skip school. A similar study in Canada showed lower levels of social competence and higher levels of antisocial behaviour among truant students (Corville-Smith et al., 1998). Are similar results observed across many schools and across countries and economies in the PISA 2015 collaborative problem-solving assessment?

Performance in collaborative problem solving

On average across OECD countries, students who had skipped a whole day of school in the two weeks prior to the PISA test score 39 points below those who had not skipped a whole day of school in collaborative problem solving (Table V.6.9a). The difference is particularly stark in Beijing-Shanghai-Jiangsu-Guangdong (China) (hereafter "B-S-J-G [China]"), Japan, Korea, Slovenia and Chinese Taipei, where it exceeds 65 score points. In four of these countries and economies, fewer than one in 30 students had skipped a whole day of school at least once in the two weeks prior to the PISA assessment. In no country/economy do students who had skipped a whole day of school during that period perform better on the collaborative problem-solving assessment than students who had not.

The performance gap remains after accounting for gender, and students' and schools' socio-economic profile. Students who had skipped a whole day of school score 29 points below students who had not after accounting for these factors (Figure V.6.6), on average across OECD countries. Similar differences are observed among students who had skipped at least one class in those two weeks (a gap of 29 score points before accounting for gender, and students' and schools' socio-economic profile; a 24 score-point gap after accounting for those factors) and among students who had arrived late for school (a 24 score-point gap before accounting for those factors; an 18 score-point gap after accounting for them) (Table V.6.9b and Table V.6.9c).

However, *PISA 2015 Results (Volume II): Policies and Practices for Successful Schools* (OECD, 2016) notes that students who had played truant from school also score lower in the science assessment. Given the relationship between collaborative problem-solving performance and performance in the three core PISA domains, is there any relationship between student truancy and lateness, and the distinctive aspects of collaborative problem solving?

The significant relationships described are not observed after accounting for student performance in science, reading and mathematics, gender, and students' and schools' socio-economic profile: there is no longer any difference in collaborative problem-solving performance between students who had and those who had not skipped a whole day of school, skipped some classes or arrived late for school when these two groups of students perform at similar levels in science, reading and mathematics (Tables V.6.9a, V.6.9b and V.6.9c). Only in Austria and Luxembourg do students who had skipped a whole day of school in the two weeks prior to the PISA assessment perform worse in collaborative problem solving (by 6 and 10 score points, respectively), after accounting for their performance in the three core PISA domains, gender, and students' and schools' socio-economic profile. By contrast, in Uruguay, students who had skipped a whole day of school score 9 points higher, and in B-S-J-G (China), they score 14 points higher than those students who had not.

It therefore appears that there is no association between student truancy and lateness, and the distinctive aspects of collaborative problem solving. This may lend support to the hypothesis that students choose to play truant from school because of factors related to their academic performance and how they view school itself, as opposed to their ability to collaborate with classmates.[7] It could also be that the antisocial behaviour and poor social competence observed by Read (1984) and Corville-Smith et al. (1998) are consequences of other factors that also lead to increased truancy.

Figure V.6.6 ■ **Skipping a whole day of school and performance in collaborative problem solving**

Difference in performance between students who had skipped a whole day of school in the two weeks prior to the PISA test and those who had not, after accounting for gender, and students' and schools' socio-economic profile[1]

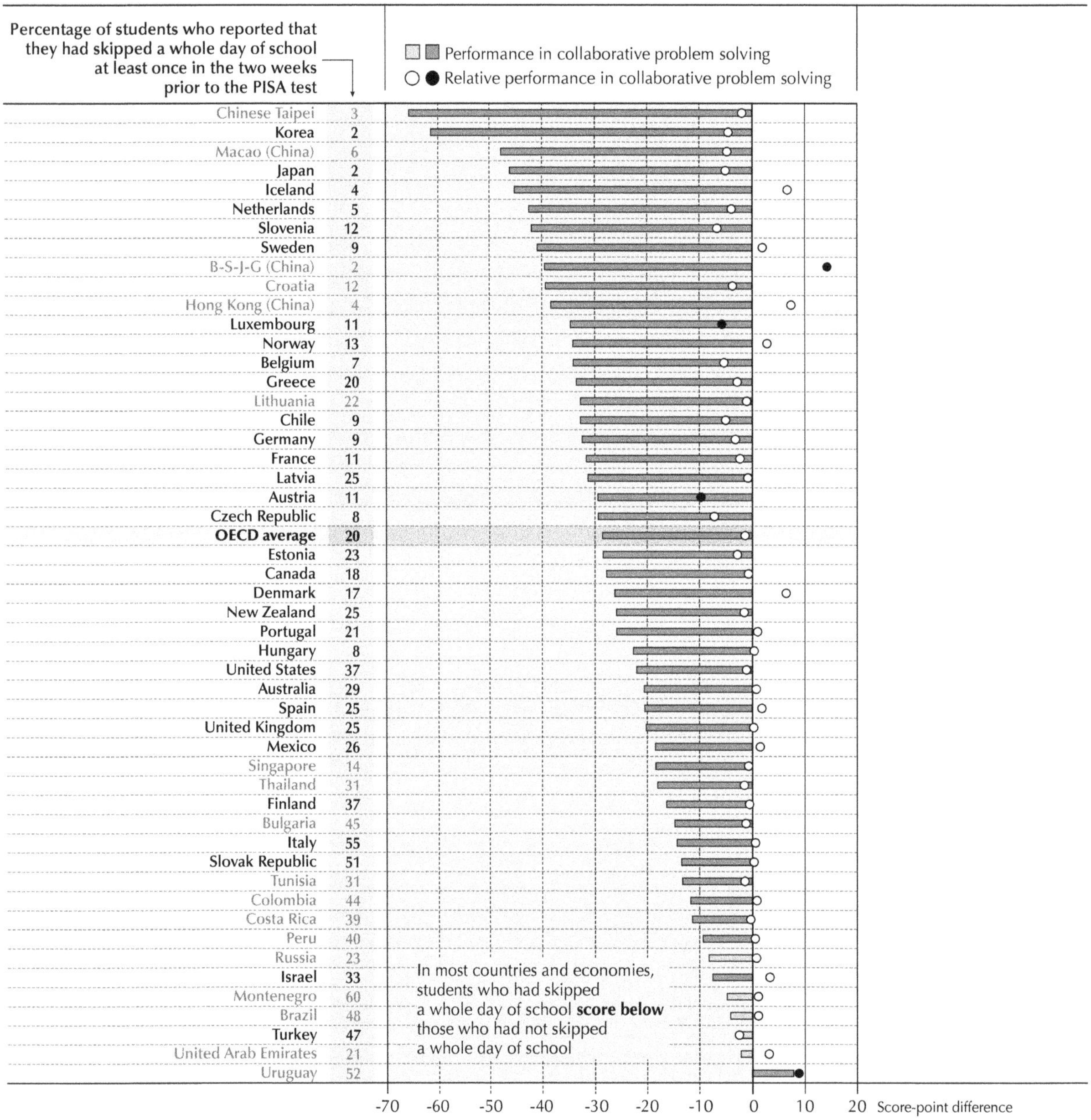

1. The socio-economic profile is measured by the PISA index of economic, social and cultural status (ESCS).

Notes: Statistically significant differences are shown in a darker tone (see Annex A3).

Relative performance refers to the residual performance, attributable to purely "collaborative problem-solving" competencies, after accounting for performance in science, reading and mathematics in a regression performed across students nationally.

Countries and economies are ranked in ascending order of the score-point difference in collaborative problem-solving performance, after accounting for gender, and students' and schools' socio-economic profile.

Source: OECD, PISA 2015 Database, Table V.6.9a.

StatLink http://dx.doi.org/10.1787/888933616427

Attitudes towards collaboration

Students who play truant or arrive late for school are also less likely to have positive attitudes towards collaboration. On average across OECD countries, students who had skipped at least one day of school or had skipped some classes in the two weeks prior to sitting the PISA assessment have significantly lower values on both the index of valuing relationships and the index of valuing teamwork. Students who had arrived late for school have a lower index of valuing relationships, but there is no difference observed in the index of valuing teamwork. After accounting for gender, and students' and schools' socio-economic profile, students who play truant or arrive late for school have lower indices of both valuing relationships and valuing teamwork (Figure V.6.7).

For example, in 53 of 56 countries and economies, students who had skipped at least one full day of school are located significantly lower on the index of valuing relationships than students who had not done so (Table V.6.10a). Differences between these two groups of students are especially large in Croatia, Iceland and Switzerland. After accounting for gender, and students' and schools' socio-economic profile, differences are still significant in 51 out of 56 countries and economies.

Figure V.6.7 ▪ **Skipping a whole day of school and attitudes towards collaboration**

Change in the index when students reported the following having taken place during the two weeks prior to the PISA assessment, OECD average

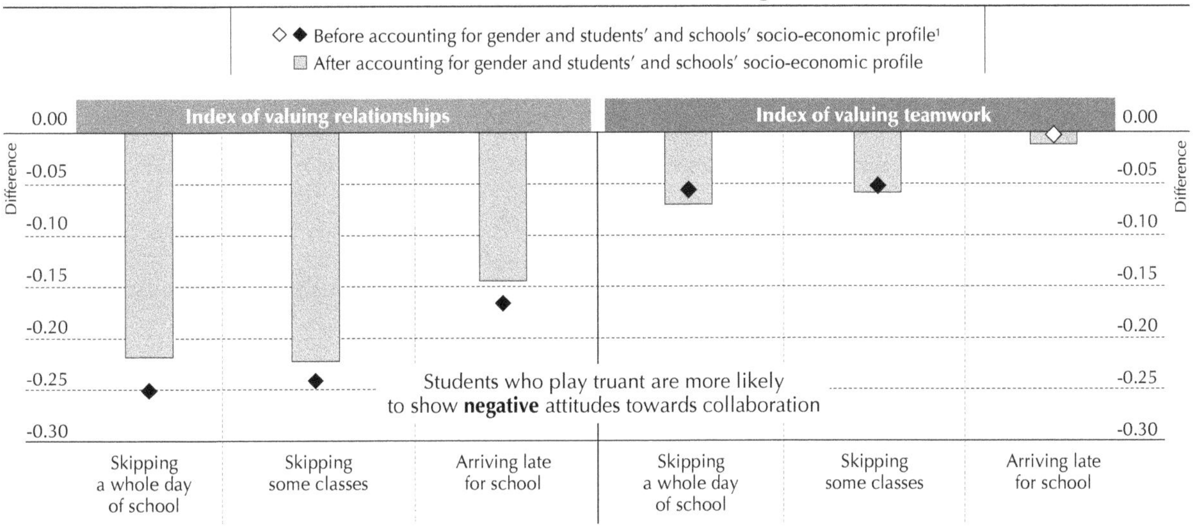

1. The socio-economic profile is measured by the PISA index of economic, social and cultural status (ESCS).

Note: Statistically significant differences are shown in a darker tone. All differences for after accounting for gender and students' and schools' socio-economic profile are statistically significant (see Annex A3).

Source: OECD, PISA 2015 Database, Tables V.6.10a-c.

StatLink http://dx.doi.org/10.1787/888933616446

The largest gaps in attitudes are observed for the statements "I am a good listener", "I enjoy seeing my classmates be successful", and "I take into account what others are interested in". On average across OECD countries, students who had skipped at least one whole day of school in the two weeks prior to the PISA assessment were over six percentage points less likely to agree or strongly agree with each of these items than students who had not done so, after accounting for gender and socio-economic profile. The gaps are particularly striking in Iceland, the Netherlands and Sweden, where they are over 9 percentage points for all three of these statements after accounting for gender and socio-economic profile (Table V.6.10a).

The largest gaps in attitudes towards collaboration are seen when considering the statements that are included in the index of valuing relationships, which are closely related to valuing others' opinions and success. It thus appears that there is a particularly strong relationship between the decision to play truant and the extent to which a student values friendships and other interpersonal relationships. This is not necessarily surprising, given that students who play truant have less time to develop such relationships and might not be as integrated into the school environment as other students.

Is there a relationship between the behaviour of a truant student and the attitudes of his or her non-truant classmates? Tables V.6.11a, V.6.11b, and V.6.11c show that, on average across OECD countries, students who had not played truant or who had not arrived late for school had lower indices of enjoying and valuing co-operation when they attended schools where more of their classmates were truant or late for school, after accounting for gender, and students' and schools' socio-economic profile. This negative association is also observed for almost all of the individual statements.[8]

In particular, the attitudes towards collaboration of students in Belgium, Lithuania and Qatar who had not played truant – they had not skipped a day of school, skipped any classes, nor had arrived late for school in the two weeks prior to the PISA assessment – were more negative when the students attend schools where more of their classmates had been truant after accounting for gender and students' and schools' socio-economic profile.

ATTENDANCE AT PRE-PRIMARY SCHOOL

Performance in collaborative problem solving

Parents often enrol their children in pre-primary school so that they can go back to work, so that their children can develop cognitive skills, and most relevant to collaboration, so that their children can begin the socialisation process before primary school. For example, parents expect their children to learn how to behave with others outside of the family, communicate, share, express themselves and observe social rules governing interpersonal interaction (Currie and Almond, 2011; Sollars, 2017; Williams, Sheridan and Sandberg, 2014). Indeed, many pre-primary schools focus on developing both empathy (Jalongo, 2013) and social skills (Ostrosky and Meadan, 2010). Does pre-primary school prepare children to collaborate and co-operate? Is the difference between those who had attended pre-primary school and those who had not still apparent ten years later, when students are 15 years old and at the age when they sit the PISA assessment?

Some 95% of 15-year-old students, on average across OECD countries, had attended some form of pre-primary school.[9] Results from the PISA 2015 collaborative problem-solving assessment and student questionnaire show that students who had attended pre-primary school score 29 points higher than students who had not attended pre-primary school. A significant difference is observed in 21 of the 47 countries for which data are available (Table V.6.12a). In four countries where at least 5% of 15-year-olds had not attended pre-primary school[10] – B-S-J-G (China), Norway, Russia and Slovenia – students who had attended pre-primary school score significantly higher in collaborative problem solving than those students who had not (Figure V.6.8). In no country or economy is the gap significant in favour of students who had not attended pre-primary school.

Figure V.6.8 ▪ **Pre-primary school and performance in collaborative problem solving**

Difference in collaborative problem-solving performance between students who had attended pre-primary school and those who had not

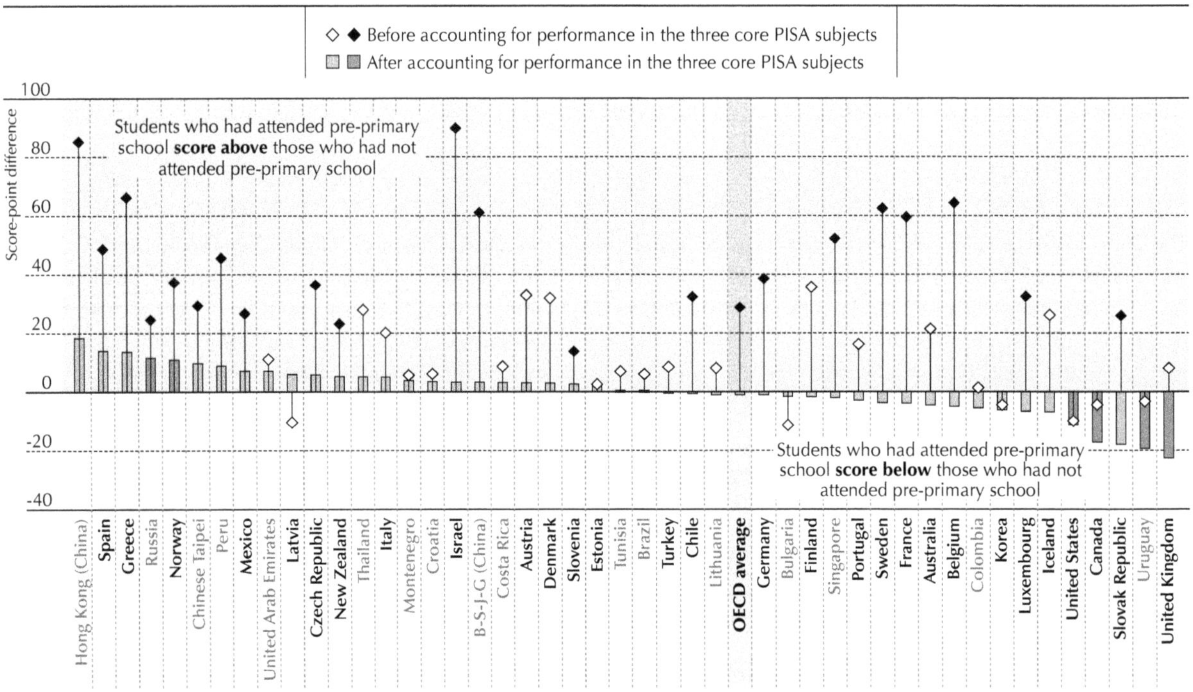

Note: Statistically significant score-point differences are shown in a darker tone (see Annex A3).

Countries and economies are ranked in descending order of the score-point difference in collaborative problem-solving performance, after accounting for the three core PISA subjects.

Source: OECD, PISA 2015 Database, Table V.6.12a.

StatLink http://dx.doi.org/10.1787/888933616465

However, this difference vanishes after accounting for student performance in science, reading and mathematics (Figure V.6.8), whether or not gender, and students' and schools' socio-economic profile are also accounted for. On average across OECD countries, there is no significant relationship between attendance at pre-primary school and the distinctive aspects of collaborative problem solving, indicating that the performance gap described above reflects the relationship between collaborative problem-solving performance and performance in science, reading and mathematics. Attendance at pre-primary school has no discernible effect on the unique aspects of collaborative problem solving (or what one would attribute to collaboration skills as opposed to general academic proficiency) ten years later.

In fact, after accounting for performance in the three core PISA subjects, a significant advantage in collaborative problem-solving performance among students who had attended pre-primary school is observed only in Norway (11 score points) and Russia (12 score points), while a significant disadvantage among students who had attended pre-primary school is found, among countries where at least 5% of 15-year-olds had not attended pre-primary school, in the United States (11 score points) (Figure V.6.8).

Different students might also gain different skills and advantages from attending pre-primary school. While advantaged families might be able to provide their children with similar learning and socialisation opportunities even if they do not attend pre-primary school, disadvantaged families might have a harder time preparing their children in the first few years of life without the help, support and structure of some form of a pre-primary school arrangement. In other words, the difference in outcomes associated with pre-primary school might differ between advantaged and disadvantaged families (Crampton and Hall, 2017; Havnes and Mogstad, 2011; Leseman, 2002; OECD, 2011; Sylva et al., 2010).[11]

On average across OECD countries, some 93% of disadvantaged[12] students and 97% of advantaged[13] students had attended some form of pre-primary education. However, on average across OECD countries, students from advantaged families appear to gain more from attendance at pre-primary school (a gap of 14 score points) than students from disadvantaged families (a gap of 9 score points) when it comes to performance in collaborative problem solving (Table V.6.12b). This gap becomes insignificant for both types of families after accounting for performance in science, reading and mathematics. Once again, this indicates that attendance at pre-primary school has no relationship with the distinctly collaborative aspects of problem solving when assessed ten years later – among both advantaged and disadvantaged students.

Attitudes towards collaboration

On average across OECD countries and after accounting for gender, and students' and schools' socio-economic profile, students who had attended pre-primary school have significantly higher values on the indices of valuing relationships and teamwork and were more likely to agree or strongly agree with all of the items that comprise these two indices (Table V.6.13). However, on average across OECD countries, less than 5% of students reported that they had not attended pre-primary school (Table V.6.12a). As a result, in most countries and economies, the standard errors of effects related to pre-primary school are large and these effects are not significant.

For example, after accounting for gender, and students' and schools' socio-economic profile, only in Chile and Finland do students who had attended pre-primary school have a higher mean index of valuing relationships, while in Australia, Lithuania, Qatar, Slovenia and Turkey, these students have a lower mean index of valuing relationships. Likewise, in only 17 of the 55 countries that took part in the student questionnaire and for which data are available do students who had attended pre-primary school have a higher mean index of valuing teamwork (Table V.6.13).

Students who had attended pre-primary school were between two and five percentage points more likely than those who had not attended to agree or strongly agree with each of the statements that are related to attitudes towards collaboration, after accounting for gender, and students' and schools' socio-economic profile. For instance, they were 4.7 percentage points more likely to agree that they "prefer working as part of a team to working alone", a gap that widens to over 15 percentage points in the Czech Republic and France. They were also 4.0 percentage points more likely to agree that they "take into account what others are interested in", a gap that grows to over 12 percentage points in the Czech Republic, Germany and Luxembourg. However, in 19 of the 52 countries that took part in the computer-based assessment and for which data are available, there is no significant difference between students who had and those who had not attended pre-primary school in their responses to all of the individual items regarding attitudes towards collaboration.

Thus, attendance at pre-primary school is positively correlated with positive attitudes towards collaboration, and while attendance at pre-primary school is also positively correlated with performance in collaborative problem solving, this relationship disappears once performance in science, reading and mathematics is accounted for. These results provide some support to the idea that pre-primary schools develop socialisation skills (through the development of cognitive skills) and positive attitudes towards co-operating with others that can have a lasting impact.

STUDENT INTERACTION IN SCIENCE CLASS

Performance in collaborative problem solving

The PISA 2015 student questionnaire asked students about how often certain activities occur during science class. Four of these activities were identified as being communication-intensive: explaining one's ideas in science class; spending time in the laboratory doing practical experiments; arguing about science questions; and taking part in class debates about investigations.

A significant negative relationship is observed between performance in the PISA 2015 collaborative problem-solving assessment and three of these activities in science class. Students who spend time in the laboratory doing practical experiments or who debate about investigations in most or all lessons score 31 points lower in collaborative problem solving than students who did so in some lessons, hardly ever or never. Similarly, they scored 23 points lower if they argue about science questions in most or all lessons (Tables V.6.14b-d). These relationships are still significant after accounting for performance in science, reading and mathematics, gender, and students' and schools' socio-economic status, although the gap shrinks to between three and four score points.

In Brazil, B-S-J-G (China), Colombia, Israel, Japan, Luxembourg, Mexico, Montenegro, Singapore, Tunisia and Uruguay, student performance in collaborative problem is lower whenever students participated in any one of these three activities in most or all science lessons, even after accounting for performance in the three core PISA subjects, gender, and students' and schools' socio-economic status (Tables V.6.14b-d).

As in all the correlations examined in this chapter, no causal relationship is claimed. Students' performance in collaborative problem solving might be influenced by the pedagogical strategies used by their teachers; but teachers might also choose certain teaching methods over others based on their students' behaviour and capabilities.

No significant relationship is observed between performance in collaborative problem solving and the fourth communication-intensive activity in science class – explaining one's ideas – after accounting for performance in the three core PISA subjects, gender, and socio-economic status (Table V.6.14a).

Attitudes towards collaboration

Significant relationships between these activities and attitudes towards collaboration are observed both on average across OECD countries and in many countries and economies. On average across OECD countries, the indices of valuing relationships and teamwork are higher among students who reported that they participate in these activities in most or all lessons than among those who reported that they participate in these activities in only some lessons or never/hardly ever (Tables V.6.15a-d).

Students who are given opportunities to explain their ideas in most or all lessons were two to six percentage points more likely to agree or strongly agree with each of the statements regarding attitudes towards collaboration. This difference is observed in most countries and economies. For example, after accounting for gender, and students' and schools' socio-economic profile, in 46 of the 56 countries and economies that administered the student questionnaire on computer, students who reported that they explain their ideas in most or all science lessons were more likely to agree that they are "a good listener"; in 37 out of 56 countries and economies, these students also agreed that they "enjoy considering different perspectives". Only in Brazil were students who reported that they explain their ideas in most or all lessons less likely to agree or strongly agree that they "enjoy considering different perspectives".

The index of student interaction in science class was created by combining student responses to how often the four communication-intensive activities described above take place. It is equal to the number of statements describing activities in which students reported that they participate during most or all lessons. Students are more likely to agree or strongly agree with each of the statements related to collaboration as they interact more in science class. The largest effects are observed for the statement "I find that teamwork raises my own efficiency". On average across OECD countries, students are 2.8 percentage points more likely to agree or strongly agree with this statement than students who do not participate in these activities for every additional communication-intensive activity in which they participate in science class, after accounting for gender, and students' and schools' socio-economic profile (Figure V.6.9).

Figure V.6.9 ▪ **Student interaction in science class and attitudes towards collaboration**

Change in the percentage of students who agree/strongly agree with the following statements per one-unit increase in the index of student interaction in science class[1], OECD average

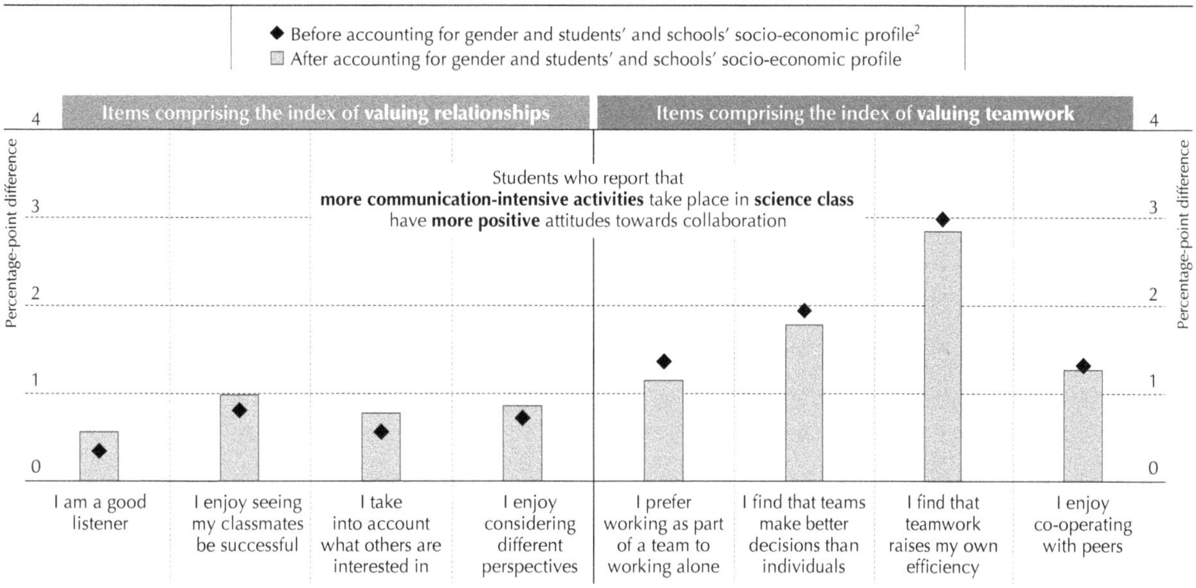

1. The index of student interaction in science class is the sum of students' responses to questions about whether their science teachers use the following teaching practices in all lessons or in most lessons: students are given opportunities to explain their ideas; students spend time in the laboratory carrying out practical experiments; students are required to argue about science questions; there is a class debate about investigations. The index ranges from 0 to 4, with all responses weighted equally.

2. The socio-economic profile is measured by the PISA index of economic, social and cultural status (ESCS).

Note: All differences are statistically significant (see Annex A3).

Source: OECD, PISA 2015 Database, Table V.6.15e.

StatLink http://dx.doi.org/10.1787/888933616484

As with performance in collaborative problem solving, attitudes towards collaboration might be influenced by pedagogical methods, but teachers might also choose certain pedagogical methods based on their students' attitudes towards collaboration. While no causal relationship can be claimed from these results, the results indicate that there is a positive and significant relationship between pedagogical methods emphasising student interaction and student attitudes towards collaboration.

The questions used in the questionnaire were specific only to science class. The interpretation of the observed relationship depends on whether the pedagogical methods used in science class are representative of the ethos prevalent throughout the school. However, Table V.6.16 shows that, on average across OECD countries, 95% of the variation in the index of student interaction in science class is observed across students in the same school, while only 5% is seen between schools. Hence, students in the same school perceive a great variety of teaching methods in their science classes, which likely also extends to other subjects. As a result, there is limited evidence to support the notion that there is a school-wide ethos of such communication-intensive pedagogy.

Notes

1. Examples of moderate physical activity are walking, climbing stairs and riding a bike to school. Students were asked whether they engage in moderate physical activity for at least 60 minutes a day.

2. Examples of vigorous physical activity are running, cycling, aerobics, soccer and skating. Students were asked whether they engage in vigorous physical activity that made them sweat and breathe hard for at least 20 minutes a day.

3. The number of days that students attended physical education class per week was top-coded down to at most five days per week.

4. The average difference across both genders is greater than the difference for either gender because of weighting: different proportions of boys and girls participated in zero and seven days of vigorous physical activity in the week prior to the PISA assessment.

5. The plateau in the index of valuing relationships after two days of vigorous physical activity per week seems to be due to boys. There is a progressive but not necessarily always significant increase in girls' attitudes towards valuing relationships with the number of days that they engage in vigorous physical activity, up to all seven days per week.

6. This distinguishes these activities from two other student activities that may have a social component to them: exercising or practicing sports outside of school, and working for pay. There is a greater barrier to taking part in these activities, as they most often occur outside the home, and students are more likely to take part in these activities on some but not all days of the week. As a result, a student's participation in these activities on the most recent school day is less likely to be representative of the average frequency of the student's participation in these activities.

7. It is not clear whether students play truant individually or in a group; truancy in a group may actually be a collaborative activity.

8. The exceptions are between students who did not skip a whole day of school and the statement "I find that teamwork raises my own efficiency"; students who did not skip any classes and the statement "I am a good listener"; and students who were never late and the statement "I am a good listener". Among students who did not display these truant behaviours, there was no significant relationship between the percentage of these students who agreed or strongly agreed to these statements and the proportion of students in their schools who did display these truant behaviours.

9. In this volume, students were deemed to have attended pre-primary school if they specified the age at which they started pre-primary school (ISCED 0). Results may differ from those in *PISA 2015 Results (Volume II): Policies and Practices for Successful Schools* (OECD, 2016), where students were deemed to have attended pre-primary school if they specified both the age at which they started pre-primary school (ISCED 0) and primary school (ISCED 1).

10. The uncertainty in the performance gap between students who did and did not attend a form of pre-primary education is large in many countries due to the relative lack of students who did not attend pre-primary school. Significant differences in these countries are therefore more difficult to ascertain. As a result, we only discuss countries where at least 5% of students (or at least one in 20 students) have not attended pre-primary school.

11. At the same time, it is noted that in some countries, notably those that do not provide this service for free, disadvantaged families may have more difficulty in affording pre-primary education.

12. Students from disadvantaged families are defined as those in the bottom quarter of the PISA index of economic, social and cultural status in their country/economy.

13. Students from advantaged families are defined as those in the top quarter of the PISA index of economic, social and cultural status in their country/economy.

References

Allen-Meares, P., R.O. Washington and **B.L. Walsh** (2000), *Social Work Services in Schools* (3rd edition), Allyn & Bacon, Boston.

Buist, M. (1980), "Truants talking", *Scottish Educational Review*, Vol. 12/1, pp. 40-51.

Centers for Disease Control and Prevention (2010), *The Association Between School Based Physical Activity, Including Physical Education, and Academic Performance*, U.S. Department of Health and Human Services, Atlanta, GA.

Corville-Smith, J. et al. (1998), "Distinguishing absentee students form regular attenders: The combined influence of personal, family, and school factors", *Journal of Youth and Adolescence*, Vol. 27/5, pp. 629-640, https://doi.org/10.1023/A:1022887124634.

Crampton, A. and **J. Hall** (2017), "Unpacking socio-economic risks for reading and academic self-concept in primary school: Differential effects and the role of the preschool home learning environment", *British Journal of Educational Psychology*, Vol. 87/3, pp. 365-382, http://dx.doi.org/10.1111/bjep.12154.

Croft, I. and **T. Grygier** (1956), "Social relationships of truants and juvenile delinquents", *Human Relations*, Vol. 9/4, pp. 439-466, https://doi.org/10.1177/001872675600900404.

Currie, J. and **D. Almond** (2011), "Chapter 15 – Human capital development before age five", in Card, D. and O. Ashenfelter (eds.), *Handbook of Labor Economics* (Volume 4, Part B), pp. 1315-1486, Elsevier, San Diego and Amsterdam, https://doi.org/10.1016/S0169-7218(11)02413-0.

Epstein, J.L. and **S.B. Sheldon** (2002), "Present and accounted for: Improving student attendance through family and community involvement", *The Journal of Educational Research*, Vol. 95/5, pp. 308-318, http://dx.doi.org/10.1080/00220670209596604.

Findlay, L.C. and **R.J. Coplan** (2008), "Come out and play: Shyness in childhood and the benefits of organised sports participation", *Canadian Journal of Behavioural Science*, Vol. 40/3, pp. 153-161, http://dx.doi.org/10.1037/0008-400X.40.3.153.

Havnes, T. and **M. Mogstad** (2011), "No child left behind: Subsidized child care and children's long-run outcomes", *American Economic Journal: Economic Policy*, Vol. 3/2, pp. 97-129, http://dx.doi.org/10.1257/pol.3.2.97.

Henry, K.L. (2007), "Who's skipping school: Characteristics of truants in 8th and 10th grade", *Journal of School Health*, Vol. 77/1, pp. 29-35, http://dx.doi.org/10.1111/j.1746-1561.2007.00159.x.

Jalongo, M.R. (2014), "Humane education and the development of empathy in early childhood: Definition, rationale, and outcomes", in Jalongo, M.R. (ed.), *Teaching Compassion: Humane Education in Early Childhood*, pp. 3-21, Springer, Dordrecht, the Netherlands.

Leseman, P.P.M. (2002), "Early childhood education and care for children from low-income or minority backgrounds", *discussion paper for OECD Oslo Workshop, June 6-7 2002*, OECD, www.oecd.org/education/school/1960663.pdf.

Mahoney, J.L. (2000), "School extracurricular activity participation as a moderator in the development of antisocial patterns", *Child Development*, Vol. 71/2, pp. 502-516, http://dx.doi.org/10.1111/1467-8624.00160.

Mahoney, J.L. and **H. Stattin** (2000), "Leisure activities and adolescent antisocial behaviour: The role of structure and social context", *Journal of Adolescence*, Vol. 23/2, pp. 113-127, https://doi.org/10.1006/jado.2000.0302.

Nielsen, A. and **D. Gerber** (1979), "Psychosocial aspects of truancy in early adolescence", *Adolescence*, Vol. 14/54, pp. 313-326.

OECD (2016), *PISA 2015 Results (Volume II): Policies and Practices for Successful Schools*, OECD Publishing, Paris, http://dx.doi.org/10.1787/9789264267510-en.

OECD (2011), "Investing in high-quality early childhood education and care (ECEC)" (brochure), Organisation for Economic Co-operation and Development, Paris, www.oecd.org/education/school/48980282.pdf.

Ostrosky, M.M. and **H. Meadan** (2010), "Helping children play and learn together", *Young Children*, Vol. 65/1, pp. 104-110.

Pascarella, E. and **J. Smart** (1991), "Impact of intercollegiate athletic participation for African American and Caucasian men: Some further evidence", *Journal of College Student Development*, Vol. 32/2, pp. 123-130.

Read, K. (1984), "The behaviour of persistent school absentees", *British Journal of Educational Psychology*, Vol. 54/3, pp. 320-330, http://dx.doi.org/10.1111/j.2044-8279.1984.tb02595.x.

Read, K. (1983), "Institutional factors and persistent school absenteeism", *Educational Management Administration & Leadership*, Vol. 11/1, pp. 17-27, https://doi.org/10.1177/174114328301100103.

Snyder, A.R. et al. (2010), "Health-related quality of life differs between adolescent athletes and adolescent nonathletes", *Journal of Sport Rehabilitation*, Vol. 19/3, pp. 237-248, https://doi.org/10.1123/jsr.19.3.237.

Sollars, V. (2017), "Parents' expectations about early years services", *Early Years: An International Research Journal*, Vol. 37/3, pp. 285-299, http://dx.doi.org/10.1080/09575146.2016.1154507.

Strickland, V.P. (1998), *Attendance and Grade Point Average: A Study (Report No. SP038147)*, National Center for Research on Teacher Learning, East Lansing, MI.

Sylva, K. et al. (eds.) (2010), *Early Childhood Matters: Evidence from the Effective Pre-School and Primary Education Project*. Routledge, Abingdon, UK.

Williams, P., **S. Sheridan** and **A. Sandberg** (2014), "Preschool – an arena for children's learning of social and cognitive knowledge", *Early Years: An International Research Journal*, Vol. 34/3, pp. 226-240, http://dx.doi.org/10.1080/09575146.2013.872605.

7

Collaborative schools, collaborative students

This chapter examines the impact of positive relationships among and between students, teachers, principals, parents and the wider community on students' proficiency in collaborative problem solving and attitudes towards collaboration. It tries to answer the question: if all school stakeholders get along well and work together to achieve common goals, does that help students develop their own collaborative problem-solving skills?

A note regarding Israel

The statistical data for Israel are supplied by and under the responsibility of the relevant Israeli authorities. The use of such data by the OECD is without prejudice to the status of the Golan Heights, East Jerusalem and Israeli settlements in the West Bank under the terms of international law.

Man is by nature a social animal – Aristotle, Politics

Collaboration and co-operation are the best, if not the only, ways in which complex organisations can address complex challenges (Gajda and Koliba, 2007) and become learning organisations (Kools and Stoll, 2016). The benefits of collaborative and co-operative behaviours have been broadly documented in various social contexts, including neighbourhoods, hospitals, companies (Coleman, 1988; Gittell et al., 2000; Sampson and Groves, 1989), and also in education. When students, teachers, parents and the school principal know and trust each other, work together, and share information, ideas and goals, students – particularly disadvantaged students – benefit (Crosnoe, Johnson and Elder, 2004; Hughes and Kwok, 2007; Jennings and Greenberg, 2009). The gains in problem-solving performance specifically could be even larger. For instance, several studies found that students who collaborate towards a common goal develop their problem-solving skills, especially when they are paired with a child of higher ability (Moshman and Geil, 1998; Samaha and De Lisi, 2000).

This chapter examines the density and quality of the relationships that students, teachers, principals, parents and the wider community build in and around secondary schools, and how they shape students' performance in collaborative problem solving and students' attitudes towards collaboration. The premise is that a socially connected school, in which all stakeholders know and respect each other and work collaboratively to achieve common goals, can help students develop their collaborative problem-solving skills and improve their attitudes towards collaboration.

What the data tell us

- Of all the relationships analysed, the strongest predictors of performance in collaborative problem solving are those involving students directly, including relationships they establish with parents, teachers and other students.
- On average across OECD countries, students who reported not being threatened by other students score 18 points higher in collaborative problem solving than students who reported being threatened at least a few times per year. Students also score 11 points higher for every 10 percentage-point increase in the number of schoolmates who reported that they are not threatened by other students.
- Across the OECD countries that distributed the parent questionnaire, parents reported knowing an average of five of their child's school friends, and four of the parents of their child's friends. The students whose parents reported knowing more of their school friends are more likely to be enrolled in socio-economically advantaged schools and score higher in collaborative problem solving.
- Students score higher in collaborative problem solving when they or their schoolmates reported that teachers treat students fairly, even after accounting for their performance in science, reading and mathematics.

Figure V.7.1 ▪ **Number and quality of relationships at school, as measured in PISA 2015**

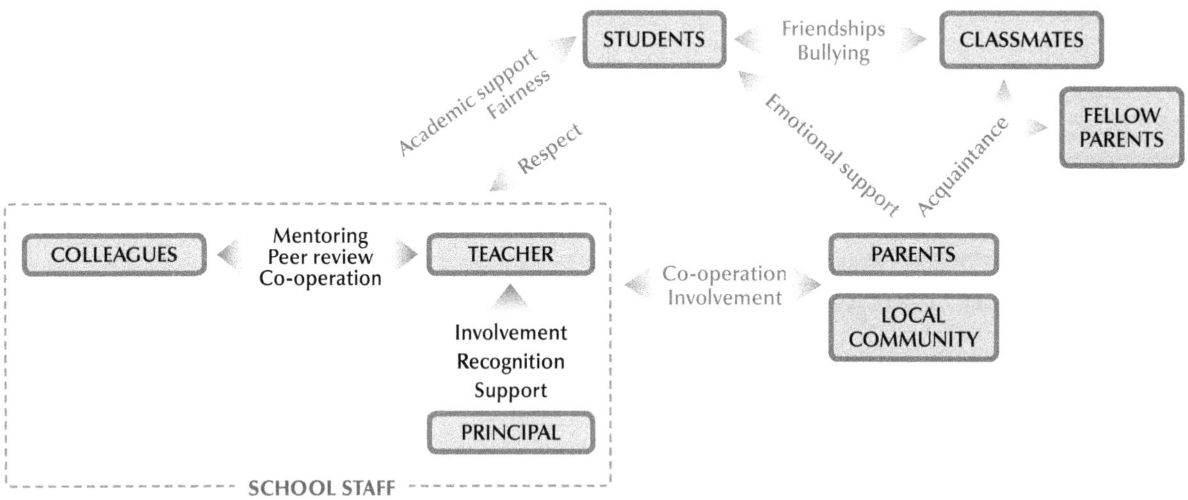

The relationships examined in this chapter are summarised in Figure V.7.1. They are classified according to the actors involved (e.g. student-student, parent-teacher, school-community) and the source of information (students, school principal, teachers and parents). Most questions measure the nature/quality of the interactions (e.g. "the principal treats teaching staff as professionals") but a few quantify the number of relationships (e.g. "How many friends of your child at school do you know by name?"). The few questions that are phrased negatively (e.g. "I was threatened by other students") have been recoded so that higher values are always interpreted as better or more relationships throughout the chapter.

STUDENT-STUDENT RELATIONSHIPS

Constructive peer relationships are essential for a healthy and productive school (Johnson, 1981). Students who feel safe and are liked by their peers can more easily concentrate on learning. These students perform better academically and are more motivated in school (Cohen et al., 2009; Sánchez, Colón and Esparza, 2005). Strong and rewarding peer relationships are particularly important for teenagers, since they spend relatively more time with friends and less time with parents than younger students do (McElhaney, Antonishak and Allen, 2008). The relationships that students establish with their schoolmates should be particularly relevant for the type of interpersonal skills evaluated in the collaborative problem-solving assessment. Lonely and bullied students may therefore be at a particular disadvantage since they have fewer opportunities to develop these collaborative skills.[1] Questions about friendships, loneliness and bullying, covering both the quantity and quality of student-student interactions, are examined in this section.

PISA asked students about their sense of belonging at school and about their experiences with bullying, and asked principals about the phenomena that hinder student learning (see also OECD, 2017). Some of these questions were retained to measure the number – "I make friends easily at school"; "I feel lonely at school" – and quality – "Other students seem to like me"; "Other students made fun of me"; "I was threatened by other students"; "I got hit or pushed around by other students"; "Student learning is hindered by students intimidating or bullying other students" – of student-student interactions.

Students feel mostly positive about their relationships with their schoolmates. On average across OECD countries, about four in five students agreed that they seemed to be liked by other students and make friends easily at school; a slightly larger proportion disagreed that they feel lonely at school (Figure V.7.2). An even greater majority reported that they are never or almost never threatened, or hit or pushed by other students. However, a smaller majority – only 70% – of students reported that other students never or almost never make fun of them.

For many students, the picture is less rosy than what is described above. For example, in Beijing-Shanghai-Jiangsu-Guangdong (China) (hereafter "B-S-J-G [China]"), Lithuania and Thailand, only six in ten students agreed that other students seem to like them and in Hong Kong (China), Latvia, Macao (China), New Zealand and Singapore, more than four out of ten students reported that other students make fun of them at least a few times per year (Figure V.7.2).

Generally, students who reported more positive student-student interactions score higher in collaborative problem solving (Table V.7.3). On average across OECD countries, students who reported that they are never or almost never threatened score 18 points higher in collaborative problem solving, after accounting for students' and schools' socio-economic profile (Figure V.7.3). Likewise, students score 14 points higher in collaborative problem solving when they reported that they are never or almost never hit or pushed by other students. These relationships are also seen in almost every school system.

At the school level, more positive student-student interactions among the student population are always associated with better student performance, even when considering those student-student interactions that are negatively related to collaborative problem-solving performance at the student level. For instance, on average across OECD countries, student performance in collaborative problem solving improves by 11 score points for every 10 percentage-point increase in the number of schoolmates who reported that they are never or almost never threatened, or never or almost never hit or pushed by other students (Figure V.7.3 and Table V.7.3).

After accounting for student performance in science, reading and mathematics – that is, among students who perform similarly in these core PISA subjects – students score higher in collaborative problem solving when they, or more of their schoolmates, reported that they are never or almost never threatened, or never or almost never hit or pushed by other students (Table V.7.4).[2] In the Czech Republic and Spain, for instance, students who reported that they are not threatened by other students score more than 14 points higher in collaborative problem solving than would be expected given their performance in other subjects. Students also score higher when more of their schoolmates agreed that other students seem to like them, disagreed that they felt lonely at school, or reported that other students never, or almost never, make fun of them.

Figure V.7.2 ▪ Student-student relationships

Less than half of students
From 50% to 75% of students
More than 75% of students

	Percentage of students who reported the following:					
	"Agree" or "strongly agree" that I make friends easily at school	"Agree" or "strongly agree" that other students seem to like me	"Disagree" or "strongly disagree" that I feel lonely at school	Other students "never or almost never" make fun of me	I am "never or almost never" threatened by other students	I "never or almost never" get hit or pushed around by other students
Netherlands	85	92	92	81	95	94
Korea	79	82	92	81	97	98
Chinese Taipei	85	72	88	83	96	98
France	86	90	91	69	92	91
Spain	83	86	91	74	92	90
Portugal	78	88	89	80	88	93
Montenegro	83	80	86	83	87	93
Greece	80	87	88	72	93	90
Ireland	81	91	88	71	89	90
Belgium	82	88	90	66	91	90
Hungary	81	83	85	75	92	91
Croatia	84	82	88	76	89	89
Switzerland	81	87	90	63	92	91
Iceland	76	83	84	78	90	92
Germany	73	85	87	67	94	94
Norway	80	83	86	75	89	87
Denmark	79	85	87	67	93	87
Luxembourg	76	81	85	73	91	91
Peru	76	77	83	78	93	89
Finland	80	82	88	69	89	86
Slovenia	77	78	85	73	92	87
United States	79	89	82	69	85	89
OECD average	**78**	**82**	**85**	**70**	**89**	**88**
Austria	78	84	85	65	92	89
Brazil	74	81	80	75	89	92
Uruguay	73	86	79	72	90	90
Chile	73	76	83	71	90	90
Slovak Republic	77	77	81	72	88	88
United Kingdom	79	88	86	62	82	85
Czech Republic	75	81	82	71	90	81
Canada	78	87	82	63	85	85
Sweden	75	78	81	71	88	83
Estonia	76	76	85	62	90	86
Australia	79	88	84	61	80	84
Poland	73	73	80	68	90	90
Japan	69	74	88	67	94	82
Singapore	80	81	82	57	87	85
Costa Rica	72	72	77	70	86	91
New Zealand	79	88	83	58	78	82
Russia	73	64	79	72	87	93
United Arab Emirates	80	79	83	63	81	81
B-S-J-G (China)	78	60	79	69	90	89
Mexico	73	72	79	66	89	85
Qatar	78	83	80	64	80	79
Tunisia	83	80	85	66	73	76
Colombia	70	69	75	68	91	87
Hong Kong (China)	81	78	81	53	85	80
Thailand	83	62	82	62	81	85
Bulgaria	75	72	75	69	84	77
Macao (China)	76	66	80	55	83	88
Turkey	62	64	65	80	87	90
Dominican Republic	66	66	69	71	82	91
Lithuania	64	63	69	74	86	87
Latvia	76	68	83	59	81	74

Note: Only countries and economies with available data for all six statements are shown.
Countries and economies are ranked in descending order of the percentage of students (average of six statements).
Source: OECD, PISA 2015 Database, Table V.7.1.
StatLink http://dx.doi.org/10.1787/888933616503

Across OECD countries, students value relationships and teamwork more whenever they reported more positive student-student interactions; they value relationships, but not necessarily teamwork, more when their schoolmates also reported more positive student-student-interactions. This positive relationship is also observed in many other countries and economies. For instance, in Japan, students who agreed or strongly agreed that other students seem to like them have an index of valuing relationships 0.43 unit higher than students who disagreed or strongly disagreed with this statement. Students in Japan who reported that they make friends easily at school have an index of valuing teamwork 0.55 unit higher than those who reported otherwise (Table V.7.5).

Figure V.7.3 ■ **Students being threatened by other students and performance in collaborative problem solving**

Change in score after accounting for students' and schools' socio-economic profile

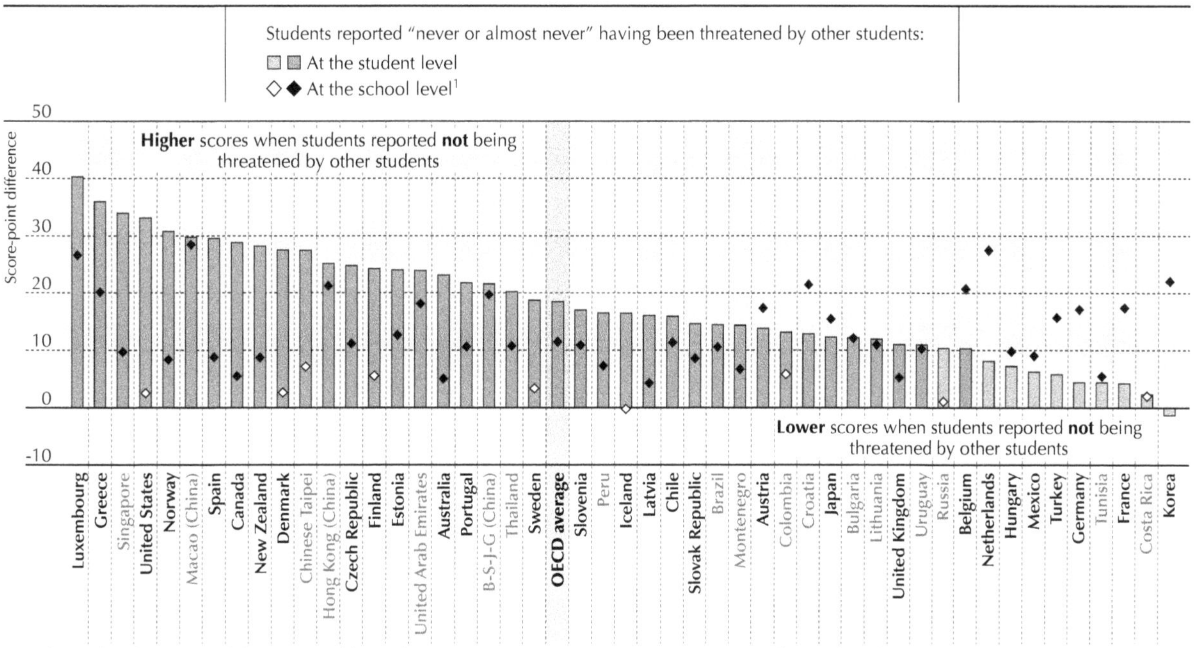

1. Refers to the change in collaborative problem-solving score per 10 percentage-point increase in the number of schoolmates who reported the above.

Notes: Statistically significant differences are shown in a darker tone (see Annex A3).

The socio-economic profile is measured by the PISA index of economic, social and cultural status (ESCS).

Countries and economies are ranked in descending order of the change in the collaborative problem-solving score when students reported that they have "never or almost never" been threatened by other students.

Source: OECD, PISA 2015 Database, Table V.7.3.

StatLink http://dx.doi.org/10.1787/888933616522

TEACHER-TEACHER RELATIONSHIPS

Teachers form a professional learning community when they engage in reflective dialogue, provide one another with feedback on teaching practices and activities, and work together to improve the school learning environment and student outcomes (Gajda and Koliba, 2007; Lomos, Hofman and Bosker, 2011). Traditionally, teachers have worked in isolation (Goddard, Goddard and Tschannen-Moran, 2007); and yet several studies suggest that teacher effectiveness and student achievement can improve when teachers co-operate with a focus on school improvement (Goddard, Goddard and Tschannen-Moran, 2007; Lomos, Hofman and Bosker, 2011; Pil and Leana, 2009; Wahlstrom and Louis, 2008), and when they teach collaboratively (Ronfeldt et al., 2015). It is worth considering whether students' collaborative skills might benefit from teachers co-operating with each other more frequently.

PISA 2015 asked teachers in the 19 school systems that distributed the teacher questionnaire how often ("never", "once a year or less", "2-4 times a year", "5-10 times a year", "1-3 times a month" or "once a week or more") they engage in the following activities: "teach jointly as a team in the same class"; "observe other teachers' classes and provide feedback"; "exchange teaching materials with colleagues"; "engage in discussions about the learning development of specific students"; "work with other teachers in [my] school to ensure common standards in evaluations for assessing

student progress"; and "take part in collaborative professional learning". PISA also asked school principals if teacher mentoring exists in the school, if teacher peer review is used to monitor the practices of teachers, and if teachers in the school co-operate by exchanging ideas or material when teaching specific units or series of lessons.

According to school leaders, teacher mentoring and teacher peer review exist as a quality-assurance arrangement in most PISA-participating schools (Table V.7.6). Only in four countries, namely Germany, Iceland, Italy and Spain, does more than one in two students attend a school whose principal reported that teacher mentoring does not exist in the school. In only eight countries (Bulgaria, Finland, Germany, Greece, Iceland, Ireland, Luxembourg and Spain) does more than one in two students attend a school where teacher peer review is not used to monitor the practices of teachers. The exchange of ideas or material among teachers is even more common. On average across OECD countries, 96% of students are enrolled in schools where the principal reported that such exchange takes place.

Figure V.7.4 ▪ **Teacher-teacher relationships**

Less than half of students
From 50% to 75% of students
More than 75% of students

	Percentage of students whose school teachers reported the following:					
	At least once a year, teach jointly as a team in the same class	At least once a year, observe other teachers' classes and provide feedback	At least five times a year, exchange teaching materials with colleagues	At least five times a year, engage in discussions about the learning development of specific students	At least five times a year, work with other teachers in my school to ensure common standards in evaluations for assessing student progress	At least five times a year, take part in collaborative professional learning
Australia	70	81	90	92	80	70
B-S-J-G (China)	95	98	79	75	69	66
United Arab Emirates	68	91	77	79	73	65
United States	45	64	75	82	69	65
Czech Republic	98	72	62	84	60	24
Dominican Republic	38	48	61	92	78	61
Germany	62	56	81	90	55	15
Hong Kong (China)	73	95	59	58	49	23
OECD average	**61**	**55**	**66**	**76**	**58**	**38**
Portugal	54	32	76	82	70	36
Brazil	62	36	57	75	60	52
Spain	40	24	64	94	71	45
Macao (China)	56	95	69	35	50	32
Peru	39	47	49	74	46	57
Chinese Taipei	59	94	37	40	37	34
Chile	58	35	55	59	49	41
Italy	60	35	54	75	49	24
Colombia	44	36	52	62	49	50
Korea	64	95	41	24	25	23

Note: Only countries and economies that distributed the general teacher questionnaire are shown.
Countries and economies are ranked in descending order of the percentage of students (average of six statements).
Source: OECD, PISA 2015 Database, Table V.7.6.
StatLink http://dx.doi.org/10.1787/888933616541

According to teachers themselves, teacher co-operation varies markedly between different types of activities and across school systems (Figure V.7.4). For instance, while almost half of students attend a school where teachers reported that they never observe other teachers' classes and provide feedback, two thirds of students attend a school where teachers exchange teaching materials and three quarters attend schools where teachers engage in discussions about the development of specific students at least five times per year. Among the countries and economies that distributed the teacher questionnaire, Australia and B-S-J-G (China) are those where teachers reported co-operating the most frequently; teachers in Colombia and Korea reported co-operating the least frequently.

Most of the questions on teacher co-operation analysed in this chapter are not related to student performance in collaborative problem solving, after accounting for the socio-economic profile of students and schools (Table V.7.8). None of the measures of teacher co-operation is associated with collaborative problem-solving performance after accounting for student performance in the core PISA subjects, on average across OECD countries (Table V.7.9). This suggests that there is no specific association between teacher co-operation, as reported by principals and teachers themselves, and students' development of collaborative skills.

Similarly, most of the questions on teacher co-operation do not show a significant relationship with students' attitudes towards collaboration, on average across OECD countries (Table V.7.10). Any significant relationships observed are tempered by the fact that the direction of these relationships differs across individual countries.

PARENTS' ACQUAINTANCES

The relationships that parents establish with students, school staff and other parents are an essential element of a collaborative school. Even when parents socialise in the school context to advance their child's academic career, they might also be contributing indirectly to the common good of the school – by reinforcing the norms of behaviour at school, spreading important information, generating trust and/or connecting the school with the wider community. Building solid parent-teacher relationships is certainly important for student behaviour (Avvisati et al., 2014), but the relationships that parents build with their child's friends and their parents can be even more important. When parents know each other – a state often referred to as intergenerational closure (Coleman, 1988) – they can develop consistent norms and guide the behaviour of their children more easily.

PISA asked parents from the 16 countries and economies that chose to distribute the parent questionnaire how many of their child's school friends they know by name, how many parents of their child's school friends they know, and how many of the school staff they would feel comfortable talking to if they had a question about their child. On average across the OECD education systems that distributed the parent questionnaire, parents reported that they would feel comfortable talking to about three of their child's teachers, and know approximately five of their child's school friends and four of the parents of their child's school friends (Figure V.7.5). There are stark variations across countries and economies. Parents in Ireland, Spain and Scotland (United Kingdom) appear to socialise the most, while parents in France, Hong Kong (China), Korea and Macao (China) socialise the least.

Figure V.7.5 ■ **Parents' acquaintances**

Fewer than 4 acquaintances
From 4 to 5 acquaintances
More than 5 acquaintances

	Number of acquaintances reported by parents[1]		
	How many parents of your child's friends at this school do you know?	How many friends of your child at school do you know by name?	How many of the school staff would you feel comfortable talking to if you had a question about your child?
Spain	5.6	6.2	4.3
Ireland	5.1	6.0	4.6
Scotland (UK)	4.8	6.0	4.4
Dominican Republic	4.8	5.0	4.2
Germany	4.8	5.7	3.4
Italy	3.7	5.1	4.5
OECD average	**4.0**	**5.2**	**3.3**
Chile	4.2	4.7	3.4
Portugal	4.5	5.3	2.3
Mexico	4.0	4.4	3.0
Croatia	3.6	4.9	3.0
Belgium (Fl.)	3.0	5.0	3.0
Luxembourg	3.1	4.7	3.0
France	2.8	4.5	2.5
Korea	3.1	4.5	1.1
Hong Kong (China)	1.9	3.4	2.2
Macao (China)	2.2	3.3	1.7

1. Parents who answered "6 or more" were assigned a value of "7".

Note: Only countries and economies that distributed the parent questionnaire are shown.

Countries and economies are ranked in descending order of the number of acquaintances (average of three questions).

Source: OECD, PISA 2015 Database, Table V.7.11.

StatLink http://dx.doi.org/10.1787/888933616560

In most countries that distributed the parent questionnaire, parents of children attending socio-economically advantaged schools socialise more than parents of children in disadvantaged schools (Figure V.7.6). For instance, in Chile, the Flemish Community (Belgium), Germany, Italy, Korea, Luxembourg and Macao (China), parents of students in advantaged schools know at least one more parent of their child's school friends than parents in disadvantaged schools do, on average. In Chile, Germany and Luxembourg, an average parent of a student in an advantaged school reported that they would be comfortable talking to at least one more teacher than a parent of a student in a disadvantaged school. However, parents of students in advantaged schools in Mexico and, to a lesser extent those in the Dominican Republic and Portugal, socialise less than parents of children who attend disadvantaged schools.

Figure V.7.6 ▪ **Differences in parents' number of acquaintances, by schools' socio-economic profile**
Difference between schools in the top and bottom quartiles of the PISA index of economic, social and cultural status

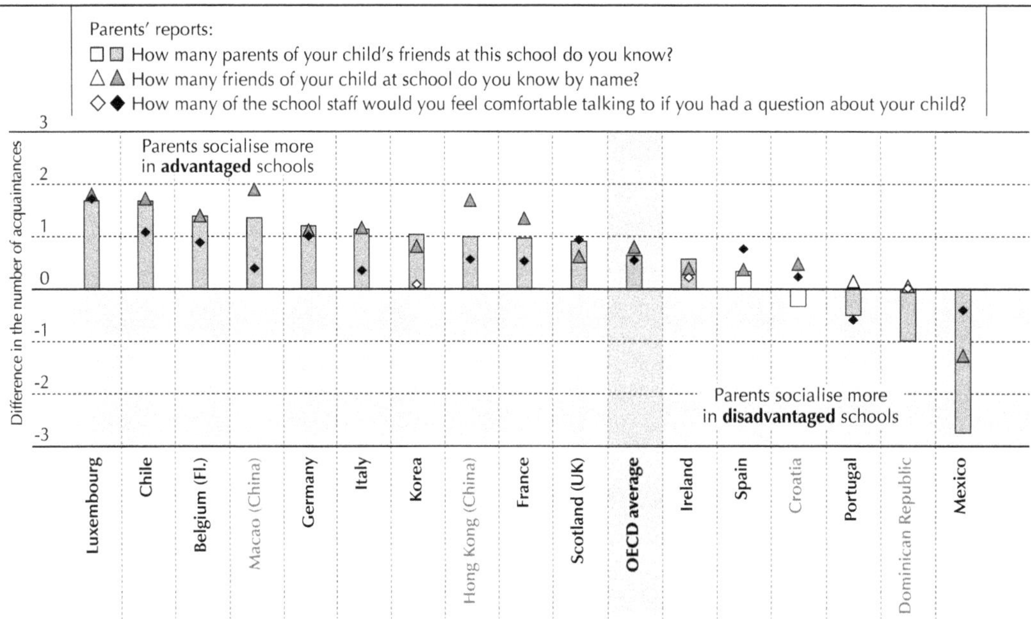

Notes: Statistically significant differences are shown in a darker tone (see Annex A3).
Only countries and economies that distributed the parent questionnaire are shown.
Countries and economies are ranked in descending order of the difference in the number of parents of their child's school friends they know.
Source: OECD, PISA 2015 Database, Table V.7.12.
StatLink http://dx.doi.org/10.1787/888933616579

On average across the OECD countries that distributed the parent questionnaire, students score higher in collaborative problem solving, after accounting for the socio-economic profile of students and schools, when their parents socialise more with their child's school friends and their school friends' parents, and also when they feel comfortable talking to more school staff (Table V.7.13). In Portugal, for instance, students score four points higher for every additional parent of their friends their parents interact with and five points higher for every additional school friend their parents know by name. Knowing more of their child's school friends may not only benefit their children, but their schoolmates too. On average across OECD countries, students score six points higher in collaborative problem solving when their classmates' parents each know another one of their school friends. Even after accounting for student performance in science, reading and mathematics, the number of school friends that parents know by name remains positively associated with student performance in the collaborative problem-solving assessment (Table V.7.14).

Students whose parents socialise more value relationships and teamwork more than students who parents socialise less. However, when their classmates' parents socialise, students seem to value relationships more but value teamwork less (Table V.7.15). All such differences in the indices are small in magnitude.

STUDENT-TEACHER RELATIONSHIPS

Since students spend a great deal of time with teachers, positive and constructive student-teacher relationships are essential for their academic achievement, sense of belonging and well-being (Anderman, 2003; Chiu et al., 2016; Hattie, 2008; OECD, 2017). When teachers care about students and provide them with the help they need, students feel safer, more competent, engaged and connected to the school (Ricard and Pelletier, 2016; Skinner, Pitzer and Steele, 2016), and these students will make greater academic gains (Furrer and Skinner, 2003). However, student-teacher relationships characterised by distrust, unfairness and disrespect are the precursor to disengagement, unco-operative behaviour and failure at school (Hamre and Pianta, 2006; OECD, 2017). Since teachers can compensate for bad experiences in other parts of students' lives, constructive student-teacher relationships are particularly important for at-risk students (Battistich et al., 1997; Crosnoe, Johnson and Elder, 2004; Gamoran, 1993; Mitchell-Copeland, Denham and DeMulder, 1997).

PISA 2015 asked students to report whether their science teacher provides support to their classmates who struggle with schoolwork or continue teaching until students understand (perceptions of teacher support); whether their teachers discipline them more harshly than others or tell them something insulting in front of others (perceptions of teacher unfairness); and whether students listen to what the teacher says and whether teachers wait a long time for students to quiet down (perceptions of disciplinary climate). In addition, principals were asked whether they believe that learning in their school is hindered by students lacking respect for teachers or teachers being too strict with students.

Students in Costa Rica, the Dominican Republic, Japan, Korea and Mexico generally reported the most positive relationships with their teachers (Figure V.7.7). For instance, in the Dominican Republic, about six in ten students reported that, in every lesson, their teachers give extra help if students need it or continue teaching until the students understand, compared to about four in ten students who so reported on average across OECD countries. In Japan, 83% of students reported that the teacher never or almost never disciplines them more harshly than other students (compared with the OECD average of 69%), and 64% reported that the teacher never or hardly ever has to wait a long time for students to quiet down, compared with the OECD average of 27%.

At the other end of the spectrum, students in many European countries, including the Czech Republic, Estonia, Hungary, Latvia and the Netherlands, reported the least positive relationships with their teachers. In these five countries, students perceived less teacher support, greater teacher unfairness, and a less positive disciplinary climate than did students in other OECD countries.

According to school principals in Peru, Qatar and the United Arab Emirates, students' lacking respect for teachers is not a particularly serious concern. In these countries, at least four in ten students attend schools whose principal reported that learning is not hindered at all by students lacking respect for teachers (Table V.7.16). By contrast, in the European countries of Belgium, Croatia, Finland, Luxembourg, the Netherlands and Norway, less than 10% of students are enrolled in schools whose principal reported that students' lack of respect does not hinder learning at all. Principals in Bulgaria, Poland and Sweden reported that teachers being too strict with students does not impede student learning, whereas in Belgium, Costa Rica, Japan, Mexico and the Netherlands, more than seven in eight students are enrolled in a school whose principal expressed at least some concern about this behaviour.

In high-performing education systems in East Asia, including those in B-S-J-G (China), Japan, Korea, Chinese Taipei and Singapore, and also in Australia and Denmark, students in advantaged schools were more likely than students in disadvantaged schools to report that their teachers give extra help when students need it. The largest difference between advantaged and disadvantaged schools is observed in principals' perceptions about the extent to which learning is hindered by students' lack of respect for teachers. This appears to be more of a problem in disadvantaged schools than in advantaged schools, particularly so in Chile and Uruguay (Table V.7.17).

Regardless of what they actually denote, students' perceptions of teachers' unfairness are among the best predictors of students' collaborative and problem-solving skills as assessed in PISA 2015. For instance, on average across OECD countries, students who reported that their teachers say something insulting to them in front of others at least a few times per year score 23 points lower in collaborative problem solving than students who reported that this never, or almost never, happened to them during the previous 12 months. Likewise, students who reported that their teachers discipline them more harshly than other students score 25 points lower in collaborative problem solving (Table V.7.18).

Students not only score higher when they reported being treated fairly by their teachers, but also when their schoolmates reported so. For instance, students score seven points higher in collaborative problem solving for every ten percentage-point increase in the number of schoolmates who reported that teachers never, or almost never, say something insulting to them in front of others, and six points higher for every ten percentage-point increase in the number of schoolmates who reported that teachers never, or almost never, discipline them more harshly than other students.

Figure V.7.7 ▪ **Student-teacher relationships**

Less than half of students
From 50% to 75% of students
More than 75% of students

	Percentage of students who reported the following:					
	In "every lesson", the teacher gives extra help when students need it	In "every lesson", the teacher continues teaching until the students understand	Teachers "never or almost never" discipline me more harshly than other students	Teachers "never or almost never" say something insulting to me in front of others	Students "never or hardly ever" don't listen to what the teacher says	The teacher "never or hardly ever" has to wait a long time for students to quiet down
Japan	35	31	83	89	49	64
Dominican Republic	58	63	84	77	22	34
Mexico	55	54	83	88	16	36
Costa Rica	53	55	65	91	22	36
Korea	29	29	81	86	48	47
United States	55	48	74	74	27	37
B-S-J-G (China)	46	36	67	87	25	39
Thailand	49	51	68	70	29	32
Iceland	46	52	75	79	24	23
Russia	46	44	71	73	24	38
Peru	47	47	56	89	18	39
Portugal	55	57	55	82	19	27
Uruguay	43	49	78	91	16	18
Colombia	43	48	74	75	18	32
Chinese Taipei	41	32	83	91	19	26
Montenegro	41	40	76	81	15	36
Brazil	47	55	70	79	16	21
Chile	47	48	67	90	15	18
Sweden	40	42	75	79	20	26
Singapore	48	44	69	72	23	25
United Arab Emirates	49	54	60	63	24	28
Hong Kong (China)	30	29	70	79	25	39
Norway	36	39	68	73	27	29
Ireland	42	44	63	69	17	33
Denmark	37	39	71	70	17	33
Spain	38	42	74	80	14	21
OECD average	**40**	**38**	**69**	**75**	**18**	**27**
Switzerland	37	34	63	79	22	31
Qatar	49	50	60	62	19	23
Turkey	41	44	68	71	18	22
Greece	40	38	77	75	10	23
Austria	31	30	58	77	33	33
Lithuania	44	41	61	68	17	29
New Zealand	50	43	62	64	17	23
Australia	49	44	64	68	14	21
Bulgaria	39	46	67	70	12	24
United Kingdom	50	44	59	63	17	22
Tunisia	37	43	69	68	14	24
France	35	36	72	77	12	21
Finland	48	36	64	74	12	20
Belgium	37	35	66	74	17	22
Luxembourg	33	34	63	76	17	27
Germany	33	30	59	84	15	24
Slovak Republic	33	28	73	75	11	24
Macao (China)	30	29	65	77	11	31
Slovenia	30	22	74	76	13	27
Poland	34	33	66	74	11	23
Croatia	31	25	73	78	8	25
Netherlands	27	23	71	84	18	14
Estonia	41	32	69	62	10	24
Czech Republic	41	24	77	65	9	21
Latvia	39	33	68	60	9	19
Hungary	32	28	63	66	13	21

Note: Only countries and economies with available data for all six statements are shown.
Countries and economies are ranked in descending order of the percentage of students (average of six statements).
Source: OECD, PISA 2015 Database, Table V.7.16.
StatLink http://dx.doi.org/10.1787/888933616598

When students, or their schoolmates, believe they have been treated unfairly, their relative performance in collaborative problem solving is significantly lower. For instance, in 25 out of 47 education systems, students who reported that their teachers never, or almost never, discipline them more harshly than other students score higher in collaborative problem solving, after accounting for their performance in core PISA subjects, than students who reported they are disciplined more harshly than other students at least a few times per year (Figure V.7.8). Students also score lower in collaborative problem solving, after accounting for performance in core PISA subjects, when more of their schoolmates reported that their classmates do not listen to the teacher or take a long time to quiet down.

Most other associations between the quality of student-teacher relationships (i.e. of teacher support and the disciplinary climate) and collaborative problem-solving scores disappear once scores in science, reading and mathematics are accounted for (Table V.7.19). This suggests that the quality of student-teacher relationships is as important for learning how to solve problems collaboratively as for acquiring knowledge and skills in science, reading and mathematics.

Figure V.7.8 ■ **Teacher discipline and relative performance in collaborative problem solving**
Change in score after accounting for performance in science, reading and mathematics

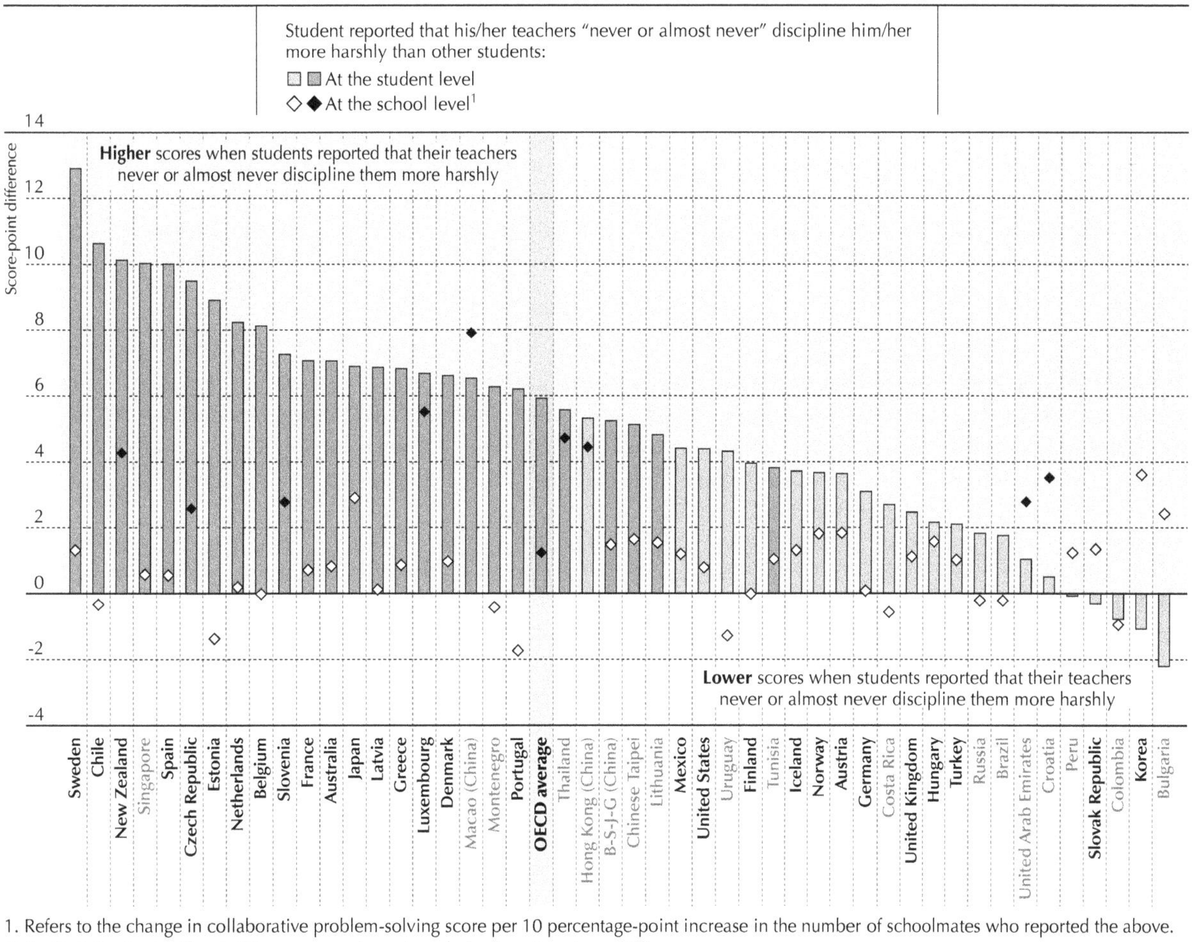

1. Refers to the change in collaborative problem-solving score per 10 percentage-point increase in the number of schoolmates who reported the above.
Note: Statistically significant differences are shown in a darker tone (see Annex A3).
Countries and economies are ranked in descending order of the score-point difference associated with students reporting that their teachers "never or almost never" discipline them more harshly than other students.
Source: OECD, PISA 2015 Database, Table V.7.19.
StatLink http://dx.doi.org/10.1787/888933616617

Students' perceptions of teacher support, teacher unfairness and the disciplinary climate are all good predictors of whether students value relationships. For example, students in every country/economy who reported that teachers give extra help when students need it or that teachers continue teaching until students understand value relationships more than other students (Table V.7.20). There are weaker but generally positive relationships between student-teacher relationships and the index of valuing teamwork.[3]

STUDENT-PARENT RELATIONSHIPS

Parents can make a major difference in their child's social and academic progress (Hattie, 2008). Several studies indicate that students do better at school when their parents get more involved in their social, emotional and academic life (Epstein, 2001; Hill and Tyson, 2009), but they also caution that the benefits depend largely on the quality of these student-parent relationships (Borgonovi and Montt, 2012; Desforges and Abouchaar, 2003; Ho and Willms, 1996). Parents can support students in their learning, develop their ability to plan and monitor the learning process, guide them on how to navigate the education system, and build their self-confidence and intrinsic motivation to learn (Fan and Williams, 2010; Pomerantz, Moorman and Litwack, 2007). However, parents can also hinder their child's social and academic progress when they hold and share negative beliefs about their child's potential to succeed (Pomerantz, Moorman and Litwack, 2007).

PISA 2015 asked students and parents about the strength and the quality of their interactions. Students were asked if they talked to their parents before and after school on the most recent day, and parents were asked if they spend time just talking with their children or eat the main meal with them. Both students and parents were also asked if they agree with the following statements about parents' emotional support: "My parents are/I am interested in my (child's) school activities"; "My parents support my/I am supportive of my child's educational efforts and achievements"; "My parents support me when I am/I support my child when he/she is facing difficulties at school"; and "My parents encourage me/I encourage my child to be confident".

In every PISA-participating country and economy except Chinese Taipei, at least seven out of ten students reported that they had talked to their parents both before and after school. In Chinese Taipei, nearly one in two students reported that they had not talked to their parents before going to school (Figure V.7.9). In the OECD countries that distributed the parent questionnaire, 83% of parents reported that, every day or almost every day, they eat the main meal with their child; 73% reported that they spend time just talking with their child (Table V.7.21).[4] In Chile, the Dominican Republic, Korea and Scotland (United Kingdom), only about seven in ten parents eat the main meal with their child, while in Chile, Macao (China) and Mexico, fewer than one in two parents spends time just talking with their child.

On average across OECD countries, about one in two students and three in four parents strongly agreed with each of the four statements related to the emotional support that parents provide to their child. In Austria, Costa Rica, Ireland and Switzerland, at least six in ten students strongly agreed with all four statements on parents' emotional support. Overall, the school systems where students reported the most positive student-parent relationships are Austria, Costa Rica, Iceland, Portugal and Switzerland. In B-S-J-G (China), Hong Kong (China), Macao (China), Poland and Chinese Taipei, students reported the least positive relationships (Figure V.7.9).

In a majority of PISA-participating education systems, the student-parent relationships among students in socio-economically advantaged schools are more positive than those among students in disadvantaged schools, according to both students and parents (Table V.7.22). For example, the proportion of students who strongly agreed that their parents are interested in their school activities is 11 percentage points larger among students in advantaged schools than among students in disadvantaged schools. Differences in how students perceive the quality of student-parent relationships between these two groups of schools – in favour of advantaged schools – are particularly large in Hungary, Korea, Singapore, the Slovak Republic and Turkey. By contrast, these differences are particularly small in Colombia, Costa Rica, the Dominican Republic, the Russian Federation (hereafter "Russia"), Sweden and Switzerland.

On average across OECD countries, students score higher in collaborative problem solving when they, their parents, their schoolmates or their schoolmates' parents reported more positive student-parent relationships, after accounting for the socio-economic profile of students and schools (Table V.7.23). For instance, students score 19 points higher in the collaborative problem-solving assessment when they reported that they had talked to their parents after school on the day prior to the PISA test, and 3 points higher after accounting for their performance in science, reading and mathematics (Figure V.7.10 and Table V.7.24).

Students who reported stronger relationships with and emotional support from their parents value both relationships and teamwork more than other students. Valuing relationships, although not necessarily valuing teamwork, is also observed when students' classmates reported stronger relationships with their parents. These positive associations are also observed, although they are weaker, when these students' parents reported stronger relationships with and emotional support for their children (Table V.7.25). For example, on average across OECD countries, students who strongly agreed that their parents encourage them to be confident have an index of valuing relationships that is 0.41 unit higher than other students – and 0.70 unit higher in the Dominican Republic.

Figure V.7.9 ▪ Student-parent relationships

Less than half of students
From 50% to 75% of students
More than 75% of students

	Percentage of students who reported the following:					
	Talked to parents before going to school on the most recent day	Talked to parents after leaving school on the most recent day	"Strongly agree" that my parents are interested in my school activities	"Strongly agree" that my parents support my educational efforts and achievements	"Strongly agree" that my parents support me when I am facing difficulties at school	"Strongly agree" that my parents encourage me to be confident
Costa Rica	84	87	70	71	73	65
Austria	84	92	74	61	70	65
Portugal	92	96	70	64	58	64
Iceland	90	97	54	70	62	66
Switzerland	83	94	69	68	62	63
Ireland	92	97	62	64	60	61
Germany	87	94	68	61	64	58
Lithuania	90	93	64	62	56	63
United States	88	94	51	70	54	62
Luxembourg	82	92	68	62	57	56
Australia	90	96	52	65	51	57
Sweden	87	95	50	61	58	59
Croatia	86	94	56	60	57	55
Canada	88	95	49	67	51	58
Spain	84	92	61	57	55	59
United Kingdom	89	95	51	64	53	56
Denmark	87	94	52	60	61	50
Norway	88	96	51	56	54	57
New Zealand	89	95	50	64	48	55
Hungary	89	94	54	57	53	54
Uruguay	81	88	59	61	55	56
Qatar	89	91	41	60	53	65
Dominican Republic	87	90	61	62	43	55
Netherlands	89	97	51	52	55	50
United Arab Emirates	91	93	32	59	53	66
Greece	88	92	51	51	49	58
Chile	81	86	54	60	54	55
France	81	91	54	62	47	53
OECD average	**86**	**92**	**52**	**56**	**51**	**52**
Mexico	80	84	60	58	51	55
Bulgaria	84	91	52	51	51	58
Belgium	85	93	50	56	51	49
Colombia	83	85	55	57	47	54
Tunisia	91	90	37	56	42	62
Slovenia	80	83	49	63	48	52
Finland	83	94	55	48	47	48
Brazil	85	89	50	53	43	52
Italy	89	94	50	44	43	52
Montenegro	80	87	40	51	49	59
Turkey	80	84	28	58	47	46
Latvia	89	94	45	41	35	33
Peru	82	84	44	44	34	49
Korea	79	86	46	43	39	40
Singapore	77	90	31	53	37	45
Thailand	93	95	21	48	33	42
Estonia	88	89	38	42	38	37
Slovak Republic	82	89	40	47	37	36
Russia	93	93	41	40	40	24
Czech Republic	86	93	38	46	38	27
Japan	90	94	30	42	37	30
Poland	83	90	40	32	34	37
B-S-J-G (China)	72	75	18	51	39	47
Chinese Taipei	56	81	18	38	37	34
Hong Kong (China)	77	89	9	31	24	27
Macao (China)	72	83	11	31	21	27

Note: Only countries and economies with available data for all six statements are shown.
Countries and economies are ranked in descending order of the percentage of students (average of six statements).
Source: OECD, PISA 2015 Database, Table V.7.21.
StatLink http://dx.doi.org/10.1787/888933616636

Figure V.7.10 ▪ **Talking to parents after school and performance in collaborative problem solving**

Change in score after accounting for students' and schools' socio-economic profile

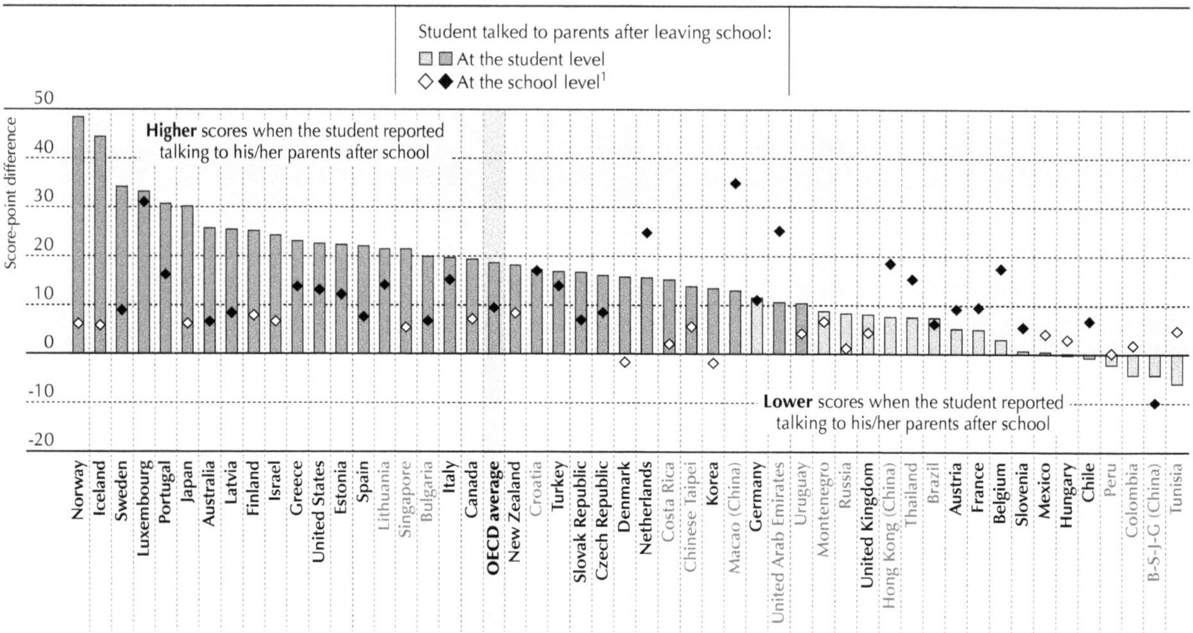

1. Refers to the change in collaborative problem-solving score per 10 percentage-point increase in the number of schoolmates who reported the above.

Notes: Statistically significant differences are shown in a darker tone (see Annex A3).

The socio-economic profile is measured by the PISA index of economic, social and cultural status (ESCS).

Countries and economies are ranked in descending order of the score-point difference associated with students reporting talking to parents after leaving school on the most recent day.

Source: OECD, PISA 2015 Database, Table V.7.23.

StatLink http://dx.doi.org/10.1787/888933616655

TEACHER-PRINCIPAL RELATIONSHIPS

School leaders not only manage administrative tasks, such as budgeting, staffing and planning the maintenance of school buildings, but also play a key role in education by actively shaping the school culture (Barber, Whelan and Clark, 2010; Hallinger and Heck, 1998; Leithwood and Jantzi, 2006; Pont, Nusche and Moorman, 2008). Building constructive relationships with teachers is key for making a school a learning organisation and creating a positive learning environment (Barnett and McCormick, 2004). For principals, this means communicating and building consensus around the school's education goals, treating teaching staff as professionals, involving them in decision making, and planning professional development activities (Bennis and Nanus, 1985; Conger and Kanungo, 1988; Grissom, Loeb and Master, 2013; Heck, Larsen and Marcoulides, 1990; Kools and Stoll, 2016). Co-operative relationships between principals and teachers may influence students' collaborative problem-solving skills and their attitudes towards collaboration only indirectly, for instance, by creating a positive and innovative school culture.

PISA 2015 asked school principals to report how frequently a series of actions and behaviours related to school management occurred during the previous academic year. The following were retained as measures of the quality of principal-teacher relationships: "providing staff with opportunities to participate in decision-making"; "engaging teachers to help build a school culture of continuous improvement"; "asking teachers to participate in reviewing management practices"; and "discussing the school's academic goals with teachers at faculty meetings". Teachers from the 19 countries and economies that distributed the teacher questionnaire were asked to respond to the following statements related to their interactions with principals: "The principal tries to achieve consensus with all staff when defining priorities and goals in school"; "The principal is aware of my needs"; "The principal treats teaching staff as professionals"; and "The principal ensures our involvement in decision making".

On average across OECD countries, about three out of four students are enrolled in schools whose principal reported that, at least once per month, he or she involves teachers in the decision-making process and engages them in the construction of a school culture of continuous improvement (Table V.7.26). About one in two students attends a school whose principal discusses the school's academic goals with teachers at faculty meetings at least once per month. Asking teachers to

review management practices is the least frequently used leadership action: only roughly one in three students is enrolled in a school whose principal reported that this happens at least once per month. These four leadership actions are most frequently practiced in the Dominican Republic, Portugal, Thailand, the United States and Uruguay, and the least frequently practiced in B-S-J-G (China), France, Luxembourg, Macao (China), Poland, Switzerland and Tunisia.

In all the education systems that distributed the teacher questionnaire, at least one in two students attends schools where the teachers agree that the principal is aware of their needs, treats them as professionals, tries to achieve consensus when defining the goals of the school, and involves them in the decision-making process (Figure V.7.11). On average across OECD countries, most students (86%) are enrolled in schools where the teachers agree that they are treated as professionals, while fewer students – but still a majority of students – attend schools where the teachers agree that the principal is aware of their needs (73%) and involve them in the decision-making process (68%). Teachers in Brazil, the Czech Republic, the Dominican Republic, Spain, the United States are particularly positive about their interactions with the school principal, while teachers in Chile, Hong Kong (China), Italy, Macao (China) and Chinese Taipei are the least positive.

Principals of disadvantaged schools reported closer and more positive relations with their teachers than principals of advantaged schools did (Table V.7.27). Principals of disadvantaged schools were more likely to report that they provide teachers with opportunities to participate in the decision-making process, review management practices and discuss the school's academic goals. Teachers in advantaged and disadvantaged schools responded similarly to statements about their principals' willingness to include them in school management and whether their principal recognises them as professionals.

On average across OECD countries, there is no significant relationship between any of the teacher-principal interactions considered and students' performance in collaborative problem solving, both before and after accounting for students' scores in science, reading and mathematics (Tables V.7.28 and V.7.29). There is also no significant relationship between any of those teacher-principal interactions and students' attitudes towards collaboration (Table V.7.30).

Figure V.7.11 ▪ **Teacher-principal relationships**

Legend: Less than half of students; From 50% to 75% of students; More than 75% of students

	Percentage of students whose school teachers reported the following:			
	"Agree" or "strongly agree" that "the principal tries to achieve consensus with all staff when defining priorities and goals in school"	"Agree" or "strongly agree" that "the principal is aware of my needs"	"Agree" or "strongly agree" that "the principal treats teaching staff as professionals"	"Agree" or "strongly agree" that "the principal ensures our involvement in decision making"
Dominican Republic	89	90	92	86
Brazil	85	86	91	79
United States	80	81	89	74
Czech Republic	82	79	89	72
Spain	76	79	91	74
United Arab Emirates	79	80	87	74
Colombia	79	77	86	74
Portugal	80	73	92	72
Peru	84	67	87	77
Germany	79	74	89	72
OECD average	**76**	**73**	**86**	**68**
B-S-J-G (China)	82	68	86	65
Australia	72	68	86	64
Korea	71	69	79	62
Italy	77	67	75	61
Chile	68	66	81	58
Hong Kong (China)	71	58	81	59
Chinese Taipei	70	60	83	55
Macao (China)	70	57	86	51

Note: Only countries and economies that distributed the general teacher questionnaire are shown.
Countries and economies are ranked in descending order of the percentage of students (average of four statements).
Source: OECD, PISA 2015 Database, Table V.7.26.
StatLink http://dx.doi.org/10.1787/888933616674

PARENT-TEACHER RELATIONSHIPS

Beyond the relationships that students form with peers, teachers and parents, few relationships are as vital for the future of students as those established between parents and teachers. When parents and teachers respect each other, communicate regularly about the child's progress, and agree on common goals, norms and planning, students benefit academically, socially and emotionally (Epstein and Salinas, 1992; Miretzky, 2004; Vosler-Hunter, 1989), especially at-risk students (Letarte, Normandeau and Allard, 2010; Spann, Kohler and Soenksen, 2003). Conversely, misunderstandings and unco-operative behaviours might have negative effects on students' well-being and life prospects. Despite the potential benefits of greater communication and co-operation among parents and teachers, many teachers receive little, if any, preparation and training on how to work effectively with families, and therefore lack the necessary communication skills for effective parent-teacher co-operation (Ferrara and Ferrar, 2005; Westergard, 2013).

Evaluating the impact of the interactions between parents and teachers on student outcomes in cross-sectional studies, including PISA, is always a challenge since problems of reverse causality may be at play. For instance, if parents participate more where they are needed more, the intensity of parent-teacher interactions could be negatively associated with student achievement, as observed in previous analyses of PISA results (OECD, 2016, 2012)".

PISA 2015 asked principals about the proportion of parents who discussed their child's progress with their teachers on the initiative of the teacher and on their own initiative during the previous academic year. It asked teachers whether parent-teacher co-operation was included as a topic in their teacher training or other professional qualification programme. PISA 2015 also asked parents whether, during the previous academic year, they discussed their child's progress with their teachers, talked with teachers about ways to support learning at home, and exchanged ideas with teachers on parenting, family support and child development.

On average across OECD countries, according to school principals, about 40% of parents had discussed their child's progress with a teacher on their own initiative (Figure V.7.12). In 11 countries and economies, including B-S-J-G (China), Greece and Italy, more than half of parents had discussed their child's progress on their own initiative, while in Japan and Tunisia, less than 25% had done so. According to principals, parents had discussed their child's progress more frequently on the initiative of their teacher. On average across OECD countries, some 57% of parents had discussed their child's progress on the teacher's initiative; in Denmark, Japan, Macao (China), Norway and Sweden, more than 75% of parents had done so.

According to parents themselves, about one in two reported that they had spoken with teachers about their child's progress and how to support learning at home, and just over one in three reported exchanging ideas on parenting, family support and child development (Table V.7.31).

PISA 2015 data show that, on average across the OECD countries that distributed the teacher questionnaire, some 40% of teachers reported that teacher-parent co-operation was included as a topic in their teacher training or other professional qualification programme. However, in some countries and economies, such as B-S-J-G (China), the Dominican Republic and the United States, more than 60% of teachers reported receiving some training on teacher-parent co-operation, whereas in Italy and Portugal, less than 30% of teachers reported so.

There are significant differences, on average across OECD countries, between socio-economically advantaged and disadvantaged schools in the nature of parent-teacher interactions (Table V.7.32). For instance, principals of advantaged schools reported more frequently than principals of disadvantaged schools that parents discuss their child's progress on their own initiative (Figure V.7.13). Conversely, when parents responded to the same question, it is the parents of students in disadvantaged schools who were more likely to report that they discuss their child's progress on their own (or on the teacher's) initiative. In these schools, parents were also more likely to report that they talk to teachers about parenting, family support and home learning than were parents of students in advantaged schools. As parents are directly involved in these relationships, their reports are likely to be more accurate than principals' estimates.

In almost all education systems that distributed the parent questionnaire, students score considerably lower in collaborative problem solving when their parents reported that, during the previous academic year, they had spoken with their child's teachers about their child's progress, home learning and homework, or parenting, family support or child development more generally (Table V.7.33). On average across OECD countries, these negative associations remain even after accounting for student performance in science, reading and mathematics (Table V.7.34).

Figure V.7.12 ▪ Parent-teacher relationships

Less than half of students
From 50% to 75% of students
More than 75% of students

	Percentage of parents who discussed their child's progress with a teacher:[1]	
	On their own initiative	On the teachers' initiative
Sweden	40	87
Spain	57	69
B-S-J-G (China)	59	62
Denmark	36	83
Russia	57	61
Norway	28	86
Portugal	50	63
Singapore	39	73
Macao (China)	33	79
United Arab Emirates	53	59
Italy	59	51
Colombia	45	65
Qatar	52	58
Israel	43	66
Thailand	49	59
Greece	65	44
Finland	44	65
Iceland	35	73
Dominican Republic	47	60
Poland	45	62
United Kingdom	41	65
Canada	49	54
Lithuania	47	55
Montenegro	56	46
Chile	40	62
Bulgaria	43	59
Hong Kong (China)	36	63
Croatia	55	43
Japan	18	80
OECD average	**40**	**57**
France	43	53
Peru	42	54
Netherlands	39	56
Korea	41	53
New Zealand	36	57
Germany	42	50
United States	41	51
Australia	39	52
Estonia	41	50
Latvia	42	49
Switzerland	30	61
Slovenia	53	37
Costa Rica	38	51
Czech Republic	38	52
Belgium	34	54
Chinese Taipei	46	41
Luxembourg	30	56
Turkey	42	43
Mexico	33	51
Brazil	33	46
Austria	36	41
Slovak Republic	38	39
Ireland	34	42
Uruguay	29	39
Hungary	34	31
Tunisia	23	32

1. Based on school principals' reports.
Countries and economies are ranked in descending order of the percentage of parents who discussed their child's progress (average of two statements).
Source: OECD, PISA 2015 Database, Table V.7.31.
StatLink http://dx.doi.org/10.1787/888933616693

Figure V.7.13 ■ **Percentage of parents who discuss their child's progress with teachers, by schools' socio-economic profile**

Difference between schools in the top and bottom quartiles of the PISA index of economic, social and cultural status

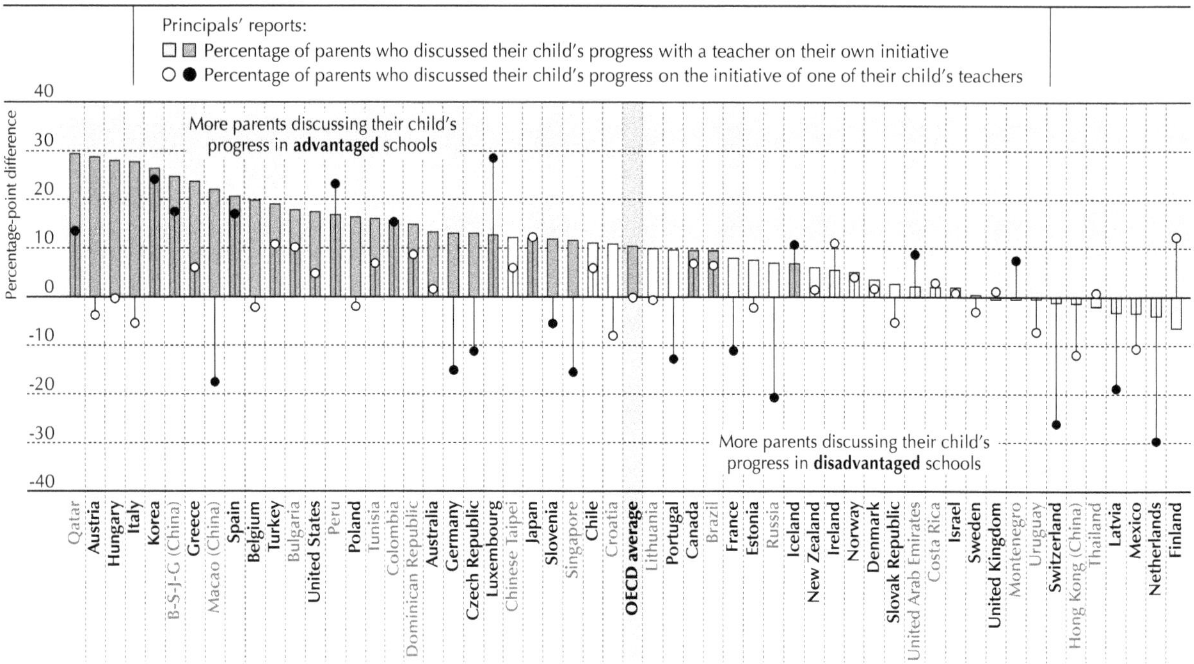

Note: Statistically significant differences are shown in a darker tone (see Annex A3).

Countries and economies are ranked in descending order of the percentage-point difference of parents who discussed their child's progress on their own initiative.

Source: OECD, PISA 2015 Database, Table V.7.32.

StatLink http://dx.doi.org/10.1787/888933616712

Students whose parents or whose classmates' parents reported that they discuss their child's progress with the child's teacher on the teacher's initiative appear to value relationships less than other students. However, the relationship is reversed for the index of valuing teamwork, which is higher among students whose parents reported that they interact with their child's teacher, on either their own or the teacher's initiative (Table V.7.35). These results might reflect the likelihood that, according to parents' reports, such interactions take place in disadvantaged schools, and as discussed in Chapter 5, disadvantaged students have higher indices of valuing teamwork but lower indices of valuing relationships (Figure V.5.6, Tables V.5.5a and V.5.5b).

However, these results do not necessarily imply that strengthening teacher-parent communications is counterproductive. More frequent interactions between parents and teachers may be the consequence, rather than the cause, of students' poor academic performance and lack of collaborative skills (i.e. reverse causality). In fact, some studies suggest that talking with teachers may be the best way to identify and solve serious behavioural problems at school (Avvisati et al., 2014; Hill and Tyson, 2009; Sirvani, 2007).

SCHOOL RELATIONSHIPS WITH PARENTS AND THE LOCAL COMMUNITY

Even if the relationships that schools establish with parents and the community influence only indirectly what happens inside the classroom, getting parents involved in school activities and decision making can improve school functioning and the academic achievement and well-being of students. It can also contribute to building healthy and socially connected communities, and allows parents to learn about and shape the school learning environment (Benson et al., 1996; Epstein et al., 2002; Henderson and Mapp, 2002; Sanders, 2003).

PISA 2015 asked principals about school efforts to involve and communicate with parents, and about the participation of parents in school activities and decision making. It also asked parents whether they agreed that the school involves parents in decision making, and whether they participate in the governance of the school, extracurricular activities or scheduled meetings and conferences. In every school system except Tunisia, a majority of students are in schools whose principal agreed that there are effective forms of school-to-home and home-to-school communications (Figure V.7.14). In all but seven countries and economies, at least one in two students is in a school that include parents in school decisions.

Figure V.7.14 ■ School relationships with parents and the community

Legend:
- Less than half of students
- From 50% to 75% of students
- More than 75% of students

	Percentage of students in schools whose principal reported the following:			Percentage of parents who:[1]	
	Our school designs effective forms of school-to-home and home-to-school communications	Our school includes parents in school decisions	Our school identifies and integrates resources and services from the community to strengthen school programmes, family practices, and student learning and development	Participated in local school government	Volunteered in physical or extracurricular activities
Dominican Republic	98	96	88	68	33
Thailand	95	95	95	52	45
Russia	99	98	86	29	48
Colombia	97	93	74	62	24
Chinese Taipei	96	84	95	39	27
Korea	95	97	91	33	19
Qatar	99	69	93	43	31
United Arab Emirates	97	82	88	38	27
Poland	96	98	83	26	24
Peru	89	74	79	52	30
Turkey	89	91	91	35	16
Estonia	99	96	80	19	24
Slovak Republic	98	88	75	39	15
Montenegro	94	91	88	28	10
Portugal	98	93	88	20	11
Hong Kong (China)	97	84	95	16	14
United States	93	81	91	16	23
Mexico	91	75	72	44	21
Latvia	89	95	86	18	14
Croatia	92	94	70	33	8
Ireland	99	99	80	11	9
Brazil	98	87	66	32	13
B-S-J-G (China)	92	53	88	33	30
Chile	93	59	80	43	20
New Zealand	98	86	86	7	15
Iceland	100	87	85	6	13
Germany	97	97	76	11	12
Slovenia	98	92	67	27	6
Spain	95	78	73	25	14
Canada	93	83	89	8	12
Australia	96	80	88	7	13
Bulgaria	89	76	73	26	17
Costa Rica	94	65	69	29	23
OECD average	**92**	**77**	**72**	**18**	**13**
Italy	96	78	58	32	9
Norway	98	76	73	10	15
Lithuania	78	97	60	16	16
United Kingdom	97	75	83	4	6
Singapore	97	47	98	10	12
Sweden	88	86	65	12	12
Hungary	88	87	62	14	12
Finland	93	68	83	8	9
Greece	100	44	68	31	16
Macao (China)	97	34	74	33	20
Denmark	91	68	58	13	16
Israel	76	56	73	22	18
Austria	86	77	49	16	11
Uruguay	92	34	74	12	8
Czech Republic	99	64	37	13	7
Netherlands	92	82	24	6	6
Japan	87	11	63	24	25
Luxembourg	66	66	63	8	5
Belgium	82	60	53	6	5
Switzerland	86	37	47	7	7
Tunisia	34	25	22	10	5

1. Based on school principals' reports.

Note: Only countries and economies with available data for all five statements are shown.

Countries and economies are ranked in descending order of the percentage of students (average of five statements).

Source: OECD, PISA 2015 Database, Table V.7.36.

StatLink http://dx.doi.org/10.1787/888933616731

However, despite efforts to include parents, on average across OECD countries, only 18% of parents participated in school government during the previous academic year, according to principals (16% according to parents) (Table V.7.36). Moreover, just 13% of parents participated in extracurricular activities, according to school principals (12% according to parents), and 76% of parents participated in a scheduled meeting or conference for parents, according to parents.[5] About seven in ten school principals and parents agreed that the school co-operates with the community to strengthen school programmes and student development.

Across OECD countries, socio-economically advantaged schools are more likely than disadvantaged schools to design effective communications with parents; but disadvantaged schools are more likely than advantaged schools to involve parents in school decisions, and co-operate with the community to strengthen school programmes and student development (Table V.7.37). On average across the OECD countries that distributed the parent questionnaire, attending scheduled meetings and conferences for parents is more common among parents of students in advantaged schools than among parents of students in disadvantaged schools.

In the OECD countries that distributed the parent questionnaire, students score lower in collaborative problem solving when parents participate in the school government, both before and after accounting for performance in science, reading and mathematics (Tables V.7.38 and V.7.39). The children of parents who reported stronger relationships between themselves and their child's school, or between their child's school and the community, also tend to place higher on the indices of both valuing relationships and valuing teamwork (Table V.7.40).

Notes

1. Bullying is a systematic abuse of power, and can be identified by three key traits: repetition, intention to harm, and an unequal power between the bully and the victim (Woods and Wolke, 2004; Olweus, 1994). See *PISA 2015 Results (Volume III): Students' Well-Being* (OECD, 2017) for a detailed discussion on bullying.

2. Relative collaborative problem-solving performance is calculated by an ordinary least squares regression of collaborative problem-solving performance over performance in science, reading and mathematics. In Chapter 3, the regression is performed at the international level in order to rank countries and economies. In Chapters 4, 5, 6 and 7, the regression is performed at the individual country or economy level, as the focus is on factors related to differential performance within each country/economy. This results in an average residual of 0 for each country/economy.

3. Students who report that teachers never, or almost never, discipline them more harshly than they do other students actually report a lower index of valuing teamwork, on average across OECD countries. However, there is substantial variation between countries: in 12 countries/economies, students who report that teachers never, or almost never, discipline them more harshly than they do other students report a lower index of valuing teamwork, while in 11 countries/economies, they report a higher index of valuing teamwork.

4. On average across the OECD countries that participated in the collaborative problem-solving assessment, 84% of students had parents who reported that they eat the main meal with their child every day or almost every day, and 72% of students had parents who reported that they spend time just talking to their child every day or almost every day.

5. On average across the OECD countries that participated in the collaborative problem-solving assessment, 75% of parents reported that they attended a scheduled meeting or conference aimed at parents in the previous academic year.

References

Anderman, L.H. (2003), "Academic and social perceptions as predictors of change in middle school students' sense of school belonging", *The Journal of Experimental Education*, Vol. 72/1, pp. 5-22, http://dx.doi.org/10.1080/00220970309600877.

Avvisati, F. et al. (2014), "Getting parents involved: A field experiment in deprived schools", *The Review of Economic Studies*, Vol. 81/1, pp. 57-83, https://doi.org/10.1093/restud/rdt027.

Barber, M., F. Whelan and **M. Clark** (2010), *Capturing the Leadership Premium: How the World's Top School Systems are Building Leadership Capacity for the Future*, McKinsey and Company.

Barnett, K. and **J. McCormick** (2004), "Leadership and individual principal-teacher relationships in schools", *Educational Administration Quarterly*, Vol. 40/3, pp. 406-434, https://doi.org/10.1177/0013161X03261742.

Battistich, V. et al. (1997), "Caring school communities", *Educational Psychologist*, Vol. 32/3, pp. 137-151, http://dx.doi.org/10.1207/s15326985ep3203_1.

Bennis, W. and **B. Nanus** (1985), *Leaders: The strategies for taking charge*, Harper and Row, New York.

Benson, P.L. et al. (1996), "Beyond the 'village' rhetoric: Creating healthy communities for children and adolescents", *Applied Developmental Science*, Vol. 2/3, pp. 138-159, http://dx.doi.org/10.1207/s1532480xads0203_3.

Borgonovi, F. and **G. Montt** (2012), "Parental involvement in selected PISA countries and economies", *OECD Education Working Papers*, No. 73, OECD Publishing, Paris, http://dx.doi.org/10.1787/5k990rk0jsjj-en.

Chiu, J. et al. (2016), "Which matters most? Perceptions of family income or parental education on academic achievement", *New York Journal of Student Affairs*, Vol. 16/2, pp. 3-16.

Cohen, J. et al. (2009), "School climate: Research, policy, practice, and teacher education", *Teachers College Record*, Vol. 111/1, pp. 180-213.

Coleman, J.S. (1988), "Social capital in the creation of human capital", *American Journal of Sociology*, Vol. 94, pp. S95-120, https://doi.org/10.1086/228943.

Conger, J.A. and **R.N. Kanungo** (1988), "The empowerment process: Integrating theory and practice", *Academy of Management Review*, Vol. 13/3, pp. 471-482.

Crosnoe, R., M.K. Johnson and **G.H. Elder, Jr.** (2004), "Intergenerational bonding in school: The behavioral and contextual correlates of student-teacher relationships", *Sociology of Education*, Vol. 77/1, pp. 60-81, https://doi.org/10.1177/003804070407700103.

Desforges, C. and **A. Abouchaar** (2003), "The impact of parental involvement, parental support and family education on pupil achievement and adjustment: A literature review", *Research report commissioned by the Department for Education and Skills, United Kingdom*, No. 433, http://dera.ioe.ac.uk/id/eprint/6305.

Epstein, J.L. (2001), *School, Family, and Community Partnerships: Preparing Educators and Improving Schools*, Westview Press, Boulder, CO.

Epstein, J.L. and **K.C. Salinas** (1992), *Promising Programs in the Middle Grades*, National Association of Secondary School Principals, Reston, VA.

Epstein, J.L. et al. (2002), *School, Family, and Community Partnerships: Your Handbook for Action (Third Edition)*, Corwin Press, Thousand Oaks, CA.

Fan, W. and **C.M. Williams** (2010), "The effects of parental involvement on students' academic self-efficacy, engagement and intrinsic motivation", *Educational Psychology*, Vol. 30/1, pp. 53-74, http://dx.doi.org/10.1080/01443410903353302.

Ferrara, M.M. and **P.J. Ferrar** (2005), "Parents as partners: Raising awareness as a teacher preparation program", *The Clearing House: A Journal of Educational Strategies, Issues and Ideas*, Vol. 79/2, pp. 77-82, http://dx.doi.org/10.3200/TCHS.79.2.77-82.

Furrer, C. and **E. Skinner** (2003), "Sense of relatedness as a factor in children's academic engagement and performance", *Journal of Educational Psychology*, Vol. 95/1, pp. 148-162, http://dx.doi.org/10.1037/0022-0663.95.1.148.

Gajda, R. and **C. Koliba** (2007), "Evaluating the imperative of intraorganizational collaboration: A school improvement perspective", *American Journal of Evaluation*, Vol. 28/1, pp. 26-44, https://doi.org/10.1177/1098214006296198.

Gamoran, A. (1993), "Alternative uses of ability grouping in secondary schools: Can we bring high-quality instruction to low-ability classes?", *American Journal of Education*, Vol. 102/1, pp. 1-22, https://doi.org/10.1086/444056.

Gittell, J.H. et al. (2000), "Impact of relational coordination on quality of care, postoperative pain and functioning, and length of stay: A nine-hospital study of surgical patients", *Medical Care*, Vol. 38/8, pp. 807-819.

Goddard, Y.L., **R.D. Goddard** and **M. Tschannen-Moran** (2007), "A theoretical and empirical investigation of teacher collaboration for school improvement and student achievement in public elementary schools", *Teachers College Record*, Vol. 109/4, pp. 877-896.

Grissom, J.A., **S. Loeb** and **B. Master** (2013), "Effective instructional time use for school leaders: Longitudinal evidence from observations of principals", *Educational Researcher*, Vol. 42/8, pp. 433-444, https://doi.org/10.3102/0013189X13510020.

Hallinger, P. and **R.H. Heck** (1998), "Exploring the principal's contribution to school effectiveness: 1980-1995", *School Effectiveness and School Improvement*, Vol. 9/2, pp. 157-191, http://dx.doi.org/10.1080/0924345980090203.

Hamre, B.K. and **R.C. Pianta** (2006), "Student-teacher relationships as a source of support and risk in schools", in G.G Bear and K.M. Minke (eds.), *Children's Needs III: Development, Prevention, and Intervention*, pp. 59-71, National Association of School Psychologists, Bethesda, MD.

Hattie, J.A.C. (2008), *Visible Learning: A Synthesis of Over 800 Meta-Analyses Relating to Achievement*, Routledge, Abingdon.

Heck, R.H., **T.J. Larsen** and **G.A. Marcoulides** (1990), "Instructional leadership and school achievement: Validation of a causal model", *Educational Administration Quarterly*, Vol. 26/2, pp. 94-125, https://doi.org/10.1177/0013161X90026002002.

Henderson, A.T. and **K.L. Mapp** (2002), *A New Wave of Evidence: The Impact of School, Family, and Community Connections on Student Achievement – Annual Synthesis 2002*, National Center for Family and Community Connections with Schools, Southwest Educational Development Laboratory, Austin, TX, www.sedl.org/connections/resources/evidence.pdf.

Hill, N.E. and **D.F. Tyson** (2009), "Parental involvement in middle school: A meta-analytic assessment of the strategies that promote achievement", *Developmental Psychology*, Vol. 45/3, pp. 740-763, http://dx.doi.org/10.1037/a0015362.

Ho, E.S.-C. and **J.D. Willms** (1996), "Effects of parental involvement on eighth-grade achievement", *Sociology of Education*, Vol. 69/2, pp. 126-141, https://doi.org/10.2307/2112802.

Hughes, J. and **O.-M. Kwok** (2007), "Influence of student-teacher and parent-teacher relationships on lower achieving readers' engagement and achievement in the primary grades", *Journal of Educational Psychology*, Vol. 99/1, pp. 39-51, https://doi.org/10.1037/0022-0663.99.1.39.

Jennings, P.A. and **M.T. Greenberg** (2009), "The prosocial classroom: Teacher social and emotional competence in relation to student and classroom outcomes", *Review of Educational Research*, Vol. 79/1, pp. 491-525, https://doi.org/10.3102/0034654308325693.

Johnson, D.W. (1981), "Student-student interaction: The neglected variable in education", *Educational Researcher*, Vol. 10/1, pp. 5-10, https://doi.org/10.3102/0013189X010001005.

Kools, M. and **L. Stoll** (2016), "What makes a school a learning organisation?" *OECD Education Working Papers*, No. 137, OECD Publishing, Paris, http://dx.doi.org/10.1787/5jlwm62b3bvh-en.

Leithwood, K. and **D. Jantzi** (2006), "Transformational school leadership for large-scale reform: Effects on students, teachers, and their classroom practices", *School Effectiveness and School Improvement*, Vol. 17/2, pp. 201-227, http://dx.doi.org/10.1080/09243450600565829.

Letarte, M.-J., S. Normandeau and **J. Allard** (2010), "Effectiveness of a parent training program 'Incredible Years' in a child protection service", *Child Abuse and Neglect*, Vol. 34/4, pp. 253-261, https://doi.org/10.1016/j.chiabu.2009.06.003.

Lomos, C., R.H. Hofman and **R.J. Bosker** (2011), "Professional communities and student achievement – a meta-analysis", *School Effectiveness and School Improvement*, Vol. 22/2, pp. 121-148, http://dx.doi.org/10.1080/09243453.2010.550467.

McElhaney, K.B., J. Antonishak and **J.P. Allen** (2008), "'They like me, they like me not': Popularity and adolescents' perceptions of acceptance predicting social functioning over time", *Child Development*, Vol. 79/3, pp. 720-731, http://dx.doi.org/10.1111/j.1467-8624.2008.01153.x.

Miretzky, D. (2004), "The communication requirements of democratic schools: Parent-teacher perspectives on their relationships", *Teachers College Record*, Vol. 106/4, pp. 814-851.

Mitchell-Copeland, J., S.A. Denham and **E.K. DeMulder** (1997), "Q-sort assessment of child-teacher attachment relationships and social competence in the preschool", *Early Education and Development*, Vol. 8/1, pp. 27-39, http://dx.doi.org/10.1207/s15566935eed0801_3.

Moshman, D. and **M. Geil** (1998), "Collaborative reasoning: Evidence for collective rationality", *Thinking and Reasoning*, Vol. 4/3, pp. 231-248, http://dx.doi.org/10.1080/135467898394148.

OECD (2017), *PISA 2015 Results (Volume III): Students' Well-Being*, OECD Publishing, Paris, http://dx.doi.org/10.1787/9789264273856-en.

OECD (2016), *PISA 2015 Results (Volume II): Policies and Practices for Successful Schools*, OECD Publishing, Paris, http://dx.doi.org/10.1787/9789264267510-en.

OECD (2012), *Let's Read Them a Story! The Parent Factor in Education*, OECD Publishing, Paris, http://dx.doi.org/10.1787/9789264176232-en.

Olweus, D. (1994), "Bullying at school", in L.R. Huesmann (ed.), *Aggressive Behavior*, pp. 97-130, *The Plenum Series in Social/Clinical Psychology*, Springer, Boston, MA.

Pil, F.K. and **C. Leana** (2009), "Applying organizational research to public school reform: The effects of teacher human and social capital on student performance", *Academy of Management Journal*, Vol. 52/6, pp. 1101-1124, http://dx.doi/org/10.5465/AMJ.2009.47084647.

Pomerantz, E.M., E.A. Moorman and **S.D. Litwack** (2007), "The how, whom, and why of parents' involvement in children's academic lives: More is not always better", *Review of Educational Research*, Vol. 77/3, pp. 373-410, https://doi.org/10.3102/003465430305567.

Pont, B., D. Nusche and **H. Moorman** (2008), *Improving School Leadership, Volume 1: Policy and Practice*, OECD Publishing, Paris, http://dx.doi.org/10.1787/9789264044715-en.

Ricard, N.C. and **L.G. Pelletier** (2016), "Dropping out of high school: The role of parent and teacher self-determination support, reciprocal friendships and academic motivation", *Contemporary Educational Psychology*, Vols. 44-45, pp. 32-40, https://doi.org/10.1016/j.cedpsych.2015.12.003.

Ronfeldt, M. et al. (2015), "Teacher collaboration in instructional teams and student achievement", *American Educational Research Journal*, Vol. 52/3, pp. 475-514, https://doi.org/10.3102/0002831215585562.

Samaha, N.V. and **R. De Lisi** (2000), "Peer collaboration on a nonverbal reasoning task by urban, minority students", *The Journal of Experimental Education*, Vol. 69/1, pp. 5-21, http://dx.doi.org/10.1080/00220970009600646.

Sampson, R.J. and **W.B. Groves** (1989), "Community structure and crime: Testing social-disorganization theory", *American Journal of Sociology*, Vol. 94/4, pp. 774-802, https://doi.org/10.1086/229068.

Sánchez, B., Y. Colón and **P. Esparza** (2005), "The role of sense of school belonging and gender in the academic adjustment of Latino adolescents", *Journal of Youth and Adolescence*, Vol. 34/6, pp. 619-628, https://doi.org/10.1007/s10964-005-8950-4.

Sanders, M.G. (2003), "Community involvement in schools: From concept to practice", *Education and Urban Society*, Vol. 35/2, pp. 161-180, https://doi.org/10.1177/0013124502239390.

Sirvani, H. (2007), "The effect of teacher communication with parents on students' mathematics achievement", *American Secondary Education*, Vol. 36/1, pp. 31-46.

Skinner, E.A., J.R. Pitzer and **J.S. Steele** (2016), "Can student engagement serve as a motivational resource for academic coping, persistence, and learning during late elementary and early middle school?", *Developmental Psychology*, Vol. 52/12, pp. 2099-2117, http://dx.doi.org/10.1037/dev0000227.

Spann, S.J., F.W. Kohler and **D. Soenksen** (2003), "Examining parents' involvement in and perceptions of special education services: An interview with families in a parent support group", *Focus on Autism and Other Developmental Disabilities*, Vol. 18/4, pp. 228-237, https://doi.org/10.1177/10883576030180040401.

Vosler-Hunter, R.W. (1989), "Changing roles, changing relationships: Parent-professional collaboration on behalf of children with emotional disabilities", *Families as Allies Project*, Portland State University, Portland, OR.

Wahlstrom, K.L. and **K.S. Louis** (2008), "How teachers experience principal leadership: The roles of professional community, trust, efficacy, and shared responsibility", *Educational Administration Quarterly*, Vol. 44/4, pp. 458-495, https://doi.org/10.1177/0013161X08321502.

Westergard, E. (2013), "Teacher competencies and parental cooperation", *International Journal about Parents in Education*, Vol. 7/2, pp. 91-99.

Woods, S. and **D. Wolke** (2004), "Direct and relational bullying among primary school children and academic achievement", *Journal of School Psychology*, Vol. 42/2, pp. 135-155, https://doi.org/10.1016/j.jsp.2003.12.002.

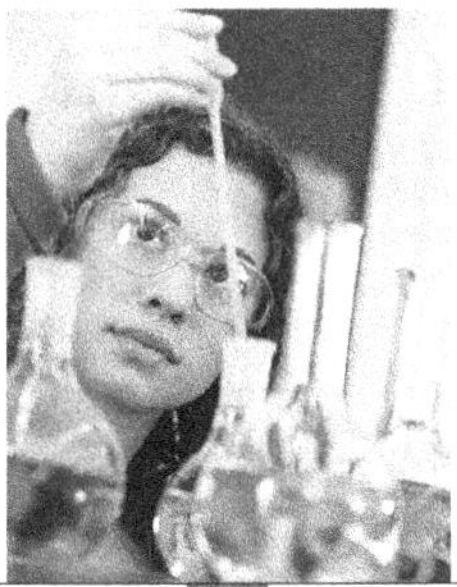

8

What the PISA 2015 results on collaborative problem solving imply for policy

Most people will have to work together with others throughout their life, in both professional and personal capacities. Addressing this need, PISA has developed an assessment that measures students' ability to solve problems collaboratively. Based on this assessment, this chapter presents some policy recommendations that might lead to improved skills in and attitudes towards collaboration.

For over 15 years, PISA has assessed 15-year-old students' literacy in science, reading and mathematics. Proficiency in these subjects is vital for tomorrow's adults. They will need to draw logical conclusions from a wide range of evidence, as scientists do; they will have to understand a variety of written material and express themselves in a clear and coherent way; and they will need to be able to find and interpret patterns and relationships in data.

But more is needed. A variety of "21st-century skills" have been identified as being crucial for the youth of today to succeed in tomorrow's world, a world that is more interconnected, digital and unpredictable than it has ever been. Although there is no commonly accepted consensus as to what these "21st-century skills" are, the list generally includes the capacity to solve problems; to think creatively and critically; and to interact productively with others.

Most people will have to work together with others frequently throughout their life, whether as members of the same team, working for supervisors, supervising others, or in their personal relationships with family and friends. The willingness and ability to understand others' points of view, to negotiate between different and perhaps conflicting objectives, and to maintain and monitor team cohesion and morale will facilitate the productivity and effectiveness of collaborative efforts and also lead to stronger interpersonal relationships.

To address this, PISA developed an assessment to measure students' ability to solve problems collaboratively, building on the assessment of individual problem-solving abilities in 2012. As an internationally-comparable assessment, PISA allows education systems to benchmark themselves and see how their students fare as collaborative team players in an increasingly interconnected world. Data from PISA can also be used to identify common attributes among students with the strongest collaboration skills, and to target at-risk populations who might need to improve their collaboration skills. This chapter presents some of the policy implications that can be gleaned from results of the PISA 2015 collaborative problem-solving assessment.

COLLABORATIVE PROBLEM SOLVING IS NOT SCIENCE, READING OR MATHEMATICS

At first glance, the results from the collaborative problem-solving assessment look broadly similar to results from the PISA assessments in the three core subjects of science, reading and mathematics. The same education systems – Canada, Estonia, Finland, Hong Kong (China), Japan, Korea, Macao (China), New Zealand and Singapore – perform at or near the top in all four assessments.

However, the results show that the PISA collaborative problem-solving assessment is clearly distinct from the assessments of the three core subjects. A student's performance in science, reading and mathematics explains less than two thirds of his or her performance in collaborative problem solving, meaning that there is still more than one third of a student's performance in collaborative problem solving that is unique to this domain. The relationship between collaborative problem-solving skills and science, reading and mathematics performance is also much weaker than the relationship between science, reading and mathematics performance themselves. In particular, in countries such as Costa Rica, Iceland, Luxembourg and the United States, students can solve problems in a collaborative fashion better than would be expected given their performance in the three core PISA subjects.

Students in many all-around top-performing countries and economies, such as Australia, Japan, Korea, New Zealand and Singapore, are even better at collaborating than expected. However, other education systems, including Beijing-Shanghai-Jiangsu-Guangdong (China) (hereafter "B-S-J-G [China]"), Croatia, Lithuania and the Russian Federation (hereafter "Russia"), perform below what would be expected given their performance in science, reading and mathematics.

PISA 2015 also asked students about their attitudes towards collaboration, particularly their thoughts about their relationships with others and about working in teams. More positive attitudes towards collaboration are found to be positively associated with students' collaboration-specific skills.

Collaborative problem solving is also distinct from individual problem solving. The correlation between education systems' performance in the 2012 individual problem-solving and 2015 collaborative problem-solving assessments is weak, as only 23% of variation in countries' and economies' performance in the 2015 collaborative problem-solving assessment is accounted for by variations in their 2012 individual problem-solving scores. Furthermore, no correlation is observed between performance in individual and collaborative problem solving after accounting for performance in science, reading and mathematics. While the 2015 collaborative problem-solving assessment was developed by building upon the framework of the 2012 individual problem-solving assessment, the skills related to individual problem solving in the more recent assessment were intentionally kept at a low or medium level, thereby further isolating skills related purely to collaboration.

BUILD INSTRUCTIONAL PRACTICE FOR COLLABORATIVE PROBLEM SOLVING

While each school has its share of stronger and weaker students, PISA assessments in science, reading and mathematics have consistently shown that education systems also have stronger and weaker schools. Similar results are observed for the collaborative problem-solving assessment. However, there is less inter-school variation in collaborative problem solving. Between-school differences account for less than 25% of total performance differences in collaborative problem solving, while they account for 30% of total performance differences in science.

Between-school differences in collaborative problem solving are further reduced – by 86% – when cognitive skills, as measured by science, reading and mathematics performance, are accounted for. Only 9% of the differences between students' "purely" collaborative problem-solving skills are observed between schools, while the remainder is observed between students who attend the same school. Whether this means that schools are more equitable in developing students' collaborative skills, or whether collaborative skills are mainly developed outside schools, cannot be discerned from PISA data.

Education systems can foster collaboration skills and attitudes in existing subjects or courses, or through new programmes, as Singapore did with its *Project Work* programme. The OECD is collecting information on how collaboration and co-operation are incorporated into school curricula through its *Education 2030* project.

MANY SCHOOL SUBJECTS PROVIDE OPPORTUNITIES TO CULTIVATE SKILLS IN AND ATTITUDES TOWARDS COLLABORATION

Collaboration skills can be taught and practiced in cognitive subjects, such as science, reading and mathematics: students can work and present in groups and can help each other learn the subject. However, much of the effort to master the material taught is typically made individually by the student. In contrast, collaboration is vital to many activities in physical education class, most obviously team sports, which require individuals to work together in groups to achieve a common goal.

However, there is variation across countries in what is emphasised in physical education class. Some countries, including Finland and Japan, emphasise collaboration instead of competition in physical education class (European Commission/EACEA/Eurydice, 2013; Nakai and Metzler, 2005). Other countries, such as Germany, Hungary, Latvia and the United Kingdom, place greater emphasis on competition and attaining one's personal best (European Commission/EACEA/Eurydice, 2013). For example, in Germany, the *Bundesjugendspiele* or Federal Youth Games are an annual individual sports competition in athletics, gymnastics, and swimming that is obligatory for all students between Years 1 and 10 (BMFSF-J, 2017).

Unfortunately, cross-sectional data from PISA cannot indicate which approach is more effective at developing collaboration skills.

What the data do show, though, is that students who attend physical education class once or twice per week score highest in collaborative problem solving. After accounting for performance in the three core PISA subjects, students who attend between zero and three days of physical education class per week score similarly, and score above students who attend four or more days per week.

ENCOURAGE STUDENTS TO MINGLE WITH OTHERS FROM DIFFERENT BACKGROUNDS

Previous PISA volumes have consistently documented that socio-economically advantaged students perform better in science, reading and mathematics than disadvantaged students. This is also true for performance in collaborative problem solving.

However, this relationship with socio-economic status is not consistently observed across education systems when looking solely at the collaborative aspect of students' collaborative problem-solving scores (i.e. once performance in science, reading and mathematics is accounted for). If anything, students of lower socio-economic status often do better than students of higher socio-economic status relative to their performance in the three core PISA subjects – although this relationship is highly variable across education systems.

In other words, students who are materially disadvantaged seem less disadvantaged when it comes to being able to work productively with others. Disadvantaged students are more likely to value teamwork, perhaps because they value more the extra boost that teamwork can bring to their own performance. Likewise, there are no large differences between the collaborative skills of immigrant and non-immigrant students.

One of the demographic factors related to the collaborative aspect of performance in this assessment is the concentration of immigrant students in a student's school. Non-immigrant students tend to perform better in the collaboration-specific aspects of the assessment when they attend schools with a larger proportion of immigrant students. This result cannot be generalised to socio-economic diversity within schools, however. Education systems should investigate whether, in their own context, diversity and students' contact with those who are different from them and who may hold different points of view can aid in developing collaboration skills.

BOYS NEED HELP IN DEVELOPING STRONGER COLLABORATION SKILLS, BUT DON'T FORGET GIRLS

Girls outperform boys in collaborative problem solving in every education system, both before and after accounting for performance in science, reading and mathematics. The relative size of the gender gap in collaborative problem-solving performance is even larger than it is in reading, where girls also outperform boys in every education system. This gender gap contrasts with that in the PISA 2012 individual problem-solving assessment, where boys outperform girls.

Hence, boys need particular support in enhancing their ability to solve problems collaboratively. This might come through developing boys' attitudes towards collaboration. Girls are found to hold more positive attitudes towards relationships, meaning that they tend to be interested in others' opinions and want others to succeed. Boys, on the other hand, are found to hold more positive attitudes towards teamwork: they see the instrumental benefits of teamwork and how collaboration can help them work more effectively and efficiently.

As positive attitudes towards collaboration – whether towards relationships or towards teamwork – are positively correlated with the collaboration-related component of performance in this assessment, education systems should look into fostering boys' appreciation of others, and their interpersonal friendships and relationships. In order to work effectively in a team and solve problems or achieve something in a collaborative fashion, boys must be able to listen to others and take their viewpoints into account. Only in this manner can teams make full use of the range of perspectives and experiences that team members offer.

However, although girls outperform boys, on average, there is a large overlap in their score distribution, with many girls also attaining only low levels of proficiency in collaborative problem solving. Schools should support both boys and girls who have trouble in forming healthy, positive and mutually supportive relationships with others.

HOW CAN STUDENTS DEVELOP STRONG RELATIONSHIPS? ON LINE, AT HOME, BUT NOT THROUGH VIDEO GAMES

One way in which children develop relationships is on line, through Internet chat rooms or social media. In the past, students would meet friends face-to-face during the lunch break or after school, or would call them and talk on the phone from home. Today, students use Facebook, WeChat, WhatsApp, Twitter, Instagram, Tumblr, and other applications to get in immediate touch with their friends. If their friends are not on line, they can leave messages that their friends can read whenever they log on again.

This might seem like a superficial method of developing relationships, one that goes against the received wisdom that it is the time spent together that forges friendships. However, in an increasingly virtual world, perhaps today's children are inadvertently training themselves to become better collaborative problem solvers simply by going on line.

Another way through which students can develop stronger relationships without leaving their own home is to develop better relationships with those at home. Many students do chores or take care of a family member. These tasks might allow them to develop a greater sense of responsibility towards others, as their family members count on them to contribute to the household. Spending time with the family members that one is caring for also gives students an opportunity to develop relationships with others – much like the concept of "opportunity to learn" in the core PISA subjects.

It is difficult to see how students develop stronger relationships when playing video games. While video games use the same virtual method of interaction as the Internet, chat rooms and social networks, students who play video games often do so under assumed names and characters, not as their true personalities. These relationships might therefore be less consequential; students have less of an incentive to maintain these relationships. If one of these relationships breaks down, there are always other avatars in this online world with whom to interact.

Of course, the type of video game that students play might be particularly important. First-person shooter games (such as *Counter-Strike*) have a goal, or perhaps a problem that players must solve, but do not give players the time to develop deeper relationships with each other. Social simulation games (such as *The Sims* series) often do not have a goal, but focus on the relationships between players' avatars.

In any case, the evidence from PISA show that students who play video games perform worse in the collaborative elements of the assessment than students who do not, something that is seen in almost every participating education system. In contrast, students who use the Internet, chat or social networks outside of school are better (or at least just as good) collaborators than students who do not. This is observed repeatedly across education systems, except in the United States. Finally, while students who use the Internet, chat or social networks, play video games, or work in the household or take care of family members all value teamwork more than students who do not, students who use these online forms of communication or who help out at home are also more likely to value relationships, while students who play video games are less likely to value relationships.

Participation in these activities is typically beyond the reach of the school curriculum. Each of these activities also comes with consequences not necessarily related to collaboration. For example, the proliferation of online networks means that students can continue to be bullied while at home, while in the past, bullying mostly ended once students left school grounds. Policy makers should consider the benefits and drawbacks of each of these activities (using the Internet, chat rooms and social networks; working in the household and taking care of family members; playing video games) and what they mean for children's collaboration skills and their ability to use these skills to solve problems.

PROMOTE POSITIVE RELATIONSHIPS AT SCHOOL

Previous OECD reports indicate that a socially connected school, in which all stakeholders know and respect each other, can be beneficial to the academic performance and well-being of students (OECD, 2017; OECD, 2016). Similarly, this report shows that fostering positive relationships at school can benefit students' collaborative problem-solving skills and their attitudes towards collaboration, especially when these relationships involve students directly. Students who establish more positive relationships with peers, teachers and parents tend to score higher in collaborative problem solving, and so do other students in the school. Even after accounting for their academic performance in reading, mathematics and science, students still perform higher in collaborative problem solving when more of their peers agreed that other students seem to like them, disagreed that they feel lonely at school, and reported that they never, or almost never, had been threatened or attacked by other students or insulted by teachers.

The good news is that most students, teachers and principals report a positive learning environment in their schools. However, too many students report that they feel isolated at school, are bullied repeatedly or are treated unfairly by teachers. While ensuring that all students are happy, safe and socially integrated at school is easier said than done, schools can start by identifying students who are socially isolated, organising activities to foster constructive relationships and school attachment, providing teacher training on classroom management, and adopting a whole-school approach to prevent and address school bullying (Borba, 2016). For their part, parents should provide academic and emotional support to their children, and talk regularly with them.

References

BMFSF-J (2017), *Bundesjugendspiele: Handbuch (Wettkampf, Wettbewerb, Mehrkampf)*, Bundesministerium für Familie, Senioren, Frauen und Jugend, Berlin, www.bundesjugendspiele.de/downloads/handbuch/handbuch_komplett_15_07_2017.pdf.

Borba, M. (2016), *The 6Rs of Bullying Prevention: Best Proven Practices to Combat Cruelty and Build Respect*, Free Spirit Publishing, Minneapolis, MN.

European Commission/EACEA/Eurydice (2013), *Physical Education and Sport at School in Europe*, Publications Office of the European Union, Luxembourg.

Nakai, T. and **M.W. Metzler** (2005), "Standards and practice for K-12 physical education in Japan", *Journal of Physical Education, Recreation & Dance*, Vol. 76/7, pp.17-22, http://dx.doi.org/10.1080/07303084.2005.10609307.

OECD (2017), *PISA 2015 Results (Volume III): Students' Well-Being*, OECD Publishing, Paris, http://dx.doi.org/10.1787/9789264273856-en.

OECD (2016), *PISA 2015 Results (Volume II): Policies and Practices for Successful Schools*, OECD Publishing, Paris, http://dx.doi.org/10.1787/9789264267510-en.

Annex A

PISA 2015 TECHNICAL BACKGROUND

All tables in Annex A are available on line

Note regarding B-S-J-G (China)

B-S-J-G (China) refers to the four PISA participating Chinese provinces of Beijing, Shanghai, Jiangsu, Guangdong.

Note regarding CABA (Argentina)

CABA (Argentina) refers to the Ciudad Autónoma de Buenos Aires, Argentina.

Note regarding FYROM

FYROM refers to the Former Yugoslav Republic of Macedonia.

Notes regarding Cyprus

Note by Turkey: The information in this document with reference to "Cyprus" relates to the southern part of the Island. There is no single authority representing both Turkish and Greek Cypriot people on the Island. Turkey recognises the Turkish Republic of Northern Cyprus (TRNC). Until a lasting and equitable solution is found within the context of the United Nations, Turkey shall preserve its position concerning the "Cyprus issue".

Note by all the European Union Member States of the OECD and the European Union: The Republic of Cyprus is recognised by all members of the United Nations with the exception of Turkey. The information in this document relates to the area under the effective control of the Government of the Republic of Cyprus.

A note regarding Israel

The statistical data for Israel are supplied by and under the responsibility of the relevant Israeli authorities. The use of such data by the OECD is without prejudice to the status of the Golan Heights, East Jerusalem and Israeli settlements in the West Bank under the terms of international law.

ANNEX A1

CONSTRUCTION OF INDICES AND MISSING OBSERVATIONS

Explanation of the indices

This section explains the indices derived from the PISA 2015 student, school, and information and communications technology (ICT) questionnaires used in this volume.

Several PISA measures reflect indices that summarise responses from students, their parents, teachers or school representatives (typically principals) to a series of related questions. The questions were selected from a larger pool of questions on the basis of theoretical considerations and previous research. The *PISA 2015 Assessment and Analytical Framework* (OECD, 2017a) provides an in-depth description of this conceptual framework. Structural equation modelling was used to confirm the theoretically expected behaviour of most indices and to validate their comparability across countries. For this purpose, a model was estimated separately for each country and collectively for all OECD countries. For a detailed description of other PISA indices and details on the methods, see the *PISA 2015 Technical Report* (OECD, 2017b).

There are two types of indices used in this volume: simple indices and scale indices.

Simple indices are variables that are constructed through the arithmetic transformation or recoding of one or more items, in exactly the same way across assessments. Here, item responses are used to calculate meaningful variables, such as the recoding of the four-digit ISCO-08 codes into "Highest parents' socio-economic index (HISEI)" or, teacher-student ratio based on information from the school questionnaire.

Scale indices are variables constructed through the scaling of multiple items. Unless otherwise indicated, the index was scaled using a two-parameter item response model (a generalised partial credit model was used in the case of items with more than two categories) and values of the index correspond to Warm likelihood estimates (WLE) (Warm, 1985). For details on how each scale index was constructed, see the *PISA 2015 Technical Report* (OECD, 2017b). In general, the scaling was done in three stages:

1. The item parameters were estimated from equally-weighted samples of students from all countries and economies; only cases with a minimum number of three valid responses to items that are part of the index were included.
2. The estimates were computed for all students and all schools by anchoring the item parameters obtained in the preceding step.
3. The Warm likelihood estimates were then standardised so that the mean of the index value for the OECD student population was zero and the standard deviation was one, countries being given equal weight in the standardisation process.

Sequential codes were assigned to the different response categories of the questions in the sequence in which the latter appeared in the student, school or parent questionnaires. Where indicated in this section, these codes were inverted for the purpose of constructing indices or scales. Negative values for an index do not necessarily imply that students responded negatively to the underlying questions. A negative value merely indicates that the respondents answered less positively than all respondents did, on average across OECD countries. Likewise, a positive value on an index indicates that the respondents answered more favourably, or more positively, than respondents did, on average in OECD countries. Terms enclosed in brackets < > in the following descriptions were replaced in the national versions of the student, school and parent questionnaires by the appropriate national equivalent. For example, the term <qualification at ISCED level 5A> was translated in the United States into "Bachelor's degree, post-graduate certificate program, Master's degree program or first professional degree program". Similarly the term <classes in the language of assessment> in Luxembourg was translated into "German classes" or "French classes" depending on whether students received the German or French version of the assessment instruments.

In addition to the simple and scaled indices described in this annex, there are a number of variables from the questionnaires that were used in this volume and correspond to single items not used to construct indices. These non-recoded variables have prefix of "ST" for items in the student questionnaire, "SC" for items in the school questionnaire, "PA" for items from the parent questionnaire, "IC" for items from the ICT questionnaire, and "TC" for items from the teacher questionnaire. All the context questionnaires as well as the PISA international database, including all variables, are available through www.oecd.org/pisa.

Student-level simple indices

Student age

The age of a student (AGE) was calculated as the difference between the year and month of testing and the year and month of a student's birth. Data on students' age were obtained from both the questionnaire (ST003) and student tracking forms. If the month of testing was not known for a particular student, the median month for that country was used in the calculation.

Immigration background

The PISA database contains three country-specific variables relating to the country of birth of the student, their mother and their father (COBN_S, COBN_M, and COBN_F). The items ST019Q01TA, ST019Q01TB and ST019Q01TC were recoded into the following categories: (1) country of birth is the same as country of assessment and (2) other. The index of immigrant background (IMMIG) was calculated from these variables with the following categories: (0) non-immigrant students (those students who had at least one parent born in the country), and (1) first- and second-generation immigrant students (those born outside the country of assessment and whose parent(s) were also born in another country, and those born in the country of assessment but whose parent(s) were born in another country). Students with missing responses for either the student or for both parents were assigned missing values for this variable.

Language spoken at home

Students indicated what language they usually speak at home (ST022), and the database includes a derived variable (LANGN) containing a country-specific code for each language. In addition, an internationally comparable variable was derived from this information with the following categories: (1) language at home is the same as the language of assessment for that student and (2) language at home is another language.

Attendance at pre-primary school

Students indicated the age at which they began pre-primary school (ISCED 0) in the student questionnaire (ST125). Students who did not remember whether they attended pre-primary school were not considered in analyses comparing students who attended and who did not attend pre-primary school. This definition differs slightly from the definition of the years of pre-primary school attendance used in *PISA 2015 Results (Volume II): Policies and Practices for Successful Schools* (OECD, 2016), which defined pre-primary school attendance through a derived variable that also relied on the age at which students began primary school (ISCED 1) (ST126).

Learning time

Learning time in total (TMINS) was computed using information about the average minutes in a <class period> (ST061) and information about the number of class periods per week attended in total (ST060). For convenience purposes, the information on learning time has been transformed into hours.

Index of student interaction in science class

The index of student interaction in science class was constructed from students' responses to question (ST098) on how often various communication-intensive activities take place in science class: "Students are given opportunities to explain their ideas"; "Students spend time in the laboratory doing practical experiments"; "Students are required to argue about science questions"; and "There is a class debate about investigations". Students can respond that these events take place "in all lessons", "in most lessons", "in some lessons", or "never or hardly ever". The index of student interaction in science class is calculated as the number of these activities that students say take place "in all lessons" or "in most lessons", and can vary from 0 to 4. Higher values indicate that students take part in communication- and interaction-intensive activities more often in science class.

Student-level scale indices

Sense of belonging

The index of sense of belonging (BELONG) was constructed from students' responses to a trend question about their sense of belonging at school. Students reported, on a four-point Likert scale with the response categories "strongly agree", "agree", "disagree", and "strongly disagree", their agreement with the following statements (ST034): "I feel like an outsider (or left out of things) at school"; "I make friends easily at school"; "I feel like I belong at school"; "I feel awkward and out of place in my school"; "Other students seem to like me"; and "I feel lonely at school". The answers to three items were reversed-coded so that higher values in the index indicate a greater sense of belonging.

Life satisfaction

Students' life satisfaction (ST016) level was based on their response to the question "Overall, how satisfied are you with your life as a whole these days". Their responses were limited to integers ranging from 0 (not at all satisfied) to 10 (completely satisfied). Students taking the computer-based questionnaire were asked to move the slider to the appropriate number (closer to 0 or to 10) and thus students could not respond below 0 or above 10.

Achievement motivation

The index of achievement motivation (MOTIVAT) was constructed from students' responses to a new question developed for PISA 2015 (ST119). Students reported, on a four-point Likert scale with the answering categories "strongly disagree", "disagree", "agree", and "strongly agree", their agreement with the following statements: "I want top grades in most or all of my courses"; "I want to be able to select from among the best opportunities available when I graduate"; "I want to be the best, whatever I do"; "I see myself as an ambitious person"; and "I want to be one of the best students in my class". Higher values indicate that students have greater achievement motivation.

Schoolwork-related anxiety

The index of schoolwork-related anxiety (ANXTEST) was constructed from student responses to question (ST118) over the extent to which they strongly agreed, agreed, disagreed or strongly disagreed with the following statements when asked to think about him or herself: "I often worry that it will be difficult for me taking a test"; "I worry that I will get poor <grades> at school";

"Even if I am well prepared for a test I feel very anxious"; "I get very tense when I study"; and "I get nervous when I don't know how to solve a task at school". Higher values indicate that students have more schoolwork-related anxiety.

Exposure to bullying

The index of bullying (BEINGBULLIED) was constructed from students' reports on how often ("never or almost never"; "a few times a year"; "a few times a month"; "once a week or more") the following happened (ST038): "Other students left me out of things on purpose"; "Other students made fun of me"; "I was threatened by other students"; "Other students took away or destroyed things that belonged to me"; "I got hit or pushed around by other students"; and "Other students spread nasty rumours about me". Higher values indicate that students are exposed to bullying more often.

Index of valuing relationships

The index of valuing relationships (COOPERATE) was constructed from students' responses to question (ST082) over the extent to which they strongly agreed, agreed, disagreed or strongly disagreed with the following statements: "I am a good listener"; "I enjoy seeing my classmates be successful"; "I take into account what others are interested in"; and "I enjoy considering different perspectives". Higher values indicate that students responded more affirmatively to these statements.

Index of valuing teamwork

The index of valuing teamwork (CPSVALUE) was constructed from students' responses to question (ST082) over the extent to which they strongly agreed, agreed, disagreed or strongly disagreed with the following statements: "I prefer working as part of a team to working alone"; "I find that teams make better decisions than individuals"; "I find that teamwork raises my own efficiency"; and "I enjoy co-operating with peers". Higher values indicate that students responded more affirmatively to these statements.

Index of ICT use at school

The index of ICT (information and communications technology) use at school (USESCH) was constructed using students' responses to question (IC011) regarding how often they use digital devices for the following activities: "<chatting online> at school"; "using email at school"; "browsing the Internet for schoolwork"; "downloading, uploading or browsing material from the school's website (e.g. <Intranet>)"; "posting [their] work on the school's website"; "playing simulations at school"; "practicing and drilling, such as for foreign language learning or mathematics"; "doing homework on a school computer"; and "using school computers for group work and communication with other students". Students could respond that they performed these activities "never or hardly ever", "once or twice a month", "once or twice a week", "almost every day" or "every day". Higher values indicate that students use ICT more often at school.

Index of students' perceived ICT competence

The index of students' perceived ICT competence (COMPICT) was constructed using students' responses to question (IC014) regarding their comfort with various digital devices. They were asked to state whether they "strongly agree", "agree", "disagree", or "strongly disagree" with the following statements: "I feel comfortable using digital devices that I am less familiar with"; "If my friends and relatives want to buy new digital devices or applications, I can give them advice"; "I feel comfortable using my digital devices at home"; "When I come across problems with digital devices, I think I can solve them"; "If my friends and relatives have a problem with digital devices, I can help them". Higher values indicate that students feel more comfortable and competent with digital devices and ICT.

Scaling of indices related to the PISA index of economic, social and cultural status

The PISA index of economic, social and cultural status (ESCS) was derived, as in previous cycles, from three variables related to family background: highest parental education (PARED), highest parental occupation (HISEI), and home possessions (HOMEPOS) including books in the home. PARED and HISEI are simple indices, described above. HOMEPOS is a proxy measure for family wealth.

Household possessions

In PISA 2015, students reported the availability of 16 household items at home (ST011) including three country-specific household items that were seen as appropriate measures of family wealth within the country's context. In addition, students reported the amount of possessions and books at home (ST012, ST013).

HOMEPOS is a summary index of all household items and possessions (ST011, ST012 and ST013). The home possessions scale for PISA 2015 was computed differently than in the previous cycles, to align the IRT model to the one used for all cognitive and non-cognitive scales. Categories for the number of books in the home are unchanged in PISA 2015. The items in ST011 (1 = "yes", 2 = "no") were reverse-coded so that a higher level indicates the presence of the indicator.

Computation of ESCS

For the purpose of computing the PISA index of economic, social and cultural status (ESCS), values for students with missing PARED, HISEI or HOMEPOS were imputed with predicted values plus a random component based on a regression on the other two variables. If there were missing data on more than one of the three variables, ESCS was not computed and a missing value was assigned for ESCS.

The PISA index of economic, social and cultural status was derived from a principal component analysis of standardised variables (each variable has an OECD mean of zero and a standard deviation of one), taking the factor scores for the first

principal component as measures of the PISA index of economic, social and cultural status. All countries and economies (both OECD and partner countries/economies) contributed equally to the principal component analysis, while in previous cycles, the principal component analysis was based on OECD countries only. However, for the purpose of reporting, the ESCS scale has been transformed with zero being the score of an average OECD student and one being the standard deviation across equally weighted OECD countries.

Principal component analysis was also performed for each participating country or economy separately, to determine to what extent the components of the index operate in similar ways across countries and economies.

School-level simple indices

School type

Schools are classified as either public or private according to whether a private entity or a public agency has the ultimate power for decision making concerning its affairs (SC013). As in previous PISA surveys, the index on school type (SCHLTYPE) has three categories, based on two questions: SC013 which asks if the school is a public or a private school, and SC016 which asks about the sources of funding. This index was calculated in 2015 and in all previous cycles.

Class size and student-teacher ratio

The average class size (CLSIZE) is derived from one of nine possible categories in question SC003, ranging from "15 students or fewer" to "more than 50 students".

The student-teacher ratio (STRATIO) was obtained by dividing the number of enrolled students (SC002) by the total number of teachers (TOTAT).

Group-based extracurricular activities at school

School principals were asked to report what extracurricular activities their schools offered to 15-year old students (SC053). The index of group-based extracurricular activities at school was computed as the total number of the following activities that occurred at school: band, orchestra or choir; a school play or school musical; a school yearbook, newspaper or magazine; volunteering or service activities; and sports teams/activities. The index varied from 0 to 5, with each activity weighted equally.

Proportion of missing observations for variables used in this volume

Unless otherwise indicated, no adjustment is made for non-response to questionnaires in analyses included in this volume. The reported percentages and estimates based on indices refer to the proportion of the sample with valid responses to the corresponding questionnaire items. Table A1.1, available on line, reports the proportion of the sample covered by analyses based on the additional background questionnaire variables used in this volume. Similar tables are available in Annex A1 of PISA Volumes I and III for variables already used in analyses in earlier volumes. Where this proportion shows large variation across countries/economies or across time, caution is required when comparing results on these dimensions.

Tables available online

Table A1.1 Weighted share of responding students covered by analyses of collaborative problem-solving performance based on PISA questionnaires (http://dx.doi.org/10.1787/888933623761)

See also Table A1.3 from PISA Volume I for data on the weighted share of responding students covered by analyses based on the student, school and parent questionnaires: http://dx.doi.org/10.1787/888933433112.

In addition, see the following tables from PISA Volume III for data on the weighted share of responding students covered by additional analyses based on the student, educational career and parent questionnaires:

- Table A1.8a Weighted share of responding students covered by analyses based on the student and educational career questionnaires: http://dx.doi.org/10.1787/888933473606
- Table A1.8c Weighted share of responding students covered by analyses based on the parent questionnaire: http://dx.doi.org/10.1787/888933473622

References

OECD (2017a), *PISA 2015 Assessment and Analytical Framework: Science, Reading, Mathematic, Financial Literacy and Collaborative Problem Solving*, OECD Publishing, Paris, http://dx.doi.org/10.1787/9789264281820-en.

OECD (2017b), *PISA 2015 Technical Report,* OECD Publishing, Paris.

OECD (2016), *PISA 2015 Results (Volume II): Policies and Practices for Successful Schools,* OECD Publishing, Paris, http://dx.doi.org/10.1787/9789264267510-en.

Warm, T.A. (1985), "Weighted Maximum Likelihood Estimation of Ability in Item Response Theory with Tests of Finite Length", Technical Report CGI-TR-85-08, U.S. Coast Guard Institute, Oklahoma City.

ANNEX A2

THE PISA TARGET POPULATION, THE PISA SAMPLES AND THE DEFINITION OF SCHOOLS

Definition of the PISA target population

PISA 2015 provides an assessment of the cumulative outcomes of education and learning at a point at which most young adults are still enrolled in initial education.

A major challenge for an international survey is to ensure that international comparability of national target populations is guaranteed.

Differences between countries in the nature and extent of pre-primary education and care, the age of entry into formal schooling and the institutional structure of education systems do not allow for a definition of internationally comparable grade levels. Consequently, international comparisons of performance in education typically define their populations with reference to a target age group. Some previous international assessments have defined their target population on the basis of the grade level that provides maximum coverage of a particular age cohort. A disadvantage of this approach is that slight variations in the age distribution of students across grade levels often lead to the selection of different target grades in different countries, or between education systems within countries, raising serious questions about the comparability of results across, and at times within, countries. In addition, because not all students of the desired age are usually represented in grade-based samples, there may be a more serious potential bias in the results if the unrepresented students are typically enrolled in the next higher grade in some countries and the next lower grade in others. This would exclude students with potentially higher levels of performance in the former countries and students with potentially lower levels of performance in the latter.

In order to address this problem, PISA uses an age-based definition for its target population, i.e. a definition that is not tied to the institutional structures of national education systems. PISA assesses students who were aged between 15 years and 3 (complete) months and 16 years and 2 (complete) months at the beginning of the assessment period, plus or minus a 1-month allowable variation, and who were enrolled in an educational institution with grade 7 or higher, regardless of the grade level or type of institution in which they were enrolled, and regardless of whether they were in full-time or part-time education. Educational institutions are generally referred to as schools in this publication, although some educational institutions (in particular, some types of vocational education establishments) may not be termed schools in certain countries. As expected from this definition, the average age of students across OECD countries was 15 years and 9 months. The range in country means was 2 months and 18 days (0.20 years), from the minimum country mean of 15 years and 8 months to the maximum country mean of 15 years and 10 months.

Given this definition of population, PISA makes statements about the knowledge and skills of a group of individuals who were born within a comparable reference period, but who may have undergone different educational experiences both in and outside school. In PISA, these knowledge and skills are referred to as the outcomes of education at an age that is common across countries. Depending on countries' policies on school entry, selection and promotion, these students may be distributed over a narrower or a wider range of grades across different education systems, tracks or streams. It is important to consider these differences when comparing PISA results across countries, as observed differences between students at age 15 may no longer appear later on as/if students' educational experiences converge over time.

If a country's scores in science, reading or mathematics are significantly higher than those in another country, it cannot automatically be inferred that the schools or particular parts of the education system in the first country are more effective than those in the second. However, one can legitimately conclude that the cumulative impact of learning experiences in the first country, starting in early childhood and up to the age of 15, and encompassing experiences in school, home and beyond, have resulted in higher outcomes in the literacy in the domains that PISA measures.

The PISA target population does not include residents attending schools in a foreign country. It does, however, include foreign nationals attending schools in the country of assessment.

To accommodate countries that requested grade-based results for the purpose of national analyses, PISA 2015 provided a sampling option to supplement age-based sampling with grade-based sampling.

Population coverage

All countries and economies attempted to maximise the coverage of 15-year-olds enrolled in education in their national samples, including students enrolled in special-education institutions. As a result, PISA 2015 reached standards of population coverage that are unprecedented in international surveys of this kind.

The sampling standards used in PISA permitted countries to exclude up to a total of 5% of the relevant population either by excluding schools or by excluding students within schools. All but 12 countries – the United Kingdom (8.22%), Luxembourg (8.16%), Canada (7.49%), Norway (6.75%), New Zealand (6.54%), Sweden (5.71%), Estonia (5.52%), Australia (5.31%),

Montenegro (5.17%), Lithuania (5.12%), Latvia (5.07%), and Denmark (5.04%) – achieved this standard, and in 29 countries and economies, the overall exclusion rate was less than 2%. When language exclusions were accounted for (i.e. removed from the overall exclusion rate), Denmark, Latvia, New Zealand and Sweden no longer had an exclusion rate greater than 5%. For details, see www.oecd.org/pisa.

Exclusions within the above limits include:

- At the school level: schools that were geographically inaccessible or where the administration of the PISA assessment was not considered feasible; and schools that provided teaching only for students in the categories defined under "within-school exclusions", such as schools for the blind. The percentage of 15-year-olds enrolled in such schools had to be less than 2.5% of the nationally desired target population (0.5% maximum for the former group and 2% maximum for the latter group). The magnitude, nature and justification of school-level exclusions are documented in the *PISA 2015 Technical Report* (OECD, 2017).
- At the student level: students with an intellectual disability; students with a functional disability; students with limited assessment language proficiency; other (a category defined by the national centres and approved by the international centre); and students taught in a language of instruction for the main domain for which no materials were available. Students could not be excluded solely because of low proficiency or common disciplinary problems. The percentage of 15-year-olds excluded within schools had to be less than 2.5% of the nationally desired target population.

Table A2.1 describes the target population of the countries participating in PISA 2015. Further information on the target population and the implementation of PISA sampling standards can be found in the *PISA 2015 Technical Report* (OECD, 2017).

- **Column 1** shows the total number of 15-year-olds according to the most recent available information, which in most countries means the year 2014 as the year before the assessment.
- **Column 2** shows the number of 15-year-olds enrolled in schools in grade 7 or above (as defined above), which is referred to as the "eligible population".
- **Column 3** shows the national desired target population. Countries were allowed to exclude up to 0.5% of students a priori from the eligible population, essentially for practical reasons. The following a priori exclusions exceed this limit but were agreed with the PISA Consortium: Belgium excluded 0.21% of its population for a particular type of student educated while working; Canada excluded 1.22% of its population from Territories and Aboriginal reserves; Chile excluded 0.04% of its students who live in Easter Island, Juan Fernandez Archipelago and Antarctica; and the United Arab Emirates excluded 0.04% of its students who had no information available. The adjudicated region of Massachusetts in the United States excluded 13.11% of its students, and North Carolina excluded 5.64% of its students. For these two regions, the desired target populations cover 15-year-old students in grade 7 or above in public schools only. The students excluded from the desired population are private school students.
- **Column 4** shows the number of students enrolled in schools that were excluded from the national desired target population, either from the sampling frame or later in the field during data collection.
- **Column 5** shows the size of the national desired target population after subtracting the students enrolled in excluded schools. This is obtained by subtracting Column 4 from Column 3.
- **Column 6** shows the percentage of students enrolled in excluded schools. This is obtained by dividing Column 4 by Column 3 and multiplying by 100.
- **Column 7** shows the number of students participating in PISA 2015. Note that in some cases this number does not account for 15-year-olds assessed as part of additional national options.
- **Column 8** shows the weighted number of participating students, i.e. the number of students in the nationally defined target population that the PISA sample represents.
- Each country attempted to maximise the coverage of PISA's target population within the sampled schools. In the case of each sampled school, all eligible students, namely those 15 years of age, regardless of grade, were first listed. Sampled students who were to be excluded had still to be included in the sampling documentation, and a list drawn up stating the reason for their exclusion. Column 9 indicates the total number of excluded students, which is further described and classified into specific categories in Table A2.2.
- **Column 10** indicates the weighted number of excluded students, i.e. the overall number of students in the nationally defined target population represented by the number of students excluded from the sample, which is also described and classified by exclusion categories in Table A2.2. Excluded students were excluded based on five categories: students with an intellectual disability (the student has a mental or emotional disability and is cognitively delayed such that he/she cannot perform in the PISA testing situation); students with a functional disability (the student has a moderate to severe permanent physical disability such that he/she cannot perform in the PISA testing situation); students with limited proficiency in the assessment language (the student is unable to read or speak any of the languages of the assessment in the country and would be unable to overcome the language barrier in the testing situation – typically a student who has received less than one year of instruction in the languages of assessment may be excluded); other (a category defined by the national centres and approved by the international centre); and students taught in a language of instruction for the main domain for which no materials were available.

[Part 1/1]

Table A2.1 PISA target populations and samples

		Population and sample information												Coverage indices		
		Total population of 15-year-olds	Total enrolled population of 15-year-olds at grade 7 or above	Total in national desired target population	Total school-level exclusions	Total in national desired target population after all school exclusions and before within-school exclusions	School-level exclusion rate (%)	Number of participating students	Weighted number of participating students	Number of excluded students	Weighted number of excluded students	Within-school exclusion rate (%)	Overall exclusion rate (%)	Coverage Index 1: Coverage of national desired population	Coverage Index 2: Coverage of national enrolled population	Coverage Index 3: Coverage of 15-year-old population
		(1)	(2)	(3)	(4)	(5)	(6)	(7)	(8)	(9)	(10)	(11)	(12)	(13)	(14)	(15)
OECD	Australia	282 888	282 547	282 547	6 940	275 607	2.46	14 530	256 329	681	7 736	2.93	5.31	0.947	0.947	0.906
	Austria	88 013	82 683	82 683	790	81 893	0.96	7 007	73 379	84	866	1.17	2.11	0.979	0.979	0.834
	Belgium	123 630	121 954	121 694	1 597	120 097	1.31	9 651	114 902	39	410	0.36	1.66	0.983	0.981	0.929
	Canada	396 966	381 660	376 994	1 590	375 404	0.42	20 058	331 546	1 830	25 340	7.10	7.49	0.925	0.914	0.835
	Chile	255 440	245 947	245 852	2 641	243 211	1.07	7 053	203 782	37	1 393	0.68	1.75	0.983	0.982	0.798
	Czech Republic	90 391	90 076	90 076	1 814	88 262	2.01	6 894	84 519	25	368	0.43	2.44	0.976	0.976	0.935
	Denmark	68 174	67 466	67 466	605	66 861	0.90	7 161	60 655	514	2 644	4.18	5.04	0.950	0.950	0.890
	Estonia	11 676	11 491	11 491	416	11 075	3.62	5 587	10 834	116	218	1.97	5.52	0.945	0.945	0.928
	Finland	58 526	58 955	58 955	472	58 483	0.80	5 882	56 934	124	1 157	1.99	2.78	0.972	0.972	0.973
	France	807 867	778 679	778 679	28 742	749 937	3.69	6 108	734 944	35	3 620	0.49	4.16	0.958	0.958	0.910
	Germany	774 149	774 149	774 149	11 150	762 999	1.44	6 522	743 969	54	5 342	0.71	2.14	0.979	0.979	0.961
	Greece	105 530	105 253	105 253	953	104 300	0.91	5 532	96 157	58	965	0.99	1.89	0.981	0.981	0.911
	Hungary	94 515	90 065	90 065	1 945	88 120	2.16	5 658	84 644	55	1 009	1.18	3.31	0.967	0.967	0.896
	Iceland	4 250	4 195	4 195	17	4 178	0.41	3 374	3 966	131	132	3.23	3.62	0.964	0.964	0.933
	Ireland	61 234	59 811	59 811	72	59 739	0.12	5 741	59 082	197	1 825	3.00	3.11	0.969	0.969	0.965
	Israel	124 852	118 997	118 997	2 310	116 687	1.94	6 598	117 031	115	1 803	1.52	3.43	0.966	0.966	0.937
	Italy	616 761	567 268	567 268	11 190	556 078	1.97	11 583	495 093	246	9 395	1.86	3.80	0.962	0.962	0.803
	Japan	1 201 615	1 175 907	1 175 907	27 323	1 148 584	2.32	6 647	1 138 349	2	318	0.03	2.35	0.976	0.976	0.947
	Korea	620 687	619 950	619 950	3 555	616 395	0.57	5 581	569 106	20	1 806	0.32	0.89	0.991	0.991	0.917
	Latvia	17 255	16 955	16 955	677	16 278	3.99	4 869	15 320	70	174	1.12	5.07	0.949	0.949	0.888
	Luxembourg	6 327	6 053	6 053	162	5 891	2.68	5 299	5 540	331	331	5.64	8.16	0.918	0.918	0.876
	Mexico	2 257 399	1 401 247	1 401 247	5 905	1 395 342	0.42	7 568	1 392 995	30	6 810	0.49	0.91	0.991	0.991	0.617
	Netherlands	201 670	200 976	200 976	6 866	194 110	3.42	5 385	191 817	14	502	0.26	3.67	0.963	0.963	0.951
	New Zealand	60 162	57 448	57 448	681	56 767	1.19	4 520	54 274	333	3 112	5.42	6.54	0.935	0.935	0.902
	Norway	63 642	63 491	63 491	854	62 637	1.35	5 456	58 083	345	3 366	5.48	6.75	0.933	0.933	0.913
	Poland	380 366	361 600	361 600	6 122	355 478	1.69	4 478	345 709	34	2 418	0.69	2.38	0.976	0.976	0.909
	Portugal	110 939	101 107	101 107	424	100 683	0.42	7 325	97 214	105	860	0.88	1.29	0.987	0.987	0.876
	Slovak Republic	55 674	55 203	55 203	1 376	53 827	2.49	6 350	49 654	114	912	1.80	4.25	0.957	0.957	0.892
	Slovenia	18 078	17 689	17 689	290	17 399	1.64	6 406	16 773	114	247	1.45	3.07	0.969	0.969	0.928
	Spain	440 084	414 276	414 276	2 175	412 101	0.53	6 736	399 935	200	10 893	2.65	3.16	0.968	0.968	0.909
	Sweden	97 749	97 210	97 210	1 214	95 996	1.25	5 458	91 491	275	4 324	4.51	5.71	0.943	0.943	0.936
	Switzerland	85 495	83 655	83 655	2 320	81 335	2.77	5 860	82 223	107	1 357	1.62	4.35	0.956	0.956	0.962
	Turkey	1 324 089	1 100 074	1 100 074	5 746	1 094 328	0.52	5 895	925 366	31	5 359	0.58	1.10	0.989	0.989	0.699
	United Kingdom	747 593	746 328	746 328	23 412	722 916	3.14	14 157	627 703	870	34 747	5.25	8.22	0.918	0.918	0.840
	United States	4 220 325	3 992 053	3 992 053	12 001	3 980 052	0.30	5 712	3 524 497	193	109 580	3.02	3.31	0.967	0.967	0.835
Partners	Albania	48 610	45 163	45 163	10	45 153	0.02	5 215	40 896	0	0	0.00	0.02	1.000	1.000	0.841
	Algeria	389 315	354 936	354 936	0	354 936	0.00	5 519	306 647	0	0	0.00	0.00	1.000	1.000	0.788
	Argentina	718 635	578 308	578 308	2 617	575 691	0.45	6 349	394 917	21	1 367	0.34	0.80	0.992	0.992	0.550
	Brazil	3 803 681	2 853 388	2 853 388	64 392	2 788 996	2.26	23 141	2 425 961	119	13 543	0.56	2.80	0.972	0.972	0.638
	B-S-J-G (China)	2 084 958	1 507 518	1 507 518	58 639	1 448 879	3.89	9 841	1 331 794	33	3 609	0.27	4.15	0.959	0.959	0.639
	Bulgaria	66 601	59 397	59 397	1 124	58 273	1.89	5 928	53 685	49	433	0.80	2.68	0.973	0.973	0.806
	Colombia	760 919	674 079	674 079	37	674 042	0.01	11 795	567 848	9	507	0.09	0.09	0.999	0.999	0.746
	Costa Rica	81 773	66 524	66 524	0	66 524	0.00	6 866	51 897	13	98	0.19	0.19	0.998	0.998	0.635
	Croatia	45 031	35 920	35 920	805	35 115	2.24	5 809	40 899	86	589	1.42	3.63	0.964	0.964	0.908
	Cyprus*	9 255	9 255	9 253	109	9 144	1.18	5 571	8 785	228	292	3.22	4.36	0.956	0.956	0.949
	Dominican Republic	193 153	139 555	139 555	2 382	137 173	1.71	4 740	132 300	4	106	0.08	1.79	0.982	0.982	0.685
	FYROM	16 719	16 717	16 717	259	16 458	1.55	5 324	15 847	8	19	0.12	1.67	0.983	0.983	0.948
	Georgia	48 695	43 197	43 197	1 675	41 522	3.88	5 316	38 334	35	230	0.60	4.45	0.955	0.955	0.787
	Hong Kong (China)	65 100	61 630	61 630	708	60 922	1.15	5 359	57 662	36	374	0.65	1.79	0.982	0.982	0.886
	Indonesia	4 534 216	3 182 816	3 182 816	4 046	3 178 770	0.13	6 513	3 092 773	0	0	0.00	0.13	0.999	0.999	0.682
	Jordan	126 399	121 729	121 729	71	121 658	0.06	7 267	108 669	70	1 006	0.92	0.97	0.990	0.990	0.860
	Kazakhstan	211 407	209 555	209 555	7 475	202 080	3.57	7 841	192 909	0	0	0.00	3.57	0.964	0.964	0.912
	Kosovo	31 546	28 229	28 229	1 156	27 073	4.10	4 826	22 333	50	174	0.77	4.84	0.952	0.952	0.708
	Lebanon	64 044	62 281	62 281	1 300	60 981	2.09	4 546	42 331	0	0	0.00	2.09	0.979	0.979	0.661
	Lithuania	33 163	32 097	32 097	573	31 524	1.79	6 525	29 915	227	1 050	3.39	5.12	0.949	0.949	0.902
	Macao (China)	5 100	4 417	4 417	3	4 414	0.07	4 476	4 507	0	0	0.00	0.07	0.999	0.999	0.884
	Malaysia	540 000	448 838	448 838	2 418	446 420	0.54	8 861	412 524	41	2 344	0.56	1.10	0.989	0.989	0.764
	Malta	4 397	4 406	4 406	63	4 343	1.43	3 634	4 296	41	41	0.95	2.36	0.976	0.976	0.977
	Moldova	31 576	30 601	30 601	182	30 419	0.59	5 325	29 341	21	118	0.40	0.99	0.990	0.990	0.929
	Montenegro	7 524	7 506	7 506	40	7 466	0.53	5 665	6 777	300	332	4.66	5.17	0.948	0.948	0.901
	Peru	580 371	478 229	478 229	6 355	471 874	1.33	6 971	431 738	13	745	0.17	1.50	0.985	0.985	0.744
	Qatar	13 871	13 850	13 850	380	13 470	2.74	12 083	12 951	193	193	1.47	4.17	0.958	0.958	0.934
	Romania	176 334	176 334	176 334	1 823	174 511	1.03	4 876	164 216	3	120	0.07	1.11	0.989	0.989	0.931
	Russia	1 176 473	1 172 943	1 172 943	24 217	1 148 726	2.06	6 036	1 120 932	13	2 469	0.22	2.28	0.977	0.977	0.953
	Singapore	48 218	47 050	47 050	445	46 605	0.95	6 115	46 224	25	179	0.39	1.33	0.987	0.987	0.959
	Chinese Taipei	295 056	287 783	287 783	1 179	286 604	0.41	7 708	251 424	22	647	0.26	0.67	0.993	0.993	0.852
	Thailand	895 513	756 917	756 917	9 646	747 271	1.27	8 249	634 795	22	2 107	0.33	1.60	0.984	0.984	0.709
	Trinidad and Tobago	17 371	17 371	17 371	0	17 371	0.00	4 692	13 197	0	0	0.00	0.00	1.000	1.000	0.760
	Tunisia	122 186	122 186	122 186	679	121 507	0.56	5 375	113 599	3	61	0.05	0.61	0.994	0.994	0.930
	United Arab Emirates	51 687	51 518	51 499	994	50 505	1.93	14 167	46 950	63	152	0.32	2.25	0.978	0.977	0.908
	Uruguay	53 533	43 865	43 865	4	43 861	0.01	6 062	38 287	6	32	0.08	0.09	0.999	0.999	0.715
	Viet Nam	1 803 552	1 032 599	1 032 599	6 557	1 026 042	0.63	5 826	874 859	0	0	0.00	0.63	0.994	0.994	0.485

Notes: For a full explanation of the details in this table please refer to the *PISA 2015 Technical Report* (OECD, 2017).
The figure for total national population of 15-year-olds enrolled in Column 2 may occasionally be larger than the total number of 15-year-olds in Column 1 due to differing data sources.
For Mexico, in 2015, the Total population of 15-year-olds enrolled in grade 7 or above is an estimate of the target population size of the sample frame from which the 15-year-olds students were selected for the PISA test. At the time Mexico provided the information to PISA, the official figure for this population was 1 573 952.
* See note at the beginning of this Annex.

StatLink http://dx.doi.org/10.1787/888933433129

[Part 1/2]

Table A2.2 Exclusions

		Student exclusions (unweighted)					
		Number of excluded students with functional disability (Code 1)	Number of excluded students with intellectual disability (Code 2)	Number of excluded students because of language (Code 3)	Number of excluded students for other reasons (Code 4)	Number of excluded students because of no materials available in the language of instruction (Code 5)	School-level exclusion rate (%)
		(1)	(2)	(3)	(4)	(5)	(6)
OECD	Australia	85	528	68	0	0	681
	Austria	8	15	61	0	0	84
	Belgium	4	18	17	0	0	39
	Canada	156	1 308	366	0	0	1 830
	Chile	6	30	1	0	0	37
	Czech Republic	2	9	14	0	0	25
	Denmark	18	269	156	70	1	514
	Estonia	17	93	6	0	0	116
	Finland	2	90	17	8	7	124
	France	5	21	9	0	0	35
	Germany	4	25	25	0	0	54
	Greece	3	44	11	0	0	58
	Hungary	3	13	9	30	0	55
	Iceland	9	66	47	9	0	131
	Ireland	25	57	55	60	0	197
	Israel	22	68	25	0	0	115
	Italy	78	147	21	0	0	246
	Japan	0	2	0	0	0	2
	Korea	3	17	0	0	0	20
	Latvia	7	47	16	0	0	70
	Luxembourg	4	254	73	0	0	331
	Mexico	4	23	3	0	0	30
	Netherlands	1	13	0	0	0	14
	New Zealand	23	140	167	0	3	333
	Norway	11	253	81	0	0	345
	Poland	11	20	0	3	0	34
	Portugal	4	99	2	0	0	105
	Slovak Republic	7	71	2	34	0	114
	Slovenia	33	36	45	0	0	114
	Spain	9	144	47	0	0	200
	Sweden	154	0	121	0	0	275
	Switzerland	8	42	57	0	0	107
	Turkey	1	23	7	0	0	31
	United Kingdom	77	690	102	0	1	870
	United States	16	120	44	13	0	193
Partners	Albania	0	0	0	0	0	0
	Algeria	0	0	0	0	0	0
	Argentina	10	10	1	0	0	21
	Brazil	20	99	0	0	0	119
	B-S-J-G (China)	6	25	2	0	0	33
	Bulgaria	39	6	4	0	0	49
	Colombia	3	4	2	0	0	9
	Costa Rica	3	1	0	9	0	13
	Croatia	2	75	9	0	0	86
	Cyprus*	12	164	52	0	0	228
	Dominican Republic	1	3	0	0	0	4
	FYROM	7	1	0	0	0	8
	Georgia	3	25	7	0	0	35
	Hong Kong (China)	0	35	1	0	0	36
	Indonesia	0	0	0	0	0	0
	Jordan	43	17	10	0	0	70
	Kazakhstan	0	0	0	0	0	0
	Kosovo	9	13	27	0	0	50
	Lebanon	0	0	0	0	0	0
	Lithuania	12	213	2	0	0	227
	Macao (China)	0	0	0	0	0	0
	Malaysia	10	22	9	0	0	41
	Malta	8	27	6	0	0	41
	Moldova	12	8	1	0	0	21
	Montenegro	14	23	5	0	258	300
	Peru	4	9	0	0	0	13
	Qatar	76	110	7	0	0	193
	Romania	1	1	1	0	0	3
	Russia	3	10	0	0	0	13
	Singapore	3	15	7	0	0	25
	Chinese Taipei	3	19	0	0	0	22
	Thailand	1	19	2	0	0	22
	Trinidad and Tobago	0	0	0	0	0	0
	Tunisia	0	0	3	0	0	3
	United Arab Emirates	16	24	23	0	0	63
	Uruguay	2	4	0	0	0	6
	Viet Nam	0	0	0	0	0	0

Exclusion codes:
Code 1: Functional disability – student has a moderate to severe permanent physical disability.
Code 2: Intellectual disability – student has a mental or emotional disability and has either been tested as cognitively delayed or is considered in the professional opinion of qualified staff to be cognitively delayed.
Code 3: Limited assessment language proficiency – student is not a native speaker of any of the languages of the assessment in the country and has been resident in the country for less than one year.
Code 4: Other reasons defined by the national centres and approved by the international centre.
Code 5: No materials available in the language of instruction.
Note: For a full explanation of the details in this table please refer to the *PISA 2015 Technical Report* (OECD, 2017).
* See note at the beginning of this Annex.
StatLink http://dx.doi.org/10.1787/888933433129

[Part 2/2]

Table A2.2 Exclusions

		Student exclusion (weighted)					
		Weighted number of excluded students with functional disability (Code 1)	Weighted number of excluded students with intellectual disability (Code 2)	Weighted number of excluded students because of language (Code 3)	Weighted number of excluded students for other reasons (Code 4)	Weighted number of excluded students because of no materials available in the language of instruction (Code 5)	Total weighted number of excluded students
		(7)	(8)	(9)	(10)	(11)	(12)
OECD	Australia	932	6 011	793	0	0	7 736
	Austria	74	117	675	0	0	866
	Belgium	33	192	185	0	0	410
	Canada	1 901	18 018	5 421	0	0	25 340
	Chile	194	1 190	9	0	0	1 393
	Czech Republic	40	140	188	0	0	368
	Denmark	122	1 539	551	421	11	2 644
	Estonia	29	176	13	0	0	218
	Finland	18	858	156	67	58	1 157
	France	562	2 144	914	0	0	3 620
	Germany	423	2 562	2 357	0	0	5 342
	Greece	43	729	193	0	0	965
	Hungary	57	284	114	554	0	1 009
	Iceland	9	67	47	9	0	132
	Ireland	213	526	516	570	0	1 825
	Israel	349	1 070	384	0	0	1 803
	Italy	3 316	5 199	880	0	0	9 395
	Japan	0	318	0	0	0	318
	Korea	291	1 515	0	0	0	1 806
	Latvia	21	115	38	0	0	174
	Luxembourg	4	254	73	0	0	331
	Mexico	842	4 802	1 165	0	0	6 810
	Netherlands	33	469	0	0	0	502
	New Zealand	233	1 287	1 568	0	24	3 112
	Norway	105	2 471	790	0	0	3 366
	Poland	876	1 339	0	203	0	2 418
	Portugal	29	818	13	0	0	860
	Slovak Republic	44	567	12	288	0	912
	Slovenia	84	71	92	0	0	247
	Spain	511	7 662	2 720	0	0	10 893
	Sweden	2 380	0	1 944	0	0	4 324
	Switzerland	91	540	726	0	0	1 357
	Turkey	43	4 094	1 222	0	0	5 359
	United Kingdom	2 724	27 808	4 001	0	214	34 747
	United States	7 873	67 816	26 525	7 366	0	109 580
Partners	Albania	0	0	0	0	0	0
	Algeria	0	0	0	0	0	0
	Argentina	579	770	18	0	0	1 367
	Brazil	1 743	11 800	0	0	0	13 543
	B-S-J-G (China)	438	2 970	201	0	0	3 609
	Bulgaria	347	51	35	0	0	433
	Colombia	181	309	17	0	0	507
	Costa Rica	22	5	0	71	0	98
	Croatia	13	501	75	0	0	589
	Cyprus*	16	212	65	0	0	292
	Dominican Republic	24	82	0	0	0	106
	FYROM	15	4	0	0	0	19
	Georgia	19	170	41	0	0	230
	Hong Kong (China)	0	363	11	0	0	374
	Indonesia	0	0	0	0	0	0
	Jordan	656	227	122	0	0	1 006
	Kazakhstan	0	0	0	0	0	0
	Kosovo	28	37	104	0	0	174
	Lebanon	0	0	0	0	0	0
	Lithuania	40	1 000	10	0	0	1 050
	Macao (China)	0	0	0	0	0	0
	Malaysia	663	1 100	580	0	0	2 344
	Malta	8	27	6	0	0	41
	Moldova	66	51	1	0	0	118
	Montenegro	27	38	6	0	261	332
	Peru	224	520	0	0	0	745
	Qatar	76	110	7	0	0	193
	Romania	31	63	26	0	0	120
	Russia	425	2 044	0	0	0	2 469
	Singapore	22	115	43	0	0	179
	Chinese Taipei	78	568	0	0	0	647
	Thailand	114	1 830	163	0	0	2 107
	Trinidad and Tobago	0	0	0	0	0	0
	Tunisia	0	0	61	0	0	61
	United Arab Emirates	30	75	47	0	0	152
	Uruguay	10	22	0	0	0	32
	Viet Nam	0	0	0	0	0	0

Exclusion codes:
Code 1: Functional disability – student has a moderate to severe permanent physical disability.
Code 2: Intellectual disability – student has a mental or emotional disability and has either been tested as cognitively delayed or is considered in the professional opinion of qualified staff to be cognitively delayed.
Code 3: Limited assessment language proficiency – student is not a native speaker of any of the languages of the assessment in the country and has been resident in the country for less than one year.
Code 4: Other reasons defined by the national centres and approved by the international centre.
Code 5: No materials available in the language of instruction.
Note: For a full explanation of the details in this table please refer to the *PISA 2015 Technical Report* (OECD, 2017).
* See note at the beginning of this Annex.
StatLink http://dx.doi.org/10.1787/888933433129

- **Column 11** shows the percentage of students excluded within schools. This is calculated as the weighted number of excluded students (Column 10), divided by the weighted number of excluded and participating students (Column 8 plus Column 10), then multiplied by 100.
- **Column 12** shows the overall exclusion rate, which represents the weighted percentage of the national desired target population excluded from PISA either through school-level exclusions or through the exclusion of students within schools. It is calculated as the school-level exclusion rate (Column 6 divided by 100) plus within-school exclusion rate (Column 11 divided by 100) multiplied by 1 minus the school-level exclusion rate (Column 6 divided by 100). This result is then multiplied by 100.
- **Column 13** presents an index of the extent to which the national desired target population is covered by the PISA sample. Australia, Canada, Denmark, Estonia, Latvia, Lithuania, Luxembourg, Montenegro, New Zealand, Norway, Sweden and the United Kingdom were the only countries where the coverage is below 95%.
- **Column 14** presents an index of the extent to which 15-year-olds enrolled in schools are covered by the PISA sample. The index measures the overall proportion of the national enrolled population that is covered by the non-excluded portion of the student sample. The index takes into account both school-level and student-level exclusions. Values close to 100 indicate that the PISA sample represents the entire education system as defined for PISA 2015. The index is the weighted number of participating students (Column 8) divided by the weighted number of participating and excluded students (Column 8 plus Column 10), times the nationally defined target population (Column 5) divided by the eligible population (Column 2) (times 100).
- **Column 15** presents an index of the coverage of the 15-year-old population. This index is the weighted number of participating students (Column 8) divided by the total population of 15-year-old students (Column 1).

This high level of coverage contributes to the comparability of the assessment results. For example, even assuming that the excluded students would have systematically scored worse than those who participated, and that this relationship is moderately strong, an exclusion rate on the order of 5% would likely lead to an overestimation of national mean scores of less than 5 score points (on a scale with an international mean of 500 score points and a standard deviation of 100 score points). This assessment is based on the following calculations: if the correlation between the propensity of exclusions and student performance is 0.3, resulting mean scores would likely be overestimated by 1 score point if the exclusion rate is 1%, by 3 score points if the exclusion rate is 5%, and by 6 score points if the exclusion rate is 10%. If the correlation between the propensity of exclusions and student performance is 0.5, resulting mean scores would be overestimated by 1 score point if the exclusion rate is 1%, by 5 score points if the exclusion rate is 5%, and by 10 score points if the exclusion rate is 10%. For this calculation, a model was used that assumes a bivariate normal distribution for performance and the propensity to participate. For details, see the *PISA 2015 Technical Report* (OECD, 2017).

Sampling procedures and response rates

The accuracy of any survey results depends on the quality of the information on which national samples are based as well as on the sampling procedures. Quality standards, procedures, instruments and verification mechanisms were developed for PISA that ensured that national samples yielded comparable data and that the results could be compared with confidence.

Most PISA samples were designed as two-stage stratified samples (where countries applied different sampling designs, these are documented in the *PISA 2015 Technical Report* [OECD, 2017]). The first stage consisted of sampling individual schools in which 15-year-old students could be enrolled. Schools were sampled systematically with probabilities proportional to size, the measure of size being a function of the estimated number of eligible (15-year-old) students enrolled. At least 150 schools were selected in each country (where this number existed), although the requirements for national analyses often required a somewhat larger sample. As the schools were sampled, replacement schools were simultaneously identified, in case a sampled school chose not to participate in PISA 2015.

In the case of Iceland, Luxembourg, Macao (China), Malta and Qatar, all schools and all eligible students within schools were included in the sample.

Experts from the PISA Consortium performed the sample selection process for most participating countries and monitored it closely in those countries that selected their own samples. The second stage of the selection process sampled students within sampled schools. Once schools were selected, a list of each sampled school's 15-year-old students was prepared. From this list, 42 students were then selected with equal probability (all 15-year-old students were selected if fewer than 42 were enrolled). The number of students to be sampled per school could deviate from 42, but could not be less than 20.

Data-quality standards in PISA required minimum participation rates for schools as well as for students. These standards were established to minimise the potential for response biases. In the case of countries meeting these standards, it was likely that any bias resulting from non-response would be negligible, i.e. typically smaller than the sampling error.

A minimum response rate of 85% was required for the schools initially selected. Where the initial response rate of schools was between 65% and 85%, however, an acceptable school-response rate could still be achieved through the use of replacement schools.

This procedure brought with it a risk of increased response bias. Participating countries were, therefore, encouraged to persuade as many of the schools in the original sample as possible to participate. Schools with a student participation rate between 25% and 50% were not regarded as participating schools, but data from these schools were included in the database and contributed to the various estimations. Data from schools with a student participation rate of less than 25% were excluded from the database.

PISA 2015 also required a minimum participation rate of 80% of students within participating schools. This minimum participation rate had to be met at the national level, not necessarily by each participating school. Follow-up sessions were required in schools in which too few students had participated in the original assessment sessions. Student participation rates were calculated over all original schools, and also over all schools, whether original sample or replacement schools, and from the participation of students in both the original assessment and any follow-up sessions. A student who participated in the original or follow-up cognitive sessions was regarded as a participant. Those who attended only the questionnaire session were included in the international database and contributed to the statistics presented in this publication if they provided at least a description of their father's or mother's occupation.

Table A2.3 shows the response rates for students and schools, before and after replacement.

- **Column 1** shows the weighted participation rate of schools before replacement. This is obtained by dividing Column 2 by Column 3.
- **Column 2** shows the weighted number of responding schools before school replacement (weighted by student enrolment).
- **Column 3** shows the weighted number of sampled schools before school replacement (including both responding and non-responding schools, weighted by student enrolment).
- **Column 4** shows the unweighted number of responding schools before school replacement.
- **Column 5** shows the unweighted number of responding and non-responding schools before school replacement.
- **Column 6** shows the weighted participation rate of schools after replacement. This is obtained by dividing Column 7 by Column 8.
- **Column 7** shows the weighted number of responding schools after school replacement (weighted by student enrolment).
- **Column 8** shows the weighted number of schools sampled after school replacement (including both responding and non-responding schools, weighted by student enrolment).
- **Column 9** shows the unweighted number of responding schools after school replacement.
- **Column 10** shows the unweighted number of responding and non-responding schools after school replacement.
- **Column 11** shows the weighted student participation rate after replacement. This is obtained by dividing Column 12 by Column 13.
- **Column 12** shows the weighted number of students assessed.
- **Column 13** shows the weighted number of students sampled (including both students who were assessed and students who were absent on the day of the assessment).
- **Column 14** shows the unweighted number of students assessed. Note that any students in schools with student-response rates of less than 50% were not included in these rates (both weighted and unweighted).
- **Column 15** shows the unweighted number of students sampled (including both students that were assessed and students who were absent on the day of the assessment). Note that any students in schools where fewer than half of the eligible students were assessed were not included in these rates (neither weighted nor unweighted).

Definition of schools

In some countries, subunits within schools were sampled instead of schools, and this may affect the estimation of the between-school variance components. In Austria, the Czech Republic, Germany, Hungary, Japan, Romania and Slovenia, schools with more than one study programme were split into the units delivering these programmes. In the Netherlands, for schools with both lower and upper secondary programmes, schools were split into units delivering each programme level. In the Flemish community of Belgium, in the case of multi-campus schools, implantations (campuses) were sampled, whereas in the French community, in the case of multi-campus schools, the larger administrative units were sampled. In Australia, for schools with more than one campus, the individual campuses were listed for sampling. In Argentina and Croatia, schools that had more than one campus had the locations listed for sampling. In Spain, the schools in the Basque region with multi-linguistic models were split into linguistic models for sampling. In Luxembourg, a school on the border with Germany was split according to the country in which the students resided. In addition, the International schools in Luxembourg were split into the students who were instructed in any of the three official languages, and those in the part of the schools that was excluded because no materials were available in the languages of instruction. The United Arab Emirates had schools split by curricula, and sometimes by gender, with other schools remaining whole. Because of reorganisation, some of Sweden's schools were split into parts, with each part having one principal. In Portugal, schools were reorganised into clusters, with teachers and the principal shared by all units in the school cluster.

[Part 1/1]

Table A2.3 Response rates

		Initial sample – before school replacement					Final sample – after school replacement					Final sample – students within schools after school replacement				
		Weighted school participation rate before replacement (%)	Weighted number of responding schools (weighted also by enrolment)	Weighted number of schools sampled (responding and non-responding) (weighted also by enrolment)	Number of responding and non-responding schools (unweighted)	Total in national desired target population after all school exclusions and before within-school exclusions	Weighted school participation rate after replacement (%)	Weighted number of responding schools (weighted also by enrolment)	Weighted number of schools sampled (responding and non-responding) (weighted also by enrolment)	Number of responding schools (unweighted)	Number of responding and non-responding schools (unweighted)	Weighted student participation rate after replacement (%)	Number of students assessed (weighted)	Number of students sampled (assessed and absent) (weighted)	Number of students assessed (unweighted)	Number of students sampled (assessed and absent) (unweighted)
		(1)	(2)	(3)	(4)	(5)	(6)	(7)	(8)	(9)	(10)	(11)	(12)	(13)	(14)	(15)
OECD	Australia	94	260 657	276 072	720	788	95	262 130	276 072	723	788	84	204 763	243 789	14 089	17 477
	Austria	100	81 690	81 730	269	273	100	81 690	81 730	269	273	87	63 660	73 521	7 007	9 868
	Belgium	83	98 786	118 915	244	301	95	113 435	118 936	286	301	91	99 760	110 075	9 635	10 602
	Canada	74	283 853	381 133	703	1 008	79	299 512	381 189	726	1 008	81	210 476	260 487	19 604	24 129
	Chile	92	215 139	232 756	207	232	99	230 749	232 757	226	232	93	189 206	202 774	7 039	7 515
	Czech Republic	98	86 354	87 999	339	344	98	86 354	87 999	339	344	89	73 386	82 672	6 835	7 693
	Denmark	90	57 803	63 897	327	371	92	58 837	63 931	331	371	89	49 732	55 830	7 149	8 184
	Estonia	100	11 142	11 154	206	207	100	11 142	11 154	206	207	93	10 088	10 822	5 587	5 994
	Finland	100	58 653	58 782	167	168	100	58 800	58 800	168	168	93	53 198	56 934	5 882	6 294
	France	91	679 984	749 284	232	255	94	706 838	749 284	241	255	88	611 563	693 336	5 980	6 783
	Germany	96	764 423	794 206	245	256	99	785 813	794 206	253	256	93	685 972	735 487	6 476	6 944
	Greece	92	95 030	103 031	190	212	98	101 653	103 218	209	212	94	89 588	94 986	5 511	5 838
	Hungary	93	83 897	89 808	231	251	99	88 751	89 825	244	251	92	77 212	83 657	5 643	6 101
	Iceland	99	4 114	4 163	122	129	99	4 114	4 163	122	129	86	3 365	3 908	3 365	3 908
	Ireland	99	61 023	61 461	167	169	99	61 023	61 461	167	169	89	51 947	58 630	5 741	6 478
	Israel	91	105 192	115 717	169	190	93	107 570	115 717	173	190	90	98 572	108 940	6 598	7 294
	Italy	74	383 933	516 113	414	532	88	451 098	515 515	464	532	88	377 011	430 041	11 477	12 841
	Japan	94	1 087 414	1 151 305	189	200	99	1 139 734	1 151 305	198	200	97	1 096 193	1 127 265	6 647	6 838
	Korea	100	612 937	615 107	168	169	100	612 937	615 107	168	169	99	559 121	567 284	5 581	5 664
	Latvia	86	14 122	16 334	231	269	93	15 103	16 324	248	269	90	12 799	14 155	4 845	5 368
	Luxembourg	100	5 891	5 891	44	44	100	5 891	5 891	44	44	96	5 299	5 540	5 299	5 540
	Mexico	95	1 311 608	1 373 919	269	284	98	1 339 901	1 373 919	275	284	95	1 290 435	1 352 237	7 568	7 938
	Netherlands	63	121 527	191 966	125	201	93	178 929	191 966	184	201	85	152 346	178 985	5 345	6 269
	New Zealand	71	40 623	56 875	145	210	85	48 094	56 913	176	210	80	36 860	45 897	4 453	5 547
	Norway	95	58 824	61 809	229	241	95	58 824	61 809	229	241	91	50 163	55 277	5 456	6 016
	Poland	88	314 288	355 158	151	170	99	352 754	355 158	168	170	88	300 617	343 405	4 466	5 108
	Portugal	86	87 756	102 193	213	254	95	97 516	102 537	238	254	82	75 391	91 916	7 180	8 732
	Slovak Republic	93	50 513	54 499	272	295	99	53 908	54 562	288	295	92	45 357	49 103	6 342	6 900
	Slovenia	98	16 886	17 286	332	349	98	16 896	17 286	333	349	92	15 072	16 424	6 406	7 009
	Spain	99	404 640	409 246	199	201	100	409 246	409 246	201	201	89	356 509	399 935	6 736	7 540
	Sweden	100	93 819	94 097	202	205	100	93 819	94 097	202	205	91	82 582	91 081	5 458	6 013
	Switzerland	93	75 482	81 026	212	232	98	79 481	81 375	225	232	92	74 465	80 544	5 838	6 305
	Turkey	97	1 057 318	1 091 317	175	195	99	1 081 935	1 091 528	187	195	95	874 609	918 816	5 895	6 211
	United Kingdom	84	591 757	707 415	506	598	93	654 992	707 415	547	598	89	517 426	581 252	14 120	16 123
	United States	67	2 601 386	3 902 089	142	213	83	3 244 399	3 893 828	177	213	90	2 629 707	2 929 771	5 712	6 376
Partners	Albania	100	43 809	43 919	229	230	100	43 809	43 919	229	230	94	38 174	40 814	5 213	5 555
	Algeria	96	341 463	355 216	159	166	96	341 463	355 216	159	166	92	274 121	296 434	5 494	5 934
	Argentina	89	508 448	572 941	212	238	97	556 478	572 941	231	238	90	345 508	382 352	6 311	7 016
	Brazil	93	2 509 198	2 692 686	806	889	94	2 533 711	2 693 137	815	889	87	1 996 574	2 286 505	22 791	26 586
	B-S-J-G (China)	88	1 259 845	1 437 201	248	268	100	1 437 652	1 437 652	268	268	97	1 287 710	1 331 794	9 841	10 097
	Bulgaria	100	56 265	56 483	179	180	100	56 600	56 600	180	180	95	50 931	53 685	5 928	6 240
	Colombia	99	664 664	673 817	364	375	100	672 526	673 835	371	375	95	535 682	566 734	11 777	12 611
	Costa Rica	99	66 485	67 073	204	206	99	66 485	67 073	204	206	92	47 494	51 369	6 846	7 411
	Croatia	100	34 575	34 652	160	162	100	34 575	34 652	160	162	91	37 275	40 803	5 809	6 354
	Cyprus*	97	8 830	9 126	122	132	97	8 830	9 126	122	132	94	8 016	8 526	5 561	5 957
	Dominican Republic	99	136 669	138 187	193	195	99	136 669	138 187	193	195	94	122 620	130 700	4 731	5 026
	FYROM	100	16 426	16 472	106	107	100	16 426	16 472	106	107	95	14 999	15 802	5 324	5 617
	Georgia	97	40 552	41 595	256	267	99	41 081	41 566	262	267	94	35 567	37 873	5 316	5 689
	Hong Kong (China)	75	45 603	60 716	115	153	90	54 795	60 715	138	153	93	48 222	51 806	5 359	5 747
	Indonesia	98	3 126 468	3 176 076	232	236	100	3 176 076	3 176 076	236	236	98	3 015 844	3 092 773	6 513	6 694
	Jordan	100	119 024	119 024	250	250	100	119 024	119 024	250	250	97	105 868	108 669	7 267	7 462
	Kazakhstan	100	202 701	202 701	232	232	100	202 701	202 701	232	232	97	187 683	192 921	7 841	8 059
	Kosovo	100	26 924	26 924	224	224	100	26 924	26 924	224	224	99	22 016	22 333	4 826	4 896
	Lebanon	67	40 542	60 882	208	308	87	53 091	60 797	270	308	95	36 052	38 143	4 546	4 788
	Lithuania	99	31 386	31 588	309	311	100	31 543	31 588	310	311	91	27 070	29 889	6 523	7 202
	Macao (China)	100	4 414	4 414	45	45	100	4 414	4 414	45	45	99	4 476	4 507	4 476	4 507
	Malaysia	51	229 340	446 237	147	230	98	437 424	446 100	224	230	97	393 785	407 396	8 843	9 097
	Malta	100	4 341	4 343	59	61	100	4 341	4 343	59	61	85	3 634	4 294	3 634	4 294
	Moldova	100	30 145	30 145	229	229	100	30 145	30 145	229	229	98	28 754	29 341	5 325	5 436
	Montenegro	100	7 301	7 312	64	65	100	7 301	7 312	64	65	94	6 346	6 766	5 665	6 043
	Peru	100	468 406	470 651	280	282	100	469 662	470 651	281	282	99	426 205	430 959	6 971	7 054
	Qatar	99	13 333	13 470	166	168	99	13 333	13 470	166	168	94	12 061	12 819	12 061	12 819
	Romania	99	171 553	172 652	181	182	100	172 495	172 495	182	182	99	162 918	164 216	4 876	4 910
	Russia	99	1 181 937	1 189 441	209	210	99	1 181 937	1 189 441	209	210	97	1 072 914	1 108 068	6 021	6 215
	Singapore	97	45 299	46 620	175	179	98	45 553	46 620	176	179	93	42 241	45 259	6 105	6 555
	Chinese Taipei	100	286 778	286 778	214	214	100	286 778	286 778	214	214	98	246 408	251 424	7 708	7 871
	Thailand	99	739 772	751 010	269	273	100	751 010	751 010	273	273	97	614 996	634 795	8 249	8 491
	Trinidad and Tobago	92	15 904	17 371	141	163	92	15 904	17 371	141	163	79	9 674	12 188	4 587	5 745
	Tunisia	99	121 751	122 767	162	165	99	121 838	122 792	163	165	86	97 337	112 665	5 340	6 175
	United Arab Emirates	99	49 310	50 060	473	477	99	49 310	50 060	473	477	95	43 774	46 263	14 167	15 014
	Uruguay	98	42 986	43 737	217	221	99	43 442	43 737	219	221	86	32 762	38 023	6 059	7 026
	Viet Nam	100	996 757	996 757	188	188	100	996 757	996 757	188	188	100	871 353	874 859	5 826	5 849

* See note at the beginning of this Annex.

StatLink http://dx.doi.org/10.1787/888933433129

Grade levels

Students assessed in PISA 2015 are at various grade levels. The percentage of students at each grade level is presented by country in Table A2.4a and by gender within each country in Table A2.4b.

[Part 1/1]

Table A2.4a Percentage of students at each grade level

		All students											
		7th grade		8th grade		9th grade		10th grade		11th grade		12th grade and above	
		%	S.E.	%	S.E.	%	S.E.	%	S.E.	%	S.E.	%	S.E.
OECD	Australia	0.0	(0.0)	0.1	(0.0)	11.2	(0.3)	74.6	(0.4)	14.0	(0.4)	0.1	(0.0)
	Austria	0.0	(0.0)	2.0	(0.6)	20.8	(0.9)	71.2	(1.0)	5.9	(0.3)	0.0	(0.0)
	Belgium	0.6	(0.1)	6.4	(0.5)	30.7	(0.7)	61.0	(0.9)	1.3	(0.1)	0.0	(0.0)
	Canada	0.1	(0.0)	0.7	(0.1)	10.8	(0.5)	87.6	(0.6)	0.8	(0.1)	0.0	(0.0)
	Chile	1.7	(0.3)	4.1	(0.6)	24.0	(0.7)	68.1	(1.0)	2.1	(0.2)	0.0	(0.0)
	Czech Republic	0.5	(0.1)	3.9	(0.3)	49.4	(1.2)	46.2	(1.2)	0.0	(0.0)	0.0	c
	Denmark	0.2	(0.1)	16.4	(0.6)	81.9	(0.7)	1.4	(0.5)	0.0	c	0.0	c
	Estonia	0.8	(0.2)	21.3	(0.6)	76.6	(0.6)	1.3	(0.3)	0.0	c	0.0	(0.0)
	Finland	0.5	(0.1)	13.6	(0.4)	85.7	(0.4)	0.0	(0.0)	0.2	(0.1)	0.0	c
	France	0.0	(0.0)	1.0	(0.2)	23.1	(0.6)	72.5	(0.7)	3.2	(0.2)	0.1	(0.1)
	Germany	0.5	(0.1)	7.7	(0.4)	47.3	(0.8)	43.1	(0.8)	1.5	(0.5)	0.0	(0.0)
	Greece	0.2	(0.1)	0.7	(0.2)	3.8	(0.8)	95.3	(0.9)	0.0	c	0.0	c
	Hungary	1.7	(0.3)	8.5	(0.5)	75.8	(0.7)	14.0	(0.5)	0.0	c	0.0	c
	Iceland	0.0	c	0.0	c	0.0	c	100.0	c	0.0	c	0.0	c
	Ireland	0.0	(0.0)	1.8	(0.2)	60.6	(0.7)	26.5	(1.1)	11.1	(0.9)	0.0	c
	Israel	0.0	c	0.1	(0.0)	16.4	(0.9)	82.7	(0.9)	0.9	(0.3)	0.0	c
	Italy	0.1	(0.0)	1.0	(0.2)	15.2	(0.6)	77.2	(0.7)	6.6	(0.3)	0.0	c
	Japan	0.0	c	0.0	c	0.0	c	100.0	(0.0)	0.0	c	0.0	c
	Korea	0.0	c	0.0	c	9.1	(0.8)	90.4	(0.8)	0.5	(0.1)	0.0	c
	Latvia	0.9	(0.2)	11.7	(0.5)	84.4	(0.6)	2.9	(0.3)	0.0	(0.0)	0.0	c
	Luxembourg	0.3	(0.1)	7.9	(0.1)	50.9	(0.1)	40.3	(0.1)	0.6	(0.0)	0.0	c
	Mexico	2.3	(0.3)	4.8	(0.4)	31.9	(1.4)	60.3	(1.6)	0.5	(0.1)	0.2	(0.0)
	Netherlands	0.1	(0.0)	2.8	(0.3)	41.6	(0.6)	54.8	(0.6)	0.8	(0.2)	0.0	(0.0)
	New Zealand	0.0	c	0.0	c	0.0	(0.0)	6.2	(0.3)	88.8	(0.5)	5.0	(0.5)
	Norway	0.0	c	0.0	c	0.6	(0.1)	99.3	(0.2)	0.1	(0.1)	0.0	c
	Poland	0.6	(0.1)	4.9	(0.3)	93.8	(0.4)	0.6	(0.2)	0.0	c	0.0	c
	Portugal	3.2	(0.3)	8.4	(0.5)	22.9	(0.9)	65.1	(1.2)	0.4	(0.1)	0.0	c
	Slovak Republic	2.2	(0.4)	4.6	(0.4)	42.6	(1.3)	50.6	(1.2)	0.1	(0.0)	0.0	c
	Slovenia	0.0	c	0.3	(0.1)	4.8	(0.3)	94.6	(0.4)	0.3	(0.1)	0.0	c
	Spain	0.1	(0.0)	8.6	(0.5)	23.4	(0.6)	67.9	(0.9)	0.1	(0.1)	0.0	c
	Sweden	0.1	(0.1)	3.1	(0.4)	94.9	(0.8)	1.8	(0.7)	0.1	(0.1)	0.0	c
	Switzerland	0.5	(0.1)	11.8	(0.7)	61.3	(1.2)	25.9	(1.3)	0.5	(0.1)	0.0	(0.0)
	Turkey	0.6	(0.1)	2.6	(0.4)	20.7	(1.0)	72.9	(1.2)	3.0	(0.3)	0.1	(0.0)
	United Kingdom	0.0	c	0.0	c	0.0	c	1.6	(0.3)	97.4	(0.4)	1.0	(0.3)
	United States	0.0	(0.0)	0.5	(0.3)	9.6	(0.7)	72.4	(0.9)	17.3	(0.6)	0.1	(0.0)
Partners	Albania	0.2	(0.1)	1.0	(0.2)	35.8	(2.3)	61.7	(2.3)	1.2	(0.7)	0.0	(0.0)
	Algeria	18.8	(1.0)	23.5	(1.1)	35.1	(1.5)	19.4	(2.1)	3.2	(0.7)	0.0	c
	Brazil	3.5	(0.2)	6.4	(0.4)	12.5	(0.5)	35.9	(0.9)	39.2	(0.8)	2.5	(0.2)
	B-S-J-G (China)	1.1	(0.2)	9.2	(0.7)	52.7	(1.7)	34.6	(2.0)	2.2	(0.5)	0.1	(0.0)
	Bulgaria	0.5	(0.2)	3.0	(0.6)	92.2	(0.8)	4.3	(0.4)	0.0	c	0.0	c
	Colombia	5.3	(0.4)	12.3	(0.6)	22.7	(0.6)	40.2	(0.7)	19.5	(0.6)	0.0	c
	Costa Rica	6.2	(0.7)	14.0	(0.7)	33.0	(1.2)	46.5	(1.6)	0.2	(0.1)	0.1	(0.1)
	Croatia	0.0	c	0.2	(0.2)	79.2	(0.5)	20.6	(0.4)	0.0	c	0.0	c
	Cyprus*	0.0	c	0.3	(0.0)	5.8	(0.1)	93.1	(0.1)	0.7	(0.1)	0.0	c
	Dominican Republic	7.1	(0.8)	13.8	(1.2)	20.6	(0.8)	41.9	(1.1)	14.2	(0.7)	2.4	(0.3)
	FYROM	0.1	(0.1)	0.1	(0.1)	70.2	(0.2)	29.7	(0.2)	0.0	c	0.0	c
	Georgia	0.1	(0.0)	0.8	(0.2)	22.0	(0.8)	76.0	(0.9)	1.1	(0.3)	0.0	c
	Hong Kong (China)	1.1	(0.1)	5.6	(0.4)	26.0	(0.7)	66.7	(0.7)	0.6	(0.5)	0.0	c
	Indonesia	2.1	(0.3)	8.1	(0.7)	42.1	(1.5)	45.5	(1.6)	2.3	(0.4)	0.0	(0.0)
	Jordan	0.2	(0.1)	0.6	(0.1)	6.6	(0.4)	92.6	(0.4)	0.0	c	0.0	c
	Kosovo	0.0	(0.1)	0.6	(0.1)	24.9	(0.8)	72.4	(0.9)	2.1	(0.2)	0.0	c
	Lebanon	3.7	(0.5)	8.3	(0.8)	16.6	(1.1)	62.3	(1.4)	9.0	(0.8)	0.1	(0.1)
	Lithuania	0.1	(0.0)	2.6	(0.2)	86.3	(0.4)	11.0	(0.4)	0.0	(0.0)	0.0	c
	Macao (China)	2.9	(0.1)	12.2	(0.2)	29.7	(0.2)	54.5	(0.1)	0.6	(0.1)	0.0	c
	Malta	0.0	c	0.0	c	0.3	(0.1)	6.1	(0.2)	93.6	(0.1)	0.1	(0.0)
	Moldova	0.2	(0.1)	7.6	(0.5)	84.5	(0.8)	7.5	(0.8)	0.0	(0.0)	0.0	c
	Montenegro	0.0	c	0.0	c	83.7	(0.1)	16.3	(0.1)	0.0	c	0.0	c
	Peru	2.5	(0.3)	6.6	(0.4)	15.9	(0.5)	50.2	(0.8)	24.8	(0.8)	0.0	c
	Qatar	0.9	(0.1)	3.5	(0.1)	16.3	(0.1)	60.7	(0.1)	18.0	(0.1)	0.6	(0.0)
	Romania	1.4	(0.3)	8.9	(0.5)	74.8	(0.9)	14.9	(0.7)	0.0	c	0.0	c
	Russia	0.2	(0.1)	6.6	(0.3)	79.7	(1.5)	13.4	(1.5)	0.1	(0.0)	0.0	c
	Singapore	0.0	(0.0)	1.9	(0.3)	7.9	(0.8)	90.0	(1.0)	0.1	(0.0)	0.1	(0.0)
	Chinese Taipei	0.0	c	0.0	c	35.4	(0.7)	64.6	(0.7)	0.0	c	0.0	c
	Thailand	0.2	(0.1)	0.6	(0.2)	23.8	(1.0)	72.9	(1.0)	2.4	(0.4)	0.0	c
	Trinidad and Tobago	3.3	(0.2)	10.8	(0.3)	27.3	(0.3)	56.5	(0.3)	2.2	(0.2)	0.0	c
	Tunisia	4.3	(0.3)	10.6	(0.8)	19.6	(1.3)	60.9	(1.7)	4.6	(0.4)	0.0	c
	United Arab Emirates	0.6	(0.1)	2.5	(0.3)	10.6	(0.7)	53.4	(0.8)	31.4	(0.8)	1.5	(0.1)
	Uruguay	7.5	(0.6)	9.7	(0.5)	20.7	(0.7)	61.3	(1.2)	0.8	(0.1)	0.0	c
	Viet Nam	0.3	(0.1)	1.7	(0.4)	7.7	(1.8)	90.4	(2.2)	0.0	(0.0)	0.0	c
	Argentina**	1.6	(0.4)	9.7	(0.8)	27.4	(1.2)	58.5	(1.6)	2.8	(0.3)	0.0	c
	Kazakhstan**	0.1	(0.1)	2.7	(0.3)	60.4	(1.7)	36.2	(1.8)	0.6	(0.1)	0.0	c
	Malaysia**	0.0	c	0.0	c	3.2	(0.6)	96.4	(0.7)	0.4	(0.3)	0.0	c

* See note at the beginning of this Annex.
** Coverage is too small to ensure comparability (see Annex A4).
StatLink http://dx.doi.org/10.1787/888933433129

[Part 1/1]

Table A2.4b Percentage of students at each grade level

	Boys												Girls											
	7th grade		8th grade		9th grade		10th grade		11th grade		12th grade and above		7th grade		8th grade		9th grade		10th grade		11th grade		12th grade and above	
	%	S.E.	%	S.E.	%	S.E.	%	S.E.	%	S.E.	%	S.E.	%	S.E.	%	S.E.	%	S.E.	%	S.E.	%	S.E.	%	S.E.
OECD																								
Australia	0.0	(0.0)	0.2	(0.1)	13.2	(0.4)	73.5	(0.5)	13.1	(0.5)	0.0	(0.0)	0.0	(0.0)	0.1	(0.0)	9.2	(0.3)	75.7	(0.5)	14.9	(0.6)	0.1	(0.1)
Austria	0.1	(0.1)	2.0	(0.4)	21.6	(1.2)	71.1	(1.2)	5.2	(0.4)	0.0	(0.0)	0.0	c	2.0	(0.9)	20.0	(1.0)	71.4	(1.3)	6.6	(0.4)	0.0	(0.0)
Belgium	0.7	(0.1)	6.7	(0.5)	33.6	(1.0)	57.9	(1.1)	1.2	(0.2)	0.0	c	0.6	(0.1)	6.2	(0.5)	27.7	(0.8)	64.2	(1.1)	1.3	(0.1)	0.0	(0.0)
Canada	0.1	(0.1)	1.0	(0.2)	11.7	(0.6)	86.5	(0.6)	0.7	(0.1)	0.0	(0.0)	0.1	(0.0)	0.4	(0.1)	9.9	(0.6)	88.8	(0.6)	0.8	(0.1)	0.0	(0.0)
Chile	2.2	(0.5)	4.8	(0.8)	26.4	(0.9)	64.8	(1.3)	1.8	(0.2)	0.1	(0.1)	1.2	(0.4)	3.5	(0.7)	21.5	(0.8)	71.4	(1.1)	2.4	(0.3)	0.0	c
Czech Republic	0.6	(0.2)	5.5	(0.5)	52.3	(1.5)	41.5	(1.6)	0.0	(0.0)	0.0	c	0.4	(0.2)	2.2	(0.3)	46.2	(1.5)	51.2	(1.6)	0.0	c	0.0	c
Denmark	0.3	(0.1)	21.9	(0.9)	76.6	(1.0)	1.2	(0.5)	0.0	c	0.0	c	0.1	(0.1)	10.8	(0.5)	87.3	(0.7)	1.7	(0.6)	0.0	c	0.0	c
Estonia	1.3	(0.3)	23.7	(0.9)	74.2	(0.8)	0.8	(0.3)	0.0	c	0.0	(0.0)	0.2	(0.1)	18.8	(0.8)	79.1	(0.8)	1.9	(0.4)	0.0	c	0.0	c
Finland	0.4	(0.1)	15.5	(0.6)	83.9	(0.6)	0.0	(0.0)	0.2	(0.1)	0.0	c	0.5	(0.1)	11.5	(0.5)	87.7	(0.5)	0.0	c	0.3	(0.2)	0.0	c
France	0.0	c	1.0	(0.2)	26.1	(0.9)	69.6	(1.0)	3.1	(0.3)	0.2	(0.1)	0.1	(0.1)	1.0	(0.2)	20.1	(0.6)	75.4	(0.8)	3.3	(0.3)	0.1	(0.0)
Germany	0.7	(0.2)	9.0	(0.5)	50.1	(1.0)	38.8	(1.0)	1.4	(0.4)	0.0	(0.0)	0.3	(0.1)	6.3	(0.6)	44.3	(0.9)	47.5	(1.0)	1.6	(0.6)	0.0	c
Greece	0.4	(0.2)	1.1	(0.3)	4.7	(1.0)	93.8	(1.2)	0.0	c	0.0	c	0.1	(0.1)	0.2	(0.1)	2.8	(0.8)	96.9	(0.8)	0.0	c	0.0	c
Hungary	1.8	(0.4)	10.1	(0.6)	75.6	(0.9)	12.5	(0.6)	0.0	c	0.0	c	1.6	(0.4)	6.9	(0.8)	76.0	(0.9)	15.5	(0.7)	0.0	c	0.0	c
Iceland	0.0	c	0.0	c	0.0	c	100.0	c	0.0	c	0.0	c	0.0	c	0.0	c	0.0	c	100.0	c	0.0	c	0.0	c
Ireland	0.0	c	2.2	(0.3)	62.8	(0.9)	24.1	(1.2)	10.9	(1.0)	0.0	c	0.0	(0.0)	1.4	(0.2)	58.2	(0.9)	29.0	(1.4)	11.3	(1.1)	0.0	c
Israel	0.0	c	0.1	(0.1)	18.0	(1.2)	80.9	(1.3)	1.1	(0.6)	0.0	c	0.0	c	0.1	(0.0)	14.9	(0.8)	84.4	(0.8)	0.7	(0.1)	0.0	c
Italy	0.2	(0.1)	1.3	(0.3)	18.1	(0.8)	75.0	(0.9)	5.4	(0.4)	0.0	c	0.1	(0.0)	0.7	(0.2)	12.2	(0.8)	79.3	(1.0)	7.7	(0.5)	0.0	c
Japan	0.0	c	0.0	c	0.0	c	100.0	c	0.0	c	0.0	c	0.0	c	0.0	c	0.0	c	100.0	c	0.0	c	0.0	c
Korea	0.0	c	0.0	c	10.1	(1.4)	89.4	(1.4)	0.5	(0.1)	0.0	c	0.0	c	0.0	c	8.0	(0.8)	91.5	(0.8)	0.5	(0.1)	0.0	c
Latvia	1.5	(0.4)	14.7	(0.8)	81.8	(0.9)	1.9	(0.3)	0.0	(0.0)	0.0	c	0.4	(0.2)	8.7	(0.7)	87.0	(0.7)	3.9	(0.4)	0.0	c	0.0	c
Luxembourg	0.2	(0.1)	9.4	(0.2)	52.4	(0.3)	37.3	(0.2)	0.7	(0.1)	0.0	c	0.3	(0.1)	6.4	(0.2)	49.4	(0.2)	43.3	(0.2)	0.6	(0.1)	0.0	c
Mexico	3.1	(0.5)	5.9	(0.6)	32.2	(1.5)	58.0	(1.6)	0.6	(0.2)	0.2	(0.0)	1.5	(0.3)	3.7	(0.4)	31.6	(1.7)	62.5	(1.7)	0.4	(0.1)	0.2	(0.1)
Netherlands	0.0	(0.0)	3.8	(0.4)	45.3	(0.8)	50.2	(0.8)	0.8	(0.3)	0.0	c	0.1	(0.0)	1.9	(0.3)	38.0	(0.7)	59.3	(0.7)	0.7	(0.2)	0.0	(0.0)
New Zealand	0.0	c	0.0	c	0.0	c	6.9	(0.5)	88.6	(0.8)	4.5	(0.5)	0.0	c	0.0	c	0.0	(0.0)	5.4	(0.4)	89.1	(0.6)	5.5	(0.6)
Norway	0.0	c	0.0	c	0.8	(0.2)	99.1	(0.2)	0.1	(0.1)	0.0	c	0.0	c	0.0	c	0.3	(0.1)	99.6	(0.1)	0.1	(0.1)	0.0	c
Poland	0.9	(0.2)	6.8	(0.5)	92.1	(0.6)	0.2	(0.2)	0.0	c	0.0	c	0.4	(0.1)	3.0	(0.3)	95.6	(0.5)	1.1	(0.3)	0.0	c	0.0	c
Portugal	4.2	(0.4)	10.5	(0.7)	25.4	(1.0)	59.6	(1.4)	0.3	(0.1)	0.0	c	2.1	(0.4)	6.4	(0.5)	20.5	(0.9)	70.5	(1.2)	0.5	(0.1)	0.0	c
Slovak Republic	2.4	(0.4)	4.8	(0.5)	43.5	(1.6)	49.4	(1.8)	0.0	c	0.0	c	1.9	(0.5)	4.3	(0.6)	41.7	(1.8)	51.9	(1.8)	0.1	(0.1)	0.0	c
Slovenia	0.0	c	0.5	(0.2)	5.4	(0.7)	93.9	(0.7)	0.2	(0.1)	0.0	c	0.0	c	0.2	(0.1)	4.1	(0.6)	95.3	(0.6)	0.4	(0.2)	0.0	c
Spain	0.1	(0.1)	10.7	(0.7)	25.4	(0.8)	63.7	(1.1)	0.1	(0.1)	0.0	c	0.0	c	6.5	(0.5)	21.3	(0.8)	72.1	(1.0)	0.1	(0.1)	0.0	c
Sweden	0.1	(0.1)	3.5	(0.5)	95.0	(0.9)	1.4	(0.7)	0.1	(0.1)	0.0	c	0.2	(0.1)	2.6	(0.4)	94.9	(1.0)	2.3	(0.9)	0.1	(0.1)	0.0	c
Switzerland	0.7	(0.2)	13.4	(0.8)	60.7	(1.1)	24.7	(1.2)	0.5	(0.1)	0.0	c	0.3	(0.1)	10.1	(0.8)	62.0	(1.7)	27.2	(1.9)	0.5	(0.2)	0.0	(0.0)
Turkey	0.8	(0.3)	3.1	(0.6)	25.4	(1.2)	68.4	(1.6)	2.2	(0.4)	0.1	(0.1)	0.4	(0.2)	2.1	(0.4)	16.1	(1.1)	77.5	(1.3)	3.8	(0.4)	0.1	(0.0)
United Kingdom	0.0	c	0.0	c	0.0	c	1.9	(0.5)	97.3	(0.6)	0.9	(0.3)	0.0	c	0.0	c	0.0	c	1.4	(0.2)	97.5	(0.3)	1.1	(0.3)
United States	0.0	c	0.5	(0.4)	11.6	(0.8)	72.4	(1.0)	15.3	(0.7)	0.2	(0.1)	0.1	(0.1)	0.5	(0.2)	7.6	(0.6)	72.4	(0.9)	19.4	(0.7)	0.1	(0.0)
Partners																								
Albania	0.2	(0.2)	0.9	(0.2)	41.2	(2.7)	56.3	(2.6)	1.3	(0.9)	0.0	(0.0)	0.1	(0.1)	1.1	(0.3)	30.4	(2.1)	67.1	(2.2)	1.2	(0.5)	0.1	(0.0)
Algeria	24.4	(1.3)	25.7	(1.2)	32.6	(1.5)	14.7	(1.9)	2.6	(0.7)	0.0	c	12.6	(1.1)	21.0	(1.2)	37.9	(2.0)	24.6	(2.5)	3.9	(0.8)	0.0	c
Brazil	4.6	(0.3)	7.8	(0.6)	13.9	(0.6)	36.5	(1.0)	35.3	(0.9)	1.8	(0.2)	2.4	(0.2)	5.0	(0.4)	11.1	(0.6)	35.3	(0.9)	43.0	(0.9)	3.1	(0.2)
B-S-J-G (China)	1.2	(0.2)	9.9	(0.7)	55.4	(1.7)	31.6	(1.9)	1.9	(0.5)	0.1	(0.0)	1.1	(0.2)	8.4	(0.8)	49.6	(1.8)	38.1	(2.2)	2.6	(0.5)	0.1	(0.1)
Bulgaria	0.6	(0.2)	4.1	(0.8)	91.8	(1.0)	3.5	(0.4)	0.0	c	0.0	c	0.4	(0.2)	1.8	(0.4)	92.7	(0.7)	5.2	(0.4)	0.0	c	0.0	c
Colombia	7.2	(0.6)	14.3	(0.8)	25.2	(0.8)	37.1	(0.9)	16.2	(0.8)	0.0	c	3.6	(0.4)	10.5	(0.7)	20.5	(0.9)	42.9	(1.0)	22.5	(0.8)	0.0	c
Costa Rica	7.8	(0.8)	16.7	(0.8)	34.3	(1.2)	41.2	(1.5)	0.1	(0.0)	0.0	c	4.7	(0.7)	11.4	(0.7)	31.8	(1.4)	51.6	(1.8)	0.3	(0.1)	0.2	(0.1)
Croatia	0.0	c	0.2	(0.1)	80.5	(0.5)	19.4	(0.5)	0.0	c	0.0	c	0.0	c	0.3	(0.2)	78.0	(0.7)	21.7	(0.7)	0.0	c	0.0	c
Cyprus*	0.0	c	0.3	(0.1)	6.6	(0.2)	92.4	(0.2)	0.6	(0.1)	0.0	c	0.0	c	0.3	(0.1)	5.1	(0.2)	93.8	(0.2)	0.8	(0.1)	0.0	c
Dominican Republic	10.3	(1.1)	16.4	(1.5)	23.3	(1.2)	37.2	(1.4)	11.1	(0.8)	1.7	(0.3)	4.0	(0.6)	11.2	(1.1)	18.1	(0.8)	46.5	(1.1)	17.2	(0.8)	3.0	(0.3)
FYROM	0.2	(0.2)	0.2	(0.2)	70.9	(0.3)	28.8	(0.2)	0.0	c	0.0	c	0.0	c	0.0	c	69.4	(0.3)	30.6	(0.3)	0.0	c	0.0	c
Georgia	0.1	(0.0)	0.9	(0.2)	23.0	(1.0)	75.2	(1.0)	0.8	(0.2)	0.0	c	0.1	(0.1)	0.7	(0.2)	20.9	(0.9)	76.8	(1.0)	1.5	(0.4)	0.0	c
Hong Kong (China)	1.3	(0.2)	6.4	(0.5)	28.5	(0.8)	63.3	(0.9)	0.5	(0.4)	0.0	c	1.0	(0.2)	4.7	(0.4)	23.5	(0.8)	70.2	(0.9)	0.6	(0.6)	0.0	c
Indonesia	2.5	(0.4)	8.9	(0.9)	44.3	(1.9)	42.1	(2.0)	2.1	(0.4)	0.0	(0.0)	1.7	(0.3)	7.2	(1.0)	39.8	(1.9)	48.9	(2.1)	2.4	(0.4)	0.0	c
Jordan	0.1	(0.1)	0.5	(0.1)	6.6	(0.7)	92.9	(0.7)	0.0	c	0.0	c	0.2	(0.1)	0.7	(0.1)	6.6	(0.6)	92.4	(0.6)	0.0	c	0.0	c
Kosovo	0.1	(0.1)	0.5	(0.1)	26.4	(0.9)	71.5	(1.0)	1.6	(0.3)	0.0	c	0.0	c	0.7	(0.2)	23.5	(1.0)	73.3	(1.0)	2.5	(0.3)	0.0	c
Lebanon	4.0	(0.6)	8.2	(0.9)	17.2	(1.4)	63.5	(1.7)	6.9	(0.7)	0.2	(0.1)	3.4	(0.6)	8.3	(1.0)	16.1	(1.2)	61.2	(1.8)	10.8	(1.2)	0.1	(0.1)
Lithuania	0.2	(0.1)	3.5	(0.3)	87.4	(0.6)	8.8	(0.5)	0.0	(0.0)	0.0	c	0.0	(0.0)	1.7	(0.2)	85.1	(0.7)	13.1	(0.6)	0.0	(0.0)	0.0	c
Macao (China)	4.3	(0.2)	16.4	(0.3)	30.8	(0.2)	48.2	(0.2)	0.4	(0.1)	0.0	c	1.6	(0.2)	8.0	(0.2)	28.7	(0.3)	60.8	(0.3)	0.9	(0.2)	0.0	c
Malta	0.0	c	0.0	c	0.5	(0.1)	6.8	(0.3)	92.7	(0.2)	0.0	c	0.0	c	0.0	c	0.1	(0.0)	5.4	(0.2)	94.4	(0.2)	0.1	(0.1)
Moldova	0.3	(0.1)	8.2	(0.7)	86.3	(0.9)	5.0	(0.9)	0.1	(0.1)	0.0	c	0.2	(0.1)	7.0	(0.6)	82.8	(1.2)	10.1	(1.2)	0.0	c	0.0	c
Montenegro	0.0	c	0.0	c	85.2	(0.2)	14.8	(0.2)	0.0	c	0.0	c	0.0	c	0.0	c	82.2	(0.2)	17.8	(0.2)	0.0	c	0.0	c
Peru	3.0	(0.5)	7.5	(0.5)	17.9	(0.7)	48.7	(0.9)	22.9	(1.0)	0.0	c	1.9	(0.3)	5.6	(0.5)	14.0	(0.6)	51.7	(1.0)	26.8	(0.9)	0.0	c
Qatar	0.8	(0.1)	3.6	(0.1)	18.0	(0.2)	59.3	(0.2)	17.6	(0.2)	0.6	(0.1)	1.0	(0.1)	3.4	(0.1)	14.5	(0.1)	62.1	(0.2)	18.4	(0.2)	0.6	(0.1)
Romania	1.7	(0.4)	10.7	(0.8)	74.3	(1.0)	13.3	(0.7)	0.0	c	0.0	c	1.1	(0.4)	7.2	(0.8)	75.3	(1.1)	16.4	(0.8)	0.0	c	0.0	c
Russia	0.2	(0.1)	7.2	(0.5)	80.1	(1.7)	12.4	(1.7)	0.0	(0.0)	0.0	c	0.1	(0.1)	6.0	(0.4)	79.3	(1.5)	14.4	(1.6)	0.1	(0.1)	0.0	c
Singapore	0.1	(0.0)	1.8	(0.3)	8.9	(0.9)	89.1	(1.1)	0.1	(0.1)	0.0	(0.0)	0.0	(0.0)	2.0	(0.4)	6.9	(0.8)	90.8	(1.1)	0.2	(0.1)	0.1	(0.0)
Chinese Taipei	0.0	c	0.0	c	36.5	(1.3)	63.5	(1.3)	0.0	c	0.0	c	0.0	c	0.0	c	34.3	(1.3)	65.7	(1.3)	0.0	c	0.0	c
Thailand	0.2	(0.1)	0.8	(0.3)	25.4	(1.2)	71.4	(1.2)	2.3	(0.4)	0.0	c	0.3	(0.1)	0.5	(0.2)	22.5	(1.3)	74.1	(1.3)	2.6	(0.4)	0.0	c
Trinidad and Tobago	3.7	(0.3)	14.2	(0.5)	30.8	(0.5)	48.9	(0.5)	2.4	(0.2)	0.0	c	2.8	(0.2)	7.5	(0.4)	23.8	(0.4)	63.9	(0.5)	2.0	(0.3)	0.0	c
Tunisia	5.9	(0.5)	13.8	(1.0)	22.0	(1.4)	54.0	(1.9)	4.3	(0.5)	0.0	c	3.0	(0.3)	7.8	(0.7)	17.5	(1.4)	67.0	(1.8)	4.8	(0.5)	0.0	c
United Arab Emirates	0.7	(0.1)	2.9	(0.4)	11.4	(1.1)	54.0	(1.3)	29.6	(1.0)	1.4	(0.2)	0.4	(0.1)	2.2	(0.5)	9.9	(0.9)	52.8	(0.9)	33.1	(1.1)	1.6	(0.2)
Uruguay	9.2	(0.8)	11.2	(0.7)	22.5	(0.9)	56.5	(1.5)	0.5	(0.1)	0.0	c	6.0	(0.7)	8.3	(0.6)	19.0	(0.8)	65.6	(1.1)	1.1	(0.2)	0.0	c
Viet Nam	0.5	(0.2)	2.3	(0.6)	11.1	(2.6)	86.1	(3.2)	0.0	c	0.0	c	0.1	(0.0)	1.1	(0.4)	4.6	(1.2)	94.2	(1.4)	0.0	(0.0)	0.0	c
Argentina**	2.3	(0.6)	11.5	(0.9)	27.8	(1.3)	56.0	(1.8)	2.4	(0.3)	0.0	c	1.0	(0.3)	8.1	(0.9)	26.9	(1.4)	60.8	(1.7)	3.2	(0.3)	0.0	c
Kazakhstan**	0.1	(0.1)	3.1	(0.4)	62.8	(2.3)	33.5	(2.4)	0.5	(0.1)	0.0	c	0.1	(0.1)	2.3	(0.3)	57.8	(1.7)	39.0	(1.8)	0.7	(0.1)	0.0	c
Malaysia**	0.0	c	0.0	c	4.2	(0.8)	95.4	(0.9)	0.4	(0.3)	0.0	c	0.0	c	0.0	c	2.3	(0.5)	97.2	(0.6)	0.4	(0.4)	0.0	c

* See note at the beginning of this Annex.
** Coverage is too small to ensure comparability (see Annex A4).
StatLink http://dx.doi.org/10.1787/888933433129

Reference

OECD (2017), *PISA 2015 Technical Report*, PISA, OECD Publishing, Paris.

ANNEX A3

TECHNICAL NOTES ON ANALYSES IN THIS VOLUME

Methods and definitions

Relative performance in collaborative problem solving

Relative performance in collaborative problem solving is defined as the difference between a student's actual performance in collaborative problem solving and his or her expected performance, based on performance in other domains:

$$RP_i^{cps} = y_i^{cps} - E(y_i^{cps} \mid y_i^{srm})$$

where y_i^{cps} represents student *i*'s performance in collaborative problem solving, and y_i^{srm} is a vector of student *i*'s performance in other domains (such as science, reading and mathematics).

A student's (conditionally) expected performance is estimated using regression models; relative performance is therefore based on residuals from regression models. All analyses of relative performance in this volume derive residuals from linear parametric regression models. However, different regression methods can be used, including ones that allow for curvilinear relationships and non-parametric regression models.

In some analyses, the regression model is calibrated on an international sample of students, in order to compare students' performance across countries. In others, when differences between different groups of students within the same country or economy (for example, within-country gender differences or the relationship between performance and the certain out-of-school student activities), the regression model is calibrated on national samples. In all cases, ten distinct regression models are estimated to compute ten plausible values of relative performance.

Relative risk

The relative risk is a measure of the association between an antecedent factor and an outcome factor. The relative risk is simply the ratio of two risks, i.e. the risk of observing the outcome when the antecedent is present and the risk of observing the outcome when the antecedent is not present. Figure A3.1 presents the notation that is used in the following.

Figure A3.1 ▪ **Labels used in a two-way table**

p_{11}	p_{12}	$p_{1.}$
p_{21}	p_{22}	$p_{2.}$
$p_{.1}$	$p_{.2}$	$p_{..}$

p_{ij} represents the probabilities for each cell and is equal to the number of observations in a particular cell divided by the total number of observations. $p_{i.}$, $p_{.j}$ respectively represent the marginal probabilities for each row and for each column. The marginal probabilities are equal to the marginal frequencies divided by the total number of students.

Assuming that rows represent the antecedent factor, with the first row for "having the antecedent" and the second row for "not having the antecedent", and that the columns represent the outcome: the first column for "having the outcome" and the second column for "not having the outcome", the relative risk is then equal to:

$$RR = \frac{(p_{11}/p_{1.})}{(p_{21}/p_{2.})}$$

Odds ratio

The same notation can be used to define the odds ratio, another measure of the relative likelihood of a particular outcome across two groups. The odds ratio for observing the outcome when an antecedent is present is simply

$$OR = \frac{(p_{11}/p_{12})}{(p_{21}/p_{22})}$$

where p_{11}/p_{12} represents the "odds" of observing the outcome when the antecedent is present, and p_{21}/p_{22} represents the "odds" of observing the outcome when the antecedent is not present.

A logistic regression can be used to estimate the odds ratio: the exponentiated logit coefficient for a binary variable is equivalent to the odds ratio. A "generalised" odds ratio, after accounting for other differences across groups, can be estimated by introducing control variables in the logistic regression.

Statistics based on multilevel models

Statistics based on multilevel models include variance components (between- and within-school variance), the index of intra-class correlation derived from these components, and regression coefficients where this has been indicated. Multilevel models are generally specified as two-level regression models (the student and school levels), with normally distributed residuals, and estimated with maximum likelihood estimation. Where the dependent variable is science, reading, mathematics or collaborative problem-solving performance, the estimation uses ten plausible values for each student's performance on the performance scale. Models were estimated using the Stata ® (version 14.1) "mixed" module.

In multilevel models, weights are used at both the student and school levels. The purpose of these weights is to account for differences in the probabilities of students being selected in the sample. Since PISA applies a two-stage sampling procedure, these differences are due to factors at both the school and the student levels. For the multilevel models, student final weights (W_FSTUWT) were used. Students' within-school weights correspond to student final weights, rescaled to amount to the sample size within each school. School weights correspond to the sum of final student weights (W_FSTUWT) within each school. This definition of school weights is the same used in the PISA 2012 Initial Report.

The index of intra-class correlation is defined and estimated as:

$$100 * \frac{\sigma_w^2}{\sigma_w^2 + \sigma_b^2}$$

where σ_w^2 and σ_b^2, respectively, represent the within- and between-variance estimates.

The results in multilevel models, and the between-school variance estimate in particular, depend on how schools are defined and organised within countries and by the units that were chosen for sampling purposes. For example, in some countries, some of the schools in the PISA sample were defined as administrative units (even if they spanned several geographically separate institutions, as in Italy); in others they were defined as those parts of larger educational institutions that serve 15-year-olds; in still others they were defined as physical school buildings; and in others they were defined from a management perspective (e.g. entities having a principal). The *PISA 2015 Technical Report* (OECD, 2017) and Annex A2 provide an overview of how schools are defined. In Slovenia, for example, the primary sampling unit is defined as a group of students who follow the same study programme within a school (an education track within a school). So in this case, the between-school variation is actually the within-school, between-track difference. The use of stratification variables in the selection of schools may also affect the estimate of the between-school variation, particularly if stratification variables are associated with between-school differences.

Because of the manner in which students were sampled, the within-school variation includes variation between classes as well as between students.

Effect sizes

Sometimes it is useful to compare differences in an index between groups, such as boys and girls, across countries. A problem that may occur in such instances is that the distribution of the index varies across groups or countries. One way to resolve this is to calculate an effect size that accounts for differences in the distributions. An effect size measures the difference between, say, the collaborative problem-solving performance of male and female students in a given country, relative to the average variation in collaborative problem-solving performance among all students in the country.

The effect size between two subgroups is calculated as:

$$\frac{m_1 - m_2}{\sqrt{\sigma^2}}$$

where m_1 and m_2, respectively, represent the mean values for the subgroups 1 and 2 and σ^2 represents the overall (between and within-group) variance.

Concentration of immigrant students

The concentration of immigrant students in schools is equal to the share of students in a school who are immigrants. It is defined as:

$$C_i = \frac{N_i^{immig}}{N_i^{immig} + N_i^{non\text{-}immig}}$$

with N_i^{immig} equal to the number of immigrant students in school i and $N_i^{non\text{-}immig}$ equal to the number of non-immigrant students in school *i*.

Similar concentration indices were defined for advantaged students (those students in the top quarter of the PISA index for economic, social and cultural status [ESCS] in their country or economy), disadvantaged students (those students in the bottom quarter of ESCS in their country or economy) and students who speak a different language at home. The proportion of students with special needs in a school was reported by school principals.

Standard errors and significance tests

The statistics in this report represent estimates of national performance based on samples of students, rather than values that could be calculated if every student in every country had answered every question. Consequently, it is important to measure the degree of uncertainty of the estimates. In PISA, each estimate has an associated degree of uncertainty, which is expressed through a standard error. The use of confidence intervals provides a way to make inferences about the population means and proportions in a manner that reflects the uncertainty associated with the sample estimates. From an observed sample statistic and assuming a normal distribution, it can be inferred that the corresponding population result would lie within the confidence interval in 95 out of 100 replications of the measurement on different samples drawn from the same population.

In many cases, readers are primarily interested in whether a given value in a particular country is different from a second value in the same or another country, e.g. whether girls in a country perform better than boys in the same country. In the tables and charts used in this report, differences are labelled as statistically significant when a difference of that magnitude or larger would be observed less than 5% of the time, if there were actually no difference in corresponding population values. Similarly, the risk of reporting a correlation as significant if there is, in fact, no correlation between two measures, is contained at 5%.

Throughout the report, significance tests were undertaken to assess the statistical significance of the comparisons made.

Gender differences and differences between subgroup means

Gender differences in student performance or other indices were tested for statistical significance. Positive differences indicate higher scores for boys while negative differences indicate higher scores for girls. Generally, differences marked in bold in the tables in this volume are statistically significant at the 95% confidence level.

Similarly, differences between other groups of students (e.g. non-immigrant students and students with an immigrant background) or categories of schools (e.g. advantaged and disadvantaged schools) were tested for statistical significance. The definitions of the subgroups can, in general, be found in the tables and the text accompanying the analysis. Socio-economically (dis) advantaged school are defined as schools in the (bottom) top quarter of the distribution of the average PISA index of economic, social and cultural status (ESCS) across schools within each country/economy. All differences marked in bold in the tables presented in Annex B of this report are statistically significant at the 95% level.

Differences between subgroup means, after accounting for other variables

For many tables, subgroup comparisons were performed both on the observed difference ("before accounting for other variables") and after accounting for other variables, such as the PISA index of economic, social and cultural status of students, gender, and performance in the three core PISA domains of science, reading and mathematics. The adjusted differences were estimated using linear regression and tested for significance at the 95% confidence level. Significant differences are marked in bold.

Performance differences between the top and bottom quartiles of PISA indices and scales

Differences in average performance between the top and bottom quarters of the PISA indices and scales were tested for statistical significance. Figures marked in bold indicate that performance between the top and bottom quarters of students on the respective index is statistically significantly different at the 95% confidence level.

Change in the performance per unit of the index

For many tables, the difference in student performance per unit on the index shown was calculated. Figures in bold indicate that the differences are statistically significantly different from zero at the 95% confidence level.

Relative risk and odds ratio

Figures in bold in the data tables presented in Annex B of this report indicate that the relative risk/odds ratio is statistically significantly different from 1 at the 95% confidence level. To compute statistical significance around the value of 1 (the null hypothesis), the relative-risk/odds-ratio statistic is assumed to follow a log-normal distribution, rather than a normal distribution, under the null hypothesis.

For many tables, "generalised" odds ratios (after accounting for other variables) are also presented. These odds ratios were estimated using logistic regression and tested for significance against the null hypothesis of an odds ratio equal to 1 (i.e. equal likelihoods, after accounting for other variables).

Range of ranks

To calculate the range of ranks for countries, data are simulated using the mean and standard error of the mean for each relevant country to generate a distribution of possible values. Some 10 000 simulations are implemented and, based on these values, 10 000 possible rankings for each country are produced. For each country, the counts for each rank are aggregated from largest to smallest until they equal 9 500 or more. Then the range of ranks per country is reported, including all the ranks that have been aggregated. This means that there is at least 95% confidence about the range of ranks, and it is safe to assume unimodality in this distribution of ranks. This method has been used in all cycles of PISA since 2003, including PISA 2015.

The main difference between the range of ranks (e.g. Figure V.3.4) and the comparison of countries' mean performance (e.g. Figure V.3.3) is that the former takes account of the multiple comparisons involved in ranking countries/economies, while the latter does not. Therefore, sometimes there is a slight difference between the range of ranks and counting the number of countries above a given country, based on pairwise comparisons of the selected countries' performance. For instance, Canada and Finland have similar mean performance and the same set of countries whose mean score is not statistically different from theirs, based on Figure V.3.3; but the rank for Canada can be restricted to be, with 95% confidence, between 2nd and 6th among OECD countries, while the range of ranks for Finland is wider (between 2nd and 7th) (Figure V.3.4). Since it is safe to assume that the distribution of rank estimates for each country has a single mode (unimodality), the results of range of ranks for countries should be used when examining countries' rankings.

Standard errors in statistics estimated from multilevel models

For statistics based on multilevel models (such as the estimates of variance components and regression coefficients from two-level regression models) the standard errors are not estimated with the usual replication method, which accounts for stratification and sampling rates from finite populations. Instead, standard errors are "model-based": their computation assumes that schools, and students within schools, are sampled at random (with sampling probabilities reflected in school and student weights) from a theoretical, infinite population of schools and students which complies with the model's parametric assumptions.

The standard error for the estimated index of intra-class correlation is calculated by deriving an approximate distribution for it from the (model-based) standard errors for the variance components, using the delta-method.

References

OECD (2017), *PISA 2015 Technical Report,* PISA, OECD Publishing, Paris.

ANNEX A4

QUALITY ASSURANCE

Quality assurance procedures were implemented in all parts of PISA 2015, as was done for all previous PISA surveys. The PISA 2015 Technical Standards (www.oecd.org/pisa) specify the way in which PISA must be implemented in each country, economy and adjudicated region. International contractors monitor the implementation in each of these and adjudicate on their adherence to the standards.

The consistent quality and linguistic equivalence of the PISA 2015 assessment instruments were facilitated by assessing the ease with which the original English version could be translated. Two source versions of the assessment instruments, in English and French were prepared (except for the financial literacy assessment and the operational manuals, which were provided only in English) in order for countries to conduct a double translation design, i.e. two independent translations from the source language(s), and reconciliation by a third person. Detailed instructions for the localisation (adaptation, translation and validation) of the instruments for the field trial and for their review for the main survey, and translation/adaptation guidelines were supplied. An independent team of expert verifiers, appointed and trained by the PISA Consortium, verified each national version against the English and/or French source versions. These translators' mother tongue was the language of instruction in the country concerned, and the translators were knowledgeable about education systems. For further information on PISA translation procedures, see the *PISA 2015 Technical Report* (OECD, 2017).

The survey was implemented through standardised procedures. The PISA Consortium provided comprehensive manuals that explained the implementation of the survey, including precise instructions for the work of school co-ordinators and scripts for test administrators to use during the assessment sessions. Proposed adaptations to survey procedures, or proposed modifications to the assessment session script, were submitted to the PISA Consortium for approval prior to verification. The PISA Consortium then verified the national translation and adaptation of these manuals.

To establish the credibility of PISA as valid and unbiased and to encourage uniformity in administering the assessment sessions, test administrators in participating countries were selected using the following criteria: it was required that the test administrator not be the science, reading or mathematics instructor of any students in the sessions he or she would conduct for PISA; and it was considered preferable that the test administrator not be a member of the staff of any school in the PISA sample. Participating countries organised an in-person training session for test administrators.

Participating countries and economies were required to ensure that test administrators worked with the school co-ordinator to prepare the assessment session, including reviewing and updating the Student Tracking Form; completing the Session Attendance Form, which is designed to record students' attendance and instruments allocation; completing the Session Report Form, which is designed to summarise session times, any disturbance to the session, etc.; ensuring that the number of test booklets and questionnaires collected from students tallied with the number sent to the school (paper-based assessment countries) or ensuring that the number of USB sticks used for the assessment were accounted for (computer-based assessment countries); and sending the school questionnaire, student questionnaires, parent and teacher questionnaires (if applicable), and all test materials (both completed and not completed) to the national centre after the testing.

The PISA Consortium responsible for overseeing survey operations implemented all phases of the PISA Quality Monitor (PQM) process: interviewing and hiring PQM candidates in each of the countries, organising their training, selecting the schools to visit, and collecting information from the PQM visits. PQMs are independent contractors located in participating countries who are hired by the international survey operations contractor. They visit a sample of schools to observe test administration and to record the implementation of the documented field-operations procedures in the main survey.

Typically, two or three PQMs were hired for each country, and they visited an average of 15 schools in each country. If there were adjudicated regions in a country, it was usually necessary to hire additional PQMs, as a minimum of five schools were observed in adjudicated regions.

All quality-assurance data collected throughout the PISA 2015 assessment were entered and collated in a central data-adjudication database on the quality of field operations, printing, translation, school and student sampling, and coding. Comprehensive reports were then generated for the PISA Adjudication Group. This group was formed by the Technical Advisory Group and the Sampling Referee. Its role is to review the adjudication database and reports to recommend adequate treatment to preserve the quality of PISA data. For further information, see the *PISA 2015 Technical Report* (OECD, 2017).

The results of adjudication and subsequent further examinations showed that the PISA Technical Standards were met in all countries and economies that participated in PISA 2015 collaborative problem-solving assessment except for Malaysia where the PISA assessment was conducted in accordance with the operational standards and guidelines of the OECD. However, the weighted response rate among the initially sampled Malaysian schools (51%) falls well short of the standard PISA response rate of 85%. Therefore, the results may not be comparable to those of other countries or to results for Malaysia from previous years.

Reference

OECD (2017), *PISA 2015 Technical Report,* PISA, OECD Publishing, Paris.

Annex B

PISA 2015 DATA

All tables in Annex B are available on line

Annex B1: Results for countries and economies

Annex B2: Results for regions within countries

Note regarding B-S-J-G (China)

B-S-J-G (China) refers to the four PISA participating Chinese provinces of Beijing, Shanghai, Jiangsu, Guangdong.

Note regarding CABA (Argentina)

CABA (Argentina) refers to the Ciudad Autónoma de Buenos Aires, Argentina.

Note regarding FYROM

FYROM refers to the Former Yugoslav Republic of Macedonia.

Notes regarding Cyprus

Note by Turkey: The information in this document with reference to "Cyprus" relates to the southern part of the Island. There is no single authority representing both Turkish and Greek Cypriot people on the Island. Turkey recognises the Turkish Republic of Northern Cyprus (TRNC). Until a lasting and equitable solution is found within the context of the United Nations, Turkey shall preserve its position concerning the "Cyprus issue".

Note by all the European Union Member States of the OECD and the European Union: The Republic of Cyprus is recognised by all members of the United Nations with the exception of Turkey. The information in this document relates to the area under the effective control of the Government of the Republic of Cyprus.

A note regarding Israel

The statistical data for Israel are supplied by and under the responsibility of the relevant Israeli authorities. The use of such data by the OECD is without prejudice to the status of the Golan Heights, East Jerusalem and Israeli settlements in the West Bank under the terms of international law.

ANNEX B1

RESULTS FOR COUNTRIES AND ECONOMIES

[Part 1/1]

Table V.3.1 Percentage of students at each proficiency level of collaborative problem solving

		All students									
		Below Level 1 (below 340 score points)		Level 1 (from 340 to less than 440 score points)		Level 2 (from 440 to less than 540 score points)		Level 3 (from 540 to less than 640 score points)		Level 4 (at or above 640 score points)	
		%	S.E.	%	S.E.	%	S.E.	%	S.E.	%	S.E.
OECD	Australia	4.3	(0.3)	15.6	(0.6)	31.2	(0.6)	33.6	(0.8)	15.3	(0.7)
	Austria	4.5	(0.4)	20.2	(0.9)	35.8	(1.0)	30.4	(1.0)	9.1	(0.7)
	Belgium	5.7	(0.5)	21.1	(0.8)	36.7	(0.7)	29.3	(0.8)	7.1	(0.6)
	Canada	3.4	(0.3)	15.0	(0.7)	32.0	(0.8)	33.8	(0.9)	15.7	(0.7)
	Chile	8.4	(0.7)	33.9	(1.2)	40.5	(1.0)	16.0	(1.0)	1.2	(0.2)
	Czech Republic	4.6	(0.5)	21.6	(0.8)	39.6	(1.0)	28.8	(1.0)	5.4	(0.4)
	Denmark	2.7	(0.3)	16.3	(0.8)	38.8	(0.9)	33.4	(0.9)	8.9	(0.7)
	Estonia	1.8	(0.3)	13.5	(0.7)	35.4	(1.1)	37.2	(1.0)	12.2	(0.8)
	Finland	3.4	(0.4)	14.7	(0.8)	32.2	(1.0)	35.2	(1.0)	14.4	(0.8)
	France	7.0	(0.5)	22.6	(0.7)	36.2	(0.9)	27.6	(1.0)	6.6	(0.5)
	Germany	3.6	(0.4)	16.9	(0.8)	34.3	(0.9)	32.4	(0.8)	12.7	(0.7)
	Greece	10.4	(1.0)	31.6	(1.2)	37.9	(1.1)	18.1	(1.0)	2.0	(0.3)
	Hungary	8.7	(0.6)	28.6	(1.0)	37.4	(0.9)	22.0	(0.9)	3.3	(0.4)
	Iceland	4.6	(0.5)	22.5	(1.0)	38.1	(1.2)	28.2	(1.0)	6.5	(0.6)
	Ireland	m	m	m	m	m	m	m	m	m	m
	Israel	11.5	(0.9)	30.2	(1.1)	30.7	(1.2)	22.1	(1.0)	5.4	(0.5)
	Italy	7.8	(0.6)	26.9	(1.0)	38.5	(1.0)	22.6	(0.9)	4.2	(0.5)
	Japan	1.2	(0.2)	8.9	(0.7)	31.4	(1.0)	44.4	(1.1)	14.0	(0.8)
	Korea	1.5	(0.3)	11.4	(0.7)	35.1	(0.9)	41.6	(1.0)	10.4	(0.8)
	Latvia	5.6	(0.5)	25.4	(0.9)	41.3	(0.9)	23.8	(1.0)	3.9	(0.5)
	Luxembourg	6.5	(0.5)	24.8	(0.7)	36.3	(0.7)	25.5	(0.7)	6.8	(0.4)
	Mexico	12.2	(0.9)	41.2	(1.4)	37.4	(1.2)	8.8	(0.6)	0.4	(0.1)
	Netherlands	3.4	(0.4)	18.6	(0.9)	35.7	(0.9)	32.3	(1.0)	10.0	(0.7)
	New Zealand	3.8	(0.4)	15.9	(0.7)	31.3	(0.9)	33.2	(1.0)	15.8	(0.9)
	Norway	4.4	(0.5)	21.0	(0.8)	39.5	(1.1)	28.3	(1.0)	6.8	(0.6)
	Poland	m	m	m	m	m	m	m	m	m	m
	Portugal	4.6	(0.4)	21.5	(0.9)	40.2	(0.8)	28.4	(1.0)	5.2	(0.5)
	Slovak Republic	9.5	(0.7)	31.1	(1.0)	38.4	(1.1)	18.4	(0.9)	2.6	(0.4)
	Slovenia	4.4	(0.4)	21.2	(0.8)	38.6	(1.2)	29.3	(0.9)	6.4	(0.7)
	Spain	4.4	(0.4)	21.4	(0.9)	41.6	(0.8)	28.3	(0.8)	4.3	(0.4)
	Sweden	4.5	(0.5)	20.1	(1.0)	35.9	(1.1)	30.3	(1.1)	9.1	(0.9)
	Switzerland	m	m	m	m	m	m	m	m	m	m
	Turkey	14.9	(1.1)	44.5	(1.4)	33.6	(1.5)	6.9	(0.8)	0.2	(0.1)
	United Kingdom	4.2	(0.4)	18.3	(0.8)	34.6	(0.8)	30.9	(0.9)	12.0	(0.7)
	United States	4.9	(0.5)	18.9	(1.0)	32.7	(0.8)	29.7	(1.0)	13.8	(1.0)
	OECD average	5.7	(0.1)	22.4	(0.2)	36.2	(0.2)	27.8	(0.2)	7.9	(0.1)
Partners	Brazil	21.2	(0.8)	43.0	(0.7)	27.7	(0.7)	7.5	(0.5)	0.6	(0.1)
	B-S-J-G (China)	5.8	(0.7)	22.4	(1.1)	37.9	(1.2)	27.4	(1.3)	6.4	(0.9)
	Bulgaria	15.3	(1.1)	34.1	(1.2)	32.6	(1.2)	16.0	(1.0)	2.0	(0.3)
	Colombia	14.1	(0.9)	42.3	(1.0)	33.8	(1.0)	9.2	(0.6)	0.6	(0.2)
	Costa Rica	9.4	(0.6)	40.6	(1.1)	39.6	(1.1)	9.9	(0.7)	0.5	(0.2)
	Croatia	6.6	(0.6)	28.7	(1.0)	41.8	(1.0)	20.4	(0.9)	2.4	(0.3)
	Cyprus*	13.0	(0.6)	36.0	(1.1)	35.5	(1.0)	14.0	(0.7)	1.5	(0.2)
	Dominican Republic	m	m	m	m	m	m	m	m	m	m
	Hong Kong (China)	1.9	(0.3)	11.7	(0.8)	33.6	(1.1)	39.7	(1.1)	13.0	(0.8)
	Lithuania	8.3	(0.6)	30.2	(0.9)	39.3	(1.0)	19.7	(0.9)	2.5	(0.3)
	Macao (China)	2.2	(0.3)	12.7	(0.5)	35.6	(0.9)	38.4	(0.9)	11.1	(0.6)
	Montenegro	17.6	(0.6)	44.7	(0.9)	31.6	(0.8)	5.9	(0.5)	0.2	(0.1)
	Peru	18.1	(1.0)	43.3	(1.1)	30.6	(1.1)	7.6	(0.7)	0.4	(0.1)
	Qatar	m	m	m	m	m	m	m	m	m	m
	Russia	7.3	(0.7)	29.2	(1.3)	39.6	(1.2)	20.3	(1.2)	3.6	(0.5)
	Singapore	1.6	(0.2)	9.7	(0.5)	27.8	(0.6)	39.5	(0.7)	21.4	(0.6)
	Chinese Taipei	2.7	(0.3)	14.2	(0.7)	37.2	(1.0)	36.3	(1.0)	9.6	(0.8)
	Thailand	12.2	(1.0)	41.9	(1.2)	34.5	(1.2)	10.4	(0.9)	0.9	(0.3)
	Tunisia	24.5	(1.3)	59.5	(1.5)	15.2	(1.1)	0.8	(0.2)	0.0	(0.0)
	United Arab Emirates	16.2	(0.8)	37.7	(0.9)	31.6	(1.0)	12.8	(0.6)	1.8	(0.2)
	Uruguay	12.9	(0.7)	37.7	(0.9)	34.2	(0.9)	13.6	(0.7)	1.7	(0.3)
	Malaysia**	10.7	(0.9)	39.1	(1.4)	39.6	(1.3)	10.1	(1.0)	0.4	(0.2)

* See note at the beginning of this Annex.
**Malaysia: Coverage is too small to ensure comparability (see Annex A4).
StatLink http://dx.doi.org/10.1787/888933616769

[Part 1/1]

Table V.3.2 Mean score and variation in collaborative problem-solving performance

		Mean score		Standard deviation		Percentiles														
						5th		10th		25th		Median (50th)		75th		90th		95th		
		Mean	S.E.	S.D.	S.E.	Score	S.E.	Score	S.E.	Score	S.E.	Score	S.E.	Score	S.E.	Score	S.E.	Score	S.E.	
OECD	Australia	531	(1.9)	107	(1.3)	347	(3.2)	388	(3.8)	460	(2.7)	537	(2.3)	607	(2.2)	664	(2.7)	698	(3.2)	
	Austria	509	(2.6)	98	(1.5)	345	(4.0)	379	(3.8)	441	(3.4)	512	(3.3)	580	(3.1)	635	(3.4)	667	(4.3)	
	Belgium	501	(2.4)	99	(1.4)	334	(4.2)	369	(3.6)	434	(3.2)	506	(2.4)	572	(2.4)	625	(3.0)	655	(3.3)	
	Canada	535	(2.3)	104	(1.0)	358	(3.5)	397	(3.5)	465	(2.8)	539	(2.7)	607	(2.4)	667	(3.2)	702	(3.1)	
	Chile	457	(2.7)	84	(1.3)	319	(3.6)	348	(3.4)	398	(3.3)	457	(3.2)	516	(3.3)	567	(3.6)	596	(4.0)	
	Czech Republic	499	(2.2)	91	(1.4)	344	(4.2)	377	(3.7)	436	(3.0)	502	(2.7)	563	(2.6)	614	(2.9)	643	(3.1)	
	Denmark	520	(2.5)	90	(1.2)	367	(3.9)	402	(3.7)	460	(3.3)	522	(2.9)	583	(3.1)	634	(3.6)	663	(4.3)	
	Estonia	535	(2.5)	90	(1.3)	382	(3.9)	416	(3.5)	475	(3.1)	538	(3.0)	598	(3.4)	650	(3.8)	679	(3.7)	
	Finland	534	(2.6)	101	(1.5)	359	(5.0)	399	(4.4)	466	(3.4)	539	(2.9)	605	(2.9)	660	(3.4)	693	(3.9)	
	France	494	(2.4)	100	(1.5)	325	(4.0)	359	(3.5)	424	(3.2)	499	(2.9)	566	(2.8)	620	(3.1)	651	(4.0)	
	Germany	525	(2.8)	101	(1.5)	354	(4.8)	390	(4.5)	456	(3.7)	527	(3.0)	595	(3.4)	653	(3.2)	686	(3.5)	
	Greece	459	(3.6)	92	(1.6)	307	(5.6)	338	(5.1)	394	(4.5)	459	(4.0)	524	(3.7)	578	(4.1)	609	(4.1)	
	Hungary	472	(2.4)	95	(1.6)	316	(4.3)	347	(3.4)	404	(3.0)	475	(3.1)	541	(2.8)	594	(3.5)	625	(3.5)	
	Iceland	499	(2.3)	94	(1.9)	343	(4.3)	375	(4.1)	433	(3.3)	502	(3.0)	566	(3.4)	620	(4.3)	652	(5.1)	
	Ireland	m	m	m	m	m	m	m	m	m	m	m	m	m	m	m	m	m	m	
	Israel	469	(3.6)	105	(1.8)	307	(3.9)	334	(4.0)	386	(4.6)	467	(5.0)	548	(4.2)	609	(4.4)	643	(4.6)	
	Italy	478	(2.5)	96	(1.6)	319	(4.6)	353	(3.7)	412	(3.3)	479	(3.0)	545	(2.9)	601	(4.0)	633	(4.5)	
	Japan	552	(2.7)	85	(1.8)	402	(5.5)	440	(4.6)	499	(3.3)	558	(2.8)	610	(2.6)	655	(3.1)	680	(3.9)	
	Korea	538	(2.5)	84	(1.5)	390	(4.9)	425	(3.8)	484	(3.3)	544	(2.6)	598	(2.5)	641	(3.1)	667	(3.4)	
	Latvia	485	(2.3)	90	(1.3)	335	(3.7)	367	(3.8)	423	(3.1)	487	(2.6)	547	(2.8)	599	(3.2)	631	(4.4)	
	Luxembourg	491	(1.5)	100	(1.0)	328	(3.6)	361	(2.5)	420	(2.0)	492	(2.1)	561	(2.0)	621	(2.5)	654	(3.7)	
	Mexico	433	(2.5)	79	(1.5)	305	(3.9)	331	(3.3)	378	(3.1)	433	(3.1)	488	(3.2)	536	(3.4)	564	(3.7)	
	Netherlands	518	(2.4)	97	(1.5)	355	(4.3)	389	(4.2)	450	(3.5)	521	(3.1)	586	(2.9)	640	(3.8)	672	(4.4)	
	New Zealand	533	(2.4)	106	(1.7)	353	(5.1)	391	(4.1)	460	(3.5)	537	(3.1)	608	(3.6)	666	(3.5)	700	(4.0)	
	Norway	502	(2.5)	94	(1.6)	345	(4.9)	380	(3.5)	439	(3.1)	505	(2.9)	568	(3.2)	621	(3.4)	653	(4.3)	
	Poland	m	m	m	m	m	m	m	m	m	m	m	m	m	m	m	m	m	m	
	Portugal	498	(2.6)	91	(1.3)	343	(4.3)	377	(4.0)	437	(3.2)	502	(2.9)	562	(3.2)	613	(2.9)	641	(3.7)	
	Slovak Republic	463	(2.4)	93	(1.5)	311	(4.0)	343	(3.4)	398	(2.9)	463	(2.8)	528	(3.1)	583	(4.0)	615	(4.4)	
	Slovenia	502	(1.8)	93	(1.3)	345	(3.6)	378	(3.0)	438	(2.8)	505	(2.4)	568	(2.7)	620	(3.7)	649	(4.3)	
	Spain	496	(2.1)	88	(1.1)	345	(3.9)	379	(3.6)	438	(3.0)	500	(2.6)	559	(2.3)	607	(2.6)	635	(2.9)	
	Sweden	510	(3.4)	98	(1.8)	344	(5.1)	379	(4.4)	441	(4.3)	513	(3.8)	579	(4.4)	635	(5.0)	667	(6.1)	
	Switzerland	m	m	m	m	m	m	m	m	m	m	m	m	m	m	m	m	m	m	
	Turkey	422	(3.4)	78	(1.6)	298	(4.0)	323	(3.8)	367	(3.6)	420	(4.0)	477	(4.4)	526	(4.3)	553	(5.0)	
	United Kingdom	519	(2.7)	103	(1.1)	348	(4.1)	384	(3.9)	449	(3.4)	521	(3.1)	591	(3.4)	651	(3.4)	686	(3.9)	
	United States	520	(3.6)	108	(1.7)	341	(4.6)	376	(4.4)	445	(4.3)	522	(4.1)	596	(4.2)	659	(4.6)	696	(5.6)	
	OECD average	500	(0.5)	95	(0.3)	341	(0.8)	375	(0.7)	435	(0.6)	503	(0.5)	567	(0.6)	621	(0.6)	652	(0.7)	
Partners	Brazil	412	(2.3)	87	(1.3)	277	(2.4)	304	(2.2)	350	(2.1)	406	(2.6)	470	(3.1)	529	(3.9)	564	(4.8)	
	B-S-J-G (China)	496	(4.0)	97	(2.1)	333	(5.4)	368	(5.0)	429	(4.7)	499	(4.3)	564	(4.9)	620	(5.2)	651	(6.0)	
	Bulgaria	444	(3.9)	98	(1.7)	290	(5.5)	319	(4.0)	370	(4.5)	442	(5.1)	515	(4.8)	575	(4.1)	606	(4.3)	
	Colombia	429	(2.3)	83	(1.4)	300	(3.6)	325	(3.2)	370	(2.7)	426	(2.7)	486	(2.9)	539	(3.2)	571	(3.7)	
	Costa Rica	441	(2.4)	78	(1.3)	316	(3.8)	343	(2.9)	387	(2.6)	440	(2.8)	494	(2.8)	542	(3.6)	570	(4.3)	
	Croatia	473	(2.5)	87	(1.5)	328	(4.3)	359	(4.1)	412	(3.3)	474	(2.8)	534	(2.6)	585	(3.3)	614	(3.7)	
	Cyprus*	444	(1.7)	91	(1.3)	298	(2.9)	328	(2.5)	379	(2.0)	443	(2.9)	508	(2.7)	564	(3.3)	596	(3.4)	
	Dominican Republic	m	m	m	m	m	m	m	m	m	m	m	m	m	m	m	m	m	m	
	Hong Kong (China)	541	(2.9)	90	(1.6)	382	(4.9)	420	(5.0)	483	(4.0)	546	(3.4)	604	(3.2)	652	(3.2)	681	(3.6)	
	Lithuania	467	(2.5)	91	(1.4)	319	(4.0)	349	(3.1)	404	(3.2)	468	(3.1)	532	(3.0)	584	(3.7)	613	(4.4)	
	Macao (China)	534	(1.2)	90	(1.1)	377	(3.4)	415	(2.8)	476	(2.1)	539	(1.9)	596	(1.8)	645	(2.6)	672	(3.4)	
	Montenegro	416	(1.3)	79	(1.2)	291	(2.5)	315	(2.3)	359	(1.5)	414	(1.7)	471	(2.4)	520	(2.8)	548	(3.4)	
	Peru	418	(2.5)	83	(1.6)	287	(2.9)	313	(2.8)	358	(2.5)	414	(2.9)	475	(3.7)	529	(4.6)	561	(4.6)	
	Qatar	m	m	m	m	m	m	m	m	m	m	m	m	m	m	m	m	m	m	
	Russia	473	(3.4)	92	(1.4)	324	(4.6)	355	(4.2)	410	(3.7)	472	(4.1)	537	(4.5)	593	(4.4)	626	(5.7)	
	Singapore	561	(1.2)	97	(1.2)	392	(3.2)	432	(2.6)	499	(1.9)	568	(1.9)	630	(1.9)	680	(2.8)	709	(3.2)	
	Chinese Taipei	527	(2.5)	90	(1.5)	370	(3.9)	407	(3.5)	468	(2.9)	531	(2.8)	590	(3.0)	639	(3.5)	667	(4.1)	
	Thailand	436	(3.5)	83	(1.7)	307	(4.0)	332	(3.4)	375	(3.4)	431	(3.9)	492	(4.5)	547	(5.1)	580	(5.7)	
	Tunisia	382	(1.9)	59	(1.4)	291	(2.8)	310	(2.6)	341	(2.1)	378	(2.2)	419	(2.8)	459	(3.6)	485	(4.4)	
	United Arab Emirates	435	(2.4)	95	(1.0)	289	(3.2)	317	(3.0)	366	(2.6)	430	(3.0)	500	(3.2)	563	(2.7)	598	(3.4)	
	Uruguay	443	(2.3)	91	(1.3)	301	(3.4)	328	(2.7)	376	(2.5)	439	(2.5)	506	(3.1)	564	(3.7)	597	(4.8)	
	Malaysia**	440	(3.3)	80	(1.7)	310	(3.9)	337	(3.6)	384	(3.5)	440	(3.7)	495	(3.8)	543	(4.8)	569	(4.7)	

* See note at the beginning of this Annex.
**Malaysia: Coverage is too small to ensure comparability (see Annex A4).
StatLink http://dx.doi.org/10.1787/888933616769

[Part 1/2]

Table V.3.3a Top performers in four PISA subjects

		Percentage of 15-year-old students who are:															
		Not top performers in any of the four subjects		Top performers[1] in only one of science, reading or mathematics		Top performers in only two of science, reading and mathematics		Top performers in science, reading and mathematics		Top performers in only collaborative problem solving		Top performers in collaborative problem solving and science		Top performers in collaborative problem solving and reading		Top performers in collaborative problem solving and mathematics	
		%	S.E.	%	S.E.	%	S.E.	%	S.E.	%	S.E.	%	S.E.	%	S.E.	%	S.E.
OECD	Australia	75.3	(0.7)	5.4	(0.4)	2.5	(0.2)	1.5	(0.2)	6.3	(0.4)	0.8	(0.1)	1.3	(0.2)	0.7	(0.2)
	Austria	80.7	(1.1)	6.5	(0.6)	2.5	(0.2)	1.3	(0.2)	3.2	(0.4)	0.3	(0.1)	0.6	(0.1)	1.0	(0.2)
	Belgium	78.4	(0.8)	8.4	(0.4)	3.8	(0.3)	2.4	(0.2)	1.9	(0.3)	0.2	(0.1)	0.4	(0.1)	0.9	(0.1)
	Canada	72.0	(0.9)	7.2	(0.4)	3.1	(0.3)	2.0	(0.2)	5.4	(0.3)	0.6	(0.1)	1.5	(0.2)	1.0	(0.2)
	Chile	96.0	(0.4)	2.0	(0.3)	0.6	(0.1)	0.3	(0.1)	0.6	(0.2)	0.0	(0.0)	0.2	(0.1)	0.0	(0.0)
	Czech Republic	84.1	(0.8)	5.5	(0.5)	2.7	(0.3)	2.4	(0.3)	1.9	(0.2)	0.2	(0.1)	0.3	(0.1)	0.4	(0.1)
	Denmark	81.6	(0.9)	6.0	(0.5)	2.4	(0.3)	1.2	(0.3)	3.5	(0.4)	0.4	(0.1)	0.5	(0.2)	1.0	(0.2)
	Estonia	76.2	(1.0)	6.2	(0.6)	3.3	(0.5)	2.1	(0.3)	3.4	(0.4)	0.7	(0.2)	0.5	(0.2)	0.7	(0.2)
	Finland	74.1	(0.9)	6.4	(0.5)	3.1	(0.3)	2.0	(0.3)	4.5	(0.4)	1.1	(0.2)	1.1	(0.2)	0.6	(0.1)
	France	79.6	(0.8)	8.0	(0.6)	3.4	(0.3)	2.5	(0.3)	2.0	(0.3)	0.2	(0.1)	0.8	(0.2)	0.4	(0.1)
	Germany	76.5	(1.0)	6.1	(0.5)	2.8	(0.3)	1.9	(0.3)	4.3	(0.4)	0.5	(0.1)	1.1	(0.2)	0.9	(0.2)
	Greece	92.4	(0.7)	3.9	(0.4)	1.1	(0.2)	0.6	(0.1)	0.8	(0.2)	0.1	(0.0)	0.2	(0.1)	0.2	(0.1)
	Hungary	88.6	(0.7)	5.0	(0.4)	1.8	(0.3)	1.2	(0.2)	1.1	(0.2)	0.1	(0.1)	0.2	(0.1)	0.3	(0.1)
	Iceland	84.5	(0.8)	6.2	(0.7)	1.9	(0.3)	0.8	(0.2)	2.3	(0.4)	0.1	(0.1)	0.6	(0.2)	0.9	(0.2)
	Ireland	m	m	m	m	m	m	m	m	m	m	m	m	m	m	m	m
	Israel	83.5	(1.2)	6.5	(0.6)	2.7	(0.4)	1.9	(0.2)	1.6	(0.3)	0.2	(0.1)	0.6	(0.2)	0.4	(0.1)
	Italy	84.8	(0.9)	7.5	(0.6)	2.3	(0.3)	1.2	(0.2)	1.7	(0.4)	0.1	(0.1)	0.3	(0.1)	0.6	(0.2)
	Japan	69.9	(1.3)	8.8	(0.6)	4.7	(0.4)	2.6	(0.4)	4.3	(0.4)	0.7	(0.2)	0.6	(0.1)	1.5	(0.3)
	Korea	72.0	(1.4)	10.6	(0.8)	4.5	(0.5)	2.6	(0.4)	2.4	(0.3)	0.2	(0.1)	0.8	(0.2)	1.5	(0.3)
	Latvia	89.9	(0.6)	4.0	(0.3)	1.3	(0.2)	0.8	(0.2)	1.8	(0.3)	0.2	(0.1)	0.3	(0.2)	0.3	(0.1)
	Luxembourg	83.7	(0.5)	5.5	(0.4)	2.4	(0.3)	1.7	(0.3)	2.2	(0.3)	0.2	(0.1)	0.6	(0.2)	0.6	(0.1)
	Mexico	99.1	(0.2)	0.4	(0.1)	0.1	(0.0)	0.0	(0.0)	0.3	(0.1)	0.0	(0.0)	0.0	(0.0)	0.0	(0.0)
	Netherlands	77.5	(0.9)	6.6	(0.5)	3.4	(0.3)	2.5	(0.3)	2.5	(0.4)	0.3	(0.1)	0.6	(0.2)	0.9	(0.3)
	New Zealand	74.0	(0.9)	5.9	(0.5)	2.5	(0.3)	1.7	(0.3)	5.5	(0.6)	1.0	(0.2)	1.6	(0.3)	0.6	(0.2)
	Norway	80.4	(0.9)	7.5	(0.6)	3.1	(0.4)	2.2	(0.3)	1.9	(0.3)	0.1	(0.1)	0.8	(0.2)	0.4	(0.2)
	Poland	m	m	m	m	m	m	m	m	m	m	m	m	m	m	m	m
	Portugal	82.9	(0.8)	7.0	(0.5)	3.2	(0.3)	1.8	(0.3)	1.5	(0.3)	0.2	(0.1)	0.4	(0.1)	0.4	(0.1)
	Slovak Republic	89.3	(0.6)	5.4	(0.5)	1.9	(0.3)	0.8	(0.2)	1.0	(0.2)	0.1	(0.1)	0.1	(0.1)	0.3	(0.1)
	Slovenia	80.1	(0.8)	6.9	(0.7)	3.9	(0.4)	2.8	(0.4)	1.9	(0.3)	0.2	(0.1)	0.4	(0.1)	0.5	(0.2)
	Spain	87.3	(0.7)	5.1	(0.5)	2.2	(0.3)	1.1	(0.2)	1.8	(0.2)	0.2	(0.1)	0.3	(0.1)	0.3	(0.1)
	Sweden	80.6	(1.2)	6.3	(0.6)	2.6	(0.3)	1.5	(0.2)	2.7	(0.4)	0.4	(0.1)	1.1	(0.2)	0.7	(0.2)
	Switzerland	m	m	m	m	m	m	m	m	m	m	m	m	m	m	m	m
	Turkey	98.3	(0.4)	1.2	(0.4)	0.2	(0.1)	0.1	(0.1)	0.1	(0.1)	0.0	(0.0)	0.0	(0.0)	0.0	(0.0)
	United Kingdom	78.6	(0.9)	5.4	(0.4)	2.6	(0.3)	1.3	(0.2)	4.4	(0.4)	0.8	(0.2)	0.7	(0.2)	0.7	(0.2)
	United States	81.1	(1.1)	3.3	(0.4)	1.2	(0.2)	0.5	(0.2)	5.7	(0.6)	0.9	(0.2)	1.3	(0.2)	0.4	(0.2)
	OECD average	82.3	(0.2)	5.8	(0.1)	2.5	(0.1)	1.5	(0.0)	2.6	(0.1)	0.4	(0.0)	0.6	(0.0)	0.6	(0.0)
Partners	Brazil	97.5	(0.3)	1.4	(0.2)	0.3	(0.1)	0.1	(0.1)	0.3	(0.1)	0.0	(0.0)	0.1	(0.0)	0.0	(0.0)
	B-S-J-G (China)	71.5	(1.9)	11.9	(0.9)	5.8	(0.5)	4.4	(0.6)	0.8	(0.2)	0.1	(0.1)	0.1	(0.1)	0.8	(0.2)
	Bulgaria	92.4	(0.8)	3.6	(0.5)	1.3	(0.3)	0.7	(0.2)	0.8	(0.2)	0.1	(0.1)	0.2	(0.1)	0.1	(0.1)
	Colombia	98.4	(0.2)	0.7	(0.1)	0.2	(0.1)	0.1	(0.0)	0.4	(0.1)	0.0	(0.0)	0.1	(0.0)	0.0	(0.0)
	Costa Rica	98.7	(0.3)	0.6	(0.1)	0.1	(0.1)	0.0	(0.0)	0.4	(0.1)	0.0	(0.0)	0.1	(0.1)	0.0	(0.0)
	Croatia	89.9	(0.7)	4.6	(0.4)	1.8	(0.3)	1.2	(0.2)	0.8	(0.2)	0.1	(0.1)	0.3	(0.1)	0.1	(0.1)
	Cyprus*	93.7	(0.4)	3.5	(0.4)	0.8	(0.2)	0.4	(0.1)	0.7	(0.1)	0.1	(0.0)	0.2	(0.1)	0.1	(0.1)
	Dominican Republic	m	m	m	m	m	m	m	m	m	m	m	m	m	m	m	m
	Hong Kong (China)	67.0	(1.2)	14.5	(0.9)	3.8	(0.4)	1.8	(0.3)	3.7	(0.4)	0.1	(0.1)	0.8	(0.2)	2.6	(0.3)
	Lithuania	89.8	(0.8)	4.8	(0.5)	1.8	(0.3)	1.1	(0.2)	0.7	(0.1)	0.1	(0.1)	0.1	(0.1)	0.3	(0.1)
	Macao (China)	72.8	(0.7)	11.7	(0.6)	3.1	(0.3)	1.3	(0.2)	3.3	(0.4)	0.3	(0.1)	0.3	(0.1)	2.1	(0.3)
	Montenegro	97.4	(0.3)	1.9	(0.3)	0.4	(0.1)	0.2	(0.1)	0.1	(0.1)	0.0	(0.0)	0.0	(0.0)	0.0	(0.0)
	Peru	99.1	(0.2)	0.4	(0.1)	0.1	(0.0)	0.0	(0.0)	0.3	(0.1)	0.0	(0.0)	0.0	(0.0)	0.0	(0.0)
	Qatar	m	m	m	m	m	m	m	m	m	m	m	m	m	m	m	m
	Russia	85.7	(1.0)	7.6	(0.7)	2.1	(0.3)	1.0	(0.2)	1.3	(0.3)	0.1	(0.1)	0.5	(0.2)	0.3	(0.1)
	Singapore	57.3	(0.7)	11.1	(0.5)	6.0	(0.5)	4.1	(0.4)	3.5	(0.4)	0.6	(0.1)	0.5	(0.2)	2.3	(0.3)
	Chinese Taipei	68.4	(1.2)	13.2	(0.6)	6.5	(0.6)	2.3	(0.4)	1.7	(0.2)	0.2	(0.1)	0.1	(0.1)	1.5	(0.3)
	Thailand	97.7	(0.5)	1.1	(0.2)	0.2	(0.1)	0.1	(0.0)	0.6	(0.2)	0.0	(0.0)	0.0	(0.0)	0.1	(0.1)
	Tunisia	99.4	(0.2)	0.5	(0.2)	0.0	(0.0)	0.0	(0.0)	0.0	(0.0)	0.0	c	0.0	c	0.0	c
	United Arab Emirates	93.6	(0.4)	2.9	(0.3)	1.1	(0.1)	0.6	(0.1)	0.6	(0.1)	0.1	(0.0)	0.1	(0.0)	0.1	(0.1)
	Uruguay	95.5	(0.5)	2.0	(0.3)	0.5	(0.1)	0.3	(0.1)	0.9	(0.2)	0.0	(0.0)	0.1	(0.1)	0.1	(0.0)
	Malaysia**	97.6	(0.5)	1.6	(0.3)	0.3	(0.1)	0.1	(0.1)	0.2	(0.1)	0.0	(0.0)	0.0	(0.0)	0.1	(0.1)

1. Top performers in collaborative problem solving are students who score at Level 4. Top performers in science, reading or mathematics score at Level 5 or 6 in the subject.
* See note at the beginning of this Annex.
**Malaysia: Coverage is too small to ensure comparability (see Annex A4).
StatLink http://dx.doi.org/10.1787/888933616769

[Part 2/2]

Table V.3.3a Top performers in four PISA subjects

	Percentage of 15-year-old students who are:								Percentage of top performers in collaborative problem solving among top performers in…							
	Top performers[1] in collaborative problem solving, science and reading		Top performers in collaborative problem solving, science and mathematics		Top performers in collaborative problem solving, reading and mathematics		Top performers in all four subjects		Science		Reading		Mathematics		Science, reading and mathematics	
	%	S.E.	%	S.E.	%	S.E.	%	S.E.	%	S.E.	%	S.E.	%	S.E.	%	S.E.
OECD																
Australia	1.0	(0.2)	1.2	(0.2)	0.4	(0.1)	3.6	(0.3)	58.5	(2.1)	56.8	(2.4)	51.9	(2.4)	70.5	(3.3)
Austria	0.4	(0.1)	1.1	(0.2)	0.4	(0.1)	2.1	(0.3)	50.5	(3.8)	48.5	(4.1)	37.2	(2.9)	61.7	(5.6)
Belgium	0.3	(0.1)	0.8	(0.1)	0.5	(0.1)	2.2	(0.2)	38.1	(2.9)	35.7	(2.7)	27.5	(2.0)	47.9	(3.6)
Canada	1.2	(0.2)	1.0	(0.2)	0.6	(0.1)	4.4	(0.3)	58.7	(2.2)	55.1	(2.2)	47.1	(1.7)	69.2	(2.7)
Chile	0.1	(0.1)	0.0	(0.0)	0.0	(0.0)	0.1	(0.0)	22.8	(5.5)	18.0	(3.7)	16.5	(4.7)	29.3	(9.2)
Czech Republic	0.2	(0.1)	0.5	(0.1)	0.2	(0.1)	1.5	(0.2)	33.7	(3.3)	29.7	(2.9)	26.0	(2.7)	39.4	(4.4)
Denmark	0.3	(0.1)	1.0	(0.2)	0.3	(0.1)	1.9	(0.3)	51.1	(4.1)	47.3	(4.2)	36.2	(2.7)	62.1	(6.1)
Estonia	0.9	(0.2)	1.6	(0.3)	0.3	(0.1)	4.0	(0.4)	53.5	(3.1)	51.8	(3.5)	46.2	(3.2)	65.0	(4.0)
Finland	1.5	(0.3)	1.2	(0.2)	0.3	(0.1)	4.1	(0.4)	55.3	(2.9)	51.5	(3.2)	52.8	(3.5)	67.3	(4.5)
France	0.5	(0.1)	0.4	(0.1)	0.3	(0.1)	2.0	(0.3)	38.1	(3.1)	28.5	(3.1)	27.2	(2.5)	44.5	(5.1)
Germany	0.7	(0.1)	1.3	(0.2)	0.5	(0.2)	3.5	(0.3)	56.2	(2.9)	49.2	(3.1)	47.4	(2.9)	64.4	(3.9)
Greece	0.1	(0.1)	0.1	(0.1)	0.1	(0.1)	0.4	(0.1)	31.7	(6.8)	19.6	(3.2)	19.7	(3.9)	38.7	(9.3)
Hungary	0.1	(0.1)	0.4	(0.1)	0.1	(0.1)	0.9	(0.2)	35.1	(5.0)	30.6	(4.4)	21.5	(3.0)	42.1	(6.9)
Iceland	0.1	(0.1)	0.4	(0.2)	0.9	(0.3)	1.3	(0.3)	49.8	(8.7)	43.4	(5.7)	33.8	(4.1)	60.9	(11.0)
Ireland	m	m	m	m	m	m	m	m	m	m	m	m	m	m	m	m
Israel	0.4	(0.1)	0.3	(0.1)	0.3	(0.1)	1.7	(0.3)	39.7	(3.5)	30.3	(2.4)	28.5	(3.0)	46.7	(4.2)
Italy	0.1	(0.1)	0.4	(0.1)	0.2	(0.1)	0.7	(0.2)	32.5	(4.7)	24.0	(3.3)	18.4	(2.5)	37.0	(6.4)
Japan	0.6	(0.1)	1.8	(0.3)	0.5	(0.2)	3.9	(0.4)	46.0	(2.5)	52.7	(3.0)	38.3	(2.3)	60.7	(3.6)
Korea	0.3	(0.1)	1.0	(0.2)	1.0	(0.2)	3.3	(0.4)	45.1	(4.0)	42.5	(3.9)	32.3	(2.8)	56.0	(4.8)
Latvia	0.2	(0.1)	0.3	(0.1)	0.1	(0.1)	0.7	(0.1)	39.0	(4.9)	31.2	(5.4)	27.1	(3.6)	47.4	(7.3)
Luxembourg	0.4	(0.1)	0.5	(0.1)	0.3	(0.1)	2.0	(0.2)	44.2	(4.1)	40.2	(3.8)	33.7	(3.4)	53.8	(5.9)
Mexico	0.0	(0.0)	0.0	(0.0)	0.0	(0.0)	0.0	(0.0)	c	c	c	c	c	c	c	c
Netherlands	0.4	(0.1)	0.9	(0.2)	0.7	(0.2)	3.6	(0.4)	46.9	(3.4)	49.2	(3.1)	39.9	(2.5)	59.7	(4.2)
New Zealand	1.5	(0.2)	1.1	(0.3)	0.4	(0.2)	4.3	(0.4)	60.9	(3.3)	56.3	(3.1)	55.5	(3.3)	71.7	(3.9)
Norway	0.4	(0.1)	0.4	(0.1)	0.4	(0.1)	2.3	(0.3)	41.1	(3.8)	32.2	(3.0)	32.2	(3.4)	51.4	(5.4)
Poland	m	m	m	m	m	m	m	m	m	m	m	m	m	m	m	m
Portugal	0.3	(0.1)	0.6	(0.1)	0.2	(0.1)	1.5	(0.2)	35.2	(3.5)	31.7	(3.2)	24.7	(2.4)	46.2	(5.2)
Slovak Republic	0.1	(0.1)	0.2	(0.1)	0.1	(0.1)	0.6	(0.1)	27.8	(3.9)	28.3	(5.0)	16.1	(2.2)	41.2	(7.6)
Slovenia	0.3	(0.1)	0.8	(0.2)	0.2	(0.1)	2.0	(0.3)	32.3	(3.2)	33.3	(3.4)	26.5	(3.0)	42.6	(5.3)
Spain	0.2	(0.1)	0.4	(0.1)	0.1	(0.1)	0.8	(0.2)	33.5	(4.3)	28.4	(4.2)	23.8	(2.6)	43.2	(6.0)
Sweden	0.6	(0.2)	0.9	(0.2)	0.4	(0.1)	2.5	(0.4)	49.8	(3.4)	45.2	(3.3)	41.9	(3.4)	62.7	(4.5)
Switzerland	m	m	m	m	m	m	m	m	m	m	m	m	m	m	m	m
Turkey	0.0	(0.0)	0.0	(0.0)	0.0	c	0.0	(0.0)	c	c	3.7	(4.4)	2.3	(2.7)	c	c
United Kingdom	1.0	(0.2)	1.0	(0.2)	0.3	(0.1)	3.1	(0.3)	54.4	(3.0)	55.5	(3.5)	47.3	(3.6)	69.4	(4.3)
United States	1.7	(0.3)	0.6	(0.2)	0.3	(0.1)	2.9	(0.4)	72.5	(3.6)	64.5	(3.1)	71.6	(5.3)	84.4	(4.9)
OECD average	0.5	(0.0)	0.7	(0.0)	0.3	(0.0)	2.1	(0.1)	44.5	(0.7)	39.2	(0.6)	33.9	(0.6)	54.6	(1.0)
Partners																
Brazil	0.0	(0.0)	0.0	(0.0)	0.0	(0.0)	0.1	(0.0)	25.7	(5.4)	15.2	(3.5)	16.6	(4.6)	31.9	(17.1)
B-S-J-G (China)	0.1	(0.1)	1.0	(0.2)	0.3	(0.1)	3.2	(0.7)	32.2	(3.6)	33.9	(4.3)	21.0	(2.5)	42.2	(4.6)
Bulgaria	0.1	(0.1)	0.2	(0.1)	0.1	(0.0)	0.4	(0.1)	29.3	(4.0)	22.6	(4.9)	18.4	(3.1)	36.9	(7.9)
Colombia	0.0	(0.0)	0.0	(0.0)	0.0	(0.0)	0.1	(0.0)	35.7	(15.8)	18.3	(7.5)	32.2	(16.3)	c	c
Costa Rica	0.0	(0.0)	0.0	(0.0)	0.0	(0.0)	0.0	(0.0)	c	c	19.9	(7.2)	c	c	c	c
Croatia	0.1	(0.1)	0.1	(0.1)	0.1	(0.1)	0.7	(0.2)	26.5	(4.3)	21.7	(3.3)	20.0	(3.1)	36.4	(7.3)
Cyprus*	0.1	(0.1)	0.1	(0.1)	0.1	(0.1)	0.2	(0.1)	31.3	(9.3)	17.7	(4.4)	15.5	(4.5)	c	c
Dominican Republic	m	m	m	m	m	m	m	m	m	m	m	m	m	m	m	m
Hong Kong (China)	0.1	(0.1)	1.0	(0.2)	1.6	(0.3)	3.1	(0.4)	57.4	(3.6)	48.3	(3.1)	31.4	(2.1)	63.4	(4.8)
Lithuania	0.1	(0.1)	0.4	(0.1)	0.1	(0.1)	0.7	(0.2)	30.8	(4.0)	21.1	(3.6)	20.3	(2.9)	36.7	(7.8)
Macao (China)	0.2	(0.1)	1.5	(0.2)	0.4	(0.1)	2.9	(0.3)	53.6	(3.3)	58.2	(3.5)	31.9	(2.0)	68.5	(4.2)
Montenegro	0.0	(0.0)	0.0	(0.0)	0.0	(0.0)	0.0	(0.0)	c	c	5.2	(3.8)	3.8	(2.6)	c	c
Peru	0.0	(0.0)	0.0	(0.0)	0.0	(0.0)	0.0	(0.0)	c	c	c	c	c	c	c	c
Qatar	m	m	m	m	m	m	m	m	m	m	m	m	m	m	m	m
Russia	0.2	(0.1)	0.2	(0.1)	0.2	(0.1)	0.7	(0.2)	33.0	(5.7)	25.3	(3.9)	16.3	(2.5)	40.7	(7.4)
Singapore	0.6	(0.1)	3.5	(0.3)	0.8	(0.2)	9.6	(0.4)	59.0	(1.6)	62.3	(2.4)	46.5	(1.5)	69.9	(2.2)
Chinese Taipei	0.1	(0.0)	2.5	(0.3)	0.2	(0.1)	3.3	(0.5)	40.1	(3.1)	53.3	(4.0)	26.5	(2.0)	58.9	(4.2)
Thailand	0.0	(0.0)	0.1	(0.1)	0.0	(0.0)	0.1	(0.1)	43.1	(11.7)	35.9	(14.2)	19.7	(6.5)	c	c
Tunisia	0.0	c	0.0	c	0.0	(0.0)	0.0	c	c	c	c	c	0.5	(2.0)	c	c
United Arab Emirates	0.2	(0.1)	0.2	(0.0)	0.1	(0.0)	0.5	(0.1)	31.7	(3.9)	28.0	(3.2)	22.3	(3.7)	42.7	(7.5)
Uruguay	0.1	(0.1)	0.1	(0.0)	0.1	(0.0)	0.2	(0.1)	37.3	(7.6)	22.3	(5.3)	24.1	(5.8)	41.3	(13.7)
Malaysia**	0.0	(0.0)	0.1	(0.0)	0.0	(0.0)	0.1	(0.0)	22.5	(9.8)	22.4	(11.1)	11.1	(4.3)	c	c

1. Top performers in collaborative problem solving are students who score at Level 4. Top performers in science, reading or mathematics score at Level 5 or 6 in the subject.
* See note at the beginning of this Annex.
**Malaysia: Coverage is too small to ensure comparability (see Annex A4).

StatLink http://dx.doi.org/10.1787/888933616769

[Part 1/2]

Table V.3.3b Low achievers in four PISA subjects

	Percentage of 15-year-old students who are:															
	Not low achievers in any of the four subjects		Low achievers[1] in only one of science, reading or mathematics		Low achievers in only two of science, reading and mathematics		Low achievers in science, reading and mathematics		Low achievers in only collaborative problem solving		Low achievers in collaborative problem solving and science		Low achievers in collaborative problem solving and reading		Low achievers in collaborative problem solving and mathematics	
	%	S.E.	%	S.E.	%	S.E.	%	S.E.	%	S.E.	%	S.E.	%	S.E.	%	S.E.
OECD																
Australia	67.1	(0.7)	7.0	(0.4)	3.5	(0.3)	2.5	(0.2)	4.6	(0.4)	0.5	(0.1)	1.3	(0.2)	1.3	(0.2)
Austria	63.5	(1.2)	5.9	(0.4)	3.1	(0.3)	2.8	(0.4)	5.9	(0.5)	0.7	(0.2)	2.0	(0.3)	1.0	(0.2)
Belgium	64.8	(1.1)	4.1	(0.4)	2.2	(0.3)	2.1	(0.2)	7.9	(0.4)	1.1	(0.1)	1.4	(0.2)	1.4	(0.2)
Canada	73.8	(0.9)	4.8	(0.4)	1.9	(0.2)	1.0	(0.1)	7.0	(0.5)	0.6	(0.1)	1.2	(0.1)	1.5	(0.2)
Chile	40.3	(1.3)	10.0	(0.6)	4.3	(0.4)	3.0	(0.4)	6.6	(0.5)	0.7	(0.2)	0.8	(0.2)	5.3	(0.6)
Czech Republic	62.7	(1.1)	5.4	(0.5)	2.8	(0.4)	2.9	(0.4)	7.3	(0.5)	0.9	(0.2)	1.7	(0.3)	1.3	(0.2)
Denmark	71.3	(1.1)	5.4	(0.5)	2.8	(0.4)	1.6	(0.3)	5.9	(0.5)	1.2	(0.2)	1.3	(0.2)	0.7	(0.2)
Estonia	77.6	(0.9)	4.7	(0.4)	1.6	(0.3)	0.9	(0.2)	5.5	(0.5)	0.6	(0.1)	1.3	(0.3)	1.3	(0.3)
Finland	75.0	(1.0)	4.3	(0.4)	1.7	(0.3)	1.0	(0.2)	6.4	(0.5)	0.8	(0.2)	0.9	(0.2)	1.4	(0.2)
France	61.4	(0.9)	4.5	(0.3)	2.4	(0.3)	2.1	(0.3)	8.3	(0.6)	1.1	(0.2)	1.5	(0.2)	1.3	(0.2)
Germany	69.2	(1.2)	5.1	(0.5)	2.7	(0.3)	2.5	(0.4)	6.3	(0.5)	1.0	(0.2)	1.2	(0.2)	1.1	(0.2)
Greece	47.6	(1.7)	5.3	(0.5)	3.1	(0.4)	2.0	(0.3)	9.1	(0.6)	1.7	(0.3)	1.2	(0.2)	3.3	(0.4)
Hungary	54.7	(1.2)	4.4	(0.4)	1.9	(0.3)	1.8	(0.3)	9.1	(0.6)	1.0	(0.2)	2.2	(0.4)	1.9	(0.3)
Iceland	59.2	(1.1)	7.1	(0.6)	4.0	(0.5)	2.4	(0.4)	6.0	(0.6)	1.7	(0.3)	1.5	(0.3)	1.3	(0.3)
Ireland	m	m	m	m	m	m	m	m	m	m	m	m	m	m	m	m
Israel	50.1	(1.6)	4.2	(0.4)	2.3	(0.2)	1.7	(0.3)	9.7	(0.6)	1.6	(0.3)	1.5	(0.3)	2.8	(0.3)
Italy	55.2	(1.2)	5.6	(0.6)	2.8	(0.4)	1.6	(0.3)	11.4	(0.7)	1.8	(0.3)	1.9	(0.3)	2.2	(0.3)
Japan	79.8	(1.1)	5.7	(0.5)	2.5	(0.3)	1.9	(0.3)	2.7	(0.3)	0.2	(0.1)	1.2	(0.2)	0.4	(0.1)
Korea	75.5	(1.2)	6.3	(0.4)	3.3	(0.3)	2.0	(0.3)	2.4	(0.3)	0.6	(0.1)	0.8	(0.2)	0.7	(0.2)
Latvia	60.4	(1.0)	5.4	(0.5)	2.0	(0.3)	1.2	(0.2)	11.2	(0.6)	1.0	(0.2)	2.0	(0.3)	2.6	(0.4)
Luxembourg	57.7	(0.6)	5.1	(0.5)	3.1	(0.4)	2.7	(0.3)	7.4	(0.5)	1.0	(0.2)	1.8	(0.3)	1.5	(0.3)
Mexico	29.5	(1.3)	9.0	(0.5)	4.6	(0.4)	3.4	(0.4)	6.4	(0.5)	1.5	(0.2)	1.3	(0.2)	4.0	(0.4)
Netherlands	68.7	(1.1)	4.4	(0.5)	2.5	(0.4)	2.4	(0.3)	6.2	(0.5)	1.0	(0.3)	1.6	(0.3)	0.8	(0.2)
New Zealand	67.6	(1.1)	7.1	(0.5)	3.3	(0.4)	2.4	(0.3)	4.4	(0.4)	0.6	(0.2)	1.3	(0.3)	1.4	(0.2)
Norway	65.7	(1.1)	4.8	(0.4)	2.6	(0.3)	1.5	(0.2)	8.9	(0.7)	1.6	(0.2)	1.4	(0.3)	1.2	(0.2)
Poland	m	m	m	m	m	m	m	m	m	m	m	m	m	m	m	m
Portugal	63.5	(1.2)	6.0	(0.5)	2.7	(0.4)	1.6	(0.2)	7.3	(0.6)	0.8	(0.1)	1.4	(0.2)	2.4	(0.3)
Slovak Republic	48.9	(1.2)	5.1	(0.5)	2.8	(0.3)	2.5	(0.4)	10.2	(0.6)	1.7	(0.2)	3.2	(0.4)	1.2	(0.2)
Slovenia	67.0	(0.8)	4.2	(0.3)	1.9	(0.3)	1.3	(0.2)	9.8	(0.5)	1.0	(0.2)	1.8	(0.3)	1.5	(0.3)
Spain	63.6	(1.1)	5.9	(0.5)	2.8	(0.4)	1.8	(0.3)	8.1	(0.6)	0.8	(0.1)	1.3	(0.2)	2.1	(0.2)
Sweden	64.2	(1.5)	5.9	(0.5)	3.5	(0.4)	1.8	(0.3)	6.1	(0.6)	1.3	(0.2)	1.7	(0.2)	1.1	(0.2)
Switzerland	m	m	m	m	m	m	m	m	m	m	m	m	m	m	m	m
Turkey	30.1	(2.0)	5.7	(0.5)	2.7	(0.3)	2.1	(0.3)	10.5	(0.7)	1.6	(0.3)	1.9	(0.4)	4.7	(0.4)
United Kingdom	65.1	(1.0)	7.0	(0.5)	3.3	(0.4)	2.1	(0.3)	5.9	(0.6)	0.7	(0.2)	1.5	(0.3)	1.7	(0.2)
United States	62.1	(1.5)	8.4	(0.8)	3.4	(0.4)	2.4	(0.3)	4.3	(0.4)	0.6	(0.1)	0.7	(0.2)	2.3	(0.4)
OECD average	61.3	(0.2)	5.7	(0.1)	2.8	(0.1)	2.0	(0.1)	7.2	(0.1)	1.0	(0.0)	1.5	(0.0)	1.8	(0.0)
Partners																
Brazil	19.7	(0.9)	8.3	(0.4)	4.3	(0.3)	3.5	(0.3)	5.5	(0.5)	0.8	(0.1)	1.0	(0.1)	5.6	(0.4)
B-S-J-G (China)	64.7	(1.7)	4.2	(0.4)	1.6	(0.2)	1.3	(0.3)	9.2	(0.6)	0.7	(0.2)	3.2	(0.5)	1.0	(0.2)
Bulgaria	40.4	(1.8)	5.8	(0.4)	2.4	(0.3)	1.9	(0.2)	7.6	(0.6)	0.9	(0.2)	3.0	(0.4)	2.5	(0.4)
Colombia	26.6	(1.0)	9.6	(0.6)	3.9	(0.3)	3.5	(0.4)	4.9	(0.4)	0.4	(0.1)	0.5	(0.1)	6.6	(0.5)
Costa Rica	26.5	(1.2)	11.4	(0.7)	6.2	(0.5)	6.0	(0.6)	6.1	(0.5)	0.8	(0.2)	1.0	(0.2)	5.4	(0.4)
Croatia	53.1	(1.4)	6.8	(0.5)	3.2	(0.4)	1.6	(0.3)	9.5	(0.5)	1.2	(0.2)	1.1	(0.2)	3.7	(0.4)
Cyprus*	36.9	(0.8)	7.1	(0.5)	4.2	(0.4)	2.8	(0.4)	9.0	(0.8)	2.3	(0.3)	2.0	(0.4)	2.6	(0.3)
Dominican Republic	m	m	m	m	m	m	m	m	m	m	m	m	m	m	m	m
Hong Kong (China)	80.2	(1.1)	3.4	(0.3)	1.7	(0.3)	1.0	(0.2)	5.4	(0.6)	0.6	(0.2)	1.0	(0.2)	0.6	(0.1)
Lithuania	53.1	(1.2)	4.7	(0.5)	2.2	(0.3)	1.5	(0.2)	11.5	(0.7)	1.4	(0.3)	2.6	(0.4)	2.1	(0.3)
Macao (China)	79.4	(0.6)	3.8	(0.4)	1.3	(0.3)	0.6	(0.2)	5.6	(0.4)	0.5	(0.1)	2.4	(0.3)	0.5	(0.2)
Montenegro	26.6	(0.7)	5.7	(0.4)	3.3	(0.3)	2.1	(0.3)	10.4	(0.7)	3.1	(0.3)	1.7	(0.2)	3.6	(0.5)
Peru	23.2	(1.3)	7.4	(0.6)	4.3	(0.3)	3.7	(0.3)	4.4	(0.5)	1.0	(0.2)	1.0	(0.2)	3.5	(0.3)
Qatar	m	m	m	m	m	m	m	m	m	m	m	m	m	m	m	m
Russia	54.9	(1.7)	5.6	(0.5)	2.1	(0.3)	0.9	(0.2)	15.9	(0.9)	2.0	(0.3)	2.7	(0.5)	2.5	(0.4)
Singapore	82.2	(0.6)	3.6	(0.3)	1.7	(0.2)	1.2	(0.2)	3.3	(0.3)	0.5	(0.2)	1.1	(0.2)	0.3	(0.1)
Chinese Taipei	74.5	(0.9)	4.7	(0.4)	2.1	(0.2)	1.8	(0.2)	4.7	(0.4)	0.3	(0.1)	2.0	(0.2)	0.5	(0.1)
Thailand	29.0	(1.5)	8.7	(0.5)	4.5	(0.5)	3.7	(0.4)	5.9	(0.6)	1.1	(0.2)	2.8	(0.4)	2.9	(0.3)
Tunisia	8.4	(0.8)	3.4	(0.4)	2.1	(0.3)	2.1	(0.4)	7.8	(0.8)	0.8	(0.3)	3.3	(0.4)	5.1	(0.5)
United Arab Emirates	35.5	(1.1)	6.2	(0.4)	2.7	(0.3)	1.8	(0.2)	8.0	(0.5)	1.3	(0.2)	2.0	(0.2)	4.1	(0.4)
Uruguay	34.7	(1.1)	7.8	(0.5)	3.7	(0.4)	3.3	(0.3)	7.2	(0.5)	0.8	(0.2)	1.4	(0.2)	4.8	(0.4)
Malaysia**	40.5	(1.8)	5.4	(0.6)	2.3	(0.3)	1.8	(0.3)	11.3	(0.7)	1.1	(0.2)	3.0	(0.4)	3.2	(0.4)

1. Low achievers in collaborative problem solving, science, reading or mathematics score below Level 2 in the subject.
* See note at the beginning of this Annex.
**Malaysia: Coverage is too small to ensure comparability (see Annex A4).
StatLink http://dx.doi.org/10.1787/888933616769

[Part 2/2]

Table V.3.3b Low achievers in four PISA subjects

		Percentage of 15-year-old students who are:								Percentage of low achievers in collaborative problem solving among low achievers in ...							
		Low achievers[1] in collaborative problem solving, science and reading		Low achievers in collaborative problem solving, science and mathematics		Low achievers in collaborative problem solving, reading and mathematics		Low achievers in all four subjects		Science		Reading		Mathematics		Science, reading and mathematics	
		%	S.E.	%	S.E.	%	S.E.	%	S.E.	%	S.E.	%	S.E.	%	S.E.	%	S.E.
OECD	Australia	1.3	(0.2)	1.4	(0.2)	0.9	(0.1)	8.6	(0.4)	66.9	(1.5)	66.6	(1.3)	55.9	(1.6)	77.1	(1.6)
	Austria	2.0	(0.4)	1.4	(0.2)	1.0	(0.2)	10.7	(0.7)	71.1	(1.8)	69.7	(2.0)	65.2	(2.5)	79.5	(2.3)
	Belgium	1.9	(0.3)	1.7	(0.2)	0.9	(0.2)	10.6	(0.7)	76.9	(1.4)	75.7	(1.6)	72.8	(1.7)	83.6	(1.6)
	Canada	1.0	(0.2)	1.5	(0.2)	0.7	(0.1)	4.9	(0.4)	72.9	(2.2)	72.6	(2.1)	60.2	(2.0)	82.4	(1.8)
	Chile	0.8	(0.2)	6.2	(0.6)	1.6	(0.3)	20.3	(1.0)	80.5	(1.7)	82.6	(1.4)	67.6	(1.6)	87.1	(1.5)
	Czech Republic	1.9	(0.3)	1.4	(0.3)	1.0	(0.2)	10.7	(0.7)	72.2	(2.1)	69.4	(2.3)	66.6	(2.2)	78.5	(2.2)
	Denmark	2.1	(0.3)	1.4	(0.2)	0.4	(0.1)	5.9	(0.5)	67.0	(2.2)	64.6	(2.4)	62.2	(2.8)	79.0	(3.2)
	Estonia	1.1	(0.2)	1.0	(0.2)	0.6	(0.2)	3.8	(0.4)	73.9	(3.0)	64.5	(3.1)	60.1	(2.7)	81.1	(3.9)
	Finland	1.2	(0.2)	1.4	(0.2)	0.7	(0.2)	5.3	(0.5)	75.2	(3.0)	72.9	(3.3)	64.6	(2.9)	84.1	(3.1)
	France	1.8	(0.2)	2.0	(0.2)	0.9	(0.2)	12.7	(0.8)	79.5	(1.6)	78.5	(1.7)	72.3	(1.8)	85.8	(1.6)
	Germany	1.5	(0.3)	1.5	(0.2)	0.5	(0.2)	7.4	(0.6)	67.1	(2.7)	65.6	(2.8)	60.9	(2.6)	74.9	(3.2)
	Greece	2.1	(0.3)	4.7	(0.5)	1.1	(0.2)	18.7	(1.6)	83.3	(1.8)	84.9	(1.5)	77.8	(1.9)	90.3	(1.2)
	Hungary	2.6	(0.3)	2.3	(0.3)	1.5	(0.2)	16.8	(0.9)	86.8	(1.3)	83.7	(1.3)	80.3	(1.4)	90.5	(1.3)
	Iceland	2.4	(0.5)	2.6	(0.5)	0.9	(0.3)	10.7	(0.6)	68.8	(2.3)	70.6	(2.4)	65.8	(3.2)	81.5	(2.7)
	Ireland	m	m	m	m	m	m	m	m	m	m	m	m	m	m	m	m
	Israel	2.2	(0.3)	3.5	(0.4)	1.3	(0.3)	19.2	(1.1)	85.0	(1.5)	87.7	(1.3)	82.5	(1.7)	91.9	(1.2)
	Italy	2.6	(0.3)	3.2	(0.4)	1.1	(0.2)	10.6	(0.7)	78.3	(1.9)	77.2	(2.1)	73.1	(2.3)	86.8	(2.1)
	Japan	1.0	(0.2)	0.4	(0.1)	0.5	(0.2)	3.7	(0.5)	55.4	(3.3)	49.6	(2.9)	46.9	(3.8)	65.8	(4.3)
	Korea	1.0	(0.2)	1.1	(0.2)	0.6	(0.2)	5.6	(0.6)	58.2	(2.6)	58.9	(3.3)	52.6	(2.7)	73.5	(3.7)
	Latvia	1.7	(0.3)	2.1	(0.3)	1.2	(0.3)	9.2	(0.6)	81.4	(2.0)	80.0	(2.0)	70.6	(2.4)	88.4	(2.0)
	Luxembourg	2.5	(0.3)	2.0	(0.3)	1.0	(0.2)	14.3	(0.5)	76.0	(1.4)	76.3	(1.7)	72.6	(1.8)	84.0	(1.5)
	Mexico	2.0	(0.3)	6.0	(0.5)	2.0	(0.3)	30.3	(1.2)	83.3	(1.2)	85.1	(1.3)	74.7	(1.5)	89.8	(1.1)
	Netherlands	1.9	(0.3)	1.2	(0.2)	0.8	(0.2)	8.5	(0.7)	68.2	(2.6)	70.6	(2.7)	67.4	(2.9)	77.7	(2.5)
	New Zealand	1.2	(0.2)	1.8	(0.3)	0.8	(0.2)	8.2	(0.6)	68.3	(2.5)	66.6	(2.5)	56.4	(2.5)	77.8	(2.8)
	Norway	1.8	(0.2)	2.5	(0.3)	0.5	(0.1)	7.5	(0.5)	71.6	(2.0)	74.9	(2.0)	68.5	(2.4)	83.6	(2.1)
	Poland	m	m	m	m	m	m	m	m	m	m	m	m	m	m	m	m
	Portugal	1.1	(0.2)	2.5	(0.3)	1.5	(0.3)	9.1	(0.6)	77.4	(2.3)	75.8	(2.4)	65.4	(2.6)	84.8	(2.1)
	Slovak Republic	3.6	(0.4)	1.7	(0.3)	1.3	(0.2)	17.6	(0.9)	80.3	(1.3)	80.0	(1.5)	78.8	(1.5)	87.4	(1.6)
	Slovenia	1.8	(0.2)	2.0	(0.3)	0.9	(0.2)	6.9	(0.4)	77.5	(2.2)	75.4	(2.0)	70.2	(2.2)	84.2	(1.9)
	Spain	1.4	(0.2)	2.8	(0.4)	0.8	(0.2)	8.5	(0.6)	73.9	(2.2)	74.1	(1.9)	63.8	(2.3)	82.3	(2.1)
	Sweden	1.9	(0.3)	2.4	(0.3)	0.6	(0.2)	9.5	(0.7)	69.9	(2.3)	74.8	(1.9)	65.4	(2.0)	83.7	(1.9)
	Switzerland	m	m	m	m	m	m	m	m	m	m	m	m	m	m	m	m
	Turkey	2.4	(0.3)	6.8	(0.6)	2.3	(0.4)	29.1	(1.8)	89.8	(0.9)	89.4	(1.0)	83.5	(1.3)	93.4	(0.9)
	United Kingdom	1.5	(0.3)	2.1	(0.3)	1.2	(0.2)	7.9	(0.6)	69.8	(1.9)	67.3	(2.2)	59.1	(2.2)	78.7	(2.4)
	United States	0.8	(0.2)	2.5	(0.3)	1.3	(0.3)	11.1	(0.8)	74.3	(2.4)	73.5	(2.2)	58.8	(2.5)	82.1	(2.3)
	OECD average	1.7	(0.1)	2.4	(0.1)	1.0	(0.0)	11.4	(0.1)	74.4	(0.4)	73.7	(0.4)	67.0	(0.4)	82.9	(0.4)
Partners	Brazil	1.3	(0.2)	6.8	(0.5)	2.5	(0.2)	40.6	(1.1)	87.4	(0.8)	89.1	(0.9)	79.1	(0.9)	92.1	(0.7)
	B-S-J-G (China)	2.4	(0.3)	0.9	(0.2)	1.2	(0.2)	9.6	(0.9)	83.8	(1.8)	75.1	(1.8)	81.0	(1.9)	88.5	(2.0)
	Bulgaria	3.1	(0.3)	2.5	(0.3)	2.2	(0.3)	27.7	(1.7)	90.3	(0.9)	86.9	(1.0)	82.8	(1.3)	93.6	(0.7)
	Colombia	0.4	(0.1)	7.2	(0.5)	1.8	(0.3)	34.7	(1.4)	87.0	(0.9)	87.2	(0.9)	75.7	(1.1)	90.7	(0.9)
	Costa Rica	1.1	(0.2)	6.1	(0.5)	2.3	(0.4)	27.0	(1.1)	75.6	(1.4)	78.0	(1.5)	65.5	(1.6)	81.8	(1.6)
	Croatia	1.2	(0.2)	4.3	(0.4)	1.4	(0.3)	12.9	(0.9)	79.6	(1.9)	83.6	(2.0)	69.8	(1.9)	88.9	(1.7)
	Cyprus*	3.2	(0.4)	5.4	(0.4)	1.2	(0.2)	23.3	(0.6)	81.1	(1.5)	83.4	(1.5)	76.2	(1.3)	89.2	(1.4)
	Dominican Republic	m	m	m	m	m	m	m	m	m	m	m	m	m	m	m	m
	Hong Kong (China)	1.3	(0.2)	0.9	(0.2)	0.3	(0.1)	3.6	(0.4)	67.8	(3.4)	66.4	(3.4)	60.2	(3.5)	78.4	(3.7)
	Lithuania	2.7	(0.3)	3.0	(0.4)	1.3	(0.2)	13.9	(0.8)	85.1	(1.5)	81.5	(1.5)	79.8	(1.4)	90.4	(1.4)
	Macao (China)	2.3	(0.4)	0.4	(0.1)	0.4	(0.1)	2.9	(0.4)	75.3	(3.9)	68.2	(2.7)	63.4	(4.6)	82.5	(5.0)
	Montenegro	3.4	(0.4)	7.5	(0.4)	1.6	(0.2)	30.9	(0.7)	88.1	(0.9)	89.7	(1.0)	84.1	(1.2)	93.6	(0.9)
	Peru	1.6	(0.2)	4.9	(0.6)	2.0	(0.3)	43.0	(1.3)	86.4	(0.9)	88.2	(0.8)	80.6	(1.0)	92.0	(0.7)
	Qatar	m	m	m	m	m	m	m	m	m	m	m	m	m	m	m	m
	Russia	2.7	(0.4)	3.0	(0.4)	0.9	(0.2)	6.8	(0.6)	79.8	(2.2)	80.8	(2.4)	69.6	(2.6)	88.1	(2.9)
	Singapore	1.7	(0.2)	0.5	(0.1)	0.3	(0.1)	3.6	(0.3)	65.9	(2.4)	60.5	(2.5)	62.6	(3.3)	75.7	(3.6)
	Chinese Taipei	1.6	(0.2)	0.5	(0.1)	0.8	(0.2)	6.6	(0.5)	71.9	(2.1)	63.1	(2.5)	65.1	(2.0)	78.7	(2.3)
	Thailand	3.6	(0.4)	3.0	(0.4)	2.8	(0.3)	32.0	(1.4)	85.1	(1.2)	82.5	(1.5)	75.6	(1.4)	89.6	(1.0)
	Tunisia	2.9	(0.4)	3.8	(0.4)	5.2	(0.6)	55.1	(1.4)	95.0	(0.8)	92.9	(0.8)	92.6	(0.8)	96.3	(0.6)
	United Arab Emirates	2.5	(0.4)	4.3	(0.4)	2.4	(0.3)	29.4	(1.0)	89.7	(0.8)	89.8	(1.0)	82.4	(1.2)	94.2	(0.6)
	Uruguay	1.3	(0.2)	5.0	(0.4)	2.5	(0.3)	27.5	(1.0)	84.9	(1.0)	84.0	(1.2)	76.0	(1.1)	89.3	(1.1)
	Malaysia**	3.2	(0.5)	2.8	(0.3)	2.2	(0.4)	23.1	(1.3)	89.4	(1.1)	84.6	(1.6)	83.2	(1.5)	92.6	(1.2)

1. Low achievers in collaborative problem solving, science, reading or mathematics score below Level 2 in the subject.
* See note at the beginning of this Annex.
**Malaysia: Coverage is too small to ensure comparability (see Annex A4).
StatLink http://dx.doi.org/10.1787/888933616769

[Part 1/2]

Table V.3.9a Relative performance in collaborative problem solving

Based on residual scores after accounting for performance in the core PISA subjects in regressions involving all OECD and partner countries/economies

		Relative performance in collaborative problem solving based on performance in...															
		Science				Reading				Mathematics				Science, reading and mathematics			
		Average relative score[1]		Percentage of students who score higher than expected[2, 3]		Average relative score		Percentage of students who score higher than expected		Average relative score		Percentage of students who score higher than expected		Average relative score		Percentage of students who score higher than expected	
		Score dif.	S.E.	%	S.E.	Score dif.	S.E.	%	S.E.	Score dif.	S.E.	%	S.E.	Score dif.	S.E.	%	S.E.
OECD	Australia	**21**	(1.6)	**62.2**	(1.0)	**26**	(1.5)	**64.7**	(0.9)	**33**	(1.9)	**66.7**	(1.1)	**23**	(1.5)	**63.4**	(1.0)
	Austria	**11**	(1.8)	**57.6**	(1.2)	**18**	(2.1)	**61.5**	(1.4)	**9**	(2.1)	**55.3**	(1.4)	**13**	(1.8)	**58.6**	(1.3)
	Belgium	-3	(1.5)	48.6	(1.0)	-1	(1.5)	49.6	(1.0)	**-7**	(1.6)	**45.7**	(0.9)	**-4**	(1.4)	**47.5**	(0.9)
	Canada	**11**	(1.6)	**56.8**	(1.0)	**12**	(1.9)	**57.1**	(1.1)	**21**	(1.9)	**60.5**	(1.1)	**10**	(1.6)	**56.1**	(1.1)
	Chile	-2	(2.0)	48.7	(1.5)	**-14**	(2.0)	**39.9**	(1.5)	**11**	(2.1)	**57.9**	(1.7)	-3	(1.9)	47.6	(1.5)
	Czech Republic	2	(1.8)	51.7	(1.3)	**5**	(1.9)	**53.1**	(1.2)	1	(1.7)	50.7	(1.1)	3	(1.7)	51.8	(1.2)
	Denmark	**16**	(1.6)	**61.5**	(1.2)	**17**	(1.9)	**61.0**	(1.3)	**8**	(2.0)	**55.4**	(1.3)	**14**	(1.7)	**60.3**	(1.1)
	Estonia	**6**	(1.7)	**54.7**	(1.5)	**18**	(2.0)	**61.9**	(1.6)	**18**	(1.8)	**61.6**	(1.2)	**8**	(1.7)	**56.6**	(1.4)
	Finland	**7**	(1.8)	**54.9**	(1.3)	**11**	(1.9)	**56.7**	(1.2)	**22**	(2.1)	**63.0**	(1.3)	**7**	(1.7)	**54.9**	(1.3)
	France	-4	(2.0)	47.8	(1.3)	**-8**	(1.7)	**45.2**	(1.3)	-4	(2.2)	48.1	(1.5)	**-7**	(1.9)	**46.0**	(1.3)
	Germany	**15**	(1.9)	**59.3**	(1.2)	**15**	(2.0)	**58.4**	(1.2)	**17**	(2.2)	**59.5**	(1.2)	**14**	(1.8)	**58.3**	(1.3)
	Greece	**-7**	(1.7)	**45.3**	(1.3)	**-19**	(1.8)	**37.6**	(1.2)	**-10**	(2.0)	**44.5**	(1.4)	**-10**	(1.6)	**42.6**	(1.3)
	Hungary	**-11**	(1.3)	**42.0**	(1.1)	**-8**	(1.6)	**45.1**	(1.2)	**-14**	(1.7)	**41.6**	(1.2)	**-10**	(1.3)	**42.9**	(1.1)
	Iceland	**19**	(1.7)	**62.2**	(1.3)	**11**	(1.7)	**56.7**	(1.2)	5	(2.0)	**53.2**	(1.3)	**15**	(1.6)	**59.9**	(1.3)
	Ireland	m	m	m	m	m	m	m	m	m	m	m	m	m	m	m	m
	Israel	**-7**	(1.7)	**44.3**	(1.2)	**-17**	(1.8)	**39.0**	(1.2)	**-12**	(2.2)	**42.6**	(1.4)	**-11**	(1.6)	**42.2**	(1.2)
	Italy	**-8**	(1.9)	**44.6**	(1.3)	**-14**	(2.1)	**42.3**	(1.3)	**-18**	(2.4)	**40.2**	(1.3)	**-11**	(1.8)	**42.8**	(1.3)
	Japan	**19**	(1.8)	**62.9**	(1.2)	**37**	(1.7)	**74.1**	(1.1)	**24**	(2.0)	**65.7**	(1.2)	**23**	(1.6)	**65.9**	(1.2)
	Korea	**24**	(1.8)	**66.6**	(1.3)	**22**	(1.9)	**65.8**	(1.4)	**17**	(2.1)	**61.7**	(1.5)	**20**	(1.8)	**65.4**	(1.4)
	Latvia	**-9**	(1.7)	**44.2**	(1.3)	**-9**	(1.9)	**44.0**	(1.5)	**-5**	(1.6)	**47.3**	(1.3)	**-9**	(1.7)	**43.8**	(1.4)
	Luxembourg	3	(1.5)	52.2	(1.2)	2	(1.4)	51.6	(1.1)	-2	(1.7)	49.2	(1.1)	2	(1.4)	51.4	(1.3)
	Mexico	-1	(1.7)	49.4	(1.2)	**-11**	(1.6)	**41.6**	(1.1)	-2	(1.8)	49.0	(1.2)	-1	(1.6)	49.1	(1.2)
	Netherlands	**9**	(1.6)	**55.6**	(1.3)	**12**	(1.8)	**58.2**	(1.4)	**5**	(1.9)	**53.6**	(1.4)	**8**	(1.5)	**55.5**	(1.3)
	New Zealand	**20**	(1.8)	**62.4**	(1.1)	**23**	(2.1)	**62.9**	(1.3)	**33**	(1.9)	**67.3**	(1.1)	**20**	(1.8)	**62.8**	(1.1)
	Norway	2	(1.9)	50.9	(1.3)	**-11**	(2.3)	**43.5**	(1.5)	-2	(2.1)	49.0	(1.2)	**-5**	(2.0)	**46.9**	(1.5)
	Poland	m	m	m	m	m	m	m	m	m	m	m	m	m	m	m	m
	Portugal	**-5**	(2.0)	**47.0**	(1.5)	-4	(2.3)	47.7	(1.6)	1	(2.0)	51.0	(1.3)	**-5**	(2.0)	**46.8**	(1.6)
	Slovak Republic	**-8**	(1.7)	**45.2**	(1.2)	**-4**	(1.8)	**47.0**	(1.2)	**-22**	(1.9)	**37.4**	(1.2)	**-7**	(1.6)	**45.4**	(1.2)
	Slovenia	**-10**	(1.7)	**43.9**	(1.1)	**-5**	(1.6)	**47.1**	(1.1)	**-9**	(1.7)	**45.4**	(1.0)	**-10**	(1.6)	**43.8**	(1.1)
	Spain	0	(1.5)	50.6	(1.3)	-3	(1.6)	48.2	(1.1)	**4**	(1.8)	**52.7**	(1.4)	-1	(1.5)	49.2	(1.3)
	Sweden	**13**	(2.0)	**58.4**	(1.3)	**7**	(2.1)	**54.5**	(1.5)	**11**	(2.0)	**56.9**	(1.4)	**9**	(1.9)	**56.7**	(1.3)
	Switzerland	m	m	m	m	m	m	m	m	m	m	m	m	m	m	m	m
	Turkey	**-20**	(1.5)	**34.9**	(1.2)	**-26**	(1.8)	**31.9**	(1.3)	**-22**	(1.8)	**35.4**	(1.3)	**-19**	(1.5)	**34.9**	(1.3)
	United Kingdom	**10**	(1.9)	**56.1**	(1.3)	**18**	(2.4)	**60.3**	(1.6)	**22**	(2.2)	**61.8**	(1.4)	**12**	(2.0)	**57.8**	(1.3)
	United States	**21**	(2.2)	**63.6**	(1.5)	**20**	(2.4)	**61.6**	(1.6)	**40**	(2.6)	**71.0**	(1.4)	**22**	(2.1)	**63.9**	(1.4)
	OECD average	**4**	(0.3)	**52.7**	(0.2)	**4**	(0.3)	**52.2**	(0.2)	**5**	(0.4)	**53.2**	(0.2)	**3**	(0.3)	**52.2**	(0.2)
Partners	Brazil	**-10**	(1.5)	**42.7**	(1.2)	**-21**	(1.9)	**36.5**	(1.2)	0	(2.0)	49.5	(1.4)	**-9**	(1.5)	**43.8**	(1.2)
	B-S-J-G (China)	**-20**	(1.8)	**36.4**	(1.2)	-2	(2.0)	48.6	(1.5)	**-30**	(2.0)	**31.7**	(1.3)	**-17**	(1.8)	**38.3**	(1.3)
	Bulgaria	**-14**	(1.5)	**39.5**	(1.2)	**-7**	(1.5)	**45.5**	(1.2)	**-15**	(2.0)	**40.5**	(1.3)	**-10**	(1.4)	**42.9**	(1.2)
	Colombia	**-5**	(1.3)	**46.1**	(1.3)	**-16**	(1.5)	**38.3**	(1.2)	**8**	(1.4)	**55.6**	(1.1)	**-4**	(1.2)	**46.6**	(1.2)
	Costa Rica	**4**	(1.9)	52.6	(1.6)	**-6**	(2.0)	**45.4**	(1.4)	**12**	(2.3)	**57.5**	(1.6)	**4**	(1.9)	**53.2**	(1.5)
	Croatia	**-9**	(1.4)	**44.0**	(1.0)	**-20**	(1.7)	**36.6**	(1.3)	**-4**	(1.7)	47.9	(1.2)	**-12**	(1.4)	**41.2**	(1.0)
	Cyprus*	**-4**	(1.6)	**47.7**	(1.1)	**-15**	(1.6)	**40.5**	(1.1)	**-12**	(1.8)	**43.1**	(1.2)	**-6**	(1.5)	**46.0**	(1.2)
	Dominican Republic	m	m	m	m	m	m	m	m	m	m	m	m	m	m	m	m
	Hong Kong (China)	**20**	(2.0)	**63.7**	(1.4)	**17**	(1.8)	**61.8**	(1.3)	2	(2.0)	52.0	(1.3)	**15**	(1.8)	**60.6**	(1.4)
	Lithuania	**-15**	(1.5)	**39.4**	(1.2)	**-14**	(1.5)	**40.5**	(1.0)	**-20**	(1.6)	**37.9**	(1.2)	**-15**	(1.4)	**39.1**	(1.1)
	Macao (China)	**9**	(1.1)	**56.9**	(0.9)	**24**	(1.0)	**67.1**	(0.9)	-2	(1.4)	50.1	(1.0)	**11**	(1.0)	**58.3**	(0.9)
	Montenegro	**-15**	(1.2)	**39.2**	(1.2)	**-32**	(1.5)	**29.5**	(1.1)	**-26**	(1.3)	**33.1**	(1.0)	**-18**	(1.2)	**36.4**	(1.1)
	Peru	-1	(1.6)	49.0	(1.4)	**-7**	(1.7)	**44.5**	(1.4)	-1	(1.8)	49.0	(1.3)	2	(1.5)	51.1	(1.5)
	Qatar	m	m	m	m	m	m	m	m	m	m	m	m	m	m	m	m
	Russia	**-18**	(2.3)	**39.1**	(1.5)	**-25**	(2.1)	**35.4**	(1.4)	**-25**	(2.8)	**37.2**	(1.6)	**-22**	(2.1)	**36.5**	(1.5)
	Singapore	**15**	(1.0)	**60.3**	(0.9)	**32**	(1.1)	**70.4**	(1.0)	**11**	(1.2)	**57.0**	(1.0)	**16**	(0.9)	**61.4**	(0.9)
	Chinese Taipei	-1	(2.0)	49.1	(1.5)	**26**	(2.0)	**67.8**	(1.3)	**-8**	(2.1)	**45.1**	(1.3)	**5**	(1.9)	**53.7**	(1.5)
	Thailand	-3	(2.0)	47.8	(1.6)	2	(2.0)	51.3	(1.6)	-5	(2.6)	47.1	(1.6)	2	(1.9)	51.6	(1.5)
	Tunisia	**-29**	(1.6)	**26.7**	(1.2)	**-15**	(2.2)	**38.4**	(1.6)	**-23**	(2.0)	**33.7**	(1.3)	**-18**	(1.7)	**35.3**	(1.5)
	United Arab Emirates	**-16**	(1.4)	**38.5**	(1.1)	**-17**	(1.8)	**38.1**	(1.4)	**-14**	(1.8)	**40.8**	(1.2)	**-14**	(1.5)	**39.6**	(1.3)
	Uruguay	**-7**	(1.4)	**44.6**	(1.2)	**-12**	(1.8)	**42.2**	(1.3)	0	(1.9)	50.0	(1.3)	**-6**	(1.5)	**45.7**	(1.2)
	Malaysia**	**-16**	(1.8)	**36.9**	(1.5)	**-10**	(2.0)	**42.4**	(1.5)	**-23**	(2.3)	**33.6**	(1.7)	**-13**	(1.7)	**39.6**	(1.5)

1. Relative scores are the residuals obtained from a pooled linear regression, across all participating countries/economies, of performance in collaborative problem solving over performance in science, reading and/or mathematics.
2. Students who score higher than expected are those with positive relative scores.
3. The percentage of students who score higher than expected is bolded when it differs significantly from 50%.
4. Top performers in science, reading or mathematics are those who attain Level 5 or above in those subjects.
5. Low achievers in science, reading or mathematics are those who attain below Level 2 in those subjects.

Notes: Students in PISA 2015 completed four clusters of test material: two in science and two distributed among reading, mathematics and collaborative problem solving. Hence, no student completed all four of science, reading, mathematics and collaborative problem solving. Scores were imputed in the domains in which students were not tested.

Values that are statistically significant are indicated in bold (see Annex A3).

* See note at the beginning of this Annex.

**Malaysia: Coverage is too small to ensure comparability (see Annex A4).

StatLink http://dx.doi.org/10.1787/888933616769

[Part 2/2]

Table V.3.9a Relative performance in collaborative problem solving

Based on residual scores after accounting for performance in the core PISA subjects in regressions involving all OECD and partner countries/economies

		Relative performance in collaborative problem solving based on performance among top performers[4] in...												Relative performance in collaborative problem solving based on performance among low achievers[5] in...											
		Science				Reading				Mathematics				Science				Reading				Mathematics			
		Average relative score[1]		Percentage of students who score higher than expected[2,3]		Average relative score		Percentage of students who score higher than expected		Average relative score		Percentage of students who score higher than expected		Average relative score		Percentage of students who score higher than expected		Average relative score		Percentage of students who score higher than expected		Average relative score		Percentage of students who score higher than expected	
		Score dif.	S.E.	%	S.E.	Score dif.	S.E.	%	S.E.	Score dif.	S.E.	%	S.E.	Score dif.	S.E.	%	S.E.	Score dif.	S.E.	%	S.E.	Score dif.	S.E.	%	S.E.
OECD	Australia	**11**	(3.3)	**56.7**	(2.3)	**22**	(3.3)	**62.8**	(2.1)	**30**	(3.8)	**66.4**	(2.1)	**19**	(2.8)	**59.5**	(2.0)	**20**	(2.4)	**60.0**	(1.6)	**22**	(2.9)	**60.3**	(1.8)
	Austria	2	(3.8)	52.1	(3.3)	**13**	(4.8)	**58.2**	(4.0)	4	(4.4)	52.5	(3.0)	**11**	(3.1)	**58.0**	(2.2)	**20**	(3.2)	**62.8**	(2.3)	**8**	(3.7)	54.0	(2.1)
	Belgium	**-15**	(3.2)	**39.8**	(2.5)	-7	(3.5)	45.6	(2.8)	**-12**	(3.2)	**42.8**	(2.1)	1	(2.5)	51.0	(1.9)	1	(3.0)	50.8	(1.8)	**-10**	(2.9)	**44.2**	(2.0)
	Canada	**15**	(3.6)	**58.6**	(2.4)	**20**	(3.1)	**61.7**	(2.0)	**21**	(3.7)	**61.3**	(1.9)	2	(3.1)	50.8	(2.3)	0	(3.8)	49.4	(2.3)	**9**	(2.8)	53.7	(1.9)
	Chile	**-26**	(7.2)	**30.3**	(6.4)	**-28**	(5.4)	**30.0**	(4.9)	-15	(8.4)	38.4	(7.5)	2	(2.6)	51.2	(2.2)	**-8**	(2.4)	**43.5**	(2.1)	**14**	(2.4)	**59.3**	(2.0)
	Czech Republic	**-24**	(4.6)	**34.0**	(3.8)	**-20**	(4.3)	**37.9**	(3.2)	**-13**	(4.3)	**42.2**	(3.1)	**10**	(3.1)	**56.5**	(2.9)	**18**	(3.7)	**60.3**	(2.6)	4	(3.6)	51.4	(2.4)
	Denmark	3	(4.3)	53.1	(3.3)	12	(6.3)	**58.8**	(4.2)	**8**	(3.6)	**56.3**	(2.8)	**18**	(2.8)	**62.5**	(2.6)	**19**	(3.1)	**62.2**	(2.4)	4	(4.0)	52.5	(2.8)
	Estonia	3	(3.2)	53.1	(2.9)	**15**	(4.1)	**61.0**	(3.1)	**21**	(4.3)	**64.0**	(3.7)	4	(4.4)	53.7	(3.7)	**17**	(4.0)	**62.3**	(3.0)	**8**	(4.0)	54.6	(2.9)
	Finland	**7**	(3.4)	54.0	(2.8)	**16**	(4.7)	**59.7**	(3.3)	**35**	(4.9)	**70.6**	(3.6)	-1	(4.2)	49.3	(3.2)	4	(4.9)	52.5	(3.2)	-1	(4.4)	49.5	(3.3)
	France	**-16**	(4.5)	**40.1**	(3.0)	**-28**	(5.0)	**33.9**	(2.8)	**-12**	(4.3)	**43.1**	(2.5)	-1	(3.2)	49.7	(2.5)	5	(3.3)	52.8	(2.3)	**-7**	(3.1)	**45.2**	(2.0)
	Germany	**8**	(3.6)	**54.9**	(2.4)	**9**	(3.9)	55.2	(3.0)	**22**	(3.8)	**63.4**	(2.6)	**19**	(3.6)	**60.5**	(2.6)	**21**	(4.3)	**60.6**	(2.5)	**11**	(4.0)	54.8	(2.6)
	Greece	**-18**	(7.9)	**36.5**	(6.2)	**-31**	(4.5)	**29.2**	(4.5)	**-15**	(6.2)	40.3	(5.5)	-6	(3.5)	45.9	(2.6)	**-11**	(3.8)	**42.3**	(2.7)	**-12**	(3.7)	**43.1**	(2.3)
	Hungary	**-15**	(5.1)	**39.4**	(4.9)	**-12**	(5.7)	41.8	(4.6)	**-18**	(4.7)	**38.2**	(3.7)	**-13**	(3.0)	**40.6**	(2.4)	**-9**	(3.6)	**43.9**	(2.5)	**-17**	(3.0)	**38.9**	(1.7)
	Iceland	6	(9.9)	54.1	(8.7)	3	(6.8)	52.0	(5.2)	0	(6.2)	50.0	(5.6)	**20**	(3.4)	**62.3**	(2.4)	**20**	(3.6)	**61.7**	(2.7)	8	(4.6)	54.2	(3.0)
	Ireland	m	m	m	m	m	m	m	m	m	m	m	m	m	m	m	m	m	m	m	m	m	m	m	m
	Israel	**-16**	(4.4)	**39.3**	(3.2)	**-24**	(4.4)	**35.0**	(3.2)	**-13**	(5.4)	**42.9**	(3.4)	-4	(3.4)	**44.5**	(2.6)	**-8**	(3.3)	**42.6**	(2.2)	**-14**	(3.4)	**39.0**	(2.2)
	Italy	**-19**	(5.8)	**38.2**	(4.7)	**-29**	(5.2)	**33.0**	(4.2)	**-34**	(4.0)	**30.9**	(2.5)	-4	(4.2)	47.3	(2.8)	-5	(4.2)	47.6	(2.5)	**-11**	(4.6)	**43.8**	(3.0)
	Japan	**-8**	(3.6)	**43.6**	(2.9)	**18**	(4.2)	**63.3**	(3.0)	**7**	(3.4)	55.2	(2.7)	**36**	(5.1)	**72.8**	(2.9)	**48**	(4.1)	**77.9**	(2.5)	**35**	(5.6)	**70.1**	(3.2)
	Korea	-5	(4.1)	45.2	(3.6)	2	(3.6)	51.6	(3.6)	-6	(3.6)	47.1	(2.7)	**36**	(3.7)	**73.4**	(2.3)	**35**	(3.4)	**73.5**	(2.5)	**33**	(3.8)	**70.1**	(2.4)
	Latvia	-12	(6.2)	41.3	(5.3)	-11	(7.7)	43.2	(7.1)	-5	(5.8)	46.8	(4.6)	**-13**	(3.5)	**41.0**	(3.0)	**-10**	(3.9)	**43.0**	(3.1)	**-9**	(4.6)	44.1	(3.8)
	Luxembourg	-8	(5.9)	44.5	(4.1)	-2	(6.6)	47.8	(4.6)	1	(5.5)	49.5	(4.0)	5	(2.5)	53.0	(1.8)	**8**	(2.7)	**55.1**	(1.7)	**-8**	(3.1)	**44.8**	(2.2)
	Mexico	-26	(15.2)	26.7	(19.1)	-18	(14.6)	34.4	(14.2)	-19	(14.6)	39.0	(14.5)	**-4**	(2.2)	**46.4**	(1.6)	**-11**	(2.6)	**41.8**	(1.7)	-1	(2.3)	49.4	(1.6)
	Netherlands	-6	(4.5)	46.3	(3.5)	**12**	(4.1)	**57.7**	(3.2)	**12**	(3.7)	**58.7**	(2.7)	**18**	(3.7)	**60.5**	(2.4)	**16**	(3.3)	**58.9**	(2.5)	2	(4.4)	50.6	(3.1)
	New Zealand	**11**	(4.0)	**57.4**	(2.8)	**19**	(4.7)	**61.1**	(3.3)	**35**	(4.2)	**69.5**	(2.8)	**17**	(4.2)	**59.5**	(2.5)	**21**	(4.2)	**61.6**	(2.7)	**22**	(4.0)	**60.4**	(2.4)
	Norway	**-15**	(5.2)	**39.7**	(3.8)	**-22**	(4.0)	**36.8**	(3.0)	-2	(4.7)	49.0	(3.4)	**12**	(3.5)	**56.9**	(2.7)	3	(4.3)	51.1	(2.8)	-5	(3.5)	47.0	(2.3)
	Poland	m	m	m	m	m	m	m	m	m	m	m	m	m	m	m	m	m	m	m	m	m	m	m	m
	Portugal	**-17**	(4.5)	**37.2**	(3.6)	**-11**	(4.5)	**42.5**	(3.6)	**-16**	(3.7)	**40.2**	(2.9)	-3	(3.7)	48.1	(2.7)	-1	(3.7)	48.3	(2.4)	**8**	(3.3)	**55.1**	(2.5)
	Slovak Republic	**-33**	(6.6)	**31.2**	(4.3)	**-18**	(6.9)	**38.1**	(5.8)	**-37**	(4.1)	**29.4**	(2.8)	4	(2.7)	52.4	(2.1)	**8**	(2.7)	**53.7**	(1.6)	**-14**	(2.9)	**41.4**	(1.9)
	Slovenia	**-31**	(5.0)	**30.8**	(3.4)	**-11**	(4.1)	42.8	(3.8)	**-16**	(4.8)	**40.9**	(4.1)	-2	(3.3)	48.5	(2.8)	0	(3.2)	48.9	(2.4)	**-8**	(3.4)	**44.8**	(2.4)
	Spain	**-17**	(5.5)	**38.5**	(4.4)	**-16**	(6.1)	40.6	(5.9)	**-11**	(4.3)	44.1	(4.1)	**6**	(3.0)	**53.9**	(2.2)	2	(3.0)	50.5	(2.3)	**7**	(3.3)	54.2	(2.4)
	Sweden	-3	(4.5)	48.4	(4.0)	5	(4.1)	53.2	(2.9)	**14**	(5.5)	**59.6**	(4.2)	**20**	(3.5)	**61.7**	(2.3)	**9**	(3.8)	**55.1**	(2.6)	6	(3.1)	52.4	(2.0)
	Switzerland	m	m	m	m	m	m	m	m	m	m	m	m	m	m	m	m	m	m	m	m	m	m	m	m
	Turkey	**-45**	(18.0)	**18.0**	(14.0)	**-52**	(13.1)	**14.8**	(11.4)	**-55**	(10.4)	**14.4**	(7.3)	**-17**	(2.2)	**37.2**	(2.0)	**-19**	(2.9)	**35.8**	(2.2)	**-17**	(2.5)	**38.2**	(1.9)
	United Kingdom	6	(3.6)	53.5	(2.7)	**20**	(5.5)	**62.2**	(3.9)	**22**	(5.1)	**63.2**	(2.9)	**12**	(3.2)	**56.2**	(2.5)	**15**	(3.8)	**58.2**	(2.5)	**19**	(3.4)	**60.1**	(2.2)
	United States	**36**	(4.9)	**73.7**	(3.7)	**37**	(4.3)	**72.3**	(2.8)	**70**	(8.4)	**86.5**	(3.6)	6	(3.4)	52.7	(2.4)	7	(3.2)	53.5	(2.6)	**20**	(3.6)	**60.2**	(2.2)
	OECD average	**-8**	(1.1)	**44.1**	(1.0)	**-4**	(1.0)	**47.4**	(0.9)	0	(1.0)	49.9	(0.8)	**7**	(0.6)	**53.7**	(0.4)	**7**	(0.6)	**53.8**	(0.4)	**3**	(0.6)	**51.3**	(0.4)
Partners	Brazil	**-31**	(8.3)	**29.7**	(5.9)	**-47**	(7.3)	**22.7**	(5.1)	**-28**	(11.4)	**33.8**	(7.5)	**-6**	(1.4)	**44.8**	(1.2)	**-11**	(2.0)	**41.6**	(1.4)	3	(1.9)	51.1	(1.4)
	B-S-J-G (China)	**-30**	(3.9)	**29.8**	(2.7)	**-17**	(5.2)	**39.4**	(4.5)	**-36**	(3.6)	**28.0**	(2.1)	**-11**	(4.0)	**42.7**	(3.0)	**10**	(3.5)	**55.5**	(2.5)	**-21**	(4.3)	**37.0**	(3.1)
	Bulgaria	**-24**	(6.9)	**33.9**	(5.5)	**-30**	(6.8)	**31.1**	(5.3)	**-25**	(5.9)	**34.9**	(3.8)	**-15**	(2.1)	**38.4**	(1.8)	1	(2.0)	49.8	(1.7)	**-18**	(2.8)	**37.8**	(1.9)
	Colombia	-7	(13.8)	47.4	(12.5)	**-27**	(8.8)	**29.1**	(7.1)	16	(20.3)	65.7	(16.8)	**-7**	(1.7)	**44.2**	(1.8)	**-10**	(1.9)	**42.3**	(1.7)	**5**	(1.5)	**53.0**	(1.3)
	Costa Rica	4	(30.1)	49.9	(20.9)	**-29**	(12.2)	**30.5**	(9.8)	-20	(26.1)	38.7	(15.9)	**7**	(2.3)	**54.3**	(2.0)	2	(2.9)	50.6	(2.0)	**15**	(2.7)	**58.6**	(1.7)
	Croatia	**-32**	(5.9)	**29.6**	(4.2)	**-30**	(4.6)	**30.1**	(4.1)	**-21**	(5.0)	**36.1**	(3.6)	-4	(2.7)	47.5	(2.1)	**-16**	(3.0)	**39.1**	(2.5)	0	(3.3)	49.9	(2.1)
	Cyprus*	**-22**	(10.2)	36.6	(9.0)	**-40**	(7.4)	**26.8**	(5.2)	**-36**	(9.0)	**30.3**	(5.6)	2	(2.6)	50.8	(1.8)	-2	(2.8)	48.1	(2.1)	**-5**	(2.2)	**46.5**	(1.5)
	Dominican Republic	m	m	m	m	m	m	m	m	m	m	m	m	m	m	m	m	m	m	m	m	m	m	m	m
	Hong Kong (China)	**19**	(4.2)	**63.3**	(3.3)	**14**	(4.1)	**59.9**	(3.3)	**-12**	(3.3)	**43.5**	(2.3)	**13**	(5.1)	**58.1**	(4.0)	**14**	(5.4)	**58.9**	(3.3)	11	(6.1)	56.2	(4.2)
	Lithuania	**-22**	(6.4)	**33.6**	(4.7)	**-28**	(6.4)	**29.9**	(3.9)	**-20**	(4.3)	**35.7**	(3.9)	**-14**	(2.9)	**39.9**	(2.7)	**-8**	(2.5)	**44.8**	(2.0)	**-21**	(2.5)	**36.3**	(2.0)
	Macao (China)	**9**	(3.3)	**56.8**	(2.8)	**30**	(4.1)	**73.9**	(3.2)	-6	(2.9)	47.9	(2.1)	-5	(4.6)	45.9	(3.4)	**8**	(3.5)	54.6	(3.0)	-3	(6.7)	48.5	(3.9)
	Montenegro	**-57**	(13.8)	**11.9**	(8.8)	**-71**	(12.1)	**10.8**	(5.8)	**-65**	(9.6)	**14.7**	(5.8)	**-8**	(1.4)	**43.7**	(1.4)	**-17**	(1.7)	**37.9**	(1.6)	**-18**	(2.0)	**37.8**	(1.6)
	Peru	0	(20.6)	51.6	(22.5)	-17	(13.4)	39.0	(15.1)	-7	(13.9)	46.3	(12.8)	**-5**	(1.9)	**45.6**	(1.8)	**-6**	(1.8)	**45.1**	(1.6)	-2	(1.7)	47.9	(1.4)
	Qatar	m	m	m	m	m	m	m	m	m	m	m	m	m	m	m	m	m	m	m	m	m	m	m	m
	Russia	**-24**	(6.8)	**36.4**	(4.8)	**-33**	(5.9)	**31.1**	(4.6)	**-45**	(5.7)	**27.7**	(3.3)	**-14**	(3.7)	**40.7**	(2.6)	**-17**	(3.3)	**39.6**	(2.4)	-10	(5.1)	**44.6**	(2.6)
	Singapore	4	(2.3)	53.2	(2.1)	**27**	(3.3)	**68.6**	(2.3)	**9**	(2.2)	**56.3**	(1.8)	**20**	(2.8)	**63.1**	(2.3)	**26**	(4.6)	**65.3**	(2.8)	6	(5.1)	52.3	(3.2)
	Chinese Taipei	**-18**	(3.7)	**37.2**	(2.7)	**21**	(4.4)	**66.0**	(3.4)	**-24**	(3.0)	**35.0**	(1.8)	**13**	(2.9)	**58.2**	(2.3)	**28**	(3.2)	**67.6**	(2.2)	**9**	(3.4)	54.8	(2.5)
	Thailand	4	(13.3)	52.8	(12.8)	5	(17.9)	54.5	(14.2)	-18	(10.3)	39.1	(7.4)	**-5**	(2.2)	**45.9**	(2.0)	-1	(2.2)	49.1	(1.9)	-1	(2.6)	48.8	(1.8)
	Tunisia	m	m	m	m	m	m	m	m	**-86**	(14.4)	**3.3**	(3.8)	**-21**	(1.6)	**31.4**	(1.5)	-3	(2.0)	**46.3**	(1.7)	**-11**	(2.0)	**40.5**	(1.5)
	United Arab Emirates	**-23**	(5.3)	**33.0**	(4.2)	**-20**	(4.8)	**37.0**	(3.7)	**-18**	(6.4)	**38.6**	(4.4)	**-14**	(1.7)	**39.1**	(1.6)	**-12**	(2.1)	**40.5**	(1.9)	**-15**	(2.2)	**39.8**	(1.5)
	Uruguay	-11	(8.8)	40.8	(7.3)	**-31**	(9.5)	**30.5**	(6.2)	-7	(7.8)	45.7	(6.6)	**-9**	(1.7)	**43.2**	(1.4)	**-6**	(2.2)	**46.0**	(1.9)	-2	(2.2)	48.2	(1.6)
	Malaysia**	**-26**	(11.9)	30.1	(10.3)	-20	(18.0)	34.2	(15.0)	**-33**	(7.3)	**27.4**	(6.7)	**-20**	(2.5)	**34.5**	(2.0)	**-8**	(2.5)	**44.0**	(2.1)	**-22**	(3.0)	**34.7**	(2.2)

1. Relative scores are the residuals obtained from a pooled linear regression, across all participating countries/economies, of performance in collaborative problem solving over performance in science, reading and/or mathematics.
2. Students who score higher than expected are those with positive relative scores.
3. The percentage of students who score higher than expected is bolded when it differs significantly from 50%.
4. Top performers in science, reading or mathematics are those who attain Level 5 or above in those subjects.
5. Low achievers in science, reading or mathematics are those who attain below Level 2 in those subjects.

Notes: Students in PISA 2015 completed four clusters of test material: two in science and two distributed among reading, mathematics and collaborative problem solving. Hence, no student completed all four of science, reading, mathematics and collaborative problem solving. Scores were imputed in the domains in which students were not tested.

Values that are statistically significant are indicated in bold (see Annex A3).

* See note at the beginning of this Annex.

**Malaysia: Coverage is too small to ensure comparability (see Annex A4).

StatLink http://dx.doi.org/10.1787/888933616769

[Part 1/1]

Table V.3.10a Index of ICT use at school

Results based on students' self-reports

		Index of ICT use at school		Percentage of students who use digital devices for the following activities at school at least once or twice a week:																	
				Chatting on line at school		Using e-mail at school		Browsing the Internet for schoolwork		Downloading, uploading or browsing material from the school's website (e.g. Intranet)		Posting work on the school's website		Playing simulations at school		Practicing and drilling, such as for foreign language learning or mathematics		Doing homework on a school computer		Using school computers for group work and communication with other students	
		Mean index	S.E.	%	S.E.	%	S.E.	%	S.E.	%	S.E.	%	S.E.	%	S.E.	%	S.E.	%	S.E.	%	S.E.
OECD	Australia	0.56	(0.01)	36.1	(0.6)	60.8	(0.8)	79.7	(0.5)	44.3	(0.9)	21.9	(0.7)	16.4	(0.4)	31.8	(0.6)	56.4	(0.8)	45.7	(0.8)
	Austria	0.11	(0.02)	55.0	(0.8)	29.6	(1.1)	54.9	(1.0)	25.7	(1.0)	17.5	(0.9)	14.7	(0.8)	28.4	(0.7)	20.8	(0.9)	22.3	(0.9)
	Belgium	-0.20	(0.02)	29.2	(0.9)	19.7	(0.8)	33.1	(0.8)	22.3	(0.6)	20.3	(0.6)	10.7	(0.5)	19.2	(0.5)	16.2	(0.6)	17.9	(0.6)
	Canada	m	m	m	m	m	m	m	m	m	m	m	m	m	m	m	m	m	m	m	m
	Chile	0.14	(0.02)	47.1	(1.0)	23.2	(1.0)	50.5	(1.0)	23.4	(0.7)	13.2	(0.7)	12.1	(0.6)	26.7	(0.7)	35.8	(1.5)	32.3	(1.3)
	Czech Republic	0.27	(0.02)	63.7	(1.0)	39.1	(1.0)	54.3	(0.9)	36.5	(0.9)	15.7	(0.7)	17.6	(0.8)	33.4	(0.8)	21.5	(0.7)	36.4	(0.8)
	Denmark	0.74	(0.01)	75.9	(0.7)	33.7	(1.0)	86.7	(0.6)	52.6	(1.1)	34.4	(1.1)	20.7	(0.7)	50.2	(0.9)	65.2	(1.1)	40.3	(1.1)
	Estonia	-0.11	(0.02)	26.1	(0.7)	31.1	(0.7)	44.0	(0.8)	23.2	(0.7)	11.1	(0.5)	13.2	(0.5)	19.4	(0.6)	14.5	(0.6)	16.3	(0.6)
	Finland	0.11	(0.01)	76.3	(0.7)	35.4	(0.7)	47.7	(1.0)	18.2	(0.8)	13.1	(0.7)	13.1	(0.7)	14.8	(0.8)	9.5	(0.7)	16.6	(0.7)
	France	0.02	(0.02)	28.3	(0.8)	20.4	(0.9)	40.5	(1.0)	22.6	(0.7)	16.2	(0.7)	17.9	(0.7)	24.3	(0.8)	19.6	(0.7)	24.1	(0.8)
	Germany	-0.42	(0.02)	21.1	(0.7)	8.1	(0.4)	31.6	(0.8)	8.6	(0.5)	5.7	(0.4)	6.7	(0.4)	13.9	(0.8)	7.0	(0.5)	12.3	(0.7)
	Greece	0.02	(0.03)	38.1	(1.1)	25.5	(0.9)	39.1	(0.8)	24.7	(1.0)	20.5	(1.0)	21.2	(1.0)	25.0	(1.0)	31.5	(0.9)	32.7	(0.9)
	Hungary	-0.04	(0.02)	51.4	(1.1)	21.1	(0.9)	40.0	(0.8)	24.6	(0.9)	18.8	(0.8)	18.6	(0.8)	27.4	(0.8)	18.6	(0.8)	24.1	(0.8)
	Iceland	0.15	(0.02)	55.8	(0.8)	23.9	(0.8)	58.0	(0.8)	22.6	(0.7)	9.9	(0.5)	11.8	(0.6)	35.0	(0.9)	24.6	(0.7)	27.3	(0.8)
	Ireland	-0.38	(0.03)	28.4	(1.0)	20.1	(1.2)	29.2	(1.0)	8.7	(0.5)	4.7	(0.5)	5.4	(0.4)	15.6	(0.7)	12.7	(0.8)	16.5	(0.6)
	Israel	-0.10	(0.03)	20.5	(0.9)	21.1	(0.9)	37.3	(1.3)	23.8	(0.9)	17.7	(0.8)	17.5	(0.8)	29.2	(1.0)	21.9	(0.8)	21.2	(0.8)
	Italy	0.00	(0.02)	46.6	(0.9)	18.0	(0.8)	45.6	(1.1)	25.3	(0.9)	17.0	(0.8)	19.8	(0.8)	31.5	(0.9)	19.6	(0.8)	23.4	(0.8)
	Japan	-1.05	(0.02)	17.5	(1.2)	6.4	(0.5)	13.3	(0.7)	3.0	(0.3)	2.5	(0.3)	6.7	(0.4)	5.9	(0.4)	2.6	(0.4)	3.7	(0.3)
	Korea	-0.95	(0.03)	13.8	(0.8)	7.9	(0.7)	16.6	(1.1)	8.5	(0.9)	5.5	(0.6)	5.4	(0.4)	9.4	(0.6)	8.8	(0.9)	8.0	(0.8)
	Latvia	0.16	(0.02)	57.9	(1.0)	32.4	(0.8)	49.1	(0.9)	31.5	(0.8)	15.9	(0.7)	23.2	(0.7)	34.8	(0.9)	17.4	(0.7)	23.7	(0.8)
	Luxembourg	-0.04	(0.01)	37.0	(0.7)	25.7	(0.6)	39.5	(0.7)	19.7	(0.5)	17.1	(0.5)	16.0	(0.5)	23.7	(0.5)	22.9	(0.6)	25.2	(0.6)
	Mexico	-0.16	(0.03)	25.1	(0.9)	17.2	(0.8)	38.1	(1.2)	22.4	(1.0)	13.9	(0.8)	14.1	(0.8)	24.6	(0.8)	29.7	(1.1)	24.7	(0.9)
	Netherlands	0.44	(0.02)	60.0	(1.3)	34.7	(1.0)	74.5	(1.2)	44.4	(1.1)	20.2	(0.7)	15.8	(0.5)	45.8	(1.0)	36.5	(1.2)	35.6	(0.9)
	New Zealand	0.42	(0.02)	49.3	(1.2)	56.8	(1.5)	71.9	(1.1)	36.2	(1.2)	18.4	(1.1)	15.8	(0.9)	25.7	(1.0)	43.4	(1.1)	36.2	(1.2)
	Norway	m	m	m	m	m	m	m	m	m	m	m	m	m	m	m	m	m	m	m	m
	Poland	-0.21	(0.03)	28.0	(0.9)	17.2	(0.7)	44.5	(1.1)	22.9	(0.8)	11.8	(0.7)	12.4	(0.6)	29.1	(0.9)	14.5	(0.7)	17.8	(0.8)
	Portugal	0.08	(0.02)	49.5	(1.0)	37.9	(0.8)	40.6	(1.1)	28.4	(0.8)	15.0	(0.7)	18.2	(0.7)	27.8	(0.8)	20.3	(0.8)	27.6	(0.9)
	Slovak Republic	0.22	(0.02)	51.9	(1.0)	31.6	(0.8)	46.2	(0.8)	29.5	(0.8)	23.9	(0.8)	22.1	(0.8)	35.0	(0.9)	22.7	(0.8)	27.0	(0.9)
	Slovenia	0.02	(0.01)	47.4	(0.8)	34.5	(0.8)	42.4	(0.8)	26.3	(0.7)	17.0	(0.6)	18.5	(0.6)	22.1	(0.7)	18.0	(0.6)	22.5	(0.7)
	Spain	-0.04	(0.02)	26.8	(1.0)	25.5	(1.0)	44.2	(1.2)	22.3	(1.0)	14.9	(1.0)	12.2	(0.6)	25.1	(0.9)	20.7	(1.1)	26.8	(1.0)
	Sweden	0.52	(0.02)	50.6	(1.1)	47.8	(1.3)	81.6	(1.1)	38.5	(1.4)	27.0	(1.2)	17.9	(0.9)	42.2	(1.4)	34.1	(1.5)	37.2	(1.3)
	Switzerland	-0.12	(0.02)	33.1	(1.2)	25.3	(1.0)	37.0	(0.8)	17.4	(0.9)	12.3	(0.8)	10.5	(0.7)	23.2	(0.9)	13.9	(0.7)	18.2	(0.7)
	Turkey	m	m	m	m	m	m	m	m	m	m	m	m	m	m	m	m	m	m	m	m
	United Kingdom[1]	0.29	(0.02)	30.2	(1.2)	47.3	(1.9)	69.0	(0.9)	29.3	(1.2)	11.1	(0.8)	10.3	(0.6)	27.8	(1.1)	44.2	(1.3)	28.0	(1.0)
	United States	m	m	m	m	m	m	m	m	m	m	m	m	m	m	m	m	m	m	m	m
	OECD average	0.01	(0.00)	41.2	(0.2)	28.4	(0.2)	47.8	(0.2)	25.4	(0.2)	15.6	(0.1)	14.7	(0.1)	26.7	(0.1)	24.0	(0.2)	24.9	(0.2)
Partners	Brazil	-0.14	(0.02)	29.4	(0.8)	19.5	(0.6)	39.9	(0.8)	24.3	(0.8)	15.3	(0.5)	18.1	(0.5)	29.0	(0.7)	18.9	(0.6)	22.4	(0.6)
	B-S-J-G (China)	-0.65	(0.02)	26.8	(1.1)	7.0	(0.4)	17.0	(0.6)	11.5	(0.6)	6.0	(0.5)	10.4	(0.6)	24.8	(0.8)	7.9	(0.5)	12.6	(0.6)
	Bulgaria	0.39	(0.03)	60.9	(0.8)	34.4	(0.9)	52.2	(0.9)	33.8	(1.1)	28.8	(1.0)	27.7	(1.0)	45.6	(0.9)	31.4	(1.1)	38.1	(1.0)
	Colombia	0.18	(0.02)	36.5	(1.1)	32.9	(0.9)	51.8	(1.1)	31.1	(0.9)	23.5	(0.8)	22.0	(0.7)	36.5	(0.8)	30.4	(0.8)	32.7	(0.9)
	Costa Rica	0.11	(0.02)	51.9	(1.0)	26.8	(1.0)	55.3	(1.0)	27.0	(0.8)	15.6	(0.8)	12.9	(0.6)	37.7	(0.9)	27.8	(0.9)	28.0	(0.9)
	Croatia	-0.16	(0.02)	49.7	(0.9)	20.7	(0.8)	37.8	(0.9)	20.6	(0.8)	13.4	(0.7)	14.9	(0.7)	24.5	(0.7)	16.0	(0.8)	21.1	(0.7)
	Cyprus*	m	m	m	m	m	m	m	m	m	m	m	m	m	m	m	m	m	m	m	m
	Dominican Republic	-0.12	(0.03)	16.2	(0.8)	12.9	(0.8)	38.7	(1.1)	23.2	(0.9)	18.4	(0.8)	21.4	(0.9)	34.2	(1.0)	26.8	(1.0)	25.6	(1.0)
	Hong Kong (China)	-0.20	(0.03)	23.0	(0.8)	21.0	(0.8)	32.5	(1.0)	25.7	(1.1)	11.6	(0.7)	19.8	(0.9)	19.3	(0.8)	20.8	(1.0)	17.8	(1.0)
	Lithuania	-0.02	(0.02)	19.2	(0.7)	31.4	(0.8)	40.7	(0.8)	25.2	(0.8)	18.0	(0.7)	20.2	(0.7)	34.7	(0.8)	20.2	(0.7)	23.2	(0.8)
	Macao (China)	-0.09	(0.01)	21.5	(0.5)	12.3	(0.5)	30.1	(0.7)	24.0	(0.6)	32.0	(0.6)	10.7	(0.4)	19.1	(0.5)	22.2	(0.6)	18.7	(0.5)
	Montenegro	m	m	m	m	m	m	m	m	m	m	m	m	m	m	m	m	m	m	m	m
	Peru	-0.26	(0.02)	16.1	(0.8)	10.9	(0.7)	34.0	(1.0)	16.3	(0.7)	9.6	(0.6)	14.7	(0.5)	24.2	(0.8)	19.6	(0.8)	17.2	(0.8)
	Qatar	m	m	m	m	m	m	m	m	m	m	m	m	m	m	m	m	m	m	m	m
	Russia	0.12	(0.03)	35.2	(1.1)	29.1	(1.0)	44.5	(1.1)	31.8	(1.2)	25.7	(1.1)	26.5	(1.1)	38.7	(1.1)	31.0	(1.1)	33.6	(0.9)
	Singapore	0.01	(0.03)	45.3	(0.8)	29.7	(1.4)	45.9	(1.2)	24.2	(0.9)	14.1	(0.9)	12.8	(0.5)	24.0	(0.9)	21.5	(0.8)	22.4	(0.9)
	Chinese Taipei	-0.39	(0.02)	35.1	(1.1)	12.9	(0.6)	26.0	(0.9)	17.7	(0.8)	4.4	(0.3)	10.9	(0.5)	13.9	(0.6)	17.1	(0.8)	12.9	(0.7)
	Thailand	0.62	(0.02)	58.3	(1.1)	44.7	(1.2)	67.5	(0.9)	54.1	(0.9)	46.7	(1.2)	37.5	(0.9)	50.1	(0.9)	46.7	(0.9)	50.3	(0.9)
	Tunisia	m	m	m	m	m	m	m	m	m	m	m	m	m	m	m	m	m	m	m	m
	United Arab Emirates	m	m	m	m	m	m	m	m	m	m	m	m	m	m	m	m	m	m	m	m
	Uruguay	0.16	(0.02)	42.7	(0.9)	23.8	(1.2)	53.6	(0.8)	36.0	(0.8)	23.9	(0.9)	22.8	(0.8)	33.1	(0.7)	29.2	(0.9)	29.8	(0.9)
	Malaysia**	m	m	m	m	m	m	m	m	m	m	m	m	m	m	m	m	m	m	m	m

1. Only the United Kingdom subnational entities of England, Northern Ireland and Wales participated in the ICT questionnaire.
* See note at the beginning of this Annex.
**Malaysia: Coverage is too small to ensure comparability (see Annex A4).
StatLink http://dx.doi.org/10.1787/888933616769

[Part 1/1]

Table V.3.10b Index of students' self-reported ICT competence

Results based on students' self-reports

		Index of students' self-reported ICT competence		Percentage of students who agreed/strongly agreed with the following statements: I feel comfortable using digital devices that I am less familiar with		If my friends and relatives want to buy new digital devices or applications, I can give them advice		I feel comfortable using my digital devices at home		When I come across problems with digital devices, I can solve them		If my friends and relatives have a problem with digital devices, I can help them	
		Mean index	S.E.	%	S.E.	%	S.E.	%	S.E.	%	S.E.	%	S.E.
OECD	Australia	0.21	(0.01)	72.0	(0.5)	78.1	(0.5)	96.0	(0.2)	82.6	(0.4)	79.7	(0.4)
	Austria	-0.08	(0.02)	44.7	(0.9)	61.0	(0.8)	86.2	(0.6)	71.5	(0.7)	68.0	(0.8)
	Belgium	0.05	(0.01)	71.0	(0.6)	74.3	(0.5)	93.6	(0.3)	75.5	(0.5)	75.0	(0.5)
	Canada	m	m	m	m	m	m	m	m	m	m	m	m
	Chile	0.09	(0.01)	71.4	(0.6)	73.9	(0.7)	91.1	(0.4)	77.9	(0.7)	77.3	(0.6)
	Czech Republic	-0.10	(0.01)	74.1	(0.7)	69.9	(0.6)	91.2	(0.4)	69.5	(0.7)	67.8	(0.7)
	Denmark	0.25	(0.02)	81.5	(0.6)	79.9	(0.6)	96.7	(0.3)	83.0	(0.5)	79.1	(0.8)
	Estonia	-0.05	(0.01)	66.8	(0.7)	69.9	(0.6)	92.0	(0.5)	76.5	(0.7)	68.1	(0.7)
	Finland	-0.08	(0.01)	47.2	(0.8)	77.4	(0.5)	93.0	(0.4)	76.0	(0.6)	74.9	(0.5)
	France	0.23	(0.01)	78.0	(0.7)	78.5	(0.6)	94.0	(0.4)	76.3	(0.6)	77.5	(0.5)
	Germany	-0.05	(0.01)	65.6	(0.6)	65.6	(0.6)	86.2	(0.6)	71.1	(0.6)	67.2	(0.6)
	Greece	0.05	(0.01)	66.2	(0.8)	78.0	(0.8)	90.2	(0.6)	74.3	(0.7)	76.9	(0.7)
	Hungary	0.07	(0.02)	77.8	(0.7)	69.6	(0.9)	89.9	(0.5)	79.0	(0.6)	75.6	(0.7)
	Iceland	-0.01	(0.02)	47.2	(1.0)	76.3	(0.8)	91.8	(0.5)	80.2	(0.6)	78.0	(0.7)
	Ireland	0.21	(0.01)	71.1	(0.8)	80.7	(0.6)	97.3	(0.2)	83.1	(0.6)	79.3	(0.6)
	Israel	-0.02	(0.02)	64.5	(0.8)	69.4	(1.2)	86.4	(0.6)	74.3	(1.0)	73.6	(1.1)
	Italy	-0.02	(0.01)	62.8	(0.6)	76.1	(0.6)	89.7	(0.5)	76.2	(0.6)	74.0	(0.6)
	Japan	-0.94	(0.02)	48.3	(0.8)	40.8	(0.6)	57.2	(0.7)	29.8	(0.7)	29.8	(0.6)
	Korea	-0.57	(0.02)	51.6	(0.7)	51.6	(0.9)	87.8	(0.5)	52.5	(0.9)	46.5	(0.9)
	Latvia	-0.13	(0.01)	53.0	(0.8)	73.7	(0.7)	86.1	(0.6)	75.5	(0.7)	69.1	(0.7)
	Luxembourg	0.01	(0.02)	61.6	(0.7)	65.8	(0.8)	87.2	(0.5)	74.3	(0.7)	71.8	(0.7)
	Mexico	-0.09	(0.02)	71.1	(0.8)	69.2	(0.6)	77.3	(0.8)	71.1	(0.7)	72.6	(0.7)
	Netherlands	-0.04	(0.01)	63.7	(0.7)	72.8	(0.6)	93.5	(0.4)	78.1	(0.6)	77.0	(0.6)
	New Zealand	0.21	(0.02)	76.1	(0.7)	79.2	(0.8)	96.0	(0.4)	83.6	(0.7)	80.1	(0.8)
	Norway	m	m	m	m	m	m	m	m	m	m	m	m
	Poland	0.02	(0.01)	74.8	(0.7)	69.7	(0.7)	91.9	(0.5)	81.2	(0.7)	74.2	(0.7)
	Portugal	0.39	(0.01)	83.5	(0.5)	86.6	(0.5)	96.6	(0.3)	87.3	(0.5)	85.7	(0.6)
	Slovak Republic	-0.13	(0.02)	68.6	(0.8)	67.7	(0.7)	86.6	(0.5)	72.1	(0.6)	69.8	(0.8)
	Slovenia	0.06	(0.02)	75.8	(0.7)	69.7	(0.8)	93.1	(0.4)	79.2	(0.6)	74.5	(0.7)
	Spain	0.15	(0.01)	72.0	(0.7)	77.4	(0.5)	93.8	(0.5)	77.6	(0.7)	78.1	(0.6)
	Sweden	0.27	(0.02)	76.5	(0.8)	78.5	(0.7)	94.3	(0.4)	82.8	(0.6)	76.8	(0.8)
	Switzerland	0.05	(0.02)	61.5	(1.0)	67.4	(0.9)	90.2	(0.6)	75.1	(0.8)	70.8	(1.0)
	Turkey	m	m	m	m	m	m	m	m	m	m	m	m
	United Kingdom[1]	0.34	(0.02)	77.1	(0.7)	84.4	(0.6)	96.9	(0.4)	85.8	(0.6)	84.1	(0.6)
	United States	m	m	m	m	m	m	m	m	m	m	m	m
	OECD average	0.01	(0.00)	67.0	(0.1)	72.0	(0.1)	90.1	(0.1)	75.3	(0.1)	72.7	(0.1)
Partners	Brazil	-0.01	(0.02)	68.3	(0.6)	78.4	(0.6)	89.0	(0.5)	73.3	(0.7)	75.4	(0.6)
	B-S-J-G (China)	-0.50	(0.01)	32.6	(0.8)	65.9	(0.8)	80.7	(0.8)	56.1	(0.8)	54.5	(0.8)
	Bulgaria	-0.01	(0.02)	64.4	(0.8)	75.8	(0.8)	86.2	(0.8)	75.0	(0.8)	76.5	(0.7)
	Colombia	-0.02	(0.01)	69.7	(0.7)	71.7	(0.6)	84.1	(0.6)	81.1	(0.7)	77.6	(0.6)
	Costa Rica	0.06	(0.02)	74.1	(0.5)	76.1	(0.7)	89.5	(0.5)	72.1	(0.6)	78.4	(0.6)
	Croatia	0.17	(0.01)	81.8	(0.6)	75.8	(0.6)	94.1	(0.4)	81.0	(0.5)	74.7	(0.6)
	Cyprus*	m	m	m	m	m	m	m	m	m	m	m	m
	Dominican Republic	-0.05	(0.02)	58.5	(0.9)	72.5	(0.9)	82.4	(1.0)	70.5	(0.8)	75.8	(0.8)
	Hong Kong (China)	-0.07	(0.01)	71.3	(0.8)	70.1	(0.6)	91.8	(0.5)	83.0	(0.6)	76.4	(0.5)
	Lithuania	0.01	(0.02)	57.0	(0.8)	70.4	(0.7)	75.2	(0.7)	73.9	(0.7)	73.7	(0.7)
	Macao (China)	-0.16	(0.01)	68.4	(0.7)	71.7	(0.8)	92.6	(0.4)	74.8	(0.7)	66.8	(0.7)
	Montenegro	m	m	m	m	m	m	m	m	m	m	m	m
	Peru	-0.27	(0.01)	67.9	(0.6)	66.6	(0.7)	82.8	(0.7)	62.2	(0.8)	65.0	(0.7)
	Qatar	m	m	m	m	m	m	m	m	m	m	m	m
	Russia	-0.04	(0.01)	70.7	(0.7)	78.8	(0.6)	90.1	(0.6)	77.6	(0.6)	76.2	(0.6)
	Singapore	-0.01	(0.01)	61.5	(0.7)	67.7	(0.7)	95.9	(0.3)	78.4	(0.7)	72.6	(0.6)
	Chinese Taipei	-0.16	(0.01)	62.4	(0.6)	67.0	(0.6)	89.4	(0.4)	72.4	(0.6)	68.7	(0.6)
	Thailand	-0.25	(0.02)	67.5	(0.7)	73.5	(0.6)	76.7	(0.8)	69.5	(0.8)	72.0	(0.7)
	Tunisia	m	m	m	m	m	m	m	m	m	m	m	m
	United Arab Emirates	m	m	m	m	m	m	m	m	m	m	m	m
	Uruguay	0.07	(0.02)	68.8	(0.7)	77.2	(0.6)	86.7	(0.5)	77.1	(0.7)	79.9	(0.7)
	Malaysia**	m	m	m	m	m	m	m	m	m	m	m	m

1. Only the United Kingdom subnational entities of England, Northern Ireland and Wales participated in the ICT questionnaire.
* See note at the beginning of this Annex.
**Malaysia: Coverage is too small to ensure comparability (see Annex A4).
StatLink http://dx.doi.org/10.1787/888933616769

[Part 1/2]

Table V.3.11a Index of ICT use at school and performance in collaborative problem solving

Results based on students' self-reports

		Index of ICT use at school												Performance in collaborative problem solving, by national quarter of the index of ICT use at school									
		All students		Variability of the index		Bottom quarter		Second quarter		Third quarter		Top quarter		Bottom quarter		Second quarter		Third quarter		Top quarter		Top – bottom quarter	
		Mean index	S.E.	S.D.	S.E.	Mean index	S.E.	Mean index	S.E.	Mean index	S.E.	Mean index	S.E.	Mean score	S.E.	Mean score	S.E.	Mean score	S.E.	Mean score	S.E.	Score dif.	S.E.
OECD	Australia	0.56	(0.01)	0.77	(0.01)	-0.35	(0.02)	0.42	(0.01)	0.78	(0.01)	1.40	(0.02)	520	(3.1)	543	(3.5)	553	(2.7)	534	(3.7)	**14**	(4.5)
	Austria	0.11	(0.02)	0.88	(0.02)	-0.95	(0.02)	-0.09	(0.02)	0.35	(0.02)	1.14	(0.04)	516	(3.7)	532	(3.2)	526	(3.8)	486	(5.9)	**-30**	(6.8)
	Belgium	-0.20	(0.02)	1.03	(0.01)	-1.54	(0.02)	-0.46	(0.03)	0.17	(0.02)	1.04	(0.02)	500	(3.3)	517	(3.5)	529	(3.9)	488	(3.9)	**-12**	(4.4)
	Canada	m	m	m	m	m	m	m	m	m	m	m	m	m	m	m	m	m	m	m	m	m	m
	Chile	0.14	(0.02)	0.85	(0.02)	-0.93	(0.04)	0.00	(0.02)	0.39	(0.01)	1.10	(0.03)	465	(3.7)	483	(3.8)	468	(3.4)	429	(4.0)	**-36**	(4.8)
	Czech Republic	0.27	(0.02)	1.03	(0.02)	-1.01	(0.04)	0.09	(0.02)	0.56	(0.01)	1.46	(0.04)	517	(3.0)	517	(3.2)	507	(3.2)	472	(4.6)	**-46**	(5.3)
	Denmark	0.74	(0.01)	0.64	(0.02)	0.06	(0.02)	0.58	(0.01)	0.86	(0.01)	1.45	(0.02)	529	(3.7)	537	(4.1)	532	(4.0)	508	(4.1)	**-21**	(5.5)
	Estonia	-0.11	(0.02)	0.98	(0.02)	-1.37	(0.02)	-0.31	(0.02)	0.19	(0.02)	1.04	(0.03)	542	(4.3)	560	(3.6)	550	(4.3)	500	(4.1)	**-42**	(6.1)
	Finland	0.11	(0.01)	0.74	(0.02)	-0.70	(0.02)	-0.07	(0.01)	0.25	(0.01)	0.97	(0.04)	535	(4.2)	559	(3.9)	554	(4.2)	506	(4.1)	**-29**	(5.1)
	France	0.02	(0.02)	0.94	(0.01)	-1.17	(0.03)	-0.15	(0.02)	0.29	(0.02)	1.10	(0.03)	499	(4.6)	525	(3.4)	515	(4.1)	480	(3.7)	**-19**	(5.8)
	Germany	-0.42	(0.02)	0.77	(0.01)	-1.40	(0.02)	-0.59	(0.02)	-0.17	(0.01)	0.50	(0.03)	535	(3.7)	549	(3.5)	547	(4.1)	514	(5.1)	**-22**	(5.4)
	Greece	0.02	(0.03)	1.17	(0.02)	-1.46	(0.03)	-0.28	(0.03)	0.35	(0.03)	1.46	(0.05)	483	(3.7)	496	(3.5)	470	(6.0)	415	(4.4)	**-68**	(4.5)
	Hungary	-0.04	(0.02)	1.05	(0.02)	-1.35	(0.02)	-0.31	(0.03)	0.26	(0.02)	1.26	(0.04)	485	(3.7)	500	(3.7)	483	(4.3)	437	(3.9)	**-48**	(5.0)
	Iceland	0.15	(0.02)	0.83	(0.02)	-0.85	(0.03)	0.00	(0.01)	0.37	(0.01)	1.09	(0.03)	503	(3.8)	521	(4.1)	513	(4.4)	478	(4.9)	**-25**	(6.0)
	Ireland	-0.38	(0.03)	0.89	(0.01)	-1.54	(0.03)	-0.62	(0.03)	-0.05	(0.03)	0.68	(0.03)	m	m	m	m	m	m	m	m	m	m
	Israel	-0.10	(0.03)	1.12	(0.02)	-1.52	(0.03)	-0.39	(0.05)	0.25	(0.03)	1.27	(0.04)	488	(5.9)	516	(5.0)	491	(5.5)	428	(4.6)	**-60**	(7.0)
	Italy	0.00	(0.02)	0.97	(0.02)	-1.23	(0.03)	-0.21	(0.02)	0.28	(0.02)	1.17	(0.03)	492	(3.8)	502	(4.3)	491	(3.4)	452	(4.5)	**-40**	(4.7)
	Japan	-1.05	(0.02)	0.78	(0.02)	-1.67	(0.00)	-1.67	(0.00)	-0.92	(0.06)	0.04	(0.03)	548	(3.8)	547	(3.5)	559	(3.6)	562	(4.4)	14	(5.4)
	Korea	-0.95	(0.03)	0.93	(0.02)	-1.67	(0.00)	-1.67	(0.00)	-0.89	(0.07)	0.41	(0.05)	545	(3.4)	546	(3.2)	545	(3.3)	521	(4.6)	**-24**	(5.2)
	Latvia	0.16	(0.02)	0.96	(0.02)	-1.04	(0.03)	-0.02	(0.02)	0.43	(0.01)	1.26	(0.03)	501	(3.8)	507	(3.6)	491	(3.8)	450	(4.4)	**-51**	(5.0)
	Luxembourg	-0.04	(0.01)	1.02	(0.01)	-1.32	(0.02)	-0.28	(0.01)	0.25	(0.01)	1.19	(0.03)	506	(3.4)	523	(4.2)	508	(3.2)	460	(3.7)	**-46**	(5.5)
	Mexico	-0.16	(0.03)	1.00	(0.01)	-1.51	(0.03)	-0.39	(0.03)	0.22	(0.02)	1.04	(0.04)	428	(3.4)	441	(3.6)	444	(3.3)	433	(4.1)	5	(5.0)
	Netherlands	0.44	(0.02)	0.72	(0.02)	-0.42	(0.03)	0.32	(0.02)	0.63	(0.01)	1.24	(0.02)	517	(4.6)	532	(3.4)	535	(3.3)	493	(4.8)	**-24**	(6.4)
	New Zealand	0.42	(0.02)	0.82	(0.02)	-0.52	(0.04)	0.25	(0.02)	0.61	(0.02)	1.35	(0.04)	542	(4.7)	562	(4.3)	553	(4.3)	513	(5.2)	**-29**	(7.1)
	Norway	m	m	m	m	m	m	m	m	m	m	m	m	m	m	m	m	m	m	m	m	m	m
	Poland	-0.21	(0.03)	1.03	(0.02)	-1.54	(0.03)	-0.47	(0.03)	0.12	(0.02)	1.05	(0.04)	m	m	m	m	m	m	m	m	m	m
	Portugal	0.08	(0.02)	0.99	(0.01)	-1.17	(0.03)	-0.14	(0.02)	0.37	(0.02)	1.25	(0.03)	515	(3.8)	523	(3.4)	502	(3.6)	464	(4.0)	**-50**	(4.8)
	Slovak Republic	0.22	(0.02)	1.01	(0.02)	-0.99	(0.03)	-0.01	(0.02)	0.46	(0.02)	1.43	(0.04)	473	(4.0)	489	(3.5)	472	(4.0)	438	(3.5)	**-35**	(5.3)
	Slovenia	0.02	(0.01)	0.97	(0.01)	-1.22	(0.02)	-0.20	(0.02)	0.32	(0.01)	1.17	(0.03)	505	(4.0)	527	(3.3)	518	(3.8)	476	(3.3)	**-28**	(5.4)
	Spain	-0.04	(0.02)	0.88	(0.02)	-1.20	(0.04)	-0.20	(0.02)	0.27	(0.02)	0.98	(0.03)	494	(3.3)	509	(3.0)	506	(3.4)	491	(3.9)	-3	(4.9)
	Sweden	0.52	(0.02)	0.84	(0.02)	-0.41	(0.04)	0.31	(0.02)	0.68	(0.02)	1.51	(0.04)	525	(4.9)	537	(4.3)	530	(4.7)	486	(4.7)	**-39**	(5.5)
	Switzerland	-0.12	(0.02)	0.89	(0.02)	-1.25	(0.04)	-0.29	(0.02)	0.16	(0.02)	0.92	(0.04)	m	m	m	m	m	m	m	m	m	m
	Turkey	m	m	m	m	m	m	m	m	m	m	m	m	m	m	m	m	m	m	m	m	m	m
	United Kingdom[2]	0.29	(0.02)	0.75	(0.02)	-0.59	(0.04)	0.16	(0.02)	0.48	(0.02)	1.11	(0.04)	521	(4.3)	541	(4.3)	543	(4.4)	507	(4.9)	**-14**	(6.1)
	United States	m	m	m	m	m	m	m	m	m	m	m	m	m	m	m	m	m	m	m	m	m	m
	OECD average-28	0.04	(0.00)	0.91	(0.00)	-1.05	(0.01)	-0.19	(0.00)	0.29	(0.00)	1.12	(0.01)	508	(0.7)	523	(0.7)	516	(0.8)	479	(0.8)	**-29**	(1.0)
	OECD average-31	0.01	(0.00)	0.91	(0.00)	-1.09	(0.01)	-0.22	(0.00)	0.27	(0.00)	1.10	(0.01)	m	m	m	m	m	m	m	m	m	m
Partners	Brazil	-0.14	(0.02)	1.15	(0.02)	-1.62	(0.02)	-0.47	(0.03)	0.23	(0.02)	1.28	(0.03)	432	(4.3)	435	(4.0)	430	(4.1)	408	(4.5)	**-24**	(5.1)
	B-S-J-G (China)	-0.65	(0.02)	0.94	(0.01)	-1.67	(0.00)	-1.20	(0.04)	-0.30	(0.02)	0.58	(0.03)	512	(4.2)	506	(5.1)	500	(4.6)	479	(6.3)	**-33**	(5.9)
	Bulgaria	0.39	(0.03)	1.20	(0.02)	-1.03	(0.03)	0.07	(0.02)	0.63	(0.03)	1.87	(0.05)	478	(4.4)	490	(4.8)	446	(6.4)	413	(4.5)	**-65**	(5.5)
	Colombia	0.18	(0.02)	1.01	(0.01)	-1.14	(0.03)	0.01	(0.02)	0.51	(0.02)	1.35	(0.03)	437	(3.9)	446	(3.3)	441	(3.2)	421	(3.5)	**-16**	(4.5)
	Costa Rica	0.11	(0.02)	0.98	(0.02)	-1.13	(0.04)	-0.09	(0.02)	0.39	(0.02)	1.26	(0.03)	446	(3.9)	456	(3.2)	450	(3.3)	427	(4.4)	**-19**	(5.2)
	Croatia	-0.16	(0.02)	1.04	(0.02)	-1.46	(0.02)	-0.44	(0.03)	0.15	(0.02)	1.12	(0.04)	482	(3.7)	498	(3.1)	486	(4.5)	443	(4.0)	**-38**	(4.9)
	Cyprus*	m	m	m	m	m	m	m	m	m	m	m	m	m	m	m	m	m	m	m	m	m	m
	Dominican Republic	-0.12	(0.03)	1.12	(0.02)	-1.62	(0.03)	-0.41	(0.04)	0.29	(0.03)	1.26	(0.04)	m	m	m	m	m	m	m	m	m	m
	Hong Kong (China)	-0.20	(0.03)	1.08	(0.02)	-1.64	(0.03)	-0.45	(0.04)	0.22	(0.02)	1.08	(0.04)	545	(4.0)	565	(4.3)	550	(4.2)	512	(4.5)	**-34**	(5.2)
	Lithuania	-0.02	(0.02)	1.08	(0.02)	-1.38	(0.02)	-0.27	(0.02)	0.30	(0.02)	1.30	(0.04)	479	(3.7)	504	(3.6)	483	(3.5)	426	(4.0)	**-53**	(4.9)
	Macao (China)	-0.09	(0.01)	0.88	(0.01)	-1.31	(0.02)	-0.19	(0.01)	0.26	(0.01)	0.89	(0.02)	523	(3.1)	545	(3.0)	546	(2.8)	525	(3.5)	2	(5.2)
	Montenegro	m	m	m	m	m	m	m	m	m	m	m	m	m	m	m	m	m	m	m	m	m	m
	Peru	-0.26	(0.02)	0.88	(0.01)	-1.48	(0.03)	-0.43	(0.03)	0.10	(0.02)	0.78	(0.02)	440	(4.5)	427	(3.7)	428	(3.1)	408	(3.8)	**-33**	(5.3)
	Qatar	m	m	m	m	m	m	m	m	m	m	m	m	m	m	m	m	m	m	m	m	m	m
	Russia	0.12	(0.03)	1.21	(0.02)	-1.47	(0.03)	-0.17	(0.03)	0.51	(0.03)	1.59	(0.04)	488	(4.7)	504	(4.6)	474	(4.6)	448	(4.7)	**-40**	(5.9)
	Singapore	0.01	(0.03)	0.94	(0.01)	-1.23	(0.04)	-0.16	(0.03)	0.35	(0.02)	1.09	(0.04)	565	(3.4)	573	(2.9)	567	(3.2)	547	(3.5)	**-18**	(5.2)
	Chinese Taipei	-0.39	(0.02)	0.91	(0.01)	-1.65	(0.02)	-0.61	(0.04)	0.03	(0.02)	0.68	(0.02)	518	(3.6)	526	(3.4)	541	(3.7)	524	(4.2)	6	(5.5)
	Thailand	0.62	(0.02)	0.91	(0.02)	-0.50	(0.04)	0.48	(0.02)	0.89	(0.01)	1.61	(0.03)	450	(4.4)	449	(4.7)	436	(5.1)	421	(4.2)	**-29**	(5.2)
	Tunisia	m	m	m	m	m	m	m	m	m	m	m	m	m	m	m	m	m	m	m	m	m	m
	United Arab Emirates	m	m	m	m	m	m	m	m	m	m	m	m	m	m	m	m	m	m	m	m	m	m
	Uruguay	0.16	(0.02)	1.13	(0.02)	-1.28	(0.03)	-0.10	(0.02)	0.48	(0.02)	1.53	(0.04)	465	(3.6)	479	(4.0)	462	(4.0)	418	(4.8)	**-47**	(5.7)
	Malaysia**	m	m	m	m	m	m	m	m	m	m	m	m	m	m	m	m	m	m	m	m	m	m

1. Socio-economic profile is measured by the PISA index of economic, social and cultural status.
2. Only the United Kingdom subnational entities of England, Northern Ireland and Wales participated in the ICT questionnaire.
Note: Values that are statistically significant are indicated in bold (see Annex A3).
* See note at the beginning of this Annex.
**Malaysia: Coverage is too small to ensure comparability (see Annex A4).

StatLink http://dx.doi.org/10.1787/888933616769

[Part 2/2]

Table V.3.11a Index of ICT use at school and performance in collaborative problem solving

Results based on students' self-reports

		Change in collaborative problem-solving performance per one-unit change on the index of ICT use at school				Increased likelihood of students in the bottom quarter of the index of ICT use at school scoring below Level 2 on the collaborative problem-solving scale (below 440 score points)		Increased likelihood of students in the top quarter of the index of ICT use at school scoring at Level 4 on the collaborative problem-solving scale (at or above 640 score points)	
		Before accounting for students' and schools' socio-economic profile[1]		After accounting for students' and schools' socio-economic profile					
		Score dif.	S.E.	Score dif.	S.E.	Relative risk	S.E.	Relative risk	S.E.
OECD	Australia	7	(2.2)	**-5**	(2.1)	**1.36**	(0.08)	1.14	(0.11)
	Austria	**-14**	(2.4)	**-10**	(2.1)	0.96	(0.09)	**0.57**	(0.10)
	Belgium	**-6**	(1.4)	**-5**	(1.2)	1.10	(0.09)	**0.69**	(0.10)
	Canada	m	m	m	m	m	m	m	m
	Chile	**-16**	(1.9)	**-14**	(1.6)	0.93	(0.06)	0.39	(0.20)
	Czech Republic	**-17**	(1.8)	**-15**	(1.8)	**0.71**	(0.06)	**0.37**	(0.10)
	Denmark	**-14**	(2.5)	**-15**	(2.4)	0.91	(0.10)	**0.70**	(0.12)
	Estonia	**-17**	(2.0)	**-17**	(2.0)	0.91	(0.11)	**0.43**	(0.08)
	Finland	**-15**	(2.6)	**-18**	(2.5)	1.02	(0.09)	**0.56**	(0.07)
	France	**-7**	(2.0)	**-7**	(1.9)	1.11	(0.09)	**0.53**	(0.11)
	Germany	**-13**	(2.7)	**-8**	(2.6)	0.95	(0.10)	**0.73**	(0.08)
	Greece	**-21**	(1.2)	**-18**	(1.1)	**0.74**	(0.04)	**0.17**	(0.12)
	Hungary	**-19**	(1.8)	**-13**	(1.7)	**0.85**	(0.05)	**0.29**	(0.12)
	Iceland	**-12**	(2.4)	**-13**	(2.4)	0.98	(0.08)	**0.60**	(0.15)
	Ireland	m	m	m	m	m	m	m	m
	Israel	**-21**	(2.1)	**-18**	(1.9)	0.87	(0.07)	**0.30**	(0.09)
	Italy	**-15**	(1.8)	**-12**	(1.6)	**0.87**	(0.06)	**0.47**	(0.12)
	Japan	2	(3.1)	2	(2.6)	1.21	(0.15)	**1.43**	(0.15)
	Korea	**-13**	(2.6)	**-14**	(1.8)	**0.72**	(0.07)	**0.71**	(0.12)
	Latvia	**-18**	(1.9)	**-17**	(1.8)	**0.74**	(0.06)	**0.36**	(0.15)
	Luxembourg	**-18**	(1.8)	**-14**	(1.6)	**0.86**	(0.06)	**0.50**	(0.10)
	Mexico	1	(1.8)	**-5**	(1.4)	**1.10**	(0.05)	1.51	(1.01)
	Netherlands	**-10**	(3.0)	**-10**	(2.4)	1.06	(0.09)	**0.67**	(0.12)
	New Zealand	**-13**	(2.9)	**-16**	(2.6)	0.89	(0.10)	**0.69**	(0.10)
	Norway	m	m	m	m	m	m	m	m
	Poland	m	m	m	m	m	m	m	m
	Portugal	**-19**	(1.7)	**-14**	(1.5)	**0.72**	(0.06)	**0.29**	(0.09)
	Slovak Republic	**-11**	(1.9)	**-9**	(1.7)	0.92	(0.05)	**0.21**	(0.12)
	Slovenia	**-12**	(2.0)	**-9**	(1.9)	0.96	(0.09)	**0.36**	(0.11)
	Spain	-3	(1.9)	**-4**	(1.8)	1.15	(0.08)	0.78	(0.18)
	Sweden	**-17**	(2.4)	**-20**	(2.2)	0.85	(0.08)	**0.56**	(0.11)
	Switzerland	m	m	m	m	m	m	m	m
	Turkey	m	m	m	m	m	m	m	m
	United Kingdom[2]	**-8**	(2.9)	**-10**	(2.8)	1.16	(0.11)	**0.71**	(0.09)
	United States	m	m	m	m	m	m	m	m
	OECD average-28	**-12**	(0.4)	**-12**	(0.4)	**0.95**	(0.02)	**0.60**	(0.04)
	OECD average-31	m	m	m	m	m	m	m	m
Partners	Brazil	**-8**	(1.6)	**-11**	(1.4)	0.93	(0.04)	0.66	(0.35)
	B-S-J-G (China)	**-16**	(2.1)	**-15**	(1.6)	**0.72**	(0.05)	0.77	(0.19)
	Bulgaria	**-18**	(1.7)	**-12**	(1.7)	**0.72**	(0.05)	**0.09**	(0.08)
	Colombia	**-5**	(1.5)	**-10**	(1.3)	1.01	(0.04)	0.69	(0.41)
	Costa Rica	**-8**	(1.8)	**-10**	(1.4)	0.99	(0.05)	0.36	(0.32)
	Croatia	**-15**	(1.7)	**-11**	(1.6)	0.94	(0.06)	**0.27**	(0.13)
	Cyprus*	m	m	m	m	m	m	m	m
	Dominican Republic	m	m	m	m	m	m	m	m
	Hong Kong (China)	**-14**	(1.7)	**-14**	(1.7)	0.87	(0.10)	**0.46**	(0.07)
	Lithuania	**-18**	(1.5)	**-16**	(1.5)	**0.86**	(0.05)	**0.15**	(0.10)
	Macao (China)	-1	(2.2)	-2	(2.2)	**1.37**	(0.16)	0.86	(0.11)
	Montenegro	m	m	m	m	m	m	m	m
	Peru	**-14**	(2.1)	**-12**	(1.7)	**0.82**	(0.04)	0.56	(0.38)
	Qatar	m	m	m	m	m	m	m	m
	Russia	**-12**	(1.6)	**-12**	(1.5)	0.87	(0.07)	**0.38**	(0.11)
	Singapore	**-8**	(1.8)	**-15**	(2.2)	0.83	(0.11)	0.89	(0.07)
	Chinese Taipei	2	(2.1)	0	(1.6)	**1.23**	(0.11)	1.06	(0.15)
	Thailand	**-9**	(1.9)	**-10**	(1.7)	**0.85**	(0.04)	0.44	(0.20)
	Tunisia	m	m	m	m	m	m	m	m
	United Arab Emirates	m	m	m	m	m	m	m	m
	Uruguay	**-14**	(1.8)	**-14**	(1.6)	**0.86**	(0.04)	**0.29**	(0.16)
	Malaysia**	m	m	m	m	m	m	m	m

1. Socio-economic profile is measured by the PISA index of economic, social and cultural status.
2. Only the United Kingdom subnational entities of England, Northern Ireland and Wales participated in the ICT questionnaire.
Note: Values that are statistically significant are indicated in bold (see Annex A3).
* See note at the beginning of this Annex.
**Malaysia: Coverage is too small to ensure comparability (see Annex A4).
StatLink http://dx.doi.org/10.1787/888933616769

[Part 1/2]

Table V.3.11b Index of students' self-reported ICT competence and performance in collaborative problem solving

Results based on students' self-reports

		Index of students' self-reported ICT competence												Performance in collaborative problem solving, by national quarter of the index of students' self-reported ICT competence									
		All students		Variability of the index		Bottom quarter		Second quarter		Third quarter		Top quarter		Bottom quarter		Second quarter		Third quarter		Top quarter		Top – bottom quarter	
		Mean index	S.E.	S.D.	S.E.	Mean index	S.E.	Mean index	S.E.	Mean index	S.E.	Mean index	S.E.	Mean score	S.E.	Mean score	S.E.	Mean score	S.E.	Mean score	S.E.	Score dif.	S.E.
OECD	Australia	0.21	(0.01)	0.94	(0.01)	-0.92	(0.01)	-0.09	(0.01)	0.33	(0.01)	1.51	(0.02)	535	(3.3)	523	(3.3)	548	(3.2)	547	(3.7)	**12**	(5.2)
	Austria	-0.08	(0.02)	1.07	(0.01)	-1.37	(0.02)	-0.51	(0.02)	0.21	(0.03)	1.36	(0.02)	504	(4.0)	520	(4.3)	519	(4.2)	520	(3.8)	**16**	(5.3)
	Belgium	0.05	(0.01)	0.96	(0.01)	-1.07	(0.02)	-0.26	(0.01)	0.14	(0.01)	1.39	(0.03)	518	(3.3)	510	(3.5)	509	(3.2)	501	(3.5)	**-17**	(4.0)
	Canada	m	m	m	m	m	m	m	m	m	m	m	m	m	m	m	m	m	m	m	m	m	m
	Chile	0.09	(0.01)	0.96	(0.01)	-1.06	(0.02)	-0.22	(0.01)	0.23	(0.02)	1.39	(0.02)	451	(3.9)	464	(3.9)	463	(4.0)	474	(3.9)	**23**	(5.2)
	Czech Republic	-0.10	(0.01)	0.96	(0.01)	-1.22	(0.02)	-0.45	(0.02)	0.07	(0.01)	1.19	(0.02)	498	(3.4)	503	(3.3)	504	(3.4)	510	(4.1)	**12**	(4.6)
	Denmark	0.25	(0.02)	0.95	(0.01)	-0.88	(0.02)	-0.08	(0.01)	0.38	(0.02)	1.56	(0.02)	528	(3.9)	518	(3.0)	530	(3.8)	533	(3.6)	5	(4.4)
	Estonia	-0.05	(0.01)	0.95	(0.01)	-1.13	(0.02)	-0.39	(0.02)	0.09	(0.01)	1.25	(0.02)	538	(4.3)	544	(3.9)	527	(3.6)	544	(4.0)	6	(5.0)
	Finland	-0.08	(0.01)	0.90	(0.01)	-1.16	(0.02)	-0.34	(0.01)	0.04	(0.01)	1.13	(0.03)	536	(4.0)	551	(3.7)	528	(3.7)	540	(3.6)	3	(4.5)
	France	0.23	(0.01)	1.03	(0.01)	-1.01	(0.02)	-0.15	(0.01)	0.41	(0.02)	1.67	(0.02)	506	(3.7)	501	(3.6)	514	(3.5)	499	(4.8)	-7	(4.6)
	Germany	-0.05	(0.01)	1.02	(0.01)	-1.28	(0.02)	-0.47	(0.01)	0.20	(0.02)	1.35	(0.02)	539	(3.6)	540	(4.7)	535	(3.9)	534	(4.7)	-5	(5.2)
	Greece	0.05	(0.01)	0.96	(0.01)	-1.08	(0.02)	-0.25	(0.02)	0.19	(0.02)	1.35	(0.02)	449	(4.6)	465	(4.4)	470	(4.1)	478	(4.5)	**30**	(5.2)
	Hungary	0.07	(0.02)	0.99	(0.01)	-1.10	(0.02)	-0.23	(0.02)	0.16	(0.02)	1.44	(0.03)	467	(4.5)	474	(4.2)	483	(3.9)	485	(3.8)	**19**	(5.7)
	Iceland	-0.01	(0.02)	0.93	(0.01)	-1.11	(0.03)	-0.29	(0.02)	0.11	(0.02)	1.26	(0.03)	504	(4.8)	507	(3.9)	493	(4.3)	515	(3.9)	**12**	(5.1)
	Ireland	0.21	(0.01)	0.90	(0.01)	-0.86	(0.02)	-0.10	(0.01)	0.35	(0.02)	1.46	(0.02)	m	m	m	m	m	m	m	m	m	m
	Israel	-0.02	(0.02)	1.09	(0.01)	-1.35	(0.03)	-0.33	(0.03)	0.15	(0.02)	1.44	(0.03)	464	(6.2)	484	(5.2)	483	(5.2)	494	(4.5)	**31**	(7.0)
	Italy	-0.02	(0.01)	0.91	(0.01)	-1.09	(0.02)	-0.31	(0.02)	0.10	(0.01)	1.22	(0.02)	482	(4.0)	488	(4.3)	482	(4.0)	485	(3.5)	2	(4.6)
	Japan	-0.94	(0.02)	1.02	(0.01)	-2.16	(0.02)	-1.20	(0.01)	-0.79	(0.01)	0.39	(0.03)	543	(3.9)	559	(3.5)	563	(3.3)	550	(3.8)	7	(4.6)
	Korea	-0.57	(0.02)	0.89	(0.01)	-1.58	(0.02)	-0.89	(0.01)	-0.33	(0.02)	0.52	(0.03)	529	(3.7)	550	(2.9)	538	(3.4)	539	(3.7)	**9**	(3.7)
	Latvia	-0.13	(0.01)	0.90	(0.01)	-1.18	(0.02)	-0.43	(0.01)	0.00	(0.01)	1.07	(0.03)	478	(3.4)	485	(4.1)	484	(4.4)	503	(3.4)	**25**	(4.5)
	Luxembourg	0.01	(0.02)	1.07	(0.01)	-1.28	(0.02)	-0.37	(0.02)	0.23	(0.02)	1.47	(0.02)	494	(3.7)	502	(3.6)	501	(3.9)	509	(3.1)	**15**	(5.1)
	Mexico	-0.09	(0.02)	1.04	(0.01)	-1.34	(0.02)	-0.43	(0.02)	0.09	(0.01)	1.32	(0.03)	418	(3.1)	433	(3.0)	439	(3.1)	457	(3.7)	**39**	(3.8)
	Netherlands	-0.04	(0.01)	0.85	(0.01)	-1.01	(0.02)	-0.31	(0.02)	0.05	(0.01)	1.12	(0.02)	522	(4.2)	518	(3.1)	513	(3.5)	526	(4.0)	4	(4.6)
	New Zealand	0.21	(0.02)	0.91	(0.01)	-0.87	(0.02)	-0.07	(0.01)	0.31	(0.03)	1.46	(0.02)	537	(4.8)	529	(4.9)	556	(4.6)	552	(4.1)	**15**	(6.1)
	Norway	m	m	m	m	m	m	m	m	m	m	m	m	m	m	m	m	m	m	m	m	m	m
	Poland	0.02	(0.01)	0.94	(0.01)	-1.07	(0.02)	-0.25	(0.02)	0.10	(0.01)	1.30	(0.03)	m	m	m	m	m	m	m	m	m	m
	Portugal	0.39	(0.01)	0.92	(0.01)	-0.68	(0.02)	0.02	(0.00)	0.50	(0.03)	1.70	(0.02)	501	(3.7)	480	(3.7)	517	(4.3)	505	(3.9)	3	(5.4)
	Slovak Republic	-0.13	(0.02)	0.96	(0.01)	-1.25	(0.02)	-0.43	(0.02)	0.02	(0.00)	1.14	(0.03)	458	(4.3)	468	(3.5)	468	(3.6)	479	(3.6)	**22**	(5.1)
	Slovenia	0.06	(0.02)	0.96	(0.01)	-1.07	(0.02)	-0.24	(0.02)	0.15	(0.02)	1.39	(0.03)	508	(4.0)	503	(3.8)	507	(4.1)	510	(4.2)	2	(5.4)
	Spain	0.15	(0.01)	0.96	(0.01)	-0.98	(0.02)	-0.19	(0.01)	0.32	(0.02)	1.46	(0.02)	495	(3.6)	495	(3.4)	506	(3.1)	506	(3.1)	**11**	(4.5)
	Sweden	0.27	(0.02)	1.03	(0.01)	-1.00	(0.02)	-0.07	(0.01)	0.46	(0.03)	1.68	(0.02)	520	(4.4)	502	(4.0)	537	(5.3)	521	(4.4)	1	(5.0)
	Switzerland	0.05	(0.02)	1.03	(0.01)	-1.20	(0.03)	-0.36	(0.02)	0.29	(0.02)	1.46	(0.02)	m	m	m	m	m	m	m	m	m	m
	Turkey	m	m	m	m	m	m	m	m	m	m	m	m	m	m	m	m	m	m	m	m	m	m
	United Kingdom[2]	0.34	(0.02)	0.93	(0.01)	-0.76	(0.02)	-0.01	(0.01)	0.51	(0.03)	1.63	(0.02)	528	(5.0)	514	(4.4)	544	(4.5)	531	(4.6)	3	(6.1)
	United States	m	m	m	m	m	m	m	m	m	m	m	m	m	m	m	m	m	m	m	m	m	m
	OECD average-28	0.00	(0.00)	0.97	(0.00)	-1.14	(0.00)	-0.32	(0.00)	0.16	(0.00)	1.32	(0.00)	502	(0.8)	505	(0.7)	509	(0.7)	512	(0.7)	**11**	(1.0)
	OECD average-31	0.01	(0.00)	0.97	(0.00)	-1.13	(0.00)	-0.31	(0.00)	0.16	(0.00)	1.32	(0.00)	m	m	m	m	m	m	m	m	m	m
Partners	Brazil	-0.01	(0.02)	0.97	(0.01)	-1.15	(0.02)	-0.28	(0.02)	0.08	(0.01)	1.30	(0.03)	410	(4.3)	426	(4.3)	428	(4.9)	445	(4.0)	**34**	(4.1)
	B-S-J-G (China)	-0.50	(0.01)	0.78	(0.01)	-1.37	(0.02)	-0.77	(0.01)	-0.32	(0.02)	0.47	(0.02)	491	(5.3)	503	(4.4)	505	(4.8)	497	(5.2)	6	(5.5)
	Bulgaria	-0.01	(0.02)	1.02	(0.01)	-1.23	(0.03)	-0.25	(0.02)	0.09	(0.02)	1.35	(0.03)	438	(5.7)	465	(4.2)	452	(5.2)	481	(5.4)	**43**	(6.5)
	Colombia	-0.02	(0.01)	0.96	(0.01)	-1.16	(0.03)	-0.25	(0.02)	0.08	(0.01)	1.25	(0.02)	414	(3.9)	434	(3.3)	440	(3.2)	459	(3.7)	**45**	(4.5)
	Costa Rica	0.06	(0.02)	1.00	(0.01)	-1.13	(0.02)	-0.25	(0.02)	0.18	(0.02)	1.43	(0.02)	434	(3.5)	443	(3.5)	449	(3.1)	457	(3.6)	**23**	(4.1)
	Croatia	0.17	(0.01)	0.99	(0.01)	-1.02	(0.02)	-0.12	(0.01)	0.28	(0.02)	1.53	(0.02)	464	(3.7)	472	(3.6)	488	(3.8)	488	(3.3)	**23**	(3.9)
	Cyprus*	m	m	m	m	m	m	m	m	m	m	m	m	m	m	m	m	m	m	m	m	m	m
	Dominican Republic	-0.05	(0.02)	1.13	(0.02)	-1.47	(0.04)	-0.35	(0.03)	0.20	(0.03)	1.42	(0.03)	m	m	m	m	m	m	m	m	m	m
	Hong Kong (China)	-0.07	(0.01)	0.82	(0.01)	-1.01	(0.02)	-0.24	(0.01)	0.02	(0.00)	0.96	(0.03)	547	(4.0)	543	(4.1)	534	(3.6)	549	(4.1)	3	(4.2)
	Lithuania	0.01	(0.02)	1.11	(0.01)	-1.36	(0.02)	-0.37	(0.02)	0.31	(0.02)	1.47	(0.02)	443	(3.4)	464	(3.5)	483	(3.7)	504	(3.4)	**61**	(3.9)
	Macao (China)	-0.16	(0.01)	0.77	(0.01)	-1.03	(0.01)	-0.44	(0.01)	0.00	(0.01)	0.82	(0.03)	544	(2.5)	537	(3.1)	521	(3.1)	536	(3.3)	-8	(4.3)
	Montenegro	m	m	m	m	m	m	m	m	m	m	m	m	m	m	m	m	m	m	m	m	m	m
	Peru	-0.27	(0.01)	0.88	(0.01)	-1.28	(0.02)	-0.59	(0.01)	-0.09	(0.01)	0.88	(0.03)	413	(3.8)	428	(3.9)	432	(3.1)	448	(4.8)	**35**	(5.4)
	Qatar	m	m	m	m	m	m	m	m	m	m	m	m	m	m	m	m	m	m	m	m	m	m
	Russia	-0.04	(0.01)	0.88	(0.01)	-1.05	(0.02)	-0.24	(0.02)	0.02	(0.00)	1.11	(0.04)	477	(4.8)	476	(5.3)	472	(4.4)	488	(4.4)	**11**	(5.1)
	Singapore	-0.01	(0.01)	0.91	(0.01)	-1.07	(0.02)	-0.31	(0.02)	0.09	(0.01)	1.25	(0.02)	568	(2.8)	566	(2.7)	547	(3.0)	570	(3.2)	2	(4.6)
	Chinese Taipei	-0.16	(0.01)	0.88	(0.01)	-1.16	(0.01)	-0.46	(0.01)	0.00	(0.01)	0.99	(0.03)	530	(3.8)	531	(3.3)	511	(3.8)	538	(3.6)	8	(4.3)
	Thailand	-0.25	(0.02)	0.81	(0.01)	-1.22	(0.02)	-0.44	(0.02)	0.02	(0.01)	0.66	(0.03)	430	(4.7)	440	(4.5)	430	(3.6)	455	(5.0)	**24**	(4.7)
	Tunisia	m	m	m	m	m	m	m	m	m	m	m	m	m	m	m	m	m	m	m	m	m	m
	United Arab Emirates	m	m	m	m	m	m	m	m	m	m	m	m	m	m	m	m	m	m	m	m	m	m
	Uruguay	0.07	(0.02)	1.03	(0.01)	-1.15	(0.03)	-0.19	(0.01)	0.18	(0.02)	1.45	(0.02)	444	(3.4)	461	(3.4)	460	(3.6)	461	(5.2)	**17**	(5.3)
	Malaysia**	m	m	m	m	m	m	m	m	m	m	m	m	m	m	m	m	m	m	m	m	m	m

1. Socio-economic profile is measured by the PISA index of economic, social and cultural status.
2. Only the United Kingdom subnational entities of England, Northern Ireland and Wales participated in the ICT questionnaire.
Note: Values that are statistically significant are indicated in bold (see Annex A3).
* See note at the beginning of this Annex.
**Malaysia: Coverage is too small to ensure comparability (see Annex A4).
StatLink http://dx.doi.org/10.1787/888933616769

[Part 2/2]

Table V.3.11b Index of students' self-reported ICT competence and performance in collaborative problem solving

Results based on students' self-reports

	Change in collaborative problem-solving performance per one-unit change on the index of students' self-reported ICT competence				Increased likelihood of students in the bottom quarter of the index of students' self-reported ICT competence scoring below Level 2 on the collaborative problem-solving scale (below 440 score points)		Increased likelihood of students in the top quarter of students' self-reported ICT competence scoring at Level 4 on the collaborative problem-solving scale (at or above 640 score points)	
	Before accounting for students' and schools' socio-economic profile[1]		After accounting for students' and schools' socio-economic profile					
	Score dif.	S.E.	Score dif.	S.E.	Relative risk	S.E.	Relative risk	S.E.
OECD								
Australia	**8**	(1.9)	**5**	(1.9)	1.1	(0.1)	1.1	(0.1)
Austria	**5**	(1.9)	3	(1.7)	**1.4**	(0.1)	1.1	(0.1)
Belgium	**-5**	(1.4)	**-3**	(1.3)	0.9	(0.1)	**0.8**	(0.1)
Canada	m	m	m	m	m	m	m	m
Chile	**9**	(1.7)	**5**	(1.6)	**1.2**	(0.1)	1.1	(0.5)
Czech Republic	**5**	(1.7)	3	(1.7)	1.1	(0.1)	1.1	(0.2)
Denmark	**4**	(1.6)	2	(1.6)	1.0	(0.1)	1.1	(0.2)
Estonia	2	(1.9)	0	(1.9)	1.0	(0.1)	1.1	(0.1)
Finland	0	(1.8)	-2	(1.7)	1.1	(0.1)	1.0	(0.1)
France	0	(1.5)	-1	(1.4)	1.0	(0.1)	0.8	(0.2)
Germany	-1	(1.8)	-1	(1.7)	1.0	(0.1)	0.9	(0.1)
Greece	**11**	(1.9)	**7**	(1.8)	**1.3**	(0.1)	**1.7**	(0.5)
Hungary	**9**	(2.0)	**5**	(1.5)	**1.2**	(0.1)	1.0	(0.2)
Iceland	**5**	(1.8)	**4**	(1.8)	1.1	(0.1)	1.3	(0.2)
Ireland	m	m	m	m	m	m	m	m
Israel	**12**	(2.1)	**8**	(1.7)	**1.3**	(0.1)	1.1	(0.2)
Italy	2	(1.7)	3	(1.6)	1.0	(0.1)	0.9	(0.2)
Japan	**4**	(1.7)	**3**	(1.6)	**1.5**	(0.2)	1.0	(0.1)
Korea	**6**	(1.6)	**3**	(1.5)	**1.2**	(0.1)	**1.6**	(0.2)
Latvia	**10**	(1.8)	**7**	(1.8)	**1.2**	(0.1)	**1.6**	(0.4)
Luxembourg	**6**	(1.6)	**3**	(1.5)	**1.2**	(0.1)	1.2	(0.2)
Mexico	**15**	(1.2)	**6**	(1.1)	**1.3**	(0.0)	3.6	(2.8)
Netherlands	1	(1.9)	-1	(1.7)	1.0	(0.1)	1.0	(0.2)
New Zealand	**9**	(2.6)	**6**	(2.6)	1.2	(0.1)	1.1	(0.1)
Norway	m	m	m	m	m	m	m	m
Poland	m	m	m	m	m	m	m	m
Portugal	**5**	(2.2)	2	(2.1)	1.0	(0.2)	1.1	(0.3)
Slovak Republic	**8**	(1.8)	1	(1.6)	**1.2**	(0.1)	1.1	(0.3)
Slovenia	2	(1.8)	2	(1.7)	1.1	(0.1)	1.0	(0.2)
Spain	**6**	(1.6)	**5**	(1.5)	**1.2**	(0.1)	1.1	(0.2)
Sweden	**5**	(1.7)	1	(1.6)	1.0	(0.1)	1.0	(0.1)
Switzerland	m	m	m	m	m	m	m	m
Turkey	m	m	m	m	m	m	m	m
United Kingdom[2]	**4**	(2.2)	3	(2.0)	1.1	(0.1)	1.0	(0.1)
United States	m	m	m	m	m	m	m	m
OECD average-28	**5**	(0.3)	**3**	(0.3)	**1.1**	(0.0)	**1.2**	(0.1)
OECD average-31	m	m	m	m	m	m	m	m
Partners								
Brazil	**14**	(1.5)	**6**	(1.3)	**1.2**	(0.0)	1.6	(0.7)
B-S-J-G (China)	**9**	(2.4)	**-6**	(1.9)	**1.2**	(0.1)	1.4	(0.6)
Bulgaria	**16**	(2.1)	**10**	(1.8)	**1.3**	(0.1)	**1.9**	(0.5)
Colombia	**18**	(1.7)	**10**	(1.6)	**1.3**	(0.0)	**2.8**	(1.1)
Costa Rica	**10**	(1.4)	**5**	(1.3)	**1.2**	(0.0)	1.1	(0.7)
Croatia	**10**	(1.4)	**7**	(1.3)	**1.3**	(0.1)	1.3	(0.4)
Cyprus*	m	m	m	m	m	m	m	m
Dominican Republic	m	m	m	m	m	m	m	m
Hong Kong (China)	3	(1.8)	2	(1.7)	0.9	(0.1)	**1.3**	(0.1)
Lithuania	**22**	(1.2)	**16**	(1.1)	**1.7**	(0.1)	**2.6**	(0.6)
Macao (China)	-3	(2.4)	-4	(2.4)	**0.8**	(0.1)	1.2	(0.2)
Montenegro	m	m	m	m	m	m	m	m
Peru	**15**	(2.1)	3	(1.7)	**1.2**	(0.0)	2.2	(1.1)
Qatar	m	m	m	m	m	m	m	m
Russia	**6**	(1.9)	1	(1.8)	1.1	(0.1)	1.3	(0.3)
Singapore	1	(1.8)	-3	(1.8)	0.8	(0.1)	**1.2**	(0.1)
Chinese Taipei	**4**	(1.5)	1	(1.4)	1.0	(0.1)	**1.4**	(0.2)
Thailand	**13**	(2.0)	**5**	(1.8)	**1.1**	(0.0)	**3.0**	(1.0)
Tunisia	m	m	m	m	m	m	m	m
United Arab Emirates	m	m	m	m	m	m	m	m
Uruguay	**7**	(1.8)	3	(1.7)	**1.2**	(0.1)	1.4	(0.5)
Malaysia**	m	m	m	m	m	m	m	m

1. Socio-economic profile is measured by the PISA index of economic, social and cultural status.
2. Only the United Kingdom subnational entities of England, Northern Ireland and Wales participated in the ICT questionnaire.
Note: Values that are statistically significant are indicated in bold (see Annex A3).
* See note at the beginning of this Annex.
**Malaysia: Coverage is too small to ensure comparability (see Annex A4).
StatLink http://dx.doi.org/10.1787/888933616769

[Part 1/1]

Table V.3.12 Low self-reported ICT competence and performance in collaborative problem solving

Results based on students' self-reports

		Percentage of students whose index of self-reported ICT competence is...				Performance in collaborative problem solving among students whose self-reported ICT competence is...								Relative performance[1] in collaborative problem solving among students whose self-reported ICT competence is...					
		... below -1.00		... above -1.00		... below -1.00		... above -1.00		Difference (above -1.00 minus below -1.00)		Increased likelihood of students with an index of self-reported ICT competence below -1.00 scoring below Level 2 on the collaborative problem-solving scale (below 440 score points)		... below -1.00		... above -1.00		Difference (above -1.00 minus below -1.00)	
		%	S.E.	%	S.E.	Mean score	S.E.	Mean score	S.E.	Score dif.	S.E.	Relative risk	S.E.	Score dif.	S.E.	Score dif.	S.E.	Score dif.	S.E.
OECD	Australia	7.8	(0.3)	92.2	(0.3)	517	(5.3)	540	(2.0)	**23**	(5.5)	**1.3**	(0.1)	**18**	(4.0)	**21**	(1.6)	3	(4.4)
	Austria	19.4	(0.6)	80.6	(0.6)	501	(4.3)	519	(2.8)	**18**	(4.9)	**1.2**	(0.1)	**10**	(2.7)	**11**	(2.2)	1	(3.0)
	Belgium	10.2	(0.3)	89.8	(0.3)	505	(5.1)	510	(2.3)	5	(4.7)	1.0	(0.1)	0	(2.9)	**-7**	(1.4)	**-6**	(3.1)
	Canada	m	m	m	m	m	m	m	m	m	m	m	m	m	m	m	m	m	m
	Chile	10.6	(0.4)	89.4	(0.4)	442	(4.8)	465	(2.7)	**23**	(4.8)	**1.2**	(0.1)	-6	(3.3)	**-5**	(2.2)	1	(3.7)
	Czech Republic	13.2	(0.5)	86.8	(0.5)	487	(4.5)	506	(2.2)	**20**	(4.7)	**1.3**	(0.1)	-2	(3.3)	0	(1.9)	2	(3.0)
	Denmark	6.4	(0.4)	93.6	(0.4)	512	(6.9)	528	(2.4)	**17**	(6.6)	1.2	(0.2)	**16**	(5.1)	**13**	(1.7)	-3	(5.1)
	Estonia	12.3	(0.5)	87.7	(0.5)	531	(5.4)	539	(2.5)	8	(5.6)	1.1	(0.2)	**11**	(3.8)	5	(1.9)	-6	(3.6)
	Finland	12.9	(0.5)	87.1	(0.5)	525	(5.2)	541	(2.4)	**15**	(4.7)	1.2	(0.1)	7	(3.5)	4	(1.9)	-3	(3.1)
	France	9.1	(0.4)	90.9	(0.4)	491	(5.3)	506	(2.6)	**15**	(5.4)	1.1	(0.1)	**-8**	(4.1)	**-9**	(2.2)	-1	(4.5)
	Germany	16.6	(0.5)	83.4	(0.5)	538	(3.9)	537	(3.0)	-1	(4.0)	**0.8**	(0.1)	**22**	(2.8)	**11**	(2.1)	**-10**	(2.9)
	Greece	10.2	(0.5)	89.8	(0.5)	441	(6.4)	468	(3.2)	**27**	(5.6)	**1.2**	(0.1)	**-15**	(4.0)	**-11**	(1.6)	4	(3.8)
	Hungary	10.9	(0.4)	89.1	(0.4)	441	(5.7)	482	(2.6)	**41**	(5.7)	**1.5**	(0.1)	**-15**	(3.9)	**-11**	(1.7)	4	(3.8)
	Iceland	11.7	(0.6)	88.3	(0.6)	493	(6.7)	506	(2.3)	**13**	(6.4)	1.2	(0.1)	**15**	(4.7)	**15**	(1.7)	0	(4.6)
	Ireland	6.6	(0.3)	93.4	(0.3)	m	m	m	m	m	m	m	m	m	m	m	m	m	m
	Israel	16.0	(0.8)	84.0	(0.8)	450	(7.7)	487	(3.6)	**37**	(6.8)	**1.3**	(0.1)	**-14**	(3.9)	**-12**	(2.0)	1	(4.2)
	Italy	11.3	(0.5)	88.7	(0.5)	474	(5.6)	485	(2.9)	11	(6.0)	1.1	(0.1)	**-10**	(4.1)	**-13**	(2.1)	-3	(4.4)
	Japan	49.3	(0.8)	50.7	(0.8)	551	(3.2)	557	(2.7)	**6**	(2.8)	1.1	(0.1)	**22**	(1.9)	**18**	(2.2)	-3	(2.1)
	Korea	30.8	(0.8)	69.2	(0.8)	534	(3.2)	541	(2.6)	**8**	(2.7)	1.1	(0.1)	**22**	(2.3)	**17**	(2.0)	**-5**	(1.9)
	Latvia	12.7	(0.5)	87.3	(0.5)	472	(4.6)	490	(2.3)	**17**	(4.7)	**1.2**	(0.1)	**-12**	(3.6)	**-10**	(1.7)	1	(3.6)
	Luxembourg	15.7	(0.6)	84.3	(0.6)	485	(4.4)	504	(1.9)	**20**	(4.9)	1.1	(0.1)	4	(3.5)	1	(1.8)	-4	(3.6)
	Mexico	16.0	(0.6)	84.0	(0.6)	408	(3.4)	442	(2.5)	**34**	(3.2)	**1.3**	(0.0)	**-6**	(2.5)	-1	(1.6)	4	(2.5)
	Netherlands	9.8	(0.4)	90.2	(0.4)	517	(5.1)	520	(2.4)	3	(4.8)	1.1	(0.1)	**19**	(4.2)	**5**	(1.6)	**-14**	(4.0)
	New Zealand	7.1	(0.5)	92.9	(0.5)	522	(8.6)	545	(2.6)	**23**	(8.4)	1.3	(0.2)	9	(5.5)	**19**	(2.2)	10	(5.8)
	Norway	m	m	m	m	m	m	m	m	m	m	m	m	m	m	m	m	m	m
	Poland	10.0	(0.5)	90.0	(0.5)	m	m	m	m	m	m	m	m	m	m	m	m	m	m
	Portugal	4.7	(0.3)	95.3	(0.3)	480	(8.7)	502	(2.6)	**22**	(8.4)	**1.3**	(0.2)	-10	(5.2)	**-7**	(2.0)	3	(5.2)
	Slovak Republic	15.0	(0.6)	85.0	(0.6)	448	(4.9)	472	(2.3)	**24**	(4.6)	**1.2**	(0.1)	-2	(3.4)	**-11**	(1.7)	**-9**	(3.3)
	Slovenia	10.9	(0.5)	89.1	(0.5)	502	(5.1)	507	(1.8)	6	(5.0)	1.0	(0.1)	**-15**	(4.1)	**-12**	(1.9)	3	(3.8)
	Spain	8.7	(0.4)	91.3	(0.4)	484	(5.1)	502	(2.1)	**18**	(4.7)	**1.3**	(0.1)	-4	(3.4)	**-3**	(1.7)	1	(3.4)
	Sweden	9.2	(0.5)	90.8	(0.5)	501	(5.9)	522	(3.3)	**21**	(5.7)	**1.2**	(0.1)	**13**	(3.9)	**7**	(2.1)	-6	(3.5)
	Switzerland	14.2	(0.8)	85.8	(0.8)	m	m	m	m	m	m	m	m	m	m	m	m	m	m
	Turkey	m	m	m	m	m	m	m	m	m	m	m	m	m	m	m	m	m	m
	United Kingdom[2]	5.3	(0.4)	94.7	(0.4)	500	(9.0)	531	(3.0)	**31**	(8.9)	**1.4**	(0.2)	10	(6.3)	**11**	(2.5)	1	(6.4)
	United States	m	m	m	m	m	m	m	m	m	m	m	m	m	m	m	m	m	m
	OECD average-28	13.4	(0.1)	86.6	(0.1)	491	(1.1)	509	(0.5)	**18**	(1.1)	**1.2**	(0.0)	**3**	(0.7)	**2**	(0.4)	-1	(0.7)
	OECD average-31	13.1	(0.1)	86.9	(0.1)	m	m	m	m	m	m	m	m	m	m	m	m	m	m
Partners	Brazil	11.4	(0.5)	88.6	(0.5)	393	(4.4)	432	(3.5)	**39**	(4.4)	**1.1**	(0.0)	**-10**	(3.6)	**-9**	(2.4)	0	(3.9)
	B-S-J-G (China)	22.3	(0.7)	77.7	(0.7)	491	(5.0)	502	(4.0)	**11**	(4.1)	**1.1**	(0.1)	**-8**	(2.9)	**-22**	(1.7)	**-13**	(2.7)
	Bulgaria	12.1	(0.6)	87.9	(0.6)	411	(5.7)	466	(3.5)	**55**	(5.2)	**1.3**	(0.1)	**-15**	(3.0)	**-11**	(2.0)	4	(3.5)
	Colombia	11.7	(0.5)	88.3	(0.5)	394	(4.3)	443	(2.3)	**48**	(4.3)	**1.4**	(0.0)	**-10**	(3.0)	**-6**	(1.6)	4	(3.1)
	Costa Rica	11.0	(0.4)	89.0	(0.4)	424	(4.0)	449	(2.5)	**25**	(3.7)	**1.2**	(0.0)	3	(3.5)	3	(2.0)	0	(3.4)
	Croatia	8.4	(0.4)	91.6	(0.4)	445	(5.4)	481	(2.5)	**36**	(5.2)	**1.4**	(0.1)	**-20**	(3.8)	**-13**	(1.6)	6	(4.0)
	Cyprus*	m	m	m	m	m	m	m	m	m	m	m	m	m	m	m	m	m	m
	Dominican Republic	17.3	(0.8)	82.7	(0.8)	m	m	m	m	m	m	m	m	m	m	m	m	m	m
	Hong Kong (China)	9.5	(0.4)	90.5	(0.4)	523	(6.1)	545	(2.9)	**22**	(5.5)	**1.5**	(0.2)	**13**	(4.2)	**15**	(2.2)	1	(3.9)
	Lithuania	16.7	(0.6)	83.3	(0.6)	435	(3.9)	481	(2.4)	**46**	(3.7)	**1.5**	(0.1)	**-16**	(2.5)	**-16**	(1.4)	0	(2.4)
	Macao (China)	9.5	(0.5)	90.5	(0.5)	537	(4.8)	534	(1.5)	-2	(5.5)	1.0	(0.1)	**13**	(3.3)	**9**	(1.4)	-4	(3.8)
	Montenegro	m	m	m	m	m	m	m	m	m	m	m	m	m	m	m	m	m	m
	Peru	16.1	(0.6)	83.9	(0.6)	406	(3.8)	435	(2.9)	**29**	(3.8)	**1.1**	(0.0)	1	(2.7)	2	(1.9)	1	(2.7)
	Qatar	m	m	m	m	m	m	m	m	m	m	m	m	m	m	m	m	m	m
	Russia	9.2	(0.4)	90.8	(0.4)	454	(5.3)	481	(3.5)	**26**	(5.5)	**1.3**	(0.1)	**-27**	(3.9)	**-22**	(2.4)	5	(4.5)
	Singapore	11.5	(0.5)	88.5	(0.5)	558	(4.0)	564	(1.3)	6	(4.3)	1.1	(0.1)	**18**	(3.6)	**14**	(1.3)	-4	(3.7)
	Chinese Taipei	14.0	(0.4)	86.0	(0.4)	520	(4.6)	529	(2.5)	**9**	(4.3)	**1.3**	(0.1)	4	(3.5)	3	(2.0)	-1	(3.4)
	Thailand	15.0	(0.5)	85.0	(0.5)	419	(4.4)	443	(3.6)	**24**	(3.6)	**1.2**	(0.0)	-4	(3.2)	3	(2.0)	**7**	(3.0)
	Tunisia	m	m	m	m	m	m	m	m	m	m	m	m	m	m	m	m	m	m
	United Arab Emirates	m	m	m	m	m	m	m	m	m	m	m	m	m	m	m	m	m	m
	Uruguay	11.0	(0.5)	89.0	(0.5)	423	(4.7)	461	(2.6)	**38**	(4.5)	**1.2**	(0.1)	**-9**	(3.4)	**-8**	(2.0)	0	(3.5)
	Malaysia**	m	m	m	m	m	m	m	m	m	m	m	m	m	m	m	m	m	m

1. Relative scores are the residuals obtained from a pooled linear regression, across all participating countries/economies, of performance in collaborative problem solving over performance in science, reading and/or mathematics.
2. Only the United Kingdom subnational entities of England, Northern Ireland and Wales participated in the ICT questionnaire.
Note: Values that are statistically significant are indicated in bold (see Annex A3).
* See note at the beginning of this Annex.
**Malaysia: Coverage is too small to ensure comparability (see Annex A4).
StatLink http://dx.doi.org/10.1787/888933616769

[Part 1/1]

Table V.4.1a Variation in collaborative problem-solving performance

		Mean performance in collaborative problem solving		Variation in collaborative problem-solving performance						As a percentage of the average total variation in collaborative problem-solving performance across OECD countries			Index of intra-class correlation[3]	
				Total variation[1]		Between-school variation[2]		Within-school variation		Total variation	Between-school variation	Within-school variation		
		Mean score	S.E.	Variance	S.E.	Variance	S.E.	Variance	S.E.	%	%	%	Overall	S.E.
OECD	Australia	531	(1.9)	11 374	(283)	1 975	(164)	9 536	(211)	125.6	21.8	105.3	17.2	(1.2)
	Austria	509	(2.6)	9 680	(293)	3 274	(291)	6 333	(197)	106.9	36.1	69.9	34.1	(2.2)
	Belgium	501	(2.4)	9 731	(284)	3 407	(292)	6 265	(144)	107.4	37.6	69.2	35.2	(2.1)
	Canada	535	(2.3)	10 861	(204)	1 546	(135)	9 266	(179)	119.9	17.1	102.3	14.3	(1.1)
	Chile	457	(2.7)	7 065	(219)	2 000	(197)	4 999	(145)	78.0	22.1	55.2	28.6	(2.1)
	Czech Republic	499	(2.2)	8 277	(255)	2 534	(248)	5 594	(188)	91.4	28.0	61.8	31.2	(2.3)
	Denmark	520	(2.5)	8 139	(220)	1 081	(144)	7 009	(189)	89.9	11.9	77.4	13.4	(1.6)
	Estonia	535	(2.5)	8 160	(237)	1 437	(201)	6 656	(194)	90.1	15.9	73.5	17.8	(2.2)
	Finland	534	(2.6)	10 298	(298)	638	(132)	9 555	(247)	113.7	7.0	105.5	6.3	(1.2)
	France	494	(2.4)	w	w	w	w	w	w	w	w	w	w	w
	Germany	525	(2.8)	10 198	(294)	3 199	(270)	6 987	(192)	112.6	35.3	77.1	31.4	(2.0)
	Greece	459	(3.6)	8 489	(287)	2 329	(304)	6 047	(189)	93.7	25.7	66.8	27.8	(2.8)
	Hungary	472	(2.4)	9 101	(312)	4 088	(366)	4 791	(119)	100.5	45.1	52.9	46.0	(2.4)
	Iceland	499	(2.3)	8 926	(351)	387	(162)	8 704	(441)	98.5	4.3	96.1	4.3	(1.8)
	Ireland	m	m	m	m	m	m	m	m	m	m	m	m	m
	Israel	469	(3.6)	11 058	(381)	4 777	(419)	6 280	(298)	122.1	52.7	69.3	43.2	(2.8)
	Italy	478	(2.5)	9 263	(309)	3 084	(279)	6 132	(168)	102.3	34.1	67.7	33.5	(2.1)
	Japan	552	(2.7)	7 152	(296)	2 013	(226)	5 107	(163)	79.0	22.2	56.4	28.3	(2.3)
	Korea	538	(2.5)	7 033	(249)	1 469	(207)	5 529	(174)	77.6	16.2	61.0	21.0	(2.4)
	Latvia	485	(2.3)	8 078	(237)	979	(152)	6 911	(189)	89.2	10.8	76.3	12.4	(1.7)
	Luxembourg	491	(1.5)	9 958	(207)	2 549	(423)	7 494	(300)	109.9	28.1	82.7	25.4	(3.5)
	Mexico	433	(2.5)	6 262	(235)	1 806	(203)	4 431	(137)	69.1	19.9	48.9	28.9	(2.4)
	Netherlands	518	(2.4)	9 347	(289)	3 584	(320)	5 759	(167)	103.2	39.6	63.6	38.4	(2.3)
	New Zealand	533	(2.4)	11 192	(354)	1 483	(225)	9 689	(303)	123.6	16.4	107.0	13.3	(1.8)
	Norway	502	(2.5)	8 806	(292)	819	(136)	7 976	(258)	97.2	9.0	88.1	9.3	(1.4)
	Poland	m	m	m	m	m	m	m	m	m	m	m	m	m
	Portugal	498	(2.6)	8 317	(233)	1 593	(178)	6 724	(183)	91.8	17.6	74.2	19.1	(1.8)
	Slovak Republic	463	(2.4)	8 637	(286)	2 945	(302)	5 592	(155)	95.4	32.5	61.7	34.5	(2.4)
	Slovenia	502	(1.8)	8 592	(246)	3 091	(304)	5 339	(166)	94.9	34.1	58.9	36.7	(2.4)
	Spain	496	(2.1)	7 749	(198)	835	(118)	6 902	(167)	85.6	9.2	76.2	10.8	(1.4)
	Sweden	510	(3.4)	9 659	(356)	1 309	(203)	8 228	(253)	106.6	14.5	90.8	13.7	(1.9)
	Switzerland	m	m	m	m	m	m	m	m	m	m	m	m	m
	Turkey	422	(3.4)	6 100	(245)	2 560	(259)	3 529	(91)	67.3	28.3	39.0	42.0	(2.6)
	United Kingdom	519	(2.7)	10 609	(231)	1 883	(203)	8 727	(197)	117.1	20.8	96.3	17.7	(1.7)
	United States	520	(3.6)	11 698	(380)	1 880	(269)	9 847	(268)	129.1	20.8	108.7	16.0	(1.9)
	OECD average	500	(0.5)	9 058	(50)	2 191	(45)	6 825	(38)	100.0	24.2	75.3	24.6	(0.4)
Partners	Brazil	412	(2.3)	7 653	(231)	2 460	(232)	5 247	(118)	84.5	27.2	57.9	31.9	(2.1)
	B-S-J-G (China)	496	(4.0)	9 383	(408)	3 875	(377)	5 470	(163)	103.6	42.8	60.4	41.5	(2.5)
	Bulgaria	444	(3.9)	9 563	(327)	4 189	(366)	5 404	(150)	105.6	46.2	59.7	43.7	(2.4)
	Colombia	429	(2.3)	6 852	(238)	2 111	(223)	4 758	(165)	75.6	23.3	52.5	30.7	(2.4)
	Costa Rica	441	(2.4)	6 026	(205)	1 403	(197)	4 608	(120)	66.5	15.5	50.9	23.3	(2.5)
	Croatia	473	(2.5)	7 590	(260)	2 222	(232)	5 336	(168)	83.8	24.5	58.9	29.4	(2.3)
	Cyprus*	444	(1.7)	8 326	(238)	1 461	(250)	6 820	(224)	91.9	16.1	75.3	17.6	(2.6)
	Dominican Republic	m	m	m	m	m	m	m	m	m	m	m	m	m
	Hong Kong (China)	541	(2.9)	8 176	(288)	1 985	(219)	6 184	(190)	90.3	21.9	68.3	24.3	(2.0)
	Lithuania	467	(2.5)	8 205	(261)	2 367	(275)	5 788	(176)	90.6	26.1	63.9	29.0	(2.6)
	Macao (China)	534	(1.2)	8 011	(188)	1 700	(505)	6 219	(230)	88.4	18.8	68.7	21.5	(5.2)
	Montenegro	416	(1.3)	6 249	(190)	1 203	(228)	5 061	(202)	69.0	13.3	55.9	19.2	(3.0)
	Peru	418	(2.5)	6 961	(266)	2 677	(251)	4 297	(108)	76.9	29.6	47.4	38.4	(2.2)
	Qatar	m	m	m	m	m	m	m	m	m	m	m	m	m
	Russia	473	(3.4)	8 493	(266)	1 763	(233)	6 780	(164)	93.8	19.5	74.9	20.6	(2.2)
	Singapore	561	(1.2)	9 330	(236)	2 205	(269)	7 111	(216)	103.0	24.3	78.5	23.7	(2.4)
	Chinese Taipei	527	(2.5)	8 136	(264)	2 113	(249)	6 005	(163)	89.8	23.3	66.3	26.0	(2.4)
	Thailand	436	(3.5)	6 948	(283)	2 472	(299)	4 570	(154)	76.7	27.3	50.5	35.1	(2.9)
	Tunisia	382	(1.9)	3 470	(170)	1 109	(223)	2 363	(69)	38.3	12.2	26.1	31.9	(4.4)
	United Arab Emirates	435	(2.4)	8 979	(192)	3 706	(292)	5 307	(110)	99.1	40.9	58.6	41.1	(2.0)
	Uruguay	443	(2.3)	8 275	(238)	2 381	(221)	5 945	(185)	91.4	26.3	65.6	28.6	(2.1)
	Malaysia**	440	(3.3)	6 330	(272)	1 593	(201)	4 722	(178)	69.9	17.6	52.1	25.2	(2.5)

1. The total variation in student performance is calculated from the square of the standard deviation for all students. Due to the unbalanced, clustered nature of the data, the sum of the between- and within-school components, as an estimate from a sample, does not necessarily add up to the total variation.
2. In some countries/economies, subunits within schools were sampled instead of schools; this may affect the estimation of between-school variation components (see Annex A3).
3. The intra-class correlation is the variation in student performance between schools, divided by the sum of the variation in student performance between schools and the variation in student performance within schools, and multiplied by 100.
* See note at the beginning of this Annex.
**Malaysia: Coverage is too small to ensure comparability (see Annex A4).
StatLink http://dx.doi.org/10.1787/888933616788

[Part 1/1]

Table V.4.1b Variation in relative collaborative problem-solving performance

		Variation in relative collaborative problem-solving performance[1]					The percentage of the variation in collaborative problem-solving performance explained by performance in science, reading and mathematics				
	Total variation[2]		Between-school variation[3]		Within-school variation		Total variation	Between-school variation	Within-school variation	Index of intra-class correlation[4]	
	Variance	S.E.	Variance	S.E.	Variance	S.E.	%	%	%	Overall	S.E.
OECD											
Australia	4 429	(134)	473	(69)	4 018	(116)	61.1	76.1	57.9	10.5	(1.4)
Austria	3 462	(146)	355	(58)	3 094	(120)	64.2	89.2	51.1	10.3	(1.5)
Belgium	3 633	(106)	293	(43)	3 301	(89)	62.7	91.4	47.3	8.2	(1.1)
Canada	4 389	(107)	594	(65)	3 812	(91)	59.6	61.6	58.9	13.5	(1.3)
Chile	2 734	(127)	217	(46)	2 513	(103)	61.3	89.1	49.7	7.9	(1.5)
Czech Republic	3 536	(149)	291	(43)	3 200	(125)	57.3	88.5	42.8	8.3	(1.1)
Denmark	3 213	(116)	290	(53)	2 914	(104)	60.5	73.1	58.4	9.1	(1.6)
Estonia	2 993	(120)	231	(51)	2 738	(91)	63.3	83.9	58.9	7.8	(1.6)
Finland	3 770	(128)	201	(42)	3 570	(109)	63.4	68.5	62.6	5.3	(1.0)
France	w	w	w	w	w	w	w	w	w	w	w
Germany	4 089	(111)	299	(47)	3 763	(109)	59.9	90.6	46.1	7.4	(1.1)
Greece	3 082	(100)	153	(37)	2 886	(93)	63.7	93.4	52.3	5.0	(1.2)
Hungary	3 007	(97)	196	(36)	2 770	(76)	67.0	95.2	42.2	6.6	(1.2)
Iceland	3 445	(124)	143	(44)	3 269	(157)	61.4	63.0	62.4	4.2	(1.3)
Ireland	m	m	m	m	m	m	m	m	m	m	m
Israel	3 748	(156)	549	(78)	3 193	(135)	66.1	88.5	49.2	14.7	(1.8)
Italy	4 163	(161)	639	(85)	3 502	(125)	55.1	79.3	42.9	15.4	(1.7)
Japan	3 108	(105)	350	(53)	2 755	(83)	56.5	82.6	46.1	11.3	(1.5)
Korea	2 540	(98)	173	(38)	2 359	(80)	63.9	88.2	57.3	6.8	(1.3)
Latvia	3 354	(104)	124	(36)	3 213	(103)	58.5	87.3	53.5	3.7	(1.0)
Luxembourg	3 617	(136)	86	(38)	3 476	(124)	63.7	96.6	53.6	2.4	(1.0)
Mexico	2 486	(93)	212	(39)	2 258	(64)	60.3	88.3	49.0	8.6	(1.4)
Netherlands	3 406	(110)	314	(61)	3 087	(99)	63.6	91.2	46.4	9.2	(1.7)
New Zealand	4 134	(151)	295	(62)	3 810	(147)	63.1	80.1	60.7	7.2	(1.4)
Norway	3 699	(139)	438	(73)	3 260	(99)	58.0	46.5	59.1	11.8	(1.7)
Poland	m	m	m	m	m	m	m	m	m	m	m
Portugal	3 215	(112)	254	(46)	2 936	(89)	61.3	84.1	56.3	7.9	(1.3)
Slovak Republic	3 590	(145)	381	(63)	3 169	(105)	58.4	87.1	43.3	10.7	(1.5)
Slovenia	3 618	(122)	347	(70)	3 251	(97)	57.9	88.8	39.1	9.6	(1.7)
Spain	3 349	(100)	227	(40)	3 122	(93)	56.8	72.9	54.8	6.8	(1.1)
Sweden	3 353	(135)	234	(52)	3 119	(97)	65.3	82.1	62.1	7.0	(1.4)
Switzerland	m	m	m	m	m	m	m	m	m	m	m
Turkey	2 459	(72)	282	(49)	2 176	(53)	59.7	89.0	38.4	11.5	(1.8)
United Kingdom	4 178	(121)	471	(66)	3 694	(88)	60.6	75.0	57.7	11.3	(1.4)
United States	3 576	(180)	398	(84)	3 172	(145)	69.4	78.9	67.8	11.1	(2.0)
OECD average	3 476	(22)	304	(10)	3 157	(19)	61.6	86.1	53.7	8.7	(0.3)
Partners											
Brazil	3 143	(119)	521	(71)	2 657	(79)	58.9	78.8	49.4	16.4	(1.8)
B-S-J-G (China)	3 311	(109)	370	(60)	2 931	(86)	64.7	90.5	46.4	11.2	(1.6)
Bulgaria	2 848	(97)	203	(39)	2 656	(85)	70.2	95.2	50.8	7.1	(1.3)
Colombia	2 422	(87)	243	(34)	2 174	(75)	64.6	88.5	54.3	10.0	(1.3)
Costa Rica	3 064	(94)	304	(45)	2 745	(79)	49.2	78.3	40.4	10.0	(1.3)
Croatia	2 961	(95)	172	(36)	2 779	(90)	61.0	92.3	47.9	5.8	(1.2)
Cyprus*	3 495	(106)	170	(53)	3 337	(100)	58.0	88.4	51.1	4.8	(1.4)
Dominican Republic	m	m	m	m	m	m	m	m	m	m	m
Hong Kong (China)	3 449	(113)	222	(55)	3 226	(99)	57.8	88.8	47.8	6.4	(1.5)
Lithuania	2 961	(84)	236	(45)	2 704	(79)	63.9	90.0	53.3	8.0	(1.4)
Macao (China)	2 847	(127)	71	(46)	2 776	(138)	64.5	95.8	55.4	2.5	(1.5)
Montenegro	2 670	(107)	90	(26)	2 591	(111)	57.3	92.5	48.8	3.3	(0.9)
Peru	2 381	(79)	283	(39)	2 083	(64)	65.8	89.4	51.5	12.0	(1.4)
Qatar	m	m	m	m	m	m	m	m	m	m	m
Russia	4 038	(140)	461	(99)	3 578	(110)	52.5	73.9	47.2	11.4	(2.2)
Singapore	3 173	(83)	255	(56)	2 916	(73)	66.0	88.4	59.0	8.0	(1.6)
Chinese Taipei	3 019	(90)	363	(56)	2 653	(70)	62.9	82.8	55.8	12.0	(1.6)
Thailand	2 514	(109)	442	(72)	2 071	(87)	63.8	82.1	54.7	17.6	(2.4)
Tunisia	1 949	(58)	261	(49)	1 684	(42)	43.8	76.5	28.7	13.4	(2.2)
United Arab Emirates	2 796	(79)	578	(65)	2 231	(53)	68.9	84.4	58.0	20.6	(1.8)
Uruguay	3 199	(138)	326	(59)	2 890	(113)	61.3	86.3	51.4	10.1	(1.6)
Malaysia**	2 338	(96)	393	(61)	1 943	(69)	63.1	75.3	58.8	16.8	(2.2)

1. Relative performance refers to the residual performance, attributable to purely «collaborative problem-solving» competencies, after accounting for performance in science, reading and mathematics in a regression performed across students at the national level.
2. The total variation in student performance is calculated from the square of the standard deviation for all students. Due to the unbalanced, clustered nature of the data, the sum of the between- and within-school components, as an estimate from a sample, does not necessarily add up to the total variation.
3. In some countries/economies, subunits within schools were sampled instead of schools; this may affect the estimation of between-school variation components (see Annex A3).
4. The intra-class correlation is the variation in student performance between schools, divided by the sum of the variation in student performance between schools and the variation in student performance within schools, and multiplied by 100.
* See note at the beginning of this Annex.
**Malaysia: Coverage is too small to ensure comparability (see Annex A4).

StatLink http://dx.doi.org/10.1787/888933616788

[Part 1/2]

Table V.4.2 Percentage of students at each proficiency level in collaborative problem solving, by gender

	Boys										Girls									
	Below Level 1 (below 340 score points)		Level 1 (from 340 to less than 440 score points)		Level 2 (from 440 to less than 540 score points)		Level 3 (from 540 to less than 640 score points)		Level 4 (at or above 640 score points)		Below Level 1 (below 340 score points)		Level 1 (from 340 to less than 440 score points)		Level 2 (from 440 to less than 540 score points)		Level 3 (from 540 to less than 640 score points)		Level 4 (at or above 640 score points)	
	%	S.E.	%	S.E.	%	S.E.	%	S.E.	%	S.E.	%	S.E.	%	S.E.	%	S.E.	%	S.E.	%	S.E.
OECD																				
Australia	6.5	(0.5)	19.5	(0.8)	32.2	(0.9)	30.5	(1.0)	11.3	(0.6)	2.1	(0.3)	11.6	(0.7)	30.1	(0.8)	36.8	(1.1)	19.3	(1.2)
Austria	5.7	(0.6)	23.4	(1.1)	35.9	(1.3)	27.3	(1.2)	7.7	(0.8)	3.3	(0.6)	16.9	(1.2)	35.7	(1.4)	33.5	(1.4)	10.5	(1.0)
Belgium	7.1	(0.6)	23.7	(1.0)	37.4	(1.0)	26.3	(1.0)	5.4	(0.6)	4.3	(0.5)	18.3	(1.1)	36.0	(1.0)	32.5	(1.1)	8.9	(0.8)
Canada	4.9	(0.4)	19.1	(0.9)	34.0	(0.9)	30.4	(1.0)	11.7	(0.7)	1.9	(0.3)	11.0	(0.8)	30.1	(1.0)	37.2	(1.0)	19.8	(0.8)
Chile	10.0	(1.1)	36.0	(1.7)	38.2	(1.3)	14.8	(1.0)	1.0	(0.3)	6.9	(0.7)	31.7	(1.4)	42.8	(1.6)	17.3	(1.2)	1.3	(0.3)
Czech Republic	6.5	(0.7)	24.9	(1.2)	39.2	(1.2)	25.1	(1.2)	4.4	(0.5)	2.7	(0.4)	18.2	(1.1)	40.2	(1.5)	32.6	(1.4)	6.4	(0.6)
Denmark	3.5	(0.4)	18.8	(1.1)	39.8	(1.4)	30.5	(1.2)	7.4	(0.8)	1.8	(0.4)	13.7	(1.1)	37.8	(1.4)	36.4	(1.5)	10.4	(0.9)
Estonia	2.6	(0.4)	16.7	(1.0)	37.1	(1.3)	33.6	(1.2)	10.0	(0.9)	0.9	(0.3)	10.1	(0.8)	33.6	(1.5)	40.9	(1.5)	14.5	(1.1)
Finland	5.2	(0.6)	19.9	(1.1)	35.0	(1.2)	29.8	(1.2)	10.1	(0.9)	1.6	(0.3)	9.0	(0.7)	29.3	(1.3)	41.0	(1.3)	19.1	(1.2)
France	9.5	(0.9)	25.9	(1.1)	35.1	(1.4)	24.1	(1.5)	5.4	(0.6)	4.5	(0.5)	19.2	(1.1)	37.4	(1.3)	31.1	(1.2)	7.8	(0.8)
Germany	4.7	(0.6)	20.1	(1.1)	35.9	(1.1)	29.2	(1.2)	10.1	(0.8)	2.4	(0.4)	13.7	(0.9)	32.8	(1.1)	35.7	(1.0)	15.5	(0.9)
Greece	13.7	(1.4)	35.0	(1.4)	35.1	(1.5)	14.7	(1.0)	1.5	(0.3)	6.7	(0.9)	28.0	(1.7)	41.1	(1.3)	21.7	(1.4)	2.5	(0.5)
Hungary	10.5	(0.9)	32.4	(1.6)	36.0	(1.3)	18.8	(1.3)	2.3	(0.4)	6.9	(0.8)	24.8	(1.3)	38.8	(1.4)	25.2	(1.3)	4.4	(0.6)
Iceland	6.7	(0.8)	26.2	(1.5)	36.8	(1.8)	25.2	(1.3)	5.2	(0.8)	2.8	(0.5)	19.1	(1.3)	39.3	(1.6)	31.1	(1.5)	7.8	(0.9)
Ireland	m	m	m	m	m	m	m	m	m	m	m	m	m	m	m	m	m	m	m	m
Israel	13.9	(1.3)	32.0	(1.3)	29.5	(1.5)	20.1	(1.2)	4.5	(0.7)	9.0	(1.1)	28.3	(1.3)	32.0	(1.5)	24.3	(1.4)	6.3	(0.8)
Italy	10.1	(0.9)	29.6	(1.2)	36.7	(1.3)	20.3	(1.2)	3.2	(0.5)	5.6	(0.6)	24.2	(1.5)	40.3	(1.5)	24.8	(1.2)	5.2	(0.8)
Japan	1.8	(0.3)	11.5	(1.0)	34.9	(1.5)	40.5	(1.4)	11.4	(1.2)	0.7	(0.3)	6.2	(0.5)	27.8	(1.1)	48.5	(1.3)	16.7	(1.1)
Korea	2.3	(0.4)	15.3	(1.1)	38.0	(1.3)	36.5	(1.5)	7.9	(0.8)	0.6	(0.2)	7.2	(0.9)	32.0	(1.4)	47.2	(1.4)	13.1	(1.3)
Latvia	8.1	(0.8)	31.8	(1.4)	39.5	(1.3)	18.1	(0.9)	2.5	(0.5)	3.1	(0.5)	19.0	(1.0)	43.0	(1.3)	29.5	(1.6)	5.4	(0.8)
Luxembourg	8.5	(0.7)	27.9	(1.0)	35.5	(1.2)	22.4	(1.1)	5.6	(0.6)	4.6	(0.6)	21.8	(1.0)	37.1	(1.3)	28.6	(1.0)	7.9	(0.6)
Mexico	15.1	(1.1)	41.9	(1.6)	34.2	(1.5)	8.5	(0.7)	0.4	(0.2)	9.3	(0.8)	40.6	(1.8)	40.7	(1.4)	9.1	(0.9)	0.4	(0.2)
Netherlands	4.6	(0.5)	22.3	(1.3)	36.2	(1.3)	28.8	(1.4)	8.2	(0.9)	2.2	(0.4)	14.9	(1.0)	35.2	(1.4)	35.8	(1.3)	11.9	(1.1)
New Zealand	5.8	(0.6)	20.0	(1.2)	32.3	(1.2)	29.8	(1.4)	12.1	(1.0)	1.7	(0.4)	11.7	(0.9)	30.2	(1.2)	36.7	(1.3)	19.7	(1.3)
Norway	6.4	(0.8)	25.0	(1.1)	38.9	(1.3)	24.5	(1.3)	5.3	(0.7)	2.4	(0.4)	16.9	(1.0)	40.2	(1.4)	32.2	(1.6)	8.4	(0.7)
Poland	m	m	m	m	m	m	m	m	m	m	m	m	m	m	m	m	m	m	m	m
Portugal	6.1	(0.6)	24.2	(1.3)	38.9	(1.3)	26.1	(1.2)	4.7	(0.7)	3.1	(0.4)	18.7	(1.0)	41.6	(1.2)	30.9	(1.2)	5.7	(0.6)
Slovak Republic	11.5	(0.9)	36.1	(1.3)	35.7	(1.6)	14.9	(1.1)	1.7	(0.3)	7.4	(0.7)	25.7	(1.2)	41.3	(1.3)	22.0	(1.2)	3.5	(0.6)
Slovenia	6.0	(0.6)	26.3	(1.2)	39.2	(1.3)	23.8	(1.1)	4.6	(0.8)	2.7	(0.4)	15.8	(1.0)	38.0	(1.7)	35.2	(1.4)	8.3	(0.9)
Spain	5.5	(0.7)	25.1	(1.2)	41.1	(1.3)	24.8	(1.2)	3.5	(0.5)	3.3	(0.4)	17.7	(1.0)	42.1	(1.2)	31.8	(1.2)	5.1	(0.5)
Sweden	6.6	(0.7)	25.7	(1.3)	36.4	(1.4)	24.9	(1.5)	6.4	(0.9)	2.4	(0.4)	14.4	(1.2)	35.5	(1.6)	35.9	(1.2)	11.8	(1.3)
Switzerland	m	m	m	m	m	m	m	m	m	m	m	m	m	m	m	m	m	m	m	m
Turkey	18.4	(1.5)	46.9	(1.6)	29.5	(1.8)	5.1	(0.8)	0.1	(0.1)	11.3	(1.3)	42.1	(2.0)	37.6	(1.9)	8.7	(1.0)	0.2	(0.2)
United Kingdom	5.5	(0.5)	21.8	(1.2)	36.3	(1.0)	27.4	(1.0)	8.9	(1.0)	2.8	(0.4)	14.6	(0.9)	32.8	(1.1)	34.5	(1.3)	15.2	(1.0)
United States	6.7	(0.9)	21.7	(1.2)	32.5	(1.1)	27.0	(1.4)	12.1	(1.1)	3.1	(0.6)	16.0	(1.1)	33.0	(1.2)	32.4	(1.4)	15.6	(1.3)
OECD average	7.5	(0.1)	25.8	(0.2)	36.0	(0.2)	24.5	(0.2)	6.1	(0.1)	3.9	(0.1)	18.8	(0.2)	36.4	(0.2)	31.3	(0.2)	9.6	(0.2)
Partners																				
Brazil	25.3	(0.9)	42.7	(0.8)	24.7	(0.9)	6.8	(0.6)	0.5	(0.1)	17.4	(0.9)	43.3	(0.9)	30.5	(0.9)	8.2	(0.6)	0.7	(0.2)
B-S-J-G (China)	6.9	(0.8)	24.8	(1.3)	38.1	(1.4)	25.2	(1.3)	4.9	(0.7)	4.6	(0.7)	19.7	(1.4)	37.7	(1.4)	29.9	(1.7)	8.2	(1.2)
Bulgaria	18.7	(1.5)	37.3	(1.5)	29.6	(1.4)	12.9	(1.2)	1.5	(0.3)	11.4	(1.1)	30.6	(1.4)	36.0	(1.4)	19.4	(1.3)	2.6	(0.6)
Colombia	15.3	(1.3)	43.0	(1.4)	32.8	(1.2)	8.3	(0.8)	0.5	(0.2)	13.0	(1.0)	41.6	(1.1)	34.7	(1.4)	10.0	(0.9)	0.7	(0.2)
Costa Rica	10.6	(0.8)	41.5	(1.4)	37.8	(1.5)	9.7	(0.9)	0.5	(0.2)	8.2	(0.7)	39.6	(1.3)	41.3	(1.3)	10.2	(0.9)	0.6	(0.2)
Croatia	9.1	(1.0)	32.9	(1.3)	39.4	(1.5)	16.7	(1.0)	1.8	(0.4)	4.4	(0.6)	24.9	(1.2)	44.0	(1.2)	23.8	(1.1)	2.9	(0.5)
Cyprus*	18.6	(0.9)	39.7	(1.7)	30.3	(1.3)	10.4	(0.8)	1.0	(0.3)	7.4	(0.7)	32.3	(1.1)	40.7	(1.3)	17.5	(0.9)	2.1	(0.4)
Dominican Republic	m	m	m	m	m	m	m	m	m	m	m	m	m	m	m	m	m	m	m	m
Hong Kong (China)	2.9	(0.5)	15.3	(1.2)	37.3	(1.4)	35.4	(1.5)	9.1	(0.7)	1.0	(0.3)	8.1	(0.8)	29.9	(1.7)	44.1	(1.6)	17.0	(1.2)
Lithuania	11.4	(0.8)	33.6	(1.2)	36.7	(1.2)	16.4	(1.2)	1.9	(0.4)	5.2	(0.6)	26.8	(1.1)	42.0	(1.5)	23.1	(1.1)	3.0	(0.5)
Macao (China)	3.6	(0.4)	17.4	(0.9)	37.8	(1.5)	33.1	(1.6)	8.1	(0.8)	0.8	(0.3)	8.0	(0.7)	33.3	(1.2)	43.7	(1.2)	14.1	(0.9)
Montenegro	22.2	(1.0)	46.5	(1.3)	26.7	(1.2)	4.5	(0.6)	0.1	(0.1)	12.7	(0.9)	42.9	(1.3)	36.7	(1.3)	7.5	(0.7)	0.2	(0.1)
Peru	19.1	(1.2)	44.1	(1.4)	29.3	(1.2)	7.1	(0.8)	0.4	(0.2)	17.1	(1.1)	42.5	(1.4)	32.0	(1.5)	8.1	(0.9)	0.4	(0.2)
Qatar	m	m	m	m	m	m	m	m	m	m	m	m	m	m	m	m	m	m	m	m
Russia	9.7	(0.9)	32.4	(1.6)	37.9	(1.3)	17.6	(1.3)	2.5	(0.5)	5.0	(0.8)	26.1	(1.7)	41.2	(1.6)	23.0	(1.5)	4.7	(0.7)
Singapore	2.2	(0.3)	11.7	(0.8)	29.1	(1.0)	38.0	(1.2)	19.0	(0.9)	1.0	(0.2)	7.6	(0.6)	26.4	(1.0)	41.1	(1.3)	24.0	(1.1)
Chinese Taipei	3.7	(0.5)	17.7	(1.1)	38.6	(1.4)	32.4	(1.2)	7.6	(1.0)	1.5	(0.3)	10.7	(0.8)	35.7	(1.3)	40.2	(1.5)	11.8	(1.2)
Thailand	17.8	(1.5)	45.8	(1.7)	29.0	(1.6)	7.1	(1.0)	0.4	(0.2)	7.9	(0.9)	39.0	(1.5)	38.7	(1.4)	13.0	(1.1)	1.4	(0.4)
Tunisia	28.3	(1.9)	57.8	(1.9)	13.2	(1.2)	0.7	(0.3)	0.0	c	21.3	(1.3)	61.0	(1.6)	16.9	(1.4)	0.9	(0.3)	0.0	(0.0)
United Arab Emirates	22.9	(1.2)	39.9	(1.1)	25.5	(1.1)	10.2	(0.7)	1.6	(0.3)	9.7	(0.8)	35.5	(1.3)	37.5	(1.2)	15.3	(1.0)	2.0	(0.2)
Uruguay	15.4	(1.1)	39.2	(1.2)	32.0	(1.1)	12.0	(1.0)	1.4	(0.4)	10.6	(0.8)	36.3	(1.1)	36.2	(1.2)	15.1	(1.0)	1.9	(0.3)
Malaysia**	13.8	(1.3)	42.1	(1.6)	35.2	(1.5)	8.7	(1.1)	0.3	(0.2)	8.0	(0.8)	36.5	(1.7)	43.5	(1.6)	11.5	(1.2)	0.5	(0.2)

Note: Values that are statistically significant are indicated in bold (see Annex A3).
* See note at the beginning of this Annex.
**Malaysia: Coverage is too small to ensure comparability (see Annex A4).
StatLink http://dx.doi.org/10.1787/888933616788

[Part 2/2]

Table V.4.2 Percentage of students at each proficiency level in collaborative problem solving, by gender

	Gender differences (boys - girls)										Increased risk of ...					
	Below Level 1 (below 340 score points)		Level 1 (from 340 to less than 440 score points)		Level 2 (from 440 to less than 540 score points)		Level 3 (from 540 to less than 640 score points)		Level 4 (at or above 640 score points)		Boys scoring below Level 1 on the collaborative problem-solving scale (below 340 score points)		Boys scoring below Level 2 on the collaborative problem-solving scale (below 440 score points)		Girls scoring at Level 4 on the collaborative problem-solving scale (at or above 640 score points)	
	% dif.	S.E.	% dif.	S.E.	% dif.	S.E.	% dif.	S.E.	% dif.	S.E.	Relative risk	S.E.	Relative risk	S.E.	Relative risk	S.E.
OECD																
Australia	**4.4**	(0.5)	**7.9**	(0.9)	2.1	(1.2)	**-6.3**	(1.3)	**-8.0**	(1.2)	**3.1**	(0.5)	**1.9**	(0.1)	**1.7**	(0.1)
Austria	**2.4**	(0.8)	**6.5**	(1.7)	0.2	(1.7)	**-6.2**	(1.6)	**-2.9**	(1.2)	**1.7**	(0.4)	**1.4**	(0.1)	**1.4**	(0.2)
Belgium	**2.9**	(0.7)	**5.4**	(1.4)	1.4	(1.4)	**-6.2**	(1.4)	**-3.5**	(0.9)	**1.7**	(0.2)	**1.4**	(0.1)	**1.6**	(0.2)
Canada	**3.0**	(0.5)	**8.0**	(0.9)	**3.9**	(1.1)	**-6.8**	(1.1)	**-8.1**	(0.9)	**2.6**	(0.4)	**1.9**	(0.1)	**1.7**	(0.1)
Chile	**3.1**	(1.2)	**4.3**	(2.1)	**-4.6**	(2.0)	**-2.4**	(1.2)	-0.4	(0.4)	**1.5**	(0.2)	**1.2**	(0.1)	1.4	(0.5)
Czech Republic	**3.8**	(0.8)	**6.7**	(1.6)	-1.0	(1.9)	**-7.5**	(1.6)	**-2.0**	(0.9)	**2.5**	(0.5)	**1.5**	(0.1)	**1.5**	(0.2)
Denmark	**1.8**	(0.6)	**5.1**	(1.5)	2.0	(2.3)	**-5.9**	(2.0)	**-3.0**	(1.1)	**2.0**	(0.5)	**1.4**	(0.1)	**1.4**	(0.2)
Estonia	**1.7**	(0.5)	**6.6**	(1.2)	**3.6**	(1.7)	**-7.2**	(1.8)	**-4.6**	(1.2)	**3.0**	(1.0)	**1.7**	(0.1)	**1.5**	(0.1)
Finland	**3.6**	(0.6)	**10.8**	(1.2)	**5.6**	(1.4)	**-11.1**	(1.6)	**-8.9**	(1.5)	**3.3**	(0.8)	**2.4**	(0.2)	**1.9**	(0.2)
France	**5.0**	(0.9)	**6.7**	(1.7)	-2.3	(1.9)	**-7.0**	(1.9)	**-2.4**	(0.9)	**2.1**	(0.3)	**1.5**	(0.1)	**1.5**	(0.2)
Germany	**2.3**	(0.5)	**6.4**	(1.2)	**3.1**	(1.4)	**-6.4**	(1.5)	**-5.4**	(1.0)	**1.9**	(0.3)	**1.5**	(0.1)	**1.5**	(0.1)
Greece	**7.0**	(1.2)	**7.0**	(1.9)	**-6.0**	(1.9)	**-7.0**	(1.5)	-1.0	(0.6)	**2.0**	(0.2)	**1.4**	(0.1)	1.7	(0.5)
Hungary	**3.6**	(1.2)	**7.6**	(2.2)	-2.8	(2.0)	**-6.3**	(1.8)	**-2.1**	(0.6)	**1.5**	(0.2)	**1.4**	(0.1)	**1.9**	(0.4)
Iceland	**3.9**	(0.9)	**7.1**	(2.0)	-2.5	(2.4)	**-5.9**	(1.9)	**-2.7**	(1.1)	**2.4**	(0.5)	**1.5**	(0.1)	**1.5**	(0.3)
Ireland	m	m	m	m	m	m	m	m	m	m	m	m	m	m	m	m
Israel	**4.8**	(1.4)	**3.7**	(1.5)	-2.5	(1.8)	**-4.2**	(1.7)	-1.8	(1.0)	**1.5**	(0.2)	**1.2**	(0.1)	1.4	(0.3)
Italy	**4.5**	(1.0)	**5.5**	(1.9)	-3.6	(1.9)	**-4.5**	(1.6)	**-1.9**	(0.8)	**1.8**	(0.2)	**1.3**	(0.1)	**1.6**	(0.3)
Japan	**1.1**	(0.4)	**5.3**	(0.9)	**7.1**	(1.6)	**-8.0**	(1.7)	**-5.4**	(1.6)	**2.6**	(1.2)	**1.9**	(0.2)	**1.5**	(0.2)
Korea	**1.7**	(0.5)	**8.1**	(1.4)	**6.0**	(1.9)	**-10.8**	(2.0)	**-5.1**	(1.3)	**4.2**	(1.7)	**2.3**	(0.3)	**1.6**	(0.2)
Latvia	**5.0**	(0.9)	**12.8**	(1.7)	-3.5	(1.9)	**-11.5**	(1.7)	**-2.9**	(0.8)	**2.7**	(0.5)	**1.8**	(0.1)	**2.2**	(0.5)
Luxembourg	**4.0**	(0.9)	**6.1**	(1.5)	-1.6	(2.1)	**-6.2**	(1.6)	**-2.4**	(0.9)	**1.9**	(0.3)	**1.4**	(0.1)	**1.4**	(0.2)
Mexico	**5.8**	(1.0)	1.3	(1.7)	**-6.5**	(1.6)	-0.6	(0.9)	0.0	(0.2)	**1.6**	(0.1)	**1.1**	(0.0)	1.1	(0.7)
Netherlands	**2.4**	(0.6)	**7.4**	(1.5)	1.0	(2.0)	**-7.0**	(1.7)	**-3.8**	(1.4)	**2.1**	(0.4)	**1.6**	(0.1)	**1.5**	(0.2)
New Zealand	**4.1**	(0.7)	**8.4**	(1.6)	2.1	(1.6)	**-6.9**	(1.8)	**-7.6**	(1.4)	**3.4**	(0.9)	**1.9**	(0.2)	**1.6**	(0.2)
Norway	**4.0**	(0.9)	**8.1**	(1.2)	-1.3	(1.7)	**-7.7**	(2.1)	**-3.1**	(0.8)	**2.7**	(0.6)	**1.6**	(0.1)	**1.6**	(0.2)
Poland	m	m	m	m	m	m	m	m	m	m	m	m	m	m	m	m
Portugal	**3.0**	(0.6)	**5.5**	(1.5)	-2.7	(1.8)	**-4.8**	(1.4)	-1.0	(0.8)	**2.0**	(0.3)	**1.4**	(0.1)	1.2	(0.2)
Slovak Republic	**4.2**	(1.1)	**10.4**	(1.8)	**-5.6**	(1.9)	**-7.1**	(1.4)	**-1.8**	(0.7)	**1.6**	(0.2)	**1.4**	(0.1)	**2.1**	(0.5)
Slovenia	**3.3**	(0.7)	**10.5**	(1.4)	1.2	(1.8)	**-11.3**	(1.7)	**-3.7**	(1.0)	**2.2**	(0.4)	**1.8**	(0.1)	**1.8**	(0.3)
Spain	**2.2**	(0.7)	**7.4**	(1.2)	-1.0	(1.9)	**-7.0**	(1.7)	**-1.5**	(0.7)	**1.7**	(0.3)	**1.5**	(0.1)	**1.4**	(0.2)
Sweden	**4.2**	(0.8)	**11.3**	(1.6)	0.9	(2.0)	**-11.0**	(1.5)	**-5.4**	(1.5)	**2.7**	(0.5)	**1.9**	(0.1)	**1.9**	(0.3)
Switzerland	m	m	m	m	m	m	m	m	m	m	m	m	m	m	m	m
Turkey	**7.1**	(1.8)	**4.7**	(2.3)	**-8.1**	(2.2)	**-3.6**	(1.0)	-0.1	(0.2)	**1.6**	(0.2)	**1.2**	(0.1)	m	m
United Kingdom	**2.7**	(0.6)	**7.2**	(1.3)	**3.5**	(1.5)	**-7.1**	(1.4)	**-6.3**	(1.3)	**1.9**	(0.3)	**1.6**	(0.1)	**1.7**	(0.2)
United States	**3.6**	(1.1)	**5.8**	(1.3)	-0.5	(1.7)	**-5.4**	(1.9)	**-3.5**	(1.3)	**2.2**	(0.5)	**1.5**	(0.1)	**1.3**	(0.1)
OECD average	**3.6**	(0.2)	**7.1**	(0.3)	-0.4	(0.3)	**-6.8**	(0.3)	**-3.5**	(0.2)	**2.2**	(0.1)	**1.6**	(0.0)	**1.6**	(0.1)
Partners																
Brazil	**7.9**	(1.0)	-0.6	(1.0)	**-5.7**	(1.1)	**-1.4**	(0.6)	-0.2	(0.2)	**1.5**	(0.1)	**1.1**	(0.0)	1.4	(0.5)
B-S-J-G (China)	**2.3**	(0.8)	**5.2**	(1.5)	0.4	(1.5)	**-4.7**	(1.4)	**-3.2**	(0.8)	**1.5**	(0.2)	**1.3**	(0.1)	**1.6**	(0.2)
Bulgaria	**7.3**	(1.4)	**6.7**	(1.5)	**-6.4**	(1.7)	**-6.5**	(1.5)	-1.2	(0.6)	**1.6**	(0.2)	**1.3**	(0.1)	**1.8**	(0.5)
Colombia	2.4	(1.2)	1.4	(1.6)	-1.9	(1.6)	-1.7	(1.2)	-0.2	(0.3)	1.2	(0.1)	**1.1**	(0.0)	1.4	(0.7)
Costa Rica	**2.4**	(0.9)	1.9	(1.5)	**-3.6**	(1.7)	-0.5	(1.1)	-0.2	(0.2)	**1.3**	(0.1)	**1.1**	(0.0)	1.4	(0.7)
Croatia	**4.7**	(1.0)	**8.0**	(1.6)	**-4.6**	(1.8)	**-7.1**	(1.3)	-1.1	(0.6)	**2.1**	(0.3)	**1.4**	(0.1)	1.6	(0.4)
Cyprus*	**11.1**	(1.0)	**7.4**	(1.9)	**-10.4**	(1.7)	**-7.1**	(1.1)	**-1.1**	(0.5)	**2.5**	(0.2)	**1.5**	(0.1)	2.3	(1.0)
Dominican Republic	m	m	m	m	m	m	m	m	m	m	m	m	m	m	m	m
Hong Kong (China)	**1.8**	(0.5)	**7.3**	(1.2)	**7.5**	(2.1)	**-8.7**	(2.1)	**-7.9**	(1.4)	**2.9**	(1.0)	**2.0**	(0.2)	**1.9**	(0.2)
Lithuania	**6.2**	(0.8)	**6.8**	(1.5)	**-5.3**	(1.7)	**-6.6**	(1.5)	-1.1	(0.6)	**2.2**	(0.2)	**1.4**	(0.1)	1.6	(0.4)
Macao (China)	**2.8**	(0.5)	**9.4**	(1.2)	**4.4**	(1.9)	**-10.6**	(2.0)	**-6.0**	(1.2)	**4.8**	(2.0)	**2.4**	(0.2)	**1.7**	(0.2)
Montenegro	**9.5**	(1.5)	**3.6**	(1.8)	**-10.0**	(1.9)	**-3.0**	(0.8)	-0.1	(0.2)	**1.8**	(0.2)	**1.2**	(0.0)	m	m
Peru	2.1	(1.2)	1.6	(1.6)	-2.6	(1.6)	-1.0	(0.9)	0.0	(0.2)	1.1	(0.1)	**1.1**	(0.0)	1.0	(0.7)
Qatar	m	m	m	m	m	m	m	m	m	m	m	m	m	m	m	m
Russia	**4.7**	(1.0)	**6.3**	(1.9)	**-3.4**	(1.7)	**-5.4**	(1.5)	**-2.2**	(0.7)	**1.9**	(0.3)	**1.4**	(0.1)	**1.9**	(0.4)
Singapore	**1.2**	(0.4)	**4.1**	(1.1)	2.7	(1.6)	-3.1	(2.0)	**-5.0**	(1.6)	**2.3**	(0.7)	**1.6**	(0.2)	**1.3**	(0.1)
Chinese Taipei	**2.2**	(0.5)	**7.0**	(1.3)	2.9	(1.8)	**-7.8**	(1.8)	**-4.2**	(1.5)	**2.5**	(0.6)	**1.7**	(0.2)	**1.6**	(0.3)
Thailand	**9.9**	(1.4)	**6.8**	(2.0)	**-9.8**	(1.8)	**-5.9**	(1.2)	**-1.0**	(0.4)	**2.3**	(0.3)	**1.4**	(0.1)	**4.2**	(2.4)
Tunisia	**7.0**	(1.7)	-3.1	(1.9)	**-3.7**	(1.5)	-0.2	(0.3)	0.0	(0.0)	**1.3**	(0.1)	**1.0**	(0.0)	m	m
United Arab Emirates	**13.2**	(1.4)	**4.4**	(1.6)	**-12.0**	(1.5)	**-5.2**	(1.2)	-0.4	(0.3)	**2.4**	(0.2)	**1.4**	(0.1)	1.3	(0.3)
Uruguay	**4.7**	(1.4)	2.9	(1.5)	**-4.2**	(1.5)	**-3.0**	(1.3)	-0.4	(0.5)	**1.4**	(0.2)	**1.2**	(0.0)	1.3	(0.4)
Malaysia**	**5.8**	(1.2)	**5.5**	(1.9)	**-8.3**	(1.7)	**-2.8**	(1.0)	-0.2	(0.2)	**1.7**	(0.2)	**1.3**	(0.0)	1.8	(1.0)

Note: Values that are statistically significant are indicated in bold (see Annex A3).
* See note at the beginning of this Annex.
**Malaysia: Coverage is too small to ensure comparability (see Annex A4).
StatLink http://dx.doi.org/10.1787/888933616788

[Part 1/3]

Table V.4.3a Mean score and variation in collaborative problem-solving performance, by gender

	Boys																	
	Mean score		Standard deviation		Percentiles													
					5th		10th		25th		Median (50th)		75th		90th		95th	
	Mean score	S.E.	S.D.	S.E.	Score	S.E.	Score	S.E.	Score	S.E.	Score	S.E.	Score	S.E.	Score	S.E.	Score	S.E.
OECD																		
Australia	511	(2.5)	109	(1.4)	327	(3.9)	364	(3.9)	436	(3.8)	516	(3.5)	589	(2.7)	647	(3.0)	681	(3.4)
Austria	498	(3.4)	99	(1.8)	334	(5.2)	367	(4.6)	427	(4.7)	499	(4.5)	570	(4.2)	627	(5.1)	657	(5.2)
Belgium	489	(3.0)	99	(1.6)	323	(5.4)	358	(4.3)	421	(4.5)	492	(3.5)	559	(3.3)	613	(3.5)	643	(5.1)
Canada	516	(2.8)	104	(1.3)	341	(4.1)	378	(3.4)	444	(3.9)	519	(3.4)	590	(3.6)	649	(3.8)	684	(4.6)
Chile	450	(3.1)	85	(1.7)	312	(5.1)	340	(4.8)	390	(3.8)	449	(3.8)	510	(4.2)	563	(4.6)	592	(5.5)
Czech Republic	486	(2.9)	93	(1.6)	329	(5.1)	362	(4.7)	421	(4.4)	489	(3.6)	552	(3.6)	606	(4.3)	635	(4.8)
Denmark	509	(2.9)	92	(1.8)	356	(5.7)	389	(5.0)	448	(3.9)	512	(3.4)	573	(4.1)	625	(4.5)	656	(5.2)
Estonia	522	(2.9)	92	(1.6)	367	(5.5)	402	(3.9)	459	(4.2)	525	(3.5)	587	(4.0)	640	(4.6)	669	(4.9)
Finland	511	(3.2)	103	(1.7)	338	(6.1)	375	(4.9)	440	(4.0)	513	(3.9)	584	(3.8)	641	(4.6)	675	(6.1)
France	480	(3.4)	103	(1.9)	311	(5.9)	343	(5.0)	406	(5.0)	483	(4.3)	553	(4.4)	612	(4.2)	643	(4.6)
Germany	510	(3.4)	101	(1.6)	343	(5.0)	376	(4.9)	441	(4.4)	511	(3.9)	581	(3.9)	640	(4.6)	674	(4.9)
Greece	444	(4.2)	93	(1.9)	294	(6.7)	324	(6.0)	378	(5.1)	443	(5.3)	510	(4.8)	567	(4.7)	598	(5.9)
Hungary	459	(3.3)	94	(2.2)	308	(6.1)	338	(4.0)	391	(4.0)	459	(4.4)	528	(4.5)	582	(5.5)	612	(4.9)
Iceland	485	(3.0)	96	(2.4)	328	(5.7)	359	(5.1)	417	(4.1)	486	(4.9)	554	(4.2)	609	(5.6)	640	(6.6)
Ireland	m	m	m	m	m	m	m	m	m	m	m	m	m	m	m	m	m	m
Israel	459	(4.3)	106	(2.2)	300	(4.2)	326	(5.0)	375	(4.9)	453	(6.0)	539	(5.8)	602	(6.1)	635	(6.6)
Italy	466	(3.4)	98	(1.8)	306	(6.9)	340	(5.0)	398	(4.4)	466	(4.5)	536	(3.8)	592	(5.0)	623	(5.1)
Japan	539	(3.6)	87	(2.0)	387	(6.8)	423	(6.0)	483	(4.5)	544	(4.0)	599	(3.8)	646	(4.8)	673	(6.1)
Korea	522	(3.5)	87	(1.8)	371	(5.8)	406	(5.7)	465	(4.8)	528	(4.0)	584	(3.7)	631	(4.0)	657	(5.0)
Latvia	465	(2.6)	90	(1.8)	320	(4.9)	349	(4.0)	400	(4.3)	464	(3.9)	527	(3.2)	581	(4.4)	613	(5.2)
Luxembourg	478	(2.5)	101	(1.5)	316	(5.4)	348	(3.8)	405	(3.0)	477	(3.2)	549	(3.6)	611	(4.2)	644	(5.3)
Mexico	426	(2.9)	82	(1.7)	297	(5.2)	323	(4.3)	367	(3.7)	425	(3.4)	483	(3.8)	534	(4.1)	563	(4.8)
Netherlands	504	(3.0)	98	(1.9)	343	(5.2)	375	(4.8)	434	(4.1)	505	(3.8)	574	(3.9)	631	(4.8)	663	(6.5)
New Zealand	513	(3.2)	108	(2.0)	332	(6.1)	367	(5.5)	437	(4.8)	516	(4.4)	590	(4.1)	651	(5.3)	686	(6.2)
Norway	487	(3.0)	96	(2.2)	329	(6.4)	362	(5.1)	421	(4.1)	490	(3.8)	554	(4.3)	610	(5.0)	642	(6.9)
Poland	m	m	m	m	m	m	m	m	m	m	m	m	m	m	m	m	m	m
Portugal	489	(3.2)	94	(1.6)	331	(4.7)	364	(5.3)	424	(4.2)	492	(3.7)	556	(3.7)	607	(4.4)	638	(5.3)
Slovak Republic	448	(2.8)	91	(1.7)	304	(4.9)	333	(4.0)	384	(3.5)	446	(3.8)	512	(3.9)	568	(4.6)	600	(5.5)
Slovenia	484	(2.2)	93	(1.5)	332	(4.1)	363	(4.1)	419	(3.0)	485	(3.4)	550	(3.7)	605	(4.4)	636	(6.1)
Spain	485	(2.7)	89	(1.4)	336	(5.1)	368	(3.9)	424	(3.5)	487	(3.2)	549	(3.6)	600	(3.6)	628	(3.9)
Sweden	489	(4.0)	99	(2.2)	329	(5.3)	360	(5.1)	419	(4.4)	489	(4.6)	558	(4.9)	616	(6.3)	651	(7.6)
Switzerland	m	m	m	m	m	m	m	m	m	m	m	m	m	m	m	m	m	m
Turkey	411	(4.0)	77	(1.9)	289	(5.3)	314	(4.6)	356	(4.5)	408	(4.9)	464	(5.0)	513	(5.9)	541	(5.9)
United Kingdom	503	(3.1)	102	(1.7)	336	(4.7)	370	(4.7)	432	(4.1)	503	(4.0)	573	(3.7)	634	(5.5)	669	(5.9)
United States	507	(4.4)	111	(2.0)	326	(7.4)	360	(6.2)	428	(5.4)	508	(5.2)	586	(5.7)	651	(6.2)	688	(6.3)
OECD average	486	(0.6)	96	(0.3)	328	(1.0)	360	(0.8)	418	(0.8)	487	(0.7)	554	(0.7)	609	(0.8)	641	(1.0)
Partners																		
Brazil	402	(2.5)	89	(1.3)	266	(2.8)	294	(2.7)	339	(2.2)	395	(3.0)	461	(3.6)	523	(4.3)	559	(4.9)
B-S-J-G (China)	486	(3.9)	96	(2.3)	325	(6.3)	358	(5.5)	419	(5.5)	489	(4.3)	555	(4.8)	609	(5.6)	640	(6.8)
Bulgaria	429	(4.6)	97	(2.0)	281	(6.4)	309	(5.0)	357	(4.8)	423	(5.9)	499	(6.0)	562	(5.6)	595	(6.0)
Colombia	425	(2.9)	83	(1.7)	295	(5.3)	321	(3.8)	366	(3.5)	422	(3.4)	481	(4.2)	535	(4.3)	566	(5.0)
Costa Rica	437	(2.8)	79	(1.8)	311	(4.6)	337	(3.6)	381	(3.3)	436	(3.4)	492	(3.4)	541	(4.6)	569	(6.1)
Croatia	459	(3.3)	89	(1.8)	315	(5.8)	345	(4.9)	396	(4.6)	459	(3.8)	521	(3.9)	576	(5.1)	606	(4.7)
Cyprus*	424	(2.0)	91	(1.8)	282	(3.7)	310	(2.7)	358	(2.6)	419	(3.4)	488	(4.2)	547	(4.5)	578	(5.8)
Dominican Republic	m	m	m	m	m	m	m	m	m	m	m	m	m	m	m	m	m	m
Hong Kong (China)	523	(3.7)	91	(2.0)	365	(7.5)	401	(5.2)	464	(5.1)	528	(4.2)	587	(4.4)	636	(3.5)	665	(5.0)
Lithuania	453	(2.9)	92	(1.7)	306	(4.2)	335	(3.4)	387	(3.6)	453	(4.0)	520	(3.9)	573	(4.3)	605	(5.3)
Macao (China)	515	(1.9)	93	(1.5)	354	(5.1)	390	(4.3)	453	(2.6)	520	(2.9)	580	(3.0)	630	(4.0)	660	(4.9)
Montenegro	403	(1.8)	79	(1.6)	281	(3.8)	305	(2.7)	346	(2.5)	399	(2.9)	457	(3.3)	508	(3.9)	537	(4.4)
Peru	414	(2.8)	83	(1.9)	285	(4.2)	310	(3.4)	355	(2.7)	410	(3.3)	470	(4.0)	525	(5.6)	559	(6.3)
Qatar	m	m	m	m	m	m	m	m	m	m	m	m	m	m	m	m	m	m
Russia	460	(3.8)	93	(1.7)	311	(5.7)	341	(4.3)	396	(4.2)	459	(4.7)	524	(5.3)	582	(5.6)	614	(5.8)
Singapore	552	(1.7)	99	(1.7)	378	(4.7)	418	(4.0)	486	(3.5)	558	(2.6)	622	(2.9)	674	(3.0)	704	(4.4)
Chinese Taipei	513	(3.4)	92	(1.9)	353	(5.0)	390	(4.3)	452	(3.6)	517	(3.8)	577	(4.4)	628	(5.6)	657	(6.4)
Thailand	416	(4.1)	81	(1.8)	293	(4.0)	316	(4.0)	357	(4.1)	410	(5.0)	470	(5.8)	526	(7.0)	558	(7.0)
Tunisia	375	(2.3)	59	(1.7)	285	(3.6)	305	(3.2)	335	(2.8)	371	(2.6)	412	(3.2)	454	(4.4)	479	(5.2)
United Arab Emirates	416	(2.9)	97	(1.5)	274	(4.9)	300	(3.7)	345	(3.1)	406	(3.5)	479	(4.3)	551	(4.3)	590	(5.6)
Uruguay	434	(3.3)	92	(1.9)	292	(5.0)	319	(3.7)	367	(3.5)	429	(3.8)	499	(4.8)	557	(5.3)	590	(5.9)
Malaysia**	429	(3.6)	81	(2.1)	299	(4.7)	326	(4.0)	371	(4.0)	427	(4.4)	485	(4.8)	535	(5.7)	565	(6.1)

Note: Values that are statistically significant are indicated in bold (see Annex A3).
* See note at the beginning of this Annex.
**Malaysia: Coverage is too small to ensure comparability (see Annex A4).
StatLink http://dx.doi.org/10.1787/888933616788

[Part 2/3]

Table V.4.3a Mean score and variation in collaborative problem-solving performance, by gender

	Girls																	
	Mean score		Standard deviation		Percentiles													
					5th		10th		25th		Median (50th)		75th		90th		95th	
	Mean score	S.E.	S.D.	S.E.	Score	S.E.	Score	S.E.	Score	S.E.	Score	S.E.	Score	S.E.	Score	S.E.	Score	S.E.
OECD																		
Australia	552	(2.5)	100	(1.8)	379	(6.3)	420	(4.6)	486	(3.0)	556	(2.8)	622	(3.3)	678	(3.5)	710	(4.6)
Austria	521	(3.4)	96	(2.2)	358	(6.8)	395	(5.4)	456	(4.5)	525	(4.3)	589	(3.8)	643	(5.3)	675	(5.6)
Belgium	514	(2.9)	97	(1.8)	347	(5.3)	383	(4.5)	448	(4.0)	518	(3.2)	583	(3.4)	635	(3.8)	664	(4.7)
Canada	555	(2.4)	100	(1.2)	384	(4.5)	424	(4.6)	489	(3.0)	557	(3.1)	623	(2.8)	681	(3.8)	717	(4.0)
Chile	464	(3.1)	82	(1.6)	328	(4.5)	356	(3.9)	406	(3.8)	465	(4.0)	521	(4.0)	571	(4.5)	600	(5.6)
Czech Republic	512	(2.7)	87	(1.8)	365	(5.4)	397	(4.3)	453	(4.3)	515	(3.1)	573	(3.3)	621	(4.1)	649	(4.9)
Denmark	530	(3.3)	88	(1.5)	380	(5.5)	416	(4.7)	471	(4.2)	533	(3.8)	592	(3.8)	642	(4.6)	669	(6.1)
Estonia	549	(2.7)	86	(1.6)	402	(4.7)	435	(4.4)	491	(3.2)	551	(3.8)	608	(4.0)	659	(4.2)	688	(4.9)
Finland	559	(3.0)	94	(2.0)	397	(6.6)	436	(5.5)	499	(4.0)	565	(3.3)	623	(3.6)	675	(4.1)	706	(6.1)
France	508	(2.8)	96	(1.7)	344	(4.5)	380	(3.9)	444	(4.0)	513	(3.5)	577	(3.6)	628	(4.3)	658	(5.4)
Germany	540	(3.0)	98	(1.9)	372	(5.7)	409	(5.2)	474	(4.0)	543	(3.5)	608	(3.7)	663	(3.9)	696	(5.4)
Greece	475	(3.7)	88	(1.7)	328	(6.3)	358	(5.4)	415	(4.3)	476	(4.8)	538	(4.5)	589	(4.7)	618	(5.1)
Hungary	485	(2.8)	95	(1.9)	325	(6.2)	358	(4.9)	419	(4.2)	490	(3.7)	552	(3.6)	605	(4.2)	635	(4.5)
Iceland	512	(2.6)	91	(2.4)	364	(5.5)	393	(4.8)	450	(4.1)	514	(3.4)	575	(4.3)	628	(5.6)	659	(6.7)
Ireland	m	m	m	m	m	m	m	m	m	m	m	m	m	m	m	m	m	m
Israel	481	(4.7)	104	(2.3)	316	(6.4)	345	(5.8)	401	(6.6)	480	(6.0)	558	(5.4)	616	(5.7)	650	(5.1)
Italy	489	(3.4)	93	(2.1)	335	(4.9)	368	(5.2)	426	(4.9)	490	(3.9)	554	(4.0)	610	(5.3)	641	(6.6)
Japan	565	(2.6)	80	(2.3)	424	(6.4)	461	(4.6)	516	(3.3)	571	(2.7)	619	(2.9)	662	(4.2)	687	(4.8)
Korea	556	(3.3)	77	(1.8)	419	(6.1)	453	(5.8)	507	(4.3)	560	(3.3)	609	(3.9)	650	(3.6)	673	(4.8)
Latvia	505	(2.9)	85	(1.8)	361	(6.0)	393	(4.8)	448	(3.8)	507	(4.0)	563	(3.9)	614	(4.3)	642	(5.0)
Luxembourg	504	(1.9)	97	(1.7)	343	(5.3)	375	(4.0)	435	(3.1)	506	(3.4)	572	(2.5)	628	(3.3)	660	(4.8)
Mexico	440	(2.7)	76	(1.7)	316	(4.4)	343	(3.9)	388	(3.4)	440	(3.7)	492	(3.5)	537	(4.2)	564	(4.6)
Netherlands	531	(2.8)	93	(1.8)	372	(5.8)	407	(5.5)	468	(3.7)	534	(3.6)	597	(3.6)	648	(4.8)	680	(5.6)
New Zealand	553	(3.0)	99	(2.0)	386	(6.5)	421	(4.4)	486	(4.5)	556	(3.5)	624	(4.8)	678	(5.0)	711	(6.1)
Norway	518	(3.2)	89	(1.6)	371	(5.0)	402	(4.3)	458	(4.2)	518	(4.0)	579	(4.0)	631	(3.9)	662	(4.7)
Poland	m	m	m	m	m	m	m	m	m	m	m	m	m	m	m	m	m	m
Portugal	507	(2.7)	87	(1.6)	360	(5.1)	393	(4.3)	450	(3.4)	511	(3.3)	569	(3.7)	617	(4.1)	645	(4.8)
Slovak Republic	478	(3.4)	92	(2.3)	320	(6.3)	356	(5.4)	416	(4.8)	480	(3.6)	542	(4.5)	596	(5.8)	627	(6.4)
Slovenia	521	(2.2)	89	(2.1)	367	(5.9)	402	(4.9)	461	(3.5)	525	(3.0)	583	(3.9)	632	(3.8)	660	(6.3)
Spain	508	(2.6)	86	(1.5)	359	(5.6)	394	(4.8)	452	(3.6)	512	(3.1)	567	(2.5)	614	(3.5)	640	(4.0)
Sweden	531	(3.8)	93	(2.0)	371	(6.5)	408	(5.7)	469	(4.7)	535	(4.0)	596	(5.1)	647	(5.5)	678	(7.2)
Switzerland	m	m	m	m	m	m	m	m	m	m	m	m	m	m	m	m	m	m
Turkey	434	(4.1)	77	(2.1)	310	(5.2)	335	(4.9)	379	(4.8)	433	(4.8)	489	(4.7)	535	(4.7)	561	(6.3)
United Kingdom	536	(3.3)	101	(1.6)	365	(5.9)	403	(5.2)	469	(4.4)	539	(3.7)	607	(3.6)	664	(4.6)	700	(5.3)
United States	533	(4.0)	104	(2.4)	360	(5.1)	395	(5.3)	462	(5.1)	535	(4.6)	605	(4.5)	667	(5.9)	702	(6.4)
OECD average	515	(0.5)	91	(0.3)	360	(1.0)	394	(0.9)	453	(0.7)	517	(0.7)	578	(0.7)	630	(0.8)	660	(1.0)
Partners																		
Brazil	421	(2.6)	85	(1.7)	289	(3.4)	315	(2.9)	360	(2.6)	416	(2.9)	477	(3.4)	534	(4.4)	568	(5.8)
B-S-J-G (China)	508	(4.6)	96	(2.3)	344	(6.8)	380	(5.5)	443	(5.5)	510	(5.2)	575	(5.7)	630	(6.3)	661	(7.3)
Bulgaria	461	(3.9)	96	(2.1)	304	(6.8)	333	(5.1)	390	(5.3)	461	(5.2)	531	(4.7)	586	(4.3)	616	(5.7)
Colombia	433	(2.7)	83	(1.8)	304	(4.0)	329	(3.8)	374	(3.3)	430	(3.4)	490	(3.6)	543	(4.5)	575	(5.3)
Costa Rica	445	(2.7)	76	(1.4)	321	(5.0)	349	(3.5)	393	(2.9)	444	(3.2)	496	(3.6)	544	(4.2)	572	(3.9)
Croatia	486	(2.6)	84	(1.8)	346	(5.7)	376	(4.6)	429	(3.4)	488	(3.4)	545	(3.2)	592	(3.9)	621	(5.3)
Cyprus*	464	(2.2)	87	(1.5)	324	(4.1)	353	(3.8)	404	(3.3)	463	(3.2)	524	(3.5)	577	(4.0)	608	(4.5)
Dominican Republic	m	m	m	m	m	m	m	m	m	m	m	m	m	m	m	m	m	m
Hong Kong (China)	559	(3.4)	86	(1.9)	407	(7.1)	446	(5.6)	505	(4.2)	564	(3.9)	618	(3.6)	665	(4.3)	693	(5.1)
Lithuania	482	(2.8)	87	(1.9)	338	(5.3)	370	(4.6)	421	(3.9)	484	(3.3)	543	(3.1)	592	(4.8)	621	(5.6)
Macao (China)	553	(2.0)	82	(1.3)	412	(5.9)	447	(4.5)	499	(3.1)	556	(2.4)	610	(2.4)	654	(3.5)	681	(4.3)
Montenegro	429	(2.0)	77	(1.5)	305	(4.2)	330	(3.3)	374	(2.4)	428	(2.9)	483	(3.0)	530	(3.6)	556	(4.3)
Peru	421	(3.0)	83	(1.9)	289	(3.8)	315	(3.4)	361	(3.4)	419	(3.7)	479	(4.6)	533	(5.4)	562	(5.2)
Qatar	m	m	m	m	m	m	m	m	m	m	m	m	m	m	m	m	m	m
Russia	486	(3.9)	90	(2.2)	340	(7.2)	372	(5.1)	424	(4.7)	485	(4.5)	548	(5.3)	602	(5.8)	637	(7.2)
Singapore	572	(2.1)	93	(1.6)	411	(5.3)	449	(4.0)	512	(3.1)	577	(2.7)	637	(3.1)	687	(4.5)	715	(4.8)
Chinese Taipei	541	(3.4)	86	(1.9)	392	(4.7)	428	(4.8)	486	(4.5)	544	(3.7)	600	(4.3)	647	(5.0)	675	(5.4)
Thailand	451	(3.6)	82	(2.2)	324	(4.9)	349	(3.8)	392	(3.8)	447	(4.2)	505	(4.6)	560	(5.7)	593	(7.7)
Tunisia	387	(2.3)	58	(1.5)	297	(3.3)	316	(3.2)	346	(2.1)	384	(2.9)	424	(3.5)	463	(3.9)	489	(5.3)
United Arab Emirates	454	(3.1)	89	(1.5)	314	(4.6)	341	(3.7)	390	(3.7)	452	(3.8)	515	(4.0)	571	(4.0)	603	(4.6)
Uruguay	451	(2.7)	89	(1.5)	310	(5.0)	337	(3.4)	386	(3.1)	447	(3.3)	512	(3.3)	570	(4.2)	603	(5.5)
Malaysia**	450	(3.4)	77	(1.6)	323	(4.6)	349	(4.0)	397	(4.1)	451	(3.9)	503	(4.2)	548	(4.7)	573	(4.9)

Note: Values that are statistically significant are indicated in bold (see Annex A3).
* See note at the beginning of this Annex.
**Malaysia: Coverage is too small to ensure comparability (see Annex A4).
StatLink http://dx.doi.org/10.1787/888933616788

[Part 3/3]

Table V.4.3a Mean score and variation in collaborative problem-solving performance, by gender

		Gender difference (boys - girls)																	
		Mean score		Standard deviation		Percentiles													
						5th		10th		25th		Median (50th)		75th		90th		95th	
		Score dif.	S.E.	S.D. dif.	S.E.	Score dif.	S.E.	Score dif.	S.E.	Score dif.	S.E.	Score dif.	S.E.	Score dif.	S.E.	Score dif.	S.E.	Score dif.	S.E.
OECD	Australia	-41	(3.1)	8	(1.9)	-52	(6.6)	-56	(5.3)	-50	(4.1)	-40	(4.1)	-33	(3.9)	-31	(4.2)	-29	(5.3)
	Austria	-24	(4.4)	3	(2.7)	-24	(8.5)	-28	(6.6)	-29	(6.2)	-26	(5.7)	-20	(5.3)	-17	(7.0)	-17	(7.2)
	Belgium	-25	(3.7)	1	(2.0)	-25	(6.0)	-25	(5.5)	-28	(5.4)	-26	(4.3)	-24	(4.7)	-21	(4.6)	-21	(6.1)
	Canada	-39	(2.6)	4	(1.6)	-43	(5.3)	-46	(5.1)	-45	(3.7)	-39	(3.5)	-33	(3.7)	-33	(4.6)	-33	(5.6)
	Chile	-14	(3.0)	3	(2.1)	-17	(6.9)	-15	(5.3)	-16	(4.3)	-16	(4.6)	-11	(4.1)	-8	(5.2)	-8	(5.8)
	Czech Republic	-26	(3.6)	7	(2.0)	-36	(6.5)	-36	(5.1)	-32	(5.5)	-26	(4.3)	-21	(5.0)	-16	(5.7)	-14	(7.5)
	Denmark	-21	(3.5)	4	(2.4)	-24	(7.9)	-26	(6.1)	-23	(5.0)	-21	(4.4)	-19	(5.1)	-17	(5.9)	-13	(6.7)
	Estonia	-27	(2.8)	6	(1.8)	-36	(6.1)	-33	(4.8)	-33	(4.5)	-26	(4.6)	-20	(4.2)	-19	(5.4)	-18	(5.9)
	Finland	-48	(3.6)	9	(2.4)	-59	(7.9)	-61	(6.1)	-59	(4.8)	-51	(4.1)	-39	(4.9)	-34	(6.0)	-32	(8.8)
	France	-29	(3.9)	7	(2.1)	-34	(7.3)	-37	(6.2)	-38	(6.2)	-30	(5.1)	-23	(4.7)	-17	(5.2)	-15	(7.2)
	Germany	-30	(3.2)	3	(2.1)	-29	(5.9)	-33	(5.6)	-33	(4.6)	-32	(4.1)	-27	(4.1)	-23	(4.9)	-22	(7.6)
	Greece	-31	(3.7)	5	(2.0)	-34	(7.7)	-35	(6.0)	-37	(5.2)	-33	(5.5)	-28	(5.6)	-22	(5.3)	-20	(7.0)
	Hungary	-26	(4.1)	-1	(2.2)	-16	(7.8)	-20	(6.2)	-28	(5.9)	-32	(5.5)	-24	(5.4)	-23	(6.7)	-23	(6.5)
	Iceland	-27	(3.4)	6	(2.9)	-35	(7.4)	-34	(7.0)	-32	(5.5)	-28	(5.6)	-21	(5.5)	-19	(6.5)	-18	(8.0)
	Ireland	m	m	m	m	m	m	m	m	m	m	m	m	m	m	m	m	m	m
	Israel	-22	(5.4)	2	(2.6)	-16	(7.2)	-19	(6.7)	-27	(6.9)	-27	(7.1)	-19	(7.0)	-15	(7.9)	-15	(7.9)
	Italy	-23	(4.5)	4	(2.4)	-29	(7.9)	-29	(7.1)	-28	(6.1)	-24	(5.4)	-18	(5.3)	-17	(7.2)	-18	(7.8)
	Japan	-26	(3.7)	7	(2.4)	-38	(8.2)	-37	(6.1)	-33	(4.8)	-27	(4.3)	-21	(4.3)	-16	(6.7)	-14	(6.7)
	Korea	-33	(4.4)	10	(2.3)	-48	(8.3)	-47	(7.8)	-43	(6.4)	-32	(5.1)	-25	(5.2)	-19	(4.9)	-16	(6.1)
	Latvia	-40	(3.2)	4	(2.3)	-42	(8.0)	-44	(5.8)	-48	(4.9)	-43	(5.0)	-36	(4.7)	-33	(5.5)	-29	(6.3)
	Luxembourg	-25	(3.3)	4	(2.4)	-27	(7.1)	-27	(5.9)	-30	(4.7)	-28	(5.0)	-22	(4.4)	-17	(5.5)	-16	(6.7)
	Mexico	-14	(2.9)	6	(1.6)	-19	(6.2)	-20	(4.3)	-22	(3.7)	-15	(3.7)	-9	(3.8)	-3	(5.0)	-1	(6.2)
	Netherlands	-27	(3.3)	5	(2.3)	-28	(6.7)	-32	(5.7)	-34	(4.6)	-29	(4.8)	-23	(4.5)	-18	(6.5)	-17	(7.8)
	New Zealand	-41	(3.8)	9	(2.4)	-53	(8.3)	-54	(6.1)	-49	(6.3)	-40	(5.2)	-33	(5.2)	-26	(6.5)	-25	(9.1)
	Norway	-30	(3.7)	7	(2.3)	-42	(7.6)	-40	(6.1)	-37	(5.3)	-29	(4.8)	-25	(5.4)	-21	(5.1)	-20	(7.3)
	Poland	m	m	m	m	m	m	m	m	m	m	m	m	m	m	m	m	m	m
	Portugal	-19	(2.8)	7	(1.9)	-29	(5.9)	-29	(5.8)	-26	(4.5)	-18	(3.8)	-13	(3.7)	-9	(5.0)	-7	(5.9)
	Slovak Republic	-30	(4.2)	-1	(2.7)	-16	(7.1)	-23	(6.4)	-32	(6.4)	-35	(5.2)	-30	(5.4)	-28	(6.6)	-27	(8.0)
	Slovenia	-36	(2.6)	3	(2.4)	-35	(7.5)	-39	(5.9)	-43	(4.5)	-40	(4.4)	-33	(5.3)	-28	(5.5)	-24	(7.9)
	Spain	-22	(3.0)	3	(1.9)	-23	(7.4)	-27	(5.3)	-28	(3.7)	-25	(3.7)	-18	(3.8)	-14	(4.7)	-12	(5.1)
	Sweden	-42	(3.9)	6	(2.3)	-43	(7.4)	-48	(6.4)	-51	(4.8)	-46	(4.8)	-38	(5.6)	-31	(6.6)	-27	(9.0)
	Switzerland	m	m	m	m	m	m	m	m	m	m	m	m	m	m	m	m	m	m
	Turkey	-23	(4.3)	0	(2.4)	-20	(7.2)	-21	(6.3)	-23	(5.4)	-25	(5.3)	-25	(4.6)	-22	(5.3)	-20	(7.3)
	United Kingdom	-34	(3.5)	1	(2.4)	-30	(7.0)	-33	(5.7)	-36	(4.8)	-36	(4.2)	-34	(4.2)	-29	(7.1)	-31	(7.8)
	United States	-26	(4.3)	7	(2.8)	-33	(8.5)	-35	(7.9)	-34	(6.0)	-27	(4.9)	-19	(5.5)	-15	(6.5)	-14	(7.1)
	OECD average	-29	(0.6)	5	(0.4)	-32	(1.3)	-34	(1.1)	-35	(0.9)	-30	(0.8)	-24	(0.9)	-21	(1.0)	-19	(1.3)
Partners	Brazil	-18	(2.3)	4	(1.4)	-23	(4.2)	-21	(3.5)	-21	(2.6)	-20	(3.1)	-16	(3.5)	-11	(3.8)	-9	(5.0)
	B-S-J-G (China)	-22	(3.2)	0	(2.0)	-19	(7.3)	-22	(5.4)	-24	(5.4)	-21	(4.2)	-21	(4.1)	-22	(5.3)	-21	(6.2)
	Bulgaria	-31	(4.2)	1	(2.4)	-23	(7.7)	-24	(5.7)	-33	(5.2)	-38	(5.9)	-32	(6.5)	-24	(6.2)	-21	(7.9)
	Colombia	-8	(3.3)	0	(1.9)	-8	(5.9)	-8	(4.4)	-8	(4.0)	-8	(4.0)	-8	(4.9)	-9	(6.0)	-9	(6.9)
	Costa Rica	-7	(2.7)	3	(1.9)	-10	(6.3)	-11	(4.0)	-12	(3.3)	-8	(3.5)	-4	(4.0)	-3	(5.4)	-3	(5.8)
	Croatia	-27	(3.3)	5	(2.1)	-31	(7.0)	-31	(5.3)	-33	(4.9)	-29	(4.4)	-24	(4.3)	-17	(6.0)	-15	(6.5)
	Cyprus*	-40	(2.4)	5	(2.1)	-42	(5.9)	-43	(4.2)	-46	(3.8)	-44	(3.9)	-35	(4.1)	-30	(6.0)	-29	(6.9)
	Dominican Republic	m	m	m	m	m	m	m	m	m	m	m	m	m	m	m	m	m	m
	Hong Kong (China)	-36	(4.4)	5	(2.6)	-43	(9.5)	-44	(6.9)	-41	(5.7)	-36	(5.3)	-32	(5.4)	-29	(5.2)	-27	(7.5)
	Lithuania	-29	(3.1)	5	(2.0)	-32	(5.9)	-35	(4.7)	-34	(4.4)	-32	(4.4)	-23	(4.0)	-19	(5.0)	-16	(6.6)
	Macao (China)	-38	(2.9)	11	(2.0)	-58	(7.7)	-56	(7.0)	-46	(4.2)	-37	(3.8)	-30	(4.0)	-24	(5.6)	-21	(6.4)
	Montenegro	-26	(2.9)	1	(1.8)	-24	(5.4)	-25	(4.5)	-28	(3.6)	-29	(4.8)	-26	(3.9)	-21	(4.4)	-19	(5.4)
	Peru	-7	(3.0)	0	(1.9)	-4	(5.0)	-5	(4.1)	-7	(3.7)	-8	(3.9)	-9	(4.5)	-8	(5.7)	-3	(6.7)
	Qatar	m	m	m	m	m	m	m	m	m	m	m	m	m	m	m	m	m	m
	Russia	-25	(3.9)	3	(2.7)	-29	(7.7)	-31	(6.0)	-27	(5.3)	-26	(4.6)	-23	(5.2)	-20	(7.5)	-23	(8.1)
	Singapore	-20	(2.9)	7	(2.4)	-33	(7.1)	-30	(6.1)	-26	(5.1)	-19	(3.9)	-15	(4.8)	-13	(5.5)	-10	(6.7)
	Chinese Taipei	-28	(4.9)	6	(2.3)	-39	(6.5)	-38	(5.4)	-34	(5.7)	-27	(5.1)	-23	(6.2)	-20	(7.5)	-18	(8.2)
	Thailand	-35	(3.6)	-1	(2.4)	-31	(5.7)	-32	(4.3)	-35	(3.9)	-37	(4.9)	-35	(5.6)	-34	(7.0)	-34	(9.0)
	Tunisia	-12	(2.4)	1	(1.5)	-11	(4.3)	-11	(3.5)	-11	(2.8)	-13	(3.4)	-12	(4.0)	-9	(4.7)	-10	(5.1)
	United Arab Emirates	-38	(4.1)	8	(2.3)	-41	(5.7)	-41	(5.1)	-45	(4.7)	-46	(4.9)	-36	(5.8)	-20	(6.2)	-13	(7.7)
	Uruguay	-17	(3.9)	3	(2.1)	-18	(7.4)	-18	(5.4)	-20	(4.7)	-18	(4.8)	-13	(4.9)	-13	(6.0)	-13	(6.6)
	Malaysia**	-21	(2.7)	5	(1.5)	-24	(4.8)	-23	(3.9)	-25	(3.7)	-24	(3.9)	-19	(4.4)	-13	(4.4)	-8	(4.9)

Note: Values that are statistically significant are indicated in bold (see Annex A3).
* See note at the beginning of this Annex.
**Malaysia: Coverage is too small to ensure comparability (see Annex A4).
StatLink http://dx.doi.org/10.1787/888933616788

[Part 1/1]

Table V.4.3b Gender differences in relative performance in collaborative problem solving

After accounting for performance in science, reading and mathematics

		Score-point difference in relative performance[1] in collaborative problem solving (boys - girls)			
		Before accounting for students' socio-economic status		After accounting for students' socio-economic status	
		Score dif.	S.E.	Score dif.	S.E.
OECD	Australia	**-34**	(2.8)	**-34**	(2.8)
	Austria	**-31**	(3.3)	**-31**	(3.3)
	Belgium	**-30**	(2.3)	**-30**	(2.3)
	Canada	**-33**	(2.2)	**-33**	(2.2)
	Chile	**-21**	(2.2)	**-21**	(2.2)
	Czech Republic	**-29**	(3.2)	**-29**	(3.2)
	Denmark	**-21**	(3.1)	**-22**	(3.1)
	Estonia	**-26**	(2.5)	**-26**	(2.7)
	Finland	**-28**	(3.5)	**-28**	(3.6)
	France	**-25**	(3.2)	**-25**	(3.2)
	Germany	**-35**	(2.6)	**-37**	(2.7)
	Greece	**-20**	(2.4)	**-20**	(2.3)
	Hungary	**-24**	(3.1)	**-24**	(3.1)
	Iceland	**-15**	(2.8)	**-14**	(2.8)
	Ireland	m	m	m	m
	Israel	**-22**	(2.9)	**-24**	(3.1)
	Italy	**-34**	(2.7)	**-34**	(2.8)
	Japan	**-28**	(2.8)	**-29**	(2.8)
	Korea	**-18**	(3.3)	**-18**	(3.3)
	Latvia	**-25**	(2.5)	**-25**	(2.5)
	Luxembourg	**-24**	(3.2)	**-24**	(3.2)
	Mexico	**-15**	(2.5)	**-16**	(2.5)
	Netherlands	**-21**	(2.5)	**-22**	(2.6)
	New Zealand	**-39**	(3.2)	**-39**	(3.4)
	Norway	**-24**	(3.2)	**-24**	(3.4)
	Poland	m	m	m	m
	Portugal	**-20**	(2.5)	**-19**	(2.4)
	Slovak Republic	**-21**	(3.4)	**-21**	(3.3)
	Slovenia	**-24**	(2.9)	**-24**	(2.8)
	Spain	**-23**	(2.4)	**-23**	(2.4)
	Sweden	**-27**	(3.0)	**-27**	(3.1)
	Switzerland	m	m	m	m
	Turkey	**-17**	(3.3)	**-17**	(3.2)
	United Kingdom	**-30**	(2.3)	**-30**	(2.5)
	United States	**-27**	(4.0)	**-27**	(3.9)
	OECD average	**-25**	(0.5)	**-25**	(0.5)
Partners	Brazil	**-15**	(2.5)	**-15**	(2.4)
	B-S-J-G (China)	**-25**	(2.8)	**-25**	(2.7)
	Bulgaria	**-13**	(2.5)	**-13**	(2.5)
	Colombia	**-16**	(2.4)	**-16**	(2.5)
	Costa Rica	**-13**	(3.3)	**-13**	(3.3)
	Croatia	**-23**	(2.2)	**-24**	(2.4)
	Cyprus*	**-21**	(2.3)	**-21**	(2.4)
	Dominican Republic	m	m	m	m
	Hong Kong (China)	**-27**	(2.8)	**-28**	(2.8)
	Lithuania	**-19**	(2.8)	**-20**	(2.8)
	Macao (China)	**-23**	(2.4)	**-23**	(2.4)
	Montenegro	**-19**	(2.6)	**-19**	(2.6)
	Peru	**-11**	(2.0)	**-11**	(1.9)
	Qatar	m	m	m	m
	Russia	**-21**	(2.9)	**-21**	(2.9)
	Singapore	**-19**	(2.4)	**-19**	(2.5)
	Chinese Taipei	**-24**	(2.5)	**-24**	(2.6)
	Thailand	**-22**	(2.5)	**-24**	(2.4)
	Tunisia	**-13**	(2.2)	**-14**	(2.2)
	United Arab Emirates	**-14**	(2.9)	**-15**	(3.0)
	Uruguay	**-20**	(2.9)	**-20**	(2.9)
	Malaysia**	-14	(2.3)	-15	(2.4)

1. Relative performance refers to the residual performance, attributable to purely "collaborative problem-solving" competencies, after accounting for performance in science, reading and mathematics in a regression performed across students at the national level.
Note: Values that are statistically significant are indicated in bold (see Annex A3).
* See note at the beginning of this Annex.
**Malaysia: Coverage is too small to ensure comparability (see Annex A4).
StatLink http://dx.doi.org/10.1787/888933616788

[Part 1/2]

Table V.4.6a Performance in collaborative problem solving, by students' socio-economic status

		Mean ESCS[1]		National quarters of student ESCS							
				Bottom quarter		Second quarter		Third quarter		Top quarter	
		Mean index	S.E.	Mean index	S.E.	Mean index	S.E.	Mean index	S.E.	Mean index	S.E.
OECD	Australia	0.27	(0.01)	-0.81	(0.02)	0.06	(0.01)	0.65	(0.01)	1.18	(0.01)
	Austria	0.09	(0.02)	-0.97	(0.03)	-0.24	(0.02)	0.37	(0.03)	1.21	(0.02)
	Belgium	0.16	(0.02)	-1.05	(0.03)	-0.13	(0.03)	0.59	(0.03)	1.25	(0.02)
	Canada	0.53	(0.02)	-0.58	(0.02)	0.34	(0.02)	0.91	(0.02)	1.46	(0.01)
	Chile	-0.49	(0.03)	-1.86	(0.04)	-0.92	(0.03)	-0.12	(0.04)	0.96	(0.03)
	Czech Republic	-0.21	(0.01)	-1.19	(0.02)	-0.53	(0.02)	0.04	(0.02)	0.85	(0.02)
	Denmark	0.59	(0.02)	-0.64	(0.03)	0.41	(0.03)	1.07	(0.02)	1.53	(0.01)
	Estonia	0.05	(0.01)	-0.96	(0.02)	-0.25	(0.02)	0.39	(0.02)	1.01	(0.01)
	Finland	0.25	(0.02)	-0.73	(0.02)	-0.02	(0.03)	0.60	(0.03)	1.17	(0.02)
	France	-0.14	(0.02)	-1.17	(0.02)	-0.42	(0.02)	0.19	(0.02)	0.85	(0.02)
	Germany	0.12	(0.02)	-1.07	(0.02)	-0.24	(0.02)	0.43	(0.03)	1.36	(0.02)
	Greece	-0.08	(0.03)	-1.31	(0.03)	-0.47	(0.04)	0.32	(0.04)	1.14	(0.02)
	Hungary	-0.23	(0.02)	-1.44	(0.02)	-0.62	(0.03)	0.13	(0.03)	1.02	(0.02)
	Iceland	0.73	(0.01)	-0.28	(0.02)	0.57	(0.02)	1.10	(0.01)	1.55	(0.01)
	Ireland	0.16	(0.02)	-0.94	(0.02)	-0.15	(0.03)	0.52	(0.03)	1.21	(0.02)
	Israel	0.16	(0.03)	-0.99	(0.05)	0.00	(0.04)	0.55	(0.02)	1.10	(0.02)
	Italy	-0.07	(0.02)	-1.31	(0.02)	-0.38	(0.02)	0.27	(0.02)	1.16	(0.02)
	Japan	-0.18	(0.01)	-1.10	(0.02)	-0.44	(0.02)	0.08	(0.02)	0.72	(0.01)
	Korea	-0.20	(0.02)	-1.06	(0.02)	-0.45	(0.03)	0.04	(0.03)	0.68	(0.03)
	Latvia	-0.44	(0.02)	-1.62	(0.02)	-0.82	(0.03)	-0.03	(0.03)	0.72	(0.02)
	Luxembourg	0.07	(0.01)	-1.42	(0.02)	-0.26	(0.02)	0.56	(0.02)	1.41	(0.01)
	Mexico	-1.22	(0.04)	-2.73	(0.04)	-1.73	(0.04)	-0.86	(0.05)	0.42	(0.05)
	Netherlands	0.16	(0.02)	-0.85	(0.03)	-0.07	(0.02)	0.50	(0.02)	1.07	(0.02)
	New Zealand	0.17	(0.02)	-0.89	(0.02)	-0.06	(0.02)	0.52	(0.02)	1.09	(0.02)
	Norway	0.48	(0.02)	-0.53	(0.03)	0.33	(0.02)	0.82	(0.02)	1.31	(0.01)
	Poland	-0.39	(0.02)	-1.34	(0.02)	-0.81	(0.02)	-0.18	(0.03)	0.75	(0.02)
	Portugal	-0.39	(0.03)	-1.83	(0.02)	-0.88	(0.03)	0.00	(0.05)	1.16	(0.03)
	Slovak Republic	-0.11	(0.02)	-1.24	(0.04)	-0.47	(0.02)	0.18	(0.03)	1.10	(0.02)
	Slovenia	0.03	(0.01)	-1.04	(0.01)	-0.30	(0.02)	0.40	(0.02)	1.07	(0.01)
	Spain	-0.51	(0.04)	-2.05	(0.03)	-0.98	(0.04)	-0.04	(0.05)	1.03	(0.03)
	Sweden	0.33	(0.02)	-0.78	(0.03)	0.12	(0.03)	0.72	(0.02)	1.27	(0.01)
	Switzerland	0.14	(0.02)	-1.05	(0.03)	-0.18	(0.03)	0.50	(0.03)	1.30	(0.02)
	Turkey	-1.43	(0.05)	-2.87	(0.04)	-1.91	(0.05)	-1.06	(0.06)	0.14	(0.07)
	United Kingdom	0.21	(0.02)	-0.92	(0.02)	-0.09	(0.03)	0.58	(0.03)	1.27	(0.02)
	United States	0.10	(0.04)	-1.25	(0.06)	-0.18	(0.04)	0.55	(0.04)	1.29	(0.02)
	OECD average-32	-0.04	(0.00)	-1.20	(0.00)	-0.34	(0.00)	0.33	(0.01)	1.08	(0.00)
	OECD average-35	-0.04	(0.00)	-1.20	(0.00)	-0.35	(0.00)	0.32	(0.01)	1.08	(0.00)
Partners	Brazil	-0.96	(0.03)	-2.43	(0.03)	-1.36	(0.03)	-0.61	(0.03)	0.57	(0.04)
	B-S-J-G (China)	-1.07	(0.04)	-2.36	(0.03)	-1.57	(0.03)	-0.83	(0.06)	0.47	(0.07)
	Bulgaria	-0.08	(0.03)	-1.37	(0.04)	-0.46	(0.04)	0.37	(0.04)	1.14	(0.02)
	Colombia	-0.99	(0.04)	-2.41	(0.04)	-1.36	(0.03)	-0.62	(0.04)	0.44	(0.05)
	Costa Rica	-0.80	(0.04)	-2.29	(0.03)	-1.23	(0.04)	-0.41	(0.05)	0.73	(0.03)
	Croatia	-0.24	(0.02)	-1.22	(0.02)	-0.59	(0.02)	-0.03	(0.03)	0.89	(0.02)
	Cyprus*	0.20	(0.01)	-1.02	(0.01)	-0.15	(0.02)	0.62	(0.02)	1.33	(0.01)
	Dominican Republic	-0.90	(0.03)	-2.23	(0.04)	-1.27	(0.03)	-0.57	(0.03)	0.46	(0.03)
	Hong Kong (China)	-0.53	(0.03)	-1.73	(0.02)	-0.91	(0.03)	-0.18	(0.04)	0.69	(0.03)
	Lithuania	-0.06	(0.02)	-1.24	(0.02)	-0.37	(0.03)	0.38	(0.03)	0.97	(0.02)
	Macao (China)	-0.54	(0.01)	-1.59	(0.02)	-0.87	(0.01)	-0.30	(0.01)	0.60	(0.01)
	Montenegro	-0.18	(0.01)	-1.23	(0.01)	-0.48	(0.01)	0.13	(0.01)	0.88	(0.01)
	Peru	-1.08	(0.04)	-2.56	(0.03)	-1.58	(0.04)	-0.73	(0.05)	0.55	(0.05)
	Qatar	0.58	(0.01)	-0.47	(0.01)	0.47	(0.01)	0.89	(0.01)	1.42	(0.01)
	Russia	0.05	(0.02)	-0.95	(0.03)	-0.20	(0.03)	0.40	(0.03)	0.95	(0.02)
	Singapore	0.03	(0.01)	-1.22	(0.02)	-0.20	(0.02)	0.45	(0.02)	1.09	(0.01)
	Chinese Taipei	-0.21	(0.02)	-1.28	(0.02)	-0.51	(0.02)	0.11	(0.03)	0.84	(0.02)
	Thailand	-1.23	(0.04)	-2.53	(0.02)	-1.70	(0.03)	-0.98	(0.04)	0.29	(0.07)
	Tunisia	-0.83	(0.03)	-2.31	(0.04)	-1.24	(0.03)	-0.48	(0.04)	0.69	(0.04)
	United Arab Emirates	0.50	(0.01)	-0.49	(0.03)	0.37	(0.02)	0.79	(0.01)	1.32	(0.01)
	Uruguay	-0.78	(0.02)	-2.12	(0.02)	-1.25	(0.02)	-0.46	(0.03)	0.71	(0.04)
	Malaysia**	-0.47	(0.04)	-1.82	(0.04)	-0.91	(0.04)	-0.12	(0.05)	0.96	(0.04)

1. ESCS refers to the PISA index of economic, social and cultural status.
Note: Values that are statistically significant are indicated in bold (see Annex A3).
* See note at the beginning of this Annex.
**Malaysia: Coverage is too small to ensure comparability (see Annex A4).
StatLink http://dx.doi.org/10.1787/888933616788

[Part 2/2]

Table V.4.6a Performance in collaborative problem solving, by students' socio-economic status

	Performance in collaborative problem solving, by national quarter of student ESCS[1]												When accounting for students' socio-economic status			
	Mean		Bottom quarter		Second quarter		Third quarter		Top quarter		Difference (top - bottom quarter)		Change in collaborative problem-solving performance per unit of student ESCS		Explained variance in student performance (r-squared × 100)	
	Mean score	S.E.	Mean score	S.E.	Mean score	S.E.	Mean score	S.E.	Mean score	S.E.	Score dif.	S.E.	Score dif.	S.E.	%	S.E.
OECD																
Australia	531	(1.9)	498	(2.8)	522	(3.0)	544	(3.0)	570	(3.4)	72	(4.4)	35	(1.9)	6.7	(0.8)
Austria	509	(2.6)	474	(3.9)	497	(4.0)	523	(3.2)	548	(4.4)	74	(5.4)	35	(2.1)	9.0	(1.1)
Belgium	501	(2.4)	458	(3.9)	486	(3.0)	517	(3.3)	548	(3.7)	89	(5.2)	39	(2.0)	12.8	(1.2)
Canada	535	(2.3)	504	(3.3)	528	(2.9)	548	(3.5)	567	(3.1)	63	(4.1)	29	(1.7)	5.3	(0.6)
Chile	457	(2.7)	420	(3.6)	455	(4.1)	461	(3.8)	496	(4.0)	76	(5.0)	26	(1.5)	11.3	(1.3)
Czech Republic	499	(2.2)	461	(4.4)	488	(3.6)	509	(3.5)	539	(3.2)	78	(6.1)	38	(2.6)	11.2	(1.4)
Denmark	520	(2.5)	493	(3.5)	511	(3.6)	527	(4.1)	551	(3.8)	58	(4.8)	25	(2.0)	6.0	(0.9)
Estonia	535	(2.5)	508	(3.9)	529	(4.1)	542	(3.6)	565	(3.1)	56	(4.6)	26	(2.1)	5.0	(0.8)
Finland	534	(2.6)	504	(4.4)	522	(4.1)	543	(4.1)	566	(4.0)	62	(5.9)	33	(2.7)	5.8	(0.9)
France	494	(2.4)	454	(3.5)	480	(3.9)	508	(3.8)	543	(4.1)	90	(5.0)	44	(2.1)	12.3	(1.1)
Germany	525	(2.8)	497	(4.5)	524	(4.1)	539	(4.1)	571	(4.2)	74	(5.6)	29	(2.0)	7.6	(1.0)
Greece	459	(3.6)	427	(4.9)	448	(4.7)	465	(4.9)	497	(4.5)	71	(5.6)	28	(2.0)	8.3	(1.1)
Hungary	472	(2.4)	425	(3.8)	462	(4.0)	479	(3.9)	524	(3.9)	99	(5.5)	40	(1.9)	15.9	(1.3)
Iceland	499	(2.3)	485	(4.4)	494	(4.4)	508	(4.1)	515	(4.1)	29	(5.4)	17	(2.9)	1.7	(0.6)
Ireland	m	m	m	m	m	m	m	m	m	m	m	m	m	m	m	m
Israel	469	(3.6)	422	(5.4)	460	(4.9)	495	(5.5)	505	(4.5)	83	(7.0)	38	(2.9)	9.4	(1.4)
Italy	478	(2.5)	445	(4.3)	474	(3.5)	488	(3.5)	510	(3.7)	65	(5.4)	26	(1.9)	6.7	(1.0)
Japan	552	(2.7)	524	(3.5)	548	(3.7)	559	(3.7)	577	(3.1)	52	(4.0)	27	(2.0)	5.2	(0.7)
Korea	538	(2.5)	515	(3.5)	530	(3.4)	546	(3.9)	563	(4.2)	49	(5.3)	28	(2.6)	5.1	(1.0)
Latvia	485	(2.3)	458	(3.5)	476	(3.7)	494	(4.1)	513	(3.5)	55	(5.0)	23	(2.1)	5.6	(0.9)
Luxembourg	491	(1.5)	448	(3.3)	480	(3.3)	501	(3.1)	541	(3.1)	93	(4.4)	30	(1.4)	11.3	(0.9)
Mexico	433	(2.5)	400	(3.6)	423	(3.2)	443	(3.9)	468	(3.8)	68	(5.1)	22	(1.4)	11.1	(1.4)
Netherlands	518	(2.4)	489	(3.5)	504	(3.7)	525	(3.7)	555	(4.5)	66	(5.8)	33	(2.7)	6.6	(1.1)
New Zealand	533	(2.4)	496	(4.8)	528	(4.8)	547	(4.0)	572	(4.2)	76	(6.9)	37	(3.2)	7.4	(1.2)
Norway	502	(2.5)	479	(3.5)	497	(3.7)	512	(4.2)	527	(3.6)	47	(4.2)	25	(2.1)	3.8	(0.6)
Poland	m	m	m	m	m	m	m	m	m	m	m	m	m	m	m	m
Portugal	498	(2.6)	465	(3.7)	489	(3.7)	502	(4.4)	538	(4.5)	73	(5.4)	23	(1.7)	8.8	(1.3)
Slovak Republic	463	(2.4)	427	(4.2)	455	(2.8)	470	(3.3)	503	(4.4)	76	(5.9)	30	(2.1)	9.7	(1.2)
Slovenia	502	(1.8)	472	(3.7)	487	(3.4)	512	(3.3)	538	(2.9)	67	(5.0)	32	(2.1)	8.0	(1.0)
Spain	496	(2.1)	469	(3.5)	486	(3.2)	505	(3.2)	528	(3.2)	59	(4.5)	20	(1.3)	7.0	(0.9)
Sweden	510	(3.4)	477	(3.5)	497	(4.0)	527	(4.3)	546	(5.9)	69	(5.9)	33	(2.5)	7.7	(1.1)
Switzerland	m	m	m	m	m	m	m	m	m	m	m	m	m	m	m	m
Turkey	422	(3.4)	398	(4.8)	416	(4.1)	424	(4.0)	453	(6.4)	55	(7.4)	19	(2.0)	7.9	(1.7)
United Kingdom	519	(2.7)	489	(3.6)	503	(4.6)	532	(3.7)	559	(4.2)	69	(5.2)	30	(2.2)	6.3	(0.9)
United States	520	(3.6)	486	(4.4)	503	(4.3)	533	(6.0)	565	(5.3)	79	(6.5)	29	(2.1)	7.5	(1.0)
OECD average-32	500	(0.5)	468	(0.7)	491	(0.7)	510	(0.7)	536	(0.7)	69	(1.0)	30	(0.4)	7.9	(0.2)
OECD average-35	m	m	m	m	m	m	m	m	m	m	m	m	m	m	m	m
Partners																
Brazil	412	(2.3)	384	(2.6)	403	(2.5)	414	(3.3)	454	(4.7)	70	(5.0)	23	(1.4)	9.5	(1.1)
B-S-J-G (China)	496	(4.0)	447	(4.8)	485	(5.4)	504	(4.5)	549	(7.4)	101	(8.6)	35	(2.4)	15.9	(2.2)
Bulgaria	444	(3.9)	398	(5.5)	429	(4.9)	460	(4.9)	495	(4.4)	97	(6.4)	37	(2.1)	14.2	(1.4)
Colombia	429	(2.3)	392	(3.2)	414	(3.2)	436	(3.2)	474	(4.8)	82	(6.0)	29	(1.7)	14.8	(1.8)
Costa Rica	441	(2.4)	416	(3.3)	427	(3.1)	444	(3.7)	478	(4.1)	63	(5.1)	21	(1.6)	10.0	(1.4)
Croatia	473	(2.5)	446	(3.6)	461	(3.7)	475	(3.5)	511	(4.2)	64	(5.2)	31	(2.1)	8.6	(1.0)
Cyprus*	444	(1.7)	423	(3.4)	436	(3.3)	447	(3.3)	473	(3.9)	50	(5.2)	20	(2.1)	4.1	(0.8)
Dominican Republic	m	m	m	m	m	m	m	m	m	m	m	m	m	m	m	m
Hong Kong (China)	541	(2.9)	525	(3.9)	539	(4.0)	542	(4.2)	560	(4.7)	35	(6.0)	14	(2.2)	2.1	(0.6)
Lithuania	467	(2.5)	434	(3.3)	455	(3.1)	479	(4.5)	505	(3.7)	71	(4.9)	31	(2.2)	8.5	(1.1)
Macao (China)	534	(1.2)	524	(3.0)	535	(2.7)	536	(3.2)	541	(3.0)	17	(4.5)	8	(1.9)	0.6	(0.3)
Montenegro	416	(1.3)	395	(2.2)	412	(2.6)	420	(2.5)	438	(2.4)	43	(3.5)	19	(1.4)	4.1	(0.6)
Peru	418	(2.5)	364	(2.7)	409	(3.8)	431	(3.7)	467	(4.7)	103	(5.5)	32	(1.6)	21.6	(1.8)
Qatar	m	m	m	m	m	m	m	m	m	m	m	m	m	m	m	m
Russia	473	(3.4)	440	(4.4)	468	(5.0)	489	(5.2)	502	(4.2)	62	(5.4)	31	(2.7)	6.3	(1.0)
Singapore	561	(1.2)	519	(2.7)	552	(2.8)	575	(3.1)	600	(3.2)	81	(4.2)	33	(1.7)	9.8	(0.9)
Chinese Taipei	527	(2.5)	495	(3.8)	517	(3.2)	535	(3.8)	560	(4.2)	65	(5.8)	30	(2.5)	7.5	(1.1)
Thailand	436	(3.5)	414	(4.0)	419	(3.6)	436	(4.4)	477	(7.7)	64	(8.7)	24	(2.5)	9.7	(2.0)
Tunisia	382	(1.9)	363	(2.4)	372	(2.6)	381	(2.8)	412	(4.1)	48	(4.5)	16	(1.5)	9.2	(1.5)
United Arab Emirates	435	(2.4)	402	(3.2)	430	(3.8)	453	(3.0)	459	(3.1)	58	(3.8)	28	(1.8)	4.9	(0.6)
Uruguay	443	(2.3)	407	(3.0)	428	(3.3)	449	(3.9)	489	(4.5)	82	(5.4)	29	(1.7)	12.4	(1.4)
Malaysia**	440	(3.3)	408	(4.2)	428	(3.6)	448	(5.0)	476	(5.4)	68	(6.2)	24	(1.9)	10.8	(1.5)

1. ESCS refers to the PISA index of economic, social and cultural status.
Note: Values that are statistically significant are indicated in bold (see Annex A3).
* See note at the beginning of this Annex.
**Malaysia: Coverage is too small to ensure comparability (see Annex A4).
StatLink http://dx.doi.org/10.1787/888933616788

[Part 1/2]

Table V.4.6b Performance in collaborative problem solving, by schools' socio-economic profile

		Mean ESCS[1]		National quarters of school ESCS							
				Bottom quarter		Second quarter		Third quarter		Top quarter	
		Mean index	S.E.	Mean index	S.E.	Mean index	S.E.	Mean index	S.E.	Mean index	S.E.
OECD	Australia	0.27	(0.01)	-0.30	(0.02)	0.13	(0.02)	0.44	(0.01)	0.81	(0.02)
	Austria	0.09	(0.02)	-0.48	(0.03)	-0.10	(0.03)	0.24	(0.03)	0.71	(0.03)
	Belgium	0.16	(0.02)	-0.48	(0.04)	0.01	(0.03)	0.35	(0.02)	0.79	(0.03)
	Canada	0.53	(0.02)	0.05	(0.02)	0.42	(0.02)	0.67	(0.02)	0.99	(0.02)
	Chile	-0.49	(0.03)	-1.35	(0.04)	-0.84	(0.04)	-0.26	(0.05)	0.50	(0.04)
	Czech Republic	-0.21	(0.01)	-0.72	(0.02)	-0.39	(0.02)	-0.12	(0.03)	0.41	(0.02)
	Denmark	0.59	(0.02)	0.09	(0.03)	0.47	(0.02)	0.73	(0.03)	1.08	(0.03)
	Estonia	0.05	(0.01)	-0.44	(0.03)	-0.08	(0.02)	0.15	(0.02)	0.56	(0.02)
	Finland	0.25	(0.02)	-0.10	(0.03)	0.14	(0.02)	0.32	(0.03)	0.66	(0.04)
	France	-0.14	(0.02)	-0.72	(0.02)	-0.27	(0.02)	0.02	(0.03)	0.43	(0.03)
	Germany	0.12	(0.02)	-0.50	(0.03)	-0.07	(0.03)	0.28	(0.03)	0.77	(0.03)
	Greece	-0.08	(0.03)	-0.72	(0.04)	-0.23	(0.04)	0.08	(0.03)	0.56	(0.04)
	Hungary	-0.23	(0.02)	-1.03	(0.03)	-0.44	(0.03)	-0.01	(0.04)	0.58	(0.03)
	Iceland	0.73	(0.00)	0.35	(0.00)	0.68	(0.00)	0.84	(0.00)	1.06	(0.00)
	Ireland	0.16	(0.02)	-0.29	(0.03)	0.02	(0.02)	0.25	(0.03)	0.66	(0.05)
	Israel	0.16	(0.03)	-0.38	(0.06)	0.05	(0.04)	0.33	(0.02)	0.66	(0.03)
	Italy	-0.07	(0.02)	-0.69	(0.03)	-0.25	(0.03)	0.09	(0.02)	0.58	(0.03)
	Japan	-0.18	(0.01)	-0.63	(0.02)	-0.32	(0.02)	-0.06	(0.02)	0.27	(0.02)
	Korea	-0.20	(0.02)	-0.59	(0.03)	-0.33	(0.02)	-0.12	(0.03)	0.25	(0.04)
	Latvia	-0.44	(0.02)	-1.04	(0.03)	-0.62	(0.03)	-0.29	(0.04)	0.20	(0.02)
	Luxembourg	0.07	(0.00)	-0.58	(0.00)	-0.24	(0.00)	0.22	(0.00)	0.90	(0.00)
	Mexico	-1.22	(0.04)	-2.22	(0.06)	-1.47	(0.05)	-1.02	(0.04)	-0.19	(0.07)
	Netherlands	0.16	(0.02)	-0.31	(0.04)	0.03	(0.02)	0.28	(0.02)	0.64	(0.03)
	New Zealand	0.17	(0.02)	-0.28	(0.02)	0.02	(0.02)	0.29	(0.03)	0.63	(0.03)
	Norway	0.48	(0.02)	0.14	(0.03)	0.40	(0.02)	0.56	(0.02)	0.83	(0.03)
	Poland	-0.39	(0.02)	-0.85	(0.03)	-0.53	(0.03)	-0.29	(0.02)	0.10	(0.04)
	Portugal	-0.39	(0.03)	-1.14	(0.04)	-0.60	(0.04)	-0.26	(0.05)	0.44	(0.05)
	Slovak Republic	-0.11	(0.02)	-0.81	(0.05)	-0.22	(0.02)	0.06	(0.03)	0.54	(0.03)
	Slovenia	0.03	(0.00)	-0.51	(0.01)	-0.16	(0.01)	0.17	(0.01)	0.63	(0.00)
	Spain	-0.51	(0.04)	-1.32	(0.04)	-0.81	(0.05)	-0.39	(0.05)	0.47	(0.07)
	Sweden	0.33	(0.02)	-0.08	(0.03)	0.21	(0.03)	0.43	(0.02)	0.79	(0.03)
	Switzerland	0.14	(0.02)	-0.36	(0.03)	-0.03	(0.03)	0.21	(0.04)	0.75	(0.04)
	Turkey	-1.43	(0.05)	-2.22	(0.06)	-1.62	(0.05)	-1.26	(0.05)	-0.61	(0.10)
	United Kingdom	0.21	(0.02)	-0.30	(0.02)	0.04	(0.03)	0.32	(0.03)	0.77	(0.04)
	United States	0.10	(0.04)	-0.60	(0.07)	-0.04	(0.04)	0.28	(0.04)	0.77	(0.04)
	OECD average-32	-0.04	(0.00)	-0.62	(0.01)	-0.20	(0.01)	0.10	(0.01)	0.58	(0.01)
	OECD average-35	-0.04	(0.00)	-0.61	(0.01)	-0.20	(0.00)	0.10	(0.01)	0.57	(0.01)
Partners	Brazil	-0.96	(0.03)	-1.76	(0.03)	-1.21	(0.03)	-0.86	(0.03)	0.00	(0.05)
	B-S-J-G (China)	-1.07	(0.04)	-1.89	(0.03)	-1.41	(0.05)	-0.95	(0.06)	-0.04	(0.10)
	Bulgaria	-0.08	(0.03)	-0.85	(0.05)	-0.26	(0.04)	0.14	(0.04)	0.64	(0.03)
	Colombia	-0.99	(0.04)	-1.83	(0.05)	-1.26	(0.03)	-0.90	(0.04)	0.03	(0.07)
	Costa Rica	-0.80	(0.04)	-1.62	(0.05)	-1.08	(0.04)	-0.72	(0.04)	0.21	(0.07)
	Croatia	-0.24	(0.02)	-0.69	(0.02)	-0.42	(0.02)	-0.17	(0.02)	0.32	(0.04)
	Cyprus*	0.20	(0.00)	-0.38	(0.00)	0.04	(0.00)	0.30	(0.00)	0.83	(0.00)
	Dominican Republic	-0.90	(0.03)	-1.56	(0.04)	-1.17	(0.04)	-0.81	(0.05)	-0.06	(0.05)
	Hong Kong (China)	-0.53	(0.03)	-1.05	(0.02)	-0.81	(0.03)	-0.44	(0.04)	0.16	(0.06)
	Lithuania	-0.06	(0.02)	-0.67	(0.03)	-0.20	(0.03)	0.09	(0.03)	0.52	(0.04)
	Macao (China)	-0.54	(0.00)	-1.06	(0.00)	-0.76	(0.00)	-0.49	(0.00)	0.15	(0.00)
	Montenegro	-0.18	(0.00)	-0.58	(0.01)	-0.31	(0.00)	-0.06	(0.00)	0.25	(0.00)
	Peru	-1.08	(0.04)	-2.19	(0.04)	-1.40	(0.05)	-0.80	(0.05)	0.07	(0.07)
	Qatar	0.58	(0.00)	0.09	(0.00)	0.51	(0.00)	0.71	(0.00)	1.00	(0.00)
	Russia	0.05	(0.02)	-0.47	(0.04)	-0.03	(0.03)	0.20	(0.03)	0.49	(0.02)
	Singapore	0.03	(0.01)	-0.51	(0.00)	-0.21	(0.00)	0.13	(0.02)	0.71	(0.01)
	Chinese Taipei	-0.21	(0.02)	-0.72	(0.03)	-0.36	(0.03)	-0.11	(0.03)	0.33	(0.04)
	Thailand	-1.23	(0.04)	-1.99	(0.04)	-1.53	(0.04)	-1.13	(0.05)	-0.26	(0.10)
	Tunisia	-0.83	(0.03)	-1.62	(0.05)	-1.09	(0.04)	-0.68	(0.04)	0.05	(0.07)
	United Arab Emirates	0.50	(0.01)	0.04	(0.03)	0.38	(0.02)	0.62	(0.01)	0.96	(0.01)
	Uruguay	-0.78	(0.02)	-1.46	(0.02)	-1.12	(0.03)	-0.71	(0.03)	0.18	(0.06)
	Malaysia**	-0.47	(0.04)	-1.20	(0.05)	-0.70	(0.05)	-0.30	(0.06)	0.32	(0.06)

1. ESCS refers to the PISA index of economic, social and cultural status.
Note: Values that are statistically significant are indicated in bold (see Annex A3).
* See note at the beginning of this Annex.
**Malaysia: Coverage is too small to ensure comparability (see Annex A4).
StatLink http://dx.doi.org/10.1787/888933616788

[Part 2/2]

Table V.4.6b Performance in collaborative problem solving, by schools' socio-economic profile

	Performance in collaborative problem solving, by national quarter of school ESCS[1]												When accounting for schools' socio-economic profile			
	Mean		Bottom quarter		Second quarter		Third quarter		Top quarter		Difference (top - bottom quarter)		Change in collaborative problem-solving performance per unit of school ESCS		Explained variance in student performance (r-squared × 100)	
	Mean score	S.E.	Mean score	S.E.	Mean score	S.E.	Mean score	S.E.	Mean score	S.E.	Score dif.	S.E.	Score dif.	S.E.	%	S.E.
OECD																
Australia	531	(1.9)	496	(4.1)	523	(4.5)	540	(4.0)	575	(3.7)	**80**	(5.4)	**70**	(4.3)	8.1	(1.0)
Austria	509	(2.6)	451	(5.0)	492	(7.7)	534	(5.5)	564	(4.4)	**113**	(6.7)	**93**	(5.0)	19.9	(1.8)
Belgium	501	(2.4)	440	(5.1)	482	(5.0)	523	(5.6)	564	(4.5)	**124**	(7.1)	**99**	(4.9)	24.4	(2.0)
Canada	535	(2.3)	505	(3.9)	530	(4.2)	545	(4.8)	566	(4.2)	**61**	(5.4)	**64**	(4.5)	5.1	(0.7)
Chile	457	(2.7)	413	(5.0)	441	(4.9)	472	(6.8)	505	(5.4)	**92**	(7.5)	**47**	(2.5)	17.5	(1.7)
Czech Republic	499	(2.2)	451	(5.1)	483	(4.7)	505	(5.0)	558	(4.0)	**107**	(6.7)	**90**	(4.9)	19.5	(1.9)
Denmark	520	(2.5)	497	(4.1)	511	(5.1)	528	(5.3)	547	(5.2)	**50**	(6.5)	**51**	(6.1)	4.9	(1.2)
Estonia	535	(2.5)	510	(5.0)	527	(6.3)	541	(4.3)	567	(4.4)	**58**	(6.4)	**62**	(5.6)	7.1	(1.3)
Finland	534	(2.6)	518	(5.5)	527	(5.6)	540	(4.6)	551	(5.2)	**33**	(7.6)	**52**	(9.2)	2.4	(0.9)
France	494	(2.4)	423	(6.7)	485	(6.1)	528	(4.8)	549	(4.0)	**126**	(7.4)	**110**	(4.5)	23.8	(1.9)
Germany	525	(2.8)	473	(5.6)	511	(6.9)	562	(6.8)	585	(4.2)	**112**	(7.3)	**88**	(5.0)	18.6	(2.0)
Greece	459	(3.6)	404	(8.0)	455	(6.5)	475	(4.4)	503	(5.7)	**99**	(9.3)	**73**	(5.5)	15.9	(2.2)
Hungary	472	(2.4)	395	(4.5)	453	(5.6)	497	(5.7)	545	(4.9)	**149**	(6.7)	**91**	(3.6)	34.9	(1.9)
Iceland	499	(2.3)	491	(4.0)	497	(3.7)	502	(4.5)	511	(4.1)	**20**	(5.9)	**28**	(6.6)	0.7	(0.3)
Ireland	m	m	m	m	m	m	m	m	m	m	m	m	m	m	m	m
Israel	469	(3.6)	403	(10.5)	452	(10.4)	500	(7.1)	534	(6.6)	**131**	(12.8)	**113**	(11.0)	21.0	(2.9)
Italy	478	(2.5)	418	(6.3)	474	(6.0)	502	(6.7)	524	(4.7)	**106**	(7.8)	**80**	(4.3)	17.2	(1.7)
Japan	552	(2.7)	511	(4.9)	540	(6.2)	565	(8.0)	592	(5.1)	**81**	(7.0)	**89**	(6.4)	13.4	(1.8)
Korea	538	(2.5)	501	(5.2)	535	(4.9)	548	(5.5)	569	(5.3)	**68**	(7.7)	**81**	(6.8)	10.1	(1.9)
Latvia	485	(2.3)	456	(4.8)	476	(4.1)	492	(4.8)	518	(4.7)	**62**	(6.7)	**49**	(4.4)	7.0	(1.3)
Luxembourg	491	(1.5)	439	(2.6)	470	(2.6)	504	(2.7)	556	(3.2)	**117**	(4.1)	**79**	(2.6)	21.2	(1.2)
Mexico	433	(2.5)	393	(4.4)	418	(5.2)	442	(5.7)	481	(5.0)	**87**	(7.3)	**40**	(2.6)	16.7	(1.9)
Netherlands	518	(2.4)	456	(5.2)	491	(7.0)	541	(6.7)	584	(4.6)	**128**	(6.9)	**121**	(9.8)	22.5	(2.4)
New Zealand	533	(2.4)	498	(5.8)	525	(5.4)	547	(6.3)	573	(4.8)	**75**	(7.7)	**79**	(7.1)	7.1	(1.2)
Norway	502	(2.5)	489	(4.5)	500	(5.7)	506	(5.4)	520	(4.7)	**31**	(6.4)	**43**	(7.7)	1.6	(0.6)
Poland	m	m	m	m	m	m	m	m	m	m	m	m	m	m	m	m
Portugal	498	(2.6)	454	(5.0)	495	(5.5)	511	(5.8)	535	(4.2)	**81**	(6.2)	**49**	(3.9)	11.1	(1.7)
Slovak Republic	463	(2.4)	412	(4.5)	445	(4.5)	469	(4.8)	528	(5.7)	**116**	(7.2)	**75**	(6.0)	20.5	(1.8)
Slovenia	502	(1.8)	446	(2.7)	481	(3.9)	522	(4.2)	559	(3.5)	**113**	(4.4)	**101**	(3.7)	23.9	(1.5)
Spain	496	(2.1)	473	(4.6)	490	(4.4)	505	(5.4)	521	(4.4)	**49**	(5.9)	**27**	(2.8)	4.6	(0.9)
Sweden	510	(3.4)	480	(4.2)	502	(4.9)	511	(6.2)	553	(7.4)	**73**	(7.7)	**82**	(8.5)	8.1	(1.7)
Switzerland	m	m	m	m	m	m	m	m	m	m	m	m	m	m	m	m
Turkey	422	(3.4)	378	(5.5)	403	(6.7)	442	(9.4)	469	(7.2)	**91**	(9.6)	**55**	(4.8)	20.7	(3.3)
United Kingdom	519	(2.7)	485	(5.6)	508	(5.3)	523	(5.8)	568	(5.0)	**83**	(7.9)	**74**	(5.6)	8.8	(1.5)
United States	520	(3.6)	478	(6.7)	512	(6.4)	533	(7.1)	563	(6.2)	**86**	(8.8)	**55**	(5.8)	7.9	(1.4)
OECD average-32	500	(0.5)	457	(0.9)	489	(1.0)	514	(1.0)	545	(0.9)	**88**	(1.3)	**72**	(1.0)	13.9	(0.3)
OECD average-35	m	m	m	m	m	m	m	m	m	m	m	m	m	m	m	m
Partners																
Brazil	412	(2.3)	375	(3.4)	400	(4.5)	411	(4.2)	468	(5.5)	**92**	(6.2)	**51**	(2.5)	16.6	(1.7)
B-S-J-G (China)	496	(4.0)	429	(6.1)	472	(8.1)	523	(8.9)	560	(8.0)	**131**	(9.9)	**70**	(3.1)	27.6	(2.8)
Bulgaria	444	(3.9)	376	(6.7)	415	(7.2)	469	(7.2)	522	(5.8)	**147**	(9.0)	**97**	(5.5)	33.2	(2.7)
Colombia	429	(2.3)	385	(4.7)	413	(4.2)	436	(4.1)	483	(5.4)	**98**	(7.1)	**52**	(2.8)	21.2	(2.2)
Costa Rica	441	(2.4)	413	(3.8)	426	(5.5)	442	(4.7)	483	(5.5)	**70**	(6.9)	**39**	(3.1)	13.5	(1.9)
Croatia	473	(2.5)	432	(6.7)	456	(7.8)	478	(5.8)	527	(5.0)	**94**	(8.3)	**90**	(6.5)	16.9	(2.0)
Cyprus*	444	(1.7)	404	(3.1)	449	(3.0)	450	(3.9)	476	(3.1)	**73**	(4.2)	**57**	(3.1)	8.6	(0.9)
Dominican Republic	m	m	m	m	m	m	m	m	m	m	m	m	m	m	m	m
Hong Kong (China)	541	(2.9)	505	(6.9)	529	(6.7)	558	(8.2)	574	(4.7)	**70**	(8.6)	**50**	(6.1)	7.3	(1.6)
Lithuania	467	(2.5)	424	(4.3)	457	(5.0)	472	(5.5)	519	(5.5)	**95**	(7.4)	**79**	(4.8)	16.3	(2.0)
Macao (China)	534	(1.2)	518	(2.5)	546	(2.8)	536	(2.8)	536	(3.0)	**18**	(4.1)	**16**	(3.3)	0.8	(0.3)
Montenegro	416	(1.3)	383	(2.8)	400	(2.5)	427	(2.4)	455	(2.7)	**72**	(3.6)	**87**	(3.9)	13.2	(1.1)
Peru	418	(2.5)	360	(3.3)	399	(5.8)	431	(3.8)	480	(6.5)	**120**	(7.5)	**51**	(2.3)	29.3	(2.1)
Qatar	m	m	m	m	m	m	m	m	m	m	m	m	m	m	m	m
Russia	473	(3.4)	433	(5.6)	463	(5.3)	485	(6.2)	517	(6.8)	**84**	(8.5)	**80**	(7.1)	10.7	(1.7)
Singapore	561	(1.2)	519	(2.9)	537	(2.7)	572	(3.8)	618	(5.1)	**99**	(6.1)	**77**	(3.9)	14.5	(1.2)
Chinese Taipei	527	(2.5)	479	(5.6)	515	(5.3)	537	(4.6)	575	(6.7)	**96**	(9.2)	**89**	(5.8)	16.1	(2.2)
Thailand	436	(3.5)	404	(5.1)	413	(7.0)	439	(7.0)	491	(6.8)	**87**	(8.5)	**50**	(3.7)	17.5	(2.9)
Tunisia	382	(1.9)	357	(4.1)	370	(5.1)	386	(5.0)	415	(4.6)	**58**	(6.1)	**36**	(3.7)	16.1	(2.9)
United Arab Emirates	435	(2.4)	394	(6.0)	420	(6.4)	445	(5.4)	486	(4.7)	**92**	(7.6)	**99**	(6.1)	14.2	(1.7)
Uruguay	443	(2.3)	398	(4.4)	416	(4.0)	464	(6.0)	495	(5.2)	**97**	(6.7)	**59**	(2.9)	18.5	(1.8)
Malaysia**	440	(3.3)	406	(4.6)	427	(6.6)	448	(6.8)	479	(7.4)	**74**	(9.0)	**49**	(4.4)	13.2	(2.5)

1. ESCS refers to the PISA index of economic, social and cultural status.
Note: Values that are statistically significant are indicated in bold (see Annex A3).
* See note at the beginning of this Annex.
**Malaysia: Coverage is too small to ensure comparability (see Annex A4).
StatLink http://dx.doi.org/10.1787/888933616788

[Part 1/1]

Table V.4.6c Impact of socio-economic status on collaborative problem-solving performance

Results based on students' self-reports

	When accounting for students' socio-economic status				When accounting for schools' socio-economic profile[1]				When accounting for students' and schools' socio-economic profile					
	Change in collaborative problem-solving score per unit of student ESCS		Explained variance in student performance (r-squared × 100)		Change in collaborative problem-solving score per unit of school ESCS		Explained variance in student performance (r-squared × 100)		Change in collaborative problem-solving score per unit of student ESCS		Change in collaborative problem-solving score per unit of school ESCS		Explained variance in student performance (r-squared × 100)	
	Score dif.	S.E.	%	S.E.	Score dif.	S.E.	%	S.E.	Score dif.	S.E.	Score dif.	S.E.	%	S.E.
OECD														
Australia	35	(1.9)	6.7	(0.8)	70	(4.3)	8.1	(1.0)	20	(2.0)	50	(4.8)	9.6	(1.0)
Austria	35	(2.1)	9.0	(1.1)	93	(5.0)	19.9	(1.8)	9	(1.8)	84	(5.2)	20.3	(1.8)
Belgium	39	(2.0)	12.8	(1.2)	99	(4.9)	24.4	(2.0)	14	(1.6)	85	(5.2)	25.6	(2.0)
Canada	29	(1.7)	5.3	(0.6)	64	(4.5)	5.1	(0.7)	20	(1.7)	44	(4.8)	7.1	(0.8)
Chile	26	(1.5)	11.3	(1.3)	47	(2.5)	17.5	(1.7)	7	(1.5)	40	(2.8)	17.9	(1.7)
Czech Republic	38	(2.6)	11.2	(1.4)	90	(4.9)	19.5	(1.9)	14	(2.4)	75	(4.7)	20.6	(2.0)
Denmark	25	(2.0)	6.0	(0.9)	51	(6.1)	4.9	(1.2)	19	(2.1)	33	(6.7)	7.6	(1.2)
Estonia	26	(2.1)	5.0	(0.8)	62	(5.6)	7.1	(1.3)	14	(2.3)	48	(6.5)	8.2	(1.3)
Finland	33	(2.7)	5.8	(0.9)	52	(9.2)	2.4	(0.9)	29	(2.7)	23	(9.4)	6.2	(1.1)
France	44	(2.1)	12.3	(1.1)	110	(4.5)	23.8	(1.9)	15	(2.0)	96	(4.9)	24.8	(1.8)
Germany	29	(2.0)	7.6	(1.0)	88	(5.0)	18.6	(2.0)	8	(1.6)	81	(5.3)	19.0	(2.0)
Greece	28	(2.0)	8.3	(1.1)	73	(5.5)	15.9	(2.2)	10	(1.7)	62	(5.6)	16.8	(2.2)
Hungary	40	(1.9)	15.9	(1.3)	91	(3.6)	34.9	(1.9)	2	(1.5)	88	(3.9)	34.9	(1.8)
Iceland	17	(2.9)	1.7	(0.6)	28	(6.6)	0.7	(0.3)	15	(3.1)	14	(7.2)	1.8	(0.6)
Ireland	m	m	m	m	m	m	m	m	m	m	m	m	m	m
Israel	38	(2.9)	9.4	(1.4)	113	(11.0)	21.0	(2.9)	13	(2.4)	100	(12.0)	21.8	(2.8)
Italy	26	(1.9)	6.7	(1.0)	80	(4.3)	17.2	(1.7)	6	(1.6)	74	(4.6)	17.4	(1.7)
Japan	27	(2.0)	5.2	(0.7)	89	(6.4)	13.4	(1.8)	8	(1.9)	81	(6.8)	13.7	(1.7)
Korea	28	(2.6)	5.1	(1.0)	81	(6.8)	10.1	(1.9)	12	(2.0)	69	(7.0)	10.8	(1.9)
Latvia	23	(2.1)	5.6	(0.9)	49	(4.4)	7.0	(1.3)	13	(2.1)	36	(4.7)	8.3	(1.3)
Luxembourg	30	(1.4)	11.3	(0.9)	79	(2.6)	21.2	(1.2)	12	(1.5)	67	(2.8)	22.4	(1.3)
Mexico	22	(1.4)	11.1	(1.4)	40	(2.6)	16.7	(1.9)	7	(1.3)	33	(2.9)	17.4	(1.9)
Netherlands	33	(2.7)	6.6	(1.1)	121	(9.8)	22.5	(2.4)	4	(2.1)	118	(9.9)	22.5	(2.4)
New Zealand	37	(3.2)	7.4	(1.2)	79	(7.1)	7.1	(1.2)	26	(3.1)	53	(7.4)	10.0	(1.4)
Norway	25	(2.1)	3.8	(0.6)	43	(7.7)	1.6	(0.6)	22	(2.2)	21	(8.2)	4.2	(0.7)
Poland	m	m	m	m	m	m	m	m	m	m	m	m	m	m
Portugal	23	(1.7)	8.8	(1.3)	49	(3.9)	11.1	(1.7)	13	(1.7)	36	(4.2)	13.0	(1.8)
Slovak Republic	30	(2.1)	9.7	(1.2)	75	(6.0)	20.5	(1.8)	6	(1.9)	68	(6.2)	20.8	(1.9)
Slovenia	32	(2.1)	8.0	(1.0)	101	(3.7)	23.9	(1.5)	2	(2.6)	98	(4.8)	24.0	(1.4)
Spain	20	(1.3)	7.0	(0.9)	27	(2.8)	4.6	(0.9)	16	(1.4)	12	(3.0)	7.6	(1.0)
Sweden	33	(2.5)	7.7	(1.1)	82	(8.5)	8.1	(1.7)	23	(2.2)	59	(8.7)	11.1	(1.7)
Switzerland	m	m	m	m	m	m	m	m	m	m	m	m	m	m
Turkey	19	(2.0)	7.9	(1.7)	55	(4.8)	20.7	(3.3)	3	(1.3)	52	(5.0)	20.8	(3.3)
United Kingdom	30	(2.2)	6.3	(0.9)	74	(5.6)	8.8	(1.5)	17	(1.8)	57	(5.8)	10.3	(1.5)
United States	29	(2.1)	7.5	(1.0)	55	(5.8)	7.9	(1.4)	18	(2.1)	37	(6.3)	9.9	(1.4)
OECD average	30	(0.4)	7.9	(0.2)	72	(1.0)	13.9	(0.3)	13	(0.4)	59	(1.1)	15.2	(0.3)
Partners														
Brazil	23	(1.4)	9.5	(1.1)	51	(2.5)	16.6	(1.7)	7	(1.2)	44	(2.6)	17.1	(1.7)
B-S-J-G (China)	35	(2.4)	15.9	(2.2)	70	(3.1)	27.6	(2.8)	8	(1.6)	62	(3.3)	28.1	(2.9)
Bulgaria	37	(2.1)	14.2	(1.4)	97	(5.5)	33.2	(2.7)	6	(1.4)	91	(5.7)	33.5	(2.7)
Colombia	29	(1.7)	14.8	(1.8)	52	(2.8)	21.2	(2.2)	10	(1.6)	41	(3.1)	22.3	(2.3)
Costa Rica	21	(1.6)	10.0	(1.4)	39	(3.1)	13.5	(1.9)	9	(1.4)	30	(3.1)	14.7	(1.9)
Croatia	31	(2.1)	8.6	(1.0)	90	(6.5)	16.9	(2.0)	13	(1.8)	77	(6.7)	18.1	(2.0)
Cyprus*	20	(2.1)	4.1	(0.8)	57	(3.1)	8.6	(0.9)	7	(2.5)	50	(3.8)	9.0	(0.9)
Dominican Republic	m	m	m	m	m	m	m	m	m	m	m	m	m	m
Hong Kong (China)	14	(2.2)	2.1	(0.6)	50	(6.1)	7.3	(1.6)	1	(1.7)	50	(6.1)	7.3	(1.6)
Lithuania	31	(2.2)	8.5	(1.1)	79	(4.8)	16.3	(2.0)	11	(2.0)	68	(5.3)	17.1	(2.0)
Macao (China)	8	(1.9)	0.6	(0.3)	16	(3.3)	0.8	(0.3)	5	(2.4)	12	(4.1)	0.9	(0.3)
Montenegro	19	(1.4)	4.1	(0.6)	87	(3.9)	13.2	(1.1)	6	(1.6)	80	(4.6)	13.6	(1.1)
Peru	32	(1.6)	21.6	(1.8)	51	(2.3)	29.3	(2.1)	10	(1.5)	41	(2.6)	30.4	(2.1)
Qatar	m	m	m	m	m	m	m	m	m	m	m	m	m	m
Russia	31	(2.7)	6.3	(1.0)	80	(7.1)	10.7	(1.7)	14	(2.2)	66	(7.1)	11.7	(1.8)
Singapore	33	(1.7)	9.8	(0.9)	77	(3.9)	14.5	(1.2)	17	(1.8)	61	(4.1)	16.3	(1.3)
Chinese Taipei	30	(2.5)	7.5	(1.1)	89	(5.8)	16.1	(2.2)	11	(1.8)	78	(5.8)	16.9	(2.2)
Thailand	24	(2.5)	9.7	(2.0)	50	(3.7)	17.5	(2.9)	6	(1.9)	44	(3.9)	17.9	(2.9)
Tunisia	16	(1.5)	9.2	(1.5)	36	(3.7)	16.1	(2.9)	6	(1.1)	30	(3.9)	16.9	(2.9)
United Arab Emirates	28	(1.8)	4.9	(0.6)	99	(6.1)	14.2	(1.7)	6	(1.6)	93	(6.4)	14.4	(1.7)
Uruguay	29	(1.7)	12.4	(1.4)	59	(2.9)	18.5	(1.8)	12	(1.6)	47	(3.1)	19.8	(1.8)
Malaysia**	24	(1.9)	10.8	(1.5)	49	(4.4)	13.2	(2.5)	14	(1.4)	35	(4.6)	15.6	(2.4)

1. The socio-economic profile is measured by the PISA index of economic, social and cultural status (ESCS).
Note: Values that are statistically significant are indicated in bold (see Annex A3).
* See note at the beginning of this Annex.
**Malaysia: Coverage is too small to ensure comparability (see Annex A4).
StatLink http://dx.doi.org/10.1787/888933616788

[Part 1/2]

Table V.4.8 Percentage of low and top performers in collaborative problem solving, by students' socio-economic status

		All students				Students in the bottom quarter of ESCS[1]				Students in the second quarter of ESCS			
		Below Level 2 (below 440 score points)		Level 4 (at or above 640 score points)		Below Level 2 (below 440 score points)		Level 4 (at or above 640 score points)		Below Level 2 (below 440 score points)		Level 4 (at or above 640 score points)	
		%	S.E.	%	S.E.	%	S.E.	%	S.E.	%	S.E.	%	S.E.
OECD	Australia	19.2	(0.6)	15.7	(0.7)	29.8	(1.2)	9.1	(0.8)	22.1	(1.1)	12.6	(1.1)
	Austria	24.4	(1.0)	9.2	(0.7)	36.2	(2.0)	3.7	(0.6)	27.9	(1.8)	6.4	(1.0)
	Belgium	26.3	(1.0)	7.2	(0.6)	42.7	(2.0)	2.5	(0.4)	30.8	(1.4)	4.1	(0.6)
	Canada	18.1	(0.8)	16.0	(0.7)	26.8	(1.4)	8.8	(0.8)	19.7	(1.5)	13.4	(0.9)
	Chile	41.8	(1.4)	1.2	(0.2)	61.1	(2.2)	0.2	(0.2)	41.8	(2.3)	0.8	(0.4)
	Czech Republic	25.9	(1.0)	5.4	(0.4)	40.7	(2.1)	1.6	(0.4)	29.2	(1.8)	3.4	(0.7)
	Denmark	18.5	(0.9)	9.0	(0.7)	26.6	(1.4)	4.5	(0.9)	21.0	(1.6)	7.1	(1.2)
	Estonia	15.0	(0.8)	12.3	(0.8)	22.4	(1.7)	6.0	(1.1)	16.3	(1.6)	10.6	(1.5)
	Finland	18.1	(0.9)	14.5	(0.8)	26.9	(1.8)	8.9	(1.2)	20.5	(1.7)	11.7	(1.2)
	France	28.6	(0.9)	6.8	(0.5)	44.7	(1.9)	2.4	(0.5)	33.6	(1.8)	4.4	(0.8)
	Germany	18.1	(1.0)	14.3	(0.8)	27.3	(2.1)	6.5	(0.9)	19.7	(1.4)	11.8	(1.3)
	Greece	41.9	(1.7)	2.0	(0.3)	56.4	(2.5)	0.5	(0.3)	46.8	(2.4)	1.4	(0.4)
	Hungary	37.2	(1.1)	3.4	(0.4)	57.8	(2.1)	0.6	(0.3)	40.3	(2.1)	2.3	(0.6)
	Iceland	26.8	(1.2)	6.7	(0.6)	32.4	(2.4)	5.2	(1.0)	28.6	(2.0)	5.1	(1.0)
	Ireland	m	m	m	m	m	m	m	m	m	m	m	m
	Israel	41.2	(1.6)	5.5	(0.5)	61.3	(2.6)	1.4	(0.4)	43.5	(2.2)	3.5	(0.8)
	Italy	34.0	(1.2)	4.3	(0.5)	47.7	(2.1)	1.9	(0.6)	35.9	(2.0)	3.7	(0.6)
	Japan	10.0	(0.8)	14.1	(0.8)	15.9	(1.5)	7.4	(1.0)	10.0	(1.1)	12.6	(1.3)
	Korea	12.9	(0.8)	10.4	(0.8)	19.2	(1.6)	6.1	(0.8)	14.5	(1.3)	7.7	(1.0)
	Latvia	30.7	(1.0)	3.9	(0.5)	41.6	(2.0)	1.5	(0.6)	34.2	(2.0)	2.6	(0.7)
	Luxembourg	30.8	(0.7)	6.9	(0.4)	47.0	(1.9)	1.9	(0.7)	34.5	(1.5)	4.3	(0.8)
	Mexico	53.3	(1.5)	0.4	(0.1)	71.6	(2.4)	0.0	(0.0)	58.4	(2.0)	0.1	(0.1)
	Netherlands	21.8	(1.0)	10.1	(0.7)	30.2	(1.9)	4.5	(0.8)	25.5	(1.6)	6.9	(1.1)
	New Zealand	18.9	(0.9)	16.4	(0.9)	29.3	(2.0)	7.5	(1.1)	20.0	(1.6)	13.3	(1.6)
	Norway	24.8	(1.0)	7.0	(0.6)	33.8	(1.7)	4.1	(0.9)	25.9	(1.8)	4.9	(0.9)
	Poland	m	m	m	m	m	m	m	m	m	m	m	m
	Portugal	25.9	(1.1)	5.3	(0.5)	39.5	(2.1)	2.3	(0.6)	28.4	(1.9)	3.4	(0.6)
	Slovak Republic	40.2	(1.2)	2.6	(0.4)	56.7	(2.3)	0.7	(0.4)	42.9	(1.5)	1.4	(0.4)
	Slovenia	25.6	(0.8)	6.4	(0.7)	36.6	(2.1)	2.6	(0.7)	31.0	(1.5)	4.6	(1.1)
	Spain	25.5	(1.0)	4.3	(0.4)	36.5	(1.8)	1.8	(0.4)	29.5	(1.5)	3.0	(0.7)
	Sweden	23.8	(1.2)	9.3	(0.9)	34.7	(1.9)	3.2	(0.6)	26.8	(1.8)	5.8	(1.0)
	Switzerland	m	m	m	m	m	m	m	m	m	m	m	m
	Turkey	59.2	(1.9)	0.2	(0.1)	72.7	(2.9)	0.0	(0.1)	63.1	(2.5)	0.1	(0.2)
	United Kingdom	22.0	(1.0)	12.4	(0.8)	31.2	(1.7)	6.6	(1.0)	26.6	(1.8)	8.7	(1.0)
	United States	23.3	(1.1)	14.0	(1.0)	33.3	(2.1)	6.6	(0.9)	27.5	(1.7)	8.9	(1.4)
	OECD average	27.6	(0.2)	8.0	(0.1)	39.7	(0.4)	3.8	(0.1)	30.5	(0.3)	6.0	(0.2)
Partners	Brazil	63.3	(1.1)	0.7	(0.1)	77.7	(1.0)	0.1	(0.1)	68.4	(1.4)	0.3	(0.2)
	B-S-J-G (China)	28.3	(1.5)	6.5	(0.9)	47.3	(2.6)	1.5	(0.5)	30.1	(2.5)	3.6	(1.0)
	Bulgaria	48.7	(1.8)	2.0	(0.3)	70.3	(2.5)	0.4	(0.2)	55.2	(2.5)	1.0	(0.4)
	Colombia	56.5	(1.3)	0.6	(0.2)	75.7	(1.8)	0.0	(0.0)	63.9	(1.9)	0.1	(0.1)
	Costa Rica	49.9	(1.4)	0.6	(0.2)	63.6	(2.2)	0.1	(0.1)	57.5	(2.0)	0.2	(0.2)
	Croatia	35.3	(1.3)	2.4	(0.3)	46.8	(1.9)	0.7	(0.3)	39.7	(2.1)	1.6	(0.4)
	Cyprus*	48.7	(1.1)	1.5	(0.3)	58.5	(2.2)	0.6	(0.4)	52.9	(1.9)	1.1	(0.4)
	Dominican Republic	m	m	m	m	m	m	m	m	m	m	m	m
	Hong Kong (China)	13.5	(0.9)	13.2	(0.8)	17.5	(1.6)	10.2	(1.0)	14.2	(1.6)	12.3	(1.3)
	Lithuania	38.2	(1.2)	2.5	(0.3)	53.3	(1.8)	0.6	(0.3)	43.3	(1.8)	1.3	(0.4)
	Macao (China)	14.9	(0.5)	11.1	(0.6)	16.8	(1.3)	8.8	(1.1)	14.0	(1.4)	10.5	(1.1)
	Montenegro	61.9	(0.8)	0.2	(0.1)	72.7	(1.4)	0.0	(0.1)	64.8	(1.9)	0.1	(0.1)
	Peru	61.4	(1.4)	0.4	(0.1)	87.8	(1.2)	0.0	c	66.8	(2.5)	0.1	(0.1)
	Qatar	m	m	m	m	m	m	m	m	m	m	m	m
	Russia	36.1	(1.6)	3.7	(0.5)	51.5	(2.6)	1.4	(0.5)	38.0	(2.7)	2.8	(0.6)
	Singapore	11.3	(0.4)	21.5	(0.6)	20.7	(1.2)	10.3	(0.9)	11.9	(1.0)	17.2	(1.2)
	Chinese Taipei	16.9	(0.8)	9.7	(0.8)	26.2	(1.6)	4.3	(0.7)	18.8	(1.3)	7.0	(0.9)
	Thailand	53.5	(1.7)	1.0	(0.3)	65.2	(2.3)	0.1	(0.1)	61.5	(2.1)	0.3	(0.2)
	Tunisia	83.6	(1.1)	0.0	(0.0)	92.0	(1.3)	0.0	c	89.3	(1.6)	0.0	c
	United Arab Emirates	53.4	(1.2)	1.8	(0.2)	69.0	(1.9)	0.3	(0.1)	55.5	(1.8)	1.2	(0.3)
	Uruguay	50.2	(1.1)	1.7	(0.3)	67.8	(2.0)	0.2	(0.1)	57.1	(1.8)	0.7	(0.4)
	Malaysia**	49.6	(1.8)	0.4	(0.2)	66.9	(2.3)	0.1	(0.1)	55.9	(2.2)	0.1	(0.1)

1. ESCS refers to the PISA index of economic, social and cultural status.

Note: Values that are statistically significant are indicated in bold (see Annex A3).

* See note at the beginning of this Annex.

**Malaysia: Coverage is too small to ensure comparability (see Annex A4).

StatLink http://dx.doi.org/10.1787/888933616788

[Part 2/2]

Table V.4.8 Percentage of low and top performers in collaborative problem solving, by students' socio-economic status

	Students in the third quarter of ESCS[1]				Students in the top quarter of ESCS				Increased likelihood of students in the bottom quarter of ESCS scoring below Level 2 on the collaborative problem-solving scale (below 440 score points)		Increased likelihood of students in the top quarter of this index scoring at Level 4 on the collaborative problem-solving scale (at or above 640 score points)	
	Below Level 2 (below 440 score points)		Level 4 (at or above 640 score points)		Below Level 2 (below 440 score points)		Level 4 (at or above 640 score points)					
	%	S.E.	%	S.E.	%	S.E.	%	S.E.	Relative risk	S.E.	Relative risk	S.E.
OECD												
Australia	15.0	(0.9)	16.7	(1.3)	9.9	(0.9)	24.2	(1.4)	**1.9**	(0.1)	**1.9**	(0.1)
Austria	19.8	(1.3)	10.2	(1.1)	13.6	(1.4)	16.5	(1.7)	**1.8**	(0.1)	**2.5**	(0.3)
Belgium	20.3	(1.3)	8.3	(0.9)	11.5	(1.0)	14.2	(1.5)	**2.0**	(0.1)	**2.9**	(0.3)
Canada	14.3	(1.0)	18.2	(1.3)	11.5	(1.0)	23.6	(1.4)	**1.8**	(0.1)	**1.8**	(0.1)
Chile	40.1	(2.3)	1.0	(0.4)	24.3	(1.7)	2.8	(0.6)	**1.7**	(0.1)	**4.4**	(1.6)
Czech Republic	21.8	(1.7)	6.2	(0.9)	12.0	(1.2)	10.5	(1.3)	**1.9**	(0.1)	**2.9**	(0.6)
Denmark	15.7	(1.6)	9.3	(1.1)	10.9	(1.2)	15.0	(1.5)	**1.7**	(0.1)	**2.2**	(0.3)
Estonia	13.3	(1.3)	13.8	(1.3)	8.1	(0.9)	18.9	(1.5)	**1.8**	(0.2)	**1.9**	(0.2)
Finland	15.2	(1.5)	16.0	(1.4)	9.8	(1.1)	21.6	(1.9)	**1.8**	(0.2)	**1.8**	(0.2)
France	23.4	(1.5)	7.5	(1.0)	12.5	(1.2)	12.9	(1.5)	**1.9**	(0.1)	**2.7**	(0.4)
Germany	16.2	(1.5)	15.5	(1.5)	9.3	(1.2)	23.6	(1.5)	**1.8**	(0.1)	**2.1**	(0.2)
Greece	38.5	(2.3)	2.0	(0.6)	25.9	(1.9)	4.1	(0.8)	**1.5**	(0.1)	**3.2**	(0.7)
Hungary	33.6	(1.9)	2.7	(0.6)	17.1	(1.5)	7.9	(1.1)	**1.9**	(0.1)	**4.2**	(0.7)
Iceland	23.5	(2.0)	7.1	(1.2)	22.5	(1.7)	9.3	(1.7)	**1.3**	(0.1)	**1.6**	(0.3)
Ireland	m	m	m	m	m	m	m	m	m	m	m	m
Israel	30.8	(2.2)	7.0	(1.1)	29.0	(1.8)	10.1	(1.2)	**1.8**	(0.1)	**2.6**	(0.4)
Italy	30.4	(1.8)	4.8	(0.8)	22.1	(1.7)	6.8	(1.1)	**1.6**	(0.1)	**2.0**	(0.3)
Japan	8.4	(1.0)	15.5	(1.3)	5.6	(0.9)	20.9	(1.5)	**2.0**	(0.2)	**1.8**	(0.1)
Korea	10.3	(1.4)	11.8	(1.4)	7.5	(1.1)	16.1	(2.1)	**1.8**	(0.2)	**1.9**	(0.3)
Latvia	26.8	(1.9)	4.4	(0.9)	20.4	(1.6)	7.3	(1.1)	**1.5**	(0.1)	**2.6**	(0.5)
Luxembourg	27.0	(1.5)	7.1	(1.1)	14.7	(1.3)	14.2	(1.2)	**1.8**	(0.1)	**3.2**	(0.4)
Mexico	47.6	(2.4)	0.3	(0.2)	35.5	(2.2)	1.0	(0.4)	**1.5**	(0.1)	**6.9**	(4.9)
Netherlands	19.3	(1.7)	10.6	(1.2)	12.2	(1.3)	18.5	(1.7)	**1.6**	(0.1)	**2.5**	(0.3)
New Zealand	15.3	(1.3)	18.4	(1.8)	10.9	(1.2)	26.4	(2.0)	**1.9**	(0.2)	**2.0**	(0.2)
Norway	21.8	(1.6)	7.9	(1.2)	17.9	(1.4)	11.0	(1.1)	**1.5**	(0.1)	**2.0**	(0.3)
Poland	m	m	m	m	m	m	m	m	m	m	m	m
Portugal	23.8	(1.7)	5.2	(0.9)	11.9	(1.4)	10.1	(1.5)	**1.8**	(0.1)	**2.8**	(0.5)
Slovak Republic	36.8	(1.9)	2.7	(0.7)	24.5	(2.0)	5.8	(1.0)	**1.6**	(0.1)	**3.6**	(0.7)
Slovenia	21.1	(1.5)	6.9	(1.2)	13.7	(1.3)	11.6	(1.5)	**1.7**	(0.1)	**2.5**	(0.4)
Spain	22.1	(1.8)	5.0	(0.7)	13.9	(1.5)	7.5	(0.9)	**1.7**	(0.1)	**2.3**	(0.4)
Sweden	17.9	(1.7)	11.2	(1.4)	15.7	(1.6)	17.1	(2.3)	**1.7**	(0.1)	**2.5**	(0.3)
Switzerland	m	m	m	m	m	m	m	m	m	m	m	m
Turkey	58.3	(2.5)	0.1	(0.1)	42.9	(3.5)	0.4	(0.2)	**1.3**	(0.1)	4.5	(7.0)
United Kingdom	17.8	(1.3)	13.9	(1.3)	12.2	(1.3)	20.5	(1.7)	**1.7**	(0.1)	**2.1**	(0.2)
United States	19.3	(2.0)	15.1	(1.6)	13.2	(1.4)	25.2	(2.0)	**1.7**	(0.1)	**2.5**	(0.2)
OECD average	23.9	(0.3)	8.8	(0.2)	16.3	(0.3)	13.6	(0.3)	**1.7**	(0.0)	**2.7**	(0.3)
Partners												
Brazil	62.7	(1.7)	0.5	(0.2)	44.3	(2.0)	1.8	(0.4)	**1.3**	(0.0)	**7.1**	(3.0)
B-S-J-G (China)	23.7	(1.7)	6.1	(1.1)	12.1	(1.9)	14.8	(2.5)	**2.2**	(0.2)	**4.0**	(0.8)
Bulgaria	41.4	(2.5)	2.0	(0.6)	27.9	(2.0)	4.9	(0.9)	**1.7**	(0.1)	**4.4**	(1.1)
Colombia	52.5	(1.9)	0.4	(0.2)	33.9	(2.3)	1.8	(0.6)	**1.5**	(0.0)	**9.2**	(5.0)
Costa Rica	48.5	(2.4)	0.5	(0.3)	30.1	(2.4)	1.5	(0.4)	**1.4**	(0.1)	**6.1**	(3.3)
Croatia	34.3	(2.0)	2.0	(0.5)	20.4	(1.7)	5.3	(1.0)	**1.5**	(0.1)	**3.7**	(0.9)
Cyprus*	47.8	(1.8)	1.6	(0.7)	35.6	(2.2)	2.9	(0.7)	**1.3**	(0.1)	**2.6**	(0.8)
Dominican Republic	m	m	m	m	m	m	m	m	m	m	m	m
Hong Kong (China)	12.0	(1.6)	11.9	(1.2)	10.2	(1.2)	18.6	(1.7)	**1.4**	(0.1)	**1.6**	(0.2)
Lithuania	33.0	(2.2)	2.9	(0.7)	23.2	(1.6)	5.3	(0.9)	**1.6**	(0.1)	**3.4**	(0.9)
Macao (China)	14.3	(1.3)	11.6	(1.6)	14.4	(1.3)	13.6	(1.3)	1.2	(0.1)	**1.3**	(0.2)
Montenegro	59.6	(1.7)	0.2	(0.1)	50.5	(1.7)	0.4	(0.3)	**1.2**	(0.0)	5.7	(10.6)
Peru	54.6	(2.1)	0.4	(0.2)	36.5	(2.6)	1.2	(0.4)	**1.7**	(0.1)	10.8	(18.5)
Qatar	m	m	m	m	m	m	m	m	m	m	m	m
Russia	29.0	(2.4)	4.4	(1.0)	25.7	(1.6)	6.4	(1.1)	**1.7**	(0.1)	**2.3**	(0.5)
Singapore	8.4	(0.9)	24.4	(1.5)	4.4	(0.6)	34.0	(1.8)	**2.5**	(0.2)	**2.0**	(0.1)
Chinese Taipei	14.2	(1.2)	10.8	(1.3)	8.4	(0.9)	16.6	(2.0)	**1.9**	(0.1)	**2.3**	(0.3)
Thailand	52.9	(2.5)	0.5	(0.3)	34.2	(3.4)	3.0	(1.0)	**1.3**	(0.1)	**10.5**	(6.2)
Tunisia	84.9	(1.7)	0.0	c	68.0	(2.5)	0.0	(0.1)	**1.1**	(0.0)	m	m
United Arab Emirates	45.7	(1.6)	2.3	(0.5)	43.3	(1.6)	3.5	(0.5)	**1.4**	(0.0)	**2.8**	(0.6)
Uruguay	47.0	(2.0)	1.7	(0.5)	29.0	(2.0)	4.2	(0.8)	**1.5**	(0.1)	**4.9**	(1.4)
Malaysia**	44.4	(3.0)	0.2	(0.2)	31.3	(2.6)	1.3	(0.5)	**1.5**	(0.1)	11.6	(19.3)

1. ESCS refers to the PISA index of economic, social and cultural status.
Note: Values that are statistically significant are indicated in bold (see Annex A3).
* See note at the beginning of this Annex.
**Malaysia: Coverage is too small to ensure comparability (see Annex A4).
StatLink http://dx.doi.org/10.1787/888933616788

[Part 1/2]

Table V.4.14a Performance in collaborative problem solving, by immigrant background

		Percentage of immigrant students in PISA 2015		Performance in collaborative problem solving							
				Non-immigrant students		Immigrant students		Second-generation immigrants		First-generation immigrants	
		%	S.E.	Mean score	S.E.	Mean score	S.E.	Mean score	S.E.	Mean score	S.E.
OECD	Australia	25.0	(0.7)	534	(2.1)	534	(3.4)	547	(4.4)	521	(4.5)
	Austria	20.3	(1.1)	521	(2.8)	468	(5.1)	477	(4.8)	453	(8.5)
	Belgium	17.7	(0.9)	513	(2.3)	456	(4.9)	459	(5.9)	453	(6.6)
	Canada	30.1	(1.3)	539	(2.4)	536	(3.6)	540	(4.7)	532	(4.2)
	Chile	2.1	(0.5)	459	(2.7)	436	(12.9)	449	(27.2)	431	(13.1)
	Czech Republic	3.4	(0.3)	500	(2.1)	488	(11.2)	505	(13.4)	472	(13.7)
	Denmark	10.7	(0.6)	527	(2.7)	466	(3.8)	470	(4.2)	455	(9.1)
	Estonia	10.0	(0.5)	542	(2.7)	493	(4.4)	491	(4.5)	511	(20.6)
	Finland	4.0	(0.4)	538	(2.5)	457	(9.9)	468	(12.2)	447	(12.1)
	France	13.2	(1.0)	503	(2.5)	452	(6.7)	464	(7.5)	430	(9.1)
	Germany	16.9	(0.9)	540	(2.8)	491	(6.1)	497	(6.1)	470	(10.6)
	Greece	10.8	(0.7)	465	(3.8)	424	(5.4)	433	(7.0)	407	(9.0)
	Hungary	2.7	(0.2)	472	(2.4)	484	(11.5)	496	(12.8)	469	(19.9)
	Iceland	4.1	(0.3)	503	(2.4)	449	(9.2)	469	(18.3)	440	(11.8)
	Ireland	14.4	(1.0)	m	m	m	m	m	m	m	m
	Israel	17.5	(1.0)	473	(3.6)	468	(7.5)	488	(6.9)	411	(12.7)
	Italy	8.0	(0.5)	481	(2.6)	468	(5.1)	467	(7.7)	468	(6.9)
	Japan	0.5	(0.1)	553	(2.6)	432	(38.1)	c	c	c	c
	Korea	0.1	(0.0)	539	(2.6)	c	c	m	m	c	c
	Latvia	5.0	(0.4)	487	(2.2)	472	(7.4)	476	(7.2)	455	(20.8)
	Luxembourg	52.0	(0.6)	506	(2.2)	481	(2.1)	482	(2.9)	479	(3.4)
	Mexico	1.2	(0.1)	435	(2.5)	372	(11.9)	c	c	367	(14.0)
	Netherlands	10.7	(0.9)	523	(2.6)	483	(6.5)	488	(6.9)	464	(11.9)
	New Zealand	27.1	(1.2)	539	(2.8)	529	(4.6)	531	(6.8)	528	(5.3)
	Norway	12.0	(1.0)	510	(2.5)	462	(5.7)	476	(7.6)	449	(7.4)
	Poland	0.3	(0.1)	m	m	m	m	m	m	m	m
	Portugal	7.3	(0.4)	501	(2.7)	481	(6.1)	501	(9.2)	464	(8.2)
	Slovak Republic	1.2	(0.2)	466	(2.3)	398	(14.8)	400	(21.2)	396	(21.7)
	Slovenia	7.8	(0.5)	507	(1.8)	457	(6.4)	471	(8.1)	439	(9.4)
	Spain	11.0	(0.8)	502	(2.0)	473	(6.3)	487	(12.1)	470	(6.5)
	Sweden	17.4	(1.2)	522	(3.1)	463	(6.9)	479	(9.0)	443	(8.4)
	Switzerland	31.1	(1.2)	m	m	m	m	m	m	m	m
	Turkey	0.8	(0.2)	424	(3.4)	435	(15.6)	442	(17.5)	c	c
	United Kingdom	16.7	(1.0)	524	(2.8)	511	(6.4)	519	(6.4)	503	(8.4)
	United States	23.1	(1.5)	528	(3.7)	508	(5.9)	515	(6.9)	493	(7.5)
	OECD average-32	12.2	(0.1)	505	(0.5)	469	(1.9)	482	(2.0)	459	(2.2)
	OECD average-35	12.5	(0.1)	m	m	m	m	m	m	m	m
Partners	Brazil	0.8	(0.1)	416	(2.4)	365	(12.6)	370	(14.5)	356	(20.9)
	B-S-J-G (China)	0.3	(0.1)	498	(3.9)	373	(24.8)	c	c	c	c
	Bulgaria	1.0	(0.1)	448	(3.7)	406	(14.2)	c	c	c	c
	Colombia	0.6	(0.1)	431	(2.3)	404	(16.4)	393	(18.1)	c	c
	Costa Rica	8.0	(0.6)	443	(2.4)	427	(5.6)	420	(5.5)	442	(12.0)
	Croatia	10.8	(0.6)	477	(2.5)	454	(4.9)	456	(5.5)	444	(10.8)
	Cyprus*	11.3	(0.4)	446	(1.8)	446	(4.9)	468	(7.6)	437	(6.0)
	Dominican Republic	1.8	(0.3)	m	m	m	m	m	m	m	m
	Hong Kong (China)	35.1	(1.3)	547	(3.2)	533	(3.9)	536	(4.4)	529	(4.6)
	Lithuania	1.8	(0.2)	470	(2.4)	459	(11.0)	470	(10.5)	420	(29.7)
	Macao (China)	62.2	(0.7)	523	(2.2)	540	(1.9)	541	(2.4)	538	(3.2)
	Montenegro	5.6	(0.3)	417	(1.3)	431	(6.1)	438	(7.5)	419	(9.6)
	Peru	0.5	(0.1)	419	(2.5)	386	(18.6)	c	c	c	c
	Qatar	55.2	(0.4)	m	m	m	m	m	m	m	m
	Russia	6.9	(0.5)	475	(3.6)	477	(8.4)	473	(11.7)	483	(12.1)
	Singapore	20.9	(1.0)	559	(1.4)	575	(3.6)	588	(5.7)	569	(4.4)
	Chinese Taipei	0.3	(0.1)	527	(2.5)	c	c	c	c	c	c
	Thailand	0.8	(0.3)	438	(3.5)	416	(15.7)	413	(16.0)	c	c
	Tunisia	1.5	(0.2)	384	(1.9)	355	(7.6)	347	(8.2)	c	c
	United Arab Emirates	57.6	(0.9)	404	(2.4)	464	(3.1)	451	(3.6)	472	(3.7)
	Uruguay	0.6	(0.1)	444	(2.3)	463	(24.3)	c	c	c	c
	Malaysia**	0.9	(0.2)	442	(3.3)	432	(14.7)	428	(15.3)	c	c

Notes: Values that are statistically significant are indicated in bold (see Annex A3).
The differences in performance after accounting for socio-economic status were obtained through regressions using dummy variables for first- and second-generation immigrants simultaneously, instead of through performing separate regressions on restricted samples of non-immigrants and first-generation immigrants, and of non-immigrants and second-generation immigrants.
* See note at the beginning of this Annex.
**Malaysia: Coverage is too small to ensure comparability (see Annex A4).
StatLink http://dx.doi.org/10.1787/888933616788

[Part 2/2]

Table V.4.14a Performance in collaborative problem solving, by immigrant background

		Score-point difference in collaborative problem-solving performance																	
		Before accounting for gender and students' socio-economic status						After accounting for gender and students' socio-economic status						After accounting for gender, language spoken at home, and students' socio-economic status					
		Non-immigrants minus Immigrants		Non-immigrants minus Second-generation immigrants		Non-immigrants minus First-generation immigrants		Non-immigrants minus Immigrants		Non-immigrants minus Second-generation immigrants		Non-immigrants minus First-generation immigrants		Non-immigrants minus Immigrants		Non-immigrants minus Second-generation immigrants		Non-immigrants minus First-generation immigrants	
		Score dif.	S.E.	Score dif.	S.E.	Score dif.	S.E.	Score dif.	S.E.	Score dif.	S.E.	Score dif.	S.E.	Score dif.	S.E.	Score dif.	S.E.	Score dif.	S.E.
OECD	Australia	0	(3.7)	**-13**	(4.7)	**13**	(4.7)	-2	(3.4)	**-15**	(4.6)	**11**	(4.2)	**-12**	(3.2)	**-22**	(4.4)	0	(4.3)
	Austria	**52**	(6.0)	**43**	(5.6)	**68**	(9.1)	**34**	(5.5)	**25**	(5.8)	**48**	(7.6)	10	(5.7)	2	(6.2)	**24**	(7.4)
	Belgium	**57**	(4.9)	**54**	(5.6)	**60**	(6.9)	**39**	(4.5)	**36**	(5.2)	**43**	(6.2)	**24**	(5.1)	**22**	(5.4)	**26**	(6.9)
	Canada	3	(3.8)	-1	(4.8)	7	(4.4)	3	(3.6)	-4	(4.5)	**10**	(4.2)	-3	(4.1)	-7	(4.7)	4	(4.9)
	Chile	23	(13.2)	9	(27.3)	**28**	(13.5)	15	(11.8)	12	(24.3)	17	(12.7)	14	(11.9)	10	(24.3)	16	(12.5)
	Czech Republic	11	(10.7)	-5	(12.7)	**27**	(13.5)	6	(10.7)	-17	(12.8)	**27**	(13.5)	-9	(12.4)	-27	(14.1)	12	(15.7)
	Denmark	**61**	(4.3)	**57**	(4.4)	**72**	(9.6)	**48**	(4.8)	**42**	(5.4)	**63**	(9.5)	**38**	(5.4)	**34**	(5.8)	**51**	(10.7)
	Estonia	**49**	(5.0)	**50**	(5.0)	30	(20.8)	**46**	(4.8)	**46**	(4.9)	35	(20.6)	**42**	(5.0)	**43**	(5.1)	27	(21.7)
	Finland	**81**	(9.8)	**69**	(11.9)	**91**	(12.2)	**63**	(9.9)	**51**	(11.4)	**73**	(12.8)	**31**	(11.5)	20	(12.0)	**40**	(14.7)
	France	**51**	(6.9)	**39**	(7.6)	**73**	(9.3)	**28**	(7.0)	**19**	(7.7)	**47**	(9.6)	**20**	(7.3)	13	(7.8)	**37**	(10.6)
	Germany	**49**	(6.2)	**43**	(6.1)	**70**	(10.6)	**32**	(5.8)	**25**	(5.8)	**57**	(10.4)	**12**	(5.9)	9	(6.0)	**30**	(10.7)
	Greece	**40**	(5.9)	**31**	(7.4)	**57**	(9.4)	**21**	(6.3)	**16**	(7.6)	**32**	(10.1)	**15**	(7.0)	12	(7.9)	**22**	(10.8)
	Hungary	-12	(11.5)	-23	(12.7)	3	(19.9)	-1	(10.7)	-2	(12.4)	-1	(19.2)	-5	(10.4)	-7	(12.5)	-4	(18.8)
	Iceland	**54**	(9.7)	35	(18.7)	**63**	(12.0)	**46**	(9.8)	25	(19.0)	**54**	(12.4)	25	(13.1)	9	(20.0)	**34**	(15.6)
	Ireland	m	m	m	m	m	m	m	m	m	m	m	m	m	m	m	m	m	m
	Israel	4	(7.1)	**-15**	(6.8)	**62**	(12.3)	-8	(6.0)	**-23**	(6.4)	**40**	(9.7)	**-20**	(6.2)	**-31**	(6.5)	**24**	(10.4)
	Italy	**13**	(4.9)	14	(8.0)	**13**	(6.5)	1	(5.1)	5	(8.5)	-1	(6.9)	-7	(5.6)	-1	(8.8)	-12	(7.2)
	Japan	**121**	(37.6)	c	c	c	c	**121**	(36.8)	c	c	c	c	62	(37.3)	c	c	c	c
	Korea	c	c	m	m	c	c	c	c	m	m	c	c	c	c	m	m	c	c
	Latvia	15	(7.4)	10	(7.6)	32	(20.3)	**20**	(7.1)	**16**	(7.3)	37	(19.9)	**15**	(7.0)	13	(7.2)	25	(20.1)
	Luxembourg	**25**	(2.9)	**24**	(3.8)	**27**	(3.7)	4	(3.4)	1	(4.1)	**9**	(3.9)	**13**	(3.5)	**9**	(4.0)	**19**	(4.3)
	Mexico	**63**	(12.2)	c	c	**68**	(14.4)	**48**	(12.2)	c	c	**48**	(14.8)	**42**	(12.7)	c	c	**42**	(15.1)
	Netherlands	**40**	(7.1)	**35**	(7.6)	**60**	(12.0)	**22**	(6.5)	**17**	(7.1)	**42**	(11.4)	14	(7.1)	10	(7.5)	**31**	(12.0)
	New Zealand	10	(5.3)	9	(7.3)	11	(5.8)	**10**	(4.9)	3	(6.7)	**15**	(5.4)	0	(5.7)	-5	(7.4)	4	(6.0)
	Norway	**48**	(5.7)	**34**	(7.9)	**61**	(7.1)	**36**	(5.7)	**24**	(7.9)	**48**	(6.8)	**22**	(8.2)	15	(9.6)	**33**	(9.3)
	Poland	m	m	m	m	m	m	m	m	m	m	m	m	m	m	m	m	m	m
	Portugal	**20**	(6.2)	-1	(8.9)	**36**	(8.6)	**19**	(6.1)	5	(8.9)	**31**	(8.7)	13	(6.9)	3	(9.1)	**22**	(10.2)
	Slovak Republic	**68**	(14.8)	**65**	(21.5)	**70**	(21.5)	**66**	(14.2)	**57**	(20.9)	**75**	(21.8)	**45**	(14.9)	**46**	(20.4)	43	(23.8)
	Slovenia	**50**	(6.7)	**36**	(8.2)	**68**	(9.8)	**30**	(7.1)	**17**	(8.3)	**46**	(10.3)	8	(9.4)	2	(10.4)	22	(12.1)
	Spain	**29**	(6.0)	15	(12.1)	**32**	(6.2)	**19**	(6.1)	5	(12.1)	**22**	(6.3)	**16**	(6.0)	2	(11.9)	**19**	(6.2)
	Sweden	**59**	(6.3)	**43**	(8.1)	**79**	(8.6)	**43**	(6.1)	**31**	(7.5)	**59**	(8.4)	**26**	(7.2)	**19**	(8.3)	**41**	(9.1)
	Switzerland	m	m	m	m	m	m	m	m	m	m	m	m	m	m	m	m	m	m
	Turkey	-11	(15.4)	-18	(17.2)	c	c	4	(15.9)	-3	(17.0)	c	c	-4	(16.1)	-8	(16.7)	c	c
	United Kingdom	**13**	(6.6)	5	(6.4)	**21**	(8.8)	10	(5.9)	1	(6.1)	**18**	(7.8)	5	(5.7)	-1	(6.1)	14	(7.8)
	United States	**20**	(6.0)	13	(7.0)	**35**	(7.7)	-3	(6.1)	-9	(7.0)	9	(8.5)	**-13**	(6.5)	**-16**	(7.0)	-2	(9.8)
	OECD average-32	**36**	(1.9)	**23**	(2.0)	**46**	(2.2)	**26**	(1.8)	**14**	(2.0)	**35**	(2.1)	**14**	(1.9)	**6**	(2.0)	**22**	(2.3)
	OECD average-35	m	m	m	m	m	m	m	m	m	m	m	m	m	m	m	m	m	m
Partners	Brazil	**51**	(12.6)	**46**	(14.5)	**60**	(20.8)	**48**	(12.5)	**44**	(14.8)	**58**	(20.7)	**49**	(12.7)	**45**	(14.7)	**55**	(21.2)
	B-S-J-G (China)	**125**	(24.9)	c	c	c	c	**126**	(23.7)	c	c	c	c	**120**	(23.9)	c	c	c	c
	Bulgaria	**42**	(13.6)	c	c	c	c	**32**	(13.9)	c	c	c	c	16	(13.8)	c	c	c	c
	Colombia	27	(16.1)	**37**	(17.9)	c	c	**39**	(14.9)	**43**	(17.2)	c	c	**37**	(15.2)	**41**	(17.3)	c	c
	Costa Rica	**16**	(4.9)	**23**	(4.9)	1	(11.6)	3	(4.8)	8	(4.8)	-6	(10.8)	3	(4.8)	8	(4.7)	-6	(10.8)
	Croatia	**23**	(4.6)	**21**	(5.2)	**33**	(10.7)	**14**	(4.2)	**12**	(4.8)	**27**	(9.8)	**13**	(4.3)	**11**	(4.9)	**24**	(9.8)
	Cyprus*	0	(4.8)	**-22**	(7.8)	9	(5.8)	-2	(4.7)	**-20**	(7.5)	5	(5.8)	-1	(5.1)	**-20**	(7.5)	6	(6.2)
	Dominican Republic	m	m	m	m	m	m	m	m	m	m	m	m	m	m	m	m	m	m
	Hong Kong (China)	**14**	(3.9)	**11**	(4.2)	**18**	(4.7)	7	(3.9)	5	(4.3)	**10**	(4.7)	3	(3.6)	1	(3.9)	7	(4.6)
	Lithuania	11	(10.6)	0	(10.4)	50	(29.1)	11	(10.0)	4	(10.4)	37	(22.1)	3	(10.1)	-1	(10.6)	18	(22.1)
	Macao (China)	**-17**	(3.3)	**-18**	(3.7)	**-15**	(4.0)	**-19**	(3.4)	**-21**	(3.8)	**-16**	(4.0)	**-16**	(3.4)	**-18**	(3.8)	**-13**	(3.9)
	Montenegro	**-15**	(6.3)	**-21**	(7.5)	-2	(9.9)	-10	(6.2)	**-15**	(7.4)	-2	(9.5)	**-13**	(6.3)	**-16**	(7.5)	-7	(9.3)
	Peru	32	(18.1)	c	c	c	c	**38**	(16.1)	c	c	c	c	**34**	(16.5)	c	c	c	c
	Qatar	m	m	m	m	m	m	m	m	m	m	m	m	m	m	m	m	m	m
	Russia	-3	(8.9)	2	(12.9)	-9	(11.3)	-6	(8.8)	-1	(12.9)	-12	(11.6)	-9	(8.8)	-4	(12.7)	-16	(11.4)
	Singapore	**-16**	(4.0)	**-29**	(5.9)	**-10**	(4.7)	0	(4.0)	**-18**	(5.7)	9	(4.8)	-6	(3.9)	**-23**	(5.5)	3	(4.8)
	Chinese Taipei	c	c	c	c	c	c	c	c	c	c	c	c	c	c	c	c	c	c
	Thailand	23	(16.0)	25	(16.2)	c	c	1	(20.3)	9	(18.3)	c	c	-6	(21.4)	4	(19.3)	c	c
	Tunisia	**29**	(7.6)	**37**	(8.1)	c	c	**34**	(7.1)	**41**	(8.0)	c	c	**33**	(7.1)	**40**	(8.0)	c	c
	United Arab Emirates	**-60**	(3.6)	**-47**	(4.1)	**-68**	(4.0)	**-61**	(3.3)	**-50**	(4.0)	**-68**	(3.7)	**-58**	(3.6)	**-48**	(4.1)	**-66**	(4.0)
	Uruguay	-19	(24.3)	c	c	c	c	-6	(22.3)	c	c	c	c	-14	(22.5)	c	c	c	c
	Malaysia**	10	(14.9)	13	(15.4)	c	c	-4	(15.1)	-8	(15.9)	c	c	-4	(14.9)	-6	(15.8)	c	c

Notes: Values that are statistically significant are indicated in bold (see Annex A3).
The differences in performance after accounting for socio-economic status were obtained through regressions using dummy variables for first- and second-generation immigrants simultaneously, instead of through performing separate regressions on restricted samples of non-immigrants and first-generation immigrants, and of non-immigrants and second-generation immigrants.
* See note at the beginning of this Annex.
**Malaysia: Coverage is too small to ensure comparability (see Annex A4).

StatLink http://dx.doi.org/10.1787/888933616788

[Part 1/1]

Table V.4.14b Relative performance in collaborative problem solving, by immigrant background

After accounting for performance in science, reading and mathematics

		Percentage of immigrant students in PISA 2015		Score-point difference in relative performance[1] in collaborative problem solving																	
				Before accounting for gender and students' socio-economic status						After accounting for gender and students' socio-economic status						After accounting for gender, language spoken at home, and students' socio-economic status					
				Non-immigrants minus Immigrants		Non-immigrants minus Second-generation immigrants		Non-immigrants minus First-generation immigrants		Non-immigrants minus Immigrants		Non-immigrants minus Second-generation immigrants		Non-immigrants minus First-generation immigrants		Non-immigrants minus Immigrants		Non-immigrants minus Second-generation immigrants		Non-immigrants minus First-generation immigrants	
		%	S.E.	Score dif.	S.E.	Score dif.	S.E.	Score dif.	S.E.	Score dif.	S.E.	Score dif.	S.E.	Score dif.	S.E.	Score dif.	S.E.	Score dif.	S.E.	Score dif.	S.E.
OECD	Australia	25.0	(0.7)	4	(2.7)	0	(3.7)	**9**	(3.5)	4	(2.6)	0	(3.4)	**8**	(3.4)	1	(2.4)	-2	(3.2)	5	(3.4)
	Austria	20.3	(1.1)	-4	(4.4)	-5	(4.3)	-2	(6.9)	-3	(4.5)	-4	(4.4)	-1	(6.8)	-5	(4.4)	-6	(4.6)	-3	(6.3)
	Belgium	17.7	(0.9)	6	(3.2)	6	(3.6)	6	(4.8)	6	(3.1)	7	(3.6)	5	(4.7)	3	(3.4)	4	(4.0)	2	(4.7)
	Canada	30.1	(1.3)	**7**	(3.0)	5	(4.0)	**8**	(3.6)	**7**	(3.0)	5	(4.0)	**8**	(3.5)	4	(3.2)	3	(4.0)	6	(3.8)
	Chile	2.1	(0.5)	2	(10.0)	5	(16.3)	1	(10.9)	0	(9.7)	4	(15.5)	-1	(10.7)	0	(9.7)	4	(15.5)	-1	(10.7)
	Czech Republic	3.4	(0.3)	-13	(7.5)	**-20**	(8.9)	-6	(10.4)	-12	(8.0)	**-19**	(9.2)	-6	(10.5)	-10	(8.9)	-17	(9.6)	-3	(11.9)
	Denmark	10.7	(0.6)	**8**	(2.9)	4	(3.3)	**19**	(6.5)	**8**	(3.3)	5	(3.8)	**19**	(6.4)	**10**	(3.6)	6	(3.8)	**22**	(7.4)
	Estonia	10.0	(0.5)	**23**	(4.0)	**24**	(4.0)	11	(14.6)	**21**	(3.8)	**22**	(3.8)	8	(14.2)	**20**	(3.9)	**21**	(3.9)	7	(14.4)
	Finland	4.0	(0.4)	9	(7.5)	16	(8.4)	4	(10.1)	10	(7.4)	15	(8.3)	6	(10.0)	3	(9.2)	8	(9.4)	-2	(11.8)
	France	13.2	(1.0)	5	(3.7)	4	(3.7)	7	(7.3)	5	(3.8)	4	(3.8)	8	(7.4)	6	(4.0)	5	(4.0)	10	(7.9)
	Germany	16.9	(0.9)	-6	(3.5)	-6	(3.8)	-5	(6.4)	**-7**	(3.3)	**-7**	(3.7)	-6	(6.6)	**-9**	(3.9)	**-9**	(4.0)	-9	(7.6)
	Greece	10.8	(0.7)	4	(4.6)	1	(5.4)	9	(7.5)	3	(4.7)	1	(5.4)	8	(7.8)	3	(5.0)	1	(5.5)	8	(8.5)
	Hungary	2.7	(0.2)	3	(9.0)	3	(7.5)	2	(17.2)	3	(9.0)	4	(7.5)	1	(17.4)	4	(8.9)	6	(7.5)	2	(17.3)
	Iceland	4.1	(0.3)	**-17**	(7.3)	-14	(13.2)	**-18**	(9.1)	-12	(7.5)	-12	(13.1)	-13	(9.3)	**-19**	(9.4)	-18	(14.5)	-20	(10.5)
	Ireland	14.4	(1.0)	m	m	m	m	m	m	m	m	m	m	m	m	m	m	m	m	m	m
	Israel	17.5	(1.0)	-9	(4.5)	**-15**	(5.0)	9	(7.2)	**-9**	(4.5)	**-15**	(5.0)	10	(7.0)	**-10**	(4.7)	**-15**	(5.0)	10	(7.5)
	Italy	8.0	(0.5)	**-17**	(4.4)	-5	(5.8)	**-25**	(5.9)	**-16**	(4.5)	-4	(5.9)	**-24**	(5.9)	**-17**	(4.8)	-5	(6.1)	**-25**	(6.2)
	Japan	0.5	(0.1)	**60**	(19.1)	c	c	c	c	**66**	(19.9)	c	c	c	c	32	(24.9)	c	c	c	c
	Korea	0.1	(0.0)	c	c	m	m	c	c	c	c	m	m	c	c	c	c	m	m	c	c
	Latvia	5.0	(0.4)	3	(5.4)	3	(5.0)	3	(15.9)	3	(5.4)	3	(4.9)	2	(16.6)	3	(5.5)	3	(5.0)	3	(17.0)
	Luxembourg	52.0	(0.6)	**-6**	(2.3)	**-7**	(2.6)	-6	(2.9)	**-5**	(2.5)	**-6**	(2.8)	-5	(3.0)	-3	(2.6)	-4	(2.8)	-3	(3.4)
	Mexico	1.2	(0.1)	-7	(10.8)	c	c	-10	(13.2)	-7	(10.6)	c	c	-11	(13.0)	-7	(10.8)	c	c	-11	(13.0)
	Netherlands	10.7	(0.9)	-2	(4.9)	-2	(5.8)	-1	(8.3)	0	(4.6)	-1	(5.7)	2	(8.1)	1	(5.6)	0	(6.3)	3	(8.8)
	New Zealand	27.1	(1.2)	6	(3.7)	1	(5.0)	**9**	(4.3)	6	(3.5)	2	(5.0)	**9**	(3.9)	4	(4.1)	0	(5.6)	6	(4.3)
	Norway	12.0	(1.0)	**11**	(4.9)	7	(6.8)	**15**	(5.1)	**11**	(4.7)	7	(6.5)	**16**	(4.9)	7	(6.2)	4	(7.2)	12	(6.9)
	Poland	0.3	(0.1)	m	m	m	m	m	m	m	m	m	m	m	m	m	m	m	m	m	m
	Portugal	7.3	(0.4)	10	(5.4)	3	(6.4)	**15**	(7.2)	9	(5.5)	3	(6.5)	**14**	(7.3)	8	(5.6)	3	(6.3)	14	(8.1)
	Slovak Republic	1.2	(0.2)	10	(10.3)	15	(14.7)	5	(15.8)	9	(10.2)	13	(14.5)	5	(16.2)	13	(10.5)	16	(14.9)	10	(16.5)
	Slovenia	7.8	(0.5)	2	(5.3)	1	(6.0)	2	(8.2)	0	(5.2)	-1	(5.8)	2	(8.0)	2	(6.2)	1	(6.8)	4	(8.8)
	Spain	11.0	(0.8)	-4	(5.5)	-5	(9.5)	-3	(5.6)	-3	(5.6)	-5	(9.4)	-2	(5.8)	-4	(5.4)	-6	(9.2)	-3	(5.6)
	Sweden	17.4	(1.2)	7	(4.2)	7	(5.1)	6	(5.6)	7	(4.0)	7	(5.0)	7	(5.5)	0	(4.7)	1	(5.4)	-2	(6.4)
	Switzerland	31.1	(1.2)	m	m	m	m	m	m	m	m	m	m	m	m	m	m	m	m	m	m
	Turkey	0.8	(0.2)	-23	(13.7)	-10	(14.1)	c	c	-20	(13.8)	-9	(14.6)	c	c	-22	(13.9)	-10	(14.5)	c	c
	United Kingdom	16.7	(1.0)	-4	(4.9)	-3	(5.3)	-5	(6.1)	-3	(4.8)	-1	(5.4)	-4	(5.8)	-5	(4.7)	-3	(5.3)	-7	(6.0)
	United States	23.1	(1.5)	-7	(3.9)	-6	(3.4)	-10	(7.1)	-7	(4.3)	-6	(3.9)	-11	(7.2)	-6	(4.7)	-5	(4.3)	-9	(8.0)
	OECD average-32	12.2	(0.1)	2	(1.3)	0	(1.4)	2	(1.7)	2	(1.3)	0	(1.4)	2	(1.7)	0	(1.4)	0	(1.4)	1	(1.8)
	OECD average-35	12.5	(0.1)	m	m	m	m	m	m	m	m	m	m	m	m	m	m	m	m	m	m
Partners	Brazil	0.8	(0.1)	-10	(9.7)	-16	(11.7)	0	(15.6)	-10	(9.4)	-14	(11.7)	-1	(16.0)	-8	(9.6)	-14	(11.7)	2	(16.6)
	B-S-J-G (China)	0.3	(0.1)	15	(24.2)	c	c	c	c	20	(22.4)	c	c	c	c	21	(22.2)	c	c	c	c
	Bulgaria	1.0	(0.1)	**-22**	(8.8)	c	c	c	c	**-22**	(9.0)	c	c	c	c	**-23**	(8.3)	c	c	c	c
	Colombia	0.6	(0.1)	-16	(14.0)	-20	(13.5)	c	c	-8	(13.2)	-11	(12.8)	c	c	-8	(13.3)	-11	(12.8)	c	c
	Costa Rica	8.0	(0.6)	-2	(3.9)	3	(4.4)	-12	(7.7)	-3	(4.0)	2	(4.5)	-12	(7.7)	-2	(4.1)	2	(4.6)	-12	(7.6)
	Croatia	10.8	(0.6)	5	(3.5)	2	(3.7)	18	(9.5)	4	(3.5)	2	(3.7)	17	(9.1)	4	(3.4)	2	(3.7)	**18**	(8.9)
	Cyprus*	11.3	(0.4)	-3	(4.0)	**-14**	(5.5)	2	(5.0)	-2	(3.9)	**-13**	(5.5)	3	(4.9)	-4	(4.2)	**-15**	(5.4)	1	(5.4)
	Dominican Republic	1.8	(0.3)	m	m	m	m	m	m	m	m	m	m	m	m	m	m	m	m	m	m
	Hong Kong (China)	35.1	(1.3)	4	(2.6)	4	(2.8)	5	(3.8)	**6**	(2.6)	5	(2.8)	7	(3.7)	**6**	(2.6)	5	(2.7)	7	(3.6)
	Lithuania	1.8	(0.2)	6	(8.2)	2	(7.6)	20	(20.0)	4	(8.2)	0	(7.7)	17	(19.2)	3	(8.4)	0	(7.9)	16	(19.3)
	Macao (China)	62.2	(0.7)	-1	(3.0)	-2	(3.1)	0	(3.4)	1	(2.9)	0	(3.1)	2	(3.2)	1	(2.9)	1	(3.2)	3	(3.2)
	Montenegro	5.6	(0.3)	-4	(5.5)	-8	(6.2)	5	(9.5)	-5	(5.3)	-8	(6.1)	2	(9.2)	-5	(5.4)	-8	(6.2)	1	(9.1)
	Peru	0.5	(0.1)	-5	(10.7)	c	c	c	c	0	(11.1)	c	c	c	c	0	(11.1)	c	c	c	c
	Qatar	55.2	(0.4)	m	m	m	m	m	m	m	m	m	m	m	m	m	m	m	m	m	m
	Russia	6.9	(0.5)	-9	(7.0)	-5	(9.1)	-14	(9.1)	-11	(7.0)	-7	(9.1)	-16	(9.3)	-12	(7.1)	-7	(9.1)	-17	(9.4)
	Singapore	20.9	(1.0)	5	(2.8)	2	(4.0)	7	(3.6)	4	(2.8)	1	(4.0)	6	(3.6)	4	(2.6)	1	(4.0)	6	(3.4)
	Chinese Taipei	0.3	(0.1)	c	c	c	c	c	c	c	c	c	c	c	c	c	c	c	c	c	c
	Thailand	0.8	(0.3)	13	(12.0)	13	(13.1)	c	c	7	(12.4)	8	(12.7)	c	c	4	(12.9)	6	(13.3)	c	c
	Tunisia	1.5	(0.2)	-6	(7.1)	-2	(7.7)	c	c	0	(6.6)	4	(7.4)	c	c	1	(6.5)	5	(7.3)	c	c
	United Arab Emirates	57.6	(0.9)	5	(2.7)	**7**	(3.2)	3	(3.1)	3	(2.6)	5	(3.2)	1	(2.9)	3	(2.5)	5	(3.1)	1	(2.9)
	Uruguay	0.6	(0.1)	-24	(15.3)	c	c	c	c	-21	(15.0)	c	c	c	c	-23	(15.1)	c	c	c	c
	Malaysia**	0.9	(0.2)	-5	(12.4)	-8	(12.4)	c	c	-7	(12.9)	-11	(12.9)	c	c	-7	(12.8)	-11	(12.9)	c	c

1. Relative performance refers to the residual performance, attributable to purely «collaborative problem-solving» competencies, after accounting for performance in science, reading and mathematics in a regression performed across students at the national level.

Notes: Values that are statistically significant are indicated in bold (see Annex A3).

The differences in performance after accounting for socio-economic status were obtained through regressions using dummy variables for first- and second-generation immigrants simultaneously, instead of through performing separate regressions on restricted samples of non-immigrants and first-generation immigrants, and of non-immigrants and second-generation immigrants.

* See note at the beginning of this Annex.

**Malaysia: Coverage is too small to ensure comparability (see Annex A4).

StatLink http://dx.doi.org/10.1787/888933616788

[Part 1/2]

Table V.4.22 Performance in collaborative problem solving and the concentration of immigrant students

Results are for non-immigrant students

	School-level proportion of immigrant students[1]										Performance in collaborative problem solving, by school-level proportion of immigrant students							
	Mean[2]		Bottom quarter[3]		Second quarter		Third quarter		Top quarter		Bottom quarter		Second quarter		Third quarter		Top quarter	
	%	S.E.	%	S.E.	%	S.E.	%	S.E.	%	S.E.	Mean score	S.E.	Mean score	S.E.	Mean score	S.E.	Mean score	S.E.
OECD																		
Australia	17.8	(0.5)	0.4	(0.4)	8.5	(0.5)	19.1	(0.8)	42.9	(1.0)	520	(4.5)	533	(4.1)	545	(4.2)	542	(4.0)
Austria	14.4	(0.6)	2.3	(0.5)	7.3	(0.5)	14.0	(1.0)	34.2	(1.3)	520	(7.5)	530	(8.9)	522	(9.4)	513	(7.0)
Belgium	13.1	(0.7)	1.2	(0.2)	5.4	(0.5)	11.6	(0.9)	34.4	(1.6)	523	(6.5)	520	(8.5)	515	(7.5)	497	(7.3)
Canada	18.3	(0.9)	0.5	(0.2)	5.4	(0.5)	16.9	(1.5)	50.5	(1.8)	523	(4.7)	530	(5.8)	549	(5.4)	555	(4.3)
Chile	1.8	(0.3)	0.0	c	0.0	c	0.3	(0.4)	6.7	(1.1)	454	(4.0)	455	(4.7)	467	(5.6)	461	(7.3)
Czech Republic	2.9	(0.3)	0.0	c	0.0	c	1.9	(0.5)	9.8	(0.8)	499	(3.9)	497	(3.7)	504	(4.9)	502	(6.6)
Denmark	8.1	(0.4)	0.2	(0.2)	3.5	(0.4)	7.8	(0.6)	21.0	(0.9)	530	(6.6)	529	(4.8)	526	(5.3)	525	(4.8)
Estonia	8.2	(0.3)	0.0	c	2.3	(0.4)	6.2	(0.4)	24.3	(0.8)	540	(6.0)	553	(4.5)	558	(3.6)	515	(4.2)
Finland	3.6	(0.4)	0.0	c	0.8	(0.4)	3.1	(0.4)	10.6	(1.0)	533	(4.9)	538	(5.8)	534	(6.8)	545	(6.2)
France	10.2	(0.7)	0.1	(0.3)	3.8	(0.4)	9.2	(0.9)	27.7	(1.8)	507	(6.8)	515	(6.9)	504	(8.8)	490	(8.2)
Germany	13.3	(0.7)	0.9	(0.3)	5.8	(0.6)	13.2	(0.9)	33.1	(1.6)	541	(8.3)	543	(7.7)	561	(7.6)	519	(6.5)
Greece	8.9	(0.5)	0.3	(0.3)	4.0	(0.4)	8.9	(0.6)	22.2	(1.4)	477	(6.0)	475	(8.0)	462	(11.1)	446	(7.3)
Hungary	2.5	(0.2)	0.0	c	0.0	c	2.1	(0.4)	7.8	(0.6)	461	(5.2)	449	(5.3)	487	(8.3)	494	(8.6)
Iceland	3.7	(0.1)	0.0	c	0.7	(0.0)	3.6	(0.0)	10.4	(0.2)	500	(4.2)	499	(3.7)	511	(3.9)	504	(4.1)
Ireland	12.7	(0.7)	2.9	(0.4)	7.8	(0.5)	13.7	(1.0)	26.5	(1.7)	m	m	m	m	m	m	m	m
Israel	14.3	(0.7)	1.5	(0.3)	6.5	(0.8)	15.8	(1.0)	33.3	(1.7)	399	(10.1)	496	(15.0)	505	(11.6)	497	(8.1)
Italy	6.8	(0.4)	0.0	c	2.7	(0.5)	7.3	(0.6)	17.2	(0.9)	467	(6.7)	497	(8.6)	480	(8.4)	479	(5.6)
Japan	0.5	(0.1)	0.0	c	0.0	c	0.0	c	1.9	(0.4)	553	(3.3)	556	(3.6)	555	(3.7)	549	(5.7)
Korea	0.1	(0.0)	0.0	c	0.0	c	0.0	c	0.3	(0.1)	540	(3.4)	536	(3.6)	537	(3.7)	541	(3.5)
Latvia	4.4	(0.4)	0.0	c	0.0	c	2.9	(0.7)	14.8	(0.9)	485	(4.2)	486	(4.0)	486	(4.4)	489	(4.7)
Luxembourg	43.1	(0.2)	25.1	(0.1)	33.4	(0.3)	47.1	(0.2)	66.7	(0.5)	523	(3.9)	539	(3.9)	499	(4.8)	466	(4.8)
Mexico	1.2	(0.1)	0.0	c	0.0	c	0.0	(0.1)	4.6	(0.5)	443	(3.2)	443	(3.9)	442	(4.2)	413	(5.8)
Netherlands	8.2	(0.7)	0.0	(0.0)	2.7	(0.5)	7.1	(1.0)	22.9	(1.6)	534	(9.1)	534	(8.4)	517	(8.8)	509	(8.7)
New Zealand	21.5	(0.9)	4.6	(0.8)	14.4	(1.1)	22.8	(1.4)	44.4	(1.5)	527	(6.5)	542	(8.6)	541	(8.7)	552	(6.4)
Norway	9.8	(0.6)	1.0	(0.4)	5.0	(0.4)	9.7	(0.6)	23.3	(1.5)	512	(5.6)	508	(6.3)	504	(5.2)	518	(4.9)
Poland	0.2	(0.1)	0.0	c	0.0	c	0.0	c	0.9	(0.3)	m	m	m	m	m	m	m	m
Portugal	6.5	(0.4)	0.0	c	2.3	(0.5)	6.5	(0.6)	17.2	(0.9)	493	(5.8)	496	(6.9)	508	(6.5)	506	(6.2)
Slovak Republic	1.1	(0.1)	0.0	c	0.0	c	0.0	(0.1)	4.4	(0.5)	467	(4.1)	467	(3.7)	469	(4.3)	461	(6.6)
Slovenia	6.5	(0.1)	0.0	c	2.3	(0.1)	6.1	(0.1)	17.7	(0.4)	511	(3.9)	522	(3.2)	511	(3.2)	484	(3.6)
Spain	9.2	(0.5)	0.0	(0.1)	3.3	(0.4)	8.7	(1.0)	24.7	(1.3)	497	(4.4)	510	(5.1)	500	(5.2)	501	(4.0)
Sweden	12.9	(0.7)	1.1	(0.4)	6.4	(0.7)	12.7	(0.8)	31.4	(1.7)	527	(6.8)	514	(6.5)	521	(4.6)	528	(6.2)
Switzerland	26.1	(0.9)	8.9	(1.0)	18.6	(1.2)	29.0	(1.6)	48.2	(1.6)	m	m	m	m	m	m	m	m
Turkey	0.7	(0.1)	0.0	c	0.0	c	0.0	c	2.9	(0.6)	423	(4.8)	423	(4.8)	424	(5.2)	425	(7.6)
United Kingdom	11.5	(0.6)	0.0	(0.0)	3.7	(0.6)	10.0	(0.9)	32.4	(1.6)	526	(6.2)	529	(6.0)	530	(7.3)	516	(7.5)
United States	16.1	(0.9)	0.8	(0.4)	7.0	(0.8)	15.4	(1.2)	41.0	(2.3)	522	(7.1)	530	(9.1)	539	(12.0)	522	(7.5)
OECD average-32	9.4	(0.1)	1.2	(0.0)	4.3	(0.1)	9.1	(0.1)	23.0	(0.2)	502	(1.0)	509	(1.2)	510	(1.2)	502	(1.1)
OECD average-35	9.7	(0.1)	1.5	(0.1)	4.7	(0.1)	9.5	(0.1)	23.2	(0.2)	m	m	m	m	m	m	m	m
Partners																		
Brazil	0.7	(0.1)	0.0	c	0.0	c	0.0	c	3.0	(0.3)	417	(3.1)	417	(3.4)	416	(3.2)	414	(4.8)
B-S-J-G (China)	0.3	(0.1)	0.0	c	0.0	c	0.0	c	1.1	(0.2)	504	(5.1)	503	(5.4)	498	(4.4)	487	(5.6)
Bulgaria	1.0	(0.1)	0.0	c	0.0	c	0.1	(0.3)	3.8	(0.3)	456	(5.2)	448	(5.6)	455	(6.6)	433	(10.6)
Colombia	0.6	(0.1)	0.0	c	0.0	c	0.0	c	2.3	(0.4)	435	(3.2)	428	(3.1)	431	(3.5)	429	(5.9)
Costa Rica	7.1	(0.5)	0.0	c	2.5	(0.6)	7.2	(0.7)	18.8	(1.2)	443	(5.5)	443	(8.1)	450	(7.6)	436	(6.2)
Croatia	9.9	(0.5)	1.5	(0.4)	6.0	(0.6)	10.8	(0.6)	21.2	(1.2)	483	(7.8)	478	(8.9)	479	(10.0)	468	(7.0)
Cyprus*	8.5	(0.1)	1.9	(0.0)	4.1	(0.0)	6.7	(0.0)	21.2	(0.3)	452	(3.0)	433	(3.7)	451	(3.4)	448	(3.6)
Dominican Republic	1.7	(0.2)	0.0	c	0.0	c	0.5	(0.4)	6.3	(0.7)	m	m	m	m	m	m	m	m
Hong Kong (China)	31.0	(1.1)	13.0	(1.5)	25.4	(1.4)	34.4	(1.7)	51.1	(1.2)	559	(8.8)	555	(9.9)	551	(10.1)	526	(9.5)
Lithuania	1.4	(0.1)	0.0	c	0.0	c	0.0	c	5.7	(0.5)	467	(3.5)	470	(3.4)	472	(3.9)	472	(5.7)
Macao (China)	56.3	(0.3)	40.2	(0.2)	48.2	(0.2)	61.2	(0.7)	75.8	(0.3)	529	(5.3)	523	(4.8)	510	(5.1)	533	(4.8)
Montenegro	5.3	(0.1)	0.9	(0.0)	2.8	(0.0)	5.3	(0.1)	12.3	(0.2)	407	(2.8)	409	(2.5)	422	(2.7)	428	(2.7)
Peru	0.4	(0.1)	0.0	c	0.0	c	0.0	c	1.7	(0.4)	420	(3.7)	418	(3.5)	418	(3.3)	418	(4.8)
Qatar	33.4	(0.2)	11.6	(0.1)	22.7	(0.1)	36.7	(0.3)	62.5	(0.5)	m	m	m	m	m	m	m	m
Russia	6.2	(0.5)	0.1	(0.2)	3.4	(0.4)	6.7	(0.4)	14.8	(1.2)	460	(6.7)	474	(7.5)	481	(8.5)	485	(9.0)
Singapore	17.1	(0.2)	7.4	(0.1)	13.4	(0.1)	18.6	(0.1)	29.2	(0.7)	540	(3.1)	547	(3.2)	562	(3.5)	587	(3.4)
Chinese Taipei	0.3	(0.1)	0.0	c	0.0	c	0.0	c	1.1	(0.2)	529	(3.5)	527	(3.7)	525	(3.5)	527	(4.3)
Thailand	0.7	(0.2)	0.0	c	0.0	c	0.0	c	2.9	(0.9)	441	(4.7)	437	(4.7)	438	(4.8)	437	(4.9)
Tunisia	1.4	(0.2)	0.0	c	0.0	c	0.8	(0.4)	4.9	(0.5)	390	(3.2)	392	(3.8)	385	(4.2)	369	(5.6)
United Arab Emirates	27.0	(1.1)	3.2	(0.8)	14.6	(1.2)	28.4	(1.7)	61.7	(1.9)	413	(3.8)	395	(7.0)	400	(6.1)	409	(5.8)
Uruguay	0.6	(0.1)	0.0	c	0.0	c	0.0	c	2.3	(0.4)	447	(3.7)	442	(3.8)	443	(3.4)	446	(5.1)
Malaysia**	0.9	(0.2)	0.0	c	0.0	c	0.0	c	3.4	(0.7)	439	(4.1)	442	(4.6)	441	(4.4)	444	(6.0)

1. The school-level proportion of immigrant students is the proportion of students in each school who have an immigrant background.
2. The mean school-level proportion of immigrant students is equal to the average proportion of immigrant students in a school that a non-immigrant student attends.
3. Non-immigrant students are ranked according to the proportion of immigrant students in the school that they attend. The bottom quarter of this ranking are those non-immigrant students who attend schools with the smallest proportion of immigrant students, i.e. lowest immigrant diversity.
4. The socio-economic profile is measured by the PISA index of economic, social, and cultural status (ESCS).
5. Relative performance refers to the residual performance, attributable to purely «collaborative problem solving» competencies, after accounting for performance in science, reading and mathematics in a regression performed across students at the national level.
Note: Values that are statistically significant are indicated in bold (see Annex A3).
* See note at the beginning of this Annex.
**Malaysia: Coverage is too small to ensure comparability (see Annex A4).
StatLink http://dx.doi.org/10.1787/888933616788

[Part 2/2]

Table V.4.22 Performance in collaborative problem solving and the concentration of immigrant students

Results are for non-immigrant students

		Performance in collaborative problem solving, by school-level proportion of immigrant students[1]				Relative performance in collaborative problem solving[5], by school-level proportion of immigrant students			
		Difference (top - bottom quarter)				Difference (top - bottom quarter)			
		Before accounting for gender, and students' and schools' socio-economic profile[4]		After accounting for gender, and students' and schools' socio-economic profile		Before accounting for gender, and students' and schools' socio-economic profile		After accounting for gender, and students' and schools' socio-economic profile	
		Score dif.	S.E.	Score dif.	S.E.	Score dif.	S.E.	Score dif.	S.E.
OECD	Australia	**21**	(6.0)	8	(5.3)	2	(4.2)	1	(4.0)
	Austria	-8	(10.0)	8	(8.1)	4	(4.2)	4	(4.2)
	Belgium	**-25**	(9.7)	-9	(6.5)	-1	(4.4)	-2	(4.3)
	Canada	**32**	(6.0)	9	(6.6)	5	(5.5)	5	(5.7)
	Chile	7	(8.7)	-2	(6.6)	1	(4.3)	0	(4.1)
	Czech Republic	3	(8.1)	-8	(5.7)	1	(3.8)	2	(3.7)
	Denmark	-5	(8.2)	1	(7.1)	-3	(4.6)	-2	(4.8)
	Estonia	**-25**	(6.6)	**-29**	(6.5)	-8	(4.6)	-8	(4.5)
	Finland	12	(7.9)	2	(5.9)	-1	(4.8)	0	(4.8)
	France	-17	(12.4)	-7	(6.6)	0	(3.9)	2	(3.9)
	Germany	**-21**	(10.7)	1	(9.1)	5	(5.8)	6	(5.5)
	Greece	**-31**	(9.8)	-4	(8.8)	-4	(4.6)	-1	(5.0)
	Hungary	**34**	(11.3)	-3	(6.3)	4	(3.5)	1	(3.4)
	Iceland	4	(5.2)	4	(4.7)	4	(4.1)	4	(4.1)
	Ireland	m	m	m	m	m	m	m	m
	Israel	**98**	(13.0)	**84**	(8.6)	**41**	(6.1)	**47**	(5.8)
	Italy	11	(8.6)	**21**	(6.2)	6	(5.8)	6	(5.2)
	Japan	-5	(6.4)	-3	(7.8)	5	(4.4)	3	(3.8)
	Korea	0	(4.1)	-10	(11.3)	-4	(9.4)	-3	(6.9)
	Latvia	3	(6.1)	-8	(5.2)	-3	(3.7)	-3	(3.7)
	Luxembourg	**-57**	(5.8)	2	(7.8)	2	(4.5)	8	(5.0)
	Mexico	**-30**	(7.1)	**-11**	(4.7)	-5	(3.8)	-2	(3.5)
	Netherlands	-25	(13.7)	3	(8.7)	-1	(4.7)	-1	(4.5)
	New Zealand	**25**	(8.5)	8	(8.2)	2	(5.4)	4	(5.1)
	Norway	5	(7.4)	4	(6.8)	-3	(5.6)	-2	(5.6)
	Poland	m	m	m	m	m	m	m	m
	Portugal	13	(8.1)	-1	(5.9)	7	(5.0)	7	(5.0)
	Slovak Republic	-6	(8.3)	-4	(5.5)	-1	(3.9)	-1	(3.6)
	Slovenia	**-27**	(4.8)	**-10**	(4.5)	0	(3.6)	0	(3.6)
	Spain	4	(5.9)	**12**	(5.5)	4	(3.8)	5	(3.9)
	Sweden	1	(8.6)	**20**	(8.5)	7	(5.8)	8	(6.2)
	Switzerland	m	m	m	m	m	m	m	m
	Turkey	1	(9.6)	-13	(8.5)	2	(5.4)	1	(4.9)
	United Kingdom	-10	(9.9)	-3	(8.7)	-4	(5.8)	-3	(5.5)
	United States	0	(10.1)	14	(8.4)	7	(5.8)	8	(6.2)
	OECD average-32	0	(1.5)	2	(1.3)	**2**	(0.9)	**3**	(0.8)
	OECD average-35	m	m	m	m	m	m	m	m
Partners	Brazil	-3	(5.6)	-6	(5.0)	3	(3.7)	3	(3.5)
	B-S-J-G (China)	**-16**	(6.7)	-16	(8.8)	-1	(6.0)	0	(6.1)
	Bulgaria	-24	(12.7)	-7	(6.4)	3	(3.4)	4	(3.2)
	Colombia	-7	(6.9)	**-12**	(6.0)	4	(3.2)	2	(3.2)
	Costa Rica	-7	(8.4)	-4	(6.1)	-2	(5.3)	-1	(5.2)
	Croatia	-16	(9.9)	-3	(6.9)	5	(4.4)	4	(4.2)
	Cyprus*	-4	(4.5)	-9	(4.8)	-3	(4.2)	-2	(4.1)
	Dominican Republic	m	m	m	m	m	m	m	m
	Hong Kong (China)	**-33**	(13.1)	11	(14.2)	4	(5.1)	2	(6.6)
	Lithuania	5	(6.9)	-8	(6.0)	2	(3.3)	1	(3.3)
	Macao (China)	4	(7.3)	**39**	(7.4)	6	(4.8)	4	(5.0)
	Montenegro	**21**	(4.1)	**-11**	(4.9)	4	(3.5)	2	(4.0)
	Peru	-3	(5.8)	-5	(5.8)	-2	(4.4)	-3	(4.6)
	Qatar	m	m	m	m	m	m	m	m
	Russia	**26**	(11.3)	8	(8.1)	**17**	(6.5)	**12**	(5.5)
	Singapore	**47**	(4.8)	6	(4.8)	-3	(3.9)	0	(3.9)
	Chinese Taipei	-2	(5.2)	-3	(6.9)	1	(5.1)	0	(5.3)
	Thailand	-3	(6.1)	6	(6.8)	2	(5.8)	5	(5.4)
	Tunisia	**-20**	(7.1)	**-15**	(4.7)	-4	(3.4)	-3	(3.4)
	United Arab Emirates	-4	(7.0)	**52**	(14.6)	12	(11.5)	12	(10.8)
	Uruguay	0	(6.4)	-3	(5.0)	-4	(4.1)	-3	(4.0)
	Malaysia**	5	(6.9)	-11	(6.3)	0	(5.3)	-2	(5.4)

1. The school-level proportion of immigrant students is the proportion of students in each school who have an immigrant background.
2. The mean school-level proportion of immigrant students is equal to the average proportion of immigrant students in a school that a non-immigrant student attends.
3. Non-immigrant students are ranked according to the proportion of immigrant students in the school that they attend. The bottom quarter of this ranking are those non-immigrant students who attend schools with the smallest proportion of immigrant students, i.e. lowest immigrant diversity.
4. The socio-economic profile is measured by the PISA index of economic, social, and cultural status (ESCS).
5. Relative performance refers to the residual performance, attributable to purely «collaborative problem solving» competencies, after accounting for performance in science, reading and mathematics in a regression performed across students at the national level.
Note: Values that are statistically significant are indicated in bold (see Annex A3).
* See note at the beginning of this Annex.
**Malaysia: Coverage is too small to ensure comparability (see Annex A4).
StatLink http://dx.doi.org/10.1787/888933616788

[Part 1/1]

Table V.5.1 Attitudes towards collaboration

		Valuing relationships										Valuing teamwork									
		Index of valuing relationships		Percentage of students who agreed/strongly agreed with the following statements:								Index of valuing teamwork		Percentage of students who agreed/strongly agreed with the following statements:							
				I am a good listener		I enjoy seeing my classmates be successful		I take into account what others are interested in		I enjoy considering different perspectives				I prefer working as part of a team to working alone		I find that teams make better decisions than individuals		I find that teamwork raises my own efficiency		I enjoy co-operating with peers	
		Mean index	S.E.	%	S.E.	%	S.E.	%	S.E.	%	S.E.	Mean index	S.E.	%	S.E.	%	S.E.	%	S.E.	%	S.E.
OECD	Australia	0.09	(0.01)	87.5	(0.3)	91.6	(0.3)	91.1	(0.3)	90.7	(0.3)	0.01	(0.01)	66.1	(0.5)	73.7	(0.5)	72.4	(0.4)	89.0	(0.3)
	Austria	0.24	(0.01)	88.6	(0.4)	82.8	(0.6)	88.2	(0.4)	81.5	(0.5)	0.19	(0.01)	69.1	(0.7)	75.1	(0.6)	67.2	(0.6)	87.4	(0.5)
	Belgium	-0.06	(0.01)	84.9	(0.4)	90.6	(0.4)	85.7	(0.5)	88.9	(0.4)	-0.11	(0.01)	66.2	(0.6)	71.1	(0.5)	63.0	(0.5)	84.9	(0.5)
	Canada	0.11	(0.01)	89.2	(0.3)	90.5	(0.3)	89.5	(0.3)	90.3	(0.4)	0.00	(0.01)	66.6	(0.4)	71.9	(0.5)	69.8	(0.4)	87.3	(0.3)
	Chile	0.08	(0.02)	86.5	(0.6)	90.5	(0.4)	79.9	(0.6)	90.2	(0.5)	0.21	(0.02)	71.8	(0.6)	74.7	(0.7)	81.1	(0.6)	93.1	(0.3)
	Czech Republic	-0.20	(0.01)	91.8	(0.4)	77.6	(0.6)	86.0	(0.6)	85.8	(0.6)	0.00	(0.02)	72.2	(0.7)	76.4	(0.7)	66.5	(0.7)	89.3	(0.5)
	Denmark	0.01	(0.01)	91.2	(0.4)	91.1	(0.4)	86.5	(0.5)	89.4	(0.4)	-0.12	(0.01)	64.5	(0.8)	66.8	(0.8)	60.8	(0.8)	90.1	(0.5)
	Estonia	0.03	(0.02)	88.0	(0.5)	89.0	(0.5)	91.7	(0.4)	87.1	(0.6)	-0.10	(0.02)	61.6	(0.8)	72.5	(0.7)	70.8	(0.7)	80.8	(0.6)
	Finland	-0.08	(0.01)	90.6	(0.5)	86.4	(0.6)	92.3	(0.4)	79.2	(0.7)	-0.22	(0.02)	62.9	(0.7)	71.7	(0.6)	59.5	(0.8)	82.9	(0.6)
	France	-0.07	(0.01)	86.3	(0.5)	86.8	(0.5)	82.7	(0.5)	88.3	(0.4)	0.11	(0.02)	70.6	(0.7)	72.1	(0.6)	76.4	(0.5)	85.2	(0.5)
	Germany	0.15	(0.02)	89.8	(0.4)	82.3	(0.5)	89.4	(0.4)	81.5	(0.5)	0.14	(0.02)	65.8	(0.7)	71.7	(0.6)	65.3	(0.6)	91.7	(0.4)
	Greece	0.03	(0.02)	85.2	(0.6)	90.0	(0.5)	86.8	(0.5)	90.9	(0.5)	0.18	(0.01)	71.9	(0.6)	82.7	(0.6)	75.7	(0.6)	88.5	(0.4)
	Hungary	-0.03	(0.02)	84.1	(0.6)	87.2	(0.5)	84.9	(0.5)	87.9	(0.5)	-0.02	(0.02)	74.0	(0.7)	77.0	(0.7)	66.8	(0.7)	85.7	(0.6)
	Iceland	-0.09	(0.02)	81.6	(0.7)	87.1	(0.5)	79.3	(0.6)	88.8	(0.6)	-0.20	(0.02)	58.2	(0.8)	62.6	(0.8)	64.9	(0.9)	86.7	(0.7)
	Ireland	0.03	(0.01)	84.5	(0.5)	93.0	(0.4)	89.5	(0.4)	89.1	(0.4)	0.04	(0.01)	67.9	(0.7)	74.1	(0.6)	72.0	(0.6)	87.6	(0.5)
	Israel	0.24	(0.02)	92.3	(0.5)	91.2	(0.5)	88.3	(0.5)	83.4	(0.6)	-0.03	(0.02)	63.7	(0.8)	73.4	(0.6)	63.9	(0.8)	87.9	(0.4)
	Italy	-0.14	(0.01)	85.5	(0.5)	85.2	(0.5)	77.6	(0.5)	91.0	(0.4)	0.02	(0.02)	71.5	(0.6)	73.6	(0.6)	70.9	(0.6)	87.7	(0.5)
	Japan	-0.22	(0.02)	76.8	(0.6)	86.0	(0.5)	78.0	(0.5)	67.5	(0.7)	-0.03	(0.02)	65.6	(0.7)	80.5	(0.6)	53.6	(0.7)	89.2	(0.4)
	Korea	-0.02	(0.02)	95.0	(0.3)	82.2	(0.6)	89.2	(0.5)	91.2	(0.4)	0.14	(0.01)	75.5	(0.7)	83.0	(0.5)	84.4	(0.5)	86.8	(0.5)
	Latvia	-0.30	(0.02)	80.7	(0.7)	83.8	(0.6)	81.5	(0.7)	82.0	(0.5)	-0.14	(0.02)	69.0	(0.7)	70.6	(0.8)	65.6	(0.8)	81.8	(0.6)
	Luxembourg	0.03	(0.01)	86.0	(0.5)	83.7	(0.5)	84.2	(0.5)	82.8	(0.5)	0.00	(0.01)	67.8	(0.7)	71.1	(0.7)	66.8	(0.6)	85.3	(0.5)
	Mexico	0.16	(0.02)	88.7	(0.4)	92.7	(0.4)	84.3	(0.5)	92.7	(0.4)	0.23	(0.01)	70.2	(0.6)	82.3	(0.6)	83.0	(0.5)	90.2	(0.4)
	Netherlands	-0.18	(0.01)	89.0	(0.5)	91.3	(0.4)	94.0	(0.3)	80.7	(0.5)	-0.26	(0.01)	63.9	(0.7)	62.8	(0.7)	68.1	(0.8)	84.1	(0.5)
	New Zealand	0.01	(0.02)	82.9	(0.7)	91.2	(0.5)	89.2	(0.5)	89.6	(0.4)	0.07	(0.02)	69.6	(0.7)	75.9	(0.7)	73.0	(0.7)	89.7	(0.5)
	Norway	0.11	(0.02)	87.7	(0.5)	88.0	(0.5)	92.5	(0.4)	88.6	(0.5)	-0.23	(0.02)	60.3	(0.8)	66.4	(0.8)	56.0	(0.8)	83.8	(0.6)
	Poland	-0.21	(0.02)	88.3	(0.6)	83.0	(0.7)	78.7	(0.8)	88.1	(0.5)	-0.06	(0.02)	73.5	(0.7)	71.4	(0.7)	68.7	(0.8)	85.2	(0.5)
	Portugal	0.37	(0.02)	93.2	(0.4)	96.1	(0.3)	93.0	(0.3)	93.7	(0.4)	0.32	(0.02)	71.8	(0.7)	83.0	(0.6)	81.0	(0.5)	94.9	(0.3)
	Slovak Republic	-0.34	(0.01)	77.8	(0.6)	78.5	(0.6)	83.7	(0.6)	82.8	(0.6)	-0.12	(0.02)	71.8	(0.6)	74.3	(0.7)	69.6	(0.6)	80.5	(0.6)
	Slovenia	-0.04	(0.01)	82.1	(0.7)	92.3	(0.4)	89.8	(0.5)	83.6	(0.6)	0.02	(0.01)	69.4	(0.7)	75.2	(0.7)	71.2	(0.7)	89.0	(0.5)
	Spain	0.19	(0.02)	93.3	(0.4)	90.2	(0.5)	85.5	(0.6)	92.0	(0.4)	0.15	(0.02)	66.8	(0.7)	75.4	(0.7)	72.2	(0.6)	92.6	(0.3)
	Sweden	0.05	(0.02)	87.0	(0.5)	87.0	(0.5)	89.6	(0.4)	86.0	(0.5)	-0.19	(0.02)	58.2	(0.8)	63.3	(0.7)	66.9	(0.7)	83.0	(0.6)
	Switzerland	0.19	(0.02)	87.0	(0.6)	88.3	(0.5)	88.2	(0.5)	86.2	(0.6)	0.22	(0.02)	73.1	(0.7)	75.5	(0.7)	71.6	(0.8)	91.1	(0.5)
	Turkey	0.00	(0.02)	86.4	(0.6)	83.3	(0.7)	75.6	(0.6)	88.3	(0.5)	-0.04	(0.01)	47.9	(0.7)	71.0	(0.7)	78.9	(0.7)	80.7	(0.6)
	United Kingdom	-0.04	(0.02)	86.9	(0.5)	89.2	(0.5)	88.2	(0.5)	87.3	(0.5)	-0.04	(0.01)	68.4	(0.7)	73.9	(0.6)	71.6	(0.6)	85.6	(0.6)
	United States	0.13	(0.02)	89.8	(0.4)	93.0	(0.4)	86.3	(0.5)	90.8	(0.5)	0.06	(0.02)	69.0	(0.7)	75.0	(0.7)	74.2	(0.6)	87.0	(0.4)
	OECD average-32	0.01	(0.00)	87.1	(0.1)	87.8	(0.1)	86.4	(0.1)	86.7	(0.1)	0.00	(0.00)	66.9	(0.1)	73.5	(0.1)	69.7	(0.1)	86.9	(0.1)
	OECD average-35	0.01	(0.00)	87.0	(0.1)	87.8	(0.1)	86.3	(0.1)	86.8	(0.1)	0.01	(0.00)	67.3	(0.1)	73.5	(0.1)	69.8	(0.1)	87.0	(0.1)
Partners	Brazil	-0.04	(0.01)	84.2	(0.3)	94.1	(0.2)	83.6	(0.4)	87.4	(0.3)	0.20	(0.01)	70.6	(0.5)	79.5	(0.4)	83.1	(0.4)	93.7	(0.3)
	B-S-J-G (China)	0.01	(0.02)	87.1	(0.6)	88.9	(0.5)	88.9	(0.5)	90.8	(0.4)	0.39	(0.01)	87.1	(0.5)	86.5	(0.4)	89.2	(0.5)	92.6	(0.4)
	Bulgaria	-0.03	(0.02)	88.1	(0.5)	86.6	(0.6)	79.9	(0.7)	89.2	(0.5)	-0.07	(0.02)	66.7	(0.8)	73.0	(0.7)	74.1	(0.8)	82.0	(0.7)
	Colombia	0.05	(0.01)	90.0	(0.4)	93.2	(0.3)	78.8	(0.6)	83.8	(0.6)	0.23	(0.01)	68.1	(0.6)	83.5	(0.5)	76.7	(0.5)	93.9	(0.3)
	Costa Rica	0.35	(0.02)	89.5	(0.5)	94.6	(0.3)	83.7	(0.5)	93.8	(0.4)	0.34	(0.02)	70.8	(0.6)	82.3	(0.6)	77.8	(0.6)	92.7	(0.3)
	Croatia	0.01	(0.02)	92.8	(0.4)	92.3	(0.4)	77.5	(0.7)	87.2	(0.5)	0.21	(0.02)	76.2	(0.6)	80.9	(0.6)	79.3	(0.7)	90.2	(0.5)
	Cyprus*	0.07	(0.01)	84.2	(0.5)	90.0	(0.4)	84.4	(0.5)	89.1	(0.4)	0.10	(0.01)	67.8	(0.6)	77.8	(0.5)	76.1	(0.6)	86.8	(0.5)
	Dominican Republic	0.27	(0.02)	88.3	(0.5)	90.1	(0.6)	84.1	(0.8)	82.9	(0.7)	0.51	(0.02)	73.5	(0.8)	81.9	(0.7)	82.4	(0.7)	93.8	(0.5)
	Hong Kong (China)	-0.04	(0.02)	89.8	(0.5)	84.8	(0.6)	89.7	(0.5)	91.7	(0.5)	0.05	(0.02)	71.0	(0.7)	80.2	(0.6)	76.9	(0.6)	84.5	(0.5)
	Lithuania	0.16	(0.02)	85.7	(0.5)	85.1	(0.7)	77.3	(0.6)	88.4	(0.5)	0.33	(0.02)	73.3	(0.6)	78.6	(0.6)	79.5	(0.6)	85.7	(0.5)
	Macao (China)	-0.15	(0.01)	84.1	(0.5)	84.9	(0.5)	85.7	(0.6)	89.5	(0.5)	0.01	(0.01)	69.0	(0.7)	74.2	(0.6)	79.8	(0.6)	84.0	(0.5)
	Montenegro	-0.05	(0.01)	82.6	(0.5)	94.7	(0.3)	80.9	(0.6)	84.2	(0.6)	-0.09	(0.01)	43.7	(0.7)	76.0	(0.6)	74.4	(0.7)	89.5	(0.4)
	Peru	-0.08	(0.01)	90.2	(0.4)	84.5	(0.5)	78.1	(0.6)	90.8	(0.4)	0.09	(0.01)	67.8	(0.7)	79.3	(0.6)	76.5	(0.6)	90.5	(0.4)
	Qatar	0.12	(0.01)	85.0	(0.4)	91.6	(0.2)	74.9	(0.4)	87.5	(0.3)	0.23	(0.01)	61.8	(0.5)	80.4	(0.4)	83.1	(0.4)	87.8	(0.3)
	Russia	-0.25	(0.02)	91.5	(0.5)	78.0	(0.8)	84.4	(0.6)	81.7	(0.6)	-0.18	(0.02)	71.7	(0.8)	67.7	(0.8)	70.4	(0.8)	80.3	(0.9)
	Singapore	0.32	(0.01)	91.8	(0.4)	91.4	(0.3)	91.5	(0.5)	95.4	(0.2)	0.27	(0.01)	72.6	(0.6)	82.3	(0.6)	80.1	(0.6)	92.1	(0.4)
	Chinese Taipei	0.22	(0.02)	92.4	(0.4)	90.6	(0.4)	92.4	(0.3)	92.8	(0.3)	0.37	(0.02)	84.8	(0.5)	84.1	(0.5)	85.2	(0.5)	90.5	(0.3)
	Thailand	0.10	(0.02)	90.4	(0.6)	97.8	(0.2)	92.7	(0.4)	88.9	(0.4)	0.37	(0.02)	83.0	(0.5)	90.5	(0.4)	87.2	(0.5)	96.4	(0.3)
	Tunisia	0.12	(0.02)	89.1	(0.5)	94.1	(0.4)	73.7	(0.7)	87.0	(0.6)	0.43	(0.02)	78.1	(0.7)	84.3	(0.6)	85.7	(0.6)	92.3	(0.4)
	United Arab Emirates	0.32	(0.01)	88.3	(0.4)	92.6	(0.3)	86.2	(0.4)	91.1	(0.3)	0.45	(0.02)	68.8	(0.5)	86.5	(0.4)	85.5	(0.4)	91.5	(0.3)
	Uruguay	0.11	(0.02)	83.6	(0.5)	95.5	(0.3)	81.8	(0.6)	90.4	(0.4)	0.20	(0.01)	70.3	(0.6)	80.0	(0.5)	75.2	(0.7)	92.9	(0.4)
	Malaysia**	-0.02	(0.02)	87.4	(0.5)	94.1	(0.3)	75.4	(0.6)	90.1	(0.5)	0.59	(0.02)	87.5	(0.6)	91.0	(0.4)	92.3	(0.4)	95.7	(0.3)

* See note at the beginning of this Annex.

**Malaysia: Coverage is too small to ensure comparability (see Annex A4).

StatLink http://dx.doi.org/10.1787/888933616807

[Part 1/1]

Table V.5.2d Taking into account others' interests and performance in collaborative problem solving

"I take into account what others are interested in"

	Percentage of students who agreed/strongly agreed with the statement		Performance in collaborative problem solving				Difference (agreed/strongly agreed – disagreed/strongly disagreed)							
							Before accounting for gender, and students' and schools' socio-economic profile[1]				After accounting for gender, and students' and schools' socio-economic profile			
			Disagreed/ strongly disagreed		Agreed/ strongly agreed		Performance in collaborative problem solving		Relative performance in collaborative problem solving[2]		Performance in collaborative problem solving		Relative performance in collaborative problem solving	
	%	S.E.	Mean score	S.E.	Mean score	S.E.	Score dif.	S.E.	Score dif.	S.E.	Score dif.	S.E.	Score dif.	S.E.
OECD														
Australia	91.2	(0.3)	493	(5.5)	539	(1.9)	**46**	(5.6)	7	(5.0)	**29**	(5.5)	5	(4.9)
Austria	88.2	(0.4)	485	(5.2)	515	(2.6)	**30**	(5.1)	7	(4.1)	**22**	(4.9)	2	(4.0)
Belgium	85.8	(0.5)	466	(3.7)	513	(2.4)	**47**	(3.3)	**14**	(2.5)	**32**	(3.1)	**12**	(2.5)
Canada	89.5	(0.3)	498	(4.9)	543	(2.2)	**44**	(4.9)	**13**	(4.2)	**34**	(4.7)	**11**	(4.0)
Chile	80.1	(0.6)	429	(4.1)	466	(2.7)	**37**	(4.1)	**11**	(3.0)	**25**	(3.8)	**10**	(2.8)
Czech Republic	86.0	(0.5)	468	(5.0)	507	(2.0)	**39**	(4.7)	**12**	(3.5)	**25**	(4.2)	**8**	(3.6)
Denmark	86.5	(0.5)	491	(3.7)	528	(2.7)	**37**	(4.1)	6	(3.4)	**29**	(4.1)	5	(3.3)
Estonia	91.7	(0.4)	488	(6.0)	541	(2.5)	**54**	(5.8)	**27**	(4.3)	**43**	(5.3)	**24**	(4.0)
Finland	92.3	(0.4)	498	(6.4)	539	(2.5)	**41**	(6.2)	**11**	(4.8)	**32**	(6.3)	8	(4.6)
France	83.0	(0.5)	463	(4.6)	507	(2.5)	**44**	(4.8)	5	(4.1)	**24**	(4.3)	3	(3.9)
Germany	89.7	(0.4)	506	(6.3)	538	(2.7)	**32**	(5.6)	8	(4.4)	**24**	(5.3)	3	(4.3)
Greece	86.8	(0.5)	434	(5.9)	465	(3.4)	**31**	(5.0)	**12**	(3.3)	**24**	(4.7)	**10**	(3.3)
Hungary	85.0	(0.5)	446	(4.4)	478	(2.6)	**31**	(4.8)	5	(3.2)	**14**	(4.3)	3	(3.2)
Iceland	79.3	(0.6)	488	(4.7)	506	(2.5)	**18**	(4.9)	5	(3.6)	**14**	(4.8)	6	(3.6)
Ireland	89.5	(0.4)	m	m	m	m	m	m	m	m	m	m	m	m
Israel	88.3	(0.5)	436	(5.0)	478	(3.6)	**42**	(4.6)	-1	(3.4)	**27**	(4.3)	-3	(3.4)
Italy	77.6	(0.5)	449	(4.6)	489	(2.4)	**41**	(4.3)	**13**	(3.7)	**29**	(3.9)	**10**	(3.5)
Japan	78.3	(0.5)	541	(4.1)	556	(2.7)	**15**	(3.8)	**8**	(3.0)	**9**	(3.5)	**6**	(2.9)
Korea	89.2	(0.5)	514	(4.5)	542	(2.6)	**27**	(4.5)	4	(3.0)	**16**	(4.3)	3	(2.9)
Latvia	81.6	(0.7)	464	(4.6)	491	(2.4)	**26**	(5.0)	4	(3.5)	**17**	(4.6)	1	(3.4)
Luxembourg	84.2	(0.5)	455	(3.8)	501	(1.5)	**46**	(4.0)	**10**	(3.1)	**31**	(3.5)	**7**	(2.9)
Mexico	84.3	(0.5)	415	(3.8)	437	(2.6)	**22**	(3.6)	3	(3.0)	**16**	(3.4)	2	(2.9)
Netherlands	94.0	(0.3)	485	(7.1)	524	(2.4)	**38**	(6.9)	**10**	(5.1)	**25**	(6.2)	8	(5.0)
New Zealand	89.3	(0.5)	486	(6.9)	543	(2.6)	**57**	(7.4)	**21**	(6.2)	**46**	(7.3)	**21**	(6.1)
Norway	92.5	(0.4)	459	(6.6)	509	(2.6)	**50**	(7.0)	**18**	(5.1)	**41**	(6.7)	**14**	(5.0)
Poland	78.7	(0.8)	m	m	m	m	m	m	m	m	m	m	m	m
Portugal	93.0	(0.3)	485	(7.0)	500	(2.5)	**15**	(5.9)	**12**	(4.3)	11	(6.0)	**9**	(4.3)
Slovak Republic	83.8	(0.6)	432	(3.9)	474	(2.4)	**42**	(4.0)	**9**	(2.9)	**25**	(3.6)	**8**	(2.9)
Slovenia	89.9	(0.5)	463	(5.0)	508	(1.8)	**45**	(5.0)	**12**	(4.5)	**30**	(5.2)	**9**	(4.5)
Spain	85.5	(0.6)	460	(4.4)	504	(2.2)	**44**	(4.4)	**12**	(4.1)	**35**	(4.2)	**12**	(3.9)
Sweden	89.7	(0.4)	471	(5.7)	519	(3.3)	**48**	(5.4)	**12**	(4.0)	**35**	(4.9)	**9**	(4.1)
Switzerland	88.2	(0.5)	m	m	m	m	m	m	m	m	m	m	m	m
Turkey	75.6	(0.6)	405	(4.2)	429	(3.4)	**25**	(2.6)	4	(2.3)	**17**	(2.6)	4	(2.3)
United Kingdom	88.4	(0.5)	481	(4.7)	528	(2.7)	**46**	(4.8)	**14**	(3.9)	**36**	(4.5)	**13**	(3.8)
United States	86.4	(0.5)	489	(6.7)	529	(3.4)	**40**	(6.0)	1	(4.1)	**28**	(5.7)	1	(4.0)
OECD average-32	86.5	(0.1)	470	(0.9)	508	(0.5)	**38**	(0.9)	**10**	(0.7)	**26**	(0.8)	**8**	(0.7)
OECD average-35	86.4	(0.1)	m	m	m	m	m	m	m	m	m	m	m	m
Partners														
Brazil	83.6	(0.4)	406	(3.1)	421	(2.5)	**15**	(3.1)	4	(3.2)	**12**	(3.0)	4	(3.2)
B-S-J-G (China)	88.9	(0.5)	452	(5.8)	502	(3.9)	**50**	(5.1)	8	(4.0)	**29**	(4.5)	6	(4.2)
Bulgaria	80.0	(0.7)	426	(4.8)	457	(3.6)	**31**	(4.3)	**10**	(3.2)	**21**	(3.8)	**10**	(3.3)
Colombia	78.9	(0.6)	409	(3.1)	436	(2.3)	**26**	(2.8)	-2	(2.2)	**15**	(2.5)	**-4**	(2.2)
Costa Rica	83.7	(0.5)	408	(4.1)	445	(2.6)	**37**	(4.0)	**12**	(3.9)	**30**	(3.8)	**11**	(3.9)
Croatia	77.5	(0.7)	443	(3.8)	483	(2.4)	**40**	(3.5)	5	(2.9)	**27**	(3.4)	3	(2.9)
Cyprus*	84.4	(0.5)	422	(3.8)	451	(1.9)	**29**	(3.9)	3	(3.3)	**25**	(3.6)	2	(3.3)
Dominican Republic	84.1	(0.7)	m	m	m	m	m	m	m	m	m	m	m	m
Hong Kong (China)	89.8	(0.5)	524	(5.1)	544	(3.0)	**19**	(4.7)	5	(3.9)	**13**	(5.0)	3	(3.9)
Lithuania	77.4	(0.6)	445	(3.1)	477	(2.6)	**32**	(3.4)	**6**	(2.8)	**21**	(3.2)	5	(2.8)
Macao (China)	85.7	(0.6)	513	(4.6)	538	(1.4)	**24**	(5.0)	6	(4.0)	**25**	(4.9)	6	(4.0)
Montenegro	81.0	(0.6)	400	(3.0)	424	(1.5)	**23**	(3.5)	**7**	(2.8)	**19**	(3.4)	5	(2.8)
Peru	78.1	(0.6)	390	(3.1)	428	(2.6)	**38**	(3.1)	1	(2.4)	**22**	(2.8)	0	(2.3)
Qatar	74.9	(0.4)	m	m	m	m	m	m	m	m	m	m	m	m
Russia	84.4	(0.6)	443	(5.1)	482	(3.5)	**39**	(3.9)	**20**	(3.4)	**34**	(3.7)	**18**	(3.2)
Singapore	91.5	(0.5)	517	(4.9)	566	(1.4)	**49**	(5.2)	4	(3.9)	**35**	(4.8)	3	(3.9)
Chinese Taipei	92.4	(0.3)	507	(4.9)	528	(2.5)	**21**	(4.4)	1	(3.7)	**12**	(4.2)	0	(3.6)
Thailand	92.7	(0.4)	413	(7.0)	439	(3.4)	**26**	(5.7)	7	(4.5)	**20**	(5.1)	7	(4.5)
Tunisia	73.7	(0.7)	371	(2.7)	388	(2.2)	**18**	(3.0)	4	(2.8)	**14**	(2.7)	4	(2.7)
United Arab Emirates	86.2	(0.4)	421	(4.2)	441	(2.5)	**20**	(4.0)	4	(3.1)	**16**	(3.8)	3	(3.1)
Uruguay	81.8	(0.6)	425	(3.6)	451	(2.3)	**26**	(3.7)	6	(3.5)	**14**	(3.4)	4	(3.4)
Malaysia**	75.4	(0.6)	423	(3.7)	446	(3.5)	**24**	(3.2)	4	(2.5)	**19**	(3.0)	5	(2.5)

1. Socio-economic profile is measured by the PISA index of economic, social and cultural status (ESCS).
2. Relative performance refers to the residual performance, attributable to purely "collaborative problem-solving" competencies, after accounting for performance in science, reading and mathematics in a regression performed across students at the national level. Whether a student agreed/strongly agreed with the statement "I take into account what others are interested in" was included as an explanatory variable in this regression.
Note: Values that are statistically significant are indicated in bold (see Annex A3).
* See note at the beginning of this Annex.
**Malaysia: Coverage is too small to ensure comparability (see Annex A4).
StatLink http://dx.doi.org/10.1787/888933616807

[Part 1/1]

Table V.5.2e Finding that teams make better decisions and performance in collaborative problem solving

		"I find that teams make better decisions than individuals"													
							Difference (agreed/strongly agreed – disagreed/strongly disagreed)								
		Percentage of students who agreed/ strongly agreed with the statement		Performance in collaborative problem solving				Before accounting for gender, and students' and schools' socio-economic profile[1]				After accounting for gender, and students' and schools' socio-economic profile			
				Disagreed/ strongly disagreed		Agreed/ strongly agreed		Performance in collaborative problem solving		Relative performance in collaborative problem solving[2]		Performance in collaborative problem solving		Relative performance in collaborative problem solving	
		%	S.E.	Mean score	S.E.	Mean score	S.E.	Score dif.	S.E.	Score dif.	S.E.	Score dif.	S.E.	Score dif.	S.E.
OECD	Australia	73.6	(0.5)	547	(3.2)	530	(1.9)	**-16**	(3.0)	**6**	(2.6)	**-9**	(2.8)	**8**	(2.5)
	Austria	75.1	(0.6)	521	(3.8)	509	(2.8)	**-13**	(4.1)	3	(3.5)	-3	(4.0)	3	(3.3)
	Belgium	71.1	(0.5)	512	(3.1)	505	(2.6)	**-7**	(2.8)	3	(1.9)	-1	(2.5)	**4**	(2.0)
	Canada	71.9	(0.5)	553	(2.9)	532	(2.4)	**-21**	(2.8)	3	(2.7)	**-16**	(2.8)	**5**	(2.5)
	Chile	74.7	(0.7)	457	(4.3)	459	(2.7)	2	(3.9)	4	(3.1)	6	(3.8)	**6**	(3.1)
	Czech Republic	76.4	(0.7)	502	(4.1)	502	(2.2)	0	(4.1)	**8**	(3.7)	6	(3.6)	**9**	(3.6)
	Denmark	66.8	(0.8)	529	(3.4)	520	(2.6)	**-9**	(3.3)	3	(2.6)	-4	(3.3)	3	(2.6)
	Estonia	72.5	(0.7)	541	(3.4)	535	(2.8)	-6	(3.7)	**6**	(2.7)	-3	(3.6)	**7**	(2.6)
	Finland	71.7	(0.6)	542	(3.4)	534	(2.8)	**-8**	(3.4)	0	(2.3)	-1	(3.3)	3	(2.4)
	France	72.1	(0.6)	507	(3.8)	496	(2.3)	**-11**	(3.4)	0	(3.0)	-4	(3.3)	1	(3.1)
	Germany	71.8	(0.7)	545	(3.8)	531	(2.8)	**-14**	(3.2)	-2	(2.6)	**-8**	(2.9)	0	(2.4)
	Greece	82.7	(0.6)	454	(5.4)	462	(3.4)	8	(4.5)	**8**	(2.9)	**10**	(3.6)	**8**	(2.8)
	Hungary	77.0	(0.7)	482	(3.8)	470	(2.6)	**-12**	(4.1)	4	(2.8)	-5	(3.3)	4	(2.9)
	Iceland	62.6	(0.9)	511	(3.6)	496	(2.6)	**-16**	(4.0)	0	(2.4)	**-12**	(3.9)	1	(2.4)
	Ireland	74.2	(0.7)	m	m	m	m	m	m	m	m	m	m	m	m
	Israel	73.4	(0.6)	484	(4.3)	469	(4.0)	**-14**	(4.3)	-4	(3.5)	-7	(3.9)	-3	(3.5)
	Italy	73.6	(0.6)	487	(4.3)	478	(2.4)	**-9**	(4.0)	1	(3.5)	-3	(3.9)	1	(3.6)
	Japan	80.6	(0.6)	545	(4.1)	554	(2.7)	**9**	(3.9)	**8**	(3.2)	**8**	(3.5)	**6**	(3.2)
	Korea	83.0	(0.5)	540	(4.2)	538	(2.6)	-2	(3.7)	**8**	(2.7)	0	(3.5)	**9**	(2.6)
	Latvia	70.6	(0.7)	499	(3.3)	480	(2.4)	**-19**	(3.2)	0	(2.3)	**-13**	(3.2)	1	(2.3)
	Luxembourg	71.1	(0.7)	503	(3.0)	490	(1.8)	**-13**	(3.6)	1	(3.1)	**-8**	(3.4)	1	(3.1)
	Mexico	82.3	(0.6)	436	(4.2)	433	(2.5)	-3	(3.8)	-1	(3.3)	4	(3.4)	1	(3.3)
	Netherlands	62.7	(0.7)	529	(3.1)	517	(2.9)	**-12**	(3.4)	-2	(2.0)	-6	(3.1)	0	(2.0)
	New Zealand	75.9	(0.7)	545	(4.4)	534	(2.6)	**-11**	(4.5)	**6**	(3.2)	-5	(4.0)	**9**	(3.1)
	Norway	66.4	(0.8)	508	(3.1)	504	(2.8)	-5	(3.3)	**8**	(2.3)	-2	(3.1)	**9**	(2.4)
	Poland	71.5	(0.7)	m	m	m	m	m	m	m	m	m	m	m	m
	Portugal	83.0	(0.6)	506	(4.3)	498	(2.7)	**-8**	(3.7)	**9**	(3.2)	-1	(3.6)	**10**	(3.1)
	Slovak Republic	74.3	(0.7)	463	(3.7)	469	(2.4)	7	(3.5)	5	(2.5)	5	(2.9)	**5**	(2.4)
	Slovenia	75.2	(0.7)	511	(3.1)	501	(2.2)	**-9**	(3.8)	**6**	(2.8)	1	(3.5)	**8**	(2.8)
	Spain	75.4	(0.7)	497	(3.2)	498	(2.4)	2	(3.4)	4	(2.8)	4	(3.4)	6	(2.9)
	Sweden	63.3	(0.7)	520	(4.4)	510	(3.4)	**-10**	(3.7)	5	(3.2)	-5	(3.5)	**7**	(3.1)
	Switzerland	75.5	(0.7)	m	m	m	m	m	m	m	m	m	m	m	m
	Turkey	71.0	(0.7)	419	(4.1)	425	(3.5)	5	(2.9)	-1	(2.3)	**5**	(2.8)	0	(2.3)
	United Kingdom	74.0	(0.6)	535	(3.8)	518	(2.8)	**-17**	(3.5)	1	(2.6)	**-13**	(3.3)	2	(2.6)
	United States	74.9	(0.7)	539	(5.1)	518	(3.6)	**-22**	(4.3)	3	(3.2)	**-17**	(4.0)	5	(3.3)
	OECD average-32	73.5	(0.1)	508	(0.7)	501	(0.5)	**-8**	(0.7)	**3**	(0.5)	**-3**	(0.6)	**4**	(0.5)
	OECD average-35	73.5	(0.1)	m	m	m	m	m	m	m	m	m	m	m	m
Partners	Brazil	79.5	(0.4)	422	(3.5)	418	(2.4)	-4	(3.0)	1	(2.7)	2	(2.8)	2	(2.7)
	B-S-J-G (China)	86.5	(0.4)	488	(6.2)	498	(3.9)	**10**	(4.5)	6	(3.5)	**10**	(4.0)	6	(3.4)
	Bulgaria	73.0	(0.7)	458	(4.4)	448	(3.7)	**-10**	(3.6)	1	(2.5)	-1	(3.3)	2	(2.5)
	Colombia	83.5	(0.5)	430	(3.9)	430	(2.3)	0	(3.6)	0	(2.5)	6	(3.0)	1	(2.4)
	Costa Rica	82.3	(0.6)	448	(4.3)	437	(2.6)	**-11**	(3.9)	6	(3.4)	-3	(3.9)	6	(3.5)
	Croatia	80.9	(0.6)	472	(4.0)	475	(2.5)	3	(3.6)	**11**	(2.3)	**10**	(3.2)	**12**	(2.3)
	Cyprus*	77.8	(0.5)	447	(4.1)	447	(1.9)	0	(4.2)	1	(3.6)	6	(3.9)	1	(3.7)
	Dominican Republic	82.0	(0.7)	m	m	m	m	m	m	m	m	m	m	m	m
	Hong Kong (China)	80.3	(0.6)	547	(3.7)	540	(3.2)	-7	(3.7)	1	(2.7)	**-7**	(3.6)	1	(2.7)
	Lithuania	78.6	(0.6)	472	(4.5)	469	(2.5)	-4	(4.5)	1	(3.3)	1	(4.2)	2	(3.3)
	Macao (China)	74.2	(0.6)	533	(2.8)	534	(1.6)	2	(3.6)	2	(2.9)	0	(3.6)	1	(2.9)
	Montenegro	76.0	(0.6)	425	(2.8)	417	(1.4)	**-8**	(2.9)	2	(2.7)	-1	(2.8)	3	(2.6)
	Peru	79.3	(0.6)	417	(3.9)	420	(2.5)	4	(3.2)	-2	(2.5)	4	(2.7)	-1	(2.4)
	Qatar	80.4	(0.4)	m	m	m	m	m	m	m	m	m	m	m	m
	Russia	67.7	(0.8)	478	(4.2)	475	(3.6)	-2	(3.5)	5	(2.7)	4	(3.1)	**7**	(2.6)
	Singapore	82.3	(0.6)	578	(2.9)	558	(1.4)	**-20**	(3.4)	**7**	(2.6)	**-11**	(3.1)	**7**	(2.5)
	Chinese Taipei	84.1	(0.5)	543	(4.0)	524	(2.4)	**-20**	(3.2)	-1	(2.2)	**-12**	(2.8)	0	(2.2)
	Thailand	90.5	(0.4)	428	(6.6)	438	(3.4)	10	(5.4)	0	(3.7)	**10**	(5.0)	1	(3.8)
	Tunisia	84.4	(0.5)	389	(3.4)	383	(2.0)	**-6**	(2.9)	**-8**	(2.4)	-2	(2.7)	**-6**	(2.4)
	United Arab Emirates	86.5	(0.4)	451	(4.1)	436	(2.5)	**-15**	(3.7)	-6	(3.6)	-7	(3.4)	-5	(3.5)
	Uruguay	80.0	(0.5)	463	(3.7)	443	(2.3)	**-20**	(3.7)	**6**	(2.6)	**-11**	(3.4)	**7**	(2.6)
	Malaysia**	91.0	(0.4)	426	(6.1)	442	(3.3)	**16**	(5.2)	2	(3.0)	**17**	(4.8)	2	(2.9)

1. Socio-economic profile is measured by the PISA index of economic, social and cultural status (ESCS).
2. Relative performance refers to the residual performance, attributable to purely "collaborative problem-solving" competencies, after accounting for performance in science, reading and mathematics in a regression performed across students at the national level. Whether a student agreed/strongly agreed with the statement "I find that teams make better decisions than individuals" was included as an explanatory variable in this regression.
Note: Values that are statistically significant are indicated in bold (see Annex A3).
* See note at the beginning of this Annex.
**Malaysia: Coverage is too small to ensure comparability (see Annex A4).
StatLink http://dx.doi.org/10.1787/888933616807

[Part 1/1]

Table V.5.3 Variation in attitudes towards co-operation

	Index of valuing relationships		Variation in the index of valuing relationships: Total variation[1]		Between-school variation[2]		Within-school variation		Percentage of variation that lies within schools[3]		Index of valuing teamwork		Variation in the index of valuing teamwork: Total variation		Between-school variation		Within-school variation		Percentage of variation that lies within schools	
	Mean index	S.E.	Variance	S.E.	Variance	S.E.	Variance	S.E.	%	S.E.	Mean index	S.E.	Variance	S.E.	Variance	S.E.	Variance	S.E.	%	S.E.
OECD																				
Australia	0.09	(0.01)	0.93	(0.01)	0.03	(0.01)	0.89	(0.01)	96.5	(0.5)	0.01	(0.01)	0.96	(0.01)	0.01	(0.00)	0.94	(0.02)	98.6	(0.4)
Austria	0.24	(0.01)	1.22	(0.02)	0.03	(0.01)	1.19	(0.02)	97.7	(0.5)	0.19	(0.01)	1.20	(0.02)	0.04	(0.01)	1.16	(0.02)	96.9	(0.6)
Belgium	-0.06	(0.01)	0.89	(0.02)	0.02	(0.00)	0.86	(0.02)	97.2	(0.5)	-0.11	(0.01)	0.98	(0.02)	0.03	(0.01)	0.95	(0.02)	97.0	(0.5)
Canada	0.11	(0.01)	1.03	(0.02)	0.02	(0.00)	1.03	(0.02)	98.3	(0.4)	0.00	(0.01)	1.09	(0.02)	0.01	(0.00)	1.08	(0.02)	99.2	(0.3)
Chile	0.08	(0.02)	1.10	(0.02)	0.04	(0.01)	1.05	(0.02)	96.2	(0.7)	0.21	(0.02)	0.93	(0.02)	0.02	(0.00)	0.92	(0.02)	98.3	(0.5)
Czech Republic	-0.20	(0.01)	0.82	(0.02)	0.03	(0.01)	0.76	(0.02)	96.2	(0.9)	0.00	(0.02)	0.90	(0.02)	0.02	(0.01)	0.88	(0.02)	98.3	(0.6)
Denmark	0.01	(0.01)	0.83	(0.02)	0.01	(0.00)	0.81	(0.02)	98.5	(0.6)	-0.12	(0.01)	0.90	(0.02)	0.02	(0.01)	0.88	(0.02)	98.0	(0.6)
Estonia	0.03	(0.02)	0.90	(0.02)	0.02	(0.01)	0.89	(0.02)	97.7	(0.6)	-0.10	(0.02)	0.93	(0.02)	0.01	(0.00)	0.93	(0.02)	98.5	(0.5)
Finland	-0.08	(0.01)	0.84	(0.02)	0.01	(0.00)	0.83	(0.02)	98.9	(0.6)	-0.22	(0.02)	0.86	(0.02)	0.01	(0.00)	0.85	(0.02)	98.8	(0.4)
France	-0.07	(0.01)	1.03	(0.02)	0.03	(0.01)	1.00	(0.02)	97.3	(0.6)	0.11	(0.02)	1.17	(0.02)	0.02	(0.01)	1.13	(0.02)	98.5	(0.5)
Germany	0.15	(0.02)	1.10	(0.02)	0.03	(0.01)	1.07	(0.02)	97.6	(0.7)	0.14	(0.02)	1.04	(0.02)	0.01	(0.01)	1.02	(0.02)	98.7	(0.6)
Greece	0.03	(0.02)	0.94	(0.02)	0.02	(0.01)	0.92	(0.02)	98.2	(0.6)	0.18	(0.01)	1.01	(0.02)	0.00	(0.00)	1.01	(0.02)	99.5	(0.4)
Hungary	-0.03	(0.02)	1.02	(0.02)	0.04	(0.01)	0.96	(0.02)	95.8	(0.7)	-0.02	(0.02)	1.02	(0.02)	0.01	(0.00)	1.01	(0.02)	99.3	(0.4)
Iceland	-0.09	(0.02)	1.10	(0.03)	0.02	(0.01)	1.10	(0.05)	98.5	(0.6)	-0.20	(0.02)	0.99	(0.03)	0.00	(0.01)	1.00	(0.04)	99.7	(0.5)
Ireland	0.03	(0.01)	0.87	(0.02)	0.01	(0.00)	0.86	(0.02)	98.8	(0.5)	0.04	(0.01)	1.01	(0.02)	0.01	(0.01)	1.01	(0.02)	99.2	(0.6)
Israel	0.24	(0.02)	1.20	(0.02)	0.03	(0.01)	1.16	(0.03)	97.8	(0.6)	-0.03	(0.02)	1.03	(0.02)	0.04	(0.01)	0.99	(0.02)	96.5	(0.6)
Italy	-0.14	(0.01)	0.90	(0.02)	0.02	(0.00)	0.88	(0.02)	98.0	(0.5)	0.02	(0.02)	0.95	(0.02)	0.02	(0.01)	0.92	(0.02)	97.5	(0.6)
Japan	-0.22	(0.02)	1.12	(0.02)	0.03	(0.01)	1.09	(0.02)	97.3	(0.6)	-0.03	(0.02)	1.01	(0.02)	0.02	(0.00)	0.99	(0.02)	97.6	(0.5)
Korea	-0.02	(0.02)	0.88	(0.02)	0.02	(0.00)	0.85	(0.02)	97.4	(0.5)	0.14	(0.01)	0.83	(0.02)	0.01	(0.00)	0.81	(0.02)	98.6	(0.5)
Latvia	-0.30	(0.02)	0.82	(0.03)	0.02	(0.01)	0.80	(0.02)	97.2	(0.7)	-0.14	(0.02)	1.00	(0.02)	0.02	(0.01)	0.97	(0.03)	98.4	(0.7)
Luxembourg	0.03	(0.01)	1.19	(0.02)	0.02	(0.01)	1.20	(0.05)	98.6	(0.4)	0.00	(0.01)	1.22	(0.02)	0.00	(0.00)	1.22	(0.04)	99.7	(0.2)
Mexico	0.16	(0.02)	1.08	(0.02)	0.04	(0.01)	1.04	(0.02)	96.7	(0.6)	0.23	(0.01)	0.91	(0.02)	0.02	(0.01)	0.90	(0.02)	98.1	(0.6)
Netherlands	-0.18	(0.01)	0.60	(0.02)	0.01	(0.00)	0.58	(0.02)	97.7	(0.7)	-0.26	(0.01)	0.63	(0.02)	0.01	(0.00)	0.63	(0.02)	98.9	(0.6)
New Zealand	0.01	(0.02)	0.93	(0.02)	0.03	(0.01)	0.90	(0.02)	96.8	(0.8)	0.07	(0.02)	0.99	(0.02)	0.02	(0.01)	0.96	(0.02)	98.1	(0.7)
Norway	0.11	(0.02)	1.04	(0.02)	0.03	(0.01)	1.02	(0.02)	97.6	(0.7)	-0.23	(0.02)	1.12	(0.02)	0.02	(0.01)	1.10	(0.02)	98.1	(0.6)
Poland	-0.21	(0.02)	0.84	(0.03)	0.01	(0.00)	0.83	(0.02)	99.1	(0.5)	-0.06	(0.02)	0.98	(0.03)	0.01	(0.01)	0.98	(0.03)	98.7	(0.5)
Portugal	0.37	(0.02)	0.96	(0.01)	0.02	(0.01)	0.92	(0.02)	97.5	(0.7)	0.32	(0.02)	0.98	(0.02)	0.01	(0.00)	0.96	(0.02)	98.7	(0.5)
Slovak Republic	-0.34	(0.01)	0.86	(0.02)	0.04	(0.01)	0.82	(0.02)	95.0	(1.0)	-0.12	(0.02)	0.90	(0.02)	0.02	(0.01)	0.88	(0.02)	97.8	(0.6)
Slovenia	-0.04	(0.01)	0.88	(0.02)	0.04	(0.01)	0.84	(0.02)	95.3	(0.9)	0.02	(0.01)	0.90	(0.02)	0.02	(0.01)	0.88	(0.02)	97.9	(0.7)
Spain	0.19	(0.02)	0.99	(0.02)	0.02	(0.00)	0.96	(0.02)	97.5	(0.5)	0.15	(0.02)	1.00	(0.02)	0.03	(0.01)	0.98	(0.02)	97.4	(0.6)
Sweden	0.05	(0.02)	1.09	(0.03)	0.02	(0.01)	1.08	(0.02)	97.9	(0.6)	-0.19	(0.02)	0.99	(0.02)	0.02	(0.01)	0.97	(0.02)	98.1	(0.7)
Switzerland	0.19	(0.02)	1.12	(0.02)	0.04	(0.01)	1.06	(0.02)	96.0	(0.7)	0.22	(0.02)	0.99	(0.02)	0.04	(0.01)	0.94	(0.02)	96.0	(0.7)
Turkey	0.00	(0.02)	1.27	(0.03)	0.04	(0.01)	1.19	(0.03)	96.6	(0.7)	-0.04	(0.01)	0.88	(0.02)	0.00	(0.00)	0.87	(0.02)	99.5	(0.3)
United Kingdom	-0.04	(0.02)	0.93	(0.02)	0.02	(0.00)	0.91	(0.02)	97.5	(0.5)	-0.04	(0.01)	0.96	(0.02)	0.01	(0.01)	0.94	(0.02)	98.6	(0.6)
United States	0.13	(0.02)	1.01	(0.02)	0.02	(0.01)	1.00	(0.02)	98.4	(0.5)	0.06	(0.02)	1.05	(0.02)	0.01	(0.00)	1.04	(0.02)	98.6	(0.4)
OECD average-32	0.01	(0.00)	0.98	(0.00)	0.03	(0.00)	0.96	(0.00)	97.4	(0.1)	0.00	(0.00)	0.98	(0.00)	0.02	(0.00)	0.96	(0.00)	98.4	(0.1)
OECD average-35	0.01	(0.00)	0.98	(0.00)	0.03	(0.00)	0.95	(0.00)	97.4	(0.1)	0.01	(0.00)	0.98	(0.00)	0.02	(0.00)	0.96	(0.00)	98.3	(0.1)
Partners																				
Brazil	-0.04	(0.01)	0.92	(0.02)	0.02	(0.00)	0.89	(0.01)	97.5	(0.5)	0.20	(0.01)	0.82	(0.01)	0.01	(0.00)	0.80	(0.01)	99.2	(0.3)
B-S-J-G (China)	0.01	(0.02)	0.92	(0.02)	0.04	(0.01)	0.88	(0.02)	95.4	(0.9)	0.39	(0.01)	0.86	(0.02)	0.01	(0.00)	0.85	(0.02)	98.3	(0.5)
Bulgaria	-0.03	(0.02)	1.12	(0.03)	0.03	(0.01)	1.05	(0.03)	97.1	(0.7)	-0.07	(0.02)	1.06	(0.03)	0.02	(0.01)	1.02	(0.02)	98.4	(0.5)
Colombia	0.05	(0.01)	1.05	(0.02)	0.02	(0.01)	1.02	(0.02)	97.9	(0.5)	0.23	(0.01)	0.85	(0.02)	0.01	(0.00)	0.84	(0.02)	98.6	(0.5)
Costa Rica	0.35	(0.02)	1.17	(0.02)	0.01	(0.00)	1.14	(0.02)	98.8	(0.4)	0.34	(0.02)	1.06	(0.02)	0.02	(0.01)	1.03	(0.02)	98.0	(0.6)
Croatia	0.01	(0.02)	1.03	(0.02)	0.04	(0.01)	0.99	(0.02)	96.1	(0.6)	0.21	(0.02)	0.97	(0.02)	0.01	(0.00)	0.95	(0.02)	98.7	(0.5)
Cyprus*	0.07	(0.01)	1.14	(0.02)	0.04	(0.01)	1.11	(0.03)	96.9	(1.0)	0.10	(0.01)	1.03	(0.02)	0.02	(0.01)	1.01	(0.02)	97.8	(0.7)
Dominican Republic	0.27	(0.02)	1.56	(0.04)	0.02	(0.01)	1.53	(0.05)	99.0	(0.8)	0.51	(0.02)	1.21	(0.04)	0.01	(0.01)	1.17	(0.03)	99.6	(0.5)
Hong Kong (China)	-0.04	(0.02)	0.93	(0.03)	0.01	(0.00)	0.93	(0.03)	99.3	(0.4)	0.05	(0.02)	1.03	(0.03)	0.00	(0.00)	1.02	(0.03)	99.8	(0.3)
Lithuania	0.16	(0.02)	1.39	(0.03)	0.05	(0.01)	1.33	(0.03)	96.5	(0.8)	0.33	(0.02)	1.35	(0.03)	0.02	(0.01)	1.34	(0.03)	98.5	(0.5)
Macao (China)	-0.15	(0.01)	0.77	(0.02)	0.01	(0.00)	0.76	(0.03)	98.4	(0.5)	0.01	(0.01)	0.78	(0.02)	0.00	(0.00)	0.77	(0.03)	99.9	(0.3)
Montenegro	-0.05	(0.01)	1.05	(0.02)	0.01	(0.00)	1.03	(0.03)	99.1	(0.4)	-0.09	(0.01)	0.94	(0.02)	0.01	(0.00)	0.93	(0.03)	99.0	(0.5)
Peru	-0.08	(0.01)	0.96	(0.02)	0.05	(0.01)	0.91	(0.02)	94.8	(0.7)	0.09	(0.01)	0.77	(0.02)	0.02	(0.00)	0.75	(0.02)	97.9	(0.5)
Qatar	0.12	(0.01)	1.36	(0.02)	0.02	(0.01)	1.20	(0.08)	98.0	(0.4)	0.23	(0.01)	1.07	(0.01)	0.04	(0.01)	0.95	(0.05)	96.0	(1.0)
Russia	-0.25	(0.02)	0.86	(0.02)	0.01	(0.00)	0.86	(0.02)	98.9	(0.5)	-0.18	(0.02)	0.82	(0.02)	0.02	(0.00)	0.82	(0.02)	98.2	(0.5)
Singapore	0.32	(0.01)	1.02	(0.02)	0.01	(0.00)	1.01	(0.02)	98.8	(0.5)	0.27	(0.01)	1.06	(0.02)	0.02	(0.01)	1.05	(0.02)	98.4	(0.6)
Chinese Taipei	0.22	(0.02)	1.00	(0.01)	0.02	(0.00)	0.98	(0.02)	98.3	(0.4)	0.37	(0.02)	1.00	(0.02)	0.02	(0.00)	0.98	(0.02)	98.4	(0.4)
Thailand	0.10	(0.02)	0.71	(0.02)	0.02	(0.00)	0.69	(0.02)	97.2	(0.7)	0.37	(0.02)	0.66	(0.02)	0.02	(0.00)	0.64	(0.02)	97.4	(0.6)
Tunisia	0.12	(0.02)	1.11	(0.02)	0.03	(0.01)	1.08	(0.02)	97.2	(0.7)	0.43	(0.02)	1.05	(0.03)	0.02	(0.01)	1.03	(0.03)	98.1	(0.6)
United Arab Emirates	0.32	(0.01)	1.22	(0.02)	0.04	(0.01)	1.17	(0.02)	96.7	(0.5)	0.45	(0.02)	1.08	(0.02)	0.04	(0.01)	1.03	(0.02)	95.9	(0.5)
Uruguay	0.11	(0.02)	1.04	(0.02)	0.01	(0.01)	1.01	(0.02)	99.0	(0.5)	0.20	(0.01)	1.01	(0.02)	0.01	(0.00)	0.99	(0.02)	99.1	(0.4)
Malaysia**	-0.02	(0.02)	0.83	(0.01)	0.04	(0.01)	0.80	(0.02)	95.5	(0.8)	0.59	(0.02)	0.78	(0.01)	0.04	(0.01)	0.73	(0.01)	94.4	(0.9)

1. The total variation in student performance is calculated from the square of the standard deviation for all students. Due to the unbalanced, clustered nature of the data, the sum of the between- and within-school components, as an estimate from a sample, does not necessarily add up to the total.
2. In some countries/economies, subunits within schools were sampled instead of schools; this may affect the estimation of between-school variation components (see Annex A3).
3. The percentage of variation that lies within schools is calculated as the ratio of the within-school variation over the sum of the within- and between-school variations.
* See note at the beginning of this Annex.
**Malaysia: Coverage is too small to ensure comparability (see Annex A4).
StatLink http://dx.doi.org/10.1787/888933616807

[Part 1/2]

Table V.5.4a Index of valuing relationships, by gender

		Boys										Girls									
				Percentage of students who agreed/strongly agreed with the following statements:										Percentage of students who agreed/strongly agreed with the following statements:							
		Index of valuing relationships		I am a good listener		I enjoy seeing my classmates be successful		I take into account what others are interested in		I enjoy considering different perspectives		Index of valuing relationships		I am a good listener		I enjoy seeing my classmates be successful		I take into account what others are interested in		I enjoy considering different perspectives	
		Mean index	S.E.	%	S.E.	%	S.E.	%	S.E.	%	S.E.	Mean index	S.E.	%	S.E.	%	S.E.	%	S.E.	%	S.E.
OECD	Australia	0.00	(0.01)	84.4	(0.5)	90.1	(0.4)	89.6	(0.5)	88.9	(0.5)	0.17	(0.01)	90.7	(0.4)	93.2	(0.4)	92.5	(0.3)	92.4	(0.4)
	Austria	0.04	(0.02)	86.0	(0.6)	78.2	(0.9)	84.8	(0.7)	80.6	(0.7)	0.45	(0.02)	91.3	(0.5)	87.5	(0.8)	91.5	(0.6)	82.3	(0.7)
	Belgium	-0.16	(0.02)	82.2	(0.6)	88.2	(0.6)	84.2	(0.7)	88.5	(0.4)	0.03	(0.02)	87.7	(0.5)	92.9	(0.4)	87.1	(0.6)	89.4	(0.5)
	Canada	0.02	(0.02)	87.0	(0.5)	88.7	(0.4)	88.0	(0.5)	88.4	(0.5)	0.19	(0.02)	91.4	(0.4)	92.2	(0.4)	90.9	(0.4)	92.1	(0.4)
	Chile	-0.02	(0.02)	84.7	(0.7)	88.1	(0.6)	78.8	(0.9)	89.4	(0.7)	0.18	(0.02)	88.3	(0.7)	92.8	(0.6)	81.0	(0.8)	90.9	(0.6)
	Czech Republic	-0.33	(0.02)	88.5	(0.6)	74.0	(0.9)	82.0	(0.8)	83.8	(0.9)	-0.06	(0.02)	95.2	(0.5)	81.4	(0.9)	90.2	(0.7)	87.9	(0.7)
	Denmark	-0.08	(0.02)	88.6	(0.6)	90.0	(0.6)	84.9	(0.7)	86.8	(0.7)	0.10	(0.02)	93.8	(0.5)	92.3	(0.5)	88.1	(0.7)	92.0	(0.6)
	Estonia	-0.11	(0.02)	84.4	(0.7)	86.6	(0.8)	89.4	(0.7)	85.8	(0.9)	0.17	(0.02)	91.7	(0.5)	91.4	(0.6)	94.0	(0.4)	88.5	(0.6)
	Finland	-0.22	(0.02)	86.9	(0.8)	84.0	(0.8)	90.5	(0.6)	77.4	(1.0)	0.06	(0.02)	94.5	(0.4)	89.1	(0.7)	94.2	(0.5)	81.2	(0.9)
	France	-0.14	(0.02)	84.8	(0.8)	84.1	(0.7)	81.6	(0.7)	87.7	(0.7)	0.00	(0.02)	87.7	(0.6)	89.5	(0.6)	83.9	(0.8)	88.9	(0.6)
	Germany	0.01	(0.02)	87.7	(0.6)	78.4	(0.9)	86.9	(0.7)	81.6	(0.7)	0.30	(0.02)	91.8	(0.5)	86.1	(0.6)	91.8	(0.5)	81.3	(0.8)
	Greece	-0.06	(0.02)	81.6	(0.9)	88.7	(0.7)	84.3	(0.7)	88.5	(0.7)	0.13	(0.02)	89.0	(0.7)	91.4	(0.6)	89.3	(0.6)	93.3	(0.5)
	Hungary	-0.13	(0.02)	80.9	(0.9)	85.7	(0.8)	82.1	(0.8)	87.0	(0.6)	0.07	(0.02)	87.3	(0.7)	88.6	(0.7)	87.8	(0.6)	88.8	(0.7)
	Iceland	-0.11	(0.03)	81.1	(1.0)	85.2	(0.8)	77.8	(1.0)	87.1	(0.9)	-0.06	(0.02)	82.0	(0.9)	88.8	(0.7)	80.7	(1.0)	90.5	(0.7)
	Ireland	-0.12	(0.02)	80.7	(0.7)	90.4	(0.7)	87.4	(0.6)	87.7	(0.7)	0.18	(0.02)	88.6	(0.6)	95.7	(0.4)	91.7	(0.5)	90.4	(0.6)
	Israel	0.09	(0.03)	89.7	(0.7)	88.8	(0.7)	86.2	(0.9)	81.6	(0.9)	0.38	(0.02)	94.8	(0.5)	93.6	(0.5)	90.2	(0.5)	85.0	(0.7)
	Italy	-0.25	(0.02)	80.5	(0.7)	82.1	(0.8)	74.8	(0.8)	89.4	(0.6)	-0.02	(0.02)	90.3	(0.6)	88.2	(0.6)	80.4	(0.7)	92.6	(0.5)
	Japan	-0.32	(0.02)	73.3	(1.0)	81.4	(0.8)	75.9	(0.8)	68.8	(0.8)	-0.13	(0.02)	80.4	(0.9)	90.7	(0.6)	80.2	(0.6)	66.1	(0.9)
	Korea	-0.02	(0.02)	94.4	(0.4)	83.7	(0.8)	87.0	(0.7)	90.7	(0.6)	-0.01	(0.02)	95.7	(0.4)	80.6	(0.8)	91.5	(0.6)	91.7	(0.5)
	Latvia	-0.43	(0.02)	75.6	(0.9)	79.6	(0.8)	77.1	(0.9)	78.9	(0.9)	-0.17	(0.02)	85.7	(0.9)	87.9	(0.8)	85.7	(0.9)	85.0	(0.7)
	Luxembourg	-0.10	(0.02)	83.2	(0.7)	79.6	(0.8)	80.6	(0.7)	81.3	(0.8)	0.16	(0.02)	88.6	(0.6)	87.7	(0.6)	87.7	(0.7)	84.2	(0.8)
	Mexico	0.06	(0.02)	87.5	(0.6)	91.8	(0.6)	82.5	(0.8)	91.7	(0.5)	0.27	(0.02)	89.9	(0.7)	93.5	(0.5)	86.3	(0.6)	93.7	(0.5)
	Netherlands	-0.24	(0.02)	86.0	(0.8)	89.9	(0.6)	92.6	(0.5)	79.8	(0.8)	-0.13	(0.02)	91.9	(0.5)	92.7	(0.5)	95.3	(0.4)	81.5	(0.7)
	New Zealand	-0.11	(0.02)	80.0	(1.0)	89.3	(0.7)	88.5	(0.7)	87.8	(0.8)	0.13	(0.02)	85.7	(0.9)	93.0	(0.6)	89.9	(0.7)	91.4	(0.6)
	Norway	-0.06	(0.02)	84.5	(0.8)	84.7	(0.8)	89.8	(0.7)	85.1	(0.9)	0.28	(0.02)	90.9	(0.6)	91.2	(0.6)	95.1	(0.5)	92.1	(0.5)
	Poland	-0.26	(0.02)	87.0	(0.8)	82.1	(0.9)	77.2	(1.0)	86.8	(0.7)	-0.15	(0.02)	89.6	(0.7)	83.9	(0.9)	80.2	(1.0)	89.5	(0.6)
	Portugal	0.23	(0.02)	90.3	(0.6)	94.4	(0.5)	91.2	(0.6)	92.6	(0.6)	0.52	(0.02)	96.2	(0.3)	97.9	(0.3)	94.8	(0.4)	94.8	(0.4)
	Slovak Republic	-0.41	(0.02)	76.4	(0.8)	75.8	(1.0)	80.8	(0.8)	81.6	(0.8)	-0.27	(0.02)	79.4	(0.9)	81.3	(0.9)	86.8	(0.7)	84.1	(0.8)
	Slovenia	-0.17	(0.02)	78.6	(1.0)	90.6	(0.6)	87.0	(0.7)	80.4	(0.9)	0.10	(0.02)	85.8	(0.8)	94.0	(0.6)	92.7	(0.6)	86.9	(0.8)
	Spain	0.09	(0.02)	91.6	(0.6)	89.6	(0.7)	83.3	(0.9)	90.1	(0.6)	0.28	(0.02)	95.0	(0.5)	90.9	(0.6)	87.6	(0.7)	94.0	(0.4)
	Sweden	-0.03	(0.03)	85.8	(0.7)	85.1	(0.9)	87.2	(0.8)	84.0	(0.8)	0.13	(0.02)	88.3	(0.6)	88.8	(0.5)	92.0	(0.4)	87.9	(0.7)
	Switzerland	0.01	(0.03)	84.9	(0.8)	85.2	(0.8)	85.5	(0.9)	84.9	(0.9)	0.39	(0.02)	89.4	(0.7)	91.8	(0.6)	91.0	(0.5)	87.7	(0.6)
	Turkey	-0.11	(0.03)	84.1	(0.8)	83.6	(0.9)	74.5	(0.9)	86.1	(0.9)	0.10	(0.03)	88.7	(0.7)	83.1	(1.0)	76.6	(0.9)	90.4	(0.5)
	United Kingdom	-0.14	(0.02)	83.4	(0.8)	86.6	(0.7)	86.8	(0.6)	85.8	(0.7)	0.07	(0.02)	90.5	(0.6)	91.9	(0.6)	89.6	(0.6)	88.7	(0.6)
	United States	0.08	(0.03)	87.7	(0.7)	91.8	(0.5)	85.3	(0.8)	89.8	(0.7)	0.17	(0.02)	91.9	(0.6)	94.2	(0.4)	87.3	(0.7)	91.7	(0.6)
	OECD average-32	-0.10	(0.00)	84.4	(0.1)	85.6	(0.1)	84.3	(0.1)	85.2	(0.1)	0.11	(0.00)	89.8	(0.1)	90.0	(0.1)	88.5	(0.1)	88.2	(0.1)
	OECD average-35	-0.10	(0.00)	84.4	(0.1)	85.6	(0.1)	84.2	(0.1)	85.3	(0.1)	0.11	(0.00)	89.7	(0.1)	90.0	(0.1)	88.5	(0.1)	88.3	(0.1)
Partners	Brazil	-0.04	(0.02)	83.8	(0.5)	93.2	(0.4)	82.6	(0.5)	85.7	(0.4)	-0.05	(0.01)	84.5	(0.5)	95.0	(0.3)	84.5	(0.5)	88.8	(0.4)
	B-S-J-G (China)	-0.01	(0.02)	84.2	(0.8)	87.9	(0.6)	88.2	(0.6)	91.3	(0.5)	0.03	(0.02)	90.4	(0.6)	90.1	(0.7)	89.7	(0.6)	90.4	(0.6)
	Bulgaria	-0.13	(0.02)	84.1	(0.8)	84.2	(0.8)	78.0	(1.0)	87.4	(0.7)	0.07	(0.02)	92.4	(0.5)	89.3	(0.6)	82.0	(0.9)	91.2	(0.6)
	Colombia	-0.06	(0.02)	89.0	(0.6)	92.1	(0.6)	74.9	(0.8)	82.3	(1.0)	0.16	(0.02)	90.9	(0.4)	94.2	(0.4)	82.3	(0.6)	85.1	(0.7)
	Costa Rica	0.28	(0.02)	88.8	(0.6)	93.2	(0.4)	81.8	(0.8)	92.1	(0.5)	0.41	(0.02)	90.2	(0.6)	95.8	(0.4)	85.5	(0.7)	95.4	(0.5)
	Croatia	-0.16	(0.02)	90.4	(0.6)	89.9	(0.7)	74.0	(1.0)	84.2	(0.8)	0.16	(0.02)	95.1	(0.4)	94.5	(0.5)	80.7	(0.9)	90.1	(0.7)
	Cyprus*	-0.09	(0.02)	79.4	(0.8)	86.2	(0.6)	82.2	(0.8)	86.3	(0.6)	0.22	(0.02)	88.7	(0.6)	93.7	(0.5)	86.4	(0.7)	91.7	(0.6)
	Dominican Republic	0.17	(0.03)	86.7	(0.8)	89.6	(0.8)	81.9	(0.9)	80.5	(1.0)	0.37	(0.03)	89.8	(0.6)	90.5	(0.7)	86.2	(0.9)	85.1	(0.9)
	Hong Kong (China)	-0.06	(0.03)	86.8	(0.6)	81.8	(0.9)	87.6	(0.7)	90.8	(0.7)	-0.02	(0.02)	92.9	(0.6)	87.7	(0.7)	91.9	(0.7)	92.7	(0.5)
	Lithuania	0.02	(0.03)	81.6	(0.9)	82.2	(1.0)	74.3	(0.8)	86.1	(0.8)	0.30	(0.03)	89.9	(0.6)	88.1	(0.7)	80.3	(0.8)	90.7	(0.5)
	Macao (China)	-0.13	(0.02)	80.8	(0.7)	82.8	(0.7)	85.3	(0.7)	89.9	(0.6)	-0.17	(0.02)	87.5	(0.7)	87.0	(0.7)	86.0	(0.8)	89.1	(0.7)
	Montenegro	-0.17	(0.02)	80.2	(0.6)	93.2	(0.4)	78.1	(0.8)	80.4	(0.8)	0.07	(0.02)	84.9	(0.7)	96.3	(0.3)	83.7	(0.9)	87.9	(0.7)
	Peru	-0.15	(0.02)	89.1	(0.5)	83.5	(0.7)	76.6	(0.8)	90.0	(0.5)	-0.01	(0.02)	91.2	(0.5)	85.5	(0.7)	79.7	(0.8)	91.5	(0.6)
	Qatar	0.05	(0.02)	83.4	(0.5)	88.0	(0.4)	76.7	(0.6)	85.7	(0.4)	0.19	(0.01)	86.6	(0.5)	95.0	(0.3)	73.2	(0.5)	89.2	(0.4)
	Russia	-0.29	(0.02)	90.7	(0.7)	76.4	(1.0)	81.6	(1.1)	82.0	(0.6)	-0.21	(0.02)	92.2	(0.6)	79.5	(1.1)	87.1	(0.6)	81.3	(1.0)
	Singapore	0.30	(0.02)	89.5	(0.6)	90.3	(0.5)	90.8	(0.7)	95.2	(0.4)	0.33	(0.02)	94.2	(0.5)	92.6	(0.5)	92.3	(0.5)	95.6	(0.4)
	Chinese Taipei	0.16	(0.02)	89.7	(0.6)	89.1	(0.6)	91.3	(0.5)	92.6	(0.5)	0.28	(0.02)	95.2	(0.3)	92.1	(0.4)	93.5	(0.5)	93.0	(0.5)
	Thailand	0.07	(0.02)	87.3	(0.9)	96.4	(0.4)	91.9	(0.7)	87.3	(0.7)	0.12	(0.02)	92.8	(0.5)	98.8	(0.2)	93.3	(0.5)	90.2	(0.6)
	Tunisia	0.04	(0.02)	87.4	(0.7)	93.9	(0.6)	73.2	(1.1)	84.9	(0.9)	0.18	(0.02)	90.5	(0.6)	94.3	(0.4)	74.2	(0.8)	88.7	(0.7)
	United Arab Emirates	0.22	(0.02)	86.3	(0.6)	90.0	(0.5)	84.1	(0.5)	89.2	(0.5)	0.41	(0.03)	90.2	(0.5)	95.1	(0.4)	88.1	(0.7)	92.8	(0.4)
	Uruguay	0.05	(0.02)	81.7	(0.7)	94.6	(0.5)	79.1	(0.9)	88.8	(0.7)	0.17	(0.02)	85.2	(0.7)	96.3	(0.4)	84.2	(0.8)	91.8	(0.5)
	Malaysia**	-0.09	(0.02)	84.7	(0.7)	93.7	(0.5)	76.4	(0.7)	89.1	(0.6)	0.04	(0.02)	89.8	(0.6)	94.4	(0.5)	74.6	(0.9)	91.0	(0.5)

Note: Values that are statistically significant are indicated in bold (see Annex A3).
* See note at the beginning of this Annex.
**Malaysia: Coverage is too small to ensure comparability (see Annex A4).
StatLink http://dx.doi.org/10.1787/888933616807

[Part 2/2]

Table V.5.4a Index of valuing relationships, by gender

		Gender difference (boys - girls):									
				Percentage of students who agreed/strongly agreed with the following statements:							
		Index of valuing relationships		I am a good listener		I enjoy seeing my classmates be successful		I take into account what others are interested in		I enjoy considering different perspectives	
		Dif.	S.E.	% dif.	S.E.	% dif.	S.E.	% dif.	S.E.	% dif.	S.E.
OECD	Australia	**-0.17**	(0.02)	**-6.3**	(0.6)	**-3.1**	(0.5)	**-2.9**	(0.5)	**-3.5**	(0.6)
	Austria	**-0.42**	(0.03)	**-5.3**	(0.9)	**-9.3**	(1.2)	**-6.7**	(0.9)	-1.7	(0.9)
	Belgium	**-0.19**	(0.03)	**-5.5**	(0.8)	**-4.6**	(0.7)	**-2.9**	(0.9)	-0.9	(0.6)
	Canada	**-0.17**	(0.02)	**-4.4**	(0.6)	**-3.5**	(0.6)	**-2.9**	(0.6)	**-3.7**	(0.6)
	Chile	**-0.19**	(0.03)	**-3.6**	(0.9)	**-4.7**	(0.9)	-2.2	(1.2)	-1.5	(0.9)
	Czech Republic	**-0.27**	(0.03)	**-6.7**	(0.8)	**-7.4**	(1.2)	**-8.2**	(1.0)	**-4.1**	(1.1)
	Denmark	**-0.17**	(0.03)	**-5.2**	(0.8)	**-2.2**	(0.7)	**-3.2**	(1.0)	**-5.2**	(0.9)
	Estonia	**-0.29**	(0.03)	**-7.3**	(0.9)	**-4.7**	(0.9)	**-4.7**	(0.8)	**-2.6**	(1.0)
	Finland	**-0.28**	(0.03)	**-7.7**	(0.8)	**-5.1**	(1.0)	**-3.7**	(0.8)	**-3.8**	(1.4)
	France	**-0.15**	(0.03)	**-2.9**	(0.9)	**-5.4**	(0.8)	**-2.3**	(1.1)	-1.2	(0.9)
	Germany	**-0.29**	(0.03)	**-4.1**	(0.8)	**-7.7**	(1.1)	**-4.9**	(0.9)	0.3	(1.1)
	Greece	**-0.20**	(0.03)	**-7.4**	(1.0)	**-2.7**	(0.9)	**-5.0**	(0.9)	**-4.8**	(0.7)
	Hungary	**-0.19**	(0.03)	**-6.4**	(1.0)	**-3.0**	(1.1)	**-5.7**	(1.1)	**-1.8**	(0.9)
	Iceland	-0.05	(0.04)	-0.9	(1.3)	**-3.5**	(1.1)	-2.9	(1.5)	**-3.4**	(1.0)
	Ireland	**-0.29**	(0.02)	**-7.9**	(1.0)	**-5.2**	(0.7)	**-4.3**	(0.7)	**-2.7**	(0.8)
	Israel	**-0.29**	(0.03)	**-5.1**	(0.8)	**-4.8**	(0.8)	**-4.0**	(1.0)	**-3.4**	(1.1)
	Italy	**-0.23**	(0.03)	**-9.8**	(0.9)	**-6.1**	(0.8)	**-5.6**	(1.1)	**-3.2**	(0.8)
	Japan	**-0.19**	(0.03)	**-7.0**	(1.3)	**-9.3**	(0.9)	**-4.2**	(1.1)	**2.7**	(1.1)
	Korea	-0.02	(0.03)	**-1.3**	(0.6)	**3.1**	(1.1)	**-4.5**	(1.0)	-0.9	(0.8)
	Latvia	**-0.26**	(0.03)	**-10.1**	(1.1)	**-8.4**	(1.2)	**-8.6**	(1.1)	**-6.1**	(1.2)
	Luxembourg	**-0.26**	(0.03)	**-5.4**	(0.9)	**-8.2**	(1.0)	**-7.1**	(1.0)	**-2.9**	(1.2)
	Mexico	**-0.22**	(0.02)	**-2.4**	(0.9)	**-1.7**	(0.7)	**-3.8**	(0.9)	**-2.0**	(0.6)
	Netherlands	**-0.11**	(0.02)	**-5.9**	(0.9)	**-2.8**	(0.7)	**-2.7**	(0.6)	-1.7	(1.0)
	New Zealand	**-0.24**	(0.03)	**-5.6**	(1.3)	**-3.8**	(0.8)	-1.4	(1.0)	**-3.6**	(1.1)
	Norway	**-0.34**	(0.03)	**-6.4**	(1.0)	**-6.5**	(0.9)	**-5.4**	(0.8)	**-7.0**	(1.0)
	Poland	**-0.11**	(0.03)	**-2.6**	(1.0)	-1.8	(1.3)	**-2.9**	(1.4)	**-2.8**	(0.9)
	Portugal	**-0.30**	(0.03)	**-5.9**	(0.7)	**-3.5**	(0.5)	**-3.6**	(0.8)	**-2.3**	(0.7)
	Slovak Republic	**-0.14**	(0.03)	**-3.0**	(1.3)	**-5.5**	(1.3)	**-6.1**	(1.0)	**-2.4**	(1.1)
	Slovenia	**-0.27**	(0.02)	**-7.3**	(1.2)	**-3.4**	(0.8)	**-5.7**	(0.9)	**-6.5**	(1.2)
	Spain	**-0.19**	(0.02)	**-3.3**	(0.7)	-1.2	(0.8)	**-4.3**	(0.9)	**-3.9**	(0.7)
	Sweden	**-0.17**	(0.03)	**-2.4**	(0.9)	**-3.7**	(1.1)	**-4.8**	(1.0)	**-4.0**	(1.1)
	Switzerland	**-0.38**	(0.03)	**-4.5**	(1.0)	**-6.6**	(1.0)	**-5.5**	(1.1)	**-2.8**	(1.0)
	Turkey	**-0.21**	(0.04)	**-4.6**	(1.0)	0.4	(1.2)	-2.1	(1.3)	**-4.2**	(1.0)
	United Kingdom	**-0.21**	(0.02)	**-7.1**	(0.9)	**-5.4**	(0.9)	**-2.8**	(0.7)	**-2.8**	(0.7)
	United States	**-0.09**	(0.03)	**-4.2**	(1.0)	**-2.4**	(0.6)	-2.0	(1.1)	**-1.9**	(0.8)
	OECD average-32	**-0.21**	(0.01)	**-5.3**	(0.2)	**-4.4**	(0.2)	**-4.3**	(0.2)	**-2.9**	(0.2)
	OECD average-35	**-0.21**	(0.00)	**-5.3**	(0.2)	**-4.4**	(0.2)	**-4.3**	(0.2)	**-2.9**	(0.2)
Partners	Brazil	0.01	(0.02)	-0.7	(0.7)	**-1.8**	(0.5)	**-1.9**	(0.6)	**-3.1**	(0.6)
	B-S-J-G (China)	-0.04	(0.02)	**-6.2**	(0.8)	**-2.2**	(0.9)	-1.5	(0.8)	0.9	(0.7)
	Bulgaria	**-0.20**	(0.03)	**-8.3**	(1.0)	**-5.1**	(1.0)	**-4.0**	(1.3)	**-3.7**	(1.0)
	Colombia	**-0.22**	(0.02)	**-1.9**	(0.7)	**-2.1**	(0.7)	**-7.4**	(0.9)	**-2.8**	(1.1)
	Costa Rica	**-0.13**	(0.03)	**-1.4**	(0.7)	**-2.6**	(0.5)	**-3.7**	(1.1)	**-3.3**	(0.6)
	Croatia	**-0.32**	(0.03)	**-4.6**	(0.7)	**-4.6**	(0.8)	**-6.7**	(1.3)	**-5.9**	(1.1)
	Cyprus*	**-0.31**	(0.03)	**-9.3**	(1.0)	**-7.5**	(0.8)	**-4.2**	(1.1)	**-5.4**	(0.9)
	Dominican Republic	**-0.19**	(0.04)	**-3.0**	(1.1)	-0.9	(1.0)	**-4.3**	(1.1)	**-4.6**	(1.4)
	Hong Kong (China)	-0.04	(0.03)	**-6.1**	(0.9)	**-5.9**	(1.1)	**-4.3**	(0.9)	**-1.9**	(0.8)
	Lithuania	**-0.28**	(0.04)	**-8.3**	(1.1)	**-5.9**	(1.1)	**-6.0**	(1.1)	**-4.6**	(0.9)
	Macao (China)	0.04	(0.02)	**-6.7**	(0.9)	**-4.2**	(1.0)	-0.7	(1.0)	0.8	(0.9)
	Montenegro	**-0.25**	(0.03)	**-4.7**	(1.0)	**-3.1**	(0.5)	**-5.6**	(1.1)	**-7.5**	(1.0)
	Peru	**-0.14**	(0.02)	**-2.0**	(0.6)	**-2.0**	(0.8)	**-3.1**	(1.0)	**-1.5**	(0.7)
	Qatar	**-0.14**	(0.02)	**-3.3**	(0.7)	**-7.0**	(0.5)	3.5	(0.8)	**-3.6**	(0.6)
	Russia	**-0.08**	(0.03)	**-1.5**	(0.8)	**-3.0**	(1.4)	**-5.6**	(1.2)	0.7	(1.1)
	Singapore	-0.03	(0.03)	**-4.6**	(0.8)	**-2.3**	(0.7)	**-1.6**	(0.8)	-0.4	(0.7)
	Chinese Taipei	**-0.12**	(0.02)	**-5.5**	(0.6)	**-3.0**	(0.7)	**-2.2**	(0.7)	-0.4	(0.6)
	Thailand	**-0.05**	(0.03)	**-5.4**	(1.0)	**-2.4**	(0.4)	-1.4	(0.8)	**-2.9**	(0.8)
	Tunisia	**-0.14**	(0.03)	**-3.2**	(0.9)	-0.4	(0.7)	-1.0	(1.2)	**-3.7**	(1.0)
	United Arab Emirates	**-0.18**	(0.03)	**-3.9**	(0.8)	**-5.1**	(0.6)	**-4.0**	(0.9)	**-3.6**	(0.7)
	Uruguay	**-0.11**	(0.03)	**-3.5**	(0.9)	**-1.8**	(0.6)	**-5.1**	(1.1)	**-2.9**	(0.8)
	Malaysia**	**-0.13**	(0.03)	**-5.0**	(0.8)	-0.7	(0.7)	1.8	(0.9)	**-1.9**	(0.7)

Note: Values that are statistically significant are indicated in bold (see Annex A3).
* See note at the beginning of this Annex.
**Malaysia: Coverage is too small to ensure comparability (see Annex A4).
StatLink http://dx.doi.org/10.1787/888933616807

[Part 1/2]

Table V.5.4b Index of valuing teamwork, by gender

		Boys										Girls									
				Percentage of students who agreed/strongly agreed with the following statements:										Percentage of students who agreed/strongly agreed with the following statements:							
		Index of valuing teamwork		I prefer working as part of a team to working alone		I find that teams make better decisions than individuals		I find that teamwork raises my own efficiency		I enjoy co-operating with peers		Index of valuing teamwork		I prefer working as part of a team to working alone		I find that teams make better decisions than individuals		I find that teamwork raises my own efficiency		I enjoy co-operating with peers	
		Mean index	S.E.	%	S.E.	%	S.E.	%	S.E.	%	S.E.	Mean index	S.E.	%	S.E.	%	S.E.	%	S.E.	%	S.E.
OECD	Australia	0.09	(0.01)	70.4	(0.7)	77.2	(0.6)	74.0	(0.6)	89.4	(0.5)	-0.08	(0.01)	61.8	(0.6)	70.2	(0.7)	70.8	(0.6)	88.5	(0.5)
	Austria	0.22	(0.02)	70.9	(0.8)	76.1	(0.8)	67.6	(1.0)	87.7	(0.7)	0.16	(0.02)	67.2	(1.1)	74.1	(1.0)	66.7	(0.8)	87.0	(0.7)
	Belgium	-0.04	(0.02)	68.9	(0.8)	74.1	(0.7)	64.0	(0.9)	85.7	(0.7)	-0.17	(0.02)	63.4	(0.7)	68.1	(0.8)	61.9	(0.6)	84.1	(0.5)
	Canada	0.12	(0.02)	72.7	(0.6)	75.5	(0.7)	72.9	(0.6)	88.2	(0.5)	-0.11	(0.01)	60.6	(0.7)	68.3	(0.7)	66.8	(0.7)	86.4	(0.5)
	Chile	0.26	(0.02)	73.9	(1.0)	77.7	(0.9)	82.2	(0.8)	93.1	(0.4)	0.15	(0.02)	69.7	(0.9)	71.6	(0.9)	80.1	(0.8)	93.2	(0.5)
	Czech Republic	0.03	(0.02)	72.6	(1.0)	77.7	(1.0)	68.2	(1.0)	88.4	(0.6)	-0.03	(0.02)	71.8	(0.9)	75.0	(0.9)	64.9	(1.0)	90.2	(0.7)
	Denmark	-0.04	(0.02)	67.7	(0.9)	69.6	(0.9)	63.2	(1.0)	91.2	(0.5)	-0.20	(0.02)	61.3	(1.1)	63.9	(1.1)	58.4	(1.1)	89.1	(0.7)
	Estonia	-0.05	(0.02)	63.8	(0.9)	74.8	(1.0)	72.0	(0.9)	82.5	(0.8)	-0.15	(0.02)	59.3	(1.1)	70.0	(0.9)	69.7	(1.0)	79.1	(0.9)
	Finland	-0.13	(0.02)	67.6	(1.0)	77.1	(0.7)	63.5	(1.0)	85.7	(0.8)	-0.31	(0.02)	57.8	(1.0)	66.0	(0.9)	55.3	(1.1)	79.9	(0.9)
	France	0.14	(0.02)	71.3	(0.9)	74.3	(0.9)	76.4	(0.7)	85.6	(0.6)	0.08	(0.02)	70.0	(1.0)	70.0	(0.9)	76.4	(0.8)	84.7	(0.7)
	Germany	0.18	(0.02)	68.1	(1.0)	73.3	(0.8)	65.0	(0.8)	91.9	(0.5)	0.11	(0.02)	63.6	(0.9)	70.1	(1.0)	65.6	(0.9)	91.5	(0.5)
	Greece	0.21	(0.02)	73.6	(0.9)	82.7	(0.8)	77.3	(0.8)	88.3	(0.6)	0.14	(0.02)	70.1	(0.8)	82.6	(0.8)	74.0	(0.9)	88.8	(0.6)
	Hungary	0.03	(0.02)	74.7	(0.9)	77.7	(0.9)	68.6	(0.9)	85.4	(0.8)	-0.06	(0.02)	73.4	(1.1)	76.4	(1.0)	65.0	(1.0)	86.0	(0.8)
	Iceland	-0.10	(0.03)	63.5	(1.2)	68.0	(1.3)	67.2	(1.2)	87.1	(1.0)	-0.29	(0.02)	53.4	(1.0)	57.7	(1.2)	62.8	(1.2)	86.3	(0.9)
	Ireland	0.07	(0.02)	70.3	(1.0)	75.3	(0.9)	71.9	(0.9)	88.8	(0.6)	0.01	(0.02)	65.4	(1.0)	72.8	(0.8)	72.1	(0.8)	86.4	(0.7)
	Israel	-0.04	(0.02)	63.7	(1.1)	74.1	(1.0)	65.4	(1.0)	86.1	(0.6)	-0.02	(0.02)	63.8	(1.0)	72.8	(0.8)	62.5	(1.0)	89.6	(0.6)
	Italy	0.09	(0.02)	73.7	(0.9)	75.0	(0.9)	72.1	(0.9)	88.1	(0.7)	-0.04	(0.02)	69.2	(0.8)	72.2	(0.9)	69.7	(0.8)	87.3	(0.7)
	Japan	-0.06	(0.02)	64.9	(0.9)	78.5	(0.9)	53.5	(0.9)	87.6	(0.7)	0.00	(0.02)	66.2	(0.9)	82.5	(0.7)	53.6	(1.0)	90.8	(0.5)
	Korea	0.22	(0.02)	80.0	(0.9)	84.4	(0.7)	85.5	(0.7)	87.9	(0.6)	0.06	(0.02)	70.6	(1.0)	81.5	(0.8)	83.3	(0.7)	85.6	(0.8)
	Latvia	-0.08	(0.02)	71.2	(0.8)	72.6	(1.0)	67.0	(1.1)	82.4	(0.8)	-0.19	(0.02)	66.8	(1.1)	68.6	(1.0)	64.2	(1.0)	81.1	(0.9)
	Luxembourg	0.05	(0.02)	69.8	(0.9)	71.8	(0.8)	67.1	(1.0)	86.2	(0.7)	-0.04	(0.02)	65.9	(0.9)	70.4	(0.9)	66.5	(0.8)	84.5	(0.7)
	Mexico	0.27	(0.02)	72.4	(0.8)	84.2	(0.8)	83.6	(0.8)	89.6	(0.6)	0.19	(0.02)	67.9	(0.8)	80.3	(0.7)	82.3	(0.8)	90.9	(0.6)
	Netherlands	-0.17	(0.02)	68.2	(0.9)	67.8	(1.1)	70.3	(1.0)	85.9	(0.7)	-0.34	(0.02)	59.8	(1.0)	57.9	(1.0)	66.0	(1.0)	82.3	(0.8)
	New Zealand	0.14	(0.02)	73.9	(0.8)	78.7	(0.9)	74.6	(1.0)	90.3	(0.7)	-0.01	(0.02)	65.3	(1.1)	73.1	(1.0)	71.4	(0.9)	89.1	(0.7)
	Norway	-0.15	(0.02)	64.5	(0.9)	68.9	(1.0)	58.6	(1.1)	85.9	(0.8)	-0.30	(0.02)	56.1	(1.1)	63.9	(1.1)	53.4	(1.2)	81.7	(0.8)
	Poland	0.00	(0.02)	75.1	(1.0)	73.1	(1.0)	70.8	(1.0)	86.2	(0.7)	-0.11	(0.02)	71.9	(1.0)	69.7	(1.0)	66.7	(1.0)	84.1	(0.8)
	Portugal	0.36	(0.02)	73.6	(0.9)	84.9	(0.8)	82.7	(0.7)	93.7	(0.5)	0.27	(0.02)	70.0	(0.8)	81.0	(0.9)	79.2	(0.7)	96.0	(0.4)
	Slovak Republic	-0.09	(0.02)	71.6	(0.9)	75.2	(0.9)	69.7	(0.9)	80.1	(0.8)	-0.16	(0.02)	72.0	(0.9)	73.3	(0.9)	69.5	(0.9)	81.0	(0.7)
	Slovenia	0.05	(0.02)	71.7	(1.0)	77.0	(0.9)	72.7	(1.0)	89.2	(0.7)	-0.01	(0.02)	67.0	(1.1)	73.3	(1.0)	69.6	(1.1)	88.8	(0.8)
	Spain	0.17	(0.02)	67.7	(0.9)	76.9	(0.9)	72.7	(0.9)	92.5	(0.5)	0.13	(0.02)	66.0	(1.1)	73.9	(1.0)	71.8	(0.9)	92.6	(0.5)
	Sweden	-0.06	(0.02)	64.5	(1.0)	67.5	(0.9)	70.3	(0.9)	86.6	(0.7)	-0.32	(0.02)	52.0	(1.3)	59.2	(1.1)	63.4	(1.0)	79.4	(1.1)
	Switzerland	0.26	(0.03)	76.0	(0.8)	76.6	(0.8)	72.4	(1.1)	90.9	(0.7)	0.18	(0.03)	70.0	(1.2)	74.4	(1.0)	70.8	(1.0)	91.3	(0.6)
	Turkey	-0.02	(0.02)	48.9	(1.1)	73.2	(0.9)	80.9	(0.9)	80.4	(0.7)	-0.07	(0.02)	47.0	(0.9)	68.8	(1.0)	76.9	(0.9)	80.9	(0.9)
	United Kingdom	0.01	(0.02)	71.3	(0.8)	75.9	(0.8)	71.6	(0.9)	85.8	(0.8)	-0.10	(0.02)	65.5	(0.9)	71.9	(0.8)	71.5	(0.8)	85.3	(0.7)
	United States	0.17	(0.02)	72.3	(0.9)	78.8	(1.0)	77.6	(0.9)	89.1	(0.7)	-0.05	(0.02)	65.7	(1.0)	71.2	(0.8)	70.9	(0.8)	85.0	(0.6)
	OECD average-32	0.06	(0.00)	69.5	(0.2)	75.7	(0.2)	71.2	(0.2)	87.4	(0.1)	-0.06	(0.00)	64.4	(0.2)	71.2	(0.2)	68.3	(0.2)	86.5	(0.1)
	OECD average-35	0.06	(0.00)	69.9	(0.2)	75.6	(0.2)	71.2	(0.2)	87.5	(0.1)	-0.05	(0.00)	64.8	(0.2)	71.3	(0.2)	68.4	(0.2)	86.5	(0.1)
Partners	Brazil	0.25	(0.01)	71.7	(0.8)	80.2	(0.5)	84.4	(0.5)	92.7	(0.4)	0.17	(0.01)	69.6	(0.6)	78.9	(0.5)	81.8	(0.5)	94.6	(0.3)
	B-S-J-G (China)	0.40	(0.02)	85.2	(0.6)	86.2	(0.5)	88.8	(0.6)	91.6	(0.6)	0.38	(0.01)	89.3	(0.6)	86.8	(0.6)	89.7	(0.6)	93.6	(0.5)
	Bulgaria	-0.02	(0.03)	69.3	(1.1)	74.7	(0.9)	74.7	(1.1)	80.8	(0.9)	-0.13	(0.02)	63.8	(1.1)	71.1	(1.0)	73.4	(0.9)	83.4	(0.9)
	Colombia	0.26	(0.02)	67.8	(1.0)	84.2	(0.6)	79.6	(0.8)	92.9	(0.5)	0.21	(0.02)	68.4	(0.8)	82.9	(0.7)	74.2	(0.9)	94.7	(0.4)
	Costa Rica	0.39	(0.02)	73.1	(0.8)	82.9	(0.9)	79.6	(0.7)	91.9	(0.5)	0.29	(0.03)	68.5	(1.0)	81.7	(0.8)	76.0	(1.0)	93.6	(0.5)
	Croatia	0.26	(0.02)	77.8	(0.8)	82.4	(0.7)	80.7	(1.0)	89.3	(0.7)	0.17	(0.02)	74.8	(0.9)	79.5	(0.9)	78.0	(0.8)	91.2	(0.6)
	Cyprus*	0.11	(0.02)	69.6	(0.8)	78.2	(0.9)	76.6	(0.9)	84.5	(0.8)	0.09	(0.02)	66.2	(0.8)	77.5	(0.8)	75.6	(0.7)	88.9	(0.6)
	Dominican Republic	0.54	(0.03)	73.3	(1.2)	82.0	(1.0)	83.9	(1.0)	93.5	(0.7)	0.48	(0.03)	73.7	(1.0)	81.8	(0.9)	81.0	(1.0)	94.2	(0.6)
	Hong Kong (China)	0.08	(0.02)	71.8	(1.0)	79.1	(0.8)	77.9	(0.8)	83.2	(0.8)	0.03	(0.02)	70.2	(1.0)	81.3	(0.8)	75.8	(0.8)	85.8	(0.7)
	Lithuania	0.38	(0.03)	75.7	(1.0)	80.4	(0.8)	78.7	(1.0)	85.6	(0.8)	0.28	(0.02)	71.0	(0.8)	76.8	(0.8)	80.4	(0.8)	85.9	(0.7)
	Macao (China)	0.02	(0.02)	68.5	(0.9)	73.0	(0.9)	79.5	(0.9)	84.1	(0.7)	-0.01	(0.02)	69.5	(1.0)	75.5	(1.0)	80.1	(0.8)	83.9	(0.7)
	Montenegro	-0.09	(0.02)	44.9	(1.0)	77.0	(0.8)	75.6	(0.8)	88.1	(0.6)	-0.09	(0.02)	42.6	(0.9)	75.0	(0.9)	73.2	(1.0)	91.0	(0.6)
	Peru	0.14	(0.02)	71.6	(0.9)	81.9	(0.7)	79.1	(0.7)	89.6	(0.5)	0.04	(0.02)	63.9	(1.0)	76.7	(0.9)	74.0	(0.8)	91.4	(0.5)
	Qatar	0.21	(0.02)	63.9	(0.6)	81.0	(0.6)	81.0	(0.6)	85.3	(0.5)	0.26	(0.01)	59.8	(0.6)	79.8	(0.5)	85.0	(0.4)	90.1	(0.3)
	Russia	-0.12	(0.02)	73.2	(1.2)	68.7	(0.9)	73.1	(0.9)	82.4	(1.0)	-0.24	(0.02)	70.4	(1.1)	66.7	(1.0)	67.9	(1.2)	78.3	(1.1)
	Singapore	0.34	(0.02)	75.3	(0.7)	81.9	(0.8)	80.5	(0.7)	91.7	(0.5)	0.20	(0.02)	69.7	(1.0)	82.7	(0.8)	79.7	(0.8)	92.6	(0.7)
	Chinese Taipei	0.42	(0.02)	85.1	(0.7)	85.0	(0.7)	86.4	(0.5)	90.4	(0.4)	0.31	(0.02)	84.4	(0.7)	83.3	(0.7)	84.0	(0.8)	90.6	(0.5)
	Thailand	0.42	(0.02)	83.2	(0.8)	90.6	(0.5)	89.6	(0.6)	95.4	(0.5)	0.33	(0.02)	82.9	(0.7)	90.5	(0.5)	85.5	(0.8)	97.1	(0.3)
	Tunisia	0.44	(0.02)	79.7	(0.9)	85.3	(0.8)	85.5	(0.8)	91.5	(0.6)	0.42	(0.02)	76.7	(0.9)	83.5	(0.8)	86.0	(0.7)	92.9	(0.5)
	United Arab Emirates	0.44	(0.02)	71.0	(0.7)	86.7	(0.5)	84.9	(0.6)	90.0	(0.5)	0.45	(0.02)	66.7	(0.7)	86.3	(0.5)	86.1	(0.6)	92.8	(0.5)
	Uruguay	0.25	(0.02)	71.5	(1.0)	80.8	(0.8)	76.0	(1.0)	91.9	(0.5)	0.16	(0.02)	69.2	(0.8)	79.2	(0.7)	74.5	(0.8)	93.7	(0.4)
	Malaysia**	0.58	(0.02)	88.7	(0.7)	91.1	(0.5)	92.4	(0.5)	95.3	(0.4)	0.59	(0.02)	86.4	(0.7)	90.9	(0.5)	92.2	(0.4)	96.1	(0.4)

Note: Values that are statistically significant are indicated in bold (see Annex A3).
* See note at the beginning of this Annex.
**Malaysia: Coverage is too small to ensure comparability (see Annex A4).
StatLink http://dx.doi.org/10.1787/888933616807

[Part 2/2]

Table V.5.4b Index of valuing teamwork, by gender

		Gender difference (boys - girls):									
				Percentage of students who agreed/strongly agreed with the following statements:							
		Index of valuing teamwork		I prefer working as part of a team to working alone		I find that teams make better decisions than individuals		I find that teamwork raises my own efficiency		I enjoy co-operating with peers	
		Dif.	S.E.	% dif.	S.E.	% dif.	S.E.	% dif.	S.E.	% dif.	S.E.
OECD	Australia	**0.17**	(0.02)	**8.7**	(0.8)	**7.0**	(1.0)	**3.2**	(0.9)	0.9	(0.6)
	Austria	0.06	(0.03)	**3.7**	(1.4)	2.0	(1.4)	0.8	(1.3)	0.6	(1.0)
	Belgium	**0.13**	(0.03)	**5.5**	(1.0)	**6.0**	(1.1)	2.1	(1.1)	**1.6**	(0.8)
	Canada	**0.23**	(0.02)	**12.1**	(0.9)	**7.2**	(1.0)	**6.1**	(0.9)	**1.8**	(0.8)
	Chile	**0.11**	(0.03)	**4.2**	(1.5)	**6.1**	(1.1)	2.1	(1.1)	-0.1	(0.6)
	Czech Republic	**0.06**	(0.03)	0.7	(1.3)	**2.8**	(1.3)	**3.3**	(1.3)	**-1.8**	(0.9)
	Denmark	**0.17**	(0.03)	**6.4**	(1.4)	**5.7**	(1.3)	**4.8**	(1.5)	**2.1**	(0.8)
	Estonia	**0.10**	(0.03)	**4.5**	(1.2)	**4.8**	(1.3)	2.4	(1.3)	**3.4**	(1.2)
	Finland	**0.18**	(0.03)	**9.8**	(1.3)	**11.1**	(1.1)	**8.3**	(1.2)	**5.9**	(1.0)
	France	**0.07**	(0.03)	1.3	(1.3)	**4.3**	(1.3)	0.0	(1.1)	0.9	(0.9)
	Germany	**0.06**	(0.03)	**4.4**	(1.3)	**3.2**	(1.3)	-0.6	(1.1)	0.5	(0.7)
	Greece	**0.07**	(0.03)	**3.5**	(1.1)	0.1	(1.1)	**3.3**	(1.2)	-0.5	(0.8)
	Hungary	**0.09**	(0.03)	1.3	(1.4)	1.3	(1.3)	**3.5**	(1.2)	-0.7	(1.1)
	Iceland	**0.19**	(0.04)	**10.1**	(1.6)	**10.3**	(1.8)	**4.4**	(1.7)	0.9	(1.2)
	Ireland	**0.06**	(0.02)	**4.9**	(1.4)	**2.5**	(1.2)	-0.2	(1.2)	**2.4**	(0.8)
	Israel	-0.02	(0.03)	-0.1	(1.5)	1.4	(1.2)	**2.9**	(1.3)	**-3.4**	(0.9)
	Italy	**0.13**	(0.03)	**4.5**	(1.2)	**2.9**	(1.2)	2.4	(1.3)	0.8	(0.8)
	Japan	**-0.06**	(0.03)	-1.2	(1.2)	**-3.9**	(1.1)	-0.1	(1.3)	**-3.2**	(0.8)
	Korea	**0.17**	(0.03)	**9.4**	(1.4)	**2.8**	(1.2)	**2.3**	(1.0)	**2.3**	(0.9)
	Latvia	**0.11**	(0.03)	**4.4**	(1.4)	**3.9**	(1.3)	2.9	(1.5)	1.3	(1.1)
	Luxembourg	**0.09**	(0.03)	**3.9**	(1.2)	1.4	(1.2)	0.6	(1.4)	**1.7**	(0.9)
	Mexico	**0.07**	(0.03)	**4.5**	(1.2)	**3.9**	(1.1)	1.3	(1.2)	-1.3	(0.9)
	Netherlands	**0.17**	(0.02)	**8.4**	(1.3)	**9.9**	(1.5)	**4.3**	(1.3)	**3.6**	(1.0)
	New Zealand	**0.15**	(0.02)	**8.6**	(1.2)	**5.5**	(1.2)	**3.1**	(1.2)	1.2	(0.8)
	Norway	**0.15**	(0.03)	**8.4**	(1.4)	**5.1**	(1.4)	**5.3**	(1.6)	**4.3**	(1.0)
	Poland	**0.11**	(0.03)	**3.2**	(1.5)	**3.4**	(1.5)	**4.1**	(1.2)	**2.1**	(0.9)
	Portugal	**0.09**	(0.03)	**3.6**	(1.1)	**3.9**	(1.2)	**3.4**	(0.9)	**-2.3**	(0.6)
	Slovak Republic	**0.07**	(0.03)	-0.4	(1.4)	1.9	(1.2)	0.2	(1.3)	-0.9	(1.0)
	Slovenia	**0.05**	(0.03)	**4.7**	(1.6)	**3.7**	(1.3)	**3.1**	(1.6)	0.4	(1.0)
	Spain	0.04	(0.03)	1.7	(1.3)	**3.0**	(1.1)	0.9	(1.2)	-0.1	(0.7)
	Sweden	**0.26**	(0.03)	**12.5**	(1.6)	**8.3**	(1.5)	**6.9**	(1.4)	**7.2**	(1.3)
	Switzerland	**0.08**	(0.03)	**6.0**	(1.4)	**2.2**	(1.1)	1.6	(1.3)	-0.4	(0.8)
	Turkey	0.05	(0.03)	2.0	(1.3)	**4.4**	(1.3)	**4.0**	(1.1)	-0.5	(1.0)
	United Kingdom	**0.12**	(0.03)	**5.8**	(1.1)	**4.0**	(1.1)	0.1	(1.2)	0.5	(1.1)
	United States	**0.22**	(0.03)	**6.6**	(1.3)	**7.6**	(1.1)	**6.7**	(1.1)	**4.1**	(1.0)
	OECD average-32	**0.11**	(0.00)	**5.1**	(0.2)	**4.4**	(0.2)	**2.9**	(0.2)	**1.0**	(0.2)
	OECD average-35	**0.11**	(0.00)	**5.1**	(0.2)	**4.3**	(0.2)	**2.8**	(0.2)	**1.0**	(0.2)
Partners	Brazil	**0.08**	(0.01)	**2.1**	(0.8)	1.3	(0.7)	**2.6**	(0.7)	**-1.9**	(0.5)
	B-S-J-G (China)	0.02	(0.02)	**-4.1**	(0.8)	-0.5	(0.9)	-0.9	(0.6)	**-2.0**	(0.7)
	Bulgaria	**0.11**	(0.03)	**5.5**	(1.4)	**3.6**	(1.4)	1.4	(1.3)	**-2.6**	(1.2)
	Colombia	0.04	(0.02)	-0.6	(1.2)	1.3	(0.8)	**5.3**	(1.3)	**-1.9**	(0.6)
	Costa Rica	**0.10**	(0.03)	**4.5**	(1.2)	1.1	(1.1)	**3.6**	(1.2)	**-1.7**	(0.7)
	Croatia	**0.09**	(0.02)	**3.0**	(1.2)	**2.9**	(1.0)	**2.7**	(1.1)	**-1.9**	(0.9)
	Cyprus*	0.02	(0.03)	**3.3**	(1.1)	0.6	(1.3)	0.9	(1.2)	**-4.4**	(1.1)
	Dominican Republic	0.05	(0.04)	-0.4	(1.5)	0.2	(1.2)	**2.9**	(1.5)	-0.7	(0.9)
	Hong Kong (China)	0.05	(0.03)	1.5	(1.3)	**-2.2**	(1.1)	2.1	(1.2)	**-2.6**	(1.1)
	Lithuania	**0.10**	(0.04)	**4.7**	(1.3)	**3.6**	(1.1)	-1.7	(1.2)	-0.3	(1.0)
	Macao (China)	0.02	(0.03)	-1.0	(1.3)	-2.4	(1.5)	-0.7	(1.2)	0.2	(1.0)
	Montenegro	0.00	(0.03)	2.3	(1.2)	2.0	(1.2)	**2.4**	(1.2)	**-2.9**	(1.0)
	Peru	**0.10**	(0.02)	**7.6**	(1.4)	**5.2**	(1.1)	**5.1**	(1.0)	**-1.8**	(0.7)
	Qatar	**-0.05**	(0.02)	**4.2**	(0.8)	1.1	(0.8)	**-4.0**	(0.7)	**-4.8**	(0.6)
	Russia	**0.12**	(0.03)	2.8	(1.7)	2.0	(1.1)	**5.2**	(1.3)	**4.2**	(1.1)
	Singapore	**0.15**	(0.03)	**5.5**	(1.2)	-0.9	(1.1)	0.9	(1.0)	-0.9	(0.8)
	Chinese Taipei	**0.11**	(0.02)	0.8	(0.9)	1.7	(0.9)	**2.4**	(0.8)	-0.2	(0.6)
	Thailand	**0.09**	(0.03)	0.3	(1.0)	0.1	(0.7)	**4.1**	(1.0)	**-1.8**	(0.6)
	Tunisia	0.01	(0.03)	**2.9**	(1.3)	1.8	(1.1)	-0.5	(0.9)	-1.4	(0.7)
	United Arab Emirates	-0.01	(0.02)	**4.4**	(1.1)	0.4	(0.7)	-1.2	(0.8)	**-2.9**	(0.7)
	Uruguay	**0.08**	(0.03)	2.2	(1.3)	1.7	(1.1)	1.6	(1.3)	**-1.8**	(0.7)
	Malaysia**	-0.01	(0.03)	**2.3**	(0.8)	0.2	(0.6)	0.3	(0.6)	-0.8	(0.6)

Note: Values that are statistically significant are indicated in bold (see Annex A3).
* See note at the beginning of this Annex.
**Malaysia: Coverage is too small to ensure comparability (see Annex A4).
StatLink http://dx.doi.org/10.1787/888933616807

[Part 1/2]

Table V.5.5a Index of valuing relationships, by socio-economic status

	Index of valuing relationships		Index of valuing relationships, by national quarter of student ESCS[1]										Index of valuing relationships, by national quarter of school ESCS									
			Bottom quarter		Second quarter		Third quarter		Top quarter		Top - bottom quarter		Bottom quarter		Second quarter		Third quarter		Top quarter		Top - bottom quarter	
	Mean index	S.E.	Mean index	S.E.	Mean index	S.E.	Mean index	S.E.	Mean index	S.E.	Index dif.	S.E.	Mean index	S.E.	Mean index	S.E.	Mean index	S.E.	Mean index	S.E.	Index dif.	S.E.
OECD																						
Australia	0.09	(0.01)	-0.06	(0.02)	0.05	(0.02)	0.13	(0.02)	0.24	(0.02)	**0.31**	(0.03)	-0.02	(0.03)	0.07	(0.02)	0.13	(0.03)	0.18	(0.02)	**0.20**	(0.03)
Austria	0.24	(0.01)	0.12	(0.03)	0.20	(0.03)	0.29	(0.03)	0.36	(0.04)	**0.24**	(0.05)	0.17	(0.04)	0.21	(0.04)	0.22	(0.03)	0.37	(0.03)	**0.20**	(0.05)
Belgium	-0.06	(0.01)	-0.16	(0.02)	-0.11	(0.03)	-0.03	(0.03)	0.04	(0.02)	**0.20**	(0.03)	-0.15	(0.03)	-0.14	(0.03)	-0.02	(0.03)	0.06	(0.03)	**0.21**	(0.04)
Canada	0.11	(0.01)	-0.03	(0.02)	0.06	(0.02)	0.17	(0.02)	0.24	(0.02)	**0.27**	(0.03)	0.00	(0.02)	0.11	(0.03)	0.11	(0.03)	0.21	(0.03)	**0.21**	(0.04)
Chile	0.09	(0.02)	-0.11	(0.03)	0.11	(0.04)	0.12	(0.04)	0.23	(0.03)	**0.34**	(0.04)	-0.13	(0.03)	0.07	(0.04)	0.17	(0.04)	0.23	(0.04)	**0.37**	(0.05)
Czech Republic	-0.20	(0.01)	-0.36	(0.03)	-0.23	(0.03)	-0.14	(0.03)	-0.06	(0.03)	**0.29**	(0.04)	-0.35	(0.03)	-0.27	(0.03)	-0.10	(0.03)	-0.08	(0.03)	**0.27**	(0.04)
Denmark	0.01	(0.01)	-0.12	(0.03)	-0.07	(0.03)	0.04	(0.03)	0.19	(0.03)	**0.31**	(0.04)	-0.12	(0.03)	-0.01	(0.03)	0.06	(0.02)	0.10	(0.03)	**0.22**	(0.04)
Estonia	0.03	(0.02)	-0.09	(0.04)	-0.02	(0.03)	0.06	(0.03)	0.17	(0.03)	**0.26**	(0.05)	-0.08	(0.04)	0.04	(0.03)	0.02	(0.04)	0.14	(0.04)	**0.22**	(0.05)
Finland	-0.08	(0.01)	-0.22	(0.03)	-0.12	(0.02)	-0.06	(0.03)	0.06	(0.03)	**0.28**	(0.04)	-0.18	(0.03)	-0.07	(0.03)	-0.07	(0.03)	-0.01	(0.03)	**0.17**	(0.04)
France	-0.07	(0.01)	-0.25	(0.03)	-0.14	(0.03)	-0.02	(0.03)	0.13	(0.03)	**0.38**	(0.04)	-0.27	(0.03)	-0.16	(0.03)	0.01	(0.03)	0.14	(0.03)	**0.41**	(0.04)
Germany	0.16	(0.02)	0.01	(0.04)	0.12	(0.03)	0.20	(0.03)	0.32	(0.03)	**0.31**	(0.05)	0.05	(0.04)	0.07	(0.05)	0.23	(0.04)	0.29	(0.03)	**0.25**	(0.05)
Greece	0.03	(0.02)	0.00	(0.03)	-0.05	(0.03)	0.05	(0.03)	0.13	(0.03)	**0.13**	(0.04)	-0.08	(0.03)	-0.01	(0.03)	0.06	(0.03)	0.15	(0.03)	**0.23**	(0.05)
Hungary	-0.03	(0.02)	-0.20	(0.03)	-0.04	(0.03)	0.01	(0.03)	0.11	(0.03)	**0.30**	(0.04)	-0.29	(0.04)	-0.05	(0.03)	0.01	(0.04)	0.20	(0.03)	**0.49**	(0.05)
Iceland	-0.09	(0.02)	-0.23	(0.04)	-0.18	(0.04)	-0.10	(0.04)	0.17	(0.04)	**0.39**	(0.06)	-0.22	(0.04)	-0.14	(0.04)	-0.05	(0.04)	0.07	(0.04)	**0.29**	(0.06)
Ireland	0.03	(0.01)	-0.09	(0.03)	0.03	(0.03)	0.05	(0.03)	0.13	(0.03)	**0.22**	(0.04)	-0.01	(0.03)	0.04	(0.03)	0.03	(0.04)	0.05	(0.04)	0.06	(0.05)
Israel	0.24	(0.02)	0.22	(0.03)	0.17	(0.03)	0.21	(0.03)	0.35	(0.03)	**0.13**	(0.05)	0.23	(0.05)	0.25	(0.04)	0.22	(0.04)	0.25	(0.04)	0.02	(0.06)
Italy	-0.13	(0.01)	-0.27	(0.03)	-0.13	(0.03)	-0.09	(0.03)	-0.06	(0.03)	**0.21**	(0.04)	-0.27	(0.03)	-0.16	(0.03)	-0.08	(0.03)	-0.03	(0.03)	**0.23**	(0.04)
Japan	-0.22	(0.02)	-0.34	(0.03)	-0.25	(0.03)	-0.18	(0.03)	-0.10	(0.03)	**0.24**	(0.04)	-0.37	(0.04)	-0.19	(0.04)	-0.16	(0.03)	-0.15	(0.04)	**0.22**	(0.06)
Korea	-0.02	(0.02)	-0.19	(0.03)	-0.04	(0.03)	0.00	(0.03)	0.17	(0.04)	**0.36**	(0.04)	-0.19	(0.04)	-0.02	(0.04)	0.03	(0.03)	0.11	(0.03)	**0.31**	(0.04)
Latvia	-0.30	(0.02)	-0.45	(0.03)	-0.32	(0.03)	-0.26	(0.03)	-0.16	(0.03)	**0.29**	(0.04)	-0.44	(0.04)	-0.33	(0.03)	-0.27	(0.03)	-0.17	(0.04)	**0.27**	(0.06)
Luxembourg	0.04	(0.01)	-0.06	(0.03)	-0.02	(0.03)	0.04	(0.03)	0.19	(0.03)	**0.25**	(0.04)	-0.08	(0.03)	-0.01	(0.03)	0.07	(0.03)	0.16	(0.03)	**0.24**	(0.04)
Mexico	0.16	(0.02)	0.08	(0.03)	0.10	(0.03)	0.15	(0.03)	0.33	(0.03)	**0.25**	(0.04)	0.03	(0.03)	0.05	(0.03)	0.22	(0.03)	0.35	(0.03)	**0.32**	(0.04)
Netherlands	-0.18	(0.01)	-0.23	(0.02)	-0.20	(0.02)	-0.17	(0.02)	-0.11	(0.03)	**0.12**	(0.04)	-0.22	(0.03)	-0.21	(0.03)	-0.18	(0.02)	-0.11	(0.03)	**0.11**	(0.04)
New Zealand	0.01	(0.02)	-0.10	(0.04)	-0.03	(0.03)	0.04	(0.03)	0.14	(0.03)	**0.24**	(0.04)	-0.04	(0.05)	-0.06	(0.04)	0.06	(0.03)	0.10	(0.04)	**0.14**	(0.06)
Norway	0.11	(0.02)	-0.02	(0.03)	0.10	(0.03)	0.14	(0.03)	0.21	(0.03)	**0.22**	(0.04)	0.06	(0.04)	0.15	(0.04)	0.08	(0.04)	0.14	(0.04)	0.07	(0.06)
Poland	-0.20	(0.02)	-0.37	(0.03)	-0.22	(0.03)	-0.14	(0.03)	-0.08	(0.03)	**0.29**	(0.04)	-0.21	(0.03)	-0.24	(0.04)	-0.17	(0.04)	-0.19	(0.04)	0.01	(0.05)
Portugal	0.38	(0.02)	0.27	(0.03)	0.32	(0.02)	0.44	(0.03)	0.47	(0.03)	**0.20**	(0.04)	0.32	(0.03)	0.32	(0.04)	0.39	(0.04)	0.46	(0.04)	**0.14**	(0.05)
Slovak Republic	-0.34	(0.01)	-0.53	(0.03)	-0.33	(0.02)	-0.34	(0.03)	-0.18	(0.03)	**0.35**	(0.04)	-0.50	(0.03)	-0.41	(0.04)	-0.33	(0.04)	-0.14	(0.03)	**0.36**	(0.05)
Slovenia	-0.04	(0.01)	-0.17	(0.03)	-0.04	(0.03)	-0.05	(0.03)	0.10	(0.03)	**0.27**	(0.04)	-0.17	(0.02)	-0.16	(0.03)	0.05	(0.03)	0.11	(0.03)	**0.28**	(0.04)
Spain	0.19	(0.02)	0.07	(0.03)	0.14	(0.03)	0.22	(0.03)	0.34	(0.03)	**0.27**	(0.04)	0.11	(0.03)	0.17	(0.04)	0.22	(0.03)	0.27	(0.04)	**0.16**	(0.05)
Sweden	0.05	(0.02)	-0.10	(0.03)	0.01	(0.03)	0.08	(0.03)	0.21	(0.03)	**0.31**	(0.05)	-0.03	(0.04)	0.03	(0.05)	0.08	(0.05)	0.13	(0.04)	**0.16**	(0.06)
Switzerland	0.20	(0.02)	0.15	(0.04)	0.14	(0.04)	0.14	(0.04)	0.35	(0.03)	**0.20**	(0.04)	0.19	(0.04)	0.13	(0.05)	0.16	(0.06)	0.30	(0.03)	**0.11**	(0.05)
Turkey	0.00	(0.02)	-0.02	(0.05)	-0.04	(0.03)	0.03	(0.04)	0.01	(0.04)	0.03	(0.06)	-0.11	(0.05)	0.02	(0.05)	0.02	(0.05)	0.05	(0.05)	**0.16**	(0.08)
United Kingdom	-0.03	(0.02)	-0.17	(0.03)	-0.05	(0.03)	0.00	(0.03)	0.09	(0.03)	**0.25**	(0.04)	-0.04	(0.03)	-0.10	(0.04)	-0.05	(0.04)	0.06	(0.03)	**0.09**	(0.05)
United States	0.13	(0.02)	-0.04	(0.03)	0.10	(0.03)	0.18	(0.03)	0.28	(0.03)	**0.32**	(0.04)	0.05	(0.04)	0.17	(0.04)	0.10	(0.04)	0.19	(0.03)	**0.14**	(0.05)
OECD average-32	0.01	(0.00)	-0.12	(0.01)	-0.03	(0.01)	0.04	(0.01)	0.14	(0.01)	**0.26**	(0.01)	-0.10	(0.01)	-0.02	(0.01)	0.04	(0.01)	0.12	(0.01)	**0.22**	(0.01)
OECD average-35	0.01	(0.00)	-0.12	(0.01)	-0.03	(0.01)	0.03	(0.01)	0.14	(0.01)	**0.26**	(0.01)	-0.10	(0.01)	-0.02	(0.01)	0.04	(0.01)	0.11	(0.01)	**0.21**	(0.01)
Partners																						
Brazil	-0.04	(0.01)	-0.13	(0.02)	-0.11	(0.02)	-0.03	(0.02)	0.11	(0.02)	**0.24**	(0.03)	-0.15	(0.02)	-0.11	(0.02)	-0.03	(0.03)	0.12	(0.02)	**0.28**	(0.03)
B-S-J-G (China)	0.01	(0.02)	-0.17	(0.03)	-0.07	(0.03)	0.06	(0.03)	0.22	(0.03)	**0.38**	(0.04)	-0.22	(0.02)	-0.05	(0.04)	0.09	(0.03)	0.21	(0.04)	**0.43**	(0.05)
Bulgaria	-0.03	(0.02)	-0.22	(0.03)	-0.03	(0.04)	0.01	(0.03)	0.11	(0.03)	**0.34**	(0.04)	-0.18	(0.05)	-0.11	(0.05)	0.01	(0.04)	0.14	(0.02)	**0.32**	(0.06)
Colombia	0.06	(0.01)	0.01	(0.03)	-0.04	(0.03)	0.05	(0.03)	0.20	(0.03)	**0.19**	(0.04)	-0.03	(0.03)	0.04	(0.03)	0.02	(0.02)	0.19	(0.03)	**0.22**	(0.04)
Costa Rica	0.35	(0.02)	0.31	(0.03)	0.31	(0.03)	0.31	(0.04)	0.45	(0.03)	**0.14**	(0.05)	0.31	(0.03)	0.32	(0.03)	0.33	(0.03)	0.43	(0.04)	**0.12**	(0.05)
Croatia	0.01	(0.02)	-0.08	(0.03)	-0.04	(0.03)	0.04	(0.03)	0.10	(0.03)	**0.18**	(0.04)	-0.08	(0.04)	-0.05	(0.05)	0.00	(0.05)	0.16	(0.04)	**0.24**	(0.05)
Cyprus*	0.07	(0.01)	-0.01	(0.03)	0.06	(0.03)	0.05	(0.03)	0.16	(0.03)	**0.17**	(0.05)	-0.08	(0.03)	0.19	(0.03)	0.17	(0.03)	-0.01	(0.03)	0.07	(0.04)
Dominican Republic	0.27	(0.02)	0.27	(0.05)	0.21	(0.04)	0.24	(0.04)	0.36	(0.04)	0.09	(0.05)	0.17	(0.06)	0.21	(0.08)	0.32	(0.05)	0.37	(0.03)	**0.20**	(0.07)
Hong Kong (China)	-0.04	(0.02)	-0.16	(0.03)	-0.01	(0.03)	-0.07	(0.03)	0.09	(0.03)	**0.25**	(0.04)	-0.12	(0.03)	-0.01	(0.04)	0.00	(0.02)	-0.02	(0.04)	**0.10**	(0.05)
Lithuania	0.16	(0.02)	-0.04	(0.03)	0.14	(0.03)	0.13	(0.04)	0.40	(0.04)	**0.43**	(0.05)	-0.02	(0.04)	0.09	(0.04)	0.20	(0.03)	0.36	(0.04)	**0.39**	(0.06)
Macao (China)	-0.15	(0.01)	-0.19	(0.03)	-0.14	(0.02)	-0.19	(0.03)	-0.08	(0.02)	**0.10**	(0.04)	-0.15	(0.03)	-0.08	(0.02)	-0.16	(0.02)	-0.21	(0.02)	-0.06	(0.04)
Montenegro	-0.05	(0.01)	-0.08	(0.03)	-0.09	(0.03)	-0.07	(0.03)	0.04	(0.03)	**0.12**	(0.04)	-0.07	(0.03)	-0.06	(0.03)	-0.10	(0.02)	0.03	(0.03)	**0.09**	(0.04)
Peru	-0.08	(0.01)	-0.29	(0.03)	-0.14	(0.03)	0.01	(0.02)	0.09	(0.03)	**0.38**	(0.05)	-0.30	(0.03)	-0.16	(0.04)	0.02	(0.03)	0.12	(0.04)	**0.42**	(0.06)
Qatar	0.12	(0.01)	-0.02	(0.03)	0.05	(0.02)	0.17	(0.02)	0.29	(0.03)	**0.31**	(0.03)	0.05	(0.03)	0.07	(0.02)	0.20	(0.02)	0.16	(0.02)	**0.12**	(0.03)
Russia	-0.25	(0.02)	-0.38	(0.04)	-0.29	(0.03)	-0.22	(0.04)	-0.13	(0.03)	**0.25**	(0.04)	-0.31	(0.03)	-0.27	(0.04)	-0.20	(0.03)	-0.22	(0.03)	0.09	(0.04)
Singapore	0.32	(0.02)	0.22	(0.03)	0.32	(0.03)	0.31	(0.03)	0.42	(0.03)	**0.20**	(0.04)	0.28	(0.02)	0.28	(0.02)	0.36	(0.03)	0.35	(0.05)	0.07	(0.05)
Chinese Taipei	0.22	(0.02)	0.07	(0.03)	0.20	(0.03)	0.30	(0.03)	0.31	(0.03)	**0.24**	(0.04)	0.13	(0.03)	0.18	(0.04)	0.28	(0.03)	0.28	(0.03)	**0.15**	(0.04)
Thailand	0.10	(0.02)	-0.01	(0.02)	0.10	(0.02)	0.11	(0.03)	0.18	(0.03)	**0.19**	(0.03)	0.06	(0.03)	0.07	(0.04)	0.06	(0.03)	0.19	(0.02)	**0.13**	(0.04)
Tunisia	0.12	(0.02)	0.12	(0.03)	0.15	(0.03)	0.09	(0.03)	0.12	(0.03)	0.00	(0.05)	0.04	(0.05)	0.14	(0.05)	0.19	(0.04)	0.11	(0.03)	0.07	(0.05)
United Arab Emirates	0.32	(0.01)	0.26	(0.03)	0.28	(0.03)	0.33	(0.02)	0.41	(0.03)	**0.16**	(0.04)	0.33	(0.04)	0.41	(0.04)	0.34	(0.03)	0.20	(0.03)	**-0.13**	(0.05)
Uruguay	0.11	(0.02)	0.01	(0.03)	0.05	(0.03)	0.15	(0.03)	0.25	(0.03)	**0.24**	(0.04)	-0.01	(0.04)	0.15	(0.03)	0.11	(0.03)	0.20	(0.03)	**0.21**	(0.05)
Malaysia**	-0.02	(0.02)	-0.14	(0.03)	-0.04	(0.03)	-0.04	(0.03)	0.12	(0.03)	**0.26**	(0.04)	-0.08	(0.05)	-0.11	(0.04)	0.06	(0.03)	0.04	(0.04)	**0.12**	(0.06)

1. ESCS refers to the PISA index of economic, social and cultural status.
2. Socio-economic profile is measured by the PISA index of economic, social and cultural status (ESCS).
Note: Values that are statistically significant are indicated in bold (see Annex A3).
* See note at the beginning of this Annex.
**Malaysia: Coverage is too small to ensure comparability (see Annex A4).
StatLink http://dx.doi.org/10.1787/888933616807

[Part 2/2]

Table V.5.5a Index of valuing relationships, by socio-economic status

	When accounting for student socio-economic status				When accounting for schools' socio-economic profile[2]				When accounting for students' and schools' socio-economic profile					
	Change in the index of valuing relationships per unit of student ESCS[1]		Explained variance in the index of valuing relationships (r-squared × 100)		Change in the index of valuing relationships per unit of school ESCS		Explained variance in the index of valuing relationships (r-squared × 100)		Change in the index of valuing relationships per unit of student ESCS		Change the index of valuing relationships per unit of school ESCS		Explained variance in the index of valuing relationships (r-squared × 100)	
	Index dif.	S.E.	%	S.E.	Index dif.	S.E.	%	S.E.	Index dif.	S.E.	Index dif.	S.E.	%	S.E.
OECD														
Australia	**0.15**	(0.01)	1.4	(0.3)	**0.16**	(0.03)	0.5	(0.2)	**0.14**	(0.02)	0.02	(0.03)	1.4	(0.3)
Austria	**0.11**	(0.02)	0.7	(0.2)	**0.11**	(0.04)	0.2	(0.2)	**0.10**	(0.02)	0.01	(0.04)	0.7	(0.2)
Belgium	**0.09**	(0.01)	0.8	(0.2)	**0.17**	(0.03)	0.7	(0.2)	**0.06**	(0.01)	**0.11**	(0.03)	1.0	(0.2)
Canada	**0.14**	(0.01)	1.3	(0.2)	**0.20**	(0.03)	0.5	(0.2)	**0.13**	(0.01)	**0.07**	(0.03)	1.4	(0.2)
Chile	**0.12**	(0.01)	1.5	(0.3)	**0.17**	(0.02)	1.6	(0.3)	**0.07**	(0.02)	**0.11**	(0.03)	1.8	(0.3)
Czech Republic	**0.15**	(0.02)	1.6	(0.4)	**0.21**	(0.03)	1.1	(0.3)	**0.12**	(0.02)	**0.10**	(0.03)	1.8	(0.4)
Denmark	**0.13**	(0.02)	1.6	(0.4)	**0.20**	(0.03)	0.7	(0.3)	**0.12**	(0.02)	**0.09**	(0.04)	1.7	(0.4)
Estonia	**0.13**	(0.02)	1.1	(0.3)	**0.21**	(0.04)	0.8	(0.3)	**0.10**	(0.02)	**0.11**	(0.05)	1.3	(0.4)
Finland	**0.15**	(0.02)	1.4	(0.3)	**0.22**	(0.05)	0.5	(0.2)	**0.13**	(0.02)	0.08	(0.05)	1.5	(0.4)
France	**0.19**	(0.02)	2.2	(0.4)	**0.35**	(0.03)	2.3	(0.4)	**0.12**	(0.02)	**0.23**	(0.04)	3.0	(0.5)
Germany	**0.12**	(0.02)	1.2	(0.3)	**0.23**	(0.03)	1.1	(0.3)	**0.09**	(0.02)	**0.14**	(0.04)	1.5	(0.4)
Greece	**0.05**	(0.02)	0.3	(0.2)	**0.17**	(0.03)	0.7	(0.3)	0.01	(0.02)	**0.16**	(0.04)	0.7	(0.3)
Hungary	**0.12**	(0.01)	1.4	(0.3)	**0.27**	(0.03)	2.7	(0.6)	0.02	(0.02)	**0.25**	(0.04)	2.7	(0.6)
Iceland	**0.21**	(0.03)	2.2	(0.6)	**0.37**	(0.07)	1.0	(0.4)	**0.18**	(0.03)	**0.19**	(0.08)	2.4	(0.6)
Ireland	**0.11**	(0.02)	1.0	(0.3)	0.04	(0.04)	0.0	(0.1)	**0.13**	(0.02)	-0.08	(0.04)	1.0	(0.3)
Israel	**0.06**	(0.02)	0.2	(0.2)	0.02	(0.05)	0.0	(0.0)	**0.07**	(0.02)	-0.06	(0.06)	0.3	(0.2)
Italy	**0.08**	(0.01)	0.6	(0.2)	**0.17**	(0.03)	0.8	(0.2)	**0.04**	(0.02)	**0.13**	(0.03)	0.9	(0.2)
Japan	**0.13**	(0.02)	0.7	(0.2)	**0.22**	(0.05)	0.5	(0.2)	**0.10**	(0.02)	**0.12**	(0.06)	0.9	(0.2)
Korea	**0.21**	(0.02)	2.3	(0.5)	**0.33**	(0.04)	1.4	(0.4)	**0.17**	(0.02)	**0.17**	(0.05)	2.5	(0.5)
Latvia	**0.12**	(0.02)	1.4	(0.4)	**0.21**	(0.04)	1.2	(0.5)	**0.08**	(0.02)	**0.13**	(0.05)	1.7	(0.5)
Luxembourg	**0.09**	(0.01)	0.8	(0.2)	**0.15**	(0.02)	0.6	(0.2)	**0.06**	(0.02)	**0.08**	(0.03)	0.9	(0.3)
Mexico	**0.08**	(0.01)	0.9	(0.3)	**0.16**	(0.02)	1.5	(0.4)	0.02	(0.01)	**0.13**	(0.03)	1.5	(0.4)
Netherlands	**0.05**	(0.02)	0.2	(0.2)	0.07	(0.05)	0.1	(0.1)	**0.04**	(0.02)	0.03	(0.05)	0.2	(0.2)
New Zealand	**0.13**	(0.02)	1.0	(0.3)	**0.15**	(0.05)	0.3	(0.2)	**0.12**	(0.02)	0.03	(0.06)	1.1	(0.3)
Norway	**0.12**	(0.02)	0.7	(0.3)	0.05	(0.07)	0.0	(0.1)	**0.13**	(0.02)	-0.07	(0.07)	0.7	(0.3)
Poland	**0.13**	(0.02)	1.4	(0.4)	**0.09**	(0.04)	0.2	(0.2)	**0.14**	(0.02)	-0.05	(0.05)	1.5	(0.4)
Portugal	**0.07**	(0.01)	0.7	(0.3)	**0.10**	(0.03)	0.4	(0.2)	**0.06**	(0.01)	0.03	(0.03)	0.8	(0.3)
Slovak Republic	**0.16**	(0.02)	2.3	(0.6)	**0.31**	(0.03)	3.1	(0.8)	**0.08**	(0.02)	**0.23**	(0.03)	3.5	(0.8)
Slovenia	**0.13**	(0.02)	1.2	(0.3)	**0.29**	(0.03)	1.9	(0.4)	**0.06**	(0.02)	**0.23**	(0.04)	2.1	(0.4)
Spain	**0.09**	(0.01)	1.3	(0.3)	**0.09**	(0.02)	0.4	(0.2)	**0.10**	(0.01)	0.00	(0.03)	1.3	(0.3)
Sweden	**0.14**	(0.02)	1.2	(0.4)	**0.20**	(0.05)	0.4	(0.2)	**0.13**	(0.02)	0.07	(0.05)	1.3	(0.4)
Switzerland	**0.08**	(0.02)	0.4	(0.2)	**0.09**	(0.04)	0.1	(0.1)	**0.07**	(0.02)	0.02	(0.05)	0.4	(0.2)
Turkey	0.02	(0.02)	0.1	(0.1)	**0.09**	(0.04)	0.3	(0.3)	0.00	(0.02)	**0.10**	(0.04)	0.3	(0.3)
United Kingdom	**0.11**	(0.02)	0.9	(0.3)	**0.09**	(0.04)	0.2	(0.1)	**0.11**	(0.02)	-0.02	(0.04)	0.9	(0.3)
United States	**0.12**	(0.01)	1.3	(0.3)	**0.11**	(0.03)	0.4	(0.2)	**0.12**	(0.02)	-0.01	(0.03)	1.3	(0.3)
OECD average-32	**0.12**	(0.00)	1.1	(0.1)	**0.18**	(0.01)	0.9	(0.1)	**0.09**	(0.00)	**0.09**	(0.01)	1.4	(0.1)
OECD average-35	**0.12**	(0.00)	1.1	(0.1)	**0.17**	(0.01)	0.8	(0.1)	**0.09**	(0.00)	**0.08**	(0.01)	1.4	(0.1)
Partners														
Brazil	**0.09**	(0.01)	1.1	(0.2)	**0.15**	(0.02)	1.3	(0.3)	**0.05**	(0.01)	**0.11**	(0.02)	1.5	(0.3)
B-S-J-G (China)	**0.14**	(0.01)	2.6	(0.6)	**0.22**	(0.02)	2.9	(0.6)	**0.08**	(0.02)	**0.15**	(0.03)	3.3	(0.6)
Bulgaria	**0.13**	(0.02)	1.5	(0.4)	**0.22**	(0.04)	1.4	(0.4)	**0.09**	(0.02)	**0.13**	(0.04)	1.8	(0.4)
Colombia	**0.07**	(0.01)	0.6	(0.2)	**0.12**	(0.02)	0.8	(0.3)	**0.03**	(0.01)	**0.09**	(0.02)	0.8	(0.3)
Costa Rica	**0.05**	(0.01)	0.3	(0.2)	**0.06**	(0.03)	0.2	(0.1)	**0.05**	(0.02)	0.02	(0.03)	0.3	(0.2)
Croatia	**0.08**	(0.02)	0.5	(0.2)	**0.21**	(0.05)	0.7	(0.3)	**0.04**	(0.02)	**0.17**	(0.05)	0.8	(0.3)
Cyprus*	**0.07**	(0.02)	0.4	(0.2)	0.04	(0.03)	0.0	(0.0)	**0.08**	(0.02)	-0.05	(0.04)	0.4	(0.2)
Dominican Republic	**0.05**	(0.02)	0.2	(0.1)	**0.13**	(0.03)	0.4	(0.2)	0.01	(0.02)	**0.12**	(0.04)	0.4	(0.2)
Hong Kong (China)	**0.10**	(0.02)	0.9	(0.3)	**0.09**	(0.03)	0.2	(0.1)	**0.10**	(0.02)	-0.01	(0.04)	0.9	(0.3)
Lithuania	**0.19**	(0.02)	2.0	(0.4)	**0.31**	(0.04)	1.5	(0.4)	**0.15**	(0.02)	**0.16**	(0.04)	2.3	(0.5)
Macao (China)	**0.04**	(0.02)	0.2	(0.1)	-0.03	(0.03)	0.0	(0.0)	**0.08**	(0.02)	**-0.10**	(0.03)	0.4	(0.2)
Montenegro	**0.05**	(0.02)	0.2	(0.1)	0.07	(0.04)	0.0	(0.1)	**0.05**	(0.02)	0.02	(0.05)	0.2	(0.1)
Peru	**0.13**	(0.01)	2.4	(0.5)	**0.19**	(0.02)	2.8	(0.6)	**0.06**	(0.01)	**0.13**	(0.02)	3.0	(0.6)
Qatar	**0.14**	(0.02)	0.8	(0.2)	**0.17**	(0.03)	0.3	(0.1)	**0.13**	(0.02)	0.04	(0.04)	0.8	(0.2)
Russia	**0.13**	(0.02)	1.1	(0.3)	**0.11**	(0.04)	0.2	(0.1)	**0.14**	(0.02)	-0.03	(0.05)	1.1	(0.3)
Singapore	**0.08**	(0.02)	0.5	(0.2)	**0.07**	(0.04)	0.1	(0.1)	**0.08**	(0.02)	-0.01	(0.04)	0.5	(0.2)
Chinese Taipei	**0.12**	(0.02)	1.1	(0.3)	**0.16**	(0.04)	0.4	(0.2)	**0.11**	(0.02)	0.05	(0.04)	1.1	(0.3)
Thailand	**0.07**	(0.01)	0.7	(0.2)	**0.08**	(0.02)	0.4	(0.2)	**0.06**	(0.01)	0.02	(0.03)	0.8	(0.3)
Tunisia	0.00	(0.01)	0.0	(0.0)	0.04	(0.03)	0.1	(0.1)	-0.02	(0.01)	0.06	(0.03)	0.1	(0.1)
United Arab Emirates	**0.08**	(0.02)	0.3	(0.1)	**-0.14**	(0.05)	0.2	(0.1)	**0.15**	(0.02)	**-0.28**	(0.06)	0.9	(0.3)
Uruguay	**0.08**	(0.01)	0.8	(0.2)	**0.09**	(0.02)	0.3	(0.2)	**0.08**	(0.02)	0.01	(0.03)	0.8	(0.2)
Malaysia**	**0.09**	(0.01)	1.1	(0.3)	**0.10**	(0.03)	0.5	(0.3)	**0.08**	(0.01)	0.02	(0.04)	1.1	(0.3)

1. ESCS refers to the PISA index of economic, social and cultural status.
2. Socio-economic profile is measured by the PISA index of economic, social and cultural status (ESCS).
Note: Values that are statistically significant are indicated in bold (see Annex A3).
* See note at the beginning of this Annex.
**Malaysia: Coverage is too small to ensure comparability (see Annex A4).
StatLink http://dx.doi.org/10.1787/888933616807

[Part 1/2]

Table V.5.5b Index of valuing teamwork, by socio-economic status

		Index of valuing teamwork		Index of valuing teamwork, by national quarter of student ESCS[1]										Index of valuing teamwork, by national quarter of school ESCS									
				Bottom quarter		Second quarter		Third quarter		Top quarter		Top - bottom quarter		Bottom quarter		Second quarter		Third quarter		Top quarter		Top - bottom quarter	
		Mean index	S.E.	Mean index	S.E.	Mean index	S.E.	Mean index	S.E.	Mean index	S.E.	Index dif.	S.E.	Mean index	S.E.	Mean index	S.E.	Mean index	S.E.	Mean index	S.E.	Index dif.	S.E.
OECD	Australia	0.01	(0.01)	0.04	(0.02)	0.01	(0.02)	0.01	(0.02)	-0.05	(0.02)	**-0.09**	(0.03)	0.03	(0.02)	0.03	(0.02)	0.01	(0.02)	-0.05	(0.02)	**-0.08**	(0.03)
	Austria	0.19	(0.01)	0.30	(0.03)	0.25	(0.03)	0.18	(0.03)	0.02	(0.03)	**-0.28**	(0.04)	0.40	(0.04)	0.23	(0.04)	0.12	(0.04)	0.00	(0.04)	**-0.41**	(0.05)
	Belgium	-0.11	(0.01)	-0.04	(0.03)	-0.07	(0.02)	-0.09	(0.03)	-0.22	(0.02)	**-0.18**	(0.03)	0.01	(0.03)	-0.04	(0.03)	-0.14	(0.04)	-0.24	(0.02)	**-0.25**	(0.04)
	Canada	0.00	(0.01)	-0.01	(0.02)	0.00	(0.02)	0.03	(0.02)	-0.01	(0.02)	0.00	(0.03)	-0.02	(0.02)	0.02	(0.03)	-0.01	(0.03)	0.01	(0.02)	0.04	(0.03)
	Chile	0.21	(0.02)	0.19	(0.03)	0.19	(0.03)	0.24	(0.03)	0.21	(0.03)	0.02	(0.04)	0.20	(0.03)	0.23	(0.04)	0.20	(0.03)	0.20	(0.03)	0.00	(0.04)
	Czech Republic	0.00	(0.02)	0.01	(0.03)	0.05	(0.03)	0.01	(0.03)	-0.06	(0.03)	-0.07	(0.04)	0.05	(0.04)	0.00	(0.03)	0.05	(0.04)	-0.08	(0.03)	**-0.13**	(0.05)
	Denmark	-0.12	(0.01)	-0.01	(0.03)	-0.11	(0.03)	-0.12	(0.03)	-0.24	(0.03)	**-0.22**	(0.04)	-0.02	(0.03)	-0.11	(0.03)	-0.13	(0.03)	-0.23	(0.03)	**-0.21**	(0.04)
	Estonia	-0.10	(0.02)	-0.05	(0.03)	-0.11	(0.03)	-0.10	(0.03)	-0.13	(0.03)	-0.08	(0.05)	-0.06	(0.04)	-0.05	(0.03)	-0.11	(0.03)	-0.16	(0.03)	**-0.11**	(0.04)
	Finland	-0.22	(0.02)	-0.21	(0.03)	-0.21	(0.03)	-0.21	(0.03)	-0.23	(0.02)	-0.02	(0.04)	-0.25	(0.04)	-0.15	(0.03)	-0.25	(0.03)	-0.22	(0.02)	0.03	(0.05)
	France	0.11	(0.02)	0.19	(0.03)	0.19	(0.03)	0.08	(0.03)	-0.03	(0.02)	**-0.22**	(0.04)	0.26	(0.04)	0.13	(0.04)	0.05	(0.03)	0.01	(0.03)	**-0.25**	(0.04)
	Germany	0.15	(0.02)	0.16	(0.03)	0.17	(0.03)	0.12	(0.03)	0.13	(0.03)	-0.03	(0.04)	0.21	(0.04)	0.16	(0.04)	0.14	(0.03)	0.09	(0.03)	**-0.12**	(0.05)
	Greece	0.18	(0.01)	0.30	(0.03)	0.17	(0.03)	0.18	(0.03)	0.08	(0.03)	**-0.22**	(0.04)	0.20	(0.04)	0.25	(0.03)	0.15	(0.03)	0.13	(0.03)	-0.07	(0.05)
	Hungary	-0.02	(0.02)	-0.01	(0.03)	0.01	(0.03)	-0.03	(0.03)	-0.06	(0.03)	-0.05	(0.04)	0.00	(0.03)	0.03	(0.04)	-0.03	(0.03)	-0.08	(0.03)	-0.08	(0.04)
	Iceland	-0.20	(0.02)	-0.24	(0.04)	-0.20	(0.03)	-0.17	(0.04)	-0.18	(0.04)	0.06	(0.06)	-0.24	(0.04)	-0.16	(0.03)	-0.19	(0.04)	-0.21	(0.04)	0.03	(0.05)
	Ireland	0.04	(0.01)	0.10	(0.03)	0.09	(0.03)	0.06	(0.03)	-0.07	(0.03)	**-0.17**	(0.04)	0.07	(0.03)	0.10	(0.04)	0.02	(0.04)	-0.02	(0.04)	-0.09	(0.06)
	Israel	-0.03	(0.02)	0.05	(0.03)	-0.01	(0.03)	-0.10	(0.03)	-0.07	(0.03)	**-0.13**	(0.04)	0.06	(0.05)	0.04	(0.04)	-0.09	(0.04)	-0.15	(0.04)	**-0.21**	(0.07)
	Italy	0.02	(0.02)	0.10	(0.03)	0.03	(0.03)	0.03	(0.03)	-0.06	(0.02)	**-0.16**	(0.03)	0.12	(0.04)	0.05	(0.04)	0.00	(0.03)	-0.07	(0.03)	**-0.19**	(0.05)
	Japan	-0.02	(0.02)	-0.03	(0.03)	0.00	(0.03)	-0.04	(0.03)	-0.03	(0.03)	0.00	(0.04)	-0.09	(0.04)	0.04	(0.04)	0.00	(0.03)	-0.05	(0.04)	0.03	(0.06)
	Korea	0.14	(0.01)	0.05	(0.03)	0.14	(0.02)	0.18	(0.02)	0.20	(0.03)	**0.16**	(0.04)	0.07	(0.03)	0.17	(0.03)	0.15	(0.03)	0.19	(0.03)	**0.12**	(0.04)
	Latvia	-0.14	(0.02)	-0.10	(0.04)	-0.06	(0.04)	-0.17	(0.03)	-0.21	(0.04)	**-0.11**	(0.05)	-0.08	(0.04)	-0.11	(0.04)	-0.14	(0.03)	-0.20	(0.04)	**-0.12**	(0.06)
	Luxembourg	0.00	(0.01)	0.10	(0.03)	0.04	(0.03)	-0.04	(0.03)	-0.09	(0.03)	**-0.18**	(0.04)	0.06	(0.03)	0.00	(0.03)	0.01	(0.03)	-0.06	(0.03)	**-0.12**	(0.04)
	Mexico	0.23	(0.01)	0.30	(0.03)	0.25	(0.03)	0.19	(0.03)	0.18	(0.03)	**-0.12**	(0.04)	0.28	(0.04)	0.20	(0.03)	0.25	(0.03)	0.19	(0.02)	**-0.09**	(0.04)
	Netherlands	-0.26	(0.01)	-0.23	(0.02)	-0.21	(0.02)	-0.26	(0.03)	-0.34	(0.02)	**-0.10**	(0.03)	-0.17	(0.03)	-0.24	(0.03)	-0.28	(0.03)	-0.34	(0.02)	**-0.17**	(0.04)
	New Zealand	0.06	(0.02)	0.11	(0.03)	0.13	(0.03)	0.01	(0.03)	0.01	(0.03)	-0.10	(0.05)	0.11	(0.05)	0.05	(0.04)	0.08	(0.04)	0.02	(0.03)	-0.10	(0.06)
	Norway	-0.23	(0.02)	-0.16	(0.03)	-0.18	(0.03)	-0.26	(0.03)	-0.31	(0.03)	**-0.15**	(0.04)	-0.21	(0.04)	-0.19	(0.04)	-0.27	(0.04)	-0.24	(0.04)	-0.04	(0.05)
	Poland	-0.05	(0.02)	0.03	(0.03)	0.02	(0.03)	-0.06	(0.03)	-0.20	(0.03)	**-0.23**	(0.05)	0.05	(0.03)	0.00	(0.03)	-0.04	(0.04)	-0.22	(0.03)	**-0.26**	(0.04)
	Portugal	0.32	(0.02)	0.37	(0.03)	0.36	(0.03)	0.33	(0.03)	0.22	(0.03)	**-0.15**	(0.04)	0.42	(0.03)	0.29	(0.04)	0.32	(0.03)	0.24	(0.03)	**-0.17**	(0.05)
	Slovak Republic	-0.12	(0.02)	-0.20	(0.03)	-0.05	(0.03)	-0.10	(0.02)	-0.13	(0.03)	0.07	(0.04)	-0.22	(0.04)	-0.09	(0.03)	-0.06	(0.03)	-0.13	(0.03)	0.09	(0.05)
	Slovenia	0.02	(0.01)	0.07	(0.02)	0.06	(0.03)	0.00	(0.03)	-0.04	(0.04)	**-0.12**	(0.04)	0.07	(0.02)	0.08	(0.03)	0.03	(0.03)	-0.09	(0.03)	**-0.16**	(0.04)
	Spain	0.15	(0.02)	0.22	(0.03)	0.16	(0.03)	0.09	(0.04)	0.12	(0.03)	**-0.10**	(0.04)	0.21	(0.03)	0.13	(0.04)	0.12	(0.03)	0.13	(0.04)	-0.07	(0.05)
	Sweden	-0.19	(0.02)	-0.17	(0.04)	-0.12	(0.05)	-0.21	(0.03)	-0.25	(0.03)	-0.08	(0.05)	-0.13	(0.04)	-0.19	(0.04)	-0.21	(0.03)	-0.23	(0.04)	-0.10	(0.06)
	Switzerland	0.22	(0.02)	0.36	(0.03)	0.25	(0.03)	0.21	(0.03)	0.06	(0.03)	**-0.30**	(0.04)	0.37	(0.03)	0.26	(0.05)	0.22	(0.05)	0.02	(0.03)	**-0.35**	(0.04)
	Turkey	-0.04	(0.01)	-0.11	(0.03)	-0.04	(0.03)	-0.02	(0.03)	-0.01	(0.03)	**0.10**	(0.04)	-0.14	(0.03)	0.00	(0.03)	0.00	(0.04)	-0.03	(0.03)	**0.11**	(0.05)
	United Kingdom	-0.04	(0.01)	-0.06	(0.02)	0.03	(0.03)	-0.06	(0.03)	-0.07	(0.03)	0.00	(0.04)	0.00	(0.03)	-0.07	(0.03)	-0.02	(0.03)	-0.08	(0.02)	**-0.09**	(0.04)
	United States	0.06	(0.02)	0.06	(0.03)	0.06	(0.03)	0.10	(0.03)	0.02	(0.04)	-0.04	(0.05)	0.07	(0.04)	0.07	(0.05)	0.04	(0.04)	0.05	(0.04)	-0.02	(0.06)
	OECD average-32	0.00	(0.00)	0.03	(0.01)	0.03	(0.01)	-0.01	(0.01)	-0.05	(0.01)	**-0.08**	(0.01)	0.04	(0.01)	0.02	(0.01)	-0.01	(0.01)	-0.05	(0.01)	**-0.09**	(0.01)
	OECD average-35	0.01	(0.00)	0.04	(0.01)	0.04	(0.01)	0.00	(0.00)	-0.05	(0.01)	**-0.09**	(0.01)	0.05	(0.01)	0.03	(0.01)	0.00	(0.01)	-0.05	(0.01)	**-0.10**	(0.01)
Partners	Brazil	0.21	(0.01)	0.23	(0.02)	0.20	(0.02)	0.17	(0.02)	0.22	(0.02)	-0.01	(0.03)	0.22	(0.02)	0.18	(0.02)	0.21	(0.02)	0.22	(0.02)	0.01	(0.03)
	B-S-J-G (China)	0.39	(0.01)	0.35	(0.02)	0.39	(0.03)	0.43	(0.03)	0.40	(0.03)	0.05	(0.04)	0.36	(0.02)	0.39	(0.03)	0.44	(0.04)	0.38	(0.03)	0.02	(0.04)
	Bulgaria	-0.07	(0.02)	-0.09	(0.03)	-0.03	(0.04)	-0.08	(0.04)	-0.07	(0.03)	0.03	(0.04)	-0.04	(0.05)	-0.06	(0.05)	-0.05	(0.04)	-0.13	(0.03)	-0.09	(0.06)
	Colombia	0.23	(0.01)	0.28	(0.02)	0.22	(0.02)	0.21	(0.02)	0.22	(0.02)	-0.06	(0.03)	0.28	(0.03)	0.25	(0.03)	0.21	(0.03)	0.20	(0.03)	**-0.08**	(0.04)
	Costa Rica	0.34	(0.02)	0.46	(0.03)	0.39	(0.03)	0.28	(0.03)	0.22	(0.04)	**-0.24**	(0.05)	0.49	(0.03)	0.39	(0.04)	0.26	(0.04)	0.20	(0.04)	**-0.28**	(0.05)
	Croatia	0.21	(0.02)	0.28	(0.03)	0.24	(0.03)	0.22	(0.03)	0.12	(0.03)	**-0.16**	(0.04)	0.31	(0.04)	0.23	(0.03)	0.20	(0.04)	0.11	(0.03)	**-0.21**	(0.05)
	Cyprus*	0.10	(0.01)	0.11	(0.03)	0.14	(0.03)	0.07	(0.03)	0.06	(0.03)	-0.05	(0.04)	0.11	(0.03)	0.20	(0.03)	0.14	(0.03)	-0.07	(0.03)	**-0.17**	(0.05)
	Dominican Republic	0.51	(0.02)	0.49	(0.05)	0.46	(0.04)	0.51	(0.03)	0.58	(0.04)	0.09	(0.06)	0.41	(0.05)	0.47	(0.06)	0.58	(0.04)	0.56	(0.04)	**0.15**	(0.07)
	Hong Kong (China)	0.06	(0.02)	-0.03	(0.03)	0.11	(0.03)	0.05	(0.03)	0.09	(0.03)	**0.11**	(0.04)	0.01	(0.03)	0.08	(0.04)	0.09	(0.04)	0.05	(0.04)	0.03	(0.05)
	Lithuania	0.33	(0.02)	0.35	(0.03)	0.42	(0.03)	0.29	(0.03)	0.27	(0.04)	-0.07	(0.05)	0.38	(0.04)	0.37	(0.03)	0.36	(0.04)	0.22	(0.04)	**-0.16**	(0.06)
	Macao (China)	0.01	(0.01)	-0.02	(0.02)	0.02	(0.02)	-0.01	(0.03)	0.03	(0.03)	0.05	(0.03)	0.00	(0.02)	0.02	(0.03)	0.03	(0.02)	-0.04	(0.03)	-0.04	(0.04)
	Montenegro	-0.09	(0.01)	-0.11	(0.02)	-0.04	(0.02)	-0.04	(0.03)	-0.16	(0.03)	-0.05	(0.03)	0.01	(0.03)	-0.05	(0.03)	-0.10	(0.03)	-0.19	(0.03)	**-0.20**	(0.04)
	Peru	0.09	(0.01)	-0.04	(0.02)	0.12	(0.02)	0.16	(0.03)	0.10	(0.02)	**0.15**	(0.03)	-0.05	(0.03)	0.10	(0.03)	0.16	(0.03)	0.13	(0.02)	**0.18**	(0.04)
	Qatar	0.24	(0.01)	0.17	(0.02)	0.25	(0.02)	0.26	(0.02)	0.27	(0.02)	**0.10**	(0.03)	0.22	(0.02)	0.29	(0.02)	0.29	(0.02)	0.15	(0.02)	**-0.07**	(0.03)
	Russia	-0.18	(0.02)	-0.16	(0.03)	-0.14	(0.03)	-0.18	(0.03)	-0.24	(0.04)	-0.08	(0.05)	-0.08	(0.03)	-0.13	(0.03)	-0.19	(0.04)	-0.31	(0.03)	**-0.23**	(0.05)
	Singapore	0.27	(0.01)	0.35	(0.03)	0.31	(0.03)	0.23	(0.04)	0.19	(0.03)	**-0.16**	(0.04)	0.37	(0.02)	0.32	(0.03)	0.31	(0.03)	0.08	(0.04)	**-0.30**	(0.05)
	Chinese Taipei	0.37	(0.02)	0.35	(0.03)	0.41	(0.02)	0.38	(0.03)	0.33	(0.03)	-0.02	(0.04)	0.41	(0.02)	0.35	(0.03)	0.41	(0.04)	0.31	(0.04)	**-0.11**	(0.04)
	Thailand	0.37	(0.02)	0.31	(0.02)	0.36	(0.02)	0.38	(0.03)	0.43	(0.03)	**0.12**	(0.03)	0.36	(0.03)	0.37	(0.04)	0.35	(0.03)	0.41	(0.02)	0.05	(0.04)
	Tunisia	0.43	(0.02)	0.54	(0.03)	0.51	(0.03)	0.42	(0.03)	0.25	(0.03)	**-0.28**	(0.05)	0.56	(0.04)	0.47	(0.04)	0.43	(0.04)	0.25	(0.03)	**-0.31**	(0.05)
	United Arab Emirates	0.45	(0.01)	0.47	(0.02)	0.46	(0.02)	0.47	(0.03)	0.40	(0.03)	**-0.07**	(0.03)	0.51	(0.03)	0.54	(0.03)	0.50	(0.03)	0.25	(0.03)	**-0.26**	(0.04)
	Uruguay	0.20	(0.01)	0.22	(0.03)	0.25	(0.03)	0.23	(0.03)	0.12	(0.03)	**-0.10**	(0.04)	0.27	(0.04)	0.26	(0.03)	0.18	(0.03)	0.12	(0.02)	**-0.15**	(0.04)
	Malaysia**	0.59	(0.02)	0.59	(0.03)	0.61	(0.03)	0.57	(0.03)	0.58	(0.03)	-0.01	(0.04)	0.65	(0.05)	0.54	(0.04)	0.64	(0.05)	0.52	(0.04)	**-0.13**	(0.06)

1. ESCS refers to the PISA index of economic, social and cultural status.
2. Socio-economic profile is measured by the PISA index of economic, social and cultural status (ESCS).
Note: Values that are statistically significant are indicated in bold (see Annex A3).
* See note at the beginning of this Annex.
**Malaysia: Coverage is too small to ensure comparability (see Annex A4).
StatLink http://dx.doi.org/10.1787/888933616807

[Part 2/2]

Table V.5.5b Index of valuing teamwork, by socio-economic status

		When accounting for student socio-economic status				When accounting for schools' socio-economic profile[2]				When accounting for students' and schools' socio-economic profile					
		Change in the index of valuing teamwork per unit of student ESCS[1]		Explained variance in the index of valuing teamwork (r-squared × 100)		Change in the index of valuing teamwork per unit of school ESCS		Explained variance in the index of valuing teamwork (r-squared × 100)		Change in the index of valuing teamwork per unit of student ESCS		Change in the index of valuing teamwork per unit of school ESCS		Explained variance in the index of valuing teamwork (r-squared × 100)	
		Index dif.	S.E.	%	S.E.	Index dif.	S.E.	%	S.E.	Index dif.	S.E.	Index dif.	S.E.	%	S.E.
OECD	Australia	**-0.03**	(0.01)	0.1	(0.0)	**-0.07**	(0.02)	0.1	(0.1)	-0.02	(0.01)	-0.05	(0.02)	0.1	(0.1)
	Austria	**-0.12**	(0.02)	0.9	(0.2)	**-0.34**	(0.03)	2.1	(0.4)	-0.02	(0.02)	**-0.31**	(0.04)	2.1	(0.4)
	Belgium	**-0.07**	(0.01)	0.4	(0.2)	**-0.21**	(0.03)	1.0	(0.3)	-0.02	(0.01)	**-0.19**	(0.03)	1.0	(0.3)
	Canada	0.01	(0.01)	0.0	(0.0)	0.02	(0.03)	0.0	(0.0)	0.01	(0.01)	0.01	(0.03)	0.0	(0.0)
	Chile	0.01	(0.01)	0.0	(0.0)	-0.01	(0.02)	0.0	(0.0)	0.03	(0.02)	-0.04	(0.02)	0.1	(0.1)
	Czech Republic	-0.03	(0.02)	0.0	(0.1)	**-0.12**	(0.03)	0.3	(0.1)	0.01	(0.02)	**-0.13**	(0.04)	0.3	(0.1)
	Denmark	**-0.09**	(0.02)	0.7	(0.3)	**-0.20**	(0.03)	0.7	(0.2)	**-0.06**	(0.02)	**-0.14**	(0.04)	0.9	(0.3)
	Estonia	-0.03	(0.02)	0.1	(0.1)	**-0.09**	(0.04)	0.1	(0.1)	-0.01	(0.02)	-0.08	(0.05)	0.1	(0.1)
	Finland	0.00	(0.02)	0.0	(0.0)	0.01	(0.04)	0.0	(0.0)	-0.01	(0.02)	0.02	(0.05)	0.0	(0.0)
	France	**-0.10**	(0.02)	0.5	(0.2)	**-0.21**	(0.04)	0.7	(0.2)	**-0.05**	(0.02)	**-0.15**	(0.05)	0.8	(0.2)
	Germany	-0.02	(0.01)	0.0	(0.1)	**-0.09**	(0.04)	0.2	(0.2)	0.00	(0.02)	**-0.10**	(0.04)	0.2	(0.2)
	Greece	**-0.07**	(0.02)	0.5	(0.2)	**-0.08**	(0.03)	0.2	(0.1)	**-0.07**	(0.02)	-0.01	(0.03)	0.5	(0.2)
	Hungary	-0.02	(0.02)	0.0	(0.1)	**-0.06**	(0.03)	0.1	(0.1)	0.01	(0.02)	**-0.07**	(0.04)	0.2	(0.1)
	Iceland	0.04	(0.03)	0.1	(0.1)	0.09	(0.06)	0.1	(0.1)	0.03	(0.03)	0.05	(0.07)	0.1	(0.2)
	Ireland	**-0.07**	(0.02)	0.3	(0.2)	**-0.11**	(0.04)	0.2	(0.1)	**-0.06**	(0.02)	-0.05	(0.04)	0.4	(0.2)
	Israel	**-0.06**	(0.02)	0.2	(0.1)	**-0.21**	(0.05)	0.7	(0.3)	-0.01	(0.02)	**-0.20**	(0.06)	0.7	(0.3)
	Italy	**-0.06**	(0.01)	0.4	(0.2)	**-0.15**	(0.03)	0.6	(0.2)	**-0.03**	(0.01)	**-0.12**	(0.03)	0.6	(0.2)
	Japan	-0.01	(0.02)	0.0	(0.0)	0.00	(0.06)	0.0	(0.0)	-0.01	(0.02)	0.01	(0.06)	0.0	(0.0)
	Korea	**0.09**	(0.02)	0.4	(0.2)	**0.11**	(0.05)	0.2	(0.1)	**0.08**	(0.02)	0.03	(0.05)	0.4	(0.2)
	Latvia	**-0.05**	(0.02)	0.2	(0.2)	**-0.10**	(0.05)	0.2	(0.2)	-0.03	(0.02)	-0.07	(0.05)	0.3	(0.2)
	Luxembourg	**-0.06**	(0.01)	0.3	(0.2)	**-0.08**	(0.02)	0.2	(0.1)	**-0.05**	(0.02)	-0.04	(0.03)	0.4	(0.2)
	Mexico	**-0.04**	(0.01)	0.2	(0.1)	**-0.03**	(0.02)	0.1	(0.1)	**-0.04**	(0.01)	0.00	(0.02)	0.2	(0.1)
	Netherlands	**-0.05**	(0.02)	0.3	(0.2)	**-0.20**	(0.04)	0.8	(0.3)	-0.01	(0.02)	**-0.18**	(0.04)	0.8	(0.3)
	New Zealand	-0.05	(0.02)	0.1	(0.1)	-0.10	(0.05)	0.1	(0.1)	-0.03	(0.03)	-0.06	(0.06)	0.2	(0.2)
	Norway	**-0.06**	(0.02)	0.2	(0.1)	-0.11	(0.07)	0.1	(0.1)	**-0.05**	(0.02)	-0.06	(0.07)	0.2	(0.2)
	Poland	**-0.12**	(0.02)	0.9	(0.3)	**-0.25**	(0.05)	0.9	(0.3)	**-0.08**	(0.02)	**-0.17**	(0.06)	1.3	(0.4)
	Portugal	**-0.05**	(0.01)	0.3	(0.1)	**-0.09**	(0.02)	0.3	(0.1)	**-0.03**	(0.02)	**-0.06**	(0.03)	0.4	(0.2)
	Slovak Republic	0.04	(0.02)	0.1	(0.1)	**0.11**	(0.04)	0.4	(0.3)	0.00	(0.02)	**0.11**	(0.04)	0.4	(0.3)
	Slovenia	**-0.05**	(0.02)	0.2	(0.1)	**-0.15**	(0.03)	0.5	(0.2)	0.00	(0.02)	**-0.15**	(0.04)	0.5	(0.2)
	Spain	**-0.03**	(0.01)	0.1	(0.1)	-0.03	(0.03)	0.0	(0.1)	**-0.03**	(0.01)	-0.01	(0.03)	0.1	(0.1)
	Sweden	**-0.04**	(0.02)	0.1	(0.1)	-0.08	(0.06)	0.1	(0.1)	-0.03	(0.02)	-0.05	(0.06)	0.1	(0.1)
	Switzerland	**-0.12**	(0.02)	1.2	(0.3)	**-0.31**	(0.04)	1.8	(0.5)	**-0.07**	(0.02)	**-0.24**	(0.05)	2.0	(0.5)
	Turkey	**0.03**	(0.01)	0.2	(0.1)	**0.07**	(0.02)	0.2	(0.1)	0.02	(0.01)	**0.05**	(0.03)	0.3	(0.2)
	United Kingdom	-0.01	(0.02)	0.0	(0.0)	-0.06	(0.03)	0.1	(0.1)	0.01	(0.02)	-0.07	(0.04)	0.1	(0.1)
	United States	-0.01	(0.02)	0.0	(0.0)	-0.03	(0.04)	0.0	(0.1)	-0.01	(0.02)	-0.02	(0.04)	0.0	(0.1)
	OECD average-32	**-0.03**	(0.00)	0.2	(0.0)	**-0.08**	(0.01)	0.3	(0.0)	**-0.01**	(0.00)	**-0.06**	(0.01)	0.4	(0.0)
	OECD average-35	**-0.04**	(0.00)	0.3	(0.0)	**-0.09**	(0.01)	0.4	(0.0)	**-0.02**	(0.00)	**-0.07**	(0.01)	0.5	(0.0)
Partners	Brazil	0.00	(0.01)	0.0	(0.0)	0.00	(0.01)	0.0	(0.0)	0.00	(0.01)	0.00	(0.02)	0.0	(0.0)
	B-S-J-G (China)	0.02	(0.01)	0.1	(0.1)	0.00	(0.02)	0.0	(0.0)	**0.03**	(0.01)	-0.03	(0.02)	0.1	(0.1)
	Bulgaria	0.01	(0.02)	0.0	(0.0)	-0.04	(0.03)	0.0	(0.1)	0.04	(0.02)	-0.08	(0.04)	0.1	(0.1)
	Colombia	**-0.02**	(0.01)	0.1	(0.1)	**-0.05**	(0.02)	0.1	(0.1)	0.00	(0.01)	-0.04	(0.02)	0.1	(0.1)
	Costa Rica	**-0.08**	(0.01)	0.9	(0.3)	**-0.15**	(0.03)	1.1	(0.4)	**-0.04**	(0.02)	**-0.11**	(0.04)	1.3	(0.4)
	Croatia	**-0.07**	(0.02)	0.4	(0.2)	**-0.19**	(0.03)	0.6	(0.2)	**-0.04**	(0.02)	**-0.14**	(0.04)	0.7	(0.2)
	Cyprus*	-0.03	(0.02)	0.1	(0.1)	**-0.14**	(0.03)	0.4	(0.2)	0.01	(0.02)	**-0.15**	(0.04)	0.4	(0.2)
	Dominican Republic	**0.04**	(0.02)	0.2	(0.1)	**0.09**	(0.03)	0.2	(0.2)	0.02	(0.02)	0.07	(0.04)	0.3	(0.2)
	Hong Kong (China)	**0.04**	(0.02)	0.2	(0.1)	0.05	(0.03)	0.0	(0.1)	**0.04**	(0.02)	0.00	(0.04)	0.2	(0.1)
	Lithuania	-0.01	(0.02)	0.0	(0.0)	**-0.14**	(0.04)	0.3	(0.2)	0.04	(0.02)	**-0.18**	(0.05)	0.4	(0.2)
	Macao (China)	0.01	(0.02)	0.0	(0.0)	-0.02	(0.03)	0.0	(0.0)	0.02	(0.02)	-0.04	(0.03)	0.0	(0.1)
	Montenegro	-0.03	(0.02)	0.1	(0.1)	**-0.28**	(0.04)	0.9	(0.3)	0.02	(0.02)	**-0.30**	(0.05)	0.9	(0.3)
	Peru	**0.05**	(0.01)	0.5	(0.2)	**0.07**	(0.02)	0.5	(0.2)	**0.03**	(0.01)	**0.04**	(0.02)	0.5	(0.3)
	Qatar	**0.05**	(0.01)	0.2	(0.1)	-0.02	(0.03)	0.0	(0.0)	**0.07**	(0.01)	**-0.09**	(0.03)	0.2	(0.1)
	Russia	**-0.05**	(0.02)	0.2	(0.2)	**-0.20**	(0.05)	0.7	(0.3)	0.00	(0.02)	**-0.20**	(0.05)	0.7	(0.3)
	Singapore	**-0.07**	(0.02)	0.4	(0.2)	**-0.22**	(0.03)	1.0	(0.3)	-0.01	(0.02)	**-0.21**	(0.03)	1.1	(0.3)
	Chinese Taipei	0.00	(0.01)	0.0	(0.0)	**-0.08**	(0.03)	0.1	(0.1)	0.03	(0.02)	**-0.11**	(0.04)	0.2	(0.1)
	Thailand	**0.04**	(0.01)	0.3	(0.2)	0.03	(0.02)	0.1	(0.1)	**0.05**	(0.01)	-0.01	(0.02)	0.3	(0.2)
	Tunisia	**-0.09**	(0.01)	1.1	(0.3)	**-0.17**	(0.03)	1.3	(0.4)	**-0.05**	(0.02)	**-0.12**	(0.03)	1.5	(0.4)
	United Arab Emirates	-0.02	(0.02)	0.0	(0.0)	**-0.25**	(0.05)	0.8	(0.3)	**0.06**	(0.02)	**-0.31**	(0.06)	0.9	(0.3)
	Uruguay	**-0.04**	(0.01)	0.2	(0.1)	**-0.10**	(0.02)	0.4	(0.1)	0.00	(0.02)	**-0.10**	(0.02)	0.4	(0.1)
	Malaysia**	0.00	(0.01)	0.0	(0.0)	-0.07	(0.03)	0.2	(0.2)	0.02	(0.01)	**-0.09**	(0.04)	0.3	(0.2)

1. ESCS refers to the PISA index of economic, social and cultural status.
2. Socio-economic profile is measured by the PISA index of economic, social and cultural status (ESCS).
Note: Values that are statistically significant are indicated in bold (see Annex A3).
* See note at the beginning of this Annex.
**Malaysia: Coverage is too small to ensure comparability (see Annex A4).
StatLink http://dx.doi.org/10.1787/888933616807

[Part 1/1]

Table V.5.8a Index of valuing relationships, by immigrant background

		Index of valuing relationships										Difference in the index of valuing relationships					
		All students		Non-immigrant students		Immigrant students		Second-generation immigrants		First-generation immigrants		Non-immigrants minus immigrants		Non-immigrants minus second-generation immigrants		Non-immigrants minus first-generation immigrants	
		Mean index	S.E.	Mean index	S.E.	Mean index	S.E.	Mean index	S.E.	Mean index	S.E.	Index dif.	S.E.	Index dif.	S.E.	Index dif.	S.E.
OECD	Australia	0.09	(0.01)	0.05	(0.01)	0.19	(0.03)	0.18	(0.03)	0.20	(0.03)	**-0.13**	(0.03)	**-0.12**	(0.03)	**-0.14**	(0.04)
	Austria	0.24	(0.01)	0.25	(0.02)	0.21	(0.03)	0.23	(0.04)	0.17	(0.06)	0.04	(0.04)	0.02	(0.05)	0.09	(0.06)
	Belgium	-0.06	(0.01)	-0.07	(0.01)	-0.04	(0.03)	-0.02	(0.04)	-0.06	(0.04)	-0.03	(0.03)	-0.04	(0.04)	-0.01	(0.05)
	Canada	0.11	(0.01)	0.07	(0.01)	0.21	(0.02)	0.20	(0.02)	0.23	(0.04)	**-0.14**	(0.02)	**-0.13**	(0.02)	**-0.16**	(0.04)
	Chile	0.09	(0.02)	0.09	(0.02)	-0.09	(0.09)	0.13	(0.18)	-0.17	(0.12)	0.18	(0.10)	-0.04	(0.18)	**0.26**	(0.13)
	Czech Republic	-0.19	(0.01)	-0.19	(0.01)	-0.42	(0.08)	-0.36	(0.12)	-0.47	(0.10)	**0.23**	(0.08)	0.17	(0.12)	**0.29**	(0.10)
	Denmark	0.01	(0.01)	0.02	(0.02)	-0.03	(0.03)	0.00	(0.04)	-0.13	(0.07)	0.05	(0.04)	0.01	(0.05)	**0.15**	(0.07)
	Estonia	0.03	(0.02)	0.05	(0.02)	-0.12	(0.04)	-0.13	(0.05)	0.06	(0.23)	**0.17**	(0.05)	**0.18**	(0.05)	-0.01	(0.23)
	Finland	-0.08	(0.01)	-0.08	(0.01)	-0.06	(0.07)	0.06	(0.08)	-0.16	(0.10)	-0.02	(0.07)	-0.14	(0.08)	0.07	(0.10)
	France	-0.07	(0.01)	-0.06	(0.02)	-0.09	(0.04)	-0.10	(0.05)	-0.06	(0.06)	0.02	(0.04)	0.03	(0.05)	0.00	(0.06)
	Germany	0.16	(0.02)	0.15	(0.02)	0.18	(0.04)	0.16	(0.04)	0.23	(0.09)	-0.02	(0.05)	-0.01	(0.05)	-0.07	(0.09)
	Greece	0.03	(0.02)	0.05	(0.02)	-0.10	(0.06)	-0.06	(0.07)	-0.19	(0.11)	**0.15**	(0.07)	0.11	(0.08)	**0.24**	(0.11)
	Hungary	-0.03	(0.02)	-0.03	(0.02)	0.06	(0.10)	0.13	(0.12)	-0.02	(0.15)	-0.09	(0.09)	-0.16	(0.12)	0.00	(0.15)
	Iceland	-0.09	(0.02)	-0.08	(0.02)	-0.15	(0.08)	0.03	(0.15)	-0.23	(0.10)	0.07	(0.08)	-0.12	(0.16)	0.15	(0.10)
	Ireland	0.03	(0.01)	0.03	(0.01)	0.02	(0.03)	-0.10	(0.07)	0.06	(0.04)	0.01	(0.03)	0.13	(0.07)	-0.03	(0.04)
	Israel	0.24	(0.02)	0.26	(0.02)	0.17	(0.05)	0.16	(0.06)	0.20	(0.09)	0.09	(0.05)	0.10	(0.06)	0.06	(0.09)
	Italy	-0.13	(0.01)	-0.14	(0.02)	-0.09	(0.05)	-0.09	(0.07)	-0.09	(0.07)	-0.05	(0.05)	-0.04	(0.07)	-0.05	(0.08)
	Japan	-0.22	(0.02)	-0.22	(0.02)	-0.37	(0.24)	c	c	c	c	0.15	(0.24)	c	c	c	c
	Korea	-0.02	(0.02)	-0.02	(0.02)	c	c	m	m	c	c	c	c	m	m	c	c
	Latvia	-0.30	(0.02)	-0.30	(0.02)	-0.36	(0.06)	-0.32	(0.06)	-0.53	(0.24)	0.07	(0.06)	0.03	(0.06)	0.23	(0.24)
	Luxembourg	0.04	(0.01)	0.06	(0.02)	0.01	(0.02)	0.04	(0.02)	-0.04	(0.03)	**0.05**	(0.03)	0.02	(0.03)	**0.10**	(0.03)
	Mexico	0.17	(0.02)	0.17	(0.02)	0.15	(0.15)	c	c	0.30	(0.18)	0.01	(0.15)	c	c	-0.13	(0.18)
	Netherlands	-0.18	(0.01)	-0.20	(0.01)	-0.05	(0.04)	-0.04	(0.04)	-0.12	(0.11)	**-0.14**	(0.04)	**-0.16**	(0.04)	-0.08	(0.11)
	New Zealand	0.02	(0.02)	-0.02	(0.02)	0.11	(0.04)	0.15	(0.05)	0.09	(0.04)	**-0.13**	(0.04)	**-0.17**	(0.05)	**-0.11**	(0.05)
	Norway	0.11	(0.02)	0.11	(0.02)	0.08	(0.05)	0.17	(0.06)	-0.01	(0.09)	0.03	(0.05)	-0.06	(0.06)	0.12	(0.09)
	Poland	-0.20	(0.02)	-0.20	(0.02)	c	c	c	c	c	c	c	c	c	c	c	c
	Portugal	0.37	(0.02)	0.38	(0.02)	0.30	(0.05)	0.30	(0.07)	0.31	(0.07)	0.07	(0.05)	0.08	(0.07)	0.07	(0.07)
	Slovak Republic	-0.34	(0.01)	-0.33	(0.01)	-0.61	(0.20)	-0.47	(0.23)	c	c	0.27	(0.20)	0.13	(0.23)	c	c
	Slovenia	-0.04	(0.01)	-0.03	(0.02)	-0.14	(0.06)	-0.16	(0.06)	-0.12	(0.10)	0.11	(0.06)	**0.13**	(0.06)	0.09	(0.10)
	Spain	0.19	(0.02)	0.18	(0.02)	0.26	(0.04)	0.33	(0.10)	0.25	(0.05)	-0.08	(0.04)	-0.15	(0.10)	-0.07	(0.05)
	Sweden	0.05	(0.02)	0.04	(0.02)	0.08	(0.04)	0.09	(0.05)	0.07	(0.07)	-0.04	(0.05)	-0.05	(0.05)	-0.02	(0.07)
	Switzerland	0.20	(0.02)	0.21	(0.03)	0.17	(0.03)	0.22	(0.04)	0.07	(0.05)	0.04	(0.04)	-0.01	(0.04)	**0.14**	(0.06)
	Turkey	0.01	(0.02)	0.01	(0.02)	-0.44	(0.24)	0.08	(0.23)	c	c	0.45	(0.24)	-0.07	(0.23)	c	c
	United Kingdom	-0.03	(0.02)	-0.05	(0.02)	0.07	(0.03)	0.14	(0.05)	0.00	(0.06)	**-0.12**	(0.04)	**-0.19**	(0.05)	-0.05	(0.06)
	United States	0.13	(0.02)	0.14	(0.02)	0.13	(0.03)	0.13	(0.03)	0.13	(0.05)	0.01	(0.03)	0.01	(0.04)	0.01	(0.05)
	OECD average-32	0.01	(0.00)	0.01	(0.00)	-0.03	(0.02)	0.03	(0.02)	-0.01	(0.02)	**0.04**	(0.02)	-0.02	(0.02)	0.04	(0.02)
	OECD average-35	0.01	(0.00)	0.01	(0.00)	-0.02	(0.02)	0.04	(0.02)	0.00	(0.02)	**0.04**	(0.02)	-0.02	(0.02)	**0.04**	(0.02)
Partners	Brazil	-0.04	(0.01)	-0.04	(0.01)	-0.16	(0.15)	-0.18	(0.20)	-0.12	(0.19)	0.13	(0.15)	0.15	(0.21)	0.08	(0.19)
	B-S-J-G (China)	0.02	(0.02)	0.02	(0.02)	c	c	c	c	c	c	c	c	c	c	c	c
	Bulgaria	-0.03	(0.02)	-0.03	(0.02)	-0.17	(0.19)	c	c	c	c	0.14	(0.19)	c	c	c	c
	Colombia	0.06	(0.02)	0.06	(0.02)	-0.10	(0.20)	-0.06	(0.25)	c	c	0.16	(0.20)	0.12	(0.25)	c	c
	Costa Rica	0.35	(0.02)	0.35	(0.02)	0.35	(0.05)	0.44	(0.07)	0.17	(0.08)	0.00	(0.06)	-0.09	(0.07)	**0.18**	(0.09)
	Croatia	0.01	(0.02)	0.01	(0.02)	-0.02	(0.05)	-0.07	(0.05)	0.20	(0.11)	0.03	(0.05)	0.08	(0.05)	-0.19	(0.11)
	Cyprus*	0.07	(0.01)	0.08	(0.01)	-0.03	(0.05)	-0.03	(0.09)	-0.02	(0.05)	**0.11**	(0.05)	0.12	(0.09)	**0.11**	(0.05)
	Dominican Republic	0.29	(0.02)	0.30	(0.02)	0.01	(0.16)	-0.05	(0.20)	0.10	(0.26)	0.28	(0.17)	0.35	(0.20)	0.20	(0.26)
	Hong Kong (China)	-0.04	(0.02)	-0.04	(0.02)	-0.04	(0.02)	0.00	(0.03)	-0.11	(0.04)	0.00	(0.03)	-0.04	(0.04)	0.08	(0.04)
	Lithuania	0.17	(0.02)	0.17	(0.02)	-0.13	(0.14)	0.02	(0.12)	-0.65	(0.43)	**0.30**	(0.14)	0.15	(0.12)	0.83	(0.43)
	Macao (China)	-0.15	(0.01)	-0.18	(0.02)	-0.13	(0.02)	-0.14	(0.02)	-0.12	(0.03)	-0.05	(0.02)	-0.04	(0.03)	-0.06	(0.04)
	Montenegro	-0.04	(0.01)	-0.04	(0.01)	-0.17	(0.06)	-0.09	(0.08)	-0.31	(0.09)	**0.13**	(0.06)	0.05	(0.08)	**0.28**	(0.09)
	Peru	-0.08	(0.02)	-0.08	(0.01)	-0.28	(0.26)	c	c	c	c	0.20	(0.26)	c	c	c	c
	Qatar	0.13	(0.01)	0.03	(0.02)	0.20	(0.01)	0.20	(0.03)	0.20	(0.02)	**-0.17**	(0.02)	**-0.17**	(0.03)	**-0.17**	(0.03)
	Russia	-0.25	(0.02)	-0.26	(0.02)	-0.14	(0.06)	-0.14	(0.08)	-0.13	(0.10)	**-0.12**	(0.06)	-0.11	(0.08)	-0.13	(0.09)
	Singapore	0.32	(0.02)	0.32	(0.02)	0.28	(0.03)	0.29	(0.05)	0.28	(0.04)	0.04	(0.03)	0.03	(0.05)	0.05	(0.04)
	Chinese Taipei	0.22	(0.02)	0.22	(0.02)	c	c	c	c	c	c	c	c	c	c	c	c
	Thailand	0.10	(0.02)	0.10	(0.02)	0.07	(0.15)	-0.04	(0.16)	c	c	0.04	(0.15)	0.15	(0.16)	c	c
	Tunisia	0.13	(0.02)	0.14	(0.02)	-0.42	(0.13)	-0.55	(0.14)	c	c	**0.57**	(0.13)	**0.70**	(0.14)	c	c
	United Arab Emirates	0.33	(0.02)	0.37	(0.02)	0.30	(0.02)	0.34	(0.03)	0.27	(0.02)	**0.07**	(0.03)	0.03	(0.03)	**0.10**	(0.03)
	Uruguay	0.11	(0.02)	0.11	(0.02)	0.34	(0.21)	c	c	c	c	-0.23	(0.21)	c	c	c	c
	Malaysia**	-0.02	(0.02)	-0.02	(0.02)	-0.20	(0.14)	-0.20	(0.15)	c	c	0.18	(0.14)	0.18	(0.15)	c	c

Note: Values that are statistically significant are indicated in bold (see Annex A3).
* See note at the beginning of this Annex.
**Malaysia: Coverage is too small to ensure comparability (see Annex A4).
StatLink http://dx.doi.org/10.1787/888933616807

[Part 1/1]

Table V.5.8b Index of valuing teamwork, by immigrant background

		Index of valuing teamwork										Difference in the index of valuing teamwork					
		All students		Non-immigrant students		Immigrant students		Second-generation immigrants		First-generation immigrants		Non-immigrants minus immigrants		Non-immigrants minus second-generation immigrants		Non-immigrants minus first-generation immigrants	
		Mean index	S.E.	Mean index	S.E.	Mean index	S.E.	Mean index	S.E.	Mean index	S.E.	Index dif.	S.E.	Index dif.	S.E.	Index dif.	S.E.
OECD	Australia	0.01	(0.01)	-0.03	(0.01)	0.10	(0.02)	0.08	(0.03)	0.12	(0.03)	**-0.13**	(0.02)	**-0.10**	(0.03)	**-0.15**	(0.03)
	Austria	0.19	(0.01)	0.16	(0.02)	0.27	(0.03)	0.32	(0.04)	0.19	(0.06)	**-0.11**	(0.04)	**-0.16**	(0.04)	-0.03	(0.06)
	Belgium	-0.11	(0.01)	-0.13	(0.02)	0.00	(0.04)	0.02	(0.04)	-0.02	(0.06)	**-0.13**	(0.04)	**-0.15**	(0.04)	-0.11	(0.07)
	Canada	0.00	(0.01)	-0.03	(0.01)	0.06	(0.02)	0.05	(0.03)	0.07	(0.03)	**-0.09**	(0.03)	**-0.08**	(0.03)	**-0.10**	(0.03)
	Chile	0.21	(0.02)	0.21	(0.02)	0.11	(0.09)	0.38	(0.20)	0.02	(0.10)	0.10	(0.09)	-0.17	(0.20)	0.19	(0.11)
	Czech Republic	0.01	(0.02)	0.01	(0.02)	-0.01	(0.09)	0.17	(0.13)	-0.18	(0.10)	0.02	(0.09)	-0.16	(0.13)	0.19	(0.10)
	Denmark	-0.12	(0.02)	-0.12	(0.02)	-0.12	(0.03)	-0.10	(0.03)	-0.15	(0.07)	-0.01	(0.03)	-0.02	(0.04)	0.03	(0.07)
	Estonia	-0.10	(0.02)	-0.10	(0.02)	-0.09	(0.05)	-0.09	(0.05)	-0.07	(0.26)	-0.01	(0.05)	0.00	(0.05)	-0.02	(0.26)
	Finland	-0.21	(0.02)	-0.22	(0.02)	-0.12	(0.09)	-0.12	(0.12)	-0.12	(0.11)	-0.10	(0.09)	-0.10	(0.12)	-0.10	(0.11)
	France	0.11	(0.02)	0.11	(0.02)	0.10	(0.04)	0.07	(0.04)	0.16	(0.07)	0.00	(0.04)	0.03	(0.04)	-0.05	(0.08)
	Germany	0.15	(0.02)	0.14	(0.02)	0.16	(0.04)	0.16	(0.04)	0.19	(0.09)	-0.02	(0.04)	-0.01	(0.04)	-0.04	(0.09)
	Greece	0.18	(0.01)	0.17	(0.01)	0.23	(0.05)	0.29	(0.07)	0.11	(0.09)	-0.06	(0.06)	-0.12	(0.07)	0.06	(0.09)
	Hungary	-0.02	(0.02)	-0.02	(0.02)	-0.02	(0.09)	-0.02	(0.10)	-0.01	(0.18)	0.00	(0.09)	0.00	(0.11)	-0.01	(0.18)
	Iceland	-0.21	(0.02)	-0.21	(0.02)	-0.01	(0.08)	0.10	(0.16)	-0.06	(0.11)	**-0.20**	(0.09)	**-0.32**	(0.16)	-0.15	(0.11)
	Ireland	0.04	(0.02)	0.05	(0.02)	0.01	(0.04)	-0.07	(0.08)	0.04	(0.04)	0.04	(0.04)	0.12	(0.07)	0.01	(0.04)
	Israel	-0.03	(0.02)	-0.01	(0.02)	-0.15	(0.04)	-0.16	(0.05)	-0.12	(0.08)	**0.14**	(0.05)	**0.15**	(0.05)	0.11	(0.09)
	Italy	0.02	(0.02)	0.01	(0.02)	0.17	(0.06)	0.08	(0.10)	0.23	(0.06)	**-0.16**	(0.06)	-0.07	(0.10)	**-0.22**	(0.07)
	Japan	-0.03	(0.02)	-0.03	(0.02)	-0.23	(0.20)	c	c	c	c	0.20	(0.20)	c	c	c	c
	Korea	0.14	(0.01)	0.14	(0.01)	c	c	m	m	c	c	c	c	m	m	c	c
	Latvia	-0.14	(0.02)	-0.14	(0.02)	-0.22	(0.08)	-0.16	(0.08)	-0.46	(0.24)	0.08	(0.08)	0.03	(0.08)	0.32	(0.24)
	Luxembourg	0.00	(0.01)	-0.03	(0.02)	0.02	(0.02)	0.07	(0.03)	-0.03	(0.03)	-0.05	(0.03)	**-0.09**	(0.03)	0.01	(0.04)
	Mexico	0.23	(0.01)	0.23	(0.01)	0.29	(0.11)	c	c	0.45	(0.11)	-0.05	(0.11)	c	c	-0.22	(0.12)
	Netherlands	-0.26	(0.01)	-0.27	(0.01)	-0.17	(0.04)	-0.18	(0.05)	-0.13	(0.08)	**-0.09**	(0.04)	-0.09	(0.05)	-0.14	(0.09)
	New Zealand	0.07	(0.02)	0.05	(0.02)	0.11	(0.04)	0.22	(0.06)	0.04	(0.05)	-0.06	(0.04)	**-0.17**	(0.06)	0.02	(0.05)
	Norway	-0.23	(0.02)	-0.23	(0.02)	-0.20	(0.04)	-0.18	(0.06)	-0.22	(0.07)	-0.03	(0.05)	-0.06	(0.07)	-0.01	(0.07)
	Poland	-0.05	(0.02)	-0.05	(0.02)	c	c	c	c	c	c	c	c	c	c	c	c
	Portugal	0.32	(0.02)	0.32	(0.02)	0.24	(0.05)	0.23	(0.07)	0.25	(0.07)	0.08	(0.05)	0.09	(0.07)	0.07	(0.07)
	Slovak Republic	-0.12	(0.02)	-0.11	(0.02)	-0.59	(0.17)	-0.53	(0.17)	c	c	**0.48**	(0.17)	**0.41**	(0.17)	c	c
	Slovenia	0.02	(0.01)	0.02	(0.02)	0.09	(0.06)	0.07	(0.07)	0.12	(0.09)	-0.07	(0.06)	-0.05	(0.07)	-0.10	(0.09)
	Spain	0.15	(0.02)	0.15	(0.02)	0.12	(0.04)	0.20	(0.11)	0.10	(0.04)	0.03	(0.04)	-0.05	(0.10)	0.05	(0.05)
	Sweden	-0.19	(0.02)	-0.21	(0.02)	-0.07	(0.05)	-0.10	(0.07)	-0.04	(0.06)	**-0.14**	(0.05)	-0.11	(0.07)	**-0.17**	(0.06)
	Switzerland	0.22	(0.02)	0.18	(0.03)	0.30	(0.03)	0.36	(0.04)	0.18	(0.04)	**-0.12**	(0.04)	**-0.18**	(0.04)	0.01	(0.05)
	Turkey	-0.04	(0.02)	-0.03	(0.02)	-0.34	(0.26)	-0.06	(0.33)	c	c	0.31	(0.26)	0.03	(0.34)	c	c
	United Kingdom	-0.04	(0.01)	-0.06	(0.02)	0.06	(0.03)	0.13	(0.05)	0.00	(0.05)	**-0.13**	(0.04)	**-0.19**	(0.05)	-0.07	(0.06)
	United States	0.06	(0.02)	0.04	(0.02)	0.11	(0.03)	0.13	(0.03)	0.08	(0.06)	**-0.07**	(0.03)	**-0.09**	(0.04)	-0.04	(0.06)
	OECD average-32	0.00	(0.00)	-0.01	(0.00)	0.00	(0.02)	0.04	(0.02)	0.02	(0.02)	-0.01	(0.02)	**-0.06**	(0.02)	-0.02	(0.02)
	OECD average-35	0.01	(0.00)	0.00	(0.00)	0.01	(0.01)	0.04	(0.02)	0.02	(0.02)	-0.01	(0.01)	**-0.05**	(0.02)	-0.02	(0.02)
Partners	Brazil	0.21	(0.01)	0.21	(0.01)	0.14	(0.16)	0.24	(0.20)	-0.11	(0.19)	0.07	(0.16)	-0.03	(0.20)	0.32	(0.19)
	B-S-J-G (China)	0.40	(0.01)	0.40	(0.01)	0.04	(0.27)	c	c	c	c	0.36	(0.27)	c	c	c	c
	Bulgaria	-0.07	(0.02)	-0.07	(0.02)	-0.29	(0.14)	c	c	c	c	0.22	(0.15)	c	c	c	c
	Colombia	0.24	(0.01)	0.24	(0.01)	-0.06	(0.18)	-0.01	(0.25)	c	c	0.30	(0.18)	0.25	(0.25)	c	c
	Costa Rica	0.34	(0.02)	0.34	(0.02)	0.36	(0.05)	0.37	(0.06)	0.32	(0.08)	-0.02	(0.05)	-0.03	(0.06)	0.01	(0.08)
	Croatia	0.21	(0.02)	0.20	(0.02)	0.35	(0.04)	0.35	(0.05)	0.34	(0.10)	**-0.15**	(0.04)	**-0.15**	(0.05)	-0.15	(0.09)
	Cyprus*	0.10	(0.01)	0.12	(0.01)	-0.07	(0.04)	0.01	(0.08)	-0.10	(0.05)	**0.19**	(0.05)	0.11	(0.08)	**0.22**	(0.05)
	Dominican Republic	0.52	(0.02)	0.53	(0.02)	0.25	(0.13)	0.11	(0.16)	0.43	(0.21)	**0.28**	(0.14)	**0.41**	(0.16)	0.09	(0.22)
	Hong Kong (China)	0.05	(0.02)	0.07	(0.02)	0.01	(0.02)	0.03	(0.04)	-0.03	(0.04)	**0.07**	(0.03)	0.04	(0.04)	**0.11**	(0.04)
	Lithuania	0.34	(0.02)	0.34	(0.02)	-0.02	(0.13)	0.12	(0.11)	-0.51	(0.40)	**0.36**	(0.13)	0.22	(0.11)	**0.85**	(0.40)
	Macao (China)	0.00	(0.01)	0.02	(0.02)	0.00	(0.01)	-0.01	(0.02)	0.02	(0.03)	0.02	(0.03)	0.03	(0.03)	0.00	(0.04)
	Montenegro	-0.08	(0.01)	-0.07	(0.01)	-0.23	(0.06)	-0.15	(0.08)	-0.38	(0.10)	**0.16**	(0.06)	0.08	(0.08)	**0.31**	(0.10)
	Peru	0.09	(0.01)	0.09	(0.01)	-0.44	(0.21)	c	c	c	c	**0.53**	(0.21)	c	c	c	c
	Qatar	0.24	(0.01)	0.16	(0.01)	0.31	(0.01)	0.33	(0.02)	0.30	(0.01)	**-0.15**	(0.02)	**-0.17**	(0.02)	**-0.14**	(0.02)
	Russia	-0.18	(0.02)	-0.18	(0.02)	-0.08	(0.08)	-0.11	(0.09)	-0.04	(0.10)	-0.10	(0.08)	-0.07	(0.09)	-0.14	(0.10)
	Singapore	0.27	(0.01)	0.30	(0.01)	0.16	(0.04)	0.14	(0.06)	0.16	(0.05)	**0.14**	(0.04)	**0.16**	(0.06)	**0.14**	(0.06)
	Chinese Taipei	0.37	(0.02)	0.37	(0.02)	c	c	c	c	c	c	c	c	c	c	c	c
	Thailand	0.38	(0.02)	0.38	(0.02)	0.36	(0.13)	0.37	(0.15)	c	c	0.01	(0.13)	0.00	(0.15)	c	c
	Tunisia	0.43	(0.02)	0.43	(0.02)	0.35	(0.13)	0.28	(0.13)	c	c	0.09	(0.13)	0.15	(0.13)	c	c
	United Arab Emirates	0.46	(0.02)	0.51	(0.02)	0.42	(0.02)	0.47	(0.02)	0.39	(0.02)	**0.09**	(0.02)	0.04	(0.02)	**0.12**	(0.03)
	Uruguay	0.20	(0.01)	0.20	(0.01)	0.16	(0.19)	c	c	c	c	0.03	(0.19)	c	c	c	c
	Malaysia**	0.59	(0.02)	0.59	(0.02)	0.42	(0.13)	0.38	(0.15)	c	c	0.18	(0.13)	0.21	(0.15)	c	c

Note: Values that are statistically significant are indicated in bold (see Annex A3).
* See note at the beginning of this Annex.
**Malaysia: Coverage is too small to ensure comparability (see Annex A4).
StatLink http://dx.doi.org/10.1787/888933616807

[Part 1/1]

Table V.5.12 Correlation between indices of attitudes towards collaboration and indices of well-being

	Correlation between... and...																					
	Index of valuing relationships		Index of valuing relationships										Index of valuing teamwork									
	Index of valuing teamwork		Life satisfaction		Index of schoolwork-related anxiety		Index of achievement motivation		Index of sense of belonging		Index of exposure to bullying		Life satisfaction		Index of schoolwork-related anxiety		Index of achievement motivation		Index of sense of belonging		Index of exposure to bullying	
	Corr.	S.E.	Corr.	S.E.	Corr.	S.E.	Corr.	S.E.	Corr.	S.E.	Corr.	S.E.	Corr.	S.E.	Corr.	S.E.	Corr.	S.E.	Corr.	S.E.	Corr.	S.E.
OECD Australia	0.41	(0.01)	m	m	0.07	(0.01)	0.27	(0.01)	0.18	(0.01)	-0.09	(0.01)	m	m	0.06	(0.01)	0.09	(0.01)	0.19	(0.01)	-0.07	(0.01)
Austria	0.36	(0.01)	0.10	(0.02)	-0.01	(0.02)	0.12	(0.01)	0.20	(0.01)	-0.15	(0.02)	0.11	(0.01)	0.08	(0.02)	0.01	(0.01)	0.14	(0.02)	-0.09	(0.01)
Belgium[1]	0.32	(0.01)	0.11	(0.02)	0.07	(0.01)	0.13	(0.01)	0.16	(0.01)	-0.08	(0.01)	0.08	(0.02)	0.06	(0.01)	0.03	(0.01)	0.17	(0.01)	-0.06	(0.01)
Canada	0.45	(0.01)	m	m	0.04	(0.01)	0.25	(0.01)	0.23	(0.01)	-0.11	(0.01)	m	m	0.05	(0.01)	0.07	(0.01)	0.25	(0.01)	-0.07	(0.01)
Chile	0.48	(0.01)	0.13	(0.02)	0.04	(0.02)	0.24	(0.02)	0.17	(0.02)	-0.07	(0.02)	0.17	(0.02)	0.10	(0.02)	0.20	(0.02)	0.19	(0.02)	-0.06	(0.02)
Czech Republic	0.35	(0.02)	0.06	(0.02)	0.07	(0.02)	0.12	(0.02)	0.15	(0.02)	-0.09	(0.02)	0.12	(0.01)	0.10	(0.02)	0.07	(0.02)	0.19	(0.02)	-0.10	(0.01)
Denmark	0.31	(0.01)	m	m	0.00	(0.01)	0.18	(0.02)	0.20	(0.02)	-0.14	(0.02)	m	m	0.09	(0.01)	-0.06	(0.02)	0.14	(0.02)	-0.08	(0.02)
Estonia	0.39	(0.02)	0.13	(0.01)	0.02	(0.02)	0.22	(0.02)	0.18	(0.02)	-0.08	(0.01)	0.15	(0.01)	0.08	(0.02)	0.10	(0.02)	0.21	(0.02)	-0.07	(0.02)
Finland	0.39	(0.01)	0.13	(0.02)	-0.06	(0.02)	0.16	(0.02)	0.18	(0.02)	-0.08	(0.02)	0.18	(0.01)	0.00	(0.02)	0.00	(0.01)	0.25	(0.01)	-0.10	(0.02)
France	0.34	(0.01)	0.09	(0.01)	0.11	(0.02)	0.20	(0.01)	0.17	(0.02)	-0.04	(0.02)	0.07	(0.02)	0.10	(0.01)	0.00	(0.02)	0.14	(0.01)	-0.06	(0.02)
Germany	0.34	(0.01)	0.13	(0.02)	-0.01	(0.02)	0.13	(0.01)	0.17	(0.02)	-0.12	(0.02)	0.12	(0.01)	0.07	(0.01)	-0.05	(0.02)	0.19	(0.02)	-0.11	(0.02)
Greece	0.46	(0.02)	0.10	(0.02)	0.05	(0.02)	0.11	(0.02)	0.19	(0.01)	-0.13	(0.02)	0.10	(0.02)	0.08	(0.02)	0.05	(0.02)	0.22	(0.02)	-0.12	(0.02)
Hungary	0.41	(0.01)	0.11	(0.02)	0.09	(0.02)	0.23	(0.02)	0.17	(0.01)	-0.06	(0.02)	0.12	(0.02)	0.12	(0.02)	0.11	(0.02)	0.17	(0.02)	-0.08	(0.02)
Iceland	0.43	(0.02)	0.21	(0.01)	-0.14	(0.02)	0.29	(0.02)	0.15	(0.02)	-0.14	(0.02)	0.15	(0.02)	0.01	(0.02)	0.05	(0.02)	0.12	(0.02)	-0.05	(0.02)
Ireland	0.36	(0.02)	0.11	(0.01)	0.04	(0.02)	0.24	(0.02)	0.17	(0.01)	-0.06	(0.01)	0.18	(0.01)	0.06	(0.02)	0.08	(0.01)	0.24	(0.01)	-0.09	(0.02)
Israel	0.45	(0.01)	m	m	-0.05	(0.02)	0.27	(0.02)	m	m	m	m	m	m	0.01	(0.01)	0.16	(0.02)	m	m	m	m
Italy	0.37	(0.01)	0.06	(0.02)	0.15	(0.02)	0.17	(0.01)	0.14	(0.01)	m	m	0.10	(0.02)	0.12	(0.01)	0.08	(0.01)	0.16	(0.02)	m	m
Japan	0.60	(0.01)	0.23	(0.01)	0.13	(0.01)	0.19	(0.01)	0.35	(0.01)	-0.07	(0.02)	0.28	(0.01)	0.09	(0.01)	0.20	(0.01)	0.41	(0.01)	-0.12	(0.02)
Korea	0.57	(0.01)	0.20	(0.01)	-0.01	(0.02)	0.22	(0.02)	0.36	(0.02)	-0.04	(0.01)	0.20	(0.01)	0.00	(0.02)	0.17	(0.02)	0.36	(0.01)	-0.04	(0.02)
Latvia	0.40	(0.02)	0.13	(0.02)	0.09	(0.02)	0.23	(0.02)	0.14	(0.02)	-0.10	(0.02)	0.12	(0.02)	0.16	(0.02)	0.13	(0.02)	0.18	(0.02)	-0.06	(0.02)
Luxembourg	0.41	(0.01)	0.12	(0.02)	0.04	(0.02)	0.18	(0.02)	0.18	(0.02)	-0.08	(0.02)	0.11	(0.02)	0.08	(0.01)	0.02	(0.02)	0.16	(0.02)	-0.07	(0.02)
Mexico	0.52	(0.01)	0.13	(0.01)	0.09	(0.01)	0.33	(0.02)	0.13	(0.02)	-0.07	(0.01)	0.13	(0.01)	0.14	(0.02)	0.24	(0.02)	0.11	(0.02)	-0.05	(0.01)
Netherlands	0.29	(0.02)	0.08	(0.02)	0.00	(0.02)	0.18	(0.02)	0.18	(0.02)	-0.03	(0.02)	0.15	(0.02)	0.01	(0.02)	0.03	(0.02)	0.16	(0.01)	-0.08	(0.02)
New Zealand	0.41	(0.02)	m	m	0.07	(0.02)	0.31	(0.02)	0.19	(0.02)	-0.09	(0.02)	m	m	0.11	(0.02)	0.14	(0.02)	0.22	(0.02)	-0.04	(0.02)
Norway	0.31	(0.02)	m	m	0.06	(0.02)	0.18	(0.02)	0.18	(0.02)	-0.12	(0.02)	m	m	0.07	(0.02)	-0.03	(0.02)	0.15	(0.01)	-0.05	(0.02)
Poland	0.35	(0.01)	0.15	(0.02)	-0.01	(0.02)	0.18	(0.02)	0.11	(0.02)	-0.10	(0.02)	0.16	(0.02)	0.08	(0.02)	0.01	(0.02)	0.14	(0.02)	-0.13	(0.02)
Portugal	0.45	(0.01)	0.11	(0.02)	0.19	(0.02)	0.22	(0.01)	0.19	(0.01)	-0.09	(0.02)	0.15	(0.02)	0.11	(0.02)	0.06	(0.02)	0.18	(0.02)	-0.07	(0.02)
Slovak Republic	0.42	(0.02)	0.09	(0.02)	0.07	(0.02)	0.27	(0.02)	0.17	(0.02)	-0.06	(0.01)	0.11	(0.02)	0.14	(0.02)	0.16	(0.02)	0.14	(0.02)	-0.06	(0.01)
Slovenia	0.39	(0.01)	0.10	(0.02)	0.04	(0.02)	0.23	(0.02)	0.17	(0.02)	-0.08	(0.02)	0.13	(0.02)	0.10	(0.02)	0.08	(0.02)	0.14	(0.02)	-0.09	(0.02)
Spain	0.35	(0.01)	0.10	(0.02)	0.16	(0.01)	0.18	(0.01)	0.12	(0.02)	-0.03	(0.01)	0.13	(0.01)	0.15	(0.01)	0.05	(0.02)	0.17	(0.01)	-0.07	(0.01)
Sweden	0.38	(0.01)	m	m	-0.03	(0.02)	0.19	(0.02)	0.12	(0.02)	-0.11	(0.02)	m	m	0.03	(0.02)	0.02	(0.02)	0.11	(0.02)	-0.08	(0.02)
Switzerland	0.33	(0.02)	0.12	(0.02)	0.00	(0.02)	0.09	(0.02)	0.18	(0.02)	-0.12	(0.02)	0.11	(0.02)	0.05	(0.02)	-0.03	(0.02)	0.18	(0.02)	-0.11	(0.02)
Turkey	0.53	(0.01)	0.11	(0.01)	0.11	(0.02)	0.36	(0.02)	0.10	(0.02)	-0.11	(0.02)	0.11	(0.01)	0.10	(0.02)	0.31	(0.02)	0.07	(0.02)	-0.06	(0.02)
United Kingdom	0.43	(0.01)	0.12	(0.01)	0.03	(0.02)	0.23	(0.01)	0.18	(0.02)	-0.07	(0.01)	0.18	(0.02)	0.00	(0.02)	0.10	(0.01)	0.24	(0.02)	-0.10	(0.02)
United States	0.44	(0.02)	0.13	(0.01)	0.00	(0.02)	0.31	(0.01)	0.24	(0.02)	-0.07	(0.02)	0.19	(0.01)	0.05	(0.02)	0.19	(0.01)	0.27	(0.02)	-0.05	(0.01)
OECD average-32	0.41	(0.00)	0.12	(0.00)	0.05	(0.00)	0.22	(0.00)	0.18	(0.00)	-0.09	(0.00)	0.14	(0.00)	0.08	(0.00)	0.09	(0.00)	0.19	(0.00)	-0.07	(0.00)
OECD average-35	0.41	(0.00)	0.12	(0.00)	0.04	(0.00)	0.21	(0.00)	0.18	(0.00)	-0.09	(0.00)	0.14	(0.00)	0.08	(0.00)	0.08	(0.00)	0.19	(0.00)	-0.08	(0.00)
Partners Brazil	0.53	(0.01)	0.11	(0.01)	0.22	(0.01)	0.35	(0.01)	0.17	(0.01)	-0.01	(0.01)	0.13	(0.01)	0.21	(0.01)	0.22	(0.01)	0.17	(0.01)	-0.03	(0.01)
B-S-J-G (China)	0.55	(0.01)	0.15	(0.01)	0.02	(0.02)	0.31	(0.01)	0.29	(0.02)	-0.07	(0.01)	0.18	(0.01)	0.09	(0.02)	0.25	(0.01)	0.32	(0.01)	-0.08	(0.01)
Bulgaria	0.52	(0.02)	0.14	(0.02)	0.14	(0.02)	0.29	(0.02)	0.12	(0.02)	-0.04	(0.02)	0.14	(0.02)	0.13	(0.02)	0.20	(0.02)	0.08	(0.02)	-0.04	(0.02)
Colombia	0.48	(0.01)	0.08	(0.01)	0.24	(0.02)	0.33	(0.01)	0.08	(0.02)	-0.05	(0.01)	0.13	(0.01)	0.24	(0.01)	0.26	(0.01)	0.09	(0.01)	-0.02	(0.01)
Costa Rica	0.45	(0.01)	0.14	(0.01)	0.15	(0.02)	0.30	(0.01)	0.09	(0.02)	-0.06	(0.01)	0.22	(0.01)	0.15	(0.02)	0.17	(0.01)	0.12	(0.01)	-0.15	(0.01)
Croatia	0.46	(0.01)	0.09	(0.02)	0.12	(0.02)	0.18	(0.02)	0.17	(0.02)	-0.08	(0.02)	0.18	(0.02)	0.11	(0.01)	0.10	(0.01)	0.18	(0.02)	-0.08	(0.02)
Cyprus*	0.54	(0.01)	0.14	(0.01)	0.04	(0.02)	0.25	(0.01)	0.24	(0.02)	m	m	0.11	(0.02)	0.10	(0.02)	0.12	(0.02)	0.20	(0.02)	m	m
Dominican Republic	0.66	(0.01)	0.11	(0.02)	0.34	(0.02)	0.46	(0.02)	0.07	(0.02)	-0.03	(0.02)	0.12	(0.02)	0.32	(0.02)	0.45	(0.02)	0.05	(0.02)	-0.02	(0.02)
Hong Kong (China)	0.55	(0.02)	0.17	(0.02)	0.06	(0.02)	0.21	(0.02)	0.29	(0.01)	-0.03	(0.01)	0.22	(0.01)	0.08	(0.02)	0.14	(0.02)	0.33	(0.01)	-0.01	(0.02)
Lithuania	0.44	(0.01)	0.15	(0.01)	0.08	(0.02)	0.25	(0.02)	0.10	(0.01)	-0.08	(0.02)	0.16	(0.01)	0.07	(0.02)	0.08	(0.02)	0.08	(0.01)	-0.09	(0.02)
Macao (China)	0.44	(0.01)	0.12	(0.02)	0.04	(0.02)	0.13	(0.02)	0.22	(0.02)	-0.04	(0.02)	0.16	(0.01)	0.10	(0.02)	0.10	(0.02)	0.26	(0.02)	-0.05	(0.02)
Montenegro	0.52	(0.01)	0.12	(0.01)	0.16	(0.02)	0.32	(0.01)	0.18	(0.02)	-0.01	(0.02)	0.10	(0.01)	0.17	(0.02)	0.17	(0.02)	0.12	(0.02)	-0.03	(0.02)
Peru	0.46	(0.01)	0.11	(0.01)	0.10	(0.02)	0.31	(0.01)	0.25	(0.02)	-0.08	(0.01)	0.13	(0.01)	0.17	(0.01)	0.23	(0.01)	0.21	(0.02)	-0.08	(0.02)
Qatar	0.61	(0.01)	0.14	(0.01)	0.10	(0.01)	0.35	(0.01)	0.22	(0.01)	-0.05	(0.01)	0.12	(0.01)	0.11	(0.01)	0.30	(0.01)	0.22	(0.01)	-0.03	(0.01)
Russia	0.47	(0.02)	0.14	(0.01)	0.01	(0.02)	0.21	(0.02)	0.15	(0.02)	-0.10	(0.02)	0.17	(0.01)	0.05	(0.02)	0.16	(0.02)	0.17	(0.02)	-0.12	(0.02)
Singapore	0.50	(0.01)	m	m	0.04	(0.02)	0.19	(0.02)	0.23	(0.01)	-0.07	(0.01)	m	m	0.11	(0.02)	0.13	(0.01)	0.23	(0.02)	-0.04	(0.01)
Chinese Taipei	0.56	(0.01)	0.16	(0.01)	0.08	(0.01)	0.23	(0.01)	0.31	(0.01)	-0.06	(0.01)	0.20	(0.01)	0.11	(0.01)	0.13	(0.01)	0.31	(0.01)	-0.08	(0.01)
Thailand	0.57	(0.01)	0.11	(0.01)	0.04	(0.02)	0.38	(0.02)	0.23	(0.02)	-0.03	(0.01)	0.14	(0.02)	0.04	(0.02)	0.28	(0.02)	0.25	(0.02)	-0.04	(0.01)
Tunisia	0.48	(0.01)	0.04	(0.02)	0.09	(0.02)	0.33	(0.02)	0.22	(0.01)	-0.06	(0.02)	0.06	(0.02)	0.12	(0.01)	0.21	(0.02)	0.21	(0.02)	-0.04	(0.02)
United Arab Emirates	0.55	(0.01)	0.15	(0.01)	0.04	(0.01)	0.34	(0.01)	0.26	(0.01)	-0.09	(0.01)	0.15	(0.01)	0.08	(0.01)	0.25	(0.01)	0.26	(0.01)	-0.07	(0.02)
Uruguay	0.44	(0.01)	0.11	(0.01)	0.17	(0.01)	0.22	(0.02)	0.13	(0.02)	-0.02	(0.02)	0.14	(0.02)	0.20	(0.02)	0.12	(0.02)	0.12	(0.02)	-0.07	(0.02)
Malaysia**	0.48	(0.01)	0.13	(0.01)	0.07	(0.01)	0.35	(0.01)	0.26	(0.01)	-0.08	(0.02)	0.17	(0.01)	0.06	(0.02)	0.34	(0.01)	0.33	(0.02)	-0.09	(0.02)

1. Data on life satisfaction are not available for the Flemish community of Belgium.
* See note at the beginning of this Annex.
**Malaysia: Coverage is too small to ensure comparability (see Annex A4).
StatLink http://dx.doi.org/10.1787/888933616807

[Part 1/2]

Table V.5.14a Index of valuing relationships and performance in collaborative problem solving

	Index of valuing relationships												Collaborative problem-solving performance, by national quarter of the index of valuing relationships									
	All students		Variability of the index		Bottom quarter		Second quarter		Third quarter		Top quarter		Bottom quarter		Second quarter		Third quarter		Top quarter		Difference (top – bottom quarter)	
	Mean index	S.E.	S.D.	S.E.	Mean index	S.E.	Mean index	S.E.	Mean index	S.E.	Mean index	S.E.	Mean score	S.E.	Mean score	S.E.	Mean score	S.E.	Mean score	S.E.	Score dif.	S.E.
OECD																						
Australia	0.09	(0.01)	0.96	(0.01)	-0.96	(0.01)	-0.29	(0.00)	0.16	(0.02)	1.44	(0.02)	507	(3.4)	531	(2.9)	543	(2.8)	555	(3.5)	**48**	(4.3)
Austria	0.24	(0.01)	1.11	(0.01)	-1.16	(0.02)	-0.21	(0.02)	0.67	(0.02)	1.68	(0.02)	489	(3.9)	505	(3.8)	525	(3.8)	524	(4.2)	**35**	(5.0)
Belgium	-0.06	(0.01)	0.94	(0.01)	-1.14	(0.01)	-0.35	(0.01)	0.02	(0.02)	1.22	(0.02)	474	(3.4)	510	(3.4)	518	(3.6)	523	(3.0)	**49**	(3.9)
Canada	0.11	(0.01)	1.02	(0.01)	-1.01	(0.02)	-0.29	(0.00)	0.20	(0.02)	1.53	(0.02)	518	(3.6)	536	(3.2)	547	(2.8)	551	(3.0)	**33**	(3.9)
Chile	0.08	(0.02)	1.05	(0.01)	-1.16	(0.02)	-0.35	(0.01)	0.33	(0.03)	1.50	(0.02)	430	(3.8)	457	(3.7)	471	(3.7)	475	(3.2)	**46**	(4.1)
Czech Republic	-0.20	(0.01)	0.90	(0.01)	-1.24	(0.02)	-0.43	(0.02)	-0.13	(0.02)	1.02	(0.02)	473	(4.4)	500	(3.4)	508	(2.9)	525	(3.2)	**53**	(4.7)
Denmark	0.01	(0.01)	0.91	(0.01)	-1.04	(0.02)	-0.29	(0.00)	0.13	(0.02)	1.24	(0.02)	498	(3.3)	523	(3.3)	533	(3.5)	538	(3.8)	**39**	(4.0)
Estonia	0.03	(0.02)	0.95	(0.01)	-1.06	(0.02)	-0.29	(0.00)	0.15	(0.03)	1.32	(0.03)	507	(4.6)	533	(3.8)	549	(3.6)	557	(3.8)	**50**	(5.1)
Finland	-0.08	(0.01)	0.91	(0.01)	-1.10	(0.01)	-0.36	(0.01)	-0.04	(0.02)	1.17	(0.03)	513	(3.8)	533	(3.7)	541	(3.8)	557	(4.0)	**44**	(5.2)
France	-0.07	(0.01)	1.01	(0.01)	-1.23	(0.02)	-0.40	(0.01)	0.03	(0.02)	1.33	(0.02)	468	(3.7)	496	(3.1)	513	(4.5)	517	(3.6)	**49**	(4.5)
Germany	0.15	(0.02)	1.05	(0.01)	-1.14	(0.01)	-0.32	(0.02)	0.54	(0.02)	1.54	(0.02)	507	(4.3)	524	(3.9)	553	(3.4)	549	(4.7)	**42**	(5.5)
Greece	0.03	(0.02)	0.97	(0.01)	-1.10	(0.02)	-0.30	(0.01)	0.19	(0.03)	1.34	(0.03)	434	(5.0)	464	(4.5)	468	(3.8)	476	(4.1)	**41**	(4.8)
Hungary	-0.03	(0.02)	1.01	(0.01)	-1.19	(0.02)	-0.37	(0.01)	0.09	(0.03)	1.36	(0.03)	443	(4.1)	468	(3.8)	483	(3.5)	495	(3.6)	**52**	(5.2)
Iceland	-0.09	(0.02)	1.05	(0.01)	-1.26	(0.02)	-0.46	(0.02)	0.01	(0.03)	1.37	(0.04)	486	(4.5)	492	(4.1)	506	(4.0)	522	(4.2)	**37**	(5.5)
Ireland	0.03	(0.01)	0.93	(0.01)	-1.03	(0.01)	-0.30	(0.01)	0.11	(0.02)	1.33	(0.03)	m	m	m	m	m	m	m	m	m	m
Israel	0.24	(0.02)	1.09	(0.01)	-1.05	(0.03)	-0.28	(0.01)	0.59	(0.02)	1.70	(0.02)	455	(4.6)	474	(4.8)	485	(5.0)	477	(4.7)	**22**	(5.0)
Italy	-0.14	(0.01)	0.95	(0.01)	-1.25	(0.01)	-0.48	(0.02)	0.05	(0.02)	1.14	(0.02)	452	(4.6)	477	(3.5)	494	(3.4)	499	(3.6)	**46**	(5.4)
Japan	-0.22	(0.02)	1.06	(0.01)	-1.40	(0.02)	-0.67	(0.02)	-0.07	(0.02)	1.25	(0.03)	534	(3.8)	547	(3.5)	558	(3.5)	570	(3.8)	**36**	(4.4)
Korea	-0.02	(0.02)	0.94	(0.01)	-1.04	(0.02)	-0.30	(0.01)	-0.02	(0.02)	1.30	(0.04)	529	(3.6)	529	(3.4)	538	(3.8)	558	(3.4)	**29**	(4.1)
Latvia	-0.30	(0.02)	0.91	(0.02)	-1.34	(0.02)	-0.57	(0.02)	-0.19	(0.02)	0.90	(0.03)	461	(4.4)	480	(3.8)	493	(3.6)	508	(3.7)	**47**	(5.5)
Luxembourg	0.03	(0.01)	1.09	(0.01)	-1.27	(0.02)	-0.40	(0.01)	0.31	(0.03)	1.49	(0.02)	468	(3.1)	489	(3.0)	501	(3.3)	516	(3.0)	**49**	(4.8)
Mexico	0.16	(0.02)	1.04	(0.01)	-1.05	(0.03)	-0.29	(0.00)	0.44	(0.03)	1.56	(0.02)	413	(3.3)	432	(3.3)	440	(3.5)	449	(3.6)	**35**	(4.2)
Netherlands	-0.18	(0.01)	0.77	(0.01)	-1.01	(0.01)	-0.35	(0.01)	-0.28	(0.01)	0.92	(0.03)	502	(3.7)	520	(4.1)	523	(3.6)	540	(4.4)	**39**	(5.2)
New Zealand	0.01	(0.02)	0.97	(0.01)	-1.08	(0.02)	-0.30	(0.01)	0.08	(0.03)	1.35	(0.03)	508	(4.6)	534	(4.3)	550	(4.2)	550	(3.7)	**42**	(5.8)
Norway	0.11	(0.02)	1.02	(0.01)	-1.05	(0.03)	-0.29	(0.00)	0.27	(0.03)	1.50	(0.02)	483	(3.9)	503	(3.7)	516	(3.9)	517	(3.8)	**34**	(5.4)
Poland	-0.21	(0.02)	0.92	(0.01)	-1.25	(0.02)	-0.49	(0.02)	-0.11	(0.02)	1.03	(0.03)	m	m	m	m	m	m	m	m	m	m
Portugal	0.37	(0.02)	0.98	(0.01)	-0.68	(0.02)	-0.19	(0.02)	0.66	(0.02)	1.71	(0.02)	482	(4.0)	493	(3.3)	512	(3.6)	511	(3.6)	**30**	(4.2)
Slovak Republic	-0.34	(0.01)	0.93	(0.01)	-1.39	(0.02)	-0.61	(0.02)	-0.28	(0.01)	0.91	(0.03)	435	(3.7)	462	(3.3)	475	(3.5)	498	(3.5)	**63**	(4.6)
Slovenia	-0.04	(0.01)	0.94	(0.01)	-1.11	(0.01)	-0.37	(0.01)	0.07	(0.03)	1.23	(0.02)	470	(3.5)	502	(4.0)	514	(2.7)	528	(3.1)	**59**	(4.5)
Spain	0.19	(0.02)	1.00	(0.01)	-0.98	(0.03)	-0.28	(0.01)	0.52	(0.02)	1.51	(0.02)	470	(3.6)	501	(3.2)	509	(3.3)	511	(3.0)	**41**	(4.1)
Sweden	0.05	(0.02)	1.05	(0.01)	-1.15	(0.02)	-0.32	(0.01)	0.16	(0.03)	1.51	(0.03)	488	(4.3)	509	(3.8)	526	(4.5)	529	(4.9)	**41**	(5.1)
Switzerland	0.19	(0.02)	1.06	(0.01)	-1.11	(0.03)	-0.28	(0.02)	0.59	(0.03)	1.58	(0.03)	m	m	m	m	m	m	m	m	m	m
Turkey	0.00	(0.02)	1.13	(0.01)	-1.33	(0.03)	-0.44	(0.02)	0.27	(0.04)	1.50	(0.02)	404	(4.4)	420	(4.0)	434	(4.4)	435	(4.4)	**30**	(4.1)
United Kingdom	-0.04	(0.02)	0.96	(0.01)	-1.13	(0.02)	-0.33	(0.01)	0.01	(0.02)	1.30	(0.03)	496	(3.8)	519	(4.0)	525	(4.4)	545	(3.7)	**50**	(4.5)
United States	0.13	(0.02)	1.00	(0.01)	-0.99	(0.02)	-0.29	(0.00)	0.25	(0.04)	1.54	(0.03)	495	(5.4)	517	(4.1)	535	(5.1)	545	(4.4)	**51**	(5.5)
OECD average-32	0.01	(0.00)	0.99	(0.00)	-1.13	(0.00)	-0.36	(0.00)	0.16	(0.00)	1.35	(0.00)	478	(0.7)	499	(0.7)	512	(0.7)	520	(0.7)	**43**	(0.8)
OECD average-35	0.01	(0.00)	0.99	(0.00)	-1.13	(0.00)	-0.36	(0.00)	0.16	(0.00)	1.35	(0.00)	m	m	m	m	m	m	m	m	m	m
Partners																						
Brazil	-0.04	(0.01)	0.96	(0.01)	-1.09	(0.01)	-0.37	(0.01)	-0.01	(0.02)	1.30	(0.02)	397	(2.9)	416	(2.9)	424	(2.9)	438	(3.4)	**41**	(3.1)
B-S-J-G (China)	0.01	(0.02)	0.96	(0.01)	-1.04	(0.01)	-0.31	(0.01)	0.01	(0.02)	1.38	(0.03)	468	(5.1)	496	(4.3)	504	(5.4)	518	(5.3)	**50**	(5.5)
Bulgaria	-0.03	(0.02)	1.06	(0.01)	-1.27	(0.03)	-0.36	(0.01)	0.11	(0.03)	1.39	(0.03)	424	(4.4)	444	(4.8)	464	(4.9)	471	(4.5)	**47**	(4.9)
Colombia	0.05	(0.01)	1.02	(0.01)	-1.15	(0.01)	-0.36	(0.01)	0.28	(0.03)	1.45	(0.02)	411	(3.0)	434	(3.1)	435	(2.9)	440	(3.3)	**29**	(3.5)
Costa Rica	0.35	(0.02)	1.08	(0.01)	-0.94	(0.02)	-0.18	(0.02)	0.71	(0.03)	1.79	(0.02)	416	(3.6)	438	(3.8)	447	(3.7)	454	(3.1)	**37**	(3.7)
Croatia	0.01	(0.02)	1.01	(0.01)	-1.17	(0.02)	-0.35	(0.02)	0.16	(0.03)	1.40	(0.03)	446	(3.9)	472	(3.4)	483	(3.4)	494	(3.3)	**48**	(4.2)
Cyprus*	0.07	(0.01)	1.07	(0.01)	-1.19	(0.02)	-0.31	(0.01)	0.25	(0.03)	1.51	(0.02)	419	(3.4)	445	(2.6)	457	(3.2)	465	(3.4)	**46**	(4.4)
Dominican Republic	0.27	(0.02)	1.25	(0.02)	-1.26	(0.04)	-0.26	(0.02)	0.69	(0.03)	1.91	(0.03)	m	m	m	m	m	m	m	m	m	m
Hong Kong (China)	-0.04	(0.02)	0.97	(0.01)	-1.09	(0.03)	-0.29	(0.00)	-0.08	(0.02)	1.29	(0.03)	532	(4.1)	537	(4.4)	548	(3.9)	548	(4.4)	**15**	(4.7)
Lithuania	0.16	(0.02)	1.18	(0.01)	-1.32	(0.02)	-0.33	(0.03)	0.63	(0.02)	1.66	(0.03)	440	(3.4)	465	(3.7)	481	(3.7)	492	(3.6)	**52**	(4.5)
Macao (China)	-0.15	(0.01)	0.88	(0.01)	-1.12	(0.01)	-0.43	(0.02)	-0.12	(0.02)	1.07	(0.02)	512	(3.4)	533	(2.9)	543	(2.8)	547	(3.3)	**34**	(5.3)
Montenegro	-0.05	(0.01)	1.02	(0.01)	-1.21	(0.01)	-0.39	(0.01)	0.08	(0.02)	1.33	(0.02)	398	(2.3)	421	(2.4)	425	(2.5)	432	(3.0)	**34**	(3.5)
Peru	-0.08	(0.01)	0.98	(0.01)	-1.21	(0.01)	-0.43	(0.02)	0.06	(0.02)	1.26	(0.02)	391	(3.3)	416	(3.3)	432	(3.8)	440	(3.5)	**50**	(4.1)
Qatar	0.12	(0.01)	1.17	(0.01)	-1.29	(0.01)	-0.34	(0.01)	0.45	(0.02)	1.65	(0.02)	m	m	m	m	m	m	m	m	m	m
Russia	-0.25	(0.02)	0.93	(0.01)	-1.26	(0.02)	-0.54	(0.02)	-0.24	(0.02)	1.03	(0.03)	454	(4.8)	473	(4.6)	476	(4.2)	499	(4.0)	**46**	(5.5)
Singapore	0.32	(0.01)	1.01	(0.01)	-0.79	(0.02)	-0.26	(0.02)	0.61	(0.02)	1.70	(0.03)	549	(3.4)	556	(3.6)	573	(2.9)	569	(2.8)	**20**	(4.9)
Chinese Taipei	0.22	(0.02)	1.00	(0.01)	-0.83	(0.02)	-0.29	(0.00)	0.36	(0.03)	1.63	(0.02)	517	(3.4)	512	(3.5)	538	(3.3)	539	(3.3)	**22**	(3.5)
Thailand	0.10	(0.02)	0.85	(0.01)	-0.75	(0.02)	-0.29	(0.00)	0.16	(0.03)	1.25	(0.03)	421	(4.4)	433	(4.2)	444	(4.2)	450	(4.5)	**29**	(4.6)
Tunisia	0.12	(0.02)	1.05	(0.01)	-1.15	(0.02)	-0.35	(0.01)	0.45	(0.03)	1.53	(0.02)	369	(2.9)	385	(2.9)	391	(2.8)	390	(3.0)	**21**	(3.5)
United Arab Emirates	0.32	(0.01)	1.10	(0.01)	-0.99	(0.02)	-0.20	(0.01)	0.68	(0.01)	1.78	(0.02)	423	(3.1)	434	(3.5)	451	(3.4)	443	(3.6)	**20**	(3.8)
Uruguay	0.11	(0.02)	1.02	(0.01)	-1.08	(0.02)	-0.32	(0.01)	0.35	(0.03)	1.51	(0.03)	429	(3.0)	455	(3.5)	452	(3.3)	451	(4.0)	**22**	(4.9)
Malaysia**	-0.02	(0.02)	0.91	(0.01)	-1.08	(0.01)	-0.38	(0.01)	0.14	(0.03)	1.22	(0.03)	416	(4.0)	440	(3.8)	447	(4.0)	458	(4.4)	**42**	(4.8)

1. Socio-economic profile is measured by the PISA index of economic, social and cultural status (ESCS).
2. Relative performance refers to the residual performance, attributable to purely "collaborative problem-solving" competencies, after accounting for performance in science, reading and mathematics in a regression performed across students at the national level.
Note: Values that are statistically significant are indicated in bold (see Annex A3).
* See note at the beginning of this Annex.
**Malaysia: Coverage is too small to ensure comparability (see Annex A4).
StatLink http://dx.doi.org/10.1787/888933616807

[Part 2/2]

Table V.5.14a Index of valuing relationships and performance in collaborative problem solving

	Before accounting for students' and schools' socio-economic profile[1]								After accounting for students' and schools' socio-economic profile											
	Change in collaborative problem-solving performance per unit change in the index of valuing relationships		Explained variance in student performance (r-squared × 100)		Change in relative collaborative problem-solving performance[2] per unit change in the index of valuing relationships		Explained variance in relative student performance (r-squared × 100)		Change in collaborative problem-solving performance per unit change in the index of valuing relationships		Explained variance in student performance (r-squared × 100)		Change in relative collaborative problem-solving performance per unit change in the index of valuing relationships		Explained variance in relative student performance (r-squared × 100)		Increased likelihood of students in the bottom quarter of the index of valuing relationships scoring below Level 2 on the collaborative problem-solving scale (below 440 score points)		Increased likelihood of students in the top quarter of the index of valuing relationships scoring at Level 4 on the collaborative problem-solving scale (at or above 640 score points)	
	Score dif.	S.E.	%	S.E.	Score dif.	S.E.	%	S.E.	Score dif.	S.E.	%	S.E.	Score dif.	S.E.	%	S.E.	Relative risk	S.E.	Relative risk	S.E.
OECD																				
Australia	**18**	(1.6)	2.5	(0.5)	**4**	(1.4)	0.4	(0.3)	**14**	(1.6)	11.2	(1.0)	**4**	(1.5)	0.5	(0.3)	**1.6**	(0.1)	**1.4**	(0.1)
Austria	**13**	(1.6)	2.2	(0.5)	**5**	(1.3)	0.8	(0.4)	**11**	(1.5)	21.8	(1.8)	**5**	(1.3)	1.1	(0.5)	**1.5**	(0.1)	**1.5**	(0.2)
Belgium	**18**	(1.3)	3.2	(0.5)	**5**	(1.2)	0.7	(0.3)	**14**	(1.3)	25.4	(1.8)	**5**	(1.2)	0.8	(0.3)	**1.7**	(0.1)	**1.3**	(0.2)
Canada	**12**	(1.4)	1.4	(0.3)	2	(1.1)	0.1	(0.1)	**9**	(1.3)	7.8	(0.8)	2	(1.1)	0.1	(0.1)	**1.5**	(0.1)	**1.2**	(0.1)
Chile	**15**	(1.5)	3.7	(0.7)	**3**	(1.2)	0.4	(0.3)	**11**	(1.5)	19.8	(1.6)	**3**	(1.2)	0.6	(0.3)	**1.5**	(0.1)	1.9	(0.7)
Czech Republic	**19**	(1.8)	3.8	(0.6)	**7**	(1.4)	1.0	(0.4)	**14**	(1.8)	21.8	(1.9)	**7**	(1.4)	1.2	(0.4)	**1.8**	(0.1)	**1.6**	(0.2)
Denmark	**16**	(1.7)	2.6	(0.5)	**4**	(1.3)	0.4	(0.2)	**13**	(1.7)	8.8	(1.1)	**4**	(1.3)	0.6	(0.4)	**1.7**	(0.1)	**1.3**	(0.2)
Estonia	**19**	(1.8)	4.0	(0.8)	**6**	(1.6)	1.2	(0.6)	**16**	(1.8)	11.3	(1.5)	**6**	(1.6)	1.5	(0.6)	**2.0**	(0.2)	**1.6**	(0.2)
Finland	**16**	(2.0)	2.0	(0.5)	2	(1.3)	0.1	(0.1)	**13**	(1.9)	6.9	(1.0)	2	(1.3)	0.5	(0.3)	**1.6**	(0.1)	**1.4**	(0.2)
France	**19**	(1.5)	3.8	(0.6)	**3**	(1.2)	0.3	(0.2)	**11**	(1.4)	25.1	(1.8)	**3**	(1.2)	0.3	(0.2)	**1.6**	(0.1)	**1.5**	(0.3)
Germany	**16**	(2.0)	2.6	(0.7)	**4**	(1.4)	0.5	(0.4)	**11**	(1.9)	20.6	(1.8)	**4**	(1.6)	0.7	(0.4)	**1.7**	(0.1)	**1.4**	(0.1)
Greece	**15**	(1.7)	2.4	(0.5)	**4**	(1.0)	0.5	(0.2)	**11**	(1.5)	18.2	(2.1)	**4**	(1.0)	0.5	(0.2)	**1.4**	(0.1)	1.4	(0.4)
Hungary	**18**	(1.8)	3.6	(0.7)	**2**	(1.1)	0.2	(0.2)	**9**	(1.7)	35.8	(1.8)	2	(1.2)	0.8	(0.3)	**1.5**	(0.1)	**1.8**	(0.4)
Iceland	**15**	(1.7)	2.7	(0.6)	0	(1.2)	0.0	(0.1)	**13**	(1.7)	4.0	(0.7)	1	(1.2)	0.9	(0.4)	**1.2**	(0.1)	**1.7**	(0.4)
Ireland	m	m	m	m	m	m	m	m	m	m	m	m	m	m	m	m	m	m	m	m
Israel	**7**	(1.7)	0.6	(0.3)	1	(1.2)	0.1	(0.1)	**7**	(1.5)	22.3	(2.9)	1	(1.3)	1.1	(0.6)	1.1	(0.1)	1.2	(0.2)
Italy	**18**	(2.0)	3.0	(0.6)	**6**	(1.5)	0.8	(0.4)	**14**	(1.9)	19.3	(1.8)	**6**	(1.5)	1.1	(0.5)	**1.5**	(0.1)	**1.7**	(0.3)
Japan	**12**	(1.5)	2.4	(0.6)	**7**	(1.4)	1.6	(0.7)	**10**	(1.4)	15.4	(1.7)	**7**	(1.4)	2.1	(0.8)	**1.7**	(0.2)	**1.5**	(0.2)
Korea	**12**	(1.7)	1.8	(0.5)	**4**	(1.2)	0.5	(0.3)	**8**	(1.5)	11.5	(1.8)	**4**	(1.2)	1.3	(0.5)	**1.3**	(0.1)	**1.5**	(0.2)
Latvia	**20**	(1.9)	3.9	(0.7)	2	(1.4)	0.1	(0.2)	**16**	(1.9)	10.9	(1.5)	2	(1.4)	0.2	(0.2)	**1.5**	(0.1)	**2.1**	(0.4)
Luxembourg	**16**	(1.6)	3.0	(0.6)	**3**	(1.3)	0.4	(0.3)	**12**	(1.5)	23.8	(1.5)	**3**	(1.2)	1.1	(0.4)	**1.5**	(0.1)	**1.7**	(0.3)
Mexico	**13**	(1.5)	2.9	(0.6)	**3**	(1.3)	0.5	(0.3)	**9**	(1.4)	18.8	(2.0)	**3**	(1.3)	1.8	(0.7)	**1.3**	(0.0)	1.5	(0.8)
Netherlands	**17**	(2.3)	1.8	(0.5)	**7**	(1.5)	0.9	(0.4)	**15**	(1.9)	23.1	(2.5)	**7**	(1.5)	1.0	(0.4)	**1.5**	(0.1)	**1.5**	(0.2)
New Zealand	**17**	(2.2)	2.5	(0.6)	**6**	(1.6)	0.9	(0.4)	**14**	(2.1)	11.3	(1.4)	**7**	(1.6)	1.3	(0.6)	**1.6**	(0.1)	**1.4**	(0.1)
Norway	**13**	(1.9)	2.0	(0.6)	2	(1.5)	0.2	(0.3)	**11**	(1.9)	5.7	(0.9)	3	(1.5)	0.3	(0.3)	**1.5**	(0.1)	1.2	(0.2)
Poland	m	m	m	m	m	m	m	m	m	m	m	m	m	m	m	m	m	m	m	m
Portugal	**12**	(1.5)	1.6	(0.4)	**6**	(1.2)	1.1	(0.4)	**9**	(1.5)	14.2	(1.8)	**6**	(1.2)	1.5	(0.4)	**1.5**	(0.1)	1.4	(0.3)
Slovak Republic	**23**	(1.6)	5.6	(0.7)	**5**	(1.1)	0.7	(0.3)	**16**	(1.4)	22.3	(1.7)	**4**	(1.2)	1.2	(0.4)	**1.5**	(0.1)	**2.5**	(0.5)
Slovenia	**24**	(1.7)	5.7	(0.8)	**6**	(1.3)	1.0	(0.4)	**17**	(1.6)	26.8	(1.5)	**6**	(1.3)	1.2	(0.4)	**1.9**	(0.1)	**1.9**	(0.3)
Spain	**14**	(1.5)	2.7	(0.6)	**4**	(1.2)	0.6	(0.3)	**12**	(1.5)	9.4	(1.1)	**5**	(1.2)	0.8	(0.4)	**1.5**	(0.1)	**1.4**	(0.2)
Sweden	**16**	(1.7)	2.9	(0.6)	**4**	(1.3)	0.6	(0.3)	**13**	(1.7)	12.6	(1.7)	**4**	(1.4)	0.9	(0.5)	**1.6**	(0.1)	**1.4**	(0.2)
Switzerland	m	m	m	m	m	m	m	m	m	m	m	m	m	m	m	m	m	m	m	m
Turkey	**10**	(1.3)	2.1	(0.6)	1	(0.9)	0.1	(0.1)	**8**	(1.2)	22.2	(3.2)	1	(0.9)	0.8	(0.5)	**1.2**	(0.0)	1.2	(2.1)
United Kingdom	**18**	(1.6)	2.9	(0.5)	**6**	(1.6)	0.9	(0.4)	**16**	(1.5)	12.4	(1.5)	**6**	(1.6)	1.0	(0.4)	**1.6**	(0.1)	**1.5**	(0.2)
United States	**17**	(1.8)	2.6	(0.5)	**4**	(1.2)	0.6	(0.3)	**14**	(1.7)	11.7	(1.3)	**5**	(1.2)	0.8	(0.4)	**1.7**	(0.1)	**1.3**	(0.1)
OECD average-32	**16**	(0.3)	2.8	(0.1)	**4**	(0.2)	0.6	(0.1)	**12**	(0.3)	16.6	(0.3)	**4**	(0.2)	0.9	(0.1)	**1.5**	(0.0)	**1.5**	(0.1)
OECD average-35	m	m	m	m	m	m	m	m	m	m	m	m	m	m	m	m	m	m	m	m
Partners																				
Brazil	**15**	(1.1)	2.9	(0.4)	**3**	(1.0)	0.3	(0.2)	**11**	(0.9)	18.3	(1.7)	**2**	(1.0)	0.8	(0.4)	**1.2**	(0.0)	**2.5**	(0.8)
B-S-J-G (China)	**19**	(1.6)	3.4	(0.5)	**4**	(1.2)	0.4	(0.3)	**9**	(1.5)	29.0	(2.8)	**3**	(1.3)	0.9	(0.4)	**1.6**	(0.1)	**1.8**	(0.3)
Bulgaria	**17**	(1.5)	3.3	(0.6)	**4**	(0.9)	0.7	(0.3)	**10**	(1.3)	33.6	(2.5)	**4**	(0.9)	1.4	(0.4)	**1.4**	(0.1)	**1.9**	(0.5)
Colombia	**9**	(1.3)	1.3	(0.3)	0	(0.9)	0.0	(0.0)	**6**	(1.2)	22.8	(2.2)	-1	(0.9)	2.7	(0.9)	**1.2**	(0.0)	1.8	(0.7)
Costa Rica	**13**	(1.2)	3.0	(0.5)	**6**	(0.9)	1.5	(0.4)	**11**	(1.1)	16.7	(1.9)	**6**	(0.9)	1.6	(0.4)	**1.3**	(0.0)	2.6	(1.3)
Croatia	**17**	(1.4)	3.8	(0.6)	**6**	(1.2)	1.2	(0.4)	**13**	(1.4)	20.3	(1.8)	**6**	(1.2)	1.3	(0.5)	**1.6**	(0.1)	**1.6**	(0.4)
Cyprus*	**15**	(1.5)	3.2	(0.6)	**3**	(1.0)	0.3	(0.2)	**15**	(1.4)	11.8	(1.1)	**3**	(1.0)	0.6	(0.3)	**1.4**	(0.1)	1.5	(0.6)
Dominican Republic	m	m	m	m	m	m	m	m	m	m	m	m	m	m	m	m	m	m	m	m
Hong Kong (China)	5	(1.6)	0.2	(0.2)	**2**	(1.1)	0.1	(0.1)	3	(1.7)	7.4	(1.6)	2	(1.1)	0.3	(0.2)	1.2	(0.2)	1.2	(0.1)
Lithuania	**17**	(1.3)	4.9	(0.8)	**3**	(1.1)	0.4	(0.3)	**13**	(1.4)	20.0	(1.8)	**2**	(1.2)	0.7	(0.3)	**1.6**	(0.1)	**2.0**	(0.4)
Macao (China)	**13**	(2.1)	1.7	(0.5)	3	(1.7)	0.3	(0.3)	**13**	(2.1)	2.6	(0.6)	3	(1.7)	0.8	(0.4)	**1.6**	(0.2)	1.1	(0.2)
Montenegro	**11**	(1.2)	2.0	(0.4)	1	(1.1)	0.1	(0.1)	**10**	(1.1)	15.0	(1.1)	1	(1.1)	0.4	(0.3)	**1.2**	(0.0)	3.3	(4.7)
Peru	**19**	(1.4)	5.0	(0.7)	**4**	(1.2)	0.6	(0.4)	**11**	(1.2)	31.6	(2.0)	**3**	(1.3)	2.3	(0.5)	**1.4**	(0.0)	2.1	(1.2)
Qatar	m	m	m	m	m	m	m	m	m	m	m	m	m	m	m	m	m	m	m	m
Russia	**16**	(2.0)	2.6	(0.7)	**5**	(1.7)	0.6	(0.4)	**14**	(2.0)	13.7	(1.6)	**5**	(1.7)	3.1	(1.0)	**1.4**	(0.1)	**1.9**	(0.3)
Singapore	**8**	(1.5)	0.7	(0.3)	1	(1.1)	0.0	(0.1)	**6**	(1.3)	16.7	(1.2)	1	(1.1)	0.3	(0.2)	**1.5**	(0.1)	1.1	(0.1)
Chinese Taipei	**11**	(1.3)	1.5	(0.4)	**4**	(1.0)	0.4	(0.3)	**8**	(1.2)	17.7	(2.2)	**4**	(1.1)	0.6	(0.4)	**1.7**	(0.1)	**1.3**	(0.1)
Thailand	**13**	(2.2)	1.8	(0.6)	**4**	(1.5)	0.5	(0.3)	**10**	(2.0)	19.0	(2.8)	**3**	(1.5)	1.9	(0.9)	**1.2**	(0.1)	1.9	(0.7)
Tunisia	**8**	(1.1)	1.9	(0.5)	2	(0.9)	0.2	(0.2)	**7**	(1.0)	18.6	(2.9)	2	(0.9)	2.3	(0.8)	**1.1**	(0.0)	m	m
United Arab Emirates	**8**	(1.2)	0.8	(0.3)	1	(1.0)	0.1	(0.1)	**9**	(1.2)	15.5	(1.7)	1	(1.0)	1.2	(0.5)	**1.2**	(0.0)	1.2	(0.2)
Uruguay	**6**	(1.7)	0.4	(0.3)	0	(1.2)	0.0	(0.1)	3	(1.6)	19.5	(1.8)	0	(1.2)	0.3	(0.3)	**1.2**	(0.1)	1.4	(0.5)
Malaysia**	**17**	(1.9)	3.7	(0.8)	**4**	(1.5)	0.7	(0.5)	**14**	(1.7)	18.2	(2.4)	**4**	(1.5)	1.2	(0.7)	**1.3**	(0.0)	2.3	(1.1)

1. Socio-economic profile is measured by the PISA index of economic, social and cultural status (ESCS).
2. Relative performance refers to the residual performance, attributable to purely "collaborative problem-solving" competencies, after accounting for performance in science, reading and mathematics in a regression performed across students at the national level.
Note: Values that are statistically significant are indicated in bold (see Annex A3).
* See note at the beginning of this Annex.
**Malaysia: Coverage is too small to ensure comparability (see Annex A4).
StatLink http://dx.doi.org/10.1787/888933616807

[Part 1/2]

Table V.5.14b Index of valuing teamwork and performance in collaborative problem solving

		Index of valuing teamwork											Collaborative problem-solving performance, by national quarter of the index of valuing teamwork									
		All students		Variability of the index		Bottom quarter		Second quarter		Third quarter		Top quarter		Bottom quarter		Second quarter		Third quarter		Top quarter		Difference (top - bottom quarter)
		Mean index	S.E.	S.D.	S.E.	Mean index	S.E.	Mean index	S.E.	Mean index	S.E.	Mean index	S.E.	Mean score	S.E.	Mean score	S.E.	Mean score	S.E.	Mean score	S.E.	Score dif.	S.E.
OECD	Australia	0.01	(0.01)	0.98	(0.01)	-1.19	(0.01)	-0.27	(0.01)	0.17	(0.01)	1.30	(0.02)	555	(2.9)	533	(3.2)	521	(2.9)	527	(3.7)	**-28**	(4.0)
	Austria	0.19	(0.01)	1.10	(0.01)	-1.22	(0.02)	-0.20	(0.02)	0.59	(0.02)	1.59	(0.02)	531	(3.9)	513	(4.4)	508	(3.9)	492	(3.9)	**-39**	(5.7)
	Belgium	-0.11	(0.01)	0.99	(0.01)	-1.28	(0.02)	-0.47	(0.02)	0.12	(0.01)	1.21	(0.02)	521	(3.3)	518	(3.5)	499	(3.2)	487	(3.6)	**-34**	(3.9)
	Canada	0.00	(0.01)	1.05	(0.01)	-1.27	(0.01)	-0.31	(0.01)	0.18	(0.01)	1.41	(0.02)	568	(3.2)	538	(3.4)	524	(2.9)	521	(3.0)	**-47**	(3.9)
	Chile	0.21	(0.02)	0.97	(0.01)	-0.98	(0.02)	-0.09	(0.01)	0.42	(0.02)	1.48	(0.02)	464	(3.9)	450	(3.9)	459	(3.3)	461	(3.9)	-3	(4.1)
	Czech Republic	0.00	(0.02)	0.95	(0.01)	-1.15	(0.02)	-0.28	(0.02)	0.21	(0.01)	1.24	(0.02)	508	(3.7)	501	(3.0)	493	(3.3)	504	(3.2)	-4	(3.5)
	Denmark	-0.12	(0.01)	0.95	(0.01)	-1.24	(0.02)	-0.50	(0.02)	0.11	(0.01)	1.15	(0.02)	538	(3.7)	533	(3.6)	510	(3.4)	512	(3.8)	**-26**	(4.7)
	Estonia	-0.10	(0.02)	0.96	(0.01)	-1.26	(0.02)	-0.41	(0.02)	0.13	(0.01)	1.16	(0.03)	547	(4.1)	534	(3.9)	529	(3.9)	537	(3.7)	**-10**	(4.9)
	Finland	-0.22	(0.02)	0.93	(0.01)	-1.31	(0.02)	-0.55	(0.02)	-0.01	(0.01)	1.00	(0.03)	552	(4.1)	545	(4.0)	523	(3.8)	526	(3.7)	**-26**	(5.3)
	France	0.11	(0.02)	1.08	(0.01)	-1.21	(0.02)	-0.22	(0.02)	0.31	(0.02)	1.56	(0.02)	510	(4.5)	498	(3.4)	497	(3.6)	488	(4.1)	**-22**	(5.2)
	Germany	0.14	(0.02)	1.02	(0.01)	-1.14	(0.02)	-0.22	(0.02)	0.51	(0.02)	1.44	(0.02)	545	(3.8)	527	(4.8)	536	(3.7)	525	(4.2)	**-19**	(4.7)
	Greece	0.18	(0.01)	1.01	(0.01)	-1.06	(0.02)	-0.11	(0.01)	0.40	(0.02)	1.49	(0.02)	473	(5.0)	456	(4.6)	459	(4.6)	455	(3.7)	**-18**	(5.1)
	Hungary	-0.02	(0.02)	1.01	(0.01)	-1.27	(0.02)	-0.27	(0.02)	0.18	(0.01)	1.29	(0.02)	489	(3.6)	470	(4.0)	463	(4.1)	468	(3.9)	**-21**	(4.9)
	Iceland	-0.20	(0.02)	0.99	(0.01)	-1.40	(0.03)	-0.52	(0.02)	0.03	(0.02)	1.08	(0.03)	519	(4.5)	508	(3.6)	486	(4.0)	492	(3.8)	**-27**	(5.3)
	Ireland	0.04	(0.01)	1.01	(0.01)	-1.20	(0.02)	-0.25	(0.02)	0.24	(0.02)	1.38	(0.02)	m	m	m	m	m	m	m	m	m	m
	Israel	-0.03	(0.02)	1.01	(0.01)	-1.27	(0.02)	-0.38	(0.02)	0.22	(0.01)	1.30	(0.03)	491	(4.7)	475	(4.8)	464	(5.2)	459	(4.9)	**-32**	(6.0)
	Italy	0.02	(0.02)	0.98	(0.01)	-1.19	(0.02)	-0.25	(0.02)	0.24	(0.01)	1.29	(0.03)	490	(3.6)	481	(4.0)	479	(3.3)	470	(3.2)	**-20**	(4.3)
	Japan	-0.03	(0.02)	1.01	(0.01)	-1.24	(0.02)	-0.41	(0.02)	0.25	(0.02)	1.29	(0.02)	554	(3.6)	553	(3.5)	549	(3.9)	552	(4.0)	-2	(4.8)
	Korea	0.14	(0.01)	0.91	(0.01)	-0.93	(0.02)	-0.04	(0.01)	0.17	(0.01)	1.37	(0.03)	543	(3.8)	532	(3.4)	532	(3.6)	547	(3.0)	4	(4.2)
	Latvia	-0.14	(0.02)	1.00	(0.01)	-1.37	(0.02)	-0.44	(0.02)	0.11	(0.01)	1.15	(0.02)	502	(4.2)	494	(4.3)	475	(3.4)	473	(3.2)	**-29**	(5.3)
	Luxembourg	0.00	(0.01)	1.11	(0.01)	-1.39	(0.02)	-0.31	(0.02)	0.28	(0.02)	1.43	(0.02)	509	(3.3)	495	(3.3)	488	(2.9)	481	(3.0)	**-28**	(5.0)
	Mexico	0.23	(0.01)	0.95	(0.01)	-0.94	(0.02)	-0.07	(0.01)	0.44	(0.02)	1.48	(0.02)	436	(3.4)	430	(3.3)	432	(3.0)	438	(3.6)	2	(3.3)
	Netherlands	-0.26	(0.01)	0.80	(0.01)	-1.22	(0.02)	-0.50	(0.01)	-0.02	(0.01)	0.70	(0.03)	539	(3.9)	523	(3.7)	511	(3.9)	512	(3.9)	**-27**	(4.6)
	New Zealand	0.07	(0.02)	0.99	(0.01)	-1.15	(0.02)	-0.20	(0.02)	0.23	(0.02)	1.39	(0.03)	557	(4.3)	535	(4.0)	530	(4.2)	519	(4.2)	**-38**	(5.3)
	Norway	-0.23	(0.02)	1.06	(0.01)	-1.49	(0.02)	-0.62	(0.02)	0.02	(0.02)	1.18	(0.03)	521	(3.4)	517	(3.7)	492	(3.8)	489	(3.9)	**-31**	(4.7)
	Poland	-0.06	(0.02)	0.99	(0.01)	-1.28	(0.03)	-0.30	(0.02)	0.14	(0.02)	1.22	(0.03)	m	m	m	m	m	m	m	m	m	m
	Portugal	0.32	(0.02)	0.99	(0.01)	-0.90	(0.02)	-0.02	(0.01)	0.53	(0.03)	1.65	(0.02)	514	(3.6)	490	(3.5)	497	(4.0)	495	(3.7)	**-19**	(4.0)
	Slovak Republic	-0.12	(0.02)	0.95	(0.01)	-1.28	(0.02)	-0.36	(0.02)	0.06	(0.01)	1.10	(0.03)	467	(3.6)	464	(3.5)	464	(3.5)	475	(3.3)	**8**	(3.9)
	Slovenia	0.02	(0.01)	0.95	(0.01)	-1.15	(0.02)	-0.23	(0.02)	0.22	(0.01)	1.25	(0.02)	515	(3.7)	497	(3.6)	498	(3.2)	504	(3.5)	**-11**	(5.4)
	Spain	0.15	(0.02)	1.00	(0.01)	-1.08	(0.02)	-0.20	(0.02)	0.41	(0.02)	1.47	(0.02)	505	(3.1)	499	(3.5)	492	(3.1)	494	(3.5)	**-12**	(4.3)
	Sweden	-0.19	(0.02)	0.99	(0.01)	-1.39	(0.02)	-0.53	(0.01)	0.05	(0.02)	1.11	(0.03)	524	(4.7)	525	(4.3)	503	(5.0)	501	(4.1)	**-23**	(5.0)
	Switzerland	0.22	(0.02)	0.99	(0.01)	-1.04	(0.02)	-0.12	(0.02)	0.54	(0.03)	1.49	(0.03)	m	m	m	m	m	m	m	m	m	m
	Turkey	-0.04	(0.01)	0.94	(0.01)	-1.19	(0.02)	-0.37	(0.01)	0.19	(0.02)	1.19	(0.02)	416	(4.4)	418	(4.0)	423	(4.3)	436	(4.2)	**20**	(4.4)
	United Kingdom	-0.04	(0.01)	0.98	(0.01)	-1.24	(0.02)	-0.29	(0.02)	0.13	(0.01)	1.23	(0.02)	542	(3.9)	521	(3.4)	509	(3.6)	514	(4.2)	**-28**	(4.4)
	United States	0.06	(0.02)	1.03	(0.01)	-1.21	(0.02)	-0.21	(0.02)	0.22	(0.02)	1.43	(0.02)	550	(5.1)	509	(4.7)	514	(5.1)	519	(4.2)	**-31**	(5.3)
	OECD average-32	0.00	(0.00)	0.99	(0.00)	-1.21	(0.00)	-0.31	(0.00)	0.22	(0.00)	1.29	(0.00)	515	(0.7)	503	(0.7)	496	(0.7)	496	(0.7)	**-19**	(0.8)
	OECD average-35	0.01	(0.00)	0.99	(0.00)	-1.20	(0.00)	-0.30	(0.00)	0.23	(0.00)	1.30	(0.00)	m	m	m	m	m	m	m	m	m	m
Partners	Brazil	0.20	(0.01)	0.90	(0.01)	-0.86	(0.01)	-0.08	(0.01)	0.33	(0.01)	1.42	(0.01)	422	(3.7)	409	(3.0)	418	(2.8)	428	(2.7)	6	(3.6)
	B-S-J-G (China)	0.39	(0.01)	0.93	(0.01)	-0.61	(0.02)	0.03	c	0.45	(0.03)	1.70	(0.02)	498	(5.1)	493	(5.0)	492	(5.1)	503	(4.2)	6	(4.1)
	Bulgaria	-0.07	(0.02)	1.03	(0.01)	-1.34	(0.03)	-0.32	(0.03)	0.11	(0.01)	1.27	(0.03)	456	(4.8)	452	(4.6)	443	(4.7)	453	(4.4)	-3	(4.7)
	Colombia	0.23	(0.01)	0.92	(0.01)	-0.89	(0.02)	-0.09	(0.01)	0.47	(0.02)	1.44	(0.02)	432	(3.5)	431	(3.3)	429	(3.0)	429	(3.3)	-3	(4.0)
	Costa Rica	0.34	(0.02)	1.03	(0.01)	-0.96	(0.02)	-0.02	(0.01)	0.64	(0.02)	1.69	(0.02)	448	(4.2)	439	(3.9)	438	(3.4)	430	(3.4)	**-19**	(4.4)
	Croatia	0.21	(0.02)	0.98	(0.01)	-0.98	(0.02)	-0.07	(0.01)	0.38	(0.02)	1.53	(0.02)	482	(3.4)	469	(4.1)	474	(3.1)	470	(3.4)	**-11**	(4.0)
	Cyprus*	0.10	(0.01)	1.02	(0.01)	-1.15	(0.02)	-0.19	(0.01)	0.29	(0.02)	1.43	(0.02)	455	(3.7)	442	(2.8)	445	(3.3)	445	(3.5)	**-10**	(4.6)
	Dominican Republic	0.51	(0.02)	1.10	(0.02)	-0.88	(0.03)	0.14	(0.03)	0.87	(0.02)	1.90	(0.02)	m	m	m	m	m	m	m	m	m	m
	Hong Kong (China)	0.05	(0.02)	1.01	(0.01)	-1.20	(0.02)	-0.12	(0.02)	0.14	(0.02)	1.39	(0.04)	549	(4.2)	539	(4.2)	538	(4.1)	538	(4.4)	**-11**	(4.7)
	Lithuania	0.33	(0.02)	1.16	(0.01)	-1.21	(0.03)	0.00	(0.02)	0.76	(0.02)	1.77	(0.02)	478	(4.4)	466	(3.5)	473	(3.4)	462	(3.6)	**-16**	(5.5)
	Macao (China)	0.01	(0.01)	0.88	(0.01)	-1.04	(0.02)	-0.24	(0.01)	0.12	(0.01)	1.17	(0.02)	538	(3.3)	526	(3.0)	532	(3.2)	539	(3.7)	0	(5.0)
	Montenegro	-0.09	(0.01)	0.97	(0.01)	-1.25	(0.02)	-0.40	(0.01)	0.11	(0.01)	1.19	(0.02)	428	(2.7)	416	(2.5)	414	(2.8)	418	(2.7)	**-10**	(3.0)
	Peru	0.09	(0.01)	0.88	(0.01)	-0.99	(0.02)	-0.17	(0.01)	0.26	(0.01)	1.25	(0.02)	409	(3.6)	413	(3.3)	427	(3.4)	430	(3.1)	**21**	(3.9)
	Qatar	0.23	(0.01)	1.03	(0.01)	-1.05	(0.02)	-0.08	(0.01)	0.51	(0.01)	1.55	(0.01)	m	m	m	m	m	m	m	m	m	m
	Russia	-0.18	(0.02)	0.91	(0.01)	-1.26	(0.03)	-0.43	(0.03)	0.03	(0.00)	0.95	(0.03)	486	(4.2)	475	(5.0)	467	(4.6)	474	(4.2)	**-12**	(4.5)
	Singapore	0.27	(0.01)	1.03	(0.01)	-0.98	(0.02)	-0.05	(0.01)	0.45	(0.02)	1.67	(0.02)	584	(2.5)	554	(3.1)	557	(2.9)	551	(3.0)	**-33**	(4.4)
	Chinese Taipei	0.37	(0.02)	1.00	(0.01)	-0.81	(0.03)	0.03	c	0.50	(0.03)	1.75	(0.02)	543	(3.6)	511	(3.4)	529	(3.4)	523	(3.3)	**-20**	(3.6)
	Thailand	0.37	(0.02)	0.81	(0.01)	-0.51	(0.02)	0.03	c	0.46	(0.03)	1.49	(0.03)	430	(4.8)	427	(4.4)	442	(4.2)	449	(3.9)	**19**	(4.5)
	Tunisia	0.43	(0.02)	1.02	(0.01)	-0.85	(0.03)	0.07	(0.01)	0.75	(0.02)	1.74	(0.02)	391	(2.9)	380	(2.8)	384	(2.9)	380	(3.0)	**-11**	(3.6)
	United Arab Emirates	0.45	(0.02)	1.04	(0.01)	-0.86	(0.02)	0.08	(0.02)	0.80	(0.02)	1.77	(0.02)	444	(3.6)	435	(3.5)	437	(3.0)	436	(2.9)	**-8**	(3.7)
	Uruguay	0.20	(0.01)	1.01	(0.01)	-1.03	(0.02)	-0.12	(0.01)	0.42	(0.02)	1.55	(0.02)	464	(3.8)	448	(3.2)	445	(3.1)	429	(3.8)	**-35**	(4.9)
	Malaysia**	0.59	(0.02)	0.88	(0.01)	-0.40	(0.02)	0.13	(0.02)	0.84	(0.03)	1.79	(0.02)	434	(4.5)	439	(3.9)	439	(3.9)	450	(4.1)	**16**	(4.1)

1. Socio-economic profile is measured by the PISA index of economic, social and cultural status (ESCS).
2. Relative performance refers to the residual performance, attributable to purely "collaborative problem-solving" competencies, after accounting for performance in science, reading and mathematics in a regression performed across students at the national level.
Note: Values that are statistically significant are indicated in bold (see Annex A3).
* See note at the beginning of this Annex.
**Malaysia: Coverage is too small to ensure comparability (see Annex A4).
StatLink http://dx.doi.org/10.1787/888933616807

[Part 2/2]

Table V.5.14b Index of valuing teamwork and performance in collaborative problem solving

		Before accounting for students' and schools' socio-economic profile[1]							After accounting for students' and schools' socio-economic profile											
		Change in collaborative problem-solving performance per unit change in the index of valuing teamwork		Explained variance in student performance (r-squared × 100)		Change in relative collaborative problem-solving performance[2] per unit change in the index of valuing teamwork		Explained variance in student performance (r-squared × 100)		Change in collaborative problem-solving performance per unit change in the index of valuing teamwork		Explained variance in relative student performance (r-squared × 100)		Change in relative collaborative problem-solving performance per unit change in the index of valuing teamwork		Explained variance in relative student performance (r-squared × 100)		Increased likelihood of students in the bottom quarter of the index of valuing teamwork scoring below Level 2 on the collaborative problem-solving scale (below 440 score points)		Increased likelihood of students in the top quarter of the index of valuing teamwork scoring at Level 4 on the collaborative problem-solving scale (at or above 640 score points)	
		Score dif.	S.E.	%	S.E.	Score dif.	S.E.	%	S.E.	Score dif.	S.E.	%	S.E.	Score dif.	S.E.	%	S.E.	Relative risk	S.E.	Relative risk	S.E.
OECD	Australia	**-11**	(1.6)	1.0	(0.3)	2	(1.4)	0.1	(0.1)	**-10**	(1.6)	10.3	(1.0)	2	(1.4)	0.2	(0.1)	**0.7**	(0.0)	**0.8**	(0.1)
	Austria	**-12**	(1.7)	2.0	(0.5)	2	(1.3)	0.1	(0.2)	**-7**	(1.6)	20.9	(1.9)	2	(1.3)	0.3	(0.2)	**0.7**	(0.1)	**0.7**	(0.1)
	Belgium	**-14**	(1.3)	2.0	(0.4)	-2	(0.9)	0.1	(0.1)	**-9**	(1.1)	24.6	(1.9)	-1	(1.0)	0.2	(0.1)	**0.7**	(0.0)	**0.6**	(0.1)
	Canada	**-15**	(1.3)	2.4	(0.4)	**-3**	(1.3)	0.3	(0.2)	**-16**	(1.3)	9.5	(0.8)	**-3**	(1.3)	0.3	(0.2)	**0.6**	(0.0)	**0.6**	(0.1)
	Chile	0	(1.5)	0.0	(0.0)	2	(1.0)	0.1	(0.1)	0	(1.5)	17.8	(1.7)	2	(1.0)	0.3	(0.2)	0.9	(0.0)	1.2	(0.5)
	Czech Republic	-2	(1.4)	0.1	(0.1)	**4**	(1.2)	0.4	(0.3)	0	(1.4)	19.7	(1.9)	**4**	(1.3)	0.6	(0.3)	0.9	(0.1)	0.9	(0.1)
	Denmark	**-11**	(1.7)	1.4	(0.4)	0	(1.2)	0.0	(0.1)	**-9**	(1.7)	8.1	(1.2)	0	(1.2)	0.2	(0.2)	**0.6**	(0.1)	**0.7**	(0.1)
	Estonia	-4	(1.9)	0.2	(0.2)	**3**	(1.5)	0.4	(0.4)	-3	(2.0)	8.4	(1.3)	**3**	(1.5)	0.7	(0.4)	0.9	(0.1)	0.9	(0.1)
	Finland	**-11**	(2.0)	1.0	(0.4)	2	(1.5)	0.2	(0.2)	**-11**	(2.0)	6.5	(1.0)	2	(1.5)	0.5	(0.3)	**0.7**	(0.1)	**0.7**	(0.1)
	France	**-7**	(1.5)	0.6	(0.3)	2	(1.3)	0.2	(0.2)	**-3**	(1.4)	23.9	(1.8)	2	(1.3)	0.2	(0.2)	**0.8**	(0.1)	0.7	(0.2)
	Germany	**-7**	(1.6)	0.5	(0.2)	1	(1.1)	0.0	(0.0)	**-5**	(1.4)	19.5	(1.9)	0	(1.1)	0.2	(0.1)	0.8	(0.1)	0.8	(0.1)
	Greece	**-5**	(1.7)	0.3	(0.2)	1	(1.0)	0.1	(0.1)	-3	(1.5)	16.9	(2.2)	1	(1.0)	0.1	(0.1)	**0.8**	(0.0)	0.6	(0.2)
	Hungary	**-7**	(1.7)	0.5	(0.2)	1	(1.2)	0.0	(0.1)	**-5**	(1.5)	35.1	(1.9)	1	(1.2)	0.7	(0.3)	**0.8**	(0.0)	0.8	(0.2)
	Iceland	**-11**	(1.8)	1.3	(0.4)	-1	(1.2)	0.0	(0.1)	**-11**	(1.8)	3.3	(0.7)	0	(1.2)	0.9	(0.4)	**0.8**	(0.1)	0.7	(0.2)
	Ireland	m	m	m	m	m	m	m	m	m	m	m	m	m	m	m	m	m	m	m	m
	Israel	**-10**	(2.1)	1.0	(0.4)	-1	(1.4)	0.0	(0.1)	**-6**	(1.9)	22.0	(2.8)	0	(1.5)	1.1	(0.6)	**0.8**	(0.0)	0.7	(0.2)
	Italy	**-7**	(1.5)	0.5	(0.2)	1	(1.3)	0.0	(0.1)	**-3**	(1.5)	17.5	(1.7)	1	(1.4)	0.4	(0.3)	**0.8**	(0.0)	0.7	(0.2)
	Japan	1	(1.7)	0.0	(0.1)	3	(1.6)	0.3	(0.3)	1	(1.6)	13.8	(1.7)	3	(1.6)	0.7	(0.4)	0.9	(0.1)	1.0	(0.1)
	Korea	2	(1.7)	0.1	(0.1)	**4**	(1.3)	0.5	(0.4)	0	(1.6)	10.7	(1.9)	**4**	(1.4)	1.2	(0.6)	1.0	(0.1)	1.1	(0.1)
	Latvia	**-10**	(1.7)	1.2	(0.4)	-1	(1.2)	0.1	(0.1)	**-8**	(1.6)	9.1	(1.3)	-1	(1.2)	0.1	(0.1)	**0.7**	(0.1)	**0.5**	(0.2)
	Luxembourg	**-8**	(1.5)	0.8	(0.3)	0	(1.2)	0.0	(0.1)	**-6**	(1.5)	22.5	(1.3)	-1	(1.2)	0.7	(0.3)	**0.8**	(0.1)	0.7	(0.2)
	Mexico	1	(1.4)	0.0	(0.0)	2	(1.5)	0.2	(0.2)	2	(1.4)	17.4	(1.9)	2	(1.5)	1.7	(0.7)	1.0	(0.0)	1.0	(0.6)
	Netherlands	**-11**	(2.0)	0.9	(0.3)	-1	(1.3)	0.0	(0.0)	**-7**	(1.9)	22.0	(2.5)	-1	(1.3)	0.1	(0.1)	**0.7**	(0.1)	0.8	(0.1)
	New Zealand	**-12**	(2.1)	1.4	(0.5)	1	(1.6)	0.0	(0.1)	**-11**	(1.8)	10.7	(1.5)	0	(1.6)	0.3	(0.3)	**0.7**	(0.1)	**0.6**	(0.1)
	Norway	**-13**	(1.3)	2.1	(0.5)	1	(1.0)	0.1	(0.1)	**-12**	(1.3)	5.9	(0.8)	1	(1.0)	0.2	(0.1)	**0.8**	(0.1)	**0.6**	(0.1)
	Poland	m	m	m	m	m	m	m	m	m	m	m	m	m	m	m	m	m	m	m	m
	Portugal	**-6**	(1.4)	0.5	(0.2)	**3**	(1.0)	0.2	(0.2)	**-4**	(1.4)	13.4	(1.8)	**3**	(1.0)	0.5	(0.3)	**0.8**	(0.1)	0.9	(0.2)
	Slovak Republic	3	(1.6)	0.1	(0.1)	1	(1.3)	0.0	(0.1)	1	(1.6)	19.8	(1.8)	1	(1.3)	0.8	(0.4)	1.0	(0.0)	1.2	(0.3)
	Slovenia	-4	(1.9)	0.1	(0.1)	**4**	(1.6)	0.5	(0.3)	0	(1.7)	23.8	(1.5)	**5**	(1.6)	0.9	(0.5)	**0.8**	(0.1)	0.9	(0.2)
	Spain	**-4**	(1.5)	0.2	(0.2)	**3**	(1.5)	0.4	(0.3)	**-3**	(1.5)	7.7	(1.0)	**3**	(1.5)	0.5	(0.3)	0.9	(0.1)	0.7	(0.1)
	Sweden	**-10**	(1.7)	1.1	(0.4)	**3**	(1.3)	0.2	(0.2)	**-9**	(1.7)	11.7	(1.8)	**3**	(1.3)	0.5	(0.3)	**0.8**	(0.1)	**0.7**	(0.1)
	Switzerland	m	m	m	m	m	m	m	m	m	m	m	m	m	m	m	m	m	m	m	m
	Turkey	**8**	(1.5)	1.0	(0.4)	1	(1.2)	0.1	(0.1)	**6**	(1.5)	21.3	(3.2)	1	(1.2)	0.8	(0.5)	**1.1**	(0.0)	2.5	(5.2)
	United Kingdom	**-9**	(1.5)	0.8	(0.3)	1	(1.2)	0.1	(0.1)	**-9**	(1.4)	10.9	(1.5)	1	(1.2)	0.1	(0.1)	**0.8**	(0.1)	**0.8**	(0.1)
	United States	**-10**	(1.7)	0.9	(0.3)	**3**	(1.0)	0.3	(0.2)	**-9**	(1.5)	10.8	(1.4)	**3**	(1.0)	0.5	(0.3)	**0.7**	(0.1)	**0.7**	(0.1)
	OECD average-32	**-7**	(0.3)	0.8	(0.1)	**1**	(0.2)	0.2	(0.0)	**-5**	(0.3)	15.5	(0.3)	**1**	(0.2)	0.5	(0.1)	**0.8**	(0.0)	0.8	(0.2)
	OECD average-35	m	m	m	m	m	m	m	m	m	m	m	m	m	m	m	m	m	m	m	m
Partners	Brazil	5	(1.3)	0.3	(0.1)	**3**	(1.2)	0.2	(0.2)	5	(1.2)	17.1	(1.7)	**3**	(1.2)	0.8	(0.4)	1.0	(0.1)	1.0	(0.3)
	B-S-J-G (China)	2	(1.6)	0.0	(0.1)	2	(1.1)	0.1	(0.1)	2	(1.4)	28.1	(2.8)	2	(1.1)	0.7	(0.4)	1.1	(0.1)	1.0	(0.1)
	Bulgaria	-2	(1.6)	0.1	(0.1)	1	(0.9)	0.0	(0.1)	-1	(1.3)	32.4	(2.6)	1	(0.9)	1.0	(0.4)	**0.9**	(0.0)	0.9	(0.2)
	Colombia	-2	(1.4)	0.0	(0.1)	-2	(1.2)	0.2	(0.2)	0	(1.4)	22.2	(2.2)	-2	(1.2)	2.8	(0.9)	1.0	(0.0)	0.7	(0.4)
	Costa Rica	**-6**	(1.4)	0.6	(0.3)	2	(1.2)	0.2	(0.2)	**-3**	(1.4)	14.5	(1.9)	2	(1.3)	0.4	(0.3)	**0.9**	(0.0)	0.7	(0.5)
	Croatia	**-4**	(1.5)	0.2	(0.1)	**4**	(1.1)	0.5	(0.3)	-1	(1.4)	17.9	(2.0)	**4**	(1.1)	0.6	(0.3)	0.9	(0.0)	0.9	(0.2)
	Cyprus*	-3	(1.7)	0.1	(0.1)	0	(1.5)	0.0	(0.1)	-1	(1.6)	8.9	(0.9)	0	(1.5)	0.3	(0.3)	**0.9**	(0.0)	1.0	(0.4)
	Dominican Republic	m	m	m	m	m	m	m	m	m	m	m	m	m	m	m	m	m	m	m	m
	Hong Kong (China)	**-4**	(1.7)	0.2	(0.2)	1	(1.1)	0.0	(0.1)	**-4**	(1.7)	7.5	(1.6)	0	(1.1)	0.2	(0.2)	**0.8**	(0.1)	0.9	(0.1)
	Lithuania	**-4**	(1.7)	0.3	(0.2)	1	(1.2)	0.1	(0.1)	-2	(1.6)	17.3	(2.0)	1	(1.2)	0.5	(0.3)	0.9	(0.1)	**0.5**	(0.2)
	Macao (China)	1	(1.8)	0.0	(0.0)	3	(1.6)	0.3	(0.3)	1	(1.8)	0.9	(0.3)	3	(1.6)	0.9	(0.4)	1.0	(0.1)	1.0	(0.1)
	Montenegro	**-3**	(1.2)	0.1	(0.1)	0	(1.0)	0.0	(0.0)	0	(1.2)	13.4	(1.0)	1	(1.0)	0.4	(0.3)	**0.9**	(0.0)	0.7	(1.1)
	Peru	**9**	(1.5)	1.0	(0.3)	**3**	(1.2)	0.3	(0.2)	**6**	(1.3)	30.2	(2.1)	2	(1.3)	2.2	(0.5)	**1.1**	(0.0)	1.2	(0.7)
	Qatar	m	m	m	m	m	m	m	m	m	m	m	m	m	m	m	m	m	m	m	m
	Russia	-3	(1.7)	0.1	(0.1)	2	(1.3)	0.1	(0.1)	-1	(1.7)	11.7	(1.7)	**3**	(1.3)	2.8	(1.0)	**0.9**	(0.0)	0.9	(0.2)
	Singapore	**-10**	(1.5)	1.2	(0.3)	1	(1.1)	0.0	(0.1)	**-6**	(1.3)	16.8	(1.3)	0	(1.1)	0.3	(0.2)	**0.7**	(0.1)	**0.8**	(0.1)
	Chinese Taipei	**-5**	(1.3)	0.3	(0.1)	-1	(1.2)	0.0	(0.1)	**-4**	(1.3)	17.1	(2.1)	-1	(1.2)	0.2	(0.2)	**1.2**	(0.1)	**0.7**	(0.1)
	Thailand	**9**	(2.0)	0.7	(0.3)	**3**	(1.4)	0.3	(0.3)	**7**	(1.9)	18.4	(2.9)	**3**	(1.4)	1.8	(0.9)	**1.2**	(0.0)	1.2	(0.5)
	Tunisia	**-4**	(1.1)	0.5	(0.3)	-2	(1.0)	0.1	(0.2)	-1	(1.1)	17.0	(2.9)	-1	(1.0)	2.2	(0.8)	**0.9**	(0.0)	m	m
	United Arab Emirates	-3	(1.4)	0.1	(0.1)	-1	(1.2)	0.1	(0.1)	0	(1.4)	14.4	(1.7)	0	(1.2)	1.1	(0.4)	0.9	(0.0)	**0.5**	(0.2)
	Uruguay	**-12**	(1.7)	1.9	(0.5)	0	(1.4)	0.0	(0.1)	**-10**	(1.7)	20.7	(1.9)	0	(1.4)	0.3	(0.3)	**0.8**	(0.0)	0.5	(0.2)
	Malaysia**	**7**	(1.7)	0.6	(0.3)	**4**	(1.2)	0.6	(0.3)	**8**	(1.5)	16.6	(2.5)	**4**	(1.2)	1.2	(0.6)	**1.1**	(0.0)	1.1	(0.7)

1. Socio-economic profile is measured by the PISA index of economic, social and cultural status (ESCS).
2. Relative performance refers to the residual performance, attributable to purely "collaborative problem-solving" competencies, after accounting for performance in science, reading and mathematics in a regression performed across students at the national level.
Note: Values that are statistically significant are indicated in bold (see Annex A3).
* See note at the beginning of this Annex.
**Malaysia: Coverage is too small to ensure comparability (see Annex A4).
StatLink http://dx.doi.org/10.1787/888933616807

[Part 1/3]

Table V.6.1a Days engaged in moderate physical activity and performance in collaborative problem solving

Results based on students' self-reports

		Days engaged in moderate physical activity[1] in an average week				Performance in collaborative problem solving – Days of moderate physical activity per week – All students															
		Average number of days		Variability		0		1		2		3		4		5		6		7	
		Days	S.E.	S.D.	S.E.	Mean score	S.E.	Mean score	S.E.	Mean score	S.E.	Mean score	S.E.	Mean score	S.E.	Mean score	S.E.	Mean score	S.E.	Mean score	S.E.
OECD	Australia	4.6	(0.03)	2.3	(0.01)	532	(3.9)	539	(3.9)	535	(4.4)	539	(4.2)	532	(4.4)	542	(4.5)	552	(6.7)	528	(3.3)
	Austria	5.2	(0.04)	2.6	(0.01)	497	(5.6)	502	(5.0)	504	(5.6)	516	(5.6)	513	(6.2)	513	(5.7)	533	(7.6)	520	(3.2)
	Belgium	4.6	(0.03)	2.5	(0.01)	482	(4.6)	487	(4.0)	505	(4.2)	507	(4.5)	510	(4.5)	528	(3.8)	538	(6.2)	521	(3.2)
	Canada	5.3	(0.02)	2.3	(0.01)	530	(4.8)	546	(5.9)	541	(4.1)	539	(3.5)	525	(4.8)	540	(4.6)	552	(5.1)	540	(3.1)
	Chile	4.4	(0.03)	2.4	(0.01)	470	(4.3)	459	(4.0)	458	(4.7)	449	(4.6)	457	(4.8)	468	(4.9)	471	(7.1)	457	(4.2)
	Czech Republic	5.2	(0.04)	2.4	(0.02)	466	(6.9)	490	(4.5)	493	(4.2)	503	(3.8)	499	(5.2)	508	(4.1)	523	(7.0)	515	(3.2)
	Denmark	5.6	(0.04)	2.3	(0.02)	502	(6.4)	514	(7.4)	525	(6.5)	524	(5.4)	520	(5.9)	534	(3.9)	535	(5.1)	524	(3.8)
	Estonia	4.7	(0.04)	2.3	(0.01)	535	(5.2)	525	(5.8)	540	(4.8)	540	(4.5)	537	(5.3)	549	(4.8)	550	(7.6)	527	(3.4)
	Finland	5.2	(0.04)	2.2	(0.01)	522	(6.4)	524	(6.1)	536	(5.3)	539	(5.2)	547	(5.0)	543	(4.4)	554	(4.7)	531	(4.5)
	France	4.6	(0.04)	2.6	(0.01)	485	(5.0)	490	(4.1)	496	(5.1)	494	(4.5)	498	(5.8)	513	(6.7)	524	(7.4)	514	(3.6)
	Germany	5.6	(0.04)	2.4	(0.02)	516	(7.4)	525	(6.2)	528	(6.3)	528	(5.6)	521	(6.5)	550	(4.9)	560	(8.3)	543	(4.0)
	Greece	4.3	(0.04)	2.4	(0.02)	462	(5.1)	450	(4.7)	463	(4.5)	454	(5.5)	456	(7.0)	475	(6.8)	470	(7.1)	467	(4.8)
	Hungary	5.2	(0.04)	2.4	(0.01)	460	(5.4)	449	(5.7)	464	(5.5)	466	(4.9)	464	(7.3)	479	(4.7)	497	(7.7)	487	(3.9)
	Iceland	5.2	(0.04)	2.4	(0.02)	504	(7.9)	503	(6.5)	511	(5.7)	498	(5.8)	501	(5.9)	500	(5.2)	511	(5.8)	499	(4.1)
	Ireland	4.5	(0.04)	2.3	(0.02)	m	m	m	m	m	m	m	m	m	m	m	m	m	m	m	m
	Israel	4.2	(0.05)	2.5	(0.01)	480	(5.4)	458	(5.3)	472	(6.2)	458	(5.8)	467	(5.6)	476	(6.5)	493	(6.7)	486	(4.9)
	Italy	m	m	m	m	m	m	m	m	m	m	m	m	m	m	m	m	m	m	m	m
	Japan	4.7	(0.06)	2.8	(0.01)	563	(3.1)	538	(6.1)	547	(6.6)	546	(5.5)	559	(8.6)	558	(4.4)	568	(3.8)	541	(3.8)
	Korea	4.3	(0.05)	2.6	(0.02)	552	(3.6)	532	(4.2)	542	(4.2)	534	(4.3)	537	(6.2)	540	(3.9)	541	(8.3)	529	(4.5)
	Latvia	5.2	(0.04)	2.4	(0.02)	472	(6.4)	462	(5.8)	484	(4.6)	483	(4.4)	492	(5.3)	491	(4.2)	488	(6.4)	496	(3.8)
	Luxembourg	4.4	(0.04)	2.4	(0.01)	489	(4.8)	486	(4.5)	492	(4.2)	499	(4.0)	486	(4.7)	500	(5.8)	510	(9.1)	506	(3.6)
	Mexico	4.3	(0.03)	2.3	(0.02)	434	(4.5)	418	(3.4)	422	(3.9)	439	(3.6)	443	(5.9)	445	(4.5)	445	(5.7)	447	(3.7)
	Netherlands	5.6	(0.04)	2.2	(0.02)	498	(7.2)	496	(8.3)	499	(5.7)	493	(5.4)	521	(7.9)	534	(4.1)	542	(4.7)	529	(3.6)
	New Zealand	4.8	(0.04)	2.4	(0.02)	523	(6.6)	542	(6.2)	534	(5.4)	534	(6.0)	526	(6.4)	540	(5.0)	564	(6.7)	540	(5.2)
	Norway	5.6	(0.04)	2.3	(0.02)	496	(5.7)	475	(7.0)	494	(5.5)	493	(5.7)	516	(5.7)	514	(3.9)	534	(5.6)	512	(3.5)
	Poland	5.6	(0.04)	2.4	(0.02)	m	m	m	m	m	m	m	m	m	m	m	m	m	m	m	m
	Portugal	4.4	(0.04)	2.5	(0.02)	498	(4.9)	491	(5.3)	492	(4.6)	498	(4.3)	501	(5.1)	517	(5.2)	522	(10.4)	503	(3.5)
	Slovak Republic	5.1	(0.04)	2.4	(0.02)	436	(5.9)	446	(5.8)	459	(5.2)	468	(4.3)	477	(5.3)	477	(4.9)	479	(6.9)	479	(3.3)
	Slovenia	4.9	(0.04)	2.3	(0.02)	496	(5.8)	488	(4.3)	497	(4.3)	502	(4.8)	511	(5.6)	519	(5.2)	520	(7.8)	507	(3.7)
	Spain	4.2	(0.03)	2.4	(0.01)	484	(4.2)	496	(4.3)	502	(3.9)	499	(4.0)	500	(5.4)	504	(4.4)	503	(6.2)	505	(3.4)
	Sweden	5.2	(0.05)	2.4	(0.02)	484	(6.2)	509	(6.3)	503	(5.3)	513	(6.3)	521	(6.2)	522	(4.6)	530	(7.4)	525	(4.5)
	Switzerland	5.2	(0.04)	2.5	(0.02)	m	m	m	m	m	m	m	m	m	m	m	m	m	m	m	m
	Turkey	4.0	(0.05)	2.5	(0.02)	416	(4.3)	405	(4.4)	416	(4.8)	423	(5.4)	421	(8.0)	443	(5.7)	450	(10.3)	445	(4.1)
	United Kingdom	4.7	(0.04)	2.5	(0.01)	506	(4.9)	508	(6.1)	528	(5.5)	534	(5.0)	516	(6.6)	534	(4.6)	549	(7.2)	525	(4.2)
	United States	5.2	(0.04)	2.4	(0.02)	514	(6.5)	512	(8.7)	533	(6.8)	527	(6.7)	524	(7.5)	525	(4.9)	535	(6.8)	524	(4.1)
	OECD average-32	4.9	(0.01)	2.4	(0.00)	494	(1.0)	492	(1.0)	500	(0.9)	501	(0.9)	503	(1.1)	512	(0.9)	521	(1.3)	509	(0.7)
	OECD average-35	4.9	(0.01)	2.4	(0.00)	m	m	m	m	m	m	m	m	m	m	m	m	m	m	m	m
Partners	Brazil	3.7	(0.03)	2.4	(0.01)	434	(3.4)	408	(4.0)	408	(3.7)	425	(3.7)	423	(5.1)	428	(4.5)	421	(8.1)	435	(3.7)
	B-S-J-G (China)	4.2	(0.05)	2.5	(0.02)	513	(5.4)	481	(6.7)	490	(6.0)	484	(6.5)	505	(7.5)	486	(4.5)	533	(9.3)	508	(5.3)
	Bulgaria	4.5	(0.04)	2.4	(0.02)	429	(5.1)	424	(5.7)	435	(5.4)	440	(6.2)	477	(6.0)	465	(6.3)	482	(6.8)	478	(4.3)
	Colombia	3.6	(0.04)	2.4	(0.02)	422	(3.2)	417	(3.5)	426	(4.2)	427	(4.2)	443	(6.6)	435	(5.9)	455	(7.0)	462	(4.0)
	Costa Rica	3.9	(0.04)	2.3	(0.02)	444	(4.9)	438	(4.3)	433	(4.4)	440	(5.4)	438	(5.6)	438	(4.8)	455	(8.1)	440	(4.2)
	Croatia	4.7	(0.04)	2.5	(0.01)	460	(4.1)	458	(4.3)	464	(4.1)	469	(4.6)	474	(6.6)	486	(4.7)	494	(7.7)	490	(3.7)
	Cyprus*	4.3	(0.03)	2.3	(0.01)	442	(4.8)	442	(3.9)	441	(4.1)	446	(4.9)	451	(5.5)	453	(5.3)	469	(7.0)	454	(3.8)
	Dominican Republic	4.2	(0.04)	2.4	(0.02)	m	m	m	m	m	m	m	m	m	m	m	m	m	m	m	m
	Hong Kong (China)	4.4	(0.05)	2.6	(0.01)	556	(4.5)	538	(4.1)	536	(5.2)	538	(4.7)	528	(8.1)	548	(4.9)	544	(7.1)	537	(4.1)
	Lithuania	5.1	(0.04)	2.4	(0.01)	448	(5.8)	452	(4.9)	460	(5.4)	468	(4.2)	462	(6.0)	480	(5.1)	495	(6.5)	484	(3.3)
	Macao (China)	4.2	(0.04)	2.6	(0.01)	543	(3.6)	524	(3.7)	530	(3.7)	531	(6.2)	537	(7.8)	537	(4.8)	552	(6.9)	534	(3.3)
	Montenegro	5.1	(0.04)	2.3	(0.01)	410	(5.8)	406	(4.8)	407	(4.0)	423	(3.0)	416	(4.2)	425	(4.0)	439	(6.9)	432	(3.0)
	Peru	4.2	(0.04)	2.3	(0.02)	417	(5.5)	401	(3.6)	413	(3.9)	431	(4.2)	428	(6.1)	432	(4.5)	450	(8.1)	443	(4.3)
	Qatar	3.7	(0.02)	2.4	(0.01)	m	m	m	m	m	m	m	m	m	m	m	m	m	m	m	m
	Russia	5.2	(0.04)	2.3	(0.02)	473	(7.1)	465	(7.0)	466	(6.2)	465	(5.1)	468	(6.3)	486	(7.5)	485	(7.0)	488	(4.5)
	Singapore	4.5	(0.03)	2.6	(0.01)	574	(3.9)	546	(3.8)	543	(3.6)	553	(4.7)	557	(6.4)	568	(4.2)	578	(8.3)	575	(2.7)
	Chinese Taipei	4.7	(0.03)	2.6	(0.01)	531	(3.8)	523	(4.8)	526	(4.1)	523	(6.6)	540	(5.6)	526	(3.6)	544	(7.8)	524	(3.1)
	Thailand	4.8	(0.04)	2.3	(0.01)	439	(7.0)	417	(4.3)	428	(4.4)	440	(5.0)	435	(5.5)	438	(4.8)	462	(10.9)	453	(4.1)
	Tunisia	3.5	(0.04)	2.2	(0.02)	395	(3.0)	382	(3.1)	374	(3.4)	379	(3.3)	369	(4.6)	387	(6.8)	379	(6.2)	397	(3.4)
	United Arab Emirates	3.5	(0.03)	2.4	(0.01)	432	(3.1)	423	(4.4)	438	(4.4)	436	(5.0)	445	(5.3)	449	(5.4)	473	(11.1)	460	(4.4)
	Uruguay	4.3	(0.04)	2.4	(0.01)	445	(4.2)	434	(4.8)	443	(4.5)	455	(5.0)	448	(5.6)	461	(5.0)	444	(7.2)	459	(4.4)
	Malaysia**	5.1	(0.05)	2.4	(0.01)	426	(6.1)	421	(5.4)	429	(4.5)	436	(4.5)	432	(6.4)	437	(4.6)	442	(9.1)	461	(3.9)

1. Examples of moderate physical activity include walking, climbing stairs and riding a bike to school. One day of moderate physical activity consists of at least 60 minutes of such activities.
* See note at the beginning of this Annex.
**Malaysia: Coverage is too small to ensure comparability (see Annex A4).
StatLink http://dx.doi.org/10.1787/888933616826

[Part 2/3]

Table V.6.1a Days engaged in moderate physical activity and performance in collaborative problem solving

Results based on students' self-reports

		Performance in collaborative problem solving															
		Days of moderate physical activity[1] per week															
		Boys															
		0		1		2		3		4		5		6		7	
		Mean score	S.E.	Mean score	S.E.	Mean score	S.E.	Mean score	S.E.	Mean score	S.E.	Mean score	S.E.	Mean score	S.E.	Mean score	S.E.
OECD	Australia	515	(5.9)	516	(5.9)	508	(6.1)	519	(6.0)	515	(6.5)	523	(5.4)	526	(8.0)	514	(3.9)
	Austria	485	(7.1)	493	(6.8)	487	(7.6)	503	(6.8)	497	(9.2)	506	(6.9)	530	(9.3)	509	(4.6)
	Belgium	475	(5.8)	470	(5.6)	487	(6.3)	491	(6.0)	494	(6.2)	517	(5.0)	522	(7.6)	512	(4.6)
	Canada	517	(7.3)	529	(8.3)	519	(6.0)	516	(5.1)	502	(5.8)	522	(5.1)	534	(6.3)	523	(3.9)
	Chile	472	(6.0)	453	(6.3)	451	(6.1)	440	(5.8)	449	(6.8)	465	(5.9)	468	(9.2)	448	(4.7)
	Czech Republic	452	(8.9)	481	(5.7)	482	(6.9)	492	(6.0)	481	(7.5)	497	(5.5)	509	(9.8)	506	(4.1)
	Denmark	496	(7.3)	495	(9.5)	519	(8.3)	512	(7.7)	509	(8.7)	526	(5.1)	524	(6.9)	515	(4.5)
	Estonia	525	(6.5)	516	(8.1)	524	(6.2)	528	(6.2)	523	(7.3)	540	(6.0)	532	(10.6)	513	(5.0)
	Finland	506	(8.2)	496	(7.6)	512	(6.9)	515	(7.3)	520	(7.5)	523	(5.4)	531	(7.1)	511	(5.2)
	France	478	(6.3)	472	(6.5)	483	(7.0)	481	(6.4)	483	(8.4)	503	(9.1)	501	(9.0)	501	(5.0)
	Germany	501	(10.1)	516	(8.7)	517	(8.8)	511	(8.0)	494	(9.2)	538	(6.3)	537	(10.3)	531	(4.6)
	Greece	448	(7.1)	436	(5.9)	449	(7.1)	437	(6.6)	438	(8.7)	455	(8.6)	463	(9.5)	455	(5.9)
	Hungary	457	(7.4)	437	(7.5)	452	(6.8)	452	(6.8)	446	(10.2)	465	(6.8)	480	(10.9)	472	(5.4)
	Iceland	498	(11.7)	493	(10.1)	503	(7.3)	484	(10.2)	490	(9.5)	490	(7.3)	501	(9.0)	481	(5.2)
	Ireland	m	m	m	m	m	m	m	m	m	m	m	m	m	m	m	m
	Israel	478	(9.6)	450	(7.0)	464	(8.3)	446	(7.7)	457	(6.8)	458	(8.8)	473	(8.9)	473	(6.5)
	Italy	m	m	m	m	m	m	m	m	m	m	m	m	m	m	m	m
	Japan	551	(5.1)	528	(7.5)	546	(6.6)	526	(7.8)	546	(11.1)	547	(6.4)	555	(5.8)	528	(4.7)
	Korea	526	(6.5)	511	(6.6)	528	(5.4)	521	(5.8)	517	(8.7)	529	(4.9)	533	(9.8)	521	(5.3)
	Latvia	459	(8.1)	449	(7.1)	468	(6.8)	460	(6.3)	468	(8.1)	471	(6.0)	471	(9.1)	475	(5.0)
	Luxembourg	484	(6.9)	478	(6.4)	478	(5.9)	482	(6.5)	469	(6.4)	492	(7.6)	484	(11.3)	492	(5.3)
	Mexico	429	(6.5)	412	(4.5)	412	(5.5)	431	(5.2)	430	(7.4)	442	(5.5)	445	(7.3)	442	(4.7)
	Netherlands	492	(9.0)	477	(9.6)	481	(7.9)	472	(7.9)	485	(11.4)	525	(4.9)	527	(6.4)	519	(5.3)
	New Zealand	509	(9.0)	520	(10.1)	511	(7.0)	506	(9.8)	500	(8.9)	524	(7.3)	548	(7.8)	522	(6.0)
	Norway	483	(7.8)	461	(9.3)	479	(7.6)	468	(8.2)	503	(9.1)	506	(5.3)	520	(7.0)	499	(4.2)
	Poland	m	m	m	m	m	m	m	m	m	m	m	m	m	m	m	m
	Portugal	493	(7.4)	480	(6.9)	479	(6.4)	483	(5.8)	487	(6.5)	506	(7.7)	519	(13.1)	498	(4.4)
	Slovak Republic	437	(6.8)	424	(7.3)	443	(5.8)	454	(5.8)	467	(7.9)	463	(6.3)	465	(9.5)	463	(4.3)
	Slovenia	479	(8.8)	468	(6.2)	481	(6.6)	480	(6.2)	492	(7.8)	502	(6.0)	503	(11.0)	492	(5.0)
	Spain	477	(5.5)	483	(5.6)	487	(5.1)	487	(5.9)	488	(7.5)	492	(6.1)	497	(8.6)	496	(4.4)
	Sweden	475	(7.9)	488	(8.7)	484	(6.8)	497	(7.5)	496	(8.2)	503	(6.8)	510	(10.5)	504	(6.0)
	Switzerland	m	m	m	m	m	m	m	m	m	m	m	m	m	m	m	m
	Turkey	402	(5.4)	389	(5.7)	404	(6.4)	414	(6.5)	409	(10.5)	433	(7.1)	437	(14.9)	437	(5.2)
	United Kingdom	504	(7.3)	489	(7.7)	506	(7.4)	511	(6.6)	492	(7.8)	514	(6.4)	530	(9.4)	514	(5.0)
	United States	506	(10.0)	504	(12.1)	519	(9.6)	514	(9.2)	508	(10.6)	509	(6.2)	524	(7.5)	514	(5.2)
	OECD average-32	484	(1.4)	478	(1.4)	486	(1.2)	485	(1.3)	486	(1.5)	500	(1.2)	506	(1.7)	496	(0.9)
	OECD average-35	m	m	m	m	m	m	m	m	m	m	m	m	m	m	m	m
Partners	Brazil	428	(5.0)	399	(4.6)	397	(5.1)	414	(4.9)	416	(6.7)	417	(5.6)	419	(9.8)	431	(4.2)
	B-S-J-G (China)	490	(5.7)	465	(7.2)	479	(6.8)	475	(8.3)	496	(9.2)	483	(5.0)	530	(12.3)	503	(5.7)
	Bulgaria	430	(7.9)	420	(7.1)	424	(6.3)	418	(7.4)	452	(8.2)	449	(9.0)	457	(9.7)	460	(5.7)
	Colombia	417	(4.5)	411	(4.6)	419	(5.4)	422	(5.2)	434	(7.9)	433	(6.9)	454	(8.3)	460	(5.8)
	Costa Rica	440	(7.4)	434	(5.3)	426	(4.7)	437	(6.8)	436	(7.1)	438	(5.9)	457	(12.0)	437	(5.6)
	Croatia	450	(6.2)	446	(5.7)	447	(5.4)	452	(7.1)	457	(8.7)	466	(6.1)	481	(10.6)	478	(4.4)
	Cyprus*	424	(6.4)	420	(6.4)	422	(5.5)	422	(6.3)	433	(6.4)	433	(6.7)	453	(9.6)	436	(4.9)
	Dominican Republic	m	m	m	m	m	m	m	m	m	m	m	m	m	m	m	m
	Hong Kong (China)	534	(5.6)	520	(6.2)	516	(6.4)	517	(6.3)	512	(9.9)	535	(6.5)	527	(11.0)	522	(5.6)
	Lithuania	438	(7.5)	437	(6.9)	439	(6.7)	453	(6.0)	446	(7.7)	467	(5.8)	489	(8.7)	474	(4.2)
	Macao (China)	522	(5.7)	501	(5.4)	510	(5.4)	510	(7.2)	517	(10.2)	520	(6.7)	538	(10.2)	519	(4.3)
	Montenegro	398	(9.4)	391	(6.1)	392	(4.6)	408	(5.0)	403	(5.4)	415	(5.6)	426	(8.0)	422	(3.6)
	Peru	413	(7.5)	394	(4.4)	405	(4.7)	428	(5.8)	420	(7.8)	426	(6.0)	455	(10.7)	440	(4.8)
	Qatar	m	m	m	m	m	m	m	m	m	m	m	m	m	m	m	m
	Russia	467	(9.2)	454	(10.3)	455	(7.5)	453	(5.4)	449	(8.4)	471	(7.1)	470	(8.2)	476	(5.7)
	Singapore	559	(6.7)	530	(6.1)	531	(5.2)	545	(6.2)	545	(9.9)	557	(6.2)	576	(11.7)	571	(3.3)
	Chinese Taipei	513	(6.1)	499	(6.6)	509	(5.5)	508	(8.0)	528	(8.2)	516	(4.9)	532	(10.0)	514	(4.1)
	Thailand	413	(9.9)	402	(6.2)	410	(6.6)	424	(6.1)	416	(7.2)	411	(6.3)	443	(16.1)	431	(4.9)
	Tunisia	387	(4.6)	373	(4.2)	369	(4.1)	376	(4.1)	363	(6.1)	387	(7.6)	371	(7.8)	393	(4.3)
	United Arab Emirates	413	(3.9)	399	(5.2)	417	(5.2)	417	(6.5)	424	(7.2)	434	(7.4)	453	(12.3)	445	(6.2)
	Uruguay	438	(6.7)	430	(8.2)	433	(6.3)	445	(7.5)	432	(7.4)	447	(6.1)	439	(8.9)	454	(5.6)
	Malaysia**	411	(7.9)	408	(6.1)	415	(5.3)	423	(5.5)	423	(8.5)	430	(6.6)	439	(10.7)	456	(4.1)

1. Examples of moderate physical activity include walking, climbing stairs and riding a bike to school. One day of moderate physical activity consists of at least 60 minutes of such activities.
* See note at the beginning of this Annex.
**Malaysia: Coverage is too small to ensure comparability (see Annex A4).
StatLink http://dx.doi.org/10.1787/888933616826

[Part 3/3]

Table V.6.1a Days engaged in moderate physical activity and performance in collaborative problem solving

Results based on students' self-reports

		Performance in collaborative problem solving															
		Days of moderate physical activity[1] per week															
		Girls															
		0		1		2		3		4		5		6		7	
		Mean score	S.E.	Mean score	S.E.	Mean score	S.E.	Mean score	S.E.	Mean score	S.E.	Mean score	S.E.	Mean score	S.E.	Mean score	S.E.
OECD	Australia	545	(5.6)	557	(4.8)	556	(4.9)	556	(5.0)	549	(5.5)	561	(5.6)	579	(8.6)	552	(4.5)
	Austria	511	(8.5)	509	(6.6)	518	(7.6)	527	(7.6)	528	(8.4)	521	(7.9)	536	(11.1)	532	(4.1)
	Belgium	488	(5.5)	501	(5.1)	520	(5.6)	524	(6.0)	529	(6.6)	540	(5.2)	556	(9.4)	531	(4.3)
	Canada	541	(6.2)	557	(6.5)	557	(4.9)	557	(4.3)	547	(5.6)	558	(5.8)	574	(7.3)	564	(3.9)
	Chile	469	(5.9)	463	(4.6)	465	(5.5)	458	(5.6)	466	(6.4)	472	(7.3)	478	(11.3)	468	(5.7)
	Czech Republic	488	(9.6)	503	(7.0)	504	(5.4)	514	(4.3)	516	(6.1)	519	(5.9)	535	(9.8)	524	(4.3)
	Denmark	511	(10.3)	529	(8.3)	529	(7.7)	532	(6.3)	530	(7.0)	543	(5.4)	547	(7.5)	535	(4.8)
	Estonia	546	(7.4)	535	(6.3)	557	(6.4)	551	(6.0)	549	(6.6)	558	(7.4)	569	(9.2)	541	(4.6)
	Finland	550	(10.5)	553	(8.7)	561	(6.7)	560	(6.3)	571	(6.0)	564	(6.5)	576	(6.5)	555	(5.3)
	France	491	(6.7)	505	(5.1)	507	(6.6)	509	(7.4)	516	(7.8)	526	(8.1)	543	(9.9)	526	(4.6)
	Germany	536	(10.4)	532	(7.8)	537	(7.1)	542	(7.3)	544	(8.0)	563	(5.9)	583	(10.8)	554	(4.7)
	Greece	475	(5.9)	463	(6.7)	475	(4.8)	472	(6.3)	476	(9.4)	499	(8.3)	479	(10.6)	482	(5.5)
	Hungary	464	(8.1)	460	(8.8)	474	(7.7)	480	(7.1)	478	(10.2)	493	(6.3)	515	(9.2)	502	(4.1)
	Iceland	510	(9.4)	513	(8.0)	517	(8.1)	508	(6.8)	510	(6.8)	508	(6.8)	519	(7.3)	519	(5.5)
	Ireland	m	m	m	m	m	m	m	m	m	m	m	m	m	m	m	m
	Israel	481	(6.1)	464	(7.0)	478	(7.3)	471	(8.0)	481	(9.2)	502	(7.2)	520	(12.1)	507	(7.2)
	Italy	m	m	m	m	m	m	m	m	m	m	m	m	m	m	m	m
	Japan	572	(3.4)	546	(8.1)	548	(10.0)	563	(6.4)	573	(10.3)	567	(4.4)	581	(5.6)	563	(4.0)
	Korea	566	(4.0)	549	(5.3)	556	(5.8)	553	(6.3)	559	(8.4)	553	(5.7)	554	(11.2)	546	(6.3)
	Latvia	492	(9.2)	478	(9.4)	501	(6.4)	504	(6.2)	514	(6.9)	511	(5.8)	502	(8.9)	515	(4.7)
	Luxembourg	493	(6.0)	493	(5.2)	503	(5.8)	515	(5.5)	505	(6.4)	511	(7.9)	545	(12.6)	523	(4.8)
	Mexico	437	(4.9)	424	(4.4)	433	(4.2)	447	(4.6)	458	(7.5)	448	(5.6)	446	(8.9)	454	(4.5)
	Netherlands	505	(9.5)	512	(10.6)	517	(7.6)	515	(6.6)	549	(7.9)	544	(4.8)	558	(6.8)	538	(4.0)
	New Zealand	537	(8.7)	558	(6.7)	553	(7.3)	558	(6.8)	551	(7.7)	557	(6.7)	585	(10.1)	566	(7.0)
	Norway	516	(8.8)	491	(8.7)	510	(7.2)	512	(6.2)	525	(7.1)	522	(5.0)	544	(7.6)	525	(5.0)
	Poland	m	m	m	m	m	m	m	m	m	m	m	m	m	m	m	m
	Portugal	501	(5.7)	500	(6.5)	503	(4.9)	514	(5.2)	516	(8.8)	528	(5.4)	526	(11.4)	510	(4.9)
	Slovak Republic	435	(9.5)	466	(6.9)	475	(7.0)	482	(6.2)	487	(6.3)	490	(6.8)	492	(8.9)	497	(4.4)
	Slovenia	517	(8.7)	508	(6.3)	510	(5.8)	521	(6.4)	531	(7.3)	538	(8.0)	538	(9.1)	526	(4.5)
	Spain	492	(4.9)	507	(5.3)	513	(4.8)	509	(4.8)	511	(5.9)	516	(5.2)	511	(9.2)	517	(5.8)
	Sweden	499	(8.8)	529	(8.1)	522	(6.7)	528	(8.3)	543	(7.0)	541	(5.7)	545	(8.9)	545	(4.7)
	Switzerland	m	m	m	m	m	m	m	m	m	m	m	m	m	m	m	m
	Turkey	428	(5.5)	422	(5.2)	429	(5.4)	435	(7.6)	435	(9.2)	451	(7.6)	466	(14.2)	453	(4.9)
	United Kingdom	509	(5.7)	523	(6.8)	547	(6.8)	558	(7.2)	544	(8.4)	554	(6.0)	574	(9.4)	538	(5.0)
	United States	520	(7.4)	518	(11.2)	541	(7.6)	535	(8.2)	539	(8.8)	541	(6.6)	549	(11.0)	540	(5.6)
	OECD average-32	504	(1.4)	505	(1.3)	513	(1.2)	516	(1.2)	520	(1.4)	526	(1.2)	536	(1.7)	524	(0.9)
	OECD average-35	m	m	m	m	m	m	m	m	m	m	m	m	m	m	m	m
Partners	Brazil	437	(3.7)	416	(4.7)	417	(4.3)	436	(4.7)	430	(6.1)	438	(5.3)	424	(10.6)	439	(5.1)
	B-S-J-G (China)	536	(6.5)	500	(7.6)	501	(7.1)	493	(7.7)	519	(9.7)	490	(6.0)	537	(12.7)	515	(6.5)
	Bulgaria	428	(5.8)	429	(7.4)	449	(6.8)	462	(6.3)	502	(7.3)	483	(7.6)	505	(8.6)	499	(5.4)
	Colombia	425	(3.7)	422	(4.5)	432	(5.2)	433	(5.9)	453	(9.1)	437	(6.7)	456	(10.4)	464	(4.9)
	Costa Rica	447	(4.8)	442	(5.5)	440	(5.8)	443	(6.9)	442	(7.3)	439	(6.0)	452	(10.1)	444	(5.2)
	Croatia	467	(5.7)	468	(6.3)	478	(4.9)	483	(5.4)	493	(8.0)	504	(6.0)	512	(9.1)	504	(4.4)
	Cyprus*	459	(6.1)	461	(4.9)	457	(4.9)	467	(5.3)	467	(7.2)	475	(7.4)	487	(9.3)	477	(5.2)
	Dominican Republic	m	m	m	m	m	m	m	m	m	m	m	m	m	m	m	m
	Hong Kong (China)	571	(5.6)	555	(4.7)	553	(6.2)	557	(6.3)	547	(11.9)	560	(6.6)	561	(9.5)	559	(4.9)
	Lithuania	462	(7.9)	467	(6.9)	480	(6.0)	480	(5.4)	479	(8.2)	493	(6.4)	501	(7.8)	494	(4.1)
	Macao (China)	558	(5.0)	545	(4.1)	549	(5.1)	554	(8.3)	561	(10.2)	556	(6.2)	566	(8.5)	553	(4.4)
	Montenegro	420	(7.2)	419	(6.3)	421	(5.4)	435	(4.3)	427	(5.9)	434	(5.0)	455	(8.8)	444	(4.1)
	Peru	422	(6.9)	408	(4.5)	423	(4.8)	433	(5.0)	435	(7.2)	440	(5.6)	444	(9.1)	448	(5.2)
	Qatar	m	m	m	m	m	m	m	m	m	m	m	m	m	m	m	m
	Russia	480	(9.4)	474	(7.8)	476	(8.7)	477	(7.2)	487	(6.8)	498	(10.0)	499	(8.9)	500	(4.6)
	Singapore	587	(5.4)	560	(5.2)	553	(4.8)	563	(6.8)	571	(8.8)	578	(6.0)	580	(12.6)	582	(4.3)
	Chinese Taipei	544	(4.7)	539	(6.0)	539	(5.6)	536	(7.6)	553	(7.8)	537	(5.4)	562	(10.2)	540	(4.2)
	Thailand	459	(7.9)	430	(4.9)	440	(5.1)	450	(5.3)	452	(7.1)	455	(5.4)	477	(12.1)	471	(4.8)
	Tunisia	399	(3.4)	390	(3.5)	378	(4.1)	382	(4.2)	377	(5.1)	388	(8.9)	388	(8.5)	400	(5.0)
	United Arab Emirates	444	(4.0)	445	(4.9)	458	(5.2)	456	(6.1)	469	(6.7)	464	(6.1)	502	(15.6)	480	(5.3)
	Uruguay	448	(5.3)	437	(5.9)	449	(5.0)	464	(5.9)	463	(7.7)	475	(7.1)	452	(9.9)	466	(5.8)
	Malaysia**	439	(7.5)	436	(6.6)	443	(5.5)	450	(5.4)	441	(7.4)	442	(4.9)	445	(11.7)	466	(4.4)

1. Examples of moderate physical activity include walking, climbing stairs and riding a bike to school. One day of moderate physical activity consists of at least 60 minutes of such activities.
* See note at the beginning of this Annex.
**Malaysia: Coverage is too small to ensure comparability (see Annex A4).
StatLink http://dx.doi.org/10.1787/888933616826

[Part 1/3]

Table V.6.1b Days engaged in vigorous physical activity and performance in collaborative problem solving

Results based on students' self-reports

		Days engaged in vigorous physical activity[1] in an average week				Performance in collaborative problem solving – Days of vigorous physical activity per week – All students															
		Average number of days		Variability		0		1		2		3		4		5		6		7	
		Days	S.E.	S.D.	S.E.	Mean score	S.E.	Mean score	S.E.	Mean score	S.E.	Mean score	S.E.	Mean score	S.E.	Mean score	S.E.	Mean score	S.E.	Mean score	S.E.
OECD	Australia	3.9	(0.03)	2.2	(0.01)	548	(3.2)	545	(3.4)	541	(3.7)	532	(3.7)	542	(4.5)	527	(4.4)	541	(6.6)	503	(4.2)
	Austria	3.4	(0.05)	2.1	(0.03)	515	(3.8)	517	(4.6)	518	(4.1)	523	(5.0)	525	(4.8)	497	(6.4)	497	(8.7)	465	(7.1)
	Belgium	3.5	(0.03)	2.1	(0.01)	500	(3.8)	499	(3.7)	515	(3.7)	523	(3.8)	519	(5.1)	511	(4.8)	508	(8.6)	490	(4.7)
	Canada	4.3	(0.03)	2.3	(0.01)	551	(3.8)	548	(4.7)	550	(4.0)	538	(3.7)	539	(4.0)	534	(3.5)	541	(6.1)	512	(4.5)
	Chile	3.4	(0.03)	2.1	(0.02)	478	(4.0)	460	(4.2)	461	(5.0)	458	(4.7)	455	(5.1)	450	(6.4)	448	(9.0)	431	(5.8)
	Czech Republic	4.1	(0.04)	2.2	(0.02)	497	(4.7)	503	(4.0)	508	(4.1)	503	(4.7)	501	(4.2)	515	(4.6)	513	(5.8)	486	(4.1)
	Denmark	4.4	(0.05)	2.2	(0.02)	519	(5.4)	532	(5.5)	523	(4.4)	535	(4.1)	529	(4.6)	529	(4.8)	514	(5.9)	504	(4.4)
	Estonia	4.1	(0.03)	2.1	(0.02)	547	(4.8)	543	(4.5)	537	(4.4)	535	(4.8)	541	(4.5)	540	(4.7)	541	(6.7)	509	(4.7)
	Finland	4.0	(0.04)	2.1	(0.02)	530	(5.1)	540	(5.3)	544	(4.8)	535	(4.7)	550	(5.2)	537	(5.2)	543	(6.2)	507	(8.3)
	France	3.2	(0.03)	2.0	(0.02)	499	(3.5)	512	(4.1)	506	(4.1)	505	(4.6)	505	(5.8)	491	(7.8)	493	(10.7)	462	(6.4)
	Germany	3.9	(0.03)	2.0	(0.02)	534	(5.0)	540	(5.2)	541	(4.7)	543	(4.4)	539	(4.5)	547	(5.7)	534	(9.2)	495	(7.2)
	Greece	3.9	(0.03)	2.2	(0.02)	476	(4.6)	457	(5.7)	467	(5.2)	458	(5.0)	467	(5.9)	465	(6.6)	451	(6.7)	435	(5.9)
	Hungary	4.2	(0.05)	2.2	(0.02)	468	(4.5)	466	(5.1)	480	(4.2)	486	(4.3)	474	(5.1)	473	(4.8)	490	(7.0)	461	(5.2)
	Iceland	5.0	(0.04)	2.3	(0.02)	513	(6.1)	509	(7.0)	516	(6.1)	493	(5.5)	505	(6.0)	510	(5.5)	505	(5.6)	484	(4.5)
	Ireland	4.1	(0.03)	2.2	(0.02)	m	m	m	m	m	m	m	m	m	m	m	m	m	m	m	m
	Israel	3.9	(0.05)	2.3	(0.02)	486	(5.5)	466	(4.9)	480	(5.7)	474	(5.7)	465	(5.8)	462	(6.7)	472	(7.4)	451	(6.3)
	Italy	m	m	m	m	m	m	m	m	m	m	m	m	m	m	m	m	m	m	m	m
	Japan	3.9	(0.06)	2.7	(0.02)	567	(3.3)	559	(4.6)	552	(4.8)	547	(5.4)	549	(7.2)	555	(7.1)	555	(3.6)	527	(3.9)
	Korea	3.2	(0.04)	2.2	(0.03)	555	(3.4)	537	(3.5)	545	(3.6)	535	(4.5)	530	(5.7)	520	(5.6)	519	(8.6)	508	(6.9)
	Latvia	4.2	(0.04)	2.1	(0.02)	503	(4.9)	486	(4.7)	493	(4.1)	487	(3.7)	490	(5.4)	479	(4.9)	480	(7.8)	464	(6.0)
	Luxembourg	3.9	(0.03)	2.2	(0.02)	494	(4.6)	496	(4.4)	502	(3.7)	508	(5.0)	500	(4.7)	504	(5.3)	496	(8.6)	464	(5.2)
	Mexico	3.8	(0.03)	2.2	(0.02)	443	(3.9)	423	(3.7)	427	(3.3)	440	(3.9)	450	(4.8)	441	(5.4)	444	(6.0)	430	(4.4)
	Netherlands	3.7	(0.03)	1.9	(0.02)	519	(5.4)	511	(3.9)	529	(5.1)	528	(4.0)	533	(4.6)	519	(6.6)	517	(8.8)	494	(8.0)
	New Zealand	3.9	(0.04)	2.2	(0.02)	544	(4.8)	553	(5.9)	548	(4.9)	529	(5.3)	537	(5.7)	530	(6.0)	541	(7.4)	506	(6.7)
	Norway	4.4	(0.04)	2.2	(0.02)	506	(4.4)	501	(5.0)	506	(4.6)	520	(4.3)	513	(4.7)	508	(4.8)	507	(6.5)	487	(4.7)
	Poland	4.6	(0.04)	2.3	(0.02)	m	m	m	m	m	m	m	m	m	m	m	m	m	m	m	m
	Portugal	3.6	(0.04)	2.1	(0.02)	510	(4.2)	491	(4.1)	495	(4.4)	505	(4.4)	510	(5.5)	499	(5.6)	526	(9.6)	474	(5.3)
	Slovak Republic	4.2	(0.04)	2.3	(0.02)	471	(5.1)	464	(4.8)	471	(4.4)	477	(3.6)	473	(5.3)	463	(4.6)	475	(6.6)	452	(3.6)
	Slovenia	4.3	(0.04)	2.3	(0.02)	506	(4.6)	493	(4.8)	524	(4.3)	506	(4.4)	507	(5.2)	514	(4.6)	506	(6.4)	483	(4.6)
	Spain	3.5	(0.03)	2.1	(0.02)	501	(3.3)	498	(3.9)	501	(3.4)	500	(3.2)	492	(3.9)	503	(5.3)	501	(6.6)	485	(6.4)
	Sweden	4.3	(0.04)	2.2	(0.02)	504	(5.7)	514	(6.0)	521	(5.2)	527	(4.5)	529	(5.4)	511	(5.9)	521	(5.4)	497	(6.4)
	Switzerland	3.9	(0.03)	2.0	(0.02)	m	m	m	m	m	m	m	m	m	m	m	m	m	m	m	m
	Turkey	3.4	(0.04)	2.2	(0.02)	432	(4.8)	414	(4.4)	421	(5.1)	432	(5.3)	415	(6.2)	428	(6.6)	428	(11.4)	425	(5.1)
	United Kingdom	3.4	(0.03)	2.1	(0.02)	528	(4.2)	527	(4.0)	538	(4.5)	521	(4.4)	515	(5.6)	515	(6.2)	512	(8.7)	497	(6.2)
	United States	4.5	(0.04)	2.4	(0.01)	540	(5.1)	528	(7.0)	538	(7.5)	526	(6.5)	523	(8.1)	520	(4.7)	531	(7.0)	499	(5.5)
	OECD average-32	3.9	(0.01)	2.2	(0.00)	509	(0.8)	504	(0.9)	510	(0.8)	507	(0.8)	507	(1.0)	503	(1.0)	505	(1.4)	480	(1.0)
	OECD average-35	3.9	(0.01)	2.2	(0.00)	m	m	m	m	m	m	m	m	m	m	m	m	m	m	m	m
Partners	Brazil	3.2	(0.03)	2.3	(0.02)	438	(2.9)	407	(4.6)	415	(4.7)	423	(3.8)	415	(5.7)	424	(5.0)	422	(7.3)	416	(4.9)
	B-S-J-G (China)	4.0	(0.05)	2.2	(0.02)	515	(6.7)	485	(6.2)	490	(5.5)	494	(5.2)	493	(7.4)	499	(5.9)	517	(9.0)	497	(4.5)
	Bulgaria	3.9	(0.04)	2.3	(0.02)	452	(4.7)	443	(5.5)	453	(4.2)	449	(5.7)	465	(6.4)	462	(6.2)	466	(8.2)	447	(5.0)
	Colombia	3.5	(0.03)	2.2	(0.02)	429	(3.4)	418	(3.5)	433	(3.9)	443	(4.3)	441	(5.4)	435	(5.4)	431	(6.9)	435	(5.2)
	Costa Rica	3.2	(0.04)	2.1	(0.02)	450	(3.9)	436	(3.8)	436	(5.1)	444	(5.3)	437	(6.0)	434	(5.0)	444	(8.5)	413	(5.2)
	Croatia	3.8	(0.04)	2.3	(0.02)	480	(3.3)	467	(4.1)	476	(3.8)	487	(4.8)	479	(4.7)	471	(5.1)	482	(7.1)	459	(5.0)
	Cyprus*	4.0	(0.03)	2.3	(0.02)	460	(3.9)	443	(3.8)	454	(4.5)	437	(4.4)	453	(4.2)	446	(5.2)	456	(6.8)	436	(4.4)
	Dominican Republic	3.9	(0.05)	2.3	(0.02)	m	m	m	m	m	m	m	m	m	m	m	m	m	m	m	m
	Hong Kong (China)	3.3	(0.04)	2.1	(0.02)	559	(4.2)	547	(3.8)	538	(4.5)	540	(5.9)	538	(6.4)	537	(6.1)	528	(10.2)	500	(6.5)
	Lithuania	4.1	(0.03)	2.2	(0.02)	471	(4.5)	470	(4.7)	471	(3.9)	466	(4.7)	478	(4.7)	480	(5.1)	483	(6.4)	455	(5.1)
	Macao (China)	3.0	(0.03)	2.0	(0.03)	551	(2.8)	534	(2.5)	533	(3.3)	532	(5.6)	534	(6.4)	509	(7.6)	521	(8.7)	495	(6.0)
	Montenegro	4.3	(0.03)	2.4	(0.02)	431	(3.6)	413	(4.1)	419	(3.6)	427	(3.4)	424	(4.9)	421	(4.7)	427	(5.0)	414	(3.2)
	Peru	3.6	(0.03)	2.1	(0.02)	446	(4.0)	414	(3.8)	420	(4.3)	429	(4.2)	417	(5.1)	417	(5.7)	430	(7.4)	415	(4.4)
	Qatar	3.4	(0.02)	2.2	(0.01)	m	m	m	m	m	m	m	m	m	m	m	m	m	m	m	m
	Russia	4.2	(0.04)	2.2	(0.02)	496	(6.2)	475	(5.0)	483	(4.8)	477	(5.1)	469	(6.3)	478	(6.2)	470	(7.8)	457	(5.1)
	Singapore	3.2	(0.02)	1.9	(0.02)	579	(3.8)	561	(2.7)	559	(3.1)	564	(3.2)	565	(4.8)	545	(5.6)	552	(12.8)	533	(5.8)
	Chinese Taipei	3.6	(0.03)	2.2	(0.02)	530	(3.3)	526	(5.2)	536	(3.5)	531	(4.6)	533	(6.0)	513	(5.1)	530	(9.4)	502	(4.0)
	Thailand	3.7	(0.03)	2.1	(0.02)	457	(5.3)	437	(4.4)	439	(4.0)	442	(4.8)	436	(7.0)	425	(4.3)	421	(8.1)	421	(4.9)
	Tunisia	3.3	(0.03)	2.1	(0.02)	399	(2.8)	380	(3.1)	381	(3.3)	377	(3.7)	375	(4.9)	376	(5.4)	376	(7.0)	382	(4.2)
	United Arab Emirates	3.4	(0.03)	2.2	(0.02)	442	(3.3)	435	(3.7)	438	(4.0)	440	(4.9)	452	(5.9)	443	(5.5)	445	(7.4)	426	(4.4)
	Uruguay	3.7	(0.04)	2.2	(0.02)	458	(3.7)	444	(4.4)	451	(3.9)	457	(4.7)	451	(5.4)	450	(4.9)	440	(6.3)	428	(5.5)
	Malaysia**	4.0	(0.04)	2.1	(0.02)	445	(4.7)	440	(4.7)	443	(4.0)	444	(4.0)	445	(6.0)	434	(5.1)	425	(9.4)	434	(4.6)

1. Vigorous physical activities are those that make a student sweat and breathe hard, such as running, cycling, aerobics, soccer or skating. One day of vigorous physical activity consists of at least 20 minutes of such activities.
* See note at the beginning of this Annex.
**Malaysia: Coverage is too small to ensure comparability (see Annex A4).
StatLink http://dx.doi.org/10.1787/888933616826

[Part 2/3]

Table V.6.1b Days engaged in vigorous physical activity and performance in collaborative problem solving

Results based on students' self-reports

	Performance in collaborative problem solving – Days of vigorous physical activity[1] per week – Boys															
	0		1		2		3		4		5		6		7	
	Mean score	S.E.	Mean score	S.E.	Mean score	S.E.	Mean score	S.E.	Mean score	S.E.	Mean score	S.E.	Mean score	S.E.	Mean score	S.E.
OECD																
Australia	531	(4.7)	522	(5.4)	523	(6.0)	515	(4.7)	523	(5.4)	509	(6.3)	527	(8.7)	489	(5.2)
Austria	508	(6.3)	508	(6.0)	509	(5.8)	517	(6.1)	516	(6.0)	484	(6.8)	490	(10.9)	453	(8.5)
Belgium	490	(5.7)	484	(5.0)	500	(5.2)	511	(5.3)	505	(5.9)	501	(5.7)	492	(11.0)	480	(5.9)
Canada	538	(5.4)	530	(6.7)	528	(5.4)	525	(5.7)	518	(5.3)	517	(4.2)	528	(7.0)	498	(5.3)
Chile	480	(5.6)	454	(6.1)	459	(6.3)	456	(5.7)	450	(6.0)	449	(7.1)	444	(10.5)	426	(6.4)
Czech Republic	487	(6.8)	487	(6.2)	499	(5.1)	495	(5.7)	485	(6.0)	499	(6.4)	501	(7.8)	474	(5.3)
Denmark	506	(6.1)	515	(8.2)	515	(6.2)	525	(6.1)	524	(6.1)	519	(6.4)	510	(7.1)	501	(5.6)
Estonia	540	(7.2)	528	(7.4)	527	(5.8)	524	(5.9)	529	(5.8)	529	(5.5)	528	(8.9)	497	(5.8)
Finland	508	(6.3)	513	(7.7)	524	(6.0)	513	(6.1)	527	(6.7)	516	(6.6)	519	(8.5)	490	(8.8)
France	490	(6.1)	500	(6.7)	494	(5.5)	492	(5.5)	492	(7.7)	476	(9.6)	480	(13.1)	456	(7.5)
Germany	526	(8.3)	527	(7.5)	522	(7.0)	531	(5.4)	532	(5.8)	534	(7.0)	517	(11.3)	481	(8.8)
Greece	461	(7.2)	444	(8.0)	452	(7.1)	440	(5.6)	455	(7.0)	454	(8.6)	452	(8.6)	428	(6.4)
Hungary	462	(6.8)	448	(7.2)	464	(7.6)	466	(6.1)	460	(7.5)	469	(6.3)	481	(8.5)	451	(6.7)
Iceland	509	(10.6)	498	(11.2)	514	(10.5)	483	(8.5)	486	(7.8)	496	(7.7)	496	(7.4)	472	(5.5)
Ireland	m	m	m	m	m	m	m	m	m	m	m	m	m	m	m	m
Israel	483	(11.6)	463	(6.5)	470	(8.8)	466	(6.7)	458	(7.8)	453	(7.4)	462	(9.1)	443	(7.9)
Italy	m	m	m	m	m	m	m	m	m	m	m	m	m	m	m	m
Japan	555	(5.5)	554	(6.1)	542	(7.2)	533	(7.6)	538	(9.2)	544	(8.2)	547	(5.1)	519	(4.6)
Korea	537	(5.5)	518	(5.6)	532	(4.7)	524	(6.0)	523	(5.9)	514	(6.6)	518	(9.8)	506	(7.0)
Latvia	481	(8.2)	463	(6.1)	478	(6.3)	472	(5.6)	470	(6.8)	463	(6.0)	470	(8.7)	445	(7.0)
Luxembourg	489	(7.6)	473	(6.9)	491	(5.6)	497	(6.9)	491	(6.2)	497	(7.0)	481	(9.7)	455	(6.0)
Mexico	431	(5.5)	412	(4.7)	417	(5.3)	433	(5.4)	443	(6.5)	439	(6.0)	442	(7.8)	429	(5.0)
Netherlands	506	(7.7)	491	(6.4)	510	(7.0)	516	(4.6)	519	(5.6)	514	(8.2)	511	(9.7)	485	(9.8)
New Zealand	533	(7.0)	528	(8.9)	523	(6.7)	513	(8.0)	522	(7.2)	516	(7.9)	525	(8.9)	484	(7.6)
Norway	492	(6.4)	485	(7.3)	493	(6.2)	504	(7.0)	497	(6.6)	499	(6.0)	497	(7.9)	479	(6.0)
Poland	m	m	m	m	m	m	m	m	m	m	m	m	m	m	m	m
Portugal	504	(7.0)	476	(6.9)	484	(4.9)	497	(5.2)	505	(6.8)	493	(6.6)	523	(11.2)	468	(5.9)
Slovak Republic	457	(7.3)	440	(7.1)	452	(5.7)	466	(5.3)	458	(6.8)	454	(5.6)	467	(7.6)	444	(4.4)
Slovenia	489	(6.5)	470	(6.7)	503	(6.4)	488	(6.1)	488	(6.8)	497	(5.8)	488	(7.0)	478	(5.9)
Spain	489	(5.3)	480	(6.0)	490	(5.2)	492	(4.0)	484	(5.0)	497	(5.8)	486	(8.5)	476	(7.3)
Sweden	493	(7.5)	497	(8.1)	504	(6.7)	501	(6.5)	504	(7.7)	492	(8.3)	501	(7.2)	482	(7.8)
Switzerland	m	m	m	m	m	m	m	m	m	m	m	m	m	m	m	m
Turkey	406	(6.4)	393	(5.5)	410	(5.8)	422	(6.5)	414	(7.9)	425	(8.7)	433	(14.9)	422	(6.0)
United Kingdom	516	(5.6)	503	(5.9)	525	(6.0)	507	(5.3)	502	(6.8)	506	(7.6)	493	(9.9)	489	(6.6)
United States	536	(8.2)	517	(9.9)	536	(10.4)	513	(8.7)	516	(8.7)	508	(6.6)	514	(8.5)	494	(6.0)
OECD average-32	498	(1.3)	488	(1.3)	496	(1.2)	495	(1.1)	495	(1.2)	492	(1.2)	494	(1.7)	471	(1.2)
OECD average-35	m	m	m	m	m	m	m	m	m	m	m	m	m	m	m	m
Partners																
Brazil	431	(4.4)	399	(4.9)	412	(5.3)	420	(5.0)	412	(6.4)	415	(6.2)	421	(8.8)	413	(5.0)
B-S-J-G (China)	496	(9.6)	470	(7.3)	483	(5.5)	483	(6.2)	489	(9.1)	485	(5.8)	509	(10.1)	495	(5.4)
Bulgaria	434	(7.0)	423	(7.8)	435	(6.0)	432	(7.6)	448	(8.5)	456	(7.5)	458	(10.5)	438	(5.5)
Colombia	416	(5.3)	414	(4.4)	426	(4.8)	439	(6.2)	435	(7.2)	434	(6.7)	434	(7.1)	435	(5.6)
Costa Rica	453	(6.5)	430	(5.5)	438	(6.1)	443	(6.1)	439	(6.3)	435	(6.4)	433	(9.4)	412	(5.8)
Croatia	467	(6.0)	455	(6.3)	457	(5.8)	477	(6.3)	459	(6.1)	462	(6.8)	468	(8.0)	451	(5.6)
Cyprus*	442	(6.9)	417	(5.9)	433	(6.3)	414	(6.5)	438	(5.6)	429	(6.7)	446	(7.6)	425	(5.7)
Dominican Republic	m	m	m	m	m	m	m	m	m	m	m	m	m	m	m	m
Hong Kong (China)	538	(5.2)	529	(5.0)	522	(5.8)	529	(7.2)	525	(7.0)	529	(7.6)	510	(13.0)	490	(7.2)
Lithuania	445	(7.4)	446	(6.7)	457	(6.1)	455	(6.8)	464	(5.5)	470	(5.1)	476	(8.5)	450	(6.0)
Macao (China)	533	(5.6)	512	(3.8)	520	(4.9)	511	(6.7)	525	(7.0)	503	(8.8)	508	(10.6)	489	(6.9)
Montenegro	407	(6.8)	394	(6.1)	407	(5.1)	413	(4.5)	410	(6.7)	418	(6.0)	423	(6.8)	411	(3.7)
Peru	437	(7.5)	406	(4.3)	415	(5.3)	427	(4.9)	419	(5.8)	418	(6.8)	434	(8.9)	414	(4.5)
Qatar	m	m	m	m	m	m	m	m	m	m	m	m	m	m	m	m
Russia	484	(8.5)	461	(7.8)	470	(6.5)	465	(6.4)	461	(10.0)	471	(7.6)	455	(9.2)	449	(5.3)
Singapore	568	(6.2)	553	(4.2)	552	(4.2)	559	(4.7)	554	(5.5)	541	(6.8)	535	(14.5)	531	(6.7)
Chinese Taipei	512	(5.6)	509	(6.8)	523	(5.2)	523	(6.1)	525	(8.0)	500	(6.3)	521	(11.7)	495	(4.4)
Thailand	435	(9.7)	413	(6.1)	416	(5.3)	425	(6.4)	419	(8.0)	414	(5.7)	413	(10.7)	413	(5.2)
Tunisia	390	(4.6)	374	(4.1)	377	(4.5)	372	(4.8)	372	(6.4)	379	(6.1)	377	(8.0)	382	(5.0)
United Arab Emirates	415	(4.1)	413	(4.3)	424	(4.9)	424	(6.5)	433	(7.1)	433	(6.9)	432	(7.9)	415	(5.2)
Uruguay	451	(6.2)	436	(6.5)	441	(6.9)	447	(7.0)	449	(7.3)	450	(5.9)	435	(7.3)	425	(6.5)
Malaysia**	416	(7.9)	430	(6.4)	427	(5.6)	433	(4.9)	435	(7.0)	430	(6.3)	428	(10.5)	431	(4.8)

1. Vigorous physical activities are those that make a student sweat and breathe hard, such as running, cycling, aerobics, soccer or skating. One day of vigorous physical activity consists of at least 20 minutes of such activities.
* See note at the beginning of this Annex.
**Malaysia: Coverage is too small to ensure comparability (see Annex A4).
StatLink http://dx.doi.org/10.1787/888933616826

[Part 3/3]

Table V.6.1b Days engaged in vigorous physical activity and performance in collaborative problem solving

Results based on students' self-reports

	Performance in collaborative problem solving															
	Days of vigorous physical activity[1] per week															
	Girls															
	0		1		2		3		4		5		6		7	
	Mean score	S.E.	Mean score	S.E.	Mean score	S.E.	Mean score	S.E.	Mean score	S.E.	Mean score	S.E.	Mean score	S.E.	Mean score	S.E.
OECD																
Australia	558	(4.4)	561	(4.4)	555	(4.0)	550	(5.0)	565	(5.9)	553	(5.7)	562	(7.9)	538	(6.4)
Austria	520	(5.0)	524	(6.2)	526	(6.1)	530	(6.7)	538	(7.0)	523	(10.5)	515	(14.9)	499	(11.0)
Belgium	505	(4.5)	510	(4.3)	528	(4.7)	539	(4.3)	542	(6.8)	527	(8.0)	539	(10.7)	510	(8.5)
Canada	560	(4.3)	558	(5.1)	566	(4.7)	551	(4.2)	559	(5.1)	555	(5.3)	559	(8.9)	545	(6.6)
Chile	478	(4.7)	464	(4.4)	462	(5.7)	459	(6.0)	468	(8.5)	452	(10.3)	460	(12.9)	444	(8.6)
Czech Republic	507	(6.2)	516	(4.4)	516	(5.5)	511	(5.7)	518	(5.3)	533	(5.5)	530	(8.8)	505	(6.3)
Denmark	530	(7.6)	544	(5.5)	529	(5.1)	543	(4.9)	535	(6.5)	541	(5.9)	520	(9.2)	513	(7.4)
Estonia	552	(5.9)	557	(5.4)	545	(5.2)	547	(6.3)	554	(6.1)	553	(6.4)	560	(10.9)	529	(8.1)
Finland	555	(7.0)	564	(5.9)	562	(5.9)	555	(5.9)	572	(6.3)	561	(6.3)	572	(7.8)	543	(12.0)
France	504	(4.4)	521	(4.7)	517	(5.4)	524	(7.5)	523	(8.5)	514	(11.0)	522	(15.6)	479	(10.6)
Germany	540	(6.9)	549	(6.1)	554	(5.0)	555	(5.5)	549	(6.4)	567	(7.9)	566	(15.1)	522	(10.7)
Greece	484	(4.7)	467	(6.8)	480	(5.1)	480	(6.5)	487	(8.1)	483	(7.8)	450	(11.2)	452	(10.1)
Hungary	472	(6.3)	478	(6.8)	491	(4.6)	505	(5.3)	490	(7.5)	481	(7.2)	508	(10.1)	479	(7.6)
Iceland	515	(7.4)	517	(8.0)	517	(7.2)	502	(7.0)	520	(8.0)	523	(6.4)	514	(7.2)	504	(6.9)
Ireland	m	m	m	m	m	m	m	m	m	m	m	m	m	m	m	m
Israel	488	(5.9)	468	(6.9)	490	(5.9)	486	(7.9)	476	(8.4)	483	(11.1)	495	(12.6)	472	(10.3)
Italy	m	m	m	m	m	m	m	m	m	m	m	m	m	m	m	m
Japan	573	(3.6)	562	(6.2)	560	(5.2)	562	(5.7)	565	(9.1)	570	(8.2)	568	(6.3)	548	(4.6)
Korea	562	(4.0)	552	(4.4)	562	(4.4)	554	(6.5)	555	(10.5)	533	(8.6)	526	(18.5)	514	(11.0)
Latvia	515	(5.7)	504	(6.2)	505	(5.1)	503	(5.1)	512	(6.4)	500	(6.9)	496	(12.8)	502	(9.1)
Luxembourg	497	(5.0)	511	(4.5)	510	(4.9)	517	(6.1)	513	(6.5)	516	(9.1)	522	(11.7)	487	(8.6)
Mexico	450	(4.9)	432	(4.6)	436	(3.8)	448	(4.6)	458	(6.4)	444	(7.4)	447	(8.8)	431	(5.9)
Netherlands	526	(5.8)	525	(4.5)	544	(5.2)	542	(5.7)	550	(5.7)	526	(8.8)	527	(13.6)	512	(13.3)
New Zealand	553	(6.2)	573	(7.6)	567	(5.6)	544	(6.9)	553	(7.6)	551	(8.8)	565	(10.8)	548	(10.7)
Norway	518	(6.2)	515	(6.0)	518	(5.7)	530	(5.0)	526	(5.5)	521	(6.7)	521	(8.4)	503	(6.4)
Poland	m	m	m	m	m	m	m	m	m	m	m	m	m	m	m	m
Portugal	514	(4.3)	502	(4.6)	504	(6.0)	515	(5.4)	519	(7.4)	511	(8.0)	533	(12.9)	489	(10.1)
Slovak Republic	481	(5.9)	480	(6.1)	486	(5.5)	487	(4.6)	491	(6.8)	479	(7.5)	486	(9.6)	470	(6.9)
Slovenia	518	(6.1)	508	(6.1)	540	(5.0)	521	(5.7)	531	(7.5)	541	(6.9)	535	(10.2)	494	(6.8)
Spain	508	(3.6)	511	(4.5)	510	(4.5)	508	(5.2)	505	(5.8)	512	(8.4)	524	(9.8)	509	(11.1)
Sweden	515	(6.7)	526	(7.4)	535	(6.6)	546	(6.0)	547	(5.6)	537	(7.6)	544	(7.7)	528	(7.7)
Switzerland	m	m	m	m	m	m	m	m	m	m	m	m	m	m	m	m
Turkey	442	(5.4)	432	(5.5)	433	(6.0)	443	(5.9)	416	(8.8)	433	(8.8)	412	(15.8)	430	(7.4)
United Kingdom	534	(5.2)	542	(4.7)	552	(6.3)	538	(6.1)	538	(7.8)	535	(10.1)	544	(13.9)	523	(11.6)
United States	542	(5.5)	535	(8.3)	539	(7.7)	537	(7.1)	530	(10.5)	535	(6.2)	553	(10.6)	514	(7.8)
OECD average-32	517	(1.0)	516	(1.0)	521	(1.0)	520	(1.1)	523	(1.3)	519	(1.4)	522	(2.1)	501	(1.6)
OECD average-35	m	m	m	m	m	m	m	m	m	m	m	m	m	m	m	m
Partners																
Brazil	441	(2.9)	415	(5.8)	419	(5.3)	426	(4.8)	421	(8.0)	434	(6.3)	424	(11.6)	422	(7.3)
B-S-J-G (China)	529	(6.8)	500	(7.7)	497	(7.1)	507	(6.1)	499	(9.2)	514	(8.5)	536	(17.0)	501	(7.1)
Bulgaria	463	(5.4)	461	(5.9)	470	(5.2)	469	(6.5)	486	(8.3)	474	(8.6)	481	(11.1)	469	(7.7)
Colombia	435	(3.7)	421	(4.1)	439	(4.9)	446	(5.5)	451	(7.8)	436	(7.4)	426	(12.5)	436	(8.2)
Costa Rica	449	(4.0)	441	(4.3)	433	(6.0)	447	(6.1)	433	(11.7)	432	(8.0)	464	(13.5)	417	(9.6)
Croatia	486	(4.0)	474	(4.4)	490	(4.4)	497	(6.0)	505	(6.6)	488	(6.6)	517	(11.5)	476	(7.3)
Cyprus*	469	(4.0)	462	(4.5)	470	(5.4)	458	(5.5)	470	(6.2)	473	(6.4)	476	(10.0)	457	(6.5)
Dominican Republic	m	m	m	m	m	m	m	m	m	m	m	m	m	m	m	m
Hong Kong (China)	572	(4.8)	560	(4.7)	552	(5.6)	553	(7.4)	559	(12.5)	553	(8.0)	570	(13.0)	533	(10.4)
Lithuania	486	(4.7)	484	(5.5)	483	(5.2)	477	(5.2)	496	(6.2)	497	(8.6)	495	(8.6)	465	(7.9)
Macao (China)	561	(3.4)	553	(3.3)	545	(4.3)	561	(6.9)	549	(10.9)	525	(12.1)	547	(15.2)	533	(15.2)
Montenegro	441	(4.3)	427	(5.0)	429	(5.2)	438	(4.8)	442	(6.6)	426	(5.8)	433	(6.7)	423	(4.9)
Peru	448	(4.3)	420	(4.7)	425	(5.1)	433	(5.3)	414	(7.2)	414	(8.9)	423	(11.5)	419	(9.1)
Qatar	m	m	m	m	m	m	m	m	m	m	m	m	m	m	m	m
Russia	502	(7.4)	485	(6.4)	493	(5.5)	489	(5.7)	478	(6.7)	485	(9.4)	492	(9.9)	472	(9.1)
Singapore	586	(4.7)	568	(3.6)	565	(3.9)	570	(4.8)	585	(10.4)	561	(11.0)	601	(20.2)	539	(11.0)
Chinese Taipei	540	(4.2)	536	(6.1)	547	(4.3)	541	(6.6)	548	(7.9)	535	(7.3)	549	(12.4)	526	(7.8)
Thailand	468	(5.4)	450	(4.8)	450	(4.3)	454	(4.9)	453	(8.6)	442	(6.5)	432	(10.9)	441	(7.2)
Tunisia	402	(3.1)	385	(3.7)	385	(3.9)	381	(4.1)	380	(6.2)	370	(7.5)	373	(11.6)	383	(5.6)
United Arab Emirates	455	(4.2)	451	(4.8)	453	(5.0)	457	(5.9)	480	(7.9)	459	(7.0)	476	(14.1)	453	(6.2)
Uruguay	460	(3.9)	449	(5.3)	458	(3.8)	466	(5.5)	453	(8.4)	450	(8.7)	453	(10.7)	437	(10.5)
Malaysia**	459	(5.1)	446	(5.1)	452	(4.2)	453	(4.7)	458	(6.9)	440	(7.1)	417	(13.8)	441	(7.5)

1. Vigorous physical activities are those that make a student sweat and breathe hard, such as running, cycling, aerobics, soccer or skating. One day of vigorous physical activity consists of at least 20 minutes of such activities.
* See note at the beginning of this Annex.
**Malaysia: Coverage is too small to ensure comparability (see Annex A4).

StatLink http://dx.doi.org/10.1787/888933616826

[Part 1/3]

Table V.6.1c Days of physical education class and performance in collaborative problem solving

Results based on students' self-reports

		Days attending physical education class in an average week				Performance in collaborative problem solving — Days of physical education class per week — All students											
		Average number of days		Variability		0		1		2		3		4		5+	
		Days	S.E.	S.D.	S.E.	Mean score	S.E.	Mean score	S.E.	Mean score	S.E.	Mean score	S.E.	Mean score	S.E.	Mean score	S.E.
OECD	Australia	2.2	(0.02)	1.4	(0.01)	552	(3.9)	558	(4.8)	542	(2.7)	532	(3.3)	520	(5.0)	461	(4.9)
	Austria	1.3	(0.03)	1.0	(0.03)	469	(5.1)	526	(3.1)	511	(8.0)	469	(16.6)	482	(17.6)	442	(9.8)
	Belgium	1.6	(0.03)	0.9	(0.03)	456	(9.2)	506	(3.2)	518	(4.2)	452	(9.0)	484	(10.3)	468	(12.1)
	Canada	2.7	(0.03)	2.0	(0.01)	555	(4.1)	550	(4.9)	545	(5.4)	558	(4.2)	524	(6.9)	516	(3.1)
	Chile	1.8	(0.03)	1.2	(0.02)	458	(12.3)	464	(3.6)	471	(5.1)	447	(10.9)	432	(10.0)	406	(5.6)
	Czech Republic	1.7	(0.03)	0.9	(0.03)	484	(7.2)	508	(3.5)	508	(3.1)	491	(9.0)	445	(12.5)	441	(8.0)
	Denmark	1.4	(0.04)	1.0	(0.06)	517	(13.8)	529	(2.7)	514	(5.2)	504	(8.7)	516	(14.0)	493	(10.1)
	Estonia	1.7	(0.02)	0.8	(0.02)	529	(7.8)	543	(3.9)	538	(3.2)	499	(15.5)	c	c	456	(12.3)
	Finland	1.8	(0.02)	1.1	(0.02)	534	(15.1)	556	(2.9)	537	(3.1)	510	(6.9)	483	(10.2)	458	(7.8)
	France	1.4	(0.02)	1.0	(0.02)	464	(9.3)	520	(2.9)	459	(4.9)	475	(9.8)	422	(16.0)	411	(8.1)
	Germany	1.4	(0.02)	0.8	(0.02)	520	(18.3)	546	(2.9)	528	(5.8)	477	(14.9)	452	(15.6)	460	(11.4)
	Greece	2.3	(0.02)	1.1	(0.02)	447	(8.7)	469	(7.8)	472	(3.3)	431	(7.5)	413	(12.8)	416	(5.2)
	Hungary	3.7	(0.04)	1.2	(0.02)	441	(13.7)	399	(13.6)	437	(12.5)	487	(4.8)	474	(5.9)	475	(4.9)
	Iceland	2.4	(0.02)	1.2	(0.01)	495	(11.7)	504	(5.5)	509	(3.0)	509	(5.2)	486	(7.5)	460	(6.4)
	Ireland	1.1	(0.02)	0.8	(0.03)	m	m	m	m	m	m	m	m	m	m	m	m
	Israel	2.0	(0.04)	1.3	(0.02)	473	(13.4)	463	(6.3)	500	(4.5)	428	(10.6)	408	(8.7)	392	(4.5)
	Italy	m	m	m	m	m	m	m	m	m	m	m	m	m	m	m	m
	Japan	2.5	(0.03)	0.7	(0.02)	c	c	566	(8.6)	560	(4.4)	548	(3.2)	543	(17.6)	463	(24.4)
	Korea	2.2	(0.03)	0.7	(0.04)	481	(22.3)	522	(9.4)	544	(2.7)	532	(6.5)	525	(7.7)	488	(9.7)
	Latvia	2.0	(0.03)	1.0	(0.02)	489	(7.7)	496	(4.9)	493	(2.7)	457	(7.4)	458	(13.9)	434	(6.3)
	Luxembourg	1.6	(0.01)	1.0	(0.01)	441	(9.5)	509	(2.2)	481	(2.8)	466	(7.7)	486	(9.9)	447	(6.3)
	Mexico	1.6	(0.05)	1.4	(0.02)	455	(5.0)	437	(4.7)	427	(4.3)	441	(6.5)	427	(11.6)	414	(5.8)
	Netherlands	1.4	(0.03)	0.8	(0.03)	495	(9.5)	538	(3.6)	499	(4.6)	481	(10.0)	490	(15.4)	459	(17.0)
	New Zealand	2.0	(0.05)	1.9	(0.02)	561	(3.1)	547	(9.2)	540	(6.7)	530	(5.9)	513	(5.4)	491	(6.1)
	Norway	1.8	(0.04)	0.8	(0.03)	461	(23.1)	502	(4.2)	513	(2.8)	495	(6.4)	479	(14.6)	468	(13.3)
	Poland	3.2	(0.06)	0.9	(0.02)	m	m	m	m	m	m	m	m	m	m	m	m
	Portugal	2.1	(0.02)	0.7	(0.02)	451	(21.7)	477	(6.8)	508	(2.7)	494	(10.4)	425	(18.3)	428	(8.8)
	Slovak Republic	2.0	(0.03)	0.9	(0.02)	451	(7.6)	468	(8.2)	473	(3.2)	464	(7.5)	403	(9.5)	401	(7.8)
	Slovenia	2.1	(0.01)	0.9	(0.01)	433	(13.6)	471	(3.4)	516	(2.9)	513	(3.9)	477	(11.2)	455	(8.1)
	Spain	1.9	(0.02)	0.5	(0.03)	452	(12.9)	509	(6.7)	500	(2.1)	487	(19.9)	c	c	436	(12.1)
	Sweden	2.2	(0.03)	1.1	(0.02)	486	(15.8)	545	(7.4)	513	(3.7)	514	(8.6)	505	(11.0)	468	(5.8)
	Switzerland	2.0	(0.03)	1.0	(0.02)	m	m	m	m	m	m	m	m	m	m	m	m
	Turkey	2.1	(0.04)	1.6	(0.03)	446	(12.8)	427	(4.4)	430	(5.2)	422	(12.4)	452	(8.8)	399	(4.2)
	United Kingdom	1.9	(0.03)	1.2	(0.02)	506	(8.2)	531	(4.2)	535	(4.2)	507	(5.1)	494	(5.8)	455	(6.7)
	United States	2.4	(0.08)	2.2	(0.03)	542	(4.5)	506	(14.2)	516	(10.5)	520	(7.5)	510	(8.6)	511	(5.0)
	OECD average-32	2.0	(0.01)	1.1	(0.00)	485	(2.2)	506	(1.1)	504	(0.9)	488	(1.7)	473	(2.2)	451	(1.7)
	OECD average-35	2.0	(0.01)	1.1	(0.00)	m	m	m	m	m	m	m	m	m	m	m	m
Partners	Brazil	1.8	(0.02)	1.3	(0.02)	431	(6.3)	435	(3.8)	420	(3.1)	386	(7.4)	398	(11.9)	379	(3.7)
	B-S-J-G (China)	2.3	(0.04)	1.0	(0.03)	445	(13.4)	471	(7.9)	496	(6.3)	508	(5.6)	532	(12.8)	497	(11.3)
	Bulgaria	2.6	(0.03)	1.2	(0.02)	408	(10.7)	486	(14.6)	462	(4.2)	445	(5.6)	419	(10.6)	423	(5.7)
	Colombia	1.6	(0.03)	1.3	(0.02)	416	(14.6)	442	(2.6)	426	(6.1)	415	(11.6)	410	(13.7)	386	(4.5)
	Costa Rica	1.0	(0.02)	0.5	(0.03)	417	(7.6)	444	(2.8)	415	(12.5)	c	c	c	c	384	(15.4)
	Croatia	1.7	(0.03)	0.6	(0.02)	462	(14.0)	468	(4.5)	480	(3.5)	413	(13.0)	c	c	413	(15.5)
	Cyprus*	2.2	(0.01)	1.1	(0.01)	437	(8.5)	440	(3.4)	464	(2.5)	421	(4.1)	441	(8.8)	404	(5.2)
	Dominican Republic	2.5	(0.04)	1.7	(0.02)	m	m	m	m	m	m	m	m	m	m	m	m
	Hong Kong (China)	1.1	(0.01)	0.5	(0.03)	505	(16.8)	544	(2.7)	531	(12.9)	464	(20.1)	c	c	460	(18.9)
	Lithuania	2.0	(0.02)	1.0	(0.02)	457	(5.8)	465	(7.8)	477	(2.6)	445	(8.1)	423	(13.3)	429	(6.2)
	Macao (China)	1.7	(0.01)	0.8	(0.01)	458	(16.2)	540	(2.3)	541	(2.0)	468	(7.8)	435	(16.0)	465	(11.0)
	Montenegro	2.8	(0.02)	1.4	(0.01)	420	(7.0)	428	(5.7)	431	(1.7)	430	(3.7)	400	(7.1)	397	(2.9)
	Peru	1.7	(0.03)	1.4	(0.02)	434	(12.6)	434	(3.1)	425	(6.0)	403	(13.4)	362	(12.3)	374	(3.8)
	Qatar	1.9	(0.01)	1.6	(0.01)	m	m	m	m	m	m	m	m	m	m	m	m
	Russia	2.9	(0.04)	1.0	(0.03)	475	(15.5)	499	(10.5)	489	(5.8)	479	(3.7)	445	(9.4)	424	(7.3)
	Singapore	1.7	(0.01)	0.8	(0.01)	548	(13.5)	578	(2.0)	554	(1.9)	564	(6.0)	516	(15.4)	457	(10.7)
	Chinese Taipei	1.8	(0.02)	0.7	(0.02)	447	(12.9)	524	(6.4)	531	(3.0)	513	(8.2)	533	(35.9)	481	(11.6)
	Thailand	1.3	(0.02)	1.0	(0.03)	420	(7.6)	450	(3.7)	421	(6.4)	388	(8.9)	381	(15.3)	369	(5.3)
	Tunisia	1.9	(0.03)	1.3	(0.02)	396	(4.7)	401	(3.3)	373	(2.9)	366	(4.4)	376	(6.9)	364	(4.2)
	United Arab Emirates	1.9	(0.02)	1.4	(0.01)	456	(6.4)	455	(3.8)	433	(3.1)	444	(6.2)	402	(7.4)	386	(4.3)
	Uruguay	1.9	(0.03)	1.4	(0.02)	448	(4.6)	464	(6.2)	455	(2.9)	422	(8.2)	437	(11.1)	398	(4.0)
	Malaysia**	1.8	(0.03)	1.2	(0.03)	433	(11.7)	452	(4.4)	438	(4.5)	425	(9.4)	431	(11.7)	399	(6.1)

* See note at the beginning of this Annex.
**Malaysia: Coverage is too small to ensure comparability (see Annex A4).
StatLink http://dx.doi.org/10.1787/888933616826

[Part 2/3]

Table V.6.1c Days of physical education class and performance in collaborative problem solving

Results based on students' self-reports

		Performance in collaborative problem solving											
		Days of physical education class per week											
		Boys											
		0		1		2		3		4		5+	
		Mean score	S.E.	Mean score	S.E.	Mean score	S.E.	Mean score	S.E.	Mean score	S.E.	Mean score	S.E.
OECD	Australia	541	(5.2)	538	(6.0)	527	(3.9)	513	(4.4)	504	(6.3)	442	(5.8)
	Austria	463	(8.2)	516	(4.1)	506	(8.6)	456	(16.2)	467	(17.2)	434	(9.7)
	Belgium	423	(14.3)	494	(4.1)	506	(4.9)	450	(9.5)	486	(11.6)	464	(13.1)
	Canada	537	(5.5)	541	(6.5)	533	(7.7)	539	(5.7)	507	(9.8)	496	(3.6)
	Chile	c	c	455	(4.5)	465	(5.1)	450	(15.6)	430	(15.5)	405	(7.6)
	Czech Republic	476	(11.8)	494	(4.8)	499	(4.6)	479	(9.3)	435	(13.2)	430	(8.5)
	Denmark	510	(18.8)	518	(3.3)	509	(6.5)	501	(11.9)	496	(14.1)	485	(12.5)
	Estonia	518	(10.3)	531	(4.6)	526	(3.7)	498	(20.5)	c	c	456	(13.9)
	Finland	488	(21.8)	534	(4.2)	521	(4.1)	494	(7.4)	468	(11.6)	442	(8.8)
	France	429	(12.8)	510	(3.8)	449	(6.9)	458	(11.7)	413	(17.9)	396	(9.0)
	Germany	481	(18.8)	533	(3.6)	514	(6.4)	470	(16.8)	c	c	457	(15.5)
	Greece	421	(11.3)	446	(11.9)	459	(4.1)	426	(8.9)	403	(17.9)	396	(7.5)
	Hungary	c	c	393	(18.9)	425	(11.3)	472	(6.2)	461	(7.3)	466	(5.8)
	Iceland	484	(20.1)	487	(8.0)	498	(3.8)	494	(6.9)	472	(11.2)	451	(9.0)
	Ireland	m	m	m	m	m	m	m	m	m	m	m	m
	Israel	472	(22.3)	454	(7.8)	493	(4.5)	423	(13.8)	409	(12.0)	386	(5.6)
	Italy	m	m	m	m	m	m	m	m	m	m	m	m
	Japan	c	c	555	(9.4)	547	(5.6)	535	(4.0)	543	(27.2)	461	(28.7)
	Korea	c	c	495	(12.7)	528	(3.6)	524	(9.5)	522	(10.4)	481	(11.5)
	Latvia	449	(13.7)	474	(7.0)	476	(3.3)	440	(9.0)	447	(16.6)	428	(7.0)
	Luxembourg	432	(11.5)	501	(3.5)	469	(4.3)	447	(9.8)	480	(11.7)	439	(7.6)
	Mexico	452	(5.5)	431	(5.3)	421	(5.0)	433	(8.3)	404	(14.4)	405	(7.0)
	Netherlands	482	(12.0)	527	(4.7)	485	(5.0)	472	(11.0)	486	(19.3)	447	(17.7)
	New Zealand	547	(4.8)	538	(11.6)	525	(9.4)	505	(8.2)	493	(7.7)	474	(7.2)
	Norway	c	c	489	(5.3)	498	(3.4)	485	(8.0)	484	(18.2)	451	(15.6)
	Poland	m	m	m	m	m	m	m	m	m	m	m	m
	Portugal	c	c	479	(7.2)	499	(3.3)	482	(11.9)	421	(23.3)	406	(12.1)
	Slovak Republic	424	(10.4)	453	(9.1)	460	(3.6)	450	(8.5)	398	(11.0)	395	(8.8)
	Slovenia	417	(15.8)	465	(4.2)	500	(3.6)	492	(5.9)	447	(14.1)	442	(10.6)
	Spain	431	(15.6)	497	(7.1)	490	(2.7)	c	c	c	c	434	(13.8)
	Sweden	463	(20.2)	527	(10.3)	494	(4.1)	504	(11.3)	488	(12.6)	455	(6.8)
	Switzerland	m	m	m	m	m	m	m	m	m	m	m	m
	Turkey	422	(14.1)	414	(5.1)	423	(5.9)	415	(19.4)	447	(11.7)	391	(5.4)
	United Kingdom	494	(11.6)	517	(5.1)	518	(5.4)	490	(5.4)	483	(6.5)	452	(8.6)
	United States	533	(5.8)	507	(21.0)	503	(12.8)	502	(10.7)	492	(9.5)	502	(5.6)
	OECD average-32	472	(2.8)	494	(1.5)	492	(1.1)	477	(2.0)	464	(2.7)	441	(2.0)
	OECD average-35	m	m	m	m	m	m	m	m	m	m	m	m
Partners	Brazil	425	(8.0)	428	(3.9)	412	(3.5)	378	(7.9)	396	(12.8)	375	(5.1)
	B-S-J-G (China)	426	(17.1)	462	(7.2)	485	(6.0)	500	(6.2)	527	(11.5)	482	(13.1)
	Bulgaria	390	(14.9)	476	(18.2)	447	(5.0)	431	(6.5)	402	(11.7)	414	(6.2)
	Colombia	415	(17.2)	440	(3.3)	423	(6.9)	409	(14.6)	421	(19.0)	380	(6.4)
	Costa Rica	417	(8.9)	440	(3.3)	411	(19.3)	c	c	c	c	395	(15.8)
	Croatia	455	(17.8)	455	(5.0)	467	(4.4)	390	(15.2)	c	c	399	(17.6)
	Cyprus*	416	(12.5)	418	(3.9)	449	(3.4)	402	(5.6)	429	(13.4)	381	(6.3)
	Dominican Republic	m	m	m	m	m	m	m	m	m	m	m	m
	Hong Kong (China)	489	(16.1)	526	(3.5)	521	(14.2)	c	c	c	c	436	(18.3)
	Lithuania	440	(7.5)	444	(10.2)	466	(3.4)	434	(8.0)	414	(14.4)	425	(7.2)
	Macao (China)	437	(20.8)	521	(2.9)	526	(3.1)	460	(8.8)	428	(18.8)	448	(13.7)
	Montenegro	401	(9.5)	416	(8.1)	419	(2.4)	418	(5.8)	395	(8.2)	389	(4.0)
	Peru	433	(14.2)	430	(3.6)	417	(6.8)	398	(18.8)	354	(17.4)	376	(4.5)
	Qatar	m	m	m	m	m	m	m	m	m	m	m	m
	Russia	452	(18.7)	486	(13.4)	479	(6.8)	468	(4.6)	439	(10.6)	417	(8.3)
	Singapore	536	(26.7)	575	(2.9)	543	(2.4)	528	(9.0)	490	(18.1)	451	(12.4)
	Chinese Taipei	437	(16.6)	511	(7.4)	517	(4.3)	502	(9.9)	c	c	460	(13.2)
	Thailand	402	(8.0)	432	(4.5)	405	(7.2)	376	(10.4)	371	(15.5)	359	(7.3)
	Tunisia	384	(6.0)	394	(3.9)	368	(3.6)	367	(6.0)	369	(10.5)	363	(5.7)
	United Arab Emirates	432	(8.8)	440	(4.7)	416	(4.8)	432	(7.5)	393	(9.6)	373	(4.6)
	Uruguay	444	(7.7)	459	(8.9)	449	(3.9)	417	(10.6)	435	(13.8)	393	(5.4)
	Malaysia**	425	(13.6)	443	(4.8)	428	(5.3)	405	(9.9)	416	(12.8)	387	(7.4)

* See note at the beginning of this Annex.
**Malaysia: Coverage is too small to ensure comparability (see Annex A4).
StatLink http://dx.doi.org/10.1787/888933616826

[Part 3/3]

Table V.6.1c Days of physical education class and performance in collaborative problem solving

Results based on students' self-reports

		Performance in collaborative problem solving											
		Days of physical education class per week											
		Girls											
		0		1		2		3		4		5+	
		Mean score	S.E.	Mean score	S.E.	Mean score	S.E.	Mean score	S.E.	Mean score	S.E.	Mean score	S.E.
OECD	Australia	560	(4.9)	575	(5.7)	557	(3.7)	551	(3.8)	542	(6.9)	495	(7.4)
	Austria	476	(6.7)	535	(3.9)	514	(10.1)	483	(21.5)	503	(27.3)	471	(19.6)
	Belgium	488	(16.1)	517	(3.6)	530	(4.6)	455	(15.0)	477	(16.8)	473	(17.7)
	Canada	567	(4.5)	558	(6.7)	557	(5.7)	576	(4.3)	542	(7.3)	541	(3.7)
	Chile	457	(16.1)	471	(4.1)	476	(6.3)	445	(13.7)	434	(12.3)	407	(7.2)
	Czech Republic	490	(9.9)	520	(3.7)	518	(3.5)	508	(12.1)	470	(18.8)	469	(14.1)
	Denmark	523	(15.3)	539	(3.3)	520	(5.9)	508	(10.9)	539	(22.5)	501	(12.5)
	Estonia	541	(11.9)	554	(4.6)	550	(3.6)	501	(27.3)	c	c	c	c
	Finland	586	(16.2)	571	(3.4)	558	(4.5)	541	(11.5)	510	(14.5)	491	(10.6)
	France	490	(11.4)	529	(3.5)	471	(4.8)	492	(12.7)	c	c	431	(12.0)
	Germany	553	(20.2)	558	(3.1)	542	(6.8)	486	(16.8)	c	c	465	(15.0)
	Greece	465	(11.8)	490	(9.2)	487	(3.3)	437	(12.4)	426	(16.5)	435	(6.2)
	Hungary	450	(17.9)	405	(16.4)	454	(17.8)	504	(5.2)	485	(6.1)	484	(5.3)
	Iceland	501	(12.9)	517	(7.5)	519	(3.6)	525	(6.2)	500	(9.3)	472	(8.1)
	Ireland	m	m	m	m	m	m	m	m	m	m	m	m
	Israel	473	(9.1)	471	(8.9)	507	(6.0)	435	(14.2)	407	(12.3)	400	(6.3)
	Italy	m	m	m	m	m	m	m	m	m	m	m	m
	Japan	c	c	581	(11.1)	571	(4.5)	561	(3.4)	545	(14.2)	c	c
	Korea	c	c	548	(8.7)	560	(3.6)	543	(6.6)	529	(9.3)	c	c
	Latvia	509	(7.7)	511	(6.1)	510	(3.5)	480	(9.3)	c	c	453	(13.3)
	Luxembourg	457	(16.3)	517	(2.5)	494	(4.0)	486	(11.3)	500	(18.4)	466	(12.0)
	Mexico	458	(5.4)	444	(5.2)	434	(4.5)	448	(6.9)	454	(10.5)	423	(7.3)
	Netherlands	515	(11.5)	547	(3.7)	514	(5.8)	493	(12.2)	493	(19.8)	c	c
	New Zealand	571	(3.9)	558	(11.5)	555	(7.6)	554	(7.2)	537	(5.5)	524	(8.9)
	Norway	c	c	514	(4.9)	527	(3.9)	512	(9.0)	c	c	c	c
	Poland	m	m	m	m	m	m	m	m	m	m	m	m
	Portugal	c	c	474	(9.7)	516	(2.8)	505	(10.2)	c	c	455	(11.0)
	Slovak Republic	469	(10.1)	480	(8.7)	486	(4.2)	479	(9.3)	419	(15.2)	418	(14.2)
	Slovenia	c	c	481	(4.8)	531	(3.5)	531	(4.4)	516	(15.6)	490	(12.8)
	Spain	477	(20.5)	519	(8.4)	510	(2.5)	496	(22.0)	c	c	c	c
	Sweden	497	(19.3)	558	(6.8)	531	(4.3)	529	(10.7)	524	(18.5)	494	(7.7)
	Switzerland	m	m	m	m	m	m	m	m	m	m	m	m
	Turkey	456	(13.2)	440	(5.0)	437	(6.2)	427	(14.4)	455	(11.9)	410	(5.2)
	United Kingdom	515	(9.5)	542	(4.9)	551	(4.8)	533	(7.1)	514	(11.1)	460	(10.1)
	United States	548	(4.8)	505	(13.9)	527	(12.2)	537	(7.6)	526	(11.5)	524	(7.0)
	OECD average-32	504	(2.5)	517	(1.3)	517	(1.1)	502	(2.2)	494	(3.0)	466	(2.2)
	OECD average-35	m	m	m	m	m	m	m	m	m	m	m	m
Partners	Brazil	436	(6.2)	442	(4.3)	428	(3.3)	394	(9.3)	400	(14.9)	386	(4.5)
	B-S-J-G (China)	483	(20.3)	481	(10.2)	507	(7.3)	518	(6.0)	541	(17.7)	515	(14.0)
	Bulgaria	434	(16.2)	501	(14.8)	475	(4.6)	461	(5.9)	442	(15.4)	440	(8.1)
	Colombia	417	(15.9)	445	(3.2)	429	(7.3)	420	(15.9)	395	(15.6)	392	(5.5)
	Costa Rica	417	(9.4)	447	(3.2)	419	(11.5)	c	c	c	c	c	c
	Croatia	c	c	481	(5.3)	491	(3.7)	c	c	c	c	c	c
	Cyprus*	458	(12.0)	469	(5.2)	477	(2.8)	438	(5.5)	449	(10.3)	431	(6.9)
	Dominican Republic	m	m	m	m	m	m	m	m	m	m	m	m
	Hong Kong (China)	523	(27.1)	562	(3.0)	543	(18.0)	c	c	c	c	c	c
	Lithuania	474	(8.8)	481	(8.9)	487	(3.0)	461	(13.6)	448	(34.0)	442	(12.3)
	Macao (China)	c	c	559	(3.0)	554	(3.0)	492	(18.3)	c	c	497	(15.5)
	Montenegro	442	(9.7)	442	(7.5)	442	(2.5)	442	(5.7)	409	(11.6)	405	(4.1)
	Peru	435	(14.0)	438	(3.5)	431	(7.5)	409	(14.8)	371	(15.4)	370	(5.6)
	Qatar	m	m	m	m	m	m	m	m	m	m	m	m
	Russia	492	(14.5)	506	(12.8)	498	(6.7)	489	(4.3)	451	(15.6)	436	(9.5)
	Singapore	556	(12.8)	582	(3.1)	566	(2.8)	590	(7.2)	544	(18.7)	c	c
	Chinese Taipei	c	c	536	(6.6)	544	(4.3)	527	(11.7)	c	c	515	(13.8)
	Thailand	436	(8.3)	462	(4.1)	435	(8.3)	399	(12.5)	c	c	383	(8.3)
	Tunisia	404	(5.9)	405	(3.6)	378	(3.6)	366	(4.6)	385	(8.7)	366	(5.2)
	United Arab Emirates	471	(8.4)	468	(4.8)	447	(3.6)	460	(9.2)	414	(10.7)	413	(6.4)
	Uruguay	450	(5.3)	469	(7.0)	460	(3.6)	430	(10.1)	441	(17.0)	407	(6.4)
	Malaysia**	440	(13.7)	460	(4.6)	446	(5.0)	443	(11.8)	456	(16.8)	417	(7.5)

* See note at the beginning of this Annex.
**Malaysia: Coverage is too small to ensure comparability (see Annex A4).
StatLink http://dx.doi.org/10.1787/888933616826

[Part 1/1]

Table V.6.7a Accessing the Internet/chat/social networks and performance in collaborative problem solving

Results based on students' self-reports

	Percentage of students who reported accessing the Internet/chat/ social networks before or after school on the most recent school day		Performance in collaborative problem solving				Difference (accessing - not accessing the Internet/chat/social networks)							
			Students who reported not accessing the Internet/chat/social networks before or after school		Students who reported accessing the Internet/chat/ social networks before or after school		Performance in collaborative problem solving				Relative performance in collaborative problem solving[2]			
							Before accounting for gender, and students' and schools' socio-economic profile[1]		After accounting for gender, and students' and schools' socio-economic profile		Before accounting for gender, and students' and schools' socio-economic profile		After accounting for gender, and students' and schools' socio-economic profile	
	%	S.E.	Mean score	S.E.	Mean score	S.E.	Score dif.	S.E.	Score dif.	S.E.	Score dif.	S.E.	Score dif.	S.E.
OECD														
Australia	94.3	(0.3)	542	(6.1)	536	(2.0)	-6	(6.3)	**-14**	(6.3)	5	(4.9)	3	(4.8)
Austria	93.1	(0.3)	516	(7.6)	512	(2.7)	-5	(7.6)	-3	(7.0)	6	(5.6)	5	(5.5)
Belgium	95.2	(0.3)	497	(5.3)	509	(2.5)	**12**	(5.2)	3	(4.8)	6	(3.6)	4	(3.5)
Canada	91.7	(0.3)	546	(4.9)	539	(2.2)	-7	(4.5)	**-13**	(4.2)	**15**	(3.3)	**10**	(3.2)
Chile	93.6	(0.4)	439	(7.3)	462	(2.9)	**23**	(7.8)	10	(7.6)	7	(6.7)	6	(6.9)
Czech Republic	94.8	(0.4)	486	(7.5)	504	(2.2)	**18**	(8.0)	13	(7.7)	**20**	(7.1)	**19**	(7.1)
Denmark	97.5	(0.3)	508	(10.5)	525	(2.5)	17	(10.9)	12	(10.1)	**13**	(6.5)	13	(6.5)
Estonia	94.0	(0.4)	526	(7.8)	538	(2.5)	12	(7.7)	2	(6.7)	10	(5.6)	6	(5.4)
Finland	96.8	(0.2)	513	(10.9)	538	(2.4)	**25**	(10.2)	11	(10.5)	12	(7.4)	10	(7.7)
France	88.3	(0.5)	512	(5.1)	499	(2.5)	**-13**	(5.0)	**-13**	(4.5)	0	(3.4)	-1	(3.5)
Germany	92.6	(0.5)	526	(8.4)	537	(3.6)	11	(8.4)	14	(8.0)	**14**	(6.6)	**16**	(6.6)
Greece	93.1	(0.4)	459	(7.0)	462	(3.5)	4	(7.2)	-2	(6.8)	-3	(4.4)	-3	(4.5)
Hungary	95.6	(0.4)	454	(9.8)	478	(2.5)	**24**	(9.8)	7	(8.0)	10	(6.2)	9	(5.9)
Iceland	97.3	(0.3)	511	(11.8)	502	(2.2)	-9	(11.4)	-14	(11.4)	7	(8.3)	5	(8.2)
Ireland	92.5	(0.4)	m	m	m	m	m	m	m	m	m	m	m	m
Israel	87.3	(1.3)	473	(10.8)	474	(3.4)	2	(10.1)	-3	(7.7)	5	(4.9)	3	(4.8)
Italy	94.4	(0.4)	469	(7.0)	482	(2.6)	12	(7.2)	7	(6.5)	3	(5.0)	2	(4.8)
Japan	84.5	(0.5)	545	(4.2)	555	(2.7)	**10**	(4.0)	**9**	(3.8)	1	(3.6)	2	(3.5)
Korea	91.5	(0.6)	550	(6.1)	538	(2.5)	**-12**	(5.5)	-4	(5.2)	**11**	(3.8)	**9**	(3.8)
Latvia	95.1	(0.4)	472	(7.4)	487	(2.3)	**15**	(7.3)	11	(7.3)	**16**	(5.6)	**13**	(5.6)
Luxembourg	93.4	(0.3)	499	(6.8)	496	(1.6)	-3	(7.1)	1	(6.4)	6	(5.4)	6	(5.4)
Mexico	83.9	(1.0)	410	(4.3)	443	(2.6)	**33**	(4.2)	3	(4.2)	**6**	(3.1)	1	(3.3)
Netherlands	96.3	(0.3)	511	(9.5)	522	(2.4)	10	(9.4)	6	(8.4)	**13**	(5.9)	8	(6.0)
New Zealand	93.0	(0.4)	545	(7.5)	538	(2.7)	-7	(7.8)	-10	(6.8)	**16**	(5.4)	**15**	(5.0)
Norway	98.0	(0.2)	470	(12.7)	508	(2.5)	**38**	(12.9)	**29**	(12.8)	11	(9.5)	9	(9.7)
Poland	94.9	(0.4)	m	m	m	m	m	m	m	m	m	m	m	m
Portugal	94.6	(0.3)	497	(7.2)	500	(2.6)	3	(6.7)	0	(6.5)	10	(5.1)	**10**	(4.9)
Slovak Republic	94.5	(0.3)	453	(8.1)	469	(2.4)	**16**	(7.8)	3	(7.2)	1	(6.8)	2	(6.6)
Slovenia	82.5	(0.6)	513	(4.4)	503	(2.2)	**-10**	(5.2)	-8	(5.1)	9	(4.8)	7	(4.7)
Spain	94.6	(0.3)	478	(6.0)	501	(2.2)	**23**	(5.7)	**17**	(5.6)	8	(4.4)	7	(4.5)
Sweden	95.8	(0.3)	503	(10.6)	518	(3.4)	15	(9.7)	5	(8.0)	-6	(6.9)	-8	(7.0)
Switzerland	93.5	(0.5)	m	m	m	m	m	m	m	m	m	m	m	m
Turkey	83.7	(0.8)	412	(4.8)	426	(3.6)	**14**	(4.2)	-5	(4.0)	0	(2.6)	0	(2.6)
United Kingdom	94.8	(0.3)	533	(8.6)	523	(2.7)	-10	(8.1)	-11	(7.2)	**16**	(5.8)	**13**	(5.5)
United States	92.1	(0.4)	557	(6.5)	521	(3.6)	**-35**	(6.1)	**-39**	(5.8)	-8	(4.0)	**-10**	(3.9)
OECD average-32	92.7	(0.1)	498	(1.4)	505	(0.5)	**7**	(1.4)	1	(1.3)	**8**	(1.0)	**6**	(1.0)
OECD average-35	92.8	(0.1)	m	m	m	m	m	m	m	m	m	m	m	m
Partners														
Brazil	89.8	(0.4)	388	(4.2)	427	(2.9)	**39**	(4.1)	**13**	(3.7)	**10**	(3.8)	**7**	(3.6)
B-S-J-G (China)	74.0	(1.3)	514	(5.6)	490	(4.3)	**-23**	(5.6)	**-16**	(4.2)	**9**	(3.0)	**11**	(2.9)
Bulgaria	94.0	(0.3)	434	(7.7)	457	(3.7)	**23**	(6.8)	4	(5.6)	7	(4.5)	4	(4.6)
Colombia	85.6	(0.7)	402	(4.3)	438	(2.3)	**36**	(4.2)	7	(3.8)	**12**	(2.9)	**7**	(2.8)
Costa Rica	91.4	(0.5)	416	(5.3)	443	(2.8)	**26**	(5.0)	6	(5.7)	-3	(5.1)	-4	(5.5)
Croatia	96.9	(0.2)	459	(8.6)	475	(2.5)	17	(8.6)	14	(7.8)	**12**	(5.5)	10	(5.5)
Cyprus*	93.9	(0.4)	424	(6.3)	451	(2.0)	**27**	(6.3)	**16**	(5.9)	5	(5.4)	4	(5.3)
Dominican Republic	82.4	(0.9)	m	m	m	m	m	m	m	m	m	m	m	m
Hong Kong (China)	97.3	(0.2)	518	(10.2)	543	(2.9)	**25**	(10.3)	16	(9.9)	11	(8.6)	6	(8.6)
Lithuania	95.5	(0.3)	442	(8.3)	472	(2.3)	**30**	(7.9)	**18**	(7.3)	**13**	(5.3)	**11**	(5.1)
Macao (China)	98.0	(0.2)	518	(11.2)	535	(1.3)	17	(11.5)	12	(11.3)	13	(9.0)	12	(8.9)
Montenegro	91.6	(0.4)	418	(4.9)	422	(1.5)	4	(5.2)	0	(5.0)	6	(4.6)	5	(4.6)
Peru	75.1	(0.9)	412	(3.6)	440	(3.0)	**28**	(3.8)	-2	(3.0)	**5**	(2.3)	1	(2.3)
Qatar	90.8	(0.3)	m	m	m	m	m	m	m	m	m	m	m	m
Russia	95.7	(0.3)	466	(8.8)	477	(3.4)	11	(8.7)	-3	(8.8)	6	(6.4)	2	(6.6)
Singapore	93.6	(0.3)	572	(6.0)	561	(1.3)	-10	(6.5)	-12	(6.7)	8	(4.7)	6	(4.6)
Chinese Taipei	91.1	(0.4)	542	(5.1)	525	(2.6)	**-16**	(5.4)	-2	(4.7)	**12**	(4.2)	**13**	(4.2)
Thailand	95.0	(0.3)	409	(5.7)	439	(3.6)	**30**	(6.2)	6	(5.5)	6	(4.2)	2	(4.2)
Tunisia	84.6	(0.8)	377	(3.3)	388	(2.3)	**10**	(3.6)	-4	(3.4)	2	(2.8)	-2	(2.9)
United Arab Emirates	93.7	(0.3)	433	(6.4)	440	(2.5)	7	(5.7)	-4	(4.7)	**9**	(3.8)	7	(3.8)
Uruguay	94.4	(0.4)	419	(6.7)	451	(2.7)	**33**	(7.3)	**14**	(6.9)	7	(5.1)	7	(5.1)
Malaysia**	87.2	(0.7)	441	(6.8)	441	(3.3)	0	(6.2)	-4	(4.8)	**7**	(3.3)	**7**	(3.4)

1. The socio-economic profile is measured by the PISA index of economic, social and cultural status (ESCS).
2. Relative performance refers to the residual performance, attributable to purely "collaborative problem-solving" competencies, after accounting for science, reading and mathematics performance in a regression performed across students at a national level. Whether students reported accessing the Internet, chat, or social networks outside of school was included as an explanatory variable in this regression.
Note: Values that are statistically significant are indicated in bold (see Annex A3).
* See note at the beginning of this Annex.
**Malaysia: Coverage is too small to ensure comparability (see Annex A4).

StatLink http://dx.doi.org/10.1787/888933616826

[Part 1/1]

Table V.6.7c Meeting friends/talking to friends on the phone and performance in collaborative problem solving

Results based on students' self-reports

	Percentage of students who reported meeting friends or talking to friends on the phone before or after school on the most recent school day		Performance in collaborative problem solving				Difference (meeting/talking to friends - not meeting/talking to friends)							
							Performance in collaborative problem solving				Relative performance in collaborative problem solving[2]			
			Students who reported neither meeting friends nor talking to friends before or after school		Students who reported meeting friends or talking to friends before or after school		Before accounting for gender, and students' and schools' socio-economic profile[1]		After accounting for gender, and students' and schools' socio-economic profile		Before accounting for gender, and students' and schools' socio-economic profile		After accounting for gender, and students' and schools' socio-economic profile	
	%	S.E.	Mean score	S.E.	Mean score	S.E.	Score dif.	S.E.	Score dif.	S.E.	Score dif.	S.E.	Score dif.	S.E.
OECD														
Australia	76.0	(0.5)	563	(3.5)	527	(2.1)	**-36**	(3.9)	**-36**	(3.8)	-2	(3.5)	-3	(3.5)
Austria	80.4	(0.7)	540	(3.6)	505	(2.9)	**-34**	(3.8)	**-24**	(3.7)	-4	(2.8)	-5	(2.8)
Belgium	81.4	(0.5)	534	(3.4)	503	(2.6)	**-31**	(3.6)	**-26**	(3.4)	-5	(2.7)	**-6**	(2.6)
Canada	79.8	(0.4)	563	(3.7)	534	(2.3)	**-29**	(3.7)	**-33**	(3.7)	3	(3.5)	1	(3.5)
Chile	76.7	(0.6)	478	(4.1)	456	(3.1)	**-22**	(4.2)	**-22**	(4.0)	-1	(3.8)	-2	(3.8)
Czech Republic	85.5	(0.5)	520	(3.9)	500	(2.3)	**-20**	(4.4)	**-15**	(4.3)	0	(4.0)	0	(4.1)
Denmark	78.6	(0.6)	540	(3.9)	520	(2.6)	**-20**	(4.1)	**-23**	(3.9)	3	(3.0)	3	(2.9)
Estonia	80.5	(0.7)	554	(4.5)	533	(2.5)	**-22**	(4.4)	**-22**	(4.3)	2	(3.6)	2	(3.6)
Finland	83.0	(0.5)	555	(4.9)	533	(2.6)	**-21**	(4.8)	**-21**	(4.5)	1	(3.1)	2	(3.2)
France	83.2	(0.5)	515	(4.1)	498	(2.6)	**-17**	(4.0)	**-16**	(3.9)	0	(3.0)	-2	(3.0)
Germany	78.5	(0.9)	550	(5.1)	532	(3.6)	**-18**	(4.7)	**-9**	(4.0)	3	(3.6)	5	(3.4)
Greece	88.6	(0.5)	480	(6.0)	460	(3.4)	**-20**	(5.6)	**-13**	(4.8)	1	(3.8)	0	(3.7)
Hungary	88.9	(0.5)	504	(5.2)	474	(2.6)	**-31**	(5.1)	**-20**	(4.8)	-2	(3.7)	-2	(3.6)
Iceland	82.9	(0.7)	526	(4.7)	498	(2.4)	**-27**	(5.0)	**-29**	(5.0)	-5	(3.9)	-4	(4.0)
Ireland	81.2	(0.6)	m	m	m	m	m	m	m	m	m	m	m	m
Israel	91.9	(0.4)	470	(7.2)	475	(3.7)	5	(6.8)	-3	(6.1)	2	(4.4)	0	(4.3)
Italy	93.4	(0.4)	483	(5.9)	481	(2.6)	-2	(5.7)	-2	(5.1)	6	(3.8)	3	(3.9)
Japan	73.7	(0.6)	578	(3.0)	545	(2.7)	**-34**	(3.0)	**-25**	(2.7)	-3	(2.1)	-3	(2.2)
Korea	76.3	(0.8)	562	(3.3)	531	(2.6)	**-31**	(3.1)	**-25**	(2.8)	2	(2.3)	1	(2.1)
Latvia	88.8	(0.5)	501	(4.8)	484	(2.3)	**-17**	(5.0)	**-16**	(4.8)	1	(4.0)	1	(3.9)
Luxembourg	83.6	(0.6)	519	(4.1)	492	(1.6)	**-27**	(4.5)	**-17**	(3.9)	3	(3.2)	2	(3.1)
Mexico	66.2	(0.7)	442	(3.5)	436	(2.8)	-6	(3.1)	**-12**	(2.9)	-1	(2.2)	-2	(2.3)
Netherlands	82.1	(0.6)	546	(4.7)	516	(2.5)	**-30**	(4.6)	**-23**	(4.5)	-3	(3.3)	-4	(3.4)
New Zealand	73.6	(0.8)	564	(4.3)	529	(2.8)	**-35**	(4.7)	**-33**	(4.3)	2	(3.9)	1	(3.9)
Norway	86.1	(0.6)	530	(5.5)	504	(2.7)	**-26**	(6.1)	**-30**	(5.9)	-6	(5.3)	-6	(5.5)
Poland	87.4	(0.5)	m	m	m	m	m	m	m	m	m	m	m	m
Portugal	85.7	(0.6)	522	(3.6)	496	(2.7)	**-26**	(3.4)	**-27**	(3.3)	0	(2.8)	-1	(2.8)
Slovak Republic	90.7	(0.4)	478	(6.1)	467	(2.3)	**-11**	(5.6)	-8	(5.0)	-2	(4.8)	-1	(4.5)
Slovenia	62.3	(0.7)	516	(3.1)	499	(2.7)	**-17**	(4.5)	**-11**	(4.4)	**9**	(4.3)	7	(4.3)
Spain	77.3	(0.7)	520	(3.2)	493	(2.3)	**-27**	(3.0)	**-21**	(2.9)	-1	(2.1)	-2	(2.0)
Sweden	81.4	(0.7)	539	(4.8)	513	(3.5)	**-26**	(4.1)	**-30**	(3.6)	-1	(2.9)	-3	(2.8)
Switzerland	80.5	(0.7)	m	m	m	m	m	m	m	m	m	m	m	m
Turkey	83.9	(0.7)	427	(4.9)	423	(3.5)	-4	(3.9)	**-11**	(3.4)	-3	(2.6)	-3	(2.4)
United Kingdom	82.5	(0.6)	562	(4.4)	516	(2.7)	**-46**	(3.8)	**-39**	(3.8)	-1	(3.0)	-1	(2.9)
United States	85.5	(0.5)	557	(5.8)	519	(3.5)	**-38**	(5.0)	**-40**	(4.5)	-6	(4.0)	-7	(3.8)
OECD average-32	81.5	(0.1)	523	(0.8)	500	(0.5)	**-23**	(0.8)	**-21**	(0.7)	0	(0.6)	-1	(0.6)
OECD average-35	81.7	(0.1)	m	m	m	m	m	m	m	m	m	m	m	m
Partners														
Brazil	84.3	(0.5)	424	(4.1)	423	(2.9)	-1	(3.5)	**-8**	(3.3)	0	(3.1)	-2	(3.0)
B-S-J-G (China)	69.2	(1.0)	515	(4.6)	488	(4.3)	**-27**	(4.0)	**-18**	(3.1)	4	(2.7)	6	(2.8)
Bulgaria	91.1	(0.5)	464	(7.9)	455	(3.7)	-9	(6.9)	-11	(5.7)	3	(5.0)	2	(5.0)
Colombia	70.5	(0.6)	442	(3.1)	429	(2.5)	**-13**	(2.9)	**-16**	(2.5)	0	(2.2)	-1	(2.0)
Costa Rica	84.2	(0.5)	452	(5.0)	438	(2.8)	**-13**	(4.6)	**-16**	(4.1)	-6	(3.6)	-6	(3.6)
Croatia	82.9	(0.5)	489	(4.0)	472	(2.6)	**-17**	(4.1)	**-13**	(3.7)	5	(3.5)	4	(3.4)
Cyprus*	91.4	(0.4)	442	(5.8)	450	(2.0)	8	(6.1)	5	(5.5)	**9**	(4.3)	8	(4.3)
Dominican Republic	81.9	(0.7)	m	m	m	m	m	m	m	m	m	m	m	m
Hong Kong (China)	82.8	(0.5)	557	(4.6)	539	(2.9)	**-18**	(4.1)	**-15**	(4.1)	0	(3.4)	2	(3.4)
Lithuania	91.1	(0.4)	490	(5.3)	469	(2.4)	**-21**	(5.0)	**-18**	(4.4)	1	(3.4)	2	(3.3)
Macao (China)	85.5	(0.6)	554	(4.0)	531	(1.4)	**-23**	(4.4)	**-24**	(4.4)	0	(3.5)	1	(3.5)
Montenegro	91.1	(0.4)	418	(5.6)	423	(1.5)	5	(6.1)	-1	(5.8)	4	(5.1)	3	(5.0)
Peru	67.2	(0.8)	451	(3.4)	425	(2.8)	**-26**	(2.8)	**-24**	(2.6)	**-6**	(2.0)	**-7**	(2.0)
Qatar	86.6	(0.4)	m	m	m	m	m	m	m	m	m	m	m	m
Russia	90.0	(0.5)	502	(6.4)	474	(3.5)	**-28**	(6.3)	**-24**	(5.6)	-2	(4.8)	-2	(4.7)
Singapore	75.9	(0.7)	582	(3.1)	555	(1.7)	**-27**	(4.0)	**-23**	(3.5)	0	(2.7)	1	(2.7)
Chinese Taipei	74.7	(0.6)	551	(3.3)	519	(2.6)	**-32**	(3.0)	**-20**	(2.6)	4	(2.3)	**6**	(2.2)
Thailand	85.4	(0.6)	466	(5.0)	433	(3.5)	**-34**	(4.1)	**-34**	(3.8)	**-9**	(3.3)	**-11**	(3.1)
Tunisia	88.3	(0.5)	390	(3.7)	386	(2.2)	-4	(3.6)	**-8**	(3.5)	-3	(3.0)	-4	(3.0)
United Arab Emirates	88.4	(0.4)	467	(4.5)	437	(2.5)	**-30**	(3.8)	**-25**	(3.6)	-2	(3.1)	-2	(3.0)
Uruguay	85.1	(0.5)	449	(4.9)	450	(2.7)	0	(4.9)	-8	(4.6)	1	(3.5)	0	(3.4)
Malaysia**	82.3	(0.7)	455	(4.4)	438	(3.4)	**-17**	(3.8)	**-12**	(3.4)	**7**	(2.7)	**7**	(2.7)

1. The socio-economic profile is measured by the PISA index of economic, social and cultural status (ESCS).
2. Relative performance refers to the residual performance, attributable to purely "collaborative problem-solving" competencies, after accounting for science, reading and mathematics performance in a regression performed across students at a national level. Whether students reported meeting friends or talking to friends outside of school was included as an explanatory variable in this regression.
Note: Values that are statistically significant are indicated in bold (see Annex A3).
* See note at the beginning of this Annex.
**Malaysia: Coverage is too small to ensure comparability (see Annex A4).
StatLink http://dx.doi.org/10.1787/888933616826

[Part 1/1]

Table V.6.9a Skipping a whole day of school and performance in collaborative problem solving

Results based on students' self-reports

		Percentage of students who reported that they had skipped a whole day of school at least once in the two weeks prior to the PISA test		Performance in collaborative problem solving				Difference (skipped - had not skipped)							
								Performance in collaborative problem solving				Relative performance in collaborative problem solving[2]			
				Had not skipped a whole day of school		Had skipped a whole day of school at least once		Before accounting for gender, and students' and schools' socio-economic profile[1]		After accounting for gender, and students' and schools' socio-economic profile		Before accounting for gender, and students' and schools' socio-economic profile		After accounting for gender, and students' and schools' socio-economic profile	
		%	S.E.	Mean score	S.E.	Mean score	S.E.	Score dif.	S.E.	Score dif.	S.E.	Score dif.	S.E.	Score dif.	S.E.
OECD	Australia	29.0	(0.6)	542	(2.0)	517	(3.1)	**-25**	(3.2)	**-21**	(3.2)	2	(2.6)	1	(2.6)
	Austria	10.9	(0.5)	515	(2.6)	479	(5.5)	**-36**	(5.9)	**-29**	(5.8)	**-11**	(4.3)	**-10**	(4.1)
	Belgium	7.1	(0.3)	511	(2.3)	452	(5.8)	**-59**	(5.7)	**-34**	(4.6)	-7	(3.9)	-5	(3.8)
	Canada	17.8	(0.5)	544	(2.3)	511	(3.7)	**-33**	(3.7)	**-28**	(3.5)	0	(3.0)	-1	(3.0)
	Chile	9.3	(0.6)	463	(2.8)	421	(5.2)	**-42**	(5.6)	**-33**	(5.2)	-6	(3.9)	-5	(3.8)
	Czech Republic	8.1	(0.4)	505	(2.0)	465	(6.0)	**-40**	(5.4)	**-29**	(4.9)	-7	(4.4)	-7	(4.3)
	Denmark	17.0	(0.6)	529	(2.5)	497	(4.4)	**-32**	(4.3)	**-26**	(4.1)	6	(3.8)	7	(3.7)
	Estonia	23.0	(0.8)	545	(2.6)	509	(3.8)	**-35**	(3.6)	**-28**	(3.5)	-3	(2.9)	-3	(2.9)
	Finland	36.6	(0.9)	542	(2.9)	525	(3.4)	**-18**	(3.7)	**-16**	(3.4)	1	(2.8)	0	(2.8)
	France	10.8	(0.6)	506	(2.5)	445	(5.4)	**-61**	(6.0)	**-32**	(5.3)	-5	(4.2)	-2	(4.2)
	Germany	8.9	(0.4)	540	(2.9)	497	(7.0)	**-43**	(7.0)	**-32**	(6.0)	-3	(5.2)	-3	(5.2)
	Greece	19.6	(0.8)	469	(3.3)	425	(5.0)	**-44**	(4.0)	**-33**	(3.7)	-5	(2.8)	-3	(2.9)
	Hungary	8.4	(0.5)	478	(2.4)	423	(5.9)	**-55**	(5.8)	**-23**	(5.5)	-2	(4.4)	0	(4.4)
	Iceland	4.5	(0.4)	504	(2.3)	452	(9.8)	**-52**	(9.8)	**-45**	(9.7)	7	(7.0)	7	(7.0)
	Ireland	24.4	(0.8)	m	m	m	m	m	m	m	m	m	m	m	m
	Israel	32.7	(0.9)	475	(4.0)	467	(4.3)	-8	(4.0)	**-7**	(3.3)	3	(2.9)	3	(2.8)
	Italy	55.2	(0.8)	493	(2.8)	469	(3.1)	**-23**	(3.3)	**-14**	(3.0)	0	(2.6)	1	(2.5)
	Japan	1.8	(0.2)	554	(2.6)	485	(13.9)	**-68**	(13.6)	**-46**	(13.5)	-7	(10.3)	-5	(10.2)
	Korea	1.9	(0.2)	540	(2.5)	460	(10.6)	**-80**	(10.8)	**-61**	(10.0)	-6	(7.8)	-4	(7.8)
	Latvia	24.7	(0.7)	496	(2.4)	457	(3.1)	**-39**	(3.4)	**-31**	(3.1)	-2	(2.4)	-1	(2.3)
	Luxembourg	11.4	(0.4)	501	(1.6)	449	(4.0)	**-52**	(4.2)	**-35**	(4.0)	**-7**	(2.9)	**-6**	(2.9)
	Mexico	25.8	(0.8)	440	(2.6)	419	(3.6)	**-21**	(3.5)	**-18**	(3.2)	1	(3.3)	2	(3.3)
	Netherlands	5.3	(0.3)	524	(2.4)	468	(6.9)	**-57**	(6.8)	**-42**	(6.6)	-4	(6.2)	-4	(6.0)
	New Zealand	25.0	(0.7)	545	(2.7)	510	(4.1)	**-35**	(4.2)	**-26**	(4.0)	-1	(3.0)	-1	(3.0)
	Norway	13.5	(0.5)	510	(2.5)	474	(4.5)	**-36**	(4.3)	**-34**	(4.1)	2	(3.5)	3	(3.4)
	Poland	20.3	(0.9)	m	m	m	m	m	m	m	m	m	m	m	m
	Portugal	20.8	(0.7)	506	(2.5)	474	(4.2)	**-32**	(3.6)	**-26**	(3.3)	1	(3.0)	1	(2.9)
	Slovak Republic	51.1	(1.0)	476	(2.8)	458	(3.1)	**-19**	(3.4)	**-13**	(3.1)	1	(2.6)	0	(2.6)
	Slovenia	12.4	(0.5)	511	(1.8)	446	(4.4)	**-66**	(4.6)	**-42**	(4.4)	**-9**	(3.5)	-7	(3.5)
	Spain	24.7	(0.7)	504	(2.3)	480	(3.3)	**-25**	(3.1)	**-20**	(3.0)	2	(2.4)	2	(2.3)
	Sweden	9.0	(0.5)	519	(3.4)	470	(5.1)	**-49**	(5.3)	**-41**	(4.9)	3	(3.6)	2	(3.6)
	Switzerland	9.6	(0.6)	m	m	m	m	m	m	m	m	m	m	m	m
	Turkey	47.0	(0.9)	423	(3.8)	423	(3.8)	0	(3.0)	-3	(2.2)	**-4**	(1.7)	-2	(1.6)
	United Kingdom	25.5	(0.6)	529	(2.7)	502	(4.5)	**-27**	(4.4)	**-20**	(3.7)	1	(2.7)	0	(2.7)
	United States	37.2	(0.8)	533	(3.6)	507	(4.2)	**-27**	(3.3)	**-22**	(3.2)	-1	(2.2)	-1	(2.1)
	OECD average-32	19.9	(0.1)	509	(0.5)	470	(1.0)	**-39**	(1.0)	**-29**	(0.9)	**-2**	(0.7)	-1	(0.7)
	OECD average-35	19.7	(0.1)	m	m	m	m	m	m	m	m	m	m	m	m
Partners	Brazil	48.0	(0.6)	423	(2.9)	417	(2.7)	**-7**	(2.7)	-4	(2.6)	1	(2.3)	1	(2.2)
	B-S-J-G (China)	2.3	(0.2)	498	(4.0)	425	(9.8)	**-73**	(9.9)	**-39**	(8.8)	9	(7.5)	**14**	(7.0)
	Bulgaria	44.7	(0.9)	462	(3.8)	435	(4.2)	**-26**	(3.7)	**-15**	(2.6)	-1	(1.8)	-1	(1.8)
	Colombia	43.8	(0.8)	437	(2.7)	422	(2.5)	**-15**	(2.6)	**-12**	(2.4)	1	(1.8)	1	(1.8)
	Costa Rica	39.1	(0.9)	445	(2.7)	429	(3.3)	**-16**	(3.1)	**-11**	(2.6)	1	(2.1)	0	(2.1)
	Croatia	12.3	(0.6)	481	(2.5)	426	(4.4)	**-54**	(4.3)	**-39**	(4.0)	-5	(2.8)	-4	(2.8)
	Cyprus*	23.4	(0.6)	455	(2.1)	421	(2.9)	**-34**	(3.4)	**-31**	(3.3)	-1	(3.3)	2	(3.3)
	Dominican Republic	51.4	(0.9)	m	m	m	m	m	m	m	m	m	m	m	m
	Hong Kong (China)	3.5	(0.2)	543	(3.0)	497	(10.1)	**-46**	(10.3)	**-38**	(10.0)	4	(7.1)	8	(6.7)
	Lithuania	22.3	(0.7)	480	(2.5)	434	(3.7)	**-45**	(3.6)	**-33**	(3.4)	-2	(2.3)	-1	(2.3)
	Macao (China)	6.4	(0.4)	537	(1.2)	490	(6.6)	**-47**	(6.6)	**-48**	(6.5)	-8	(4.9)	-5	(4.9)
	Montenegro	59.6	(0.8)	423	(2.1)	418	(1.7)	-5	(2.6)	-5	(2.5)	1	(2.5)	1	(2.4)
	Peru	40.0	(0.8)	423	(2.8)	420	(3.0)	-3	(2.9)	**-9**	(2.6)	2	(2.1)	1	(2.1)
	Qatar	40.3	(0.5)	m	m	m	m	m	m	m	m	m	m	m	m
	Russia	23.2	(0.7)	477	(3.6)	470	(5.1)	-7	(4.9)	-8	(4.5)	2	(3.6)	1	(3.4)
	Singapore	14.3	(0.5)	565	(1.3)	543	(4.1)	**-22**	(4.5)	**-18**	(4.3)	-1	(3.0)	-1	(3.1)
	Chinese Taipei	3.2	(0.2)	530	(2.5)	438	(7.6)	**-92**	(7.6)	**-65**	(7.5)	-5	(6.4)	-2	(6.2)
	Thailand	31.4	(0.9)	445	(3.7)	420	(3.6)	**-25**	(3.0)	**-18**	(2.8)	-3	(1.8)	-1	(1.8)
	Tunisia	31.0	(0.9)	389	(2.3)	371	(2.4)	**-18**	(2.6)	**-13**	(2.2)	-3	(2.0)	-1	(1.9)
	United Arab Emirates	21.0	(0.7)	438	(2.8)	441	(4.6)	3	(5.1)	-2	(4.5)	4	(3.6)	3	(3.5)
	Uruguay	51.5	(0.8)	448	(3.0)	446	(2.6)	-2	(3.2)	**8**	(2.8)	**9**	(2.6)	**9**	(2.4)
	Malaysia**	12.4	(0.7)	442	(3.3)	425	(6.1)	**-17**	(5.4)	**-18**	(4.5)	1	(3.6)	2	(3.4)

1. The socio-economic profile is measured by the PISA index of economic, social and cultural status (ESCS).
2. Relative performance refers to the residual performance, attributable to purely "collaborative problem-solving" competencies, after accounting for science, reading and mathematics performance in a regression performed across students at a national level. Whether students reported having skipped a full day of school in the two weeks prior to the PISA test was included as an explanatory variable in this regression.
Note: Values that are statistically significant are indicated in bold (see Annex A3).
* See note at the beginning of this Annex.
**Malaysia: Coverage is too small to ensure comparability (see Annex A4).
StatLink http://dx.doi.org/10.1787/888933616826

[Part 1/1]

Table V.6.9b Skipping some classes and performance in collaborative problem solving

Results based on students' self-reports

		Percentage of students who reported that they had skipped class at least once in the two weeks prior to the PISA test		Performance in collaborative problem solving				Difference (skipped at least once - had not skipped)							
								Performance in collaborative problem solving				Relative performance in collaborative problem solving[2]			
				Had not skipped any classes		Had skipped class at least once		Before accounting for gender, and students' and schools' socio-economic profile[1]		After accounting for gender, and students' and schools' socio-economic profile		Before accounting for gender, and students' and schools' socio-economic profile		After accounting for gender, and students' and schools' socio-economic profile	
		%	S.E.	Mean score	S.E.	Mean score	S.E.	Score dif.	S.E.	Score dif.	S.E.	Score dif.	S.E.	Score dif.	S.E.
OECD	Australia	16.0	(0.4)	541	(1.9)	503	(4.1)	**-38**	(4.1)	**-32**	(4.0)	-1	(3.1)	-1	(3.1)
	Austria	17.2	(0.7)	515	(2.6)	495	(4.5)	**-20**	(4.5)	**-22**	(4.1)	**-9**	(3.4)	**-8**	(3.2)
	Belgium	11.7	(0.6)	513	(2.3)	460	(4.9)	**-53**	(4.9)	**-32**	(4.0)	-6	(3.3)	-4	(3.2)
	Canada	26.5	(0.7)	546	(2.3)	517	(3.2)	**-29**	(2.8)	**-25**	(2.7)	4	(1.9)	3	(1.9)
	Chile	18.7	(0.8)	464	(2.9)	438	(4.1)	**-27**	(4.5)	**-22**	(4.1)	**-8**	(3.6)	**-7**	(3.6)
	Czech Republic	9.6	(0.5)	504	(2.0)	480	(5.5)	**-25**	(5.2)	**-20**	(5.0)	-5	(4.1)	-5	(4.0)
	Denmark	24.0	(0.8)	530	(2.6)	502	(4.0)	**-28**	(3.9)	**-27**	(3.7)	2	(3.0)	1	(3.0)
	Estonia	34.9	(0.8)	549	(2.8)	513	(3.2)	**-37**	(3.2)	**-32**	(3.2)	-5	(2.6)	-3	(2.6)
	Finland	48.2	(0.9)	539	(3.1)	532	(3.0)	**-7**	(3.4)	**-10**	(3.2)	2	(2.6)	0	(2.6)
	France	24.8	(0.8)	509	(2.6)	470	(3.9)	**-39**	(4.3)	**-23**	(3.7)	-3	(2.7)	-2	(2.7)
	Germany	15.7	(0.7)	540	(2.8)	514	(6.1)	**-26**	(5.9)	**-29**	(4.6)	-5	(4.0)	-5	(3.9)
	Greece	45.3	(1.4)	475	(3.5)	442	(4.4)	**-34**	(4.0)	**-22**	(3.2)	-3	(2.3)	-1	(2.3)
	Hungary	17.7	(0.8)	482	(2.6)	433	(4.7)	**-49**	(5.2)	**-22**	(4.1)	1	(3.1)	2	(3.0)
	Iceland	18.5	(0.7)	510	(2.5)	466	(4.7)	**-44**	(5.3)	**-40**	(5.3)	1	(4.2)	2	(4.2)
	Ireland	23.1	(0.8)	m	m	m	m	m	m	m	m	m	m	m	m
	Israel	38.0	(1.1)	469	(4.0)	479	(4.7)	**11**	(5.1)	3	(4.1)	**6**	(2.5)	**7**	(2.5)
	Italy	40.9	(0.7)	492	(2.7)	463	(3.5)	**-29**	(3.6)	**-23**	(3.3)	**-7**	(3.1)	-5	(3.1)
	Japan	3.1	(0.3)	554	(2.6)	503	(9.3)	**-51**	(9.2)	**-30**	(8.7)	7	(7.0)	7	(6.9)
	Korea	2.6	(0.3)	541	(2.5)	464	(8.9)	**-77**	(9.1)	**-57**	(8.4)	-5	(5.7)	-3	(5.7)
	Latvia	39.1	(0.9)	495	(2.4)	473	(3.1)	**-22**	(3.2)	**-20**	(3.1)	-1	(2.8)	0	(2.8)
	Luxembourg	15.3	(0.5)	500	(1.6)	463	(4.1)	**-38**	(4.2)	**-33**	(4.0)	-6	(3.4)	-5	(3.3)
	Mexico	24.9	(0.8)	436	(2.7)	431	(3.5)	-5	(3.5)	**-9**	(2.9)	2	(2.4)	1	(2.5)
	Netherlands	18.9	(0.8)	526	(2.7)	499	(4.4)	**-28**	(5.1)	**-23**	(4.2)	-4	(3.5)	-2	(3.5)
	New Zealand	22.6	(0.7)	545	(2.7)	508	(4.4)	**-38**	(4.8)	**-31**	(4.4)	2	(3.2)	0	(3.1)
	Norway	19.7	(0.7)	512	(2.6)	479	(4.6)	**-33**	(4.6)	**-32**	(4.6)	3	(4.1)	3	(4.1)
	Poland	37.4	(1.2)	m	m	m	m	m	m	m	m	m	m	m	m
	Portugal	32.9	(0.7)	509	(2.6)	481	(3.6)	**-28**	(3.1)	**-22**	(2.8)	-1	(2.8)	0	(2.7)
	Slovak Republic	49.7	(0.8)	478	(2.7)	456	(3.1)	**-22**	(3.4)	**-18**	(2.9)	2	(2.4)	2	(2.4)
	Slovenia	29.1	(0.8)	515	(2.1)	475	(3.2)	**-40**	(3.5)	**-22**	(3.2)	-3	(2.8)	0	(2.8)
	Spain	33.5	(0.9)	503	(2.5)	490	(2.8)	**-12**	(3.1)	**-12**	(2.9)	3	(2.3)	3	(2.2)
	Sweden	16.3	(0.7)	522	(3.3)	476	(5.1)	**-46**	(4.6)	**-41**	(4.5)	-2	(3.7)	-3	(3.6)
	Switzerland	17.3	(0.8)	m	m	m	m	m	m	m	m	m	m	m	m
	Turkey	44.6	(1.0)	423	(3.8)	424	(3.9)	1	(3.4)	-1	(2.4)	-4	(2.3)	-3	(2.1)
	United Kingdom	33.9	(0.8)	526	(2.9)	514	(3.6)	**-12**	(3.5)	**-14**	(3.4)	1	(3.0)	0	(2.9)
	United States	42.2	(1.1)	531	(3.8)	514	(4.4)	**-17**	(4.0)	**-16**	(3.7)	2	(3.2)	1	(3.0)
	OECD average-32	26.1	(0.1)	509	(0.5)	480	(0.8)	**-29**	(0.8)	**-24**	(0.7)	**-1**	(0.6)	**-1**	(0.6)
	OECD average-35	26.1	(0.1)	m	m	m	m	m	m	m	m	m	m	m	m
Partners	Brazil	46.0	(0.6)	433	(2.6)	405	(2.6)	**-28**	(2.2)	**-21**	(2.1)	0	(1.7)	0	(1.7)
	B-S-J-G (China)	10.1	(0.5)	502	(3.9)	449	(6.0)	**-53**	(5.4)	**-32**	(4.8)	-4	(3.5)	-1	(3.5)
	Bulgaria	47.5	(1.2)	468	(4.0)	431	(4.0)	**-37**	(4.1)	**-18**	(3.0)	-1	(2.3)	0	(2.3)
	Colombia	45.5	(0.8)	435	(2.5)	425	(2.8)	**-9**	(2.8)	**-8**	(2.7)	4	(2.3)	4	(2.3)
	Costa Rica	43.3	(0.9)	444	(2.8)	433	(3.3)	**-11**	(3.3)	**-8**	(3.0)	-1	(2.7)	-1	(2.6)
	Croatia	24.5	(0.8)	483	(2.5)	447	(3.8)	**-35**	(3.5)	**-25**	(3.1)	**-4**	(2.1)	-2	(2.1)
	Cyprus*	39.3	(0.7)	462	(2.1)	425	(2.7)	**-37**	(3.2)	**-26**	(3.1)	0	(3.0)	1	(3.1)
	Dominican Republic	55.5	(1.1)	m	m	m	m	m	m	m	m	m	m	m	m
	Hong Kong (China)	5.2	(0.3)	544	(2.9)	507	(8.2)	**-37**	(7.9)	**-33**	(7.2)	-3	(4.8)	0	(4.6)
	Lithuania	40.4	(0.9)	481	(2.3)	452	(3.2)	**-29**	(3.0)	**-24**	(2.9)	-2	(1.8)	-1	(1.8)
	Macao (China)	9.4	(0.4)	537	(1.3)	505	(5.7)	**-32**	(5.9)	**-33**	(5.8)	**-8**	(4.1)	-6	(4.0)
	Montenegro	54.9	(0.7)	429	(1.9)	412	(1.9)	**-17**	(2.8)	**-15**	(2.7)	0	(2.6)	1	(2.6)
	Peru	41.1	(0.7)	427	(2.8)	414	(3.2)	**-12**	(3.1)	**-14**	(2.7)	-1	(2.0)	-2	(2.1)
	Qatar	34.8	(0.4)	m	m	m	m	m	m	m	m	m	m	m	m
	Russia	38.6	(1.2)	481	(3.3)	466	(4.6)	**-15**	(3.8)	**-17**	(3.3)	0	(3.1)	-1	(2.9)
	Singapore	13.5	(0.5)	563	(1.3)	556	(3.9)	-7	(4.4)	**-9**	(4.0)	-5	(3.2)	-4	(3.2)
	Chinese Taipei	10.6	(0.5)	532	(2.4)	479	(5.6)	**-53**	(5.1)	**-39**	(4.1)	-1	(3.7)	3	(3.5)
	Thailand	41.9	(1.1)	438	(3.5)	436	(4.6)	-1	(4.1)	-2	(3.0)	1	(2.3)	2	(2.0)
	Tunisia	42.4	(0.9)	386	(2.4)	382	(2.2)	-4	(2.5)	-4	(2.4)	-3	(2.0)	-1	(1.9)
	United Arab Emirates	33.1	(0.7)	444	(2.9)	428	(3.0)	**-16**	(3.2)	**-11**	(3.1)	-1	(2.5)	0	(2.5)
	Uruguay	40.3	(0.9)	455	(2.6)	436	(3.2)	**-20**	(3.8)	**-13**	(3.5)	1	(2.8)	1	(2.8)
	Malaysia**	22.9	(0.9)	441	(3.3)	438	(4.6)	-3	(3.7)	-4	(3.0)	3	(2.2)	4	(2.0)

1. The socio-economic profile is measured by the PISA index of economic, social and cultural status (ESCS).
2. Relative performance refers to the residual performance, attributable to purely "collaborative problem-solving" competencies, after accounting for science, reading and mathematics performance in a regression performed across students at a national level. Whether students reported having skipped class at least once in the two weeks prior to the PISA test was included as an explanatory variable in this regression.
Note: Values that are statistically significant are indicated in bold (see Annex A3).
* See note at the beginning of this Annex.
**Malaysia: Coverage is too small to ensure comparability (see Annex A4).
StatLink http://dx.doi.org/10.1787/888933616826

[Part 1/1]

Table V.6.9c Arriving late for school and performance in collaborative problem solving

Results based on students' self-reports

		Percentage of students who reported that they had arrived late for school at least once in the two weeks prior to the PISA test		Performance in collaborative problem solving				Difference (had arrived late at least once - had not arrived late)							
				Had not arrived late		Had arrived late for school at least once		Performance in collaborative problem solving: Before accounting for gender, and students' and schools' socio-economic profile[1]		Performance in collaborative problem solving: After accounting for gender, and students' and schools' socio-economic profile		Relative performance in collaborative problem solving[2]: Before accounting for gender, and students' and schools' socio-economic profile		Relative performance in collaborative problem solving[2]: After accounting for gender, and students' and schools' socio-economic profile	
		%	S.E.	Mean score	S.E.	Mean score	S.E.	Score dif.	S.E.	Score dif.	S.E.	Score dif.	S.E.	Score dif.	S.E.
OECD	Australia	41.0	(0.6)	548	(2.2)	517	(2.5)	**-31**	(2.9)	**-25**	(2.8)	-4	(2.3)	-4	(2.3)
	Austria	35.2	(1.0)	520	(2.9)	496	(3.5)	**-24**	(3.9)	**-21**	(3.6)	**-6**	(2.7)	-4	(2.6)
	Belgium	51.5	(0.9)	527	(2.6)	488	(2.9)	**-40**	(2.9)	**-27**	(2.4)	**-5**	(1.8)	-3	(1.8)
	Canada	47.7	(0.8)	552	(2.4)	523	(2.6)	**-29**	(2.5)	**-24**	(2.4)	0	(2.1)	2	(2.1)
	Chile	66.7	(0.9)	474	(3.8)	452	(2.5)	**-22**	(3.1)	**-16**	(2.7)	-2	(2.0)	-1	(1.9)
	Czech Republic	52.0	(0.9)	516	(2.3)	489	(2.9)	**-28**	(3.2)	**-19**	(2.8)	-4	(2.1)	-2	(2.1)
	Denmark	47.6	(0.9)	529	(2.7)	517	(3.2)	**-13**	(3.2)	**-11**	(3.1)	-1	(2.4)	1	(2.3)
	Estonia	42.9	(0.9)	543	(2.8)	528	(3.3)	**-16**	(3.6)	**-16**	(3.5)	1	(2.9)	3	(2.9)
	Finland	36.2	(0.9)	546	(2.7)	519	(3.6)	**-27**	(3.6)	**-23**	(3.3)	-3	(2.6)	1	(2.6)
	France	52.6	(0.9)	521	(2.7)	479	(2.9)	**-42**	(3.3)	**-27**	(2.8)	**-5**	(2.4)	-4	(2.3)
	Germany	40.1	(1.0)	547	(3.2)	519	(3.7)	**-28**	(3.9)	**-23**	(3.2)	-4	(2.5)	-2	(2.4)
	Greece	54.2	(0.8)	465	(3.6)	457	(3.9)	**-8**	(3.0)	**-8**	(2.8)	1	(2.1)	2	(2.1)
	Hungary	35.8	(0.9)	486	(2.9)	452	(3.2)	**-34**	(3.9)	**-14**	(3.3)	-1	(2.7)	0	(2.6)
	Iceland	50.0	(1.0)	513	(3.1)	490	(2.7)	**-22**	(3.8)	**-20**	(3.8)	-3	(2.6)	-1	(2.6)
	Ireland	31.1	(0.9)	m	m	m	m	m	m	m	m	m	m	m	m
	Israel	57.9	(1.1)	478	(4.4)	469	(3.9)	**-9**	(3.9)	-2	(3.4)	3	(2.1)	**4**	(2.0)
	Italy	36.2	(0.9)	489	(2.5)	464	(3.6)	**-25**	(3.3)	**-17**	(2.9)	-1	(2.2)	1	(2.1)
	Japan	11.7	(0.6)	555	(2.7)	534	(5.7)	**-21**	(5.6)	**-10**	(4.8)	4	(4.0)	7	(4.1)
	Korea	19.4	(1.0)	546	(2.6)	509	(3.7)	**-37**	(3.4)	**-28**	(3.0)	-1	(2.3)	-1	(2.2)
	Latvia	53.1	(1.0)	489	(2.8)	485	(2.8)	-4	(3.4)	**-7**	(3.0)	1	(2.4)	2	(2.5)
	Luxembourg	54.3	(0.7)	509	(2.0)	482	(2.3)	**-28**	(3.1)	**-24**	(2.8)	-5	(2.6)	-3	(2.5)
	Mexico	48.9	(0.9)	437	(3.1)	432	(2.7)	-5	(3.0)	**-7**	(2.6)	3	(2.0)	3	(2.0)
	Netherlands	51.0	(0.8)	542	(2.8)	501	(2.9)	**-40**	(3.0)	**-23**	(2.5)	-4	(2.1)	-2	(2.2)
	New Zealand	45.3	(1.0)	552	(3.3)	519	(2.6)	**-33**	(3.6)	**-25**	(3.3)	2	(2.4)	2	(2.4)
	Norway	47.0	(0.9)	518	(2.8)	491	(2.9)	**-27**	(2.9)	**-25**	(3.0)	-2	(2.8)	0	(2.9)
	Poland	56.5	(1.2)	m	m	m	m	m	m	m	m	m	m	m	m
	Portugal	45.6	(1.0)	501	(2.6)	497	(3.5)	-4	(3.0)	**-8**	(3.0)	**5**	(1.9)	**6**	(1.8)
	Slovak Republic	37.2	(0.9)	480	(2.5)	446	(3.1)	**-33**	(3.1)	**-21**	(3.0)	-3	(2.6)	-1	(2.6)
	Slovenia	49.5	(0.9)	512	(2.6)	495	(2.6)	**-17**	(3.7)	**-12**	(3.2)	-3	(2.9)	-2	(2.8)
	Spain	42.0	(0.9)	505	(2.6)	489	(2.6)	**-16**	(2.9)	**-16**	(2.7)	1	(2.1)	2	(2.1)
	Sweden	54.5	(0.8)	529	(3.6)	501	(3.6)	**-27**	(3.1)	**-23**	(2.9)	-4	(2.1)	-2	(2.1)
	Switzerland	45.8	(1.1)	m	m	m	m	m	m	m	m	m	m	m	m
	Turkey	48.2	(1.2)	428	(4.1)	418	(3.6)	**-9**	(3.6)	**-6**	(2.7)	0	(2.1)	1	(2.0)
	United Kingdom	32.9	(0.9)	530	(3.0)	506	(3.5)	**-24**	(3.5)	**-22**	(3.2)	1	(3.0)	3	(3.0)
	United States	34.8	(1.1)	536	(3.5)	500	(4.6)	**-37**	(3.9)	**-28**	(3.9)	-1	(2.7)	0	(2.7)
	OECD average-32	44.5	(0.2)	513	(0.5)	489	(0.6)	**-24**	(0.6)	**-18**	(0.6)	**-1**	(0.4)	0	(0.4)
	OECD average-35	44.5	(0.2)	m	m	m	m	m	m	m	m	m	m	m	m
Partners	Brazil	39.9	(0.7)	422	(2.7)	419	(2.9)	-3	(2.9)	-4	(2.7)	4	(2.5)	4	(2.5)
	B-S-J-G (China)	39.8	(1.1)	512	(4.4)	472	(3.9)	**-40**	(4.0)	**-19**	(3.1)	**-5**	(2.3)	-2	(2.3)
	Bulgaria	55.7	(1.0)	466	(4.0)	438	(3.8)	**-28**	(3.3)	**-11**	(2.7)	0	(2.3)	1	(2.2)
	Colombia	42.9	(0.9)	429	(2.8)	434	(2.5)	5	(2.9)	1	(2.3)	**7**	(1.8)	**7**	(1.8)
	Costa Rica	53.7	(1.0)	440	(3.1)	438	(3.3)	-1	(3.8)	-4	(3.5)	0	(2.7)	0	(2.7)
	Croatia	42.6	(0.9)	481	(2.7)	465	(3.1)	**-16**	(2.9)	**-14**	(2.6)	-2	(1.8)	0	(1.7)
	Cyprus*	57.3	(0.7)	456	(2.2)	441	(2.3)	**-15**	(2.7)	**-13**	(2.7)	0	(2.4)	1	(2.4)
	Dominican Republic	41.5	(1.1)	m	m	m	m	m	m	m	m	m	m	m	m
	Hong Kong (China)	24.5	(0.7)	549	(3.0)	520	(4.2)	**-29**	(3.8)	**-21**	(3.5)	-2	(2.7)	1	(2.7)
	Lithuania	47.8	(0.8)	476	(2.5)	463	(3.3)	**-14**	(3.3)	**-14**	(3.2)	-1	(2.2)	1	(2.2)
	Macao (China)	29.1	(0.6)	543	(1.5)	511	(2.7)	**-32**	(3.3)	**-30**	(3.3)	-4	(2.4)	-3	(2.4)
	Montenegro	63.4	(0.8)	429	(2.2)	415	(1.6)	**-14**	(2.7)	**-13**	(2.5)	-1	(1.9)	0	(1.8)
	Peru	59.7	(0.9)	427	(3.3)	419	(2.7)	**-9**	(3.1)	**-9**	(2.4)	-3	(2.0)	-3	(1.9)
	Qatar	46.8	(0.4)	m	m	m	m	m	m	m	m	m	m	m	m
	Russia	55.5	(1.4)	479	(3.5)	473	(4.2)	-7	(3.7)	**-7**	(3.4)	6	(2.9)	5	(2.8)
	Singapore	23.9	(0.6)	574	(1.5)	524	(2.9)	**-50**	(3.5)	**-38**	(3.3)	**-7**	(2.5)	**-6**	(2.3)
	Chinese Taipei	33.8	(0.8)	534	(2.6)	512	(3.2)	**-22**	(3.0)	**-17**	(2.6)	0	(2.2)	2	(2.2)
	Thailand	36.1	(1.0)	443	(3.5)	426	(3.9)	**-17**	(2.7)	**-13**	(2.5)	-3	(1.8)	-2	(1.8)
	Tunisia	74.4	(0.8)	386	(2.8)	383	(2.0)	-3	(2.4)	**-5**	(2.3)	-1	(2.0)	-1	(2.0)
	United Arab Emirates	43.5	(0.7)	451	(3.1)	422	(2.6)	**-29**	(3.1)	**-23**	(3.0)	2	(2.3)	2	(2.3)
	Uruguay	65.0	(0.9)	453	(3.1)	444	(2.5)	**-9**	(3.2)	-5	(2.9)	**4**	(2.2)	**5**	(2.2)
	Malaysia**	34.5	(0.9)	444	(3.6)	433	(3.5)	**-10**	(3.1)	**-6**	(2.7)	3	(2.3)	4	(2.3)

1. The socio-economic profile is measured by the PISA index of economic, social and cultural status (ESCS).
2. Relative performance refers to the residual performance, attributable to purely "collaborative problem-solving" competencies, after accounting for science, reading and mathematics performance in a regression performed across students at a national level. Whether students reported having arrived late for school at least once in the two weeks prior to the PISA test was included as an explanatory variable in this regression.
Note: Values that are statistically significant are indicated in bold (see Annex A3).
* See note at the beginning of this Annex.
**Malaysia: Coverage is too small to ensure comparability (see Annex A4).
StatLink http://dx.doi.org/10.1787/888933616826

[Part 1/1]

Table V.6.12a Attendance at pre-primary school and performance in collaborative problem solving

Results based on students' self-reports

	Percentage of students who had attended pre-primary school (supervision and care; early childhood education development; or pre-primary education)		Performance in collaborative problem solving				Difference (had attended - had not attended)							
							Performance in collaborative problem solving				Relative performance in collaborative problem solving[2]			
			Had not attended pre-primary school		Had attended pre-primary school		Before accounting for gender, and students' and schools' socio-economic profile[1]		After accounting for gender, and students' and schools' socio-economic profile		Before accounting for gender, and students' and schools' socio-economic profile		After accounting for gender, and students' and schools' socio-economic profile	
	%	S.E.	Mean score	S.E.	Mean score	S.E.	Score dif.	S.E.	Score dif.	S.E.	Score dif.	S.E.	Score dif.	S.E.
OECD														
Australia	97.8	(0.2)	515	(12.6)	537	(2.0)	21	(12.8)	-2	(12.1)	-5	(9.9)	-5	(9.6)
Austria	98.7	(0.2)	479	(16.9)	512	(2.7)	33	(17.0)	8	(16.1)	3	(13.2)	5	(13.1)
Belgium	98.9	(0.2)	439	(12.7)	504	(2.4)	**64**	(12.8)	**28**	(12.0)	-5	(10.1)	-6	(10.2)
Canada	97.4	(0.2)	543	(9.6)	538	(2.4)	-4	(9.6)	-14	(9.3)	**-17**	(6.9)	**-19**	(6.7)
Chile	96.8	(0.4)	430	(10.0)	462	(2.7)	**32**	(10.1)	5	(9.9)	0	(8.2)	-2	(8.3)
Czech Republic	98.2	(0.3)	465	(12.6)	501	(2.2)	**36**	(13.0)	14	(11.8)	6	(10.4)	6	(10.5)
Denmark	99.4	(0.1)	487	(24.7)	519	(2.5)	32	(25.0)	14	(24.2)	3	(20.6)	-1	(20.3)
Estonia	94.7	(0.5)	537	(8.3)	539	(2.6)	3	(7.8)	-15	(7.8)	2	(6.0)	1	(6.1)
Finland	98.3	(0.2)	502	(17.9)	538	(2.6)	36	(18.3)	25	(16.5)	-2	(12.3)	0	(12.0)
France	99.2	(0.1)	439	(23.5)	499	(2.5)	**60**	(23.1)	20	(21.9)	-4	(17.8)	-1	(17.9)
Germany	98.7	(0.2)	497	(15.9)	535	(2.9)	**39**	(15.9)	23	(15.7)	-1	(14.3)	-5	(14.2)
Greece	97.9	(0.4)	397	(13.2)	463	(3.5)	**66**	(13.7)	**32**	(12.6)	14	(11.1)	9	(10.9)
Hungary	99.8	(0.1)	c	c	474	(2.5)	c	c	c	c	c	c	c	c
Iceland	98.3	(0.3)	473	(22.4)	499	(2.5)	26	(22.3)	14	(22.7)	-7	(12.2)	-4	(11.7)
Ireland	92.9	(0.4)	m	m	m	m	m	m	m	m	m	m	m	m
Israel	99.1	(0.3)	382	(22.0)	472	(3.5)	**90**	(21.8)	16	(20.6)	3	(15.3)	0	(16.1)
Italy	98.3	(0.2)	460	(15.7)	480	(2.6)	20	(15.5)	16	(15.3)	5	(14.8)	6	(14.1)
Japan	99.6	(0.1)	c	c	556	(2.6)	c	c	c	c	c	c	c	c
Korea	97.2	(0.3)	545	(9.1)	541	(2.6)	-4	(9.0)	-12	(8.8)	-6	(6.8)	-7	(6.6)
Latvia	94.6	(0.5)	492	(9.8)	482	(2.5)	-10	(10.1)	-11	(9.5)	6	(7.5)	6	(7.4)
Luxembourg	97.4	(0.2)	463	(11.3)	495	(1.6)	**32**	(11.2)	13	(10.2)	-7	(8.1)	-7	(8.2)
Mexico	98.3	(0.2)	407	(9.9)	434	(2.5)	**27**	(10.2)	1	(11.0)	7	(8.0)	2	(7.9)
Netherlands	m	m	m	m	m	m	m	m	m	m	m	m	m	m
New Zealand	96.2	(0.3)	514	(10.8)	537	(2.9)	**23**	(11.5)	17	(10.7)	5	(9.0)	7	(8.6)
Norway	94.1	(0.4)	469	(7.9)	506	(2.6)	**37**	(7.9)	**20**	(7.9)	**11**	(5.1)	**11**	(5.2)
Poland	82.7	(1.3)	m	m	m	m	m	m	m	m	m	m	m	m
Portugal	94.0	(0.4)	485	(9.0)	501	(2.6)	16	(8.6)	-2	(8.6)	-3	(6.6)	-3	(6.6)
Slovak Republic	96.2	(0.3)	440	(10.0)	466	(2.5)	**26**	(10.0)	-15	(10.9)	-18	(9.4)	-17	(9.4)
Slovenia	86.4	(0.5)	491	(5.1)	504	(2.2)	**14**	(6.2)	-3	(5.7)	3	(4.9)	3	(5.1)
Spain	99.0	(0.1)	450	(15.2)	498	(2.2)	**49**	(15.1)	**31**	(15.2)	14	(13.6)	15	(13.5)
Sweden	96.3	(0.4)	454	(11.9)	516	(3.6)	**62**	(11.9)	**33**	(10.7)	-4	(7.1)	-1	(7.0)
Switzerland	98.7	(0.2)	m	m	m	m	m	m	m	m	m	m	m	m
Turkey	50.5	(1.3)	422	(3.8)	430	(4.4)	8	(4.4)	**-7**	(3.6)	0	(2.9)	-2	(3.2)
United Kingdom	98.4	(0.2)	516	(13.9)	524	(2.8)	8	(13.5)	-14	(11.9)	**-23**	(11.0)	**-27**	(10.4)
United States	81.8	(0.8)	530	(5.6)	520	(3.7)	-10	(5.5)	**-23**	(5.3)	**-11**	(4.5)	**-12**	(4.3)
OECD average-32	95.2	(0.1)	473	(2.6)	503	(0.5)	**29**	(2.6)	**7**	(2.5)	-1	(2.0)	-2	(2.0)
OECD average-35	94.9	(0.1)	m	m	m	m	m	m	m	m	m	m	m	m
Partners														
Brazil	97.2	(0.2)	408	(6.3)	414	(2.4)	6	(6.3)	-6	(6.1)	1	(5.8)	-1	(5.6)
B-S-J-G (China)	82.9	(1.3)	446	(6.1)	507	(4.2)	**61**	(6.9)	**16**	(5.3)	3	(4.0)	1	(4.1)
Bulgaria	94.0	(0.4)	457	(8.2)	445	(3.7)	-11	(7.1)	**-15**	(5.6)	-2	(4.8)	-3	(4.6)
Colombia	96.7	(0.4)	428	(7.8)	430	(2.4)	1	(8.0)	**-20**	(6.6)	-5	(6.4)	-11	(6.3)
Costa Rica	90.9	(0.4)	434	(5.5)	443	(2.5)	9	(5.4)	-5	(5.0)	3	(4.6)	2	(4.5)
Croatia	80.3	(0.9)	467	(4.0)	474	(2.7)	6	(3.9)	**-9**	(3.6)	4	(2.7)	4	(2.9)
Cyprus*	98.3	(0.2)	440	(14.2)	448	(2.1)	9	(13.7)	-5	(13.0)	-13	(10.7)	-12	(10.6)
Dominican Republic	96.3	(0.4)	m	m	m	m	m	m	m	m	m	m	m	m
Hong Kong (China)	99.0	(0.2)	460	(17.3)	546	(3.2)	**85**	(16.8)	**72**	(16.6)	18	(12.2)	18	(11.8)
Lithuania	76.5	(1.0)	461	(3.5)	469	(2.9)	8	(4.3)	**-17**	(4.0)	-1	(2.5)	-3	(2.7)
Macao (China)	99.5	(0.1)	c	c	538	(1.5)	c	c	c	c	c	c	c	c
Montenegro	73.0	(0.6)	413	(2.8)	418	(1.7)	6	(3.4)	**-8**	(3.3)	4	(2.6)	3	(2.7)
Peru	95.4	(0.4)	375	(6.4)	421	(2.5)	**46**	(6.8)	2	(6.3)	9	(5.6)	3	(5.5)
Qatar	86.1	(0.3)	m	m	m	m	m	m	m	m	m	m	m	m
Russia	86.0	(1.2)	452	(7.6)	477	(3.6)	**25**	(7.7)	1	(7.4)	**12**	(5.7)	4	(5.8)
Singapore	98.9	(0.2)	514	(17.0)	566	(1.7)	**52**	(17.0)	31	(17.4)	-2	(9.5)	-3	(9.5)
Chinese Taipei	98.2	(0.2)	503	(13.5)	532	(2.7)	**29**	(13.2)	14	(10.7)	10	(9.8)	8	(9.8)
Thailand	99.4	(0.1)	410	(17.0)	438	(3.4)	28	(16.8)	28	(16.5)	5	(12.7)	7	(12.3)
Tunisia	91.3	(0.7)	377	(4.1)	384	(2.1)	7	(3.9)	**-14**	(4.1)	1	(3.6)	**-7**	(3.3)
United Arab Emirates	92.8	(0.3)	429	(5.9)	440	(2.7)	11	(5.8)	-5	(5.4)	7	(4.9)	4	(4.6)
Uruguay	99.2	(0.2)	448	(14.1)	445	(2.4)	-3	(14.2)	-27	(14.1)	**-19**	(9.8)	**-21**	(10.0)
Malaysia**	96.3	(0.4)	427	(7.7)	442	(3.3)	15	(7.6)	-10	(7.0)	0	(5.5)	-2	(5.3)

1. The socio-economic profile is measured by the PISA index of economic, social and cultural status (ESCS).
2. Relative performance refers to the residual performance, attributable to purely "collaborative problem-solving" competencies, after accounting for science, reading and mathematics performance in a regression performed across students at a national level. Whether students attended pre-primary school was included as an explanatory variable in this regression.
Notes: Values that are statistically significant are indicated in bold (see Annex A3).
Results on attendance to pre-primary school can differ from data published in Volume II due to the wider definition of pre-primary school used here.
* See note at the beginning of this Annex.
**Malaysia: Coverage is too small to ensure comparability (see Annex A4).
StatLink http://dx.doi.org/10.1787/888933616826

[Part 1/1]

Table V.6.12b Attendance at pre-primary school and performance in collaborative problem solving, by socio-economic status

Results based on students' self-reports

	PISA index of economic, social, and cultural status (ESCS)				Percentage of students who had attended pre-primary school (supervision and care; early childhood education development; or pre-primary education)				Difference between students who had attended pre-primary school and those who had not							
									Performance in collaborative problem solving				Relative performance in collaborative problem solving[1]			
	Disadvantaged students (bottom quarter of ESCS)		Advantaged students (top quarter of ESCS)		Disadvantaged students (bottom quarter of ESCS)		Advantaged students (top quarter of ESCS)		Disadvantaged students (bottom quarter of ESCS)		Advantaged students (top quarter of ESCS)		Disadvantaged students (bottom quarter of ESCS)		Advantaged students (top quarter of ESCS)	
	Mean index	S.E.	Mean index	S.E.	%	S.E.	%	S.E.	Score dif.	S.E.	Score dif.	S.E.	Score dif.	S.E.	Score dif.	S.E.
OECD																
Australia	-0.81	(0.02)	1.18	(0.01)	96.2	(0.5)	98.4	(0.3)	27	(18.3)	8	(23.0)	2	(12.4)	-12	(15.0)
Austria	-0.97	(0.03)	1.21	(0.02)	97.8	(0.5)	99.1	(0.3)	3	(21.3)	c	c	-2	(17.2)	c	c
Belgium	-1.05	(0.03)	1.25	(0.02)	97.7	(0.5)	99.6	(0.1)	**43**	(16.4)	c	c	-10	(14.1)	c	c
Canada	-0.58	(0.02)	1.46	(0.01)	96.7	(0.4)	97.5	(0.3)	-20	(12.9)	0	(19.0)	**-23**	(9.0)	-10	(12.8)
Chile	-1.86	(0.04)	0.96	(0.03)	93.4	(1.1)	98.8	(0.2)	11	(11.9)	c	c	2	(9.0)	c	c
Czech Republic	-1.19	(0.02)	0.85	(0.02)	96.9	(0.6)	98.5	(0.4)	27	(16.0)	c	c	-4	(15.1)	c	c
Denmark	-0.64	(0.03)	1.53	(0.01)	99.0	(0.2)	99.5	(0.2)	c	c	c	c	c	c	c	c
Estonia	-0.96	(0.02)	1.01	(0.01)	91.5	(1.0)	96.9	(0.6)	-7	(16.2)	0	(17.0)	-4	(9.2)	6	(12.7)
Finland	-0.73	(0.02)	1.17	(0.02)	96.8	(0.6)	98.5	(0.4)	43	(22.7)	c	c	-4	(16.6)	c	c
France	-1.17	(0.02)	0.85	(0.02)	98.7	(0.3)	99.7	(0.2)	c	c	c	c	c	c	c	c
Germany	-1.07	(0.02)	1.36	(0.02)	98.1	(0.4)	99.2	(0.3)	c	c	c	c	c	c	c	c
Greece	-1.31	(0.03)	1.14	(0.02)	95.7	(1.0)	99.0	(0.3)	**32**	(16.4)	c	c	10	(13.7)	c	c
Hungary	-1.44	(0.02)	1.02	(0.02)	99.6	(0.2)	100.0	c	c	c	m	m	c	c	m	m
Iceland	-0.28	(0.02)	1.55	(0.01)	96.7	(0.8)	98.6	(0.5)	c	c	c	c	c	c	c	c
Ireland	-0.94	(0.02)	1.21	(0.02)	87.7	(0.9)	95.8	(0.6)	m	m	m	m	m	m	m	m
Israel	-0.99	(0.05)	1.10	(0.02)	97.8	(1.0)	99.8	(0.1)	c	c	c	c	c	c	c	c
Italy	-1.31	(0.02)	1.16	(0.02)	98.6	(0.4)	98.0	(0.5)	13	(30.2)	60	(32.2)	4	(25.3)	13	(32.4)
Japan	-1.10	(0.02)	0.72	(0.01)	99.4	(0.2)	99.7	(0.1)	c	c	c	c	c	c	c	c
Korea	-1.06	(0.02)	0.68	(0.03)	95.9	(0.6)	97.9	(0.4)	-22	(13.0)	c	c	-11	(9.9)	c	c
Latvia	-1.62	(0.02)	0.72	(0.02)	93.7	(1.1)	94.6	(1.0)	-13	(15.4)	-4	(18.2)	0	(10.6)	13	(14.7)
Luxembourg	-1.42	(0.02)	1.41	(0.01)	96.4	(0.6)	98.6	(0.4)	2	(13.1)	c	c	-17	(10.0)	c	c
Mexico	-2.73	(0.04)	0.42	(0.05)	96.1	(0.6)	99.4	(0.2)	0	(11.0)	c	c	4	(9.6)	c	c
Netherlands	-0.85	(0.03)	1.07	(0.02)	m	m	m	m	m	m	m	m	m	m	m	m
New Zealand	-0.89	(0.02)	1.09	(0.02)	96.1	(0.6)	96.7	(0.6)	23	(22.2)	**40**	(20.0)	18	(18.6)	-1	(15.6)
Norway	-0.53	(0.03)	1.31	(0.01)	88.4	(1.0)	98.0	(0.4)	**26**	(12.5)	c	c	14	(8.4)	c	c
Poland	-1.34	(0.02)	0.75	(0.03)	75.7	(2.3)	90.1	(1.1)	m	m	m	m	m	m	m	m
Portugal	-1.83	(0.02)	1.16	(0.03)	89.4	(1.0)	98.5	(0.4)	-8	(10.4)	c	c	-4	(7.3)	c	c
Slovak Republic	-1.24	(0.04)	1.10	(0.02)	92.1	(0.9)	97.8	(0.5)	17	(12.0)	10	(21.6)	-17	(11.0)	-24	(17.1)
Slovenia	-1.04	(0.01)	1.07	(0.01)	77.9	(1.4)	92.0	(0.9)	-1	(9.3)	20	(13.1)	3	(8.0)	10	(10.0)
Spain	-2.05	(0.03)	1.03	(0.03)	98.1	(0.3)	99.8	(0.1)	c	c	c	c	c	c	c	c
Sweden	-0.78	(0.03)	1.27	(0.01)	91.5	(1.1)	98.4	(0.4)	**41**	(12.6)	c	c	-3	(8.8)	c	c
Switzerland	-1.05	(0.03)	1.30	(0.02)	97.9	(0.4)	99.0	(0.3)	m	m	m	m	m	m	m	m
Turkey	-2.87	(0.04)	0.14	(0.07)	33.9	(1.6)	75.0	(2.2)	-10	(6.1)	11	(6.9)	-3	(4.5)	0	(4.9)
United Kingdom	-0.92	(0.02)	1.27	(0.02)	97.2	(0.5)	99.3	(0.2)	4	(16.7)	c	c	-22	(14.4)	c	c
United States	-1.25	(0.06)	1.29	(0.02)	75.0	(1.8)	89.4	(1.0)	**-23**	(9.3)	-9	(12.1)	-13	(7.2)	**-15**	(6.5)
OECD average-32	-1.20	(0.00)	1.08	(0.00)	92.7	(0.2)	97.3	(0.1)	**9**	(3.3)	**14**	(6.1)	-3	(2.6)	-2	(5.0)
OECD average-35	-1.20	(0.00)	1.08	(0.00)	92.2	(0.2)	97.1	(0.1)	m	m	m	m	m	m	m	m
Partners																
Brazil	-2.43	(0.03)	0.57	(0.04)	96.1	(0.4)	98.4	(0.2)	-5	(9.4)	12	(12.4)	0	(9.1)	-4	(9.2)
B-S-J-G (China)	-2.36	(0.03)	0.47	(0.07)	64.9	(3.1)	96.0	(0.8)	**25**	(7.1)	**84**	(18.4)	2	(4.4)	3	(12.6)
Bulgaria	-1.37	(0.04)	1.14	(0.02)	93.1	(1.0)	94.4	(0.7)	4	(13.6)	**-26**	(12.1)	8	(9.0)	3	(8.5)
Colombia	-2.41	(0.04)	0.44	(0.05)	93.7	(1.0)	98.3	(0.4)	-17	(8.9)	-15	(20.3)	-13	(8.3)	-13	(13.9)
Costa Rica	-2.29	(0.03)	0.73	(0.03)	85.9	(1.2)	94.4	(0.6)	0	(7.3)	9	(11.4)	4	(6.7)	-6	(9.1)
Croatia	-1.22	(0.02)	0.89	(0.02)	68.1	(1.4)	90.7	(1.1)	-9	(5.7)	8	(10.9)	0	(4.6)	9	(8.1)
Cyprus*	-1.02	(0.01)	1.33	(0.01)	97.1	(0.6)	99.0	(0.3)	-7	(23.0)	c	c	-9	(20.2)	c	c
Dominican Republic	-2.23	(0.04)	0.46	(0.03)	94.2	(0.9)	98.3	(0.5)	m	m	m	m	m	m	m	m
Hong Kong (China)	-1.73	(0.02)	0.69	(0.03)	98.2	(0.4)	99.6	(0.2)	c	c	c	c	c	c	c	c
Lithuania	-1.24	(0.02)	0.97	(0.02)	62.4	(1.9)	87.2	(1.1)	**-14**	(5.8)	-6	(9.2)	-3	(4.2)	-3	(5.3)
Macao (China)	-1.59	(0.02)	0.60	(0.01)	99.1	(0.3)	99.7	(0.2)	c	c	c	c	c	c	c	c
Montenegro	-1.23	(0.01)	0.88	(0.01)	59.1	(1.4)	82.7	(1.1)	-3	(4.6)	0	(7.7)	2	(3.6)	2	(6.9)
Peru	-2.56	(0.03)	0.55	(0.05)	88.9	(1.3)	99.3	(0.2)	6	(6.8)	c	c	3	(6.5)	c	c
Qatar	-0.47	(0.01)	1.42	(0.01)	72.0	(1.0)	92.4	(0.5)	m	m	m	m	m	m	m	m
Russia	-0.95	(0.03)	0.95	(0.02)	76.5	(1.9)	91.3	(1.1)	**24**	(8.6)	5	(13.7)	**14**	(6.1)	7	(10.8)
Singapore	-1.22	(0.02)	1.09	(0.01)	98.2	(0.5)	99.7	(0.2)	c	c	c	c	c	c	c	c
Chinese Taipei	-1.28	(0.02)	0.84	(0.02)	96.9	(0.6)	98.7	(0.3)	**38**	(18.1)	c	c	16	(11.8)	c	c
Thailand	-2.53	(0.02)	0.29	(0.07)	99.4	(0.2)	99.8	(0.1)	c	c	c	c	c	c	c	c
Tunisia	-2.31	(0.04)	0.69	(0.04)	79.3	(1.9)	96.0	(0.7)	-2	(4.6)	-12	(12.1)	-1	(4.5)	-8	(9.5)
United Arab Emirates	-0.49	(0.03)	1.32	(0.01)	88.5	(0.7)	95.1	(0.5)	-3	(7.0)	7	(11.3)	6	(5.7)	8	(8.8)
Uruguay	-2.12	(0.02)	0.71	(0.04)	98.6	(0.4)	99.7	(0.2)	c	c	c	c	c	c	c	c
Malaysia**	-1.82	(0.04)	0.96	(0.04)	91.9	(1.4)	98.6	(0.3)	0	(10.0)	1	(19.0)	-2	(7.7)	-14	(12.5)

1. Relative performance refers to the residual performance, attributable to purely "collaborative problem-solving" competencies, after accounting for science, reading and mathematics performance in a regression performed across students at a national level. The years of attendance at pre-primary school was included as an explanatory variable in this regression.

Note: Values that are statistically significant are indicated in bold (see Annex A3).

* See note at the beginning of this Annex.

**Malaysia: Coverage is too small to ensure comparability (see Annex A4).

StatLink http://dx.doi.org/10.1787/888933616826

[Part 1/1]

Table V.6.14c Index of student interaction in science class and performance in collaborative problem solving

Results based on students' self-reports

		Index of student interaction in science class[1]				Change per unit increase in the index of student interaction in science class							
						Performance in collaborative problem solving				Relative performance in collaborative problem solving[3]			
		Average		Variability		Before accounting for gender, and students' and schools' socio-economic profile[2]		After accounting for gender, and students' and schools' socio-economic profile		Before accounting for gender, and students' and schools' socio-economic profile		After accounting for gender, and students' and schools' socio-economic profile	
		Mean index	S.E.	S.D.	S.E.	Score dif.	S.E.	Score dif.	S.E.	Score dif.	S.E.	Score dif.	S.E.
OECD	Australia	1.43	(0.02)	1.17	(0.01)	**-10**	(1.3)	**-9**	(1.2)	**-2**	(0.9)	-1	(0.9)
	Austria	1.36	(0.03)	1.26	(0.02)	**-7**	(1.6)	**-6**	(1.4)	**-2**	(1.0)	-1	(1.0)
	Belgium	1.24	(0.02)	1.09	(0.01)	**-9**	(1.4)	**-4**	(1.2)	-1	(0.9)	1	(0.9)
	Canada	1.61	(0.02)	1.27	(0.01)	**-15**	(1.2)	**-14**	(1.1)	**-4**	(1.0)	**-2**	(1.0)
	Chile	1.43	(0.03)	1.24	(0.01)	**-12**	(1.3)	**-10**	(1.3)	-2	(1.3)	-1	(1.4)
	Czech Republic	1.33	(0.02)	1.07	(0.01)	**-12**	(1.5)	**-9**	(1.3)	**-4**	(1.2)	**-3**	(1.2)
	Denmark	2.19	(0.03)	1.30	(0.01)	**5**	(1.5)	**4**	(1.4)	1	(1.2)	1	(1.2)
	Estonia	1.24	(0.02)	1.05	(0.02)	**-12**	(1.6)	**-11**	(1.6)	0	(1.1)	1	(1.2)
	Finland	1.20	(0.02)	1.03	(0.02)	**-9**	(1.8)	**-8**	(1.7)	-2	(1.2)	-1	(1.2)
	France	1.72	(0.02)	1.19	(0.01)	0	(1.5)	-2	(1.3)	-1	(1.1)	-1	(1.1)
	Germany	1.59	(0.02)	1.25	(0.01)	-1	(1.7)	-2	(1.5)	-1	(1.3)	0	(1.2)
	Greece	1.43	(0.03)	1.20	(0.02)	**-15**	(1.8)	**-11**	(1.5)	**-3**	(1.0)	-2	(1.0)
	Hungary	1.17	(0.02)	1.10	(0.01)	**-7**	(2.0)	**-5**	(1.8)	-1	(1.3)	0	(1.2)
	Iceland	1.37	(0.02)	1.15	(0.01)	**-5**	(1.9)	**-4**	(2.0)	-3	(1.6)	-2	(1.6)
	Ireland	1.29	(0.02)	1.14	(0.01)	m	m	m	m	m	m	m	m
	Israel	1.61	(0.03)	1.33	(0.01)	**-14**	(1.5)	**-11**	(1.4)	**-5**	(0.8)	**-5**	(0.8)
	Italy	1.41	(0.02)	1.09	(0.01)	**-11**	(1.5)	**-7**	(1.4)	**-3**	(1.2)	-2	(1.1)
	Japan	0.83	(0.03)	1.04	(0.02)	**-12**	(1.9)	**-10**	(1.7)	**-6**	(1.4)	**-4**	(1.3)
	Korea	0.79	(0.02)	1.15	(0.02)	**-15**	(1.5)	**-12**	(1.3)	**-3**	(1.1)	-2	(1.0)
	Latvia	1.32	(0.02)	1.12	(0.01)	**-11**	(1.5)	**-8**	(1.5)	-1	(1.3)	0	(1.2)
	Luxembourg	1.66	(0.02)	1.27	(0.01)	**-10**	(1.5)	**-7**	(1.3)	**-4**	(1.1)	**-3**	(1.0)
	Mexico	1.80	(0.03)	1.34	(0.01)	**-7**	(1.2)	**-7**	(1.1)	**-3**	(0.9)	**-3**	(0.9)
	Netherlands	1.15	(0.02)	1.20	(0.01)	**-9**	(1.7)	**-7**	(1.4)	0	(1.4)	0	(1.3)
	New Zealand	1.48	(0.03)	1.22	(0.01)	**-12**	(1.9)	**-11**	(1.8)	0	(1.6)	1	(1.5)
	Norway	1.42	(0.03)	1.23	(0.02)	**-9**	(1.3)	**-7**	(1.2)	**-3**	(1.0)	**-2**	(1.0)
	Poland	1.24	(0.03)	1.16	(0.01)	m	m	m	m	m	m	m	m
	Portugal	1.85	(0.03)	1.26	(0.01)	**-5**	(1.4)	**-5**	(1.3)	0	(1.0)	0	(0.9)
	Slovak Republic	1.22	(0.03)	1.14	(0.02)	**-13**	(1.5)	**-9**	(1.4)	0	(1.2)	0	(1.2)
	Slovenia	1.78	(0.03)	1.31	(0.02)	-3	(2.2)	-2	(2.0)	0	(2.0)	0	(2.0)
	Spain	1.14	(0.02)	1.00	(0.01)	**-10**	(1.5)	**-9**	(1.5)	**-3**	(1.2)	-2	(1.2)
	Sweden	1.80	(0.03)	1.35	(0.01)	**-5**	(1.7)	**-5**	(1.5)	-2	(1.2)	-1	(1.1)
	Switzerland	1.73	(0.03)	1.26	(0.01)	m	m	m	m	m	m	m	m
	Turkey	1.88	(0.03)	1.30	(0.01)	**-6**	(1.4)	**-4**	(1.2)	-1	(1.1)	0	(1.0)
	United Kingdom	1.24	(0.02)	1.05	(0.01)	**-13**	(1.5)	**-12**	(1.4)	**-4**	(1.0)	**-3**	(1.1)
	United States	1.72	(0.04)	1.34	(0.01)	**-12**	(1.4)	**-10**	(1.4)	-1	(0.9)	0	(0.9)
	OECD average-32	1.45	(0.00)	1.19	(0.00)	**-9**	(0.3)	**-7**	(0.3)	**-2**	(0.2)	**-1**	(0.2)
	OECD average-35	1.45	(0.00)	1.19	(0.00)	m	m	m	m	m	m	m	m
Partners	Brazil	1.18	(0.02)	1.28	(0.01)	**-13**	(1.0)	**-12**	(0.8)	**-3**	(0.7)	**-3**	(0.7)
	B-S-J-G (China)	1.08	(0.03)	1.11	(0.02)	2	(2.0)	**-6**	(1.6)	**-4**	(1.3)	**-5**	(1.3)
	Bulgaria	1.73	(0.03)	1.36	(0.01)	**-16**	(1.4)	**-10**	(1.0)	**-2**	(0.8)	**-2**	(0.8)
	Colombia	1.41	(0.03)	1.17	(0.01)	**-9**	(1.4)	**-10**	(1.3)	**-2**	(1.1)	**-3**	(1.1)
	Costa Rica	1.16	(0.02)	1.11	(0.01)	**-6**	(1.3)	**-7**	(1.2)	-1	(1.1)	-1	(1.0)
	Croatia	1.25	(0.02)	1.20	(0.01)	**-9**	(1.3)	**-6**	(1.1)	**-2**	(0.8)	-2	(0.8)
	Cyprus*	1.99	(0.02)	1.37	(0.01)	**-9**	(1.2)	**-6**	(1.2)	**-2**	(0.9)	-2	(0.9)
	Dominican Republic	2.24	(0.03)	1.13	(0.01)	m	m	m	m	m	m	m	m
	Hong Kong (China)	1.38	(0.03)	1.39	(0.02)	**-4**	(1.4)	**-3**	(1.3)	-1	(1.1)	-1	(1.1)
	Lithuania	1.60	(0.02)	1.21	(0.01)	**-9**	(1.3)	**-7**	(1.3)	**-2**	(1.1)	-2	(1.1)
	Macao (China)	0.94	(0.02)	1.08	(0.02)	**-5**	(1.8)	**-5**	(1.8)	-1	(1.4)	0	(1.3)
	Montenegro	1.45	(0.02)	1.35	(0.01)	**-15**	(1.1)	**-11**	(1.1)	**-5**	(0.9)	**-5**	(0.9)
	Peru	2.16	(0.03)	1.27	(0.01)	**-6**	(1.1)	**-5**	(0.9)	0	(0.8)	0	(0.8)
	Qatar	1.97	(0.02)	1.45	(0.01)	m	m	m	m	m	m	m	m
	Russia	1.97	(0.03)	1.36	(0.01)	**-8**	(1.3)	**-7**	(1.3)	**-3**	(1.0)	**-2**	(0.9)
	Singapore	1.29	(0.02)	1.14	(0.01)	**-7**	(1.5)	**-9**	(1.4)	**-4**	(1.2)	**-3**	(1.2)
	Chinese Taipei	0.93	(0.02)	1.09	(0.02)	**-5**	(1.4)	**-4**	(1.4)	0	(0.9)	0	(1.0)
	Thailand	1.15	(0.03)	1.38	(0.02)	**-3**	(1.1)	0	(0.9)	0	(0.7)	1	(0.7)
	Tunisia	2.05	(0.03)	1.35	(0.01)	**-8**	(0.8)	**-6**	(0.8)	**-3**	(0.7)	**-3**	(0.6)
	United Arab Emirates	1.91	(0.02)	1.41	(0.01)	**-12**	(1.0)	**-7**	(0.9)	-1	(0.7)	0	(0.7)
	Uruguay	1.27	(0.02)	1.17	(0.01)	**-15**	(1.5)	**-13**	(1.4)	**-6**	(1.2)	**-5**	(1.2)
	Malaysia**	1.50	(0.02)	1.24	(0.01)	**-4**	(1.4)	-2	(1.3)	-1	(1.0)	-1	(1.0)

1. The index of student interaction in science class is the sum of students' responses to questions about whether their science teachers carry out the following teaching practices: students are given opportunities to explain their ideas; students spend time in the laboratory carrying out practical experiments; students are required to argue about science questions; and there is a class debate about investigations. The index ranges from 0 to 4, with each response weighted equally.
2. The socio-economic profile is measured by the PISA index of economic, social and cultural status (ESCS).
3. Relative performance refers to the residual performance, attributable to purely "collaborative problem-solving" competencies, after accounting for science, reading and mathematics performance in a regression performed across students at a national level. The index of student interaction in science class was included as an explanatory variable in this regression.
Note: Values that are statistically significant are indicated in bold (see Annex A3).
* See note at the beginning of this Annex.
**Malaysia: Coverage is too small to ensure comparability (see Annex A4).
StatLink http://dx.doi.org/10.1787/888933616826

[Part 1/1]

Table V.7.1 Student-student relationships

		Percentage of students who reported the following:												Percentage of students in schools whose principal reported that students' learning is "not hindered at all" by students intimidating or bullying other students	
		"Agree" or "strongly agree" that "I make friends easily at school"		"Agree" or "strongly agree" that "other students seem to like me"		"Disagree" or "strongly disagree" that "I feel lonely at school"		Other students "never or almost never" make fun of me		I am "never or almost never" threatened by other students		I "never or almost never" get hit or pushed around by other students			
		%	S.E.	%	S.E.	%	S.E.	%	S.E.	%	S.E.	%	S.E.	%	S.E.
OECD	Australia	79.4	(0.5)	87.6	(0.3)	83.5	(0.4)	61.4	(0.5)	79.8	(0.5)	84.0	(0.4)	11.9	(1.6)
	Austria	77.9	(0.6)	83.8	(0.5)	84.6	(0.5)	64.5	(0.7)	92.1	(0.5)	89.0	(0.6)	18.4	(2.9)
	Belgium	81.8	(0.4)	88.2	(0.5)	90.5	(0.4)	66.4	(0.6)	91.0	(0.3)	89.5	(0.4)	13.6	(2.2)
	Canada	78.3	(0.5)	87.3	(0.4)	81.6	(0.4)	63.0	(0.5)	85.3	(0.4)	84.7	(0.4)	13.8	(1.9)
	Chile	73.2	(0.6)	76.0	(0.6)	83.1	(0.6)	70.6	(0.6)	90.2	(0.5)	90.0	(0.4)	21.0	(2.8)
	Czech Republic	75.3	(0.7)	81.2	(0.6)	81.9	(0.6)	71.1	(0.8)	89.6	(0.5)	81.2	(0.6)	28.0	(2.7)
	Denmark	79.2	(0.5)	85.4	(0.6)	87.1	(0.5)	67.4	(0.7)	92.6	(0.4)	87.3	(0.5)	27.8	(3.2)
	Estonia	76.0	(0.7)	76.5	(0.7)	85.3	(0.6)	62.1	(0.7)	90.0	(0.5)	86.0	(0.6)	15.5	(1.8)
	Finland	79.8	(0.5)	82.0	(0.5)	88.2	(0.5)	68.9	(0.8)	88.6	(0.5)	86.5	(0.6)	4.7	(1.5)
	France	86.3	(0.5)	89.7	(0.4)	90.6	(0.4)	69.2	(0.6)	91.5	(0.4)	91.3	(0.5)	29.2	(3.1)
	Germany	73.3	(0.7)	85.0	(0.5)	87.3	(0.5)	66.5	(0.8)	94.1	(0.4)	94.2	(0.4)	7.2	(1.7)
	Greece	80.2	(0.5)	87.4	(0.5)	88.0	(0.5)	71.8	(0.8)	93.3	(0.6)	89.9	(0.6)	50.5	(4.0)
	Hungary	81.1	(0.6)	82.7	(0.7)	85.5	(0.5)	75.3	(0.7)	91.6	(0.5)	90.5	(0.5)	56.7	(3.2)
	Iceland	76.1	(0.7)	82.9	(0.6)	83.6	(0.6)	77.8	(0.8)	90.0	(0.5)	92.5	(0.5)	16.1	(0.2)
	Ireland	81.1	(0.5)	90.5	(0.5)	87.8	(0.5)	71.2	(0.7)	88.7	(0.5)	89.7	(0.5)	13.0	(3.0)
	Israel	m	m	m	m	m	m	m	m	m	m	m	m	57.6	(3.4)
	Italy	83.0	(0.5)	76.6	(0.6)	89.5	(0.5)	m	m	m	m	m	m	40.5	(4.0)
	Japan	68.8	(0.7)	73.8	(0.6)	88.5	(0.5)	67.2	(0.7)	93.5	(0.4)	81.5	(0.6)	27.8	(2.8)
	Korea	79.3	(0.6)	81.9	(0.6)	91.7	(0.4)	80.6	(0.7)	97.1	(0.2)	98.0	(0.2)	25.7	(3.3)
	Latvia	75.7	(0.7)	68.2	(0.7)	82.8	(0.6)	58.9	(0.8)	80.8	(0.6)	74.4	(0.7)	40.0	(3.1)
	Luxembourg	75.9	(0.6)	81.3	(0.6)	85.1	(0.4)	73.2	(0.6)	91.1	(0.4)	91.5	(0.3)	19.3	(0.1)
	Mexico	72.7	(0.5)	72.0	(0.7)	79.3	(0.5)	66.0	(0.6)	89.4	(0.4)	84.9	(0.5)	25.8	(2.6)
	Netherlands	85.2	(0.5)	91.9	(0.5)	92.4	(0.4)	80.7	(0.6)	94.7	(0.4)	93.7	(0.4)	0.0	(0.0)
	New Zealand	78.9	(0.6)	88.2	(0.5)	83.1	(0.7)	57.6	(0.7)	78.4	(0.6)	81.9	(0.6)	13.5	(2.2)
	Norway	80.0	(0.5)	83.0	(0.6)	85.6	(0.5)	74.6	(0.7)	89.2	(0.5)	87.2	(0.5)	5.1	(1.6)
	Poland	73.5	(0.7)	73.3	(0.7)	79.8	(0.7)	67.8	(0.8)	90.0	(0.5)	89.5	(0.5)	30.4	(3.6)
	Portugal	77.8	(0.6)	87.6	(0.5)	88.8	(0.5)	80.4	(0.6)	88.2	(0.5)	93.0	(0.4)	31.3	(3.9)
	Slovak Republic	77.0	(0.5)	76.7	(0.6)	80.6	(0.6)	71.9	(0.8)	88.1	(0.5)	88.4	(0.6)	42.7	(3.5)
	Slovenia	76.8	(0.8)	78.5	(0.6)	85.4	(0.6)	73.4	(0.7)	92.0	(0.4)	86.5	(0.5)	47.3	(0.4)
	Spain	83.2	(0.5)	86.0	(0.6)	90.7	(0.4)	73.9	(0.6)	92.2	(0.4)	90.3	(0.5)	24.9	(3.3)
	Sweden	74.9	(0.6)	78.4	(0.6)	81.0	(0.6)	70.9	(0.9)	88.2	(0.6)	83.2	(0.6)	17.7	(2.8)
	Switzerland	80.6	(0.6)	87.5	(0.5)	90.1	(0.4)	63.4	(0.8)	92.3	(0.5)	90.9	(0.5)	17.5	(2.7)
	Turkey	62.3	(0.8)	63.6	(0.8)	65.0	(0.8)	80.2	(0.8)	86.6	(0.6)	90.1	(0.5)	37.2	(4.1)
	United Kingdom	78.7	(0.6)	87.7	(0.5)	86.4	(0.4)	62.3	(0.7)	81.8	(0.6)	85.3	(0.5)	20.7	(3.0)
	United States	78.6	(0.6)	88.7	(0.5)	81.8	(0.6)	68.8	(0.9)	85.4	(0.6)	89.2	(0.5)	12.9	(2.5)
	OECD average-32	77.6	(0.1)	81.9	(0.1)	85.1	(0.1)	69.9	(0.1)	89.2	(0.1)	87.9	(0.1)	25.1	(0.5)
	OECD average-35	77.7	(0.1)	82.1	(0.1)	85.2	(0.1)	69.7	(0.1)	89.3	(0.1)	88.1	(0.1)	24.7	(0.5)
Partners	Brazil	73.9	(0.5)	81.0	(0.4)	80.1	(0.4)	75.5	(0.5)	88.6	(0.3)	91.7	(0.3)	39.9	(2.4)
	B-S-J-G (China)	78.2	(0.5)	59.6	(0.7)	78.5	(0.6)	69.2	(0.9)	89.6	(0.5)	89.3	(0.5)	27.7	(3.2)
	Bulgaria	74.9	(0.6)	71.9	(0.7)	75.1	(0.8)	69.1	(0.8)	84.2	(0.7)	76.6	(0.8)	41.7	(3.8)
	Colombia	70.3	(0.6)	68.7	(0.5)	74.9	(0.6)	68.2	(0.7)	91.1	(0.4)	87.3	(0.4)	25.9	(2.8)
	Costa Rica	71.7	(0.7)	72.2	(0.7)	77.4	(0.5)	69.8	(0.6)	86.1	(0.5)	91.4	(0.4)	15.0	(2.7)
	Croatia	83.8	(0.5)	81.6	(0.6)	87.6	(0.5)	75.8	(0.7)	88.8	(0.6)	89.0	(0.5)	30.5	(3.7)
	Cyprus*	80.6	(0.5)	85.4	(0.5)	86.5	(0.4)	69.0	(0.6)	85.3	(0.4)	84.7	(0.5)	14.4	(0.1)
	Dominican Republic	66.1	(0.9)	66.2	(0.8)	69.1	(0.9)	71.0	(0.8)	82.5	(0.7)	90.8	(0.5)	17.1	(3.2)
	Hong Kong (China)	81.0	(0.7)	77.9	(0.7)	80.7	(0.7)	53.3	(1.0)	84.8	(0.6)	79.8	(0.7)	26.2	(4.2)
	Lithuania	64.5	(0.7)	62.6	(0.8)	69.0	(0.7)	74.3	(0.6)	86.4	(0.5)	87.3	(0.5)	23.4	(2.7)
	Macao (China)	76.1	(0.6)	65.9	(0.7)	80.0	(0.7)	55.5	(0.7)	83.3	(0.5)	88.4	(0.5)	37.1	(0.1)
	Montenegro	83.3	(0.5)	79.7	(0.5)	86.3	(0.4)	82.9	(0.5)	87.0	(0.4)	93.1	(0.4)	25.8	(0.3)
	Peru	75.9	(0.6)	77.2	(0.6)	82.5	(0.6)	77.8	(0.6)	92.8	(0.4)	88.5	(0.5)	36.0	(2.5)
	Qatar	77.8	(0.4)	82.9	(0.4)	80.5	(0.4)	63.7	(0.4)	79.9	(0.4)	78.9	(0.4)	65.0	(0.1)
	Russia	73.1	(0.7)	64.3	(0.7)	79.1	(0.6)	71.7	(1.1)	87.2	(0.8)	92.6	(0.6)	49.0	(3.8)
	Singapore	80.2	(0.6)	81.2	(0.5)	82.1	(0.6)	57.0	(0.6)	86.7	(0.4)	85.1	(0.4)	17.5	(1.0)
	Chinese Taipei	85.1	(0.4)	72.2	(0.5)	87.7	(0.4)	82.6	(0.5)	96.4	(0.2)	97.7	(0.2)	42.2	(3.5)
	Thailand	82.5	(0.5)	61.6	(0.8)	81.7	(0.7)	61.8	(0.8)	81.1	(0.8)	85.1	(0.8)	40.0	(4.0)
	Tunisia	83.4	(0.6)	80.3	(0.5)	85.0	(0.6)	65.9	(0.7)	73.2	(0.8)	75.5	(0.8)	16.3	(3.4)
	United Arab Emirates	79.8	(0.5)	79.1	(0.5)	82.6	(0.4)	62.9	(0.6)	80.9	(0.5)	80.6	(0.6)	51.1	(2.8)
	Uruguay	73.1	(0.6)	85.6	(0.5)	79.4	(0.6)	72.1	(0.6)	89.7	(0.4)	89.6	(0.4)	41.9	(2.8)
	Malaysia**	87.5	(0.6)	76.7	(0.7)	83.1	(0.6)	56.4	(0.9)	84.4	(0.8)	84.6	(0.6)	35.7	(3.4)

* See note at the beginning of this Annex.
**Malaysia: Coverage is too small to ensure comparability (see Annex A4).
StatLink http://dx.doi.org/10.1787/888933616845

[Part 1/2]

Table V.7.3 Student-student relationships and performance in collaborative problem solving

	After accounting for students' and schools' socio-economic profile[1]															
	Change in collaborative problem-solving score when students reported the following:															
	"Agree" or "strongly agree" that "I make friends easily at school"				"Agree" or "strongly agree" that "other students seem to like me"				"Disagree" or "strongly disagree" that "I feel lonely at school"				Other students "never or almost never" make fun of me			
	Student-level[2]		School-level[3]		Student-level		School-level		Student-level		School-level		Student-level		School-level	
	Score dif.	S.E.	Score dif.	S.E.	Score dif.	S.E.	Score dif.	S.E.	Score dif.	S.E.	Score dif.	S.E.	Score dif.	S.E.	Score dif.	S.E.
OECD																
Australia	**-12**	(3.2)	1	(1.4)	8	(4.7)	**5**	(2.1)	-3	(4.5)	3	(1.8)	2	(2.4)	**3**	(1.1)
Austria	4	(3.4)	**8**	(3.6)	**15**	(3.7)	**13**	(3.2)	**16**	(3.9)	**13**	(4.2)	**-8**	(3.2)	1	(2.8)
Belgium	**-18**	(2.9)	-3	(3.1)	-7	(3.8)	**12**	(3.2)	-2	(4.0)	**13**	(2.8)	**-7**	(2.0)	**5**	(2.3)
Canada	**-12**	(4.2)	-2	(2.0)	**22**	(4.8)	**7**	(2.4)	2	(4.1)	0	(2.0)	2	(2.3)	3	(1.5)
Chile	-1	(3.0)	1	(3.0)	**12**	(2.9)	4	(2.9)	**11**	(3.7)	4	(3.1)	1	(2.7)	2	(2.3)
Czech Republic	-1	(2.6)	0	(1.8)	**9**	(3.7)	**5**	(2.4)	7	(4.0)	**4**	(2.2)	2	(3.3)	3	(1.4)
Denmark	**-11**	(3.8)	1	(2.8)	**12**	(4.5)	4	(2.6)	2	(4.2)	0	(2.8)	-4	(3.0)	-1	(1.7)
Estonia	**-14**	(4.6)	**8**	(2.4)	**17**	(4.1)	**12**	(2.2)	3	(3.9)	**10**	(2.6)	-6	(3.1)	**5**	(2.0)
Finland	**-14**	(3.6)	-2	(3.1)	-3	(4.3)	5	(3.7)	1	(5.7)	3	(3.4)	0	(3.2)	1	(2.7)
France	**-12**	(4.6)	5	(3.1)	-1	(5.0)	**15**	(3.8)	-4	(4.8)	**7**	(3.6)	**-7**	(2.8)	**5**	(2.3)
Germany	**-12**	(3.2)	3	(3.0)	4	(4.7)	**14**	(3.7)	2	(4.8)	**13**	(3.1)	**-14**	(3.3)	0	(2.4)
Greece	-1	(3.9)	-1	(2.9)	**15**	(4.4)	**10**	(2.9)	**11**	(4.8)	3	(4.1)	2	(3.0)	**6**	(2.4)
Hungary	**-13**	(3.2)	1	(3.3)	-3	(3.4)	**7**	(3.0)	-3	(3.6)	6	(3.4)	-2	(3.0)	3	(2.2)
Iceland	-9	(5.0)	0	(1.9)	**13**	(5.8)	0	(2.4)	**14**	(5.7)	-4	(2.6)	5	(4.7)	-1	(1.9)
Ireland	m	m	m	m	m	m	m	m	m	m	m	m	m	m	m	m
Israel	m	m	m	m	m	m	m	m	m	m	m	m	m	m	m	m
Italy	-5	(4.1)	-7	(3.7)	**10**	(3.5)	1	(2.4)	**13**	(4.6)	5	(4.1)	m	m	m	m
Japan	-5	(2.9)	2	(3.5)	5	(2.7)	**12**	(2.4)	4	(3.9)	**14**	(3.8)	**-11**	(2.2)	-1	(2.3)
Korea	**-11**	(3.1)	-2	(2.7)	1	(2.9)	**8**	(3.7)	-2	(4.8)	1	(5.2)	**-13**	(3.1)	4	(2.8)
Latvia	**-12**	(3.6)	-2	(1.9)	4	(3.2)	1	(1.4)	0	(5.2)	2	(2.2)	0	(3.1)	1	(1.1)
Luxembourg	-3	(4.3)	**9**	(3.6)	**18**	(4.5)	**30**	(3.7)	**13**	(5.2)	**29**	(4.1)	1	(3.5)	**9**	(2.6)
Mexico	**8**	(2.9)	2	(2.1)	**9**	(2.4)	**7**	(2.0)	**15**	(2.9)	**10**	(2.4)	-4	(2.4)	**4**	(1.5)
Netherlands	-8	(4.6)	**9**	(4.2)	**16**	(4.9)	**23**	(5.5)	**18**	(4.7)	**24**	(6.6)	**-10**	(3.5)	3	(4.5)
New Zealand	**-9**	(4.0)	-2	(2.7)	**24**	(5.9)	0	(4.0)	9	(4.4)	**-6**	(2.7)	**8**	(3.6)	**5**	(1.9)
Norway	**-10**	(4.6)	3	(2.4)	**14**	(4.6)	4	(2.7)	6	(4.8)	3	(2.7)	1	(4.2)	4	(2.5)
Poland	m	m	m	m	m	m	m	m	m	m	m	m	m	m	m	m
Portugal	**-9**	(3.0)	1	(2.6)	**9**	(4.5)	**12**	(3.7)	**9**	(4.5)	7	(3.9)	2	(4.0)	**7**	(2.6)
Slovak Republic	-1	(3.0)	-1	(2.2)	3	(3.3)	1	(2.1)	**13**	(3.5)	4	(2.4)	-3	(2.8)	**5**	(1.7)
Slovenia	7	(4.0)	0	(2.0)	6	(3.3)	**6**	(1.9)	**13**	(4.4)	**8**	(2.8)	-2	(3.1)	**4**	(1.5)
Spain	1	(3.3)	3	(2.7)	**18**	(3.8)	3	(2.6)	**22**	(3.7)	7	(3.8)	2	(2.9)	2	(1.8)
Sweden	6	(3.9)	2	(2.6)	**22**	(3.7)	2	(2.8)	**16**	(3.7)	1	(2.7)	-5	(3.5)	1	(2.2)
Switzerland	m	m	m	m	m	m	m	m	m	m	m	m	m	m	m	m
Turkey	0	(2.5)	**12**	(3.0)	-2	(3.0)	**13**	(2.9)	2	(3.2)	**12**	(3.0)	2	(3.0)	3	(3.5)
United Kingdom	**-14**	(4.3)	3	(2.8)	1	(4.3)	5	(3.7)	**-11**	(4.7)	5	(3.2)	-5	(3.3)	0	(2.1)
United States	**-9**	(4.4)	-5	(3.5)	**14**	(6.0)	1	(3.9)	-8	(4.5)	0	(3.5)	2	(3.7)	0	(2.4)
OECD average	**-6**	(0.7)	**2**	(0.5)	**9**	(0.7)	**8**	(0.6)	**6**	(0.8)	**7**	(0.6)	**-2**	(0.6)	**3**	(0.4)
Partners																
Brazil	**-5**	(1.9)	2	(1.8)	**14**	(2.4)	**9**	(1.7)	**17**	(2.9)	**10**	(1.6)	3	(2.9)	3	(1.8)
B-S-J-G (China)	**-9**	(3.2)	4	(4.6)	-4	(2.9)	1	(3.2)	-1	(3.0)	4	(4.5)	**8**	(3.1)	7	(4.2)
Bulgaria	-2	(2.9)	-1	(3.0)	1	(2.6)	2	(2.3)	**9**	(3.8)	**8**	(2.7)	-1	(2.8)	4	(2.1)
Colombia	**8**	(2.4)	4	(2.2)	**16**	(2.5)	2	(2.3)	**13**	(2.5)	4	(2.0)	**-7**	(2.3)	0	(2.3)
Costa Rica	4	(3.1)	-1	(2.0)	**11**	(2.8)	3	(2.0)	**11**	(3.2)	-1	(2.7)	-6	(3.7)	-2	(2.0)
Croatia	-3	(3.5)	5	(4.1)	-2	(3.1)	**12**	(3.6)	**8**	(3.6)	**20**	(3.8)	-3	(3.0)	**10**	(3.0)
Cyprus*	1	(4.1)	**5**	(1.9)	**21**	(4.5)	**24**	(2.2)	**22**	(5.4)	**14**	(2.4)	7	(3.8)	**12**	(1.5)
Dominican Republic	m	m	m	m	m	m	m	m	m	m	m	m	m	m	m	m
Hong Kong (China)	5	(4.0)	**13**	(3.9)	**10**	(3.9)	**19**	(3.2)	**15**	(3.9)	7	(4.4)	2	(2.9)	6	(3.3)
Lithuania	**8**	(3.3)	2	(2.3)	**12**	(3.3)	3	(2.6)	**8**	(3.2)	**4**	(2.1)	**-9**	(2.7)	1	(1.8)
Macao (China)	**-8**	(3.9)	**19**	(3.0)	**13**	(3.8)	**7**	(1.9)	5	(4.4)	**19**	(2.7)	**10**	(3.6)	**19**	(1.2)
Montenegro	-1	(4.4)	7	(3.9)	**11**	(3.6)	**8**	(2.8)	**18**	(5.2)	**19**	(3.5)	-1	(3.3)	2	(2.2)
Peru	2	(3.3)	2	(1.7)	**11**	(3.6)	**5**	(2.0)	**17**	(2.9)	**8**	(2.1)	-4	(2.9)	-1	(1.6)
Qatar	m	m	m	m	m	m	m	m	m	m	m	m	m	m	m	m
Russia	**-15**	(3.6)	-2	(2.2)	0	(3.7)	-1	(2.4)	6	(3.5)	4	(2.7)	-4	(3.0)	1	(2.4)
Singapore	-6	(3.9)	1	(4.5)	**21**	(4.1)	5	(2.7)	3	(3.5)	**9**	(2.9)	**9**	(3.7)	**5**	(1.4)
Chinese Taipei	**-8**	(3.4)	0	(4.3)	0	(2.9)	0	(2.9)	**13**	(3.8)	3	(4.1)	0	(2.6)	5	(2.9)
Thailand	**11**	(3.6)	**9**	(3.2)	**7**	(2.5)	**7**	(2.3)	**18**	(3.1)	**11**	(2.8)	**10**	(2.5)	**8**	(2.0)
Tunisia	-5	(3.2)	2	(3.1)	1	(2.8)	-3	(2.8)	4	(3.0)	4	(2.3)	-2	(2.0)	-1	(2.0)
United Arab Emirates	-2	(3.0)	4	(3.6)	**13**	(3.0)	**20**	(2.5)	**14**	(3.0)	**18**	(2.7)	**7**	(2.4)	**6**	(2.1)
Uruguay	2	(3.5)	-1	(2.4)	**31**	(4.0)	**10**	(2.8)	**16**	(3.1)	**7**	(2.0)	**-10**	(2.9)	0	(2.0)
Malaysia**	5	(4.2)	5	(4.0)	**14**	(3.1)	1	(3.1)	**20**	(3.6)	**6**	(2.8)	**6**	(2.0)	-1	(1.9)

1. Socio-economic profile is measured by the PISA index of economic, social and cultural status (ESCS).
2. Student-level refers to the change in collaborative problem-solving score associated with students reporting the above.
3. School-level refers to the change in collaborative problem-solving score per 10 percentage-point increase in the number of schoolmates who reported the above.

Notes: Values that are statistically significant are indicated in bold (see Annex A3).
Questionnaire items that are measured at both the student and school levels are included in the same regression model.
* See note at the beginning of this Annex.
**Malaysia: Coverage is too small to ensure comparability (see Annex A4).

StatLink http://dx.doi.org/10.1787/888933616845

[Part 2/2]

Table V.7.3 Student-student relationships and performance in collaborative problem solving

		After accounting for students' and schools' socio-economic profile[1]									
		Change in collaborative problem-solving score when students reported the following:								Change in collaborative problem-solving score when principals reported that students' learning is not hindered "at all" by students intimidating or bullying other students	
		I am "never or almost never" threatened by other students				I "never or almost never" get hit or pushed around by other students					
		Student-level[2]		School-level[3]		Student-level		School-level			
		Score dif.	S.E.	Score dif.	S.E.	Score dif.	S.E.	Score dif.	S.E.	Score dif.	S.E.
OECD	Australia	**23**	(3.5)	**5**	(1.3)	**22**	(3.9)	**7**	(1.4)	12	(6.4)
	Austria	**14**	(5.7)	**17**	(4.1)	9	(5.4)	**19**	(2.8)	4	(7.6)
	Belgium	**10**	(4.6)	**21**	(2.8)	**9**	(3.6)	**15**	(3.3)	**-18**	(8.4)
	Canada	**29**	(3.9)	**6**	(2.0)	**22**	(3.5)	4	(2.6)	-1	(5.7)
	Chile	**16**	(4.9)	**11**	(3.0)	**13**	(5.3)	**10**	(2.9)	5	(6.5)
	Czech Republic	**25**	(4.5)	**11**	(2.1)	**15**	(3.8)	**4**	(1.9)	**11**	(4.6)
	Denmark	**28**	(6.4)	3	(3.5)	**17**	(4.7)	4	(2.1)	-1	(5.5)
	Estonia	**24**	(5.0)	**13**	(3.1)	**11**	(4.6)	2	(3.0)	-5	(6.0)
	Finland	**24**	(5.3)	6	(3.9)	**25**	(4.8)	5	(3.2)	9	(12.2)
	France	4	(4.6)	**17**	(3.3)	0	(4.8)	**15**	(2.8)	8	(6.2)
	Germany	4	(7.7)	**17**	(4.0)	**19**	(7.0)	**17**	(4.4)	13	(15.4)
	Greece	**36**	(5.7)	**20**	(4.1)	**15**	(5.0)	**13**	(3.1)	**14**	(5.5)
	Hungary	7	(6.1)	**10**	(3.8)	8	(4.5)	**12**	(3.2)	**11**	(5.6)
	Iceland	**16**	(6.9)	0	(2.2)	**17**	(7.1)	4	(3.0)	**10**	(5.1)
	Ireland	m	m	m	m	m	m	m	m	m	m
	Israel	m	m	m	m	m	m	m	m	10	(8.2)
	Italy	m	m	m	m	m	m	m	m	7	(7.4)
	Japan	**12**	(5.0)	**15**	(4.7)	-5	(3.2)	**7**	(2.9)	6	(5.7)
	Korea	-1	(8.7)	**22**	(7.7)	1	(10.7)	**24**	(8.3)	**19**	(4.3)
	Latvia	**16**	(4.3)	**4**	(1.9)	**9**	(3.9)	1	(1.3)	1	(4.2)
	Luxembourg	**40**	(5.7)	**27**	(4.9)	**39**	(5.3)	**20**	(4.1)	7	(3.9)
	Mexico	6	(4.0)	**9**	(2.4)	2	(3.4)	**9**	(2.2)	1	(4.9)
	Netherlands	8	(6.8)	**27**	(6.3)	8	(6.7)	**28**	(6.3)	c	c
	New Zealand	**28**	(5.0)	**9**	(2.3)	**22**	(5.5)	**9**	(2.0)	-9	(6.8)
	Norway	**31**	(5.4)	**8**	(3.0)	**28**	(4.1)	**8**	(3.3)	-5	(17.0)
	Poland	m	m	m	m	m	m	m	m	m	m
	Portugal	**22**	(4.2)	**11**	(3.1)	**32**	(5.5)	**15**	(3.9)	4	(5.8)
	Slovak Republic	**15**	(4.1)	**9**	(2.3)	2	(4.2)	**9**	(2.2)	**12**	(4.8)
	Slovenia	**17**	(5.1)	**11**	(2.1)	8	(4.4)	**12**	(1.4)	**19**	(3.0)
	Spain	**30**	(5.6)	**9**	(3.7)	**26**	(4.5)	6	(3.1)	-3	(5.1)
	Sweden	**19**	(5.8)	3	(2.8)	**15**	(4.6)	4	(2.7)	7	(7.8)
	Switzerland	m	m	m	m	m	m	m	m	m	m
	Turkey	6	(4.1)	**16**	(3.0)	**12**	(4.3)	**20**	(4.1)	**24**	(6.9)
	United Kingdom	**11**	(4.6)	**5**	(2.5)	8	(5.0)	**6**	(3.3)	10	(7.0)
	United States	**33**	(4.3)	3	(3.8)	**25**	(5.3)	6	(4.2)	3	(9.1)
	OECD average	**18**	(1.0)	**11**	(0.7)	**14**	(0.9)	**11**	(0.6)	**6**	(1.3)
Partners	Brazil	**14**	(4.2)	**11**	(2.0)	**21**	(3.8)	**12**	(2.4)	1	(4.9)
	B-S-J-G (China)	**22**	(4.4)	**20**	(5.2)	**17**	(5.4)	**19**	(5.4)	8	(6.0)
	Bulgaria	**12**	(4.3)	**12**	(2.3)	6	(3.0)	**11**	(2.6)	3	(4.8)
	Colombia	**13**	(3.7)	6	(3.7)	**8**	(3.3)	**7**	(3.3)	-2	(5.5)
	Costa Rica	2	(4.0)	2	(3.0)	5	(4.9)	7	(3.7)	0	(5.7)
	Croatia	**13**	(4.5)	**22**	(3.4)	7	(4.4)	**19**	(3.3)	11	(6.9)
	Cyprus*	**34**	(3.5)	**21**	(1.8)	**26**	(4.1)	**20**	(1.8)	**8**	(4.2)
	Dominican Republic	m	m	m	m	m	m	m	m	m	m
	Hong Kong (China)	**25**	(4.4)	**21**	(3.3)	**13**	(4.1)	**18**	(3.4)	**24**	(8.6)
	Lithuania	**12**	(3.5)	**11**	(2.6)	6	(4.4)	**11**	(3.0)	**19**	(5.0)
	Macao (China)	**30**	(3.9)	**28**	(1.3)	**28**	(5.7)	**36**	(1.8)	**27**	(3.2)
	Montenegro	**14**	(3.6)	**7**	(2.1)	**21**	(5.0)	**9**	(4.2)	**13**	(3.4)
	Peru	**17**	(4.7)	**7**	(2.1)	**9**	(3.4)	3	(2.2)	0	(3.6)
	Qatar	m	m	m	m	m	m	m	m	m	m
	Russia	10	(5.3)	1	(4.0)	**21**	(6.6)	7	(6.3)	5	(4.6)
	Singapore	**34**	(4.6)	**10**	(1.9)	**26**	(4.3)	**7**	(1.8)	2	(5.1)
	Chinese Taipei	**27**	(5.5)	7	(5.9)	**20**	(8.6)	13	(8.4)	1	(5.3)
	Thailand	**20**	(3.7)	**11**	(2.5)	**31**	(3.6)	**13**	(2.2)	-3	(6.3)
	Tunisia	4	(2.6)	**5**	(2.1)	4	(3.1)	**6**	(1.9)	11	(6.7)
	United Arab Emirates	**24**	(2.6)	**18**	(1.8)	**23**	(2.6)	**15**	(1.3)	1	(5.3)
	Uruguay	**11**	(3.7)	**10**	(2.9)	9	(4.5)	**9**	(2.6)	**14**	(4.4)
	Malaysia**	**32**	(2.8)	4	(2.7)	**24**	(3.3)	**6**	(2.8)	6	(4.3)

1. Socio-economic profile is measured by the PISA index of economic, social and cultural status (ESCS).
2. Student-level refers to the change in collaborative problem-solving score associated with students reporting the above.
3. School-level refers to the change in collaborative problem-solving score per 10 percentage-point increase in the number of schoolmates who reported the above.
Notes: Values that are statistically significant are indicated in bold (see Annex A3).
Questionnaire items that are measured at both the student and school levels are included in the same regression model.
* See note at the beginning of this Annex.
**Malaysia: Coverage is too small to ensure comparability (see Annex A4).
StatLink http://dx.doi.org/10.1787/888933616845

[Part 1/2]

Table V.7.4 Student-student relationships and relative performance in collaborative problem solving

		After accounting for performance in science, reading and mathematics															
		Change in collaborative problem-solving score when students reported the following:															
		"Agree" or "strongly agree" that "I make friends easily at school"				"Agree" or "strongly agree" that "other students seem to like me"				"Disagree" or "strongly disagree" that "I feel lonely at school"				Other students "never or almost never" make fun of me			
		Student-level[1]		School-level[2]		Student-level		School-level		Student-level		School-level		Student-level		School-level	
		Score dif.	S.E.	Score dif.	S.E.	Score dif.	S.E.	Score dif.	S.E.	Score dif.	S.E.	Score dif.	S.E.	Score dif.	S.E.	Score dif.	S.E.
OECD	Australia	-4	(2.9)	0	(1.1)	-6	(3.8)	0	(1.4)	**-8**	(4.2)	1	(1.3)	-3	(2.2)	1	(0.9)
	Austria	4	(2.9)	3	(2.0)	**6**	(3.1)	**4**	(1.8)	7	(3.0)	**4**	(2.3)	1	(2.4)	**3**	(1.6)
	Belgium	**-6**	(2.3)	-3	(2.1)	**-6**	(3.2)	3	(2.0)	**-8**	(3.1)	2	(2.0)	-2	(1.7)	1	(1.5)
	Canada	-7	(4.0)	**-4**	(1.5)	6	(4.4)	-1	(1.7)	-4	(3.3)	-3	(1.4)	-3	(2.2)	-1	(1.3)
	Chile	1	(2.5)	-2	(1.8)	1	(2.2)	0	(1.4)	2	(3.6)	-2	(1.9)	**5**	(2.3)	2	(1.7)
	Czech Republic	**5**	(2.3)	0	(1.4)	4	(3.2)	1	(1.3)	2	(3.4)	1	(1.4)	4	(3.3)	1	(0.9)
	Denmark	**-7**	(2.8)	1	(1.6)	-3	(4.2)	0	(1.6)	**-9**	(3.1)	0	(1.8)	-2	(2.6)	-1	(1.4)
	Estonia	-2	(3.9)	**3**	(1.3)	6	(3.5)	**5**	(1.3)	-2	(3.1)	**3**	(1.7)	1	(2.7)	2	(1.2)
	Finland	-2	(3.0)	2	(2.4)	-4	(3.0)	2	(2.5)	-8	(3.9)	3	(3.2)	1	(2.7)	0	(1.9)
	France	-6	(4.0)	-1	(1.8)	-4	(3.6)	1	(2.0)	**-9**	(4.1)	1	(2.0)	-2	(2.6)	2	(1.2)
	Germany	**-5**	(2.4)	0	(1.9)	-3	(3.8)	2	(2.2)	-5	(3.6)	4	(2.1)	**-7**	(2.8)	0	(1.6)
	Greece	3	(3.1)	1	(1.5)	3	(3.2)	3	(1.5)	3	(4.2)	-2	(2.5)	3	(2.3)	1	(1.3)
	Hungary	**-8**	(2.6)	0	(1.8)	**-7**	(2.9)	1	(1.3)	**-7**	(3.1)	2	(1.7)	-2	(2.6)	2	(1.2)
	Iceland	**-11**	(3.7)	-1	(1.5)	-7	(4.2)	-2	(1.7)	-4	(4.0)	-2	(1.7)	0	(3.3)	1	(1.4)
	Ireland	m	m	m	m	m	m	m	m	m	m	m	m	m	m	m	m
	Israel	m	m	m	m	m	m	m	m	m	m	m	m	m	m	m	m
	Italy	1	(4.2)	**-5**	(2.5)	5	(3.3)	-3	(1.6)	5	(3.7)	0	(2.6)	m	m	m	m
	Japan	1	(3.0)	-1	(1.9)	1	(2.6)	-1	(1.6)	-3	(3.1)	-1	(2.4)	**-4**	(1.8)	0	(1.4)
	Korea	-2	(2.7)	-2	(1.8)	-1	(2.3)	-1	(1.9)	0	(3.1)	-1	(2.9)	2	(2.5)	1	(1.5)
	Latvia	-1	(2.7)	-1	(1.2)	0	(2.6)	0	(1.2)	-5	(4.2)	0	(1.4)	-2	(2.4)	1	(0.8)
	Luxembourg	-4	(3.4)	3	(2.8)	0	(4.4)	**8**	(2.2)	-2	(4.5)	**12**	(3.4)	-2	(2.9)	1	(2.1)
	Mexico	3	(2.7)	**3**	(1.3)	-1	(2.3)	**4**	(1.2)	4	(2.5)	**5**	(1.3)	0	(1.9)	1	(1.0)
	Netherlands	-1	(4.5)	**7**	(2.3)	4	(5.0)	5	(2.8)	7	(4.9)	3	(3.4)	-5	(3.1)	5	(2.5)
	New Zealand	-1	(3.0)	-1	(1.8)	4	(3.9)	-1	(2.4)	3	(3.8)	**-3**	(1.5)	1	(2.8)	**4**	(1.4)
	Norway	**-11**	(3.9)	-1	(2.0)	-4	(3.6)	1	(1.9)	-8	(4.2)	0	(2.1)	-3	(3.4)	2	(2.0)
	Poland	m	m	m	m	m	m	m	m	m	m	m	m	m	m	m	m
	Portugal	-4	(2.6)	0	(1.8)	2	(3.3)	3	(2.3)	0	(3.5)	-2	(2.6)	-2	(3.4)	-1	(2.0)
	Slovak Republic	-2	(2.8)	-1	(1.3)	-1	(3.3)	0	(1.2)	4	(3.0)	1	(1.5)	**-6**	(2.2)	0	(1.1)
	Slovenia	**7**	(3.4)	1	(1.3)	0	(3.0)	2	(1.2)	4	(3.6)	3	(2.0)	2	(2.7)	0	(1.0)
	Spain	**8**	(2.6)	0	(1.8)	**10**	(3.2)	1	(1.6)	**9**	(3.0)	3	(2.7)	**6**	(2.4)	2	(1.5)
	Sweden	2	(3.5)	0	(1.6)	4	(3.6)	-1	(2.0)	3	(3.0)	0	(1.7)	-4	(2.7)	1	(1.4)
	Switzerland	m	m	m	m	m	m	m	m	m	m	m	m	m	m	m	m
	Turkey	0	(2.3)	1	(1.6)	-2	(2.9)	**4**	(1.7)	2	(3.0)	**4**	(1.6)	3	(2.9)	2	(1.9)
	United Kingdom	-5	(3.2)	1	(1.8)	-6	(4.3)	1	(2.7)	**-10**	(3.1)	3	(2.6)	-4	(2.5)	0	(1.5)
	United States	-3	(3.1)	0	(2.2)	-2	(3.6)	0	(2.6)	**-11**	(3.6)	1	(2.2)	-1	(2.6)	2	(2.3)
	OECD average	**-2**	(0.6)	0	(0.3)	0	(0.6)	**1**	(0.3)	**-2**	(0.6)	**1**	(0.4)	-1	(0.5)	**1**	(0.3)
Partners	Brazil	-2	(1.8)	-1	(1.2)	3	(2.1)	1	(1.4)	5	(2.7)	1	(1.5)	1	(2.8)	0	(1.4)
	B-S-J-G (China)	**-6**	(3.0)	2	(2.3)	-3	(2.6)	0	(1.7)	-3	(2.5)	0	(2.1)	**7**	(2.6)	1	(2.3)
	Bulgaria	-1	(2.4)	1	(1.7)	-4	(2.2)	2	(1.5)	-1	(3.1)	**3**	(1.6)	-1	(2.3)	1	(1.4)
	Colombia	2	(2.2)	-1	(1.6)	3	(2.6)	2	(1.4)	**4**	(2.0)	1	(1.2)	-3	(2.1)	0	(1.4)
	Costa Rica	3	(2.2)	-1	(1.5)	**6**	(2.4)	0	(1.7)	**6**	(2.4)	0	(1.9)	3	(3.7)	0	(1.7)
	Croatia	-2	(2.9)	-1	(2.2)	-5	(2.6)	3	(2.1)	2	(3.0)	**5**	(2.4)	2	(2.4)	1	(1.8)
	Cyprus*	2	(3.3)	0	(1.7)	6	(3.5)	**4**	(1.9)	6	(4.1)	0	(2.2)	2	(3.0)	2	(1.3)
	Dominican Republic	m	m	m	m	m	m	m	m	m	m	m	m	m	m	m	m
	Hong Kong (China)	**11**	(3.0)	**4**	(1.7)	**8**	(2.9)	4	(2.1)	**9**	(2.9)	2	(2.2)	2	(2.2)	**5**	(1.7)
	Lithuania	5	(3.0)	2	(1.1)	**7**	(3.0)	2	(1.3)	2	(3.0)	2	(1.1)	-4	(2.4)	0	(1.2)
	Macao (China)	1	(2.7)	1	(2.4)	5	(2.8)	-1	(1.6)	2	(3.3)	3	(2.5)	5	(2.9)	**4**	(1.2)
	Montenegro	-1	(4.0)	-2	(2.8)	4	(3.7)	1	(2.0)	7	(5.0)	3	(2.5)	0	(3.1)	-3	(1.5)
	Peru	-3	(3.3)	1	(1.2)	-2	(3.5)	**3**	(1.3)	0	(2.4)	**4**	(1.5)	-1	(2.3)	1	(1.3)
	Qatar	m	m	m	m	m	m	m	m	m	m	m	m	m	m	m	m
	Russia	-3	(2.9)	**-5**	(2.1)	0	(2.8)	-1	(2.1)	2	(3.5)	0	(2.3)	3	(2.6)	-3	(1.7)
	Singapore	-2	(3.3)	-3	(1.8)	3	(2.5)	-1	(1.5)	-3	(2.9)	-1	(1.5)	4	(3.1)	**2**	(1.0)
	Chinese Taipei	0	(3.1)	-3	(2.7)	2	(2.7)	-2	(2.3)	5	(2.9)	-1	(2.8)	**5**	(2.1)	3	(2.1)
	Thailand	5	(3.8)	**5**	(2.1)	2	(1.7)	2	(1.7)	3	(2.4)	3	(1.8)	2	(2.2)	**5**	(1.8)
	Tunisia	-4	(3.2)	1	(2.3)	-1	(3.1)	-4	(1.9)	1	(3.1)	-1	(1.9)	1	(2.0)	**-4**	(1.3)
	United Arab Emirates	-3	(2.8)	-2	(1.9)	0	(2.3)	3	(1.4)	-1	(2.8)	2	(1.4)	2	(2.1)	**2**	(1.1)
	Uruguay	2	(2.8)	0	(1.6)	**11**	(3.5)	2	(1.7)	**7**	(2.4)	2	(1.7)	**-6**	(2.1)	0	(1.7)
	Malaysia**	**11**	(4.1)	-2	(2.1)	4	(2.2)	-2	(2.4)	4	(3.2)	-1	(2.0)	2	(1.4)	**-3**	(1.5)

1. Student-level refers to the change in collaborative problem-solving score associated with students reporting the above.
2. School-level refers to the change in collaborative problem-solving score per 10 percentage-point increase in the number of schoolmates who reported the above.
Notes: Values that are statistically significant are indicated in bold (see Annex A3).
Questionnaire items that are measured at both the student and school levels are included in the same regression model.
* See note at the beginning of this Annex.
**Malaysia: Coverage is too small to ensure comparability (see Annex A4).

StatLink http://dx.doi.org/10.1787/888933616845

[Part 2/2]

Table V.7.4 Student-student relationships and relative performance in collaborative problem solving

	After accounting for performance in science, reading and mathematics									
	Change in collaborative problem-solving score when students reported the following:								Change in collaborative problem-solving score when principals reported that students' learning is not hindered "at all" by students intimidating or bullying other students	
	I am "never or almost never" threatened by other students				I "never or almost never" get hit or pushed around by other students					
	Student-level[1]		School-level[2]		Student-level		School-level			
	Score dif.	S.E.	Score dif.	S.E.	Score dif.	S.E.	Score dif.	S.E.	Score dif.	S.E.
OECD										
Australia	2	(2.8)	0	(1.0)	6	(3.3)	1	(1.1)	1	(3.3)
Austria	-1	(5.1)	**5**	(2.3)	3	(4.6)	**9**	(1.9)	-2	(5.5)
Belgium	-4	(4.0)	**4**	(2.0)	1	(3.4)	**5**	(2.0)	-8	(4.5)
Canada	2	(3.2)	-3	(1.7)	**6**	(3.0)	-2	(1.8)	-9	(5.3)
Chile	3	(4.3)	-2	(2.0)	0	(4.0)	-2	(2.0)	3	(4.2)
Czech Republic	**16**	(4.2)	2	(1.6)	**12**	(3.8)	2	(1.2)	3	(3.2)
Denmark	4	(4.7)	0	(2.3)	6	(3.7)	1	(1.5)	0	(3.6)
Estonia	**10**	(3.5)	1	(1.7)	6	(3.2)	1	(1.7)	-7	(3.9)
Finland	2	(4.3)	-2	(3.0)	7	(4.0)	-2	(2.3)	0	(8.5)
France	-4	(3.9)	3	(2.1)	-5	(3.9)	2	(1.9)	-2	(3.6)
Germany	-6	(6.2)	2	(2.9)	0	(5.0)	3	(3.4)	1	(8.6)
Greece	**11**	(4.9)	2	(2.2)	6	(4.0)	2	(1.8)	-1	(2.9)
Hungary	-1	(5.9)	2	(1.8)	2	(3.9)	3	(1.8)	3	(2.5)
Iceland	-4	(4.6)	0	(1.4)	-4	(5.4)	-2	(2.0)	3	(3.4)
Ireland	m	m	m	m	m	m	m	m	m	m
Israel	m	m	m	m	m	m	m	m	-2	(4.4)
Italy	m	m	m	m	m	m	m	m	8	(4.8)
Japan	4	(4.7)	2	(2.8)	-2	(3.2)	3	(1.6)	1	(3.5)
Korea	-3	(7.4)	8	(4.4)	-12	(8.6)	5	(5.3)	3	(3.1)
Latvia	-1	(3.1)	0	(1.2)	-3	(3.1)	-1	(0.9)	-1	(2.7)
Luxembourg	2	(4.2)	**9**	(3.2)	2	(4.8)	**8**	(3.0)	**7**	(3.2)
Mexico	-3	(3.7)	**3**	(1.5)	-2	(3.1)	**3**	(1.3)	-1	(2.9)
Netherlands	-5	(5.5)	1	(4.1)	-1	(4.8)	4	(4.2)	c	c
New Zealand	5	(3.4)	**3**	(1.6)	5	(3.8)	**3**	(1.5)	-8	(5.5)
Norway	5	(4.0)	4	(2.2)	**9**	(3.3)	2	(2.5)	-6	(10.2)
Poland	m	m	m	m	m	m	m	m	m	m
Portugal	5	(3.6)	-2	(2.8)	**11**	(4.9)	-1	(3.3)	-5	(3.2)
Slovak Republic	-5	(3.1)	0	(1.3)	**-15**	(3.6)	0	(1.3)	1	(3.5)
Slovenia	5	(3.8)	3	(1.7)	4	(3.5)	**4**	(1.3)	5	(3.1)
Spain	**15**	(4.6)	4	(3.0)	**17**	(3.3)	3	(2.3)	-2	(3.2)
Sweden	-2	(5.2)	0	(1.9)	-3	(4.1)	1	(1.9)	4	(5.1)
Switzerland	m	m	m	m	m	m	m	m	m	m
Turkey	1	(3.4)	2	(2.2)	3	(4.0)	3	(2.5)	**9**	(3.4)
United Kingdom	-3	(3.9)	1	(1.9)	-3	(4.0)	4	(2.1)	5	(5.4)
United States	**6**	(3.0)	1	(3.0)	4	(3.8)	4	(3.0)	6	(6.0)
OECD average	**2**	(0.8)	**2**	(0.4)	**2**	(0.8)	**2**	(0.4)	0	(0.9)
Partners										
Brazil	-2	(3.8)	1	(1.6)	-1	(3.4)	0	(1.8)	-2	(3.8)
B-S-J-G (China)	**8**	(3.9)	2	(2.5)	7	(4.8)	1	(2.5)	1	(3.5)
Bulgaria	-1	(3.1)	**3**	(1.3)	2	(2.1)	**3**	(1.4)	2	(2.9)
Colombia	-3	(2.8)	2	(2.0)	-2	(2.8)	3	(1.8)	-4	(4.2)
Costa Rica	1	(4.2)	1	(2.2)	1	(5.0)	3	(2.8)	1	(5.3)
Croatia	3	(4.1)	**5**	(2.1)	6	(3.7)	**6**	(1.9)	0	(3.3)
Cyprus*	**7**	(2.9)	3	(1.8)	3	(2.9)	2	(1.7)	0	(3.5)
Dominican Republic	m	m	m	m	m	m	m	m	m	m
Hong Kong (China)	**8**	(3.2)	**7**	(2.0)	5	(3.1)	**7**	(1.8)	6	(4.0)
Lithuania	0	(2.7)	3	(1.4)	-1	(3.1)	2	(1.5)	**6**	(2.9)
Macao (China)	**10**	(3.1)	**6**	(1.4)	**12**	(4.8)	**8**	(1.9)	3	(3.4)
Montenegro	6	(3.4)	2	(1.9)	4	(4.4)	-2	(2.9)	0	(2.9)
Peru	4	(3.8)	**6**	(1.6)	2	(2.9)	**4**	(1.6)	2	(2.5)
Qatar	m	m	m	m	m	m	m	m	m	m
Russia	0	(5.1)	-4	(3.0)	2	(6.5)	-1	(4.4)	-2	(4.3)
Singapore	**10**	(3.8)	1	(1.3)	**8**	(3.4)	2	(1.2)	0	(2.6)
Chinese Taipei	**12**	(4.8)	0	(4.6)	11	(7.4)	4	(5.7)	-1	(3.5)
Thailand	4	(3.0)	**6**	(1.8)	5	(3.3)	**6**	(1.8)	1	(4.0)
Tunisia	3	(2.3)	1	(1.8)	4	(2.7)	1	(1.6)	4	(4.1)
United Arab Emirates	1	(2.2)	**4**	(1.1)	3	(2.2)	**4**	(1.2)	-5	(2.8)
Uruguay	-2	(2.9)	1	(2.4)	-4	(3.5)	1	(2.1)	2	(3.1)
Malaysia**	4	(2.1)	-2	(2.0)	4	(2.4)	-1	(2.2)	-3	(3.7)

1. Student-level refers to the change in collaborative problem-solving score associated with students reporting the above.
2. School-level refers to the change in collaborative problem-solving score per 10 percentage-point increase in the number of schoolmates who reported the above.
Notes: Values that are statistically significant are indicated in bold (see Annex A3).
Questionnaire items that are measured at both the student and school levels are included in the same regression model.
* See note at the beginning of this Annex.
**Malaysia: Coverage is too small to ensure comparability (see Annex A4).
StatLink http://dx.doi.org/10.1787/888933616845

[Part 1/1]

Table V.7.16 Student-teacher relationships

		Percentage of students who reported the following:												Percentage of students in schools whose principal reported the following:			
		In "every lesson", the teacher gives extra help when students need it		In "every lesson", the teacher continues teaching until the students understand		Teachers "never or almost never" discipline me more harshly than other students		Teachers "never or almost never" say something insulting to me in front of others		Students "never or hardly ever" don't listen to what the teacher says		The teacher "never or hardly ever" has to wait a long time for students to quiet down		Students' learning is "not hindered at all" by students lacking respect for teachers		Students' learning is "not hindered at all" by teachers being too strict with students	
		%	S.E.	%	S.E.	%	S.E.	%	S.E.	%	S.E.	%	S.E.	%	S.E.	%	S.E.
OECD	Australia	48.5	(0.7)	43.5	(0.7)	63.5	(0.6)	67.6	(0.5)	14.4	(0.4)	21.5	(0.6)	20.7	(1.6)	30.5	(2.1)
	Austria	30.7	(0.9)	29.6	(1.0)	58.0	(0.7)	77.4	(0.6)	33.2	(1.2)	33.4	(1.2)	28.2	(3.0)	30.9	(3.4)
	Belgium	36.7	(0.7)	35.0	(0.8)	66.4	(0.6)	74.3	(0.7)	16.9	(0.6)	22.0	(0.7)	7.3	(1.8)	19.6	(2.3)
	Canada	52.5	(0.7)	44.7	(0.6)	m	m	m	m	19.9	(0.6)	29.9	(0.7)	14.4	(1.9)	26.7	(2.3)
	Chile	46.5	(1.0)	47.8	(1.1)	66.8	(0.6)	89.7	(0.5)	14.7	(0.9)	18.5	(1.0)	28.2	(3.3)	17.7	(3.2)
	Czech Republic	40.7	(0.9)	23.6	(0.8)	76.8	(0.7)	65.2	(0.8)	8.9	(0.6)	21.1	(0.9)	17.7	(2.6)	29.1	(2.6)
	Denmark	37.0	(1.0)	39.0	(0.9)	71.2	(0.6)	69.9	(0.7)	17.4	(0.9)	33.1	(1.2)	23.5	(3.1)	41.5	(3.2)
	Estonia	40.9	(1.0)	31.7	(0.9)	68.6	(0.8)	62.2	(0.8)	9.8	(0.6)	23.9	(0.9)	29.2	(2.6)	30.6	(2.5)
	Finland	48.0	(0.8)	36.3	(0.9)	63.5	(0.8)	74.2	(0.7)	11.8	(0.6)	20.2	(0.8)	8.8	(2.0)	34.7	(3.5)
	France	34.9	(0.9)	36.5	(0.9)	72.2	(0.7)	77.0	(0.5)	12.3	(0.6)	21.2	(0.7)	19.9	(2.5)	21.1	(2.7)
	Germany	32.8	(0.9)	30.1	(0.9)	59.5	(0.8)	83.7	(0.7)	15.3	(0.6)	24.3	(0.9)	14.1	(2.6)	23.8	(3.2)
	Greece	39.7	(1.1)	38.5	(1.0)	76.9	(0.8)	74.8	(0.7)	10.2	(0.6)	22.7	(1.0)	32.7	(3.4)	32.8	(4.0)
	Hungary	32.5	(0.9)	27.9	(0.9)	62.6	(0.8)	66.4	(0.7)	13.4	(0.7)	21.2	(0.8)	25.9	(2.9)	40.8	(3.6)
	Iceland	45.8	(0.8)	52.4	(0.8)	74.8	(0.8)	78.9	(0.8)	23.5	(0.7)	23.4	(0.6)	16.3	(0.2)	49.4	(0.3)
	Ireland	41.7	(0.9)	43.7	(1.0)	63.3	(0.8)	69.5	(0.7)	17.2	(0.7)	32.5	(0.9)	21.2	(3.3)	28.1	(3.5)
	Israel	35.5	(0.8)	44.4	(1.0)	m	m	m	m	19.0	(0.9)	26.4	(1.2)	19.6	(3.2)	26.1	(3.7)
	Italy	28.9	(0.8)	29.3	(0.6)	m	m	m	m	12.2	(0.5)	25.0	(0.7)	26.6	(3.4)	12.6	(2.3)
	Japan	34.7	(0.8)	30.6	(0.8)	82.6	(0.5)	88.9	(0.4)	49.5	(1.2)	63.9	(1.4)	16.0	(2.8)	10.6	(2.3)
	Korea	29.4	(0.8)	28.8	(0.8)	80.9	(0.6)	85.7	(0.5)	48.2	(1.2)	47.4	(1.3)	18.0	(2.9)	30.4	(3.5)
	Latvia	38.6	(0.8)	33.2	(0.7)	68.3	(0.7)	60.4	(1.0)	8.8	(0.5)	19.4	(0.8)	14.2	(2.0)	21.7	(2.3)
	Luxembourg	33.1	(0.7)	33.6	(0.7)	63.0	(0.6)	76.0	(0.6)	16.7	(0.5)	26.8	(0.6)	9.0	(0.1)	24.2	(0.1)
	Mexico	54.7	(1.0)	54.2	(0.9)	82.8	(0.6)	88.2	(0.5)	16.5	(0.7)	36.4	(1.1)	26.3	(2.5)	12.4	(1.9)
	Netherlands	27.3	(1.0)	23.2	(0.9)	71.4	(0.7)	83.7	(0.6)	17.9	(0.8)	14.3	(0.7)	8.5	(3.1)	8.8	(2.9)
	New Zealand	50.3	(0.9)	42.5	(0.9)	62.4	(0.8)	64.4	(0.8)	16.5	(0.6)	23.4	(0.8)	20.1	(2.9)	29.7	(3.0)
	Norway	36.1	(0.9)	38.8	(1.0)	68.4	(0.7)	72.5	(0.7)	27.4	(1.0)	29.2	(1.1)	9.3	(2.2)	21.3	(3.0)
	Poland	34.2	(0.9)	33.2	(1.0)	65.8	(0.9)	74.4	(0.8)	10.7	(0.6)	22.8	(0.9)	23.0	(3.3)	53.1	(3.6)
	Portugal	54.8	(1.0)	56.7	(1.1)	55.2	(0.6)	81.9	(0.6)	19.1	(0.9)	27.4	(1.0)	10.6	(1.9)	32.9	(3.5)
	Slovak Republic	33.4	(0.9)	27.6	(0.9)	73.0	(0.7)	74.5	(0.8)	10.9	(0.6)	24.1	(0.9)	21.0	(2.7)	29.3	(2.5)
	Slovenia	29.6	(0.9)	21.9	(1.0)	74.1	(0.7)	76.3	(0.7)	13.2	(0.8)	26.5	(1.1)	31.0	(0.3)	28.6	(0.4)
	Spain	37.7	(1.1)	42.0	(1.0)	73.8	(0.7)	79.7	(0.7)	13.5	(0.7)	20.8	(0.9)	13.1	(2.0)	23.9	(3.0)
	Sweden	39.5	(1.2)	42.2	(1.2)	74.7	(0.7)	79.4	(0.5)	20.5	(1.0)	26.3	(1.0)	19.6	(2.8)	52.1	(3.4)
	Switzerland	37.0	(1.0)	34.3	(0.9)	62.9	(0.7)	79.2	(0.8)	21.6	(1.0)	31.3	(1.2)	18.0	(2.7)	29.2	(3.3)
	Turkey	40.7	(1.0)	44.5	(1.1)	67.9	(0.8)	71.2	(0.7)	18.2	(0.7)	21.7	(0.8)	15.9	(2.9)	48.7	(4.2)
	United Kingdom	50.4	(0.8)	43.9	(0.9)	59.5	(0.9)	63.4	(0.7)	17.2	(0.8)	21.6	(0.8)	17.4	(2.6)	41.8	(3.9)
	United States	54.7	(1.0)	47.8	(0.9)	73.9	(0.8)	74.3	(0.7)	26.7	(0.9)	37.1	(1.1)	17.8	(3.1)	26.0	(3.5)
	OECD average-32	39.9	(0.2)	37.6	(0.2)	69.4	(0.1)	75.2	(0.1)	18.5	(0.1)	26.7	(0.2)	18.8	(0.5)	28.4	(0.5)
	OECD average-35	39.7	(0.2)	37.5	(0.2)	68.9	(0.1)	75.2	(0.1)	18.4	(0.1)	26.9	(0.2)	18.9	(0.4)	29.2	(0.5)
Partners	Brazil	47.0	(0.7)	55.0	(0.6)	69.6	(0.5)	78.8	(0.5)	15.7	(0.5)	20.6	(0.5)	10.8	(1.7)	36.9	(2.2)
	B-S-J-G (China)	46.2	(1.1)	36.4	(0.9)	67.1	(1.0)	86.6	(0.5)	24.7	(1.0)	38.9	(1.1)	23.6	(3.1)	20.2	(3.1)
	Bulgaria	39.0	(0.9)	45.7	(0.8)	67.1	(0.8)	69.9	(0.9)	12.3	(0.6)	23.8	(1.0)	39.1	(3.6)	53.3	(3.9)
	Colombia	43.2	(0.8)	47.9	(0.9)	74.0	(0.7)	75.5	(0.8)	18.3	(0.6)	31.7	(1.0)	21.6	(2.9)	15.6	(2.2)
	Costa Rica	53.1	(0.9)	55.3	(1.0)	65.1	(0.7)	91.1	(0.5)	22.0	(0.7)	35.8	(1.1)	20.9	(3.2)	11.9	(2.3)
	Croatia	30.8	(0.8)	24.7	(0.9)	73.2	(0.7)	77.7	(0.7)	7.7	(0.4)	24.8	(0.9)	8.7	(2.2)	23.0	(3.2)
	Cyprus*	38.4	(0.8)	36.7	(0.7)	68.0	(0.6)	64.7	(0.6)	10.3	(0.4)	16.6	(0.6)	6.7	(0.1)	22.7	(0.1)
	Dominican Republic	58.1	(1.2)	63.3	(1.2)	83.7	(0.6)	76.6	(0.8)	21.7	(0.9)	34.3	(1.2)	11.6	(2.6)	18.6	(3.2)
	Hong Kong (China)	30.5	(0.9)	29.0	(0.8)	70.4	(0.8)	79.5	(0.8)	24.9	(1.1)	38.6	(1.1)	12.8	(3.2)	15.3	(3.4)
	Lithuania	44.5	(0.8)	40.8	(0.7)	60.5	(0.7)	68.0	(0.8)	17.3	(0.8)	29.4	(0.7)	22.0	(2.7)	49.9	(3.2)
	Macao (China)	30.0	(0.7)	29.2	(0.7)	64.9	(0.6)	76.8	(0.6)	10.6	(0.5)	31.2	(0.7)	36.0	(0.1)	35.0	(0.1)
	Montenegro	40.9	(0.8)	40.4	(0.8)	75.9	(0.6)	81.1	(0.6)	15.1	(0.5)	36.3	(0.7)	10.6	(0.1)	25.2	(0.3)
	Peru	47.4	(0.8)	47.0	(0.8)	56.1	(0.6)	89.0	(0.5)	18.1	(0.6)	38.6	(0.9)	42.3	(2.8)	16.8	(2.4)
	Qatar	49.2	(0.5)	50.4	(0.5)	60.4	(0.4)	62.2	(0.4)	19.4	(0.4)	23.1	(0.4)	42.5	(0.1)	46.5	(0.1)
	Russia	45.9	(1.1)	44.2	(1.1)	71.2	(1.0)	73.1	(1.0)	24.2	(1.6)	37.8	(1.8)	30.6	(3.0)	27.5	(3.6)
	Singapore	48.2	(0.6)	44.1	(0.6)	68.6	(0.7)	72.0	(0.6)	23.1	(0.6)	25.1	(0.5)	30.3	(1.5)	24.4	(1.0)
	Chinese Taipei	40.8	(0.7)	32.0	(0.7)	82.7	(0.6)	90.6	(0.4)	18.5	(0.5)	25.9	(0.8)	28.0	(3.4)	23.1	(3.4)
	Thailand	49.0	(0.9)	51.1	(0.9)	67.6	(0.9)	70.2	(0.8)	29.1	(0.7)	31.8	(0.8)	36.0	(4.0)	26.2	(3.6)
	Tunisia	36.6	(0.9)	43.3	(1.0)	69.3	(0.7)	68.4	(0.8)	14.0	(0.6)	24.0	(0.9)	15.4	(3.2)	11.7	(3.0)
	United Arab Emirates	48.9	(0.6)	53.6	(0.6)	59.9	(0.7)	63.4	(0.6)	23.9	(0.6)	27.7	(0.7)	45.9	(2.6)	39.8	(2.7)
	Uruguay	43.1	(0.8)	48.6	(0.9)	78.0	(0.7)	90.7	(0.4)	16.0	(0.6)	17.6	(0.7)	30.3	(2.6)	29.1	(2.8)
	Malaysia**	52.0	(1.1)	51.7	(1.0)	43.8	(0.9)	71.9	(0.9)	15.9	(0.6)	29.4	(0.9)	19.4	(2.8)	26.9	(3.8)

* See note at the beginning of this Annex.
**Malaysia: Coverage is too small to ensure comparability (see Annex A4).
StatLink http://dx.doi.org/10.1787/888933616845

[Part 1/2]

Table V.7.18 Student-teacher relationships and performance in collaborative problem solving

		After accounting for students' and schools' socio-economic profile[1]															
		Change in collaborative problem-solving score when students reported the following:															
		In "every lesson", the teacher gives extra help when students need it				In "every lesson", the teacher continues teaching until the students understand				Teachers "never or almost never" discipline me more harshly than other students				Teachers "never or almost never" say something insulting to me in front of others			
		Student-level[2]		School-level[3]		Student-level		School-level		Student-level		School-level		Student-level		School-level	
		Score dif.	S.E.	Score dif.	S.E.	Score dif.	S.E.	Score dif.	S.E.	Score dif.	S.E.	Score dif.	S.E.	Score dif.	S.E.	Score dif.	S.E.
OECD	Australia	**12**	(2.9)	1	(1.0)	**9**	(3.1)	0	(1.1)	**39**	(3.1)	**4**	(1.3)	**33**	(3.0)	**3**	(1.2)
	Austria	0	(3.5)	**-6**	(2.1)	**8**	(3.4)	**-5**	(2.2)	**14**	(3.0)	3	(2.4)	**19**	(3.9)	**11**	(2.4)
	Belgium	4	(2.5)	-2	(1.9)	4	(2.4)	-2	(1.7)	**22**	(2.5)	4	(1.9)	**16**	(2.2)	**9**	(2.1)
	Canada	**9**	(2.6)	-1	(1.3)	4	(2.7)	-2	(1.4)	m	m	m	m	m	m	m	m
	Chile	-5	(2.9)	1	(2.0)	-2	(2.9)	3	(1.8)	**24**	(2.4)	**8**	(2.2)	**32**	(4.8)	**10**	(2.2)
	Czech Republic	-1	(2.9)	1	(1.2)	-2	(3.0)	-1	(1.6)	**22**	(3.7)	**8**	(1.6)	**12**	(3.1)	**6**	(1.4)
	Denmark	**9**	(3.4)	2	(1.4)	**11**	(3.2)	2	(1.6)	**36**	(3.3)	3	(2.1)	**28**	(3.5)	2	(1.9)
	Estonia	**8**	(3.0)	**5**	(1.4)	4	(3.5)	**5**	(1.9)	**30**	(3.3)	1	(2.4)	**19**	(3.2)	2	(2.1)
	Finland	**14**	(3.8)	3	(1.9)	5	(3.8)	3	(2.0)	**30**	(2.9)	0	(2.7)	**29**	(3.4)	2	(2.8)
	France	4	(3.3)	-4	(2.1)	**6**	(2.9)	-2	(1.9)	**23**	(3.4)	**9**	(2.1)	**19**	(3.5)	**13**	(2.1)
	Germany	-1	(3.3)	-1	(1.9)	6	(3.9)	0	(2.4)	**18**	(2.7)	3	(2.1)	**23**	(4.4)	**9**	(2.5)
	Greece	-4	(3.5)	0	(2.2)	-5	(2.9)	-2	(2.1)	**17**	(3.3)	**9**	(2.4)	**15**	(3.4)	**10**	(2.4)
	Hungary	1	(3.2)	-2	(1.9)	1	(3.4)	-1	(2.1)	**11**	(2.5)	**6**	(1.6)	**11**	(3.0)	**6**	(1.8)
	Iceland	4	(4.6)	0	(1.3)	2	(4.3)	1	(1.2)	**33**	(5.3)	1	(2.0)	**31**	(5.1)	2	(2.0)
	Ireland	m	m	m	m	m	m	m	m	m	m	m	m	m	m	m	m
	Israel	2	(3.0)	**-21**	(2.9)	**9**	(2.6)	**-12**	(3.6)	m	m	m	m	m	m	m	m
	Italy	-2	(2.7)	**-5**	(1.9)	3	(2.7)	**-5**	(1.7)	m	m	m	m	m	m	m	m
	Japan	-4	(3.1)	0	(1.9)	-5	(2.9)	-2	(2.1)	**16**	(3.4)	**9**	(3.8)	**19**	(4.5)	**15**	(4.1)
	Korea	5	(3.2)	**4**	(1.8)	4	(3.7)	3	(1.6)	**14**	(3.5)	**14**	(3.6)	**15**	(3.7)	**10**	(3.9)
	Latvia	7	(3.4)	0	(1.4)	7	(3.6)	-1	(1.6)	**34**	(3.2)	3	(1.8)	**17**	(3.0)	-1	(1.4)
	Luxembourg	-6	(3.1)	**-6**	(2.1)	1	(3.6)	-2	(2.2)	**25**	(2.8)	**16**	(2.3)	**34**	(3.1)	**11**	(2.2)
	Mexico	**-5**	(2.3)	-1	(1.4)	**-7**	(2.5)	-1	(1.6)	**19**	(3.4)	**7**	(1.9)	**19**	(3.2)	**8**	(2.4)
	Netherlands	**12**	(3.4)	-1	(2.3)	**13**	(3.7)	-4	(2.9)	**25**	(3.3)	5	(2.8)	**18**	(4.4)	**9**	(4.4)
	New Zealand	**8**	(4.1)	1	(2.0)	4	(4.1)	0	(2.0)	**41**	(3.8)	**8**	(1.9)	**36**	(4.2)	**6**	(2.1)
	Norway	-1	(3.4)	**4**	(1.5)	3	(3.5)	3	(1.5)	**36**	(3.2)	3	(1.8)	**27**	(3.8)	2	(2.1)
	Poland	m	m	m	m	m	m	m	m	m	m	m	m	m	m	m	m
	Portugal	3	(3.2)	**-5**	(1.7)	6	(3.5)	**-4**	(1.7)	**20**	(2.5)	**6**	(2.3)	**41**	(3.4)	**10**	(2.3)
	Slovak Republic	-5	(3.1)	-1	(1.7)	**-7**	(3.0)	-1	(1.7)	**16**	(3.2)	**7**	(1.5)	**13**	(3.4)	**6**	(1.8)
	Slovenia	6	(5.5)	0	(1.5)	-1	(6.3)	-1	(2.2)	**20**	(3.8)	**8**	(1.7)	**17**	(3.3)	**8**	(1.7)
	Spain	0	(2.7)	0	(1.6)	4	(3.0)	-1	(1.8)	**27**	(2.7)	2	(2.0)	**27**	(3.2)	3	(2.0)
	Sweden	-1	(3.5)	0	(1.7)	3	(3.6)	-1	(1.9)	**44**	(2.9)	**6**	(2.5)	**34**	(4.2)	4	(2.4)
	Switzerland	m	m	m	m	m	m	m	m	m	m	m	m	m	m	m	m
	Turkey	3	(2.4)	-1	(3.5)	1	(2.2)	-1	(3.3)	**8**	(2.6)	**11**	(2.1)	**12**	(2.7)	**9**	(2.9)
	United Kingdom	**9**	(3.5)	1	(1.9)	5	(3.0)	1	(1.9)	**27**	(3.0)	4	(2.1)	**24**	(2.9)	**7**	(2.1)
	United States	**13**	(3.6)	2	(2.4)	**11**	(3.9)	-3	(2.1)	**38**	(3.5)	**8**	(3.0)	**27**	(3.9)	4	(3.1)
	OECD average	**3**	(0.6)	**-1**	(0.3)	**3**	(0.6)	**-1**	(0.4)	**25**	(0.6)	**6**	(0.4)	**23**	(0.7)	**7**	(0.5)
Partners	Brazil	**-8**	(2.6)	0	(1.4)	**-6**	(2.5)	0	(1.3)	**23**	(2.2)	**6**	(1.4)	**23**	(2.4)	**7**	(1.6)
	B-S-J-G (China)	**8**	(2.8)	3	(2.5)	-1	(2.8)	-3	(2.4)	**14**	(3.3)	**6**	(2.3)	**25**	(4.6)	**8**	(3.8)
	Bulgaria	-4	(3.0)	1	(2.2)	-1	(3.3)	1	(1.9)	**12**	(2.4)	**9**	(1.8)	**17**	(2.4)	**5**	(2.6)
	Colombia	**-7**	(2.5)	**-5**	(1.6)	-2	(2.9)	**-3**	(1.5)	**9**	(2.8)	3	(2.4)	**6**	(2.6)	-2	(2.1)
	Costa Rica	4	(2.6)	3	(1.6)	2	(2.7)	2	(1.9)	**6**	(2.6)	1	(2.0)	**15**	(5.1)	5	(3.8)
	Croatia	2	(2.9)	2	(3.1)	**6**	(2.4)	-1	(2.4)	5	(3.3)	**15**	(2.8)	1	(3.5)	**11**	(3.1)
	Cyprus*	**11**	(3.8)	1	(1.6)	**8**	(3.5)	3	(1.7)	**33**	(3.3)	**6**	(1.3)	**20**	(3.3)	**10**	(1.5)
	Dominican Republic	m	m	m	m	m	m	m	m	m	m	m	m	m	m	m	m
	Hong Kong (China)	7	(3.8)	1	(3.9)	5	(3.9)	0	(4.2)	**26**	(3.5)	**19**	(2.4)	**30**	(3.9)	**22**	(3.4)
	Lithuania	**8**	(2.5)	**4**	(1.7)	4	(3.0)	**4**	(1.8)	**20**	(2.7)	**6**	(1.5)	**15**	(2.7)	**7**	(1.6)
	Macao (China)	7	(3.9)	**14**	(2.0)	3	(3.5)	**9**	(2.4)	**10**	(3.1)	**34**	(2.0)	**21**	(3.7)	**28**	(1.5)
	Montenegro	-4	(2.8)	3	(1.7)	-4	(2.7)	1	(2.0)	**20**	(2.6)	**8**	(2.5)	**17**	(2.9)	**7**	(2.6)
	Peru	**-7**	(2.2)	-1	(1.4)	**-7**	(2.3)	0	(1.3)	**9**	(2.3)	**4**	(1.3)	**16**	(3.3)	**8**	(2.0)
	Qatar	m	m	m	m	m	m	m	m	m	m	m	m	m	m	m	m
	Russia	**-8**	(3.2)	0	(2.0)	**-10**	(3.3)	0	(2.0)	**20**	(3.3)	**6**	(2.2)	**16**	(3.5)	**5**	(2.4)
	Singapore	**10**	(3.5)	**4**	(1.3)	6	(3.3)	**4**	(1.2)	**31**	(2.6)	**12**	(1.6)	**25**	(3.0)	**8**	(1.8)
	Chinese Taipei	**9**	(2.7)	3	(2.2)	3	(2.9)	1	(2.3)	**9**	(3.3)	**6**	(2.6)	**23**	(4.2)	**8**	(3.5)
	Thailand	3	(2.6)	1	(2.0)	1	(2.5)	1	(2.0)	**24**	(2.3)	**12**	(2.2)	**17**	(2.4)	**11**	(2.2)
	Tunisia	**-7**	(1.8)	-3	(1.8)	**-7**	(2.0)	-3	(1.7)	**9**	(2.0)	**7**	(1.8)	**7**	(2.1)	**7**	(2.2)
	United Arab Emirates	**6**	(2.2)	3	(1.6)	**7**	(2.7)	-1	(1.5)	**25**	(2.7)	**14**	(1.2)	**25**	(2.4)	**10**	(1.4)
	Uruguay	**-11**	(3.1)	**-6**	(1.7)	**-8**	(3.1)	**-5**	(1.7)	**18**	(3.8)	5	(1.9)	**32**	(5.0)	**11**	(3.1)
	Malaysia**	**10**	(2.6)	2	(1.6)	1	(2.2)	3	(1.8)	**20**	(2.4)	5	(2.2)	**20**	(3.5)	3	(2.1)

1. The socio-economic profile is measured by the PISA index of economic, social and cultural status (ESCS).
2. Student-level refers to the change in collaborative problem-solving score associated with students reporting the above.
3. School-level refers to the change in collaborative problem-solving score per 10 percentage-point increase in the number of schoolmates who reported the above.
Notes: Values that are statistically significant are indicated in bold (see Annex A3).
Questionnaire items that are measured at both the student and school levels are included in the same regression model.
* See note at the beginning of this Annex.
**Malaysia: Coverage is too small to ensure comparability (see Annex A4).
StatLink http://dx.doi.org/10.1787/888933616845

[Part 2/2]

Table V.7.18 Student-teacher relationships and performance in collaborative problem solving

		After accounting for students' and schools' socio-economic profile[1]											
		Change in collaborative problem-solving score when students reported the following:								Change in collaborative problem-solving score when principals reported the following:			
		Students "never or hardly ever" don't listen to what the teacher says				The teacher "never or hardly ever" has to wait a long time for students to quiet down				Students' learning is "not hindered at all" by students lacking respect for teachers		Students' learning is "not hindered at all" by teachers being too strict with students	
		Student-level[2]		School-level[3]		Student-level		School-level					
		Score dif.	S.E.	Score dif.	S.E.	Score dif.	S.E.	Score dif.	S.E.	Score dif.	S.E.	Score dif.	S.E.
OECD	Australia	**16**	(4.4)	**6**	(1.6)	**18**	(4.0)	**5**	(1.4)	**17**	(4.4)	4	(4.1)
	Austria	7	(4.1)	**6**	(1.7)	7	(4.0)	3	(1.8)	11	(7.0)	-6	(6.8)
	Belgium	**7**	(3.3)	**7**	(2.3)	**12**	(3.2)	0	(1.6)	4	(13.2)	2	(7.0)
	Canada	**10**	(3.4)	1	(1.6)	**16**	(2.7)	2	(1.4)	6	(6.0)	-5	(4.5)
	Chile	5	(4.2)	**8**	(2.8)	**9**	(3.8)	**5**	(2.4)	7	(6.6)	3	(6.7)
	Czech Republic	-4	(5.3)	3	(2.0)	5	(3.8)	**5**	(1.2)	7	(5.6)	-4	(4.4)
	Denmark	4	(4.4)	2	(1.8)	2	(3.5)	2	(1.4)	**14**	(6.4)	6	(5.7)
	Estonia	-1	(5.2)	1	(2.1)	**19**	(3.3)	3	(1.6)	-1	(4.8)	4	(4.8)
	Finland	3	(5.5)	2	(2.8)	**12**	(4.3)	0	(2.0)	11	(9.7)	-1	(4.4)
	France	1	(5.0)	2	(3.0)	**10**	(3.5)	**4**	(2.1)	2	(7.1)	-6	(6.3)
	Germany	-9	(5.4)	2	(2.8)	2	(4.4)	**4**	(2.1)	5	(10.1)	-2	(7.3)
	Greece	-4	(5.0)	6	(3.7)	**9**	(3.3)	**7**	(2.4)	5	(6.7)	-3	(6.3)
	Hungary	-5	(4.3)	3	(2.8)	1	(4.0)	**5**	(2.2)	9	(6.1)	**-17**	(5.2)
	Iceland	2	(5.2)	**5**	(1.5)	3	(5.0)	**3**	(1.3)	7	(4.6)	-5	(3.9)
	Ireland	m	m	m	m	m	m	m	m	m	m	m	m
	Israel	4	(3.5)	4	(4.6)	**9**	(2.8)	3	(3.6)	9	(11.4)	-17	(12.0)
	Italy	3	(5.1)	3	(2.6)	2	(3.6)	**4**	(1.9)	1	(7.7)	**-20**	(6.9)
	Japan	-1	(3.1)	**6**	(1.6)	1	(2.6)	**6**	(1.2)	-8	(6.8)	-8	(7.7)
	Korea	-2	(2.7)	**8**	(1.2)	0	(2.9)	**8**	(1.3)	**16**	(5.3)	-1	(4.8)
	Latvia	-4	(5.8)	1	(2.9)	4	(4.4)	2	(1.7)	0	(5.8)	**-11**	(4.4)
	Luxembourg	**13**	(4.5)	**7**	(2.7)	**13**	(3.4)	**7**	(2.2)	**13**	(5.4)	**-9**	(2.8)
	Mexico	0	(3.5)	**6**	(1.6)	4	(2.9)	**3**	(1.2)	0	(4.8)	-9	(6.0)
	Netherlands	0	(3.9)	**8**	(2.6)	3	(4.5)	**10**	(3.4)	1	(15.2)	5	(16.4)
	New Zealand	**23**	(4.7)	2	(2.6)	**27**	(4.4)	2	(2.0)	1	(7.6)	-5	(6.3)
	Norway	1	(3.4)	**4**	(1.4)	2	(4.0)	**5**	(1.2)	15	(10.4)	-3	(6.9)
	Poland	m	m	m	m	m	m	m	m	m	m	m	m
	Portugal	6	(4.2)	3	(1.9)	**12**	(3.7)	**4**	(1.9)	9	(7.3)	-2	(4.9)
	Slovak Republic	-1	(4.7)	**6**	(2.6)	4	(3.7)	**8**	(1.6)	**14**	(5.7)	-8	(5.2)
	Slovenia	-2	(8.8)	1	(2.1)	5	(6.0)	**5**	(1.6)	**17**	(3.7)	2	(3.2)
	Spain	-1	(4.5)	3	(2.4)	**11**	(3.7)	2	(1.7)	-2	(7.8)	2	(4.4)
	Sweden	3	(4.5)	3	(1.8)	**9**	(3.9)	3	(1.9)	6	(7.1)	-5	(4.9)
	Switzerland	m	m	m	m	m	m	m	m	m	m	m	m
	Turkey	**8**	(2.9)	**9**	(2.6)	**11**	(2.8)	**9**	(2.5)	**27**	(8.3)	7	(5.9)
	United Kingdom	**19**	(4.3)	**5**	(1.9)	**11**	(4.4)	**4**	(1.8)	**13**	(6.3)	9	(5.4)
	United States	**19**	(4.5)	4	(2.6)	**28**	(3.8)	**5**	(2.5)	4	(7.5)	10	(6.5)
	OECD average	**4**	(0.8)	**4**	(0.4)	**9**	(0.7)	**4**	(0.3)	**7**	(1.4)	**-3**	(1.1)
Partners	Brazil	3	(4.4)	**5**	(1.8)	-1	(3.6)	3	(1.6)	1	(6.6)	-2	(4.5)
	B-S-J-G (China)	3	(3.3)	1	(2.7)	6	(3.2)	**7**	(2.5)	1	(6.2)	2	(7.4)
	Bulgaria	-8	(5.6)	**8**	(3.4)	3	(4.3)	**8**	(2.2)	5	(4.6)	3	(5.5)
	Colombia	3	(4.0)	0	(1.8)	4	(2.5)	1	(1.4)	0	(4.8)	5	(5.0)
	Costa Rica	**6**	(3.0)	3	(2.0)	**9**	(2.5)	2	(1.8)	4	(4.7)	8	(7.7)
	Croatia	-1	(5.5)	**11**	(4.7)	**11**	(3.1)	**12**	(2.0)	3	(8.7)	6	(6.0)
	Cyprus*	9	(5.5)	3	(2.8)	**17**	(4.6)	**9**	(1.9)	3	(6.5)	**10**	(4.5)
	Dominican Republic	m	m	m	m	m	m	m	m	m	m	m	m
	Hong Kong (China)	3	(4.1)	**8**	(3.4)	**12**	(3.3)	**11**	(2.5)	21	(11.8)	21	(11.7)
	Lithuania	-5	(3.5)	**6**	(1.6)	0	(3.2)	**7**	(1.4)	5	(5.8)	1	(4.5)
	Macao (China)	-6	(5.4)	5	(3.0)	**14**	(3.6)	**23**	(1.7)	**21**	(2.8)	**8**	(2.8)
	Montenegro	-1	(3.8)	4	(2.5)	**12**	(3.3)	**5**	(1.3)	4	(3.7)	0	(2.5)
	Peru	5	(3.5)	2	(1.8)	**6**	(2.3)	0	(1.3)	0	(3.9)	7	(5.3)
	Qatar	m	m	m	m	m	m	m	m	m	m	m	m
	Russia	-1	(4.0)	1	(1.6)	3	(3.5)	1	(1.7)	3	(5.8)	1	(5.6)
	Singapore	**13**	(3.7)	**7**	(1.8)	**13**	(3.4)	**4**	(1.5)	1	(4.6)	3	(4.0)
	Chinese Taipei	-4	(3.3)	**9**	(2.6)	5	(2.9)	**9**	(1.9)	6	(6.6)	0	(7.0)
	Thailand	**7**	(2.7)	-1	(2.0)	**9**	(2.9)	4	(2.1)	1	(6.3)	4	(6.2)
	Tunisia	**-12**	(3.1)	**-6**	(2.7)	**-7**	(2.6)	1	(2.0)	0	(5.5)	**17**	(7.1)
	United Arab Emirates	-2	(3.1)	0	(2.1)	2	(3.0)	**4**	(2.2)	**22**	(5.4)	9	(5.9)
	Uruguay	-9	(5.0)	-1	(2.3)	0	(4.3)	2	(2.0)	**13**	(5.4)	2	(4.4)
	Malaysia**	5	(3.2)	-1	(2.6)	**16**	(2.7)	2	(1.7)	10	(6.3)	3	(6.4)

1. The socio-economic profile is measured by the PISA index of economic, social and cultural status (ESCS).
2. Student-level refers to the change in collaborative problem-solving score associated with students reporting the above.
3. School-level refers to the change in collaborative problem-solving score per 10 percentage-point increase in the number of schoolmates who reported the above.

Notes: Values that are statistically significant are indicated in bold (see Annex A3).
Questionnaire items that are measured at both the student and school levels are included in the same regression model.
* See note at the beginning of this Annex.
**Malaysia: Coverage is too small to ensure comparability (see Annex A4).

StatLink http://dx.doi.org/10.1787/888933616845

[Part 1/2]

Table V.7.19 Student-teacher relationships and relative performance in collaborative problem solving

After accounting for performance in science, reading and mathematics — Change in collaborative problem-solving score when students reported the following:

		In "every lesson", the teacher gives extra help when students need it				In "every lesson", the teacher continues teaching until the students understand				Teachers "never or almost never" discipline me more harshly than other students				Teachers "never or almost never" say something insulting to me in front of others			
		Student-level[1]		School-level[2]		Student-level		School-level		Student-level		School-level		Student-level		School-level	
		Score dif.	S.E.	Score dif.	S.E.	Score dif.	S.E.	Score dif.	S.E.	Score dif.	S.E.	Score dif.	S.E.	Score dif.	S.E.	Score dif.	S.E.
OECD	Australia	2	(2.4)	0	(0.8)	3	(2.3)	0	(0.8)	**7**	(2.4)	1	(0.8)	4	(2.4)	1	(0.8)
	Austria	2	(3.0)	0	(1.2)	4	(2.5)	0	(1.3)	4	(2.4)	2	(1.5)	3	(3.5)	**5**	(1.6)
	Belgium	3	(1.9)	1	(1.2)	4	(1.9)	0	(1.1)	**8**	(1.8)	0	(1.2)	**4**	(1.9)	2	(1.4)
	Canada	3	(1.9)	0	(0.9)	3	(2.5)	-1	(1.0)	m	m	m	m	m	m	m	m
	Chile	2	(2.7)	-1	(1.2)	2	(2.9)	1	(1.1)	**11**	(2.1)	0	(1.2)	**10**	(3.9)	0	(1.8)
	Czech Republic	3	(2.6)	1	(0.8)	1	(2.7)	0	(1.0)	**9**	(3.1)	**3**	(1.3)	2	(2.6)	**2**	(0.9)
	Denmark	0	(2.7)	1	(1.1)	1	(2.3)	0	(1.2)	**7**	(2.6)	1	(1.4)	0	(2.8)	0	(1.3)
	Estonia	4	(2.4)	1	(0.9)	4	(2.8)	1	(1.2)	**9**	(2.6)	-1	(1.3)	1	(2.3)	1	(1.1)
	Finland	1	(3.5)	1	(1.4)	0	(3.2)	2	(1.3)	4	(2.1)	0	(1.7)	4	(2.3)	0	(2.0)
	France	2	(2.7)	-1	(1.2)	3	(2.6)	0	(1.2)	**7**	(2.9)	1	(1.4)	5	(3.0)	3	(1.4)
	Germany	-6	(3.0)	1	(1.4)	-4	(3.3)	1	(1.4)	3	(2.1)	0	(1.5)	0	(3.8)	1	(1.7)
	Greece	-2	(3.0)	0	(1.2)	-4	(2.4)	0	(1.1)	**7**	(2.8)	1	(1.6)	5	(3.0)	0	(1.4)
	Hungary	-2	(2.7)	-2	(1.2)	-2	(3.1)	-1	(1.2)	2	(2.0)	2	(1.1)	0	(2.5)	1	(1.2)
	Iceland	-3	(3.7)	0	(1.0)	-4	(3.5)	1	(0.8)	4	(3.5)	1	(1.6)	1	(3.9)	2	(1.4)
	Ireland	m	m	m	m	m	m	m	m	m	m	m	m	m	m	m	m
	Israel	-2	(2.1)	**-10**	(1.6)	-1	(1.9)	**-7**	(1.8)	m	m	m	m	m	m	m	m
	Italy	1	(2.3)	0	(1.5)	1	(2.2)	1	(1.4)	m	m	m	m	m	m	m	m
	Japan	-3	(2.9)	-1	(1.4)	-3	(2.6)	-1	(1.3)	**7**	(2.3)	3	(2.4)	6	(3.8)	3	(2.7)
	Korea	3	(3.2)	0	(1.2)	2	(3.5)	1	(1.0)	-1	(2.8)	4	(2.0)	1	(2.9)	2	(2.1)
	Latvia	0	(2.5)	1	(0.9)	0	(2.2)	1	(1.0)	**7**	(2.9)	0	(1.1)	1	(2.3)	-1	(0.9)
	Luxembourg	-3	(2.8)	0	(1.8)	-2	(3.0)	1	(1.8)	**7**	(2.5)	**6**	(2.0)	**6**	(2.7)	2	(1.7)
	Mexico	-1	(2.0)	-2	(0.8)	-4	(2.0)	-2	(0.9)	4	(3.0)	1	(1.3)	-1	(2.8)	0	(1.6)
	Netherlands	4	(2.4)	1	(1.6)	4	(2.5)	2	(1.7)	**8**	(2.8)	0	(2.0)	3	(3.8)	0	(2.0)
	New Zealand	4	(3.2)	0	(1.5)	6	(3.3)	1	(1.4)	**10**	(3.3)	**4**	(1.6)	**6**	(3.2)	3	(1.6)
	Norway	**-7**	(2.6)	1	(1.2)	-5	(3.0)	1	(1.2)	4	(2.9)	2	(1.5)	-2	(3.3)	0	(1.6)
	Poland	m	m	m	m	m	m	m	m	m	m	m	m	m	m	m	m
	Portugal	-2	(2.8)	-1	(1.4)	-1	(3.0)	-1	(1.3)	**6**	(1.9)	-2	(1.6)	**12**	(3.5)	1	(1.6)
	Slovak Republic	-2	(2.9)	0	(1.1)	-2	(2.5)	0	(1.2)	0	(2.7)	1	(1.0)	-4	(2.9)	0	(1.3)
	Slovenia	1	(4.7)	1	(1.1)	-1	(5.3)	2	(1.5)	**7**	(3.2)	**3**	(1.2)	5	(3.0)	2	(1.4)
	Spain	3	(2.1)	-1	(1.1)	2	(2.4)	-1	(1.3)	**10**	(2.3)	1	(1.7)	**8**	(2.5)	2	(1.6)
	Sweden	-5	(2.8)	0	(1.2)	-3	(3.0)	-1	(1.2)	**13**	(2.4)	1	(1.8)	6	(3.7)	0	(1.6)
	Switzerland	m	m	m	m	m	m	m	m	m	m	m	m	m	m	m	m
	Turkey	1	(2.6)	-1	(1.6)	0	(2.4)	0	(1.3)	2	(2.0)	1	(1.6)	3	(2.2)	1	(1.9)
	United Kingdom	0	(3.2)	1	(1.5)	-1	(2.8)	1	(1.4)	2	(2.6)	1	(1.7)	2	(2.4)	2	(1.6)
	United States	3	(2.3)	-2	(1.7)	3	(2.9)	-2	(1.6)	4	(2.7)	1	(2.4)	0	(3.3)	1	(2.3)
	OECD average	0	(0.5)	0	(0.2)	0	(0.5)	0	(0.2)	**6**	(0.5)	**1**	(0.3)	**3**	(0.6)	**1**	(0.3)
Partners	Brazil	-4	(2.5)	-1	(1.2)	-3	(2.3)	-1	(1.0)	2	(2.1)	0	(1.1)	2	(2.3)	0	(1.2)
	B-S-J-G (China)	2	(2.5)	-1	(1.4)	1	(2.5)	-1	(1.6)	**5**	(2.5)	1	(1.4)	**11**	(4.4)	3	(2.3)
	Bulgaria	**-5**	(2.3)	-2	(1.3)	-4	(2.8)	-1	(1.3)	-2	(2.2)	2	(1.3)	-1	(1.8)	1	(1.5)
	Colombia	-3	(1.9)	0	(1.2)	-1	(2.5)	0	(1.0)	-1	(2.2)	-1	(1.4)	**-4**	(2.0)	-1	(1.2)
	Costa Rica	**6**	(2.3)	1	(1.3)	4	(2.3)	0	(1.5)	3	(2.4)	-1	(1.4)	2	(4.9)	0	(2.8)
	Croatia	0	(2.7)	3	(1.9)	1	(2.3)	1	(1.6)	0	(2.7)	**4**	(1.7)	-2	(3.1)	2	(1.9)
	Cyprus*	1	(2.8)	-1	(1.3)	1	(2.9)	0	(1.4)	3	(2.6)	0	(1.1)	-2	(2.6)	2	(1.3)
	Dominican Republic	m	m	m	m	m	m	m	m	m	m	m	m	m	m	m	m
	Hong Kong (China)	**-6**	(2.9)	0	(1.7)	**-8**	(2.8)	0	(1.7)	5	(2.9)	**4**	(1.6)	**7**	(3.0)	**5**	(2.2)
	Lithuania	2	(1.9)	1	(1.0)	-1	(2.4)	0	(1.0)	**5**	(2.0)	2	(1.1)	1	(2.2)	0	(1.0)
	Macao (China)	3	(2.6)	3	(1.5)	3	(2.2)	3	(1.8)	**7**	(2.1)	**8**	(2.0)	5	(2.9)	**6**	(1.5)
	Montenegro	-4	(2.4)	1	(1.2)	-4	(2.3)	0	(1.1)	**6**	(2.2)	0	(2.2)	4	(2.7)	-2	(1.7)
	Peru	1	(1.9)	-1	(0.9)	1	(1.7)	-1	(0.8)	0	(1.9)	1	(0.9)	-4	(2.7)	**4**	(1.3)
	Qatar	m	m	m	m	m	m	m	m	m	m	m	m	m	m	m	m
	Russia	-3	(2.6)	**-3**	(1.5)	**-6**	(2.7)	**-5**	(1.3)	2	(3.2)	0	(1.8)	-2	(3.1)	-2	(1.7)
	Singapore	2	(2.7)	0	(0.9)	3	(2.6)	0	(0.8)	**10**	(2.2)	1	(1.0)	**10**	(2.3)	0	(1.1)
	Chinese Taipei	1	(2.3)	-1	(1.4)	1	(2.4)	-1	(1.5)	**5**	(2.6)	2	(2.1)	6	(3.5)	1	(2.9)
	Thailand	0	(2.4)	2	(1.3)	-1	(2.4)	0	(1.1)	**6**	(2.0)	**5**	(1.7)	2	(1.7)	**5**	(1.8)
	Tunisia	-3	(1.7)	-2	(1.4)	**-3**	(1.7)	-3	(1.3)	**4**	(1.8)	1	(1.5)	2	(2.0)	2	(1.6)
	United Arab Emirates	2	(1.7)	-1	(1.0)	2	(2.1)	**-2**	(1.0)	1	(2.5)	**3**	(1.1)	0	(2.2)	1	(1.0)
	Uruguay	-2	(2.2)	-1	(1.1)	-2	(2.4)	-2	(1.1)	4	(2.6)	-1	(1.4)	8	(4.0)	1	(2.0)
	Malaysia**	1	(2.2)	-2	(1.3)	0	(2.0)	-2	(1.5)	3	(2.3)	2	(1.7)	0	(3.2)	-2	(1.6)

1. Student-level refers to the change in collaborative problem-solving score associated with students reporting the above.
2. School-level refers to the change in collaborative problem-solving score per 10 percentage-point increase in the number of schoolmates who reported the above.
Notes: Values that are statistically significant are indicated in bold (see Annex A3).
Questionnaire items that are measured at both the student and school levels are included in the same regression model.
* See note at the beginning of this Annex.
**Malaysia: Coverage is too small to ensure comparability (see Annex A4).
StatLink http://dx.doi.org/10.1787/888933616845

[Part 2/2]

Table V.7.19 Student-teacher relationships and relative performance in collaborative problem solving

	After accounting for performance in science, reading and mathematics											
	Change in collaborative problem-solving score when students reported the following:								Change in collaborative problem-solving score when principals reported the following:			
	Students "never or hardly ever" don't listen to what the teacher says				The teacher "never or hardly ever" has to wait a long time for students to quiet down				Students' learning is "not hindered at all" by students lacking respect for teachers		Students' learning is "not hindered at all" by teachers being too strict with students	
	Student-level		School-level		Student-level		School-level					
	Score dif.	S.E.	Score dif.	S.E.	Score dif.	S.E.	Score dif.	S.E.	Score dif.	S.E.	Score dif.	S.E.
OECD												
Australia	-1	(4.1)	2	(1.1)	2	(3.2)	1	(1.0)	2	(2.6)	1	(2.8)
Austria	1	(3.9)	1	(1.2)	2	(3.6)	0	(1.0)	0	(4.3)	-3	(3.9)
Belgium	4	(3.1)	**4**	(1.3)	**6**	(2.9)	0	(1.2)	-3	(6.0)	3	(3.9)
Canada	-3	(3.2)	0	(1.4)	-1	(2.3)	0	(1.1)	-7	(4.5)	-3	(3.7)
Chile	3	(3.6)	1	(1.3)	3	(3.1)	0	(1.2)	3	(3.7)	4	(4.6)
Czech Republic	-3	(4.6)	0	(1.5)	3	(3.3)	0	(0.8)	2	(4.0)	-2	(3.3)
Denmark	-3	(3.7)	0	(1.2)	-4	(2.6)	1	(0.9)	3	(4.1)	2	(3.4)
Estonia	0	(4.2)	-1	(1.6)	**10**	(2.7)	0	(1.0)	-3	(2.7)	0	(3.0)
Finland	6	(4.5)	-2	(1.8)	6	(3.2)	-1	(1.4)	0	(6.4)	5	(3.0)
France	4	(4.0)	0	(1.7)	**8**	(3.0)	1	(1.3)	1	(3.8)	-2	(3.5)
Germany	**-12**	(4.9)	3	(1.9)	**-7**	(3.6)	2	(1.3)	-2	(5.8)	2	(4.3)
Greece	-5	(4.2)	0	(1.9)	3	(2.8)	1	(1.1)	-1	(3.4)	2	(3.0)
Hungary	-3	(3.9)	0	(1.7)	0	(3.3)	2	(1.2)	0	(3.1)	-5	(3.0)
Iceland	3	(4.0)	1	(1.0)	-1	(3.8)	1	(0.8)	6	(3.6)	-2	(3.0)
Ireland	m	m	m	m	m	m	m	m	m	m	m	m
Israel	-2	(3.3)	0	(2.5)	-2	(2.7)	-1	(1.9)	2	(6.4)	-12	(6.8)
Italy	-1	(4.2)	**4**	(1.8)	-3	(3.1)	2	(1.3)	1	(5.0)	-2	(5.7)
Japan	**-5**	(2.5)	0	(1.0)	**-4**	(2.1)	1	(0.9)	-8	(5.1)	3	(5.6)
Korea	4	(2.1)	1	(0.9)	3	(2.5)	1	(1.0)	3	(3.8)	0	(2.7)
Latvia	-1	(4.8)	0	(1.8)	-1	(3.3)	0	(1.1)	1	(3.7)	-4	(2.8)
Luxembourg	0	(3.9)	1	(2.1)	0	(2.8)	0	(1.8)	**11**	(4.4)	-1	(2.4)
Mexico	-3	(2.9)	1	(1.2)	-2	(2.6)	-1	(0.8)	-3	(2.8)	-3	(3.7)
Netherlands	-5	(3.6)	2	(1.8)	-2	(3.7)	1	(2.3)	7	(8.6)	10	(7.0)
New Zealand	8	(4.6)	0	(2.1)	**8**	(3.1)	1	(1.6)	-5	(5.5)	-3	(4.4)
Norway	-2	(2.6)	0	(1.1)	-1	(3.2)	1	(1.0)	-4	(7.1)	2	(5.0)
Poland	m	m	m	m	m	m	m	m	m	m	m	m
Portugal	-2	(3.5)	-1	(1.4)	1	(3.0)	0	(1.3)	0	(5.1)	-2	(3.2)
Slovak Republic	-5	(4.1)	0	(1.7)	-4	(3.0)	1	(1.0)	-3	(4.2)	-7	(3.6)
Slovenia	6	(7.4)	0	(1.5)	4	(5.5)	1	(1.3)	7	(3.5)	-1	(2.9)
Spain	-2	(2.9)	0	(1.9)	0	(2.6)	1	(1.4)	-2	(5.2)	1	(3.5)
Sweden	0	(3.6)	0	(1.4)	5	(3.0)	0	(1.4)	1	(4.4)	0	(3.2)
Switzerland	m	m	m	m	m	m	m	m	m	m	m	m
Turkey	**6**	(3.0)	0	(1.6)	**5**	(2.4)	0	(1.7)	5	(5.1)	2	(3.1)
United Kingdom	-1	(3.6)	3	(1.6)	-4	(3.6)	2	(1.5)	6	(5.9)	1	(4.2)
United States	-5	(3.7)	0	(1.9)	2	(2.9)	-1	(1.7)	-4	(6.1)	1	(5.0)
OECD average	-1	(0.7)	**1**	(0.3)	1	(0.6)	**1**	(0.2)	0	(0.9)	0	(0.7)
Partners												
Brazil	1	(4.2)	-1	(1.3)	-1	(3.6)	-2	(1.1)	-10	(6.1)	1	(3.2)
B-S-J-G (China)	-4	(2.9)	-1	(1.7)	-2	(2.9)	-1	(1.5)	-3	(4.1)	-6	(4.0)
Bulgaria	-4	(5.0)	-1	(1.9)	0	(3.8)	-1	(1.2)	4	(2.8)	-1	(2.7)
Colombia	1	(3.2)	-1	(1.4)	-1	(2.1)	**-2**	(0.9)	-3	(3.8)	-4	(4.3)
Costa Rica	5	(2.9)	2	(1.7)	**5**	(2.6)	-1	(1.3)	-1	(4.2)	6	(5.7)
Croatia	-5	(4.5)	-2	(2.6)	2	(2.1)	**2**	(1.0)	-3	(6.2)	3	(4.1)
Cyprus*	2	(4.7)	2	(2.4)	4	(3.8)	2	(1.5)	-1	(5.8)	3	(3.6)
Dominican Republic	m	m	m	m	m	m	m	m	m	m	m	m
Hong Kong (China)	-3	(3.5)	**4**	(1.7)	1	(3.0)	**4**	(1.3)	4	(5.9)	8	(5.8)
Lithuania	**-6**	(2.8)	1	(1.0)	-5	(2.7)	1	(0.7)	-2	(3.5)	-2	(2.4)
Macao (China)	5	(4.2)	1	(2.3)	**8**	(2.4)	**5**	(1.3)	-1	(2.7)	0	(2.3)
Montenegro	-1	(3.7)	0	(2.4)	3	(2.7)	0	(1.0)	**6**	(3.1)	**10**	(1.9)
Peru	1	(3.5)	1	(1.2)	3	(2.1)	-1	(0.9)	2	(2.5)	5	(3.5)
Qatar	m	m	m	m	m	m	m	m	m	m	m	m
Russia	2	(3.8)	**-3**	(1.3)	-2	(3.7)	**-3**	(1.3)	-4	(4.9)	-5	(4.3)
Singapore	-2	(3.0)	**2**	(1.0)	-2	(3.1)	**2**	(0.9)	1	(2.4)	**7**	(2.6)
Chinese Taipei	1	(2.8)	2	(1.8)	3	(2.3)	1	(1.4)	-1	(4.1)	-2	(4.1)
Thailand	-1	(2.2)	-2	(1.1)	4	(2.7)	0	(1.3)	2	(4.3)	0	(4.5)
Tunisia	**-7**	(3.0)	-4	(2.0)	**-6**	(2.6)	-2	(1.3)	-4	(4.7)	5	(5.6)
United Arab Emirates	-4	(2.9)	0	(1.3)	-2	(2.6)	0	(1.2)	0	(3.1)	4	(3.2)
Uruguay	**-11**	(4.3)	-1	(1.7)	-4	(3.9)	-1	(1.4)	3	(3.2)	1	(3.4)
Malaysia**	0	(2.2)	-3	(2.0)	0	(2.2)	0	(1.3)	-7	(5.2)	-3	(4.9)

1. Student-level refers to the change in collaborative problem-solving score associated with students reporting the above.
2. School-level refers to the change in collaborative problem-solving score per 10 percentage-point increase in the number of schoolmates who reported the above.
Notes: Values that are statistically significant are indicated in bold (see Annex A3).
Questionnaire items that are measured at both the student and school levels are included in the same regression model.
* See note at the beginning of this Annex.
**Malaysia: Coverage is too small to ensure comparability (see Annex A4).
StatLink http://dx.doi.org/10.1787/888933616845

[Part 1/2]

Table V.7.21 Student-parent relationships

		Percentage of students who reported the following:											
		Talked to parents before going to school on the most recent day		Talked to parents after leaving school on the most recent day		"Strongly agree" that my parents are interested in my school activities		"Strongly agree" that my parents support my educational efforts and achievements		"Strongly agree" that my parents support me when I am facing difficulties at school		"Strongly agree" that my parents encourage me to be confident	
		%	S.E.	%	S.E.	%	S.E.	%	S.E.	%	S.E.	%	S.E.
OECD	Australia	90.1	(0.4)	95.7	(0.2)	51.6	(0.5)	64.7	(0.5)	51.2	(0.5)	57.2	(0.5)
	Austria	84.1	(0.7)	91.7	(0.5)	74.2	(0.6)	61.4	(0.7)	69.9	(0.6)	64.9	(0.6)
	Belgium[1]	85.4	(0.5)	93.2	(0.3)	49.6	(0.6)	56.0	(0.6)	50.8	(0.6)	49.0	(0.6)
	Canada	88.2	(0.4)	95.0	(0.2)	49.1	(0.6)	66.8	(0.6)	51.1	(0.6)	57.6	(0.5)
	Chile	81.2	(0.5)	86.4	(0.5)	53.6	(0.8)	59.8	(0.7)	54.1	(0.9)	54.7	(0.8)
	Czech Republic	85.6	(0.6)	93.5	(0.4)	38.0	(0.7)	45.8	(0.8)	38.2	(0.7)	27.4	(0.7)
	Denmark	87.2	(0.6)	94.3	(0.6)	52.1	(0.8)	60.2	(0.8)	61.0	(0.7)	50.4	(0.6)
	Estonia	87.9	(0.5)	88.8	(0.5)	37.8	(0.7)	42.4	(0.8)	37.7	(0.7)	36.6	(0.7)
	Finland	82.8	(0.6)	94.5	(0.4)	54.6	(0.9)	48.3	(0.9)	46.9	(0.8)	47.7	(0.8)
	France	80.8	(0.5)	91.4	(0.4)	54.4	(0.7)	62.4	(0.6)	47.4	(0.6)	52.6	(0.8)
	Germany	86.9	(0.6)	94.5	(0.4)	67.9	(0.7)	61.1	(0.7)	64.1	(0.7)	58.3	(0.8)
	Greece	88.5	(0.5)	92.0	(0.5)	51.1	(0.9)	50.6	(0.8)	49.4	(0.8)	58.4	(0.8)
	Hungary	89.4	(0.5)	93.5	(0.4)	54.0	(0.8)	56.7	(0.8)	52.7	(0.8)	53.9	(0.8)
	Iceland	90.2	(0.5)	97.4	(0.3)	53.7	(0.9)	69.9	(0.9)	62.1	(0.9)	65.8	(0.9)
	Ireland	92.1	(0.5)	96.7	(0.3)	61.7	(0.7)	63.8	(0.7)	60.4	(0.7)	61.0	(0.7)
	Israel	88.0	(0.8)	91.1	(0.6)	m	m	m	m	m	m	m	m
	Italy	89.3	(0.4)	93.6	(0.4)	50.0	(0.7)	44.0	(0.7)	42.9	(0.7)	51.8	(0.7)
	Japan	90.2	(0.5)	93.9	(0.4)	30.1	(0.8)	42.1	(0.7)	37.4	(0.7)	30.5	(0.7)
	Korea	79.4	(0.9)	85.5	(0.7)	46.0	(1.1)	43.5	(1.1)	39.4	(1.0)	40.0	(1.1)
	Latvia	89.4	(0.5)	93.5	(0.4)	44.5	(0.9)	40.6	(1.0)	35.3	(0.9)	32.9	(0.9)
	Luxembourg	82.4	(0.6)	91.6	(0.4)	67.8	(0.6)	62.2	(0.6)	56.6	(0.6)	55.9	(0.7)
	Mexico	79.7	(0.7)	84.4	(0.5)	59.6	(0.7)	58.0	(0.7)	50.7	(0.7)	55.5	(0.6)
	Netherlands	89.0	(0.5)	96.6	(0.2)	50.6	(0.8)	52.1	(0.9)	55.1	(0.9)	50.4	(0.9)
	New Zealand	88.8	(0.4)	95.0	(0.4)	49.6	(0.8)	64.1	(0.7)	48.4	(0.8)	54.6	(0.7)
	Norway	87.6	(0.4)	96.0	(0.3)	50.5	(0.9)	55.6	(0.8)	54.1	(0.8)	57.0	(0.9)
	Poland	83.4	(0.6)	90.5	(0.4)	40.2	(1.0)	32.2	(0.8)	34.1	(0.9)	37.0	(0.9)
	Portugal	92.0	(0.4)	96.0	(0.3)	70.1	(0.7)	64.4	(0.7)	57.9	(0.8)	63.9	(0.6)
	Slovak Republic	81.8	(0.6)	88.7	(0.5)	40.4	(0.8)	47.3	(0.8)	36.9	(0.7)	35.7	(0.7)
	Slovenia	79.8	(0.7)	83.1	(0.6)	49.1	(0.8)	62.9	(0.7)	48.4	(0.8)	51.8	(0.7)
	Spain	84.0	(0.4)	92.1	(0.4)	60.6	(0.7)	56.6	(0.7)	54.8	(0.6)	58.5	(0.7)
	Sweden	87.4	(0.5)	94.8	(0.4)	49.5	(0.9)	60.8	(0.9)	58.2	(0.9)	59.5	(0.9)
	Switzerland	82.7	(0.6)	93.7	(0.5)	68.6	(0.9)	68.1	(0.9)	62.2	(0.9)	62.7	(0.9)
	Turkey	80.0	(0.8)	84.0	(0.8)	28.2	(0.9)	57.7	(0.8)	47.4	(0.8)	46.2	(0.8)
	United Kingdom[2]	88.7	(0.5)	94.9	(0.3)	50.6	(0.7)	63.5	(0.7)	52.6	(0.8)	56.2	(0.8)
	United States	88.2	(0.5)	94.3	(0.4)	51.3	(0.8)	70.4	(0.7)	53.9	(0.7)	62.2	(0.8)
	OECD average-32[3]	86.1	(0.1)	92.2	(0.1)	51.3	(0.1)	56.5	(0.1)	50.5	(0.1)	51.5	(0.1)
	OECD average-35[4]	86.1	(0.1)	92.3	(0.1)	51.8	(0.1)	56.4	(0.1)	50.7	(0.1)	51.7	(0.1)
Partners	Brazil	85.2	(0.4)	89.5	(0.5)	50.2	(0.5)	53.1	(0.5)	42.6	(0.4)	51.7	(0.5)
	B-S-J-G (China)	72.1	(0.8)	75.0	(1.0)	18.0	(0.6)	50.5	(0.8)	39.1	(0.8)	46.7	(0.8)
	Bulgaria	84.1	(0.6)	91.0	(0.6)	52.4	(0.7)	50.8	(0.8)	50.6	(0.8)	58.2	(0.8)
	Colombia	82.5	(0.5)	85.3	(0.5)	55.3	(0.7)	56.8	(0.6)	46.7	(0.7)	53.8	(0.6)
	Costa Rica	83.5	(0.6)	87.0	(0.6)	69.5	(0.8)	71.1	(0.7)	73.4	(0.7)	64.9	(0.7)
	Croatia	85.8	(0.5)	93.9	(0.4)	55.8	(0.7)	60.4	(0.8)	56.8	(0.8)	55.0	(0.7)
	Cyprus*	86.1	(0.4)	88.0	(0.5)	57.9	(0.7)	56.2	(0.7)	53.3	(0.8)	59.7	(0.8)
	Dominican Republic	86.6	(0.7)	89.8	(0.6)	61.2	(0.8)	62.3	(0.9)	43.0	(0.8)	55.2	(0.9)
	Hong Kong (China)	76.8	(0.6)	89.0	(0.5)	8.9	(0.5)	31.4	(0.9)	24.3	(0.7)	27.3	(0.9)
	Lithuania	89.7	(0.4)	92.8	(0.4)	64.4	(0.6)	61.6	(0.7)	56.1	(0.7)	63.2	(0.6)
	Macao (China)	72.5	(0.6)	83.3	(0.5)	10.7	(0.5)	31.5	(0.7)	21.2	(0.6)	27.1	(0.7)
	Montenegro	79.8	(0.6)	86.9	(0.5)	39.6	(0.7)	51.5	(0.7)	49.1	(0.7)	58.5	(0.6)
	Peru	81.7	(0.6)	84.1	(0.6)	43.8	(0.7)	44.0	(0.8)	33.6	(0.7)	48.8	(0.7)
	Qatar	88.6	(0.4)	91.0	(0.3)	40.5	(0.4)	60.4	(0.4)	53.1	(0.5)	65.1	(0.4)
	Russia	92.6	(0.4)	92.8	(0.4)	41.0	(1.0)	39.8	(0.9)	39.5	(1.1)	24.5	(0.8)
	Singapore	77.2	(0.5)	89.6	(0.4)	30.8	(0.6)	53.1	(0.6)	37.4	(0.8)	44.7	(0.7)
	Chinese Taipei	56.3	(0.7)	81.0	(0.6)	18.5	(0.6)	37.9	(0.7)	36.8	(0.8)	34.4	(0.6)
	Thailand	92.6	(0.4)	94.5	(0.3)	21.2	(0.6)	47.7	(1.0)	33.1	(0.9)	42.4	(1.0)
	Tunisia	90.6	(0.5)	90.3	(0.6)	36.7	(0.8)	56.3	(0.8)	42.1	(0.8)	62.0	(0.8)
	United Arab Emirates	90.5	(0.4)	93.3	(0.3)	31.5	(0.6)	59.0	(0.6)	52.8	(0.5)	66.5	(0.5)
	Uruguay	81.2	(0.7)	87.7	(0.6)	59.1	(0.8)	61.5	(0.8)	54.9	(0.7)	55.5	(0.7)
	Malaysia**	90.0	(0.6)	93.1	(0.4)	24.9	(1.0)	58.0	(1.0)	38.0	(1.0)	58.5	(1.1)

1. The parent questionnaire was distributed only in the Flemish Community.
2. The parent questionnaire was distributed only in Scotland.
3. For the results from the parent questionnaire, the OECD average-32 is the arithmetic mean of the OECD countries with available data from the parent questionnaire and the collaborative problem-solving assessment.
4. For the results from the parent questionnaire, the OECD average-35 is the arithmetic mean of the OECD countries with available data from the parent questionnaire.
* See note at the beginning of this Annex.
**Malaysia: Coverage is too small to ensure comparability (see Annex A4).
StatLink http://dx.doi.org/10.1787/888933616845

[Part 2/2]

Table V.7.21 Student-parent relationships

		Percentage of students whose parents reported the following:											
		"Every day or almost every day" eat the main meal with my child around a table		"Every day or almost every day" spend time just talking to my child		"Strongly agree" that I am interested in my child's school activities		"Strongly agree" that I support my child's efforts at school and his/her achievements		"Strongly agree" that I support my child when he/she is facing difficulties at school		"Strongly agree" that I encourage my child to be confident	
		%	S.E.	%	S.E.	%	S.E.	%	S.E.	%	S.E.	%	S.E.
OECD	Australia	m	m	m	m	m	m	m	m	m	m	m	m
	Austria	m	m	m	m	m	m	m	m	m	m	m	m
	Belgium[1]	90.7	(0.6)	71.2	(0.6)	64.5	(0.8)	69.0	(0.7)	74.3	(0.7)	73.7	(0.7)
	Canada	m	m	m	m	m	m	m	m	m	m	m	m
	Chile	69.0	(0.8)	48.7	(0.8)	66.2	(0.8)	77.2	(0.7)	79.1	(0.6)	82.8	(0.7)
	Czech Republic	m	m	m	m	m	m	m	m	m	m	m	m
	Denmark	m	m	m	m	m	m	m	m	m	m	m	m
	Estonia	m	m	m	m	m	m	m	m	m	m	m	m
	Finland	m	m	m	m	m	m	m	m	m	m	m	m
	France	91.4	(0.5)	73.1	(0.6)	71.4	(0.7)	83.6	(0.6)	73.6	(0.7)	79.9	(0.6)
	Germany	83.1	(0.6)	93.1	(0.4)	79.5	(0.7)	67.1	(0.9)	80.4	(0.8)	85.9	(0.6)
	Greece	m	m	m	m	m	m	m	m	m	m	m	m
	Hungary	m	m	m	m	m	m	m	m	m	m	m	m
	Iceland	m	m	m	m	m	m	m	m	m	m	m	m
	Ireland	75.3	(0.8)	80.9	(0.6)	84.4	(0.6)	84.8	(0.7)	87.0	(0.6)	86.6	(0.6)
	Israel	m	m	m	m	m	m	m	m	m	m	m	m
	Italy	94.9	(0.4)	77.1	(0.6)	53.9	(0.7)	54.2	(0.8)	56.7	(0.8)	73.9	(0.6)
	Japan	m	m	m	m	m	m	m	m	m	m	m	m
	Korea	70.2	(0.8)	53.7	(0.8)	43.9	(0.9)	41.9	(1.0)	44.2	(0.9)	46.4	(0.8)
	Latvia	m	m	m	m	m	m	m	m	m	m	m	m
	Luxembourg	87.4	(0.6)	80.8	(0.6)	78.6	(0.7)	79.8	(0.7)	78.1	(0.7)	82.7	(0.6)
	Mexico	76.5	(0.6)	43.4	(0.8)	68.5	(0.7)	72.5	(0.7)	71.0	(0.7)	75.2	(0.7)
	Netherlands	m	m	m	m	m	m	m	m	m	m	m	m
	New Zealand	m	m	m	m	m	m	m	m	m	m	m	m
	Norway	m	m	m	m	m	m	m	m	m	m	m	m
	Poland	m	m	m	m	m	m	m	m	m	m	m	m
	Portugal	94.7	(0.3)	90.2	(0.5)	68.9	(0.7)	70.3	(0.7)	77.6	(0.7)	83.6	(0.5)
	Slovak Republic	m	m	m	m	m	m	m	m	m	m	m	m
	Slovenia	m	m	m	m	m	m	m	m	m	m	m	m
	Spain	92.6	(0.5)	79.1	(0.7)	69.4	(0.8)	73.0	(0.8)	73.5	(0.8)	83.0	(0.6)
	Sweden	m	m	m	m	m	m	m	m	m	m	m	m
	Switzerland	m	m	m	m	m	m	m	m	m	m	m	m
	Turkey	m	m	m	m	m	m	m	m	m	m	m	m
	United Kingdom[2]	68.2	(1.4)	84.1	(0.9)	79.6	(0.8)	86.3	(0.8)	87.0	(0.8)	85.2	(0.8)
	United States	m	m	m	m	m	m	m	m	m	m	m	m
	OECD average-32[3]	83.5	(0.2)	72.2	(0.2)	67.7	(0.2)	70.4	(0.2)	72.3	(0.2)	77.5	(0.2)
	OECD average-35[4]	82.8	(0.2)	72.9	(0.2)	69.1	(0.2)	71.6	(0.2)	73.5	(0.2)	78.2	(0.2)
Partners	Brazil	m	m	m	m	m	m	m	m	m	m	m	m
	B-S-J-G (China)	m	m	m	m	m	m	m	m	m	m	m	m
	Bulgaria	m	m	m	m	m	m	m	m	m	m	m	m
	Colombia	m	m	m	m	m	m	m	m	m	m	m	m
	Costa Rica	m	m	m	m	m	m	m	m	m	m	m	m
	Croatia	73.4	(0.7)	65.2	(0.7)	68.6	(0.7)	79.5	(0.6)	80.1	(0.5)	81.7	(0.6)
	Cyprus*	m	m	m	m	m	m	m	m	m	m	m	m
	Dominican Republic	69.9	(1.0)	56.3	(1.0)	73.0	(0.9)	76.1	(0.9)	66.7	(1.1)	78.5	(0.8)
	Hong Kong (China)	87.1	(0.4)	67.0	(0.7)	18.6	(0.5)	50.6	(0.7)	57.3	(0.9)	66.6	(0.7)
	Lithuania	m	m	m	m	m	m	m	m	m	m	m	m
	Macao (China)	82.6	(0.5)	39.5	(0.6)	20.9	(0.6)	49.6	(0.7)	45.1	(0.7)	60.3	(0.7)
	Montenegro	m	m	m	m	m	m	m	m	m	m	m	m
	Peru	m	m	m	m	m	m	m	m	m	m	m	m
	Qatar	m	m	m	m	m	m	m	m	m	m	m	m
	Russia	m	m	m	m	m	m	m	m	m	m	m	m
	Singapore	m	m	m	m	m	m	m	m	m	m	m	m
	Chinese Taipei	m	m	m	m	m	m	m	m	m	m	m	m
	Thailand	m	m	m	m	m	m	m	m	m	m	m	m
	Tunisia	m	m	m	m	m	m	m	m	m	m	m	m
	United Arab Emirates	m	m	m	m	m	m	m	m	m	m	m	m
	Uruguay	m	m	m	m	m	m	m	m	m	m	m	m
	Malaysia**	m	m	m	m	m	m	m	m	m	m	m	m

1. The parent questionnaire was distributed only in the Flemish Community.
2. The parent questionnaire was distributed only in Scotland.
3. For the results from the parent questionnaire, the OECD average-32 is the arithmetic mean of the OECD countries with available data from the parent questionnaire and the collaborative problem-solving assessment.
4. For the results from the parent questionnaire, the OECD average-35 is the arithmetic mean of the OECD countries with available data from the parent questionnaire.
* See note at the beginning of this Annex.
**Malaysia: Coverage is too small to ensure comparability (see Annex A4).

StatLink http://dx.doi.org/10.1787/888933616845

[Part 1/2]

Table V.7.23 Student-parent relationships and performance in collaborative problem solving

		After accounting for students' and schools' socio-economic profile[1]																						
		Change in collaborative problem-solving score when students reported the following:																						
		Talked to parents before going to school on the most recent day				Talked to parents after leaving school on the most recent day				"Strongly agree" that my parents are interested in my school activities				"Strongly agree" that my parents support my educational efforts and achievements				"Strongly agree" that my parents support me when I am facing difficulties at school				"Strongly agree" that my parents encourage me to be confident			
		Student-level[2]		School-level[3]		Student-level		School-level		Student-level		School-level		Student-level		School-level		Student-level		School-level		Student-level		School-level	
		Score dif.	S.E.	Score dif.	S.E.	Score dif.	S.E.	Score dif.	S.E.	Score dif.	S.E.	Score dif.	S.E.	Score dif.	S.E.	Score dif.	S.E.	Score dif.	S.E.	Score dif.	S.E.	Score dif.	S.E.	Score dif.	S.E.
OECD	Australia	5	(4.6)	-1	(2.0)	**26**	(7.9)	**7**	(2.9)	**15**	(2.9)	1	(1.2)	**19**	(2.8)	2	(1.3)	2	(2.8)	-1	(1.4)	1	(3.3)	0	(1.5)
	Austria	-1	(4.3)	4	(2.6)	5	(6.4)	**9**	(3.6)	**-15**	(2.8)	1	(2.3)	-5	(3.0)	2	(2.4)	-5	(2.8)	-3	(2.9)	5	(2.8)	1	(2.9)
	Belgium[4]	**-10**	(3.4)	**9**	(3.0)	3	(4.8)	**17**	(3.8)	**-5**	(2.1)	0	(2.3)	-2	(2.3)	-2	(2.2)	**-8**	(2.2)	3	(2.3)	**-5**	(2.1)	0	(2.3)
	Canada	1	(3.3)	3	(2.7)	**19**	(5.7)	7	(4.3)	**13**	(2.6)	0	(1.5)	**18**	(2.7)	1	(1.8)	-2	(2.3)	1	(1.5)	1	(2.8)	-2	(1.6)
	Chile	**-12**	(3.6)	0	(3.1)	-1	(4.3)	**7**	(3.1)	-1	(2.4)	**5**	(2.3)	4	(3.1)	4	(2.3)	0	(2.6)	1	(2.6)	0	(2.6)	1	(2.6)
	Czech Republic	**-9**	(4.6)	2	(2.2)	**16**	(6.2)	**8**	(2.6)	-2	(2.9)	3	(2.0)	**8**	(2.8)	**5**	(1.6)	3	(2.7)	0	(1.7)	-3	(3.3)	-1	(1.8)
	Denmark	-5	(5.1)	0	(1.6)	**16**	(7.4)	-2	(2.4)	**10**	(3.4)	-2	(1.6)	**11**	(3.5)	-1	(1.6)	**10**	(3.2)	1	(1.8)	**9**	(2.8)	1	(1.7)
	Estonia	4	(4.8)	5	(3.1)	**22**	(4.5)	**12**	(3.6)	-3	(3.5)	1	(2.2)	**10**	(3.0)	**9**	(1.8)	-2	(3.1)	**4**	(2.0)	4	(3.0)	**8**	(1.6)
	Finland	**-9**	(4.3)	3	(3.1)	**25**	(7.6)	8	(5.5)	**12**	(3.5)	**5**	(2.3)	**9**	(3.3)	4	(2.5)	2	(3.8)	4	(2.3)	**9**	(3.5)	3	(2.6)
	France	**-8**	(3.4)	1	(2.6)	5	(6.4)	**10**	(3.6)	0	(2.6)	3	(2.7)	**7**	(2.7)	2	(2.7)	-1	(2.7)	-1	(2.6)	0	(2.8)	-2	(2.3)
	Germany	10	(6.4)	3	(3.0)	12	(8.5)	**11**	(3.3)	**-10**	(3.5)	1	(2.6)	0	(3.2)	0	(2.3)	**-7**	(3.1)	1	(2.5)	-2	(3.0)	-2	(2.5)
	Greece	**10**	(4.2)	**7**	(3.3)	**23**	(4.6)	**14**	(4.6)	**8**	(3.1)	**10**	(2.3)	**13**	(2.8)	**11**	(2.2)	0	(2.9)	**6**	(2.7)	5	(3.0)	**8**	(2.0)
	Hungary	-8	(4.6)	4	(2.8)	0	(7.2)	3	(3.5)	0	(2.7)	**6**	(2.2)	2	(2.8)	**6**	(1.8)	-4	(2.6)	**4**	(1.8)	-4	(2.7)	1	(1.8)
	Iceland	9	(6.4)	-1	(3.4)	**44**	(12.2)	6	(5.4)	**9**	(3.9)	2	(1.5)	**17**	(4.7)	**3**	(1.7)	8	(4.5)	3	(1.9)	**10**	(4.7)	0	(1.8)
	Ireland	m	m	m	m	m	m	m	m	m	m	m	m	m	m	m	m	m	m	m	m	m	m	m	m
	Israel	3	(5.5)	1	(5.7)	**24**	(5.4)	7	(10.1)	m	m	m	m	m	m	m	m	m	m	m	m	m	m	m	m
	Italy	5	(4.1)	1	(3.5)	**20**	(5.6)	**15**	(4.4)	0	(3.2)	-3	(2.1)	5	(3.3)	-2	(2.2)	-3	(3.0)	**-6**	(2.1)	**-8**	(2.9)	-4	(2.2)
	Japan	**11**	(4.1)	6	(3.8)	**30**	(6.1)	6	(4.8)	**14**	(2.7)	**7**	(2.4)	**11**	(2.4)	**7**	(2.6)	**9**	(2.4)	2	(3.0)	**7**	(2.5)	1	(3.2)
	Korea	**9**	(3.7)	-1	(1.5)	**13**	(3.2)	-2	(2.0)	**15**	(2.7)	**6**	(1.9)	**14**	(3.0)	**6**	(1.8)	**8**	(2.6)	3	(2.1)	**8**	(2.9)	2	(1.9)
	Latvia	-5	(4.9)	4	(3.0)	**25**	(7.1)	**8**	(3.3)	4	(3.3)	2	(1.7)	**12**	(3.0)	3	(1.5)	2	(4.0)	1	(1.7)	7	(3.6)	0	(1.6)
	Luxembourg	4	(4.1)	**16**	(3.0)	**33**	(6.0)	**31**	(4.2)	-2	(4.0)	**4**	(1.8)	1	(3.3)	0	(2.5)	-3	(3.2)	**5**	(1.8)	-6	(3.7)	-4	(2.4)
	Mexico	**-5**	(2.4)	0	(1.8)	0	(2.8)	4	(2.1)	-1	(2.9)	3	(2.0)	4	(2.8)	**5**	(2.1)	0	(2.5)	3	(1.8)	0	(2.7)	3	(1.8)
	Netherlands	-2	(4.6)	-1	(5.4)	**16**	(7.2)	**25**	(8.4)	**8**	(2.8)	5	(2.7)	**9**	(2.9)	5	(3.3)	**8**	(2.6)	-1	(2.8)	**10**	(3.1)	0	(2.6)
	New Zealand	4	(5.5)	5	(3.6)	**18**	(8.6)	8	(5.2)	**13**	(3.2)	-2	(2.5)	**24**	(3.5)	1	(2.5)	4	(3.7)	-2	(2.3)	3	(4.0)	-2	(2.5)
	Norway	9	(5.8)	0	(2.9)	**48**	(9.4)	6	(4.0)	3	(3.3)	2	(1.9)	6	(3.4)	**4**	(1.9)	-2	(3.4)	**4**	(1.9)	0	(2.9)	3	(1.6)
	Poland	m	m	m	m	m	m	m	m	m	m	m	m	m	m	m	m	m	m	m	m	m	m	m	m
	Portugal	8	(4.9)	5	(4.3)	**31**	(6.6)	**16**	(5.9)	1	(3.3)	2	(2.8)	4	(2.8)	**5**	(2.0)	-1	(2.5)	2	(2.4)	-3	(2.7)	1	(2.3)
	Slovak Republic	3	(3.4)	3	(2.5)	**17**	(5.1)	**7**	(2.8)	**5**	(2.6)	4	(2.0)	**15**	(2.7)	**8**	(1.6)	4	(2.8)	**5**	(2.1)	5	(2.5)	2	(1.6)
	Slovenia	-5	(4.3)	1	(2.0)	1	(4.8)	**6**	(1.8)	6	(3.5)	3	(1.8)	**11**	(4.2)	**4**	(1.6)	1	(3.2)	2	(1.6)	3	(3.5)	1	(1.8)
	Spain	-7	(3.8)	2	(2.8)	**22**	(5.8)	**8**	(3.5)	**-7**	(2.3)	0	(1.9)	-4	(2.6)	1	(1.9)	-4	(2.4)	3	(1.9)	**-9**	(3.3)	0	(1.8)
	Sweden	3	(5.2)	-1	(3.1)	**34**	(8.5)	**9**	(4.4)	4	(3.1)	**-3**	(1.7)	**19**	(3.1)	-3	(2.0)	1	(3.1)	**-5**	(2.2)	5	(3.3)	-2	(2.2)
	Switzerland	m	m	m	m	m	m	m	m	m	m	m	m	m	m	m	m	m	m	m	m	m	m	m	m
	Turkey	**13**	(3.3)	**14**	(2.8)	**17**	(4.3)	**14**	(3.4)	4	(2.5)	**8**	(2.8)	**7**	(2.7)	**15**	(2.2)	2	(2.5)	**12**	(2.5)	2	(2.6)	**11**	(3.0)
	United Kingdom[5]	-4	(5.5)	5	(3.3)	8	(8.0)	4	(5.4)	**18**	(2.9)	**5**	(2.2)	**24**	(3.5)	2	(2.0)	1	(3.2)	3	(2.1)	**7**	(3.0)	3	(2.0)
	United States	-6	(5.7)	3	(4.2)	**23**	(8.0)	**13**	(5.1)	**9**	(3.6)	-2	(2.5)	**19**	(3.9)	0	(3.4)	1	(4.1)	-2	(2.7)	0	(4.0)	-2	(2.7)
	OECD average	0	(0.8)	**3**	(0.6)	**19**	(1.2)	**9**	(0.8)	**4**	(0.6)	**2**	(0.4)	**9**	(0.6)	**3**	(0.4)	1	(0.5)	**2**	(0.4)	**2**	(0.6)	**1**	(0.4)
Partners	Brazil	-5	(3.2)	2	(2.4)	7	(4.2)	**6**	(2.4)	**7**	(2.2)	**6**	(1.4)	**13**	(2.5)	**6**	(1.5)	4	(2.1)	**4**	(1.5)	**8**	(2.0)	**3**	(1.5)
	B-S-J-G (China)	**-9**	(3.1)	**-13**	(2.6)	-4	(3.4)	**-10**	(2.6)	-3	(3.4)	-5	(3.5)	4	(2.4)	**6**	(2.6)	**6**	(2.6)	**5**	(2.7)	**6**	(2.9)	4	(2.6)
	Bulgaria	-2	(3.8)	2	(2.9)	**20**	(6.0)	**7**	(3.2)	1	(2.4)	5	(2.4)	**9**	(2.5)	3	(3.0)	-1	(2.1)	4	(2.9)	5	(2.8)	0	(2.4)
	Colombia	**-7**	(3.3)	-1	(2.4)	-4	(3.6)	2	(2.6)	-2	(2.1)	-2	(1.9)	2	(2.2)	-3	(2.2)	-4	(2.5)	1	(2.1)	-3	(2.4)	-3	(1.8)
	Costa Rica	4	(3.4)	**5**	(2.8)	**15**	(4.6)	2	(3.4)	3	(2.6)	**4**	(2.2)	1	(2.7)	**5**	(2.1)	-1	(3.0)	**7**	(1.9)	-2	(2.5)	**4**	(1.9)
	Croatia	1	(3.8)	3	(3.9)	**17**	(4.7)	**17**	(4.7)	4	(3.1)	**9**	(3.3)	**6**	(2.6)	**11**	(2.4)	-1	(2.7)	**8**	(3.1)	-4	(2.6)	**7**	(3.1)
	Cyprus*	**19**	(4.1)	**18**	(2.2)	**33**	(4.6)	**17**	(1.9)	**10**	(3.2)	**10**	(1.2)	**19**	(3.1)	**9**	(1.4)	**7**	(3.0)	**7**	(1.3)	5	(3.4)	**9**	(1.4)
	Dominican Republic	m	m	m	m	m	m	m	m	m	m	m	m	m	m	m	m	m	m	m	m	m	m	m	m
	Hong Kong (China)	**-10**	(3.4)	2	(5.2)	8	(4.4)	**19**	(4.3)	**-17**	(5.0)	-3	(5.4)	2	(3.3)	1	(4.5)	-4	(3.5)	3	(4.9)	1	(3.4)	0	(4.8)
	Lithuania	4	(4.6)	**12**	(3.0)	**21**	(5.0)	**14**	(2.8)	**8**	(3.0)	**7**	(1.5)	**16**	(3.2)	**4**	(1.3)	-1	(2.9)	**4**	(1.7)	-3	(3.4)	**5**	(1.4)
	Macao (China)	-4	(3.4)	**-5**	(2.5)	**13**	(4.2)	**35**	(3.1)	3	(5.1)	**-6**	(2.5)	**10**	(3.4)	**11**	(1.6)	2	(4.0)	**10**	(2.2)	1	(3.5)	**6**	(1.6)
	Montenegro	**-9**	(3.4)	**-10**	(2.4)	9	(5.2)	7	(4.0)	**5**	(2.7)	2	(3.0)	**25**	(2.7)	**11**	(1.9)	**21**	(2.3)	**10**	(2.5)	**17**	(2.6)	**8**	(2.5)
	Peru	**-7**	(2.9)	-1	(2.2)	-2	(3.5)	0	(2.1)	4	(2.5)	-1	(1.6)	**7**	(2.5)	1	(1.5)	1	(2.4)	0	(1.5)	3	(2.7)	2	(1.8)
	Qatar	m	m	m	m	m	m	m	m	m	m	m	m	m	m	m	m	m	m	m	m	m	m	m	m
	Russia	-2	(5.7)	-3	(4.4)	8	(5.5)	1	(4.6)	1	(3.6)	0	(2.2)	5	(3.4)	5	(2.6)	1	(3.0)	3	(2.3)	0	(3.7)	-1	(2.8)
	Singapore	2	(3.5)	-1	(2.3)	**21**	(4.6)	5	(3.0)	3	(3.1)	1	(1.9)	1	(2.9)	1	(1.7)	-4	(3.2)	1	(2.2)	**-8**	(3.0)	-2	(1.4)
	Chinese Taipei	-3	(2.4)	-2	(2.4)	**14**	(2.9)	6	(3.0)	5	(3.4)	1	(3.2)	**18**	(3.2)	2	(2.5)	**10**	(2.9)	1	(2.7)	**9**	(3.1)	1	(2.7)
	Thailand	3	(4.4)	6	(5.1)	8	(5.5)	**15**	(5.7)	**6**	(3.0)	**7**	(2.1)	**20**	(2.2)	**8**	(1.9)	**12**	(1.9)	**9**	(1.9)	**6**	(2.3)	2	(1.8)
	Tunisia	-3	(4.0)	5	(3.4)	-6	(3.2)	5	(2.6)	1	(2.6)	3	(1.9)	3	(2.5)	**4**	(1.9)	2	(2.4)	2	(1.9)	**6**	(2.3)	1	(2.3)
	United Arab Emirates	-1	(4.0)	6	(3.6)	**11**	(4.4)	**25**	(3.3)	**9**	(2.6)	**7**	(1.8)	**17**	(2.2)	**17**	(1.4)	**5**	(2.4)	**7**	(2.4)	**9**	(2.6)	**9**	(2.2)
	Uruguay	-3	(3.8)	-2	(2.5)	**10**	(4.8)	4	(2.4)	1	(2.8)	2	(1.7)	1	(2.5)	2	(2.0)	**-5**	(2.5)	-1	(1.9)	-2	(2.4)	-3	(2.1)
	Malaysia**	-2	(4.5)	-5	(4.6)	10	(5.1)	-4	(6.4)	3	(2.8)	2	(2.1)	**14**	(2.6)	**4**	(1.9)	**11**	(3.2)	2	(1.9)	**14**	(2.9)	2	(1.7)

1. The socio-economic profile is measured by the PISA index of economic, social and cultural status (ESCS).
2. Student-level refers to the change in collaborative problem-solving score associated with students or parents reporting the above.
3. School-level refers to the change in collaborative problem-solving score per 10 percentage-point increase in the number of schoolmates or school parents who reported the above.
4. The parent questionnaire was distributed only in the Flemish Community.
5. The parent questionnaire was distributed only in Scotland.

Notes: Values that are statistically significant are indicated in bold (see Annex A3).
Questionnaire items that are measured at both the student and school levels are included in the same regression model.
* See note at the beginning of this Annex.
**Malaysia: Coverage is too small to ensure comparability (see Annex A4).

StatLink http://dx.doi.org/10.1787/888933616845

[Part 2/2]

Table V.7.23 Student-parent relationships and performance in collaborative problem solving

	After accounting for students' and schools' socio-economic profile[1]																							
	Change in collaborative problem-solving score when parents reported the following:																							
	"Every day or almost every day" eat the main meal with my child around a table				"Every day or almost every day" spend time just talking to my child				"Strongly agree" that I am interested in my child's school activities				"Strongly agree" that I support my child's efforts at school and his/her achievements				"Strongly agree" that I support my child when he/she is facing difficulties at school				"Strongly agree" that I encourage my child to be confident			
	Student-level[2]		School-level[3]		Student-level		School-level		Student-level		School-level		Student-level		School-level		Student-level		School-level		Student-level		School-level	
	Score dif.	S.E.	Score dif.	S.E.	Score dif.	S.E.	Score dif.	S.E.	Score dif.	S.E.	Score dif.	S.E.	Score dif.	S.E.	Score dif.	S.E.	Score dif.	S.E.	Score dif.	S.E.	Score dif.	S.E.	Score dif.	S.E.
OECD																								
Australia	m	m	m	m	m	m	m	m	m	m	m	m	m	m	m	m	m	m	m	m	m	m	m	m
Austria	m	m	m	m	m	m	m	m	m	m	m	m	m	m	m	m	m	m	m	m	m	m	m	m
Belgium[4]	2	(6.0)	4	(4.2)	1	(3.5)	4	(3.5)	4	(3.2)	-1	(3.2)	**7**	(3.4)	**7**	(3.0)	1	(4.0)	1	(3.1)	2	(3.6)	0	(3.0)
Canada	m	m	m	m	m	m	m	m	m	m	m	m	m	m	m	m	m	m	m	m	m	m	m	m
Chile	-2	(2.6)	-2	(2.4)	0	(2.6)	0	(2.0)	**9**	(2.4)	**6**	(2.6)	**7**	(3.3)	**6**	(3.0)	4	(3.8)	4	(3.5)	6	(3.9)	3	(2.8)
Czech Republic	m	m	m	m	m	m	m	m	m	m	m	m	m	m	m	m	m	m	m	m	m	m	m	m
Denmark	m	m	m	m	m	m	m	m	m	m	m	m	m	m	m	m	m	m	m	m	m	m	m	m
Estonia	m	m	m	m	m	m	m	m	m	m	m	m	m	m	m	m	m	m	m	m	m	m	m	m
Finland	m	m	m	m	m	m	m	m	m	m	m	m	m	m	m	m	m	m	m	m	m	m	m	m
France	**13**	(5.7)	4	(3.4)	-4	(3.1)	2	(2.6)	2	(3.9)	**4**	(2.1)	5	(4.3)	0	(2.9)	-1	(3.2)	-3	(2.6)	-1	(3.5)	-2	(3.1)
Germany	-8	(4.9)	3	(2.6)	-8	(9.0)	4	(4.7)	-5	(5.2)	5	(2.5)	**-12**	(4.2)	3	(2.3)	**-14**	(4.9)	2	(2.8)	-3	(5.5)	4	(3.0)
Greece	m	m	m	m	m	m	m	m	m	m	m	m	m	m	m	m	m	m	m	m	m	m	m	m
Hungary	m	m	m	m	m	m	m	m	m	m	m	m	m	m	m	m	m	m	m	m	m	m	m	m
Iceland	m	m	m	m	m	m	m	m	m	m	m	m	m	m	m	m	m	m	m	m	m	m	m	m
Ireland	m	m	m	m	m	m	m	m	m	m	m	m	m	m	m	m	m	m	m	m	m	m	m	m
Israel	m	m	m	m	m	m	m	m	m	m	m	m	m	m	m	m	m	m	m	m	m	m	m	m
Italy	-5	(7.7)	-1	(3.9)	-7	(3.8)	-4	(2.7)	4	(3.9)	3	(2.0)	5	(4.0)	4	(2.3)	2	(4.3)	**5**	(2.3)	1	(4.2)	1	(2.3)
Japan	m	m	m	m	m	m	m	m	m	m	m	m	m	m	m	m	m	m	m	m	m	m	m	m
Korea	3	(3.1)	0	(2.3)	**7**	(2.8)	**8**	(2.6)	**8**	(2.4)	**6**	(2.6)	**14**	(2.5)	**8**	(2.3)	**6**	(2.3)	**6**	(2.7)	**8**	(2.4)	**6**	(2.3)
Latvia	m	m	m	m	m	m	m	m	m	m	m	m	m	m	m	m	m	m	m	m	m	m	m	m
Luxembourg	9	(5.9)	2	(5.3)	**14**	(4.6)	0	(3.7)	7	(5.5)	**8**	(3.3)	4	(4.6)	0	(3.6)	3	(5.5)	5	(3.4)	**12**	(5.7)	2	(3.9)
Mexico	-3	(2.5)	0	(2.2)	**-5**	(2.4)	2	(1.9)	0	(2.8)	**6**	(1.9)	4	(3.0)	**6**	(2.0)	-3	(2.9)	**5**	(2.0)	0	(2.9)	**5**	(1.9)
Netherlands	m	m	m	m	m	m	m	m	m	m	m	m	m	m	m	m	m	m	m	m	m	m	m	m
New Zealand	m	m	m	m	m	m	m	m	m	m	m	m	m	m	m	m	m	m	m	m	m	m	m	m
Norway	m	m	m	m	m	m	m	m	m	m	m	m	m	m	m	m	m	m	m	m	m	m	m	m
Poland	m	m	m	m	m	m	m	m	m	m	m	m	m	m	m	m	m	m	m	m	m	m	m	m
Portugal	0	(6.8)	10	(5.2)	1	(5.0)	6	(4.1)	**9**	(3.2)	**8**	(2.6)	**19**	(3.3)	**6**	(2.5)	**8**	(3.5)	5	(2.8)	**11**	(3.9)	5	(3.1)
Slovak Republic	m	m	m	m	m	m	m	m	m	m	m	m	m	m	m	m	m	m	m	m	m	m	m	m
Slovenia	m	m	m	m	m	m	m	m	m	m	m	m	m	m	m	m	m	m	m	m	m	m	m	m
Spain	6	(7.1)	1	(3.9)	3	(4.0)	4	(2.8)	**14**	(3.4)	4	(1.9)	**19**	(3.7)	2	(2.5)	**13**	(3.9)	4	(2.3)	**14**	(4.1)	1	(2.7)
Sweden	m	m	m	m	m	m	m	m	m	m	m	m	m	m	m	m	m	m	m	m	m	m	m	m
Switzerland	m	m	m	m	m	m	m	m	m	m	m	m	m	m	m	m	m	m	m	m	m	m	m	m
Turkey	m	m	m	m	m	m	m	m	m	m	m	m	m	m	m	m	m	m	m	m	m	m	m	m
United Kingdom[5]	2	(7.1)	3	(2.0)	7	(9.7)	2	(3.8)	-1	(6.8)	0	(3.0)	6	(9.9)	0	(3.0)	-3	(10.8)	2	(3.7)	0	(8.5)	-2	(3.3)
United States	m	m	m	m	m	m	m	m	m	m	m	m	m	m	m	m	m	m	m	m	m	m	m	m
OECD average	1	(1.7)	**2**	(1.1)	1	(1.6)	**3**	(1.0)	**5**	(1.2)	**4**	(0.8)	**7**	(1.4)	**4**	(0.8)	1	(1.5)	**3**	(0.9)	**5**	(1.4)	**2**	(0.9)
Partners																								
Brazil	m	m	m	m	m	m	m	m	m	m	m	m	m	m	m	m	m	m	m	m	m	m	m	m
B-S-J-G (China)	m	m	m	m	m	m	m	m	m	m	m	m	m	m	m	m	m	m	m	m	m	m	m	m
Bulgaria	m	m	m	m	m	m	m	m	m	m	m	m	m	m	m	m	m	m	m	m	m	m	m	m
Colombia	m	m	m	m	m	m	m	m	m	m	m	m	m	m	m	m	m	m	m	m	m	m	m	m
Costa Rica	m	m	m	m	m	m	m	m	m	m	m	m	m	m	m	m	m	m	m	m	m	m	m	m
Croatia	**-16**	(4.2)	-4	(2.7)	**-5**	(2.5)	-3	(3.4)	0	(2.8)	**7**	(3.4)	4	(3.2)	**14**	(3.2)	1	(3.6)	**9**	(4.1)	-3	(3.6)	6	(3.7)
Cyprus*	m	m	m	m	m	m	m	m	m	m	m	m	m	m	m	m	m	m	m	m	m	m	m	m
Dominican Republic	m	m	m	m	m	m	m	m	m	m	m	m	m	m	m	m	m	m	m	m	m	m	m	m
Hong Kong (China)	1	(4.6)	**15**	(5.8)	-1	(3.3)	**11**	(4.3)	**-8**	(3.5)	-4	(5.1)	5	(3.3)	3	(4.0)	2	(3.3)	**9**	(3.9)	6	(3.3)	9	(4.8)
Lithuania	m	m	m	m	m	m	m	m	m	m	m	m	m	m	m	m	m	m	m	m	m	m	m	m
Macao (China)	3	(4.4)	**25**	(3.0)	-3	(3.1)	**12**	(2.4)	0	(4.0)	-2	(1.7)	**10**	(3.5)	-1	(2.1)	2	(3.0)	**-12**	(1.8)	0	(4.0)	0	(2.6)
Montenegro	m	m	m	m	m	m	m	m	m	m	m	m	m	m	m	m	m	m	m	m	m	m	m	m
Peru	m	m	m	m	m	m	m	m	m	m	m	m	m	m	m	m	m	m	m	m	m	m	m	m
Qatar	m	m	m	m	m	m	m	m	m	m	m	m	m	m	m	m	m	m	m	m	m	m	m	m
Russia	m	m	m	m	m	m	m	m	m	m	m	m	m	m	m	m	m	m	m	m	m	m	m	m
Singapore	m	m	m	m	m	m	m	m	m	m	m	m	m	m	m	m	m	m	m	m	m	m	m	m
Chinese Taipei	m	m	m	m	m	m	m	m	m	m	m	m	m	m	m	m	m	m	m	m	m	m	m	m
Thailand	m	m	m	m	m	m	m	m	m	m	m	m	m	m	m	m	m	m	m	m	m	m	m	m
Tunisia	m	m	m	m	m	m	m	m	m	m	m	m	m	m	m	m	m	m	m	m	m	m	m	m
United Arab Emirates	m	m	m	m	m	m	m	m	m	m	m	m	m	m	m	m	m	m	m	m	m	m	m	m
Uruguay	m	m	m	m	m	m	m	m	m	m	m	m	m	m	m	m	m	m	m	m	m	m	m	m
Malaysia**	m	m	m	m	m	m	m	m	m	m	m	m	m	m	m	m	m	m	m	m	m	m	m	m

1. The socio-economic profile is measured by the PISA index of economic, social and cultural status (ESCS).
2. Student-level refers to the change in collaborative problem-solving score associated with students or parents reporting the above.
3. School-level refers to the change in collaborative problem-solving score per 10 percentage-point increase in the number of schoolmates or school parents who reported the above.
4. The parent questionnaire was distributed only in the Flemish Community.
5. The parent questionnaire was distributed only in Scotland.

Notes: Values that are statistically significant are indicated in bold (see Annex A3).
Questionnaire items that are measured at both the student and school levels are included in the same regression model.
* See note at the beginning of this Annex.
**Malaysia: Coverage is too small to ensure comparability (see Annex A4).

StatLink http://dx.doi.org/10.1787/888933616845

[Part 1/2]

Table V.7.24 Student-parent relationships and relative performance in collaborative problem solving

After accounting for performance in science, reading and mathematics

Change in collaborative problem-solving score when students reported the following:

		Talked to parents before going to school on the most recent day				Talked to parents after leaving school on the most recent day				"Strongly agree" that my parents are interested in my school activities				"Strongly agree" that my parents support my educational efforts and achievements				"Strongly agree" that my parents support me when I am facing difficulties at school				"Strongly agree" that my parents encourage me to be confident			
		Student-level[1]		School-level[2]		Student-level		School-level		Student-level		School-level		Student-level		School-level		Student-level		School-level		Student-level		School-level	
		Score dif.	S.E.	Score dif.	S.E.	Score dif.	S.E.	Score dif.	S.E.	Score dif.	S.E.	Score dif.	S.E.	Score dif.	S.E.	Score dif.	S.E.	Score dif.	S.E.	Score dif.	S.E.	Score dif.	S.E.	Score dif.	S.E.
OECD	Australia	2	(2.9)	1	(1.4)	7	(5.2)	3	(2.3)	2	(3.3)	0	(0.8)	4	(2.6)	0	(0.8)	0	(2.9)	1	(0.9)	-3	(3.0)	0	(0.9)
	Austria	-3	(3.3)	2	(2.0)	2	(5.5)	2	(2.3)	**-9**	(2.2)	-1	(1.6)	0	(2.2)	-1	(1.5)	1	(1.9)	1	(1.8)	**5**	(2.0)	2	(1.6)
	Belgium[3]	**-8**	(2.8)	1	(1.9)	-5	(3.6)	4	(2.4)	**-5**	(1.8)	-1	(1.1)	-4	(2.2)	-2	(1.1)	**-5**	(2.0)	2	(1.3)	-2	(1.9)	1	(1.2)
	Canada	-2	(2.4)	0	(2.1)	-6	(4.2)	0	(3.0)	1	(2.3)	-1	(1.1)	3	(2.3)	-2	(1.3)	-1	(2.1)	-3	(1.3)	0	(2.6)	-3	(1.5)
	Chile	-4	(2.9)	-1	(1.7)	-4	(4.1)	1	(1.8)	1	(1.9)	-1	(1.4)	4	(2.1)	-1	(1.3)	4	(1.9)	0	(1.3)	2	(2.1)	0	(1.4)
	Czech Republic	-4	(3.9)	2	(1.5)	6	(5.9)	**4**	(2.0)	-5	(2.4)	2	(1.3)	1	(2.5)	**3**	(1.2)	2	(2.0)	1	(1.1)	-2	(2.3)	2	(1.3)
	Denmark	-4	(3.0)	-1	(1.3)	3	(5.6)	-3	(1.8)	-4	(2.4)	0	(1.1)	-2	(2.5)	0	(1.2)	3	(2.1)	1	(1.2)	0	(2.3)	1	(1.2)
	Estonia	5	(4.0)	1	(1.8)	**8**	(3.6)	1	(2.3)	-4	(2.8)	0	(1.2)	-1	(2.3)	**2**	(1.1)	-1	(2.5)	2	(1.3)	3	(2.0)	**3**	(1.1)
	Finland	-2	(3.2)	1	(2.1)	2	(6.3)	5	(4.2)	2	(2.9)	0	(1.4)	1	(3.0)	-2	(1.4)	1	(3.3)	-1	(1.5)	3	(3.1)	-1	(1.7)
	France	-1	(3.1)	1	(1.5)	0	(5.8)	0	(2.1)	1	(2.3)	2	(1.4)	2	(2.7)	1	(1.3)	1	(2.6)	2	(1.4)	2	(2.8)	2	(1.2)
	Germany	1	(5.2)	1	(2.3)	6	(7.3)	3	(2.6)	-3	(3.1)	0	(1.4)	2	(2.9)	0	(1.4)	-1	(2.6)	0	(1.4)	0	(2.5)	-1	(1.6)
	Greece	0	(3.8)	1	(2.1)	3	(4.2)	2	(2.7)	-1	(2.6)	2	(1.4)	1	(2.4)	1	(1.3)	-2	(2.4)	0	(1.5)	3	(2.6)	2	(1.3)
	Hungary	-6	(4.4)	1	(1.7)	-3	(6.3)	1	(2.0)	-4	(2.4)	2	(1.2)	-3	(2.5)	2	(1.1)	-3	(2.1)	2	(1.1)	-3	(2.2)	1	(1.1)
	Iceland	2	(4.5)	-3	(2.4)	3	(9.9)	0	(3.8)	-5	(2.7)	0	(1.1)	-2	(3.2)	0	(1.4)	-4	(2.8)	0	(1.5)	0	(3.0)	0	(1.5)
	Ireland	m	m	m	m	m	m	m	m	m	m	m	m	m	m	m	m	m	m	m	m	m	m	m	m
	Israel	3	(4.4)	1	(2.8)	7	(4.3)	7	(4.4)	m	m	m	m	m	m	m	m	m	m	m	m	m	m	m	m
	Italy	3	(3.7)	1	(2.4)	9	(5.0)	**7**	(2.7)	-1	(2.8)	-1	(1.6)	0	(3.0)	1	(1.6)	0	(2.6)	-2	(1.7)	-4	(2.5)	0	(1.7)
	Japan	**9**	(3.5)	2	(2.1)	**16**	(4.8)	1	(2.4)	**7**	(2.5)	-2	(1.5)	**7**	(2.3)	-3	(1.4)	**8**	(2.2)	-1	(1.7)	**8**	(2.5)	-3	(2.1)
	Korea	**10**	(2.4)	2	(1.1)	**10**	(2.4)	2	(1.3)	**7**	(2.4)	-2	(1.2)	4	(2.6)	-2	(1.1)	**5**	(2.2)	**-3**	(1.2)	**5**	(2.4)	**-3**	(1.2)
	Latvia	0	(4.1)	-1	(1.9)	9	(5.8)	2	(2.5)	1	(3.0)	1	(1.1)	-2	(2.7)	1	(1.0)	0	(3.4)	1	(1.0)	2	(3.0)	1	(1.0)
	Luxembourg	2	(3.2)	**7**	(2.4)	9	(4.6)	**15**	(3.2)	-2	(3.6)	-1	(1.6)	-2	(3.1)	-1	(2.2)	-3	(2.9)	0	(1.6)	-2	(3.4)	-3	(2.2)
	Mexico	**-4**	(2.0)	-1	(1.3)	**-6**	(2.4)	0	(1.7)	1	(2.6)	1	(1.3)	1	(2.9)	2	(1.2)	0	(2.5)	**2**	(1.0)	1	(2.6)	1	(1.1)
	Netherlands	-1	(3.8)	0	(2.7)	0	(6.4)	0	(4.3)	4	(2.2)	0	(1.7)	**6**	(2.5)	2	(2.1)	**7**	(2.4)	1	(1.7)	**8**	(2.9)	2	(1.6)
	New Zealand	-2	(4.5)	-1	(2.7)	-6	(7.0)	-1	(3.5)	1	(2.9)	-1	(1.6)	5	(2.7)	-1	(1.7)	3	(3.0)	-1	(1.5)	4	(3.2)	-1	(1.8)
	Norway	5	(4.6)	1	(2.2)	4	(7.3)	2	(3.7)	0	(3.1)	0	(1.5)	-2	(3.2)	1	(1.6)	**-7**	(3.1)	1	(1.6)	**-7**	(2.3)	0	(1.5)
	Poland	m	m	m	m	m	m	m	m	m	m	m	m	m	m	m	m	m	m	m	m	m	m	m	m
	Portugal	**11**	(3.7)	-3	(3.1)	**17**	(5.5)	0	(4.5)	-2	(2.8)	0	(1.7)	-3	(2.5)	0	(1.6)	-1	(2.2)	0	(1.5)	-1	(2.1)	0	(1.4)
	Slovak Republic	1	(2.8)	-1	(1.7)	0	(5.0)	1	(1.4)	-2	(2.1)	**3**	(1.0)	1	(2.4)	**3**	(1.1)	-2	(2.6)	**3**	(1.1)	-1	(2.4)	2	(1.1)
	Slovenia	-3	(3.5)	0	(1.7)	-1	(4.0)	3	(1.5)	**7**	(3.1)	1	(1.1)	5	(3.7)	1	(1.3)	1	(2.8)	0	(1.2)	5	(3.0)	1	(1.3)
	Spain	-2	(3.1)	1	(1.7)	**10**	(4.4)	3	(2.8)	**-8**	(1.8)	1	(1.1)	-5	(2.4)	0	(1.2)	**-5**	(2.1)	1	(1.3)	-5	(2.9)	0	(1.3)
	Sweden	1	(3.8)	1	(2.0)	2	(6.3)	2	(3.0)	0	(3.1)	0	(1.2)	2	(2.5)	0	(1.4)	1	(2.7)	-1	(1.3)	1	(2.8)	0	(1.4)
	Switzerland	m	m	m	m	m	m	m	m	m	m	m	m	m	m	m	m	m	m	m	m	m	m	m	m
	Turkey	4	(2.5)	**4**	(1.5)	5	(3.2)	**4**	(1.6)	2	(2.2)	1	(1.4)	1	(2.3)	**3**	(1.3)	0	(2.1)	2	(1.4)	0	(2.1)	2	(1.7)
	United Kingdom[4]	-6	(4.4)	2	(2.7)	-9	(5.6)	0	(3.8)	4	(2.5)	2	(1.5)	**10**	(3.0)	0	(1.5)	1	(2.8)	1	(1.7)	4	(2.9)	2	(1.4)
	United States	-1	(4.4)	1	(2.8)	4	(5.9)	0	(3.1)	3	(2.8)	0	(1.4)	**7**	(2.7)	2	(1.9)	6	(3.1)	1	(1.5)	4	(3.1)	1	(1.8)
	OECD average	0	(0.6)	**1**	(0.4)	**3**	(1.0)	**2**	(0.5)	0	(0.5)	0	(0.2)	**1**	(0.5)	0	(0.3)	0	(0.5)	0	(0.3)	1	(0.5)	0	(0.3)
Partners	Brazil	**-6**	(2.7)	0	(1.5)	-3	(4.5)	1	(1.8)	1	(2.0)	1	(1.0)	3	(2.6)	0	(1.0)	0	(2.0)	0	(1.1)	1	(2.4)	0	(1.0)
	B-S-J-G (China)	2	(2.6)	-1	(1.5)	4	(3.1)	1	(1.7)	-1	(3.0)	0	(2.0)	**-4**	(2.2)	-2	(1.6)	1	(2.4)	-1	(1.4)	2	(2.5)	-1	(1.5)
	Bulgaria	-2	(3.2)	0	(2.0)	8	(4.6)	1	(2.1)	-3	(2.3)	2	(1.4)	-3	(2.2)	**3**	(1.5)	-2	(1.9)	**3**	(1.4)	1	(2.3)	2	(1.3)
	Colombia	**-7**	(2.7)	**-3**	(1.6)	**-7**	(3.1)	-2	(1.9)	0	(2.2)	0	(1.3)	-2	(1.8)	-1	(1.3)	-3	(2.0)	0	(1.2)	-3	(2.0)	-2	(1.3)
	Costa Rica	4	(3.2)	0	(2.3)	**8**	(3.8)	-1	(2.7)	4	(2.5)	0	(1.6)	2	(2.5)	1	(1.7)	1	(3.2)	2	(1.4)	4	(2.3)	1	(1.4)
	Croatia	4	(3.0)	0	(2.1)	**14**	(4.2)	6	(3.1)	2	(2.5)	1	(1.6)	1	(2.1)	2	(1.4)	2	(2.5)	2	(1.7)	2	(2.2)	2	(1.9)
	Cyprus*	1	(3.1)	1	(1.9)	**9**	(3.6)	1	(1.8)	0	(2.7)	2	(1.2)	1	(2.6)	1	(1.2)	1	(2.4)	1	(1.2)	0	(2.6)	2	(1.4)
	Dominican Republic	m	m	m	m	m	m	m	m	m	m	m	m	m	m	m	m	m	m	m	m	m	m	m	m
	Hong Kong (China)	-2	(2.6)	1	(2.5)	5	(3.0)	**6**	(2.3)	**-14**	(3.8)	-1	(3.8)	**-7**	(2.8)	1	(2.0)	**-7**	(2.9)	1	(2.4)	**-6**	(2.6)	1	(1.8)
	Lithuania	2	(3.8)	2	(1.6)	3	(4.0)	2	(1.7)	**6**	(2.3)	**2**	(0.8)	5	(2.8)	0	(0.8)	1	(2.5)	0	(0.9)	-1	(2.6)	0	(0.9)
	Macao (China)	-1	(2.8)	-4	(2.2)	5	(3.7)	0	(1.7)	-1	(3.5)	**-4**	(1.8)	1	(2.5)	1	(1.3)	1	(3.0)	0	(1.6)	0	(2.9)	0	(1.3)
	Montenegro	2	(2.9)	-1	(2.0)	4	(4.6)	5	(3.1)	0	(2.3)	1	(1.9)	**8**	(2.4)	2	(1.4)	**7**	(1.9)	**3**	(1.3)	**9**	(2.2)	3	(1.8)
	Peru	-4	(2.3)	-1	(1.6)	-3	(2.7)	-1	(1.7)	3	(2.2)	1	(1.2)	3	(2.5)	1	(1.0)	**5**	(2.4)	1	(1.2)	2	(2.4)	2	(1.2)
	Qatar	m	m	m	m	m	m	m	m	m	m	m	m	m	m	m	m	m	m	m	m	m	m	m	m
	Russia	-1	(4.6)	-5	(3.8)	1	(4.5)	-5	(3.7)	-4	(3.2)	2	(2.2)	-4	(3.0)	3	(2.0)	-1	(2.5)	3	(1.9)	-2	(3.0)	0	(1.9)
	Singapore	3	(2.6)	-2	(1.3)	**9**	(3.7)	-1	(1.6)	0	(2.1)	-2	(1.2)	0	(2.0)	**-3**	(1.0)	-2	(2.4)	**-3**	(1.2)	-1	(2.1)	-1	(1.1)
	Chinese Taipei	0	(1.7)	-2	(2.0)	**5**	(2.2)	0	(2.3)	1	(3.2)	0	(2.0)	3	(2.9)	-1	(1.6)	3	(2.7)	-1	(1.7)	3	(2.9)	-2	(1.8)
	Thailand	0	(4.3)	-1	(2.9)	-4	(4.8)	0	(4.0)	3	(2.1)	1	(1.4)	**6**	(1.9)	**3**	(1.2)	**7**	(1.9)	**4**	(1.3)	**5**	(2.1)	2	(1.2)
	Tunisia	-6	(3.4)	0	(2.4)	**-10**	(3.2)	1	(1.7)	1	(2.3)	0	(1.5)	0	(2.1)	0	(1.5)	0	(2.3)	0	(1.4)	3	(2.4)	0	(1.4)
	United Arab Emirates	**-6**	(2.6)	-1	(2.1)	-3	(3.9)	**5**	(2.0)	2	(2.8)	**2**	(1.0)	1	(2.2)	**3**	(1.0)	-1	(2.0)	1	(1.3)	2	(2.2)	0	(1.2)
	Uruguay	1	(3.0)	1	(1.7)	4	(4.0)	2	(1.8)	-5	(2.6)	1	(1.3)	-4	(2.0)	0	(1.4)	-3	(2.1)	-1	(1.5)	-1	(1.7)	-2	(1.4)
	Malaysia**	4	(3.7)	-3	(3.7)	7	(4.2)	-1	(4.7)	-1	(2.9)	0	(1.6)	1	(2.3)	0	(1.4)	2	(2.8)	0	(1.5)	**6**	(2.8)	-1	(1.2)

1. Student-level refers to the change in collaborative problem-solving score associated with students or parents reporting the above.
2. School-level refers to the change in collaborative problem-solving score per 10 percentage-point increase in the number of schoolmates or school parents who reported the above.
3. The parent questionnaire was distributed only in the Flemish Community.
4. The parent questionnaire was distributed only in Scotland.

Notes: Values that are statistically significant are indicated in bold (see Annex A3).

Questionnaire items that are measured at both the student and school levels are included in the same regression model.

* See note at the beginning of this Annex.

**Malaysia: Coverage is too small to ensure comparability (see Annex A4).

StatLink http://dx.doi.org/10.1787/888933616845

[Part 2/2]

Table V.7.24 Student-parent relationships and relative performance in collaborative problem solving

	After accounting for performance in science, reading and mathematics																							
	Change in collaborative problem-solving score when parents reported the following:																							
	"Every day or almost every day" eat the main meal with my child around a table				"Every day or almost every day" spend time just talking to my child				"Strongly agree" that I am interested in my child's school activities				"Strongly agree" that I support my child's efforts at school and his/her achievements				"Strongly agree" that I support my child when he/she is facing difficulties at school				"Strongly agree" that I encourage my child to be confident			
	Student-level[1]		School-level[2]		Student-level		School-level		Student-level		School-level		Student-level		School-level		Student-level		School-level		Student-level		School-level	
	Score dif.	S.E.	Score dif.	S.E.	Score dif.	S.E.	Score dif.	S.E.	Score dif.	S.E.	Score dif.	S.E.	Score dif.	S.E.	Score dif.	S.E.	Score dif.	S.E.	Score dif.	S.E.	Score dif.	S.E.	Score dif.	S.E.
OECD																								
Australia	m	m	m	m	m	m	m	m	m	m	m	m	m	m	m	m	m	m	m	m	m	m	m	m
Austria	m	m	m	m	m	m	m	m	m	m	m	m	m	m	m	m	m	m	m	m	m	m	m	m
Belgium[3]	-3	(5.3)	0	(2.3)	3	(3.1)	4	(2.0)	-2	(2.7)	0	(1.6)	1	(2.8)	2	(1.7)	1	(3.3)	1	(1.7)	2	(3.1)	0	(1.9)
Canada	m	m	m	m	m	m	m	m	m	m	m	m	m	m	m	m	m	m	m	m	m	m	m	m
Chile	**5**	(2.3)	0	(1.5)	3	(2.4)	1	(1.5)	3	(2.2)	2	(1.3)	5	(2.8)	1	(1.7)	3	(3.1)	2	(1.7)	4	(3.2)	1	(1.7)
Czech Republic	m	m	m	m	m	m	m	m	m	m	m	m	m	m	m	m	m	m	m	m	m	m	m	m
Denmark	m	m	m	m	m	m	m	m	m	m	m	m	m	m	m	m	m	m	m	m	m	m	m	m
Estonia	m	m	m	m	m	m	m	m	m	m	m	m	m	m	m	m	m	m	m	m	m	m	m	m
Finland	m	m	m	m	m	m	m	m	m	m	m	m	m	m	m	m	m	m	m	m	m	m	m	m
France	7	(4.9)	0	(2.1)	-3	(2.8)	**3**	(1.5)	4	(3.3)	1	(1.3)	5	(3.7)	3	(1.6)	1	(2.5)	0	(1.4)	3	(3.0)	1	(1.6)
Germany	-8	(4.2)	1	(1.7)	-9	(8.4)	-3	(3.2)	-6	(4.1)	1	(1.7)	**-8**	(3.4)	0	(1.5)	**-10**	(4.4)	1	(1.6)	-5	(4.3)	1	(2.1)
Greece	m	m	m	m	m	m	m	m	m	m	m	m	m	m	m	m	m	m	m	m	m	m	m	m
Hungary	m	m	m	m	m	m	m	m	m	m	m	m	m	m	m	m	m	m	m	m	m	m	m	m
Iceland	m	m	m	m	m	m	m	m	m	m	m	m	m	m	m	m	m	m	m	m	m	m	m	m
Ireland	m	m	m	m	m	m	m	m	m	m	m	m	m	m	m	m	m	m	m	m	m	m	m	m
Israel	m	m	m	m	m	m	m	m	m	m	m	m	m	m	m	m	m	m	m	m	m	m	m	m
Italy	-9	(6.1)	0	(3.4)	-4	(3.3)	1	(1.7)	0	(3.3)	**3**	(1.3)	0	(3.5)	**3**	(1.5)	-1	(3.8)	**3**	(1.4)	-3	(3.9)	2	(1.5)
Japan	m	m	m	m	m	m	m	m	m	m	m	m	m	m	m	m	m	m	m	m	m	m	m	m
Korea	1	(2.4)	1	(1.3)	3	(2.5)	2	(1.3)	0	(2.2)	0	(1.4)	-1	(2.0)	0	(1.2)	0	(1.9)	0	(1.2)	1	(2.3)	1	(1.4)
Latvia	m	m	m	m	m	m	m	m	m	m	m	m	m	m	m	m	m	m	m	m	m	m	m	m
Luxembourg	3	(4.8)	7	(3.9)	3	(3.6)	0	(2.6)	3	(4.9)	2	(2.1)	4	(4.1)	-3	(3.1)	1	(5.2)	1	(2.3)	8	(5.3)	-3	(3.3)
Mexico	-3	(2.2)	0	(1.4)	0	(2.0)	2	(1.1)	-4	(2.4)	2	(1.3)	-2	(2.9)	**3**	(1.1)	**-6**	(2.8)	**4**	(1.1)	-4	(2.5)	**3**	(1.1)
Netherlands	m	m	m	m	m	m	m	m	m	m	m	m	m	m	m	m	m	m	m	m	m	m	m	m
New Zealand	m	m	m	m	m	m	m	m	m	m	m	m	m	m	m	m	m	m	m	m	m	m	m	m
Norway	m	m	m	m	m	m	m	m	m	m	m	m	m	m	m	m	m	m	m	m	m	m	m	m
Poland	m	m	m	m	m	m	m	m	m	m	m	m	m	m	m	m	m	m	m	m	m	m	m	m
Portugal	-1	(6.2)	0	(3.6)	-1	(4.2)	2	(2.8)	4	(2.9)	**3**	(1.4)	5	(2.7)	1	(1.5)	2	(3.0)	2	(1.6)	4	(3.5)	**4**	(1.6)
Slovak Republic	m	m	m	m	m	m	m	m	m	m	m	m	m	m	m	m	m	m	m	m	m	m	m	m
Slovenia	m	m	m	m	m	m	m	m	m	m	m	m	m	m	m	m	m	m	m	m	m	m	m	m
Spain	1	(5.7)	0	(2.9)	1	(3.0)	1	(2.1)	5	(3.1)	1	(1.3)	**7**	(3.4)	0	(1.7)	4	(3.7)	1	(1.6)	4	(3.2)	0	(1.8)
Sweden	m	m	m	m	m	m	m	m	m	m	m	m	m	m	m	m	m	m	m	m	m	m	m	m
Switzerland	m	m	m	m	m	m	m	m	m	m	m	m	m	m	m	m	m	m	m	m	m	m	m	m
Turkey	m	m	m	m	m	m	m	m	m	m	m	m	m	m	m	m	m	m	m	m	m	m	m	m
United Kingdom[4]	-3	(5.1)	0	(1.5)	2	(7.1)	-1	(2.8)	-11	(6.1)	-1	(2.3)	-2	(7.0)	-3	(2.3)	2	(7.3)	-2	(2.8)	2	(6.6)	-4	(2.4)
United States	m	m	m	m	m	m	m	m	m	m	m	m	m	m	m	m	m	m	m	m	m	m	m	m
OECD average	-1	(1.4)	1	(0.8)	0	(1.3)	1	(0.6)	0	(1.1)	**1**	(0.5)	1	(1.1)	1	(0.5)	0	(1.2)	1	(0.5)	2	(1.2)	1	(0.6)
Partners																								
Brazil	m	m	m	m	m	m	m	m	m	m	m	m	m	m	m	m	m	m	m	m	m	m	m	m
B-S-J-G (China)	m	m	m	m	m	m	m	m	m	m	m	m	m	m	m	m	m	m	m	m	m	m	m	m
Bulgaria	m	m	m	m	m	m	m	m	m	m	m	m	m	m	m	m	m	m	m	m	m	m	m	m
Colombia	m	m	m	m	m	m	m	m	m	m	m	m	m	m	m	m	m	m	m	m	m	m	m	m
Costa Rica	m	m	m	m	m	m	m	m	m	m	m	m	m	m	m	m	m	m	m	m	m	m	m	m
Croatia	-7	(4.0)	-2	(1.5)	-2	(1.9)	0	(1.6)	-2	(2.8)	2	(1.6)	-2	(2.9)	**4**	(1.6)	0	(2.7)	**4**	(2.0)	-2	(2.7)	**3**	(1.7)
Cyprus*	m	m	m	m	m	m	m	m	m	m	m	m	m	m	m	m	m	m	m	m	m	m	m	m
Dominican Republic	m	m	m	m	m	m	m	m	m	m	m	m	m	m	m	m	m	m	m	m	m	m	m	m
Hong Kong (China)	-5	(3.4)	0	(2.7)	-2	(3.1)	1	(1.9)	**-12**	(3.4)	-2	(2.2)	**-7**	(3.4)	0	(1.6)	-5	(2.8)	1	(1.5)	-2	(2.8)	1	(1.7)
Lithuania	m	m	m	m	m	m	m	m	m	m	m	m	m	m	m	m	m	m	m	m	m	m	m	m
Macao (China)	-5	(3.2)	2	(2.3)	-5	(2.8)	-1	(1.2)	**-6**	(3.1)	-2	(1.4)	-3	(2.6)	-2	(1.7)	-3	(2.6)	**-3**	(1.3)	-4	(3.1)	-3	(1.7)
Montenegro	m	m	m	m	m	m	m	m	m	m	m	m	m	m	m	m	m	m	m	m	m	m	m	m
Peru	m	m	m	m	m	m	m	m	m	m	m	m	m	m	m	m	m	m	m	m	m	m	m	m
Qatar	m	m	m	m	m	m	m	m	m	m	m	m	m	m	m	m	m	m	m	m	m	m	m	m
Russia	m	m	m	m	m	m	m	m	m	m	m	m	m	m	m	m	m	m	m	m	m	m	m	m
Singapore	m	m	m	m	m	m	m	m	m	m	m	m	m	m	m	m	m	m	m	m	m	m	m	m
Chinese Taipei	m	m	m	m	m	m	m	m	m	m	m	m	m	m	m	m	m	m	m	m	m	m	m	m
Thailand	m	m	m	m	m	m	m	m	m	m	m	m	m	m	m	m	m	m	m	m	m	m	m	m
Tunisia	m	m	m	m	m	m	m	m	m	m	m	m	m	m	m	m	m	m	m	m	m	m	m	m
United Arab Emirates	m	m	m	m	m	m	m	m	m	m	m	m	m	m	m	m	m	m	m	m	m	m	m	m
Uruguay	m	m	m	m	m	m	m	m	m	m	m	m	m	m	m	m	m	m	m	m	m	m	m	m
Malaysia**	m	m	m	m	m	m	m	m	m	m	m	m	m	m	m	m	m	m	m	m	m	m	m	m

1. Student-level refers to the change in collaborative problem-solving score associated with students or parents reporting the above.
2. School-level refers to the change in collaborative problem-solving score per 10 percentage-point increase in the number of schoolmates or school parents who reported the above.
3. The parent questionnaire was distributed only in the Flemish Community.
4. The parent questionnaire was distributed only in Scotland.

Notes: Values that are statistically significant are indicated in bold (see Annex A3).
Questionnaire items that are measured at both the student and school levels are included in the same regression model.
* See note at the beginning of this Annex.
**Malaysia: Coverage is too small to ensure comparability (see Annex A4).

StatLink http://dx.doi.org/10.1787/888933616845

ANNEX B2

RESULTS FOR REGIONS WITHIN COUNTRIES

[Part 1/1]

Table B2.V.1 Percentage of students at each proficiency level of collaborative problem solving

	All students									
	Below Level 1 (below 340 score points)		Level 1 (from 340 to less than 440 score points)		Level 2 (from 440 to less than 540 score points)		Level 3 (from 540 to less than 640 score points)		Level 4 (at or above 640 score points)	
	%	S.E.	%	S.E.	%	S.E.	%	S.E.	%	S.E.
OECD										
Belgium										
Flemish community•	3.9	(0.5)	17.2	(0.9)	35.1	(0.9)	34.0	(1.0)	9.7	(0.8)
French community	8.1	(0.9)	25.8	(1.4)	38.5	(1.3)	23.6	(1.3)	4.0	(0.6)
German-speaking community	3.2	(1.1)	22.4	(2.6)	45.5	(3.6)	26.1	(3.6)	2.9	(1.2)
Canada										
Alberta	3.2	(0.7)	13.8	(1.4)	30.4	(1.8)	34.5	(2.0)	18.2	(1.7)
British Columbia	2.3	(0.7)	10.6	(1.3)	27.4	(1.8)	37.2	(1.9)	22.5	(1.9)
Manitoba	4.6	(1.0)	18.5	(1.6)	34.4	(1.8)	29.5	(1.8)	12.9	(1.5)
New Brunswick	4.3	(1.0)	18.1	(1.6)	35.8	(2.2)	30.8	(2.2)	11.1	(1.6)
Newfoundland and Labrador	4.0	(0.8)	16.8	(1.8)	35.8	(2.1)	31.7	(1.9)	11.7	(1.5)
Nova Scotia	3.3	(0.7)	15.7	(1.5)	32.7	(1.8)	33.0	(2.5)	15.3	(1.6)
Ontario	3.7	(0.5)	16.1	(1.3)	32.2	(1.5)	32.6	(1.5)	15.5	(1.4)
Prince Edward Island	3.1	(1.2)	15.4	(2.2)	34.8	(3.5)	34.4	(3.8)	12.3	(2.2)
Quebec	3.1	(0.5)	14.1	(1.4)	33.6	(1.6)	36.0	(1.6)	13.3	(1.4)
Saskatchewan	4.7	(1.0)	21.3	(1.6)	35.6	(1.3)	28.7	(1.6)	9.7	(1.0)
Italy										
Bolzano	3.0	(0.6)	18.2	(1.9)	39.6	(1.9)	32.4	(2.2)	6.9	(1.6)
Campania	13.0	(1.6)	36.8	(2.2)	34.9	(2.0)	13.4	(1.4)	1.9	(0.5)
Lombardia	4.8	(1.1)	22.0	(1.8)	39.5	(1.7)	28.0	(2.0)	5.7	(1.1)
Trento	3.7	(0.6)	20.2	(1.3)	43.1	(2.1)	28.5	(1.6)	4.4	(0.8)
Portugal										
Região Autónoma dos Açores	7.2	(0.8)	31.6	(1.6)	40.3	(2.3)	18.6	(1.6)	2.3	(0.6)
Spain										
Andalusia•	7.2	(1.0)	24.9	(1.7)	39.4	(1.5)	24.6	(1.8)	3.9	(0.6)
Aragon•	4.9	(0.9)	21.0	(1.8)	39.9	(1.7)	28.7	(1.9)	5.6	(1.2)
Asturias•	5.5	(1.6)	21.5	(2.3)	40.2	(1.8)	27.6	(2.5)	5.3	(1.8)
Balearic Islands•	5.4	(0.8)	24.4	(1.7)	40.6	(2.2)	25.4	(2.4)	4.2	(1.0)
Basque Country•	6.2	(0.9)	25.3	(1.5)	40.6	(1.5)	24.3	(1.6)	3.6	(0.6)
Canary Islands•	6.4	(1.0)	25.6	(1.5)	39.4	(1.4)	24.6	(1.7)	4.0	(0.9)
Cantabria•	5.1	(1.2)	26.5	(2.4)	40.0	(1.4)	24.6	(2.3)	3.7	(1.3)
Castile and Leon•	2.6	(0.5)	16.5	(1.5)	40.1	(1.6)	33.0	(1.6)	7.8	(1.0)
Castile-La Mancha•	4.3	(0.7)	21.2	(1.6)	42.1	(1.6)	27.6	(1.6)	4.8	(0.9)
Catalonia•	4.6	(0.8)	19.9	(1.4)	38.4	(1.4)	29.9	(1.9)	7.1	(0.9)
Comunidad Valenciana•	4.7	(0.7)	23.1	(1.5)	41.6	(1.7)	26.1	(1.7)	4.5	(0.9)
Extremadura•	7.7	(1.1)	28.3	(1.6)	39.3	(1.7)	21.5	(1.9)	3.2	(0.7)
Galicia•	5.2	(0.8)	22.6	(1.7)	39.9	(1.6)	27.8	(2.0)	4.6	(0.9)
La Rioja•	5.6	(1.1)	22.5	(2.7)	38.1	(2.1)	28.3	(2.7)	5.4	(1.8)
Madrid•	3.2	(0.8)	15.8	(1.1)	38.2	(1.6)	34.7	(1.5)	8.1	(0.9)
Murcia•	5.8	(1.0)	24.7	(1.9)	40.9	(1.6)	24.7	(1.7)	3.9	(0.7)
Navarre•	3.7	(0.8)	19.0	(1.8)	41.5	(2.0)	29.9	(2.6)	6.0	(1.1)
United Kingdom										
England	4.3	(0.5)	17.8	(1.0)	34.0	(0.9)	31.0	(1.0)	12.9	(0.9)
Northern Ireland	2.6	(0.5)	18.5	(1.4)	39.1	(1.6)	32.8	(1.4)	7.0	(0.8)
Scotland•	4.2	(0.5)	19.6	(0.8)	35.1	(1.0)	31.2	(1.0)	9.8	(0.7)
Wales	3.9	(0.5)	23.0	(1.3)	41.0	(1.3)	27.2	(1.5)	4.9	(0.5)
United States										
Massachusetts•	2.7	(0.6)	12.8	(1.5)	29.6	(1.8)	35.0	(1.9)	19.9	(1.9)
North Carolina•	3.9	(0.6)	18.2	(1.5)	32.4	(1.7)	31.7	(2.0)	13.8	(1.6)
Partners										
Colombia										
Bogotá	5.1	(0.9)	29.3	(1.9)	44.3	(2.0)	19.4	(1.9)	1.9	(0.8)
Cali	9.5	(1.2)	41.9	(2.0)	37.6	(1.8)	10.5	(1.4)	0.6	(0.2)
Manizales	7.1	(1.0)	37.7	(2.2)	42.5	(1.8)	11.9	(1.6)	0.7	(0.4)
Medellín	7.8	(1.2)	36.8	(2.0)	41.1	(2.0)	13.3	(1.6)	1.0	(0.4)
United Arab Emirates										
Abu Dhabi•	18.2	(1.4)	41.7	(1.5)	30.3	(1.7)	9.0	(1.1)	0.8	(0.2)
Ajman	21.5	(2.2)	42.2	(2.1)	28.1	(2.2)	7.7	(1.4)	0.4	(0.4)
Dubai•	9.3	(0.6)	26.8	(0.8)	35.6	(1.1)	23.5	(0.9)	4.7	(0.5)
Fujairah	24.1	(2.7)	45.1	(2.7)	24.9	(2.2)	5.3	(1.5)	0.6	(0.4)
Ras Al Khaimah	24.5	(3.2)	45.4	(3.2)	24.4	(2.5)	5.2	(1.5)	0.6	(0.5)
Sharjah	16.0	(2.7)	39.3	(3.1)	33.6	(3.0)	10.5	(2.4)	0.6	(0.4)
Umm Al Quwain	25.1	(3.6)	48.8	(3.9)	22.0	(2.8)	4.0	(1.3)	0.1	(0.3)

• PISA for adjudicated region.
Notes: Results for the province of Quebec in this table should be treated with caution due to a possible non-response bias.
In Massachusetts and North Carolina, the desired target population covers 15-year-old students in grade 7 or above in public schools only (see Annex A2).
See Table V.3.1 for national data.
StatLink http://dx.doi.org/10.1787/888933616750

[Part 1/1]

Table B2.V.2 Mean score and variation in collaborative problem-solving performance

	Mean score		Standard deviation		Percentiles													
					5th		10th		25th		Median (50th)		75th		90th		95th	
	Mean	S.E.	S.D.	S.E.	Score	S.E.	Score	S.E.	Score	S.E.	Score	S.E.	Score	S.E.	Score	S.E.	Score	S.E.
OECD																		
Belgium																		
Flemish community•	519	(2.8)	97	(2.0)	351	(5.1)	387	(5.1)	454	(4.1)	525	(2.8)	588	(2.9)	639	(4.1)	667	(4.4)
French community	479	(4.2)	97	(2.0)	318	(6.3)	352	(6.3)	412	(6.2)	483	(4.8)	548	(4.5)	602	(5.0)	632	(5.1)
German-speaking community	493	(6.4)	81	(3.4)	357	(12.1)	385	(10.1)	438	(8.3)	495	(7.3)	548	(8.7)	595	(12.1)	620	(12.4)
Canada																		
Alberta	543	(5.8)	105	(2.7)	363	(8.8)	402	(8.6)	471	(7.9)	547	(6.9)	616	(6.6)	676	(7.2)	711	(8.8)
British Columbia	561	(5.8)	105	(3.0)	380	(11.2)	421	(10.0)	494	(7.4)	565	(5.6)	632	(6.5)	692	(6.7)	728	(9.7)
Manitoba	519	(5.5)	105	(2.5)	343	(10.3)	381	(7.4)	446	(6.8)	520	(5.8)	593	(6.3)	655	(8.1)	690	(11.0)
New Brunswick	517	(5.5)	101	(2.9)	347	(10.6)	385	(7.7)	449	(7.7)	520	(7.2)	588	(7.2)	645	(9.0)	679	(7.8)
Newfoundland and Labrador	521	(4.4)	100	(2.4)	352	(8.7)	391	(8.0)	454	(6.2)	525	(6.1)	591	(5.9)	647	(6.7)	681	(8.3)
Nova Scotia	533	(4.6)	104	(3.0)	358	(8.0)	393	(7.7)	462	(6.1)	535	(6.0)	606	(5.8)	665	(7.7)	699	(8.8)
Ontario	532	(4.4)	106	(1.8)	353	(6.1)	393	(5.6)	460	(5.3)	535	(5.0)	605	(4.9)	666	(6.6)	702	(6.6)
Prince Edward Island	529	(5.9)	100	(5.0)	362	(17.2)	394	(14.4)	463	(9.4)	533	(8.8)	597	(9.2)	651	(14.4)	689	(16.8)
Quebec	534	(4.7)	98	(2.3)	363	(7.7)	403	(7.3)	470	(5.9)	538	(4.9)	601	(5.3)	655	(5.9)	688	(7.3)
Saskatchewan	508	(3.7)	101	(2.3)	342	(7.6)	376	(5.7)	436	(5.6)	509	(4.9)	580	(4.9)	638	(5.9)	673	(5.8)
Italy																		
Bolzano	512	(7.3)	88	(2.1)	361	(8.6)	395	(7.9)	452	(6.9)	516	(7.0)	575	(8.9)	624	(9.5)	652	(10.9)
Campania	443	(5.4)	93	(3.2)	297	(10.4)	327	(7.8)	378	(5.6)	440	(5.9)	505	(7.2)	566	(8.6)	601	(9.4)
Lombardia	498	(5.6)	93	(2.8)	342	(11.2)	377	(8.5)	434	(7.2)	500	(6.3)	563	(6.8)	615	(7.2)	645	(7.8)
Trento	500	(2.8)	86	(2.0)	353	(6.0)	385	(4.2)	443	(3.5)	504	(3.7)	558	(3.8)	606	(6.1)	635	(7.2)
Portugal																		
Região Autónoma dos Açores	467	(2.8)	87	(2.2)	327	(5.2)	354	(4.7)	404	(4.8)	467	(4.1)	528	(4.0)	580	(5.8)	609	(5.5)
Spain																		
Andalusia•	483	(4.4)	94	(2.2)	322	(8.4)	357	(6.4)	419	(5.4)	484	(5.2)	550	(5.1)	603	(5.4)	631	(5.9)
Aragon•	499	(6.1)	91	(2.1)	341	(8.4)	379	(8.3)	438	(7.1)	502	(6.9)	564	(6.2)	615	(7.0)	644	(8.4)
Asturias•	496	(10.7)	92	(1.9)	337	(11.8)	370	(13.4)	434	(11.2)	500	(10.4)	560	(10.8)	612	(10.3)	641	(12.4)
Balearic Islands•	488	(5.6)	91	(2.1)	337	(8.0)	370	(6.2)	426	(5.5)	490	(6.0)	552	(7.2)	605	(6.8)	634	(7.8)
Basque Country•	484	(4.8)	91	(1.5)	331	(6.8)	363	(5.6)	421	(5.2)	487	(5.7)	548	(5.0)	600	(4.9)	628	(5.7)
Canary Islands•	484	(5.0)	93	(2.3)	329	(8.2)	362	(6.7)	420	(5.5)	486	(5.8)	551	(4.8)	603	(6.7)	632	(7.1)
Cantabria•	485	(8.2)	89	(2.0)	339	(8.9)	367	(7.4)	421	(8.9)	487	(8.8)	548	(8.0)	598	(9.4)	627	(11.9)
Castile and Leon•	517	(4.2)	88	(1.8)	366	(7.2)	400	(6.8)	459	(5.1)	519	(5.3)	578	(5.0)	630	(5.4)	657	(5.7)
Castile-La Mancha•	497	(4.3)	89	(1.9)	347	(7.1)	379	(7.2)	438	(5.6)	499	(4.8)	559	(4.8)	610	(5.8)	639	(7.0)
Catalonia•	505	(4.7)	94	(2.1)	343	(8.1)	379	(7.1)	441	(6.3)	509	(5.5)	572	(4.9)	625	(5.7)	653	(5.8)
Comunidad Valenciana•	492	(3.8)	89	(2.3)	342	(5.8)	375	(5.9)	432	(4.9)	494	(5.3)	554	(5.0)	605	(6.4)	635	(7.4)
Extremadura•	474	(4.7)	92	(2.0)	321	(7.3)	354	(6.4)	409	(5.5)	476	(5.1)	539	(6.2)	593	(6.3)	623	(6.8)
Galicia•	494	(5.7)	91	(2.1)	339	(7.1)	373	(6.8)	431	(6.9)	499	(6.1)	559	(6.8)	610	(7.0)	636	(7.4)
La Rioja•	495	(9.1)	94	(2.5)	335	(8.5)	369	(9.3)	430	(10.7)	499	(9.7)	562	(9.8)	611	(11.1)	642	(13.2)
Madrid•	519	(3.4)	90	(2.4)	361	(9.5)	398	(7.3)	461	(4.7)	524	(4.1)	581	(5.2)	631	(5.0)	658	(5.6)
Murcia•	486	(5.0)	90	(2.0)	334	(8.0)	366	(6.2)	424	(6.5)	490	(5.5)	550	(5.4)	601	(5.2)	631	(5.9)
Navarre•	505	(6.5)	89	(2.0)	353	(8.5)	389	(7.6)	447	(7.0)	508	(6.8)	568	(7.2)	618	(7.4)	647	(7.1)
United Kingdom																		
England	521	(3.1)	104	(1.3)	347	(4.8)	384	(4.6)	450	(4.2)	523	(3.7)	594	(3.9)	654	(3.6)	690	(4.2)
Northern Ireland	514	(3.7)	88	(1.9)	366	(6.6)	398	(5.5)	452	(5.5)	517	(4.3)	577	(4.5)	626	(5.0)	654	(5.2)
Scotland•	513	(2.5)	99	(1.7)	347	(5.0)	381	(4.4)	444	(3.7)	516	(3.0)	585	(3.5)	639	(3.7)	670	(4.4)
Wales	496	(3.5)	89	(1.5)	349	(5.1)	378	(4.9)	434	(4.6)	498	(4.0)	559	(4.2)	611	(4.2)	639	(4.3)
United States																		
Massachusetts•	549	(6.2)	105	(2.8)	368	(9.5)	408	(8.7)	478	(8.1)	553	(7.6)	624	(7.1)	682	(7.6)	714	(8.9)
North Carolina•	525	(5.3)	104	(2.4)	351	(6.9)	387	(6.5)	450	(6.0)	527	(7.4)	601	(6.5)	657	(5.9)	690	(7.6)
Partners																		
Colombia																		
Bogotá	474	(4.8)	82	(2.9)	340	(6.8)	368	(5.4)	417	(5.2)	474	(5.6)	530	(6.6)	580	(7.9)	608	(9.6)
Cali	440	(4.4)	78	(2.0)	317	(5.1)	342	(4.9)	386	(4.6)	437	(5.1)	494	(6.4)	545	(6.7)	573	(7.6)
Manizales	451	(3.9)	77	(2.2)	327	(6.0)	353	(4.3)	397	(4.2)	450	(4.4)	504	(5.4)	552	(6.8)	580	(9.0)
Medellín	453	(4.5)	80	(2.0)	324	(6.9)	351	(5.6)	396	(5.0)	451	(5.1)	508	(5.5)	557	(7.1)	586	(7.2)
United Arab Emirates																		
Abu Dhabi•	422	(4.2)	88	(1.9)	287	(5.2)	313	(4.6)	358	(4.3)	417	(5.2)	481	(5.6)	539	(6.4)	572	(7.1)
Ajman	412	(5.7)	87	(2.9)	275	(10.2)	303	(7.3)	349	(6.2)	407	(7.2)	472	(7.3)	529	(9.6)	563	(9.0)
Dubai•	477	(2.2)	100	(1.6)	313	(3.9)	343	(2.9)	404	(3.0)	479	(2.8)	550	(3.2)	605	(3.8)	638	(4.4)
Fujairah	402	(7.3)	85	(4.9)	274	(10.2)	299	(6.6)	342	(6.6)	396	(8.1)	457	(10.9)	516	(13.4)	546	(13.9)
Ras Al Khaimah	400	(9.0)	84	(5.4)	272	(11.0)	298	(9.7)	341	(8.1)	393	(8.8)	454	(11.6)	510	(14.1)	547	(18.2)
Sharjah	429	(9.4)	88	(3.1)	286	(12.2)	316	(9.6)	367	(10.6)	427	(11.1)	490	(11.9)	545	(11.3)	575	(11.8)
Umm Al Quwain	394	(6.1)	77	(4.5)	276	(12.7)	299	(9.9)	339	(8.7)	389	(7.8)	442	(8.2)	499	(11.7)	531	(14.4)

• PISA for adjudicated region.
Notes: Results for the province of Quebec in this table should be treated with caution due to a possible non-response bias.
In Massachusetts and North Carolina, the desired target population covers 15-year-old students in grade 7 or above in public schools only (see Annex A2).
See Table V.3.2 for national data.
StatLink http://dx.doi.org/10.1787/888933616750

[Part 1/2]

Table B2.V.3 Top performers in four PISA subjects

		Percentage of 15-year-old students who are:															
		Not top performers in any of the four subjects		Top performers[1] in only one of science, reading or mathematics		Top performers in only two of science, reading and mathematics		Top performers in science, reading and mathematics		Top performers in only collaborative problem solving		Top performers in collaborative problem solving and science		Top performers in collaborative problem solving and reading		Top performers in collaborative problem solving and mathematics	
		%	S.E.	%	S.E.	%	S.E.	%	S.E.	%	S.E.	%	S.E.	%	S.E.	%	S.E.
OECD	**Belgium**																
	Flemish community•	72.3	(1.0)	10.0	(0.6)	4.8	(0.5)	3.2	(0.4)	2.5	(0.4)	0.3	(0.1)	0.5	(0.1)	1.2	(0.2)
	French community	85.7	(1.2)	6.4	(0.7)	2.5	(0.3)	1.4	(0.3)	1.3	(0.3)	0.1	(0.1)	0.2	(0.1)	0.6	(0.2)
	German-speaking community	86.2	(2.3)	6.2	(1.5)	3.0	(1.7)	1.6	(0.8)	1.3	(0.8)	0.1	(0.3)	0.1	(0.3)	0.3	(0.4)
	Canada																
	Alberta	70.0	(1.8)	6.8	(1.0)	3.1	(0.6)	1.9	(0.5)	5.9	(0.9)	1.1	(0.3)	1.5	(0.4)	0.9	(0.4)
	British Columbia	66.7	(2.2)	6.5	(1.0)	2.8	(0.6)	1.5	(0.5)	8.4	(1.2)	1.0	(0.4)	2.1	(0.6)	1.3	(0.4)
	Manitoba	81.6	(1.6)	3.6	(0.6)	1.3	(0.4)	0.6	(0.3)	5.4	(1.0)	0.6	(0.3)	1.3	(0.4)	1.0	(0.5)
	New Brunswick	81.3	(1.9)	4.4	(1.0)	2.1	(0.7)	1.1	(0.4)	4.3	(0.9)	0.6	(0.3)	1.1	(0.4)	0.6	(0.4)
	Newfoundland and Labrador	82.2	(1.5)	3.6	(0.9)	1.7	(0.6)	0.9	(0.5)	5.4	(1.1)	0.7	(0.4)	1.1	(0.6)	0.5	(0.3)
	Nova Scotia	77.4	(1.7)	4.4	(0.9)	1.8	(0.6)	1.0	(0.5)	6.7	(1.2)	0.7	(0.4)	1.4	(0.5)	0.5	(0.3)
	Ontario	73.4	(1.7)	6.3	(0.9)	2.8	(0.5)	1.9	(0.4)	5.3	(0.6)	0.6	(0.2)	1.6	(0.4)	0.8	(0.2)
	Prince Edward Island	80.6	(2.9)	4.1	(1.7)	2.0	(1.0)	0.9	(0.9)	5.1	(1.6)	0.6	(0.6)	1.3	(0.8)	0.4	(0.5)
	Quebec	66.8	(2.2)	11.9	(1.3)	4.8	(0.6)	3.2	(0.6)	3.5	(0.6)	0.2	(0.1)	0.9	(0.3)	1.8	(0.5)
	Saskatchewan	85.0	(1.2)	3.2	(0.7)	1.4	(0.5)	0.7	(0.3)	4.3	(0.6)	0.4	(0.2)	0.8	(0.4)	0.7	(0.3)
	Italy																
	Bolzano	80.1	(2.0)	8.2	(1.1)	3.1	(0.7)	1.7	(0.5)	2.4	(1.1)	0.3	(0.2)	0.3	(0.2)	0.7	(0.4)
	Campania	92.3	(1.2)	4.2	(0.9)	1.0	(0.4)	0.5	(0.3)	0.8	(0.3)	0.1	(0.1)	0.2	(0.1)	0.2	(0.1)
	Lombardia	79.2	(2.0)	9.6	(1.3)	3.5	(0.7)	1.9	(0.5)	2.1	(0.6)	0.1	(0.1)	0.5	(0.2)	0.7	(0.3)
	Trento	81.1	(1.3)	9.2	(1.0)	3.5	(0.8)	1.7	(0.5)	1.6	(0.6)	0.1	(0.1)	0.3	(0.2)	0.5	(0.2)
	Portugal																
	Região Autónoma dos Açores	90.8	(1.0)	3.8	(0.8)	1.7	(0.6)	1.3	(0.5)	0.6	(0.3)	0.1	(0.1)	0.1	(0.2)	0.2	(0.2)
	Spain																
	Andalusia•	90.1	(1.0)	3.8	(0.6)	1.5	(0.4)	0.7	(0.3)	2.0	(0.4)	0.2	(0.1)	0.4	(0.2)	0.3	(0.2)
	Aragon•	83.9	(1.4)	6.1	(0.9)	2.9	(0.7)	1.6	(0.5)	2.2	(0.6)	0.3	(0.2)	0.4	(0.3)	0.4	(0.2)
	Asturias•	85.7	(1.5)	5.3	(0.9)	2.3	(0.6)	1.4	(0.6)	2.2	(1.1)	0.2	(0.2)	0.5	(0.3)	0.4	(0.3)
	Balearic Islands•	89.3	(1.4)	4.3	(0.9)	1.5	(0.4)	0.8	(0.3)	1.9	(0.6)	0.2	(0.1)	0.4	(0.3)	0.4	(0.3)
	Basque Country•	88.1	(1.0)	5.6	(0.6)	1.8	(0.4)	0.9	(0.2)	1.4	(0.4)	0.1	(0.1)	0.5	(0.2)	0.4	(0.2)
	Canary Islands•	90.4	(1.0)	3.8	(0.6)	1.2	(0.4)	0.5	(0.2)	2.0	(0.7)	0.2	(0.2)	0.7	(0.3)	0.1	(0.1)
	Cantabria•	86.4	(1.9)	6.2	(1.2)	2.4	(0.5)	1.3	(0.5)	1.4	(0.8)	0.1	(0.1)	0.4	(0.2)	0.3	(0.2)
	Castile and Leon•	81.0	(1.4)	6.4	(0.8)	3.0	(0.6)	1.9	(0.6)	2.6	(0.5)	0.5	(0.2)	0.8	(0.3)	0.5	(0.3)
	Castile-La Mancha•	87.0	(1.1)	5.1	(0.7)	2.0	(0.5)	1.1	(0.3)	2.0	(0.5)	0.2	(0.1)	0.5	(0.2)	0.3	(0.2)
	Catalonia•	83.2	(1.5)	6.0	(0.9)	2.4	(0.6)	1.3	(0.4)	2.9	(0.6)	0.3	(0.2)	0.4	(0.2)	0.7	(0.3)
	Comunidad Valenciana•	88.4	(1.2)	4.6	(0.7)	1.7	(0.4)	0.9	(0.3)	2.1	(0.6)	0.2	(0.2)	0.5	(0.3)	0.3	(0.2)
	Extremadura•	91.0	(0.9)	3.9	(0.7)	1.1	(0.4)	0.8	(0.2)	1.5	(0.5)	0.1	(0.1)	0.2	(0.2)	0.3	(0.2)
	Galicia•	84.4	(1.1)	6.3	(0.7)	3.1	(0.6)	1.6	(0.4)	1.8	(0.5)	0.3	(0.2)	0.5	(0.2)	0.3	(0.2)
	La Rioja•	83.5	(2.2)	7.0	(2.0)	2.9	(0.7)	1.2	(0.6)	2.0	(1.0)	0.1	(0.1)	0.4	(0.2)	0.7	(0.4)
	Madrid•	80.2	(1.4)	7.3	(1.1)	2.9	(0.5)	1.5	(0.5)	3.0	(0.7)	0.3	(0.2)	1.1	(0.4)	0.6	(0.3)
	Murcia•	90.0	(1.0)	4.0	(0.8)	1.4	(0.4)	0.8	(0.2)	1.7	(0.5)	0.2	(0.2)	0.4	(0.2)	0.2	(0.2)
	Navarre•	80.7	(2.2)	8.4	(1.7)	3.2	(0.8)	1.7	(0.5)	1.8	(0.6)	0.1	(0.1)	0.6	(0.3)	0.6	(0.3)
	United Kingdom																
	England	77.3	(1.1)	5.6	(0.5)	2.8	(0.4)	1.4	(0.3)	4.6	(0.4)	0.9	(0.2)	0.8	(0.2)	0.7	(0.2)
	Northern Ireland	86.1	(1.3)	4.0	(0.6)	2.0	(0.4)	0.9	(0.3)	2.8	(0.5)	0.4	(0.3)	0.5	(0.2)	0.4	(0.2)
	Scotland•	82.5	(0.9)	4.6	(0.5)	2.1	(0.4)	1.0	(0.3)	4.4	(0.5)	0.5	(0.2)	0.7	(0.3)	0.7	(0.3)
	Wales	90.1	(0.8)	3.2	(0.5)	1.2	(0.3)	0.6	(0.2)	2.1	(0.4)	0.4	(0.2)	0.3	(0.2)	0.3	(0.2)
	United States																
	Massachusetts•	73.3	(2.3)	4.1	(0.8)	1.9	(0.5)	0.9	(0.3)	6.8	(0.8)	1.3	(0.5)	1.6	(0.5)	0.5	(0.3)
	North Carolina•	80.6	(1.7)	3.4	(0.6)	1.5	(0.4)	0.7	(0.3)	5.7	(0.9)	1.1	(0.4)	1.6	(0.4)	0.2	(0.2)
Partners	**Colombia**																
	Bogotá	95.8	(0.9)	1.7	(0.6)	0.4	(0.2)	0.2	(0.2)	1.1	(0.6)	0.1	(0.1)	0.2	(0.2)	0.1	(0.1)
	Cali	98.6	(0.4)	0.6	(0.3)	0.1	(0.2)	0.1	(0.1)	0.4	(0.2)	0.0	(0.0)	0.1	(0.1)	0.0	(0.1)
	Manizales	98.0	(0.7)	0.9	(0.4)	0.3	(0.2)	0.1	(0.1)	0.4	(0.3)	0.0	(0.1)	0.1	(0.1)	0.0	(0.0)
	Medellín	97.3	(0.6)	1.4	(0.4)	0.2	(0.2)	0.1	(0.1)	0.5	(0.2)	0.0	(0.0)	0.1	(0.1)	0.0	(0.0)
	United Arab Emirates																
	Abu Dhabi•	95.8	(0.6)	2.1	(0.4)	0.8	(0.2)	0.5	(0.2)	0.3	(0.1)	0.0	(0.0)	0.1	(0.1)	0.1	(0.1)
	Ajman	98.7	(0.5)	0.6	(0.4)	0.2	(0.2)	0.0	(0.0)	0.3	(0.4)	0.0	c	0.1	(0.1)	0.0	(0.1)
	Dubai•	86.5	(0.6)	5.3	(0.5)	2.2	(0.3)	1.3	(0.3)	1.3	(0.3)	0.3	(0.1)	0.3	(0.1)	0.3	(0.2)
	Fujairah	97.7	(0.9)	1.2	(0.6)	0.3	(0.3)	0.1	(0.2)	0.1	(0.1)	0.0	(0.0)	0.1	(0.1)	0.0	(0.0)
	Ras Al Khaimah	98.4	(1.0)	0.8	(0.4)	0.2	(0.2)	0.1	(0.1)	0.2	(0.2)	0.0	(0.1)	0.0	(0.1)	0.1	(0.2)
	Sharjah	95.4	(1.4)	2.7	(0.9)	0.8	(0.5)	0.4	(0.4)	0.3	(0.3)	0.1	(0.1)	0.1	(0.1)	0.0	(0.1)
	Umm Al Quwain	99.2	(0.6)	0.6	(0.5)	0.1	(0.2)	0.1	(0.2)	0.0	(0.2)	0.0	(0.1)	0.0	(0.1)	0.0	c

• PISA for adjudicated region.
1. Top performers in collaborative problem solving are students who score at Level 4. Top performers in science, reading or mathematics score at Level 5 or 6 in the subject.
Notes: Results for the province of Quebec in this table should be treated with caution due to a possible non-response bias.
In Massachusetts and North Carolina, the desired target population covers 15-year-old students in grade 7 or above in public schools only (see Annex A2).
See Table V.3.3a for national data.
StatLink http://dx.doi.org/10.1787/888933616750

[Part 2/2]

Table B2.V.3 Top performers in four PISA subjects

	Percentage of 15-year-old students who are:								Percentage of top performers in collaborative problem solving among top performers in...							
	Top performers[1] in collaborative problem solving, science and reading		Top performers in collaborative problem solving, science and mathematics		Top performers in collaborative problem solving, reading and mathematics		Top performers in all four subjects		Science		Reading		Mathematics		Science, reading and mathematics	
	%	S.E.	%	S.E.	%	S.E.	%	S.E.	%	S.E.	%	S.E.	%	S.E.	%	S.E.
OECD																
Belgium																
Flemish community•	0.4	(0.1)	1.1	(0.2)	0.7	(0.2)	3.2	(0.4)	40.9	(3.7)	38.7	(3.4)	29.5	(2.7)	50.1	(4.4)
French community	0.1	(0.1)	0.4	(0.1)	0.3	(0.1)	1.0	(0.2)	30.5	(3.9)	28.3	(3.9)	22.8	(2.8)	41.5	(6.5)
German-speaking community	0.1	(0.2)	0.2	(0.3)	0.1	(0.2)	0.7	(0.5)	c	c	c	c	13.6	(7.2)	c	c
Canada																
Alberta	2.1	(0.5)	1.4	(0.5)	0.5	(0.3)	4.9	(0.7)	59.3	(5.5)	58.2	(5.4)	56.8	(5.0)	72.2	(6.9)
British Columbia	1.6	(0.5)	1.6	(0.5)	0.7	(0.3)	5.8	(0.9)	68.0	(4.6)	65.4	(4.7)	59.4	(4.5)	79.4	(5.1)
Manitoba	0.8	(0.3)	1.0	(0.5)	0.4	(0.2)	2.4	(0.6)	67.9	(6.2)	65.1	(6.6)	59.7	(7.2)	79.0	(8.3)
New Brunswick	1.0	(0.4)	0.7	(0.4)	0.4	(0.3)	2.4	(0.6)	58.4	(6.7)	56.7	(7.4)	45.4	(8.7)	68.7	(10.8)
Newfoundland and Labrador	0.9	(0.5)	0.7	(0.4)	0.3	(0.2)	2.2	(0.6)	57.9	(8.2)	56.7	(8.7)	56.9	(8.4)	c	c
Nova Scotia	1.4	(0.5)	0.8	(0.4)	0.3	(0.2)	3.6	(0.7)	65.7	(6.5)	62.5	(7.6)	56.9	(7.1)	77.6	(8.5)
Ontario	1.3	(0.4)	0.7	(0.2)	0.6	(0.2)	4.6	(0.6)	59.8	(4.3)	55.1	(4.5)	51.3	(3.9)	70.4	(4.3)
Prince Edward Island	0.9	(0.6)	0.8	(0.7)	0.3	(0.6)	2.8	(1.4)	58.0	(15.5)	60.2	(14.0)	c	c	c	c
Quebec	0.4	(0.2)	1.2	(0.4)	0.9	(0.3)	4.4	(0.8)	48.6	(4.9)	44.7	(4.1)	33.7	(3.6)	58.2	(6.1)
Saskatchewan	0.7	(0.3)	0.6	(0.2)	0.2	(0.2)	1.9	(0.4)	59.5	(7.7)	59.4	(8.6)	52.2	(6.9)	73.4	(9.5)
Italy																
Bolzano	0.3	(0.2)	1.0	(0.3)	0.3	(0.2)	1.6	(0.5)	41.1	(7.3)	36.8	(7.5)	25.8	(4.7)	49.4	(10.4)
Campania	0.0	(0.0)	0.2	(0.2)	0.1	(0.1)	0.3	(0.2)	33.9	(14.3)	21.1	(8.2)	18.9	(6.5)	c	c
Lombardia	0.2	(0.2)	0.6	(0.2)	0.4	(0.2)	1.2	(0.3)	32.2	(6.5)	26.0	(4.7)	19.6	(3.4)	38.1	(8.1)
Trento	0.1	(0.1)	0.5	(0.3)	0.3	(0.2)	1.0	(0.4)	29.4	(7.9)	23.9	(6.5)	16.1	(3.8)	35.5	(11.5)
Portugal																
Região Autónoma dos Açores	0.1	(0.1)	0.3	(0.3)	0.1	(0.1)	0.8	(0.5)	30.6	(10.5)	27.6	(10.7)	21.4	(8.0)	38.0	(16.3)
Spain																
Andalusia•	0.2	(0.1)	0.2	(0.1)	0.2	(0.1)	0.6	(0.2)	34.3	(8.0)	28.8	(5.4)	26.2	(6.6)	c	c
Aragon•	0.3	(0.2)	0.4	(0.2)	0.3	(0.2)	1.2	(0.5)	33.6	(10.4)	30.0	(6.5)	25.7	(8.0)	43.5	(13.8)
Asturias•	0.2	(0.1)	0.4	(0.3)	0.2	(0.2)	1.2	(0.4)	34.3	(10.7)	33.1	(9.9)	27.0	(8.7)	47.4	(16.7)
Balearic Islands•	0.3	(0.2)	0.4	(0.2)	0.2	(0.2)	0.5	(0.2)	34.2	(8.0)	29.7	(7.6)	28.8	(6.9)	c	c
Basque Country•	0.1	(0.1)	0.2	(0.1)	0.3	(0.1)	0.6	(0.2)	31.4	(5.6)	28.2	(4.9)	20.3	(3.6)	41.3	(10.3)
Canary Islands•	0.3	(0.2)	0.1	(0.1)	0.1	(0.1)	0.4	(0.3)	34.7	(9.3)	30.4	(8.7)	27.1	(7.7)	c	c
Cantabria•	0.2	(0.2)	0.3	(0.2)	0.2	(0.1)	0.9	(0.3)	30.0	(8.2)	24.9	(7.7)	20.9	(6.8)	41.0	(12.8)
Castile and Leon•	0.5	(0.3)	0.6	(0.3)	0.3	(0.2)	2.0	(0.4)	42.1	(5.5)	36.5	(5.4)	33.4	(5.5)	52.4	(9.3)
Castile-La Mancha•	0.2	(0.2)	0.3	(0.2)	0.2	(0.1)	0.9	(0.3)	34.8	(8.0)	30.5	(7.3)	27.5	(5.7)	45.6	(11.1)
Catalonia•	0.2	(0.1)	0.7	(0.3)	0.3	(0.2)	1.5	(0.4)	40.2	(5.5)	39.9	(8.1)	31.6	(4.5)	53.1	(12.0)
Comunidad Valenciana•	0.3	(0.2)	0.2	(0.1)	0.2	(0.1)	0.7	(0.3)	35.0	(6.4)	31.1	(6.2)	26.1	(6.4)	45.6	(14.1)
Extremadura•	0.1	(0.1)	0.2	(0.2)	0.2	(0.1)	0.6	(0.3)	34.2	(9.3)	30.6	(8.1)	24.3	(5.7)	c	c
Galicia•	0.3	(0.2)	0.3	(0.2)	0.1	(0.1)	1.1	(0.3)	26.0	(5.7)	25.2	(6.2)	22.4	(5.0)	39.3	(9.5)
La Rioja•	0.2	(0.2)	0.7	(0.5)	0.3	(0.3)	1.1	(0.5)	34.9	(11.4)	35.6	(9.7)	24.2	(8.9)	c	c
Madrid•	0.6	(0.3)	0.5	(0.3)	0.3	(0.2)	1.7	(0.5)	41.1	(6.5)	37.7	(6.0)	31.6	(5.5)	54.0	(12.1)
Murcia•	0.2	(0.2)	0.3	(0.2)	0.1	(0.1)	0.7	(0.3)	36.0	(7.4)	29.1	(7.1)	28.8	(6.9)	c	c
Navarre•	0.2	(0.2)	0.5	(0.3)	0.3	(0.2)	1.7	(0.4)	38.5	(6.3)	34.4	(5.3)	24.3	(5.0)	50.2	(9.2)
United Kingdom																
England	1.1	(0.2)	1.1	(0.3)	0.3	(0.1)	3.3	(0.4)	55.1	(3.3)	55.9	(3.8)	48.1	(4.1)	70.0	(4.7)
Northern Ireland	0.6	(0.2)	0.6	(0.2)	0.2	(0.1)	1.5	(0.3)	46.9	(5.3)	47.9	(6.4)	40.9	(6.1)	62.5	(9.2)
Scotland•	0.6	(0.2)	0.7	(0.2)	0.3	(0.1)	1.9	(0.3)	49.5	(5.0)	54.8	(5.3)	41.1	(4.5)	66.0	(6.8)
Wales	0.3	(0.2)	0.4	(0.1)	0.1	(0.1)	1.0	(0.3)	44.6	(5.3)	46.0	(7.8)	38.5	(6.0)	61.3	(11.3)
United States																
Massachusetts•	2.5	(0.6)	1.3	(0.5)	0.4	(0.2)	5.4	(1.1)	74.4	(3.8)	69.0	(5.1)	75.8	(4.6)	86.0	(5.1)
North Carolina•	1.9	(0.4)	0.6	(0.2)	0.2	(0.2)	2.5	(0.5)	66.6	(5.0)	64.3	(5.0)	64.6	(7.0)	78.9	(7.4)
Partners																
Colombia																
Bogotá	0.1	(0.1)	0.1	(0.1)	0.1	(0.1)	0.2	(0.2)	c	c	c	c	c	c	c	c
Cali	0.0	(0.1)	0.0	(0.0)	0.0	(0.0)	0.0	(0.1)	c	c	c	c	c	c	c	c
Manizales	0.0	(0.1)	0.0	(0.0)	0.0	(0.0)	0.1	(0.1)	c	c	c	c	c	c	c	c
Medellín	0.1	(0.1)	0.0	(0.0)	0.0	(0.1)	0.2	(0.2)	c	c	21.7	(10.9)	c	c	c	c
United Arab Emirates																
Abu Dhabi•	0.0	(0.1)	0.1	(0.1)	0.0	(0.1)	0.2	(0.1)	18.8	(7.0)	18.2	(6.4)	13.5	(5.2)	c	c
Ajman	0.0	c	0.0	c	0.0	c	0.0	(0.0)	c	c	c	c	c	c	c	c
Dubai•	0.4	(0.2)	0.5	(0.2)	0.2	(0.1)	1.3	(0.2)	39.7	(4.3)	34.8	(4.4)	29.5	(5.2)	50.7	(7.9)
Fujairah	0.0	(0.1)	0.0	c	0.0	(0.0)	0.3	(0.3)	c	c	c	c	c	c	c	c
Ras Al Khaimah	0.0	(0.1)	0.1	(0.1)	0.0	(0.1)	0.1	(0.2)	c	c	c	c	c	c	c	c
Sharjah	0.0	(0.1)	0.0	(0.1)	0.1	(0.1)	0.1	(0.1)	c	c	c	c	c	c	c	c
Umm Al Quwain	0.0	(0.1)	0.0	c	0.0	c	0.0	c	c	c	c	c	c	c	c	c

• PISA for adjudicated region.
1. Top performers in collaborative problem solving are students who score at Level 4. Top performers in science, reading or mathematics score at Level 5 or 6 in the subject.
Notes: Results for the province of Quebec in this table should be treated with caution due to a possible non-response bias.
In Massachusetts and North Carolina, the desired target population covers 15-year-old students in grade 7 or above in public schools only (see Annex A2).
See Table V.3.3a for national data.
StatLink http://dx.doi.org/10.1787/888933616750

[Part 1/2]

Table B2.V.4 Low achievers in four PISA subjects

		Percentage of 15-year-old students who are:															
		Not low achievers in any of the four subjects		Low achievers[1] in only one of science, reading or mathematics		Low achievers in only two of science, reading and mathematics		Low achievers in science, reading and mathematics		Low achievers in only collaborative problem solving		Low achievers in collaborative problem solving and science		Low achievers in collaborative problem solving and reading		Low achievers in collaborative problem solving and mathematics	
		%	S.E.	%	S.E.	%	S.E.	%	S.E.	%	S.E.	%	S.E.	%	S.E.	%	S.E.
OECD	**Belgium**																
	Flemish community•	70.5	(1.2)	4.0	(0.4)	2.2	(0.4)	2.2	(0.3)	5.9	(0.5)	0.9	(0.2)	1.2	(0.2)	0.8	(0.2)
	French community	57.7	(2.0)	4.2	(0.5)	2.3	(0.4)	1.9	(0.3)	10.2	(0.6)	1.2	(0.3)	1.7	(0.4)	2.1	(0.4)
	German-speaking community	67.3	(2.5)	3.7	(1.4)	2.1	(0.9)	1.4	(0.9)	10.6	(2.3)	0.7	(0.7)	1.3	(0.8)	1.9	(1.4)
	Canada																
	Alberta	74.9	(1.9)	5.7	(0.9)	1.5	(0.5)	0.9	(0.3)	6.7	(1.0)	0.4	(0.2)	0.9	(0.3)	2.1	(0.6)
	British Columbia	79.0	(1.6)	5.2	(1.0)	1.9	(0.5)	0.9	(0.4)	4.8	(0.8)	0.6	(0.3)	1.1	(0.4)	0.9	(0.4)
	Manitoba	66.0	(2.0)	6.0	(1.0)	3.0	(0.7)	1.9	(0.5)	6.6	(1.0)	0.9	(0.4)	1.4	(0.5)	1.7	(0.5)
	New Brunswick	66.7	(2.3)	6.2	(0.9)	2.9	(0.8)	1.9	(0.8)	7.2	(1.2)	0.7	(0.4)	1.2	(0.4)	1.9	(0.5)
	Newfoundland and Labrador	69.1	(1.8)	5.9	(0.9)	2.5	(0.8)	1.8	(0.6)	6.1	(1.4)	0.5	(0.3)	0.7	(0.3)	1.7	(0.5)
	Nova Scotia	72.0	(2.1)	5.6	(0.8)	2.2	(0.5)	1.2	(0.5)	6.1	(0.9)	0.6	(0.3)	1.0	(0.4)	1.8	(0.6)
	Ontario	72.3	(1.7)	4.9	(0.8)	2.0	(0.4)	1.1	(0.2)	7.2	(0.8)	0.7	(0.2)	1.1	(0.3)	1.7	(0.4)
	Prince Edward Island	73.7	(3.1)	4.9	(1.7)	1.9	(1.0)	1.0	(0.8)	6.7	(1.8)	0.5	(0.5)	1.0	(0.6)	1.7	(1.0)
	Quebec	77.6	(1.8)	3.2	(0.6)	1.3	(0.3)	0.7	(0.2)	7.9	(0.9)	0.6	(0.2)	1.5	(0.4)	1.0	(0.3)
	Saskatchewan	63.7	(1.7)	6.2	(0.9)	2.6	(0.6)	1.5	(0.5)	8.4	(1.0)	1.0	(0.4)	1.5	(0.5)	2.3	(0.5)
	Italy																
	Bolzano	71.0	(1.6)	4.8	(0.9)	1.9	(0.6)	1.1	(0.4)	8.8	(1.5)	1.0	(0.4)	1.6	(0.5)	1.3	(0.5)
	Campania	37.6	(2.4)	6.5	(1.1)	3.8	(0.7)	2.2	(0.6)	12.8	(1.5)	3.0	(0.7)	2.4	(0.6)	3.4	(0.8)
	Lombardia	63.4	(2.3)	5.5	(0.9)	2.6	(0.8)	1.7	(0.6)	10.8	(1.4)	1.2	(0.4)	1.4	(0.4)	2.1	(0.5)
	Trento	70.0	(1.3)	3.7	(0.7)	1.4	(0.3)	1.0	(0.3)	11.1	(1.0)	1.2	(0.4)	1.2	(0.3)	1.5	(0.4)
	Portugal																
	Região Autónoma dos Açores	49.8	(1.4)	6.1	(0.9)	3.0	(0.6)	2.3	(0.5)	8.8	(1.1)	1.1	(0.4)	1.6	(0.5)	3.3	(0.8)
	Spain																
	Andalusia•	54.7	(2.0)	6.9	(0.9)	3.7	(0.7)	2.6	(0.6)	7.9	(1.0)	1.3	(0.4)	1.3	(0.3)	2.5	(0.6)
	Aragon•	67.0	(2.4)	4.2	(0.8)	1.9	(0.5)	1.0	(0.5)	10.3	(1.6)	0.8	(0.3)	1.4	(0.4)	1.8	(0.6)
	Asturias•	64.6	(2.5)	4.9	(1.0)	2.3	(0.6)	1.3	(0.6)	9.1	(2.1)	0.9	(0.3)	1.6	(0.4)	2.3	(0.7)
	Balearic Islands•	59.1	(2.1)	6.5	(1.1)	3.0	(0.7)	1.7	(0.4)	8.8	(1.2)	1.0	(0.3)	1.6	(0.7)	2.5	(0.8)
	Basque Country•	60.0	(1.8)	4.7	(0.5)	2.4	(0.5)	1.3	(0.3)	11.5	(1.4)	1.8	(0.3)	1.8	(0.3)	1.8	(0.4)
	Canary Islands•	52.9	(1.9)	8.7	(1.2)	4.1	(0.7)	2.4	(0.6)	7.0	(1.0)	0.8	(0.3)	1.1	(0.4)	3.9	(0.7)
	Cantabria•	61.3	(2.8)	4.1	(0.9)	1.9	(0.5)	1.1	(0.4)	12.8	(2.0)	1.3	(0.5)	1.5	(0.4)	2.4	(0.9)
	Castile and Leon•	73.6	(1.7)	4.7	(0.8)	1.8	(0.4)	0.8	(0.3)	8.0	(1.1)	0.6	(0.3)	0.9	(0.4)	1.9	(0.5)
	Castile-La Mancha•	64.2	(1.6)	6.1	(0.9)	2.7	(0.6)	1.5	(0.5)	8.7	(1.1)	0.9	(0.3)	1.4	(0.4)	2.2	(0.6)
	Catalonia•	66.8	(2.2)	5.1	(0.8)	2.2	(0.5)	1.4	(0.4)	8.7	(1.0)	0.9	(0.3)	1.6	(0.4)	1.4	(0.4)
	Comunidad Valenciana•	63.0	(1.8)	5.5	(0.8)	2.4	(0.6)	1.2	(0.4)	10.6	(1.0)	1.1	(0.4)	1.4	(0.5)	2.6	(0.6)
	Extremadura•	54.3	(1.9)	5.3	(0.8)	2.7	(0.6)	1.6	(0.4)	10.0	(1.3)	1.4	(0.4)	2.3	(0.6)	2.7	(0.6)
	Galicia•	65.8	(2.1)	4.3	(0.7)	1.4	(0.4)	0.8	(0.4)	11.3	(1.5)	0.7	(0.3)	1.5	(0.5)	2.6	(0.6)
	La Rioja•	64.6	(2.1)	4.3	(1.1)	1.8	(0.6)	1.2	(0.5)	10.2	(2.9)	1.1	(0.6)	2.2	(0.7)	1.2	(0.7)
	Madrid•	72.6	(1.7)	5.1	(0.9)	2.1	(0.5)	1.2	(0.3)	6.6	(1.0)	0.7	(0.3)	0.9	(0.4)	1.8	(0.5)
	Murcia•	57.6	(2.1)	6.9	(1.3)	2.8	(0.5)	2.2	(0.6)	8.8	(1.4)	1.0	(0.4)	1.3	(0.4)	2.8	(0.8)
	Navarre•	70.7	(2.0)	4.0	(0.7)	1.8	(0.5)	0.8	(0.3)	10.5	(2.1)	1.1	(0.3)	1.7	(0.7)	1.2	(0.4)
	United Kingdom																
	England	65.2	(1.2)	7.2	(0.6)	3.4	(0.4)	2.2	(0.3)	5.8	(0.7)	0.6	(0.2)	1.5	(0.3)	1.8	(0.3)
	Northern Ireland	69.6	(1.5)	4.8	(0.8)	2.6	(0.4)	2.0	(0.5)	5.5	(1.0)	1.0	(0.3)	1.0	(0.3)	1.2	(0.3)
	Scotland•	65.0	(1.1)	6.2	(0.6)	3.2	(0.5)	1.8	(0.3)	6.4	(0.6)	0.9	(0.3)	1.7	(0.3)	1.3	(0.3)
	Wales	61.3	(1.4)	6.2	(0.7)	3.3	(0.4)	2.4	(0.5)	7.2	(0.9)	1.2	(0.3)	1.6	(0.4)	1.6	(0.3)
	United States																
	Massachusetts•	75.8	(2.4)	5.4	(0.9)	2.1	(0.6)	1.3	(0.4)	3.9	(0.6)	0.4	(0.2)	0.6	(0.3)	1.4	(0.4)
	North Carolina•	63.8	(2.3)	8.7	(1.0)	3.3	(0.6)	2.2	(0.5)	3.8	(0.7)	0.3	(0.2)	0.8	(0.3)	2.6	(0.7)
Partners	**Colombia**																
	Bogotá	44.7	(2.5)	13.4	(1.6)	4.5	(0.6)	3.0	(0.7)	4.6	(0.8)	0.3	(0.2)	0.4	(0.3)	6.2	(0.8)
	Cali	28.6	(2.6)	11.0	(1.3)	4.7	(0.9)	4.4	(0.8)	4.0	(0.6)	0.4	(0.2)	0.3	(0.2)	6.4	(0.8)
	Manizales	35.4	(2.4)	11.8	(1.1)	4.3	(0.8)	3.7	(0.7)	5.3	(0.9)	0.4	(0.2)	0.3	(0.2)	6.1	(0.9)
	Medellín	35.8	(2.4)	11.0	(1.4)	4.7	(0.8)	3.9	(0.7)	4.5	(0.9)	0.4	(0.2)	0.2	(0.2)	5.9	(0.8)
	United Arab Emirates																
	Abu Dhabi•	29.1	(1.9)	6.1	(0.7)	2.8	(0.6)	2.1	(0.4)	8.0	(0.8)	1.2	(0.3)	2.0	(0.4)	4.6	(0.6)
	Ajman	21.4	(1.9)	7.6	(1.2)	4.2	(1.1)	3.1	(0.9)	5.8	(1.3)	0.9	(0.5)	1.9	(0.8)	5.2	(1.2)
	Dubai•	54.3	(0.7)	5.9	(0.6)	2.3	(0.4)	1.4	(0.3)	7.4	(0.7)	0.9	(0.2)	1.9	(0.3)	2.9	(0.4)
	Fujairah	20.7	(2.8)	5.7	(1.3)	2.5	(0.7)	1.9	(0.7)	7.0	(1.3)	1.3	(0.6)	2.2	(0.8)	4.9	(1.5)
	Ras Al Khaimah	19.8	(3.6)	5.5	(1.2)	2.7	(0.9)	2.2	(1.0)	7.9	(1.2)	1.5	(0.7)	3.1	(1.1)	3.7	(1.1)
	Sharjah	34.1	(4.1)	6.8	(1.6)	2.6	(0.8)	1.3	(0.5)	9.9	(1.4)	2.0	(0.7)	1.7	(0.7)	4.4	(0.9)
	Umm Al Quwain	16.7	(2.2)	4.7	(1.4)	2.6	(1.2)	2.1	(1.6)	6.1	(1.6)	1.2	(1.0)	1.9	(1.0)	4.4	(1.3)

• PISA for adjudicated region.
1. Low achievers in collaborative problem solving, science, reading or mathematics score below Level 2 in the subject.
Notes: Results for the province of Quebec in this table should be treated with caution due to a possible non-response bias.
In Massachusetts and North Carolina, the desired target population covers 15-year-old students in grade 7 or above in public schools only (see Annex A2).
See Table V.3.3b for national data.
StatLink http://dx.doi.org/10.1787/888933616750

[Part 2/2]

Table B2.V.4 Low achievers in four PISA subjects

	Percentage of 15-year-old students who are:								Percentage of low achievers in collaborative problem solving among low achievers in...							
	Low achievers[1] in collaborative problem solving, science and reading		Low achievers in collaborative problem solving, science and mathematics		Low achievers in collaborative problem solving, reading and mathematics		Low achievers in all four subjects		Science		Reading		Mathematics		Science, reading and mathematics	
	%	S.E.	%	S.E.	%	S.E.	%	S.E.	%	S.E.	%	S.E.	%	S.E.	%	S.E.
OECD																
Belgium																
Flemish community•	1.7	(0.3)	1.2	(0.2)	0.6	(0.2)	8.7	(0.8)	73.3	(2.3)	71.2	(2.8)	67.1	(2.7)	79.6	(2.7)
French community	2.0	(0.4)	2.3	(0.4)	1.3	(0.3)	13.0	(1.3)	80.1	(2.2)	79.9	(2.2)	77.8	(2.3)	87.2	(1.9)
German-speaking community	1.1	(0.8)	1.4	(0.9)	1.2	(1.0)	7.4	(1.5)	74.6	(7.6)	77.4	(7.2)	69.3	(7.2)	84.0	(8.8)
Canada																
Alberta	0.6	(0.3)	1.3	(0.4)	1.0	(0.3)	4.1	(0.7)	74.4	(5.2)	71.8	(5.6)	56.2	(5.4)	82.0	(5.7)
British Columbia	0.9	(0.4)	1.1	(0.5)	0.4	(0.3)	3.1	(0.7)	65.2	(5.6)	67.5	(8.0)	47.6	(6.4)	76.6	(8.1)
Manitoba	1.6	(0.6)	2.0	(0.5)	1.0	(0.4)	8.0	(1.1)	71.6	(4.3)	71.9	(5.7)	61.4	(4.1)	81.0	(4.3)
New Brunswick	1.2	(0.3)	1.7	(0.5)	1.0	(0.4)	7.4	(1.5)	70.9	(5.7)	73.1	(5.5)	57.2	(6.0)	79.9	(7.3)
Newfoundland and Labrador	0.8	(0.4)	2.0	(0.8)	0.8	(0.5)	8.1	(1.0)	73.5	(4.5)	73.9	(5.8)	60.0	(3.9)	82.1	(5.8)
Nova Scotia	0.9	(0.4)	1.9	(0.7)	0.8	(0.4)	5.9	(1.1)	72.6	(4.4)	75.8	(4.8)	58.5	(3.6)	82.6	(5.7)
Ontario	1.0	(0.3)	1.9	(0.4)	0.6	(0.2)	5.4	(0.7)	74.0	(3.7)	74.0	(3.1)	61.9	(3.7)	83.4	(3.2)
Prince Edward Island	1.0	(0.7)	1.4	(0.9)	1.1	(0.8)	5.1	(1.3)	70.9	(9.3)	77.7	(9.3)	60.6	(7.9)	83.9	(11.1)
Quebec	1.2	(0.4)	0.9	(0.3)	0.5	(0.3)	3.6	(0.6)	74.0	(3.7)	71.1	(4.0)	67.0	(5.0)	83.7	(4.6)
Saskatchewan	1.2	(0.5)	2.4	(0.6)	1.2	(0.5)	7.9	(1.0)	75.0	(3.2)	76.1	(4.4)	63.2	(3.9)	83.8	(5.0)
Italy																
Bolzano	1.6	(0.6)	1.2	(0.5)	0.7	(0.3)	4.8	(0.6)	74.6	(5.9)	65.9	(6.5)	66.3	(6.4)	82.4	(6.4)
Campania	3.8	(0.7)	5.2	(0.9)	1.5	(0.5)	17.7	(2.0)	81.6	(3.1)	81.4	(3.0)	77.0	(3.8)	88.9	(3.1)
Lombardia	1.5	(0.5)	2.4	(0.7)	0.8	(0.3)	6.8	(1.1)	72.4	(4.8)	69.1	(5.9)	64.4	(5.0)	80.0	(6.0)
Trento	1.3	(0.3)	1.7	(0.5)	0.5	(0.2)	5.5	(0.6)	77.9	(3.5)	75.6	(5.1)	70.6	(4.2)	84.8	(4.7)
Portugal																
Região Autónoma dos Açores	1.3	(0.4)	3.9	(0.7)	2.3	(0.6)	16.5	(1.3)	82.4	(2.5)	82.1	(2.7)	73.5	(2.9)	87.9	(3.0)
Spain																
Andalusia•	1.7	(0.6)	3.2	(0.7)	1.6	(0.5)	12.5	(1.1)	73.9	(2.9)	76.9	(3.4)	65.6	(2.5)	82.8	(3.5)
Aragon•	1.5	(0.6)	1.7	(0.6)	1.1	(0.4)	7.3	(1.0)	79.7	(3.3)	79.6	(5.1)	69.3	(5.0)	87.7	(4.9)
Asturias•	1.4	(0.5)	2.0	(0.5)	1.1	(0.3)	8.7	(1.1)	79.4	(5.0)	78.5	(6.8)	68.6	(4.9)	86.9	(5.1)
Balearic Islands•	1.5	(0.6)	2.6	(0.9)	1.4	(0.5)	10.3	(1.1)	75.6	(3.4)	77.4	(4.2)	67.1	(3.3)	85.8	(3.3)
Basque Country•	2.5	(0.5)	2.4	(0.4)	0.8	(0.3)	9.0	(0.9)	77.8	(3.0)	80.9	(2.4)	71.7	(3.3)	87.7	(2.6)
Canary Islands•	0.8	(0.3)	3.9	(0.7)	1.8	(0.5)	12.8	(1.1)	76.2	(3.6)	78.0	(3.2)	62.2	(3.3)	84.4	(3.6)
Cantabria•	1.7	(0.7)	2.7	(0.8)	0.9	(0.4)	8.2	(1.1)	80.8	(3.5)	83.0	(3.7)	73.7	(5.4)	88.4	(3.3)
Castile and Leon•	0.7	(0.2)	1.8	(0.5)	0.7	(0.2)	4.5	(0.7)	74.3	(5.1)	75.1	(4.5)	61.1	(4.4)	85.2	(5.0)
Castile-La Mancha•	1.1	(0.5)	2.5	(0.5)	1.3	(0.4)	7.4	(0.9)	73.7	(4.1)	74.8	(4.2)	62.7	(4.0)	83.3	(4.9)
Catalonia•	1.4	(0.4)	2.1	(0.5)	0.9	(0.4)	7.5	(1.2)	75.6	(3.1)	74.5	(3.7)	67.0	(4.0)	84.4	(3.3)
Comunidad Valenciana•	1.4	(0.4)	2.4	(0.5)	1.2	(0.4)	7.1	(0.9)	76.2	(4.4)	77.3	(4.3)	65.2	(3.7)	85.2	(4.2)
Extremadura•	2.2	(0.6)	2.9	(0.7)	1.4	(0.4)	13.1	(1.3)	80.6	(3.2)	82.6	(3.1)	74.2	(3.2)	89.0	(2.8)
Galicia•	0.9	(0.3)	2.1	(0.6)	1.1	(0.4)	7.6	(0.9)	84.1	(3.2)	83.5	(4.2)	72.1	(3.5)	90.3	(3.8)
La Rioja•	2.4	(1.0)	1.3	(0.7)	0.8	(0.4)	8.9	(1.3)	80.4	(5.5)	79.4	(6.2)	74.4	(7.0)	88.3	(5.1)
Madrid•	0.8	(0.3)	1.8	(0.5)	0.8	(0.3)	5.4	(0.8)	72.3	(4.1)	73.8	(3.8)	59.9	(4.3)	82.4	(4.0)
Murcia•	1.1	(0.4)	3.0	(0.7)	1.4	(0.5)	11.1	(1.0)	76.9	(3.7)	76.8	(4.2)	65.4	(4.2)	83.5	(4.2)
Navarre•	1.6	(0.6)	1.3	(0.5)	0.5	(0.3)	4.8	(0.7)	73.5	(4.2)	76.3	(4.7)	65.0	(4.9)	85.4	(4.7)
United Kingdom																
England	1.4	(0.3)	2.1	(0.4)	1.3	(0.3)	7.7	(0.7)	69.5	(2.2)	66.2	(2.4)	58.2	(2.7)	78.1	(2.8)
Northern Ireland	1.5	(0.4)	2.2	(0.7)	0.8	(0.3)	8.0	(0.8)	70.9	(3.0)	73.0	(3.9)	65.1	(4.2)	80.0	(4.0)
Scotland•	2.1	(0.3)	1.9	(0.3)	0.8	(0.2)	8.8	(0.8)	70.2	(2.5)	74.4	(2.6)	62.5	(2.8)	82.7	(2.9)
Wales	1.9	(0.6)	2.0	(0.4)	0.9	(0.2)	10.6	(0.8)	72.7	(2.3)	72.3	(3.5)	64.7	(3.3)	81.7	(3.6)
United States																
Massachusetts•	0.5	(0.3)	1.8	(0.5)	0.8	(0.3)	6.2	(0.9)	73.8	(4.1)	71.8	(3.4)	59.0	(3.0)	83.0	(4.0)
North Carolina•	0.7	(0.3)	2.2	(0.5)	1.4	(0.4)	10.2	(1.2)	74.6	(3.2)	73.3	(3.5)	56.9	(3.0)	82.6	(3.4)
Partners																
Colombia																
Bogotá	0.2	(0.2)	5.9	(0.8)	1.4	(0.4)	15.4	(1.4)	77.6	(2.9)	77.0	(3.4)	59.3	(3.0)	83.9	(3.4)
Cali	0.2	(0.2)	7.6	(1.1)	1.5	(0.6)	31.0	(2.1)	83.4	(2.0)	83.6	(2.3)	70.9	(2.3)	87.7	(2.1)
Manizales	0.3	(0.3)	7.3	(1.4)	1.3	(0.6)	23.9	(2.0)	82.0	(2.2)	82.6	(2.8)	66.9	(2.6)	86.7	(2.3)
Medellín	0.3	(0.2)	7.2	(0.9)	1.2	(0.4)	24.9	(2.0)	81.0	(2.2)	82.6	(2.4)	67.7	(2.8)	86.5	(2.2)
United Arab Emirates																
Abu Dhabi•	2.5	(0.5)	4.7	(0.7)	2.7	(0.5)	34.2	(1.9)	90.3	(1.3)	90.4	(1.5)	83.5	(1.8)	94.2	(1.0)
Ajman	1.9	(0.8)	6.0	(1.2)	2.8	(0.7)	39.2	(2.4)	87.2	(2.4)	89.0	(2.6)	81.0	(2.4)	92.8	(2.1)
Dubai•	1.8	(0.3)	2.6	(0.3)	1.8	(0.3)	16.8	(0.5)	86.3	(1.4)	86.4	(2.0)	76.0	(2.1)	92.3	(1.7)
Fujairah	2.4	(0.9)	5.5	(1.2)	3.1	(1.2)	42.7	(2.7)	93.0	(1.8)	92.2	(1.8)	87.3	(2.7)	95.8	(1.6)
Ras Al Khaimah	4.7	(1.7)	4.5	(1.5)	2.6	(0.9)	41.9	(3.8)	91.9	(2.2)	90.9	(2.2)	87.4	(2.4)	95.0	(2.1)
Sharjah	2.9	(1.0)	5.0	(1.0)	2.1	(0.6)	27.4	(3.5)	90.0	(2.7)	90.7	(2.9)	82.7	(4.0)	95.6	(1.8)
Umm Al Quwain	3.3	(1.5)	5.8	(2.0)	2.3	(1.1)	48.8	(3.2)	92.7	(3.2)	92.7	(3.0)	89.5	(3.0)	95.8	(3.1)

• PISA for adjudicated region.
1. Low achievers in collaborative problem solving, science, reading or mathematics score below Level 2 in the subject.
Notes: Results for the province of Quebec in this table should be treated with caution due to a possible non-response bias.
In Massachusetts and North Carolina, the desired target population covers 15-year-old students in grade 7 or above in public schools only (see Annex A2).
See Table V.3.3b for national data.
StatLink http://dx.doi.org/10.1787/888933616750

[Part 1/3]

Table B2.V.5 Relative performance in collaborative problem solving

Based on residual scores after accounting for performance in the core PISA subjects in regressions involving all OECD and partner countries/economies

	Relative performance in collaborative problem solving based on performance in...															
	Science				Reading				Mathematics				Science, reading and mathematics			
	Average relative score[1]		Percentage of students who score higher than expected[2, 3]		Average relative score		Percentage of students who score higher than expected		Average relative score		Percentage of students who score higher than expected		Average relative score		Percentage of students who score higher than expected	
	Score dif.	S.E.	%	S.E.	Score dif.	S.E.	%	S.E.	Score dif.	S.E.	%	S.E.	Score dif.	S.E.	%	S.E.
OECD																
Belgium																
Flemish community•	**4**	(2.0)	**53.0**	(1.2)	**8**	(1.8)	**54.7**	(1.1)	0	(2.3)	49.9	(1.2)	3	(1.8)	51.9	(1.2)
French community	**-11**	(2.1)	**43.4**	(1.5)	**-11**	(2.2)	**43.4**	(1.6)	**-16**	(2.4)	**40.6**	(1.4)	**-12**	(2.0)	**42.2**	(1.4)
German-speaking community	-14	(7.8)	41.3	(6.4)	-11	(6.9)	41.4	(4.8)	-12	(7.0)	42.5	(5.7)	-14	(7.3)	39.7	(5.7)
Canada																
Alberta	8	(4.6)	54.8	(2.9)	**14**	(5.8)	**58.4**	(3.2)	**31**	(5.7)	**65.6**	(3.3)	9	(4.9)	55.8	(3.2)
British Columbia	**28**	(4.3)	**66.6**	(2.4)	**31**	(5.4)	**67.2**	(2.9)	**42**	(5.2)	**70.5**	(2.6)	**27**	(4.3)	**66.4**	(2.5)
Manitoba	**17**	(4.6)	**60.2**	(2.7)	**17**	(4.1)	**60.0**	(2.4)	**24**	(4.2)	**62.4**	(2.4)	**17**	(4.0)	**60.1**	(2.7)
New Brunswick	**10**	(3.5)	**56.7**	(2.9)	**10**	(3.8)	**56.6**	(3.1)	**20**	(4.9)	**61.2**	(3.2)	**10**	(3.5)	**56.5**	(3.0)
Newfoundland and Labrador	**15**	(4.2)	**59.0**	(3.0)	**15**	(4.4)	**59.3**	(3.0)	**29**	(4.6)	**66.4**	(2.8)	**14**	(4.3)	**59.1**	(3.1)
Nova Scotia	**17**	(2.9)	**60.6**	(2.2)	**17**	(3.1)	**60.3**	(1.9)	**32**	(3.5)	**66.0**	(2.1)	**16**	(2.7)	**60.2**	(2.2)
Ontario	**11**	(3.1)	**56.7**	(1.9)	**8**	(3.3)	**54.9**	(2.0)	**22**	(3.3)	**61.1**	(1.7)	**8**	(3.0)	**55.4**	(2.0)
Prince Edward Island	**15**	(4.4)	**60.5**	(3.3)	**15**	(4.6)	**58.1**	(3.5)	**27**	(5.9)	**65.1**	(4.1)	**14**	(4.3)	**59.7**	(3.3)
Quebec	2	(2.9)	51.2	(2.2)	**6**	(3.0)	53.9	(2.4)	-2	(3.4)	49.1	(2.0)	0	(2.7)	50.1	(2.1)
Saskatchewan	**10**	(2.9)	**56.3**	(1.9)	**8**	(3.1)	**55.5**	(2.1)	**17**	(3.1)	**59.6**	(2.2)	**9**	(2.8)	**56.0**	(2.0)
Italy																
Bolzano	-2	(8.1)	48.7	(5.2)	7	(8.9)	55.0	(5.4)	-4	(8.6)	47.7	(5.4)	-1	(7.7)	49.6	(5.1)
Campania	**-15**	(4.6)	**41.2**	(3.0)	**-26**	(5.1)	**35.4**	(2.8)	**-27**	(5.2)	**35.9**	(2.8)	**-18**	(4.5)	**39.0**	(2.9)
Lombardia	-6	(4.7)	46.2	(3.0)	-9	(5.4)	44.9	(3.2)	**-11**	(5.7)	43.9	(3.3)	-9	(4.8)	44.2	(3.2)
Trento	**-11**	(2.2)	**42.9**	(1.6)	**-12**	(3.1)	**42.1**	(2.3)	**-15**	(2.5)	**40.3**	(2.1)	**-14**	(2.4)	**40.6**	(1.7)
Portugal																
Região Autónoma dos Açores	**-11**	(2.3)	**42.7**	(1.8)	**-13**	(3.0)	**41.1**	(2.3)	**-8**	(2.2)	**45.0**	(1.9)	**-11**	(2.3)	**42.0**	(2.1)
Spain																
Andalusia•	2	(3.0)	52.3	(2.3)	-4	(2.9)	47.9	(2.0)	5	(3.3)	53.7	(2.4)	0	(2.9)	50.8	(2.6)
Aragon•	-9	(5.2)	44.5	(3.3)	-9	(5.3)	44.5	(3.7)	-4	(7.1)	47.8	(4.2)	**-10**	(4.8)	43.8	(3.4)
Asturias•	-7	(11.1)	45.3	(7.0)	-5	(12.7)	46.5	(7.7)	-1	(10.7)	49.7	(6.3)	-7	(11.4)	44.9	(7.2)
Balearic Islands•	-1	(5.7)	49.3	(3.7)	-3	(6.2)	48.2	(4.3)	3	(6.0)	52.1	(3.5)	-2	(4.7)	49.1	(3.2)
Basque Country•	-4	(4.5)	47.4	(2.8)	**-13**	(3.6)	**41.9**	(2.3)	**-13**	(4.8)	**42.9**	(2.6)	**-9**	(3.9)	**44.4**	(2.6)
Canary Islands•	2	(4.2)	51.7	(2.7)	-6	(5.7)	46.7	(3.8)	**17**	(4.5)	**60.1**	(2.5)	1	(4.5)	50.8	(3.1)
Cantabria•	-14	(7.4)	41.1	(5.0)	**-19**	(8.8)	**37.9**	(5.8)	-15	(10.0)	41.8	(5.9)	**-17**	(7.9)	**38.6**	(5.3)
Castile and Leon•	-1	(3.1)	49.8	(2.6)	-3	(4.1)	48.7	(3.2)	**9**	(3.9)	**55.7**	(2.7)	-3	(3.3)	48.2	(2.7)
Castile-La Mancha•	-3	(3.6)	48.6	(2.4)	-5	(3.5)	47.2	(2.6)	4	(4.2)	52.9	(2.8)	-4	(3.1)	47.6	(2.3)
Catalonia•	0	(2.6)	50.5	(1.9)	2	(3.9)	52.1	(2.5)	2	(4.2)	51.8	(3.0)	0	(3.1)	50.3	(2.2)
Comunidad Valenciana•	-5	(3.0)	47.2	(2.0)	**-10**	(3.9)	**43.9**	(2.5)	0	(3.5)	50.8	(2.4)	**-7**	(3.2)	45.5	(2.3)
Extremadura•	-7	(4.1)	45.5	(3.2)	**-10**	(3.9)	**43.2**	(2.9)	-9	(4.6)	44.8	(2.8)	**-8**	(3.8)	44.5	(3.1)
Galicia•	**-18**	(5.1)	**39.2**	(3.3)	**-16**	(6.4)	**39.7**	(4.0)	-5	(5.8)	47.7	(3.8)	**-18**	(5.4)	**38.6**	(3.8)
La Rioja•	-5	(10.1)	46.6	(6.1)	-1	(13.0)	49.8	(8.4)	-12	(13.2)	44.0	(7.2)	-6	(10.7)	46.4	(6.7)
Madrid•	4	(3.3)	53.5	(2.1)	0	(4.1)	50.5	(2.9)	**13**	(3.5)	**58.2**	(2.2)	1	(3.3)	51.4	(2.6)
Murcia•	-3	(5.1)	49.3	(4.0)	-6	(5.6)	46.3	(3.7)	5	(6.1)	53.9	(3.8)	-4	(4.8)	48.7	(3.5)
Navarre•	-6	(6.0)	46.8	(4.2)	-9	(6.1)	45.0	(4.0)	-11	(10.3)	44.1	(5.6)	-10	(6.0)	44.3	(4.1)
United Kingdom																
England	**10**	(2.2)	**55.8**	(1.6)	**19**	(2.8)	**60.5**	(1.8)	**23**	(2.6)	**62.4**	(1.6)	**12**	(2.3)	**57.8**	(1.6)
Northern Ireland	**12**	(2.6)	**59.4**	(2.3)	**13**	(4.5)	**60.0**	(3.3)	**16**	(5.2)	**61.1**	(3.5)	**12**	(3.2)	**59.2**	(2.8)
Scotland•	**14**	(1.9)	**58.3**	(1.5)	**15**	(1.8)	**59.8**	(1.5)	**17**	(2.0)	**58.8**	(1.2)	**14**	(1.8)	**58.7**	(1.6)
Wales	**7**	(2.8)	**55.0**	(2.0)	**10**	(2.9)	**57.5**	(2.2)	**9**	(4.3)	**56.6**	(3.1)	**8**	(2.7)	**56.2**	(2.1)
United States																
Massachusetts•	**23**	(2.3)	**65.5**	(1.8)	**25**	(3.3)	**65.4**	(2.0)	**46**	(3.3)	**74.8**	(1.9)	**23**	(2.5)	**65.9**	(2.0)
North Carolina•	**21**	(2.6)	**64.3**	(1.8)	**22**	(3.0)	**64.1**	(2.1)	**43**	(3.1)	**73.6**	(1.7)	**22**	(2.5)	**65.7**	(1.8)
Partners																
Colombia																
Bogotá	**6**	(2.8)	**55.0**	(2.2)	**-6**	(2.8)	**45.4**	(2.2)	**26**	(3.5)	**68.6**	(2.5)	5	(2.6)	54.0	(2.4)
Cali	2	(2.1)	51.5	(2.0)	**-11**	(2.6)	**41.4**	(2.4)	**16**	(2.1)	**61.7**	(2.0)	2	(2.0)	51.5	(2.1)
Manizales	2	(1.8)	52.3	(2.1)	**-13**	(2.0)	**40.3**	(1.8)	**17**	(2.3)	**62.5**	(2.0)	1	(1.7)	50.9	(2.2)
Medellín	4	(2.7)	53.5	(2.2)	**-13**	(3.7)	**40.3**	(3.0)	**18**	(3.6)	**63.3**	(2.7)	2	(3.0)	51.0	(2.6)
United Arab Emirates																
Abu Dhabi•	**-19**	(2.6)	**36.2**	(1.9)	**-20**	(3.1)	**36.2**	(2.3)	**-17**	(3.1)	**39.0**	(2.0)	**-16**	(2.7)	**38.0**	(2.2)
Ajman	-11	(5.7)	**41.7**	(4.1)	**-16**	(6.1)	**39.5**	(4.2)	-7	(6.5)	44.5	(4.4)	-8	(5.6)	43.7	(4.3)
Dubai•	**-9**	(2.0)	**43.8**	(1.6)	**-7**	(2.7)	**44.8**	(2.1)	-2	(2.8)	48.8	(1.8)	**-8**	(2.3)	**44.3**	(1.9)
Fujairah	**-21**	(5.2)	**34.2**	(3.5)	**-23**	(4.7)	**33.8**	(3.8)	**-22**	(5.3)	**35.1**	(4.0)	**-17**	(4.6)	**35.8**	(3.5)
Ras Al Khaimah	**-22**	(5.7)	**35.1**	(3.9)	**-20**	(6.7)	**36.3**	(4.8)	**-31**	(8.1)	**31.4**	(4.4)	**-18**	(5.7)	**37.2**	(4.4)
Sharjah	**-18**	(5.8)	**36.5**	(4.0)	**-24**	(5.3)	**33.1**	(3.7)	**-21**	(6.9)	**36.5**	(4.8)	**-18**	(5.3)	**36.4**	(3.8)
Umm Al Quwain	**-17**	(5.7)	**35.7**	(5.0)	**-22**	(4.5)	**33.6**	(3.8)	**-24**	(7.6)	**33.5**	(5.2)	**-14**	(5.1)	**37.9**	(4.2)

• PISA for adjudicated region.
1. Relative scores are the residuals obtained from a pooled linear regression, across all participating countries/economies, of the performance in collaborative problem solving over performance in science, reading and/or mathematics.
2. Students who score higher than expected are those with positive relative scores.
3. The percentage of students who score higher than expected is bolded when it differs significantly from 50%.
4. Top performers in science, reading or mathematics are those who attain Level 5 or above in those subjects.
5. Low achievers in science, reading or mathematics are those who attain below Level 2 in those subjects.
Notes: Results for the province of Quebec in this table should be treated with caution due to a possible non-response bias.
In Massachusetts and North Carolina, the desired target population covers 15-year-old students in grade 7 or above in public schools only (see Annex A2).
Students in PISA 2015 completed four clusters of test material: two in science and two distributed among reading, mathematics and collaborative problem solving. Hence, no student completed all four of science, reading, mathematics and collaborative problem solving. Scores were imputed in the domains in which students were not tested.
Values that are statistically significant are indicated in bold (see Annex A3).
See Table V.3.9a for national data.
StatLink http://dx.doi.org/10.1787/888933616750

[Part 2/3]

Table B2.V.5 Relative performance in collaborative problem solving

Based on residual scores after accounting for performance in the core PISA subjects in regressions involving all OECD and partner countries/economies

		Relative performance in collaborative problem solving based on performance among top performers[4] in...											
		Science				Reading				Mathematics			
		Average relative score[1]		Percentage of students who score higher than expected[2, 3]		Average relative score		Percentage of students who score higher than expected		Average relative score		Percentage of students who score higher than expected	
		Score dif.	S.E.	%	S.E.	Score dif.	S.E.	%	S.E.	Score dif.	S.E.	%	S.E.
OECD	**Belgium**												
	Flemish community•	**-12**	(4.1)	**41.1**	(3.4)	-2	(4.2)	48.0	(3.5)	**-11**	(4.1)	**43.5**	(2.9)
	French community	**-23**	(5.4)	**36.6**	(4.6)	**-17**	(6.9)	**39.8**	(4.8)	**-15**	(5.0)	**41.3**	(3.9)
	German-speaking community	**-42**	(20.8)	**23.1**	(13.1)	-28	(15.6)	26.4	(13.4)	-27	(15.7)	31.0	(11.6)
	Canada												
	Alberta	13	(7.5)	57.8	(4.8)	**24**	(9.5)	**64.7**	(6.1)	**39**	(8.0)	**70.6**	(5.3)
	British Columbia	**30**	(6.0)	**67.4**	(4.1)	**39**	(6.4)	**71.7**	(4.3)	**43**	(8.1)	**71.7**	(4.6)
	Manitoba	**30**	(9.3)	**70.8**	(8.0)	**35**	(8.1)	**72.8**	(5.9)	**48**	(11.2)	**77.1**	(6.9)
	New Brunswick	**19**	(9.4)	61.5	(7.9)	**30**	(8.9)	**67.4**	(6.4)	**27**	(12.7)	**65.4**	(7.6)
	Newfoundland and Labrador	**21**	(10.4)	63.3	(7.2)	**33**	(10.4)	**71.2**	(8.0)	**46**	(10.5)	**76.1**	(6.9)
	Nova Scotia	**29**	(9.9)	**67.2**	(6.9)	**36**	(11.5)	**71.2**	(6.8)	**45**	(12.3)	**72.7**	(7.1)
	Ontario	**16**	(6.7)	59.2	(4.8)	**20**	(6.4)	**61.3**	(3.9)	**31**	(6.1)	**66.4**	(3.4)
	Prince Edward Island	20	(21.3)	62.2	(17.3)	**35**	(17.0)	68.4	(12.3)	42	(22.7)	72.8	(13.9)
	Quebec	-1	(6.0)	49.3	(4.9)	2	(5.7)	51.3	(4.4)	-6	(5.9)	46.7	(3.7)
	Saskatchewan	19	(10.9)	62.6	(9.4)	**33**	(9.2)	**70.7**	(7.2)	**35**	(10.0)	**70.9**	(7.7)
	Italy												
	Bolzano	-5	(7.7)	46.3	(6.4)	1	(11.5)	50.1	(8.9)	-10	(6.7)	44.1	(4.9)
	Campania	-16	(16.7)	40.5	(15.8)	**-39**	(16.4)	**29.5**	(9.6)	**-32**	(12.9)	34.5	(8.1)
	Lombardia	**-22**	(10.4)	36.0	(7.9)	**-29**	(9.6)	**32.9**	(6.3)	**-30**	(7.8)	**31.5**	(4.9)
	Trento	**-20**	(9.7)	35.8	(8.3)	**-24**	(9.2)	**35.4**	(6.9)	**-28**	(5.6)	**31.0**	(3.7)
	Portugal												
	Região Autónoma dos Açores	**-26**	(10.6)	**29.8**	(8.6)	-16	(10.8)	37.1	(11.3)	**-21**	(10.0)	**35.6**	(6.7)
	Spain												
	Andalusia•	-10	(9.4)	43.9	(9.3)	-13	(10.3)	42.9	(8.1)	-3	(10.3)	48.8	(7.9)
	Aragon•	-20	(11.9)	36.9	(10.2)	-12	(10.1)	42.0	(8.1)	-9	(12.3)	44.0	(9.4)
	Asturias•	-17	(16.8)	36.0	(11.1)	-9	(18.2)	44.1	(12.0)	-7	(14.3)	46.9	(10.2)
	Balearic Islands•	-12	(11.6)	42.3	(9.7)	-9	(12.2)	44.5	(11.5)	1	(13.0)	52.9	(10.3)
	Basque Country•	**-19**	(9.0)	37.6	(7.1)	**-17**	(8.4)	38.9	(6.7)	**-21**	(7.9)	**37.7**	(4.6)
	Canary Islands•	-13	(11.7)	38.6	(10.9)	-10	(10.5)	43.9	(8.8)	-1	(12.5)	50.9	(7.9)
	Cantabria•	**-26**	(11.5)	33.1	(9.1)	-22	(13.1)	35.5	(9.2)	-21	(14.4)	38.2	(8.6)
	Castile and Leon•	-10	(6.9)	44.0	(5.4)	-5	(6.2)	47.1	(6.1)	5	(7.3)	53.6	(6.1)
	Castile-La Mancha•	-14	(10.6)	38.6	(8.9)	-11	(10.0)	43.1	(7.4)	-4	(8.9)	47.5	(7.4)
	Catalonia•	-11	(7.0)	44.4	(5.3)	1	(8.5)	51.0	(7.7)	-1	(6.8)	50.8	(5.3)
	Comunidad Valenciana•	**-15**	(7.8)	38.2	(7.0)	-12	(8.2)	40.9	(6.5)	-8	(9.0)	45.7	(7.9)
	Extremadura•	**-19**	(9.1)	36.1	(8.5)	-12	(10.3)	41.7	(8.6)	-11	(8.0)	41.5	(5.7)
	Galicia•	**-30**	(9.1)	**29.6**	(7.1)	-21	(11.2)	36.9	(7.3)	-12	(9.3)	42.6	(7.9)
	La Rioja•	-15	(15.6)	39.6	(11.6)	-3	(15.5)	47.3	(11.4)	-16	(19.1)	41.4	(10.6)
	Madrid•	-9	(7.7)	45.4	(6.4)	-5	(6.7)	47.1	(6.2)	0	(6.4)	50.4	(5.2)
	Murcia•	-16	(11.6)	39.0	(8.6)	-15	(12.5)	42.1	(8.7)	-1	(11.9)	49.9	(8.4)
	Navarre•	-14	(8.2)	42.2	(7.7)	-8	(8.9)	45.5	(6.7)	-19	(11.5)	40.7	(7.7)
	United Kingdom												
	England	6	(3.9)	53.8	(2.9)	**20**	(6.0)	**62.0**	(4.3)	**23**	(5.8)	**63.2**	(3.3)
	Northern Ireland	1	(6.3)	51.7	(5.2)	**17**	(8.1)	63.4	(7.3)	**21**	(7.5)	**65.3**	(6.6)
	Scotland•	0	(6.9)	50.4	(5.0)	**23**	(5.7)	**65.7**	(4.8)	**17**	(6.3)	**61.1**	(5.3)
	Wales	0	(6.3)	50.1	(5.9)	13	(8.5)	61.4	(6.0)	**18**	(7.9)	**64.3**	(6.4)
	United States												
	Massachusetts•	**35**	(4.7)	**75.5**	(3.7)	**43**	(7.2)	**77.0**	(5.1)	**75**	(5.8)	**89.1**	(3.1)
	North Carolina•	**29**	(6.6)	**70.0**	(4.7)	**38**	(5.6)	**75.2**	(4.0)	**60**	(9.3)	**84.6**	(6.8)
Partners	**Colombia**												
	Bogotá	0	(14.5)	52.6	(15.3)	-15	(13.7)	36.3	(13.9)	26	(27.5)	74.0	(18.9)
	Cali	-4	(23.8)	44.4	(27.3)	-25	(17.4)	33.8	(16.8)	25	(39.1)	62.5	(35.0)
	Manizales	-4	(30.4)	48.2	(30.1)	-26	(21.7)	29.5	(19.6)	22	(31.8)	66.1	(32.8)
	Medellín	-6	(23.2)	52.9	(28.1)	**-28**	(13.7)	30.6	(11.7)	11	(24.6)	59.8	(21.4)
	United Arab Emirates												
	Abu Dhabi•	**-40**	(9.8)	**21.2**	(7.9)	**-36**	(11.5)	**26.7**	(8.8)	**-32**	(11.3)	**28.1**	(8.7)
	Ajman	m	m	m	m	-52	(51.4)	21.5	(33.9)	-34	(47.7)	15.8	(27.5)
	Dubai•	**-12**	(5.1)	**40.3**	(4.4)	-8	(5.7)	43.8	(5.1)	-3	(7.6)	47.9	(5.7)
	Fujairah	-10	(32.8)	45.4	(23.6)	-20	(21.8)	43.8	(20.3)	-8	(35.2)	40.0	(23.4)
	Ras Al Khaimah	-11	(41.3)	45.7	(31.7)	-1	(27.2)	56.9	(29.7)	-6	(35.5)	49.4	(23.3)
	Sharjah	**-51**	(18.0)	**14.4**	(12.5)	**-44**	(19.2)	22.4	(14.7)	**-55**	(21.0)	**19.5**	(11.1)
	Umm Al Quwain	m	m	m	m	m	m	m	m	m	m	m	m

• PISA for adjudicated region.
1. Relative scores are the residuals obtained from a pooled linear regression, across all participating countries/economies, of the performance in collaborative problem solving over performance in science, reading and/or mathematics.
2. Students who score higher than expected are those with positive relative scores.
3. The percentage of students who score higher than expected is bolded when it differs significantly from 50%.
4. Top performers in science, reading or mathematics are those who attain Level 5 or above in those subjects.
5. Low achievers in science, reading or mathematics are those who attain below Level 2 in those subjects.

Notes: Results for the province of Quebec in this table should be treated with caution due to a possible non-response bias.
In Massachusetts and North Carolina, the desired target population covers 15-year-old students in grade 7 or above in public schools only (see Annex A2).
Students in PISA 2015 completed four clusters of test material: two in science and two distributed among reading, mathematics and collaborative problem solving. Hence, no student completed all four of science, reading, mathematics and collaborative problem solving. Scores were imputed in the domains in which students were not tested.
Values that are statistically significant are indicated in bold (see Annex A3).
See Table V.3.9a for national data.

StatLink http://dx.doi.org/10.1787/888933616750

[Part 3/3]

Table B2.V.5 Relative performance in collaborative problem solving

Based on residual scores after accounting for performance in the core PISA subjects in regressions involving all OECD and partner countries/economies

	Relative performance in collaborative problem solving based on performance among low achievers[5] in...											
	Science				Reading				Mathematics			
	Average relative score[1]		Percentage of students who score higher than expected[2, 3]		Average relative score		Percentage of students who score higher than expected		Average relative score		Percentage of students who score higher than expected	
	Score dif.	S.E.	%	S.E.	Score dif.	S.E.	%	S.E.	Score dif.	S.E.	%	S.E.
OECD												
Belgium												
Flemish community•	**10**	(3.5)	**56.7**	(2.3)	**11**	(4.2)	**56.6**	(2.7)	3	(4.9)	51.3	(2.9)
French community	-7	(4.0)	45.9	(3.0)	**-8**	(3.5)	45.4	(2.6)	**-20**	(4.2)	**38.1**	(2.7)
German-speaking community	3	(11.9)	50.8	(9.1)	3	(10.1)	49.7	(8.4)	-6	(11.9)	47.1	(10.6)
Canada												
Alberta	-5	(8.4)	46.8	(6.4)	-2	(9.1)	47.6	(5.5)	17	(9.1)	56.7	(5.8)
British Columbia	14	(9.2)	56.7	(6.1)	9	(11.5)	52.7	(7.8)	**35**	(11.8)	**64.7**	(5.9)
Manitoba	6	(8.0)	52.2	(4.8)	2	(10.0)	50.8	(6.0)	7	(8.9)	53.4	(5.0)
New Brunswick	4	(7.2)	51.9	(6.2)	-1	(7.2)	49.5	(4.7)	14	(7.3)	58.2	(5.1)
Newfoundland and Labrador	2	(7.4)	49.9	(5.5)	-3	(9.1)	47.1	(7.3)	10	(6.5)	55.9	(4.7)
Nova Scotia	3	(6.6)	49.3	(4.9)	-5	(7.0)	45.8	(5.0)	13	(6.6)	55.7	(4.1)
Ontario	2	(5.6)	51.9	(4.0)	-2	(5.8)	48.2	(3.8)	6	(5.1)	52.3	(3.5)
Prince Edward Island	0	(12.8)	47.6	(12.4)	-12	(12.8)	40.5	(11.5)	2	(12.5)	50.7	(9.1)
Quebec	-5	(7.8)	46.1	(4.5)	5	(7.3)	52.3	(5.3)	-7	(9.0)	45.8	(5.6)
Saskatchewan	1	(6.4)	50.3	(5.5)	-7	(7.2)	46.3	(5.0)	5	(7.4)	52.9	(4.8)
Italy												
Bolzano	0	(8.9)	49.6	(6.9)	14	(9.0)	58.3	(6.0)	-4	(10.5)	46.9	(6.1)
Campania	-11	(6.4)	43.6	(3.9)	-14	(7.4)	**40.9**	(4.1)	**-18**	(7.6)	**39.6**	(4.4)
Lombardia	5	(8.8)	52.8	(5.8)	8	(10.2)	54.1	(6.7)	5	(9.9)	54.3	(6.8)
Trento	-3	(5.5)	47.5	(4.7)	-2	(6.9)	48.3	(4.9)	-8	(5.6)	43.5	(5.0)
Portugal												
Região Autónoma dos Açores	-8	(4.0)	43.9	(3.3)	**-10**	(4.6)	**42.3**	(3.5)	-3	(3.7)	47.7	(3.0)
Spain												
Andalusia•	3	(4.9)	52.4	(3.6)	-4	(4.7)	47.9	(3.3)	2	(4.3)	51.6	(3.0)
Aragon•	-11	(5.8)	42.9	(4.0)	-12	(8.7)	41.5	(5.7)	-6	(9.8)	46.9	(6.2)
Asturias•	-7	(11.1)	44.4	(7.9)	-7	(15.2)	44.9	(9.7)	-5	(10.8)	46.9	(6.0)
Balearic Islands•	2	(6.7)	50.5	(4.8)	-3	(6.7)	48.2	(4.7)	0	(6.9)	49.9	(3.9)
Basque Country•	-4	(5.5)	46.7	(4.2)	**-13**	(4.4)	**41.4**	(3.1)	**-12**	(4.9)	**41.8**	(3.5)
Canary Islands•	1	(6.1)	50.3	(4.5)	-5	(7.3)	46.2	(5.2)	**14**	(5.5)	**57.8**	(3.4)
Cantabria•	-10	(6.9)	42.8	(4.9)	**-15**	(7.5)	**39.4**	(5.2)	-13	(10.5)	42.2	(7.0)
Castile and Leon•	-1	(5.0)	48.5	(5.3)	-4	(6.2)	48.1	(5.2)	7	(6.9)	52.9	(4.8)
Castile-La Mancha•	0	(5.9)	50.1	(4.9)	-5	(5.9)	46.6	(4.3)	4	(6.4)	53.0	(4.6)
Catalonia•	2	(5.3)	50.1	(4.1)	-1	(5.6)	49.1	(4.3)	-1	(6.1)	48.6	(4.0)
Comunidad Valenciana•	-5	(7.3)	47.7	(4.9)	-8	(7.1)	45.6	(5.7)	1	(7.4)	50.6	(4.9)
Extremadura•	-6	(6.3)	45.4	(5.5)	**-11**	(5.4)	41.9	(4.8)	**-13**	(6.4)	41.8	(4.4)
Galicia•	**-16**	(5.5)	**39.2**	(4.1)	**-17**	(7.3)	**38.1**	(4.6)	-10	(7.8)	43.9	(5.3)
La Rioja•	-4	(10.7)	45.9	(6.9)	-4	(12.2)	45.5	(7.4)	-14	(10.7)	41.6	(6.5)
Madrid•	4	(6.5)	53.1	(4.9)	-3	(6.2)	48.3	(5.2)	12	(6.0)	56.8	(4.1)
Murcia•	-1	(5.8)	50.4	(4.9)	-4	(7.7)	47.1	(5.0)	4	(7.2)	52.3	(4.6)
Navarre•	-4	(7.4)	48.0	(6.0)	-9	(8.8)	45.4	(6.3)	-6	(10.4)	47.2	(6.2)
United Kingdom												
England	**13**	(3.8)	**56.3**	(2.9)	**17**	(4.3)	**59.6**	(2.8)	**22**	(4.1)	**61.6**	(2.7)
Northern Ireland	**11**	(4.9)	58.5	(4.5)	3	(6.1)	52.8	(4.3)	2	(6.4)	51.8	(5.8)
Scotland•	**12**	(4.0)	55.6	(3.0)	2	(4.0)	49.9	(2.9)	6	(5.2)	51.6	(2.9)
Wales	**8**	(3.5)	55.2	(3.0)	5	(5.1)	51.9	(4.4)	3	(5.1)	51.3	(3.6)
United States												
Massachusetts•	4	(6.1)	52.5	(4.5)	5	(5.3)	52.1	(5.3)	**15**	(4.7)	**58.7**	(3.4)
North Carolina•	5	(3.9)	52.7	(3.6)	5	(4.0)	52.7	(3.3)	**21**	(3.8)	**62.0**	(2.7)
Partners												
Colombia												
Bogotá	3	(3.8)	53.1	(3.4)	0	(4.5)	49.6	(3.9)	**22**	(4.5)	**66.1**	(3.1)
Cali	0	(2.6)	50.0	(2.8)	-4	(3.1)	46.1	(3.1)	**13**	(2.5)	**59.2**	(2.6)
Manizales	1	(2.9)	50.2	(3.0)	-6	(4.1)	45.2	(4.3)	**15**	(2.4)	**60.9**	(2.4)
Medellín	4	(2.9)	53.1	(3.3)	-5	(4.5)	46.7	(4.1)	**16**	(3.3)	**61.3**	(2.8)
United Arab Emirates												
Abu Dhabi•	**-14**	(2.9)	**39.2**	(2.6)	**-11**	(3.4)	**41.3**	(3.0)	**-14**	(3.5)	**40.1**	(2.4)
Ajman	-9	(5.5)	42.2	(4.3)	-11	(7.1)	42.4	(4.9)	-7	(6.1)	44.0	(4.3)
Dubai•	**-11**	(2.9)	**40.7**	(2.5)	**-8**	(4.0)	**43.2**	(3.0)	-7	(4.6)	45.0	(2.9)
Fujairah	**-18**	(4.6)	**35.6**	(3.3)	**-16**	(4.7)	**37.5**	(3.7)	**-20**	(5.8)	**35.8**	(4.3)
Ras Al Khaimah	**-19**	(6.3)	**36.1**	(4.8)	**-15**	(6.9)	**39.3**	(5.2)	**-28**	(8.2)	**31.4**	(5.2)
Sharjah	**-16**	(6.3)	**38.3**	(5.5)	**-19**	(5.7)	**36.4**	(4.9)	**-19**	(8.3)	**37.3**	(5.6)
Umm Al Quwain	**-13**	(6.6)	39.1	(6.0)	**-14**	(6.7)	39.1	(6.2)	**-24**	(7.8)	**33.3**	(5.6)

• PISA for adjudicated region.
1. Relative scores are the residuals obtained from a pooled linear regression, across all participating countries/economies, of the performance in collaborative problem solving over performance in science, reading and/or mathematics.
2. Students who score higher than expected are those with positive relative scores.
3. The percentage of students who score higher than expected is bolded when it differs significantly from 50%.
4. Top performers in science, reading or mathematics are those who attain Level 5 or above in those subjects.
5. Low achievers in science, reading or mathematics are those who attain below Level 2 in those subjects.
Notes: Results for the province of Quebec in this table should be treated with caution due to a possible non-response bias.
In Massachusetts and North Carolina, the desired target population covers 15-year-old students in grade 7 or above in public schools only (see Annex A2).
Students in PISA 2015 completed four clusters of test material: two in science and two distributed among reading, mathematics and collaborative problem solving. Hence, no student completed all four of science, reading, mathematics and collaborative problem solving. Scores were imputed in the domains in which students were not tested.
Values that are statistically significant are indicated in bold (see Annex A3).
See Table V.3.9a for national data.
StatLink http://dx.doi.org/10.1787/888933616750

[Part 1/2]

Table B2.V.15 Percentage of students at each proficiency level in collaborative problem solving, by gender

		Boys										Girls									
		Below Level 1 (below 340 score points)		Level 1 (from 340 to less than 440 score points)		Level 2 (from 440 to less than 540 score points)		Level 3 (from 540 to less than 640 score points)		Level 4 (at or above 640 score points)		Below Level 1 (below 340 score points)		Level 1 (from 340 to less than 440 score points)		Level 2 (from 440 to less than 540 score points)		Level 3 (from 540 to less than 640 score points)		Level 4 (at or above 640 score points)	
		%	S.E.	%	S.E.	%	S.E.	%	S.E.	%	S.E.	%	S.E.	%	S.E.	%	S.E.	%	S.E.	%	S.E.
OECD	**Belgium**																				
	Flemish community•	4.8	(0.7)	19.7	(1.2)	37.4	(1.3)	30.9	(1.3)	7.3	(1.0)	3.0	(0.5)	14.7	(1.2)	32.8	(1.3)	37.3	(1.3)	12.2	(1.3)
	French community	10.1	(1.2)	28.6	(1.9)	37.4	(1.7)	20.7	(1.6)	3.2	(0.7)	5.9	(1.0)	22.9	(1.6)	39.7	(1.6)	26.6	(1.8)	4.9	(0.8)
	German-speaking community	4.6	(1.9)	28.1	(3.6)	41.6	(5.0)	23.6	(4.4)	2.1	(1.3)	1.7	(1.3)	16.4	(3.4)	49.5	(4.9)	28.6	(5.0)	3.7	(1.8)
	Canada																				
	Alberta	4.4	(1.0)	17.5	(1.8)	33.6	(2.6)	31.6	(2.6)	13.0	(2.0)	1.9	(0.6)	10.2	(1.7)	27.2	(2.1)	37.3	(2.3)	23.4	(2.2)
	British Columbia	3.8	(1.3)	14.5	(2.0)	29.5	(2.6)	34.7	(2.3)	17.5	(2.1)	0.8	(0.4)	7.0	(1.3)	25.3	(2.3)	39.5	(2.7)	27.4	(2.8)
	Manitoba	5.8	(1.2)	23.1	(2.6)	37.1	(3.2)	24.8	(2.8)	9.2	(1.8)	3.4	(1.2)	13.7	(1.9)	31.5	(2.1)	34.5	(2.4)	16.9	(2.0)
	New Brunswick	6.5	(1.6)	23.0	(2.5)	34.3	(2.8)	27.4	(3.1)	8.7	(1.7)	1.9	(0.7)	13.0	(1.8)	37.3	(2.8)	34.2	(2.4)	13.6	(2.2)
	Newfoundland and Labrador	5.8	(1.3)	20.3	(2.5)	37.0	(3.1)	27.3	(2.8)	9.6	(1.6)	2.3	(0.8)	13.4	(2.3)	34.6	(3.1)	36.0	(2.5)	13.7	(2.2)
	Nova Scotia	4.9	(1.1)	20.4	(2.1)	34.4	(2.4)	29.5	(2.5)	10.8	(1.8)	1.7	(0.7)	11.1	(1.7)	31.0	(2.5)	36.5	(3.6)	19.8	(2.5)
	Ontario	5.3	(0.8)	20.5	(1.7)	34.3	(1.7)	29.1	(1.7)	10.8	(1.2)	2.1	(0.6)	11.5	(1.3)	30.0	(1.9)	36.1	(1.9)	20.3	(1.9)
	Prince Edward Island	5.7	(2.3)	22.0	(3.9)	37.8	(5.0)	27.6	(5.6)	6.9	(2.4)	0.4	(0.6)	8.6	(2.5)	31.7	(4.3)	41.5	(5.3)	17.8	(3.5)
	Quebec	4.3	(0.9)	16.9	(1.7)	34.9	(2.1)	32.5	(1.9)	11.4	(1.3)	1.9	(0.5)	11.5	(1.7)	32.3	(2.3)	39.2	(2.2)	15.1	(1.8)
	Saskatchewan	7.0	(1.5)	26.3	(1.9)	35.0	(2.2)	24.8	(2.4)	6.9	(1.4)	2.2	(1.0)	15.8	(2.2)	36.2	(2.6)	33.0	(2.2)	12.8	(1.5)
	Italy																				
	Bolzano	4.0	(0.9)	21.7	(2.5)	38.5	(2.8)	30.2	(2.3)	5.6	(1.4)	2.1	(0.7)	15.0	(2.1)	40.5	(2.9)	34.3	(3.0)	8.0	(2.3)
	Campania	16.2	(2.3)	38.0	(2.4)	32.8	(2.3)	11.7	(1.5)	1.3	(0.5)	9.6	(1.9)	35.5	(3.0)	37.1	(2.8)	15.2	(1.9)	2.6	(0.8)
	Lombardia	6.6	(1.7)	24.2	(2.3)	39.0	(2.6)	25.5	(2.6)	4.6	(1.2)	2.9	(1.1)	19.7	(2.5)	40.0	(2.4)	30.4	(2.9)	6.9	(1.5)
	Trento	4.6	(1.0)	23.9	(2.1)	43.9	(2.9)	24.3	(2.3)	3.3	(1.0)	2.9	(0.7)	16.9	(1.5)	42.3	(2.6)	32.4	(2.3)	5.5	(1.2)
	Portugal																				
	Região Autónoma dos Açores	8.2	(1.3)	34.9	(2.2)	37.2	(3.2)	17.5	(2.2)	2.2	(0.8)	6.2	(1.1)	28.7	(2.2)	43.1	(2.4)	19.5	(2.2)	2.5	(0.8)
	Spain																				
	Andalusia•	8.8	(1.5)	27.7	(1.9)	38.5	(1.9)	21.9	(2.2)	3.2	(0.7)	5.6	(1.2)	22.2	(2.5)	40.3	(2.3)	27.2	(2.3)	4.7	(0.9)
	Aragon•	6.6	(1.3)	24.4	(2.4)	39.7	(2.3)	24.9	(2.1)	4.4	(1.3)	3.0	(0.8)	16.8	(1.9)	40.0	(2.6)	33.2	(2.9)	7.0	(1.7)
	Asturias•	7.3	(2.0)	24.8	(2.5)	40.3	(2.4)	22.9	(2.5)	4.7	(1.8)	3.6	(1.3)	18.1	(2.7)	40.1	(2.5)	32.4	(3.1)	5.8	(2.0)
	Balearic Islands•	7.2	(1.2)	28.7	(2.5)	39.2	(2.3)	21.5	(2.3)	3.3	(1.0)	3.5	(1.0)	19.8	(1.8)	42.1	(3.0)	29.6	(3.0)	5.0	(1.3)
	Basque Country•	8.8	(1.4)	29.2	(2.0)	38.1	(2.1)	21.1	(1.7)	2.8	(0.6)	3.7	(0.8)	21.5	(1.5)	43.0	(2.4)	27.4	(2.2)	4.4	(0.9)
	Canary Islands•	8.8	(1.4)	28.2	(2.1)	37.6	(1.9)	22.1	(1.6)	3.3	(0.9)	4.0	(1.1)	22.9	(2.3)	41.2	(2.6)	27.2	(2.8)	4.8	(1.2)
	Cantabria•	7.1	(1.5)	30.4	(3.2)	39.5	(2.3)	20.4	(2.3)	2.7	(1.1)	3.2	(1.2)	22.5	(2.2)	40.6	(2.5)	28.9	(2.8)	4.8	(1.8)
	Castile and Leon•	3.8	(0.9)	21.0	(1.8)	41.1	(2.0)	28.3	(1.9)	5.9	(1.2)	1.5	(0.5)	11.9	(1.9)	39.2	(2.2)	37.7	(2.3)	9.7	(1.3)
	Castile-La Mancha•	6.0	(1.2)	24.6	(2.2)	41.6	(2.2)	24.0	(2.1)	3.8	(0.9)	2.7	(0.7)	17.7	(1.8)	42.6	(2.3)	31.2	(2.4)	5.8	(1.2)
	Catalonia•	5.5	(1.2)	23.3	(2.2)	39.0	(1.9)	26.4	(2.2)	5.8	(1.1)	3.7	(0.9)	16.2	(1.6)	37.8	(2.2)	33.8	(2.6)	8.6	(1.4)
	Comunidad Valenciana•	6.5	(1.1)	26.1	(2.0)	40.6	(2.1)	23.5	(1.9)	3.4	(1.1)	2.8	(0.9)	19.9	(2.3)	42.7	(3.1)	28.9	(2.6)	5.7	(1.3)
	Extremadura•	10.7	(1.6)	31.9	(1.9)	37.0	(1.9)	18.0	(2.2)	2.3	(0.6)	4.2	(1.0)	24.3	(2.1)	41.9	(2.7)	25.4	(2.7)	4.2	(1.0)
	Galicia•	7.0	(1.4)	27.5	(2.1)	38.5	(2.0)	23.5	(2.3)	3.5	(0.9)	3.3	(0.9)	17.7	(2.1)	41.4	(2.2)	32.0	(2.3)	5.7	(1.4)
	La Rioja•	7.0	(1.5)	27.2	(3.5)	37.8	(2.5)	24.2	(3.2)	3.8	(1.6)	4.1	(1.1)	17.7	(3.0)	38.5	(3.3)	32.6	(3.3)	7.1	(2.4)
	Madrid•	3.8	(1.1)	18.4	(1.6)	39.5	(2.6)	31.7	(2.0)	6.6	(1.2)	2.6	(0.8)	13.2	(1.5)	36.9	(2.2)	37.8	(2.3)	9.6	(1.5)
	Murcia•	7.7	(1.6)	28.9	(2.5)	39.6	(2.2)	20.5	(1.9)	3.3	(0.8)	3.9	(0.8)	20.3	(2.0)	42.3	(2.2)	29.0	(2.5)	4.5	(0.9)
	Navarre•	5.0	(1.2)	22.7	(2.4)	41.1	(2.5)	26.1	(2.9)	5.0	(1.2)	2.3	(0.8)	15.1	(2.0)	41.8	(3.1)	33.9	(3.1)	6.9	(1.5)
	United Kingdom																				
	England	5.6	(0.6)	21.4	(1.4)	35.9	(1.2)	27.6	(1.2)	9.5	(1.2)	2.9	(0.5)	14.2	(1.1)	32.1	(1.3)	34.5	(1.5)	16.3	(1.1)
	Northern Ireland	3.5	(0.8)	22.3	(1.8)	40.3	(2.3)	28.6	(2.1)	5.3	(1.0)	1.6	(0.6)	14.7	(1.8)	37.8	(1.8)	37.0	(1.9)	8.8	(1.1)
	Scotland•	5.3	(0.9)	23.7	(1.3)	37.2	(1.3)	26.5	(1.3)	7.3	(0.9)	3.1	(0.6)	15.3	(1.2)	33.0	(1.6)	36.1	(1.5)	12.4	(1.0)
	Wales	5.2	(0.8)	26.3	(1.6)	40.7	(1.6)	23.9	(1.5)	3.9	(0.6)	2.6	(0.5)	19.5	(1.5)	41.4	(1.7)	30.7	(2.0)	5.9	(0.9)
	United States																				
	Massachusetts•	3.8	(1.0)	14.9	(1.8)	31.7	(2.1)	32.8	(2.2)	16.7	(1.9)	1.5	(0.5)	10.8	(1.9)	27.5	(2.6)	37.3	(2.8)	23.0	(2.8)
	North Carolina•	5.6	(1.0)	21.7	(1.7)	32.8	(2.1)	29.0	(2.4)	10.9	(1.6)	2.1	(0.6)	14.6	(1.9)	32.0	(2.1)	34.4	(2.3)	16.8	(1.9)
Partners	**Colombia**																				
	Bogotá	5.2	(1.2)	30.8	(2.5)	45.5	(2.4)	17.1	(2.2)	1.5	(0.8)	5.0	(0.9)	27.9	(2.4)	43.3	(2.8)	21.6	(2.6)	2.2	(1.0)
	Cali	10.6	(1.8)	41.5	(2.6)	37.0	(2.7)	10.3	(1.8)	0.6	(0.4)	8.4	(1.3)	42.3	(2.6)	38.1	(2.4)	10.6	(1.7)	0.5	(0.3)
	Manizales	8.4	(1.3)	38.7	(2.7)	40.2	(2.4)	11.9	(1.9)	0.8	(0.5)	6.0	(1.4)	36.7	(3.2)	44.8	(2.7)	11.9	(2.2)	0.6	(0.4)
	Medellín	8.1	(1.7)	38.9	(2.4)	39.9	(2.6)	11.9	(2.2)	1.1	(0.7)	7.4	(1.3)	34.8	(2.6)	42.3	(2.7)	14.7	(1.9)	0.8	(0.4)
	United Arab Emirates																				
	Abu Dhabi•	24.3	(2.1)	44.0	(2.1)	24.1	(2.0)	7.0	(1.4)	0.6	(0.3)	12.1	(1.6)	39.5	(1.9)	36.3	(2.4)	11.1	(1.5)	1.0	(0.4)
	Ajman	32.1	(3.1)	48.6	(3.0)	16.8	(3.0)	2.4	(1.1)	0.0	(0.1)	11.6	(3.7)	36.3	(3.8)	38.7	(4.4)	12.6	(2.4)	0.8	(0.7)
	Dubai•	13.3	(1.0)	29.7	(1.5)	32.2	(1.5)	20.6	(1.2)	4.3	(0.8)	5.2	(0.6)	23.9	(1.2)	39.2	(1.3)	26.6	(1.4)	5.1	(0.6)
	Fujairah	37.6	(4.6)	43.8	(3.9)	15.9	(2.6)	2.7	(1.1)	0.1	(0.2)	11.8	(2.7)	46.3	(3.7)	33.3	(3.3)	7.6	(2.6)	1.1	(0.7)
	Ras Al Khaimah	35.0	(4.7)	49.1	(4.5)	14.1	(2.6)	1.6	(1.0)	0.3	(0.4)	14.8	(2.8)	42.0	(4.1)	33.9	(3.6)	8.5	(2.4)	0.8	(0.8)
	Sharjah	24.7	(4.0)	40.3	(3.2)	26.7	(3.3)	7.6	(2.0)	0.8	(0.7)	8.3	(2.4)	38.4	(4.7)	39.8	(4.0)	13.0	(3.5)	0.5	(0.4)
	Umm Al Quwain	35.4	(5.0)	49.0	(5.0)	15.0	(3.3)	0.6	(0.8)	0.0	c	14.6	(4.1)	48.6	(4.8)	29.1	(3.9)	7.5	(2.2)	0.2	(0.5)

• PISA for adjudicated region.
Notes: Results for the province of Quebec in this table should be treated with caution due to a possible non-response bias.
In Massachusetts and North Carolina, the desired target population covers 15-year-old students in grade 7 or above in public schools only (see Annex A2).
Values that are statistically significant are indicated in bold (see Annex A3).
See Table V.4.2 for national data.
StatLink http://dx.doi.org/10.1787/888933616750

[Part 2/2]

Table B2.V.15 Percentage of students at each proficiency level in collaborative problem solving, by gender

	Gender differences (boys - girls)										Increased risk of...					
	Below Level 1 (below 340 score points)		Level 1 (from 340 to less than 440 score points)		Level 2 (from 440 to less than 540 score points)		Level 3 (from 540 to less than 640 score points)		Level 4 (at or above 640 score points)		Boys scoring below Level 1 on the collaborative problem-solving scale (below 340 score points)		Boys scoring below Level 2 on the collaborative problem-solving scale (below 440 score points)		Girls scoring at Level 4 on the collaborative problem-solving scale (at or above 640 score points)	
	% dif.	S.E.	% dif.	S.E.	% dif.	S.E.	% dif.	S.E.	% dif.	S.E.	Relative risk	S.E.	Relative risk	S.E.	Relative risk	S.E.
OECD																
Belgium																
Flemish community•	**1.8**	(0.7)	**5.0**	(1.6)	**4.5**	(1.8)	**-6.4**	(1.6)	**-4.9**	(1.5)	**1.6**	(0.3)	**1.4**	(0.1)	**1.7**	(0.3)
French community	**4.2**	(1.2)	**5.7**	(2.3)	-2.3	(2.2)	**-5.9**	(2.3)	-1.7	(0.9)	**1.7**	(0.3)	**1.3**	(0.1)	1.6	(0.4)
German-speaking community	2.9	(2.4)	**11.7**	(4.7)	-7.9	(6.8)	-5.0	(5.9)	-1.6	(2.1)	3.7	(6.3)	**1.8**	(0.4)	1.9	(2.1)
Canada																
Alberta	**2.5**	(1.0)	**7.3**	(2.0)	**6.4**	(3.1)	-5.7	(3.0)	**-10.4**	(2.4)	**2.3**	(0.8)	**1.8**	(0.3)	**1.8**	(0.3)
British Columbia	**3.0**	(1.4)	**7.5**	(2.2)	4.2	(3.2)	-4.8	(3.2)	**-9.9**	(3.1)	**5.2**	(3.4)	**2.4**	(0.4)	**1.6**	(0.2)
Manitoba	2.5	(1.5)	**9.4**	(3.1)	5.6	(4.1)	**-9.8**	(3.7)	**-7.7**	(2.3)	1.8	(0.7)	**1.7**	(0.3)	**1.9**	(0.4)
New Brunswick	**4.7**	(1.6)	**10.0**	(2.9)	-2.9	(3.4)	**-6.8**	(3.4)	**-4.9**	(2.2)	**3.6**	(1.6)	**2.0**	(0.3)	**1.6**	(0.3)
Newfoundland and Labrador	**3.6**	(1.5)	**6.9**	(3.3)	2.4	(4.7)	**-8.7**	(3.6)	-4.1	(2.4)	**2.7**	(1.3)	**1.7**	(0.3)	1.4	(0.3)
Nova Scotia	**3.2**	(1.3)	**9.3**	(2.5)	3.4	(3.3)	-7.0	(3.8)	**-9.0**	(3.0)	**3.0**	(1.5)	**2.0**	(0.3)	**1.8**	(0.4)
Ontario	**3.2**	(0.8)	**9.0**	(1.7)	**4.3**	(1.9)	**-7.0**	(2.1)	**-9.6**	(1.8)	**2.6**	(0.7)	**1.9**	(0.2)	**1.9**	(0.2)
Prince Edward Island	**5.2**	(2.5)	**13.4**	(4.9)	6.1	(6.1)	-13.8	(7.8)	**-10.9**	(4.0)	m	m	**3.1**	(1.1)	**2.6**	(1.2)
Quebec	**2.4**	(0.9)	**5.3**	(1.8)	2.6	(2.9)	**-6.8**	(2.7)	**-3.6**	(1.7)	**2.3**	(0.7)	**1.6**	(0.2)	**1.3**	(0.2)
Saskatchewan	**4.8**	(1.6)	**10.5**	(2.7)	-1.3	(4.0)	**-8.2**	(3.3)	**-5.9**	(2.1)	**3.5**	(1.5)	**1.9**	(0.2)	**1.9**	(0.5)
Italy																
Bolzano	1.9	(1.0)	**6.7**	(2.8)	-2.0	(4.3)	-4.1	(3.2)	-2.4	(2.0)	1.9	(0.7)	**1.5**	(0.2)	1.4	(0.4)
Campania	**6.6**	(2.6)	2.5	(3.1)	-4.3	(3.2)	-3.5	(2.0)	-1.3	(0.9)	**1.7**	(0.4)	**1.2**	(0.1)	2.1	(1.0)
Lombardia	**3.7**	(1.9)	4.5	(3.2)	-1.0	(3.7)	-5.0	(3.8)	-2.3	(1.6)	2.4	(1.1)	1.4	(0.2)	1.5	(0.5)
Trento	1.7	(1.2)	**7.0**	(2.5)	1.6	(3.6)	**-8.1**	(3.2)	-2.2	(1.4)	1.6	(0.5)	**1.4**	(0.1)	1.7	(0.6)
Portugal																
Região Autónoma dos Açores	2.0	(1.7)	**6.2**	(3.0)	-5.9	(3.3)	-2.1	(2.9)	-0.3	(1.2)	1.3	(0.3)	**1.2**	(0.1)	1.2	(0.6)
Spain																
Andalusia•	3.2	(1.9)	5.6	(3.0)	-1.8	(2.9)	**-5.4**	(2.7)	-1.5	(1.2)	1.6	(0.5)	**1.3**	(0.1)	1.5	(0.5)
Aragon•	**3.6**	(1.5)	**7.6**	(2.4)	-0.3	(3.5)	**-8.3**	(3.3)	-2.6	(1.9)	**2.3**	(0.9)	**1.6**	(0.2)	1.7	(0.6)
Asturias•	**3.7**	(1.5)	**6.7**	(2.5)	0.1	(3.3)	**-9.5**	(2.6)	-1.1	(1.3)	**2.1**	(0.6)	**1.5**	(0.1)	1.3	(0.5)
Balearic Islands•	**3.8**	(1.3)	**8.9**	(2.9)	-2.8	(3.1)	**-8.1**	(2.4)	-1.7	(1.3)	**2.2**	(0.7)	**1.5**	(0.2)	1.5	(0.5)
Basque Country•	**5.0**	(1.3)	**7.8**	(2.0)	-4.9	(3.4)	**-6.3**	(2.3)	-1.6	(1.1)	**2.4**	(0.5)	**1.5**	(0.1)	1.6	(0.5)
Canary Islands•	**4.8**	(1.6)	5.3	(3.0)	-3.5	(3.6)	-5.1	(3.1)	-1.5	(1.1)	**2.3**	(0.7)	**1.4**	(0.1)	1.5	(0.5)
Cantabria•	**3.9**	(1.4)	**7.9**	(2.6)	-1.2	(3.8)	**-8.5**	(2.2)	-2.1	(1.3)	**2.4**	(1.0)	**1.5**	(0.1)	1.9	(0.8)
Castile and Leon•	**2.3**	(1.0)	**9.1**	(2.2)	1.9	(2.9)	**-9.4**	(2.8)	**-3.8**	(1.4)	**2.6**	(1.2)	**1.9**	(0.3)	**1.7**	(0.4)
Castile-La Mancha•	**3.3**	(1.4)	**6.9**	(2.6)	-1.0	(3.3)	**-7.2**	(3.1)	-2.0	(1.1)	**2.2**	(0.8)	**1.5**	(0.2)	1.5	(0.4)
Catalonia•	1.8	(1.6)	**7.1**	(2.4)	1.2	(3.0)	**-7.3**	(2.8)	-2.8	(1.9)	1.5	(0.6)	**1.5**	(0.2)	1.5	(0.4)
Comunidad Valenciana•	**3.7**	(1.5)	**6.2**	(3.1)	-2.1	(3.9)	-5.4	(3.1)	-2.3	(1.7)	**2.4**	(1.0)	**1.4**	(0.2)	1.8	(0.6)
Extremadura•	**6.6**	(1.6)	**7.5**	(2.4)	-4.8	(3.2)	**-7.4**	(3.2)	-1.9	(1.1)	**2.6**	(0.6)	**1.5**	(0.1)	1.8	(0.6)
Galicia•	**3.7**	(1.6)	**9.8**	(2.7)	-3.0	(2.7)	**-8.4**	(2.6)	-2.2	(1.3)	**2.2**	(0.8)	**1.7**	(0.2)	1.7	(0.5)
La Rioja•	3.0	(1.6)	**9.5**	(3.5)	-0.7	(4.2)	**-8.4**	(3.6)	-3.3	(1.8)	1.8	(0.5)	**1.6**	(0.2)	1.9	(0.7)
Madrid•	1.2	(1.2)	**5.3**	(2.3)	2.7	(3.7)	-6.1	(3.2)	-3.0	(2.0)	1.5	(0.6)	**1.4**	(0.2)	1.5	(0.4)
Murcia•	**3.8**	(1.7)	**8.6**	(2.4)	-2.7	(3.0)	**-8.5**	(2.8)	-1.2	(1.2)	**2.0**	(0.5)	**1.5**	(0.1)	1.4	(0.5)
Navarre•	**2.7**	(1.3)	**7.7**	(2.4)	-0.7	(3.9)	**-7.8**	(2.9)	-1.9	(1.6)	2.3	(1.0)	**1.6**	(0.2)	1.4	(0.4)
United Kingdom																
England	**2.7**	(0.7)	**7.1**	(1.5)	**3.8**	(1.7)	**-6.9**	(1.7)	**-6.8**	(1.5)	**2.0**	(0.4)	**1.6**	(0.1)	**1.7**	(0.2)
Northern Ireland	**1.9**	(0.8)	**7.6**	(2.2)	2.5	(2.6)	**-8.5**	(2.8)	**-3.5**	(1.5)	**2.3**	(0.9)	**1.6**	(0.2)	**1.7**	(0.4)
Scotland•	2.2	(1.1)	**8.4**	(1.8)	**4.2**	(2.0)	**-9.6**	(2.1)	**-5.1**	(1.4)	**1.7**	(0.5)	**1.6**	(0.1)	**1.7**	(0.3)
Wales	**2.5**	(0.8)	**6.8**	(1.7)	-0.7	(2.0)	**-6.8**	(1.8)	-1.9	(1.1)	**2.0**	(0.4)	**1.4**	(0.1)	1.5	(0.3)
United States																
Massachusetts•	**2.4**	(1.0)	4.2	(2.2)	4.1	(2.9)	-4.4	(3.2)	**-6.2**	(2.8)	**2.7**	(1.1)	**1.5**	(0.2)	**1.4**	(0.2)
North Carolina•	**3.4**	(1.0)	**7.1**	(2.0)	0.7	(2.6)	**-5.3**	(2.6)	**-5.9**	(1.8)	**2.7**	(0.9)	**1.6**	(0.2)	**1.6**	(0.2)
Partners																
Colombia																
Bogotá	0.2	(1.1)	3.0	(2.8)	2.2	(3.4)	-4.6	(3.0)	-0.7	(1.0)	1.0	(0.2)	1.1	(0.1)	1.5	(1.1)
Cali	2.1	(2.0)	-0.8	(3.4)	-1.1	(3.5)	-0.3	(2.1)	0.0	(0.5)	1.3	(0.3)	1.0	(0.1)	1.6	(3.9)
Manizales	2.4	(1.9)	2.0	(4.0)	-4.6	(3.5)	0.1	(2.5)	0.2	(0.6)	1.4	(0.4)	1.1	(0.1)	0.8	(1.0)
Medellín	0.7	(1.8)	4.1	(3.0)	-2.4	(3.5)	-2.7	(2.5)	0.3	(0.9)	1.1	(0.3)	1.1	(0.1)	0.9	(1.1)
United Arab Emirates																
Abu Dhabi•	**12.2**	(2.6)	4.5	(2.7)	**-12.2**	(2.7)	**-4.1**	(2.0)	-0.4	(0.4)	**2.0**	(0.3)	**1.3**	(0.1)	1.8	(1.3)
Ajman	**20.5**	(4.7)	**12.3**	(5.6)	**-21.9**	(6.1)	**-10.2**	(2.7)	-0.8	(0.7)	**2.8**	(1.0)	**1.7**	(0.2)	m	m
Dubai•	**8.1**	(1.1)	**5.8**	(2.1)	**-7.0**	(1.8)	**-6.0**	(1.7)	-0.8	(0.9)	**2.6**	(0.3)	**1.5**	(0.1)	1.2	(0.2)
Fujairah	**25.8**	(5.3)	-2.5	(5.3)	**-17.4**	(4.4)	-4.9	(2.8)	-1.0	(0.7)	**3.2**	(0.8)	**1.4**	(0.1)	m	m
Ras Al Khaimah	**20.2**	(4.8)	7.1	(6.0)	**-19.8**	(4.4)	**-6.9**	(2.3)	-0.5	(0.8)	**2.4**	(0.5)	**1.5**	(0.1)	3.1	(6.0)
Sharjah	**16.4**	(4.4)	1.9	(5.5)	**-13.1**	(5.0)	-5.4	(3.7)	0.2	(0.8)	**3.1**	(1.1)	**1.4**	(0.2)	m	m
Umm Al Quwain	**20.7**	(5.6)	0.4	(6.0)	**-14.1**	(4.7)	**-6.8**	(2.1)	-0.2	(0.5)	**2.5**	(0.8)	**1.3**	(0.1)	m	m

• PISA for adjudicated region.
Notes: Results for the province of Quebec in this table should be treated with caution due to a possible non-response bias.
In Massachusetts and North Carolina, the desired target population covers 15-year-old students in grade 7 or above in public schools only (see Annex A2).
Values that are statistically significant are indicated in bold (see Annex A3).
See Table V.4.2 for national data.
StatLink http://dx.doi.org/10.1787/888933616750

[Part 1/3]

Table B2.V.16 Mean score and variation in collaborative problem-solving performance, by gender

	Boys																	
	Mean score		Standard deviation		Percentiles													
					5th		10th		25th		Median (50th)		75th		90th		95th	
	Mean	S.E.	S.D.	S.E.	Score	S.E.	Score	S.E.	Score	S.E.	Score	S.E.	Score	S.E.	Score	S.E.	Score	S.E.
OECD																		
Belgium																		
Flemish community•	506	(3.4)	96	(2.4)	342	(7.0)	377	(6.2)	442	(5.3)	511	(3.6)	575	(3.8)	627	(5.0)	655	(5.5)
French community	467	(5.1)	98	(2.5)	306	(8.2)	339	(6.6)	398	(6.8)	469	(6.1)	537	(5.7)	592	(6.2)	623	(6.9)
German-speaking community	480	(7.2)	83	(5.0)	343	(13.4)	368	(10.1)	417	(9.4)	483	(11.1)	542	(10.1)	583	(13.3)	610	(19.3)
Canada																		
Alberta	522	(6.6)	104	(3.4)	346	(11.1)	382	(10.9)	451	(7.8)	527	(8.3)	593	(8.2)	654	(9.6)	689	(10.8)
British Columbia	541	(7.4)	108	(4.2)	354	(14.5)	395	(13.0)	469	(10.4)	546	(9.7)	615	(8.1)	674	(9.4)	710	(14.1)
Manitoba	498	(6.5)	102	(3.5)	334	(11.6)	368	(8.9)	428	(9.2)	497	(7.0)	567	(10.2)	634	(12.2)	669	(10.7)
New Brunswick	499	(6.6)	104	(4.0)	328	(12.1)	362	(9.5)	426	(9.2)	501	(10.3)	573	(9.2)	633	(10.7)	665	(11.0)
Newfoundland and Labrador	505	(6.4)	103	(3.9)	333	(13.0)	371	(11.3)	436	(7.8)	506	(10.2)	576	(9.6)	638	(11.2)	672	(11.5)
Nova Scotia	511	(6.2)	103	(3.4)	341	(10.4)	373	(9.3)	438	(9.3)	514	(8.7)	585	(9.1)	644	(9.9)	677	(12.7)
Ontario	510	(4.8)	104	(2.2)	338	(6.3)	374	(6.1)	437	(7.0)	512	(6.2)	584	(6.2)	645	(7.3)	680	(8.6)
Prince Edward Island	499	(9.0)	100	(6.5)	337	(23.1)	365	(16.9)	431	(16.7)	503	(17.1)	568	(15.6)	621	(15.0)	656	(35.1)
Quebec	521	(5.1)	100	(3.3)	347	(9.4)	387	(8.0)	455	(7.6)	526	(6.4)	591	(7.1)	647	(7.5)	681	(9.8)
Saskatchewan	489	(5.2)	102	(3.5)	325	(10.7)	358	(9.5)	414	(6.1)	487	(6.3)	563	(8.2)	621	(9.5)	655	(9.9)
Italy																		
Bolzano	502	(7.3)	91	(2.7)	349	(8.5)	381	(9.1)	438	(9.0)	505	(7.8)	569	(8.8)	617	(9.5)	645	(10.7)
Campania	432	(6.0)	92	(3.1)	288	(10.7)	316	(9.4)	365	(7.5)	430	(6.9)	493	(7.6)	555	(8.8)	590	(11.1)
Lombardia	487	(7.2)	94	(3.7)	325	(14.6)	362	(12.8)	421	(9.9)	490	(8.1)	554	(8.7)	606	(9.1)	637	(10.0)
Trento	488	(3.6)	85	(3.0)	345	(9.9)	376	(7.7)	431	(4.9)	492	(5.8)	547	(6.7)	595	(6.9)	625	(10.3)
Portugal																		
Região Autónoma dos Açores	460	(3.3)	89	(3.1)	322	(7.9)	349	(7.2)	394	(5.1)	458	(6.0)	524	(7.0)	578	(10.4)	608	(10.1)
Spain																		
Andalusia•	471	(5.1)	96	(3.0)	312	(10.8)	346	(8.3)	406	(7.2)	471	(5.4)	540	(7.4)	595	(7.4)	625	(8.3)
Aragon•	487	(6.2)	93	(3.1)	330	(8.6)	363	(9.8)	423	(7.7)	489	(7.0)	553	(7.9)	606	(9.3)	636	(9.5)
Asturias•	483	(11.2)	95	(3.1)	324	(14.3)	356	(13.0)	418	(12.0)	487	(10.5)	547	(11.3)	604	(11.9)	637	(15.3)
Balearic Islands•	474	(6.2)	92	(2.8)	323	(10.0)	356	(8.1)	411	(7.1)	474	(6.9)	539	(8.1)	596	(9.0)	625	(10.1)
Basque Country•	470	(5.2)	93	(2.1)	317	(7.4)	346	(7.1)	403	(6.5)	472	(7.7)	537	(4.9)	590	(5.0)	618	(6.0)
Canary Islands•	473	(5.0)	95	(2.8)	316	(9.4)	348	(9.1)	408	(6.5)	475	(5.9)	541	(5.8)	595	(8.0)	625	(7.9)
Cantabria•	470	(8.2)	90	(3.0)	325	(11.6)	355	(8.2)	406	(10.6)	472	(9.0)	534	(7.7)	585	(11.2)	615	(14.0)
Castile and Leon•	501	(4.6)	90	(2.5)	351	(8.4)	383	(8.2)	441	(6.4)	504	(5.2)	564	(7.3)	616	(6.7)	646	(8.1)
Castile-La Mancha•	484	(5.3)	91	(2.9)	332	(9.5)	365	(7.1)	423	(6.9)	487	(6.7)	547	(6.5)	601	(7.6)	630	(8.2)
Catalonia•	493	(6.5)	94	(2.7)	336	(10.4)	369	(9.1)	428	(8.9)	495	(8.1)	561	(7.8)	615	(7.7)	645	(8.0)
Comunidad Valenciana•	480	(4.5)	90	(3.1)	330	(8.7)	360	(7.8)	418	(6.4)	482	(6.5)	545	(5.8)	595	(8.0)	625	(10.9)
Extremadura•	459	(5.4)	94	(2.4)	308	(9.7)	336	(8.0)	393	(7.5)	461	(6.7)	526	(7.3)	579	(7.7)	611	(8.5)
Galicia•	479	(6.5)	94	(2.8)	325	(10.5)	358	(7.8)	412	(7.9)	480	(7.5)	545	(8.2)	599	(8.4)	628	(9.0)
La Rioja•	480	(10.0)	93	(3.2)	326	(11.4)	357	(10.6)	414	(11.1)	482	(11.1)	547	(10.9)	598	(12.3)	630	(16.3)
Madrid•	509	(4.3)	90	(3.4)	353	(11.6)	388	(10.1)	450	(6.5)	513	(5.5)	572	(6.9)	622	(7.1)	649	(7.8)
Murcia•	473	(6.2)	92	(2.9)	323	(11.3)	353	(9.3)	408	(7.4)	474	(7.2)	537	(6.2)	590	(7.4)	622	(9.4)
Navarre•	493	(6.9)	91	(2.6)	340	(9.4)	372	(9.5)	432	(8.2)	495	(7.4)	556	(8.6)	609	(10.2)	639	(9.1)
United Kingdom																		
England	504	(3.7)	103	(1.9)	334	(6.0)	370	(5.9)	433	(4.8)	505	(4.9)	575	(4.3)	638	(6.3)	672	(5.8)
Northern Ireland	500	(4.2)	89	(2.5)	354	(7.5)	385	(6.1)	438	(5.3)	502	(5.0)	564	(6.2)	615	(8.0)	642	(7.6)
Scotland•	497	(3.4)	98	(2.3)	337	(6.8)	369	(5.4)	427	(4.8)	498	(3.6)	566	(4.8)	625	(5.6)	656	(7.4)
Wales	485	(3.8)	90	(1.7)	339	(6.2)	367	(5.4)	422	(5.9)	486	(5.0)	548	(4.6)	602	(4.6)	631	(5.8)
United States																		
Massachusetts•	536	(6.4)	107	(3.4)	352	(10.9)	392	(11.0)	464	(8.4)	539	(7.8)	611	(7.7)	675	(10.2)	707	(11.1)
North Carolina•	509	(5.2)	106	(3.3)	336	(7.7)	369	(7.7)	432	(7.7)	511	(7.2)	586	(7.0)	645	(8.5)	678	(10.4)
Partners																		
Colombia																		
Bogotá	469	(5.6)	80	(3.1)	340	(7.8)	365	(7.6)	413	(6.8)	469	(6.8)	523	(7.4)	573	(8.3)	600	(10.0)
Cali	439	(5.1)	79	(2.7)	313	(7.8)	338	(7.2)	383	(5.9)	436	(6.6)	493	(7.2)	544	(8.3)	574	(10.2)
Manizales	448	(4.6)	80	(3.0)	321	(8.7)	347	(6.1)	391	(5.1)	446	(5.5)	502	(6.8)	553	(9.9)	582	(12.8)
Medellín	449	(5.6)	79	(3.3)	323	(9.1)	348	(7.7)	392	(6.0)	446	(5.9)	502	(6.9)	552	(10.5)	582	(12.8)
United Arab Emirates																		
Abu Dhabi•	404	(5.8)	87	(3.0)	275	(6.2)	300	(5.6)	342	(4.7)	396	(6.8)	460	(8.5)	524	(9.8)	560	(10.8)
Ajman	377	(6.4)	76	(3.5)	257	(14.1)	283	(12.2)	326	(6.1)	373	(6.6)	424	(7.8)	478	(10.3)	511	(12.3)
Dubai•	462	(3.0)	105	(2.7)	296	(5.6)	326	(4.8)	383	(3.1)	462	(3.7)	540	(5.1)	600	(6.2)	633	(7.9)
Fujairah	372	(6.9)	79	(4.4)	255	(12.4)	279	(11.6)	317	(9.2)	364	(7.1)	420	(10.1)	479	(13.6)	515	(15.7)
Ras Al Khaimah	370	(8.6)	75	(6.1)	253	(13.0)	279	(12.6)	321	(10.0)	366	(8.7)	415	(9.6)	465	(15.1)	497	(19.0)
Sharjah	406	(11.1)	92	(4.4)	265	(17.2)	292	(12.5)	341	(11.4)	402	(14.9)	467	(13.5)	530	(16.5)	567	(18.4)
Umm Al Quwain	368	(9.1)	67	(5.1)	263	(17.9)	284	(13.7)	321	(10.7)	364	(11.2)	412	(12.5)	457	(10.8)	489	(19.9)

• PISA for adjudicated region.
Notes: Results for the province of Quebec in this table should be treated with caution due to a possible non-response bias.
In Massachusetts and North Carolina, the desired target population covers 15-year-old students in grade 7 or above in public schools only (see Annex A2).
Values that are statistically significant are indicated in bold (see Annex A3).
See Table V.4.3a for national data.
StatLink http://dx.doi.org/10.1787/888933616750

[Part 2/3]

Table B2.V.16 Mean score and variation in collaborative problem-solving performance, by gender

		Girls																
						Percentiles												
		Mean score		Standard deviation		5th		10th		25th		Median (50th)		75th		90th		95th
		Mean	S.E.	S.D.	S.E.	Score	S.E.	Score	S.E.	Score	S.E.	Score	S.E.	Score	S.E.	Score	S.E.	Score	S.E.
OECD	**Belgium**																		
	Flemish community•	532	(3.7)	96	(2.4)	363	(6.9)	400	(6.5)	469	(5.5)	539	(3.9)	601	(4.1)	650	(5.5)	677	(6.8)
	French community	491	(4.3)	94	(2.5)	333	(8.4)	367	(6.6)	428	(6.8)	495	(5.2)	558	(5.1)	610	(5.5)	639	(6.2)
	German-speaking community	506	(7.8)	76	(5.1)	381	(16.5)	411	(12.5)	457	(10.0)	505	(9.8)	557	(14.1)	604	(14.3)	631	(17.4)
	Canada																		
	Alberta	563	(6.1)	103	(3.5)	386	(13.0)	426	(11.8)	494	(8.5)	567	(7.2)	635	(6.9)	693	(9.0)	729	(11.3)
	British Columbia	581	(6.1)	97	(3.0)	417	(12.4)	456	(11.4)	519	(7.6)	581	(6.5)	647	(8.1)	705	(9.1)	741	(11.9)
	Manitoba	540	(6.6)	104	(3.6)	360	(16.1)	400	(12.3)	471	(8.6)	544	(7.1)	613	(7.9)	672	(9.8)	709	(12.1)
	New Brunswick	536	(6.3)	94	(3.1)	380	(10.1)	416	(8.7)	475	(7.8)	535	(6.5)	599	(8.5)	656	(10.6)	689	(11.6)
	Newfoundland and Labrador	537	(5.0)	95	(3.5)	377	(13.1)	413	(10.2)	475	(8.8)	540	(7.1)	602	(6.9)	657	(8.7)	689	(11.9)
	Nova Scotia	555	(5.2)	100	(5.0)	384	(13.5)	424	(12.2)	487	(7.7)	557	(6.9)	623	(7.7)	682	(11.1)	714	(13.1)
	Ontario	554	(4.8)	102	(2.5)	381	(9.3)	420	(7.6)	486	(5.7)	556	(6.0)	625	(6.0)	683	(9.1)	720	(7.9)
	Prince Edward Island	560	(8.0)	89	(6.3)	411	(15.8)	443	(15.0)	500	(13.3)	560	(10.8)	618	(12.5)	675	(19.4)	707	(31.4)
	Quebec	545	(5.6)	94	(2.5)	382	(9.6)	422	(9.0)	485	(7.4)	550	(6.5)	610	(5.9)	662	(7.7)	694	(9.3)
	Saskatchewan	530	(4.5)	95	(3.1)	373	(13.5)	406	(9.6)	463	(6.8)	531	(6.4)	594	(5.5)	655	(8.2)	690	(9.9)
	Italy																		
	Bolzano	522	(8.4)	85	(3.0)	378	(9.5)	411	(8.4)	465	(8.3)	524	(8.5)	581	(10.6)	630	(13.1)	659	(14.2)
	Campania	455	(6.5)	92	(4.4)	312	(13.3)	342	(8.6)	392	(7.3)	451	(8.0)	516	(9.0)	576	(11.6)	611	(12.9)
	Lombardia	509	(7.6)	89	(3.1)	361	(12.2)	393	(10.9)	447	(9.1)	510	(9.0)	571	(8.8)	623	(8.8)	653	(9.4)
	Trento	510	(3.6)	85	(2.6)	362	(7.4)	395	(7.5)	457	(5.0)	515	(5.1)	567	(5.3)	615	(7.8)	643	(8.9)
	Portugal																		
	Região Autónoma dos Açores	473	(4.1)	86	(2.8)	332	(8.6)	359	(7.1)	414	(6.8)	474	(5.6)	532	(5.2)	581	(8.1)	611	(9.3)
	Spain																		
	Andalusia•	493	(5.2)	92	(2.6)	334	(12.4)	374	(9.6)	432	(7.5)	497	(6.8)	558	(6.1)	610	(7.0)	636	(9.0)
	Aragon•	514	(7.1)	87	(2.8)	365	(12.0)	401	(8.0)	456	(8.2)	518	(8.5)	574	(7.2)	624	(9.8)	653	(10.6)
	Asturias•	509	(10.6)	88	(2.7)	356	(14.0)	391	(13.9)	450	(11.7)	514	(10.7)	571	(11.1)	619	(11.7)	643	(12.6)
	Balearic Islands•	503	(6.2)	87	(3.0)	355	(10.8)	388	(7.4)	445	(6.0)	506	(6.8)	564	(8.6)	613	(8.7)	640	(8.8)
	Basque Country•	498	(5.3)	86	(2.0)	354	(7.3)	385	(5.8)	440	(5.6)	499	(6.1)	558	(6.9)	607	(7.0)	636	(7.7)
	Canary Islands•	496	(6.0)	88	(2.6)	349	(10.8)	380	(8.2)	435	(7.1)	497	(6.7)	559	(6.4)	609	(8.2)	639	(8.8)
	Cantabria•	499	(8.7)	86	(3.0)	355	(9.7)	384	(10.3)	438	(9.8)	503	(9.4)	560	(9.4)	609	(10.6)	636	(12.5)
	Castile and Leon•	532	(4.6)	84	(2.4)	389	(8.3)	424	(9.5)	477	(7.6)	535	(5.5)	589	(5.5)	639	(5.8)	666	(7.5)
	Castile-La Mancha•	509	(5.0)	85	(2.4)	365	(9.0)	399	(9.4)	452	(6.5)	511	(5.2)	569	(6.3)	617	(8.4)	645	(8.6)
	Catalonia•	518	(5.0)	92	(2.8)	354	(11.3)	395	(10.3)	459	(7.1)	523	(6.2)	582	(6.0)	633	(8.2)	662	(9.6)
	Comunidad Valenciana•	505	(5.2)	86	(3.2)	364	(11.7)	396	(8.3)	446	(7.3)	507	(6.2)	564	(7.0)	615	(7.2)	644	(8.4)
	Extremadura•	491	(5.2)	87	(3.0)	348	(10.5)	378	(8.3)	430	(5.9)	493	(5.7)	553	(8.0)	604	(8.8)	634	(9.0)
	Galicia•	509	(6.2)	86	(3.1)	361	(12.3)	394	(10.7)	453	(8.5)	514	(6.4)	570	(6.8)	616	(7.9)	645	(9.0)
	La Rioja•	511	(9.1)	92	(3.4)	349	(12.2)	387	(12.6)	451	(10.8)	516	(9.6)	574	(10.2)	624	(12.9)	653	(16.1)
	Madrid•	529	(4.4)	89	(2.5)	370	(10.3)	411	(8.9)	474	(5.6)	535	(5.1)	590	(5.9)	639	(6.1)	666	(7.8)
	Murcia•	500	(4.7)	87	(2.8)	351	(9.6)	385	(8.2)	443	(7.3)	504	(5.9)	562	(6.1)	610	(6.4)	637	(7.2)
	Navarre•	518	(7.0)	85	(3.3)	375	(13.1)	408	(10.2)	463	(8.4)	520	(8.3)	578	(7.7)	625	(8.2)	651	(9.8)
	United Kingdom																		
	England	539	(3.8)	103	(1.9)	365	(6.8)	404	(6.2)	470	(5.1)	542	(4.3)	610	(4.3)	668	(5.3)	704	(6.2)
	Northern Ireland	528	(4.8)	85	(2.4)	385	(9.8)	414	(8.6)	470	(8.0)	531	(5.0)	589	(5.6)	634	(5.4)	663	(6.1)
	Scotland•	530	(3.0)	98	(2.2)	362	(8.6)	399	(6.1)	465	(4.9)	536	(4.2)	599	(4.4)	651	(4.2)	682	(5.3)
	Wales	508	(4.0)	87	(2.3)	364	(6.1)	394	(5.7)	448	(5.0)	510	(5.1)	568	(5.0)	619	(5.3)	648	(8.7)
	United States																		
	Massachusetts•	562	(7.8)	101	(3.5)	389	(12.6)	427	(12.6)	492	(10.1)	567	(9.4)	634	(8.6)	688	(10.2)	720	(10.9)
	North Carolina•	540	(6.3)	99	(2.5)	375	(7.4)	409	(7.6)	469	(7.9)	543	(8.8)	613	(7.2)	667	(8.0)	697	(8.3)
Partners	**Colombia**																		
	Bogotá	478	(5.6)	83	(3.5)	339	(8.3)	372	(6.2)	421	(6.7)	479	(6.6)	537	(8.9)	586	(9.8)	615	(11.9)
	Cali	442	(5.3)	77	(2.2)	321	(7.2)	345	(6.1)	389	(6.3)	438	(6.3)	494	(8.1)	545	(8.2)	574	(8.5)
	Manizales	455	(5.3)	75	(2.8)	335	(8.3)	359	(6.2)	401	(5.7)	454	(6.1)	506	(7.4)	550	(8.6)	578	(10.6)
	Medellín	457	(5.0)	80	(2.5)	326	(8.2)	353	(7.0)	401	(6.4)	457	(6.6)	513	(5.5)	561	(7.7)	590	(8.8)
	United Arab Emirates																		
	Abu Dhabi•	439	(5.7)	85	(2.5)	305	(7.7)	332	(6.4)	378	(6.3)	437	(6.7)	497	(6.9)	551	(7.8)	582	(8.9)
	Ajman	444	(10.7)	84	(5.9)	307	(18.4)	334	(15.7)	384	(16.4)	445	(13.3)	503	(9.6)	554	(10.9)	579	(12.4)
	Dubai•	492	(2.8)	93	(1.8)	338	(4.5)	369	(3.8)	428	(4.0)	493	(3.7)	558	(4.4)	611	(5.2)	641	(4.6)
	Fujairah	430	(10.6)	80	(5.5)	310	(10.5)	334	(10.2)	372	(9.8)	424	(10.5)	483	(15.3)	533	(15.6)	563	(20.7)
	Ras Al Khaimah	427	(11.2)	83	(5.3)	300	(12.0)	326	(10.7)	366	(10.9)	424	(13.1)	483	(13.9)	536	(18.5)	569	(18.9)
	Sharjah	449	(10.4)	79	(3.9)	322	(12.7)	347	(11.3)	394	(10.5)	448	(12.3)	507	(14.7)	553	(12.9)	579	(15.2)
	Umm Al Quwain	420	(7.0)	78	(4.8)	298	(15.0)	324	(15.1)	366	(11.1)	416	(8.4)	469	(11.0)	525	(14.4)	560	(16.3)

• PISA for adjudicated region.
Notes: Results for the province of Quebec in this table should be treated with caution due to a possible non-response bias.
In Massachusetts and North Carolina, the desired target population covers 15-year-old students in grade 7 or above in public schools only (see Annex A2).
Values that are statistically significant are indicated in bold (see Annex A3).
See Table V.4.3a for national data.
StatLink http://dx.doi.org/10.1787/888933616750

[Part 3/3]

Table B2.V.16 Mean score and variation in collaborative problem-solving performance, by gender

	Gender difference (boys - girls)																	
	Mean score		Standard deviation		Percentiles													
					5th		10th		25th		Median (50th)		75th		90th		95th	
	Score dif.	S.E.	S.D. dif.	S.E.	Score dif.	S.E.	Score dif.	S.E.	Score dif.	S.E.	Score dif.	S.E.	Score dif.	S.E.	Score dif.	S.E.	Score dif.	S.E.
OECD																		
Belgium																		
Flemish community•	**-26**	(4.4)	0	(2.8)	**-21**	(8.5)	**-23**	(7.1)	**-28**	(6.5)	**-28**	(5.0)	**-26**	(5.3)	**-23**	(6.7)	**-22**	(8.2)
French community	**-24**	(4.6)	4	(2.9)	**-27**	(9.3)	**-27**	(7.3)	**-30**	(7.6)	**-26**	(6.4)	**-21**	(6.1)	**-18**	(6.4)	**-16**	(7.8)
German-speaking community	**-26**	(8.2)	7	(7.4)	-38	(20.3)	**-43**	(15.7)	**-40**	(12.8)	-22	(13.5)	-15	(15.1)	-21	(16.4)	-21	(25.6)
Canada																		
Alberta	**-42**	(5.4)	0	(4.5)	**-40**	(14.9)	**-44**	(13.6)	**-43**	(8.2)	**-40**	(8.0)	**-42**	(7.8)	**-39**	(10.6)	**-39**	(13.1)
British Columbia	**-41**	(6.5)	**11**	(4.5)	**-62**	(17.5)	**-60**	(13.8)	**-51**	(9.8)	**-35**	(9.5)	**-31**	(9.5)	**-31**	(11.6)	-31	(17.3)
Manitoba	**-42**	(6.7)	-2	(4.5)	-26	(15.7)	**-32**	(13.7)	**-43**	(11.1)	**-47**	(9.3)	**-45**	(9.7)	**-37**	(13.5)	**-39**	(15.5)
New Brunswick	**-37**	(7.4)	**10**	(4.7)	**-52**	(14.8)	**-53**	(12.0)	**-49**	(10.8)	**-34**	(10.5)	**-26**	(11.6)	-24	(14.2)	-23	(15.1)
Newfoundland and Labrador	**-32**	(7.2)	8	(5.7)	**-44**	(17.9)	**-42**	(14.5)	**-39**	(11.8)	**-34**	(11.3)	**-26**	(12.2)	-19	(13.7)	-17	(15.9)
Nova Scotia	**-44**	(6.6)	3	(6.0)	**-43**	(17.7)	**-51**	(14.9)	**-49**	(10.1)	**-43**	(9.2)	**-37**	(10.7)	**-38**	(13.0)	**-37**	(14.9)
Ontario	**-44**	(4.3)	2	(2.9)	**-43**	(10.2)	**-46**	(8.8)	**-48**	(6.8)	**-44**	(6.7)	**-40**	(7.3)	**-39**	(8.6)	**-40**	(9.2)
Prince Edward Island	**-61**	(12.4)	12	(9.4)	**-74**	(27.0)	**-78**	(21.9)	**-70**	(22.6)	-57	(21.8)	**-50**	(19.3)	**-54**	(24.4)	-52	(49.1)
Quebec	**-24**	(5.5)	6	(3.5)	**-34**	(12.5)	**-36**	(11.2)	-30	(8.4)	**-24**	(7.4)	**-18**	(7.3)	-15	(8.4)	-14	(12.0)
Saskatchewan	**-41**	(6.3)	7	(4.6)	**-48**	(17.2)	**-48**	(15.4)	-50	(8.4)	**-43**	(8.1)	**-31**	(9.7)	**-34**	(12.5)	**-35**	(14.8)
Italy																		
Bolzano	**-20**	(5.9)	6	(3.8)	**-29**	(10.2)	**-30**	(8.6)	**-27**	(9.0)	**-19**	(7.9)	-12	(8.6)	-13	(11.2)	-14	(14.2)
Campania	**-23**	(6.4)	1	(4.4)	-24	(13.9)	**-26**	(11.2)	**-26**	(9.7)	**-21**	(8.4)	**-22**	(9.5)	-21	(11.1)	-21	(13.6)
Lombardia	**-22**	(9.6)	5	(4.5)	**-37**	(18.4)	-31	(17.0)	-25	(13.5)	-20	(11.6)	-17	(10.2)	-18	(10.3)	-17	(11.8)
Trento	**-22**	(4.7)	0	(4.1)	-18	(13.0)	-18	(11.3)	**-26**	(6.7)	**-23**	(7.5)	**-21**	(8.5)	**-20**	(8.6)	-19	(12.1)
Portugal																		
Região Autónoma dos Açores	**-12**	(5.0)	3	(3.7)	-9	(10.8)	-11	(10.8)	**-20**	(7.9)	**-16**	(8.0)	-8	(8.9)	-3	(14.6)	-3	(15.6)
Spain																		
Andalusia•	**-22**	(5.3)	4	(3.4)	-22	(15.7)	**-28**	(11.8)	**-26**	(8.0)	**-26**	(6.9)	**-18**	(8.3)	-15	(9.2)	-12	(12.2)
Aragon•	**-28**	(5.3)	6	(4.5)	**-35**	(12.7)	**-38**	(12.2)	**-33**	(8.4)	**-29**	(7.9)	**-21**	(8.7)	-17	(9.2)	-17	(11.1)
Asturias•	**-26**	(4.6)	7	(4.4)	**-32**	(13.2)	**-35**	(10.4)	**-32**	(8.0)	**-27**	(6.2)	**-24**	(7.5)	-15	(9.2)	-6	(10.6)
Balearic Islands•	**-28**	(5.6)	5	(4.0)	**-33**	(12.5)	**-32**	(9.9)	**-34**	(7.7)	**-32**	(7.4)	**-25**	(7.5)	-18	(10.9)	-15	(10.7)
Basque Country•	**-28**	(4.2)	**7**	(2.9)	**-36**	(8.7)	**-38**	(7.6)	**-36**	(6.9)	**-26**	(5.9)	**-21**	(5.9)	**-17**	(7.8)	-17	(9.1)
Canary Islands•	**-23**	(4.7)	**7**	(2.9)	**-33**	(11.8)	**-32**	(10.4)	**-27**	(7.4)	**-22**	(6.4)	**-18**	(7.1)	-14	(8.9)	-14	(9.2)
Cantabria•	**-29**	(4.1)	3	(4.4)	**-31**	(13.3)	**-28**	(9.0)	**-33**	(8.1)	**-31**	(6.1)	**-26**	(6.8)	**-23**	(9.6)	-21	(12.1)
Castile and Leon•	**-31**	(4.0)	6	(3.3)	**-38**	(10.2)	**-41**	(10.5)	**-37**	(7.7)	**-31**	(6.8)	**-25**	(7.6)	**-23**	(7.8)	**-21**	(10.0)
Castile-La Mancha•	**-25**	(5.9)	6	(3.8)	**-33**	(12.9)	**-34**	(11.1)	**-30**	(8.2)	**-24**	(7.4)	**-21**	(8.5)	-16	(9.8)	-16	(9.7)
Catalonia•	**-24**	(6.9)	2	(4.0)	-18	(14.9)	**-27**	(12.4)	**-31**	(9.8)	**-28**	(8.5)	**-21**	(8.6)	-18	(10.6)	-17	(13.6)
Comunidad Valenciana•	**-25**	(6.3)	5	(4.4)	**-34**	(15.5)	**-36**	(12.1)	**-29**	(9.7)	**-25**	(7.7)	**-19**	(8.5)	**-20**	(9.2)	-19	(14.0)
Extremadura•	**-32**	(5.4)	6	(3.9)	**-41**	(12.3)	**-42**	(9.7)	**-38**	(7.7)	**-32**	(6.5)	**-27**	(9.7)	**-25**	(10.7)	-23	(11.7)
Galicia•	**-31**	(5.7)	7	(4.4)	**-36**	(14.9)	**-36**	(12.1)	**-41**	(8.7)	**-33**	(8.0)	**-25**	(6.8)	**-18**	(8.3)	-18	(11.1)
La Rioja•	**-31**	(6.4)	2	(4.1)	-23	(14.1)	**-30**	(13.3)	**-36**	(11.4)	**-35**	(9.1)	**-27**	(9.5)	**-25**	(9.8)	-24	(14.4)
Madrid•	**-20**	(5.5)	2	(3.7)	-18	(14.2)	-23	(12.5)	**-24**	(8.2)	**-21**	(7.5)	**-18**	(7.6)	-17	(9.6)	-17	(10.3)
Murcia•	**-28**	(4.5)	5	(4.1)	**-28**	(13.3)	**-32**	(12.2)	**-34**	(7.9)	**-31**	(6.9)	**-25**	(7.0)	**-20**	(8.0)	-15	(9.9)
Navarre•	**-25**	(5.2)	6	(4.4)	**-35**	(13.6)	**-36**	(11.1)	**-30**	(9.1)	**-24**	(7.9)	**-21**	(7.3)	-16	(11.3)	-12	(11.3)
United Kingdom																		
England	**-35**	(4.1)	1	(2.8)	**-31**	(8.7)	**-34**	(7.2)	**-37**	(5.6)	**-37**	(5.1)	**-35**	(5.2)	**-30**	(7.9)	**-32**	(8.6)
Northern Ireland	**-27**	(5.1)	3	(2.8)	**-32**	(11.6)	**-29**	(10.1)	**-32**	(7.5)	**-29**	(6.2)	**-24**	(7.6)	**-20**	(9.1)	**-21**	(9.5)
Scotland•	**-33**	(4.0)	0	(2.8)	**-25**	(11.4)	**-29**	(6.8)	**-38**	(6.2)	**-38**	(5.3)	**-33**	(6.2)	**-27**	(6.6)	**-25**	(9.0)
Wales	**-23**	(3.6)	3	(2.9)	**-25**	(8.2)	**-26**	(6.0)	**-26**	(6.0)	**-23**	(5.6)	**-20**	(5.5)	**-17**	(6.1)	-17	(10.0)
United States																		
Massachusetts•	**-26**	(7.1)	6	(3.9)	**-37**	(15.2)	**-34**	(13.1)	**-28**	(9.1)	**-28**	(8.9)	**-23**	(9.5)	-13	(12.4)	-14	(13.8)
North Carolina•	**-31**	(4.8)	6	(3.6)	**-39**	(10.2)	**-39**	(8.7)	**-37**	(7.8)	**-32**	(7.5)	**-26**	(7.7)	**-23**	(9.0)	-19	(12.2
Partners																		
Colombia																		
Bogotá	-10	(5.9)	-3	(3.5)	0	(8.6)	-7	(7.9)	-8	(8.4)	-9	(7.4)	-14	(9.7)	-13	(9.5)	-15	(10.1)
Cali	-3	(5.7)	3	(2.8)	-7	(11.2)	-7	(8.3)	-6	(7.6)	-2	(7.6)	-1	(8.5)	-1	(9.4)	0	(10.6)
Manizales	-7	(6.2)	5	(3.8)	-13	(11.4)	-11	(8.5)	-10	(6.8)	-8	(7.9)	-4	(9.4)	2	(12.2)	4	(14.4)
Medellín	-8	(5.5)	-1	(4.1)	-3	(10.1)	-5	(8.3)	-8	(7.0)	-10	(7.5)	-11	(7.0)	-9	(11.0)	-8	(16.2)
United Arab Emirates																		
Abu Dhabi•	**-35**	(8.0)	2	(3.7)	**-29**	(9.3)	**-32**	(8.8)	**-37**	(7.9)	**-41**	(9.2)	**-37**	(10.5)	**-27**	(12.5)	-22	(14.2)
Ajman	**-67**	(13.3)	-8	(7.3)	**-50**	(23.9)	**-51**	(20.1)	**-58**	(17.8)	**-72**	(15.8)	**-79**	(12.4)	**-77**	(15.7)	**-68**	(17.3)
Dubai•	**-30**	(3.9)	**12**	(3.0)	**-42**	(7.1)	**-42**	(6.2)	**-45**	(4.3)	**-32**	(5.8)	**-18**	(6.5)	-11	(8.0)	-8	(8.7)
Fujairah	**-58**	(12.7)	-1	(6.9)	**-55**	(15.7)	**-55**	(16.1)	**-56**	(13.5)	**-60**	(12.5)	**-62**	(20.0)	**-54**	(18.2)	-49	(26.1)
Ras Al Khaimah	**-58**	(11.7)	-8	(7.1)	**-47**	(17.9)	**-46**	(14.5)	**-45**	(14.7)	**-58**	(13.9)	**-68**	(15.1)	**-71**	(20.0)	**-72**	(21.6)
Sharjah	**-43**	(13.8)	**13**	(5.8)	**-57**	(22.0)	**-54**	(15.8)	**-54**	(14.7)	**-46**	(18.1)	**-40**	(18.4)	-24	(19.0)	-12	(22.6)
Umm Al Quwain	**-53**	(10.7)	-10	(6.1)	-35	(20.9)	**-40**	(18.9)	**-45**	(13.2)	**-53**	(13.1)	**-57**	(16.2)	**-68**	(17.6)	**-71**	(26.1)

• PISA for adjudicated region.
Notes: Results for the province of Quebec in this table should be treated with caution due to a possible non-response bias.
In Massachusetts and North Carolina, the desired target population covers 15-year-old students in grade 7 or above in public schools only (see Annex A2).
Values that are statistically significant are indicated in bold (see Annex A3).
See Table V.4.3a for national data.
StatLink http://dx.doi.org/10.1787/888933616750

[Part 1/1]

Table B2.V.17 Gender differences in relative performance in collaborative problem solving

After accounting for performance in science, reading and mathematics

		Score-point difference in relative performance[1] in collaborative problem solving (boys - girls)			
		Before accounting for students' socio-economic status		After accounting for students' socio-economic status	
		Score dif.	S.E.	Score dif.	S.E.
OECD	**Belgium**				
	Flemish community•	**-30**	(3.1)	**-31**	(3.1)
	French community	**-28**	(2.8)	**-28**	(3.0)
	German-speaking community	**-25**	(6.8)	**-25**	(6.9)
	Canada				
	Alberta	**-39**	(4.5)	**-39**	(4.6)
	British Columbia	**-35**	(5.5)	**-35**	(5.8)
	Manitoba	**-35**	(4.5)	**-35**	(4.8)
	New Brunswick	**-28**	(5.3)	**-28**	(5.3)
	Newfoundland and Labrador	**-33**	(6.0)	**-32**	(6.2)
	Nova Scotia	**-34**	(4.6)	**-35**	(4.8)
	Ontario	**-35**	(3.4)	**-36**	(3.4)
	Prince Edward Island	**-42**	(12.0)	**-42**	(12.0)
	Quebec	**-24**	(4.8)	**-24**	(5.0)
	Saskatchewan	**-38**	(5.3)	**-38**	(5.4)
	Italy				
	Bolzano	**-33**	(5.3)	**-34**	(5.2)
	Campania	**-35**	(5.0)	**-35**	(4.9)
	Lombardia	**-35**	(4.9)	**-35**	(4.6)
	Trento	**-35**	(4.0)	**-34**	(4.2)
	Portugal				
	Região Autónoma dos Açores	**-13**	(3.5)	**-13**	(3.4)
	Spain				
	Andalusia•	**-23**	(4.2)	**-23**	(4.1)
	Aragon•	**-24**	(4.9)	**-24**	(5.1)
	Asturias•	**-26**	(3.1)	**-25**	(3.2)
	Balearic Islands•	**-25**	(4.3)	**-25**	(4.2)
	Basque Country•	**-23**	(3.6)	**-23**	(3.6)
	Canary Islands•	**-23**	(4.1)	**-23**	(4.1)
	Cantabria•	**-25**	(3.7)	**-25**	(3.8)
	Castile and Leon•	**-26**	(3.3)	**-26**	(3.2)
	Castile-La Mancha•	**-24**	(4.0)	**-24**	(4.1)
	Catalonia•	**-28**	(5.1)	**-28**	(5.2)
	Comunidad Valenciana•	**-23**	(4.6)	**-23**	(4.6)
	Extremadura•	**-26**	(4.1)	**-26**	(4.1)
	Galicia•	**-29**	(4.5)	**-29**	(4.5)
	La Rioja•	**-29**	(4.8)	**-29**	(4.7)
	Madrid•	**-24**	(4.0)	**-24**	(4.0)
	Murcia•	**-22**	(4.0)	**-23**	(3.9)
	Navarre•	**-24**	(4.0)	**-25**	(4.0)
	United Kingdom				
	England	**-31**	(2.7)	**-31**	(2.9)
	Northern Ireland	**-25**	(3.8)	**-26**	(3.9)
	Scotland•	**-25**	(3.1)	**-25**	(3.3)
	Wales	**-23**	(2.8)	**-24**	(3.0)
	United States				
	Massachusetts•	**-30**	(3.9)	**-30**	(3.9)
	North Carolina•	**-27**	(3.1)	**-27**	(3.2)
Partners	**Colombia**				
	Bogotá	**-18**	(3.5)	**-17**	(3.9)
	Cali	**-20**	(3.9)	**-21**	(3.9)
	Manizales	**-20**	(4.0)	**-20**	(4.0)
	Medellín	**-20**	(3.7)	**-20**	(3.7)
	United Arab Emirates				
	Abu Dhabi•	-9	(6.0)	-10	(6.1)
	Ajman	**-27**	(11.0)	**-26**	(11.1)
	Dubai•	**-14**	(3.9)	**-15**	(3.9)
	Fujairah	-6	(8.5)	-7	(9.3)
	Ras Al Khaimah	-20	(11.3)	-21	(11.0)
	Sharjah	**-25**	(8.1)	**-25**	(7.9)
	Umm Al Quwain	-11	(9.4)	-12	(9.5)

• PISA for adjudicated region.
1. Relative performance refers to the residual performance, attributable to purely collaborative problem-solving competencies, after accounting for performance in science, reading and mathematics in a regression performed across students at the national level.
Notes: Results for the province of Quebec in this table should be treated with caution due to a possible non-response bias.
In Massachusetts and North Carolina, the desired target population covers 15-year-old students in grade 7 or above in public schools only (see Annex A2).
Values that are statistically significant are indicated in bold (see Annex A3).
See Table V.4.3b for national data.
StatLink http://dx.doi.org/10.1787/888933616750

[Part 1/1]

Table B2.V.20 Attitudes towards collaboration

Results based on students' self-reports

	Valuing relationships										Valuing teamwork									
			Percentage of students who agreed/strongly agreed with the following statements:										Percentage of students who agreed/strongly agreed with the following statements:							
	Index of valuing relationships		I am a good listener		I enjoy seeing my classmates be successful		I take into account what others are interested in		I enjoy considering different perspectives		Index of valuing teamwork		I prefer working as part of a team to working alone		I find that teams make better decisions than individuals		I find that teamwork raises my own efficiency		I enjoy co-operating with peers	
	Mean index	S.E.	%	S.E.	%	S.E.	%	S.E.	%	S.E.	Mean index	S.E.	%	S.E.	%	S.E.	%	S.E.	%	S.E.
OECD																				
Belgium																				
Flemish community•	-0.01	(0.01)	88.2	(0.5)	92.0	(0.4)	89.5	(0.5)	91.0	(0.4)	-0.20	(0.01)	63.9	(0.7)	70.3	(0.7)	57.2	(0.8)	86.5	(0.5)
French community	-0.13	(0.02)	80.9	(0.8)	88.9	(0.8)	80.8	(0.8)	86.4	(0.6)	0.00	(0.03)	68.9	(1.1)	72.0	(0.9)	70.2	(0.8)	82.9	(0.9)
German-speaking community	-0.02	(0.05)	82.5	(2.1)	79.3	(2.2)	89.6	(1.9)	81.6	(2.1)	0.05	(0.06)	67.7	(2.4)	76.1	(2.2)	56.5	(2.6)	86.9	(1.6)
Canada																				
Alberta	0.09	(0.03)	89.8	(0.7)	89.9	(0.7)	90.4	(0.7)	90.8	(0.7)	-0.01	(0.03)	67.1	(1.1)	73.9	(1.0)	69.2	(1.3)	87.2	(0.6)
British Columbia	0.10	(0.03)	89.7	(0.8)	91.7	(0.7)	89.8	(0.8)	90.5	(0.8)	-0.09	(0.02)	63.1	(1.3)	69.4	(1.3)	66.5	(1.1)	87.7	(0.7)
Manitoba	0.00	(0.03)	89.7	(0.9)	89.5	(0.8)	87.1	(0.9)	90.2	(0.9)	-0.03	(0.04)	66.1	(1.4)	74.5	(1.1)	71.5	(1.3)	86.4	(1.0)
New Brunswick	0.06	(0.03)	86.7	(0.9)	89.4	(0.9)	86.7	(0.9)	88.3	(1.0)	0.02	(0.03)	67.3	(1.5)	71.1	(1.3)	68.7	(1.2)	84.5	(1.1)
Newfoundland and Labrador	0.03	(0.04)	87.5	(1.3)	91.9	(1.0)	88.2	(1.2)	88.9	(0.9)	0.00	(0.03)	69.0	(1.7)	72.8	(1.3)	69.9	(1.5)	88.9	(1.2)
Nova Scotia	0.09	(0.03)	88.8	(0.9)	91.9	(0.8)	90.6	(0.8)	91.1	(1.0)	0.01	(0.03)	67.2	(1.4)	70.7	(1.2)	67.5	(1.4)	89.4	(0.8)
Ontario	0.09	(0.02)	90.2	(0.5)	89.6	(0.6)	89.7	(0.6)	89.4	(0.7)	-0.01	(0.02)	65.3	(0.9)	72.2	(0.8)	70.7	(0.9)	87.1	(0.5)
Prince Edward Island	0.13	(0.06)	89.6	(2.1)	93.7	(1.3)	91.9	(1.6)	92.0	(1.7)	0.13	(0.06)	68.3	(3.0)	79.2	(2.3)	76.0	(2.4)	91.7	(1.8)
Quebec	0.22	(0.03)	86.9	(1.0)	91.8	(0.7)	89.1	(0.9)	92.0	(0.6)	0.11	(0.03)	70.7	(1.0)	70.9	(1.1)	70.0	(1.0)	87.3	(0.9)
Saskatchewan	-0.03	(0.03)	89.9	(0.7)	91.3	(0.9)	88.8	(0.9)	88.9	(0.9)	-0.08	(0.03)	66.6	(1.4)	72.9	(1.1)	71.3	(1.2)	87.3	(0.9)
Italy																				
Bolzano	0.16	(0.02)	84.6	(0.9)	84.2	(0.9)	87.7	(0.7)	85.8	(0.9)	0.22	(0.02)	76.0	(0.9)	75.1	(1.2)	67.6	(1.2)	90.4	(0.7)
Campania	-0.11	(0.02)	88.1	(0.8)	89.8	(0.8)	73.5	(1.1)	91.8	(0.8)	0.09	(0.02)	73.6	(1.5)	75.4	(1.1)	77.4	(1.2)	91.2	(0.7)
Lombardia	-0.21	(0.02)	83.0	(0.8)	81.8	(0.9)	78.8	(1.0)	90.4	(0.7)	-0.06	(0.03)	70.2	(1.4)	71.6	(1.1)	68.5	(1.4)	85.0	(0.8)
Trento	-0.24	(0.02)	83.3	(1.0)	81.9	(1.0)	81.0	(1.0)	90.4	(0.7)	-0.09	(0.02)	69.4	(1.1)	71.7	(1.1)	65.4	(1.2)	84.8	(0.9)
Portugal																				
Região Autónoma dos Açores	0.23	(0.03)	91.0	(0.9)	96.4	(0.5)	91.9	(0.8)	92.0	(0.8)	0.28	(0.03)	72.4	(1.4)	82.4	(1.0)	80.8	(1.3)	94.5	(0.7)
Spain																				
Andalusia•	0.10	(0.03)	94.1	(0.8)	90.3	(0.8)	81.0	(1.2)	92.5	(0.6)	0.17	(0.03)	66.9	(1.3)	76.1	(1.4)	72.9	(1.3)	94.2	(0.6)
Aragon•	0.16	(0.04)	94.7	(0.6)	89.5	(1.0)	88.0	(0.8)	92.3	(0.7)	0.13	(0.03)	68.2	(1.0)	73.8	(1.1)	70.0	(1.1)	93.3	(0.6)
Asturias•	0.16	(0.03)	92.7	(0.5)	88.5	(0.8)	85.6	(0.8)	91.9	(0.7)	0.12	(0.02)	65.4	(1.1)	73.7	(0.9)	69.1	(0.9)	92.2	(0.6)
Balearic Islands•	0.20	(0.02)	92.8	(0.6)	92.5	(0.6)	86.3	(0.9)	91.9	(0.8)	0.06	(0.03)	61.5	(1.5)	75.0	(1.1)	72.1	(1.2)	90.6	(0.9)
Basque Country•	0.12	(0.02)	92.0	(0.5)	87.8	(0.7)	85.7	(0.8)	93.1	(0.6)	0.08	(0.02)	68.4	(0.9)	74.2	(0.8)	70.8	(0.9)	92.4	(0.5)
Canary Islands•	0.21	(0.02)	92.7	(0.7)	89.2	(0.7)	82.7	(1.1)	92.7	(0.5)	0.17	(0.03)	65.1	(1.4)	73.7	(1.3)	72.5	(1.0)	92.4	(0.7)
Cantabria•	0.16	(0.02)	93.5	(0.7)	89.3	(0.9)	87.1	(1.1)	92.5	(0.5)	0.18	(0.03)	67.8	(1.2)	74.8	(1.0)	73.0	(1.1)	92.4	(0.7)
Castile and Leon•	0.18	(0.03)	94.4	(0.5)	90.3	(0.8)	87.9	(0.9)	94.1	(0.4)	0.16	(0.03)	66.3	(1.5)	74.2	(1.3)	72.0	(1.3)	93.7	(0.5)
Castile-La Mancha•	0.20	(0.02)	94.4	(0.5)	89.0	(0.8)	86.7	(0.8)	93.7	(0.6)	0.18	(0.03)	68.1	(0.9)	75.9	(1.1)	72.0	(1.2)	92.8	(0.7)
Catalonia•	0.25	(0.03)	92.5	(0.8)	92.6	(0.8)	85.3	(1.1)	91.0	(0.9)	0.04	(0.04)	64.3	(1.2)	72.8	(0.9)	71.2	(1.1)	90.2	(0.8)
Comunidad Valenciana•	0.15	(0.03)	92.7	(0.8)	88.9	(1.0)	85.3	(0.9)	92.3	(0.8)	0.09	(0.02)	66.1	(1.1)	74.2	(1.3)	69.9	(1.2)	92.5	(0.8)
Extremadura•	0.15	(0.03)	94.5	(0.6)	89.4	(0.8)	83.7	(0.8)	93.7	(0.5)	0.20	(0.03)	67.8	(1.2)	77.1	(1.1)	74.5	(1.4)	94.1	(0.5)
Galicia•	0.25	(0.03)	94.0	(0.7)	92.2	(0.7)	89.6	(0.8)	92.8	(0.6)	0.15	(0.03)	71.6	(1.1)	75.8	(1.5)	71.7	(1.2)	90.4	(0.9)
La Rioja•	0.11	(0.03)	92.3	(0.7)	86.2	(1.0)	85.0	(1.0)	93.2	(0.8)	0.13	(0.03)	66.7	(1.6)	73.9	(1.3)	72.9	(1.2)	92.4	(0.8)
Madrid•	0.18	(0.03)	93.6	(0.5)	87.2	(0.9)	87.6	(1.1)	91.4	(0.7)	0.13	(0.04)	65.5	(1.5)	74.0	(1.5)	70.2	(1.2)	92.3	(0.7)
Murcia•	0.23	(0.03)	94.2	(0.5)	90.3	(0.7)	85.9	(0.9)	93.4	(0.7)	0.22	(0.03)	70.5	(0.8)	76.5	(0.9)	72.8	(1.2)	93.4	(0.6)
Navarre•	0.11	(0.04)	92.9	(0.7)	88.4	(1.2)	86.3	(1.0)	92.0	(0.7)	0.18	(0.04)	70.1	(1.4)	76.4	(1.4)	72.6	(1.3)	93.1	(0.7)
United Kingdom																				
England	-0.04	(0.02)	87.0	(0.6)	89.2	(0.6)	88.0	(0.6)	87.2	(0.6)	-0.05	(0.02)	68.2	(0.8)	74.0	(0.7)	71.5	(0.7)	85.4	(0.7)
Northern Ireland	-0.07	(0.02)	87.4	(0.7)	89.8	(0.8)	89.0	(0.8)	88.8	(0.7)	-0.04	(0.03)	68.0	(1.0)	72.9	(0.9)	72.4	(1.0)	87.8	(0.7)
Scotland•	0.03	(0.02)	87.9	(0.7)	89.6	(0.5)	90.2	(0.5)	87.1	(0.8)	0.02	(0.02)	71.4	(0.9)	73.5	(0.8)	71.6	(0.7)	87.8	(0.6)
Wales	-0.10	(0.02)	84.4	(0.6)	89.1	(0.6)	87.8	(0.6)	87.0	(0.6)	-0.05	(0.02)	67.0	(0.9)	73.9	(0.8)	72.6	(0.7)	83.8	(0.7)
United States																				
Massachusetts•	0.09	(0.03)	88.9	(0.9)	92.8	(0.7)	90.0	(0.9)	90.0	(0.7)	-0.01	(0.03)	68.9	(1.3)	71.9	(1.1)	71.2	(0.9)	88.7	(0.8)
North Carolina•	0.10	(0.03)	90.9	(0.9)	93.9	(0.4)	88.0	(0.7)	91.3	(0.7)	0.07	(0.03)	70.0	(1.2)	73.8	(1.2)	74.5	(1.3)	88.7	(0.8)
Partners																				
Colombia																				
Bogotá	0.08	(0.03)	89.1	(0.8)	93.4	(0.5)	80.8	(1.1)	88.3	(0.9)	0.12	(0.02)	68.4	(1.5)	77.8	(1.1)	72.8	(0.8)	93.0	(0.6)
Cali	0.06	(0.03)	89.1	(0.7)	93.0	(0.6)	81.0	(1.2)	87.6	(1.0)	0.13	(0.02)	67.5	(1.3)	81.8	(1.1)	74.2	(0.9)	92.8	(0.7)
Manizales	0.14	(0.03)	89.3	(1.0)	94.6	(0.6)	82.4	(1.2)	88.6	(0.9)	0.22	(0.03)	70.1	(1.1)	81.4	(1.1)	76.0	(1.2)	93.3	(0.7)
Medellín	0.15	(0.03)	88.5	(0.7)	94.1	(0.7)	83.2	(1.0)	88.8	(0.9)	0.22	(0.02)	68.5	(0.9)	83.2	(1.0)	76.4	(1.2)	92.3	(0.8)
United Arab Emirates																				
Abu Dhabi•	0.37	(0.02)	87.6	(0.7)	93.0	(0.5)	86.9	(0.7)	90.7	(0.5)	0.44	(0.02)	67.3	(0.9)	86.0	(0.6)	85.3	(0.7)	90.9	(0.6)
Ajman	0.28	(0.04)	88.0	(1.1)	92.6	(1.1)	87.3	(1.0)	88.8	(1.0)	0.51	(0.03)	64.3	(1.3)	89.2	(0.8)	89.3	(0.9)	93.3	(0.9)
Dubai•	0.29	(0.02)	89.6	(0.5)	91.3	(0.5)	86.3	(0.5)	91.8	(0.5)	0.38	(0.02)	71.7	(0.7)	83.7	(0.5)	81.8	(0.6)	91.3	(0.4)
Fujairah	0.39	(0.04)	88.5	(1.1)	93.3	(0.8)	88.1	(1.0)	90.8	(0.9)	0.54	(0.04)	65.8	(1.8)	87.5	(1.3)	89.9	(1.3)	93.8	(1.0)
Ras Al Khaimah	0.42	(0.05)	88.8	(1.1)	93.6	(0.6)	87.4	(1.6)	90.3	(0.8)	0.53	(0.04)	62.9	(1.7)	89.5	(1.2)	89.9	(0.9)	92.3	(0.8)
Sharjah	0.22	(0.05)	87.8	(1.5)	93.4	(1.1)	83.3	(0.9)	91.7	(1.1)	0.50	(0.05)	71.9	(1.5)	90.0	(1.0)	88.1	(1.2)	91.5	(0.7)
Umm Al Quwain	0.31	(0.06)	85.5	(1.8)	91.9	(1.5)	83.2	(2.2)	89.3	(1.7)	0.51	(0.06)	62.7	(2.5)	89.6	(1.5)	87.4	(1.7)	90.5	(1.4)

• PISA for adjudicated region.
Notes: Results for the province of Quebec in this table should be treated with caution due to a possible non-response bias.
In Massachusetts and North Carolina, the desired target population covers 15-year-old students in grade 7 or above in public schools only (see Annex A2).
See Table V.5.1 for national data.
StatLink http://dx.doi.org/10.1787/888933616750

ANNEX B3

LIST OF TABLES AVAILABLE ON LINE

The following tables are available in electronic form only, they may be found at: www.oecd.org/pisa.

Chapter 3 Performance in collaborative problem solving

http://dx.doi.org/10.1787/888933616769

Chapter 4 Student demographics and performance in collaborative problem solving

http://dx.doi.org/10.1787/888933616788

Chapter 5 Students' attitudes towards collaboration

http://dx.doi.org/10.1787/888933616807

Chapter 6 Student activities, school practices and collaboration

http://dx.doi.org/10.1787/888933616826

...

Chapter 7 Collaborative schools, collaborative students

http://dx.doi.org/10.1787/888933616845

...

Annex B2 Results for regions within countries

http://dx.doi.org/10.1787/888933616750

...

Annex C

THE DEVELOPMENT AND IMPLEMENTATION OF PISA: A COLLABORATIVE EFFORT

PISA is a collaborative effort, bringing together experts from the participating countries, steered jointly by their governments on the basis of shared, policy-driven interests.

A PISA Governing Board, representing each country, determines the policy priorities for PISA, in the context of OECD objectives, and oversees adherence to these priorities during the implementation of the programme. This includes setting priorities for the development of indicators, for establishing the assessment instruments and for reporting the results.

Experts from participating countries also serve on working groups that are charged with linking policy objectives with the best internationally available technical expertise. By participating in these expert groups, countries ensure that: the instruments are internationally valid and take into account the cultural and educational contexts in OECD countries and in partner countries and economies; the assessment materials have strong measurement properties; and the instruments emphasise authenticity and educational validity.

Participating countries and economies implement PISA at the national level through National Project Managers, subject to the agreed administration procedures. National Project Managers play a vital role in ensuring that the implementation of the survey is of high quality, and verify and evaluate the survey results, analyses, reports and publications.

External contractors are responsible for designing and implementing the surveys, within the framework established by the PISA Governing Board. Pearson developed the science and collaborative problem-solving frameworks, and adapted the frameworks for reading and mathematics, while the Deutsches Institut für Pädagogische Forschung (DIPF) designed and developed the questionnaires. Management and oversight of this survey, the development of the instruments, scaling and analyses are the responsibility of the Educational Testing Service (ETS) as is development of the electronic platform. Other partners or subcontractors involved with ETS include: cApStAn Linguistic Quality Control and the Department of Experimental and Theoretical Pedagogy at the University of Liège (SPe) in Belgium; the Center for Educational Technology (CET) in Israel; the Public Research Centre (CRP) Henri Tudor and the Educational Measurement and Research Center (EMACS) of the University of Luxembourg in Luxembourg; and GESIS – Leibniz-Institute for the Social Sciences in Germany. Westat assumed responsibility for survey operations and sampling with the subcontractor, the Australian Council for Educational Research (ACER).

The OECD Secretariat has overall managerial responsibility for the programme, monitors its implementation daily, acts as the secretariat for the PISA Governing Board, builds consensus among countries, and serves as the interlocutor between the PISA Governing Board and the international Consortium charged with implementing the activities. The OECD Secretariat also produces the indicators and analyses and prepares the international reports and publications in co-operation with the PISA Consortium and in close consultation with OECD countries and partner countries and economies at both the policy level (PISA Governing Board) and the level of implementation (National Project Managers).

PISA Governing Board

(* Former PGB member who was involved in PISA 2015)

Chair of the PISA Governing Board: Michelle Bruniges and Lorna Bertrand*

OECD countries and Associates

Australia: Rhyan Bloor, Michelle Bruniges and Tony Zanderigo*

Austria: Mark Német

Belgium: Isabelle Erauw, Geneviève Hindryckx and Christiane Blondin*

Brazil: Maria Helena Guamaraes Castro, Maria Inês Fini and Luiz Claudio Costa*

Canada: Tomasz Gluszynski, Kathryn O'Grady, Pierre Brochu* and Patrick Bussiere*

Chile: Carolina Flores, Claudia Matus and Leonor Cariola Huerta*

Czech Republic: Tomas Zatloukal and Jana Paleckova*

Denmark: Mette Hansen, Frida Poulsen, Elsebeth Aller* and Tine Bak*

Estonia: Maie Kitsing

Finland: Tommi Karjalainen

France: Thierry Rocher and Bruno Trosseille*

Germany: Martina Diedrich, Katharina Koufen, Elfriede Ohrnberger, Annemarie Klemm* and Susanne von Below*

Greece: Chryssa Sofianopoulou and Vassilia Hatzinikita*

Hungary: Sándor Brassói and Benõ Csapó*

Iceland: Stefán Baldursson and Júlíus Björnsson*

Ireland: Peter Archer, Jude Cosgrove* and Gerry Shiel*

Israel: Hagit Glickman and Michal Beller*

Italy: Roberto Ricci and Paolo Sestito*

Japan: Akiko Ono, Masaharu Shiozaki and Ryo Watanabe*

Korea: Bu Ho Nam, Jimin Cho, Jea Yun Park*, Sungsook Kim*, Keunwoo Lee* and Myungae Lee*

Latvia: Andris Kangro, Aļona Babiča, Ennata Kivrina* and Dita Traidas*

Luxembourg: Amina Kafaï

Mexico: Eduardo Backhoff Escudero, Ana María Acevess Estrada, Otto Granados Roldán and Francisco Ciscomani*

Netherlands: Marjan Zandbergen and Paul van Oijen*

New Zealand: Craig Jones, Lisa Rodgers* and Lynne Whitney*

Norway: Marthe Akselsen, Anne-Berit Kavli* and Alette Schreiner*

Poland: Piotr Mikiewicz, Jerzy Wisniewski*, Hania Bouacid* and Stanislaw Drzazdzewski*

Portugal: Hélder Manuel Diniz de Sousa, Luisa Canto* and Castro Loura*

Slovak Republic: Romana Kanovska and Paulina Korsnakova*

Slovenia: Andreja Barle Lakota, Mojca Straus and Ksenija Bregar-Golobic

Spain: Carmen Tovar Sanchez, Vicente Alcañiz Miñano* and Ismael Sanz Labrador*

Sweden: Eva Lundgren and Anita Wester*

Switzerland: Vera Husfeldt and Claudia Zahner Rossier

Turkey: Kemal Bulbul, Mustafa Nadir Çalis* and Nurcan Devici*

United Kingdom: Lorna Bertrand and Jonathan Wright

United States: Peggy Carr, Dana Kelly*, Jack Buckley* and Daniel McGrath*

Observers (Partner economies)

Albania: Zamira Gjini and Ermal Elezi*

Algeria: Samia Mezaib and Mohamed Chaibeddra Tani*

Argentina: Elena Duro, Martín Guillermo Scasso* and Liliana Pascual*

Azerbaijan (Baku City only): Emin Amrullayev

Belarus (Republic of): Aliaksandr Yakabchuk and Mikalai Fiaskou

Bosnia and Herzegovina: Maja Stojkic

Brunei Darussalam: Dr. Azman Ahmad

Bulgaria: Neda Kristanova

Beijing-Shanghai-Jiangsu-Guangdong (China): Jun Fang, Shiliang Lin, Ping Luo*

Colombia: Ximena Dueñas and Adriana Molina*

Costa Rica: Alicia Vargas and Leonardo Garnier Rimolo*

Croatia: Michelle Bras Roth

Dominican Republic: Ancell Scheker Mendoza

Former Yugoslav Republic of Macedonia: Natasha Janevska (PISA 2018) and Dejan Zlatkovski*

Georgia: Tamar Bregvadze and Natia Mzhavanadze*

Hong Kong (China): Ho-pun Choi, Fanny Yuen-fan Wan and Esther Sui-chu Ho*

Indonesia: Dr. Totok Suprayitno, Furqon Furqon* and Khairil Anwar Notodiputro*

Jordan: Khattab Mohammad Abulibdeh

Kazakhstan: Shamshieva Nurgul, Serik Irsaliyev* and Almagul Kultumanova*

Kosovo: Anila Statovci Demaj

Lebanon: Nada Ouweijan

Lithuania: Rita Dukynaite

Macao (China): Leong Lai

Malaysia: Hon. Dato' Sulaiman bin Wak, Khairil Awang* and Amin Senin*

Malta: Charles Mifsud

Moldova (Republic of): Anatolie Topala and Valeriu Gutu*

Montenegro: Dragana Dmitrovic and Zeljko Jacimovic*

Morocco: Mohammed Sassi

Panama: Marelissa Tribaldos

Peru: Humberto Hildebrando Pérez León Ibañez and Liliana Miranda Molina*

Philippines: Elvin Ivan Yaw

Qatar: Khalid Abdulla Q. Al-Harqan and Hamda Al Sulaiti*

Romania: Roxana Mihail and Daniela Bogdan

Russian Federation: Galina Kovaleva, Sergey Kravtsov and Isak Froumin*

Saudi Arabia: Mohamed Al-harthi

Serbia (Republic of): Anamarija Viček and Zorana Lužanin*

Singapore: Chern Wei Sng and Khah Gek Low*

Chinese Taipei: Tian-Ming Sheu, Peng Li-Chun*, Gwo-Dong Chen* and Chih-Wei Hue*

Thailand: Supattra Pativisan and Precharn Dechsri*

Trinidad and Tobago: Mervyn Sambucharan and Harrilal Seecharan

Tunisia: Riadh Ben Boubaker

Ukraine: Pavlo Khobzey

United Arab Emirates: Hessa Alwahhabi, Rabaa Alsumaiti, Moza al Ghufly*, Ayesha G. Khalfan Almerri*, Ali Jaber Al Yafei* and Khawla Al Mualla*

Uruguay: Andrés Peri and Maria Helvecia Sanchez Nunez*

Viet Nam: Le Thi My Ha

PISA 2015 National Project Managers

(* Former PISA 2015 NPM)

Albania: Rezana Vrapi and Alfons Harizaj*

Algeria: Samia Mezaib

Argentina: Liliana Pascual

Australia: Sue Thomson

Austria: Birgit Suchan

Beijing-Shanghai-Jiangsu-Guangdong (China): Wang Lei

Belgium: Inge De Meyer and Anne Matoul

Brazil: Aline Mara Fernandes

Bulgaria: Svetla Petrova

Canada: Pierre Brochu and Tamara Knighton*

Chile: Ema Lagos Campos

Colombia: Javier Juyar, Francisco Reyes*, Adriana Molina* and Julián P. Mariño*

Costa Rica: Lilliam Mora

Croatia: Michelle Bras Roth

Czech Republic: Radek Blažek and Jana Paleckova*

Denmark: Hans Hummelgaard, Niels Egelund* and Chantal Nielsen*

Dominican Republic: Massiel Cohen

Estonia: Gunda Tire

Finland: Jouni Välijärvi

Former Yugoslav Republic of Macedonia: Natasha Janevska and Dejan Zlatkovski

France: Irène Verlet

Georgia: Natia Mzhavanadze

Germany: Christine Sälzer and Manfred Prenzel

Greece: Chryssa Sofianopoulou
Hong Kong (China): Esther Sui-chu Ho
Hungary: László Ostorics
Iceland: Almar Midvik Halldorsson
Indonesia: Ir. Nizam
Ireland: Gerry Shiel
Israel: Joel Rapp and Inbal Ron-Kaplan
Italy: Carlo Di Chiacchio
Japan: Akiko Ono
Jordan: Emad Ababneh
Kazakhstan: Irina Imanbek and Gulmira Berdibayeva*
Korea: Jaok Ku, Jimin Cho* and Mi-Young Song*
Latvia: Andris Kangro
Lebanon: Bassem Issa and Antoine Skaf*
Lithuania: Mindaugas Stundza
Luxembourg: Bettina Boehm
Macao (China): Kwok Cheung Cheung
Malaysia: Muhammad Zaini Mohd Zain
Malta: Louis Scerri
Mexico: María Antonieta Díaz Gutierrez
Moldova (Republic of): Valeriu Gutu
Montenegro: Divna Paljevic Sturm
Netherlands: Jesse Koops and Johanna Kordes*
New Zealand: Steve May, Saila Cowles and Maree Telford*
Norway: Marit Kjaernsli
Peru: Liliana Miranda Molina
Poland: Barbara Ostrowska
Portugal: João Maroco
Qatar: Shaikha Al-Ishaq and Saada Al-Obaidli*
Romania: Silviu Cristian Mirescu
Russian Federation: Galina Kovaleva
Serbia: Dragica Pavlovic-Babic
Singapore: Chew Leng Poon, Elaine Chua and Pik Yen Lim*
Slovak Republic: Jana Ferencova
Slovenia: Mojca Straus
Spain: Lis Cercadillo Pérez
Sweden: Magnus Oskarsson
Switzerland: Christian Nidegger
Chinese Taipei: Hsiao-Ching She and Huann-Shyang Lin
Thailand: Nantawan Nantawanit and Suchada Thaithae
Trinidad and Tobago: Mervyn Sambucharan
Tunisia: Mehrez Drissi and Med Kamel Essid*
Turkey: Umut Erkin Taş
United Arab Emirates: Mouza Rashed Khalfan Al Ghufli
United Kingdom: Dawn Pollard and Juliet Sizmur
United States: Dana Kelly, Patrick Gonzales and Holly Xie*
Uruguay: Maria Helvecia Sánchez Nunez
Viet Nam: Thi My Ha Le

OECD Secretariat

Andreas Schleicher (Strategic development)
Marilyn Achiron (Editorial support)
Peter Adams (Project management)
Francesco Avvisati (Analytic services)
Yuri Belfali (Strategic development)
Marika Boiron (Translation support)
Rose Bolognini (Production support)
Guillaume Bousquet (Analytic services)
Esther Carvalhaes (Analytic services)
Claire Chetcuti (Administrative support)
Anna Choi (Analytic services)
Cassandra Davis (Dissemination co-ordination)
Alfonso Echazarra (Analytic services)
Juliet Evans (Administration and partner country/economy relations)
Hélène Guillou (Analytic services)
Carlos González-Sancho (Analytic services)
Tue Halgreen (Project management)
Miyako Ikeda (Analytic services)
Thomas Marwood (Administrative support)
Jeffrey Mo (Analytic services)
Chiara Monticone (Analytic services)
Lesley O'Sullivan (Administrative support)
Bonaventura Francesco Pacileo (Analytic services)
Judit Pál (Analytic services)
Mario Piacentini (Analytic services)
Giannina Rech (Analytic services)
Daniel Salinas (Analytic services)
Lisa Smadja (Administrative support)
Michael Stevenson (Dissemination co-ordination)
Hanna Varkki (Administrative support)
Sophie Vayssettes (Project management)

PISA 2015 science expert group

Jonathan Osborne (SEG Chair) (Stanford University, United States and United Kingdom)
Marcus Hammann (Munster University, Germany)
Sarah Howie (University of Pretoria, South Africa)
Jody Clarke-Midura (Harvard University, United States)
Robin Millar (University of York, United Kingdom)
Andrée Tiberghien (University of Lyon, France)
Russell Tytler (Deakin University, Australia)
Darren Wong (National Institute of Education, Singapore)

Extended group

Rodger Bybee (Biological Sciences Curriculum Study (BSCS), United States)
Jens Dolin (University of Copenhagen, Denmark)
Harrie Eijkelhof (Utrecht University, Netherlands)
Geneva Haertel (SRI, United States)
Michaela Mayer (University of Roma Tre., Italy)
Eric Snow (SRI, United States)
Manabu Sumida (Ehime University, Japan)
Benny Yung (University of Hong Kong, Hong Kong, China)

PISA 2015 problem solving expert group

Arthur Graesser (Chair) (The University of Memphis United States)

Eduardo Cascallar (Katholieke Universiteit Leuven, Belgium)

Pierre Dillenbourg (Ecole Polytechnique Fédérale de Lausanne, Switzerland)

Patrick Griffin (University of Melbourne, Australia)

Chee Kit Looi (Nanyang Technological University, Singapore)

Jean-François Rouet (University of Poitiers, France)

Extended group

Rafael Calvo (University of Sydney, Argentina)

Tak Wai Chan (National Central University of Taiwan, China)

Stephen Fiore (University of Central Florida, USA)

Joachim Funke (University of Heidelberg, Germany)

Manu Kapur (National Institute of Education, Singapore)

Naomi Miyake (University of Tokyo, Japan)

Yigal Rosen (University of Haifa, Israel)

Jennifer Wiley (University of Illinois at Chicago, USA)

PISA 2015 questionnaire expert group

David Kaplan (Chair as of 2014) (University of Wisconsin-Madison, United States)

Eckhard Klieme (Chair until 2013) (German Institute for International Educational Research, Germany (DIPF), Frankfurt, Germany)

Gregory Elacqua (Universidad Diego Portales, Chile)

Marit Kjærnsli (University of Oslo, Norway)

Leonidas Kyriakides (University of Cyprus, Cyprus)

Henry M. Levin (Columbia University, United States)

Naomi Miyake (University of Tokyo, Japan)

Jonathan Osborne (Stanford University, United States)

Kathleen Scalise (University of Oregon, United States)

Fons van de Vijver (Tilburg University, Netherlands)

Ludger Wößmann (University of Munich, Germany)

Technical advisory group

Keith Rust (chair) (Westat, USA)

Theo Eggen (Cito, Netherlands)

John de Jong (Pearson, UK/VU University Amsterdam, Netherlands)

Jean Dumais (Statistics Canada, Canada)

Cees Glas (University of Twente, Netherlands)

David Kaplan (University of Wisconsin-Madison, USA and DIPF, Germany)

Irwin Kirsch (ETS, USA)

Christian Monseur (Université de Liège, Belgium)

Sophia Rabe-Hesketh (University of Berkeley, USA)

Thierry Rocher (Ministère de l'Éducation Nationale, France)

Leslie A. Rutkowski (University of Oslo, Norway)

Margaret Wu (Victoria University, Australia)

Kentaro Yamamoto (ETS, USA)

PISA 2015 Lead Contractors

Educational Testing Service (UNITED STATES) – Cores 2, 3 and 7 lead contractor

Irwin Kirsch (International project director)

Claudia Tamassia (International project manager)

David Garber (Project management, paper booklets and coding)

Larry Hanover (Editorial support)

Lisa Hemat (Project support)

Isabelle Jars (Project management, questionnaires)

Judy Mendez (Project support and contracts)

Eugenio Gonzalez (Training and data products)

Kentaro Yamamoto (Director, psychometrics and analysis)

Matthias von Davier (Director, psychometrics and analysis)

Chentong Chen (Psychometrics and analysis)

Haiwen Chen (Psychometrics and analysis)

Qiwei He (Psychometrics and analysis)

Lale Khorramdel (Manager, psychometrics and analysis)

Hyo Jeong Shin (Psychometrics and analysis)

Marylou Lennon (Test Development Coordinator, Science and Collaborative Problem Solving)

Jon Weeks (Psychometrics and analysis)

Eric Steinhauer (Test Development, Lead, Science and Collaborative Problem Solving)

Janet Koster van Groos (Test Development, Science)

Marshall L Freedman (Test Development Science)

Israel Solon (Test Development Science)

Jakub Novak (Test Development Science)

Nancy Olds (Test Development Science)

Paul Borysewicz (Test Development, Collaborative Problem Solving)

William Sims (Test Development, Collaborative Problem Solving)

Peter Cooper (Test Development, Collaborative Problem Solving)

Michael Wagner (Director, platform development)

Jason Bonthron (Platform development and authoring)

Paul Brost (Platform development)

Ramin Hemat (Platform development and authoring)

Keith Keiser (Platform development and coding system)

Debbie Pisacreta (Interface design and graphics)

Janet Stumper (Graphics)

Ted Blew (Director, data analysis, research and technology)

John Barone (Director, data analysis and database preparation)

Mathew Kandathil (Leader, data analysis and data management)

Kevin Bentley (Data products)

Hezekiah Bunde (Data management)

Karen Castellano (Data analysis)

Scott Davis (Data analysis)

Chantal Delaney (Data management)

Matthew Duchnowski (Data management)

Ying Feng (Data management)

Zhumei Guo (Data analysis)
Laura Jerry (Data analysis)
Lokesh Kapur (Data analysis)
Debra Kline (Data analysis leader)
Phillip Leung (Data products leader)
Alfred Rogers (Data management leader)
Carla Tarsitano (Data management leader)
Sarah Venema (Data products)
Tao Wang (Data products)
Lingjun Wong (Data analysis)
Yan Zhang (Data management)
Wei Zhao (Data analysis)

Deutches Institue für Internationale Pädagogische Forschung (German Institute for International Educational Research **(DIPF), GERMANY) – Core 6 lead contractor**

Eckhard Klieme (Study director, questionnaire framework and development)
Nina Jude (Management and questionnaire development)
Sonja Bayer (Questionnaire development and analysis)
Janine Buchholz (Questionnaire scaling)
Frank Goldhammer (Questionnaire development)
Silke Hertel (Questionnaire development)
Franz Klingebiel (Questionnaire development)
Susanne Kuger (Questionnaire framework and development)
Ingrid Mader (Team assistance)
Tamara Marksteiner (Questionnaire analysis)
Jean-Paul Reeff (International Consultant)
Nina Roczen (Questionnaire development)
Brigitte Steinert (Questionnaire development)
Svenja Vieluf (Questionnaire development)

Pearson (UNITED KINGDOM) – Core 1 lead contractor

John de Jong (Programme director)
Catherine Hayes (Programme manager)
Elise Bromley (Programme administrator)
Rose Clesham (Content lead, scientific literacy)
Peter Foltz (Content lead, collaborative problem solving)
Christine Rozunick (Content lead, scientific literacy)
Jon Twing (Psychometric consultant)
Michael Young (Psychometric consultant)

Westat (UNITED STATES) – Cores 4 and 5 lead contractor

Keith Rust (Director of the PISA consortium for sampling and weighting)
Sheila Krawchuk (Sampling, weighting and quality monitoring)
Andrew Caporaso (Weighting)
Jessica Chan (Sampling and weighting)
William Chan (Weighting)
Susan Fuss (Sampling and weighting)
Amita Gopinath (Sampling and weighting)
Evan Gutentag (Weighting)
Jing Kang (Sampling and weighting)
Veronique Lieber (Sampling and weighting)
John Lopdell (Sampling and weighting)
Shawn Lu (Weighting)
Martha Rozsi (Weighting)
Yumiko Siegfried (Sampling and weighting)
Joel Wakesberg (Sampling and weighting)
Sipeng Wang (Weighting)
Erin Wiley (Sampling and weighting)
Sergey Yagodin (Weighting)
Merl Robinson (Director of Core 4 Contractor for Survey Operations)
Michael Lemay (Manager of Core 4 Contractor for Survey Operations)
Jessica Chan (National Centre Support, Quality Control)
Lillian Diaz-Hoffman (National Centre Support, Quality Control)
Sarah Hartge (National Centre Support, Quality Control)
Beverley McGaughan (National Centre Support, Quality Control)

PISA 2015 Contributors, working with Lead Contractors

Australian Council for Educational Research (AUSTRALIA) – Core 5 contributor

Eveline Gebhardt (Project director)
Alla Routitsky (Within-school sampling)
Charlotte Waters (Within-school sampling)
Jorge Fallas (Within-school sampling)
Renee Chow (Within-school sampling)
David Tran (Programmer)
Martin Murphy (School sampling)
Clare Ozolins (School sampling)
Greg Macaskill (School sampling)
Jennifer Hong (School sampling)
Jorge Fallas (School sampling)
Renee Chow (School sampling)
Thomas Stephen (School sampling)

Center for Educational Technology – Core 3 contributor on test development

Tali Freund (Test Development Coordinator, Science and Collaborative Problem Solving)
Rachel Mintz (Test Development, Lead, Science)
Nurit Keinan (Test Development, Science)
Hava Ben-Horin (Test Development, Science)
Sherman Rosenfeld (Test Development, Science)
Lilach Tencer-Herschkovitz (Test Development, Science)
Nadav Caspi (Test Development, Science)
Elinor Shaked-Blazer (Test Development, Science)
Sara Hershkovitz (Test Development, Lead, Collaborative Problem Solving)
Cecilia Waisman (Test Development, Collaborative Problem Solving)
Helit Heffer (Test Development, Collaborative Problem Solving)
Estela Melamed (Test Development, Science and Collaborative Problem Solving)

cApStAn Linguistic Quality Control (BELGIUM) – Core 3 contributor on linguistic quality control

Steve Dept (Project director, translatability assessment,)

Lieve Deckx (Verification management, cognitive units)

Andrea Ferrari (Linguistic quality assurance and quality control designs)

Musab Hayatli (Right-to-left scripts, cultural adaptations)

Elica Krajceva (Verification management, questionnaires)

Shinoh Lee (Verification management, cognitive units)

Irene Liberati (Verification management, cognitive units)

Roberta Lizzi (Verification management, trend content)

Laura Wayrynen (Translation and verification operations)

GESIS-Leibniz Institute for the Social Sciences (GERMANY) – Core 3 contributor on test development

Anouk Zabal (Test Development Coordinator, Science and Collaborative Problem Solving, Software Testing)

Dorothee Behr (Test Development, Science and Collaborative Problem Solving, Software Testing)

Daniela Ackermann (Test Development, Science and Collaborative Problem Solving, Software Testing)

HallStat SPRL (BELGIUM) – Core 3 contributor as the translation referee

Beatrice Halleux (Consultant, translation/verification referee, French source development)

Luxembourg Institute for Science and Technology (LUXEMBOURG) – Core 2 Contributor on the development of the computer-based platform for the background questionnaire and cognitive assessment

Jehan Bihim (Questionnaire development)

Joël Billard (Multilingual framework and questionnaire development)

Cyril Hazotte (System administration)

Anne Hendrick (Platform Leader, project co-ordination)

Raynald Jadoul (Project management and software architecture)

Isabelle Jars (Project management and testing)

Lionel Lecaque (Software quality and knowledge base administration)

Primaël Lorbat (Multilingual framework and questionnaire architecture)

Matteo Melis (Portal integration and questionnaire development)

Jean-François Merche (System integration and administration)

Vincent Porro (Lead designer and staff co-ordination)

Igor Ribassin (Workflow development and offline tools development)

Somsack Sipasseuth (Workflow development and knowledge base integration)

Nicolas Yodi (Portal integration and questionnaire development)

Statistics Canada (CANADA) – Core 6 contributor on questionnaires

Sylvie Grenier (Overall management)

Tamara Knighton (Overall management)

Isabelle Thorny (Implementation Delivery System)

Ginette Grégoire (Implementation Delivery System)

Martine Lafrenière (Implementation Delivery System)

Rosa Tatasciore (Implementation Delivery System)

Unité d'analyse des Systèmes et des Pratiques d'enseignement (aSPe, BELGIUM) – Core 3 contributor on coding training

Dominique LaFontaine (Project supervisor)

Ariane Baye (Coding training, reading)

Isabelle Demonty (Coding training, mathematics)

Annick Fagnant (Coding training, mathematics)

Geneviève Hindryckx (Coding training, science)

Anne Matoul (Coding training, reading)

Valérie Quittre (Coding training, science)

University of Heidelberg (GERMANY) – Core 3 contributor on test development

Daniel Holt (Test Development, Collaborative Problem Solving)

Andreas Fischer (Test Development, Collaborative Problem Solving)

Ursula Pöll (Test Development, Collaborative Problem Solving)

Julia Hilse (Test Development, Collaborative Problem Solving)

Saskia Kraft (Test Development, Collaborative Problem Solving)

Florian Hofmann (Test Development, Collaborative Problem Solving)

University of Luxembourg (LUXEMBOURG) – Core 3 contributor on test development

Romain Martin (Test Development Coordinator, Science)

Samuel Greiff (Test Development Coordinator, Collaborative Problem Solving)

Sara Wilmes (Test Development, Science)

Sophie Doublet (User Testing)

Vincent Koenig (User Testing)

Katja Weinerth (User Testing)

Publication layout

Fung Kwan Tam

ORGANISATION FOR ECONOMIC CO-OPERATION AND DEVELOPMENT

The OECD is a unique forum where governments work together to address the economic, social and environmental challenges of globalisation. The OECD is also at the forefront of efforts to understand and to help governments respond to new developments and concerns, such as corporate governance, the information economy and the challenges of an ageing population. The Organisation provides a setting where governments can compare policy experiences, seek answers to common problems, identify good practice and work to co-ordinate domestic and international policies.

The OECD member countries are: Australia, Austria, Belgium, Canada, Chile, the Czech Republic, Denmark, Estonia, Finland, France, Germany, Greece, Hungary, Iceland, Ireland, Israel, Italy, Japan, Korea, Latvia, Luxembourg, Mexico, the Netherlands, New Zealand, Norway, Poland, Portugal, the Slovak Republic, Slovenia, Spain, Sweden, Switzerland, Turkey, the United Kingdom and the United States. The European Union takes part in the work of the OECD.

OECD Publishing disseminates widely the results of the Organisation's statistics gathering and research on economic, social and environmental issues, as well as the conventions, guidelines and standards agreed by its members.

OECD PUBLISHING, 2, rue André-Pascal, 75775 PARIS CEDEX 16
(98 2017 05 1E) ISBN 978-92-64-28550-7 – 2017

www.ingramcontent.com/pod-product-compliance
Ingram Content Group UK Ltd.
Pitfield, Milton Keynes, MK11 3LW, UK
UKHW051458290926
15471UKWH00008B/1268

9 789264 285507